DATE DUE

			PRINTED IN U.S.A.

Literature Criticism from 1400 to 1800

Guide to Gale Literary Criticism Series

When you need to review criticism of literary works, these are the Gale series to use:

If the author's death date is: | **You should turn to:**

After Dec. 31, 1959
(or author is still living)

CONTEMPORARY LITERARY CRITICISM

for example: Jorge Luis Borges, Anthony Burgess,
William Faulkner, Mary Gordon,
Ernest Hemingway, Iris Murdoch

1900 through 1959

TWENTIETH-CENTURY LITERARY CRITICISM

for example: Willa Cather, F. Scott Fitzgerald,
Henry James, Mark Twain, Virginia Woolf

1800 through 1899

NINETEENTH-CENTURY LITERATURE CRITICISM

for example: Fedor Dostoevski, Nathaniel Hawthorne,
George Sand, William Wordsworth

1400 through 1799

LITERATURE CRITICISM FROM 1400 TO 1800
(excluding Shakespeare)

for example: Anne Bradstreet, Daniel Defoe,
Alexander Pope, François Rabelais,
Jonathan Swift, Phillis Wheatley

SHAKESPEAREAN CRITICISM

Shakespeare's plays and poetry

Antiquity through 1399

CLASSICAL AND MEDIEVAL LITERATURE CRITICISM

for example: Dante, Homer, Plato, Sophocles, Vergil,
the Beowulf Poet

Gale also publishes related criticism series:

CHILDREN'S LITERATURE REVIEW

This series covers authors of all eras who have written for the preschool through high school audience.

SHORT STORY CRITICISM

This series covers the major short fiction writers of all nationalities and periods of literary history.

ISSN 0740-2880

Volume 11

Literature Criticism from 1400 to 1800

Excerpts from Criticism of the Works
of Fifteenth-, Seventeenth-, and
Eighteenth-Century Novelists, Poets, Playwrights,
Philosophers, and Other Creative Writers, from
the First Published Critical Appraisals
to Current Evaluations

James E. Person, Jr.
Editor

James P. Draper
Shannon J. Young
Associate Editors

 Gale Research Inc.

DETROIT • NEW YORK • FORT LAUDERDALE • LONDON

STAFF

James E. Person, Jr., *Editor*

...es P. Draper, Shannon J. Young, *Associate Editors*

Claudia Loomis, *Assistant Editor*
Denise Michlewicz Broderick, Debra A. Wells, *Contributing Assistant Editors*

Jeanne A. Gough, *Permissions and Production Manager*

Linda M. Pugliese, *Production Supervisor*
Jennifer E. Gale, Suzanne Powers, Maureen A. Puhl, *Editorial Associates*
Donna Craft, David G. Oblender, Linda M. Ross, *Editorial Assistants*

Victoria B. Cariappa, *Research Supervisor*
Karen D. Kaus, Eric Priehs, Maureen R. Richards, Mary D. Wise, *Editorial Associates*
Rogene M. Fisher, Filomena Sgambati, *Editorial Assistants*

Sandra C. Davis, *Text Permissions Supervisor*
H. Diane Cooper, Kathy Grell, Josephine M. Keene, Kimberly F. Smilay, *Permissions Associates*
Maria L. Franklin, Lisa Lantz, Camille P. Robinson, Shalice Shah, Denise Singleton,
Permissions Assistants

Patricia A. Seefelt, *Permissions Supervisor (Pictures)*
Margaret A. Chamberlain, *Permissions Associate*
Pamela A. Hayes, Lillian Quickley, *Permissions Assistants*

Mary Beth Trimper, *Production Manager*
Anthony J. Scolaro, *External Production Assistant*

Arthur Chartow, *Art Director*
C. J. Jonik, *Keyliner*

Laura Bryant, *Production Supervisor*
Louise Gagné, *Internal Production Associate*
Shelly Andrews, Sharana Wier, *Internal Production Assistants*

Copyright © 1990
Gale Research Inc.
835 Penobscot Bldg.
Detroit, MI 48226-4094

Library of Congress Catalog Card Number 84-643570
ISBN 0-8103-6110-8
ISSN 0740-2880

Printed in the United States of America

Contents

Preface   vii

Acknowledgments   xi

Authors to Appear in Future Volumes   xv

Preface

"If I have seen farther," wrote Sir Isaac Newton, echoing Fulbert of Chartres and commenting on his own indebtedness to the sages who preceded him, "it is by standing on the shoulders of giants"; this is a statement as applicable to ourselves today as it was to Newton and his world. Many of the political and intellectual foundations of the modern world can be found in the art and thought of the fifteenth through eighteenth centuries. During this time the modern nation-state was born, the sciences grew tremendously, and many of the political, social, economic, and moral philosophies that are influential today were formulated. The literature of these centuries reflects this turbulent time of radical change: the period saw the rise of drama equal in critical stature to that of classical Greece, the birth of the novel and personal essay forms, the emergence of newspapers and periodicals, and significant achievements in poetry and philosophy. Much of modern literature reflects the influence of these centuries' developments. Thus the literature of this period, criticism of which appears in *Literature Criticism from 1400 to 1800,* provides insight into the universal nature of human experience, as well as into the life and thought of the past.

Scope of the Series

Literature Criticism from 1400 to 1800 (LC) is designed to serve as an introduction to the authors of the fifteenth through eighteenth centuries and to the most significant commentators on these authors. The works of the great poets, dramatists, novelists, essayists, and philosophers of those years are considered classics in every secondary school and college or university curriculum. Because criticism of this literature spans a period of up to six hundred years, an overwhelming amount of critical material confronts the student. To help students locate and select criticism of the works of authors who died between 1400 and 1800, *LC* presents significant passages from the most noteworthy published criticism of authors of these centuries. Each volume of *LC* is carefully compiled to represent the critical heritage of the most important writers from a variety of nationalities. In addition to major authors, *LC* also presents criticism of lesser-known writers whose significant contributions to literary history are reflected in continuing critical assessments of their works.

The need for *LC* among students and teachers of literature of the fifteenth through eighteenth centuries was suggested by the proven usefulness of Gale's *Contemporary Literary Criticism (CLC), Twentieth-Century Literary Criticism (TCLC),* and *Nineteenth-Century Literature Criticism (NCLC),* which excerpt criticism of works by nineteenth- and twentieth-century authors. Because of the different time periods covered, there is no duplication of authors or critical material among any of Gale's literary criticism series. For further information about these series, readers should consult the Guide to Gale Literary Criticism Series preceding the title page of this volume. Here, the reader will note that there is a separate Gale reference series devoted to Shakespearean studies. For though belonging properly to the literary period covered in *LC,* William Shakespeare has inspired such a tremendous and ever-growing corpus of secondary material that the editors have deemed it best to give his works the extensive critical coverage best served by a separate series, *Shakespearean Criticism.*

Each volume of *LC* presents:

- criticism of authors' works which represent a variety of genres and nationalities of origin

- criticism of the works of both major and lesser-known writers of the period

- 8-10 authors per volume

- historical surveys of the critical response to authors' works: early criticism is offered to indicate initial responses, later selections document any rise or decline in literary reputations and describe the effects of social or historical forces on the work of authors, and retrospective analyses provide students with modern views. The length of each author entry is intended to present the author's critical reception in English or foreign criticism in translation. Articles and books that have not been translated into English are therefore excluded. Every attempt has been made to identify and include excerpts from the seminal essays on each author's work and to include recent critical commentary providing modern perspectives.

An author may appear more than once in the series because of the great quantity of critical material available, or because of a resurgence of criticism generated by such events as an author's anniversary celebration, the republication of an author's works, or the publication of a newly translated work.

Organization of the Book

An author entry consists of the following elements: author heading, biographical and critical introduction, list of principal works, excerpts of criticism (each followed by a bibliographical citation), and a bibliography of further reading. Also, most author entries reproduce author portraits and other illustrations pertinent to the author's life and career.

- The *author heading* consists of the author's full name, followed by birth and death dates. The portion of the name not parenthesized denotes the form under which the author most commonly wrote. If an author wrote consistently under a pseudonym, the pseudonym will be used in the author heading, with the real name given in parentheses on the first line of the biographical and critical introduction. Also located at the beginning of the introduction to the author entry are any name variations under which an author wrote, including transliterated forms for authors whose native languages use nonroman alphabets. Uncertain birth or death dates are indicated by question marks.

- The *biographical and critical introduction* contains background information designed to introduce the reader to an author and to the critical discussion surrounding his or her work. Parenthetical material following many of the introductions provides references to biographical and critical reference series published by Gale in which additional material on the author may be found, including *Children's Literature Review, Dictionary of Literary Biography, Something about the Author,* and *Yesterday's Authors of Books for Children.*

- Most *LC* entries include *portraits* of the author. Many entries also contain illustrations of materials pertinent to an author's career, including selected author holographs, title pages, letters, or representations of important people, places, and events in an author's life.

- The *list of principal works* is chronological by date of first book publication and identifies the genre of each work. In the case of foreign authors whose works have been translated into English, the title and date of the first English-language edition are given in brackets following the foreign-language listing. Unless otherwise indicated, dramas are dated by first performance, not first publication.

- *Criticism* is arranged chronologically in each author entry to provide a useful perspective on changes in critical evaluation over the years. All titles by the author featured in the critical entry are printed in boldface type to enable the user to ascertain without difficulty the works being discussed. Also for purposes of easier identification, the critic's name and the composition or publication date of the critical work are given at the beginning of each excerpt. Unsigned criticism is preceded by the title of the source in which it appeared. When an anonymous essay has been attributed to a critic, the critic's name appears in brackets at the beginning of the excerpt and in the bibliographical citation. Publication information (such as publisher names and book prices) and parenthetical numerical references (such as footnotes or page and line references to specific editions of works) have been deleted at the editor's discretion to provide smoother reading of the text.

- Critical essays are prefaced by *explanatory notes* as an additional aid to students using *LC*. The explanatory notes may provide several types of useful information, including: the reputation of a critic, the importance of a work of criticism, the specific type of criticism (biographical, psychoanalytic, structuralist, etc.), the intent of the criticism, and the growth of critical controversy or changes in critical trends regarding an author's work. In some cases, these notes cross-reference the work of critics who agree or disagree with each other. Dates in parentheses within the explanatory notes refer to a book publication date when they follow a book title and to the date of an essay excerpted and reprinted elsewhere in the author entry when they follow a critic's name.

- A complete *bibliographical citation* designed to facilitate location of the original essay or book by the reader follows each piece of criticism.

- The *additional bibliography* appearing at the end of each author entry suggests further reading on the author. In a few rare cases it includes essays for which the editors could not obtain reprint rights.

An appendix lists the sources from which material in each volume has been reprinted. It does not, however, list every book and periodical consulted in the preparation of the volume.

Cumulative Indexes

Each volume of *LC* includes a cumulative index to authors listing all the authors that have appeared in *Contemporary Literary Criticism, Twentieth-Century Literary Criticism, Nineteenth-Century Literature Criticism, Literature Criticism from 1400 to 1800,* and *Classical and Medieval Literature Criticism,* along with cross-references to the Gale series *Short Story Criticism, Children's Literature Review, Authors in the News, Contemporary Authors, Contemporary Authors Autobiography Series, Contemporary Authors Bibliographical Series, Dictionary of Literary Biography, Concise Dictionary of Literary Biography, Something about the Author, Something about the Author Autobiography Series,* and *Yesterday's Authors of Books for Children.* Readers will welcome this cumulative author index as a useful tool for locating an author within the various series. The index, which includes authors' birth and death dates, is particularly valuable for those authors who are identified with a certain period but whose death dates cause them to be placed in another, or for those authors whose careers span two periods. For example, F. Scott Fitzgerald is found in *TCLC,* yet a writer often associated with him, Ernest Hemingway, is found in *CLC.*

Each volume of *LC* also includes a cumulative nationality index, in which authors' names are arranged alphabetically under their respective nationalities and followed by the numbers of the volumes in which they appear. In addition, each volume of *LC* includes a cumulative index to titles, an alphabetical listing of the literary works discussed in the series since its inception. Each title listing includes the corresponding volume and page numbers where criticism may be located. Foreign-language titles that have been translated are followed by the titles of the translations—for example, *El ingenioso hidalgo Don Quixote de la Mancha (Don Quixote).* Page numbers following these translated titles refer to all pages on which any form of the titles, either foreign-language or translated, appear. Titles of novels, dramas, nonfiction books, and poetry, short story, or essay collections are printed in italics, while all individual poems, short stories, and essays are printed in roman type within quotation marks. In cases where the same title is used by different authors, the author's surname is given in parentheses after the title, e.g., *Poems* (Bradstreet) and *Poems* (Killigrew).

Suggestions Are Welcome

Readers who wish to suggest authors to appear in future volumes, or who have other suggestions, are cordially invited to write the editors or call our toll-free number: 1-800-347-GALE.

Acknowledgments

The editors wish to thank the copyright holders of the excerpted criticism included in this volume, the permissions managers of many book and magazine publishing companies for assisting us in securing reprint rights, and Anthony Bogucki for assistance with copyright research. We are also grateful to the staffs of the Detroit Public Library, the Library of Congress, the University of Detroit Library, the University of Michigan Library, and the Wayne State University Library for making their resources available to us. Following is a list of the copyright holders who have granted us permission to reprint material in this volume of *LC*. Every effort has been made to trace copyright, but if omissions have been made, please let us know.

COPYRIGHTED EXCERPTS IN *LC*, VOLUME 11, WERE REPRINTED FROM THE FOLLOWING PERIODICALS:

COPYRIGHTED EXCERPTS IN *LC*, VOLUME 11, WERE REPRINTED FROM THE FOLLOWING BOOKS:

Authors to Appear
in Future Volumes

Abravenel, Isaac 1437-1508
Abravenel, Judah 1460-1535
Addison, Joseph 1672-1719
Agricola, Johannes 1494?-1566
Akenside, Mark 1721-1770
Alabaster, William 1567-1640
Alarcón y Mendoza, Juan Rúiz
  1581-1634
Alberti, Leon Battista 1404-1472
Alembert, Jean Le Rond d' 1717-1783
Amory, Thomas 1691?-1788
Anton Ulrich, Duke of Brunswick
  1633-1714
Aretino, Pietro 1492-1556
Ascham, Roger 1515-1568
Aubigne, Théodore Agrippa d'
  1552-1630
Aubrey, John 1620-1697
Bâbur 1483-1530
Bacon, Sir Francis 1561-1626
Bale, John 1495-1563
Barber, Mary 1690-1757
Baretti, Giuseppi 1719-1789
Barker, Jane 1652-1727?
Bartas, Guillaume de Salluste du
  1544-1590
Baxter, Richard 1615-1691
Bayle, Pierre 1647-1706
Beaumarchais, Pierre-Augustin Caron
  de 1732-1799
Beaumont, Francis 1584-1616
Belleau, Rémy 1528-1577
Berkeley, George 1685-1753
Bessarion, Johannes 1403-1472
Bijns, Anna 1493-1575
Bisticci, Vespasiano da 1421-1498
Blackmore, Sir Richard 1650-1729
Boccalini, Traiano 1556-1613
Bodin, Jean 1530-1596
Bolingbroke, Henry St. John
  1678-1751
Boyle, Roger 1621-1679
Bradford, William 1590-1657
Brant, Sebastian 1457-1521
Bredero, Gerbrand Adriaanszoon
  1585-1618
Breitinger, Johann Jakob 1701-1776
Breton, Nicholas 1545-1626
Broome, William 1689-1745
Brown, Thomas 1663-1704
Browne, Sir Thomas 1605-1682
Bruni, Leonardo 1370-1444
Bruno, Giordano 1548-1600
Buffon, George-Louis Leclerc, Comte
  de 1707-1788
Burgoyne, John 1722-1792

Burnet, Gilbert 1643-1715
Burton, Robert 1577-1640
Butler, Samuel 1612-1680
Byrd, William, II 1674-1744
Byrom, John 1692-1763
Calderón de la Barca, Pedro 1600-1681
Camden, William 1551-1623
Campion, Thomas 1567-1620
Carew, Richard 1555-1620
Carew, Thomas 1594-1640
Carver, Jonathan 1710-1780
Casanova di Seingalt, Giacomo
  Girolamo 1725-1798
Castelvetro, Lodovico 1505-1571
Castiglione, Baldassare 1478-1529
Castillejo, Cristobalde 1492-1550
Cavendish, William 1592-1676
Caxton, William 1421?-1491
Centlivre, Susanna 1667?-1723
Chapman, George 1560-1634
Charles I 1600-1649
Chartier, Alain 1390-1440
Chaucer, Geoffrey 1340?-1400
Cibber, Colley 1671-1757
Cleveland, John 1613-1658
Collyer, Mary 1716?-1763?
Colonna, Vittoria 1490-1547
Commynes, Philippe de 1445-1511
Condillac, Etienne Bonnot, Abbé de
  1714?-1780
Cook, James 1728-1779
Corneille, Pierre 1606-1684
Cortés, Hernán 1485-1547
Cotton, John 1584-1652
Courtilz de Sandras, Gatiende
  1644-1712
Cowley, Abraham 1618-1667
Cranmer, Thomas 1489-1556
Crashaw, Richard 1612-1649
Crébillon, Prosper Jolyot de 1674-1762
Cruden, Alexander 1701-1770
Curll, Edmund 1675-1747
D'Alembert, Jean le Rond 1717-1783
Dampier, William 1653-1715
Daniel, Samuel 1562-1619
Davenant, Sir William 1606-1668
Davidson, John 1549?-1603
Da Vinci, Leonardo 1452-1519
Day, John 1574-1640
Dekker, Thomas 1572-1632
Delany, Mary Pendarves 1700-1788
Denham, Sir John 1615-1669
Deloney, Thomas 1543?-1600?
Descartes, René 1596-1650
Desfontaines, Pierre François Guyot,
  Abbé 1685-1745

Diaz del Castillo, Bernal 1492?-1584
Diderot, Denis 1713-1784
Drummond, William 1585-1649
Du Guillet, Pernette 1520?-1545
Dunbar, William 1460?-1520?
Emin, Fedor ?-1770
Erasmus, Desiderius 1466-1536
Etherege, Sir George 1635-1691
Eusden, Laurence 1688-1730
Evelyn, John 1620-1706
Fabyan, Robert ?-1513
Fairfax, Thomas 1621-1671
Fanshawe, Sir Richard 1608-1666
Farquhar, George 1678-1707
Fénelon, François 1651-1715
Fergusson, Robert 1750-1774
Ficino, Marsilio 1433-1499
Fletcher, John 1579-1625
Florian, Jean Pierre Claris de
  1755-1794
Florio, John 1553?-1625
Fontaine, Charles 1514-1565
Fontenelle, Bernard Le Bovier de
  1657-1757
Fonvizin, Denis Ivanovich 1745-1792
Ford, John 1586-1640
Foxe, John 1517-1587
Franklin, Benjamin 1706-1790
Frederick the Great 1712-1786
Froissart, Jean 1337-1404?
Fuller, Thomas 1608-1661
Galilei, Galileo 1564-1642
Garrick, David 1717-1779
Gascoigne, George 1530?-1577
Gay, John 1685-1732
Gibbon, Edward 1737-1794
Gildon, Charles 1665-1724
Glanvill, Joseph 1636-1680
Góngora y Argote, Luis de 1561-1627
Gosson, Stephen 1554-1624
Gottsched, Johann Christoph
  1700-1766
Gower, John 1330?-1408
Gracian y Morales, Baltasar 1601-1658
Graham, Dougal 1724-1779
Greene, Robert 1558?-1592
Griffith, Elizabeth 1727?-1793
Guarini, Giambattista 1538-1612
Guicciardini, Francesco 1483-1540
Hakluyt, Richard 1553-1616
Hall, Edward 1498-1547
Harrington, James 1611-1677
Hartley, David 1705-1757
Helvetius, Claude Arien 1715-1771
Henslowe, Philip ?-1616

Herbert, George 1593-1633
Herrick, Robert 1591-1674
Heywood, Thomas 1574-1641
Hobbes, Thomas 1588-1679
Hogarth, William 1697-1764
Holbach, Paul Heinrich Dietrich
   1723-1789
Holinshed, Raphael ?-1582?
Hooker, Richard 1544-1600
Hooker, Thomas 1586-1647
Howard, Henry, Earl of Surrey
   1517-1547
Howell, James 1593?-1666
Hung Sheng 1646-1704
Hutcheson, Francis 1694-1746
Ibn Khaldun, Abd al-Rahman ibn
   Muhammad 1332-1406
Iriarte, Tomas de 1750-1791
Isla y Rojo, José Francisco
   de 1703-1781
Ivan IV 1533-1584
James I, King of Scotland 1394-1437
Johnson, Samuel 1709-1784
King, William 1662-1712
Knox, John 1514?-1572
Kyd, Thomas 1558-1594
La Bruyére, Jean de 1645-1696
La Fontaine, Jean de 1621-1695
Langland, William 1330?-1400
La Rochefoucauld, Francois de
   1613-1680
Law, William 1686-1761
L'Estrange, Sir Roger 1616-1704
Let-we Thon-dara 1752-1783
Lipsius, Justus 1547-1606
Littleton, Sir Thomas 1422-1481
Lo Kuan-chung c.1400
Lodge, Thomas 1558-1625
Lope de Vega 1562-1635
Lopez de Ayala, Pero 1332-1407?
Louis XIV 1638-1715
Lovelace, Richard 1618-1657
Loyola, Ignacio de 1491-1556
Lydgate, John 1370?-1452
Lyly, John 1554-1606
MacDomhnaill, Sean Clarach
   1691-1754
Macpherson, James 1736-1796
Maitland, Sir Richard 1496-1586
Mandeville, Bernard de 1670-1733
Marlowe, Christopher 1564-1593
Marston, John 1576-1634
Massinger, Philip 1583-1640
Mather, Cotton 1663-1728
Mather, Increase 1639-1723
Mendelssohn, Moses 1729-1786

Metastasio, Pietro 1698-1782
Michelangelo Buonarrotti 1475-1564
Middleton, Thomas 1580-1627
Montfort, Hugo von 1357-1423
Morton, Thomas 1575-1647
Muret, Marc-Antoine de 1526-1585
Nashe, Thomas 1567-1601
Nawa i 1441-1501
Newton, Sir Isaac 1642-1727
North, Sir Thomas 1535?-1601?
Norton, Thomas 1532-1584
Oldham, John 1653-1683
Otway, Thomas 1652-1685
Pade-tha-ya-za 1684-1754
Painter, William 1540?-1594
Paracelsus, Philippus Aureolus 1493-1541
Parr, Catharine 1512-1548
Pascal, Blaise 1623-1662
Pasek, Jan Chryzostom 1636-1701
Peele, George 1556-1596
Pembroke, Mary Sidney, Countess of
   1561-1621
Penn, William 1644-1718
Pico della Mirandola, Giovanni
   1463-1494
Poliziano, Angelo 1454-1494
Quarles, Francis 1592-1644
Quevedo y Villegas, Francisco Gomez
   de 1580-1645
Racine, Jean 1639-1699
Raleigh, Sir Walter 1552-1618
Rapin, René 1621-1687
Reuter, Christian 1665-1712
Revius, Jacobus 1586-1658
Reynolds, Sir Joshua 1723-1792
Rochester, John Wilmot, Earl of
   1648-1680
Rojas Zorilla, Francisco de 1607-1648
Rousseau, Jean-Jacques 1712-1788
Rowe, Elizabeth 1674-1737
Rutherford, Samuel 1600?-1661
Sackville, Thomas 1536-1608
Saint-Simon, Louis de Rouvroy
   1675-1755
Santeuil, Jean Baptiste de 1630-1697
Savage, Richard 1696-1742
Savonarola, Girolamo 1452-1498
Scarron, Paul 1610-1660
Scott, Sarah 1723-1795
Selden, John 1584-1654
Sewall, Samuel 1652-1730
Shadwell, Thomas 1642-1692
Shaftesbury, Anthony Ashley Cooper,
   Earl of 1671-1713
Shenstone, William 1714-1763
Shirley, James 1596-1666

Sidney, Sir Philip 1554-1586
Skelton, John 1464?-1529
Smith, Adam 1723-1790
Sorsky, Nil 1433-1508
Spee, Friedrich von 1591-1635
Sprat, Thomas 1635-1713
Stanhope, Philip 1694-1773
Steele, Sir Richard 1672-1729
Suckling, Sir John 1609-1642
Swedenborg, Emanuel 1688-1772
Takeda Izumo 1690-1756
Tasso, Bernardo 1494-1569
Taylor, Jeremy 1613-1667
Temple, Sir William 1629-1699
Tencin, Madame de 1682-1749
Teresa de Jesús 1515-1582
Testi, Fulvio 1593-1646
Thomson, James 1700-1748
Tourneur, Cyril 1570-1626
Traherne, Thomas 1637-1674
Trai, Nguyen 1380-1442
Tristan 1601-1655
Tyndale, William 1494?-1536
Urquhart, Sir Thomas 1611-1660
Ussher, James 1581-1656
Vasari, Giorgio 1511-1574
Vaughan, Henry 1621-1695
Vaughan, Thomas 1622-1666
Vico, Giambattista 1668-1744
Villiers, George 1628-1687
Villon, François 1431-1463
Voltaire 1694-1778
Waller, Edmund 1606-1687
Walton, Izaak 1593-1683
Warburton, William 1698-1779
Warner, William 1558-1609
Warton, Thomas 1728-1790
Webster, John 1580-1638
Weise, Christian 1642-1708
Wesley, Charles 1701?-1788
Wesley, John 1703-1791
Wesley, Samuel 1662?-1735
Whetstone, George 1544?-1587?
White, Gilbert 1720-1793
Wigglesworth, Michael 1631-1705
Williams, Roger 1603-1683
Winckelman, Johann Joachim
   1717-1768
Winthrop, John 1588-1649
Wyatt, Sir Thomas 1503-1542
Yuan Mei 1716-1797
Zólkiewski, Stanislaw 1547-1620
Zrinyi, Miklos 1620-1664

Readers are cordially invited to suggest additional authors to the editors.

John Dennis

1657-1734

English essayist, critic, poet, translator, and dramatist.

Dennis was an English man of letters who achieved a wide reputation in his day as an outstanding, if controversial, literary critic and theorist. Dubbed "the Critick" by his peers, he was highly esteemed for such essays as *The Impartial Critick*, *The Advancement and Reformation of Modern Poetry*, and *The Grounds of Criticism in Poetry*. His popularity declined, however, with the emergence of new critical theories in the early eighteenth century, many of which Dennis opposed in a series of heated literary quarrels. Today, though Dennis is generally remembered more as an ill-tempered literary disputant than as a writer and critic per se, scholars still cite such essays as *The Advancement and Reformation of Poetry*, *Large Account of the Taste in Poetry*, and *An Essay on the Genius and Writings of Shakespear* as examples of perceptive, well-written criticism.

Dennis was born in London in 1657 to a well-to-do saddler. He received his secondary education at Harrow and entered Caius College, Cambridge in 1675, earning his bachelor of arts degree in 1679. While at Harrow and Caius, Dennis studied the classics extensively, becoming fluent in Latin and Greek and conversant in ancient critical doctrines of literature. Some of Dennis's earliest literary endeavors included translations of Horace, Juvenal, and Ovid, and his critical theories on poetry and drama are based, in part, upon rules established by Aristotle, Horace, and Longinus. The irrational quick temper for which Dennis later became widely known was foreshadowed by an incident that occurred while he was at Caius. College records indicate that in 1680 Dennis was expelled for stabbing a fellow student over what was apparently only a minor incident. In 1683 Dennis received his master of arts degree from Trinity Hall, Cambridge, where he likely remained as a tutor until 1686. In 1685 his father died, leaving him a small inheritance that enabled him to tour Italy and France. While in France, Dennis developed an intense dislike of things French (a bias not uncommon among his fellow Englishmen) that colored much of his work. This is especially evident in *Liberty Asserted*, a drama that achieved moderate success solely as a result of its anti-French theme. In contrast to his negative assessment of his stay in France, Dennis wrote ecstatically of his passage through the Alps into Italy.

Upon returning to England, Dennis developed a close friendship with the Restoration writer John Dryden. Dryden had an enormous impact on Dennis's intellectual growth, shaping the younger scholar's early critical views and introducing him to the theories of such leading French thinkers as René Rapin, René Le Bossu, Nicolas Boileau-Despréaux, Charles Saint-Évremond, and André Dacier. Indeed, Dennis's first critical essays, *The Impartial Critick* and *Remarks on a Book, entituled "Prince Arthur"*, reflect Dryden's tutelage and defend him against such literary opponents as Thomas Rymer and Richard Blackmore. And though Dennis later faulted some of his master's work, he nonetheless championed him long after

John Dennis

Alexander Pope had succeeded Dryden as the dominant literary figure in England. Dennis's close ties to Dryden also brought him into contact with William Congreve, William Wycherley, Charles Gildon, and Joseph Addison, all members of the famous Restoration literary circle that met at Will's coffeehouse. Dennis's welcome at Will's offered him entrée to the major literary discussions of the age, thereby helping establish his reputation as a serious scholar. Like his peers, Dennis developed an avid interest in the theater as both dramatist and critic. Yet despite numerous attempts to write for the stage, all but one of his dramas failed. All the while, Dennis was notoriously dogged in asserting the high value of his dramatic achievement, maintaining in the face of hostile criticism that his works would one day be celebrated as triumphs of the stage. Dennis's failure as a dramatist proved doubly painful for him, for his dramatic endeavors were motivated partly by financial needs. In fact, throughout his life he lived far beyond his modest means, and by the turn of the century he had no income but the one provided by his pen. He thus became involved in government affairs, writing political pamphlets and commemorative verses on issues and events of national importance. These efforts brought him political preferment and private patronage. One particular poem, "Britannia Triumphans: or, The Empire Sav'd, and Europe Deliver'd," written in 1704 to commemorate the battle victories of the Duke of Marlborough, secured him a government post at the London Custom House that supplemented his income for over fifteen years.

Despite his shortcomings as a dramatist, Dennis was hailed by mid-career as one of the leading English men of letters. His reputation continued to flourish during the first decade of the eighteenth century, and in 1701 and 1704 he composed the two critical works considered his most important and original: *The Advancement and Reformation of Modern Poetry* and *The Grounds of Criticism in Poetry.* After 1710, however, as the generation of writers led by Pope, Jonathan Swift, Addison, and Richard Steele supplanted Dryden's aging literary circle, Dennis became increasingly uncompromising in his critical views. He adhered firmly—steadfastly—to critical theories that were now outdated. Convinced of his own artistic superiority and highly sensitive to any negative commentary that might conceivably pertain to him, Dennis frequently responded in a personal manner to general commentary on critics and the art of criticism. His mistrust of the emerging generation of writers, combined with his increasing arrogance, apparently kept Dennis from accepting any literary innovations. This left him vulnerable to the satires of younger writers, who ridiculed his conservative, old-school approach. Attempting to defend his waning reputation, Dennis injudiciously engaged in literary quarrels with some of the most prominent writers of the day. His various adversarial relationships included conflicts with Pope, Swift, Addison, Steele, and other writers of lesser note. The most damaging of these quarrels was with Pope. What initially instigated the bitter dispute is not known, but scholars surmise it may have begun as early as 1705, when Pope was only seventeen years old. Officially, the quarrel began with Pope's publication of *An Essay on Criticism* in 1711 and lasted over twenty years. Pope's various satires emphasized Dennis's well-known oddities of character: excessive fear of the French, overuse of certain phrases considered vulgar, and an almost paranoid belief that he was constantly being ridiculed in print. Pope's character assassination, coupled with Dennis's inability to reply in a like manner, further injured the critic's credibility. And though he still retained old friends and a few patrons, Dennis had, for the most part, lost his ability to influence contemporary critical thought. Despite producing almost thirty works in the last twenty-five years of his life, Dennis lived in almost constant poverty. Mostly blind and in ill health, he was forced on more than one occasion to seek protection to avoid debtor's prison. Finally in January 1734, only two months after friends produced William Congreve's *The Old Batchelor* (1693) for his benefit, Dennis died and was buried at St. Martin in the Fields.

Dennis's extensive literary canon may be divided into critical and noncritical works. By far his most important writings are his essays in criticism. Closely paralleling the development, peak, and subsequent decline of his reputation, Dennis's critical essays variously restate existing critical theories, explicate his own tenets, or assess the works of other authors. In his most important criticism, Dennis attempted to interpret and reconcile the classical doctrines of Aristotle, Horace, and Longinus with the precepts offered by various Restoration and Augustan schools of thought. Central to his critical perception was a fundamental belief that standards of excellence and taste in literature are universal and timeless. Of equal importance was his concept of the function of literature. Edward Niles Hooker explicates this concept in his definitive introduction to *The Critical Works of John Dennis,* noting that Dennis "recognized clear and definite bounds to each of the *genres* of verse, and believed that each *genre* has a specific purpose and aims at a specific effect, and that there is one best way of attaining the purpose and achieving the effect. This is the doctrine of the distinction of *genres.*" Dennis held that the chief function of the "major" poetic genres—epic, tragedy, comedy, and Pindaric—is to create harmony and thereby "restore the decay that happened to human Nature by the fall." To achieve this he recommended following classical rules as guidelines. At the same time, Dennis believed that not all classical traditions were appropriate for modern poetry. Thus, in his earliest critical endeavor, the dialogue *The Impartial Critick,* Dennis argued against Rymer's more rigid interpretation of the rules, presented in *A Short View of Tragedy* (1692), which insisted that English tragedy could never realize its full potential without the introduction of the Greek chorus.

Dennis further developed his critical theories concerning poetry in two important essays, *The Advancement and Reformation of Modern Poetry* and *The Grounds of Criticism in Poetry.* In these works Dennis claimed that the emotions are central to the creation of poetry and that passion "is the Characteristical mark of Poetry, and therefore it must be every where, for without Passion there can be no Poetry." Moreover, passion is best expressed in religious subjects—a fact evidenced in the works of Homer, Vergil, and John Milton. He thus concluded that religion and poetry rely upon and enhance each other—an assumption that was in direct opposition to contemporary critical thought. In *The Advancement and Reformation of Modern Poetry* Dennis argued that classical authors, the "ancients" as they were commonly known then, generally excelled the moderns solely because they treated religious rather than secular topics in their poetry. This view is amplified in *The Grounds of Criticism in Poetry,* a discussion of the aesthetics of the sublime that differentiates between the enthusiastic and vulgar passions. These two essays, in which Dennis revealed an advanced appreciation of Milton's works together with a third tract published in 1702, *Large Account of the Taste in Poetry,* present the majority of Dennis's most valued critical ideas. The critical works Dennis produced after this point are for the most part merely recapitulations of earlier doctrines. Yet despite advancing few new ideas during the final period of his career, Dennis nonetheless produced valuable criticism of individual works in such essays as *An Essay upon the Genius and Writings of Shakespear, Remarks upon "Cato",* and *Remarks upon Mr. Pope's Translation of Homer.*

Dennis's noncritical writings include commemorative, elegiac, and burlesque poetry, translations, political tracts, and drama. Although such works make up much of Dennis's total artistic output, they are generally considered less important than the author's criticism. Dennis's poetic endeavors grew chiefly out of a desire to be deemed a wit; the bulk of his poetry imitates popular themes and genres and is rarely original in style or subject. As a political writer, Dennis addressed the major issues of his day. His political verses, including "The Court of Death: a Pindaric Poem" and "Britannia Triumphans," commemorate important state occasions, while such pamphlets as *An Essay on the Navy* and *A Proposal for Putting a Speedy End to the War* treat contemporary government issues. As a dramatist, Dennis attempted to apply his dramatic theories to his own dramatic compositions as well as in adapting the works of other playwrights. He thus borrowed from such writers as Shakespeare, Torquato Tasso, Euripides, and Livy in an attempt to demonstrate that even the works of such masters as Shakespeare could be improved upon through the application of certain dramatic rules and traditions. Dennis was particularly concerned with the plot construction and moral content of the tragedy; he thus criticized Shakespeare's historical tragedies, which he felt lacked solid plots and the concluding fables necessary to instruct an audience.

Dennis's critical reputation reached both its highest and lowest points during his lifetime. Throughout much of his career Dennis was a controversial figure, variously supported and detracted by the great writers of the age. As a young scholar, his superior knowledge of Latin, Greek, and the classics earned him the honored title of "the learned Mr. Dennis." He was highly respected and well-liked by most of his seventeenth-century contemporaries, notably Dryden, Congreve, Gildon, and Wycherley. Although some scholars disagreed with Dennis's doctrines during this period, his essays were for the most part lauded as exacting yet judicious. His poetry and political pamphlets, though accorded a lesser rank than his criticism, were also well received. As a dramatist, however, Dennis was unequivocally deemed a failure. The early eighteenth-century actor Joe Miller best sums up critical opinion of Dennis the dramatist: "[Dennis was] a very fit Person to Instruct a Dramatic Poet, for he laid down Rules for writing *good* Plays, and shew'd them what were *bad*, by his own." Most of Dennis's productions closed quickly, and only rarely have they been performed since. Regardless of his dramatic failures, Dennis was for a time almost universally regarded as one of the most astute critical thinkers of his age. Many commentators of the 1690s and early 1700s agreed with Gildon's judgment that Dennis had "shewed himself a perfect Critick, and Master of a great deal of Penetration and Judgment." One notable dissenter was Jonathan Swift, who in "A Digression concerning Criticks" in *A Tale of a Tub* (1704) satirically listed Dennis (among others) as a "true critick . . . a Hero born, descending in a direct Line from a Celestial Stem," a "*Discoverer and Collector of Writers Faults.*" Dennis's reputation slowly declined after 1710, and he never again enjoyed much approbation from the critics. While he was still considered by many the leading literary theorist of the age, Dennis's elitism—his insistence that old-school doctrines be maintained and increasing rigidity in adhering to an inflexible set of literary rules—earned him far more ridicule than esteem from his eighteenth-century peers. Indeed, in Dennis's later years writers feared the potential stigma attached to anyone who concurred with his precepts. More damaging to Dennis's reputation were his quarrels with such wits as Pope and Swift, whose satires and maligning caricatures often lampooned legitimate faults in Dennis's personality and writing.

After his death and throughout much of the eighteenth and nineteenth centuries, Dennis generated little scholarly interest. His works were largely obscured by his personal history, and except for the praise of such longstanding supporters as Aaron Hill and Charles Gildon, he was usually rejected as a bad-tempered critic: an essayist who wrote more often out of spite than to advance literary theory. As a result, Dennis's works were frequently neglected or only summarily treated and then dismissed. A few early nineteenth-century scholars, most notably Robert Southey, objectively considered Dennis's works, but most commentators readily agreed with Isaac D'Israeli's scathing conclusion that Dennis had "thrown himself among the walks of genius, and aspired to fix himself on a throne to which nature had refused him a legitimate claim." D'Israeli's condemnation was further supported by H. R. Montgomery, who later claimed Dennis was "worse than a hangman, who merely executes a painful but necessary duty. Dennis, on the contrary, indulged in wanton cruelty; and if he had been the functionary referred to, he would have treated his victim to a preliminary rehearsal of his office before executing it." Countering such negative judgments, the late nineteenth-century commentator William Roberts published a series of articles on Dennis in which he attempted to assess the critic's life and work as objectively as possible. Roberts's essays led to a small resurgence of critical interest and were instrumental in beginning at least a partial reversal of Dennis's predominantly negative reputation. Foreshadowing twentieth-century views, Edmund Gosse signalled the further reevaluation of Dennis as critic and personality, concluding: "Dennis has been resolutely misjudged, in consequence of his foolish attitude towards his younger contemporaries in old age, but in his prime he was a writer of excellent judgment. He was the earliest English critic to do unstinted justice to Milton and Molière, and he was a powerful factor in preparing public opinion for the verdicts of Addison."

The limited canon of twentieth-century criticism of Dennis's works has concentrated primarily upon his critical theories and their relation to later schools of thought. Scholars have noted that while it is unlikely that Dennis directly influenced many later writers, he nonetheless anticipated the critical precepts and aesthetic tenets of such thinkers as Edmund Burke, Johann Schiller, William Hazlitt, William Wordsworth, and John Keats. Scholars now recognize that Dennis advanced several important critical principles concerning poetry—principles for which he was never credited. Of particular interest are his theories on the sublime and on the passions in poetry. David B. Morris has argued that Dennis's theories here provide "a thorough introduction to ideas concerning the religious sublime which attracted poets and critics for the next hundred years." Critics also highly esteem his advanced appreciation of the works of Milton and Shakespeare. Although Dennis is today generally considered but a minor man of letters memorable chiefly for his contentiousness, he is nevertheless recognized as an astute critical thinker who was fairly influential during his lifetime. As biographer H. G. Paul notes, "by many of his contemporaries Dennis was regarded as the foremost English critic of his times, and few or none of the writers of his age can be considered so fully representative of the manifold critical tendencies then struggling for supremacy."

PRINCIPAL WORKS

"The tenth Ode of the Second Book of Horace imitated" [translator] (poetry) 1692; published in periodical *The Gentleman's Journal; or, The Monthly Miscellany*

"Upon our Victory at Sea" (poetry) 1692; published in periodical *The Gentleman's Journal; or, The Monthly Miscellany*

The Impartial Critick; or, Some Observations upon a late book, entitul'd "A Short View of Tragedy," written by Mr. Rymer (criticism) 1693

"The Court of Death: a Pindarique Poem, dedicated to the memory of her Most Sacred Majesty, Queen Mary" (poetry) 1695

Letters upon Several Occasions: Written by and between Mr. Dryden, Mr. Wycherley, Mr. - - - - - -, Mr. Congreve, and Mr. Dennis. Published by Mr. Dennis. With a new translation of selected letters of Monsieur Voiture [translator] (letters) 1696

Remarks on a Book, entituled "Prince Arthur, an Heroick Poem," With some General Critical Observations, and Several New Remarks upon Virgil (criticism) 1696

A Plot and No Plot (drama) 1697

Rinaldo and Armida (drama) 1698

The Usefulness of the Stage to the Happiness of Mankind, to Government and to Religion (essay) 1698

Iphigenia (drama) 1699

The Advancement and Reformation of Modern Poetry. A Critical Discourse. In Two Parts. The First, Shewing that the Principal Reason why the Ancients excel'd the Moderns in the Greater Poetry, was because they mix'd Religion with Poetry. The Second, Proving that by joyning Poetry with the Religion reveal'd to us in Sacred Writ, the Modern Poets might come to equal the Ancient (essay) 1701

*The Comical Gallant: or, the Amours of Sir John Falstaffe (drama) 1702

An Essay on the Navy; or, England's Advantage and Safety, prov'd Dependant on a Formidable and well-Disciplin'd Navy: and the Encrease and Encouragement of the Seamen (essay) 1702

Large Account of the Taste in Poetry (essay) 1702

A Proposal for Putting a Speedy End to the War, by ruining the Commerce of the French and the Spaniards, and securing our own, without any additional Expence to the nation (essay) 1703

"Britannia Triumphans; or, The Empire Sav'd, and Europe Deliver'd. By the success of her Majesty's Forces under the Wise and Heroick Conduct of his Grace the Duke of Marlborough" (poetry) 1704

The Grounds of Criticism in Poetry, contain'd in some New Discoveries never made before, requisite for the Writing and Judging of Poems surely (criticism) 1704

Liberty Asserted (drama) 1704

Reflections Critical and Satyrical, upon a Late Rhapsody call'd, "An Essay upon Criticism" (criticism) 1711

An Essay on the Genius and Writings of Shakespear: with Some Letters of Criticism to the "Spectator" (essay) 1712

Remarks upon "Cato," a Tragedy (criticism) 1713

Remarks upon Mr. Pope's Translation of Homer. With Two Letters concerning Windsor Forest, and the Temple of Fame (criticism) 1717

The Select Works of Mr. John Dennis. 2 vols. (drama and poetry) 1718

†The Invader of His Country: or, The Fatal Resentment (drama) 1720

Original Letters, Familiar, Moral and Critical. 2 vols. (letters) 1721

A Treatise concerning the State of Departed Souls Before, and At, and After the Resurrection [translator] (essay) 1733

‡The Causes the Decay and Defects of Dramatick Poetry, and of the Degeneracy of the Publick Taste (essay) 1817; published in periodical *The Monthly Magazine*

The Critical Works of John Dennis. 2 vols. (criticism and letters) 1939-43

*This drama is an adaptation of Shakespeare's *The Merry Wives of Windsor*.

†This drama is an adaptation of Shakespeare's *Coriolanus*.

‡This essay was probably written in 1725.

[PETER ANTHONY MOTTEUX] (letter date 1692)

[*French-born Motteux was an English translator and dramatist who edited the* Gentleman's Journal, *an important seventeenth-century literary periodical comprised of letters addressed to an imaginary correspondent in the country. In the following excerpt from the November, 1692, issue of the* Gentleman's Journal, *Motteux commends Dennis's translations and adaptations of Ovid, Juvenal, and Jean de La Fontaine.*]

SIR, I knew that you would be of my mind, in wishing that Mr. *Dennis* had translated wholly the 8th of *Juvenal*; nor would it have been the first time that two Translations of the same thing have met each of them with Admirers: And indeed, if his late beautiful Translation of the **"Passion of Byblis"**, and some others which I have seen, did not shew that he is equally happy in touching the soft Passions, and the more rough and manly, it would be pity that he should write any thing but Satyr. But you will own in a little time, when you see a **Collection of Poems** by him which is now in the Press, that he can vary his Subjects as his Style with uncommon success. Be pleas'd not to mistake for that **Miscellany**, when it is publish'd, a little Twelve-penny Book printed many years ago, and now once more offer'd to the World with the Title of **Poems and Letters by Mr. Dennis**. It seems to consist most of Juvenile Verses, and was formerly prefix'd without any Name to it, neither doth Mr. *Dennis* own it to be his. You will find in his **Miscellany** now in the Press several of *Æsop's* Fables in Burlesque, which, what by the Improvements he hath made of Monsieur *de la Fontaine's* thoughts, and what by the advantage which *English* hath over *French* for Burlesque, may be said to be Copies at least equal to the Originals of a Master who was once reputed inimitable.

To those merry Fables he hath given us grave Morals, which will make them at least as instructive as pleasant. For, as you know, Fables have not been invented only to please; they are Paths fill'd with Roses, that lead us to the knowledge of Virtue more agreeably, and may be compar'd to Wisdom laying by for a while its Austerity to sport with Men, and instruct them while it plays. (p. 2)

[*Peter Anthony Motteux*], *in a letter in November, 1692, in* The Gentleman's Journal, *Vol. I, November, 1692, pp. 1-4.*

[PETER ANTHONY MOTTEUX] (letter date 1693)

[*In the following excerpt from a letter published in the* Gentleman's Journal *two months after his review of Dennis's translations and adaptations (see excerpt dated 1692), Motteux evaluates Dennis as a critic.*]

I speak of Mr. *Dennis*'s considerations on Mr. *Rymer's Short View of Tragedy* (1692), that have been lately published in 5 Dialogues of the bigness of a Play. He hath given them the Title of **The Impartial Critick**, very suitable truly, to the Book: For tho he has thought it necessary to examine the first Poem in Mr. *Waller*, and the Character of Mr. *Dryden*'s *Oedipus*, he hath been no less careful to do Justice to the rare merit of those two great men, and fairly considered and answered all the chief arguments that can be raised for introducing a Chorus on our Stage.

We are promised a second Part, wherein Mr. *Dennis* designs to prove, that, tho *Shakespear* had his faults, yet he was a very great Genius, which Mr. *Rymer* seems unwilling to grant. I am only sorry that the time, which the perusal of the many excellencies which are diffus'd thro *Shakespear*'s Plays, requires, will keep Mr. *Dennis* very long from giving us that Book.

That which I mentioned in my former is also published, intituled, **Miscellanies in Verse and Prose by Mr. Dennis**. You will find when you peruse it that he happily reconciles the Critic to the Poet, and while you are pleased with the Beauty and Variety of his Verse, you will also wish that you had more of his Prose. Before you have read half the Epistle you will own, tho no name is prefixed to it, that, as the Dedicator says at last, it could be address'd to none but My Lord *Dorset*. . . .

Many of the Verses in Mr. *Dennis*'s Book were written long since, and all of them before his late Translation of the **"Passion of Byblis"**; yet, tho' he has not been willing to give himself the trouble to revise some of them, you will doubtless not think the time which you employ in their Perusal ill bestow'd. (p. 26)

[*Peter Anthony Motteux*], *in a letter in 1693, in* The Gentleman's Journal, *Vol. II, January, 1693, pp. 26-7.*

CHARLES GILDON (essay date 1699)

[*An English critic and man of letters, Gildon abridged and updated Gerard Langbaine's 1691 investigation of the London stage,* Account of the English Dramatic Poets, *giving special attention to the rising dramatists of the 1690s. In the following excerpt from the 1699 revision of this work,* The Lives and Characters of the English Dramatic Poets, *Gildon briefly sketches his friend Dennis's life, evaluating* Remarks on a Book, entitul'd "Prince Arthur," *and* A Plot and No Plot.]

This Gentleman now Living [John Dennis], has made himself a Name by several Books, both in Prose and Verse, which he has Published, but for none more than his **Critical Observations** on the so much Celebrated Prince *Arthur*, writ by Sir *Richard Blackmore*, in which he has shewed himself a perfect Critick, and Master of a great deal of Penetration and Judgment; his Remarks being beyond Controversy just, and the Faults he finds undeniably such. I am not able to give any Account of his Parents. He was Born in *London*, his Education was at *Gonvile* and *Caius College* in *Cambridge*, which he improv'd afterwards by Travel and the best Conversation; but the occasion of his being mentioned here, is a Dramatick piece he has lately Publish'd, called, **A Plot and no Plot**, a Comedy, *4to.* Acted at the Theatre Royal, 1697. and Dedicated to the Right Honourable *Robert*, Earl of *Sunderland*, Lord Chamberlain of his Majesty's Houshold. The Plot of this Play is our Author's own, tho' I confess, an Incident or two are not so new as the rest of the Play may justly be said to be; for old Bulls being perswaded, that he is in *Newgate*, when he's in his own House, is not unlike an incident in the *City-Politicks*, and young Bulls being married by *Baldernoe* has been in the *Old Batchelor, The City Match, & c.* This Play is exactly regular, and discovers it self writ by a Master of the Art of the Stage, as well as by a Man of Wit; the justness, fineness, and delicacy of the Reflections, the pleasantness of the Humours, the Novelty and Distinction of the Characters, the admirable Conduct and Design of the whole, with the useful Moral of the Play, places it in the Rank of the best Comedies of this latter Age of Poetry; and tho' he himself term it low Comedy, gives us a Desire, as well as Hopes, of some more Noble Performance.

Charles Gildon, "John Dennis," *in* Momus Triumphans; or, the Plagiaries of the English Stage *and* The Lives and Characters of the English Dramatick Poets *by Gerard Langbaine, Garland Publishing, Inc., 1973, p. 38.*

SIR RICHARD BLACKMORE (poem date 1700)

[*Blackmore was an English poet and man of letters. His negative allusions to John Dryden in the preface to his epic poem* Prince Arthur *(1695) elicited censure from Dennis in one of his earliest critical essays,* Remarks on a Book, entituled "Prince Arthur." *Blackmore in turn appointed Dennis a place in the "mob of wits" in his poem "A Satyr against Wit." Despite their initial pointed exchanges, Dennis and Blackmore later existed on good terms, each praising the other's literary efforts. In the following excerpt from "A Satyr against Wit," Blackmore places Dennis among those to be melted in the pot that determines "the Masters of Essay."*]

Set forth your Edict, let it be enjoyn'd
That all defective Species be recoyn'd.
St. E(vre)m(on)t and R(yme)r both are fit
To oversee the Coining of our Wit.
Let these be made the Masters of Essay,
They'll every Piece of Metal touch and weigh,
And tell which is too light, which has too much Allay.
'Tis true that when the course and worthless Dross
Is purg'd away, there will be mighty Loss.
Ev'n C(ongrev)e, S(outher)n(e), Manly W(ycher)ly,
When thus refin'd will grievous Suff'rers be.
Into the melting Pot when D(ryde)n comes,
What horrid Stench will rise, what noisome Fumes!
How will he shrink, when all his leud Allay
And wicked Mixture shall be purg'd away!
When once his boasted Heaps are melted down,
A Chest full scarce will yield one Sterling Crown.

Those who will *D(en)n(i)s* melt and think to find
A goodly Mass of Bullion left behind,
Do as th' *Hibernian* Wit, who, as 'tis told,
Burnt his gilt Leather to collect the Gold.

But what remains will be so pure, 'twill bear
Th' Examination of the most severe;
'Twill *S(ome)r*'s Scales and *T(al)bot*'s Test abide,
And with their Mark please all the World beside.

But when our Wit's call'd in, what will remain
The Muses learned Commerce to maintain?
How pensive will our Beaus and Ladies sit!
They'll mutiny for want of ready Wit.
That such a failure no Man may incense,
Let us erect a Bank for Wit and Sense;
A Bank whose current Bills may Payment make,
Till new Mill'd Wit shall from the Mint come back.

(p. 329)

Sir Richard Blackmore, "A Satyr against Wit," in Critical Essays of the Seventeenth Century: 1685-1700, Vol. III, *edited by J. E. Spingarn, Oxford at the Clarendon Press, 1909, pp. 325-33.*

ALEXANDER POPE (poem date 1711)

[*Pope has been called the greatest English poet of his time and one of the most important in the history of world literature. As a critic and satirical commentator on eighteenth-century England, he was the author of work that epitomizes neoclassical thought. His famous remark, "The proper study of mankind is man," perfectly illustrates the temperament of his age: a time when influential thinkers severely narrowed the limits of human speculation. Pope's work demonstrates his love of restraint, clarity, order, and decorum. His greatness lies in his cultivation of style and wit—an inclination that shaped his criticism of other writers. In one of his earliest critical works,* An Essay on Criticism (1711), *Pope (for unprofessed reasons) parodied Dennis. This metrical essay, in which Dennis, alluded to as "Appius," is cited as the archetype of critics who criticize freely yet are unable to accept unfavorable criticism of their own works, instigated a long and bitter quarrel between the two writers. In the following excerpt from* An Essay on Criticism, *Pope makes reference to Dennis's volatile temperament.*]

LEARN then what MORALS Critics ought to show,
For 'tis but half a Judge's task, to know.
'Tis not enough, taste, judgment, learning, join;
In all you speak, let truth and candour shine:
That not alone what to your sense is due
All may allow; but seek your friendship too.

Be silent always when you doubt your sense;
And speak, though sure, with seeming diffidence:
Some positive, persisting fops we know,
Who, if once wrong, will needs be always so;
But you, with pleasure own your errors past,
And make each day a Critic on the last.

'Tis not enough, your counsel still be true;
Blunt truths more mischief than nice falsehoods do;
Men must be taught as if you taught them not,
And things unknown proposed as things forgot.
Without Good Breeding, truth is disapprov'd;
That only makes superior sense beloved.

Be niggards of advice on no pretence;
For the worst avarice is that of sense.
With mean complacence ne'er betray your trust,
Nor be so civil as to prove unjust.

Caricature of Dennis based upon the line in Alexander Pope's Essay on Criticism (1711), "Like some fierce Tyrant in old tapestry." Engraving after William Hogarth.

Fear not the anger of the wise to raise;
Those best can bear reproof, who merit praise.

'Twere well might Critics still this freedom take,
But Appius reddens at each word you speak,
And stares, tremendous, with a threatening eye,
Like some fierce Tyrant in old tapestry.
Fear most to tax an Honourable fool,
Whose right it is, uncensured, to be dull;
Such, without wit, are Poets when they please,
As without learning they can take Degrees.

(pp. 79-80)

Alexander Pope, "An Essay on Criticism," in his Selected Poetry & Prose, *edited by William K. Wimsatt, Jr., Holt, Rinehart and Winston, 1951, pp. 63-84.*

JOHN DENNIS (essay date 1711)

[*Dennis was infuriated by Alexander Pope's derogatory allusion in* An Essay on Criticism (*see excerpt by Pope dated 1711*) *and responded the following month with* Reflections upon a Late Rhapsody call'd "An Essay upon Criticism." *Although the essay presented some legitimate criticism that Pope later addressed in revisions of his essay, Dennis's rebuttal contained a barrage of vicious attacks on Pope and his congenitally disfigured body. In the following excerpt from the preface to* Reflections, *Dennis begins his critique with a passionate defense of himself as an honest critic unjustly attacked.*]

Things, such monstrous Things have been lately writ, and such monstrous Judgments pass'd, that what has been formerly said has been sufficiently confirm'd, that 'tis impossible an Author can be so very foolish, but he will find more stupid Admirers.

A most notorious Instance of this Depravity of Genius and Tast, is the Essay upon which the following Reflections are writ, and the Approbation which it has met with. I will not deny but that there are two or three Passages in it with which I am not displeas'd; but what are two or three Passages as to the whole?

> Fit Chærilus ille
> Quem bis terq; bonum cum risu miror.

The approving two or Three Passages amongst a multitude of bad ones, is by no means advantageous to an Author. That little that is good in him does but set off its contrary, and make it appear more extravagant. The Thoughts, Expressions, and Numbers of this Essay are for the most part but very indifferent, and indifferent and execrable in Poetry are all one. But what is worse than all the rest, we find throughout the whole a deplorable want of that very Quality, which ought principally to appear in it, which is Judgment; and I have no Notion that where there is so great a want of Judgment, there can be any Genius.

However, I had not publish'd the following Letter, but had suffer'd his Readers to have hugg'd themselves in the Approbation of a Pamphlet so very undeserving, if I had not found things in it that have provok'd my Scorn, tho' not my Indignation. For I not only found my self attack'd without any manner of Provocation on my side, and attack'd in my Person, instead of my Writings, by one who is wholly a Stranger to me, and at a time when all the World knew that I was persecuted by Fortune; I not only saw that this was attempted in a clandestine manner with the utmost Falshood and Calumny, but found that all this was done by a little affected Hypocrite, who had nothing in his mouth at the same time but *Truth, Candor, Friendship, good Nature, Humanity*, and *Magnanimity*.

'Tis for this Reason that I have publish'd the following Letter, in which if I have not treated the Author of the Essay with my usual Candor, he may thank himself and this good-natur'd Town. For having observ'd with no little Astonishment, that Persons have been censur'd for ill Nature, who have attempted to display the Errors of Authors undeservedly successful; tho', they have done this with all imaginable Candor, and with the best and noblest Designs, which are the doing Justice, the Discovery of Truth, and the Improvement of Arts; while Writers of Lampoons and infamous Libels, whose Anonymous Authors have lain lurking in the dark, sometimes in Clubs, and sometimes solitary, like so many common Rogues and Footpads, to ruin the Fortunes, and murder the Reputations of others; have been caress'd and hugg'd by their thoughtless Applauders, and treated as if they had been the most vertuous and the best natur'd Men in the World; having observ'd all this with no little astonishment, I at last found out the reason of it, which is, because the Attempts of Libellers and Lampooners hurt only those whom they attack, and delight the rest of the Readers; whereas they who expose by a just Criticism the Absurdities of foolish fortunate Authors, attack all those who commend and admire those Authors, and disturb perhaps by opening their Eyes,

no fewer than a thousand Fops in the good Opinion which they have conceiv'd of themselves. 'Tis for this Reason that I have endeavour'd to comply with this wise and good natur'd general Disposition of Minds, and to make amends for the Ill-nature of my Criticism, by the Allurements of my *Satyr*. (pp. 396-97)

> *John Dennis, " 'Reflections Critical and Satyrical, upon a Late Rhapsody, Call'd, 'An Essay upon Criticism' (1711)," in* The Critical Works of John Dennis: 1692-1711, Vol. I, *edited by Edward Niles Hooker, The Johns Hopkins Press, 1939, pp. 396-422.*

ALEXANDER POPE (essay date 1713)

[*Pope never forgave Dennis's brutal assault in* Reflections upon a Late Rhapsody call'd "An Essay upon Criticism" *(see excerpt by Dennis dated 1711) and took his revenge by mercilessly parodying the aging critic in several pieces. Pope's repeated satires utilized Dennis's reputed idiosyncracies to create an impression of the critic as more of a caricature than a real man. Over a twenty-year period, Pope systematically destroyed Dennis's credibility in such works as* The Critical Specimen *(1711),* The Dunciad *(1728), and* "Peri Bathous" *(1728). Perhaps the most damaging satire by Pope,* The Narrative of Dr. Robert Norris, concerning the Frenzy of Mr. John Dennis, *appeared anonymously in 1713. Using the name of an actual, though not particularly reputable, English doctor, Pope created the tale of Dennis's insanity as supposedly witnessed and retold by Dr. Robert Norris. The portrayal of Dennis as a virtual madman emphasized the critic's reputed ill-temper, literary arrogance, and hatred for the French and contained enough seemingly factual material to convince many readers of its legitimacy. In the following excerpt from* The Narrative of Dr. Robert Norris, *Pope employs the voice of Norris to recount alleged events and dialogue said to have led to the determination of Dennis's madness.*]

It is an acknowledg'd Truth, that nothing is so dear to an honest Man as his good Name, nor ought he to neglect the just Vindication of his Character, when it is injuriously attack'd by any Man. The Person I have at present Cause to complain of [John Dennis], is indeed in very melancholy Circumstances, it having pleas'd God to deprive him of his Senses, which may extenuate the Crime in Him. But I should be wanting in my Duty, not only to my self, but also to him who hath endu'd me with Talents for the benefit of my Fellow-Creatures, shou'd I suffer my Profession or Honesty to be undeservedly aspers'd. I have therefore resolv'd to give the Publick an account of all that has past between that unhappy Gentleman and my self.

On the 20*th* instant, while I was in my Closet pondering the Case of one of my Patients, I heard a Knocking at my Door; upon opening of which enter'd an old Woman with Tears in her Eyes, and told me, that without my Assistance her Master would be utterly ruin'd. I was forc'd to interrupt her Sorrow by enquiring her Master's Name and Place of Abode. She told me he was one Mr. *Denn[is]* an Officer of the Custom-house, who was taken ill of a violent Frenzy last *April*, and had continu'd in those melancholy Circumstances with few or no Intervals. Upon this I ask'd her some Questions relating to his Humour and Extravagancies, that I might the better know under what Regimen to put him, when the Cause of his Distemper was found out. Alass, Sir, says she, this Day fortnight in the Morning a poor simple Child came to him from the Printer's; the Boy had no sooner enter'd the Room, but he cry'd out *the Devil was come*. He often stares ghastfully, raves aloud, and mutters between his Teeth the Word *Cator*, or *Cato*, or some such thing. Now, Doctor, this *Cator* is certainly a *Witch*, and my poor Master is under an evil Tongue; for I have heard him say *Cator* has bewitch'd the whole Nation. It pitied my very Heart, to think that a Man of my Master's Understanding and great Scholarship, who, as the Child told me, had a Book of his own in Print, should talk so outragiously. Upon this I went and laid out a Groat for a Horse-shoe, which is at this time nail'd on the Threshold of his Door; but I don't find my Master is at all the better for it; he perpetually starts and runs to the Window when any one knocks, crying out, *S'death! a Messenger from the French King! I shall die in the* Bastile.

Having said this, the old Woman presented me with a Viol of his Urine; upon Examination of which I perceiv'd the whole Temperament of his Body to be exceeding hot. I therefore instantly took my Cane and my Beaver, and repair'd to the Place where he dwelt.

When I came to his Lodgings near *Charing-cross*, up three Pair of Stairs, (which I should not have publish'd in this manner, but that this Lunatick conceals the Place of his Residence on purpose to prevent the good Offices of those charitable Friends and Physicians, who might attempt his Cure) when I came into the Room, I found this unfortunate Gentleman seated on his Bed, with Mr. *Bernard Lintott*, Bookseller, on the one side of him, and a grave elderly Gentleman on the other, who, as I have since learnt, calls himself a Grammarian, the Latitude of whose Countenance was not a little eclips'd by the Fullness of his Peruke. . . . [Dennis's] Aspect was furious, his Eyes were rather fiery than lively, which he roll'd about in an uncommon manner. He often open'd his Mouth, as if he wou'd have utter'd some Matter of Importance, but the Sound seem'd lost inwardly. His Beard was grown, which they told me he would not suffer to be shav'd, believing the modern Dramatick Poets had corrupted all the Barbers in the Town to take the first Opportunity of cutting his Throat. His Eye-brows were grey, long, and grown together, which he knit with Indignation when any thing was spoken, insomuch that he seem'd not to have smoothed his Forehead for many Years. His Flannel Night Cap, which was exceedingly begrim'd with Sweat and Dirt, hung upon his Left Ear; the Flap of his Breeches dangled between his Legs, and the Rolls of his Stockings fell down to his Ankles.

I observ'd his Room was hung with *old Tapestry*, which had several Holes in it, caus'd, as the Old Woman inform'd me, by his having cut out of it the Heads of divers *Tyrants*, the Fierceness of whose Visages had much provoked him. On all sides of his Room were pinned a great many Sheets of a Tragedy called *Cato*, with Notes on the Margin with his own Hand. The Words *Absurd, Monstrous, Execrable*, were every where written in such large Characters, that I could read them without my Spectacles. By the Fire-side lay Three-farthings-worth of Small-coal in a *Spectator*, and behind the Door huge Heaps of Papers of the same Title, which his Nurse inform'd me she had convey'd thither out of his sight, believing they were Books of the Black Art; for her Master never read in them, but he was either quite mop'd, or in raving Fits: There was nothing neat in the whole Room, except some Books on his

Shelves very well bound and gilded, whose Names I had never before heard of, nor I believe are any where else to be found; such as **Gibraltar, a Comedy**; **Remarks on Prince Arthur**; **the Grounds of Criticism in Poetry**; **an Essay on publick Spirit**. The only one I had any Knowledge of was a *Paradise Lost*, interleav'd. The whole Floor was cover'd with Manuscripts, as thick as a Pastry Cook's Shop on a Christmas Eve. On his Table were some Ends of Verse and of Candles; a Gallipot of Ink with a yellow Pen in it, and a Pot of half-dead Ale cover'd with a *Longinus*.

As I was casting my Eyes round on all this odd Furniture with some Earnestness and Astonishment, and in a profound Silence, I was on a sudden surpriz'd to hear the Man speak in the following manner:

'Beware, Doctor, that it fare not with you as with your Predecessor the famous *Hippocrates*, whom the mistaken Citizens of *Abdera* sent for in this very manner to cure the Philosopher *Democritus*; he return'd full of Admiration at the Wisdom of that Person whom he had suppos'd a Lunatick. Behold, Doctor, it was thus *Aristotle* himself and all the great Antients spent their Days and Nights, wrapt up in Criticism, and beset all around with their own Writings. As for me, whom you see in the same manner, be assur'd I have none other Disease than a Swelling in my Legs, whereof I say no more, since your Art may further certify you.'

I thereupon seated my self upon his Bed-side, and placing my Patient on my Right Hand, to judge the better in what he affirm'd of his Legs, felt his Pulse. (pp. 155-60)

I began now to be in hopes that his Case had been misrepresented, and that he was not so far gone, but some timely Medicines might recover him. I therefore proceeded to the proper Queries, which with the Answers made to me, I shall set down in Form of Dialogue, in the very Words they were spoken, because I would not omit the least Circumstance in this Narrative; and I call my Conscience to witness, as if upon Oath, that I shall tell the Truth without addition or diminution.

DOCT. Pray, Sir, how did you contract this Swelling?

DENN. By a Criticism.

DOCT. A Criticism! that's a Distemper I never read of in *Galen*.

DENN. S'Death, Sir, a Distemper! It is no Distemper, but a Noble Art. I have sat fourteen Hours a Day at it; and are you a Doctor, and don't know there's a Communication between the Legs and the Brain?

DOCT. What made you sit so many Hours, Sir?

DENN. *Cato*, Sir.

DOCT. Sir, I speak of your Distemper, what gave you this Tumor?

DENN. *Cato, Cato, Cato*.

(p. 160)

DENN. S'Death, Sir, my Friend an Apothecary! a base Mechanic! He who, like my self, professes the noblest Sciences in the Universe, Criticism and Poetry. Can you think I would submit my Writings to the Judgment of an Apothecary? By the Immortals, he himself inserted three whole Paragraphs in my **Remarks,** had a Hand in my **Publick Spirit,** nay, assisted me in my Description of the Furies, and infernal Regions in my **Appius.**

MR. LINTOTT. He is an Author; you mistake the Gentleman, Doctor; he has been an Author these twenty Years, to his Bookseller's Knowledge, and no Man's else.

DENN. Is all the Town in a Combination? Shall Poetry fall to the ground? Must our Reputation be lost to all foreign Countries? O Destruction! Perdition! *Opera! Opera!* As Poetry once rais'd a City, so when Poetry fails, Cities are overturn'd, and the World is no more.

DR. He raves, he raves; Mr. *Lintott*, I pray you pinion down his Arms, that he may do no Mischief.

DENN. O I am sick, sick to Death!

DR. That is a good Symptom, a very good Symptom. To be sick to Death (say the modern Physicians) is an excellent Symptom. When a Patient is sensible of his Pain, 'tis half a Cure. Pray, Sir, of what are you sick?

DENN. Of every thing, Of every thing. I am sick of the *Sentiments*, of the *Diction*, of the *Protasis*, of the *Epitasis*, and the *Catastrophe*———Alas, what is become of the *Drama*, the *Drama*?

OLD WOM. The *Dram*, Sir? Mr. *Lintott* drank up all the Geneva just now; but I'll go fetch more presently!

DENN. O shameful Want, scandalous Omission! By all the Immortals, here is no *Peripætia*, no Change of Fortune in the Tragedy; Z———no Change at all.

OLD WOM. Pray, good Sir, be not angry, I'll fetch Change.

DR. Hold your Peace, Woman, his Fit increases; good Mr. *Lintott* hold him.

MR. LINTOTT. Plague on't! I am damnably afraid they are in the right of it, and he is mad in earnest, if he should be really mad, who the Devil will buy the **Remarks**?

(*Here Mr.* Lintott *scratched his Head.*)

DR. Sir, I shall order you the cold Bath to morrow—Mr. *Lintott*, you are a sensible Man; pray send for Mr. *Verdier's* Servant, and as you are a Friend to the Patient, be so kind as to stay this Evening whilst he is cupp'd on the Head. The Symptoms of his Madness seem to be desperate; for *Avicen* says, that if Learning be mix'd with a Brain that is not of a Contexture fit to receive it, the Brain ferments till it be totally exhausted. We must eradicate these undigested Ideas out of the *Perecranium*, and reduce the Patient to a competent Knowledge of himself.

These were all the Words that pass'd among us at this Time; nor was there need for more, it being necessary we should make use of Force in the Cure of my Patient.

I privately whisper'd the old Woman to go to *Verdier's* in *Long Acre*, with Orders to come immediately with Cupping Glasses; in the mean time, by the Assistance of Mr. *Lintott*, we lock'd his Friend into a Closet, (who 'tis plain from his last Speech was likewise toucht in his Intellects) after which we bound our Lunatick Hand and Foot down

to the Bedsted, where he continued in violent Ravings, notwithstanding the most tender Expressions we could use to perswade him to submit to the Operation, till the Servant of *Verdier* arriv'd. He had no sooner clap'd half a dozen Cupping Glasses on his Head, and behind his Ears, but the Gentleman above-mention'd bursting open the Closet, ran furiously upon us, cut Mr. *Denn[is's]* Bandages, and let drive at us with a vast Folio, which sorely bruis'd the Shin of Mr. *Lintott*; Mr. *John Denn[is]* also starting up with the Cupping Glasses on his Head, seized another Folio, and with the same dangerously wounded me in the Skull, just above my right Temple. The Truth of this Fact Mr. *Verdier's* Servant is ready to attest upon Oath, who, taking an exact Survey of the Volumes, found that which wounded my Head to be *Gruterus's Lampas Critica*, and that which broke Mr. *Lintott's* Shin was *Scaliger's* Poetices. After this, Mr. *John Denn[is]* strengthen'd at once by Rage and Madness, snatch'd up a Peruke-Block, that stood by the Bed-side, and weilded it round in so furious a Manner, that he broke three of the Cupping Glasses from the Crown of his Head, so that much Blood trickled down his Visage—He look'd so ghastly, and his Passion was grown to such a prodigious Height, that my self, Mr. *Lintott*, and *Verdier's* Servant, were oblig'd to leave the Room in all the Expedition imaginable.

I took Mr. *Lintott* home with me, in order to have our Wounds drest, and laid hold of that Opportunity of entering into Discourse with him about the Madness of this Person, of whom he gave me the following remarkable Relation:

That on the 17th of *May*, 1712. between the Hours of 10 and 11 in the Morning, Mr. *John Denn[is]* enter'd into his Shop, and opening one of the Volumes of the *Spectator*, in the large Paper, did suddenly, without the least Provocation, tear out that of N° [40] where the Author treats of Poetical Justice, and cast it into the Street. That the said Mr. *John Denn[is]* on the 27th of *March*, 1712. finding on the said Mr. *Lintott's* Counter a Book called an *Essay on Criticism*, just then publish'd, he read a Page or two with much Frowning and Gesticulation, till coming to these two Lines;

> *Some have at first for Wits, then Poets past,*
> *Turn'd Criticks next, and prov'd plain Fools at last.*

He flung down the Book in a terrible Fury, and cried out *By G—he means Me.*

That being in his Company on a certain Time, when *Shakespear* was mention'd as of a contrary Opinion to Mr. *Denn[is]* he swore the said *Shakespear* was a *Rascal*, with other defamatory Expressions, which gave Mr. *Lintott* a very ill Opinion of the said *Shakespear*.

That about two Months since, he came again into the Shop, and cast several suspicious Looks on a Gentleman that stood by him, after which he desired some Information concerning that Person. He was no sooner acquainted that the Gentleman was a new Author, and that his first Piece was to be publish'd in a few Days, but he drew his Sword upon him, and had not my Servant luckily catch'd him by the Sleeve, I might have lost one Author upon the spot, and another the next Sessions.

Upon recollecting all these Circumstances, Mr. *Lintott* was entirely of Opinion, that he had been mad for some Time;

and I doubt not but this whole Narrative must sufficiently convince the World of the Excess of his Frenzy. It now remains, that I give the Reasons which obliged me in my own Vindication to publish this whole unfortunate Transaction.

In the first place, Mr. *John Denn[is]* had industriously caused to be reported that I enter'd into his Room *Vi & Armis*, either out of a Design to deprive him of his Life, or of a new Play called **Coriolanus, [The Invader of His Country]**, which he has had ready for the Stage these four Years.

Secondly, He hath given out about *Fleetstreet* and the *Temple*, that I was an Accomplice with his Bookseller, who visited him with Intent to take away divers valuable Manuscripts, without paying him Copy-Money.

Thirdly, He hath told others, that I am no Graduate Physician, and that he had seen me upon a Mountebank Stage in *Moorfields*, when he had Lodgings in the College there.

Fourthly, Knowing that I had much Practice in the City, he reported at the *Royal Exchange, Customhouse,* and other Places adjacent, that I was a foreign Spy, employ'd by the *French* King to convey him into *France*; that I bound him Hand and Foot; and that, if his Friend had not burst from his Confinement to his Relief, he had been at this Hour in the *Bastile*.

All which several Assertions of his are so very extravagant, as well as inconsistent, that I appeal to all Mankind whether this Person be not out of his Senses. I shall not decline giving and producing further Proofs of this Truth in open Court, if he drives the Matter so far. In the mean time I heartily forgive him, and pray that the Lord may restore him to the full Enjoyment of his Understanding: So wisheth, as becometh a Christian. (pp. 162-68)

> Alexander Pope, "The Narrative of Dr. Robert Norris, concerning the Strange and Deplorable Frenzy of Mr. John Dennis," in The Prose Works of Alexander Pope: The Earlier Works, 1711-1720, Vol. I, *edited by Norman Ault, Basil Blackwell, 1936, pp. 155-68.*

[JONATHAN SWIFT] (poem date 1714)

[*Swift is considered the foremost satirist in the English language and one of the greatest in world literature. He was also an accomplished poet, a master of political journalism, and a leader of the Anglican church in Ireland. Swift was one of the first writers of Alexander Pope's generation to satirize Dennis. In the 1704 satire* A Tale of a Tub *he ridiculed critics in general, listing Dennis as a "true critick": one who is "like a* Dog *at a Feast, whose Thoughts and Stomach are wholly set upon what the Guests* fling away, *and consequently, is apt to* Snarl *most, when there are the fewest* Bones." *Swift later parodied Dennis both in essays and in the periodical the* Examiner. *Dennis, claiming never to have spoken against or even been introduced to Swift, refrained from replying until 1711 when he became embroiled in the quarrel with Pope. Swift never revealed his reasons for the apparently unprovoked attacks; scholars surmise that Dennis was merely an easy target for Swift's wit. Dennis and Swift traded insults periodically from 1711 to 1714, ending with Swift's parting shot, "John Dennis the Sheltering Poet's Invitation to Sir Richard Steele, the secluded Party Writer, to come and live with him in the Mint" (1714). Although di-*

rected for the most part against Steele, the poem ridiculed Dennis as well. Both Dennis and Steele were experiencing serious financial difficulties at this time and Swift was quick to poke fun at their misfortunes. Here, Swift presents a fictitious invitation requesting Steele to join Dennis in his luxurious dwelling.]

If thou canst lay aside spendthrift's air,
And condescend to feed on homely fare,
Such as we minters, with ragouts unstored,
Will, in defiance of the law, afford:
Quit thy patrols with Toby's Christmas box,
And come to me at The Two Fighting Cocks;
Since printing by subscription now is grown
The stalest, idlest cheat about the town;
And ev'n Charles Gildon, who, a Papist bred,
Has an alarm against that worship spread,
Is practising those beaten paths of cruising,
And for new levies on proposals musing.

'Tis true, that Bloomsbury-square's a noble place:
But what are lofty buildings in thy case?
What's a fine house embellish'd to profusion,
Where shoulder dabbers are in execution?
Or whence its timorous tenant seldom sallies,
But apprehensive of insulting bailiffs?
This once be mindful of a friend's advice,
And cease to be improvidently nice;
Exchange the prospects that delude thy sight,
From Highgate's steep ascent and Hampstead's height,
With verdant scenes, that, from St. George's Field,
More durable and safe enjoyments yield.

Here I, even I, that ne'er till now could find
Ease to my troubled and suspicious mind,
But ever was with jealousies possess'd,
Am in a state of indolence and rest;
Fearful no more of Frenchmen in disguise,
Nor looking upon strangers as on spies,
But quite divested of my former spleen,
Am unprovoked without, and calm within:
And here I'll wait thy coming, till the sun
Shall its diurnal course completely run.
Think not that thou of sturdy bub shalt fail,
My landlord's cellar stock'd with beer and ale,
With every sort of malt that is in use,
And every country's generous produce.
The ready (for here Christian faith is sick,
Which makes us seldom trespass upon tick)
Instantly brings the choicest liquors out,
Whether we ask for home-brew'd or for stout,
For mead or cider, or, with dainties fed,
Ring for a flask or two of white or red,
Such as the drawer will not fail to swear
Was drunk by Pilkington when third time mayor.
That name, methinks, so popularly known
For opposition to the church and crown,
Might make the Lusitanian grape to pass,
And almost give a sanction to the glass;
Especially with thee, whose hasty zeal
Against the late rejected commerce bill
Made thee rise up, like an audacious elf,
To do the speaker honour, not thyself.

But if thou soar'st above the common prices,
By virtue of subscription to thy Crisis,
And nothing can go down with thee but wines
Press'd from Burgundian and Campanian vines,
Bid them be brought; for, though I hate the French,
I love their liquors, as thou lovest a wench;
Else thou must humble thy expensive taste,
And, with us, hold contentment for a feast.

The fire's already lighted; and the maid
Has a clean cloth upon the table laid,
Who never on a Saturday had struck,
But for thy entertainment, up a buck.
Think of this act of grace, which by your leave
Susan would not have done on Easter Eve,
Had she not been inform'd over and over,
'Twas for th' ingenious author of The Lover.

Cease, therefore, to beguile thyself with hopes,
Which is no more than making sandy ropes,
And quit the vain pursuit of loud applause,
That must bewilder thee in faction's cause.
Pr'ythee what is't to thee who guides the state?
Why Dunkirk's demolition is so late?
Or why her majesty thinks fit to cease
The din of war, and hush the world to peace?
The clergy too, without thy aid, can tell
What texts to choose, and on what topics dwell;
And, uninstructed by thy babbling, teach
Their flocks celestial happiness to reach.
Rather let such poor souls as you and I,
Say that the holidays are drawing nigh,
And that to-morrow's sun begins the week,
Which will abound with store of ale and cake,
With hams of bacon, and with powder'd beef,
Stuff'd to give field-itinerants relief.

Then I, who have within these precincts kept,
And ne'er beyond the chimney-sweeper's stept,
Will take a loose, and venture to be seen,
Since 'twill be Sunday, upon Shanks's green;
There, with erected looks and phrase sublime,
To talk of unity of place and time,
And with much malice, mix'd with little satire,
Explode the wits on t'other side o' th' water

Why has my Lord Godolphin's special grace
Invested me with a queen's waiter's place,
If I, debarr'd of festival delights,
Am not allow'd to spend the perquisites?
He's but a short remove from being mad,
Who at a time of jubilee is sad,
And, like a griping usurer, does spare
His money to be squander'd by his heir;
Flutter'd away in liveries and in coaches,
And washy sorts of feminine debauches.
As for my part, whate'er the world may think,
I'll bid adieu to gravity, and drink;
And, though I can't put off a woful mien,
Will be all mirth and cheerfulness within:
As, in despight of a censorious race,
I most incontinently suck my face.
What mighty projects does not he design,
Whose stomach flows, and brain turns round with wine?
Wine, powerful wine, can thaw the frozen cit,
And fashion him to humour and to wit;
Makes even Somers to disclose his art
By racking every secret from his heart,
As he flings off the statesman's sly disguise,
To name the cuckold's wife with whom he lies.
Ev'n Sarum, when he quaffs it 'stead of tea,
Fancies himself in Canterbury's see,
And S****, when he has carousing reels,
Imagines that he has regain'd the seals:
W****, by virtue of his juice, can fight,
And Stanhope of commissioners make light.
Wine gives Lord Wingham aptitude of parts,
And swells him with his family's deserts:
Whom can it not make eloquent of speech;
Whom in extremest poverty not rich?
Since, by the means of the prevailing grape,
Th***n can Lechmere's warmth not only ape,

But, half seas o'er, by its inspiring bounties,
Can qualify himself in several counties.
What I have promised, thou may'st rest assured
Shall faithfully and gladly be procured.
Nay, I'm already better than my word,
New plates and knives adorn the jovial board:
And, lest you at their sight shouldst make wry faces
The girl has scour'd the pots, and wash'd the glasses
Ta'en care so excellently well to clean 'em,
That thou may'st see thine own dear picture in 'em.

Moreover, due provision has been made,
That conversation may not be betray'd;
I have no company but what is proper
To sit with the most flagrant Whig at supper.
There's not a man among them but must please,
Since they're as like each other as are pease.
Toland and Hare have jointly sent me word
They'll come; and Kennet thinks to make a third,
Provided he's no other invitation
From men of greater quality and station.
Room will for Oldmixon and J—s be left:
But their discourses smell so much of theft,
There would be no abiding in the room,
Should two such ignorant pretenders come.
However, by this trusty bearer write,
If I should any other scabs invite;
Though, if I may my serious judgment give,
I'm wholly for King Charles's number five:
That was the stint in which that monarch fix'd,
Who would not be with noisiness perplex'd:
And that, if thou'lt agree to think it best,
Shall be our tale of heads, without one other guest.

I've nothing more, now this is said, to say,
But to request thou'lt instantly away,
And leave the duties of thy present post,
To some well-skill'd retainer in a host:
Doubtless he'll carefully thy place supply,
And o'er his grace's horses have an eye.
While thou, who slunk thro' postern more than once,
Dost by that means avoid a crowd of duns,
And, crossing o'er the Thames at Temple Stairs,
Leav'st Phillips with good words to cheat their ears.

(pp. 175-79)

*[Jonathan Swift], "Dennis' Invitation to Steele,"
in his* The Poems of Jonathan Swift, Vol. II, *edited by William Ernst Browning, G. Bell and
Sons, Ltd., 1910, pp. 175-79.*

GILES JACOB (essay date 1719)

*[Jacob was an English man of letters who is best remem-
bered as a painstaking compiler of literary facts. His most
noted factual work is* The Poetical Register: or, The Lives
and Characters of the English Dramatic Poets *(1719), a
valuable source of biographical and theatrical information
for the seventeenth and eighteenth centuries. Many of the
nearly three hundred author sketches, updated and expanded by Jacob from Charles Gildon's* The Lives and Characters of the English Dramatick Poets *(1699), contain biographical material supplemented with critical discussions. In
the following excerpt from* The Poetical Register, *Jacob
characterizes Dennis's dramatic style.]*

Mr. *Dennis* is excellent at Pindarick Writings, perfectly
regular in all his Performances; and a Person of sound
Learning: And that he is Master of a great deal of Penetration and Judgment, his Criticisms, particularly on Sir
Richard Blackmore's Prince Arthur, sufficiently demonstrate. He has oblig'd the World with the following Plays.

I. *A Plot and no Plot*; a Comedy, acted at the Theatre Royal, 1697. Dedicated to the Right Honourable the Earl of *Sunderland*. This Play, I am inform'd, Mr. *Dennis* intended as a Satire upon the Credulity of the *Jacobite* Party at that Time; and, as a certain Author has observ'd, is exactly regular, and discovers it self to be written by a Master of the Art of the Stage, as well as by a Man of Wit.

II. *Rinaldo and Armida*; a Tragedy, acted at the Theatre in *Lincolns-Inn-Fields*, 1699. Dedicated to the Duke of *Ormond*.

III. *Iphigenia*; a Tragedy, acted at the Theatre in *Lincolns-Inn-Fields*, 1700.

IV. *Liberty Asserted*; a Tragedy, acted at the Theatre in *Lincolns-Inn-Fields*, by her Majesty's Servants, 1704. This Play is Dedicated to *Anthony Henley*, Esq; and was acted with very great Applause.

V. *Appius and Virginia*; a Tragedy, acted at the Theatre Royal; Dedicated to *Sidney* Earl of *Godolphin*.

VI. *The Comical Gallant; With the Humours of Sir John Falstaff*; a Comedy. Being an Alteration of *Shakespear's Merry Wives of Windsor*.

This Gentleman, in his Comedy, hath shewn a great deal of Justness, and Delicacy of Reflection, a Pleasantness of Humour, a Novelty and Distinction of Characters, an admirable Conduct and Design, and a useful Moral. When he first began to write Tragedy, he saw, with Concern, that Love had got the entire possession of the Tragick Stage, contrary to the Nature and Design of Tragedy, the Practice of *Sopbocles, Euripides,* and our Countryman *Shakespear*. As his Intentions were more to get Reputation than Money, and to gain the Approbation of the Judicious and Knowing (which he look'd upon as a certain Earnest of future Fame) rather than of a Crowd of ignorant Spectators and Readers; he resolv'd to deviate a little from the reigning Practice of the Stage; and not to make his Heroes whining Slaves in their Amours; which not only debases the Majesty of Tragedy, but confounds most of its principal Characters, by making that Passion the predominant Quality in all; and which must for ever make the present and succeeding Writers unable to attain to the Excellency of the Ancients: But he did not think it adviseable at once to shew his principal Characters wholly exempt from it, apprehending that so great and sudden an Alteration might prove disagreeable; he rather chose to steer a middle Course, and to make Love appear violent, but at the same time to give way to the force of Reason, or to the influence of some other more noble Passion; as in *Rinaldo*, it gives place to Glory; in *Iphigenia*, to Friendship; and in *Liberty Asserted,* to the publick Good. He thought by these means an Audience might be entertain'd and prepar'd for greater Alterations, whereby the Dignity of Tragedy might be supported, and its principal Characters justly distinguish'd. (pp. 68-9)

> Giles Jacob, "Mr. John Dennis," in his *The Poetical Register: or, The Lives and Characters of the English Dramatic Poets, 1719. Reprint by Garland Publishing, Inc., 1970, pp. 67-70.*

[AARON HILL] (essay date 1725)

[*Hill was an English dramatist, theater manager, and poet who helped initiate both* The Plain Dealer *(1724-25), a serial comprised of essays on literature and social matters, and the bi-weekly theatrical journal* The Prompter *(1734-36). One of a dwindling number of supporters throughout Dennis's decline in popularity, Hill repeatedly defended his old friend. In the following excerpt from* The Plain Dealer, *Hill praises the benefit performance of William Congreve's* The Old Batchelor *for the poverty-stricken critic, condemning all who maligned Dennis.*]

I was delighted, the other Day, with the Praises, in which I heard it told, at an *Assembly*, That the *Old Batchelor* is, by this Gentleman's Voluntary Offer, to be acted next *Monday*, at the *Theatre*, in *Lincoln's Inn Fields*, for the Benefit of so Learned a Benefactor to the Stage, as *Mr. Dennis*.

Upon my expressing some Concern, That it was not rather a Play, of Mr. *Dennis's* own Writing, I was inform'd, that the Master of that *Theatre*, who fought all Opportunities of shewing his Esteem of so *Excellent*, and so *Injur'd*, a Judge of Wit, and Learning, had left the Choice of the Play to Mr. *Dennis himself*; who had pitch'd upon the above-mention'd, because it was a Work of his old Friend Mr. *Congreve*.—I acknowledg'd the *Generosity* of the Master of the *Theatre*, and the *Modesty* of the *Gentleman*, whom he treats with so well-judg'd a Humanity: But I cou'd not avoid indulging a Fit of talkative *Spleen*, against that *Malice*, or *Ignorance*, which has, more than once, appear'd, in the Discountenance of some Writings, from which the *Name* of Mr. *Dennis*, will, long, continue to receive Honour, after his *Body* shall be Dust and Ashes!

The Stupidity, which follows *Prejudice*, has made Thousands of his Contemporaries insensible of his Great Merit, which, if they allow'd their Reason to examine it, they wou'd be *charm'd by*, and take a *Pride* to *encourage*.—The Terror with which young Writers have accustom'd themselves to hear, and to talk of, his *Austerity*, and of his Aversion against *Scriblers*, has spread abroad a false Opinion, that he is *Ill-natur'd*, where he is only *impartial*: And, that he is an Enemy to *Wit*, and *Learning*, while he is only such to the *Prophaners* of them.

It is pleasant to observe, to what a whimsical Degree this *Dread* of *Criticks* has been propagated; and how far down, into Low Life, we may trace the Effects of our Poet's mistaken Outcries, who, by giving their *Shepherds* the Name of *Wolves*, have taught the Clowns to set their Dogs upon 'em, and cut off the Defence of their own fold. (pp. 1-2)

> *[Aaron Hill], in an excerpt in* The Plain Dealer, *No. LXXXII, January 1, 1725, pp. 1-2.*

[AARON HILL] (poem date 1734)

[*In the following excerpt from an elegy that appeared in the* Gentleman's Magazine *soon after Dennis's death in 1734, Hill anticipates a resurgence of the critic's popularity and the eventual recognition of his literary genius.*]

Adieu, *unsocial* Excellence!—at last,
Thy foes are vanquish'd and thy fears are past!
Want the grim recompence of truth like thine,
Shall now no longer *dim* thy destin'd shine:

Th' impatient envy, the disdainful air,
The front malignant, and the captious slare!
The furious petulance, the jealous start;
The *mist* of frailties, that obscur'd thy heart!
Veil'd in thy *grave*, shall, unremember'd lye;—
For, *these* were parts, of *Dennis*, born to die!

But, there's a *nobler Seity*, behind;
His *reason* dies not: and has *friends*, to *find*.
Tho' *here*, revenge, and pride withheld his praise,
No wrongs shall reach him thro' his *future days*.
The rising ages shall redeem his name;
And nations *read* him, into lasting fame.
In his *defects* untaught, his labour'd page
Shall the slow gratitude of *time* engage.—
Perhaps, some story, of his *pitied woe*,
Mix'd in faint shades, may with his mem'ry go!
To touch futurity, with gen'rous shame,
And backward cast an unavailing blame
On times, too cold, to taste his *strength* of art;
Yet, warm contemners, of too *weak* a *heart*!

Rest in thy dust,—contented with thy lot;
Thy *good* remember'd, and thy *bad* forgot!
'Tis more, than *Cæsar*, and his *world*, cou'd give!—
Spread, o'er *his* virtues, his *few errors* live!
'Till *reas'ning brutes*, whose speck of soul wants room,
To *lodge*, the just *conception* of his doom,
Dare, with lewd license *poize* his *question'd* fame;
And *blot* the *sacred Rev'rence* of his name!

> *[Aaron Hill], "Verses, on the Death of Mr. Dennis," in* The Gentleman's Magazine; or, Monthly Intelligencer, *Vol. IV, No. XXXVII, January, 1734, p. 42*

[AARON HILL] (poem date 1735)

[*In the following excerpt from the* Prompter, *Hill imagines how Dennis might have responded to the anonymous author of the 1734 biography* The Life of Mr. John Dennis.]

By Want made peevish, and provok'd by Scorn,
By Spleen distemper'd, and by Passion torn,
Half my sad Life I pass'd, 'twixt Rage, and Pain,
'Till slighted Judgment took an envious Stain.

For this, of late, when Age dismiss'd my Breath,
My hov'ring Spirit forc'd a Pause, in Death:
With strong Reluctance shunn'd, the opening WAY;
And cast repentant Longings back at Day:
Fill'd with your Friendship, by your Pity charm'd,
And Life's last Moments by your Comfort warm'd,
Fast clung my Mind to the departing View;
And made no Haste, to HEAV'N,—*with-held, by You.*

But—e're my Soul, quite lost to worldly Care,
Flow'd formless—and dissolv'd itself, in Air;
Your LIFE OF DENNIS *shook th' unbodied Frame,*
Absolv'd my Malice past, and freed my Name.—
Come, cry'd a Cherub, with a smiling Brow,—
Such is the World thou leav'st!—Thou KNOW'ST
him, NOW!
Pride is his Pity—Artifice his Praise;
A Masque his Virtue; and His Fame a Blaze;
Insult his Charity—His Friendship FEAR;
And nothing, but his VANITY, *sincere.*

> *[Aaron Hill], "An Epistle, from Mr. Dennis's Ghost, to the Author of His Life," in* The Prompter, *No. XLVIII, April 25, 1735.*

THEOPHILUS CIBBER (essay date 1753)

[*Cibber was the son of the English actor and dramatist Colley Cibber and an actor and playwright himself. He was best known for his comedies and farces and for his revision of Shakespeare's* Henry VI. *In the following excerpt from* The Lives of the Poets of Great Britain and Ireland *(1753), he appraises Dennis's poetry.*]

[Dennis's] poem on the Battle of Ramellies ["**The Battle of Ramilla; or, The Power of Union**"], is a cold unspirited performance; it has neither fire, nor elevation, and is the true poetical sister of another poem of his, on the Battle of Blenheim ["**Brittania Triumphans**"], addressed to Queen Anne, and for which the duke of Marlborough rewarded him, says Mr. Coxeter, with a present of a hundred guineas. In these poems he has introduced a kind of machinery; good and bad angels interest themselves in the action, and his hero, the duke of Marlborough, enjoys a large share of the cœlestial protection.

Mr. Dennis had once contracted a friendship with Sir Richard Steele, whom he afterwards severely attacked. Sir Richard had promised that he would take some opportunity of mentioning his works in public with advantage, and endeavour to raise his reputation. When Sir Richard engaged in a periodical paper, there was a fair occasion of doing it, and accordingly in one of his Spectators he quotes the following couplet, which he is pleased to call humorous, but which however is a translation from Boileau.

> One fool lolls his tongue out at another,
> And shakes his empty noddle at his brother.

The citation of this couplet Mr. Dennis imagined, was rather meant to affront him, than pay a compliment to his genius, as he could discover nothing excellent in the lines, and if there was, they being only a translation, in some measure abated the merit of them. Being fired with resentment at this affront, he immediately, in a spirit of fury, wrote a letter to the *Spectator*, in which he treated him with very little ceremony, and informed him, that if he had been sincere in paying a compliment to him, he should have chosen a quotation from his poem on the Battle of Ramellies; he then points out a particular passage, of which he himself had a very high opinion, and which we shall here insert as a specimen of that performance.

A cœlestial spirit visits the duke of Marlborough the night before the battle, and after he has said several other things to him, goes on thus,

> A wondrous victory attends thy arms,
> Great in itself, and in its sequel vast;
> Whose ecchoing sound thro' all the West shall run,
> Transporting the glad nations all around,
> Who oft shall doubt, and oft suspend their joy,
> And oft imagine all an empty dream;
> The conqueror himself shall cry amaz'd,
> 'Tis not our work, alas we did it not;
> The hand of GOD, the hand of GOD is here!
> For thee, so great shall be thy high renown,
> That fame shall think no music like thy name;
> Around the circling globe it shall be spread,
> And to the world's last ages shall endure;
> And the most lofty, most aspiring man,
> Shall want th' affarance in his secret prayers
> To ask such high felicity and fame,
> As Heav'n has freely granted thee; yet this

That seems so great, so glorious to thee now,
Would look how low, how vile to thy great mind,
If I could set before th' astonish'd eyes,
Th' excess of glory, and th' excess of bliss
That is prepar'd for thy expiring soul,
When thou arriv'st at everlasting day.

The quotation by Mr. Dennis is longer, but we are persuaded the reader will not be displeased that we do not take the trouble to transcribe the whole, as it does not improve, but rather grows more languid. How strangely are people deceived in their own productions! In the language of sincerity we cannot discover a poetical conception, one striking image, or one animated line in the above, and yet Mr. Dennis observes to Sir Richard Steele, that these are the lines, by quoting which, he would really have done him honour. (pp. 217-19)

Mr. Dennis was less happy in his temper, than his genius; he possessed no inconsiderable erudition, which was joined to such natural parts, as if accompanied with prudence, or politeness, might have raised him, not only above want, but even to eminence. He was happy too in having very powerful patrons, but what could be done for a man, who declared war against all the world? Dennis has given evidence against himself in the article of politeness; for in one of his letters he says, he would not retire to a certain place in the country, lest he should be disturbed in his studies by the ladies in the house: for, says he, I am not over-fond of the conversation of women. But with all his foibles, we cannot but consider him as a good critic, and a man of genius.

His perpetual misfortune was, that he aimed at the empire of wit, for which nature had not sufficiently endowed him; and as his ambition prompted him to obtain the crown by a furious opposition to all other competitors, so, like Cæsar of old, his ambition overwhelmed him. (p. 238)

Theophilus Cibber, "Mr. John Dennis," in his The Lives of the Poets of Great Britain and Ireland, *Vol. IV, 1753. Reprint Georg Olms Verlagsbuchhandlung, 1968, pp. 215-38.*

DAVID ERSKINE BAKER (essay date 1764)

[*In the following excerpt from* Biographia Dramatica; or, A Companion to the Playhouse, *first written and compiled by David Erskine Baker in 1764 and continued to the year 1782 by Isaac Reed and 1811 by Stephen Jones, Dennis is assessed as a critic and dramatic author.*]

This gentleman [John Dennis], who though he has left many dramatic pieces behind him, was much less celebrated for them than for his critical writings. . . . (p. 183)

As a writer, he certainly was possessed of much erudition, and a considerable share of genius; and had not his self-opinion, of which perhaps no man ever possessed a larger share, induced him to aim at the empire of wit, for which he was by no means qualified, and in consequence thereof led him to treat every one as a rebel who did not subscribe to his pretended right, he would probably have been allowed, and, from the enjoyment of an easy mind, possibly possessed more merit than appears in many of his writings. In prose, he is far from a bad writer, where abuse and personal scurrility does not mingle itself with his language. In verse, he is extremely unequal, his numbers being at some times spirited and harmonious, and his subjects elevated and judicious, and at others flat, harsh, and puerile. As a dramatic author, he certainly deserves not to be held in any consideration. His plots, excepting that of his *Plot and no Plot,* which is a political play, are all borrowed, yet in the general not ill-chosen. But his characters are ill-designed and unfinished, his language prosaical, flat, and undramatic, and the conduct of his principal scenes heavy, dull, and unimpassioned. In short, though he certainly had judgment, it is evident he had no execution; and so much better a critic is he than a dramatist, that we cannot help subscribing to the opinion of a gentleman, who said of him, that he was the most complete instructor for a dramatic poet; since he could teach him to distinguish *good* plays by his *precepts,* and *bad* ones by his *examples.* (p. 185)

David Erskine Baker, in an excerpt in Biographia Dramatica; or, a Companion to the Playhouse, *Vol. I, David Erskine Baker, Isaac Reed, Stephen Jones, eds., Longman and others, 1812, pp. 183-85.*

ANDREW KIPPIS (essay date 1793)

[*Kippis was a British clergyman, essayist, and editor best known for his five-volume revision of* Biographia Britannica *(1778-93). In the following excerpt from this work, he ranks Dennis as a poet, political writer, and critic.*]

It is as a Poet that we shall first consider [John Dennis], taking his poems in the order in which they are printed in his select works, published by him, in two volumes, in the year 1721. The collection begins with some verses on the victory at sea, and the burning of the French fleet at La Hogue, in 1692; with regard to which we can only say, that their chief character is Turgidity. The paraphrase of part of the "Te Deum," in Pindaric verse, is of superior merit, though not entitled to any very high degree of praise. One of the best stanzas is the fifth, and there are some good lines in the sixth. The short Ode to Mr. Dryden, upon his translation of the Third Book of Virgil's *Georgics* . . . [exhibits] the most favourable specimen we could perhaps have selected of Mr. Dennis's poetical talents. Indeed, it stands upon a footing with many of the pieces which occur in the works of several of the minor poets, who have been allowed a place in Johnson's Collection. We cannot speak so well of the next poem; which, according to the fashion of the times, is likewise a Pindaric Ode, addressed to King William, and occasioned by the battle of Aghrim, in 1691. There is poetic spirit in the twelfth stanza; but the rest is partly turgid, and partly heavy. (p. 100)

The prayer for the King's safety in the summer-expedition of 1692, which . . . is called an epigram, is totally destitute of the point that constitutes epigrammatic beauty. This is succeeded by another Pindaric poem, dedicated to the memory of Queen Mary. The title of it is, "The Court of Death;" and Mr. Dennis evidently aims in it at rising to something great, but has not succeeded in his attempt, having mistaken the bombastic for the true sublime. The seventh stanza is remarkably turgid; and, at the same time, not very intelligible. In the conclusion our author has succeeded better than in the beginning; but, upon the whole, the poem is too long, and too tedious, to be read with much satisfaction. Passing over the **"Passion of Byblis,"** not ill translated from the Ninth Book of Ovid's *Metamorphosis*, though with some irregularity of versification, we come to **"The Monument: a Poem, sacred to the immortal Memory of the best and greatest of Kings, William the Third."** Of this performance the chief characteristics are undue length, extravagant panegyric, and prosaic composition. It is written in blank verse; but with little of that variety and harmony of which Milton hath given so beautiful an example. In fact, such blank verse as that of Dennis's is of very easy fabrication. The next production, which is entituled, **"Britannia Triumphans, or a Poem on the Battle of Blenheim,"** is not altogether so tedious as the former; but its faults are more distinguishable than its excellencies. The blank verse in which it is written has the same defects we have just mentioned; many passages are extremely turgid; and every Reader will complain that the work is too long. One thing observeable in it, to the honour of the author, is the piety which he expresses through the whole, and from which it is apparent, that he had a great reverence for Religion. How good an opinion he had of the future celebrity of his performance, is evident from his dedicating it to Queen Anne, that it might live with the immortality of her renown. Another exertion of Mr. Dennis's poetical talents was occasioned by the battle of Ramilies [**"The Battle of (Ramilla: or, The Power of Union"**], which he has celebrated at a very great length, in five books, composed likewise in blank verse. Our author, in his dedication of this performance to Lord Halifax, calls it one of the boldest poems that has been written for several years; an assertion that is undoubtedly founded on the machinery with which it abounds, and which seems to have been partly borrowed from Milton, though by no means conducted with a skill and judgment that demand approbation. In consequence, however, of this machinery, the work, though faulty enough in various respects, does not appear so tedious in the perusal as most of the productions already mentioned. The two remaining poems, which are on the Accession of King George to the British throne [**"A Poem upon the Death of Her Late Sacred Majesty Queen Anne, and the Most Happy and Most Auspicious Accession of his Sacred Majesty King George"**], and a prologue to the subscribers for *Julius Cæsar*, are unworthy of particular notice.

From the account we have given of Mr. Dennis's *Miscellaneous Poetry*, few of our Readers will be disposed to make it the object of their attention. Independently of its other deficiencies, the subjects to which it was devoted were not calculated to confer upon it any lasting degree of popularity. Political, and especially panegyrical poems (and such for the most part were our author's), are only fitted to excite a temporary admiration. The virtues of a William and Mary, and the actions of a Marlborough, undoubtedly deserved to be celebrated. But it was in or near their own time chiefly that their applauses would be heard with peculiar delight; nor can it be expected that posterity should be captivated with the productions, which, in the enthusiasm of the moment, were eagerly read and highly praised. Addison's "Campaign" was received with transport by our ancestors; but fastidious criticism is now disposed to give it the appellation of a Gazette in rhyme. (p. 101)

On Mr. Dennis's character as a political writer it is not necessary to enlarge. It is probable that, in this capacity, he may have been the author of several tracts, which are now forgotten, and with regard to which there would be no utility in endeavouring to rescue them from oblivion. In his select works are inserted the productions of this kind which he himself thought of the most consequence, and the most worthy of preservation; and of these we shall take some slight notice. The first of them was published in 1702, and is an answer to a discourse of the famous, or rather infamous, Henry Sacheverell, called, "*The Political Union.*" Mr. Dennis's piece is entituled, ***Priestcraft Dangerous to Religion and Government;*** and is a candid and moderate defence of Low-church principles and of toleration. (p. 106)

Mr. Dennis, in 1711, produced ***An Essay upon Public Spirit; being a Satire, in Prose, upon the Manners and Luxury of the Times, the chief Sources of our present Parties and Divisions***. The definition given of public Spirit is, that it is "the ardent love of one's country, affecting us with a zealous concern for its honour and interest, and inspiring us with resolution and courage to promote its service and glory." Our Author has justly called his essay a satire in prose; for it is a violent and not very judicious declamation against the vices of his own age, in contrast with the virtues of our remote ancestors. It is pleasant to observe with what zeal he expresses himself in praise of frugality and œconomy, to which he paid so little regard in his own person. We think, however, that we discover in his tract the signatures of upright and benevolent intention, though mixed with too much severity.

The last production of Mr. Dennis's, which we have to mention under the present department of our article, appeared in the beginning of King George the First's reign, and is entituled, ***Priestcraft distinguished from Christianity***. This, perhaps, may rather be considered as a theological than a political work. Our Author displays in it a very considerable knowledge of Divinity, as it was then explained, and as it still continues to be understood by the majority of believers. His views of the general nature and design of Christianity are rational and manly. (pp. 106-07)

We are now to consider Mr. Dennis in his critical capacity, in which he so frequently exerted himself, that he came to be called the Critic, by way of distinction. For sustaining this character he was well qualified by his Knowledge, Learning, and Judgment. He maintained it, likewise, with considerable reputation for some time; but the misfortune was, that, at length, he displayed his talents in this view with so much severity (we had almost said malignity), and against men of such eminence and superiority, that they succeeded in reducing him to a low degree of estimation with the publick. It was early that our Author began to shew his critical abilities. The first public proof of them of which we have any information, was exhibited in his ***Observations on Blackmore's "Prince Arthur"***; the third edition of which poem was printed in 1696. Mr. Dennis had here, without doubt, sufficient scope for a variety of strictures; but what was particularly advanced by him we are not able to say, as both the poem and the criticism are now buried in oblivion. That he did not transgress the bounds of good manners in his remarks, is probable from his afterwards corresponding with Sir Richard Blackmore on very friendly terms. (p. 107)

In 1706, our Author published ***An Essay on the Operas, after the Italian manner, which are about to be established on the English Stage: with some Reflections on the Damage*** *which they may bring to the Public.* Mr. Cibber asserts, that Mr. Dennis, in this Essay, has shewn, with an irresistible force, the extreme danger that a generous nation is exposed to, by too much indulging effeminate music [see excerpt dated 1753]. Undoubtedly, he has advanced many strong and important sentiments upon the subject; but, on the whole, he has, in our opinion, carried the matter too far. His violent declamation against operas and music is not sufficiently justified by reason and experience. Such declamation was partly the fashion of the most eminent writers of the time; and they had some cause for resentment, in the cold reception that had been given to more valuable and manly performances. Our Author declares, however, in his preface, that his Treatise is only levelled against those operas which are entirely musical; since those which are dramatical may be partly defended by the examples of the ancients. In the postscript, he celebrates, with great exultation, and in the highest strains of panegyric, the conduct of a young lady of the first quality, equally famous for her beauty, her spirit, and her virtue, who, to the glory of her own sex, and the shame of ours, had lately given very strict orders, that the *Julius Cæsar* of Shakspeare, which was acted at her request, should be done without any performance either of singing or dancing. This Lady appears to have been one of the daughters of the Duke of Marlborough.

Another of Mr. Dennis's critical publications, the exact time of the first edition of which we are not able to ascertain, but which is preserved in his *Select Works*, was, *The Grounds of Criticism in Poetry*. This tract is evidently a prosecution of the sentiments which he had maintained in his *Advancement and Reformation of modern Poetry*, and is entitled to considerable praise in the same view. The grand point he insists upon is the immense scope which Religion affords for poetic excellence. Under the word Religion he includes the whole system of supernatural machinery, the introduction of superior beings, and all the noble fictions, sentiments, addresses, and images, that may be derived from the knowledge of Revelation. That poets may hence be enabled to enrich their compositions in a very high degree, and that the descriptions of the Deity which are given in the Sacred Writings may be of peculiar advantage to them, cannot justly be denied. Epic poetry, unless it looks beyond the present world, and the mere scenes of human affairs, can never support its true dignity.

In the beginning of the year 1711, our Author produced another tract, which added farther to his reputation—as a judicious critic; we mean, his three *Letters on the Genius and Writings of Shakspeare*. In these letters he has drawn the poetical character of our immortal Dramatist with sagacity and judgment; and, in treating upon his learning, he has strongly supported the same opinion which hath since so ably, and still more decisively, been maintained by Dr. Farmer.

Thus far Mr. Dennis pursued his critical enquiries, without giving any peculiar offence. He might, indeed, occasionally deliver with freedom his sentiments concerning the writings of his contemporaries, and in some few instances might express himself with severity. But still he did not run into such excesses as to get involved in any material personal controversy. In the works already mentioned, the attack upon Mr. Collier excepted, he has stated his opinions with moderation and candour. (pp. 107-08)

The character of Mr. Dennis must, in general, be sufficiently apparent from what has already been said. Illnature has been ascribed to him with too much shew of reason; though perhaps it belonged to him more as a writer than as a man. In a letter to a friend he has endeavoured to vindicate himself from the charge; but not, we think, with entire success. This at least is certain, from several transactions, that he was very irritable in his temper. On the whole, however, there seems to be no room to doubt of his having been a person of integrity and virtue. Till he was five-and forty, he was intimately conversant with the first men of the age, both with respect to rank and abilities; and when he retired from the world, he continued to preserve some honourable connections. Such was the estimation he was held in, that he experienced the patronage of gentlemen whose political principles were extremely different from those which he always openly avowed. . . .

In the *Gentleman's Magazine* for January, 1734, some verses were inserted on the death of Mr. Dennis, in which a longer duration is promised to his reputation and his works than they will probably ever attain [see excerpt dated 1734]. (p. 114)

> *Andrew Kippis, in an excerpt in* Biographia Britannica: or, The Lives of the Most Eminent Persons Who Have Flourished in Great-Britain and Ireland, Vol. V, *edited by Andrew Kippis, second edition, 1793. Reprint by Georg Olms Verlag, 1974, pp. 99-114.*

ROBERT SOUTHEY (essay date 1807)

[*A late eighteenth- and early nineteenth-century English man of letters, Southey was a key member of the so-called Lake School of poetry, a group that included the celebrated authors William Wordsworth and Samuel Taylor Coleridge. Southey's poetry consists mainly of short verse, ballads, and epics, many of which are notable for their novel versification and meter. His prose writings—which are generally more highly praised than his poetry—include ambitious histories, biographies, and conservative social commentaries. Today Southey is primarily remembered as a conservative theorist and as the biographer of such figures as Horatio Nelson, Thomas More, and John Wesley. In the following prefatory note to a reprint of "Upon our Victory at Sea," Southey endorses Dennis's critical writings.*]

To collect the many excellent anecdotes, and to appreciate fully the merits of this remarkable man [John Dennis], would require more space than here can be allotted. An unhappy temper once hurried him to attempt murder, and the same malady provoked and exposed him to the ridicule of his contemporary wits and witlings. His critical Works should be collected. (p. 306)

> *Robert Southey, "John Dennis," in his* Specimens of the Later English Poets, Vol. I, *Longman, Hurst, Rees and Orme, 1807, pp. 306-11.*

ISAAC D'ISRAELI (essay date 1812)

[*Although probably most famous as the father of novelist and British prime minister Benjamin Disraeli, Isaac D'Israeli (also spelled Disraeli), was an essayist who wrote important works on eighteenth-century literature. His criticism is considered of particular value because of his access to source material now lost. In the following excerpt from an essay originally published in the 1812 study* Calamaties of Authors, *D'Israeli recommends the study of Dennis's works as "examples of the manner of a true mechanical critic."*]

Unfriendly to the literary character, some have imputed the brutality of certain authors to their literary habits, when it may be more truly said that they derived their literature from their brutality. (p. 51)

Dennis attained to the ambiguous honour of being distinguished as "The Critic," and he may yet instruct us how the moral influences the literary character, and how a certain talent that can never mature itself into genius, like the pale fruit that hangs in the shade, ripens only into sourness.

As a critic in his own day, party for some time kept him alive; the art of criticism was a novelty at that period of our literature. He flattered some great men, and he abused three of the greatest; this was one mode of securing popularity; because, by this contrivance, he divided the town into two parties; and the irascibility and satire of Pope and Swift were not less serviceable to him than the partial panegyrics of Dryden and Congreve. Johnson revived him, for his minute attack on Addison; and Kippis, feebly voluminous, and with the cold affectation of candour, allows him to occupy a place in our literary history too large in the eye of Truth and Taste [see excerpt dated 1793].

Let us say all the good we can of him, that we may not be interrupted in a more important inquiry. Dennis once urged fair pretensions to the office of critic. Some of his *Original Letters*, and particularly the *Remarks on "Prince Arthur,"* written in his vigour, attain even to classical criticism. Aristotle and Bossu lay open before him, and he developes and sometimes illustrates their principles with close reasoning. Passion had not yet blinded the young critic with rage; and in that happy moment, Virgil occupied his attention even more than Blackmore.

The prominent feature in his literary character was good sense; but in literature, though not in life, good sense is a penurious virtue. Dennis could not be carried beyond the cold line of a precedent, and before he ventured to be pleased, he was compelled to look into Aristotle. His learning was the bigotry of literature. It was ever Aristotle explained by Dennis. But in the explanation of the obscure text of his master, he was led into such frivolous distinctions, and tasteless propositions, that his works deserve inspection, as examples of the manner of a true mechanical critic.

This blunted feeling of the mechanical critic was at first concealed from the world in the pomp of critical erudition; but when he trusted to himself, and, destitute of taste and imagination, became a poet and a dramatist, the secret of the Royal Midas was revealed. As his evil temper prevailed, he forgot his learning, and lost the moderate sense which he seemed once to have possessed. Rage, malice, and dulness, were the heavy residuum; and now he much resembled that congenial soul whom the ever-witty South compared to the tailor's goose, which is at once hot and heavy. (pp. 51-3)

In life and in literature we meet with men who seem endowed with an obliquity of understanding, yet active and busy spirits; but, as activity is only valuable in proportion to the capacity that puts all in motion, so, when ill directed, the intellect, warped by nature, only becomes more crooked and fantastical. A kind of frantic enthusiasm breaks forth in their actions and their language, and often they seem ferocious when they are only foolish. We may thus account for the manners and style of Dennis, pushed almost to the verge of insanity, and acting on him very much like insanity itself—a circumstance which the quick vengeance of wit seized on, in the humorous *Narrative of Dr. Robert Norris, concerning the Frenzy of Mr. John Dennis, an officer of the Custom-house* [see excerpt dated 1713].

It is curious to observe that Dennis, in the definition of genius, describes himself; he says—"Genius is caused by a *furious joy* and *pride of soul* on the conception of an extraordinary hint. Many men have their *hints* without their motions of *fury and pride of soul*, because they want fire enough to agitate their spirits; and these we call cold writers. Others, who have a great deal of fire, but have not excellent organs, feel the fore-mentioned *motions*, without the extraordinary *hints*, and these we call fustian writers." His *motions* and his *hints*, as he describes them, in regard to cold or fustian writers, seem to include the extreme points of his own genius.

Another feature strongly marks the race of the Dennises. With a half-consciousness of deficient genius, they usually idolize some chimera, by adopting some extravagant principle; and they consider themselves as original when they are only absurd.

Dennis had ever some misshapen idol of the mind, which he was perpetually caressing with the zeal of perverted judgment or monstrous taste. Once his frenzy ran against the Italian Opera; and in his *Essay on Public Spirit*, he ascribes its decline to its unmanly warblings. I have seen a long letter by Dennis to the Earl of Oxford, written to congratulate his lordship on his accession to power, and the high hopes of the nation; but the greater part of the letter runs on the Italian Opera, while Dennis instructs the Minister that the national prosperity can never be effected while this general corruption of the three kingdoms lies open! (pp. 56-7)

It was not literature, then, that made the mind coarse, brutalising the habits and inflaming the style of Dennis. He had thrown himself among the walks of genius, and aspired to fix himself on a throne to which Nature had refused him a legitimate claim. (p. 58)

> *Isaac D'Israeli, "Influence of a Bad Temper in Criticism," in his* Calamities and Quarrels of Authors, *edited by the Earl of Beaconsfield, Frederick Warne and Co., 1881, pp. 51-8.*

THE MONTHLY MAGAZINE (essay date 1817)

[*In the following excerpt, the anonymous critic reviews the previously unpublished* Causes of the Decay and Defects of Dramatick Poetry, and of the Degeneracy of the Publick Taste].

Our readers will perceive that this Essay [*The Causes of the Decay and Defects of Dramatick Poetry, and of the Degeneracy of the Publick Taste*], has great merit as a composition, over and above its claim to their notice as an unpublished production. The merit of Mr. Dennis was acknowledged even by Pope, notwithstanding he treated him with so much insolence in the *Dunciad*, and many persons have ranked him among the best writers of his age. This Essay recommends itself, moreover, by its references to persons and events now almost forgotten. (p. 425)

"Memoirs and Remains of Eminent Persons," in The Monthly Magazine, *London, Vol. XLIII, No. 298, June 1, 1817, pp. 421-25.*

[SIR T. NOON TALFOURD] (essay date 1820)

[*Talfourd was a noted English literary critic, editor, poet, and dramatist. In the following excerpt from the* Retrospective Review, *he compares Dennis's adaptation of Shakespeare's* Coriolanus *(1623),* The Invader of His Country, *with the original.*]

John Dennis, the terror or the scorn of that age, which is sometimes strangely honored with the title of Augustan, has attained a lasting notoriety, to which the reviewers of our times can scarcely aspire. His name is immortalized in the *Dunciad*; his best essay is preserved in Johnson's *Lives of the Poets*; and his works yet keep their state in two substantial volumes, which are now before us. But the interest of the most poignant abuse and the severest criticism quickly perishes. We contemplate the sarcasms and the invectives which once stung into rage the irritable generation of poets, with as cold a curiosity as we look on the rusty javelins or stuffed reptiles in the glass cases of the curious. The works of Dennis will, however, assist us in forming a judgment of the criticism of his age, as compared with that of our own, and will afford us an opportunity of investigating the influences of that popular art, on literature and on the affections.

But we must not forget, that Mr. Dennis laid claims to public esteem, not only as a critic, but as a wit, a politician, and a poet. In the first and the last of these characters, he can receive but little praise. His attempts at gaiety and humour are weighty and awkward, almost without example. His poetry can only be described by negatives; it is not inharmonious, nor irregular, nor often turgid—for the author, too nice to sink into the mean, and too timid to rise into the bombastic, dwells in elaborate "decencies for ever." The climax of his admiration for Queen Mary— "Mankind extols the king—the king admires the queen"— will give a fair specimen of his architectural eulogies. He is entitled to more respect as an honest patriot. . . . He admired Shakespear, after the fashion of his age, as a wild irregular genius, who would have been ten times as great, had he known and copied the ancients. The following is a part of his general criticism on this subject, and is a very fair specimen of his best style:

Shakespear was one of the greatest geniuses that the world e'er saw for the tragick stage. Tho' he lay under greater disadvantages than any of his successors, yet had he greater and more genuine beauties than the best and greatest of them. And what makes the brightest glory of his character, those beauties were entirely his own, and owing to the force of his own nature; whereas his faults were owing to his education, and to the age that he lived in. (pp. 305-06)

Mr. Dennis proceeds very generously to apologize for Shakespear's faults, by observing, that he had neither friends to consult, nor time to make corrections. He, also, attributes his lines "utterly void of celestial fire," and passages "harsh and unmusical," to the want of opportunity to wait for felicitous hours and moments of choicest inspiration. To remedy these defects—to mend the harmony and to put life into the dulness of Shakespear—Mr. Dennis has essayed, and brought his own genius to the alteration of *Coriolanus* for the stage, under the lofty title of **The Invader of his Country, or the Fatal Resentment**. In the catastrophe, Coriolanus kills Aufidius, and is himself afterwards slain, to satisfy the requisitions of poetical justice; which, to Mr. Dennis's great distress, Shakespear so often violates. It is quite amusing to observe, with how perverted an ingenuity all the gaps in Shakespear's verses are filled up, the irregularities smoothed away, and the colloquial expressions changed for stately phrases. Thus, for example, the noble wish of Coriolanus on entering the forum—

The honoured gods
Keep Rome in safety, and the chairs of justice
Supplied with worthy men! plant love among us!
Throng our large temples with the shows of peace,
And not our streets with war—

is thus elegantly translated into classical language:

The great and tutelary gods of Rome
Keep Rome in safety, and the chairs of justice
Supplied with worthy men: plant love among you:
Adorn your temples with the pomp of peace,
And, from our streets, drive horrid war away.

The conclusion of the hero's last speech on leaving Rome—

Thus I turn my back: there is a world elsewhere,

is elevated into the following heroic lines:

For me, thus, thus, I turn my back upon you,
And make a better world where'er I go.

His fond expression of constancy to his wife—

That kiss
I carried from thee, *dear*; and my true lip
Hath virgined it e'er since,—

is thus refined:

That kiss
I carried from *my love*, and my true lip
Hath ever since preserved it like a virgin.

The icicle, which was wont to "hang on Dian's temple," here more gracefully "hangs upon the temple of Diana." The burst of mingled pride, and triumph of Coriolanus, when taunted with the word "boy," is here exalted to tragic dignity. Our readers have, doubtless, ignorantly admired the original:

Boy! False hound!
If you have writ your annals true, 'tis there,
That, like an eagle in a dove cote, I
Fluttered your Volsces in Corioli.
Alone I did it—Boy!

The following is the improved version:

This boy, that, like an eagle in a dove cote,

Flutter'd a thousand Volsces in Corioli,
And did it without second or acquittance,
Thus sends their mighty chief to mourn in hell!

Who does not now appreciate the sad lot of Shakespear—so feelingly bewailed by Mr. Dennis—that he had not a critic, of the age of King William, by his side, to refine his style and elevate his conceptions?

It is edifying to observe, how the canons of Mr. Dennis's criticism, which he regarded as the imperishable laws of genius, are now either exploded, or considered as matters of subordinate importance, wholly unaffecting the inward soul of poetry. (pp. 307-09)

> *[Sir T. Noon Talfourd], "John Dennis's Works,"
> in* The Retrospective Review, *Vol. I, No. II, 1820,
> pp. 305-22.*

WILLIAM ROBERTS (essay date 1888)

[*Roberts was an essayist and biographer whose 1888 sketch of John Dennis in* Dictionary of National Biography *was one of the first to disregard Alexander Pope's unflattering portrait. The sketch, noted by scholars for its objective portrayal, helped repair Dennis's badly tarnished reputation and led other scholars to reevaluate the critic's work. Here, Roberts comments upon Dennis's talents as a poet, dramatist, and literary critic.*]

Dennis wrote various poems, 'in the Pindaric way,' as Cibber puts it, between 1692 and 1714. They are loyal, but beneath notice....

Dennis's plays are bad, and written to illustrate a quaint theory of 'poetical justice;' but his prefaces have some interest.

Dennis is now best remembered as a critic. He was ridiculed by Swift, Theobald (in the *Censor*), and Pope; his temper became soured, and he was a general enemy of the wits. But he showed real abilities, and Southey justly observes that Dennis's critical pamphlets deserve republication (*Specimens of the Later English Poets*) [see excerpt dated 1807].

> *William Roberts, in an excerpt in* Dictionary of
> National Biography, *Vol. V,* edited by Leslie Stephen and Sidney Lee, The Macmillan Company,
> *1908, p. 820.*

EDMUND GOSSE (essay date 1889)

[*A distinguished English literary historian, critic, and biographer, Gosse wrote extensively on seventeenth- and eighteenth-century English literature. His commentary in* Seventeenth-Century Studies *(1883),* A History of Eighteenth Century Literature *(1889),* Questions at Issue *(1893), and other works is generally regarded as sound and suggestive, and he is credited with introducing the works of the Norwegian dramatist Henrik Ibsen to English readers. In the following excerpt from* A History of Eighteenth Century Literature, *Gosse assesses Dennis as critic, singling out his commentary on John Milton for special praise.*]

Of [John Dennis's] very numerous early productions there may be mentioned, *Remarks on Prince Arthur, The Advancement of Poetry, The Grounds of Criticism.* These volumes contain much sound sense, and are particularly notable for their fervent and judicious eulogy of Milton. There is nothing in them of that jealous, carping tone for which Dennis afterwards became noted. (p. 185)

In John Dennis, a writer to whom great injustice has been and still is done, a critic appeared who, with great faults of temper, had a far higher idea than Rapin or Rymer, or even Dryden, of certain classes of poetic work. The praise is due to Dennis of having been the first to dwell judicially on the sublime merits of Milton, and to give him his right place among the poets of the world. (pp. 394-95)

> *Edmund Gosse, "Defoe and the Essayists" and
> "Conclusion," in his* A History of Eighteenth
> Century Literature (1660-1780), *Macmillan and
> Co., 1889, pp. 176-206, 375-400.*

[WILLIAM ROBERTS] (essay date 1891)

[*In the following excerpt from the* Bookworm, *a London periodical that was published yearly from 1888 to 1894, Roberts offers a negative valuation of Dennis as letter writer and political essayist.*]

As a dramatist, John Dennis was an emphatic and irredeemable failure. Even if his works are estimated in connection with contemporary productions—which, indeed, is the only way of getting at their true value, and his position among dramatists—their heaviness and stupendous clumsiness are everywhere apparent. There is not a well-delineated character in the whole of his plays, and yet he is perfectly consistent to his theory of poetical justice. The cardinal point of his doctrine was that the good people should neither die nor suffer, and to this he invariably adhered, with, however, the most unhappy results. Credit must be given him for endeavouring to displace the corrupt plays at that time so much in vogue, and to this end he effected a small amount of good. But he soon became known as a writer of unsuccessful plays, and when once such a character is acquired, a man's future prospects are pretty nearly blasted. It has been wittily said that Dennis laid down excellent rules for writing good plays, and showed what were bad by his own. But if the plays are only fit for oblivion, it cannot be denied that the prefaces to them are excellent; they are, in fact, of a very high order of merit, and written in pure and flexible English, they are not only extremely pleasant reading, but important contributions to dramatic literature. (p. 353)

Dennis's political essays, like his poetry, have very little merit: his theories are much more remarkable for their extraordinary character than for their practicability. They include **An Essay on the Navy,** and **Proposals for putting a Speedy End to the War,** which, Dennis contended, could be effected by ruining the commerce of the French and Spaniards, and so recover our own without any additional expense to the nation. His **Essay on the Opera's after the Italian Manner** is a quasi-political denunciation, not so much of the Italian interlopers as of the danger which arose from encouraging their effeminate music, which, he contends, neither instructs the mind nor elevates human nature. It will perhaps be sufficient to mention that he also wrote an **Essay upon Public Spirit** ... and an answer to Mandeville's *Fables of the Bees,* under the title of **Vice and Luxury Public Mischiefs.** In the way of pure criticism his **Three Letters on the Genius and Writings of Shakespeare,** may be regarded as his best. (p. 355)

[William Roberts], "John Dennis: A Sketch," in
The Bookworm, *Vol. 4, 1891, pp. 353-58.*

GEORGE SAINTSBURY (essay date 1902)

[*Saintsbury was a late nineteenth- and early twentieth-century English literary historian and critic. Hugely prolific, he composed histories of English and European literature as well as numerous critical works on individual authors, styles, and periods. In the following excerpt from* A History of Criticism and Literary Taste in Europe *(1900-04), he considers Dennis's critical ideas and compares him with Thomas Rymer and Samuel Johnson.*]

If John Dennis had been acquainted with the poetry of Tennyson (at which he would probably have railed in his best manner, in which he would certainly have detected plagiarisms from the classics), he too might have applied to himself the words of Ulysses, "I am become a name." Everybody who has the very slightest knowledge of English literature knows, if only in connection with Dryden, Addison, and Pope, the surly, narrow, but not quite ignorant or incompetent critic, who in his younger and more genial days admired the first, and in his soured old age attacked the second and third. But it may be doubted whether very many persons have an acquaintance, at all extensive, with his works. They were never collected; the *Select Works of John Dennis* mainly consist of his utterly worthless verse. Much of the criticism is hidden away in prefaces which were seldom reprinted, and the original editions of which have become very rare. Even good libraries frequently contain only two or three out of more than a dozen or a score of separate documents: and though the British Museum itself is well furnished, it is necessary to range through a large number of publications to obtain a complete view of Dennis as a critic.

That view, when obtained, may perhaps differ not a little from those which have, in a certain general way, succeeded each other in current literary judgment. During the reign of Pope and Addison, the scurrilous assailant of the first, and the more courteous but in part severe censor of the second, was naturally regarded as at best a grumbling pedant, at worst a worthless Zoilus. The critics of the Romantic school were not likely to be much attracted by Dennis. More recently, something of a reaction has taken place in his favour; and it has become not unusual to discover in him, if not exactly a Longinus or a Coleridge, yet a serious and well-equipped critic, who actually anticipated not a little that after-criticism has had to say.

That this more charitable view is not entirely without foundation may be at once admitted. As compared with Rymer, in whose company he too often finds himself in modern appreciation, Dennis shows, indeed, pretty well. He very seldom—perhaps nowhere—exhibits that crass insensibility to poetry which distinguishes "the worst critic who ever lived." One of his earliest and not his worst pieces, *The Impartial Critic* of 1693, an answer to Rymer himself, points out with acuteness and vigour that "Tom the Second" would ruin the English stage if he had his way, and even approaches the sole causeway of criticism across the deep by advancing the argument that the circumstances of the Greek drama were perfectly different from those of the English. Yet already there are danger-signals. That the piece (which includes a Letter to a Friend and some dialogues) contains a great deal of clumsy jocu-

larity, does not much matter. But when we find Dennis devoting some of this jocularity to Antigone's lamentation over her death unwedded, we feel sadly that the man who can write thus is scarcely to be trusted on the spirit of poetry. And the admission that Rymer's censures of Shakespeare are "in most of the particulars very sensible and just" is practically ruinous.

Dennis's answer to Collier is a little later, but still earlier than most of his better known work; and it is very characteristic of his manner, which has not often, I think, been exactly described. As elsewhere, so in this tract, which is entitled *The Usefulness of the Stage to the Happiness of Mankind, to Government and to Religion*, Dennis is uncompromisingly ethical; but he had here the excuse that Collier, to whom he was replying, had taken the same line. There is less excuse here or elsewhere for his method. This is to make a loud clatter of assertions, arranged in a kind of pseudological order, which seems to have really deceived the author, and may possibly have deceived some of his readers, into believing it syllogistic and conclusive. Dennis is very great at the word "must." "As Poetry is an Art it *must* be an imitation of nature" and so forth; seldom shall you find so many "musts" anywhere as in Dennis, save perhaps in some of his modern analogues. Like all who argue in this fashion, he becomes unable to distinguish fact and his own opinion. Collier, for instance, had quoted (quite correctly) Seneca's denunciation of the Stage. To which Dennis replies, "It is not likely that Seneca should condemn the drama, . . . since . . . he wrote plays himself." That the identity of the philosopher and the dramatist is not certain does not matter: the characteristic thing is the setting of probability against fact. But with Dennis hectoring assertion is everything. "It cannot possibly be conceived that so reasonable a diversion as the drama can encourage or incline men to so unreasonable a one as gaming or so brutal a one as drunkenness." With a man who thinks this an argument, argument is impossible.

The fact is that, though he has, as has been admitted, a certain advantage over Rymer, Lord Derby's observation that "He never knew whether it was John or Thomas who answered the bell" will too often apply here. Rymer himself was not ignorant; Dennis, especially in regard to ancient criticism, was still better instructed: and though both were bad dramatists, with, in consequence, a conscious or unconscious bias on dramatic matters, Dennis was not so bad as Rymer. His devotion to Dryden does him credit, though we may suspect that it was not the best part of Dryden that he liked: and, amid the almost frantic spite and scurrility of his later attacks on Pope, he not unfrequently hits a weak place in the "young squab short gentleman's" bright but not invulnerable armour. Yet Dennis displays, as no really good critic could do, the weaknesses of his time and school both in generals and particulars. It is perfectly fair to compare him (giving weight for genius of course) with Johnson, a critic whose general views (except on port and claret) did not materially differ from his own. And, if we do so, we shall find that while Johnson is generally, if not invariably, "too good for such a breed," Dennis almost as constantly shows its worst features. He altered *The Merry Wives of Windsor* into *The Comical Gallant*—a most illaudable action certainly, yet great Dryden's self had done such things before. But he aggravated the crime by a preface, in which he finds fault with the original as having "no less than three actions" [would there were thirty-three!] by remarking that, in the second part of *Henry the Fourth*, Falstaff "does nothing but talk" [would he had talked so for five hundred acts instead of five!] and by laying down *ex cathedra* such generalities as that "Humour, not wit, is the business of comedy," a statement as false as would be its converse. In his *Essay on the Genius of Shakespeare* he is not so very far from Rymer himself in the drivelling arbitrariness of his criticism. Shakespeare has actually made Aufidius, the general of the Volscians, a base and profligate villain! Even Coriolanus himself is allowed to be called a traitor by Aufidius, and nobody contradicts! The rabble in *Julius Cæsar* and other such things "show want of Art," and there is a painful disregard of Poetical Justice. The same hopeless wrongheadedness and (if I may so say) wrong-mindedness appear in a very different work, the *Remarks on the Rape of the Lock*. I do not refer to Dennis's mere scurrilities about "AP—E" and the like. But part of the piece is quite serious criticism. Few of us in modern times care much for the "machinery" of this brilliantly artificial poem; but fewer would think of objecting to it on Dennis's grounds. Machines, it seems, must be—

i. Taken from the religion of the Poet's country.
ii. Allegorical in their application.
iii. Corresponding though opposed to each other.
iv. Justly subordinated and proportioned.
And Pope's machines, we are told, fail in all these respects.

Now, putting the fourth ground aside as being a mere matter of opinion (and some who are not fervent Papists think the machines of the *Rape* very prettily and cleverly arranged in their puppet-show way), one may ask Dennis "Who on earth told you so?" in respect of all the others. And if he alleged (as he might) this or that sixteenth or seventeenth century authority, "And who on earth told *him* so? and what authority had the authority? Why should machines be taken only from the religion of the country? Why should they be allegorical? Why should Machine Dick on the one side invariably nod to Machine Harry on the other?" And even if some sort of answer be forthcoming, "Why should the poet not do as he please if he succeeds thereby in giving the poetic pleasure?" To which last query of course neither Dennis nor any of his school could return any answer, except of the kind that requires bell, book, and candle.

Nor would he have hesitated to use this, for he is a rule-critic of the very straitest kind, a "Tantivy" of poetic Divine Right. In his three chief books of abstract criticism he endeavours to elaborate, with Longinus in part for code, and with Milton for example, a noble, indeed, and creditable, but utterly arbitrary and hopelessly narrow theory of poetry as *necessarily* religious, and as having for its sole real end the reformation of the mind, by a sort of enlarged Aristotelian *katharsis* as to spirit, and by attention to the strict laws of the art in form. Poetical Justice was a kind of mediate divinity to Dennis: as we have seen, he upbraided Shakespeare for the want of it; he remonstrated, in the *Spectator*, No. 548, and elsewhere, with Addison for taking too little account of it; part at least of his enthusiasm for Milton comes from Milton's avowed intention to make his poem a theodicy.

A noble error! let it be repeated, with no hint or shadow of sarcasm or of irreverence; but a fatal error as well. That

Poetry, like all things human, lives and moves and has its being in God, the present writer believes as fervently and unhesitatingly as any Platonic philosopher or any Patristic theologian; and he would cheerfully incur the wrath of Savonarola by applying the epithet "divine," in its fullest meaning, not merely to tragedy and epic and hymn, but to song of wine and of love. But this is not what Dennis meant at all. He meant that Poetry is to have a definitely religious, definitely moral *purpose*—not that it is and tends of itself necessarily *ad majorem Dei gloriam*, but that we are to shape it according to what our theological and ethical ideas of the glory of God are. This way easily comes bad poetry, not at all easily good; and it excludes poetic varieties which may be as good as the best written in obedience to it, and better. Moreover, putting Dennis's notion of the end of Poetry together with his notion of its method or art (which latter is to be adjusted to some at least of the straitest classical precepts), we can easily comprehend, and could easily have anticipated, the narrow intolerance and the hectoring pedantry which he shows towards all who follow not him. In a new sense—not so very different from the old mediæval one, though put with no mediæval glamour, and by an exponent full of eighteenth-century prosaism, yet destitute of eighteenth-century neatness and concinnity—Poetry becomes a part of theology; and the mere irritableness of the man of letters is aggravated into the *odium theologicum*. Bad poets (that is to say, bad according to Dennis) are not merely faulty artists but wicked men; of this Dennis is sure. "And when a man is sure," as he himself somewhere naïvely observes, "'tis his duty to speak with a modest assurance." We know, from examples more recent than poor Dennis, that, when a man is thus minded, his assurance is very apt to eat up his modesty, taking his charity, his good manners, and some other things, as condiments to the meal. (pp. 431-37)

*George Saintsbury, "From Addison to Johnson,"
in his* A History of Criticism and Literary Taste
in Europe: From the Renaissance to the Decline
of Eighteenth Century Orthodoxy, Vol. II, *William Blackwood and Sons, 1902, pp. 426-500.*

H. G. PAUL (essay date 1911)

[Paul was an American essayist and academic who wrote extensively on English studies. In the following excerpt from his 1911 biography of Dennis, he discusses Dennis's critical style.]

It is noticeable that the list of writers whom Dennis praised, . . . contains but few authors whose important works fell in his later years; and it is also significant that nearly every member of the younger generation, about 1710, whose writings were popular, came under his condemnation. Against the charge that his criticisms were ill natured, however, he was continually at warfare. Even as early as 1697 he felt it necessary to defend his practice against this charge; and for one who fought so stoutly and so unsparingly, he was extremely sensitive to the accusation. Dennis's nature contained something of the born dissenter, and he was fearless in expressing his opinions. Doubtless, too, he was somewhat soured by his failure to obtain recognition from the public and from the government. But it may be questioned whether these conditions ever consciously influenced him in his assaults upon more successful writers. For, as he repeatedly affirmed, he attacked them not because they had succeeded, but because he believed they had done so undeservedly and for the most part through the efforts of cabals. Against such combinations Dennis continually inveighed, declaring that any poet of genius would scorn these devices as destructive of the national muse. As late as 1717 he asserted that he was so far from bearing malice toward those whom he criticized [*i. e.*, Pope] that he was willing "to own their good qualities, and to do them any manner of Service that lay in [his] little Power." But in his very latest criticisms Dennis frankly took the position that he had suffered injuries which admitted of no legal redress, and that he therefore entered the lists not only for furthering the public good but also for avenging private wrongs. Dennis's earlier criticisms, however, impress the reader with his attempts to be impartial and judicial. Repeatedly he declared that he had consulted his friends about the matter in hand, and he evidently tried in his better work to state fairly and honestly the other side of the question. [Even in his] *Remarks upon Pope's Translation of Homer* he affirmed that he had attempted to write with fairness and to give no faults that he did not find in the translation. Furthermore, in these same *Remarks* he acknowledged an earlier blunder of his own.

So far as in him lay, Dennis strove in his best work not only to be logical but also to put his argument into such form as would appeal most easily and most convincingly to his readers. Some of his writings, it is true, such as the *Reflections upon an Essay on Criticism*, evince little attempt at any regular method of discussion; but most of the important critiques, including the *Remarks on Prince Arthur*, the *Large Account of the Taste in Poetry*, the *Remarks upon Cato*, and most notably the *Advancement and Reformation of Modern Poetry*, show careful planning by the writer. In his more pretentious work Dennis took pains to define the terms he employed and frequently cast his arguments into syllogistic form. The use of the dilemma, too, became characteristic of his style of argument. Restatements, summaries, and recapitulations are also frequent in Dennis's writings, especially in the *Advancement and Reformation*, where he sometimes carries them to the point of weariness in his desire that the reader may not miss the thread of the argument. Possibly at times this argument becomes, as Mr. Saintsbury describes it [see excerpt dated 1902], "a clatter of assertion;" but Dennis was at least intellectually honest and tried to convey as clearly as he could what he conceived to be the truth.

With his attempts at clearness he strove to couple a variety and elevation of style. For example, he even went so far in his desire to diversify his *Remarks on Prince Arthur* as to introduce a fragment from one of his own unfinished dramas; while to relieve the reader after a long stretch of reasoning in the *Grounds of Criticism in Poetry*, he cited several illustrative passages from the poets. In his criticisms he aimed at force and grace and attained them oftener than in either his poems or his plays. Pope seems to have recognized Dennis's attempts at elevation and to have hit at him when, in the *Essay on Criticism*, he praised Longinus for judging with fire. At any rate Dennis took the thrust to himself and retorted thus:

> [Pope] condemns his Contemporaries for no other Reason but that they are his Contemporaries. For why should not a modern critic imitate the qualities of Longinus; and when he treats of a subject that is sublime,

treat of it with Sublimity?—But pray, who are the Moderns that judge with Fury but write with Flegm? Who are they who have writ both Criticism and Poetry, who have not in their Poetry shewn a thousand times more than this Essayer's Fire?

And there is no mistaking the nature of Dennis's answer to his own question. Sometimes one is tempted to believe that he occasionally relied upon the enthusiasm of the moment to make amends for the absence of hard, consistent labor; for while, as has been stated, his more pretentious work was carefully planned and executed, time after time he declared in his shorter tracts that he had written hurriedly, and that he was thoroughly tired of his task.

But on the whole Dennis's style in his criticisms was a very good one—at times one might call it admirable, and that too after making allowance for the superabundance of strong expletives and a burly humor, which is free from slime, though not from mud. Indeed one sometimes wonders at the difference between the dull and heavy style of his dramas and the firm and often elevated style of his criticisms. But this contradiction in his style was but one of the many in the man himself.

The contradiction noticed in the preceding paragraph, indeed, is evident not only in Dennis's style but in his whole critical position, which we may now summarize. At bottom Dennis was a rationalist, or better a dogmatist who supported his positions by asserting that they were based upon reason. The age was in part responsible for his attitude, especially in his earlier years when he was very susceptible to the ideas of others. But a certain positiveness and assertiveness of nature would have made him a dogmatist in any age. His education was such as to inspire him with a love for the classics and a respect for their authority, but that respect never became a servile regard but rather the admiration of one who felt that the classics were great and good only as they conformed to the eternal dictates of reason. In the majority of his beliefs he agreed with the prevailing ideas, especially in his regard for the different classes of literature and their commonly accepted characteristics. He further agreed with current custom in that as a critic he confined himself largely to a discussion of the epic and the drama, and that as a playwright he chose nearly all his themes from the life of the court and the city and treated them with "regularity."

But there was in him another and, for the history of criticism, a more important side. For Dennis went beyond his age in appreciating that "a clear head and an accurate understanding alone are not sufficient to make a poet," and in reasserting time after time that emotion is the real basis of poetry. To his age he stood as the champion of "the furious joy and pride of soul," which he called the distinguishing mark of literary genius. In his attempt to emphasize emotion as the basis of poetry he proposed as the source of material for poetic inspiration not the Greek and Roman masterpieces venerated by the neo-classicists but the holy scriptures, a suggestion which was simply revolutionary. In his early recognition of Milton as the poet of sublime emotions, Dennis was so far in advance of his age that it is scarcely an exaggeration to maintain that his criticisms contain the first appreciation of *Paradise Lost* which may be considered as at all adequate. Dennis was also a pioneer of his times in emphasizing the relation of emotion and versification, in discussing the difference between ordinary emotion and emotion recollected in tranquility (to use Wordsworth's phrasing), as the basis of poetry, and in championing the cause of unrhymed verse when the heroic couplet was dominant. Moreover, his appreciation of Shakspere was decidedly in advance of his time. To him is also to be credited one of the earliest, if not the first, book review in a modern sense. Then too, in his better critical days he viewed literature dynamically rather than statically, recognized a standard of taste beyond judgment, and analyzed the conditions making for the taste of his age. Furthermore, though he wrote of and for the city, he manifested a keen delight in nature and seems to have gone beyond any other writer of his age in his appreciation of her sublime aspects. In a word, Dennis was possessed of a large, if not always well regulated, emotional nature and of considerable critical acumen, which frequently clashed with his respect for the rules and pointed the way to a better conception of literature.

In his later years, as has been indicated, he became more and more the champion of the rules. Such conservatism, which might well be explained by his increasing years, was fostered by the conflicts in which he engaged. The old critic who entered the lists as the champion of liberty and religion came to speak, as someone has said, with the authority of an infallible church. After he was sixty, Dennis insisted, with the assurance of one who knows himself in the right, upon the observance of the various types and even refused the name of poetry to such writings as did not conform to these standards. Against the recognition of any new class of writings he grew bitterly opposed. For example, he himself, who as a young writer had employed and defended burlesque, in his old age could scarcely find condemnation sufficiently severe for its successor, the mock epic. These later years also reveal in Dennis's work an increased attention to matters of verbal criticism, sometimes just, but more often the cavils of one looking for faults. But even in these evil days he maintained his admiration for Milton and his insistence upon emotion as the basis of poetry, and for these we may forgive many things. (pp. 197-202)

Dennis's importance for us lies not so much in the specific doctrines he maintained, as in the fact that he was one of the earliest of his nation to devote the best of a life to criticism. Through his long and toilsome career he battled loyally for what he considered right standards of judgment, encouraged the appreciation of the greater poetry, and held contemporary literature to answer for its faults. Despite his dogmatism, despite the bitter conflicts and ridicule of his later life, Dennis gained a certain recognition for the significance of the critic's work, and he helped force a consideration of the "still-vexed" question of the value and utility of criticism. (p. 212)

> *H. G. Paul, in his* John Dennis: His Life and Criticism, *1911. Reprint by AMS Press, Inc., 1966, 229 p.*

SAMUEL H. MONK (essay date 1935)

[*Monk is an American essayist and academic who has contributed to the Norton Anthology Series. In the following excerpt from his critical study* The Sublime: A Study of Critical Theories in XVIII-Century England *(1935), he traces the influence of Longinus on Dennis's critical development,* *explicating Dennis's interpretation of the role of passion in poetry in* The Advancement and Reformation of Modern Poetry *and* The Grounds of Criticism in Poetry.]

[The] eighteenth century saw various critics and philosophers take up the idea of the sublime where Boileau had left it, and develop it through a series of phases into an æsthetic concept of the first importance. The first and most interesting of these theories that we meet in the early years of the eighteenth century comes, oddly enough, from one of the minor critics of the age, Pope's sworn enemy and the target of many of that poet's barbed shafts of satire—John Dennis, who early manifested an interest in the sublime, not only in regard to natural scenery, but to theory as well. Before the end of the seventeenth century he had outlined his ideas, carrying the inquiry far beyond the region in which Longinus and Boileau had wrought, by investigating the emotional responses of individuals who experience the sublime. Boileau, following Longinus, had tried to ascertain the quality in art which may be called sublime, and had indicated generally the effect of this quality; Dennis was the first Englishman to see that if anything of value was to be learned, the inquiry must take into account not only the nature of the sublime object, but its effect also, i.e., the subjective element.

Dennis declared his intention of investigating the nature of genius, which he considered to be "nothing but a very common Passion, or a complication of common Passions." This beginning is characteristic of Dennis's view of art. His interest is always in the emotional; he can explain poetry and genius on no other ground than the passions. Thus he draws a parallel between the emotions that accompany happiness in life and those that are the result of felicity in writing. In life, when anything lucky occurs, we experience a transport of joy, which is followed by an exaltation of the mind, and frequently by astonishment. So with a fine thing in art; the soul is transported by the consciousness of its own excellence, and amazed by the view of its own surpassing power.... Thus, under the guidance of the great Greek [Longinus], Dennis is led to reduce art to the expression of passion, and to maintain that the highest art—the sublime—is the expression of the greatest passion. The sublime and the pathetic begin their long journey in each other's company. It is noticeable, also, that Dennis is the first of many writers to recognize with Longinus, in the experience of the sublime, that sense of the greatness of the human soul which Kant uses in his analysis of the sublime.

In 1701 Dennis published what Paul, his biographer, regards as his most important work—*The Advancement and Reformation of Modern Poetry*. Its sequel, *The Grounds of Criticism in Poetry*, published in 1704, was originally planned as a more extensive work which was to be his *magnum opus*, and was to contain "a Criticism upon our most Celebrated English Poets decas'd." This work never saw the light of day, since only about seventy subscriptions were taken. Of all Dennis's writings the two books with which we are concerned are his most original. They appeared shortly after the death of Dryden and before the ascendency of Pope during the brief interregnum in the realm of criticism when Dennis was known as "the Critic." They brought him a modest fame, some notoriety, and the gibes of the Martinus Scriblerus Club.

In these books Dennis stands out with startling vividness from his contemporaries. In *The Advancement and Refor-*

mation of Modern Poetry he builds up a theory of poetry based entirely on emotion, thus carrying out to some degree the plan which he had earlier announced. Hamelius gives him first place in his chapter *Anfang der Aesthetik* and does not hesitate to classify him as a romanticist. Such terms are dangerous, and we have learned not to dub a man romantic because he praised Milton or admitted emotion into his theory of art. But in spite of the fact that, taken in its totality, Dennis's criticism is quite neo-classic in method, Hamelius is not mistaken when he finds something new in these two books, and in calling attention to Dennis's departure from the strait and narrow path of criticism as practiced by his contemporaries. Dennis himself boasted of "the Newness and Boldness of the Positions" which he held.

Paul has discussed the criticism of Dennis and its relation to the various schools and movements of the early eighteenth century—a none too simple task, for Dennis's life was long and active, and his criticism is correspondingly many-sided. It is sufficient here to call attention to his religious, moralistic point of view, which Paul is inclined to attribute to the influence of Milton, and to his fondness for Longinus, which will shortly become evident. It was in *Three Hours after Marriage* that Pope and Gay satirized Dennis's discipleship of Longinus by representing the critic as "Sir Tremendous Longinus." Certainly the name of Longinus is frequently found in Dennis's criticism; it is evident that he was very much under the influence of *Peri Hupsous* and that he prided himself on his knowledge of that treatise.

Dennis, like Boileau, brings Longinus to the fore in connection with the Ancients and the Moderns. The aim of *The Advancement and Reformation* is to offer a middle ground whereby neither party need lose out irrevocably. In his second, third, and fourth chapters, Dennis proves that the ancients did not surpass the moderns either because of "external advantages" or "internal advantages," but that they derived their greatness from the nature of their subjects. He proposes a scheme whereby the moderns may equal the ancients in those kinds of poetry in which they have hitherto had the disadvantage. Dennis's opinion that "Passion is the Principal thing in Poetry," leads to his formulated definition: "Poetry then is an imitation of Nature by a Pathetick and Numerous Speech." He elaborates this view at considerable length. Passion he finds more essential to poetry than harmony, for harmony is merely the "instrument" of poetry, but passion distinguishes its very nature and character.

> For therefore Poetry is Poetry, because it is more passionate and sensual than Prose. A discourse that is writ in very good Numbers, if it wants Passion can be but measur'd Prose. But a discourse that is every where extremely pathetick, and consequently every where bold and figurative, is certainly Poetry without Numbers.

The timeworn doctrine of imitation is here, and the idea of figurative language as the proper expression of strong emotions—both old and respectable in Dennis's time. But despite the outward garb of conventional language, despite the discouraging confusion of poetry and rhetoric, Dennis's definition is out of harmony with prevailing opinion by virtue of the emphasis that it lays on the strong emotions, which he finds to be the distinguishing feature of poetry. It matters little that he adds that the function of

emotion in poetry is to facilitate the two great ends of pleasing and instructing; the fact remains that the idea of the *furor poeticus* is more prominent in Dennis's system than in that of any other critic of his day.

There follows the distinction, so important for Dennis's system, between ordinary passion and enthusiasm.

> I call that ordinary Passion, whose cause is clearly comprehended by him who feels it, whether it be Admiration, Terror, or Joy; and I call the very same Passions Enthusiasm, when their cause is not clearly comprehended by him who feels them.

This statement is extremely awkward, and standing alone would mean little. He goes on to explain that an object and the idea of an object produce the same emotions, and that some ideas "latently and unobserved by us, carry Passion along with them." All of this seems to be an attempt to account for that sense of wonder in the presence of the vast that plays so important a part in the eighteenth-century sublime. In the *Grounds of Criticism* one finds this statement, in which Dennis redefines his terms:

> Enthusiastick Passion, or Enthusiasm, is a Passion which is moved by Ideas in Contemplation, or the Meditation of things that belong not to common life. Most of our Thoughts in Meditation are naturally attended with some sort and some degree of Passion; and this Passion, if it is strong, I call Enthusiasm.

This enthusiasm is contrasted with ordinary emotion ("Vulgar Passion"), which is described as "that which is moved by the Objects themselves, or by the Ideas in the ordinary Course of Life." To illustrate his meaning, he says that the sun, mentioned in ordinary conversation, suggests "a round flat shining Body, of about two foot diameter." But occurring to the mind in meditation, it suggests "a vast and glorious Body, and the top of all the visible Creation, and the brightest material Image of the Divinity."

Despite the obvious handicap of a lack of vocabulary, it is clear that Dennis has perceived the distinction between practical emotion and æsthetic emotion, between phenomena as revealed by sense and phenomena as expressed in art. True, his concern with emotions obscures the issue, but he is certainly on the way to an æsthetic when he distinguishes between what Croce calls the theoretical and the practical.

It should be observed, also, that in this, the earliest theory of the sublime in England, the author turns to association to explain the æsthetic experience. (pp. 45-9)

Upon this enthusiastic passion Dennis seeks to found the sublime. The sixth chapter of *The Advancement and Reformation* is meant to prove "That Passion is more to be deriv'd from a Sacred Subject than from a Prophane one;" and the rest of the book is intended to show that only in their sacred poetry did the ancients excel the moderns. The poetry of the "Graecians" and the Romans failed with the decay of their religions. Let the modern poet but drink of Siloa's brook, and no longer will he have to yield to the ancients. This is Dennis's scheme for advancing and reforming the poetry of his day. Milton serves as an example of the greatness of religious poetry, and the pages of the book are strewn with passages from *Paradise Lost*. But Milton is not the only authority summoned to help Dennis prove his point, for Longinus is plainly the chief influence on the critic's mind. Almost all the examples of sublimity that Longinus gives, Dennis remarks, have as their basis religion and its emotions.

Once launched on the subject of Longinus, Dennis naturally finds his way to a discussion of the sublime. He begins by stating that enthusiasm is made up of the passions, admiration, joy, terror, and astonishment, the first giving elevation, "that Pride which exalts the Soul at the conceiving a great Hint;" the second giving transport; and the third vehemence. Elevation, transport, and vehemence were, in one form or other, to be concomitants of the sublime for many a day. They were found in the Longinian sublime, as interpreted by Boileau, and many decades later were used by Kant in his analysis of sublimity. They indicate the strongly emotional concepts that were habitually associated with the sublime, and that helped to centralize, in one idea, forces that always were considered to transcend the rules and to lie outside the realm of pure technique and within the reach only of genius.

How Longinus pointed the way to the analysis of the subjective element in æsthetic is shown in Dennis's account of his sublime.

> He takes great pains to set before us, the effects which it produces in the Minds of Men; as, for example, that it causes in them admiration and surprize; or noble Pride, and a noble Vigour, an invincible force transporting the Soul from its ordinary Situation, and a Transport, and a fulness of Joy mingled with Astonishment. These are the effects that *Longinus* tells us that the Sublime produces in the minds of men. Now I have endeavoured to shew what it is in Poetry that works these effects. So that take the Cause and the Effects together, and you have the Sublime.

When these words were written, Longinus was relatively a new force in English criticism. We therefore discover in them something of the point of view of a man who was reading him freshly. The striking thing to Dennis is that Longinus analysed the effects of the sublime on the soul. This statement would seem to support the idea that Longinus had some share in the founding of an æsthetic concept of the sublime; that he sought to turn criticism away from the rules, to turn men's minds away from the dogmas of the ancients, and to set them to analysing their own emotions in the presence of grandeur and beauty. By investigating the emotions consequent to sublimity, men began to learn that art is a matter, not of the rules, but of the individual's response to an object or an experience, and this knowledge led them gradually to that subjective view of art out of which an æsthetic was evolved. Incidentally the habit of studying the emotional effect of art was certain to emphasize the belief that the individual emotion is more valid than all the rules, and such a belief firmly held and clearly understood produces the poetry of a Wordsworth not of a Pope. Although he never forgets that poetry should teach and improve, Dennis nevertheless emphasizes the emotions, because instruction comes after the reader has been moved. The greater poetry—epic, tragedy, and ode—has as its basis poetic enthusiasm, which is evoked by religion. To Dennis, this is also the sublime emotion.

In the *Grounds of Criticism* Dennis attempted to systematize and expand some of these ideas, and in this book are found his ideas of the sublime. Remembering that Dennis is discussing epic, tragedy, and ode, *genres* that are based on enthusiasm; that enthusiasm is emotion aroused by the ideas of things that do not belong to common life, considered in contemplation, emotion whose cause is not clearly perceived; and that the sublime is found only in poetry which contains this enthusiasm, we may consider his theory.

There are six "Enthusiastic Passions"—admiration, terror, horror, joy, sadness, and desire. They are strongest when they have their origin in religious ideas. The two emotions that Dennis discussed at length are admiration and terror; if he had finished *The Grounds of Criticism* he would have treated of the others, but the failure to obtain subscribers cut short his work. It is regrettable, in the light of future developments, that we have none of his opinions on the relation of horror to the sublime. (pp. 49-51)

Dennis's sublime is made of stern stuff. Ultimately, however he might dress it in the conventional critical language of his decade, it could never harmonize with an art whose spirit was *nil admirari*. The strongest emotions are its effect; it negates reason, and transcends rules. Dennis establishes the sublime beyond the sphere of that moderate urbanity which was the ideal of Augustan literature. But it is important to remember that he did so without apparently disrupting the system. The canonization of Longinus by Boileau and Dryden had left the way open for the introduction into the neo-classic system of ideas and forces which eventually were to play an important part in its destruction. The best testimony of the need that the English felt for such ideas as Longinus's is the zeal with which they adopted and spread them. Dennis's treatment of *Peri Hupsous* is typical; he has seized on one or two statements and has expanded them, building a theory on them, and forcing Longinus to conform to his views. Paul is right in seeing the influence of Boileau's *Préface* in the passage just quoted, for the "ravishes and transports" is obviously from that critical essay; but Dennis is original in respect to the value which he attaches to powerful emotion in art and particularly in the sublime. (pp. 53-4)

With its insistence on strong emotion, [Dennis's view of the sublime] goes beyond Longinus, and is certainly quite different from Boileau's theory, for Dennis is willing to subordinate all qualities to emotion. In view of the prominence of terror, both in later theories of the sublime and in much of eighteenth-century literature, the most interesting aspect of Dennis's treatment of the sublime is his introduction of that emotion. Dennis's influence is known to have been slight, but he was certainly read, and if he helped to strengthen the cause of emotions in art, he has contributed his share to the history of English literature. (p. 54)

Samuel H. Monk, "The Sublime and the Pathetic," in his The Sublime: A Study of Critical Theories in XVIII-Century England, *1935. Reprint by The University of Michigan Press, 1960, pp. 43-62.*

HOXIE NEALE FAIRCHILD (essay date 1939)

[*An American educator, Fairchild is the author of numerous essays and books on literary and religious subjects. His major works include* The Noble Savage: A Study in Romantic

Naturalism (1928), a lengthy discussion of the depiction of the unspoiled primitive life in literature and its relationship to romantic naturalism, and the six-volume Religious Trends in English Poetry *(1939-68), which traces religious thought and feeling in English poetry from the eighteenth to the twentieth century. In the following excerpt from* Religious Trends in English Poetry, *Fairchild explores Dennis's conception of the interdependence of religion and poetry as discussed in* The Advancement and Reformation of Modern Poetry *and* The Grounds of Criticism in Poetry.]

Several of the prose works of John Dennis (1657-1734) betoken his interest in politico-ecclesiastical questions, in the moral-reform movement, and even in theology. In *The Danger to Priestcraft to Religion and Government* he opposed Sacheverell's early activities, and in *Priestcraft Distinguish'd from Christianity* he branded the Jacobite clergy as disciples of Antichrist. The reformer appeared in *An Essay upon Publick Spirit; being a Satire in Prose upon the Manners and Luxury of the Times. Vice and Luxury Public Mishaps* was a shocked attempt to refute Mandeville's paradox. The puritan and the dramatic critic united in a severe *Essay on the Operas after the Italian Manner, which are about to be establish'd on the English stage.* Among the works of his last years were translations of two Latin theological treatises by Thomas Burnet. From all this the reader will perceive that Dennis was a Whig and a Low Churchman of the half-puritanical, half-latitudinarian sort. To complete the picture, he was the son of a saddler who was prosperous enough to put him through Harrow and Cambridge.

Contrary to the expectations raised by the foregoing paragraph, very few of Dennis's cumbersome baroque poems are strictly "divine." Indeed one finds nothing of that sort except three paraphrases: of the *Te Deum*, of the Eighteenth Psalm, and of a passage from *Habbakuk*. Nevertheless all of his poems display a more or less religious earnestness and strive for both spiritual and poetic elevation. Even without acquaintance with his literary criticism it is easy to see that he has a religious conception of poetry and considers himself a *vates*. Thus in his longer, more ambitious pieces Dennis is not merley flattering his heroes or decorating his lines when he regards events in the history of England as events in the history of Protestant Christianity.

Dennis is an admirer of the Renaissance Christian epic, and especially of Tasso and Milton. **"The Battle of Ramellies"** drags its slow length along in supposedly Miltonic blank verse with the aid of councils in hell, meddlesome furies, and guardian genii. Even into the epic, however, Dennis imports the *furor poeticus* of the pindaric tradition. When preparing to celebrate Blenheim in **"Britannia Triumphans,"** he fairly foams at the mouth:

> Begin my soul, and strike the living lyre,
> O raise thy self! O rouze thy utmost pow'rs!
> Contemn the world, and ev'ry thing below,
> And soaring tow'r above mortality,
> To meet and welcome thy descending God.
> 'Tis done. O raptures never felt before!
> Tempestuous whirlwind of transporting flame!
> O whither am I caught! O whither rapt!
> To what immense unutterable heights?

These amusing lines will remind us that the contemporary opposition to "unnatural flights" was powerless to prevent writers like Dennis from admiring a poetry of "transport-ing flame." Though quite unable to write such poetry, they believed that it *should* be written.

Somewhat less afflatic but valuable for the complex of ideas which it presents is **"A Poem upon the Death of ... Queen Anne, and the ... Accession of ... King George.... With an Exhortation to all True Britons to Unity."** Woe for the Queen's death changes to joy at the coming of George. There is jubilation not only on earth but in heaven. The spirit of William III now sees the fulfilment of all his labors. (pp. 183-84)

Toleration, unity, internal peace, successful foreign wars, commercial prosperity, merchants snoring under golden canopies, liberty and virtuous activity, sound morals, "lawful" love and joy, the religion of practical charity, Augustan culture—all this without a trace of any vitalizing spiritual impulse. One could hardly find a more complete description of the Whig ideal.

In his own day no less than at present, Dennis was more widely known as a literary critic than as a poet, and his criticism bears directly upon our subject. The thesis of *The Advancement and Reformation of Modern Poetry* is clearly set forth in its sub-title: "A Critical Discourse in Two Parts. The first shewing that the Principal Reason why the Ancients excell'd the Moderns in the greater Poetry, was because they mix'd Religion with Poetry. The Second, Proving that by joining Poetry with the Religion reveal'd to us in Sacred Writ, the Modern Poets may come to equal the Ancients." True religion, Dennis insists, is not the enemy of the human passions. Her aim is rather to restore that harmony between reason and passion which was shattered by the sin of Adam. And this is precisely the aim of "the greater poetry."

The same ideas are expressed more systematically and with closer adherence to the ideal of "the rules" in *The Grounds of Criticism in Poetry*. According to Dennis the divine art of poetry "is sunk and profan'd, and miserably debas'd," not because modern poets lack ability, but because they do not know the rules. He proceeds to enlighten them. "Poetry has two Ends, a subordinate, and a final one; the subordinate one is Pleasure, and the final one is Instruction." Now not only the subordinate but the final end is attained "by exciting Passion," for poetry instructs through the feelings.

Philosophy corrects passion through reason; poetry corrects reason through passion. "And therefore," since men are swayed chiefly by their emotions, "Poetry instructs and reforms more powerfully than Philosophy can do." But religion also works upon men's reason through their passions: the method of poetry is the method of religion.

There are two kinds of passion—vulgar, and enthusiastic. The distinction is not easy to grasp, but apparently vulgar passion is the immediate response to sense-experience. It "is moved by the Objects themselves, or by the Ideas in the Ordinary Course of Life ... Enthusiastick Passion, or Enthusiasm, is a Passion which is moved by the Ideas in Contemplation, or the Meditation of things that belong not to common Life. Most of our Thoughts in Meditation are naturally attended with some sort and some degree of Passion; and this Passion, if it is strong, I call Enthusiasm." Dennis's assumption that enthusiasm is a supremely desirable quality in both poetry and religion shatters our over-simplified picture of the Age of Reason.

The principal enthusiastic passions are six: "Admiration, Terror, Horror, Joy Sadness, Desire." He proceeds to show "that the strongest Enthusiastick Passions, that are justly and reasonably rais'd, must be rais'd by religious Ideas; that is, by Ideas which either shew the Attributes of the Divinity, or relate to his Worship." Aristotle, Hermogenes, and of course Longinus are cited as authorities. Examples of great poetry inspired by religious enthusiasm are drawn from Homer, Virgil, Tasso, and Milton. Milton is by far his favorite source of illustrations, with Tasso a fairly close second.

We are to conclude that "as great Passion only is the adequate Language of the greater Poetry, so the greater Poetry is only the adequate Language of Religion; and therefore the greatest Passion is the Language of that sort of Poetry, because that sort of Poetry is the worthiest Language of Religion." The present extravagance and triviality of poetry must therefore be ascribed to its divorce from religion. Dennis rather acutely observes that "the modern Poetry being for the most part profane, has either very little Spirit; or if it has a great one, that Spirit is out of Nature because it bears no manner of Proportion to the Ideas from which it is forcibly deriv'd." In other words, the modern poet, having no religious enthusiasm, either does not attempt to be sublime or, if he *does* attempt to be sublime, has no genuine basis for the effort.

If poetry needs religion, it is equally true that religion needs poetry for "the offering of Praise and Thanksgiving, and several sorts of Prayer to God, and celebrating the Wonders of his Might. Because if the Ideas which these Subjects afford, are express'd with Passion equal to their Greatness, that which expresses them is Poetry." Not only is the Bible full of great poetry, but Christ's method of teaching "was entirely Poetical: that is, by Fables or Parables, contriv'd, and plac'd, and adapted to work very strongly upon human Passions." The cause of religion would be furthered if all the poetical parts of Scripture were rendered in verse by good poets. With astonishing *naïveté* he supposes that this would particularly attract the gentry, "For they of extraordinary Parts for the most part being extremely delighted with Poetry, and finding the greatest and most exalted Poetry upon Religious Subjects, would by degrees become more us'd to be moved by Sacred Ideas, than they would by Profane; that is, would by degrees become reform'd."

The essence of this hair-splitting analysis of imponderables is summed up by Dennis as follows: "The fundamental Rule then that we pretend to lay down for the succeeding or excelling in the greater Poetry, is that the Constitution of the Poem should be religious, that it may be throughout pathetick." He forgets a rule even more fundamental: that the constitution not only of the poem but of the poet should be religious, and religious in a deeper sense than his own poem on the accession of King George.

Both the specific and the general sources of Dennis's views have been ably discussed by Dr. Paul [in *John Dennis: His Life and Criticism* (1911)]. Dennis, like Watts, inherits the Renaissance view that poetic and religious enthusiasm are closely akin, that the poet is a divinely inspired *vates*, and that the function of poetry is to instruct through delight. He was thoroughly familiar with earlier discussions of the relationship between Christianity and poetry. The influence of Milton, Tasso, and Cowley seems to have been especially strong. Milton's entire career, of course, is a demonstration of the interfusion of the Platonic view of poetry with puritan religious feeling. In Dennis the Renaissance tradition has combined with the moral-reform interests of a sober bourgeois Whig whose puritanism has acquired a slight latitudinarian tinge, and who, without being a neoclassicist in the strict sense, has all of the neoclassical passion for "the rules." (pp. 186-89)

[The] direct influence of Dennis is not easy to estimate, for his chief importance lies in the fact that he represented tendencies widely current in the thought of his time. (p. 189)

> *Hoxie Neale Fairchild, "Middle-Classicists," in his* Religious Trends in English Poetry: Protestantism and the Cult of Sentiment, 1700-1740, *Vol. I, Columbia University Press, 1939, pp. 155-204.*

EDWARD NILES HOOKER (essay date 1943)

[*In the following excerpt from the introduction to* The Critical Works of John Dennis *(1939-43), Hooker discusses Dennis's definition of "the function and approach of a critic."*]

Like Shaftesbury Dennis looked upon criticism as essential to the health and welfare of literature. As long as criticism remains sound and vigorous, the practise of literary composition is likely to reflect its excellence; whereas bad criticism may debauch the taste of the people and consequently debase the literature by which they are entertained. Since literature flourishes most when public taste is best, a critic should watch over public taste, to correct it when it is bad and to expose the causes of its corruption. Sometimes it is corrupted by false standards embodied in specific works of art, and then it is the critic's duty to analyze these works of art so as to demonstrate the falseness of their standards by showing their esthetic inadequacy. Of course only thoroughly popular works, like *Prince Arthur, Cato,* and the *Conscious Lovers,* demand such treatment. Sometimes literary taste is corrupted by non-literary causes, such as luxury, the opera, unwise patronage, or the spirit of factionalism, and then it is the critic's duty to expose the causes, rendering them hateful or ridiculous. That it is possible to alter public taste Dennis firmly believed; he cited as examples the change in the taste for heroic tragedies brought about by the *Rehearsal,* and the change in the attitude toward the *Plain Dealer* brought about by the approbation of a small group of men blessed with taste.

Besides standing guard over the general taste a critic has another duty to his public: to make it capable of greater pleasure in literature. When criticism damns a popular work of art because it is false and hollow, it tends to restrict the pleasure of many readers. But the undiscriminating pleasures of such readers, who are in some measure pleased by anything that is printed, are ephemeral and of little subtlety or intensity. Being false, they cannot endure. By turning his readers' attention to the true and lasting beauties of art, and shaping their taste for sound artistry, the critic helps them to obtain intenser pleasure of a more lasting sort. "For Delicacy augments the Pleasure which it retrenches."

But good criticism serves the artist as well as the public. By laying down the grounds of criticism, and by examining the nature and end of art, together with the best means for attaining that end, by showing why some have failed and others have succeeded, the critic rescues art from the errors which have accrued to it in practise and restores it to its original purity. Thus, by advancing the art and by making past experiences available and readily understandable to the artist, the critic enables him to give as much genuine pleasure as his nature and talents allow.

Good criticism serves to advance polite learning, and therefore it constitutes a service to the state. "For Arts and Empire in Civiliz'd Nations have generally flourish'd together." Government, as Dennis often observed, depends for its stability upon the established religion and upon a sound ethical system. Since piety and virtue are the very basis of poetry, which aims to reconcile the soul of man to the pleasures of virtue, then criticism by insisting that poetry should fulfill its proper aim upholds morality and helps to provide for the security of the state. The political side of criticism is frequently seen in Dennis's own writings; he defended the stage partly on the grounds that it was useful to government, he urged that "the Instructions which we receive from the Stage ought to be for the Benefit of the lawful establish'd Government," and he attacked the opera not merely because its success deflected public support from poetry to a much less worthy object but also because it tended to undermine public spirit and, consequently, the state. A good critic is a patriot as well as a man of learning and virtue.

To fulfill so important a function, it is evident, the critic must be a person of considerable abilities. He must, in fact, as Dennis thought, be possessed in some measure of the same talents as were required to produce the sort of works which he criticizes. And since the first requirement in the poet who writes in the major *genres* of verse is genius, so the critic himself must have a share of genius. Ideally he should, like Longinus, be able to deal sublimely with subjects that are sublime, but Dennis never insisted strongly upon this qualification—wisely enough, since many of his own essays are hasty and careless specimens of writing. More essential, since genius is passion, he must have a capacity for great passion and for appreciating works that display great passion. Inasmuch as genius in a poem is manifested not so much in the moral, fable, or action as in the "manners" (characters), thoughts, and expression, the critic of genius will have special gifts for discerning the beauties of character and expression. Dennis associated critical genius with the ability to discover the beauties of a poem, and this ability seemed to him of a distinctly higher order than the talent of finding faults (that is, of discovering the material irregularities of a poem). With Dennis, as with many of his contemporaries, "beauties" came to signify the non-structural and less rational elements of a poem. Thus in a discussion of Shakespeare the critic of genius would be able to reveal his talent for characterization and for portraying human passions as well as his magic power of expression, the beauties which Shakespeare could achieve as the poet of nature. The purely rational critic, on the other hand, would be restricted to pointing out Shakespeare's violations of art: his frequent disregard of the moral, his structural weaknesses, and the inconsistency between his historical characters and their originals. Dennis himself, it is

true, only too often played the part of the rational critic, the critic guided by common sense and a knowledge of the rules of art, but one cannot understand his critical theory without recognizing the fact that he held in greater esteem the part of the critic possessed of genius.

Good sense, or common sense, is an ingredient in the make-up of the critic, though not of the first importance. Dennis distinguished good sense from judgment. Judgment in a critic implies both a knowledge of the art, its purpose and the means of attaining that purpose, and experience in the masterpieces of that art. Good sense, however, may exist independent of experience and taste. Good sense may suffice in detecting the faults, or the material irregularities, of a poem; that is, in noting gross faults in construction and the more obvious violations of verisimilitude. Dennis himself employed the method of good sense in pointing out wild improbabilities, such as Hoel's long speech of greeting to Prince Arthur, the action of a chorus in the tragedy planned by Rymer, or the finicky lovemaking that was carried on by Marcia, Lucia, Portia, and Juba. But Dennis was convinced that good sense, even when it was combined with experience, an inclination for poetry, and a certain measure of taste, is not enough to enable a critic to judge of the greater types of poetry.

Taste, as Dennis used the term, was much more inclusive than genius or good sense. "Taste in Writing," he said at one point, "is nothing but a fine Discernment of Truth." Yet he knew that a fine discernment of esthetic truth is the contribution of various abilities. In his clearest treatment of this subject, the *Large Account of the Taste in Poetry*, he pointed out that the three things required of a man to succeed in poetry, or to judge of poetry properly, are 1) "Great parts," 2) a "generous Education," and 3) a "due Application." By great parts he meant a lively, warm, and strong imagination and a sound and penetrating judgment. By a generous education he meant learning, comprising philosophy, a knowledge of things, and an acquaintance with the best ancient and modern authors; together with a knowledge of the world and of mankind. By a due application he meant that concentration, attended with the necessary leisure, which is required if one is to enter into the spirit of poetry. These are the components of a general taste for poetry. With such equipment one may judge of elegies, songs, love poems, and Bacchanalian odes—in short, of the "little Poetry," but to judge of the major types of poetry one must have a knowledge of the rules, and genius as well. Taste for tragedy, the epic, and the Pindaric ode, then, is the possession of a small minority. As one may gather from the above description, Dennis did not regard it as a strange and mystical property, a mysterious sixth sense unaccountably present in only a few men. Nor did he regard it as a product of good breeding and genteel company, the blessed birthright of gentlemen. Rather, he looked upon it as a normal development of experience and learning in certain individuals with superior natural faculties, especially good judgment, lively imagination, and a capacity for deep passion. A man endowed with such taste, no matter how genuine his respect for the rules, is no carpenter stolidly laying a wooden measure upon a work of art to estimate its scope, breadth, and depth. The ideal of the Augustan critic is no less sound than that of critics in any other period.

One interesting problem confronted Dennis and his contemporaries as a result of their notion of taste: if taste is the possession of a small minority, how could it be consistent with the *consensus gentium*, or the general consent of mankind, which was accepted as the stamp of truth or of esthetic excellence? Although Dennis believed that few men in any age or nation were gifted with good taste, yet, because in taste as in truth there is but one standard, he was sure that a verdict based upon good taste in one age will be valid in all other ages even as truth itself remains precious and immutable for all time. And the *consensus gentium*, accordingly, he conceived not as the common opinion of all mankind but as the enlightened opinion of men of taste in the most polite nations, past and present, of the civilized world. Thus the problem was resolved.

It is already apparent that the task of a critic in estimating the worth of a given poem is not, as Dennis saw it, a simple and mechanical one. He is to point out its beauties as well as its faults. But that is not all. Part of his obligation is to weigh the beauties against the faults. And if the beauties are more and greater than the faults, he must not be severe upon the poem's weaknesses; in the main, the work is good. If genius appears in a literary performance the critic must not discourage its author. "Wherever Genius runs thro' a Work," remarked Dennis, "I forgive its Faults, and wherever that is wanting no Beauties can touch me." It appears from this statement that there are two kinds of literary beauties: those marked by the signs of genius, and those devoid of genius. How is one to distinguish the two? Not by rule or measure but by their effects. As Dennis often pointed out, the sign of genius is its power to ravish and transport the reader. Thus the question of whether a poem contains beauties of the highest order is made subject to a pragmatic test. In the average sort of poem, where genius does not blind us to the author's weaknesses, we must weigh the beauties against the faults. But how can the two be compared? There is no quantitative measure, and Dennis does not explain how the weighing is to be performed. On the basis of his own psychology of esthetics, however, one would assume that his explanation would be something as follows: if the faults of a work are so numerous or so great as to force themselves upon the attention of the mind, the mind languishes and is therefore incapable of receiving pleasure from the performance; and since a poem can accomplish its design only by giving pleasure, a work of obtrusive faults is an esthetic failure. Alongside of this should be set Dennis's belief that if the beauties of a poem are great and overpowering, the mind is not aware of the poem's faults during the reading of it and the poem, consequently, is able to produce its designed effect. In any event the final judgment of value must be based upon an observation of the poem's effects, and we are driven back upon the pragmatic test.

Dennis explicitly recognized the need of submitting literature to the pragmatic test. Discussing sublimity and fustian, he noted that a poet could distinguish them in a given poem by submitting the work to his friends; if it struck them forcibly and warmed them, it undoubtedly contained the true sublime, for fustian cannot arouse the emotions. Before he trusted his own judgment he often read poems to men of taste among his friends, and if they were touched as he was by the passages he concluded that such works had geniune esthetic value. When he recognized the existence in art of certain "Secret, Unaccountable, Enchanting Graces," he showed his awareness of qualities

that must be judged by their effects rather than by any conceivable objective standards. It never occurred to him that the pragmatic test could result in as many judgments, and reveal as many different standards in art, as there are individual human beings. The test was valid, he believed, only when it was conducted by men of taste, and he was convinced that the judgments of men of taste concerning any given poem would invariably coincide. There were universal standards even when there were no rules.

The moral responsibility of the critic followed from Dennis's belief that one of the prime objects of poetry is to reconcile the passions to virtue. The moral element is a fundamental part of poetry. Of the various *genres* of poetry the drama is best adapted to serve as a school of public virtue. So intimate is the connection between morality and the drama, in fact, that in the past the drama and moral philosophy have risen and fallen together. In tragedy the moral lies embedded in the action and catastrophe; in comedy and the epic, in both action and characters. If the moral of an epic is not sound, or if it is not fully borne out by the action, then the poem is fundamentally weak. A bad moral in the drama may be of pernicious influence, in which event a critic is duty-bound to protest against it, as Dennis protested against Dryden's *All for Love*. For the most part Dennis's ideas about the relationship of poetry and morality were mature and sane. He demanded not that the various parts but that the total effect of the poem should be morally sound. Immodest language he deprecated, but commonly on the grounds that it violated the consistency of manners. Evil and vicious characters might be introduced in the drama and the epic, and might be shown in their true colors. Especially in comedy there was a place for corrupt characters, realistically depicted in all the baseness of their natures. Dennis even enjoyed a touch of salacity in his literature provided that it was managed with finesse and art. As for the general moral contained in the total effect of a poem, Dennis looked for nothing more than a universal truth consistent with good morality. But he expected it to be so clear as to be unmistakable even though it was never put in so many words.

Although the subtle concept of *Zeitgeist* was not yet developed, Dennis and his contemporaries were familiar with the idea that literature depends on many factors, that each poem is in some sense a product of the manners, customs, beliefs, and temperament peculiar to the people among whom it has its rise. The term *historical viewpoint* had not yet been coined, but most of the things which it signifies were commonplace. Dennis showed a constant awareness of the fact that a critic cannot judge a poem properly without being acquainted with the temper and *mores* of the audience for whom it was written. In its simplest form the historical viewpoint appears in his contention with Steele over Etherege's *Man of Mode*: to Sir Richard's argument that the comedy was unsound because the hero, though represented as a fine gentleman, was very far from being so in fact, Dennis replied that the hero represented admirably what a fine gentleman was taken to be in the court of Charles II and that the character of Dorimant therefore was justly and artistically drawn. Manners change, and that which suits one age will not entirely suit another. The complaint of Antigone was understood in Greece, where women mature early and where they were less subject to scruples, but in northern countries, where women mature at a later age, and in modern times, when virginity bears a sacred approval, the complaint would be ridiculous. Climate is the most important condition governing manners and customs, but differences in religion, systems of government, and social circumstances (such as luxury) will create differences in the manners and the attitudes of men. Since the poet writes for men of certain manners and attitudes, the critic must understand the people and times for which the poem is composed if he would judge its effect and its value. Certain episodes in Virgil which are completely probable and reasonable would, if they were copied by a modern poet, become highly improbable "by reason of the vastly different Circumstances of Times, Places, Persons, Customs, Religions, and common received Opinions." A poem may have a higher value for its own age than for any succeeding age. Homer and Virgil, for example, had a greater effect upon their contemporaries than they can have upon a modern audience, for modern readers have no faith in the pagan religion on which the great epics of Greece and Rome were based. Unless a critic understands the manners, customs, and beliefs of different periods and nations, he cannot judge properly of the reasonableness or effectiveness of the literature which developed in those periods or nations.

Being a critic, to Dennis, appeared a grave and responsible occupation, and he thought that a critic should write in a manner in keeping with his position. In treating of a sublime subject he might well write in a sublime style, as had Longinus. But for ordinary purposes he should hold to the didactic style, which is "pure, perspicuous, succinct, unaffected and grave." Since a critic's function is to instruct he must reveal the truth; and truth is plain, simple, and natural, being hidden only by ornament. Ridicule and levity of tone struck Dennis as being positively objectionable in the style of criticism, and he strongly disliked the colloquialism, affectation, and rhetorical flourish in the writings of Collier and Law. In a long and formal treatise it was sometimes desirable, he recognized, to divert the reader with raillery or verse, and in his own critical essays, notably in the *Remarks upon Cato,* he indulged freely in raillery after the manner of Rymer. But in these later treatises in which he employed raillery he was confessedly taking his revenge upon authors who had injured him, and therefore he mingled satire with criticism. The style of these essays, therefore, did not represent his idea of the style appropriate to true criticism.

Although Dennis did not go to the extreme of asserting that only a good poet is qualified to judge of poetry, he believed that a critic must possess in some degree the same qualities which go to the making of a poet. Besides a share of learning and a knowledge of the masterpieces a critic must have sensibility, a capacity for passion and imagination, and a rare discernment and judgment. The qualities which he demanded of a critic are the qualities which good critics have displayed in all ages. The mark of neoclassicism appears mainly in two assumptions: that, since art is the result of a conscious process, a more or less deliberate selection of means to attain a definite and clearly conceived end, the good critic will be able invariably to detect the author's purpose and to estimate accurately the effectiveness of the means employed; and that, since there is but one standard of truth and excellence, all good critics will agree in their judgments. (pp. cvii-cxv)

Edward Niles Hooker, "Introduction: Critical Theories," in The Critical Works of John Dennis: 1711-1729, Vol. II, *edited by Edward Niles Hooker, The Johns Hopkins Press, 1943, pp. lxxvii-cxxv.*

J. W. H. ATKINS (essay date 1951)

[*Atkins was a British literary critic and academic who wrote widely on the history of literary criticism. In the following excerpt, he surveys Dennis's career as a critic, recounting his theories on poetry and drama and ranking his literary achievements.*]

John Dennis (1657-1734), that formidable, heavy-handed critic who, respected, then feared and derided during his lifetime, has since received less than justice from later historians. In his early years as one of the 'young fry' who paid court to Dryden at Will's, his first efforts, like those of Gildon, were devoted to championing the views of the master against divers assailants; and in quick succession there appeared his readable *Impartial Critic,* consisting of five dialogues replying to various points raised in Rymer's *Short View of Tragedy;* also his *Remarks on Blackmore's Prince Arthur,* censuring Blackmore for his inadequate observance of Bossu's rules; and, again, his pamphlet *On the Usefulness of the Stage,* a reply to Collier's savagery, in which he conceded Collier's right to attack abuses but not the stage itself. In the next ten years or so his more original thinking was done; and in his *Advancement and Reformation of Modern Poetry,* his *Large Account of Taste in Poetry,* and his *Grounds of Criticism in Poetry* he submits his real message to his age, namely, the need for an impassioned poetry, fired by religious 'enthusiasm'. The one other critical work belonging to this his most fruitful period was his *Essay on the Genius and Writings of Shakespeare*: after which troubles began to accumulate for one who had previously been hailed as 'the critic'. Subsequently until his death in 1734 he became embroiled in unseemly quarrels with Pope, Addison and others. Devoid of all sympathy with the new generation of writers and embittered by lack of recognition from any quarter, he developed the character of a pugnacious and virulent Zoilus, which has since diminished his stature in the eyes of posterity. Not that these latter years were wholly without useful work; for amidst all the captious fault-finding in his judgments on Pope's *Essay on Criticism,* Addison's *Cato* and the like, there are good things, as there are also in his original *Letters* published in 1721.

That the respect paid to Dennis in his earlier years was not altogether unwarranted is shown by his sensible outlook on current questions in his *Impartial Critic,* whereas of lesser importance are his treatment of Blackmore and his reply to Collier. In the spirited dialogues of the *Impartial Critic,* however, he effectively challenges the redoubtable Rymer, calling him to account on more than one score, and censuring his crude 'pleasantries' as being neither fitting nor convincing. In the first place he disputes Rymer's demand for the restoration of the Greek Chorus to revive the English stage. The Greek Chorus, he asserts, was not adapted to a modern age, in which 'religion, climate and customs' were all different; and its success at Athens was no argument for its adoption on the English stage. It would be as absurd, he added (here alluding to another vexed question of the time), to suggest that love-themes should be banished from English plays because they were rare in Greek drama. Then, too, the same independent attitude is revealed when he counters Rymer's sneer at Dryden's *Oedipus* (1679) because the tragic hero was not strictly in accordance with Aristotelian rules. He concedes the departure from Aristotle's principles: yet Dryden, he maintains, by his 'extraordinary address' had nevertheless produced the necessary tragic effects. The rules of Aristotle, he recalled, were nothing but 'Nature and good sense reduced to a method'; and a judicious use of the rules is all that he recommends. In addition he denounces Rymer's inability to see in Shakespeare anything but faults; and in order to illustrate that critic's imperfect judgment he queries by the way the soundness of his estimate of Waller. That Waller's verse with its wit, good sense and delicate turns of thought was worthy of praise, and that he had first accustomed English ears to the music of a just cadence, this he does not dispute. Yet elsewhere in Waller, he asserted, were improprieties of expression, much prose, and an abuse of epithets; and 'every epithet', he sagely remarks, 'which does not add to the thought is to be looked upon as a botch'. These and other defects, he states, had passed unnoticed by Rymer, and his judgment was therefore of a one-sided kind. Blind to the faults of Waller, he was equally blind to the merits of Shakespeare. And on the necessity for balanced judgment, Dennis, it might be noted, lays some stress at this date. Pointing out that it was easier to find faults than to discern beauties, he explains that 'to do the first requires but common sense, but to do the last a man must have genius'; and again 'to expose a great man's faults without owning his excellences is altogether unjust'.

Of an original kind, however, were the doctrines submitted in the three noteworthy publications that followed, in which he put forward new views concerning poetry in general, and English poetry in particular. He had previously given some indication of the lines along which his mind was working. 'The poet', he had stated, 'is obliged to speak always to the heart', and therefore 'point and conceit and all they call wit is to be banished from true poetry.' And here he revealed the influence not only of 'Longinus', but also of French critics who had emphasized the emotional side of poetry. It was thus upon this emotional element that he now based his conception of poetry. That art he defined as 'an imitation of Nature by a pathctic (i.e. emotional) and numerous (i.e. rhythmical) speech'; and this idea he elsewhere elaborated when he explained that poetry excites emotion in order to delight and reform the mind, and that it performs that task more effectively than philosophy, since it stirs men's minds more powerfully. Moreover he analyses the nature of the emotional element. There are 'vulgar' or ordinary emotions, he states, that are inspired by objects in actual life; there are also 'enthusiastic' or heightened emotions inspired by 'ideas in contemplation'; as when the sun is regarded, not merely as a shining orb, but as an 'image of divinity'. And it is this 'enthusiastic', this heightened and subtler, emotion that he assigns to poetry, a conception that forestalls, if it did not inspire, Wordsworth's idea of poetry as 'emotion recollected in tranquillity'.

With this as the basis of his theory he therefore contends that for the advancement of modern poetry it was necessary to endow it with greater emotional quality. And this, he suggests, would be best achieved by infusing religious 'enthusiasm' as the ancients had done. For such a task, he argued, the Christian religion was specially suitable, since

it reconciled the old conflict between reason and passion which dated from the fall of man; and this it did by seeking not to suppress the passions but to exalt them. Moreover religious poetry necessarily dealt with the loftiest conceptions of which man was capable and was therefore calculated to inspire the most sublime emotions. Thus does he appeal to reason in support of his theory; and if his references to the authority of Aristotle, Hermogenes and 'Longinus' are less convincing, his illustrations drawn from Milton are not without their effect, for it was his admiration for that poet that had largely inspired his theory. Least important in that theory is his advocacy of religious themes, the use of which had previously been attempted in France in connexion with the epic, but without success. What, however, is of value is the stress he lays on 'fine frenzy' as the indispensable emotional element in poetry, thereby running counter to the rationalistic tendencies of his age; and for this he was dubbed 'Sir Longinus' by angry opponents in his later entanglements.

Nor is it in this respect alone that Dennis gives evidence of independent thinking, though his theorizing, for the rest, is along neo-classical lines. Thus he recognizes the necessity for rules in poetry, as well as the existence of the 'kinds'; but his adherence to orthodox principles is by no means absolute. Rules are necessary, he states, to ensure that rational order and harmony which ultimately govern the whole universe. But he notes also some irregularities in Nature which likewise contribute to the harmony of the whole; and the same, he maintains, holds good in poetry. And this he illustrates from *Paradise Lost* with its 'new thought, new images, and an original spirit, all new and different from those of Homer and Virgil'. Then, too, his conceptions of the 'kinds' are in the main neo-classical, though here again he has certain views of his own. With regard to tragedy, for instance, he notes that an observance of the Unities might strengthen the reasonableness of the action, and add clearness and grace; but then, together with Dryden, he considers it to be a 'mechanic rule', not necessarily binding, but one to be set aside in order to obtain some greater artistic beauty.

Less convincing, however, are his arguments for the need of the observance of 'poetic justice' in both tragedy and the epic, a doctrine previously advanced by Rymer, and later condemned by Addison as 'a ridiculous doctrine of modern criticism, without foundation in Nature, reason, or the practice of the ancients'. Dennis, however, asserts that if tragedy and the epic are to instruct with their fables and morals (as Bossu required) then 'poetic justice' was essential, for without it neither pity and terror in tragedy nor admiration in the epic could possibly be evoked. It was a doctrine which led to many unfortunate tamperings with Shakespeare's plays at this date. On the remaining 'kinds' he has less to say, though not without its interest is his declaration in favour of the comedy of humours with its characters of low life as against the comedy of wit with its characters of a more artificial type; or again, there is his preference for the earlier burlesque, as seen in *Hudibras*, as against the mock-heroic recently introduced by Boileau. This latter pronouncement may, however, have been inspired by his hatred of Pope, just as his disapproval of ancient ballads was definitely his retort to Addison's praise of that literary form in the *Spectator* (40).

But it is owing to his judgments in the last phase of his career that he has since incurred the wrath of later historians. And in his various **Remarks** of that period there is much that is deplorable, much scurrility, captious fault-finding and indulgence in personalities, inspired by hostility to the new school of *littérateurs*; so that he has come down as little more than 'a grumbling pedant' or 'a worthless Zoilus'. Thus Pope, for instance, is condemned as an enemy of religion who read into Homer Popish beliefs, while his verses are described as 'an eternal monotony' and 'his Pegasus, a battered Kentish jade'. Then, too, some of his judgments are lacking in insight and are of a misguided kind, as when he decries the delicate spirits in *The Rape of the Lock* on the ground that they are pagan, devoid of allegorical significance, and not justly proportioned to the main theme. On the other hand he is not without his better moments when he gives evidence of sound views and submits some penetrating judgments. Like most of his contemporaries he complains of the degeneration of literary taste, which he attributes to the growing concern of his generation with politics and business affairs; and he has some interesting suggestions to offer concerning the improvement of critical methods and standards. He had previously pointed out the need for balanced judgments; and he further explains that literature appealed not only to the intellect but to the emotions as well. It inspired 'longings which by their pleasant agitation disturb and delight the mind'. And, for actual appreciation, he adds, such things as 'a lively imagination, a piercing judgment, and an ability to enter into the various emotions', all are necessary; since 'for the judging of any sort of writing', he acutely adds, 'those talents are in some measure requisite which were necessary to produce them'.

Nor are his further judgments wholly of a destructive kind, though he has a shrewd eye for defects of various sorts. Pope's power of expression, for instance, he declares, surpassed his power of thought; and he calls attention to the equivocal manner in which that poet employed the terms 'Nature' and 'wit'. In Addison's *Cato*, again, he points out the absurdities that resulted from the strict observance of the Unities; and how lovemaking, conspiracies, debates and fighting all take place perforce in 'the large hall of the Governor's palace at Utica'. At the same time he is also capable of appreciating good things, as was shown by his rapturous and well-founded praise of Milton. That poet had not lacked earlier admirers; but Dennis was the first, after Dryden, to perceive what are perhaps his distinguishing qualities, namely, 'his sublimity and matchless harmony'. It was in virtue of its sublimity that *Paradise Lost* made its appeal to the emotions; and to Dennis it was 'the most lofty and most irregular poem ever produced by the mind of man'. Nor should it escape notice that under the same influence Dennis becomes an early champion of blank verse. That verse-form had previously won but little attention from critics; whereas Dennis now commends it for 'the diversity that distinguishes it from the heroic couplet, bringing it nearer to common use', and making it 'more proper to gain attention and also more fit for action and dialogue'. It might also be added that he notes that 'neither painting nor sculpture can show local motion', a passing glance at the sister arts not without its significance.

Such then in the main was the critical achievement of Dennis; and he is obviously something more than 'a hectoring bully' or a tame purveyor of neo-classical doctrine. From the first he gave signs of independent and even acute thinking, which opened up liberal views concerning literature and criticism as well. And it was in declining to recognize neo-classical rules as absolute and final, in calling attention to the emotional values of poetry in a rationalistic age, and in requiring from the critic poetic insight and sympathy that his best work was done. Of defects of temperament he had his share, defects that increased as time went on and transformed him into an assertive, truculent, fault-finding pedant, thus exciting the hostility and ridicule of Pope, Gay, Parnell and others. Yet to accept their estimate of his critical value is to neglect what had gone before their fierce feuds; for he had carried over into the 18th Century something of the beneficent influences of Dryden, 'Longinus', and certain French critics, and had helped his generation to realize anew the greatness of Milton. This in itself was a valuable performance. And not without its significance is the fact that later on Dr. Johnson, that most sensible of mortals, took him seriously, noting more particularly his faculty of hitting on weak points; though such testimony failed to dissipate the mists of prejudice generated by Pope and others. The truth is that Dennis, if not a great critic, is by no means negligible; for among his prolific writings are to be found many good things that marked an advance in the critical development. (pp. 149-55)

> J. W. H. Atkins, *"Neo-Classicism Challenged: Dennis, Addison, Pope, Swift, Welsted and Blackwell," in his* English Literary Criticism: 17th and 18th Centuries, *Methuen & Co. Ltd., 1951, pp. 146-85.*

EMERSON R. MARKS (essay date 1955)

[*Mark is an American essayist and academic. In the following excerpt, he explores absolutist elements in Dennis's theory of sublimity in poetry.*]

Like the old absolutism, the new variety sought to establish rules inductively derived from extant literature. It adopted much of Aristotle, Horace, and Longinus—as much as could be squared with modern literary practice. It differed in its awareness of history, that is, in recognizing that literature was shaped in part at least by the cultural conditions surrounding its production, and in its belief in literary progress (variously defined). Whether logically or not, most critics of the neoclassical period were "historical" and "comparative" without being relative. Their absolutism is apparent both when they pass judgment on specific writers and when they expound critical theory. (p. 115)

Perhaps more clearly than anyone else, Dennis combined historical analysis with strict absolutist appraisal. In a series of letters published in 1711 under the title of *An Essay on the Genius and Writings of Shakespeare,* he accounts for Shakespeare's "faults" by his times, his lack of knowledge of the rules, and his preoccupation with acting. Dennis' essay, a poor one at best, is certainly not relativist. Like Dryden, he examined new work (notably *Paradise Lost*) in the light of the old, and the old in the light of the new to evolve a critical theory that preserved the essentials of the classical system.

But this was an advance to a new absolutism, not a retreat to authority. For Dennis' eighteenth century critical thought belies his own assertion late in life that the only known rules are those of Aristotle and his interpreters, unless he was thinking of himself as one of them. Like so many others, he was impressed by what appeared to be a discrepancy between the conditions of modern science and modern literature, especially the drama. The English, he declared in 1720, have improved in architecture, music, painting, and "the Mechanick Arts" since the mid-sixteenth century. Only the drama has made no progress, because playwrights, unlike the practitioners of these other "arts," have refused to follow the rules. This dereliction was especially regrettable since, as he saw it, modern culture provided a better opportunity for producing great poetry than had obtained in ancient times—thanks above all to Christianity.

Actually, Dennis advances two arguments in support of the thesis that a Christian culture is uniquely propitious to poetic creation in the major forms: epic, tragedy, and what he called the greater ode. One . . . is part of the doctrine of progress: poetry profits by the advancement of "truth," and Christianity was an obvious advance over paganism in religious truth. This was a view widely subscribed to, even by some who were in other respects "Ancients" and classicists. The other, Dennis' own contribution, belongs in the realm of aesthetic rather than moral criticism. The greatest poetry, he believed, possessed the quality of the "sublime," and sublimity could be achieved only in a poem grounded upon religion.

This argument is not a restatement of the traditional theory of moral didacticism in pious terms. In order to be "sublime" a poem had to move passion in the reader, and every rule was valuable to the extent that it contributed to this effect. This passion was itself only a means (though a most important one) to the two ends of poetry, profit and pleasure. "But Passion answers the Two Ends of Poetry better than Harmony can do. . . . For first, it pleases more, which is evident. . . . And in Tragedy, and in Epick Poetry, a Man may instruct without Harmony, but never without Passion. . . . And as for the greater Ode, if it wants Passion, it becomes hateful and intolerable, and its Sentences grow contemptible." The religious element, in turn, was important as the most effective means of attaining passion—in other words, a means to a means to an end, not the end itself. Its value was aesthetic, not moral. "And thus we have shewn," Dennis writes, "what the chief Excellence in the Body of Poetry is, which we have prov'd to be Passion. Let us now proceed, to the Proofs of what we propounded, That Sacred Subjects, are more susceptible of Passion, than Prophane ones . . . ." And this he proceeds to do at length by examining passages from classical and modern poetry.

Dennis' theory of religion and passion as prime structural elements in poetry is clearly absolute. One notes certain earmarks of the absolutist method in his procedure. His starting point in **The Advancement and Reformation of Modern Poetry** is that found in every absolutist theory—a definition, in this case of poetry itself. "But before we proceed," he writes, "let us define Poetry; which is the first Time that a Definition has been given of that noble Art: For neither Ancient nor Modern Criticks have defin'd Poetry in general. Poetry then is an Imitation of Nature, by a pathetick and numerous Speech." In what immediately follows he distinguishes poetry from prose, concluding that "Poetry is Poetry, because it is more Passionate and Sensual than Prose." Passionless numbers are but mea-

sured prose; non-metrical discourse "that is every where extremely pathetick . . . is certainly Poetry without Numbers. . . . Passion then, is the Characteristical Mark of Poetry . . . ." (pp. 121-24)

Dennis' work is an attempt at a systematic theory setting forth a poetic in abstract terms. It displays, accordingly, both the merits and the defects of a more ambitious and deliberate undertaking. (p. 124)

Like Dryden's, Dennis' critical system does not displace the Aristotelian-Longinian aesthetic: one does not have to say that if Dennis was right the classical critics were wrong. The **Poetics** seeks primarily to reveal how tragedy functions; **On the Sublime** discovers, among other things, certain formal elements—figures of speech, stylistic devices, organic unity—as absolutes effecting that rare quality of *hypsos* which characterizes the finest literary work. Dennis, agreeing with Longinus that all truly great literature possessed something called "sublimity," sought not a different but a further source of it. In effect, his analysis probes beneath the absolutes of rhetorical detail isolated by Longinus to something he considered more fundamental. In **The Grounds of Criticism**, after paraphrasing Longinus' six "Marks" of the Sublime, he marvels "upon Reflection, how it could happen that so great a Man as *Longinus*, who whenever he met a Passage in any Discourse that was lofty enough to please him, had discernment enough to see that it had some of the preceding Marks, should miss of finding so easy a thing as this, that never any Passage had all these Marks, or so much as the Majority of them, unless it were Religious." Though he departs further from tradition than Dryden and others, his theory is rather an expansion and a complication than a substitution.

Whatever their inherent value, John Dennis' critical writings are of central significance in understanding the nature of the debate between relativist and absolutist as revealed in its first major phase in English criticism. For his work reflects with special fidelity the various and often contradictory influences upon contemporary critical thought of the new science and the new literature, of the idea of progress, and of the growing awareness of history. To dismiss the great bulk of his criticism—and that of his contemporaries—as a willful retreat to authority is to obscure the entire issue. In its failure to see that the one is largely inductive, the other deductive, such a misinterpretation establishes a wholly untenable equation between absolutist and dogmatic criticism. And this confusion, like that between historical and relativist criticism, promotes a misleading simplification of what is in reality a complex problem of literary aesthetics. (pp. 124-25)

Emerson R. Marks, "The New Absolutism," in his Relativist & Absolutist: The Early Neoclassical Debate in England, *Rutgers University Press, 1955, pp. 115-26.*

A. N. WILKINS (essay date 1958)

[*Wilkins is an American essayist and academic. In the following excerpt, he explicates Dennis's theory on the purpose and presentation of love in seventeenth- and eighteenth-century drama and examines Dennis's attempted application of this theory in* Rinaldo and Armida *and* Iphigenia.]

One of the numerous complaints of John Dennis the critic was that the theatrical audience of his day would "endure no Modern Tragedy in whose principal Character Love [was] not the predominant Quality." He was certainly not the only person who objected to the manner in which this emotion was presented on the London stage in the late seventeenth and early eighteenth centuries. Such writers as Thomas Rymer, Jeremy Collier and William Law criticised the theatres severely for their representation of love, but Dennis disagreed sharply with these men who, he thought, wanted to banish this passion altogether from the drama. He did not want to eliminate it from English tragedy; he merely wanted the dramatists to present the emotion in accordance with what he considered to be sound moral and critical principles. First, he argued that if love is to be introduced into a tragedy, it should be a genuinely "Tragical Passion, [one that] is the Cause or the Effect of a real Tragical Distress; that is, of something which is in it self terrible or deplorable." Second, it should either contribute to the resolution of the plot or should be subordinated to those emotions which do. Otherwise it will destroy the unity of action. Third, he asserted that when love is represented on the stage, it should reinforce the moral of the drama. He believed that tragedy is primarily a didactic art in which the playwright entertains the audience so that he may instruct them. When the dramatist does not present a moral in the play or when he does not provide "an exact Distribution of a Poetical Justice," he has failed, according to Dennis, in writing a tragedy worthy of the name. Too many of his contemporaries, when they made love the ruling passion of the hero, produced dramas which were "false in Morality, and of scandalous Instruction." Finally, the critic insisted, when this emotion is introduced into a play, it should be presented so that it is believable. Dramatic persons who are in love should act as human beings may be expected to act under such circumstances.

As an example of a tragedy in which love is truly a "Tragical Passion," Dennis cited Thomas Otway's *The Orphan. . . .*

By contrast, Dennis criticized John Dryden's *All for Love* because of its failure to provide the audience with a suitable moral. It is quite true that Antony's passion for Cleopatra brings about his defeat by Octavius and his suicide and that it might, therefore, be considered a "Tragical Passion," but the drama does not condemn the adultery of Antony. (p. 396)

Another play which Dennis attacked for its failure to present love properly was Joseph Addison's *Cato*. In this work, it is not the ruling passion of the hero; Cato is primarily concerned with the preservation of Roman liberty. The lovers are his sons Portius and Marcus and his daughter Marcia, as well as Lucia, Juba, and Sempronius. One of the main faults of this drama according to Dennis, is the failure of its author to subordinate the action arising from this emotion to the principal concerns of the play, the fate of Cato and of Rome. As the complications caused by love produce "no real Tragical Distress" and as they in no way hasten or retard the catastrophe, these subplots destroy the unity of action. Furthermore, the critic observed that since all of the drama takes place within twenty-four hours, it is improbable that the sons of Cato, or the others for that matter, would "play the whining

Amorous Milk-Sops" on the day which, as Portius says, is to decide the fate of Cato and of Roman liberty.

Although Dryden and Addison failed to present love in these dramas as Dennis thought it should be portrayed, he believed that in at least two of his own tragedies—*Rinaldo and Armida* and *Iphigenia*—he had been successful in representing this emotion in conformity with his own critical principles. By examining one of these plays, therefore, a person should be able to evaluate to some extent Dennis' success in applying his own precepts. Of the two tragedies, *Iphigenia* seems likely to show more of his method. *Rinaldo and Armida* is based upon Torquato Tasso's *Jerusalem Delivered*, a poem which describes the love of the Prince of Este and the niece of the King of Damascus. As the basic situation of the play was provided in his source, the most that he could do was to alter Tasso's treatment of love. In writing *Iphigenia*, however, Dennis had considerably greater freedom in presenting this emotion. It is an adaptation of Euripides' *Iphigenia in Tauris*, in which no character is motivated by love. Therefore, that part of his play involving the amours of Orestes, Pilades, Iphigenia, and the Queen of Scythia was contrived by Dennis. For this reason, *Iphigenia* provided him with a greater opportunity for applying his own principles.

Despite this addition, his version presents the same basic problem as the *Iphigenia in Tauris*. The Oracle of Delphi has informed Orestes that he may expiate the sin of slaying his mother by bringing to Athens the statue of Artemis (or Diana, as Dennis calls her) which is in a temple in the land of the Tauri. As the play opens, he and his friend Pilades have arrived in that country to carry out the instructions of the oracle and have hidden the ship in which they hope to escape. Among the Tauri, unknown to Orestes, his sister Iphigenia is the chief priestess of the temple whose duty it is to consecrate the sacrificial offerings to Artemis. As the custom of the people is to sacrifice all strangers to the goddess, it seems that Iphigenia, unaware of the identity of Orestes and Pilades, may officiate at their death. To prevent this misfortune, the playwrights bring about a mutual recognition between Iphigenia and Orestes.

Though the basic problem of *Iphigenia* is the same as that of Euripides' drama, the solution is different. In the *Iphigenia in Tauris*, the heroine reveals her identity by offering to help Orestes escape if he will bear a message to an acquaintance of her's in Argos, the city of her birth. Orestes, however, insists that he should die and that Pilades should carry the letter. When Iphigenia discloses that it is addressed to Orestes, he tells his sister who he is. Because of her office of priestess, she is able to arrange their escape by pretending that the strangers and the idol must be purified in the sea before the goddess will accept the sacrifice. Once on the seashore, Orestes, Pilades, and Iphigenia carry the image to the hidden ship and set sail for Greece. The Tauri are prevented from pursuing the fugitives when Pallas Athena appears and forbids any attempt to overtake them.

In Dennis' play, the recognition is brought about by different means. So that there may be an equal number of men and women, a Queen of Scythia was substituted for Thoas, King of Tauris, the monarch in the *Iphigenia in Tauris*. While Orestes and Pilades fall in love with Iphigenia before they discover her identity, both the priestess and the queen are attracted to Orestes. At first the queen orders that Pilades be sacrificed to the goddess and that Orestes be allowed to live, but when the Greeks resolve that both shall die if either does, she offers to release them if they will marry Scythians and, thereby, cease to be strangers before the law. Pilades is to marry Iphigenia, and the queen proposes to wed Orestes. The latter, however, refuses, and the queen discovers his affection for Iphigenia. Thereupon, the monarch tricks him into vowing that he would marry her if the woman he loves were dead. At this point, she orders that Iphigenia be sacrificed to the goddess. As her people protest against the sacrilege of slaying a priestess, the queen reveals that Iphigenia is the daughter of Agamemnon and that she has already escaped such a death at Aulis through the conspiracy of her father and mother. When Orestes learns that Iphigenia is his sister, he consents to marry the queen. Pilades is eager to wed the priestess, and the queen agrees to leave her kingdom and live in Greece. Finally she enables Orestes to expiate his sin by allowing him to carry the image of the goddess to Athens. (pp. 397-98)

Despite the introduction of love into *Iphigenia*, Dennis stated that the main purpose of his play was "to enflame the Minds of an Audience with the Love of ... Friendship," and he believed that he had "made Love a subordinate Passion, and subjected it ... to Friendship." Assuming that Orestes is the hero, one must grant that this is a "Tragedy, in whose principal Character Love is not the predominant Quality." The praise of friendship is constantly on his lips. On one occasion he asks Pilades to take shelter in the ship while he holds off the attacking Scythians. Twice he requests that he be sacrificed to the goddess so that Pilades may live. Although he does love Iphigenia, when he discovers that Pilades is also fond of her and that this rivalry threatens their friendship, Orestes does not hesitate to agree that he will relinquish his claim if the girl should prefer Pilades to him. Furthermore, though he declares at one time that he can never love the queen, he consents to marry her as the play ends. Thus, though Orestes is not indifferent to love, it is certainly not his ruling passion. Therefore, as far as the character of the hero is concerned, this emotion is subordinated to friendship.

Although Dennis achieved his purpose in this respect, he was no more successful than Addison in making love a "Tragical Passion." This emotion produces no "real Tragical Distress." Perhaps the incidents in which Orestes and Pilades encounter danger to protect one another do arouse fear and even pity, but there are no events in *Iphigenia* which are "terrible or deplorable" in the sense in which the critic used these terms. (pp. 417-18)

Perhaps more pertinent to the present inquiry is the question whether love contributes to the resolution of the plot or whether it is subordinated to an emotion which does. The affection of Iphigenia for Orestes and that of Pilades for her may be dismissed at once. She is a character who is entirely passive as far as the plot is concerned. She initiates no successful action; both her suffering and her ultimate happiness are brought about by the deeds of others. Nor do the acts of Pilades affect the plot to any great degree. It is necessary that his affection for Iphigenia be shown, for he marries her in the end, but the only other effect of his love is a minor conflict with Orestes. When Pilades learns that his friend is fond of the girl, he is jealous, but, as has been pointed out, this rivalry is short lived.

Orestes' affection for Iphigenia, however, is somewhat more important. It does not in itself bring about the resolution, but it does affect the course of the action in so far as it causes him to reject the advances of the queen and thereby moves her to act. More directly, it is the love of the queen for Orestes which leads to the conclusion of the play. First, it induces her to order that Pilades be put to death and that Orestes be permitted to live. Second, when he determines to die if his friend does, her affection for him causes her to offer the Greeks their freedom if Orestes will marry her. Finally, when he refuses and she learns that he loves Iphigenia, her passion moves the queen to command that the priestess be sacrificed to the goddess. The queen, therefore, is the most powerful character as far as the plot is concerned. She not only takes the part played by King Thoas in the *Iphigenia in Tauris*; she also assumes the function of the *deus ex machina*. In Euripides' drama, it is the appearance of Pallas Athena which prevents the pursuit and capture of Orestes and his friends when they have escaped with the idol. In the adaptation, it is the queen who permits the transportation of the image to Greece. Consequently, there is no doubt that since her ruling passion is love, this emotion contributes to the resolution of the plot.

Furthermore, love is considerably more important to the action of *Iphigenia* than friendship. It is true that Orestes is preserved from death because of Pilades' loyalty. Early in the play when he is made helpless by a seizure, his friend protects him from the attacking Scythians. In turn, Orestes' faithfulness prevents Pilades from being put to death when the queen tries to honour the custom of the country by having him sacrificed and, at the same time, to save the man she loves. Furthermore, each of these friends makes another attempt to save his companion by giving up his own life. Still, the actions of Orestes and Pilades are little more than responses to the chain of events set in motion by the queen. Therefore, instead of subordinating love to friendship, Dennis has done quite the opposite. The unity of action is preserved, but the emotion which produces the conflict and also resolves it is the love of the queen for Orestes.

In addition to contributing to the resolution of the plot, love should, the critic believed, help to reinforce the moral of a tragedy. As the avowed intention of Dennis in writing *Iphigenia* was "to enflame the Minds of an Audience with the Love of ... Friendship," the lesson which he hoped to provide for the spectators might be phrased as follows: True friendship will triumph over all obstacles and will protect friends from all danger. Obviously, the deeds of Orestes and Pilades are intended to excite admiration for friendship, and the exploits of these companions which have already been described should contribute to this purpose. Not only are these heroes willing to sacrifice their lives for one another; even when they are in love with the same woman they do not allow this rivalry to endanger their friendship. The point which their conduct is intended to illustrate, that friendship is more to be admired than love, is voiced by Orestes when he appeals to Pilades to put aside his jealousy. ... Still, however admirable the friendship of these comrades, it has comparatively little influence upon the action of the play. It is not their loyalty to one another which saves them from the fate which awaits most foreigners in the land of the Tauri. It is not their friendship which enables Orestes to fulfill the prophecy of the oracle. It is the love of the queen for Orestes. Therefore, in the same spirit in which Dennis supplied a moral for Dryden's *All for Love*, one may suggest that what the action of *Iphigenia* really tends to prove is that if an absolute monarch wants to marry a man, she can have her way if she is persistent. If the plot does not actually contradict the proposition which the drama is intended to demonstrate, it provides no support for the thesis. Consequently, as love motivates the action, one must conclude that it does not reinforce the intended moral of the play. In this respect, therefore, Dennis was not entirely successful in applying his principles.

The final criterion proposed by the critic for judging the representation of love in tragedy is credibility, and one must confess that not all the incidents in *Iphigenia* which are produced by this emotion are believable. The queen's infatuation and her attempts to win Orestes seem rather improbable, and her final decision, once she has won him, to live in Greece and allow Scythia to be ruled by a viceroy is not entirely convincing. Furthermore, the speed with which the various characters fall in love with one another seems a bit excessive. Perhaps, however, one may attribute some of these improbabilities to the dramatic conventions of the late seventeenth century. Nevertheless, one must conclude that Dennis was only partially successful in applying his principles in *Iphigenia* and that he was mistaken in believing that he had subordinated love to friendship. (pp. 418-19)

[Whether] Dennis made love a "Tragical Passion" or subordinated it to another emotion, he provides the comparatively rare instance of a critic who tried to apply his own "rules." If he failed as often as he succeeded, it should not be surprising. For as he himself wrote, it is "impossible for any Man who has not a great Genius, strictly to observe the Rules." (p. 419)

A. N. Wilkins, "John Dennis on Love as a 'Tragical Passion'," in Notes and Queries, Vol. CCIII, September and October, 1958, Pp. 396-98; 417-19.

JOAN C. GRACE (essay date 1969)

[*Grace is an American academic and essayist. In the following excerpt from a work first published in 1969, she examines Dennis's distinction between vulgar and enthusiastic passions and his interpretation of the sources of poetic genius and inspiration.*]

Although interested, as Rymer was, in the subject matter of tragedy and in the demands of the work itself, John Dennis gives more attention to the psychology of the artist and to the effect of tragedy upon the audience. His approach reveals greater historical perspective than that of Rymer, in consequence of which he is able to appreciate Shakespeare, as Rymer was not.

Dennis's most liberating critical innovation in relation to the artist is his idea of genius, first defined in the Preface to *Remarks upon "Prince Arthur"* as "the expression of a Furious Joy, or Pride, or Astonishment, or all of them caused by the conception of an extraordinary hint." Dennis's definition of the classical *furor poeticus* is partly derived from Boileau's translation in 1674 of Longinus's

Peri Hupsous. Longinus mentions two qualities of the sublime that result exclusively from the poet's innate ability rather than from art, namely, the capacity to form daring and magnificent thoughts and images, and the power to experience violent or even enthusiastic passions proceeding from these thoughts and images.

Dennis's theory of genius also bears a relationship to general Hobbesian doctrine. Hobbes, in *Leviathan*, (1:viii), indicates that the foundation of genius is passion, as it is for Dennis. One kind of joy, according to Hobbes (*Leviathan* 1:vi), springs from a sudden exaltation of the mind in its own power. Dennis, beginning with Hobbes's doctrine of the exaltation of the soul in composition, stated that the frenzy of the poet, which had formerly been considered divine, is either a common passion or a "complication of common Passions." The Preface to *Remarks upon "Prince Arthur"* expresses Dennis's views on the nature of poetic genius and on the sources of poetic inspiration. The capacity to write well and easily, says Dennis, springs from the same sources as other kinds of happiness in ordinary life. The soul becomes exalted by a hint peculiarly its own. If the hint is great and elevated, the soul expands at the sudden realization of its own unique power. A man in such a state of exaltation expresses himself differently from one who is serene.

For the genius, poetic composition is an intuitive act that simultaneously brings together strong feeling and the figurative language by which to express what the poet wants to say. Poetic creativity. Dennis holds, is marked by a kind of spontaneous, organic unity. In *The Advancement and Reformation of Modern Poetry*, Dennis identifies this quality of genius with the ability both to feel and to express passion. The successful dramatist, for instance, is one who is able to portray strong passion rather than one who constructs a well-made plot. Dennis denies, however, that genius alone is sufficient to achieve a work of stature: "Yet 'tis Art," he writes, "that makes a Subject very great, and, consequently, gives Occasion for a great Genius to shew itself." Without the control of established literary conventions, especially in tragedy and the epic, Dennis believes, poetic chaos will inevitably prevail. He insists that poetic fury be tempered by judgment, although he speaks of the forces of nature prevailing in the poet, even sometimes exalting him to the divine.

Dennis, as does Hobbes, defines vivid thoughts by calling them images. For Dennis, imagery means the material from reflection. The imagination for him is not limited to the mere power to recall images, however, or to invent a fanciful combination of images. It has aspects of a creative faculty, for as Clarence D. Thorpe notes [in *The Aesthetic Theory of Thomas Hobbes* (1940)]:

> With Dennis, as with Hobbes, ideas have their origin in sense impression. These ideas are of two sorts: those which come from ordinary objects and those which derive from the uncommon and the extraordinary. In the first case the ideas are full and clear; in the second, they are indefinite, somewhat beyond the realm of full apprehension. The first give rise to ordinary passions, the second to the enthusiastic passions.

Dennis originally made this distinction between the ordinary and enthusiastic passions in *The Advancement and Reformation of Modern Poetry*. Three years later, in *The Grounds of Criticism in Poetry*, he changed the term "ordinary" to "vulgar," and once more defined the vulgar and enthusiastic passions. Vulgar passions, giving rise to anger, pity, admiration, or wonder, are those aroused by objects themselves or by ideas in the ordinary course of life. The enthusiastic passions, leading to admiration, terror, horror, joy, sadness, or desire, are aroused by things outside common life. The enthusiastic passions are heightened by the mind's own consciousness of intense reflection. They are "caus'd by Ideas occurring to us in Meditation, and producing the same Passions that the Objects of those Ideas would raise in us, if they were set before us in the same light that those Ideas give us of them." Enthusiastic passions are moved by ideas of objects not as they actually appear to the senses but as they are shaped and changed and interpreted by the human mind. "Poetical Enthusiasm," said Dennis in *The Advancement and Reformation of Modern Poetry*, "is a Passion guided by Judgment, whose Cause is not comprehended by us." It is greater and more intense than ordinary passion. Illustrating the difference between the vulgar and enthusiastic passions in *The Grounds of Criticism in Poetry*, Dennis calls attention to the difference between the minimal effect upon the imagination of ordinary ideas in conversation and their power in meditation to arouse terror, admiration, or horror. Dennis's view of the origin of poetic creativity in this respect resembles Wordsworth's, but is different in that it emphasizes poetic fury rather than "emotion recollected in tranquillity."

Dennis changed his original definition of genius as the expression of strong feeling caused by "an extraordinary hint," contained in *Remarks upon "Prince Arthur,"* to the one he offers in *The Advancement and Reformation of Modern Poetry,* in which genius in the poet means the power worthily to express great passion, whether ordinary or enthusiastic, because he recognized that tragedy deals with the ordinary passions. Poetry arouses both vulgar and enthusiastic passions, states Dennis in *The Grounds of Criticism in Poetry,* but the vulgar passions are preferable in a way, because the poet who stirs these passions communicates to the largest audience. The enthusiastic passions are more subtle, and some people are incapable of experiencing them. The vulgar passions must particularly predominate in the parts of the epic and tragedy in which the characters converse together. (pp. 61-4)

Genius ultimately means for Dennis the power adequately to express great passion. It includes also a balanced relationship between passion and judgment. Because, in the genius, the fire of the heart and the fire of the mind are one, Dennis suggests, such a poet will express himself passionately, and give his finished work the unity of a living organism.

Dennis's view of genius and his conviction that poetry results from passion controlled by judgment are related to his philosophy of pleasure. In *The Usefulness of the Stage* Dennis states that the end of man is to achieve happiness, defined by Dennis as pleasure. It is by this principle that God maintains harmony in the universe. Happiness, he says, eludes men because they have associated it with the life of reason, and have, as a consequence, negated the importance of strong feeling. Pleasure, on the contrary, results, says Dennis, from passion—from being moved. (p. 65)

Passion, according to Dennis, is pleasurable, but requires a check by reason. Dennis, although at first under the influence of the fabulist André Dacier, was the chief English proponent of Descartes's view that the stirring of passion is itself a kind of interior sensuality.... Dennis was also influenced by the concept stemming from Book II of Lucretius's *De rerum natura*, that pleasure is associated with the viewer's realization of his own freedom from similar suffering.

Dennis sees the ends of poetry and of tragedy as the conventional ones of moral utility and pleasure. Poetry, says Dennis in *The Grounds of Criticism in Poetry*, is "an Art, by which a Poet excites Passion (and for that very Cause entertains Sense) in order to satisfy and improve, to delight and reform the Mind, and so to make Mankind happier and better: from which it appears that Poetry has two Ends, a subordinate, and a final one; the subordinate one is Pleasure, and the final one is Instruction." In the tradition of Sir Philip Sidney, Dennis believed that poetry moves us not only to want to know what is virtuous but also to want to act virtuously. Even the moral philosopher, says Dennis, cannot reform without appealing to the passionate side of man's nature. However, because poetry moves more than philosophy, it also has greater power to reform. On the basis of this reasoning, Dennis concludes that the fable, incidents, characters, sentiments, and expression in tragedy must be especially designed to move, and that since tragedy moves more than comedy, it is consequently more instructive.

Referring to Aristotle, Dennis stresses the emotional effect of surprise in tragedy, particularly in the peripety. The surprise, says Dennis, following Aristotle, should appear to result from necessity and not from chance.

Surprise is most effective when related to a pattern of apparent order. If the opponents of regularity would study Sophocles' *Oedipus*, Dennis had previously said, they would see how the structure of the play leads from surprise to surprise, from compassion to terror, and from terror to compassion again. Experience and philosophy have shown, says Dennis, that regularity of structure is required "for the surer exciting of Passion."

The Advancement and Reformation of Modern Poetry connects tragedy closely with religious experience, and notes the religious origin of Greek tragedy. Both religion (meaning for Dennis Christianity) and poetry stimulate our passions and at the same time enable us to harmonize our passions with our reason and will. Religion for the believing Christian, Dennis suggests, implies a rational order controlling the universe, an order also manifested in the design of the poet's work, even though the poet may happen to be an ancient Greek rather than a modern Christian. Just as the Christian's belief that the turbulence of life and history will ultimately be rendered meaningful by a just God enables him to control his passions, without repressing them, so the essential regularity of the dramatist's work makes our response to tragedy enlightening and harmonious, whereas it might otherwise be frenzied and disjointed. (pp. 66-8)

Three things ultimately contribute to the perfection of poetry and therefore of tragedy: nature (or genius or passion), art ("those Rules, and that Method, which capacitate us to manage every thing with the utmost Dexterity, that may contribute to the raising of Passion"), and the richness of the language. Greek tragedy, Dennis says, was great because the Greek language was perfected, the art of poetry—particularly the art of tragedy—had been cultivated, and religion moved the passions of the people. (p. 69)

The concept of genius introduces into Dennis's critical theory an idea that allows him to respond to Shakespeare in a way that Rymer could not. *An Essay on the Genius and Writings of Shakespeare* praises Shakespeare as "one of the Greatest Genius's that the World e'er saw for the Tragick Stage." His beauties were his own; his defects the result of his education and the age in which he lived. He also wrote under the pressure of theatrical deadlines, and could not wait until such time as his spirits were warm and volatile. Though unfamiliar with the ancients and with the rules, "he had a natural Discretion which never cou'd have been taught him, and his Judgment was strong and penetrating." He seemed to lack only leisure to discover the rules, of which he appeared so ignorant. Dennis pays tribute to Shakespeare's innate ability. He greatly admired Shakespeare's characterization—its justness, exactness, vividness—although he criticized his anachronisms, his failure to maintain unity of action in his historical plays, and his omission of poetic justice and a moral in some of his best tragedies. The violation of time and place, Dennis realized, was necessary for greater effect.

Shakespeare had an extraordinary talent for arousing the passions, especially terror, and his representation of them was so just, lively, and appropriate that he touches us more than other tragic poets, whose plotting and beauty of design are superior. Shakespeare's diction, in many places, is good and pure after a hundred years; his expression is "simple tho' elevated, graceful tho' bold, and easie tho' strong." He seems, says Dennis, to have originated English tragic harmony—the harmony of blank verse, diversified by dissyllabic and trisyllabic endings. This diversity distinguishes it from heroic harmony, and brings poetic expression nearer to popular usage. It gains more attention, and is better fitted for action and dialogue than heroic verse.

Shakespeare, Dennis thought, had a genius for tragedy. If he had had the art of Sophocles and Euripides, he would have surpassed them. Though he admired the French, Dennis believed, as did Dryden, that many elements in the work of Shakespeare were greater. If he had been familiar with the Greeks, he would have imitated Sophocles and Euripides instead of Plautus, whose work, Dennis believed, Shakespeare had probably read in translation.

Shakespeare's lack of learning and art caused him, according to Dennis, to make serious mistakes in characters drawn from history and in the consistency and appropriateness of his characters. Because he did not know the rules, he made his incidents less moving, less surprising, and less wonderful than they might have been. Dennis, illustrating by reference to *Coriolanus*, says that Shakespeare seems almost industriously to have avoided taking advantage of the emotional effects in tragedy that compliance with the rules makes possible. On this point, Dennis was more right than he realized. Shakespeare broke the rules, if he was conscious of them, because he realized that if the artist is to advance he must go beyond established norms. They are useful as a basis of design but stagnating when followed undeviatingly. (pp. 70-2)

Coriolanus, a play altered by Dennis to accord with his own theories, lacks, he believes, a moral, and most of Shakespeare's best tragedies violate poetic justice. As a man of his time, Dennis failed to realize what Shakespeare, no doubt, perceived—that the disproportionate consequence of the hero's action is precisely what makes his fate tragic, and that the nature of reality makes his fate what it is.

Shakespeare, concludes Dennis, was a genius who would have succeeded even better with a knowledge of the Greeks and of the rules; nonetheless, he "had none to imitate, and is himself inimitable."

Although Dennis, as we shall see, is in many ways a neoclassical critic, the concept of genius makes his critical theory freer and more viable than Rymer's. The Longinian approach to literature views literature as process, the Aristotelian as product. Shakespeare in his tragedies is always developing—breaking his own molds. (p. 73)

Although Dennis believes that poetry should imitate nature, meaning what Louis I. Bredvold has called *"la belle nature,"* and should be related to the ancient classics, he values originality most of all. Shakespeare's glory, he says, was derived from the fact that his magnificent achievements were "entirely his own, and owing to the Force of his own Nature." Dennis attempts to reconcile originality with tradition, genius with the rules, passion with reason. (p. 74)

The function of poetry and of all the arts, Dennis believes, is to help restore man's inner harmony. The rules are a means to this end. They are based upon the example of great works, tested by the response of successive generations of men, and are therefore empirical and scientific. Homer and Virgil, states Dennis in *The Advancement and Reformation of Modern Poetry*, realized the necessity of following the rules, and they did not appeal to a narrow audience of fellow countrymen but "to their Fellow-Citizens of the Universe, to all Countries, and to all Ages." The great classic writers were not without passion and imagination, yet they realized that nothing except what is great in reason and nature, meaning what reflects the harmonious order of the universe, can lastingly please mankind. The rules of poetry, like the rules of life and philosophy, are chiefly condemned, Dennis says, by those who either cannot understand them or cannot endure the labor of following them. (pp. 74-5)

The rules, according to Dennis, reflect the regularity of nature. Nothing in nature is beautiful without rule and order. The more rule and order in objects, the more they please our senses. . . . For example, Dennis finds Sophocles' *Oedipus Rex* more moving than Shakespeare's *Julius Caesar* because Sophocles' tragedy is just and regular, Shakespeare's extravagant and irregular. (p. 75)

The rules, for Dennis, applied primarily to tragedy. In contrast to Dryden, who believed the epic to be the highest form of poetry, Dennis preferred tragedy. Tragedy, Dennis believes, must contain a fable, or fictionalized version of a universal truth, exemplified in a unified action, the characters of which are generally to be historical and significant. A fable, according to Dennis, "is a Discourse invented to form the Manners by Instructions disguised under the Allegory of an Action." . . . The characters in tragedy, Dennis maintains, must also be universal and allegorical. The purpose of the action is to prove the moral, and the action cannot be completed until the moral has been exhaustively worked out. Dennis criticized Dryden's *All for Love* because it lacked a moral and a fable, and, as noted previously, he objected to the lack of a fable in Shakespeare's historical plays.

The action of tragedy, according to Dennis, must have an allegorical or universal meaning capable of instructing the audience in moral conduct by arousing and purging the emotions of pity and fear in such a way as to bring the passions into harmony with reason. The experience of tragedy, Dennis maintains, provides the emotional means to lead men to seek reasonable choices supported by the passions in harmony with the will. Witnessing a tragedy, he thought, should encourage virtuous living based on a union of rational conviction, passion, and desire. Dennis combines a fabulist and affective approach to the problem of tragic catharsis. The purgation of pity and fear contributes to moral utility.

Although Dennis occasionally develops decorum of manners as stolidly as Rymer did, he realizes that characters in tragedy cannot always reflect the ideal. He permits representation of evil characters in tragedy, provided they are shown to be what they are. Dennis acknowledges human uniqueness. A character's speech, however, he maintains, must accord with his rank and with propriety.

By reference to Horace, Freeman, the dialogist in *The Impartial Critic* who reflects Dennis's own thinking, explains, "*A Tragedy is Fabula recte morata*, in which the Manners are well painted: So that every Actor discovers immediately by what he says, his Inclinations, his Designs, and the very Bottom of his Character." Manners of epic characters, Dennis explains in *Remarks upon "Prince Arthur,"* following Le Bossu, should be *good* [well-delineated], *like* [in accord with tradition], *convenient* [appropriate], and *equal* [consistent]. In general, Dennis applies the same requirements to tragic characters. However, Dennis, in contrast to Rymer, notes that Aristotle permits the imitation of what is irregular in nature, but in this case the dramatist must make the incidents or character consistently unequal and irregular. Dennis not only follows Le Bossu's insistence that manners be well marked—with the hero's manners showing a predominant quality—but he also agrees with Le Bossu that characters should be delineated with varying degrees of intensity in proportion to their significance in the action. (pp. 77-8)

The Impartial Critic, employing arguments based on Dacier, is intended to answer Rymer's claim of superiority for the ancient method of tragedy. It also aims to refute Rymer's attacks on Shakespeare. Dennis is not hostile to Rymer, but he dislikes Rymer's style and his habit of finding only faults in Shakespeare's plays. Dennis never executed his contemplated defense of Shakespeare alluded to at the close of *The Impartial Critic,* although in 1712 he published *An Essay on the Genius and Writings of Shakespeare,* to which reference has been made earlier. The dialogue method employed in *The Impartial Critic,* by its very nature, suggests a freer, more exploratory approach to criticism than that of Rymer.

Freeman, in *The Impartial Critic,* remarking on Rymer's *The Tragedies of the Last Age* and *A Short View of Trage-*

dy, finds more learning in the latter and more good sense in the former. Dennis dislikes the design, method, and style of *A Short View of Tragedy.* Besides defining the purpose of tragedy and the nature of the tragic hero according to Aristotle, modified by Horace, *The Impartial Critic* answers Rymer's arguments in favor of the chorus, although Dennis actually devotes himself more to Dacier's comments on it than to those of Rymer, who supported the chorus largely because it was characteristic of the most effective classical tragedies. (p. 83)

Dennis is more liberal than Rymer in regard to probability. The wonderful, the "consistently inconsistent," and even the irregular are permitted in tragedy if they demonstrate an ultimate regularity. Both critics are somewhat casual about the unities of time and place. Dennis's appreciation of genius allows him to give greater weight to the total effect of tragedy than Rymer can according to his standards of common sense and the rules. Responsive to the grandeur, passion, and unity of Greek tragedy, Dennis is restricted by his belief in moral utility and poetic justice. Both critics' understanding of Aristotle is distorted by French interpretations.

Dennis's importance lies particularly in his consideration of the psychology of the artist. Furthermore, the emphasis he gives to passion as a stimulus to poetic composition shows that, in opposition to the rationalism of his age, he sensed the role in literary creation of what is now termed the unconscious. In this respect, he exhibits an openminded and probing interest in creative processes, and employs with originality the psychology of Hobbes, who had a similar interest. (pp. 85-6)

Despite his loyalty to the norms of neoclassicism, Dennis defends the necessity for originality. In contrast to the rationalists and the neoclassicists, he establishes genius as the ultimate standard by which he judges both poet and critic. His sympathetic treatment of the imagination and the passions predicts some of the changes that emerge in Romantic criticism, notably in that of Wordsworth and Coleridge. His praise of Shakespeare also attests to a shift from rigid, rationalistic criticism, particularly of the type exemplified by Rymer, to one of appreciative response.

Dennis's conservatism prevented him from developing his own insights as fully as he might have. His dependence upon *a priori* reasoning is unfortunately less stimulating and less convincing than Dryden's inductive, Socratic method of criticism, but there is no doubt that in contrast to Rymer, and even to Dryden, Dennis realized the pivotal function of passion—or the unconscious—in poetic creativity, and he insisted upon his conviction in forceful terms. In many ways his views suggest twentieth-century explanations of intuitive thinking so basic to an understanding of the poetic process. Not the graceful stylist that Dryden was, Dennis was eventually eclipsed by his more gifted contemporary. (pp. 87-8)

Joan C. Grace, "John Dennis's Theory of Tragedy: Shakespeare—'One of the Greatest Genius's That the World 'Er Saw for the Tragic Stage'," in her Tragic Theory in the Critical Works of Thomas Rymer, John Dennis, and John Dryden, *Fairleigh Dickinson University Press, 1975, pp. 61-88.*

HAROLD GUITE (essay date 1971)

[*Guite is an English essayist and academic. In the following excerpt, he disputes Dennis's thesis on ancient satire as presented in a letter written to Matthew Prior in 1721.*]

The student of Roman satire who follows his authors as far as the eighteenth century will find himself for the most part on familiar ground, but every now and then he will stumble against an oddity, such as Dennis's *To Matthew Prior, Esq; Upon the Roman Satirists* (1721), that reminds him sharply of the distance he has travelled.... (p. 113)

Dennis's main thesis is unexceptionable: the reader should savour the distinctive qualities of Horace and Juvenal without feeling obliged to champion one against the other. But his categories of comic and tragic satire argue a serious misreading of all three genres. They are an aberration nurtured by intensive controversy and do not deserve to be commended by Mr. Ian Jack [in *Augustan Satire* (1952)] as "one of the most intelligent treatments of the main point at issue, that of the style and tone most suitable satire." They read to me like a desperate defence of an untenable antithesis. Horace may have begun as an imitator of Lucilius, but Old Comedy was never a model for his *Sermones* in the sense that Greek lyric was for his *Carmina*. It is true that both Horace and Aristophanes saw themselves as teachers, but teaching was not the primary business of Old Comedy, except in those parts of the *parabasis* where the chorus shattered the dramatic illusion and spoke directly for the poet. Old Comedy is protest, not exhortation; it is a festival, not an arraignment, or even a seminar; its standard finale is a wild, erotic celebration. No one in any century can rise up from seeing or even from reading a play of Aristophanes and proceed at once to the opinion that an agreeable mixture of good sense and true pleasantry are the principal qualities of an excellent comic poet. (p. 114)

Dennis is roughly right when he says that Horace endeavours to correct the follies and errors and epidemic vices of his readers, but quite wrong to apply any such restriction to the invective of Old Comedy, which took all human life for its target, including the pernicious, outrageous passions and the abominable monstrous crimes, to attack which, says Dennis, is the business of tragedy. This last affirmation is so startling that even its author staggers back from it and tries to tone it down by adding "at least of imperfect Tragedy." The attentive reader, who has been following the sharp outlines of the antithesis, suddenly finds himself befogged. He knows that Old Comedy can only mean Aristophanes (the other writers surviving only in fragments), but he cannot pursue the argument any further until he has located at least one imperfect tragedy prior to Juvenal. If he is aware of Dennis's opinion that the only perfect Greek tragedy was Sophocles's *King Oedipus*, he will have plenty of choice, but he must now lose himself in wondering how *King Oedipus* differs from all the rest in terms of Dennis's concept of the business of tragedy. If he knows that *King Oedipus* was not written as an attack on Oedipus, he is equally aware that the *Antigone* was not an attack on Creon. It is quite true that you can find in Greek and Roman tragedy anger, indignation, rage, disdain, violent emotions and vehement style, but none of these is the essence of tragedy. The essence of Attic tragedy was compassion, as Dennis, a good Aristotelian, knew quite well when he was not writing an essay on

satire. Now there is not very much compassion in Juvenal. But here and there the harsh and grandiose rhetoric gives way to quiet and even gentle humour, just as in Horace's *Sermones* and *Epistulae* there are depths of seriousness and not a few passages of high poetry.

There are at least three general considerations that should have inhibited Dennis from making his bizarre equations. First, Attic tragedy and comedy were highly public forms, and Roman satire a rather private form, of writing. Second, tragedy and comedy were governed by such strict conventions that change came slowly, whereas *Satura*, though a true genre, was so unconfined by rules that it could be swift and sensitive in response to changes both of author and environment. Third, both Horace and Juvenal changed too much in the course of more than twenty-five years of writing to fit easily into so rigid a scheme. (pp. 115-16)

> Harold Guite, "An 18th-Century View of Roman Satire," in The Varied Pattern: Studies in the 18th Century, *edited by Peter Hughes and David Williams, A. M. Hakkert, Ltd., 1971, pp. 113-20.*

DAVID B. MORRIS (essay date 1972)

[*Morris is an American essayist and academic. In the following excerpt from* The Religious Sublime: Christian Poetry and Critical Tradition in 18th-Century England, *he explicates Dennis's precepts regarding the origins of poetic inspiration and the relation of poetry to the religious sublime.*]

Writing with a clear understanding of the tortuous cross-currents of Restoration criticism, John Dennis provided England, at the very beginning of the eighteenth century, with a thorough and articulate theory of the religious sublime. He was adept in both ancient and modern literary tradition, and he possessed in addition a pugnacious originality which allowed him to combine the old with the new in refreshing ways.... His best works, *The Advancement and Reformation of Modern Poetry* and *The Grounds of Criticism in Poetry*, argue in detail the proposition that the greatest poetry is inevitably both sublime and religious. Although some of his later criticism is marred by an eccentric inconsistency, his "argument for the religious-sublime in *The Advancement and Reformation of Modern Poetry* and in *The Grounds of Criticism in Poetry*," as Clarence DeWitt Thorpe asserts [in *The Aesthetic Theory of Thomas Hobbes* (1940)], "is his most consistent performance." Surprisingly, this important contribution to eighteenth-century criticism passes almost without comment in the histories of literary theory. In attempting to correct the omission, I will consider in some detail Dennis's ideas concerning the religious sublime. Because no eighteenth-century writer ever argued for the theory of religious sublimity with such consistent force and clarity, his criticism provides a thorough introduction to ideas concerning the religious sublime which attracted poets and critics for the next hundred years.

Dennis's theory of the religious sublime grows out of his general theory of poetry. Poetry, he believed, is "an Art, by which a Poet excites Passion." It is difficult now to appreciate the boldness of Dennis's definition; his statement simply seems an affirmation of evident truth. Further, its importance to its own time is obscured because most of his contemporaries recognized that poetry could not ignore passion, and they developed the practice of extending the definitions of particular genres by stipulating which passion each genre was designed to evoke. The irregular ode, for example, should evoke astonishment; tragedy should evoke compassion and terror; the epic should evoke admiration. Normally, however, Augustan criticism concentrated on the formal and stylistic aspects of poetry, and most critics agreed with Aristotle that poetry is fundamentally an imitation of nature, shaped by the demands of various generic forms. Dennis greatly admired Aristotle, the Rules, and the doctrine of imitation. His early work *Remarks on a Book Entituled, Prince Arthur"* is largely an orthodox Aristotelian attack on Richard Blackmore's epic irregularities. Yet Dennis went beyond Aristotle in a number of areas, particularly in defining poetry as an art of exciting passion. His assertion is revolutionary in the neoclassical period not only for what it affirms but for what it ignores. It offers a view of the nature of poetry unparalleled in its day.

Dennis rejected as inadequate the prevalent seventeenth-century theories of poetic creation: the Hobbesian theory of Fancy and Judgment and the Miltonic doctrine of inspiration. Hobbes viewed the creation of poetry, Dennis evidently believed, as too exclusively mental. Although the senses must store the memory with data, once the memory is well stocked the Hobbesian poetic process presumably takes place entirely within the mind. On the contrary, Dennis asserted, history shows that the first poetry had very little to do with the head. Among the primitive Greeks, poetry developed because "great Passions naturally threw [men] upon Harmony and figurative Language, as they must of necessity do any Poet, as long as he continues Master of them." Modern as well as primitive poetry in Dennis's view involves something more than the operation of mental processes. If Hobbes's theory of poetic creation seemed incomplete, however, Milton's theory seemed too expansive. Dennis found no difficulty in believing the Bible was inspired directly by God, but he knew it was foolish to claim as much for modern poets. His strongest support of the theory of inspiration consists of a long quotation from Milton, but most often Dennis sought a natural rather than a supernatural explanation of poetic creation. He dismissed as blasphemous the notion that pagan poets could have been truly inspired, and he doubted the ministry of demons because "'tis absurd to give a supernatural Cause of an Effect, of which we can give a very natural one." Looking to man himself for the source of poetry, Dennis concluded that history and human nature both prove that poetry originates in strong passion.

Dennis's theory of poetry, while it emphasized the passions to an unprecedented degree, by no means excluded other human faculties from a part in the poetic process. To restrict poetry to passion alone would simply reverse Hobbes's error. Rather than restricting poetry to a single faculty, Dennis demanded a poetry which would express and engage "the whole Man." By the whole man, Dennis meant man as a composite of three faculties: the reason, the passions, and the senses. When he simplified his discussion, Dennis divided man into two parts: the head and the heart. In reaching the whole man, however, poetry for Dennis must appeal primarily to the emotions. "A Poet," he insisted, " . . . is oblig'd always to speak to the Heart,"

and by engaging the passions of the reader, poetry, Dennis hoped, would ultimately instruct and reform the reason. Thus his definition of poetry as passion really conceals a theory of how the head and heart, representing the main human faculties, combine in producing an experience which offers a potentially unique form of psychic integration.

Dennis devised a complex and original discussion of the nature of human passion which he probably intended to use as the basis of his projected essay on poetic genius. He never published—and probably never wrote—the essay, but his view of the relationship between genius and passion runs through all his works, sustaining the often bizarre superstructure of his individual judgments. "Poetical Genius," he wrote, in what is perhaps the topic sentence from his unknown essay on the subject, " . . . is the true Expression of Ordinary or Enthusiastick Passions proceeding from Ideas to which it naturally belongs." This obscure distinction between Ordinary and Enthusiastic passion is central to Dennis's poetics and essential to an understanding of his theory of the religious sublime. It is probably based on Locke's discrimination between sensation and reflection as the ultimate sources of human knowledge. Explaining his terms, Dennis developed a series of differences between the two kinds of passion. First, Ordinary (or Vulgar) passion results from direct and immediate sensation—whether excited by a physical object or event or by the *idea* of a particular object or event. Enthusiastic passion always results from ideas matured and complicated through meditation. Second, the sensations arousing Ordinary passion always derive from something commonplace, but in Enthusiastic passion the ideas in meditation must be removed from the ordinary course of life. Finally, the causes of Ordinary passion are always clearly and distinctly understood, while Enthusiastic passion proceeds from complex and unfamiliar ideas which are not distinctly understood—a requirement in part explaining Dennis's overuse of the word *hint*.

Dennis illustrated the difference between Ordinary and Enthusiastic passion with a vivid example. Writing in *The Grounds of Criticism in Poetry*, he explained, "I desire the Reader to observe, that Ideas in Meditation are often very different from what Ideas of the same Objects are, in the course of common Conversation. As for example, the Sun mention'd in ordinary Conversation, gives the Idea of a round flat shining Body, of about two foot diameter. But the Sun occurring to us in Meditation, gives the Idea of a vast and glorious Body, and the top of all the visible Creation, and the brightest material Image of the Divinity." The example Dennis probably based on a passage in which Lucretius, crediting only the reports of his senses, declared that "the wheel of the sun cannot be much larger nor its glow less than is perceived by our senses." Lucretius's vision, Dennis thought, could stimulate Ordinary passion only. When the small disk perceived by the senses is transmuted by the process of meditation, however, it becomes for Dennis a source of Enthusiastic passion. Thus, when Dennis writes that poetry is an art of raising passion, he does not mean that poetry should be the source of merely visceral or nervous excitement. Rather he means that poetry should engage the mind and the passions simultaneously in a process of transforming perception. Although Dennis admits that not all men are capable of experiencing Enthusiastic passion, he believes that the epic, the Pindaric ode, and other poems which called for great thoughts and spirited verse require the experience of Enthusiastic passion in poet and reader.

Enthusiastic passion is necessary in the greater kinds of poetry, Dennis maintained, because it is the means of reforming both poetry and man. According to Dennis, poetry shared with man the corruptions of the Fall. Like Milton, he envisioned the Fall as a psychological event, a lapse from "the Harmony of the Human Faculties, and the Felicity of the first Man" into a state of inner disharmony, "a cruel War between the Passions and Senses, and the Reason." While many of Dennis's contemporaries saw the solution to man's internal disorder in the dominance of reason over sense and passion, Dennis always spoke of harmony instead of dominance. The Puritan interregnum seemed to him a powerful example of the disorder attending the mere suppression of passion by reason, and Puritan attempts to reform man failed, he wrote metaphorically, because they were "begun at the Tail, instead of the Head and the Heart." They "opprest and persecuted Mens Inclinations, instead of correcting and converting them." Man's reformation, Dennis believed, would come through the harmonious exercise of all the faculties, not through a straitjacket of reason. The vehicle of correction and conversion would be a reformed modern poetry, one able to express and to inspire Enthusiastic passion.

Poetry, for Dennis as for Milton, had the same function as all other arts: "to restore the Decays that happen'd to human Nature by the Fall." But poetry, argued Dennis, had an advantage over the other arts because it attacked the problem of man's inner disharmony most effectively: "For whereas Philosophy pretends to correct human Passions by human Reason, that is, things that are strong and ungovernable, by something that is feeble and weak: Poetry by the force of the Passion, instructs and reforms the Reason." Dennis disagreed on principle with Pope's decision to moralize his song. Poetry was to be far more than a medium for the delightful expression of moral truth. For Dennis, poetry was "the best and the noblest Art" because it made "the best Provision at the same Time for the Satisfaction of all the Faculties, the Reason, the Passions, [and] the Senses." By satisfying the whole man, not just that aspect of man which valued didactic moral truth, poetry might be the instrument for restoring the "paradise within" which Milton had predicted. "Poetry," Dennis wrote, "seems to be a noble Attempt of Nature, by which it endeavours to exalt itself to its happy primitive State; and he who is entertain'd with an accomplish'd Poem, is, for a Time, at least, restored to Paradise." The paradise is not local but psychological, referring to the condition in which man's "every Passion, in its Turn, is charm'd, while his Reason is supremely satisfied." Such a view of the usefulness and nobility of poetry is rarely encountered among the better-known Augustan writers, and it seems scarcely surprising to learn that Wordsworth and Coleridge sought Dennis's works at the beginning of the next century.

Dennis's theory of Enthusiastic passion, the foundation of his general theory of poetry, also provides the basis for his argument that the greatest sublimity derives from religious ideas. Oddly, while many of his contemporaries would have rejected Dennis's account of Enthusiastic passion, they did not reject his conclusions concerning the religious sublime. One explanation of the apparent paradox involves the thoroughness of Dennis's method of proof.

Whether he always did so consciously or not, Dennis often divided his proof into three parts, arguing from reason, from authority, and from experience. A reader, then, might well reject Dennis's arguments from reason, while being convinced or influenced by the arguments from authority and from experience. To appreciate the consistency and the thoroughness of Dennis's theory of the religious sublime requires following his own method of proof. Let us look first at his arguments from reason and from authority, and then at the arguments from experience.

Dennis based his argument from reason on the proposition that poetry should raise Enthusiastic passion in the reader. The greatest poetry, he argued, must therefore arouse the greatest Enthusiastic passion. By "greatest" Dennis meant both strongest and worthiest. Further, he insisted that religious ideas inevitably raised the strongest and worthiest Enthusiastic passion: "Religious Enthusiasm," he wrote, "must necessarily be greater than Human Enthusiasm can be, because the Passions that attend on Religious Ideas, when a Man is capable of reflecting on them as he should do, are stronger than those which attend on Prophane Ideas." To support this belief, Dennis adapted Longinus's idea that sublimity demands men with great souls. Ordinary men, he argued, are capable of Ordinary passion only. Those with great souls, however, can experience the worthier kinds of Enthusiastic passion. Thus men capable of exalted meditative reflection must discover that religious ideas move the strongest and worthiest passion. (pp. 47-53)

Dennis's association of religious Enthusiasm with the sublime becomes explicit in his arguments from authority. His long discussion of Longinus confirms that Dennis considered sublimity the highest aim and praise of poetry. (p. 54)

Although Longinus had introduced him to the idea of sublimity, Dennis was not entirely satisfied with the *Peri Hupsous*. Longinus, he believed, had failed in two essential ways. He had not fully appreciated the relationship of passion and sublimity, and he had neglected to discuss religion as the greatest source of the sublime.

Because passion was the basis of his own theory of poetry, Dennis was disturbed that Longinus had slighted the relationship between passion and sublimity. Although Longinus cited strong passion as one of the two innate requirements of the sublime writer, in the same section he also asserted that sublimity might exist in passages which evoked no passion whatsoever. This possibility contradicted Dennis's entire theory of poetry, and here he wholly disagreed with Longinus, expanding the particular objection into a criticism of Longinus's general method. In analyzing the sublime, Dennis argued, Longinus had considered its effects only—amazement, pride, terror, transport. Dennis sought to deal in causes as well, to show "what it is in Poetry that works these Effects."

The universal cause of sublimity, Dennis maintained, was passion; and in explaining Longinus's notion that sublimity could exist without passion, he attributed the "error" in part to Longinus's failure to distinguish between Ordinary and Enthusiastic passion. "The Sublime," Dennis wrote, "is indeed often without common Passion, as ordinary Passion is often without that [i.e., the Sublime]. But then it is never without Enthusiastick Passion." Dennis even argued that Longinus contradicted himself, since Longinus had already declared that strong passion was an innate requirement of the sublime writer or speaker. "Now I leave the Reader to judge," Dennis concluded after a lengthy review of the apparent contradiction, "whether *Longinus* has not been saying here all along that Sublimity is never without Passion." Despite occasional appearances to the contrary, Dennis did not imply that he and Longinus agreed completely. Instead, he believed that his own stress upon passion as the cause of sublimity complemented Longinus's treatment of the effects of the sublime. "So that, take the Cause and the Effects together," Dennis concluded, "and you have the Sublime."

Longinus's silence concerning the relationship between sublimity and religious ideas presented Dennis with an even knottier problem. "I now come to the Precepts of *Longinus*," he wrote, pursuing his argument from authority, "and pretend to shew from them that the greatest Sublimity is to be deriv'd from Religious Ideas. But why then, says the Reader, has not *Longinus* plainly told us so?" Dennis faced his dilemma honestly. His solutions, nevertheless, may seem forced. First, Dennis in johnoted, because Longinus had failed to appreciate the necessary relationship between Enthusiastic passion and sublimity, he was hardly prepared to recognize that religious ideas produce the greatest Enthusiastic passion. Second, although Longinus did not explain the relationship between sublimity and religious ideas, the *Peri Hupsous* demonstrates that he must have intuited the relationship. In support of this contention, Dennis showed that many of Longinus's examples drew their power from religious practices or beliefs. Further, Dennis cited Longinus's description of the six chief marks of the sublime, arguing that each is most powerfully attained by the use of religious ideas. This vindication, however, still left Dennis a little puzzled at the Greek critic's lack of perception. "I must confess I have wonder'd very much, upon Reflection," he mused, "how it could happen that so great a Man as *Longinus*, who whenever he met a Passage in any Discourse that was lofty enough to please him, had Discernment enough to see that it had some of the [six] preceding Marks, should miss of finding so easy a thing as this, that never any Passage had all these Marks, or so much as the Majority of them, unless it were Religious."

Dennis's bewilderment sounds much like oblique self-praise, but it also emphasizes the extent of his commitment to the theory of the religious sublime. Dennis needed Longinus's authority to support his own claim that sublimity is the unfailing mark of great poetry. But his contention that the greatest sublimity is derived from religious ideas did not depend upon the authority of Longinus. Although the theory might draw some support from ancient authorities, it was really the invention of Dennis's own reason and experience.

Dennis probably suspected that appeals to reason and authority would not convince most readers that the greatest sublimity derives from religious ideas. As he wrote on another occasion, "Men of Sense are too proud to yield to Authority, and Fools are too weak to submit to Reason, but Experience, which never deceived any one, carries Conviction both for the one and the other." Indeed, the tradition of English empiricism, from Bacon (whom Dennis quotes) to Locke (whose ideas and vocabulary he adopts), powerfully affected Dennis's critical methods.

"Nothing," he once stated categorically, "is more vain than to argue against experience." Thus, while making good use of reason and of authority, he anchored his theory of the religious sublime firmly in his own experience of literature. (pp. 55-8)

Dennis's contemporaries knew him as a champion of the Moderns. Dennis viewed himself, however, not as a combatant but as a mediator, "calming the Fury of the contending Parties." In *The Advancement and Reformation of Modern Poetry,* he approached the old question of Ancient or Modern supremacy in a spirit of compromise. "The first Part of the following Treatise," he wrote in the Epistle Dedicatory, "was intended to shew, that the Ancient Poets had that actual Pre-eminence.... The Design of the second Part is to shew, That the Moderns ... may come to equal the Ancients." Dennis's position seems moderate because he granted a large measure of praise to the Ancients without simultaneously reducing the Moderns to a race of mimic pigmies. Although he considerably oversimplified the achievement of classical literature, he based his judgment of the Ancients and his hope for Modern poetry on a proposition central to his own poetics. The Ancients, he declared, were at present superior to the Moderns primarily because they had joined "their Religion with their Poetry." The Moderns, however, "by incorporating Poetry with the Religion reveal'd to us in Sacred Writ" might eventually equal or surpass the Ancients. Pope had some reason to be irritated when Dennis vaunted "the Newness and Boldness" of his argument. Dennis's hope to restore poetry "to all its Greatness, and to all its Innocence" by returning to Christian subjects and treatment had been anticipated by Du Bartas, Herbert, Cowley, and others. In fact, although Dennis described his proposal as "a Piece of Criticism, which has, I know not how, escap'd all the *French* Criticks," his argument only repeats the basic ideas of those in France who proselytized for *le merveilleux chrétien.* The plan was not at all as original as he wished to believe.

In several respects, however, Dennis's program for poetry was new and bold. He recommended the use of Christianity in poetry as part of a more comprehensive theory. No critic who had recommended Christian poetry ever did so primarily because he believed that poetry was an art of raising passion. For Dennis, poetry and Christianity were natural partners. As he wrote in the Epistle Dedicatory to *The Advancement and Reformation of Modern Poetry*, "The ultimate End of the ensuing Discourse, is to shew, That the Intention of Poetry, and the Christian Religion, being alike to move the Affections, they may very well be made instrumental to the Advancing each other." For Dennis, the common bond between poetry and Christianity was their reliance upon passionate and suprarational persuasion and their similar designs to restore the inner harmony disrupted by the Fall. His own experience of literature convinced him that Christianity offered the most powerful source of human passion and, hence, the greatest opportunity for poetic sublimity. To prove that Christianity might elevate Modern poets to the exalted stature of the Ancients, Dennis marshaled numerous examples of sublime religious verse: from the classics, from the Bible, and especially from *Paradise Lost.*

In ransacking the classics for examples, Dennis could have simplified his task by borrowing passages cited by Longinus. Occasionally he did so. But Longinus often relied on

Homer, and Dennis preferred to support his own theory from the works of Virgil. He considered the *Aeneid* to be "the most *Religious Epick* Poem that ever was writ in the World," a judgment which deserves some explanation. Dennis's view of the *Aeneid* as the world's greatest religious epic rests upon his belief that regularity can be both a sublime and a religious quality of art. God's universe, Dennis believed, is all "Rule and Order, and Harmony" and even its seeming irregularities contribute to a providential design. The poet, whose duty is to imitate the Rule and Order and Harmony of nature, must likewise exercise a providential control over the incidents and disposition of his poem. Thus Dennis challenged any of the "Enemies to Regularity" to study the *Oedipus* of Sophocles, where he would "easily discover, how the Religion that is every where intermix'd with the Play, shews all the Surprizes . . . as so many immediate successive Effects, of a particular dreadful Providence, which make them come, like so many Thunder-claps, from a Serene Heaven, to confound and astonish him." Despite the clumsy phrasing, Dennis's meaning is plain: a poet whose careful regularity reflects the divine guidance of the universe can thereby move and astonish his readers with the force of a Longinian thunderbolt. Although for later writers sublimity became synonymous with wildness, disorder, and irregularity, Dennis found regularity a powerful source of the sublime when skillfully employed to move the passions. Yet Virgil's thoroughly praised regularity was only one aspect of his sublimity for Dennis. Like other pagan poets, Virgil frequently described the actions of various gods and goddesses. This poetic use of Greco-Roman religion seemed to Dennis a primary source of the sublimity of the Ancients.

The use of epic machinery had long been considered an important aspect of the marvellous, and the close association between the marvellous and the sublime suggested that the use of epic machinery was logically related to the sublime. Indeed, throughout the eighteenth century, epic machinery often figured in discussions of the sublime. The introduction of supernatural beings in a poem was thought to add a dimension of grandeur which human actors could not supply. (pp. 58-61)

The classics, Dennis maintained, offer abundant examples proving that the greatest sublimity derives from religious ideas. Yet, despite his admiration for Virgil, Pindar, Lucretius, and for the religious aspects of classical poetry, Dennis insisted that modern writers could not simply imitate the religious sublimity of the Ancients. With evident relish, he explicitly repudiated Pope's claim that the gods of Homer remain to this day the gods of poetry. For Dennis, one source of poetry remained available to the moderns which was more sublime than any which the pagan poets might have known.

The Bible and Christian tradition were for Dennis the ultimate sources of sublimity. *The Advancement and Reformation of Modern Poetry* and *The Grounds of Criticism in Poetry* are among the first works of English criticism to apply the tools of literary analysis to the study of biblical poetry. Dennis did not speak of rhetorical terms, as Peacham had; nor did he, like Wyther, resign completely any pretense of understanding the sources of biblical grandeur. He accepted the Scriptures as divinely inspired and inherently superior to any uninspired or falsely inspired poetry. But he also sought literary explanations for the superiority of the Bible. The sublime proved a particularly fortunate discovery for this purpose. Its emphasis upon transport and passion accounts for aspects of great poetry which cannot be wholly judged by reason. At the same time, however, it permits a nonmystical and nonmechanical appreciation of exalted poetry. The idea of sublimity illuminated the nature of biblical poetry for readers throughout the eighteenth century, and Dennis was no doubt influential in showing the way.

The Bible is the ultimate source of sublime poetry, Dennis believed, because it evokes the greatest possible Enthusiastic passion, enabling the reconciliation of all the human faculties. The inspired truth of the Bible thus becomes only one aspect of its poetical appeal. It was an important aspect, of course; paganism failed to equal the sublimity of the Christian religion partly because its falsity offended the modern reason. Yet poetry could also fail by being too reasonable. Deism, in Dennis's view, appealed exclusively to the reason and, hence, missed the sublime by preventing any strong movement of the passions. Christianity, however, appeals more strongly to the whole man than does either paganism or Deism: "it satisfies the Reason more, at the same Time that it raises a stronger Passion, and that it entertains the Senses . . . more delightfully." Thus, for Dennis, valid literary reasons (not mere piety) supported his view that Christian sublimity excels the highest achievement of the Ancients. "I could produce a hundred Passages . . . out of Sacred Writ," he affirmed, "which are infinitely superior to any Thing that can be brought upon the same Subject, from the *Grecian* and *Roman* Poets." In illustrating this conviction, he compared examples of biblical sublimity with parallel passages drawn from the classics.

Perhaps the most effective comparison of passages from the Bible and the classics juxtaposes descriptions of what Dennis considered the greatest possible subject: the power of God. The classical passage, which became a familiar illustration of sublimity in the eighteenth century, he drew from Virgil's description of the storm in the first book of the *Georgics*. The translation is Dryden's:

> *The Father of the Gods his Glory shrouds,*
> *Involv'd in Tempests, and a Night of Clouds,*
> *And from the middle Darkness, flashing out,*
> *By Fits he deals his fiery Bolts about.*
> *Earth feels the Motions of her angry God,*
> *Her Entrails tremble, and her Mountains nod,*
> *And flying Beasts in Forests seek Abode.*

Virgil's sublimity, although impressive, seems insignificant to Dennis when compared with the sublimity of Psalm 18. The portion (verses 6-15) which Dennis cites is a fine example of what eighteenth-century writers meant by the phrase *biblical sublimity*. . . . If Dennis had merely rhapsodized about the passage, his discussion would have no more value in the history of criticism than George Wyther's earlier rapture inspired by the same psalm. Earlier critics had confessed or implied the folly of analyzing God's revealed truth; Dennis subjected the Bible to literary analysis by studying its particular poetic effects.

The greater sublimity of Psalm 18, Dennis argued, could be measured by its greater engagement of all the human faculties. "Reason," he noted, "finds its Account better here than it does in *Virgil*; for the more amazing Effects that we see of Divine Displeasure, the more it answers our

Idea of infinite Wrath." The basis of this argument, as is clear in context, is qualitative: Virgil's particular details are amazing; David's are more amazing and, thus, better calculated to suggest in meditation the idea of infinite wrath. But, while reason reflects on the relationship between the finite and the infinite, the other faculties are violently excited by the quantitative succession of concrete particulars. "And that which satisfies the Reason the more here," Dennis continued, "raises the Passion more strongly, and entertains the Senses the better, because there are more and more amazing Effects of the Divine [Dis]pleasure." Dennis does not appeal to the inspired truth of the Bible as its mark of superiority; he bases his claim on poetic grounds. Both the quality and the quantity of "amazing Effects" are greater in the biblical description than in the Virgilian.

Dennis, like Bouhours, found the biblical description more sublime than the classical largely because it is more pictorial. His praise of Psalm 18 might well be written with an eye to the chapter of Longinus which Boileau entitled "Des Images.". . . For Longinus, the interaction of passion and imagination *contributed* to the sublime; for Dennis, it *created* the sublime. Demonstrating the greater passionate and imaginative appeal of the Bible, he urged his contemporaries to challenge the Ancients by utilizing the subjects and spirit of Christianity. He knew of only one powerful objection to his proposal. "For several of the Moderns have attempted Divine Poetry," he acknowledged, "and yet some of them have been contemptible to the last degree, and not one of them has excell'd the Antients." To meet this objection, Dennis drew again on his own experience of literature. He directed readers to *Paradise Lost*, "the greatest Poem that ever was written by Man."

Without *Paradise Lost*, Dennis's theory of the religious sublime might have seemed a feeble exercise in piety; only the pragmatic evidence of what works could sway a generation taught to respect the information of its senses. Practical failure, even more than Boileau's theoretical objections, had doomed *le merveilleux chrétien* in France. But *Paradise Lost* proved that Christian poetry could succeed. Dennis's main difficulty was that Milton's epic suffered from public neglect. Tonson's elegant folio edition of *Paradise Lost* in 1688 marked the first real step toward general acceptance of Milton, but not until twenty years later did Addison's *Spectator* essays successfully domesticate Milton's epic. In the interim, as Raymond D. Havens points out [in *The Influence of Milton on English Poetry* (1922)], the "first great protagonist of *Paradise Lost* was not Addison but the forgotten John Dennis." Dennis's support of *Paradise Lost* was not only earlier than Addison's but in some respects considerably bolder. Addison attempted to reconcile Milton to current Augustan tastes for regularity; Dennis praised Milton's epic despite its irregularities. While Addison recommended Milton to a general audience, Dennis elevated him especially as a model for modern poets. For Dennis, Milton was the banner of a revolution. *Paradise Lost*, he believed, offered convincing evidence that his theory of the religious sublime could transform the nature of modern poetry. (pp. 62-7)

Dennis particularly admired, among other important aspects of Milton's sublimity, the choice of blank verse, and here too he anticipated ideas which later became accepted critical dogma. Rhyme, Dennis believed, could only "debase the Majesty and weaken the Spirit of the greater Poetry." Long before nondramatic blank verse grew popular in England, Dennis wrote concerning *Paradise Lost*, "I am satisfied that something of its Excellence is owing to the Blank Verse. For Mr. *Dryden* has handled the very same Subject in Rime, but has faln so infinitely short of the Sublimity, the Majesty, the Vehemence, and the other great Qualities of *Milton*, that they are never to be nam'd together." The rhymed couplet, Dennis thought, almost inevitably required a poet to deal in point, conceit, wit, and other primarily intellectual effects. If poetry was to reconcile man's warring faculties, however, it must raise strong Enthusiastic passion; and in order to raise strong Enthusiastic passion, it must employ an appropriately passionate verse form. The most extensive writer of blank verse between Milton and Thomson, Dennis certainly followed this rule in his own poetry. The rejection of rhyme was an essential part of his general program to return poetry from its "miserably fall'n" state to "all its Greatness, and to all its Innocence." With pardonable excess he predicted that "before this Century is half expir'd, Rime will be wholly banished from our greater Poetry."

While Milton's use of blank verse contributed importantly to his sublimity, for Dennis the main cause of his superiority over both Ancients and Moderns was his use of Christian materials. In fact, Dennis expected Milton's superiority to be so evident that he offered little detailed analysis of its specific sources. (pp. 67-8)

Milton's description of Creation, one recalls, is not only visual but also vital, a picture of the world pulsing with motion. When Dennis applauds Milton's Christian version of Creation, then, he does so in the context of his earlier critical discussions of how vision and motion contribute to the sublimity of particular images. He was never content to rest his claims for Christian religious sublimity merely on the inspired truth of Christianity. When handled by a skillful poet, Christianity also supplied vivid and vigorous images which were artistically superior to anything the non-Christian religions could offer.

Dennis's admiration for Milton's religious sublimity included Milton's use of certain stylistic techniques which might be called biblical. While Augustan poets generally eschewed the biblical device of "crowding" a number of different images together, Dennis applauded this very thing in Milton's description of the Creation: "What a Number of admirable Images are here crouding upon one another?" The same idea recurs in his later comparison of Milton's adaptation of Psalm 148 with the Sternhold-Hopkins version. The homely devotion of Sternhold-Hopkins in Dennis's view utterly debased the passion and profusion of the biblical figurative language. (Pope referred to the Prayer Book psalms as winning Heaven "through Violence of Song.") Turning to Milton's adaptation, Dennis continued, "Let us now see how the Force of *Milton*'s Genius hides and conceals the Assistance of Art, while these lofty Figures, at the very time that they raise and transport his exalted Soul, are lost in his Enthusiasm and his Sublimity, as the glittering of numberless Stars is swallow'd and lost in the blaze of Day." His simile is not merely decorative. The Bible abounds with figures which might well seem as brilliant and numberless as the stars. Milton's use of this and other aspects of biblical style,

Dennis implied, gives *Paradise Lost* much of its unsurpassed sublimity.

Milton proved to Dennis that, both for its truth and for its grandeur, Christianity was the single force which could revive modern poetry. "I have reason to believe," he asserted, "that one of the principal Reasons that has made the modern Poetry so contemptible, is, That by divesting it self of Religion, it is fallen from its Dignity, and its original Nature and Excellence; and from the greatest Production of the Mind of Man, is dwindled to an extravagant and a vain Amusement." There was a vast difference for Dennis between amusement and happiness. If modern poets would only follow the example of Milton, he believed, and utilize both the sublime matter and manner of Christianity, man might yet establish a paradise within and modern poetry might yet "raise up its dejected Head, and . . . come to emulate the happiest of *Grecian* and *Roman* Ages." (pp. 69-71)

No one has succeeded fully in measuring Dennis's impact upon his age. The problem arises largely because Dennis was too quixotic to inspire the tributes and discipleship which help in retrospect to determine a writer's influence. In fact, only a critic with nothing to lose, like Charles Gildon, could afford to call Dennis "Master." For various reasons, Dennis was an abrasive presence in the Age of Pope. On some subjects, such as blank verse, he anticipated opinions which became popular only in the second and third quarters of the century. On other matters, such as comic theory, he resolutely looked backward to the Restoration. His character, like his criticism, is a blend of laudable and lamentable qualities, and he inevitably embarrasses those who attempt either to exalt or to defame him. Testimonials, therefore, are an unsatisfactory way to judge Dennis's importance to his age. A better means is to examine the ideas which he so powerfully recommended. His ultimate importance should be measured by the importance and acceptance of his ideas, not by the jibes or cheers of his contemporaries.

Dennis's positive achievements allied him with the future. He gave England its first book-length criticism of a particular work (**Remarks on Prince Arthur**) and its first systematic theory of poetry since Sidney's *Apologie*. But his most valuable contribution was his strong endorsement of Longinus and the sublime. Before Dennis's criticism appeared, no English critic had adequately explored or expounded the idea of sublimity. Indeed, sublimity was so important to Dennis's personal theory of literature that he used the adjectives *poetical* and *sublime* virtually as synonyms. The really valuable poetry, for Dennis, was always sublime. He is important, however, beyond merely helping to popularize the new idea of sublimity; through his emphasis upon the necessity of passion in poetry, he also anticipated and perhaps helped to bring about a general change in the nature of English critical thought. The poem as imitative artifact gradually ceases to control the main interest of critics, who increasingly study the mind and emotions of both poet and reader.

Dennis's treatment of the sublime in certain respects is brilliantly original. He deserves credit for applying the critical discussion of sublimity to the analysis of biblical poetry. Although Boileau's "Préface" undoubtedly spurred him to consider the general relationship between biblical poetry and the sublime, Boileau's main interest in the *fiat lux* passage (and the focus of his controversy with Jean Le Clerc and Pierre Daniel Huet) concerned the role of simplicity in the sublime. Dennis completely altered the grounds on which Boileau had associated the Bible with sublimity. Further, he initiated discussion of Milton's sublimity. Eighteenth-century critical recognition of the sublimity of *Paradise Lost* is more than a historical detail; it became a stimulus for the creation of a vast number of poems—from blank-verse fragments to ponderous epics. Finally, Dennis's discussion of sublimity devoted considerable attention to the idea of terror, and his related notions concerning Christian machinery and imaginative suggestiveness point the way to crucial future developments in English poetry and criticism. These "firsts" say nothing about the extent of Dennis's personal influence, but they do suggest that his work is full of ideas which become steadily more prominent in eighteenth-century poetry and criticism.

To a remarkable extent, individual aspects of Dennis's criticism were integrated parts of his enveloping theory of the religious sublime. Whether in Dennis's version or in some other, the notion of the religious sublime became a familiar part of eighteenth-century critical thought, and its acceptance finds a parallel in the creation of various recurring kinds of poetry. Eighteenth-century interest in the idea of religious sublimity results from combining forces, and it is impossible to decide—as Wordsworth wrote of his own growth—what portion of the river flows from what fountain. The loosely related opinions discussed in the first chapter were ready to be fused into something new and solid, especially with the appearance of Boileau's Longinus. Resentment of Milton's surly republicanism was dying, and with the light of reason illuminating new aspects of man and nature, the age was ready for a fresh approach to the literary qualities of the Bible. At the same time, the vast reaches of space and the apparent irregularities of nature—all associated with the sublime—became heady sources of devout religious awe. Dennis's real achievement was to fuse a number of such scattered ideas into a consistent and articulate theory of literature. He developed his theory of the religious sublime with such energy and resourcefulness that no writer of the first quarter of the eighteenth century could avoid some knowledge of it.

The author of the *Plain Dealer* (1725) was, for his own times, an ill prophet in predicting that "the *Name* of Mr. *Dennis*, will, long, continue to receive Honour, after his *Body* shall be Dust and Ashes" [see excerpt dated 1725]. Ironically, Dennis's name had turned to dust and ashes somewhat before his flesh. At his death in 1734, he seemed to one eulogist to have closed an era: having outlived the originality of his contributions to criticism and surviving only as a type of the ill-natured critic, he passed from memory as "the last Classick Wit of King Charles's Reign." But Dennis deserves better treatment from the historian. If . . . the idea of the religious sublime exerted a continuous pressure among eighteenth-century men-of-letters, the question of Dennis's contemporary reputation will seem relatively minor. Important ideas often watch their inventors lapse into obscurity, and general acceptance makes an idea the propertary of an age. What happens to the idea becomes the most serious question. Dennis supplied a necessary catalyst for change by introducing a fully articulated concept into the minds of his contemporaries. That act itself removed the religious sublime from any proprietary relationship with Dennis. And it simultaneously introduces us to a phenomenon which always remains mysteriously outside the laws of chemical combination or natural growth: the dynamics of literary change. (pp. 79-8)

> David B. Morris, "John Dennis and the Religious Sublime," in his The Religious Sublime: Christian Poetry and Critical Tradition in 18th-Century England, *The University Press of Kentucky, 1972, pp. 47-78.*

AVON JACK MURPHY (essay date 1984)

[*Murphy is an American essayist and educator. In the following excerpt from his full-length critical and biographical study of Dennis, he surveys the writer's career as a poet, variously assessing his numerous poetic endeavors.*]

Witty poems. Most of this early poetry is a conscious, unsuccessful attempt to become known as a witty gentleman. The completeness of the failure seems most obvious when we read *Poems in Burlesque,* twenty-two pages of rough comic verse published in 1692. The seven poems achieve the tumbling, madcap tone of most Restoration burlesques, which one writer [J. Newton in *Pendragon; or, The Carpet Knight His Kalendar* (1698)] likens to a "wanton Chamber-maid, with her Petticoats tuck'd up, in her Masque and Pattens, who walks, runs, stumbles, stops, looks about, and laughs, and perhaps all in less than a Minute." Unfortunately, this tone of itself cannot give poetry lasting value. (p. 90)

Although Dennis composes rollicking octosyllabic lines and creates amusing rhymes such as "Choler"–"maul her" and "Euridice"–"Eye did see," *Poems in Burlesque* has no lasting value. One scholar, finding Dennis's prose better than his verse, believes him to focus too much here on "curious or misshapen characters copied from life" to achieve real significance. Perhaps more helpful is another critic's feeling that worthwhile burlesque like *Hudibras* establishes "a conflict between a farcical benevolent comedy and a satirical moral and philosophical intention" [Edward A. Richards in *Hudibras in the Burlesque Tradition* (1937)]. *Poems in Burlesque* involves a much leaner combination of farce and satiric meanness; there is no sense of benevolence or philosophical depth. It is pure entertainment, as Hooker suggests, a mere trifle.

Fables. More amenable to Dennis's temperament, although still not spectacular poetry, are the ten animal fables in the 1693 *Miscellanies.* Between 1650 and 1750 the fable, a short didactic narrative usually featuring animal characters, enjoyed great popularity. Jean de La Fontaine, Roger L'Estrange, John Dryden, John Gay, Jonathan Swift, Matthew Prior, and others contributed much to a vigorous tradition. Dennis joins numerous minor poetic talents in using the tradition to compose some entertaining verse, but he adds little to it.

Locke and almost everyone else who during the seventeenth or eighteenth century discusses the fable point out its usefulness as a didactic tool. Dennis makes much of this use: "For as when *Æsop* introduces a Horse, or a Dog, or a Wolf, or a Lion, he does not pretend to shew us any singular Animal, but only to shew the Nature of that Crea-

ture.... every true Dramatick Poem is a Fable as much as any one of *Æsop*'s; it has in its Nature a direct Tendency to teach moral Virtue." The *Gentleman's Journal* praises Dennis for producing fables "at least equal to the Originals of a Master who was once reputed inimitable. To those merry Fables he hath given us grave Morals, which will make them at least as instructive as pleasant. For, as you know, Fables ... are Paths fill'd with Roses, that lead us to the knowledge of Virtue more agreeably...." An overall problem, however, lies in the great disparity between this emphasis on instruction and the burlesque comic technique used to make the instruction pleasurable.

Dennis does not go directly to Aesop for his material. Rather, although he never tells us so, he is publishing the first English translations of poems from La Fontaine's immensely popular *Fables.* A fast glance at La Fontaine's verses and then at Dennis's reveals differences great enough to make the English versions seem loose adaptations in contrast to the much closer translations found in Mandeville's *Æsop Dress'd* [1704]. Essentially, Dennis replaces La Fontaine's elegant wit with the thumping burlesque humor of Samuel Butler, and he expands the moral tag on each fable.

The action parts of Dennis's versions depict the animals as anything but dignified and restrained, as they usually are in La Fontaine. Thus the pig in "**The** *Pig,* **the** *Goat,* **and the** *Sheep*" illustrates the futility of foreseeing one's dismal end. He screeches in panic that he is one

> Whom Wastcoateer has made a Fat Pig,
> For some Cits ravenous Spouse, with Brat big.
> 'Tis for her maw I'm grown this Squab bit;
> May the Jade choak with the first gobbet.

Modish diction like "Cits," the fast octosyllabic lines, the feminine rhymes, and the lowly self-image vividly show a fool in action. Such merciless downgrading of the animal hero may provide some entertainment, but we encounter a problem of tone. Hudibrastic burlesque presupposes a wide gap between a highly dignified topic and its low comic treatment to produce mental sparks. Little such distance exists with the lowly pig, so that here the comedy does not have great power.

In the moral concluding each fable, Dennis makes certain that we recognize the maxim. His favorite procedure is to present the action and then in the moral go into implications at considerable length. (pp. 91-3)

Dennis has thought carefully about fable writing, and his versions are more able than many others, but he does not fully succeed. We can sense an unresolved conflict between what Dennis sees as hack wit writing and literature of more serious intent. He tries but cannot get where he wishes to go with this poetic vehicle.

Polite verse. Little need be said about Dennis's handful of social poems, which read like a young gallant's calling card. (p. 93)

Dennis works several topics without special distinction. "**To a Young Gentleman, Who Was Blam'd for Marrying Young**" offers several horrible couplets, such as "Tell those who blame thee that till Thirty they / The noon of Life, for Love's chief meal may stay." The strongest couplet in "**To Mr.** *E. H.* **Physician and Poet**" seems distinctive only in its lukewarmness: "Rise by vast Science and judicious rage, / Like him [Phoebus] t' enlighten and to warm our Age"—its other lines muddle along with even less inspiration. Somewhat more interesting are two poems on a lady's picture, which argue without much creativity that "Heavn's work, before the Painter's we prefer, / Since it design'd its Master-piece in her." The amorous ditty "**To Flavia Who Fear'd She Was Too Kind**" (the best of this verse) seems a pieced-together combination of Cavalier seductiveness, Whig pleading against a tyrant's "arbitrary Power," sexual description complete with "panting Breasts" and the old sex-death pun, and Neoplatonic love. It simply does not exhibit the nimbleness and wholeness of vision found in earlier love poetry like Thomas Carew's.

Dennis must write such poetry only because he feels expected to. His strengths of logic and carefully examined evidence never appear, and strong feeling seems to have no place. He obviously cannot feel his mind and soul involved.

Battle Poetry. Seeking material that would both provide him with a grand subject and let him serve his country, Dennis naturally came upon battle poetry. He wrote several pure military poems (another poem, "**The Monument,**" contains military lines within a larger structure), including one on a naval and three on land triumphs. Although marred often by awkwardness and verboseness, most of them share the strengths of vivid description, clear structure, and patriotic animation stemming from great martial victory.

"**Upon Our Victory at Sea, and Burning the *French* Fleet at *La Hogue*,**" first published in the June 1692 *Gentleman's Journal*, describes in heroic couplets the one outstanding English naval triumph since the disgrace at Beachy Head in 1691. Failing to get the proper reinforcements (or in the poet's phrase, "of treacherous Aid deceiv'd"), the French admiral Tourville attacked the combined English and Dutch fleet, losing fifteen ships and seeing his survivors dispersed. The English rejoiced, for France thereafter could launch no major fleet action, being reduced to privateering.

The poem unfolds neatly: "Immortal Fury" inspires the poet, the fleets noisily join in battle, various kinds of ammunition explode, Admiral Russell receives praise, and quiet returns after the destruction of French ships. The proud French are evil, as seen in phrases like "*Gallick* Demon" and "impious Colony." At the end their ships are likened to once proud oaks with mangled limbs, which now frighten rather than shelter.

Dennis enjoys writing furiously noisy passages:

> Their Rage by Loss of Limbs is kindled more,
> And with their Guns like Hurricanes they roar:
> Like Hurricanes the knotted Oak they tear,
> Scourge the vex'd Ocean, and torment the Air;
> While Earth, Air, Sea, in wild Confusion hurl'd,
> With universal Wrack and Chaos threat the World.

His enthusiasm can result in awkward couplets, such as "There a red Bullet from our Cannon blown, / Into a First-Rate's Powder-Room is thrown." However, perhaps because this is the shortest of his battle poems, Dennis shows here the best modulation of the sound level and the least wordiness.

He indicates his own high opinion of the poem by giving it first place in *The Select Works* (which is not arranged chronologically). A century later Robert Southey seems also to regard "**Upon Our Victory**" highly, since it is the only poem by Dennis that he prints in *Specimens of the English Poets* [see excerpt dated 1807].

The year before the great naval victory, the English army scored a land victory at the Battle of Aughrim, in which several thousand fleeing Irish Catholic rebels lost their lives. Unfortunately, Dennis's much-ridiculed poetic tribute to this martial success, "**A Pindarick Ode on the King . . . Occasion'd by the Victory at *Aghrim*,**" little enhances his reputation. Although the poem rocks with much of the "loud Cannon and tempestuous Drums" of the 1692 poem, its unsure structure and many distractingly awkward couplets do not help the poet convey a tone of national ecstasy. We should feel no surprise that readers in Coleridge's day were still smiling at such lines as "Nor *Alps* nor *Pyreneans* keep it [War] out, / Nor fortify'd Redoubt."

The other two battle poems, both much better than the Aughrim tribute yet not themselves outstanding as poetry, laud the Duke of Marlborough's victories. The first "**Britannia Triumphans: or The Empire Sav'd, and Europe Deliver'd**" (1704), recounts the thrilling Battle of Blenheim, which resulted in 15,000 Franco-Bavarian casualties, 13,000 captives, the capture of the French general Tallard, and Bavaria's withdrawal from the War of the Spanish Succession. Contemporary newspaper accounts and sermons exulted in the "Glorious Victory" by the valorous Duke, and the Queen proclaimed a day of thanksgiving. Dennis is but one of many poets rushing their verses into print to celebrate the mood.

"**Britannia Triumphans**" opens with appeals for inspiration, notably from the God of Revenge and Queen Anne, "Great Championess of Liberty and Faith." The poet then asks Germania, Austria, and Britannia to sing praise. We finally see Marlborough, wise, majestically calm, decisive. After an allied success at Schellenbourgh, the two sides poise for battle, which then rages until the enemy fall into the Danube. The poem ends with a quiet address to Death as Britannia mourns the late sons of the Duke and of the Queen.

Dennis leaves no doubts about his sympathies: the Gallic tyrant, aided by his Jacobite friends in England, opposes liberty and virtue. Marlborough, Anne's wondrous chief and Dennis's military hero, has devised a battle plan, "His Essay, an Heroick Master-piece, / Whose Brightness dazles all Spectators Eyes, / Astonishes our Friends, confounds our Foes." The hyperbolically praised Duke leads his men through the noise of "The Trumpet's Roar! The Thunder of the Drum!" to drown the enemy's pride in the horror of "the Cries, the Shrieks, the dying Groans, / The Grief, the Rage, the Fury of their Fear, / And all the Horrors of their baleful Eyes."

Dennis is really too serious. He wishes so much to praise Marlborough and Anne that he piles line upon line to produce some fustian and much verboseness. Thus his 1,381 lines make few solid points. He does not develop the skillful character analysis or directness of Addison's 470-line "The Campaign," written also to celebrate Blenheim. However, both poets received tangible returns from the grateful Duke, Dennis getting a hundred pounds and the post of royal waiter in the London Custom-House, Addison becoming undersecretary of state.

Dennis returns to Marlborough in **"The Battle of Ramillia: or, The Power of Union"** (1706), occasioned by a victory that resulted in 15,000 French deaths. He calls attention in both the dedication and the preface to his boldness in devising his Miltonesque tribute as "something of the Epick Kind." Such boldness, however, does not here produce a satisfying poem.

The blank-verse lines divide into five books. In book 1, as the Confederate troops gather, Satan enviously recounts for his troops Marlborough's success at Blenheim and praises Louis XIV, "the second Hope of Hell, / The Man, the Monarch after my own Heart"; Discord pushes the spirits to defeat Anne and the Duke. Discord and Night in book 2 rekindle Louis's ambition by reminding him of Blenheim, "Blast to my Hopes of Universal Sway." In book 3 the French leader Villeroy hears of the Confederate troops from Discord, who retells Marlborough's astounding deeds at Blenheim. An angel tells Marlborough in book 4 of his impending victory and his future joy in Heaven. Book 5 describes the Battle of Ramillies and the predicted Confederate victory.

Many elements of **"The Battle of Ramillia"** remind us too much of the Blenheim poem. Dennis ends up saying the same things about Marlborough and the satanic Louis. Strangely, we hear a great deal more about Blenheim than about Ramillies.

Two major differences between the two poems, length and epic machinery, support Cibber's judgment of the poem as "a cold unspirited performance; it has neither fire, nor elevation..." [see excerpt dated 1753]. Dennis seems unable to handle the scope of 2,040 lines, writing the most repetitive and verbose passages of his career. The great reliance on heavenly and infernal spirits leads also to tedious pages heavy on abstractions and very light on concrete detail; after four books of anticipation, we see almost nothing of the Battle of Ramillies, since Dennis by now has stated all his abstract positions. Pope seems right in lampooning Dennis's machinery in *The Critical Specimen.* (pp. 93-7)

[**Elegiac Political Verse.**] Among the more original elegies is Dennis's **"The Court of Death. A Pindarique Poem, Dedicated to the Memory of Her Most Sacred Majesty, Queen Mary."** "Bold in the design," this ode features a rare structure in a genre typified by unchanging structures. The poem contains three sections. In stanzas 1 through 4 the persona is visited at night by Pindar's Muse, who will show this poet the underworld Court of Death and help him "sing in wond'rous Rhyme / Of Things transcendently sublime." In the grim "infernal Room," of stanzas 5 through 12, Death tries to motivate his ghastly crew by describing the keen frustration felt when William III, "Th'undaunted Hero," insolently braves and defeats death. Finally, Discord introduces a plan to destroy William by killing Mary; after some description of Mary's virtues, the poet awakens with the repeated chant, "Let this Good, this Great MARIA die."

In the preface Dennis explains his wish to emulate Pindar's "vehemence, his impetuousness, and the magnificent sounds of his numbers; and ... something dreadful, something which terribly shakes us, at the very same time it transports us." He wants at the same time to imitate Milton, who shares much with Pindar. Conscious Miltonisms include the brightly shining Muse, the convocation of infernal spirits, and such phrases as "Adamantine Chains." And the style does indeed wax vehement. Death's followers roll, foam, roar, and bellow

> As when the Northern Tyrant of the Waves
> Upon the Polar Main in black *September* raves,
> The Billows, vex'd to madness, roar,
> And foaming scourge the gloomy dismal Shore.

We can sense the author's ingenuity in finding his own way to mourn the queen. Most of her elegists simply catalog her virtues, particularly her goodness and beauty. Dennis instead creates the drama of the infernal conspiracy, an interesting feature of which is the implicit linking of "the raving *French*" with the lunatic spirits. Also, England's loss is both made poignant and rationalized when the queen becomes the only logical target of the impious conspirators because of her perfection: the woman Eve involved us in the Fall, but the woman Mary restores us to immortality.

Even if its lines do not have the resonance of great poetry, **"The Court of Death"** certainly shows improvement over Dennis's early witty verse. He develops his own effective structure, and he creates the passion he finds essential in greater poetry. Appropriately, *The Mourning Poets* (1695) singles out for highest praise the boldness and daring of Dennis's Pindaric flight. (pp. 98-9)

Since he could not fail to write something on his royal hero [William III], three months after the king's death, Dennis published **"The Monument: a Poem Sacred to the Immortal Memory of the Best and Greatest of Kings, William the Third, King of Great Britain, &c."** We find here the common overall elegiac structure of (1) lamentation, (2) praise, and (3) consolation.

(1) Distraught with sudden grief, the author asks Britannia, Batavia, Europa, Liberty, Religion, guardian angels, and the earth and heavens to mourn; the universe mourns because William blessed all. (2) Unlike satanic "vulgar" heroes (read "Louis"), the heroic William asserted God's governance of man's liberty; unlike Caesar, William conquered France for liberty, not pride; he won a glorious victory at Seneffe; he delivered England in the 1688 Revolution and Ireland at Boyne, but the populace showed no gratitude. (3) Since the king accepted death from God without complaint, we must not mourn but praise him; the author summarizes William's achievements, also briefly praising Queen Anne.

The most readable passages vividly describe the action at the Battle of Seneffe. Spurred on by "Death's Bugles in the dismal Chase of Blood," the soldiers find themselves in a cacophony of fire, cornets, drums, fiery heavens, outcries, volleys, and cannonades. The fighting makes "one ghastful Charnel of the Field" until the English "Storm of Iron Hail" finally ends the noise. Dennis here writes with crispness, verve, and dramatic pacing.

The poet's main end is to praise the king. This he does in part by offering William's enemies as foils. Louis, for instance, is viewed as a prowling wolf, a lawless ocean, a bestial rapist, "the grand Destroyer." Both Louis the satanic plotter (as in **"The Court of Death"**) and those Jacobite "Sons of Darkness" plotting the king's assassination stealthily form their damnable designs in a secrecy unlike William's openness in public actions.

In his lines straightforwardly praising William's virtues, Dennis's enthusiasm for his subject creates a problem of credibility. We have no trouble assenting to the king's ability to inspire his troops, since Dennis focuses on the battle that historically best demonstrates that ability. Nor do such lines as "O Greatness, to be found on Earth no more!" prove hard to accept, since they patently belong in the elegiac tradition. However, the author too readily assumes an identification of the king with God for us fully to accept the characterization. The opening stanza laments, "The Good, the Great, the Godlike WILLIAM's dead!"—a line identical in phrasing to one on Mary except for the insertion of "Godlike." Like Ulamar in *Liberty Asserted*, William is "Like th' Offspring of the Gods, a Hero born"; but Ulamar is a totally fictional character. Still, Dennis could make such comparisons work poetically, did he not go a step beyond letting William act simply like God to make him God. We hear that William's "wondrous Zeal united Earth and Heav'n" and he sympathized even with his foes (this contradicts other lines in the poem) because he knew that all are "From one Divine Original deriv'd." Dennis's hero-worship has created a William impossible to believe in.

The quality of Dennis's poetic style fails to match his optimism about his performance. He says in the dedication, "I have less Mistrust of it than any thing I have done in Poetry. Besides, the Design and the Immortal Subject may supply in some measure the Weakness of my Performance." **"The Monument"** demonstrates, however, that if the technical control proves too weak, even the best overall designer will write only lackluster poetry. In the preface Dennis cites Milton and others to prove that blank verse lets the poet exactly phrase the intended thought, but in his hands it leads also to lack of control. This we see particularly in the overexpansiveness of descriptive passages and the repetition of numerous phrases. We might also note one of the worst lines in battle poetry, where Dennis writes alliteratively of Fortune: "She to new Slaughter lash'd on limping Fate."

We miss the compression and subtle rhythms of John Hughes's elegy on William, *The House of Nassau*. **"The Monument"** is a literary monument to Dennis's zeal, but it is not outstanding poetry.

Anne and George. Upon the 1 August 1714 death of Queen Anne, the last Stuart monarch, the crown passed to George of Hanover. A number of poems appeared to observe simultaneously the death and the accession. Many of these works mourn and praise Anne, introducing George only at the end as a consolatory motif. For instance, Edward Young devotes three-quarters of "On the Late Queen's Death, and His Majesty's Accession to the Throne" to Anne and the concluding one-quarter to George.

Dennis's **"A Poem upon the Death of Her Late Sacred Majesty Queen Anne, and the Most Happy and Most Auspicious Accession of his Sacred Majesty King George"** inverts this common structure to touch but lightly on Anne and say much about the new king. His poem divides into

three parts: (1) the narrator summons Urania to help him picture Britain's woe and fear upon Anne's death; (2) all Britons, united in politics and religion and including William as commander of "the triumphant Slain," proclaim the arrival of George, who will rule by "Reason's Law"; (3) future benefits of union under George will include victory over foreign tyrants, the sending of British ships over the world, rich citizens' helping the poor, more commerce and agriculture, "Virtue under Liberty" (embracing the disappearance of idleness, luxury, and all passions but love), strengthened religion and fidelity to the nation, and victory for true writers.

Only stanza 1, less than 10 percent of the poem, refers to Anne. Even in this stanza, the discussion is generalized. The only specified accomplishment, the land victories against France, belongs in fact to Dennis's martial hero, Marlborough, not the queen. The woman is fast forgotten in the next stanza, where we find "*Britannia* passing in an Hour / From Fear to Hope, to Joy, to Extasy." We feel no surprise, therefore, that in *The Select Works* Dennis has appropriately changed the title to **"On the Accession of King George to the British Throne."**

Dennis's slighting Anne indicates aversion to the late queen. Her Tory and High Church sympathies led her to create a Tory majority in the House of Lords and to support Henry Sacheverell, one of Dennis's bitter foes. She publicly exhibited jealousy toward George. And at the end her bewilderment about what to do made her a pathetic woman perhaps most memorable for her incredible record of twelve miscarriages and six short-lived children. Dennis cannot find much to praise. In fact, most British citizens concurred; no royal monument was erected in her memory.

Although guaranteed by the 1701 Act of Settlement, the Hanoverian right to the throne was greatly complicated by the desperate actions of Tory leaders such as Bolingbroke shortly before Anne's death. Most of Dennis's poem reflects the author's joy that at last the Hanoverian Succession will have its chance to work. He foresees a moral change so great that "the true *Britannick* Tory, and Church Whig," and the dissenter will forget their distinctions within a new union. Actually, he is re-creating the Whigs' thrilling sense of victory, which they were to enjoy politically for many years.

In prophesying the benefits to be reaped, Dennis reaches back to the principles that he has supported in earlier works. Liberty over tyranny, the importance of commerce, responsibility to one's state, and the battle against "venal, vile, accursed Pens, / That with their Lyes intoxicate the Crowd" are all here. We have before us almost a catalog of this writer's moral and political tenets.

In this, his last poem, Dennis writes a competent, interesting combination of halfhearted elegy and wholehearted anticipatory congratulation. True to his own beliefs, he looks forward to a dazzling era which he was never to enjoy. (pp. 100-03)

[Religious verse.] Dennis devoted much critical attention to the importance of religion in poetry. It may thus surprise us to discover that he wrote poetry wholly devoted to religion only three times, and all of these lines were originally incorporated into prose treatises.

We need pause but a moment over two fragmentary biblical paraphrases. In *The Advancement* Dennis had quoted the King James prose version of Psalm 18:6-15 as an instance of greatness in divine poetry. In *The Grounds,* obviously still impressed by the Psalmist, he offers his own poetic treatment of these same lines as well as of Habakkuk 3:3-15. (p. 103)

The technique of working a resounding vocabulary into unvaried, rolling blank-verse lines we have already seen in such writings as the battle poems. Unfortunately, these fragments come perilously closer to fustian than they should. They do, however, move with a strength that helps the essayist make his point; like him, we perhaps should not insist upon their being great lines.

Stronger as a poem in its own right is **"Part of the *Te Deum* Paraphras'd, in Pindarick Verse."** The original, a third-century Latin hymn by St. Ambrose beginning "Te Deum laudamus" ("We praise thee, O God"), comprises three chants. The first notes all those who praise God; the second describes Christ's deeds for man; the third prays for the Lord's blessing and mercy.

In his six-stanza version Dennis works on only the first chant, expanding upon the idea of how much in the universe praises God. The persona first bids all raise their voices to praise the eternal King, "permanent and fix'd, / Uncreated and unmix'd." In following stanzas we learn how earth's nonhuman creatures, man, and heavenly spirits "To sing Thee, Great Creator, all conspire, / All Ranks divinely touch the living Lyre." We at last find all together, worshiping the Lord of the immense universe.

The most noticeable weakness of the poem is verbose passages. Dennis tries to achieve a sense of spaciousness, expansion, and greatness by packing many lines with repetitions of phrasing or idea. . . . In terms of pure stylistics, we have here throwaway lines; however, even with their deficiencies of poetic style, the lines most surely convey Dennis's serious intent. We cannot fail to grasp his poetic logic, which derives from his philosophy of the highest poetry: if the world reflects the divine greatness, and the poet lives in the world, the greatest poetry will bring together those images, rhythms, and sounds found in the world that most tellingly suggest greatness. We may not find in the verses Milton's genius, but we can certainly feel the honest struggle of a minor poet to re-create his awe before the immensity of God's universe.

The **"Te Deum"** paraphrase enjoyed a moderately good reputation. The several editions of *A Collection of Divine Hymns and Poems upon Several Occasions,* first published in 1709, reprint the poem along with verses by the Earl of Roscommon, Dryden, and others. On 25 September 1724 the *Plain Dealer* glowingly congratulates the author for having "oblig'd the World, so nobly, in his **"Paraphrase on Te Deum,"** with Verse, and Sentiments, sublimely suited to the *Vastness* of the Occasion. . . . This is Poetry, that defies Censure, and is rais'd, even above Praise: for it is scarce possible to say so much of it, as it truly deserves." Some of Dennis's biographers temper their enthusiasm but remain positive in their overall verdict. Cibber finds the poem to confirm "that Mr. Dennis wrote with more elegance in Pindaric odes, than in blank verse," while Kippis feels that the paraphrase "is of superior merit, though not entitled to any very high degree of praise" [see excerpt dated 1793].

Dennis himself felt the highest regard for the poem. He first prints the entire paraphrase in *The Advancement,* where it helps prove the superiority of Christian to pagan poetry. In *The Grounds* he reproduces the final sixteen lines to show how the immensity of the universe can produce admiration. Still later, in a letter to the *Spectator,* he again quotes these sixteen lines to prove that in *Tatler* 119 Steele has plagiarized ideas found only in the paraphrase (unfortunately, an empty complaint, since the ideas are almost commonplaces). Dennis also argues in this letter that the translation is one of his strongest poems. However, he did not in his later years attempt religious poetry. The power of such late religious prose writings as his translations of Thomas Burnet (1728 and 1730) indicates that for Dennis prose is a more natural medium.

[The Reverse.] Dennis's most interesting poem, " **The Reverse: or, The Tables Turn'd,"** first ascribed to him in 1920, attacks John Tutchin's *The Foreigners* (1700). In many ways the Whig pamphleteer Tutchin would seem a bedfellow to Dennis. He, too, pleaded for naval reform, wrote anticlerical books, and proclaimed himself an asserter of English liberties, and he died at the hands of a pro-Sacheverell mob. Dennis, however, does not like Tutchin's discerning scandal where no evidence of wrongdoing exists. As we learn in "The Author to the Reader," he views Tutchin as a malcontent, a dull malignant, a blockhead.

Nor can Dennis accept the central point of *The Foreigners.* Evincing marked xenophobia, Tutchin attributes England's troubles to the pernicious influence of foreign-born politicians. These foreigners receive English titles, estates, wealth, and military commands as they set aside native liberties and real Englishmen become lackeys. Deep hatred seethes through lines describing the Netherlands, homeland of William III and his closest advisers:

> Its Natives void of Honesty and Grace,
> A Boorish, rude, and an inhumane Race;
> From Nature's Excrement their Life is drawn,
> Are born in Bogs, and nourish'd up from Spawn.

Tutchin also presses the Republican claims for the people's right to elect their king or to choose no king.

Dennis answers "Paragraph by Paragraph," printing his and Tutchin's verses on alternating facing pages, so that we can see "The Tables Turn'd." He argues that the foreign-born men assailed by Tutchin have actually strengthened England. Before William's accession "Impious *Israelites* were *Israel's* Foes"; as in Tutchin, "Israel" is England. Native moral corruption has long enervated the nation and shows in the influence of self-serving native politicians such as Sir Edward Seymour and in the "canker'd Malice" of Tutchin, vividly described as "a Senseless, starving Scribler." The greatest threat is posed by Republicans like the insolent "High-Priest" Gilbert Burnet.

Like most effective controversialists, Dennis uses both emotional appeals and logic. We see the former in an attack on Tutchin: "Oh may the Calves-head Rioters, our Foes, / Still use *his* Rhimes, *his* lamentable Prose." Dennis is referring to the horrible blasphemies of the possibly mythical Calves' Head Club. According to Ned Ward, this group comprised extreme Republicans who annually derided monarchical rule by wickedly celebrating the assassination of Charles I. Their supposed ritual contained incidents disgusting to all good citizens: " . . . the Anniversary *Anthem*, as they impiously call'd it, was sung, and a Calves-Skull fill'd with Wine or other Liquor, and then a Brimmer went about to the Pious Memory of those worthy Patriouts that had kill'd the Tyrant, and deliver'd their Country from his Arbitrary Sway." Such implications give Tutchin's arguments a tone of wildness and demonic conspiracy.

Dennis's logic shows best in his turning the thoughts in each of Tutchin's stanzas to the reverse thought. For example, across the page from his opponent's hateful description of the Netherlands Dennis places his most violent attack on Republicanism. Similarly, Tutchin's "If we a Foreign Slave may use in War, / Yet why in Council should that Slave appear?" turns into a strong complaint that England is shamefully disgracing her martial saviors by ostracizing them. This method is carried out in every stanza, often with imagination, until Tutchin simply has no chance.

Although published only eighteen days after *The Foreigners*, Dennis's poem effectively counters Tutchin. It does not possess the imaginative power of Defoe's answer, *The True-Born Englishman*; but it certainly has more subtlety and originality than other responses, such as the anonymously published *The Natives* (1700). Yet, as well as Dennis and Defoe wrote, they did not destroy their opponent, for next year he is still asking, "Must *Foreign* Councils manage our Intrigues, / And make our *Treaties*, and confirm our *Leagues*?"

The high quality of **"The Reverse"** does not result from Dennis's applying his critical theories about poetry. Treatises like *The Advancement* and *The Grounds* describe the ends of the highest poetry, which the lines against Tutchin clearly are not intended to achieve. The dully methodical and unimaginative "Of Prosody," first printed in the second edition of James Greenwood's *An Essay towards a Practical English Grammar* (1722), puts forward some mechanical rules for composing but gives no hint that its author could write poetry that makes us either think or feel. Rather, Dennis in **"The Reverse"** uses the couplet wit learned from Butler and Dryden and the brisk verbal aggressiveness already developing in his own controversial prose. (pp. 104-08)

> *Avon Jack Murphy, in his* John Dennis, *Twayne Publishers, 1984, 155 p.*

DAVID M. WHEELER (essay date 1986)

[*In the following excerpt, Wheeler analyzes Dennis's conception of ancient and modern poetry, relating the ideas presented in* The Advancement and Reformation of Modern Poetry *and* The Grounds of Criticism in Poetry *to those of various eighteenth- and nineteenth-century literary schools.*]

As a poet and dramatist, John Dennis is now forgotten: we would be hard-pressed to recite a line (or even the title) of one of his poems, and though a student of eighteenth-century literature might be able to name a Dennis play or two, he would need the *National Union Catalog* to locate a copy. Dennis, the literary critic, merits and receives more attention; yet, despite the reputation (perhaps the better word is power) he enjoyed during the first decade of the eighteenth century, Dennis's work generally has attracted only inclusion in histories of literary criticism rather than separate studies. (p.210)

[Here] we are concerned with the two long essays, *The Advancement and Reformation of Modern Poetry* and *The Grounds of Criticism in Poetry*, in which Dennis defines his conception of poetry and plots the course modern poetry must take if it is to equal or surpass that of the ancients.

These essays originated as part of the well-known and long-lived debate over the relative merits of the ancients and moderns, a debate that reached its finest moment in Swift's wonderful "Battle of the Books," which, as we know, advances the cause of the ancients. Dennis's *Advancement* supports the opposite side of the controversy—the moderns—and utilizes an opposite tone as well—the high seriousness appropriate to the subject, which is no less than the future, perhaps the survival, of literature.

Dennis begins the essay by endorsing the fundamental tenet of neoclassical aesthetic theory—the mimetic function of art—to justify formal regularity:

> There is nothing in Nature that is great and beautiful, without Rule and Order; and the more Rule and Order, and Harmony, we find in the Objects that strike our Senses, the more Worthy and Noble we esteem them. I humbly conceive, that it is the same in Art, and particularly in Poetry, which ought to be an exact Imitation of Nature.

In other words, since in these days of the Enlightenment, the natural ordering principles of the universe were becoming ever more apparent, the world ever more regular, though complex, art, as an imitation of nature, must be constructed on similar formal principles, principles which for most neoclassical writers were a sense of decorum, regular versification, poetic justice, and the dramatic unities. This statement appears orthodox enough, but a few things about it must be pointed out: (1) the aesthetics here is a totally objective one: greatness and beauty, rule and order, reside in the object to be imitated; (2) in imitating the divine creation, the artist himself is not merely an imitator, but a creator, an originator; and (3) the authority for Dennis's aesthetic is not Aristotelian or Horatian, but religious, as it resides in nature and ultimately in God. Though he is ostensibly discussing the rules of composition here, the objective aesthetics makes it possible for Dennis to devalue many neoclassical literary values, such as wit, harmonious versification, and well-reasoned argumentation, and shift the focus of his criticism to poetic subject matter—the object to be imitated. This argument is designed to divert modern authors from the common practice of classical imitation. (We recall that Dryden and Pope devoted a large portion of their labors to translating and rerendering Virgil, Juvenal, Ovid, Tacitus, Homer, and Horace.) Dennis considered this practice a servile and fruitless occupation that would lead only to despair of ever arriving at another Golden Age and would finally destroy literature.

Dennis then conducts a search to discover the causes of the superiority enjoyed by classical over modern poetry. Proceeding empirically, he conventionally discounts both external (climate, government, etc.) and internal (inspiration, learning, virtue, etc.) advantages and finally arrives at the only reason, given his aesthetics, possible for Dennis—the superior subjects of ancient poetry. Now, we might ask, "If the moderns were imitating the ancients, were not their subjects the same?" The answer for Dennis is "No." Though Virgil and Dryden both wrote of the exploits of Aeneas and the founding of Rome, the subjects must be distinguished because for Virgil and his audience, the subject is sacred, involving as it does the deities and divine revelation; for Dryden and his audience, the same subject is profane, being mere history and mythology.

In explaining why sacred poetry is preferable to secular, Dennis does no less than redefine poetry from the conventional "imitation of nature for the instruction and delight of mankind" to "an imitation of Nature, by a pathetick and numerous Speech" (*Advancement*). By using the word "numerous," Dennis has done no more than affirm that poetry is written in verse, but by using the word "pathetick," Dennis has broken away from neoclassical convention and is demanding the presence of emotion.... (pp. 211-13)

If Dennis establishes the prominence of passion in poetry as his major premise, his minor premise—that religion affords the most passion—follows quickly:

> Now no Subject is so capable of supplying us with Thoughts that necessarily produce these great and strong Enthusiasms, as a Religious Subject: For all which is great in Religion, is most exalted and amazing; all that is joyful, is transporting; all that is sad, is dismal; and all that is terrible, is astonishing. (*Advancement*)

The syllogistic conclusion that religious subjects produce the most passionate, and therefore the greatest, poetry proves the earlier assertion about the reason for the supremacy of the ancients and charts the course for the reformation of modern poetry. To compose great poetry, modern British poets must select religious subjects, and in this endeavor, they have the advantage over the ancients and modern Italians such as Dante and Tasso because they possess the true Protestant religion. And to illustrate by example, Dennis devotes large portions of both essays to quotations from Milton, pointing out how the Protestant epic poet surpasses his pagan and Catholic predecessors in passion and sublimity.

Such is the course that Dennis outlines for the reformation of poetry. But for Dennis, who, like nearly all neoclassical critics, perceives the function of literature to be an overtly moral one, selection of religious poetic subjects would reform not only a decadent poetry but a fallen mankind as well. He observed that

> the Misery of Man proceeded from a perpetual Conflict that is within him, and from a Discord continually reigning among the Faculties of the Soul; a cruel War between the Passions and the Senses, and the Reason. (*Advancement*)

This essential human conflict, according to Dennis, is a result of the Fall, for prior to the Fall, passion and reason cohabited in perfect harmony. The conflict was a popular theme throughout literature but especially in Restoration and eighteenth-century literature, and it can be observed, for example, in Dryden's heroic plays, in Pope's *The Rape of the Lock* and *The Essay on Man*, and in the countless sentimental comedies and tragedies that paraded across the eighteenth-century stage. In these treatments of the theme, man is unhappily placed midway between the passionate, appetitive beasts and the rational angels; in order to improve his lot, he must suppress passion and follow his godlike reason, which is the special province of man.

Dennis, however, is unconventionally suspicious of reason. In a digression in *The Advancement and Reformation of Poetry*, Dennis attacks the increasingly popular deism: since it appeals only to reason, deism is comprehensible only to an educated elite; thus lacking a requisite universality, it could not possibly be the true religion. Dennis defends revealed religion because, appealing to the passions, it is capable of being comprehended by all, and true religion must be designed for all. If we are looking for a literary illustration of Dennis's position, it seems to me that we need only recall Book IX of *Paradise Lost* where Eve succumbs not to a beastly passion (though perhaps Adam does) but to the spurious logic of a reasoning Satan.

Dennis believed that historically philosophers had understood the essential conflict, but in advocating suppression of either reason or passion, they could never attain a resolution:

> [A]ll the Passions being Natural, in the Condition in which Man is now, none of them can be wholly suppress'd without destroying the Man. (*Advancement*)

Just as Blake believed that religious suppression of emotion had destroyed man, making it necessary to perform a fanciful reconciliation of the faculties in his "Marriage of Heaven and Hell," Dennis perceives a similar kind of destruction but ascribes its cause to rationalist philosophy and philosophical, didactic poets who followed suit and eliminated passion from their works. For Dennis, of course, true religion reconciles the conflict, but so can poetry, the highest art, if it contains sufficient passion obtainable with religious subject matter: "in a sublime and accomplish'd Poem, the Reason, and Passions, and Senses are pleas'd at the same Time superlatively.... Thus, Poetry, by restoring the Harmony of the Human Faculties, provides for the Happiness of Mankind, better than any other Human Invention whatever" (*Advancement*).

Despite Dennis's insistence that religion provides the source, means, and end of the best poetry, we do not find religious verse dominating the eighteenth-century literary scene. We find Isaac Watts, but we find no more *Paradise Lost*s. Does this absence mean then that Dennis's reformative efforts failed? I think not. The cause that Dennis championed was essentially a Longinian notion of sublimity, and Samuel Holt Monk long ago chronicled the importance of the sublime as a literary value in the eighteenth century [in *The Sublime: A Study of Critical Theories in XVIII - Century England* (1935)]. In *The Grounds of Criticism in Poetry*, Dennis's list of sublime subjects, ranging from God to angels to demons, spirits, prophecies, and visions to the wonders of the created universe, anticipates similar treatments of the subject from Addison's series of *Spectator* papers on "The Pleasures of the Imagination" (1712), generally believed to be the first major British statement on aesthetic theory, to Burke's *Philosophical Enquiry into the Origins of Our Ideas of the Sublime and Beautiful* (1757). Common to nearly all items included in the lists—whether they be strewn bodies of heroic dead, allegorical personifications presented in dream visions, or descriptions of raging torrents and craggy peaks—is their ultimate reflection of the awesome and awe-inspiring majesty and power of God.

Concomitant with Dennis's contribution to an aesthetic of the sublime, and perhaps even more important, is his influential role in laying the critical groundwork for a second line of neoclassical critics and poets that existed collaterally with what we generally regard as the first line of neoclassical writers, those major figures included in the *Norton Anthology*—Dryden, Swift, Pope, Fielding, Goldsmith, Johnson—who share a nearly homogeneous poetic that affords convenient labeling. While the major figures were advocating and demonstrating an unparalleled satiric wit and remarkable literary style, other writers, now categorized into an assortment of "literary schools"—the neo-Miltonists, the antiquarians, the sentimentalists, the graveyard poets, the primitivists, the gothic novelists—were writing quite a different sort of literature. What these various schools shared was an irrepressible insistence on an emotional or imaginative impact on the reader through powerful imagery, lofty poetic diction, or morally ambiguous situation. And it is easy to overlook the fact that by mid-century, it is this second line of neoclassicists that held popular sway in poetry, fiction, drama, and criticism. And it is the very points that Dennis makes in his early essays—that literature must be emotional and must be of elevated subject matter—that form the basis for most of the literary disputes in a century known for literary disputes: not only the dispute between Pope and Dennis, but those between Fielding and Richardson in fiction, Goldsmith and Cumberland in drama, Johnson and Gray in poetry—all revolve around a debate over whether the skilled craftsmanship of the author is more or less important in a literary work than the emotional impact the work has on the reader. (pp. 213-17)

This major rift in a literary period often perceived as the most monolithic begins early and extends throughout the century. And it is John Dennis's role at the genesis of the rift that should rescue his criticism from the oblivion into which Pope had hurled him. (pp. 217-18)

> *David M. Wheeler, "John Dennis and the Religious Sublime," in* CLA Journal, *Vol. XXX, No. 2, December, 1986, pp. 210-18.*

ADDITIONAL BIBLIOGRAPHY

Albrecht, W. P. "John Dennis and the Sublime Pleasures of Tragedy." *Studies on Voltaire and the Eighteenth Century* LXXXVII (1972): 65-8.
> Relates Dennis's identification of the sublime in tragedy and the passions to the theories of such later writers as Edmund Burke, Alexander Gerard, Archibald Alison, and John Keats.

Altieri, Joanne. "Representation in Contemporary Theory." In her *The Theatre of Praise: The Panegyric Tradition in Seventeenth-Century English Drama*, pp. 175-82. Newark: University of Delaware Press, 1986.
> Considers the critical reasoning behind Dennis's opposition to opera.

Barnouw, Jeffrey. "The Morality of the Sublime to John Dennis." *Comparative Literature* 35, No. 1 (Winter 1983): 21-42.
> Compares Dennis's conception of the sublime with that of Longinus, Petrarch, Immanuel Kant, and Johann Schiller, arguing that while Dennis emphasized the importance of religion to the sublime, he in effect "reversed the main direction which had been given to its conception, and so to the experience itself, in Christian tradition starting with Saint Augustine."

Chapin, Chester F. "Addison and the Empirical Theory of Imagination." In his *Personification in Eighteenth-Century English Poetry*, pp. 8-10. New York: King's Crown Press, 1955.
> Presents Dennis's views concerning epic poetry.

Congreve, William. "Concerning Humor in Comedy." In *Critical Essays of the Seventeenth Century: 1685-1700*, edited by J. E. Spingarn, Vol. III, pp. 242-52. Oxford: Oxford University Press, Clarendon Press, 1909.
> Flattering 1695 letter from Congreve to Dennis presenting ideas on humor in comedy and requesting Dennis's critical assessment.

Graham, C. B. "The Jonsonian Tradition in the Comedies of John Dennis." *Modern Language Notes* LVI, No. 5 (May 1941): 370-72.
> Notes that Dennis's three comedies, *A Plot and No Plot, The Comical Gallant*, and *Gibraltar; Or, The Spanish Adventure*, reflect the influence of Ben Jonson.

Hirt, A. "A Question of Excess: Neo-Classical Adaptations of Greek Tragedy." *Costerus* 3 (1972): 55-119.
> Summarizes the plot of *Iphigenia* and considers how Dennis and other seventeenth- and eighteenth-century dramatists borrowed from and adapted the Euripidean original.

Hooker, Edward N. "Pope and Dennis." *ELH* 7, No. 3 (September 1940): 188-98.
> Traces part of the literary quarrel between Dennis and Alexander Pope.

[Motteux, Peter Anthony]. *The Gentleman's Journal* I (October 1692): 17.
> Praises Dennis's translation of Ovid's "The Passion of Byblis."

Pope, Alexander. "The Critical Specimen." In his *The Prose Works of Alexander Pope*, edited by Norman Ault, Vol. 1, pp. 1-18. Oxford: Shakespeare Head Press, 1936.
> 1711 satire of Dennis as "the Renown'd *Rinaldo Furioso, Critick* of the Wonderful countenance." This essay was Pope's first rejoinder to Dennis's *Reflections upon a Late Rhapsody call'd, "An Essay on Criticism"*.

R[oberts], W[illiam]. "Two Eighteenth Century Critics." *The Bookworm* 2 (1889): 145-50.
> Considers the critical reputations of Dennis and Thomas Rymer.

[Roberts, William]. "John Dennis: A Sketch." *The Bookworm* 4 (1891): 289-95.
> Brief biographical sketch treating Dennis's works and reputation.

Simon, Irène. "John Dennis and Neoclassical Criticism." *Revue belge de philologie et d'histoire* LVI, No. 3 (1978): 663-77.
> Debates possible contradictions in certain aspects of Dennis's doctrine on the sublime, examining why the critic has been called a theoretical forerunner of the Romantics.

Swift, Jonathan. "A Digression concerning Cruicks." In his *A Tale of a Tub: With Other Early Works, 1696-1707*, pp. 56-64. Oxford: Basil Blackwell, 1939.

Satirically lists Dennis as among the "true criticks" who viciously attack good writers. This brief reference was the first of several apparently unprovoked attacks by Swift upon Dennis.

Thorpe, Clarence DeWitt. "Two Augustans Cross the Alps: Dennis and Addison on Mountain Scenery." *Studies in Philology* XXXII, No. 3 (July 1935): 463-82.

Claims that Dennis and Joseph Addison were the first eighteenth-century literary men to write about their appreciation of mountain scenery.

Wilkins, A. N. "John Dennis and Poetic Justice." *Notes and Queries* CCII (October 1957): 421-24.

Discusses Dennis's application of his dramatic theory of vice and virtue in *Appius and Virginia*.

Wimsatt, William K., Jr., and Brooks, Cleanth. "Genius, Emotion, and Association." In their *Literary Criticism: A Short History*, pp. 283-312. New York: Alfred A. Knopf, 1957.

Traces the development of theories concerning "the inspirations of the authors of poetry" over approximately 200 years, commenting on the ideas of Dennis and such contemporaries of his as John Dryden, Joseph Addison, and Richard Steele.

(Sir) Thomas Elyot
1490?-1546

English philosopher, philologist, and translator.

Elyot is chiefly remembered for his influence in shaping the humanist movement in Renaissance England. The author of numerous works, he is best known for *The Boke Named the Gouernour* (most commonly referred to as *The Governour*), a voluminous discourse on statesmanship, and for *The Dictionary*, an encyclopedic Latin-English reference which measurably enhanced the prestige of his native tongue.

A judge's son, Elyot was born in Wiltshire, England around 1490. He was tutored at home and, from most evidence, was self-taught after the age of twelve. He studied the fundamentals of English common law at the Middle Temple in 1510. Beginning in 1511, Elyot accompanied his father on the western judicial circuit as clerk of assize until the latter's death in 1522. In the same year, Elyot married Margaret Barrow, a pupil of humanist Thomas More, with whose philosophy and circle of associates he became familiar. From 1523 to 1530, Elyot was clerk of the privy council under Cardinal Wolsey. In recognition of his service to the Crown, he was knighted in 1530. Elyot remarked that he had been "discharged without any recompense, rewarded only with the order of knighthode, honorable and onerouse, having moche lasse to lyve on than bifore."

Elyot published his most famous work, *The Governour*, in 1531. Dedicated to Henry VIII, this popular treatise on the education of statesmen led to the king's appointment of its author as ambassador to the court of the emperor Charles V, nephew of Catherine of Aragon. Elyot's mission was dual: he was to secure the emperor's support for Henry's divorce from Catherine and apprehend William Tyndale, a religious reformer who had fled England after denouncing Henry's intent to divorce. Elyot returned from his embassy in 1532, unsuccessful in both attempts. He published two works the following year, *Pasqvil the Playne* (which he felt most prudent to print anonymously) and *Of the Knowledeg Which Maketh a Wise Man*. Both of these dialogues address the bond between rulers and their subjects. They were oblique but, apparently, ineffectual appeals to the king's sense of sovereign responsibility, for Elyot opposed Henry's divorce and remarriage on moral and religious grounds. In 1533, Henry invalidated his marriage to Catherine and crowned Anne Boleyn queen of England.

With the flammable political climate of 1534, Elyot published English translations of two works extolling Christian fortitude in the face of adversity: *A Swete and Devovte Sermon of Holy Saynt Ciprian of Mortalitie of Man* and *The Rules of a Christian Lyfe Made by Picus Erle of Mirandula*. Because he accepted the Anglican reform, Elyot was in no danger of the martyrdom suffered by his friend More and others, yet he was shaken by the daily round of indictments and executions around him. Late in 1538 Elyot published *The Dictionary*, which provided an English vernacular equivalent for each Latin word included. About 1539 he published *The Castel of Helth*, a volume

(Sir) Thomas Elyot

devoted to proper diet and related matters of fitness written in English rather than the conventional Latin.

Although the fortunes of those around him continued to be altered by political events, the author persevered in studious application. In 1540 he again witnessed the public disgrace and execution of a powerful individual and associate, his longtime supporter Thomas Cromwell. *The Defence of Good Women*, Elyot's dialogue expounding on the capacities of women, appeared at this time. For his remaining years, Elyot oversaw editions of several extant volumes and also published new works in 1541 and 1545. These were, respectively, *The Image of Governance*, a life of the early emperor Alexander Severus, and *A Preservative agaynste Deth*, a treatise which combined Christian beliefs and classical philosophy. The circumstances of Elyot's own death at Carlton, Cambridgeshire in 1546 are unknown.

The Governour has received most of the critical attention paid its author. As an example of a literary type—the handbook for noblemen—it has been considered singular in scope and detail. Elyot's treatise outlines the proper education for sons of the ruling class from the nursery on, including recommendations outside a strictly academic province. It also encompasses such wide-ranging subjects as societal order and accountabilities for both leaders and citizens. Throughout the text, the precepts of Plato, Aristotle, Cicero, and others meld with emerging trends in humanist thought. While commentators have indicated the influence of certain Italian humanists on his work, they have noted the author's adaptation of these viewpoints to an English environment. In fact, in its union of classical perspective and secular concerns, *The Governour* has been deemed wholly representative of the spirit of English humanism. Alexander Chalmers observed that had Elyot written only *The Governour*, "it would have entitled him to the respect of posterity; as one of the best writers of his time, a man of acute observation, and of manly and liberal sentiments." Chalmers's appraisal typifies *The Governour*'s critical reception from its publication to nearly the mid-nineteenth century, when commentators came to regard the text on individual merits and not merely as a fixture of humanist literature. Some later critics have found *The Governour*'s historical analogies pedantic and its style laborious and have determined, with Isaac Disraeli, that it "must now be condemned to the solitary imprisonment of the antiquary's cell, who will pick up many curious circumstances relative to the manners of the age." Others have affirmed its lasting value despite deficiencies. While expressing reservations about Elyot's theories, C. S. Lewis warmly commended his stylistic ability. Lewis concluded: "I am not suggesting that Elyot, or a thousand such as Elyot, matter to the mind and heart of man as More matters; but the ear of man must sometimes prefer him."

With Latin-trained churchmen and scholars the nearly sole proprietors of learning in Tudor England, Elyot felt an obligation to improve the status of his own vernacular and make accessible to many what had been confined to so few. His objective is evident throughout his career in the publication in English of both original works and translations, but nowhere is it more manifest than in his dictionary. *The Dictionary* has been named Elyot's greatest legacy by some critics. When Thomas Fuller included the author in *The History of the Worthies of England* (1662), he remarked that the dictionary was, "if not the first, the best of that kind in that age," and marveled that Elyot had "hit on so necessary a subject." *The Dictionary* was an authoritative source for scholars during and after Elyot's lifetime and was instrumental in elevating English to a language of learned and practical discourse.

Such lesser writings as *The Castel of Helth* and *The Bankette of Sapience* (a collection of moral maxims culled from various authors) also reflect Elyot's far-reaching humanist concerns, but these works have generally been addressed in summary fashion. A few titles have elicited more expansive commentary. In the introduction to his edition of *Of the Knowledge Which Maketh a Wise Man*, Edwin Johnston Howard examined Elyot's dialogue form. Though inferior to Plato's, he concluded, it is handled "with skill and discretion." Current feminist issues have sparked a continuing interest in *The Defence of Good Women*. Critics have attempted to assess the author's personal estimation of a woman's role in society from the work's apologetic depiction of feminine virtue. According to Linda Woodbridge, the treatise "is a piece of literature, written out of a long literary tradition which it modifies

but whose conventions it nonetheless observes. One need not look beyond that tradition, toward dead queens or living queans, to account for Elyot's choosing to write theoretically about women."

Elyot's advancement of humanism is considered significant in the history of English thought and letters. His achievements were integral to a movement which has profoundly influenced the course of philosophy, literature, and history itself. Although Elyot's works have lost their former immediacy to the modern reader, their impact—both as the accomplishments of one individual and as valuable contributions to a vast mainstream—is still felt today. Of Elyot as man and humanist, Bernhard ten Brink has summarized: "The unselfish Renaissance-zeal for culture, the impulse to learn and to teach, live vigorously in him, and his entire literary activity testifies to the fact. In addition to this we have in him that naïve, joyous hopefulness, . . . the faith in the power of aiding the enlightenment and improvement of men by means of popular moralizing writings."

PRINCIPAL WORKS

The Boke Named the Gouernour (treatise) 1531
*The Doctrinall of Princis Made by the Noble Oratour Isocrates, and Translated out of Greke into Englishe by Syr Thomas Elyot Knyght [translator] (treatise) 1533
*The Education or Bringing Vp of Children, Translated oute of Plutarche by Syr Thomas Eliot Knyght [translator] (treatise) 1533
Of the Knowledeg Which Maketh a Wise Man (dialogue) 1533
Pasqvil the Playne (dialogue) 1533
*The Bankette of Sapience (aphorisms) 1534
A Swete and Devovte Sermon of Holy Saynt Ciprian of Mortalitie of Man. The Rules of a Christian Lyfe Made by Picus Erle of Mirandula, Bothe Translated into Englyshe by Syr T. E. [translator] (sermon and essay) 1534
The Dictionary (dictionary) 1538; also published as *Bibliotheca Eliotae: Eliotis Librarie* [revised edition], 1542
*The Castel of Helth Gathered and Made by Syr Thomas Elyot Knyghte, Out of the Chiefe Authors of Physyke, Wherby Eury Manne May Knowe the State of His Own Body, the Preseruation of Helth, and How to Instructe Welle His Physytion in Syckenes That He Be Not Deceyued (handbook) 1539
The Defence of Good Women (dialogue) 1540
The Image of Governance, Compiled of the Actes and Sentences Notable of Alexander Severus, Translated out of Greke into Englyshe by Syr T. Eliot [translator] (biography) 1541
A Preservative agaynste Deth (treatise) 1545

*First publication dates of these works are uncertain.

THOMAS FULLER (essay date 1661?)

[*Fuller was an English clergyman and historian who is best remembered for the biographical portraits collected and posthumously published in his* History of the Worthies of England *(1662). In the following excerpt from that work, he offers a thumbnail sketch of Elyot.*]

[Sir Thomas Eliot] was son to Sir Richard Eliot, and born (some say) in Suffolk; but his house and chief estate lay in this county. After his long sailing into foreign parts, he at last cast anchor at home; and being well skilled in Greek and Latin, was the author of many excellent works. Of these, one in Latin was styled, *Defensorium bonarum mulierum,* or *The defence of good women*; though some will say that such are hardly found, and easily defended.

He wrote also an excellent dictionary of Latin and English [*The Dictionary*], if not the first, the best of that kind in that age; and England then abounding with so many learned clergymen, I know not which more to wonder at, that they missed, or he hit on so necessary a subject. Let me add, Bishop Cooper grafted his dictionary on the stock of Sir Thomas Eliot; which worthy knight deceased 1546, and was buried at Carlton in this county.

> *Thomas Fuller, in an excerpt in his* The History of the Worthies of England, Vol. I, *edited by P. Austin Nuttall, revised edition, 1840. Reprint by AMS Press Inc., 1965, p. 257.*

JOHN STRYPE (essay date 1721)

[*Strype was a prolific English historian and biographer whose works, which largely address the Reformation in England, include* Ecclesiastical Memorials *(1721). In the following excerpt from that volume, he finds Elyot's life and works exemplary.*]

[Sir Thomas Elyot] was one, who as before he served his King and country in embassies and public affairs, so devoted these latter years of his life in writing discourses for the public good, and for promoting true wisdom and virtue among his countrymen. He had from his younger years a great desire after knowledge, and an earnest affectation of being beneficial to his country. When some gallants had mocked at him for writing a book of physic [*The Castel of Helth*], crying, that Sir Thomas Elyot was become a physician, in the next edition of that book, in the preface, he gave this answer; "Truly, if they will call him a physician, which is studious about the weal of his country, I vouchsafe they so name me; for during my life I will in that affection alway continue." And in the proeme of another of his books [*Of the Knowledeg Which Maketh a Wise Man*], he writ, that "he was naturally, even from his childhood, disposed to a desire of knowledge; to which he joined a constant intent to profit thereby his natural country: whereunto, according to the sentence of Tully, we be, said he, especially bounden." He applied the most part of his life in perusing diligently all ancient works, Greek and Latin, that he could come by, that treated of any piece of philosophy necessary to the institution of a man's life in virtue. And having well digested his reading, he set forth such parts of his studies as he thought might be profitable to such as should read or hear them: so that he was an excellent historian and philosopher.

Among the books he wrote, one was entitled, *The Governor*: which was a treatise instructing men, great men especially, in good morals, and reproving their vices. It consisted of divers chapters, some of them concerning *affability, benevolence, beneficence,* and of the diversity of *flatterers,* and such like. In which chapters especially were some sharp and quick sentences, which many of the sparks could not well bear. They complained of his *strange terms,*

as they called them. These Elyot compared to a galled horse abiding no plaisters, that were always knapping and kicking at such examples and sentences as they felt sharp, or did bite them. They said, it was no little presumption in him, that he would, in noting other men's vices, correct *magnificat*. By which phrase, I suppose, they meant, that however bold he made with the vices of the meaner sort of men, it was an insufferable affront to meddle with those of the nobler rank; that was, to *correct magnificat*. Others there were that conjectured he wrote to rebuke some particular person; designing thereby to bring him or his works under the indignation of some man in authority. "Thus unkindly," said he, "is my benefit received, my good will consumed, and all my labours devoured." But to this book King Henry did the honour to read it, and much liked it; making this observation upon it, "That Sir Thomas Elyot intended to augment our English tongue, whereby men should as well express more abundantly things conceived in their hearts, (wherefore language was ordained,) having words apt for the purpose; as also interpret out of Greek, Latin, or any other tongues into English, as sufficiently as out of any of the said tongues into another." The King observed also, that "throughout the book there was no new term made by him of a Latin or French word; that no sentence throughout the said book was thereby made dark, or hard to be understood."

Another book of his writing was entitled, *Of the Knowledge which maketh a wise Man,* in five Platonic dialogues between Plato and Aristippus.

He wrote divers others, but I will only mention his book of physic, called the *Castel of Health*. In what year the first edition was, I know not; but the second was in 1541. Neither for this book could he escape the detraction both of the gentry and of those of the faculty. The former sort mocked at him, saying, *A worthy matter; Sir Tho. Elyot is become a physician, and writes in physic, which beseems not a knight.* The physicians were angry, that he should meddle in their science, and write of physic in English, to make the knowledge thereof common. To the gentry he made this answer, "That many kings and emperors, and other great princes, (whose names he there sets down, as Juba, Mithridates, Artimisia, &c.) for the universal necessity and incomparable utility which they perceived to be in that science, did not only advance and honour it with special privileges, but also were therein studious themselves." And that it was no shame for a person of quality to write a book of the science of physic, any more than it was for King Henry VIII. to publish a book of the science of grammar, which he had lately done.... To the physicians he answered, "that his book of physic was intended for their benefit, that the uncertain tokens of urines and other excrements should not deceive them, but that by the true information of the sick man, by him instructed, they might be the more sure to prepare medicines convenient for the diseases." And as for those that blamed him for writing in English, he on the other hand blamed them for affecting to keep their art unknown. Insomuch that there were some of them, that would have some particular language devised, with a strange cipher, or form of letters; wherein they would have their science written. Which language or letters no man should have known, that had not professed nor practised physic. But to others of the college that made reflection upon his skill, and charged his book with errors about some herbs and medicines, them he lets understand his study in this piece of learning: that before he was twenty years old, one of the most learned physicians in England, perceiving him by nature inclined to knowledge, read to him the works of Galen, of temperaments, natural faculties, the introduction of Joannicius, and some of the aphorisms of Hippocrates, Galen, Oribasius, Paulus Celius, Alexander Trallianus, Plinius both the one and the other, with Dioscorides. He read also Avicen, Averrois, and many more. And though, he said, he had never been at Montpelier, Padua, or Salern, yet he had found something in physic, whereby he found no little profit for his own health.

The wisdom of this Knight appeared in those wise and weighty sentences that often fell from him. For example: in excuse for himself in dealing plainly with vicious men, he said, "Man is not yet so confirmed in grace, that he cannot sin: and I suppose no prince thinks himself to be exempt from mortality. And forasmuch as he shall have many occasions to fall, he ought to have the more friends, or the more instructions to warm him." Concerning our laws he had this expression; "Some do prefer the study of the laws of this realm, calling it the only study of the public weal; but a great number of persons, which have consumed in suit more than the value of that they have sued for, in their anger do call it *a common detriment.* Although undoubtedly the very self law, truly practised, passeth the laws of all other countries." Of reading the Scriptures, which in his time began to be used, he would say, "Some do chiefly extol the study of the Scriptures, as it is reason; but while they do wrest it to agree with their wills, ambition, or vain-glory, of the most noble and devout learning they do endeavour them to make it servile, and full of contention." . . . And thus we take our leave of the learned and wise Sir Tho. Elyot in that age. (pp. 342-46)

John Strype, "Chapter XXXI," in his Ecclesiastical Memorials, Relating Chiefly to Religion, and the Reformation of It, Vol. I, *1721. Reprint by Oxford at the Clarendon Press, 1822, pp. 335-46.*

A NEW AND GENERAL BIOGRAPHICAL DICTIONARY, VOL. V (essay date 1784)

[*In the following excerpt, an anonymous critic briefly but warmly commends Elyot.*]

Elyot was, as Wood observes, an excellent grammarian, poet, rhetorician, philosopher, physician, cosmographer, and historian; and distinguished as much for his candour, and the innocence and integrity of his life, as for his accomplishments. He was admired and beloved by all the men of learning who were his contemporaries; and his memory is celebrated in their respective works, particularly by Leland. (p. 87)

An excerpt in A New and General Biographical Dictionary, Vol. V, *new edition, W. Strahan and others, 1784, pp. 86-7.*

ISAAC DISRAELI (essay date 1841)

[*Although probably most famous as the father of novelist and British prime minister Benjamin Disraeli, Isaac D'Israeli (or, more commonly, Disraeli) was an essayist who wrote several important works on eighteenth-century literature. In the following excerpt from his* Amenities of Literature, *originally published in 1841, he considers Elyot a pathfinder who explored the literary potential of the English vernacular.*]

Sir Thomas Elyot is the first English prose writer who avowedly attempted to cultivate the language of his country. We track the prints of the first weak footsteps in this new path; and we detect the aberrations of a mind intent on a great popular design, but still vague and uncertain, often opposed by contemporaries, yet cheered by the little world of his readers.

Elyot for us had been little more than a name, as have been many retired students, from the negligence of contemporaries, had he not been one of those interesting authors who have let us into the history of their own minds, and either prospectively have delighted to contemplate on their future enterprises, or retrospectively have exulted in their past labours.

This amiable scholar had been introduced at Court early in life; his "great friend and crony was Sir Thomas More;" so plain Anthony à Wood indicates the familiar intercourse of two great men. Elyot was a favourite with Henry the Eighth, and employed on various embassies, particularly on the confidential one to Rome to negotiate the divorce of Queen Katherine. To his public employments he alludes in his first work, *The Governor,* which "he had gathered as well of the sayings of most noble authors, Greek and Latin, as by his own experience, he being continually trained in some daily affairs of the public weal from his childhood."

A passion for literature seems to have prevailed over the ambition of active life, and on his return from his last embassy he decided to write books "in our vulgar tongue," on a great variety of topics, to instruct his countrymen. The diversity of his reading, and an unwearied pen, happily qualified, in this early age of the literature of a nation, a student who was impatient to diffuse that knowledge which he felt he only effectually possessed in the degree, and in the space, which he communicated it.

His first elaborate work is entitled, *The Boke of the Governor, devised by Sir Thomas Elyot,* 1531,—a work once so popular, that it passed through seven or eight editions, and is still valued by the collectors of our ancient literature.

The Governor is one of those treatises which, at an early period of civilization, when general education is imperfect, becomes useful to mould the manners and to inculcate the morals which should distinguish the courtier and the statesman. Elyot takes his future *Governor* in the arms of his nurse, and places the ideal being amid all the scenes which may exercise the virtues, or the studies which he developes. The work is dedicated to Henry the Eighth. The design, the imaginary personage, the author and the patron, are equally dignified. The style is grave; and it would not be candid in a modern critic to observe that, in the progress of time, the good sense has become too obvious, and the perpetual illustrations from ancient history too familiar. The erudition in philology of that day has become a schoolboy's learning. They had then no other volumes to recur to of any authority, but what the ancients had left.

Elyot had a notion that, for the last thousand years, the world had deteriorated, and that the human mind had not expanded through the course of ages. When he compared the writers of this long series of centuries, the babbling, though the subtle, schoolmen, who had chained us down to their artificial forms, with the great authors of antiquity, there seemed an appearance of truth in his decision. Christianity had not yet exhibited to modern Europe the refined moralities of Seneca, and the curious knowledge of Plutarch, in the homilies of Saints and Fathers; nor had its histories of man, confined to our monkish annalists, emulated the narrative charms of Livy, nor the grandeur of Tacitus. Of the poets of antiquity, Elyot declared that the English language, at the time he wrote, could convey nothing equivalent, wanting even words to express the delicacies, "the turns," and the euphony of the Latin verse. (pp. 268-69)

The Boke of the Governor must now be condemned to the solitary imprisonment of the antiquary's cell, who will pick up many curious circumstances relative to the manners of the age—always an amusing subject of speculation, when we contemplate on the gradations of social life. I suspect the world owed *The Governor* to a book more famous than itself—the *Cortegiano* of Castiglione, which appeared two years before the first edition of this work of Elyot, and to whose excellence Elyot could have been no stranger in his embassies to his holiness, and to the emperor. But of *The Governor,* and *The Cortegiano,* what can we now say, but that three centuries are fatal to the immortality of volumes, which, in the infancy of literature, seemed to have flattered themselves with a perpetuity of fame.

It was, however, a generous design, in an age of Latin, to attempt to delight our countrymen by "the vulgar tongue;" but these "first fruits," as he calls them, gave their author a taste of the bitterness of "that tree of knowledge."

In a subsequent work, *Of the Knowledge which maketh a Wise Man,* Elyot has recorded how he had laid himself open to "the vulgar." In the circle of a Court there was equal peril in moralising, which was deemed to be a rebuke, as in applying rusty stories, which were considered as nothing less than disguised personalities. *The Boke* was not thankfully received. The *persifleurs,* those butterflies who carry waspish stings, accounted Sir Thomas to be of no little presumption, that "in noting other men's vices he should correct *magnificat.*" This odd neologism of "magnificat" was a mystical coinage, which circulated among these aristocratic exclusives who, as Elyot describes them, "like a galled horse abiding no plaisters, be always knapping and kicking at such examples and sentences as they do feel sharp, or do bite them." The chapters on "The Diversity of Flatterers," and similar subjects, had made many "a galled jade wince;" and in applying the salve, he got a kick for the cure. They wondered why the knight wrote at all! "Other much wiser men, and better learned than he, do forbear to write anything." They inscribed modern names to his ancient portraits. The worried author exclaims—"There be Gnathos in Spain as well as in Greece; Pasquils in England as well as in Rome, &c. If men will seek for them in England which I set in other places, I cannot let (hinder) them." But in another work—*Image of Governance,* 1540—when he detailed "the monstrous living of the Emperor Heliogabalus," and contrasted that gross epicurean with Severus, such a bold and open execration of the vices of a luxurious Court could

not avoid being obvious to the royal sensualist and his companions, however the character and the tale were removed to a bygone age.

In this early attempt to cultivate "the vulgar tongue," some cavilled at his strange terms. It is a striking instance of the simplicity of the critics at that early period of our language, that our author formally explains the word *maturity*—"a Latin word, which I am constrained to usurp, lacking a name in English, and which, though it be strange and dark, yet may be understood as other words late comen out of Italy and France, and made denizens among us." Augustus Cæsar, it seems, had frequently in his mouth this word *matura*—do maturely! as "if he should have said, Do neither too much nor too little—too swiftly nor too slowly." Elyot would confine the figurative Latin term to a metaphysical designation of the acts of men in their most perfect state, "reserving," as he says, "the word ripeness to fruit and other things, separate from affairs, as we have now in usage." Elyot exults in having augmented the English language by the introduction of this Latin term, now made English for the first time! It has flourished as well as this other, "the *redolent* savours of sweet herbs and flowers." But his ear was not always musical, and some of his neologisms are less graceful—*"an alective,"* to wit; *"fatigate,"* to fatigue; *"ostent,"* to show, and to *"sufficate* some disputation." Such were the first weak steps of the fathers of our language, who, however, culled for us many a flower among their cockle.

But a murmur more prejudicial arose than the idle cavil of new and hard words; for some asserted that "the Boke seemed to be overlong." Our primeval author considered that "knowledge of wisdom cannot be shortly declared." Elyot had not yet attained, by sufficient practice in authorship, the secret, that the volume which he had so much pleasure in writing could be over tedious in reading. "For those," he observes sarcastically, "who be well willing, it is soon learned—in good faith sooner than primero or gleek." The nation must have then consisted of young readers, when a diminutive volume in twelves was deemed to be "overlong." In this apology for his writings, he threw out an undaunted declaration of his resolution to proceed with future volumes.—"If the readers of my works, by the noble example of our most dear sovereign lord, do justly and lovingly interpret my labours, I, during the residue of my life, will now and then set forth such fruits of my study, profitable, as I trust, unto this my country, leaving malicious readers with their incurable fury." Such was the innocent criticism of our earliest writer—his pen was hardly tipped with gall.

As all subjects were equally seductive to the artless pen of a primitive author, who had yet no rivals to encounter in public, Elyot turned his useful studies to a topic very opposite to that of political ethics. He put forth *The Castle of Health,* a medical treatise, which passed through nearly as many honourable editions as *The Governor.* It did not, however, abate the number, though it changed the character of his cavillers, who were now the whole corporate body of the physicians! (pp. 270-73)

The literary history of Sir Thomas Elyot exhibits the difficulties experienced by a primitive author in the earliest attempts to open a new path to the cultivation of a vernacular literature; and it seems to have required all the magnanimity of our author to sustain his superiority among his own circle, by disdaining their petulant criticism, and by the honest confidence he gathered as he proceeded, in the successive editions of his writings. (p. 275)

Isaac Disraeli, "The Difficulties Experienced by a Primitive Author," in his Amenities of Literature, Consisting of Sketches and Characters of English Literature, *edited by the Earl of Beaconsfield, revised edition, Frederick Warne and Co., 1881, pp. 268-75.*

BERNHARD TEN BRINK (essay date 1892?)

[*In the following excerpt from the final part of his multivolume* History of English Literature *(1883-96), published after his death in 1892, ten Brink surveys Elyot's works.*]

Sir Thomas Elyot stands as a character altogether typical of the [English Renaissance], and is one of the pleasantest figures of the time; as an able lawyer and man of business, a clever diplomatist with a grand capacity for work, and an ornament to English knighthood because of his extensive knowledge, a man strictly honourable in nature, and of genuine piety. The unselfish Renaissance-zeal for culture, the impulse to learn and to teach, live vigorously in him, and his entire literary activity testifies to the fact. In addition to this we have in him that naïve, joyous hopefulness, lost for the greater part to our age, the faith in the power of aiding the enlightenment and improvement of men by means of popular moralizing writings. This middle kind of literature, which sets forth the general principles of education, of morals, of politics, not primarily in the interest of theory, but in an eminently practical sense for the educated world, has become almost unknown to our day. So far as they are found at all, the tendencies by which it was upheld are to be found now only among our poets. Scientific literature has become strictly specialized, and in popular writings we handle by preference natural science or history, rather than ethics or pedagogism. When our writers pursue practical objects, they deal with subjects sharply distinguished and narrowly defined—burning questions of the day, party interests. Whoever would, nowadays, think of writing a "dial of princes"?

It was with a species of "dial of princes" that Sir Thomas Elyot began his literary career. The year 1531 saw the publication of his *Boke named the Governour,* the dedication of which was graciously accepted by Henry VIII. (p. 194)

The abundance of subject-matter in the *The Governour* and the attractive manner it was dealt with, won for it a large circle of enthusiastic readers. In the course of half a century the book ran through eight editions, and by having influenced the intellectual culture, the opinions of a large number of Englishmen of the upper classes, it also left its mark on the literature of the day. Even though it may be doubtful whether Budé, or even Johannes Sturm, betray, in their works on the subject, any knowledge of Elyot's *Governour,* still it is certain that subsequent educational and ethical works in England are in many ways connected with his book, and that, besides this, traces of his influence are observable even in the historians and poets.

Much as Elyot wrote and published at a later date, this first work of his has remained the most famous of all his productions. And perhaps justly so, as what is peculiar to

him as a man and a writer is exhibited, probably, most fully and from the most varied points of view in his *Governour.* Many of the themes which Elyot only touches upon there, received special and fuller treatment in his subsequent works. Of his pædagogic treatises, one is a translation from Plutarch, and is entitled *The Education or bringinge up of Children,* and is dedicated "to his only entirely beloved syster Margery Puttenham;" in his Introduction he expresses the hope that she will endeavour, in accordance with Plutarch's principles, "to adapte and forme in [his] lyttel neuewes inclinacion to vertue and doctrine." Among Elyot's political treatises we have *The Doctrinal of Princes* (1534), a translation of the famous oration of Isocrates to Nicocles, and another "dial of princes" of more doubtful origin in *The Image of Governance compiled of the actes and sentences notable of the moste noble Emperour Alexander Severus, late translated out of Greke into Englyshe by syr Thomas Elyot, Knight, in the fauour of nobylitie* (1540). The first sketch of this last work belongs to the period when *The Governour* was produced, and is closely connected with it—in fact, a supplement to it. In tendency and plan it reminds us of Guevara's *Marco Aurelio,* but is superior to it in genuine richness of substance, in greater steadfastness of form, and simplicity of representation. Elyot has been reproached, as it seems wrongfully, of intentional deception with regard to this work. It is probable that he was deceived himself, and that, in fact, he fully believed the statement of a later Greek treatise—no longer extant—which claimed to be the work of Encolpius, a contemporary of Alexander Severus. This treatise was his chief authority, and the accounts given by it he afterwards supplemented from communications given by other ancient historians and other authorities.

Elyot's tendency in philosophy, as exhibited in his works, and more especially as regards moral philosophy, finds its most beautiful expression, perhaps, in his "Dialogue" between Plato and Aristippus, which had been suggested to his mind by reading Diogenes Laërtius, and which was published in 1533, and again in the following year, under the title: *Of that Knowledge which maketh a Wise Man.* Two other Dialogues by Elyot deal with subjects less far-reaching, and, if we may say so, more specific in character. His *Pasquil the Playne* (1533 and 1540), which is satirical and half jocose, deals with the theme of speech and silence, and may perhaps have been suggested by a work that had shortly before appeared in Rome, and introduced local types from that city: "Dialogus Marphorii et Pasquilli." Altogether serious, on the other hand, is his *Defence of Good Women,* which in addition to defending the weaker sex from its calumniators, was also written with the view of teaching good wives to know their duties. These dialogues exhibit a certain resemblance to the poetical contests of the Middle Ages, above all to the dramatic disputations that John Heywood and others wrote for the stage.

In the above-mentioned works Elyot moves in domains which are gladly conceded to a man of refined culture in his position in life. But his activity far exceeded the limits to which tradition or prejudice would have confined it. As a humanist he set himself a strictly philological task in undertaking to compile a Latin-English dictionary. When almost half of the first draft of this work had been set up in type, Elyot remodelled it entirely by making use of material which Henry VIII. had placed at his disposal, and then had the work published in 1538 under the title of *Biblio-*

theca. He very properly dedicated the work to the King, while one copy, with an introductory letter in Latin, was dedicated to Lord Cromwell. This Dictionary not only far surpassed everything of the kind that had hitherto appeared in England, but, in fact, in spite of all the defects attached to it, marks a very important advance in the field of Latin lexicography. A second edition appeared in 1545. After Elyot's death the work was again remodelled by Thomas Cooper, afterwards Bishop of Lincoln, and published in 1550, with various improvements and additions, under the title of *Thesaurus.* A second edition appeared in 1552.

Elyot required an even greater amount of courage than he had displayed in undertaking this work of professional philology, when, as a *dilettante,* he ventured to enter domains that are jealously guarded by members of the confraternity. He had, at an early age, become acquainted with medical literature, and was pretty well read in almost all of the authorities of antiquity and of mediæval times that had come within his reach. His own indifferent health, injured by continuous work, had led to his constantly doctoring himself, and he was somewhat skilful in treating his own ailments. Accordingly, the thought struck him to note down the results of his own observations and experience in a medical guide, his intention being to induce the public to take a rational care of their health, and in case of illnes to help them to understand the physician's reports. This treatise, which was entitled **The Castel of Helth,** must have appeared as early as 1534, was dedicated to Cromwell, and had run through at least ten subsequent editions by 1595. The professional men, who, from the outset, had looked disparagingly at Elyot's proceedings, and ridiculed the knight who tried to play the part of a physician, can hardly have become reconciled to the book considering the success it met with.

As Elyot had here entered into competition with medical men, he, on another occasion, competed with the clergy. A deeply religious temperament is evident throughout all his literary work, and he proves himself to have been as intimately acquainted with his Bible and the Fathers of the Church as he was with the classical authors. In his **Bankette of Sapience,** a collection of moral maxims from different authors dedicated to the King, he, however, draws his material chiefly from the Fathers. He translated in full a sermon which St. Cyprian had delivered on the mortality of man when a plague was raging in Africa: *A swete and devoute Sermon of Holy saynt Ciprian of Mortalitie of Man.* This was published (July 1, 1534) together with a translation of the twelve "Rules" of Mirandola— *The Rules of a Christian lyfe made by Picus erle of Mirandula*—the same author who had given occupation to the pen of Sir Thomas More at an earlier date. Elyot came forward more independently as a religious writer in another treatise. In 1544, when the close of his life was drawing near, and he may have already felt the chill of sunset upon him, he wrote a little book—in keeping with this feeling— which was intended to offer comfort, edification, and exhortation in view of death, and combined passages from the Bible and the Fathers of the Church with reflections drawn from the depth of his own heart. This treatise, which he named *A preservative agaynste deth,* was published on the 2nd of July, 1545, and dedicated to Sir Edward North, a friend made in his later years in business transactions, as a near neighbour. To such persons as may

have considered a work of this kind adapted to their position, the unwearied controversialist, in his preface to his *Governour,* addresses the following noble words which are characteristic of his whole life: "A knyght hath received that honour not onely to defende with the swerde Christis faithe and his propre countrey agaynst them whiche impugneth the one or inuadeth the other, but also, and that most chiefly, by the meane of his dignitie ... he shuld more effectually with his learning and witte assayle vice and errour, most pernicious ennemies to christen men, hauinge thereto for his swerde and speare, his tunge and his penne."

In glancing back at Elyot's literary activity, which, however, by no means fully occupied his life, we are astounded at his capacity for work and its many-sidedness. And the number of his productions is not exhausted by those that have been mentioned above. Some anonymous treatises, partly translated from Plutarch, partly compiled from various classical authors, are also assigned to him, not without good reason; and although no great weight is attached to a remark of one Bale, that "he had written many other things," still we cannot doubt the well-authenticated report, according to which he is said to have had in hand an historico-national work, *De rebus memorabilibus Angliæ.* Although Elyot occupied a less prominent position in life than Erasmus and Sir Thomas More, still—taking him all in all—he was a worthy contemporary of such men, and not undeserving of the friendship of More. By nature Elyot was more receptive and reproductive than gifted with creative power; he has rendered inestimable services to the English culture of the epoch as the contributor of popular literature, as a compiler, adapter, and communicator of rich and varied material.

Elyot's chief merit, however, at least that by which he has most distinctly influenced the development of literature, rests upon his importance as a writer of good style. And even this he did not acquire accidentally or without labour. From the commencement of his career as a writer, his endeavour was directed, not only to communicating knowledge, correct views, but as much to forming the English language into an instrument that might rival the idiom of the classics in power of expression. With this object in view he, on the one hand, introduced many new words into the language from Latin and French sources, always, however, taking into consideration that—either by their relationship to words already in use, or by the connection in which they appeared—their meaning should at once be intelligible; on the other hand, his desire was to confer upon the English formation of sentences something of the peculiar style of the Greek mode of expression, and for this his handling such writers as Isocrates must have been a good training.

Elyot's efforts, in which King Henry took a lively interest, were in the main successful. He created a style which was both thoroughly adapted to his own purpose and to the requirements of his day. For, while showing a considerable wealth of words, a complicated construction of periods, and a sufficient command of rhetorical means, he is altogether moderate in the manner he applies them, and only very rarely falls into affectation and pomposity, as, for instance, when spinning a simile into an allegory, as happens in the Preface to his *Bibliotheca.* Upon the whole, his presentation is simple, clear, and vivid, even though, as a rule, it does not exhibit that higher inspiration, that sublimer flight, which proceeds from the inward workings of a creative mind. (pp. 196-201)

Bernhard ten Brink, "Book VI: The Renaissance Up to Surrey's Death," in his History of English Literature: From the Fourteenth Century to the Death of Surrey, Vol. II, *edited by Alois Brandl, translated by L. Dora Schmitz, Henry Holt and Company, 1896, pp. 65-263.*

ALFRED AINGER (essay date 1893)

[*Ainger was an English divine, essayist, and biographer. In the following excerpt from an essay originally published in 1893, he bridges the works of Thomas More and Roger Ascham with those of Elyot.*]

Sir Thomas Elyot's place in English prose seems to fall, in other respects than mere chronological order, between Sir Thomas More and Roger Ascham. In the English that he wrote, he is somewhat less archaic than the former, and less modern than the latter. If Elyot is less cumbrous than More, he never attains the vivacity of Ascham. Charm of style was hardly as yet a gift to which English prose had attained. Elyot has many virtues—clearness and precision among them—but if he seldom falls below a certain level, he as seldom rises above it. He is measured and monotonous, and the superabundance of quotation and allusion from Greek and Latin history and literature is not relieved by any versatility of manner. But his excellent good sense and sagacity make him very readable. His pedantry—the over-weighting with ancient examples just referred to—is but the inevitable pedantry of the Renascence. And if he coins or imports many words of foreign origin that were not wanted and accordingly did not survive, this also was an epidemic of his day and is not to be charged to him personally. . . . But if Elyot is pedantic in matter, his style is free from the affectation which was so soon to possess English prose for a century to follow. The Euphuistic artificiality was not yet born, and Elyot is untouched by the spell of Guevara, the real founder of the Euphuistic manner, whose work, *The Golden Book of Marcus Aurelius,* translated by Lord Berners, appeared three years later than the *Governor.*

In yet another sense Elyot proves a kind of connecting link between More and Ascham. The object with which he undertook the *Governor*—the only work it is necessary to consider here—bears a certain resemblance to the scheme of the *Utopia.* Both writers were bent on emphasising the conditions of a perfect commonwealth. More's book was announced by his translator, Robynson, as setting forth the "best state of a public weale," and Elyot in his dedication to Henry VIII., declares the same intention, namely, to describe in the vulgar tongue "the form of a just public weal." It is true that Elyot finally concentrates his attention on a single aspect of national welfare—the fitting education of those who are to be its rulers,—but the aim of the two writers is one, and their noble effort to raise the standard of righteousness in public men and affairs was admirably seconded within a few years by Ascham and Lyly. Good sense and good morals applied to the earliest education of those destined to govern, was the starting point of Elyot's work, but as he proceeded he evidently felt that the fit training for the statesman was also the best for any other christian gentleman, and the treatise resolves itself ultimately into one on the ethics of education gener-

ally. In his chapters on the school-room, Elyot covers much of the ground afterwards trodden by Ascham, and many of the more obvious blots or defects in the elementary teaching of their day are dealt with by the two writers. It is strange that Ascham nowhere refers to, or recognises the services of his predecessor. . . . Elyot takes a line which has found ardent advocates with many educational reformers up to our own day—the advisability of allowing the young learner to acquire a general familiarity with the sense of an author before mastering the intricacies of grammatical analysis. It appears that already, so soon after the revival of learning, teachers were discovering the yet familiar truth that by the time the learner comes "to the most swete and pleasant redinge of olde authors, the sparkes of fervent desire of lernynge is extincte with the burden of grammar." . . . Elyot touches with agreeable sarcasm on another education problem, still affording plentiful material for the satirist, the unwillingness of the parent to pay salaries to the tutor or the governess at all comparable to those he is content to afford for "groom or cook." (pp. 191-93)

Alfred Ainger, "Sir Thomas Elyot," in English Prose: Fourteenth to Sixteenth Century, Vol. I, *edited by Henry Craik, The Macmillan Company, 1893, pp. 191-93.*

GEORGE SAINTSBURY (essay date 1898)

[*Saintsbury was a late-nineteenth and early-twentieth-century English literary historian and critic. Hugely prolific, he composed histories of English and European literature as well as numerous critical works on individual authors. In the following excerpt from his* Short History of English Literature, *originally published in 1898, Saintsbury offers a balanced appraisal of Elyot's literary merits.*]

Sir Thomas Elyot, who was born before 1490, was the son of a judge, and though not a member of the famous Cornish family of his name, appears to have been a West Countryman, his forebears having been connected with the district round Yeovil. He must have been well educated, but does not seem to have gone to either University, and though a student of medicine, is said not to have been a practitioner thereof. He came early into the possession of a good estate near Woodstock, and settled there; but was made by Wolsey in 1523 Clerk of the Council—an office which seems to have metaphysical connection with literature. He published the *Governour* in 1531, and seems to have been recommended by it to diplomatic employments, in which he spent the rest of his life. He died in 1546, having four years previously been elected M.P. for Cambridge.

He wrote a medical work called the *Castle of Health,* a Latin Dictionary [*The Dictionary*], some dialogues, and other things; but his fame, such as it is, rests on the *Governour.* This is one, and in England one of the first, of those curious treatises, partly of politics, partly of education, which the study of the classics, and more particularly of Plato, multiplied at the Renaissance in all countries, and not least in our own. Ascham, Lyly, Mulcaster, and many others take up from their different points of view, more and less scholastic, the theme which Elyot set them the example of handling. Incidentally the book is remarkable, because it contains the earliest version yet traced of the famous, but too probably apocryphal, story of Chief-

Justice Gascoigne and Henry V. when Prince of Wales—a pious invention very likely to flatter the powers that were. In the history of prose style Elyot is commendable rather than distinguished; free from obvious and glaring defects rather than possessed of distinct merits. He is rather too much given to long sentences; he has little or nothing of Fisher's rhetorical devices, and while the romantic grace of his not much older contemporary Berners is far from him, so also is the deliberate classical plainness of his not very much younger contemporary Ascham. He is principally valuable as an example of the kind of prose which a cultivated man of ordinary gifts would be likely to write before the definite attempts of Ascham and his school. (pp. 234-35)

> George Saintsbury, "Elizabethan Literature to the Death of Spenser," in his A Short History of English Literature, The Macmillan Company, 1898, pp. 219-306.

WILLIAM HARRISON WOODWARD (essay date 1906)

[*In the following excerpt from his* Studies in Education during the Age of the Renaissance, 1400-1600, *originally published in 1906, Woodward outlines the educational curriculum expounded in* The Governour.]

[Thomas Elyot] is a man of the world, the modern, eager world of Tudor England, claiming for its service the highest thought of antiquity. Elyot dedicated the **Governor** to the King as the first-fruits of his reading. Its object was to instruct men in such virtues as shall be expedient for them, which shall have "authority in a weal public." It is hardly a political treatise; it makes no attempt to set out the methods of government. It is not a sketch of a perfect state, Elyot has always England and Englishmen in his mind; but he undoubtedly has a forward look. He realised, as the need of an age marked by a revolution in political organisation and administration, a sounder concept of training for the sons of the governing class. The ideal of service of the state, lay and civil, was a new one in England, and Elyot saw that it would surely claim its place beside the older ideals of service through arms or "clerkship," and ultimately surpass them in importance, as the ecclesiastical and feudal territorial privileges yielded to the authority of the King's Court.

Italy alone offered examples of such political conditions, the subordination of landed right to new powers, civic, industrial and personal; it was natural, therefore, that from Italy too should come the literary presentation of the modern community, and of the education which should fit its citizens or princes for their share in it. Elyot had read deeply the politico-social writings of the Quattrocento. The **Governor** is clearly suggested by them, and without Palmieri and Patrizi, Æneas Sylvius and Pontano, the book would not have been possible. . . ."Governors" included all lay officers, paid or unpaid, involved in executive or legislative activity: royal secretaries, judges of the King's Court, justices of the peace, sheriffs, even mayors of towns, ambassadors, members of Parliament, clerks of the Exchequer or the Chancery. For with the revolution which was rapidly substituting what Sir Henry Maine has described as the basis of contract for that of status in English society, and especially in the public service, an entirely new concept of duty was, as Elyot clearly discerned,

henceforth indispensable. And for this the Italian political and educational literature provided him with most fruitful suggestion. Naturally, therefore, he condemns "that pestiferous opinion, that great learned men be inapt to ministration of things of weighty importance"; and, as a typical man of the Revival, he supports this judgment by the instances of Moses, of Alexander, of Scipio, Caesar, Hadrian, of Cato and Cicero, and even of Charles the Great.

He starts with the concept of the community as an unit organised in due order of capacity, functions, and skill, each factor in society existing as an element of an organic whole, obeying a law of proportion based on its relative importance to the State. The *Republic* has obviously suggested to him this idea of a division of labour, with honour graded according to the nature of the services rendered. That there must be one sovereign he proves from the examples of Moses and Agamemnon; from Venice and Ferrara; from Edgar, King of England, under whom prosperity and security notably advanced. Democratic Athens is a standing warning; Rome also was forced to rely upon Dictators and Emperors.

In the second chapter he proposes the necessary enquiry, which was antecedent to all larger questions of the conditions of public well-being: viz., "the best form of education or bringing up of noble children from their nativity in such manner as they may be found worthy and also able to be Governors of a public weal." Elyot expressly disclaims the idea of debarring men of humble origin from affairs, but his scheme of training demanded a certain standing of wealth and refinement in the home, and parents capable of taking large views. Further, he held that integrity in administration would be better secured if the holders of office were removed by their position from the temptation of illicit gains.

When Elyot turns to the course of education which he desires to lay down he begins, like most humanists, with the stages of infancy. The nurse must be carefully sought for and her physical and moral fitness duly assured. Her one function is the nourishing of the child; all that concerns bringing up is entrusted to a governess who is in control. No men except the physician are to be allowed within the nursery. From Plutarch, Quintilian and Erasmus, whose tract on the *Duties of the Married State* was certainly familiar to Elyot, he has learnt the importance of the instinct of imitation. For good and for evil a young child learns by imitation. (pp. 270-73)

Elyot . . . enforces three of the more important points in the training of young children upon which Erasmus had laid stress: and no doubt the English writer had studied carefully the *De Pueris* (1529) as he planned his own work. These are *(a)* the neccessity of careful attention to the habit of clear and refined speech in childhood, *(b)* the principle of instruction by methods of play in the first stages of teaching, *(c)* the value of the conversational method in learning an unknown language, in this case Latin. It is by comparing the positions advanced by Elyot with the teaching of Erasmus on early education that the statement that "Elyot interpreted Erasmus for England" carries full conviction. The same relation of the two writers is no less clear in the section which follows. "After that a child is come to seven years of age, I hold it expedient that he be taken from the company of women." This was the common opinion of the humanist, based, in the case of Elyot, upon a distrust of the companionship of serving-women, and even of the mother, seeing that the sterner side of character needs to be encouraged in the growing boy. For such reasons the most sure counsel is to withdraw him from all company of women and "to assign unto him a tutor, which should be an ancient and worshipful man," winning the boy by his gravity of temper combined with gentleness, and "such a one that the child by imitation following may grow to be excellent. And if he be also learned he is the more commendable." The essential quality of the tutor, therefore, is moral excellence. The office of a tutor, thus qualified, is, first, to know the nature of his pupil, "that is to say, whereto he is most inclined or disposed and in what thing he setteth his most delectation or appetite. If he be of nature courteous, piteous, and of a free and liberal heart, it is a principal token of grace, as it is by all Scripture determined. Then shall a wise tutor . . . declare to him what honour, what love, what commodity shall happen to him by these virtues. And if any be of disposition contrary, then to express the enormities of their vice, with as much detestation as may be."

Elyot adopts the Erasmian, and northern, idea of the necessity of a tutor to a well-born boy. (pp. 275-76)

Elyot regards as the test of the tutor's skill "that he suffer not the child to be fatigate with continual study or learning, wherewith the delicate and tender wit may be dulled or oppressed; but that there may be therewith interlaced and mixed some pleasant learning and exercise, as playing on instruments of music, which, moderately used, and without diminution of honour, that is to say, without wanton countenance and dissolute gesture, is not to be contemned." It is worth noting that Elyot realises better than Erasmus the effort involved in a hard literary and linguistic course for a boy, and the difficulty of retaining prolonged interest in the exclusive study of the rudiments of dead languages. It is apparently from this point of view that he includes music as a recreation and not as a systematic study. (p. 277)

The claims of Fine Art rest on a more secure basis than those of musical skill. Elyot feels that he must defend his position. Naturally he turns first to "ancient and excellent princes," Claudius, Titus, or Hadrian, who were educated in painting, drawing and sculpture. The direct advantages to captains in the field of a knowledge of drawing are obvious; such are the devising and improving of engines of war, the making of strategical maps, the noting of tactical positions and the lines of fortification. In the planning of houses, in mensuration, in the making of charts and maps, every man of position will find the same art necessary. Particularly, in illustration of history or travel, "I dare affirm a man shall more profit in one week by figures and charts, well and perfectly made, than he shall by the only reading or hearing the rules of that science by the space of half a year at least." Pictorial illustrations of historical narratives are of great aid to imagination. Elyot must have often had in his hands the Venetian illustrated editions of Livy, the great chronicle of Philippus Bergomensis, the Nuremberg chronicle and the Mallermi Bible, Valturius on the Art of War—the outstanding illustrated history books of his age. But such instruction is not for all. For "mine intent and meaning is only that a noble child may be induced to receive perfect instruction in these sciences." Yet although as boyhood advances literature claims all available time, yet the manual skill and artistic

and musical feeling thus early encouraged will survive and become valued factors in the personality of the grown man. For the "exquisite knowledge and understanding that he hath in those sciences hath impressed in his ears and eyes an exact and perfect judgment in respect of appreciation of beauty to the use of leisure and technical application." Elyot perceives also that the arts have been unduly depreciated by Englishmen as unpractical. But he holds that much native talent has been thereby repressed to the national loss. So far the recreactive Arts.

When he comes to lay down the curriculum of instruction to be followed by the tutor, Elyot requires that refined utterance and a knowledge of the parts of speech in his own language, at or before the age of seven, shall be already secured: the power of speaking Latin in actual practice is hardly to be looked for. Rapid progress may be expected if the tutor understands how to stimulate ambition and the desire to excel. The ancient world provides examples, in Aristotle, Antoninus, Trajan. (pp. 278-79)

In the tenth chapter he treats of the "order of learning apt for a gentleman" which is to be followed from the time when systematic instruction is entered upon. "I am of the opinion of Quintilian that I would have him learn Greek and Latin authors both at one time; or else begin with Greek. . . . And if a child do begin therein at seven years of age he may continually learn Greek authors three years, and in the meantime use the Latin tongue as a familiar language: which in a nobleman's son may well come to pass, having none other persons to serve him or keeping him company but such as can speak Latin elegantly. And what doubt is there that so may he as soon speak good Latin as he may do pure French?" Not being himself a teacher he offers no advice as to choice of a Greek grammar, but "alway I would advise him not to detain the child too long in that tedious labours either in Greek or Latin grammar. For a gentle wit is therewith soon fatigate. Grammar being but an introduction to the understanding of authors, if it be made too long or exquisite (i.e. elaborate) to the learner it in a manner mortifieth his courage. And by that time he come to the most sweet and pleasant reading of old authors the sparkes of fervent desire of learning is extinct with the burden of grammar."

This passage carries us back directly to Erasmus. The dependence upon Quintilian is exactly paralleled in the *De Ratione Studii*. The conversational use of Latin, the simultaneous study of Latin and Greek, and in especial the gradual introduction of accidence and syntax, as the pupil's need developes with the reading of texts—all is Erasmian. Elyot's belief that pure Latin may be acquired in a properly ordered home reminds us of Montaigne's experience a little later: for when he went to school at Bordeaux at the age of six he could speak only Latin, his father having insisted that the servants and the very labourers on the estate should acquire a Latin vocabulary. Palmieri on the other hand, as has been said, and the Italians generally, felt the unreality of such attempts. The adjustment of grammatical teaching which Elyot advocates was the regular humanist practice—down to the latter half of the sixteenth century.

The beginnings of Greek (begun, as he says, immediately) are made through Aesop, whose *Fables* are to be read to the pupil by the tutor. Their vocabulary is instructive, the sense easily grasped, and they possess "much moral and politic wisdom." This regard for edification in choice of authors is but one aspect of the general humanist view that classical writers are to be used always for subject-matter as well as practice in the actual language. The text will be learnt by heart as an aid to vocabulary and power in sentence structure. Aesop will be followed by "quick and merry dialogues" from Lucian. Aristophanes, being in metre, may be perhaps more quickly learnt by heart, and so may be substituted for Lucian. Aristophanes at this period held the place in classical education which Euripides was to assume a couple of centuries later. The ground of choice lay no doubt in the light thrown by his comedies upon Attic life and opinion.

Homer comes next: "from whom as from a fountain proceedeth all eloquence and learning. For in his books be contained and most perfectly expressed not only the documents martial and discipline of arms, but also incomparable wisdoms and instructions for politic governance of people." Alexander the Great is referred to as an illustration of the stimulating force of a study of Homer, since therefrom "he gathered courage and strength against his enemies, wisdom and eloquence for consultations and persuasions to his people and army." There is no instruction to be compared with that which may be enforced from Homer "if he be plainly and substantially expounded and declared by the master." So far the Greek writers. The stress laid upon their content, especially their moral purport, must be carefully noticed.

In deciding upon Latin authors, Homer suggests the poet Vergil as parallel reading. The *Aeneid* will be found attractive by its theme; and the *Eclogues* and *Georgics* hardly less so. The teacher will contrast the *Odyssey*, whose salient purpose is to commend prudence and endurance, with the feats of romance and the marvels of the *Aeneid*. The *Fasti* and *Metamorphoses* of Ovid will claim a moderate amount of time, as will the learned and sententious Horace. Associated with such construing, verse composition is to be taught, using Homer and Vergil as models, since such exercises afford "much pleasure and courage to study."

This course of reading, with work in grammar and prosody, duly adapted, is to be covered by the end of the thirteenth year. It will be noted that the authors are exclusively chosen from the poets. Elyot thinks the classical poets easier and more attractive reading than prose writers, in that they make no demand for sustained judgment or reasoning as does a political oration or historical narrative. He rightly argues that poetry is the language of childhood, both of the race and of the individual; "poetry was the first philosophy that ever was known, and through it children have always gained their first lessons in right conduct," "learning thereby not only manners and natural affections but also the wonderful works of nature, mixing serious matter with things that are pleasant." He takes occasion to protest against the "false opinion that now reigneth" that poets are but a tissue of lies and impurity. He adds as a final qualification that it "should be remembered that I require not all these works should be *thoroughly read* of a child in this time, which were almost impossible," but the purpose of such reading is to be kept in view, viz., that "of inflaming the courage of the child to attempt the imitation of great deeds." "I only desire that they (the pupils) have in every of the said books so much instruction that they may take thereby some profit."

Elyot, it is clear, regards instruction in the classics as the teaching of literature, which will be read for enjoyment. He has the humanist view of poetry as a delight. The teacher will strive to imbue the scholar with a feeling for style and rhythm, will keep grammar at arm's length, and pursue analysis or criticism only to the point where it aids enjoyment of the text. In his view the poets thus taught are easy, in that their work is pictorial and romantic and carries its intelligible moral.

The second stage of instruction is, in its turn, almost exclusively concerned with classical prose, under the heads of oratory, history, and cosmography. As an introduction to oratory the *Topica* of Cicero, or the *De Inventione Dialectica* of Rudolph Agricola will be studied. Logic is thus, in accordance with humanist judgment, reduced to its function of aiding exposition. Beyond this, Elyot has nothing to say of the claims of logic as a subject of education, following Erasmus rather than Melanchthon, and in accord generally with the practice of English schools which relegated logic to the university.

The boy of fourteen is taken straight to the orators and the writers on rhetoric: Hermogenes, a Greek rhetorician of the second century A.D., and Quintilian—"beginning at the third Book and instructing the child diligently in that part of rhetoric, principally, which concerneth persuasion for as much as it is most apt for consultations." Elyot has in view the preparation of the pupil in the art of speaking, whether deliberative or judicial. Although he uses as illustration "a great audience," or the conduct of an embassy, none the less the argument applies to duties of a much humbler type, such as pleading before a court, or the deliverances of a local magistrate. Then "a man shall not be constrained to speak words sudden and disordered but shall bestow them aptly in their places." The treatises will be read along with select orations of Cicero, Isocrates and Demosthenes as the models of logical exposition and choice diction. But as a working manual of composition he expressly commends the *De Copia* of Erasmus, "whom all gentle wits are bound to thank and support." Beyond this no allusion is made to practice in epistolary or narrative styles, though Elyot expresses contempt for the mere skill in writing grandiose adulatory letters. The reference which Elyot makes in the quotations given above is further evidence that the ultimate aim of the rhetorical training through Greek and Latin was in reality the perfecting of a man's vernacular style. Even Erasmus, though perhaps grudgingly, would not have denied this. To the humanist Reformers in Germany the strengthening of the influence of the pulpit was a leading motive of classical education, just as the Italian of the Quattrocento—a purist here and there notwithstanding—found that in respect of precision, amplitude, and grace, his power in the Tuscan speech was deeply in debt to the discipline of Latin rhetoric.

Again, Elyot is in full accord with the higher view of "eloquentia" which the humanists, as has been shown, borrowed from Cicero and Quintilian. (pp. 280-84)

Passing next to Cosmography, Elyot urges the study of geography in its relation to history. "To prepare the child to understanding of histories, which being replenished with names of countries and towns unknown to the reader, do make the history tedious or else the less pleasant, so if they be in any wise known, it increaseth an inexplicable delectation.... There is none so good learning as the demonstration of cosmography by material figures and instruments.... For what pleasure is it, in one hour to behold these realms, cities, seas, rivers, and mountains that scarcely in an old man's life cannot be journeyed and pursued: what incredible delight is taken in beholding the diversities of people, beasts, fowls, fishes, trees, fruits and herbs: to know the sundry manners and conditions of people and the variety of their natures, and that in a warm study or parlour, without peril of the sea or danger of long and painful journeys.... The commoditie thereof knew the great King Alexander, for he caused the countries whereunto he purposed any enterprise diligently and cunningly to be described and painted, that beholding the picture he might perceive which places are most dangerous and where he and his host might have most easy convenable passage." (pp. 285-86)

The general aim of historical reading is thus set out. "A young gentleman shall be taught to note and mark not only the order and elegance in declaration of the history, but also the occasion of the wars, the counsels and preparation on either part," forming a judgment on the military skill exhibited. Next, apart from war, he will ponder "the estate of the public weal if it be prosperous or in decay, what is the very occasion of the one or the other, the form and manner of the governance thereof, the good and evil qualities of them that be rulers, the commodities and good sequel of virtue, the discommodities and evil conclusion of vicious licence." Four points are here disclosed: the style of the historian, the lessons of the military events described, the causes of growth and decline in states, the political skill and moral worth of rulers, with the effects of these upon national well-being. The objection has to be met that history is sometimes "interlaced" with myth and false tradition. Elyot's answer is that the educational value of such aspects of the subject is different indeed but yet substantial. For as the moral import of history is one of its main claims to the teacher's regard, "true" things are not exclusively things that have actually occurred. "If by reading the sage counsel of Nestor, the subtle persuasions of Ulysses, the compendious gravity of Menelaus, the imperial majesty of Agamemnon, the prowess of Achilles, the valiant courage of Hector, we may apprehend anything whereby our wits may be amended and our personages be more apt to serve our public weal and our prince, what forceth it us though Homer write leasings?" No writers are so full of instruction as historians, their theme being, as it were, the mirror of man's life, expressing the attraction of virtue, and the deformity and loathliness of vice. History is thus a compendious record of military, political, and moral wisdom. (p. 287)

The boy is now presumed to have completed his seventeenth year, and with it the second stage of his literary education, which, as Elyot expounds it, revolves round the arts of exposition and oratory in Latin, geography and history, military and political. The third stage, upon which he next enters, is occupied mainly with philosophy. "By the time that the child do come to seventeen years of age, to the intent his courage be bridled with reason, it were needful to read unto him some works of philosophy, specially that part which may inform him unto virtuous manners, which part of philosophy is called moral." The choice of the *Ethics* I and II of Aristotle, in Greek, as advised by Elyot, seems of doubtful wisdom. Next may follow the *De Officiis* of Cicero; then Plato, "when the judgment of a man is come to perfection." For in this philosopher and in Cicero are joined "gravity and delectation," "excellent wisdom with divine eloquence," and "every place is so infarced with profitable counsel, joined with honesty, that those three books" (no specific dialogue of Plato is indicated) "be almost sufficient to make a perfect and excellent Governor." Elyot further advises the *Proverbs* of Solomon, *Ecclesiastes,* and *Ecclesiasticus,* and all the historical books, including the Prophets, of the Old Testament. But the New Testament is to be reverently touched as a celestial jewel or relique, not to be handled by common wits or interpreted by canons of secular knowledge. The treatment of moral duties upon the authority of classical rather than New Testament writings, on the ground that the latter were within the exclusive province of the clergy, was common in humanist practice. In conclusion he expressly commends "the little book of the most excellent Doctor Erasmus" dedicated to Charles V when Prince of Castile, entitled the *Institution of a Christian Prince,* "which should be familiar to men of station as Homer was to Alexander, or Xenophon to Scipio, for there was never book written in Latin that in so little a portion contained of sentence (i.e. principles), eloquence, and virtuous exhortation, a more compendious abundance." (pp. 288-89)

Upon exercises meet for gentlemen Elyot has much to say. There is nothing original in his enumeration of games and sports which he commends, and which are without exception drawn from current English practice. But he brings them within the circle of the humanist training by his insistence on the classical precedent by which they may be supported. He begins by claiming as the general end bodily health and fitness for study. Wherefore in the education of children, specially from the age of fourteen upwards, he will have exercises carefully prescribed; such as are "apt to the furniture of a gentleman's personage, adapting his body to hardiness, strength and agility, and to help therewith himself in peril." Galen is much relied upon, but apart from him Elyot had studied, and, later on, wrote a treatise upon, the laws of health. Wrestling, a typical English sport, heads the list; running is defended from Epaminondas, or Achilles; swimming, popular with the Romans, is useful in certain dangers, as Horatius and Caesar found. Hunting is illustrated from Xenophon's *Cyropaedeia.* The Greeks—Theseus and Alexander—hunted the lion, leopard or bear; Pompey chased wild game in Africa. In England a man is content with red deer, the fox or the hare. Hawking is not one of the nobler sports, but is good for appetite. Riding "on a great horse and a rough," with or without exercises of battle-axe or lance, is a necessary accomplishment. The long-bow is most commendable of all sports, first for its utility in national defence, archery being pre-eminently an English pursuit, and secondly as pastime and solace. It "appertaineth as well to princes and noblemen as to all others, by their example, which determine to pass forth their lives in virtue and honesty." The national obligation for defence falls upon all classes alike.

It is natural that Elyot should enquire in what consists the status of that nobility to which he has repeatedly to refer. The essence of his conclusion is that true nobility is constituted of personal merit. But, undeniably, inherited repute, title, lands, position, are accounted nobility also. Where, however, the two are united there is conspicuous distinction. Elyot (and his master Wolsey even more markedly), as an example of the new governing class, was eager to prove how right training may provide the state with trusted servants. The sentiment was an obvious one in the humanist, most of all no doubt in Italy, where personal distinction found its fullest opportunity. The "Governor" was the English aspect of the ideal Italian "Courtier." It is the motive of Erasmus' tract on the upbringing of a Prince. This doctrine Elyot will enforce through instruction. "Let young gentlemen have oftentimes told to them how Numa Pompilius was taken from his husbandry and made king of the Romans by election of the people. What caused it, suppose you, but his wisdom and virtue, which in him were very nobility, and that nobility brought him to dignity?" Now knowledge makes men apt to virtue, as Erasmus had always urged; hence the supreme worth of knowledge to one who aspires to the truest nobility which includes birth, capacity and high character. The ideal of personality, as Elyot understands it, finds its practical expression in "Prudentia," or "Sapience," which is a mental quality, compact of "natura," "scientia" and "virtus," applied to practical affairs. Rome was built up by this quality of Sapience in her citizens. This "wisdom," as distinct from "doctrine," is the flower of true education, as Elyot sees the problem in the light of the needs of England.

Amongst minor recreations Elyot advises chess, "for therein is a right subtle engine whereby the wit is made to move sharp and remembrance quickened"; cards he barely tolerates, unless games may be devised in them of moral instruction. Dice he treats as the great peril of youth and manhood.

In an interesting chapter Elyot allows dancing to be of "excellent utility, comprehending in it wonderful figures, or, as the Greeks do call them, Ideas, of virtues and noble qualities," in particular that of prudence by which he means the "knowledge of things which ought to be desired and of them that ought to be eschewed"; "and by cause that the study of virtue is tedious for the more part to them that do flourish in young years," he expounds a method by which those who join in, or even watch, rightly ordered dancing may be aroused to the understanding and the pursuit of this notable quality of prudence. This ingenious argument turns partly upon the relation between the rhythmic and harmonious movement of the body and the law of proportion and temperance in the sphere of emotion and conduct; so far it is entirely Greek in spirit. Partly, again, the dance which he describes is by way of an allegory of the complementary qualities of man and woman, or of reverence, or of deliberation, and so on. This bears again every mark of its Italian origin. The interest of Elyot's position lies, first, in his intuition of that antique feeling for rhythm which marked Alberti or Agricola, and, next, in that new sense of personality which *Il Cortegiano,* known already to Elyot, was destined to graft upon English society at large. And in this connection it is pertinent to observe how high a place he accords to the virtue of magnanimity . . . , the just consciousness of distinction, which in its form of *virtù* was the peculiar characteristic of the Italian moral type. From the Italy of the Renaissance Elyot drew also his conviction of the fitness of women for letters, and their rightful claim to real education as a preparation for worthy married life.

Like Palmieri and Erasmus, Elyot asks what it is that hinders the modern world from attaining the virtues and the

learning of the ancient time. The Englishman finds the explanation primarily in the pride, avarice and negligence of parents, and secondly in the lack of masters. By pride he means the contempt for learning openly expressed by men of estate. "It is a notable reproach to be well learned"; "the name of 'clerk' is held in base estimation." Yet such scorners should remember Henry I of England, Alexander, Hadrian, or Marcus Aurelius, whom even the owner of manors might regard as not unworthy of his esteem. This is not the answer of Palmieri; for Elyot is confronted by the special obstacle which feudal society, based on land ownership, raised in northern Europe against all ideals dissociated from arms and property. Erasmus found the same difficulty in dealing with the landed class in Germany. As regards avarice Elyot instances the parsimony of the gentry in paying their tutors, and their indifference to all qualifications except cheapness. If it be the case of a new cook or falconer no trouble is too great. Negligence is that unwillingness to continue boys' education beyond the age of fourteen. Such a state of public opinion needs radical amendment. To effect this is the purport of *The Governor.* For in the new age the future of English prosperity depended on the intelligence which could be brought to bear by all who were in a position of responsibility upon the social and political problems involved in the great changes in progress abroad and at home. Elyot realised, though, of course, imperfectly, that England had entered upon a higher stage of development, that a new governing class, a lay, professional class, was being called into existence, and that for it a freshly devised equipment was essential. That, following the example of Italy, he found in an enlightened adaptation of antique training. So he concludes his work with a confident appeal: "Now all ye readers that desire to have your children to be governors, or in any other authority, in the public weal of your country, if ye bring them up and instruct them in such form as in this book is declared, they shall then seem to all men worthy to be in authority, honour and *noblesse,* and all that is under their governance shall prosper and come to perfection." (pp. 291-94)

William Harrison Woodward, "The Renaissance and Education in England," in his Studies in Education during the Age of the Renaissance: 1400-1600, *1906. Reprint by New York: Teachers College Press, 1967, pp. 268-322.*

FOSTER WATSON (essay date 1912)

[*Watson was an English educator and the editor and author of numerous studies treating historical trends in education. In the following excerpt from a representative work,* Vives and the Renascence Education of Women *(1912), he touches on the aim of* The Defence of Good Women.]

Sir Thomas Elyot says in the **Boke named the Gouvernour,** published in 1531, "I purpose to make a book onely for ladies; wherein her laud shall be more amply expressed." In 1540, in his Preface to his *Image of Governance,* we learn that the book was certainly in existence, for he says: "My little book called the **Defence of Good Women,** not only confoundeth villainous report, but also teacheth good wives to know well their duties." In the same preface, Elyot refers to his *Dictionary* as not yet ready. Since that book was first issued in 1538, it is clear that the **Defence of Good Women** must have been written before that date.

This tractate is probably the first imitation in English of the Platonic dialogue. It is interesting in the history of education in the light of Elyot's views, expressed in the **Gouvernour,** the most distinctively Renascence treatise on education in England as to the study of Plato. "Above all other[s]," says Elyot, "the works of Plato should be most studiously read when the judgment of a man is to come to perfection, and by the other studies is instructed in the form of speaking that philosophers used. Lord God, what incomparable sweetness of words and matter shall he find in the said works of Plato and Cicero; wherein is joined gravity with delectation, excellent wisdom with divine eloquence, absolute virtue with pleasure incredible, and every place is so infarced with profitable counsel, joined with honesty," The *Defence* is further interesting, since it deals with "one example among us, as well of fortitude, as of all other virtues." Under the name of Zenobia, it surely was meant by Elyot that the discarded Queen Catharine of Aragon should be in the background of the mind of the reader; even the word *Surry* for Syria, as though a slip, may be a realistic reference to Catharine's retreat to Richmond in 1530 when Henry VIII. was with Anne Boleyn in London. Elyot thus belongs to the group of the friends of Queen Catharine of Aragon—Vives, Hyrde, and Sir Thomas More. (pp. 211-12)

[*The Defence of Good Women*] belongs to the group of books in praise of women, based on historical examples. Thus, in 1529, Cornelius Agrippa wrote *de Nobilitate et Praecellentia Foeminei Sexus,* which is the more noteworhty, since it was translated into English by David Clapham in 1542, under the title of *The Excellency of Woman-kind.* There was a considerable literature of women's books in the time of the Renascence. These books in the praise of women ordinarily were written to secure the patronage of some lady of rank. Elyot's book, it is worth noticing, is undedicated. This is negative confirmation that he had Queen Catharine in mind, for naturally her star having set, a dedication to her would be unsafe for anyone to dare. Her death in 1536 may, indeed, have been the occasion for the production of this booklet, which we have seen to have been written by 1538. The *Defence of Good Women,* apart from the interest of its imitation of the Platonic dialogue, is interesting as a document in the history of the English language. (pp. 212-13)

Foster Watson, "Sir Thomas Elyot: The Defence of Good Women," in Vives and the Renascence Education of Women, *edited by Foster Watson, Longmans, Green & Co., 1912, pp. 211-40.*

RUTH MOHL (essay date 1933)

[*Mohl is an American educator and the author of several studies of English literature. In the following excerpt from one of these works,* The Three Estates in Medieval and Renaissance Literature *(1933), she explores Elyot's views of monarchal rule and a classed society as they are presented in* The Governour.]

Sir Thomas Elyot was one of those who had small faith in the doctrine of communism. To him, those who talked of having all things in common were "fantasticall foles." His **Boke Named the Governour** is, of course, a treatise of advice for one estate only, that of rulers or magistrates. However, Elyot also, at considerable length, refutes the arguments of communists like More and preaches the old doctrine of the estates of the world—the necessity of estates and their duties. The first part of the **Boke Named the Governour** reads like a reply to the *Utopia.* Elyot is neither the political idealist that More is, nor simply a religious dogmatist, though he is finally satisfied with the explanation of divine origin of government and of classes of society. He says that he bases his arguments on "reason and commune experience" and on the authority of Plato and Aristotle, but his chief argument is that of divine order, and thereby he reaches the position of conservative adherence to the old doctrines of the necessity of monarchy and of gradations of society.

First, he has much to say, in the tone of the knightly school master that he was, of the meaning of the terms *res publica* and "publik weale." They are usually misunderstood, he says. His explanation of their real meaning is most interesting in the light of all that philosophies of estates have said before him. He defines a "publik weale" as "a body lyvyng, compacte or made of sondry astates and degrees of men, whiche is disposed by the ordre of equite and governed by the rule and moderation of reason." Thus he commits himself at once to differences in degree. The term *res publica* is nothing but the Latin word for "public weal." *Res* means more than "a thing"; it may mean also "estate, condition, substance, or profit." Now *profit* is only another word for "weal." And the word *publica* is derived from the word for "people," *populus.* "Wherefore hit semeth that men have ben longe abused in calling *Rempublicam* a commun weale," if by commonwealth they mean "that every thinge shulde be to all men in commune, without discrepance of any astate or condition." Those that give it such a meaning "be thereto moved more by sensualite than by any good reason or inclination to humanite. And that shall sone appere unto them that wyll be satisfied either with autorite or with naturall ordre and example." A very simple explanation solves the apparent contradiction: the word *populus* includes "all the inhabitantes of a realme or citie, of what astate or condition so ever they be." If one wishes to speak of the commonalty only, one must use the word *plebs,*

> wherein be contayned the base and vulgare inhabitantes not avanced to any honour or dignite, whiche is also used in our dayly communication; for in the citie of London and other cities they that be none aldermen or sheriffes be called communers. And in the countrey, at a cessions or other assembly, if no gentyl men be there at, the sayenge is that there was none but the communalte, whiche proveth in myn oppinion that *Plebs* in latine is in englisshe communaltie and *Plebeii* be communers.

Thus, he proceeds, there is as much difference between "public weal" and "common weal" as between *res publica* and *res plebeia.* If the public weal is to be a *res plebeia,* then in it the commoners only must be wealthy and the nobility needy and miserable, or all must be of one degree and sort.

In such a communism, Elyot has no interest. For it would destroy the "discrepance of degres, whereof procedeth ordre." This order runs through the whole universe, natural and supernatural. By it the incomprehensible majesty of God, as by a bright light of torch or candle, is declared to the blind inhabitants of this world. Moreover, without such order, only chaos would result and perpetual conflict. Nor can anything or anyone exist of himself; for if he destroys others on whom he depends, then he too of necessity must perish. The result is universal dissolution. All this is true of the realm supernatural, but those things within the compass of man's knowledge are similarly ordered, by "degrees and astates." The elements of the body, herbs, animals, trees, birds, fishes, all show order. Similarly order exists in the realm of humankind, "so that in every thyng is ordre, and without ordre may be nothing stable or permanent; and it may nat be called ordre, excepte it do contayne in it degrees, high and base, accordynge to the merite or estimation of the thyng that is ordred." In the "astate" of mankind, one would naturally expect more perfect order than among the inferior creatures who have not man's knowledge and wisdom and who were ordained by God for the use of man. God does not give to every man the same gifts, but some have more, some less, as pleases God's divine majesty. Therefore they cannot be all of one estate. Such as think they can have all things in common, therefore, are "fantasticall foles."

> One man excels another in understanding, and so shulde the astate of his persone be avanced in degree or place where understandynge may profite.... And unto men of suche vertue by very equitie appertaineth honour, as theyr iuste rewarde and duetie, whiche by other mennes labours must also be mainteined according to their merites. For as moche as the saide persones, excelling in knowlege wherby other be governed, be ministers for the only profite and commoditie of them whiche have nat equall understandyng: where they whiche do exercise artificiall science or corporall labour, do not travayle for theyr superiours onely but also for theyr oune necessitie. So the husbande man fedethe hym selfe and the clothe maker: the clothe maker apparayleth hym selfe and the husbande: they both socour other artificers: other artificers them: they and other artificers them that be Governours. But they that be Governours... nothinge do acquire by the sayde influence of knowlege for theyr owne necessities, but do imploye all the powers of theyr wittes, and theyr diligence, the only preservation of other theyr inferiours.

Moreover the slothful person should not share equally with the industrious; for, if he did, the industrious workman would become discouraged and idle.

> Wherefore it can none other wyse stande with reason, but that the astate of the persone in preeminence of lyvynge shulde be estemed with his understandyng, labour, and policie.

He should have honor and substance, as a reward for himself and also as an incentive to those below him. Where all things are common, there is no order, he repeats, and he enforces the repetition by an original analogy: that of household furniture. Pots and pans adorn the kitchen well enough, but they would scarcely be ornaments in the bedchamber; neither would the beds and pillows be fitting in the hall, or carpets and cushions become the stable.

> Semblably the potter and tynker, only perfecte in theyr crafte, shall littell do in the ministration of iustice. A ploughman or carter shall make but a feble answere to an ambassadour. Also a wayver (weaver) or fuller shulde be an unmete capitaine of an armie, or in any other office of a Governour.

Without these different estates there is no public weal, any more than a house is sufficiently furnished without its necessary ornaments.

Elyot similarly demonstrates the necessity of monarchy by the argument of order. A tyrant is not desirable, of course, but neither is a "communaltie." The latter "of all rules is moste to be feared." For the commons, without bridle, order everything without justice, and with vengeance and cruelty. A king or prince, on the other hand, provides the most sure governance, for he rules only for the welfare of his people, and that kind of government is best approved and has longest continued and is most ancient. With such assurance does Elyot juggle facts to further his argument. In addition to the king there should be inferior magistrates, chosen by the king and compared by Aristotle to the king's eyes, ears, hands, and legs. Such magistrates should be chosen from "that astate of men whiche be called worshipfull, if amonge them may be founden a sufficient nombre, ornate with vertue and wisedome, mete for suche purpose, and that for sondry causes." However, if such virtue and learning "do inhabite a man of the base astate of the communaltie," then he too is worthy to be so advanced.

The rest of the work is devoted chiefly to the proper training for a member of the nobility. All the finest human qualities are those of gentility. By his majesty such a one "may be espied for a Governour." Even his apparel is important. God has ordained certain apparel for certain ranks of society.

> And what enormitie shulde it nowe be thought, and a thinge to laughe at, to se a iuge or sergeant at the lawe in a short cote, garded and pounced after the galyarde facion, or an apprentice of the lawe or pleder come to the barre with a millaine bonet or frenche hatte on his heed, sette full of plumes, poudred with spangles. So is there apparaille comely to every astate and degree, and that whiche exceedeth or lackethe, procureth reproche, in a noble man especially.

Strangely enough, Elyot later asserts that in the beginning people had all things in common and that private possessions and dignities were bestowed by the consent of the people on those at whose virtue they marveled and by whose industry they received a common benefit. This readiness to labor for the common benefit was called "gentilnesse" in English, "And the persones were called gentilmen, more for the remembraunce of their vertue and benefite, than for discrepance of astates." Apparently Elyot has forgotten his earlier argument. This is another instance of how in the philosophy of estates one argument may be made to work both ways, according as the author is addressing one estate or another. On the nobility, the acquisition of estate from the commons puts a great responsibility. To the commons, nobility is said to be ordained of God, for the sake of their submission. Here Elyot proceeds to say that God is responsible for the good children of these "gentilmen," who, in turn, strove to retain the gentility of their fathers. Thus the estates of the nobility originated. Let no man think that lineage and riches make him noble: only true nobility of character can do that. The idea of divine origin of estates is asserted again toward the close of the work, however, with the same examples from nature. With equality of degree, we should, like savage beasts, desire to slay one another. (pp. 156-61)

Ruth Mohl, "The History of the Form: Later English Development," in her The Three Estates in

Medieval and Renaissance Literature, *Columbia University Press*, 1933, pp. 140-255.

EDWIN JOHNSTON HOWARD (essay date 1946)

[*Howard is an American educator and editor. In the following excerpt from the introduction to his edition of Elyot's* Of the Knowledge Which Maketh a Wise Man *(1946), he commends the author's presentation of Platonic ideals and use of the dialogue form.*]

The theme of *Of the Knowledge whiche Maketh a Wise Man* is the Platonic contention that virtue and knowledge are identical and that the man who knows what is right will always act in accordance with his knowledge. This idea Elyot could, of course, have found in a number of the authentic dialogues of Plato and also in the doubtful *Alcibiades I*. . . . As Plato was Elyot's favorite philosopher it is not surprising that his most important dialogue should deal with a typically Platonic idea and that the chief speaker in the dialogue should be Plato himself. As Elyot said in the "Proheme" of *Of the Knowledge whiche Maketh a Wise Man,* he was indebted to Diogenes Laertius's life of Plato for the exchange of remarks between Plato and Dionysius of Syracuse that stimulated him to write the work. He had already, in *The Gouernour,* manifested his interest in the subject of virtue, and it is not remarkable that he should have wished to devote an entire book to the theme. It might be said with much truth that *Of the Knowledge whiche Maketh a Wise Man* is a supplement to *The Gouernour.*

Although he makes no mention of it, Elyot drew largely upon Diogenes Laertius's life of Aristippus for the character of Plato's opponent in the dialogue. Aristippus, as depicted by Elyot, is, however, a less reputable person than he is as depicted by Diogenes Laertius. Elyot's picture is of a man of exceedingly low morals, one who cared for nothing but sensual gratification; whereas Diogenes Laertius, while admitting that Aristippus certainly had his earthly side, at the same time presented him as a philosopher of considerable stature.

Xenophon and Apuleius, both of whom Elyot elsewhere said that he had read, contain additional material that might have been drawn upon for the dialogue.

Although Plato's use of the dialogue as a means of presenting ideas undoubtedly suggested its use to Elyot, there is considerable difference between Plato's handling of the form and Elyot's. Like others of the sixteenth century, Elyot made something of the dialogue closely resembling a monologue with occasional exclamatory interjections. The chief speaker is generally clearly to be identified with the author; the other speaker serves mainly to indicate that the chief speaker's logic is irresistible in its force. There is little of Plato's subtle leading of his auditor toward the truth; instead, the author expounds his views through the mouth of the chief speaker. In the dialogue as written by Plato, the reader is presented with a question, the answer to which is not immediately apparent. In the dialogue as it was written in the sixteenth century the author's opinions are generally clear to the reader from the beginning, and the body of the dialogue consists in the main of an elaboration of these opinions. Socrates, in Plato's dialogues, makes extensive use of questions; and generally the auditor, by means of his answers, is driven to confessing that his original contention was unsound and that the truth is frequently the opposite of what he had formerly believed. Elyot proceeds, like most of those writing the dialogue in the sixteenth century, more by assertion than by question and answer. Although he does use questions, they are neither so numerous nor so important in the structure of the dialogue as Plato's. Aristippus makes a goodly number of answers to Plato's queries in *Of the Knowledge whiche Maketh a Wise Man,* but the reader often has the feeling that Plato would continue with his discourse whether Aristippus replied or not.

Even its staunchest partisans must confess that the sixteenth century dialogue is inferior to Plato's; but, when one considers that Plato has always been acknowledged the foremost writer of dialogues, such a concession seems to be minor indeed. Inferior as it was to Plato's, the sixteenth century dialogue was yet a lively and highly effective vehicle for expressing ideas of a controversial nature. The use of speakers makes the dialogue semi-dramatic in form; what might otherwise be an impersonal exposition of a theme becomes, through the agency of human speakers, a warmly personal affair. One has but to compare Elyot's dialogues with his other compositions to realize that the method of the dialogue is the more entertaining one, although the matter of, for instance, *The Gouernour* is more important than the matter of any of the dialogues. *Of the Knowledge whiche Maketh a Wise Man, Pasqvil the Playne,* and *The Defence of Good Women* deal with no more vital matters than do *The Image of Governance* and *A Preservative agaynste Deth,* but they probably are to the majority of readers more interesting and memorable.

Having been inspired to write his dialogue by reading Plato's remark to Dionysius, Elyot had but small choice of a chief speaker. His choice of a second was especially happy: Aristippus had not only been a resident of the court of Dionysius, but had been well treated there. He was, moreover, a great opponent of Plato, who apparently disliked him heartily. At the beginning of the dialogue Plato's repugnance for Aristippus's tastes and opinions is rather rancorously expressed. As, however, the argument proceeds, Plato becomes more and more concerned with the development of his thesis than with the state of Aristippus's morals.

Elyot handled the conclusion of his dialogue with skill and discretion. The historical Aristippus was, according to Plato's ethical system, a very faulty being. It is therefore a point to Elyot's credit that, although Plato had directed some weighty arguments at Aristippus and had in general bombarded him with logic, the most Aristippus would confess was that he had been to some extent influenced in his thinking. It must be admitted that this is a more artistic conclusion than the usual complete reformation on the part of the second speaker would be.

Although Sir Thomas Elyot, in the prefaces to his various works, never tired of saying that his chief purpose in writing was the improvement of his countrymen, it is perhaps permissible to wonder if he had no deeper object in view than the bettering of his compatriots in general in offering *Of the Knowledge whiche Maketh a Wise Man* to the public. In this work Elyot pictured Plato as having suffered various indignities and as having imperiled his life by proclaiming what he considered to be the truth, even though he might have won applause and favor by truckling to Dionysius of Syracuse and by refraining from pointing out wherein Dionysius was wrong. It is certain that Elyot was interested in such matters as virtue and wisdom and in the welfare of his native land. Then what could be more logical than to assume that Elyot was not writing, in *Of the Knowledge whiche Maketh a Wise Man,* merely a general treatise on wisdom, but was trying to warn his royal master, Henry VIII, of the evils of tyranny? True it is that Elyot warned his readers in "The Proheme" that he was pointing at no particular person, but that he was addressing himself to men of all kinds; but it is no less true, if we accept Elyot's word for it, that his contemporaries considered *The Gouernour* to be specifically directed at Henry. Elyot insisted that such an interpretation was the result of nothing but the malice and viciousness of his critics, and that Henry himself saw nothing of a personal nature in *The Gouernour.* If Elyot had had the good judgment to do nothing more than deny the accusations he would have been in a better position than the one in which he placed himself by giving the little anecdote about Antonine's hiring the rude fellow at double wages to criticize him. Despite Elyot's disclaimers this narrative can be interpreted only as Elyot's justification of his criticism of the king.

The reader will note that Elyot, although ostensibly writing upon the themes of wisdom and virtue, actually manages to produce a rather telling treatise on the evils of tyranny. It was to be expected, considering the inspiration of the work, that he would have something to say on the subject of tyrants, but that he would write upon it at length was not to be expected. Taken at his word he was writing for the benefit of his countrymen; if he was as wise as succeeding generations have considered him, he must have realized that only one man in England, Henry VIII, was in the position to exercise tyranny: therefore, in warning about the evils of tyranny, Elyot must have been warning Henry to act with justice.

When Elyot return to England in 1532 from his embassy to Charles V, the matter of the divorce between Henry and Catherine had advanced so far that Sir Thomas More was on the point of resigning his office: in fact, Elyot's mission to Charles terminated in March, 1532, and More resigned in May of the same year. Whether Elyot returned to England partisan toward either the queen or the king we do not know; that he came back the friend of Sir Thomas More is probable and has been assumed by biographers of More. At least Elyot was, judging from his letter to Cromwell after More's death, accused of having been a friend of More's, and this accusation he rather cravenly denied, beseeching Cromwell "now to lay apart the remembraunce of the amity betwene me and Syr Thomas More, which was but *usque ad aras,* as is the proverb." It would be only natural for a lover of wisdom and virtue such as Elyot professed himself to be to feel that More was being unjustly treated for offering what he considered good advice to his royal master. A person in a position of authority, according to the main argument of *Of the Knowledge whiche Maketh a Wise Man,* does wrong to resent honestly offered advice, even though the advice may be unpalatable.

We thus have the situation in the court of Henry's feeling resentment toward More because of More's advice and the casting out of More from the royal favor and very soon after these events Elyot's writing about a tyrant who cast off his favorite philosopher for daring to disagree with his master. Whether Elyot was actually, in the persons of Dionysius and Plato, representing Henry VIII and Sir Thomas More cannot now be determined with any degree of certainty. From the twentieth century point of view there seems to be a great similarity between Elyot's contemporaries and the persons of the dialogue, but whether the similarity was or was not intentional it is impossible to determine. In the heat of controversy issues are not always as clearly defined as they are when viewed with the perspective of more than four centuries. We may, however, say that if Elyot's treatment of the theme of the tyrant and the counselor in the year 1533 was nothing but coincidence, it was, to say the least, an extremely striking one.

If it be objected that a plea as veiled as that of Elyot's dialogue would prove ineffectual in shaking Henry's determination to have his own way, it must be admitted that there are valid grounds for the objection. If the stands of More, Fisher, and the Papacy could not influence Henry, then surely Elyot's little work could not hope to do so. But in spite of this, Elyot may have been impelled to offer his word of advice. That he contented himself with carefully cloaked allegory instead of boldly ranging himself on the side of what he considered right may be held by some to be cowardly. True as this may be, it is still true that Elyot deserves great credit, if the interpretation given above of *Of the Knowledge whiche Maketh a Wise Man* is correct, for raising his voice, however pipingly, in the cause of justice when so many others remained silent. (pp. xiv-xxxii)

> *Edwin Johnston Howard, in an introduction to* Of the Knowledge Which Maketh a Wise Man *by Sir Thomas Elyot, edited by Edwin Johnston Howard, The Anchor Press, 1946, pp. vii-xxxii.*

C. S. LEWIS (essay date 1954)

[*Lewis is considered one of the foremost Christian and mythopoeic authors of the twentieth century. He is regarded as a formidable logician and Christian polemicist, a perceptive literary critic, and—perhaps most highly—as a writer of fantasy literature. Also a noted academic and scholar, Lewis held posts at Oxford and Cambridge, where he was an aknowledged authority on medieval and Renaissance literature. In the following excerpt from his* English Literature in the Sixteenth Century, Excluding Drama, *he appraises Elyot's overall literary worth.*]

Sir Thomas Elyot (1490?-1546) though not a self-made man, for he came of a good family, boasts that he is a self-taught one who, from his twelfth year, had no instructor but himself *tam in scientiis liberalibus quam in utraque philosophia,* though he also tells us that before he was twenty a 'renoumed' physician had taken him through Galen. His earliest publication was the *Book of the Governor* (1531). This was followed in 1532 by *Pasquil the Plain* and in 1533 by *The Knowledge that maketh a Wise Man.* The former, possibly derived from an Italian source, is a dialogue in the early Platonic manner between Pasquil, the personification of free speech, and a flatterer called Gnato. Gnato represents Protestantism and is painted as an ignorant hypocrite, one of those who 'will be in the bowells of diuinitie before they know what belongeth to good humanitie'. He carries in his bosom a copy of the New Testament, but cheek by jowl with it (and 'Lorde! what discorde is bitweyne these two bokes!') Chaucer's *Troilus.* We have heard from the other side so much about idle monkes and wanton chanouns as the authors of chivalrous romance that the jibe is unexpected. The truth is that in 'advanced' circles at that time any party might accuse any other of medieval proclivities; the romances were out of fashion. In 1534 came *The Castle of Health,* a novelty in so far as it is a medical treatise written by a layman and in the vernacular. Elyot was attacked for writing it both by the doctors who resented the intrusion of an amateur and also by men of his own class who held that such work 'beseemeth not a knight, he mought haue been much better occupied'. This criticism provoked from him in the second edition a vigorous defence both of the vernacular and of the 'histories' or anecdotes with which he had plentifully besprinkled his discourse: 'they may more surely cure mens affections then diuers physitions do cure maladies'. In 1538 he brought out his *Latin-English Dictionary,* dedicated to the king whom he obediently salutes as 'supreme head of the Church under Christ' and praises for his 'evangelical faith'. In 1539 came a *Banquet of Sapience* and in 1540 an *Image of Governance.* There is evidence that he also began in Latin a book *De Rebus Memorabilibus Angliae.*

Elyot's *Dictionary* is probably the most useful thing he did, but as an English author he is chiefly remembered for the *Book of the Governor.* By a Governor he means one who rules under a king, a member of the governing classes. His book is thus a sort of blue-print for the education of the aristocracy and falls into place beside those numerous works in which humanists and others at that time endeavoured, not quite ineffectively, to alter their masters. A new type was in fact produced, even if it was not very like what the humanists wanted. Castiglione's *Il Cortegiano,* Machiavelli's *Prince,* Vives' *De Christiana Femina,* Erasmus; *Institutio Regis Christiani,* and the *De Regno et Regis Institutione* of Patricius (Francesco Patrizi) all reveal the impulse; so in its own way does the *Faerie Queene.* Patricius and Erasmus were the two that influenced Elyot most. But he is less philosophical and universal than they, more rooted in the realities of a particular time and place. Erasmus begs rulers to remember how unreasonable it is *(quam sit absurdum)* for them to be elevated above the people in splendour if they are not proportionately elevated in virtue. Elyot substitutes for *quam absurdum* 'what reproche', changing a sage's into a gentleman's censure. He borrows from Patricius the point that *res publica* means not 'common' but 'public' weal. But in Patricius this had been not much more than a philological note; in Elyot it is the starting-point for a refutation of egalitarianism and a glowing eulogy of degree which anticipates, as so many authors have done, the speech of Shakespeare's Ulysses.

Of education in its nursery stage Elyot has nothing of value to say. Like all his kind he issues rigid instructions which would be scattered to the winds by ten minutes' experience of any real child or any real nurse (he died without issue). In the later chapters of his First Book he is really laying the foundations of the system which, in a narrower but not unrecognizable form, became the 'classical education' of our public schools. He has to fight on two fronts. On the one hand he has to rebut the lingering medieval idea (Castiglione says it died hardest in France) 'that to a great gentleman it is a notable reproche to be well lerned and to be called a great clerke'. It was on this front that the humanists triumphed most completely. The

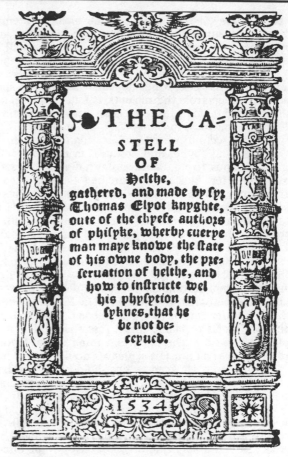

Title page of the first edition of Elyot's guide to health and fitness.

tradition of gentlemanly philistinism slowly but surely decayed and was not reinstated till compulsory games altered the whole character of school life. There was thus a long lucid interval between Squire Western and Bertie Wooster; it is arguable that during that interval England was at her greatest. On the other hand, Elyot has to fight against the current practice of his own day whereby boys having once learned 'to speake Latine elegantly' and 'to make verses without mater or sentence' are snatched away to the illiberal but lucrative study of the law, when they ought to be 'forming their minds' on the great poets, orators, and philosophers. For these Elyot expresses, and in some sense no doubt sincerely feels, a boundless enthusiasm—'I feare me to be to longe from noble Homere'. Yet his own praise of Homer does not suggest anything that would now be regarded as discriminating enjoyment. On Virgil he is more convincing.

Perhaps the most interesting thing in Elyot's advice is his plea for what we should now call aesthetic education. He laments a decay of the arts in England, by which it has come about that 'if we wyll haue any thinge well paynted, kerued, or embrawdred' we must 'resorte unto straungers'. A young nobleman who shows any talent for drawing should be given lessons in it; not only for its possible military uses, but for a deeper reason. The man who can draw will 'alway couaite congruent mater . . . and whan he happeneth to rede or here any fable or historie, forthwith he apprehendeth it more desirously and retaineth it better than any other'.

The *Book of the Governor* is thus by no means contemptible for its content; at the same time there is nothing in it which suggests a mind of the first order. Elyot is a well informed man, not a scholar; a sensible man (for the most part), not a deep thinker. As a stylist he has perhaps higher claims. His verse, which appears frequently in short translated extracts from the ancients, is Late Medieval and worthless. Within his prose we must make distinctions. The florid "Proheme", to Henry VIII, is not characteristic. Nor is . . . [the section] where his Burtonian love of 'histories' overflows all bounds and produces in the story of Titus and Gisippus (from Boccaccio) what is really a full dress *novella.* Here he is a little aureate ('Am I of that vertue that I may resiste agayne celestiall influence preordinate by prouidence diuine?'). But that is not the true Elyot. The love of long words is indeed a constant trait. In this respect Elyot is at the opposite pole from the purist Cheke. He is a convinced and conscious neologist, and is prepared to defend his practice 'for the necessary augmentation of our language'. No one will now seriously deny the necessity; and fortune so sways the destiny of words that it would be harsh to blame Elyot if his *mansuetude, pristinate,* and *levigate* have not succeeded. It is not these, whether we praise or blame them, that should determine his place as a writer. The important thing is that Elyot is aware of prose as an art. His sentences do not simply happen, they are built. He keeps a firm hold of his construction, he is nearly always lucid, and his rhythm is generally sound. In a word, his prose is, for good as well as for ill, more literary than More's. Hence some loss of race and intimacy (humour he probably had little to express) and hence also a freedom from confusion and monotony. The difference is still a very fine one, not easily to be discovered by comparing a sentence or two of his with a sentence or two of More's. After a day's reading it becomes noticeable. If it were possible for authors to be always either as lively as More or as lyrical as Tyndale at their best, the appearance of such prose as Elyot's would be a disaster. As things are, the gain almost equals the loss. I am not suggesting that Elyot, or a thousand such as Elyot, matter to the mind and heart of man as More matters; but the ear of man must sometimes prefer him. (pp. 273-76)

> C. S. Lewis, "Drab and Transitional Prose," in his English Literature in the Sixteenth Century, Excluding Drama, *Oxford at the Clarendon Press, 1954, pp. 272-317.*

FRITZ CASPARI (essay date 1954)

[*Caspari is a German diplomat, educator, and the author of numerous articles and a full-length study devoted to intellectual history,* Humanism and the Social Order in Tudor England *(1954). In the following excerpt from that work, he discusses Elyot's adaptation of humanist philosophies to suit his own conceptions of man and society.*]

There is one important and typical difference between [Sir Thomas] More's and Elyot's humanistic works: More, like Erasmus, wrote his humanistic works in Latin, whereas Elyot wrote his in English. The *Utopia* was neither published in England, nor translated into English, during More's lifetime, whereas *The boke named the Gouernour* was written in English, published in London, and went through eight editions within fifty years of the time of its first publication in 1531. Elyot, rather than More, was the great popularizer of humanism in England, and, to judge from the continued demand for his works, his efforts were popular and successful. He blended the ideas of More and Erasmus with those of a number of other humanists, mostly Italian, to arrive at his own conceptions of man and society, in which the postulates of the various humanists were so selected and modified as to become directly applicable to existing English conditions.

While Elyot was strongly influenced by the ideas current in the circle of Erasmus and More, the influence of Italian humanism is also evident in his portrayal of the perfect "Governour." The courtier, as described in Italian courtesy books, was a more distinct type than Erasmus' Christian prince and Christian knight, had a wider appeal, and was more readily imitable. As a social type, he also bore a closer relationship to contemporary reality than did More's Utopian "order of the learned." The practical concreteness of the Italian model appealed to Elyot and other sixteenth-century Englishmen who copied and transformed it to suit the needs of their own country.

Italian authors of courtesy books, such as Patrizi, Palmieri, and Castiglione, quite naturally aimed their precepts at Italian conditions. They were narrower and often shallower, more concerned with immediate, practical situations and more limited by their national horizon than Erasmus. Palmieri's *optimo cittadino* could only exist in the city states of Renaissance Italy, and Castiglione's *cortegiano* only in her courts. But the writings of classical antiquity, foremost among them those of Plato, Aristotle, Cicero, and Quintilian, formed the basis of these conceptions. In so far as the Italians revived and re-formed the classical ideal of humanity, their work was a model and a challenge for all European nations. If those features of the *cortegiano* which were suited only to his local environment could be modified, he could serve as an example in any occidental country. (pp. 149-50)

In *The boke named the Gouernour,* the best known of his works, and in his other writings, such as the *Image of Governance* and *Of the Knowledge Which Maketh a Wise Man* (described as *A disputacion Platonike*) [Elyot] was concerned with the problem of creating and educating a governing class. A typical representative of that class, Elyot lived mostly in the country, and held such offices (in Oxfordshire, Berkshire, Cambridgeshire, etc.) as justice of the peace and sheriff; . . . he was at one time (1531-32) Henry's ambassador to Charles V—an appointment perhaps connected with the success of the *Governour.* He had other experience in the central government: for more than six years (from 1523), he had been performing the duties of clerk of the council on Wolsey's recommendation, but had been "discharged without any recompense, rewarded only with the order of knighthode, honorable and onerouse, having moche lasse to lyve on than bifore." He also probably served as a member of Parliament in his later years. The rules he sat down in his books were the answers he found for the problems and questions that arose in his own life; they constitute a system that he felt would be valuable for many who were in a position similar to his own.

In the figure of the "Governour," Elyot amalgamated such chivalrous traditions as were still alive in England with humanistic ideas to form the English counterpart of the *cortegiano.* The title of Elyot's main work significantly points to the need for a man different from the Italian courtier, for an independent individual, capable of governing, able to act and decide on his own. (pp. 155-56)

Whatever the degree of Castiglione's influence, Elyot's *Governour* is the English counterpart of the *Cortegiano*—a crude counterpart, it is true, with much that sounds ponderous, commonplace, and mediocre, and without the Italian's superb mastery of form and matter; yet it is a genuine creation of Elyot's mind, not without originality, sincere in its aims and, as it turned out, highly influential in his country. The two writers are truly representative of their respective civilizations: Castiglione was the end product of a highly urbane and refined civilization and wrote with a corresponding brilliance almost brittle in its perfection; Elyot stood at the beginning of a great period in the civilization of his country and had not quite shaken off what might be termed a certain archaic heaviness in style and thought. His great achievement was the adaptation of the humanistic ideal of man and society to English needs and conditions: he created a new social norm which the English ruling class, then in its most formative period, could and did adopt as its own. The thought of Italian and northern humanists is fused in his conception. (pp. 159-60)

If the young gentlemen of his country are educated according to his plan [in the *Governour*], the result, [Elyot] thinks, will be that "undoughtedly they shuld become men of so excellent wisedome that throughout all the worlde shulde be founden in no commune weal more noble counsaylours" than in England. In this proud phrase, Elyot clearly shows the way in which humanism and patriotism had become fused in his mind: in contrast to the "internationalist" Erasmus, Elyot and most of his contemporaries among the humanists of all countries made the new learning serve patriotic ends.

Elyot's argument clearly illustrates the application of general principles to the particular problems of his country, and the manner in which humanistic learning is adapted to English purposes. The future Governours must first learn to comprehend the origin and nature of states. Through the works of Plato, Aristotle, and Xenophon, they become acquainted with different kinds of states and consitutions or, as we should say, they study philosophy and political theory. When they have acquired this philosophical foundation which enables them to see things in a wider context, they will devote themselves to the study of English jurisprudence with much greater insight and zeal. General knowledge must precede the specialized knowledge of the Common Law; the occupation with universal problems must precede the study of technical questions valid only in particular cases and in one particular country. The thorough erudition thus attained will enable them to put their best qualities at the disposal of king and country; eventually, through its medium, there will be established in England "a publike weale equivalent to the grekes or Romanes." Elyot's ambition to raise his own country to the level of the great states of antiquity shows up in the most vital passages of his work; his patriotism and humanism had fused into a burning desire to make England the equal of Greece and Rome. It should be noted here that Elyot sees the erudition of the individual as the only method by which such greatness can be achieved: this is one of the main factors that distinguish humanistic nationalism from the various diseased collectivistic na-

tionalisms of our own age. There is no other way to Elyot's goal except through the process of perfecting the single personality. At the same time, it is evident that the perfection of the individual is not only seen as an end in itself but has as its ultimate motive the greatness of England.

In his suggestions for study and teaching, Elyot adopts a number of points from Erasmus, but he places greater emphasis than the more rational Erasmus on "intuition" as a vital factor in these processes. He considers human *ratio* without recourse to something beyond it inadequate as a means of attaining knowledge. In this insistence on suprarational means of cognition, he is indebted to the Italian Neoplatonists. Elyot's ideas on the subject are scattered, but appear in their most complete form in his dialogue, *Of the Knowledge Which Maketh a Wise Man*. In that "Platonike" dialogue, he describes the attainment, function, and nature of knowledge. He declares the intuitive comprehension of spiritual things to be the last step on the way to wisdom, thus following the interpretation that had been given to Plato's doctrine at the Florentine academy. The form, as well as the subtitle, of the dialogue itself indicates his Platonism. Elyot imitates the maieutic method of discussion, Plato's famous dialectical and pedagogical device: the master leads the pupil to understanding and finally to the intuitive recognition of ultimate truths through inspired discussion. Thus Elyot speaks of the sparks by which the master lights the fire of true wisdom in his pupil. Ultimate understanding cannot be taught; it can only be aided by a wise friend and master. Socrates, Elyot says, did not teach anything to men, "but rather brought furthe that which all redy was in them." Elyot agrees with him when in the *Governour* he compares himself to the gardener who watches over the free development of a precious plant, and he uses the same comparison in his "disputacion Platonike," *Of the Knowledge Which Maketh a Wise Man,* where his Plato says to Aristippus: " . . . the sedes which Socrates had sowen in thy minde, do begyn nowe to sprynge with this lyttell waterynge: . . . thou shalte shortly perceive the frutes of wysedom . . . spryng abundantly." The intimate connection between maieutic method and inspiration is finally seen in a passage of the *Governour* adapted by Elyot from Plato's *Theaetetus,* where Socrates says: "Never man lerned of me any thinge, all thoughe by my company he became the wiser. I onely exhortynge and the good spirite inspyringe."

Intimately connected with Plato's theory of education is his doctrine of love. Like Plato, Elyot considers *eros* as a central formative power. *Eros* comes from God, and nothing that emanates from God should be more highly valued than "love, called in latine *Amor,* whereof *Amicitia* commeth, named in englisshe frendshippe or amitie." It should be noted that Elyot, by this little philological stratagem, ties love and friendship very closely together, as indeed for Plato *eros* pervades both kinds of human relationships. Elyot feels that, if friendship is taken from a man's life, the sun seems to have gone out of it. Besides basing his argument on Plato, he invokes Aristotle and Cicero to prove that true friendship is a virtue. One should strive to attain it in an age when, owing to the evil influence of ambition, it has become very rare. True friendship is possible only between good men, whose nature reveals a definite affinity of character, manners, and interests.

The value of friendship was a favorite humanistic theme. Elyot does not, as one might suspect, merely reiterate standard phrases and sentiments, but shows by original remarks and interpretations that he has thought about the question independently. In the *Governour*, he tells of various famous friendships of antiquity and dedicates a whole chapter to the story of Titus and Gysippus as a "right goodly example of frendship." (pp. 172-75)

While some of the more radical Christian reformers were preaching with revolutionary fervor that all men are equal, Elyot insisted that men are unequal because God's order is hierarchical and anti-equalitarian. God creates different kinds and higher and lower types of men. The degree of understanding, and the extent to which such understanding rules the individual and his actions, are the factors which determine a man's worth and position. As Elyot puts it in his archaic manner, understanding is "the principall parte of the soule: it is therefore congruent, and accordynge that one excelleth an other in that influence, as therby beinge next to the similitude of his maker, so shulde the astate of his persone be avanced in degree or place where understandynge may profite: whiche is also distributed in to sondry uses, faculties, and offices, necessary for the lyving and governaunce of mankynde." The individual's position in the organism of human society is to be determined by his intellectual ability and a concomitant sense of responsibility.

In the manner of the Neoplatonists, Elyot compares those of the highest intelligence—and therefore most qualified to rule—with the angels, and with fire, the purest and highest of the elements. The angels, being most fervent in their comtemplation, occupy the highest and most glorious place next to God. Similarly those mortals who most clearly partake of divine wisdom should occupy an elevated position "where they may se and also be sene," so as to be able to order human affairs in accordance with the precepts of divine reason. They show the right way to those of lower intellectual capacity and inferior social status: "by the beames of their excellent witte, shewed throughe the glasse of auctoritie, other of inferiour understandynge [are] directed to the way of vertue and commodious livynge."

Turning to the economic aspect of the question, Elyot finds it right and proper that men of such great virtue should not only be honored but maintained "according to their merites" by other people's work. There may be a faint echo of Plato's and More's Utopian commonwealths in this argument: both exempt the ruling class—More's "order of the learned"—from ordinary labor, and see to it that the necesseties of life are provided for its members by the work of the rest of the community. They also do away with economic differentiation—Plato explicitly only between members of this class, More between all—and establish communism, but while Elyot, of course, heartily agrees that the rulers should be maintained by the others, and points with great satisfaction to the beehive, where this system prevails, he is certainly far from giving any hint of communism in his scheme. He uses Plato's and More's argument, but changes it to defend the existence of a traditional aristocracy, and justifies its wealth with the hope and contention that its members have superior morals and intelligence. Being less visionary and more conservative than Plato and More, he chooses to apply his doctrine in a practical manner to the existing social order,

which he does not wish to change, rather than to invent a completely new Utopian society. What he hopes is that, in addition to their wealth and social power, persons "avanced in degree" will acquire and practice the kind of virtue he postulates.

That virtue becomes apparent in the good qualities and characteristics of a man's nature. Elyot devotes approximately half of the *Governour* to an exhaustive description of these qualities, or individual virtues. With the aid of moral tales and examples usually drawn from antiquity, he establishes a catalogue of virtues which is not distinguished by great originality. As with Plato, Aristotle, and Cicero, the highest virtue is justice. Without it, "all other qualities and vertues can nat make a man good." The essential prerequisite for the attainment of justice is the knowledge of one's self. Elyot attributes great value to the adage "nosce te ipsum." ... He who knows himself learns to know and judge other people and thus becomes just in his dealings with them. There can be no justice without faith, honesty, and truthfulness. Justice therefore prevails only in that commonwealth in which those who rule possess these and similar characteristics and practice the corresponding virtues. It is the task of the rulers to establish and maintain the divinely ordained order of society by holding their inferiors "within the bounds of reason." They preserve the organism of the state, which, like the cosmic order, is proportioned according to the value of its parts. (pp. 181-84)

After these preliminaries and a short description of aristocracy and democracy, Elyot boldly and dogmatically asserts the superiority of monarchy over all other forms of government, and thus implicitly defends the rule of Henry VIII. He advocates a benevolent monarchy, but not the kind of despotism into which his monarch's rule degenerated in its later years. He supports his argument in favor of monarchy by a comparison of the king to God, the sun, the moon—and to the queen bee! Having established the monarchical principle, he elaborates his conception by pointing out that part of the weight and responsibility of government must be borne by the aristocracy, that in practice a combination of monarchy and aristocracy will be most likely to provide good government. In keeping with the constitutional practice of his day, Elyot does not make gentry and nobility equal partners with the king in the job of governing the country. The monarch really is supreme, not just *primus inter pares*. Nevertheless, Elyot assigns very important functions to the upper class, which bears the main burden of governmental work. Its members have the duty to aid the king in performing the functions of government, primarily in "the distribution of iustice in sondry partes of a huge multitude."

Elyot always has English conditions in mind. When he speaks of "sondry meane authorities" who should help the "capitall Governour"—the king—in the administration of the country, he means the English country gentlemen, who, as justices of the peace and in other judicial and administrative functions, maintain and enforce the king's peace, or advise the king in Council and Parliament. For their instruction, Elyot writes practically all his works; their proper training is his constant concern. He frequently expresses this, in terms similar to the passage that introduces the *Image of Governance:* " ... which boke I do dedicate unto you noble lordis, gentil knightes, and other in the state of honour or worshyp, as beinge moste redy to be advanced to governance under your Prince: so that your vertues be correspondent unto your fortunes."

His educational plan presupposes a certain amount of wealth and can be carried out only in the house of a country gentleman who can afford to pay for all the requisite nurses and private tutors. Here, the interplay of actual social conditions and ideas is particularly evident; the whole system is based on the fact that a fairly wealthy landed class is the leading political group. Elyot sees this connection of economic and political power and approves of it: "It is of good congruence that they, whiche be superiour in condition or haviour, shulde have also preeminence in administration." He goes on to state that he favors this situation because "they have competent substaunce to lyve without takyng rewardes," or, in other words, because they can perform the duties imposed on them by the government without having to be paid or bribed for their services. Elyot does not think in terms of a modern, salaried civil service, but of a class which performs the functions of government essentially on an honorary and voluntary basis, which regards such service as a responsibility incident upon it on account of its wealth and superior social position. When talking of "takyng rewardes," Elyot means that men with a secure economic basis are less easily bribed than others. In any case, he described the existing situation: the duties of local government, on its higher level, were performed almost in their entirety by the unpaid country gentry. Sir Thomas Elyot himself is a good example of such service to the community. He repeatedly mentions that he works "without hope of temporall reward, only for the fervent affection, whiche I have ever borne toward the publike weale of my countrei." His claim that he has spent his own "commodity" in the process of writing books for his fellow-countrymen is probably accurate enough; but it is clear that he actually did hope for temporal rewards, and that he obtained some, for his public services.

Elyot esteems inherited position and wealth as very valuable attributes of a Governour; they are not absolutely essential, however, and they are not the main factors that determine a man's fitness to rule. Of greater consequence than the material wealth needed to insure his unselfish devotion to the service of the state, and more important than an inherited title, is a man's human quality as defined by the term "virtue." Since virtue derives from true knowledge and understanding, and since knowledge and understanding are not the special privileges of one class, a man of low birth presumably may also develop them, and thereby become qualified to serve his country in high positions. Such a parvenu, however, often lacks the aristocratic attitude and dignity necessary for one who is "above the common course of other men." He is apt to be a harsher and less kind ruler than one who has inherited the habits of tolerance and affability from family tradition. Elyot probably did not have much difficulty in arriving at this conclusion through his own observation: he must have been irked by the behavior of contemporary *nouveaux riches* and opportunistic hangers-on of the recently "arrived" house of Tudor. One wonders what he really thought of a friend like Thomas Cromwell who agreed with Elyot on the need for a strong monarchy but who definitely was not famed for noble lineage or kindness or the kind of virtue advocated by Elyot. (pp. 186-89)

[Elyot's] Governours should always bear in mind that aristocracy does not mean privilege, but responsibility. They are examples to their people, and must realize that they are being observed in all their actions, for "they sitte, as it were, on a piller on the toppe of a mountaine, where all the people do beholde them...." The "noble example of their lives" and the way in which they rule is decisive for the nature of their state. "Such as be the Governours...suche be the people." A certain attitude and corresponding manners are to be so consistently observed by a gentleman that they become part of his nature. Elyot calls this basic attitude "majesty," and describes it, the "fountaine of all excellent maners," in these words: it "is the holle proporcion and figure of noble astate, and is proprelie a beautie or comelynesse in his countenance, langage and gesture apt to his dignite, and accommodate to time, place, and company." This description resembles the definition of *grazia* given by Castiglione and others in Italy; it is derived from, and forms the counterpart of, such Italian conceptions. The gentleman should be affable, "shewyng to men a gentil and familiare visage," so that he is "easie to be spoken unto." He always controls himself and never rages in uncontrolled anger. He is placable, merciful, and beneficent, and spends liberally on the right occasions.

Reason must lead him in all his actions and rule over his emotions: a Governour must practice both inward and outward "governance"—self-control and authority. Self-control enables a man to find the mean between extremes, to see both himself and the world in which he lives with objective justice, and to apply such justice. If he thus permits reason to rule, his abilities will become virtues. If, on the other hand, he is driven by the lower part of his soul, if his emotions and passions rule without the bridle of reason, his abilities will become vices. The constant aim and goal of all his actions should be the advantage of the commonwealth, yet he must not pursue that advantage blindly and fanatically. If his actions are to be in the public interest, they should be the result of his mature and considered judgment, and should be carried out firmly but with tolerant moderation. If he acts with too much fool-hardy bravado, he cannot be called reasonable or valiant, but is "rather to be rekned with bestes savage." He must learn by experience to judge what course of action will bring the greatest benefit to the community, and act accordingly, Elyot insists that the care for the well-being of the state must take precedence over attention to any particular interests.

The "publike weale" for Elyot is always England, and it is to her greatness that he hopes to contribute. All his books are written for this purpose. Even where he does not specifically refer to it, the English background with its particular conditions is perceptible. His work is based on it and fits into it. He hopes to improve the state of England by his suggestions to such a degree that his country may measure up to the greatness of the states of antiquity. In his noble patriotism, he speaks of "the fervent zele that I have to my countrey," and adds that he desires "only to employ that poure lerning, that I have gotten, to the benefite thereof." This he did both in his judicial, administrative, and political activities, and by creating the figure of the Governour in which he amalgamated what was left of chivalrous tradition with the human norm of antiquity. (pp. 191-93)

Fritz Caspari, "Sir Thomas Elyot," in his Humanism and the Social Order in Tudor England, 1954. Reprint by New York: Teachers College Press, 1968, pp. 145-209.

JOHN M. MAJOR (essay date 1964)

[Major is an American educator and author whose particular focus is humanism in the English Renaissance. In the following excerpt from his full-length study of Elyot, Sir Thomas Elyot and Renaissance Humanism (1964), Major cites ancient authors other than Plato whose philosophies are evidenced throughout The Governour.]

No man, I suppose, ever had greater admiration for the authors of antiquity than had Sir Thomas Elyot. They were for him the creators and golden-voiced purveyors of all wisdom, excepting that sacred wisdom which is found in the Bible and Christian Fathers alone. The breadth of Elyot's reading in the classics is remarkable, even if one allows that some of the knowledge he displays—but only a small part, I think—was acquired at second hand. The *Governour* itself is a storehouse of classical quotations and allusions; the authority of ancient poets and writers of prose is invoked on every page; the wisdom of their utterance stirs the author to exclamations of praise and wonder.

As might be expected, it is the ancient philosophers and rhetoricians with whom Elyot is in greatest sympathy. To be sure, all writers are to him primarily moralists. But Plato, Cicero, Aristotle, Plutarch, Quintilian, Seneca, and Isocrates are his revered instructors in all matters pertaining to morals, government, and education—the three key topics of the *Governour* and most of Elyot's other works. Important as are the medieval and Renaissance authors of princes' mirrors and conduct books to the scheme of the *Governour,* they are in a sense intermediaries only, agents for dispensing the more precious thought of antiquity. Indeed, with a single rather large exception—the Christian orientation of their views—one wonders whether the princes' mirrors of John of Salisbury, Aquinas, or Erasmus have added anything really significant to the moral and political theory of Plato, Aristotle, and Cicero. It is not simply out of slyness or affectation that Elyot refused to acknowledge his debts to any but classical authors.

The single most powerful influence on Elyot's thought is the philosopher Plato. (pp.140-41)

Next to the divine Plato, Elyot's favorite author is unquestionably Cicero. Indeed, as one reads the *Governour,* one gains the impression that Cicero's influence is paramount, so frequently does the tag, "as Tulli saieth," meet the eye. The remarkable hold which the great Roman orator had upon Elyot and upon Petrarch, Erasmus, Ascham, and numerous other Renaissance humanists may be accounted for in somewhat the following manner. In the first place, there was his dazzling public career in the most admired state during the most admired period in history. As the philosopher in politics, Cicero was the very embodiment of the Renaissance educational ideal, while his fearless opposition to tyranny brought encouragement to men who had constantly to fight to retain their own liberties. Second, the sweetness and elevation of his ethical writings had made Cicero beloved of Christian saints and humanists alike. So close was his moral philosophy to the teachings of Christ that these faithful Christians could not help believing he had been in some way specially enlightened by God.... Finally, this moral excellence would have counted for little with Renaissance humanists had it not been that Cicero possessed in abundance the means for giving it eloquent expression. In an age in which eloquence was almost synonymous with wisdom and even with virtue, Cicero was assured of unrivaled eminence, at least among Latin authors.

Although Elyot admired Cicero for all three of the qualities described above—his statesmanship, his moral wisdom, and his eloquence—it is the last accomplishment which seems to have impressed him most. When he refers to Cicero, it is as "father of the latin eloquence" or "prince of Oratours." On one occasion, abandoning all restraint, he lauds Cicero as one "in whom it semeth that Eloquence hath sette her glorious Throne, most richely and preciously adourned for all men to wonder at, but no man to approche it." In a famous definition adopted by the Renaissance, Cicero raised eloquence to the company of supreme virtues; it is a power which comprehends all knowledge and expresses the mind's thoughts in such a way that it can compel those who listen to follow where it wishes. A power so great must therefore be directed to honest ends. By eloquence alone, he declares in a sentence cherished by humanists, man is elevated above the beasts.

The work in which this definition appears, the *De oratore,* has been described as "one of the half-dozen ancient treatises that created the formative ideal of Renaissance education." More than any other type drawn from history or literature, Elyot's governor resembles the figure of the orator set forth in this treatise and in the *Institutio oratoria* of Quintilian—the good man versed in knowledge and skilled in speech occupying public office. In a passage glowing with a fine idealism, Elyot sees the possibility that an elite of citizens endowed with high intelligence, made wise through a liberal education, and possessing an intimate knowledge of oratory and of law might bring government to such perfection that England should come in time to rival ancient Rome itself in greatness. His trust in the power of oratory and his recognition of the orator's exacting qualifications mark Elyot as a true follower of Cicero. Further, his genuine understanding of the spirit of the *De oratore* preserves him from an error common among continental humanists of mistaking the ability to speak or write cleverly for solid eloquence. The *De oratore* and Quintilian's treatise are the source for most of Elyot's statements on these matters.

In composing the *Governour,* Elyot seems to have made use of a dozen or more of the works of Cicero. Those to which he is most heavily indebted are the *De officiis, Tusculan Disputations, De amicitia,* and *De oratore,* especially the first. I have counted more than fifty passages that refer to or are translated from the *De officiis.* In the best known of these passages Elyot recommends that work of Cicero's, together with the dialogues of Plato and the *Nicomachean Ethics* of Aristotle, for the study of moral philosophy after the student has come to mature years. (pp. 141-43)

Books II and III of the *Governour* are to some extent modeled upon the *De officiis.* The virtues which take their definitions chiefly from this work of Cicero's are prudence, modesty, placability, patience, moderation, and counsel;

from the *De officiis* in conjunction with the *Nicomachean Ethics,* liberality, benificence, friendship, justice, fortitude, magnanimity, and abstinence. Elyot's treatment of friendship is of course also based on the *De amicitia,* while for his discussions of patience, fortitude, and magnanimity he borrowed some ideas from the *Tusculan Disputations* and from the Italian author Pontano. (pp. 143-44)

The third (if slightly lesser) member of Elyot's triumvirate is Aristotle. That Aristotle should occupy a position of eminence in the *Governour* may strike the reader as surprising, when he remembers the general lack of enthusiasm for the Greek philosopher on the part of many humanists. Althought the tradition of Aristotelianism continued to be very strong throughout the Renaissance period, rebellion against its authority is "a recurrent feature in the writings of many Renaissance thinkers from Petrarch to Bruno and Galileo." . . . The Renaissance humanists owed their first allegiance to Plato, Cicero, and Seneca, whom they considered superior to Aristotle both as moralists and as stylists. The name of Aristotle, moreover, was for them too closely associated with the despised Scholasticism on the one hand and on the other, Averroism, an intellectual movement which by its frankly naturalistic teachings shocked many devout Christians. The "most Aristotelian of the great humanists" was Vives. But even he, while he professed to be a little ashamed to criticize authors of long-standing reputation, especially Aristotle, "for whose mind, for whose industry, carefulness, judgment in human arts, I have an admiration and respect unique above all others," nevertheless found many opportunities for striking a blow at his favorite.

Ordinarily Elyot is full of praise for Aristotle, whom he calls a "moost sharpest witted and excellent lerned Philosopher." On one occasion he goes so far as to commend him for his eloquence. There is a hint, however, in a passage of the *Governour*. . . , that in Elyot's considered opinion it was the very lack of this quality, eloquence, which kept Aristotle as a moral teacher from attaining the greatness of Plato and Cicero. The passage in question begins with Elyot's recommending for the study of moral philosophy Books I and II of the *Nicomachean Ethics,* Cicero's *De officiis,* and the dialogues of Plato. The mere naming of such great writers so stirs his imagination that he launches forthwith into praise of their eloquence; as the eulogy gets under way, however, the reader is startled to discover that it was meant only for Plato and Cicero. Although the slighting of Aristotle may have been accidental, and although some amends are made to him in a postscript, it is likely that Elyot in this passage has let slip his true feelings. There can be no question that he respected Aristotle greatly and depended upon him for his own venture into moral philosphy. At the same time, his preference for Cicero and Plato is obvious, and is doubtless based on their superior ability to move and persuade. (pp. 144-46)

[But that Aristotle] holds a highly respected position in the *Governour* is proved in a number of ways. Having the very worthy aim of producing in English clear and accurate definitions of the important virtues, Elyot naturally turned for assistance to the *Nicomachean Ethics,* where, as Petrarch said, he would find them "egregiously defined and distinguished." For the young man who is embarking on the study of moral philosophy, Elyot recommends as an introduction Books I and II of the *Ethics,* "wherin is con-

tained the definitions and propre significations of euery vertue," Not only are many of Elyot's own analyses of individual virtues derived from this work; his basic concept of virtue itself is purely Aristotelian, taken over verbatim from the famous definition in the *Nicomachean Ethics.* Virtue, he states, is "an election annexed unto our nature, and consisteth in a meane, which is determined by reason, and that meane is the verye myddes of two thynges viciouse, the one in surplusage, the other in lacke." The essentials of this concept are never lost sight of by Elyot in his treatment of the individual virtues, even when his immediate source may be someone other than Aristotle. Thus in the chapter on mercy, which follows no particular authority, Elyot terms mercy the acceptable mean between cruelty and pity. Mercy "is alway ioyned with reason," whereas pity "is a sickenesse of the mynde"; cruelty he rejects outright as the "most odyous" of vices.

The Aristotelian doctrine of the mean becomes a kind of universal ideal in the *Governour,* applied not just to the analyses of the virtues, but to matters as diverse as the governor's apparel, the furnishings of his house, the various physical exercises, and, most interestingly of all, Elyot's theory of dancing. For him the dancing together of a man and a woman symbolizes the harmonious union of opposing traits or extremes of temperament. The masculine characteristics of fierceness, hardiness, and the rest, when joined to the milder and more tractable traits of the woman, produce "a concorde of the saide qualities," which, "signified in the personages of man and woman daunsinge, do expresse or sette out the figure of very nobilitie." Throughout several chapters Elyot explains how the different steps in the base dance *(basse danse),* intepreted according to his theory, may serve in a most pleasant fashion to illustrate to young people the meaning of the virtue prudence, a knowledge of which is necessary before they can comprehend any of the other virtues. Elyot's quaint theory of dancing, in all of its ramifications, owes almost as much to Plato, Lucian, and medieval allegory as it does to Aristotle, but the essence of it is Aristotle's doctrine of the mean. (pp. 148-49)

From Plato, Cicero, and Aristotle, Elyot acquired a knowledge of moral philosophy as well as a method of transmitting this knowledge to his English readers. Clarity and system, we may suppose, were his first concern, the subject of his discourse being rather technical and to some of his readers strange. As a guide through difficulties of this kind, Aristotle had no rival. Definitions and rules alone, however, do not always clarify, nor were they ever sufficient to make a man virtuous, as the humanists knew. To round out his explanations of the virtues, to enliven the precepts he borrowed from the philosophers, and to penetrate to the feelings of his readers, Elyot made liberal use of historical examples, many of which he selected from the favorite historian of the Renaissance, Plutarch. The popularity of this late Greek author in England increased steadily during the sixteenth century, until, by Shakespeare's time, "a knowledge of his *Lives* and his *Morals* was almost presupposed on the part of the reading Englishman." The *Governour* contains anecdotes from more than half of the total of fifty lives by Plutarch, and moreover follows very closely Plutarch's ideas on the training of young children.

The reasons are clear why Plutarch enjoyed such extreme popularity with Renaissance humanists. In the first place, history was, next to moral philosophy, the most highly prized of the liberal studies.... Of special estimation was the biographical kind of history, for this lent itself admirably to the inculcation of virtuous precepts. Elyot suggests, for instance, that in reading histories, the students should be directed not only to the descriptions of wars and governments, but also to "the good and euyll qualities of them that be rulers, the commodites and good sequele of vertue, the discommodies and euyll conclusion of vicious licence." In the biographical kind of history Plutarch was supreme. He had, in the words of his greatest translator, chosen for his *Lives* "the speciall actes of the best persons, of the famosest nations of the world." He had in addition underlined the significance of these acts by "sage precepts and frutefull instructions," by "effectuall commendation of vertue, and detestation of vice." No wonder that Erasmus could say of this paragon: "Neuer hath there been among the Greke writers (especially as touchyng matters of vertue and good behauour) any one more holy then *Plutarchus,* or better worthie of all men to be reade." (pp. 152-53)

In most of the anecdotes which he borrowed from Plutarch, Elyot shows the ... tendency to explain, supplement, or omit to suit his purpose of the moment, though he usually changes details only and leaves the outline (if not always the spirit) of the original story intact. The liberties Elyot takes are in a way a compliment to Plutarch and to the glories of that ancient history which he immortalized. Only a man to whom these things were a living force, a fertile garden of examples for the daily sustenance and pleasure of readers in every age, would have had the inclination to handle them so freely. Occasionally his alterations produce very good results. (p. 156)

Of greatest interest to us is the fact that the chapters in the *Governour* on the early training of the child reproduce almost in full the ideas of Plutarch's humane and sensible essay.... Briefly, Plutarch stresses a morally healthy environment for the child, the efficacy of education for improving character, the importance of the child's early years, standards of excellence in teaching, training in all the liberal subjects with emphasis on philosophy, exercise for the body as well as the mind, discipline to be maintained through praise and rebuke rather than corporal punishment, and a program of relaxation from studies. One special note in the essay which must have struck a responsive chord in Elyot's breast is Plutarch's magnificent tribute to learning—"truely the thynge that in vs is diuyne and immortall." (pp. 157-58)

The authority of Quintilian with Renaissance educators was even greater than that of Plutarch, perhaps because Quintilian wrote in Latin and was therefore more accessible, or because he emphasized much more strongly than did Plutarch the ideal of education for public service, or simply because his was a far weightier work than the Greek author's. Whatever the reason, the *Institutio oratoria,* from the time of its rediscovery in 1417, was taken to the hearts of humanists as the best of all treaties on education. "Every educator of the Revival," Woodward observes, "whether man of theory or man of practice, whether on Italian or Teutonic soil, Aeneas Sylvius or Patrizi, Agricola, Erasmus, Melancthon, or Elyot, steeped himself in the text and in the spirit of this treatise." The Roman orator described by Quintilian and personified by Cicero—the *vir bonus dicendi peritus* who exercises his

skill in the public interest—almost exactly accords with the Renaissance ideal of the educated man. (p. 160)

Between them, the treatises of Cicero and Quintilian provided the Renaissance with all that was thought necessary to the making of a noble orator. In the words of Petrarch, Cicero "guides his orator through the laborious tasks of legal pleading to the topmost heights of oratory," while Quintilian begins far earlier and leads the future orator "through all the turns and pitfalls of the long journey from the cradle to the impregnable citadel of eloquence." It was primarily as an educator's handbook, then—one which combined the highest ideals of learning with humane and reasonable standards of instruction—that the *Institutio oratoria* made its mark with the humanists of our period. Indeed, when Erasmus came to treat of the art of instruction generally, in his *De ratione studii,* he apologized for handling anew "a subject which has been made so conspicuously his own by the great Quintilian."

As might be expected, Quintilian's influence in the *Governour* is most clearly seen in the chapters on the early education of the gentleman, under such headings as the child's moral and intellectual environment, the qualifications of tutor and master, "educational psychology," and the range and order of the curriculum. Like the Roman author, Elyot believes strongly in the need for children to acquire good habits from the earliest (and most impressionable) age; consequently these authors insist that all persons with whom the child associates—his nurse, companions, tutor, master, and parents—not only have virtuous characters, but also at all times speak in the child's presence clearly and correctly. Elyot would even go so far as to have the child's nurse "and other women aboute hym" speak Latin, or at the least "speke none englysshe but that which is cleane, polite, perfectly and articulately pronounced." The tutor must be chosen with equal care. From an ignorant or morally lax tutor a child may learn bad habits which cling to him the rest of his life; as illustration Elyot cites Quintilian's own example of the "familiar vice" which Alexander learned from his childhood tutor Leonides.

In what he says about the qualifications and duties of the master, or grammarian, Elyot again follows Quintilian closely. Those men are not grammarians, Elyot declares, who can only teach the child how to speak "congrue" Latin and how to write mechanical verses. Rather, "I name hym a gramarien, by the autoritie of Quintilian, that speakyng latine elegantly, can expounde good autours, expressynge the inuention and disposition of the mater, their stile or fourme of eloquence, explicating the figures as well of sentences as wordes, leuyng nothyng, persone, or place, named by the autour, undeclared or hidde from his scholers." In order to do these things, the master must have read not only the poets, but every other class of writers; he must also have knowledge of music, astronomy, and philosophy and must himself be eloquent ("These be well nighe the wordes of Quintilian.").

Quintilian's remarkable understanding of the child's psychology had strong appeal for Elyot and other Renaissance educators. One very important principle which they took over from the Roman author is that pupils must be treated in different ways, according to their inclinations and abilities. "The office of a tutor," Elyot writes, "is firste to knowe the nature of his pupil" and to work with that, en-

• • • • •

couraging him in his good inclinations and causing him to detest those that are bad. Having determined the boy's dispositions, the tutor must next consider how to manage his mind. Elyot agrees with Quintilian that children should be induced to learn "with praises and such praty gyftes as children delite in," rather than by violence; cruel treatment only dulls the wits of children and makes them hate the thing for which they are beaten. All children except the most backward and recalcitrant can be made better through proper handling, as described by Quintilian and quoted by Elyot: "Quintilian, instructyng an oratour, desireth suche a childe to be giuen vnto hym, whom commendation feruently stereth [stirreth], glorie prouoketh, and beinge vainquisshed wepeth. That childe (saithe he) is to be fedde with ambition, hym a litle chiding sore biteth, in hym no parte of slouthe is to be feared." Both authors are of the opinion that the child needs some relaxation from his studies, but that it must be of a wholesome kind (Elyot advocates music, painting, and carving) and restricted, lest it lead to idleness.

As regards the actual curriculum Elyot in a general way accepts the recommendations of Quintilian, though making the necessary adjustments to his own time and country. He agrees with the Roman author that the boy shoud begin his studies before the age of seven and that he should take up Greek and Latin at the same time, or Greek first, since it is "hardest to come by." Understandably, Elyot places less emphasis on formal grammar for the child than does Quintilian, in line with more modern views of education and because the English governor of the sixteenth century is finally not an orator, however important it is that he possess eloquence. The Englishman's choice of authors to be read, on the other hand, is dictated by the same principle which guides Quintilian, namely that "care is to be taken, above all things, that tender minds . . . may learn, not only what is eloquent, but, still more, what is morally good." Furthermore, in teaching the poets to young pupils, the master is to stress matter more than style, especially whatever lessons of morality are provided. Since the orator and the governor are first of all good men, and since virtue is brought to maturity by instruction, these aspirants to high office must above all things study morality. The ultimate aim of both educators is instruction in the full "circle" of knowledge—what Elyot, following Quintilian, calls *Encyclopedia.*

The Englishman's high regard for the authority of Quintilian is shown in an interesting way in the chapter from the *Governour* defending poets, which concludes, triumphantly and rather daringly, with the assertion that all authors—ancient ones, at least—are worthy to be read: "Also no noble autour, specially of them that wrate in greke or latine before xii. C. yeres passed, is nat for any cause to be omitted. For therin I am of Quintilianes opinion, that there is fewe or none auncient warke that yeldethe nat some frute or commoditie to the diligent reders."

Finally, more than anything else, Elyot must have been inspired by Quintilian's wholehearted dedication of his splendid product, the orator, to service of the state, without regard for personal glory and in spite of the attractions of retirement. "But I should desire the orator, whom I am trying to form," Quintilian writes near the end of his work, "to be a kind of *Roman wise man,* who may prove himself a true statesman, not by discussions in retirement, but by personal experience and exertions in public life."

Next to Cicero, the favorite Roman philosopher of the Renaissance was Seneca. Even the most strict Christian educators, Erasmus affirms, would find nothing to blame in the writings of Seneca, Cicero, or Quintilian, "who not only are free of obscenity, but who also order life with the most salutary precepts, and exhort to honesty." In the course of reading which Erasmus sets up for young children, Seneca is given a place of honor right after Plutarch. Seneca's essays, Erasmus declares, "are wonderfully stimulating and excite one to enthusiasm for a life of moral integrity, raise the mind of the reader from sordid cares, and especially decry tyranny everywhere." Vives also praises the ethical teachings of Seneca, but he sees them as having a somewhat different effect. "To encourage to right manners and morals," Vives advises, "Cicero is good; to ward off what is morally bad, read Seneca."

Besides being, in Elyot's words, "a mooste graue philosopher," Seneca was greatly admired for his pithy and ingenious style, which made him one of the most frequently quoted authors in the Renaissance. In Vives' apt comment, he has "elegant, sharp and brief sentences which he hurls like thonged darts." Because of his skill as a writer of *sententiae* the Roman author was assured a prominent place in anthologies of wise sayings, a type of book which enjoyed great vogue throughout the Renaissance. In Elyot's own work of this kind, *The Banquet of Sapience,* Seneca is quoted more often than any other single writer.

Seneca's direct influence in the *Governour* is considerably less than that of some of the other classical authors discussed in this section of the present study. It is confined almost exclusively to the chapters in Book II on mercy, benevolence, and friendship, where there appear extended quotations from the *De clementia* and *De beneficiis.* These outright borrowings aside, one notices in Elyot's handling of certain of the moral virtues traces of Stoic sentiment which can probably be attributed to his familiarity with the works of writers like Seneca, Cicero, and Boethius. This imprint of Stoic philosophy is most evident, naturally enough, in Elyot's treatment of such virtues as fortitude, "painfulness," and patience. His definition of patience echoes many a passage in the essays and epistles of Seneca: "Pacience is a noble vertue, appertayninge as well to inwarde gouernaunce as to exterior gouernaunce, and is the vainquisshour of iniuries, the suer defence agayne all affectes and passions of the soule, retayninge all wayes glad semblaunt [countenance] in aduersities and doloure." Cicero is the primary source for many of the "Stoic" sentiments in the *Governour,* but Elyot also recommends for the study of patience the works of Seneca, Plutarch, and Pontano. As an example of patience in suffering he cites the ordeal of Zeno the Eleatic, founder of the Stoic philosophy, and in another context he ventures the opinion (compare Milton) that Cato Uticensis, the Stoic hero, would have been far worthier than Achilles to have been the hero of Homer's epic.

Elyot's dialogue *Of the Knowledge Which Maketh a Wise Man* shows a somewhat deeper tinge of Stoicism, in the emphasis placed on the need for controlling the passions and in the arguments advanced for a providential government of the universe. In seeking to convince "Aristippus" that the Deity is just and orders all things justly, the speaker "Plato" employs some of the following markedly

Stoic arguments: that sickness, adversity, and death, "if they happen to a good man be good"; that adversity "is not so greuous, bycause it is oute of the body, and nothynge compelleth vs to suffre but our owne wylles"; and that "nothynge is miserable, but if thou doest so thynke it." (pp. 160-65)

That there should be this element of Stoicism in Elyot's ethical and religious thought is not surprising when one considers, first, the extent to which the teachings of Stoic philosophy have been assimilated into the Christian religion itself; second, Elyot's familiarity with the ethical writings of Cicero and Seneca; and last, his probable awareness of the first stirrings, in European intellectual circles, of a revival of interest in Stoicism as a way of life, which was to culminate several decades later in the writings of Justus Lipsius and Guillaume du Vair. It must be emphasized, however, that Stoicism is a minor aspect of Elyot's thought, only a few threads woven into the solid fabric of his Christian belief.

• • • • •

Few ancient authors are closer in spirit to the author of the *Governour* than is Isocrates. It is indeed striking to discover in Isocrates' orations, expressed in their original freshness, so many of the prominent ideas of Elyot and other Renaissance humanists on morality, on education and eloquence, and on the relations between princes and subjects. Isocrates may have lacked the creative intelligence and soaring idealism of Plato, but he did possess a wonderfully sane and practical outlook on life, together with a sound ethical sense and a superb style. (p. 166)

Elyot certainly appreciated the eloquence for which Isocrates was famous. The Greek author is "so swete and delectable to rede," he affirms with pardonable exaggeration, "that, after him, almost all other seme unsauery and tedious." In combination with the soundness of Isocrates' views, this pleasing style makes him all but irresistible to the author of the *Governour:*

> Isocrates, concerning the lesson of oratours, is euery where wonderfull profitable, hauynge almost as many wyse sentences as he hath wordes: and with that is so swete and delectable to rede, that, after him, almost all other seme unsauery and tedious: and in persuadynge, as well a prince, as a priuate persone, to vertue, in two very litle and compendious warkes, wherof he made the one to kynge Nicocles, the other to his frende Demonicus, wolde be perfectly kanned [known], and had in continual memorie. (p. 168)

In the preface to *The Doctrinal of Princes* Elyot declares that the "little booke" of Isocrates "in mine opinion is to be compared in counsaile and short sentence with any booke, holy scripture excepted." Although Elyot's version adheres fairly closely to the original, his style is greatly inferior to Isocrates'. Many of his sentences are overlong and structurally weak, and in general he fails to reproduce the clarity and incisiveness of the oration. The Englishman's love of sententiousness is displayed in his breaking up of Isocrates' extended passages into short paragraphs.

• • • • •

These six classical authors—Aristotle, Cicero, Plutarch, Quintilian, Seneca, and Isocrates—together with Plato . . . , are the ultimate source of most of the important ideas in the *Governour* and in Elyot's other writings. Their appeal for him lay not only in the wisdom of their views on the great questions of education, ethics, and the art of governing, but also in the lofty moral tone that sweetened these views and made them acceptable to a sincere Christian. In addition, there were exhilaration and esthetic delight to be had from reading these masters of the polished phrase and winning cadence.

It is, I think, primarily as interpreters of classical thought and as conciliators between the pagan and Christian views of life that Erasmus and the Italian humanists were useful to Elyot. This is not to minimize the importance of their contribution, for it is doubtful that without their first having shown the way, the *Governour* could ever have been written. The same thing is true, to a lesser degree, of the medieval treatises on the art of ruling, since the *Governour,* like the *Iliad* or *Paradise Lost,* is a "traditional" book which consciously incorporates what has gone before.

Finally, in this search after the sources of Elyot's thought, we must not overlook the substantial element in his writings that directly reflects the writer's broad experience in public life. To mention this feature . . . is not amiss, because one of the most important ideas Elyot took over from his favorite classical authors was that if learning is to be brought to the proper strength, it must submit to be tempered in the forge of experience. Much of the value and charm of the *Governour* and Elyot's other works comes from his authoritative handling of matters about which he speaks from personal knowledge. The sternest pragmatist among his readers would be disarmed by the statement made early in the *Governour,* that the author has everywhere taken for his guides "the thre noble maisters, reason, lernynge, and experience." (pp. 169-70)

> *John M. Major, in his* Sir Thomas Elyot and Renaissance Humanism, *University of Nebraska Press, 1964, 276 p.*

PEARL HOGREFE (essay date 1967)

[*Hogrefe is an American educator, editor, and the author of several studies probing intellectual life in Tudor England. In the following excerpt from one such work,* The Life and Times of Sir Thomas Elyot, Englishman *(1967), she summarizes Elyot's overall character and the extent of his philosophical and literary influence.*]

[When we analyze] elements in the personality of Elyot, the human being, an outstanding quality is reticence. He has left us little evidence about personal emotions, but the lack suggests reticence. Some other qualities seem clear. He was a serious-minded, almost solemn man, though bits of humor occasionally break through the crust of solemnity. His portrait, his letters, his other writings, and the lack of any tradition about his wit or humor all tell the same story. Except for his feeling toward intimate friends, there is little evidence of warmth or charm. Of course he loved books and the classical literatures, and (as he told us himself) he was by nature prone to knowledge.

Persistence was also dominant in Elyot's personality. He was persistent in personal affairs, especially in his efforts to get payment for his work as clerk of the Council and for the extra expenses on his embassy. At times he must have seemed a nuisance to Cromwell with his requests, but so far as we know that busy official never expressed impatience. He was just as persistent in his efforts to influence his king away from dishonest affections about 1531 through 1533. One may wonder why he did not suffer a positive penalty for the ideas he emphasized in his books. Perhaps Cromwell protected him in case of need. Perhaps he escaped because, unlike More, he was not important enough: the loss of his head would not have helped Henry's "great cause." Then, too, his books, with their indirect suggestions about the behavior of the king, were subtle and philosophical; they were not the sort to inflame public opinion. Elyot was persistent and also consistent in the expression of other ideas. Though some ideas deepen, as the preference for the simple life seems to do, even minor ideas in an earlier work are likely to reappear in later works without change. His desire to honor his allegiance to his king, to support conservative doctrines in religion, to follow the teachings of the early church, to recognize a difference between rhetoric and wisdom, to emphasize exercise and diet for good health, to defend aristocracy with modifications, to stress for rulers personal morality, high ethical principles, and learning with wisdom—in all these ideas he is consistent. (pp. 343-44)

In the area of human relations Elyot had many facets. He was not the hail-fellow-well-met type. Instead he seems to have had a loneliness of spirit. Though he was about the same age as his king, he surely never felt at home, even in the innocent days of that ruler, in a court where Francis Bryan and the brawny, jovial, unsubtle Charles Brandon belonged. So far as we know, he had no skill in composing songs or playing musical instruments or turning a quick and graceful compliment—even though he had been trained at an Inn of Court as the nobles are trained. He had no taste at all for the flirtatious, the carnal, or the bawdy. He was not the typical courtier.

His attitudes toward women are strange, especially for a man whose wife had studied in More's household school. He never mentioned his wife in his extant letters or referred to her in his other writings. He never made warm, general comments, like those of Vives, for example, about the wives who share and lighten the cares of their husbands—as if he were thinking of his own wife. In the *Governour,* I, vii, when he praises Livia's counsel to her husband about mercy and patience, he adds that women should have liberty to give only this kind of counsel and no other. He followed his account of Livia with a promise to write a book only for ladies and to praise Livia amply; but when he published *The Defense of Good Women* nine years later, he did not mention Livia, and his ideas were remote and conventional. In the *Governour,* I, xviii, he says that hunting hares with greyhounds might be good for women who are not afraid of injuring their beauty in sun and wind and that the sport might cause them to be less idle than they are at home. Though his comment may be true, it does not suggest a high opinion of women. When he mentions women who live in his own world he prefers them to be gentle. Since his wife studied in More's school, he must have known Margaret More Roper and her sisters; but unlike Erasmus and Vives, who wrote of Margaret with affection and admiration, he gives no sign of friendship for an intellectual woman. (pp. 346-47)

Elyot emphasized the friendship of man for man above other human relations, in the *Governour,* in other books,

and in letters and dedications. He also cherished men friends, instead of talking in generalities. In 1533 he treated Sir John Hacket as an intimate friend when he wrote him about the dark cloud hovering over England but his own resolution to follow truth and keep his allegiance to his king. He signed himself as Hacket's son and assured friend. He considered William Raynsford a special friend for years; and though he did not name personal gifts for other relatives, his nephews, or his wife, he willed Raynsford twenty links of his chain and his best gelding. For about twenty years he considered Cromwell a trusted friend, long before the latter had become powerful. He wrote him concerning all his problems, asked help, and eventually received it. While he was dedicating books to Cromwell he stressed an interest in similar studies as the basis of friendship. In the last years of Elyot's life, Sir Edward North was a cherished friend; and as Elyot considered his last reckoning, he stated that the same religious faith is the best basis friendship, in this world and in the world to come. (pp. 347-48)

In the final analysis, why is Elyot important? From the record of his life and writings it seems clear that he exerted little or no political influence. He offered no support to the unlimited power of the king, no help in the separation from Catherine of Aragon or the break from the church of Western Europe, and no aid to Henry's shrewd handling of Parliament in the 1530's to legalize his aims. He did what he could to keep Catherine queen of England and to persuade Henry into the paths of religious orthodoxy and moral and ethical behavior, but there is no evidence that his efforts had any effect. As a member of Parliament he may have had a chance to vote for the Six Articles in 1539, but one vote was unimportant when a high tide of conservatism was rising.

Elyot was not a measurable political influence because his concept of government was an ethical system. Like other humanists of his period in England, he tended to accept a monarchy; he was not one of the bolder spirits who sometimes speculated among friends about an elective system. He was not concerned about the king's power, the controls exercised by legislative bodies, or the conflict between spiritual and temporal power. If a king acted with justice, temperance, and wisdom, and if his helpers or governors did the same, all would be well. Trying to fit Elyot to the political theories or motives of so-called "practical" men, like stretching him on a bed of Procrustes, is a common practice—and a common error.

Since Elyot had little or no political influence, then, his reputation rests on his literary work. As we look back from the twentieth century, works of lesser importance are perhaps *The Castle of Health, The Banquet of Sapience,* and *A Preservative against Death. The Castle,* with its suggestions on watching symptoms, diet, exercise, and experimentation, and its rational approach without magic or charms, doubtless had a desirable effect on the bodies of some Englishmen. *The Banquet,* with its careful organization, classical and Christian sources, and appeal to readers of English instead of Latin, gave men a thoughtful occupation for moments of leisure and furnished them quotable maxims. *A Preservative against Death,* though never reprinted and not widely known, perhaps consoled a few people in a lingering illness. But if these works had never been published, the future of English life and literature would probably have remained the same.

The translations, including two little volumes that may be Elyot's though he never acknowledged them, and two other volumes (*Saint Cyprian* with Pico's *Rules of a Christian Life* and another from Plutarch on education) are not mountain peaks in a general estimate of his work. But *The Doctrinal of Princes,* from Isocrates, carries Elyot's name and a preface stating his discoveries about the English and Greek languages. It has been evaluated by an authority, James Wortham, who examined also all other translations of classical works published before 1580 [see Additional Bibliography]. Elyot used all the methods that Erasmus had used earlier in translating Greek into Latin, he says; and Elyot succeeded in giving the thought concisely and accurately, reproducing the tone and texture of the original, and thus producing a translation that at times was a work of art. It was one of the earliest, if not the earliest, translation from Greek into English, though Elyot may have checked his work by the Latin. The question of his influence on future translators seems to be unanswered, but the individual work was an achievement.

Elyot's Platonic dialogues were an important influence. Though his later *Defense of Good Women* indicated his understanding of the inductive method, the work made no real contribution in 1540 to the Socratic method, to characterization, dramatic skill, or ideas. But *Pasquil the Plain* and *Of the Knowledge Which Maketh the Wise Man* were pioneer work in England. *Pasquil* has an earthy, satiric flavor; *Of the Knowledge* often uses everyday language but rises to large philosophic patterns. Both employ the inductive method skillfully; both avoid an English setting but convey reactions to English events of the time. These two dialogues did much to establish Socratic methods and Platonic thought in England.

Elyot exerted an outstanding influence through his *Dictionary*. He was the first man in England to analyze the need for a comprehensive work dealing with the classical Latin of the Renaissance and then to attempt a volume meeting that need. Most important of all for the future influence, he explained his Latin words in English idiom. Through his own three editions, the revisions of his work by Thomas Cooper, and the continued use of his material in Cooper's *Thesaurus,* Elyot's contribution to the English language extended through the Renaissance. As no English dictionaries existed, he influenced the language used by such writers as Spencer, Marlowe, and Shakespeare.

In the late sixteenth century and after, Elyot is often praised in a general way for his learning, enlargement of the language, and elegant style. In the *Governour* he deliberately added words of classical origin to enlarge the language. In later works he used words from his own knowledge of sheep, horses, and the general details of country life as well as words of native English origin. We need a complete, reliable study of his diction and his style before we can draw conclusions about his influence on the language. But the references to him by others suggest that he gave to many writers an awareness of words and style.

The *Governour* was an important influence because it mirrored the life of Elyot's own time in ways that have not been fully recognized. Elyot, his father, and other landed gentry carried government to all parts of England; and this practical experience must have stimulated Elyot's thinking about the qualities of good governors, though he found it expedient to use classical examples. For about seven years also, while he was clerk of the Council, Elyot had an unexcelled opportunity to watch good and bad qualities in governors, including the king himself. The court of Henry VIII and Catherine of Aragon lived in a world of music, dance, and song. Sir Thomas More, with theory and practice for both men and women, had been influencing the court to a classical education, making it desirable—almost fashionable. Colet, Grocyn, Linacre, and Lily, with their study in Italy and other Mediterranean countries, had contributed. So had Erasmus and Vives with their periods of residence in England. The Inns of Court, where most gentlemen spent at least a brief time, trained their students in song, dance, and the formalities of courtly behavior. The king had made physical pursuits, especially hunting and the use of the longbow, almost a way of life. Thus the *Governour* caught and reflected a many-sided life of England.

If Elyot did nothing but organize and report these characteristics of his time—and he probably did much more—he exerted an influence of magnitude. Though his effect on future writers is hard to measure because they drew from the classics and from other writers later than Elyot, many are indebted to him for incidents, ideas, and for idiom and diction. Some men who read the *Governour* may even have tried to shape their lives by it. Probably Elyot not only mirrored the best of his own time but did much to create Elizabethan life and the Elizabethan gentleman.

At least Elyot has a firm claim to recognition for the *Governour* because he was the first man writing in England and in English to recommend for the gentleman a combination of these things: first, a classical and literary education; second, physical development, including the use of the longbow, for peace and war; third, training for service in the government; fourth, religious and ethical development; fifth, artistic skill in painting, drawing, music, and the dance; sixth, a courtly, aristocratic behavior.

Perhaps as a literary man, in England only and in the sixteenth century only, Elyot reached and influenced a greater number of people than Sir Thomas More did. This statement is not meant to suggest that Elyot was a greater man, thinker, or writer; for he must in all ways be ranked below More. But Elyot's books were in English, and he wrote on many subjects. More's greatest single work was in Latin, his English works mainly dealt with religious controversy, and under Queen Elizabeth his life and writings were not favored for public discussion. In contrast, circumstances made it possible for Elyot to reach many people.

As a writer, Elyot lacked the creative imagination that prompted Erasmus' *Praise of Folly* and More's *Utopia*. He was not usually at home with irony or satire, though he used effective touches of it in *Pasquil the Plain.* He could not make a character live, as Erasmus was able to do, but his aims did not usually require characterization. He lacked the largeness of vision and the free play of mind that prompts men to "a speculative philosophy among friends," an intellectual mountain climbing to discover only where thought might lead. A writer who lacks these qualities may compensate by revealing himself, so that through him others discover themselves. But Elyot either lacked depths of self or he was incurably reticent—perhaps by nature and training, perhaps by the troubled times in which he lived. Hence he wrote nothing that would be chosen with no dissent as one of the great books of the world. He was for an age, not for all time. But in his age he exerted a sound, substantial influence, largely through his Platonic dialogues and Platonic thought, through his *Dictionary* and its two later editions, perhaps through his *Doctrinal of Princes* and his general concern with style and diction, and through *The Book Named the Governour.* (pp. 349-54)

> *Pearl Hogrefe, in her* The Life and Times of Sir Thomas Elyot, Englishman, *Iowa State University Press, 1967, 410 p.*

MORRISS HENRY PARTEE (essay date 1970)

[*Partee is an American Scholar of English Renaissance literature. In the following excerpt, he traces Elyot's perplexing estimation of poetry to its source of ambiguity in Plato's aesthetics.*]

Sir Thomas Elyot's discussion of poetry in *The Boke Named the Governour* (1531) and in *The Defence of Good Women* (1540) antedates by about fifty years the controversy in England over the value of poetry. His comments directly influenced such later critics as William Webbe and Sir Philip Sidney. But Elyot's use of philosophic authority contains an apparent discrepancy. This man, who studied and revered Plato, cites the philosopher to defend poetry in the *Governour.* Later, with no apologies, he alludes to Plato to condemn poetry in *The Defence of Good Women.* Similar examples of this inconsistency abound. Thomas Nashe, Stephen Gosson, and Thomas Lodge cite Plato's famous banishment of poetry from the well-run state. On the other hand, Sir Philip Sidney, William Webbe, and George Chapman think that Plato generally approves of poetry. The confusion arises not from an unavailability of his dialogues, but rather from an ambiguity inherent in Plato's aesthetics. Although the spurious *Axiochus* was the only Platonic dialogue translated into English during the sixteenth century, Marsilio Ficino's translation of the dialogues into Latin, finished in 1468 and published in 1484, had made Plato readily accessible to Western scholars. Therefore, the present examination of Elyot's ambivalent interpretation will illustrate the difficulty that Plato's aesthetics presented to the Renaissance and indeed to every critic since Plato's time.

The underlying tenets of Elyot's poetics as well as his citations of Plato reveal a basic sympathy with the philosopher's attitude toward art. The conflict between a love of poetry's beauty and a demand for mortality in art leads both men into a complex and almost contradictory statement of aesthetics. Since Plato leaves no single work devoted to art, his thought has caused unusually diverse interpretations. His aesthetics possesses a unity only within the context of the dialogues as a whole. On one hand, Plato lauds the poet's divine inspiration, and recognizes a legitimate role for myths and selected excerpts of poetry in the education of the young. On the other hand, he banishes poets from the best state imaginable. Elyot's seeming contradiction in citing Plato comes simply from his endorsing the literal statements of these dialogues with little attempt to probe into their meaning or context. But Elyot maintains—as did Plato—a consistent attitude towards poetry's value to man and society. Although Elyot ultimately accepts art, he agrees with Plato's primary concern that poetry be judged by moral standards. (pp. 327-28)

The complexity of Plato's statement on art has prevented even modern scholars from fully recognizing the basis for Elyot's interpretation of Plato. For instance, John M. Major argues that despite Elyot's broad knowledge of the dialogues, his comments on Plato's aesthetics show a mistaken reliance on the philosopher [see excerpt dated 1964]. Major assumes that Plato's expulsion of the poets in the *Republic* 10 represents a consistent position with regard to his other statements on poetry. Then, referring to Elyot's apparently paradoxical interpretation of Plato, he states, "If ever there were proof of Elyot's almost instinctive deference to the authority of Plato, it is here in this fantastic split attitude of his toward poetry, in which he invokes the philosopher's name first in order to vindicate poetry and then to condemn it. In the process, incidentally, he manages to anticipate most of the key arguments used by both sides in the controversy over poetry that arose later in the century." Elyot, however, no more has a "fantastic split attitude" than does Plato. Although rhetorically motivated, Elyot correctly states that the *Republic* banishes all poets. But he does not grapple with Plato's argument in *Republic* 10 that poetry misleads the ignorant and arouses the baser emotions of the citizens. Immediately limiting his censure of poetry in *The Defence of Good Women* to the clearly immoral, Elyot's comments here are largely consistent with those in the *Governour.* By not recognizing that Plato's explicit condemnation of poetry runs counter to his tacit sanction of its beauty, Elyot exposes a critical problem that even Sir Philip Sidney's more extensive examination of Plato in the *Defence of Poesie* does not resolve completely.

First, the *Governour.* Here Elyot alludes to that side of Plato which endeared him to poets and to the defenders of poetry. After lamenting the fortunes of poetry in England, Elyot cites the respect that antiquity gave to poetry: "Poetry was the first philosophy that euer was knowen: wherby men from their childhode were brought to the raison howe to lyue well, lernynge therby nat onely maners and naturall affections, but also the wondefull werkes of nature, mixting serious mater with thynges that were pleasaunt: as it shall be manifest to them that shall be so fortunate to rede the noble warkes of Plato and Aristotle, wherin he shall fynde the autoritie of poetes frequently alleged." Elyot may have in mind either Plato's implicit respect for poets or his explicit theory of education. When quoting poetry in the course of an argument, Plato almost always gives poets and their work high praise. In addition, although never admitting value to an entire work of art, Plato recognizes that some poetic sayings encourage a commendable harmony in the soul.

Elyot then mentions Plato's doctrine of poetic inspiration, a theory that links Muse, poet, and audience in a chain of divine influence. According to Elyot, Cicero and Plato hold that poetry springs from divine inspiration: "In poetes was supposed to be science misticall and inspired, and therfore in latine they were called *Vates,* which worde signifyeth as moche as prophetes. And therfore Tulli in his Tusculane questyons [*Tusculanae disputationes*] supposeth that a poete can nat abundantly expresse verses sufficient and complete, or that his eloquence may flowe without labour wordes wel sounyng and plentuouse, without celestiall instinction, whiche is also by Plato ratified." Although Plato indeed pays tribute to the inexplicable beauty of poetry, Elyot fails to recognize that Plato feels even the most noble inspiration to be beyond the poet's control. Evidence of Plato's reservations about poetry appears throughout his comments on inspiration. For instance, the *Ion,* a dialogue of great influence in the Renaissance, attacks the rhapsodist, the reciter of poetry, for presuming to have knowledge; the discussion of poetic inspiration is secondary. Similarly, the poet may have divine madness, but does not understand what he says. Only the *Phaedrus* 245 and *Symposium* 209 attribute to the poet an understanding similar to that of the philosopher.

Thus, in the *Governour* Elyot legitimately cites Plato's major, if qualified, approval of poetry. In *The Defence of Good Women,* on the other hand, Elyot recognizes Plato's unqualified mistrust of poetry, a doctrine found only in *Republic* 10. He follows a Platonic argument perhaps known to the Renaissance chiefly through Saint Augustine. In the *Defence,* Candidus, probably reflecting Elyot's attitude towards women, attacks Caninus's use of poetic authority against the honor of women:

> The authors whom ye so moche do set by, for the more part were poetes, which sort of persons among the latines & grekes were neuer had but in smal reputation. For I could neuer rede that in any weale publike of notable memory, Poetes were called to any honorable place, office, or dignite. Plato out of the publike weale whiche he had deuysed, wolde haue all poetes vtterly excluded. Tulli, who next vnto Plato excelled all other in vertue and eloquence, wolde not haue in his publyke weale any poetes admitted. The cause why they were soo lyttell estemed was, for as moche as the more parte of theyr inuencions consyted in leasynges, or in sterynge vp of wanton appetytes, or in pourynge oute, in raylynge, theyr poyson of malyce. For with theyr owne goddes and goddesses were they so malaparte, that with theyr aduoutries they fylled great volumes.

So Elyot not only states that Plato banishes poets, but echoes his chief objections—poets tell lies, they cater to base appetites, and they tell false tales about the gods. Elyot even refers to the lack of respect which cities have accorded to poets. Here, of course, Elyot qualifies his praise of the poet's moral lessons in the *Governour,* by suggesting that some men may incorrectly interpret the artistic presentation of immorality.

Nevertheless, Elyot, like almost all Renaissance critics, ignores the epistemological argument that Plato uses to attack poetry. When considering poetry as imitation of the Forms of virtuous action rather than as a copying of the physical world, Plato has given poetry qualified support. But in *Republic* 10.595-603 Plato analyzes poetry's relationship to the physical world, and naturally he finds poetry lacking substance. Plato reasons that a god makes the idea of a bed, a carpenter imitates this idea, and the artist copies the carpenter's product. Plato would—as Elyot states—"haue all poetes vtterly excluded" when poetry deceives the young and the inexperienced. After proposing this theory of imitation which demands complete exclusion of poetry, Plato continues his argument by stating in *Republic* 10.603-608 that all poetry, including that of Homer, panders to the lower part of man's soul.

Ignoring Plato's disparagement of poetry as an imitation of an imitation, Elyot would answer the philosopher's objections to immorality in poetry. Like Plato, he bases his mistrust of poets on the likelihood of their encouraging vice. Poetry may, however, stimulate virtue as well. More

tolerant than Plato, Candidus condemns poets only "whan they excede the termes of honestye. But if they make verses conteynynge quicke sentences, voyd of rybauldry, or in the commendation of vertue, some praty allegory, or do set forthe any notable story, than do I set by them as they be well worthy." Obviously not probing beneath the surface of Plato's final statement in *Republic* 10, Elyot's argument parallels the tentative acceptance of poetry in *Republic* 2 and 3. In *The Defence of Good Women,* therefore, Elyot would not banish all poets. He condemns only poetry devoted to the "sterynge vp of wanton appetytes."

Elyot has shown familiarity with three aspects of Plato's aesthetics: his love of poetry, his doctrine of inspiration, and his reservations about the value of poetry. An examination of his underlying principles shows, however, that Elyot consistently gives poetry more credit than does Plato. The *Governour,* like *The Defence of Good Women,* evaluates poetry in moral terms. But the *Governour* defends poetry against accusations of its occassional immorality like those suggested in the *Defence.* Despite their common orientation to morality, Elyot differs from Plato on the permissible amount of indiscriminate reading of the ancients. Plato would censure questionable passages from all past, present, and future poetry. Elyot would allow the reader to interpret and to censor for himself passages of dubious moral worth: "But sens we be nowe occupied in the defence of Poetes, it shall nat be incongruent to our mater to shewe what profite may be taken by the diligent reding of auncient poetes, contrary to the false opinion, that nowe rayneth, of them that suppose that in the warkes of poetes is contayned nothynge but baudry, (suche is their foule worde of reproche), and unprofitable leasinges." He consistently recognizes—as does Plato—that poetry may contain material besides ribaldry and lies. Elyot uses the presence of some virtuous passages to defend poetry against a somewhat hostile environment. The comments of Plato, on the other hand, spring from his defense of philosophy against a culture that commonly regarded poetry as one of the highest authorities. Accordingly, even morality in poetry cannot excuse its antagonism to philosophy.

Elyot assigns wider boundaries to the province of good poetry than does Plato. Throughout the *Republic* and the *Laws,* Plato attacks "realistic" art; only encomia and poetry directly encouraging excellence should be allowed. Elyot, on the other hand, gives the common man broader powers of interpretation. The imaginative presentation of evil deeds serves as a warning: "First, comedies, whiche they suppose to be a doctrinall of rybaudrie, they be undoutedly a picture or as it were a mirrour of man's life, wherin iuell [evil] is nat taught but discouered; to the intent that men beholdynge the promptnes of youth unto vice, the snares of harlotts and baudes laide for yonge myndes, the disceipte of seruantes, the chaunces of fortune contrary to mennes expectation, they beinge therof warned may prepare them selfe to resist or preuente occasion." By relying heavily on man's critical ability, Elyot makes the presentation of vice an integral part of poetry's moral teaching. Plato, however, condemns representations of evil, for the soul has no faculty for rejecting false impressions once implanted. (pp. 329-33)

In short, Elyot agrees with Plato that poetry must be judged for its moral worth; beauty is a secondary consideration. They are acutely aware that bad poetry does exist, and both warn against ribaldry. Similarly, both men praise poetic inspiration to some extent. Finally, they attribute some authority to poets in education and tacitly approve of poetry by their frequent allusions. The two men disagree primarily on the proper scope of poetry. Elyot divides poetry into the good and the bad; Plato into that which reveals truth and that which only mirrors the physical world. As a result, Elyot can allow complex and ambiguous art, for the wise man will easily reject the irrelevant or the evil. Plato, on the other hand, allows only poetic excerpts which directly produce harmony and virtue in the hearers.

To conclude, Elyot's apparently contradictory citation of Plato stems from a problem inherent in the philosopher's statement of aesthetics. Like most Renaissance critics, Elyot recognizes that Plato acutely felt the power and beauty of poetry. Yet he is also aware of Plato's strict regulations against immoral or frivolous poetry. But because of the tendency of the Renaissance mind to synthesize diverse ideas, Elyot glosses over a distinction between the divine beauty of poetry and the effects of poetry on fallible men, a problem never fully solved even by Plato. (p. 335)

> *Morriss Henry Partee, "Sir Thomas Elyot on Plato's Aesthetics," in* Viator, *Vol. 1, 1970, pp. 327-35.*

M. J. MacDONALD (lecture date 1971)

[*In the following excerpt from a lecture given in 1971 before the First International Congress of Neo-Latin Studies, MacDonald maintains that* The Governour *essentially promotes Elyot's defense of the English vernacular as a literary language.*]

I should like to sketch how one English humanist handled the problem of using a vernacular which he knew was inadequate, and which he felt it was his duty to augment and purify.

Thomas Elyot spent his early years as a legal clerk in the service of his father; in 1522, perhaps because of his considerable practical experience in the local courts, Cardinal Wolsey appointed him Chief Clerk of the King's Council. But with Wolsey's fall in 1529 Elyot found himself unemployed. In 1530 Henry VIII granted him a knighthood as a gesture for his years of unrewarded service; and in 1531 Thomas Berthelet, the king's printer, printed Elyot's *The Boke Named the Governour* which was dedicated to the king himself.

Now in *The Governour* Elyot is obviously persuing the most powerful of patrons. The text praises monarchy as the finest image of the order of creation; and Elyot sets out to describe what he calls "the fourme of a iuste public weale" in terms of the education of a young man: the description begins in the nursery and concludes in the counsel-house with the young Governour participating in the actual administration of the nation. Some modern scholars have found little new or out of the ordinary in *The Governour*, and many have classed it simply as a kind of early sixteenth-century *speculum principis*. Some have praised sections like the discussion of prudence in terms of the "dance"; but most have found Elyot's prose repetitive, tedious, and highly latinate. And Elyot is often tedious, repetitive, and highly latinate. But he is writing a

book which is the first of its kind in English. Furthermore he has a positive critical concern for the condition of the "vulgar tunge"—after all he is the same man who succeeded in compiling the first Latin-English dictionary in 1538.

Elyot's first concern in the *The Governour* is language, the precise and effective use of words. But if we are to take Caxton and some of the early sixteenth-century English printers and translators seriously about their attitude toward the vernacular, then we must conclude that English was in very bad shape at the beginning of the sixtheenth-century. English enjoyed little prestige as a literary language. In contrast to the "elegant" Latin of classical *auctores* and the maturity of French, Italian, and German, English is often described as "rude", "gross", "base", "low", and "barbarus". Caxton apologizes for "this symple and rude english" and complains that the vernacular is cluttered with "wordes/ which in these dayes be neither usyd nor understanden". And as late as 1527, Thomas Wyatt in his translation of Plutarch's *De tranquillitate animi* complains that English does not have enough words to convey the "grace" of the original. But in *The Governour* Elyot wastes no time in reciting these commonplace tags; rather he focuses on his English audience who "perchance for the more parte haue nat ben trayned in lerning . . .".

We must remember that in 1531 the man who read little Latin and no Greek had a very slender booklist from which to choose. To be more exact, I have counted only twelve translations printed in English before 1531 of what might be considered major classical texts. And these range in extent from Caxton's edition of Aesop's *Fables* to a 1530 edition of Julius Caesar's *Commentaryes*. And so, Elyot writes mainly for this vernacular audience; and he styles himself in one instance not as a learned authority but as one who like a "good grammarian" can "expounde good autours, expressynge the inuention and disposition of the matter, their stile or fourme of eloquence, explicating the figures as well of sentences as wordes, leuying nothing, person or place named by the author undeclared or hid from his scholars". And again he cautions that the young student should be exposed to only "pure and elegant Latin" and "none english but that which is cleane, polite, perfectly and articulately pronounced". His choice of words here is interesting. At first glance he seems to provide different standards for Latin and English. But what he does is to provide a series of synonyms which expresses the same ideal: in his *Dictionary* he defines "*elegans*" as "fresh, gorgyous, clean, polite" and "*elegantia* as gorgeousness, cleaness, beauty in words". And so, perhaps hopefully, he attempts to translate the quality of pure and elegant Latin into the vernacular.

Elyot's posture as the "good grammarian" and his method of handling the "vernacular" have much in common with Valla's *Elegantiae,* that authoritative textbook on Latin style and usage. Valla's *Elegantiae* was never printed in England; but in Erasmus's *De ratione studii,* Valla heads the list of authorities on style; in the 1520's the *Elegantiae* was used as a basic text for lectures on grammar at Oxford; Wolsey lists the *Elegantiae* as a required text in the curriculum for his new school at Ipswich; and John Dorne's record of book sales for 1520 indicates the *Elegantiae* was very popular. The *Elegantiae* is not concerned mainly with those secondary aspects of style like ornament and embellishment, but rather with those primary aspects of language like grammar, syntax, and meaning, which are

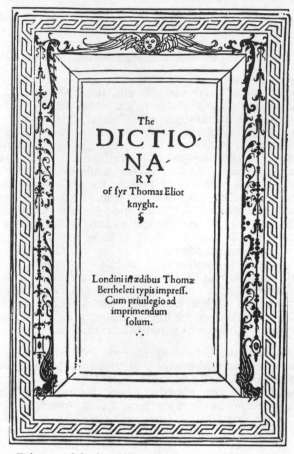

Title page of the first edition of Elyot's Dictionary *(1538).*

the basis of clarity. . . . The *Elegantiae* grows out of a concern for the precise use of words into a marvellous storehouse of knowledge and experience. And, I would suggest, it is this ideal and method which lie at the heart of an early vernacular text like *The Governour*. *The Governour* is built around a distinction between *publica, populus,* and *plebs,* and between *mens* and *intellectus;* and Elyot's critique of contemporary English education is based on a distinction between "orators, rhetoricians, and declamators". The orator is defined by his encyclopedic knowledge, whereas "they which do only teach rhetorike, which is the science whereby is taught an artificial form of speaking, wherein is the power to move, persuade, and delight, or by that science only do speak or write, without any addition of other sciences, ought to be named rhetoricians, declamators, artificial speakers or any name other than orators". (pp. 365-67)

Every major discussion, every chapter in *The Governour* begins with a discussion of the proper word, what Elyot calls the "trewe signification". It seems as if he is constantly developing his medium as he writes.

In addition he is aware that he is providing a model of vernacular composition and an argument in defence of the need for translating the classical sources of wisdom and knowledge into English. Translation is a national duty:

> lyke as the Romanes translated the wisdom of Greece in to their city, we may, if we liste, bring the learning and wisdom of them both in to this realm of England, by

the translation of their works, since like enterprise hath been taken by Frenchmen, Italians, and Germans, to our no little reproach for our negligence and sloth.

In this sense, *The Govenour* emerges as a contribution to a *translatio studii* into England.

To conclude what is just a mere sketch, it is interesting to compare *The Governour* to *A glasse of the truthe,* a curious piece of Henrician propaganda which appeared in 1530. The author, who is anonymous, declares in his introduction:

> You shall have here gentle readers, a small dialogue between the lawyer and the divine: wherein if there shall lack such eloquence, such drift or arguments and convenience of reasons, as peraventure were requisite; yet we pray you to content yourself with this our rudeness, declaring the pure truth alone . . .

In this text the author characterizes the "vulgar tunge" as a suitable vehicle for the "pure truth"; and throughout the dialogue references to "the plain truth" refer to a style which can "speak reason" and "is pithily spoken". The language with which Caxton, Norton, Barclay, Whitford, and Wyatt had struggled, and which they had so often labelled "rude" and "gross" becomes in this piece of propaganda the vehicle for pure truth and meaning alone. The publication of *The Governour* in 1531 was significant literary event because it represented a positive attempt to purify and augment, in humanist terms, the language which a text like *A glass of the truthe* took for granted. And if we are to understand the development of English prose in the sixteenth-century, and appreciate the great strides made between, for example, the publication of Caxton's translations and Ascham's *Toxophilus* and Sidney's *Apology,* we must appreciate the influence of texts like Valla's *Elengantiae* and, of course, Erasmus' *De Copia* on moulding the ideal of literary "elegance" for which Elyot strives in *The Governour.* (pp. 367-68)

> *M. J. MacDonald, "Elyot's 'The Boke Named the Governour' and the Vernacular," in* Acta Conventus Neo-Latini Lovaniensis: Proceedings of the First International Congress of Neo-Latin Studies, *edited by J. IJsewijn and E. Keßler, Leuven University Press, 1973, pp. 365-69.*

K. J. WILSON (essay date 1976)

[*In the following excerpt Wilson assesses Elyot through glimpses of the author's own prefaces to his works.*]

In 1531, Sir Thomas Elyot, his knighthood fresh upon him, asked: "What so perfectly expresseth a man as doctrine?" That a man's learning is a sufficient, indeed a perfect, expression of himself is an idea which represents Elyot in a characteristic and appealing attitude. In *The Governor* Elyot's private desire for authority, which would trouble all his works, coincided with the public necessity that the governor's authority be recognized. In the first two books he attempted to resolve the tension in his own attitude toward authority and experience precisely by determining their proper balance in the governor. *Speculum principis, speculum Eliotae.* The governor's understanding "is nat of any necessite annexed to doctrine," Elyot conceded; it is theoretically possible to rule in wisdom without learning. But what then is the office or duty of him who does possess doctrine, of the tutor or friend of the governor, for example? Elyot's response could not be more definitive: "The ende of all doctrine and studie is good counsayle."

For Elyot counsel is the center toward which "all doctrines (whiche by some autours be imagined in the fourme of a cerkle,) do sende their effectes." Counsel represents the perfection of doctrine as conceived by Elyot—the embodiment of the union of authority and experience. It is the end, the effect, of a rational process: *consultation*, "wherin counsaile is expressed . . . ." Consultation, we come to understand in the dialogue *Of the Knowledge Which Maketh a Wise Man*, is for Elyot the noblest human act. It is to this end that the reason should be educated: by consultation to weigh present experience with the authority of the past,

> than to investigate or enquire exquisitely the fourme and reason of the affaire, and in that studye to be holly resolved so effectually, that they whiche be counsailours may beare with them out of the counsayle house, as it were on their sholders, nat onely what is to be folowed and exployted, but also by what meanes or wayes hit shall be pursued. . . . Wherfore counsayle being compact of [reason, goodness, and virtue], may be named a perfecte Capitayne, a trusty companyon, a playne and unfayned frende.

The merit of this passage from the last pages of *The Governor* is two-fold. Not only is it a brilliant synthesis whereby the governor's study is justified in terms of the public good and, simultaneously, whereby Elyot's commitment to learning is directed outward into the world (these objectives he has pursued throughout the whole book)—it is not only a synthesis but also, or perhaps therefore, a moment of exultation. His profession of faith connects with a general utility.

Nevertheless, in the concluding pages the crystal forms imperfectly. Authority remains elusive, and Elyot's synthesis is flawed by his fear of exclusion, of unrecognized excellence. It is essential "that in every thinge concerning a publike weale no good counsailour be omitted or passed over, but that his reason therein be hard [i.e., heard] to an ende." The note struck here at the end of *The Governor* and intermittently throughout the book, whether plaintive or bitter one cannot be sure, suggests a strain in Elyot's character which becomes increasingly marked in the next decade and which has profound effects upon his writing. (pp. ix-xi)

In reading through his works one notices a recurrent formal element—Elyot was an inveterate prefacer. (p. xiv)

The preface or "Proheme" to *The Governor* is a lavish compliment to Henry VIII. Even on this occasion Elyot expresses the characteristic tension of *The Governor* between the authority of personal experience and that of classical authors:

> I have gathered as well of the sayenges of moste noble autours (grekes and latynes) as by myne owne experience, I beinge continually trayned in some dayly affaires of the publike weale of this your moste noble realme all mooste from my chylhode.

In dedicating to the King the "fyrste frutes of my studye," Elyot introduces a metaphor which will become habitual with him; here it ushers in the disingenuous exempla from Plutarch of the "pore husbondman" whose offering was not rejected by the Persian king, Artaxerxes, and from Horace of Choerilus, whom Alexander honorably retained "all though that the poete was but of a small estimation." If this supplicating is merely standard (Elyot would do better subsequently), the request for royal protection with which the preface closes is somehow too vehement. One feels the current of anxiety in the plea that the King defend "this litle warke agayne the assaultes of maligne interpretours whiche fayle nat to rente and deface the renoume of wryters, they them selfes beinge nothinge to the publike weale profitable." It is significant that even at this early stage in his career Elyot sees his writing as a public act and hence subject to detraction.

The Doctrinal of Princes, is dedicated generally, that is, to the reader, and perhaps specifically to Henry; for the work is a translation of Isocrates' oration to his pupil Nicocles after the latter became king. The preface conveys an attractive self-image, that of the serviceable translator, while revealing the deeper intent, as in *The Governor*, of giving authoritative counsel. Elyot begins, "This little booke (whiche in mine opinion) is to be compared in counsaile and short sentence with any booke, holy scripture excepted, I have translated out of greeke . . . ." He uses the preface to establish himself as an authority in classical languages. The chief cause of this exercise, Elyot continues, is "that thei, which do not understande greeke nor latine, shoulde not lacke the commoditee and pleasure" of the oration. But the very choice of this work indicates his persistent fascination with the governor as an individual and with the practice of good counsel. To translate Isocrates was to provide *at once* "profitable counsaile and lernyng. Fare ye well." The incomplete assimilation of personal desires within social aims in his literary works is equally apparent when one reads Elyot's early public prefatory letters in light of the private ones.

Pasquil the Playne (1533) was something of a literary experiment and a new face. Although for its first appearance the author remained anonymous, Elyot obviously expected to be recognized. Peter Quince the carpenter was schooled on prologues such as this.

> Sens plainnes in speking is of wise men commended/ and diverse do abhorre longe prohemes of Rhetorike: I have sette out this mery treatise, wherin plainnes and flateri do come in trial/ in suche wise as none honest man wil be therwith offended.

Elyot implies that he intends to be plain and brief in his preface, and that for this occasion he, like Pasquil, "is become rude and homely." His intention is to share with the reader a merry matter which "savoreth somewhat of wisedome. . . ." The preface itself is at great pains to create an aura of candor, the virtue which Pasquil embodies, adopting the tone of light acerbity found also in the dialogue. In short, the preface, like the dialogue, in giving candid advice on the snares of flattery, playfully appropriates an image of authority. Pasquil does speak his mind. Against the boldness of this gesture we must measure the anonymity of publication and the request that gentle readers defend Pasquil "ageynste venemous tunges and overthwart wittis. . . ." It is characteristic of Elyot's writing that even a jest such as the pasquinade is centered on the question of estimation and authority.

In the "Proheme" to the dialogue *Of the Knowledge Which Maketh a Wise Man* (1533), we find Elyot more outspoken, querulous, and, I think, more personal than he appears in his earlier prefaces. In this preface, written in the style of an open letter, Elyot reaffirms his commitment to learning in language which echoes the preface to *The Governor.* ... (pp. xiv-xvi)

The most revealing characteristic of the preface is that it links the personal issue of the value of Elyot's counsel with the subject of the dialogue. "Touchynge the title of my boke," he writes, "wher in [wisdom] resteth fewe menne be sure." The bounds of the inquiry are precisely those one would expect from the king's counselor recently returned from abroad. Is wisdom to be found in authority or in experience?

> One sayeth it is in moche lernynge and knowledge. An other affirmeth/ that they whiche do conducte the affayres of greatte princis or countrayes, be onely wyse men.

And to this tension, only tentatively resolved in *The Governor,* a third and homely alternative is now added:

> Nay saythe the thyrde, he is wysest that leste dothe meddle, and can sytte quietly at home and tourne a crabbe, and looke onely unto his owne busynesse.

The image of wisdom in retirement was to have a growing appeal to Elyot. In this preface, and indeed in the dialogue, it is but slightly entertained. For, as the preface shows, he is still in the fray. "And levynge malycious reders with their incurable fury," he plunges on.

The Bankette of Sapience, the commonplace book of an *érudit privé,* shows Elyot at his ease among familiar scholarly pleasures. The book is a thoroughly traditional compilation of moralistic counsels. It is also, for Elyot, the most comfortable of literary endeavors, a translation. Sayings on subjects ranging from abstinence to wrath are assembled, in alphabetical order, from the great books and the good book. The prefatory Elyot is also traditional. He is very courtly, especially in his modesty, and there is a studied charm in his little conceit of the banquet. It is dedicated "To the Kynge."

> I have provyded this lyttell banket (so is this lytle treatise intitled) composed of sondry wyse councels, gathered by me out of the warkes of moste excellent persons, as wel faithfull as gentyles. And lyke as in this lustye tyme, thinges do appere in sondrye dilectable colours and facions, so in this lytle boke shall your grace and other readers behold sentences sundry and dyvers, whiche I do applye unto bankettyng dishes, made and seasoned by Sapience her self, and served forth to the table by them, whiche dyd wryte or pronounce them. And as for me, I have no more parte in the bankette, nor deserve any more praise therfore, than one of them that beareth a torche before every course whan they come from the dresser: And yet where there is suche abundance, I may perchance for my labour have the revertion or scrappes of som of the dishes. ...

If the intent of the book is transparent, it is also, in the directness of its address, audacious. One begins to understand why Elyot's detractors could call him presumptuous. (pp. xvii-xviii)

When Elyot published his Latin-English *Dictionary* in 1538, he dedicated it to Henry. In one of his longest and grandest prefaces he celebrates the King's divine influence. The mere presence of the King, we are told, increases men's powers, a grace which Elyot himself has lately experienced. Having got to the letter M when his project came to the King's attention, Elyot found his understanding indeed augmented by a word of favor from his majesty. The result, by the logic of this complimentary conceit, was that he realized how poor what he had written so far was! He therefore completed the alphabet with greater diligence and then appended an addition to the first part. Henry had certainly taken an interest in the dictionary, to the extent that he commended Elyot on his venture and offered him use of his library. As the little world of the preface makes clear, the bestowal of royal favor could elevate Elyot to the most radiant peak of satisfaction. In the excitement of approval, Elyot pours himself out. Highly metaphorical language always indicates strong feeling in Elyot's writing. ... Looking back over all the difficulties of compiling a dictionary from innumerable sources, he recalls the stations of his travail:

> I was attached [*sic*] with an horrible feare, remembryng my dangerous enterprise (I being of so smal reputation in lernyng in comparison of them, whom I have rehersed) as well for the difficultie in the true expressynge the lyvely sence of the latine wordes, as also the importable labours in serching, expending and discussing the sentences of ancient writers. This premeditation abated my courage, and desperation was even at hand to rent all in pieces that I had written, had nat the beames of your royal majestie entred into my harte, by remembraunce of the comforte, whiche I of your grace had lately receyved, wherwith my spirite was revyved, and hath set up the sayle of good courage, and under your graces governance, your highnesse being myn onely mayster, and styrer of the shyppe of all my good fortune, I am entred the goulfe of disdaynous envie, havynge fynished for this tyme this symple Dictionarie. ...

Elyot was not only gratified by "the good estimation that your grace retayneth of my poore lerning and honestie"; he was rather content with his new *Dictionary* itself, by the aid of which "menne beinge studious, may understande better the latine tunge in syxe monethes, than they mought have doone afore in thre yeres. ..."

Elyot's expansiveness in the preface to the 1538 edition of the *Dictionary* arises, it seems, not from any material change in his fortunes (that was to come later) but from the royal recognition of his personal talent. A dictionary is indeed the perfect vessel for his learning. It contains all his interests. The translator and pedagogue, the student of law and medicine, the compiler of ancient wisdom, the serviceable counselor, Elyot has found the form toward which all his work had tended. The dictionary is distilled, defined doctrine. Its purely utilitarian purpose is to make accessible the knowledge of Latin culture. For a variety of reasons, then, the 1538 preface glows with self-confidence. In lieu of the familiar need of "quietness of mind," Elyot speaks boldly and responsibly here of "all the powers of my wytte and body."

For the enlarged 1542 edition of the *Dictionary,* renamed the *Bibliotheca Eliotae,* Elyot refined the exuberant preface of the first edition. In correcting and amplifying the *Dictionary* he seems to have grown more fully aware of how well his labor suited him. He is served not only by his learning "but also with a newe spirite of hardynesse, receyved by the often remembrance of [the King's] gracious sayde comforte...." To the reviser of the *Dictionary* the humanist ideals of *copia* and compendiousness must have appeared attainable at last, and in his new preface Elyot exults in the range of human knowledge and his own ability to survey it. (pp. xx-xxii)

The querulous themes of earlier prefaces are still present but in heightened colors and, one might say, nobler forms. Elyot justifies himself with gracious moderation, without an edge to his tone. In appealing for Henry's assistance he calls to witness "the great numbres of wonderfull lerned men" throughout history, "of whom dyverse ... were advanced to dignities, many enryched, none unrewarded." By now the King has rewarded him; more significantly, Elyot has rewarded himself with a measure of esteem. (pp. xxii-xxiii)

Between the first two editions of the dictionary, Elyot published, in 1541, *The Image of Governance.* Though he had composed or translated this life of Alexander Severus nine years earlier, the preface itself belongs to the period of Elyot's lexicography. It is significant that, after a succession of dedications to the King and to Cromwell, Elyot addresses the present work, with a certain panaché, "To Al the Nobilitie of This Flouryshynge Royalme of Englande...." The preface is often cited as a source for the chronology of Elyot's writings. A sensitive, extended self-evaluation, it focuses the image of the man projected by his letters. Particularly fascinating is the way the chronology of works is involved with Elyot's answer to detractors, and with the conflict between writing and the pursuit of wealth and reputation—in short, the way the preface reveals the mature stage of Elyot's struggle with the lifelong problem of authority and experience in the man of learning.

> I do dedicate [this book] unto you noble lordis, gentil knightes, and other in the state of honour or worship, as beinge moste redy to be advanced to governance under your Prince: so that your vertues be correspondent unto your fortunes. Yet am I not ignoraunt that diverse there be, which do not thankfully esteme my labours, dispraysinge my studies as vayne and unprofitable, sayinge in derision, that I have nothing wonne therby, but the name onely of a maker of bokes, and that I sette the trees, but the printer eateth the fruites. In dede al though disdaine and envy do cause them to speke it, yet will I not deny, but that they saye truly: for yf I wold have employed my study about the increace of my private commodity, which I have spent in wrytinge of bokes for others necessity, few men doubt (I suppose) that do knowe me, but that I shuld have attayned or this tyme to have ben moche more welthy, and in respect of the worlde in a more estimation.

The preface has the settled sobriety of a legal testament. It asks no special favors. Elyot claims his works, desiring to be judged by them. (p. xxiii)

In this retrospective view Elyot sees himself as a scholar and tutor. His personal growth during the past decade has clarified, but not changed, his ideals. The reader is meant to discern a common origin for the *Image* and the *Governor.*

> Finally, all [Alexander Severus's] lyfe is a wonderfull myrrour, if it be truely radde and justely considered, whiche if ye do often loke on, ye maye thereby attyre

your self in suche facion, as men shall therfore have you in more favour and honour, than if ye had on you as riche a garmente as the greatte Turke hathe any.

In their aim of learned counsel these two works characterize Elyot's writing as a whole. His parting request of the nobility of England is perhaps his briefest expression of a sentiment found in virtually all the prefaces:

> Onely for my good wyll in translatynge it for you, I desyre your gentyll report and assystence ageynst them, whiche do hate all thynges, whyche please not their fantasyes.

The deepest inner conflicts are never resolved, nor perhaps could they be. Yet it is gratifying to observe that Elyot's hard-won self-assertion and *amour propre....* which we find in the prefaces to the *Dictionary* and the preface to the *Image,* were as permanent as such attainments can be. (pp. xxiv-xxv)

> K. J. Wilson, in an introduction to "The Letters of Sir Thomas Elyot," in Studies in Philology, *Vol. LXXIII, No. 5, December, 1976, pp. ix-xxx.*

CONSTANCE JORDAN (essay date 1983)

[*In the following excerpt, Jordan regards characteristically humanist aspects of* The Defence of Good Women.]

Elyot's *Defence of Good Women,* published in 1540 and dedicated to Anne of Cleves, is one of many treatises on the nature and status of women which appeared during the fifteenth and sixteenth centuries. These works were of various kinds: some were written for a popular audience, others for scholars; some were composed for wives and husbands, others were intended for teachers or the clergy. Within this large body of writing, Elyot's *Defence* belongs to a special class that is particularly easy to identify. Like such works as Boccaccio's *De claris mulieribus* (1361) and Bruni's *De studiis et litteris* (1409), Elyot's *Defence* is *humanist* in character and *apologetic* in purpose. Treatises of this class argue that the cardinal virtues, celebrated in antiquity and represented in classical philosophy and history, have been (and can be) as well exemplified by women as men. Not all treatises on women by humanists can be termed feminist. Some respect traditional notions concerning the subservient place of women in society. But most are dedicated to establishing an equality between sexes. They are distinguished from other works on the subject, whether by humanists or nonhumanists, by their defensiveness, which is coupled with an interest in the secular rather than the religious aspects of the lives of women.

Humanist defenses of women fall into three general categories: defenses of women as a sex—often in the form of a catalogue of female worthies (Boccaccio's *De claris mulieribus*); discussions of marriage (Erasmus' *Encomium matrimoniae,* 1518 and *De matrimonio christiano, 1526*); and arguments for the education of women (Bruni's *De studiis et litteris*). Individual works often include material in more than one category: discussions of marriage offer examples of virtuous wives like those described in the *De claris mulieribus;* arguments for education insist that learning makes wives more tractable; chronicles of worthies dwell on the beneficial effects of education or the companionableness of a wife. Elyot's *Defence* is unusual in participating in all three categories. His theoretical defense, which refutes Aristotle's notion of the inferiority of women, is supported by evidence from "experience," or history: the Syrian Queen Zenobia who is both an examplary wife and a woman educated in philosophy and history.

The secular and more particularly the political character of these humanist defenses needs special recognition. The rules of feminine behavior that were most generally acknowledged required of women two principal virtues: silence and chastity. Of these, the first was the most decisive, for it prevented women from venturing outside their families and into public life. Humanists challenged these rules and in effect created others. Fascinated with examples of women who had taken part in the great drama of history, humanists compared them to men, praised their "virility," and entertained the possibility of a single standard for male and female virtue. (pp. 181-82)

Like two other of Elyot's works, *Pasquil the Plaine* and *The Knowledge that Maketh a Wise Man,* both written and published early in 1533, the *Defence* is in the form of a dialogue. It dramatizes an argument between three speakers: Candidus, the enlightened defender of women who adopts a Platonic position and insists that women are fit to participate in civic affairs; Caninius, their barking Aristotelian detractor; and finally Candidus' friend, Queen Zenobia, the captive of the emperor Aurelianus. Candidus' strategy is simple. He defeats Caninius by logically invalidating the criticisms of misogynists; then he confirms his position with "experience," or evidence from "history"; and in conclusion, he adduces a living example of the truth of his opinion, the captive Queen Zenobia. Reliance on "experience" to support a feminist position is common to most defenses of women. Boccaccio, Castiglione, and others, denying denunciations of women based on received opinion, resort to examples of worthies as proof. Elyot's treatment of "example" is particularly effective in this case: by representing Zenobia as a character in a dialogue, a living voice, he endows her with a kind of "vital authority"—actually defined by Socrates who prefers conversation to writing for the communication of the truth—that an account of her life alone would not provide. Zenobia offers Candidus a "perfyte conclusion" to his argument and by "the example of her lyfe vanquishethe the obstinate mynde of the frowarde Caninius" because her authority, vested in a palpable being, is so difficult to deny.

To support his attack on women Caninius draws first on the complaints of "poets" (Boccaccio seems indicated, although he is not mentioned) and second on the works of Aristotle touching the subject of women—the two most conspicuous sources of misogynist literature available to Renaissance readers. He begins the debate by declaring that women are faithless, especially in love: in women is "in the stede of fayth. falshode and trechery." Candidus dismisses the point by asserting that it is one only poets make and they are not to be believed. He alludes to the dubious "truth" of all poetic statements (reminding Caninius that Plato expelled poets from his republic for spreading falsehood), and observes—and this is his principal point—that the poets who see in "al women most beastly conditions" are either ungrateful or disappointed lovers who, rejecting women or else rejected by them, re-

vile them from spite. In effect he denies that the idea of women as faithless has a basis in observed fact and attributes it instead to compensatory fictions created by men to serve their own emotional needs. It is of theoretical importance that Candidus' reasoning here is based on the principle of induction rather than deduction. When humanists examined dogmatic concepts of womanhood by reference to "experience," they could reveal their inadequacies. . . . Insights like these subverted the orthodox doctrine on women and allowed critics to see it as an effect of psychological and social forces rather than as objectively "true."

In refuting Caninius' neo-Aristotelian misogyny, Candidus has a more difficult task. Caninius begins this phase of his attack by noting Aristotle's claim that women are a "worke of nature unperfecte," a dictum he takes from the philosopher's discussion of reproduction in *The Generation of Animals.* He continues by pointing out correlative "facts":

> They be weaker than men, and have theyr flesshe softer, lasse heare on theyr visages, and theyre voyse sharper. . . . And as concernynge the soule, they lacke hardynes, and in peryles are timerouse, more delycate than men, unapte to paynfulnesse, except they be therto constrained, or steryd by wylfullnesse: And the wytte, that they have, is not substanciall but apyshe. . . .

There are opinions Caninius discovered in the *History of Animals.* And he concludes that women cannot govern: "In the partes of wysedome and civile policy, they be founden unapte, and to have litell capacitie," a view Aristotle expresses in the *Politics.*

It would be difficult to overestimate the support Renaissance misogynists derived from Aristotle. His notion of women as fundamentally inferior to men underlay the arguments of most learned treatises limiting the activities of women to family life. His logic is circular but it was rarely rejected on this account. He derives his doctrine of the subordination of women from his belief that they are morally weaker than men, but in turn he derives this notion of moral weakness (which he correlates with such physical traits of the female as smallness of size, softness of flesh, and need for sleep) from women's subordinate place in the political economy. Despite the obvious flaw in this reasoning, commentators were generally reluctant to challenge Aristotle's conclusions, which they saw repeatedly corroborated in scripture, notably in Genesis, where Eve's transgression institutes the subordination of wives in accordance with the will of God, and in St. Paul's epistles, where women are forbidden to speak in public (especially Timothy 2: 11-12). . . . Elyot's decision to assign Aristotle's notions to a Caninius, a detractor of women, indicates a remarkable willingness to contest the philosopher's authority.

Candidus responds to Caninius' citation of Aristotle with an argument which he claims is equally Aristotelian. He points out that in the *Economics* (a work Renaissance scholars did not yet recognize as spurious) the virtues proper to men and women are, though different, yet directed to the same "purpose"; that is, these virtues are complementary. Paraphrasing his putative source, he asserts that Nature made the man "more strong and courageouse," the woman more "weake, fearefull and scrupulouse." Her "feblenesse" makes her "more circumspecte," his "strengthe" makes him more "adventurouse." A man's nature is suited to "preparynge," the acquisition of goods, the woman's to "kepying," their conservation. Yet when these occupations are compared, that of the women is perceived to be of greater value; indeed, for being less associated with mere physical skills, it is deemed more rational and therefore more characteristically human. Activities which call for circumspection exhibit "Reason", in its manifestations as "Discretion," "Election," and "Prudence," in contrast to those which exercise the body. Therefore, Candidus concludes, women are more reasonable and have stronger "wits" than men. This leads him to a final point. Because of her "economic" virtue of circumspection and the superior reason it requires, "a woman is not a creature unperfyte but as it seemeth is more perfyte than man." Here Candidus claims that women are not only equal but even superior to men. (pp. 184-88)

Having silenced Caninius, Candidus begins a counterattack and addresses directly the question of women in political life. His approach to this question, typical of defenses of women in general, is dictated by the contrasting treatments of the subject—women in politics—that appear in the *Republic* and the *Politics,* the humanists' principal sources of pro- and anti-feminist argument. The latter work, insisting that women innately possess virtues only in a mode of subordination, unlike men who possess the same virtues in a mode of command, provides authority for limiting the activity of women to the family and for placing them under the rule of their husbands. Aristotle's model of the state imitates the configuration of power within the family: at its head is the "class" of men, representing the father; under it is the "class" of women, representing the father's wife and mother of his children; and beneath these "classes" are slaves, servants, and children. For Aristotle, the family is the fundamental unit of the state, itself an aggregate of families.

Many humanists found this model of government in the state and the family insusceptible to criticism: not only did it appear to correspond to what was recognized as natural law, it also received confirmation from scripture. Plato's notion of women as endowed with the same virtue as men achieved no significant acceptance by major humanists. They might base their arguments on Socrates' statement that the virtue in men and women is the same, but they did not accept the politics that Plato then constructs on this premise. Why they did not pursue the notion of women as "guardians," rulers and governors of the state—an investigation that might have concluded in justifying in principle the right of women to govern men—is unclear. But their unwillingness to examine Plato's image of the female guardian must in part be a response to the very conditions in which Plato imagined the guardians would live, that is, with property and children in common. Such a class would violate all Christian norms of social life, and for this reason it could not be an element in a Christian politics.

To validate gynocracy, humanists took another approach which is well illustrated in the ***Defence.*** They left questions of authority aside and concentrated rather on the "evidence" in history and what it might be seen to imply. Some of the "evidence" cited as "example" is patently ridiculous. Most humanist defenses of women do not make any distinction between figures of myth (Dido) and women who are the subject of essentially "historical" accounts

(Cleopatra), but consider them all equally convincing. This lack of discrimination must often have caused Renaissance readers (as it causes modern readers) to call into question *all* the evidence supplied in such defenses. It was not until humanists developed a sense of what is really acceptable evidence that they could begin to offer cogent arguments against assertions of the "natural" inferiority of women. In this respect, the question of evidence is like the question of psychological determinants. In both cases, received opinion can only be challenged by observations based either on actual experience or "experience" for which there is some valid or verifiable historical reference.

But proofs based on "example" have another even more serious shortcoming: they produce paradoxical arguments. The women who illustrate feminine excellence are noted for acting courageously and intelligently—in short, in a manner specified as "virile." These women logically prove the worth of their sex by denying it: a strange form of defense. While it questions sexual stereotypes, i.e. some women can do men's work, it also seems to confirm gender-related values, i.e. all that is female is inferior. The regularity with which these exemplary women are labelled "manly" finally undermines their rhetorical purpose. These limitations aside, however, the practical orientation of defenses which proceed by example did permit a consideration of how women perform tasks of government customarily assigned to men even if it excluded debate on more contentious matters of principle. An account (whether fictitious or not) of a woman who was successful in speaking in council or commanding an army obviously has bearing on the larger question of gynocracy and tends to undermine theoretical denunciations of such government.

Candidus' perception of the place of women in political life is expressed in two propositions: "in armes women have been found of no lyttell reputation," and "the wyttes of women are apte . . . to wisedom and civile policie." These claims—that women have the capacity to perform in the two fields of endeavor crucial to the success of a Renaissance prince—are far-reaching, although not unusual in humanist defenses of women. (They are certainly implicit in the *De claris mulieribus* and *Il libro del cortegiano.*) If Candidus can substantiate them, he will have established the validity of the female "governor." The notion that women could take part in active warfare was supported by instances in which this actually happened. Agrippa, for example, alludes admiringly to "la Pucelle" in his *De nobilitate,* and Castiglione to Isabella of Castile in *Il libro del cortegiano.* Yet popular and learned opinion was generally opposed to the practice. A woman's comparative lack of physical strength constituted a rational basis for limiting her part in war. In some cases the prospect of women at war was regarded with angry shock. . . . The idea that women might be adept at "civile policie" was almost as often the object of criticism. The practice of "civile policie" naturally entailed the skilful use of rhetoric and oratory and in fact women were prevented from speaking in public. The prohibition originates in the literature of classical antiquity and scripture. A correlative of Aristotle's conception of a woman as emotional was a belief that her judgment was likely to be faulty. She tended to speak a great deal but little to the point. St. Paul simply forbade women to preach (speak in public), and this rule seems to have been associated in the popular imagination with

Eve's role in persuading Adam to disobey God's commandment in paradise. Women were commonly viewed as garrulous; if they were also clever they might become dangerous. In one of the earliest humanist treatises on the education of girls, Bruni explicitly denies his students instruction in eloquence: "Rhetoric in all its forms—public discussion, forensic argument, logical fence, and the like—lies absolutely outside the province of women." Vives is even more vehement: "As for eloquence I have no great care nor a woman nedeth it nat but she nedeth goodnes and wysedome." . . . Despite these rules determining feminine behavior, many defenders of women, and particularly humanists, included in their work "examples" of women who excelled in both forbidden activities. Mythical figures are cited as the founders of various arts, and certain queens, both mythical and historical, are praised for their administrative and martial achievements. Women scholars, orators, and historians are described as paragons of intellectual virtue. A survey of these panegyrical accounts suggests the extent to which their writers—almost entirely male—saw fit to question the feminine paradigms that tended decisively to deny to women a part in public life.

Queen Zenobia is among the most frequently described of female worthies: she appears in Vives' *De institutione,* in Agrippa's *De nobilitate,* in Chaucer's "Monk's Tale," and in Lydgate's *Fall of Princes,* a popular paraphrase of Boccaccio's *De casibus virorum illustrium.* Boccaccio tells her story twice. In the *De casibus virorum,* he empahasizes her fame, thus fulfilling the purpose of that work: "and if great virtue rises then it must also fall. Not even Zenobia could escape this unscathed." He barely hints that her "fall" is owing to her violation of norms of feminine behavior: "[Aurelius] having thought it unsuitable that a woman possess part of the Roman Empire, took up arms against Zenobia." In the *De claris mulieribus,* he eliminates the fortune theme and describes her simply in superlatives: most learned, most courageous, and so forth. He even manages to transform her catastrophic capture into a complimentary occasion: "Just as if he had conquered the greatest of generals and the fiercest enemy of the republic, Aurelius rejoiced in glory and kept her for a triumph and led her to Rome with her sons."

Elyot's Zenobia is in many respects the most vital of these representations; she incarnates the central paradox so often generated by the introduction of humanist ideals into the context of an essentially Christian antifeminism largely shaped by the persistence of Aristotelian norms. She demonstrates to a greater degree than many of her counterparts the qualities conventional to women, but also, by contrast, those that distinguish humanist models. She duly conforms to the expectations of conservative readers by being modest, dutiful, temperate, patient, and obedient to her husband. Yet she is also unmistakeably the product of a humanist imagination working (or playing) on the possibility that a woman can also attain a full measure of humanity.

Her education was characteristically humanist. She studied philosophy and history until she was twenty and did not marry before that time. Moreover she reports that her "lernynge was had of none honeste man in any derysyon." Learned women were frequently thought to be disposed to levity and the charge was regularly denied by their defenders. Hyrde, for example assures his readers that an educated wife is more not less tractable—a view also endorsed

by More and Erasmus. Her widowhood allowed her to demonstrate her civic virtues (the product, she asserts, of her education); immediately realizing her precarious position as regent for her sons that "I beinge a woman, shoulde nothynge be feared," she took control of the state, making speeches, establishing laws (on the basis of her acquaintance with household economy), inspecting fortifications, and even conquering territory by the extraordinary means of moral suasion. She reports "[I] added moche more to myne Empire, not soo moche by force, as by renoume of juste and politike governaunce, whiche all men had in suche admyration, that dyverse of our said ennemies . . . chase . . . to remayne in our subjection than to retourne to theyr owne countryey." But her most daring and unusual trait—one that shows her humanist origins more vividly than any other—is her real autonomy in relation to her husband. Elyot is careful to´express himself in terms as decorous as possible; nevertheless his message is clear. Zenobia obeys her husband, but only to a point. "Justice," she says, taught her to give "due obedience" to her husband and restrained her from "anythynge whiche [was] not semely." Furthermore she declares that a wife must suit her will to her husband. But she also insists that a wife is exempt from these constraints on her freedom if what her husband wishes "may tourne them bothe to losse or dyshonesty." That is, a wife must actually exercise her own judgment. (pp. 189-95)

Both Agrippa and Erasmus stress the companionableness of a wife and see marriage as a relationship of mutuality. Erasmus' remark that an ill-behaved wife is due to an ill-behaved husband—"an evyll wyfe is nat wont to chaunce but to evyll husbandes"—implies that if a husband embarks on dishonorable conduct he can expect to find his wife similarly engaged—in ways that may indeed appear "disobedient." But no humanist, to my knowledge, gives a wife as much autonomy as Elyot does by casting her in an essentially "political" role. It is not accidental that here Elyot's Zenobia resembles Castiglione's courtier because in a sense they confront the same problem. Both wife and courtier function as advisors to persons to whom they owe affection and loyalty. Both must serve their "lord," but—and this is the crucial contribution both works make to the concept of "service"—only if they are satisfied that his course of action is not one which will bring dishonor on him, his court, or his state.

Zenobia's obvious excellence, her modesty, and her competence confound Caninius who admits defeat. But the victory is Candidus' alone, for Zenobia, despite her virtue, remains the captive of the Emperor Aurelianus and among the conquered not the conquering. Her character has a certain pathos, and one is tempted to think that Elyot, who had nothing to say about courageous and intelligent women in any of his other works, wrote the *Defence* somewhat half-heartedly and perhaps to fulfill an obligation. Zenobia must nevertheless be recognized as fine example of a type, a representative of the powerful women of antiquity who first captured Boccaccio's imagination. (pp. 195-96)

Constance Jordan, "Feminism and the Humanists: The Case of Sir Thomas Elyot's 'Defence of Good Women'," in Renaissance Quarterly, *Vol. XXXVI, No. 2, Summer, 1983, pp. 181-201.*

LINDA WOODBRIDGE (essay date 1984)

[*Woodbridge is an American educator and the author of* Women and the English Renaissance *(1984). In the following excerpt from that study, she finds* The Defence of Good Women *largely typical of its literary tradition.*]

That the brief, intensive formal controversy which flourished during the early 1540s was inaugurated by an author of no less distinguished reputation than Sir Thomas Elyot is an important fact. Francis Utley has argued that the Renaissance *querelle des femmes* was carried on mainly by "hacks like Gosynhill and Pyrrye." But although popularizers were involved in the controversy, it is significant that with Sir Thomas Elyot's *The Defence of Good Women,* 1540, the Renaissance formal controversy gained at its inception the prestige of humanist credentials.

Elyot's prose dialogue was influenced by the thinking of the Spanish humanist Vives, who resided in England while tutor to Katharine of Aragon. If Elyot's ideas about women, like his mentor's, favor maidenly modesty and womanly piety too much to be called "feminist" in the modern sense, that is the case with a majority of Renaissance defenses of women: defenders and detractors alike trafficked in stereotypes which are remote from, and even antithetical to, modern feminism. Elyot's stereotype of a "good" woman suggests that modesty, piety, and home-keeping are the essence of decent womanhood, while in fact these were only the ideals of his own culture, ideals which treatises like his were designed to promote; and he insists on the subservence of wives.

According to Foster Watson, *The Defense* is "probably the first imitation in English of the Platonic dialogue" [see excerpt dated 1912], and it is easy to see why this form suggested itself: it provides a literary forum for debate and offers a method for discrediting erroneous opinion by embodying it in a speaker of questionable integrity. Elyot's antifeminist detractor, Caninius, speaks "like a cur." The literary habit of likening the misogynist to a canine, visible throughout the controversy, probably stems from the fact that the classical misogynist Diogenes was always called a dog; his followers were Cynics, a word derived from the Greek ...[word for] dog. Elyot's defender of women, Candidus, is "benigne" and "gentill." The respective temperaments of these two are a paradigm for the genre: defenders typically adopt a posture of sweet reasonableness in contrast to the vitriolic abuse of the "snarling" and "barking" detractor.

Candidus employs a strategy conventional to the formal defense: he impugns the motives of the detractor, accusing him of harboring a sour-grapes attitude. Because Caninius's advances have been repulsed by one woman, Candidus suggests, he has taken emotional refuge in the opinion that all women are worthless: he is of "the company, whiche disappointed somtime of your purpose, ar fallen in a frenesy [i.e., frenzy], and for the displesure of one, do spring on all women the poyson of infamie." He also accuses Caninius of having got his notions of feminine inconstancy from poetry; informed as it is by bawdry (the loves of the gods, and so forth), poetry gives the reader a distorted notion of what women are like. The contemporary poetry that dealt most prominently with women was Petrarchan poetry, newly imported into England at the time Elyot's *Defense* was written, but since the dialogue is set in classical times, direct allusion to Petrarchan poetry would have been inappropriate. One reference to a poetry of weeping and sighing, however, indicates that it was partly the Petrarchans Elyot had in mind.

Candidus notes that while historians and philosophers have written of some bad women like Helen of Troy, many more are good: he adduces a number of historical-literary examples from Penelope to Portia and reminds his opponent that Plato and others argued the equality of women. Caninius, not to be outdone in knowledge of Greek philosophers, brings up Aristotle's contention that women are imperfect, delight in rebuking and complaining, and are never content. Candidus discredits Aristotle by reference to his dissolute life. Caninius urges women's physical weakness, lack of courage, inconstancy, and dearth of judgment. Women are "weaker than men, . . . they lacke hardinesse, and in perilles are timerous, more delicate then men." Candidus, delighted to be able to turn Caninius's Greek philosopher against him, cites Aristotle's belief that men and women were designed as complements and that women are perfect at least for the task they were designed for: looking after the house takes neither strength nor courage. He adds, in a more palatable argument, that men are not honored for brawn, but for reason; he forces Caninius to agree that women possess reason, on the grounds that homemaking requires more reason than does breadwinning. (It would seem that Caninius gives up this point too easily.) Candidus buttresses his argument for feminine reason by adducing wise and learned women of classical literature and legend— Carmenta (alias Nicostrata), who invented the Latin alphabet, Minerva or Athena, honored as a goddess for inventing armor and introducing horticulture, the Muses as bestowers of the liberal arts, Diotima, Cassandra, and the Sybils.

Candidus now discomfits his guest by announcing he has invited a woman to dinner. "I pray you of this matter say to her nothynge," begs the embarrassed Caninius; Candidus replies, "Thus do they all that be of your facion, In wise womens absence speke reprochefullye, and whan they be present, flatter them plesauntly." The dinner guest is the martial queen Zenobia, who establishes herself as an insufferable prig by declaring that she is seldom away from home so late in the evening and expressing pious hopes that she will not be slandered or propositioned during dinner. If this means of certifying her as a "good" woman does not endear Elyot much to the modern reader, things begin to look up when she informs the company that as a young woman she held off getting married until she had studied moral philosophy. The reader is lulled into the expectation of a serious discursus on education for women—until she recounts what she learned from philosophy, the sum of which was "to honour our husbandes nexte after god: which honour resteth in due obedience." Zenobia claims that education helps a woman please her husband, which (it would appear) is the main goal of education for women. Things do not, however, remain at this feministically bleak pass forever; Zenobia tells how, after being widowed, she ruled her country, rebuilt fortifications against the besieging enemy, made good laws, and enforced them justly. Candidus holds Zenobia up as a shining example of womanhood. Caninius recants.

The closing segment of the *Defense* is noteworthy as one of the few Renaissance texts to view with approval the independence, assertiveness, and erudition of a widow—

widows being perhaps the most heavily satirized class of women in Renaissance literature. Zenobia's capability in politics and warfare demonstrates the relative freedom to act, in a man's world, that was inherent in a widow's position, as in a reigning queen's. Elyot did, however, make the portrait less threatening by softening Zenobia's aggressiveness. He has her emphasize that her learning, pursued during a protracted maidenhood, lay quiescent while she was a wife, conducing during marriage only to chastity and the defense of her sexual reputation. Only after she was widowed did her education come to the aid of more active administrative, diplomatic, and military talents. Elyot renders Zenobia acceptably "feminine," too, by altering history. The historical Zenobia had played the aggressor: after her troops conquered Egypt in A.D. 270, she claimed imperial stature, although in her husband's day her realm of Palmyra had been part of the Roman Empire. Historically, the Romans attacked Zenobia only in response to her initial acts of aggressive rebellion; Elyot creates the impression that as queen of a sovereign state Zenobia merely took the defensive against Roman incursions on the territory she held in trust for her male children. Renaissance defenders of women often take this tack when faced with military-minded females; they praise martial women only when they act in defense of their country or their children, particularly under siege. This habit was perhaps conditioned by the figurative language of Petrarchan poetry, where the lady's heart was so often a fortress under siege. But it is also a natural expression of the entrenched Western conception of woman as passive, man as active.

Elyot's treatise differs from most succeeding defenses (and attacks) in introducing no biblical examples: in the dialogue's classical setting, Christian reference would be out of place.

Foster Watson suggests that the *Defense* was written out of sympathy with Katharine of Aragon: "her death in 1536 may, indeed, have been the occasion for the production of this booklet." Posthumous sympathy, however, seems an odd motivation for defending women. Watson here displays the usual tendency of scholars to assume that works of the formal controversy were direct responses to personal emotions and contemporary events and then to look (almost always in high places) for a woman to whose actions or character the literary document can in some way be attached. But Elyot's motivation may have been purely literary. He had before him an example of the medieval formal controversy cast in dialogue, the *Interlocucyon with an argument betwyxt man and woman whiche of them could proue to be most excellẽt*, published a decade or so before he began the *Defense,* which might easily have inspired a humanist to recast the old biblically-oriented argument in classical terms. Elyot might have wished to experiment with the dialogue as he had encountered it either in Plato or in the colloquies of Erasmus, then being translated into English. Certainly Elyot's argument has a bookish quality throughout: both the *exempla* and the character of Zenobia are probably from Boccaccio's *De Claris Mulieribus;* the character of Caninius is dependent partly on the classical model of Diogenes as shaped by anecdotal traditions; references are made to classical and Petrarchan poetry. Elyot takes obvious delight in the dramatic opportunities dialogue provides: he allows Candidus to exhibit his cleverness in turning the tables on Caninius in the Aristotle

argument and enjoys staging the discomfiture of Caninius when Zenobia enters. When Candidus accuses Caninius of having got his ideas of women by reading rather than experience, Caninius argues that reading is a quite natural source of such ideas: "By the consent of al autours my wordes be confirmed, and your experience in comparison thereof is to be littel estemed." Both disputants take a recreational view of the debate: Caninius makes little jests, and Candidus replies good-humoredly: "Now in good faith that is merily spoken," "In good faith Caninius ye ar a mery companion."

Pastorals have been written by people one suspects of having hardly any interest in sheep; and Elyot's *Defense of Good Women* is a piece of literature, written out of a long literary tradition which it modifies but whose conventions it nonetheless observes. One need not look beyond that tradition, toward dead queens or living queans, to account for Elyot's choosing to write theoretically about women. (pp. 18-22)

> *Linda Woodbridge, "The Early Tudor Controversy," in her* Women and the English Renaissance: Literature and the Nature of Womankind, 1540-1620, *University of Illinois Press, 1984, pp. 18-48.*

ADDITIONAL BIBLIOGRAPHY

Bornstein, Diane. Introduction to *The Feminist Controversy of the Renaissance*, pp. v-xiii. Delmar, N. Y.: Scholar's Facsimiles & Reprints, 1980.
> Introductory remarks to a facsimile reproduction of three works: Guillaume Alexis's *An Argument betwyxt Man and Woman* (1525); Henricus Cornelius Agrippa's *De nobilitate et praecellentia foeminei sexus* (1532; Bornstein reprints its English translation, *Female Pre-eminence*, 1670); and *The Defence of Good Women*. Bornstein finds Elyot's work a reflection of the ideals of Renaissance England.

Charlton, Kenneth. *Education in Renaissance England*, pp. 82ff. London: Routledge and Kegan Paul, 1965.
> Several references to Elyot's works insofar as they fostered the awakening of educational ideals in Renaissance England.

Goode, Clement Tyson. "Sir Thomas Elyot's *Titus and Gysippus.*" *Modern Language Notes* XXXVIII, No. 1 (January 1922): 1-11.
> Probes the origin of the tale of two friends, Titus and Gysippus, in *The Governour.*

Hale, Edward E. Jr. "Ideas on Rhetoric in the Sixteenth Century." *PMLA* XVIII, No. 3 (July 1903): 424-44.
> Notes Elyot's influence, along with that of others, on evolving literary expression in the English language.

Hogrefe, Pearl. *The Sir Thomas More Circle: A Program of Ideas and Their Impact on Secular Drama*, pp. 59ff. Urbana: University of Illinois Press, 1959.
> Refers to Elyot's views of aristocracy, government, and education within a broader context of persuasions shared by Sir Thomas More and his followers.

——. *The Life and Times of Sir Thomas Elyot, Englishman.* Ames: Iowa State University Press, 1967, 410 p.

Comprehensive critical biography of the author.

Lehmberg, Stanford E. "Sir Thomas Elyot and the English Reformation." *Archiv für Reformationsgeschichte* 48, No. 1 (1957): 91-111.
Biographical summary of Elyot's importance to the English Reformation, particularly in his capacity as Henry VIII's ambassador to the emperor Charles V.

——. *Sir Thomas Elyot: Tudor Humanist.* Austin: University of Texas Press, 1960, 218 p.
Critical biography of Elyot as a chief force within the humanist movement.

Major, John M. "The Moralization of the Dance in Elyot's *Governour.*" *Studies in the Renaissance* 5 (1958): 27-36.
Links Elyot's theory of dancing in *The Governour* to the humanist preoccupation with ethics and its foundation in classical and medieval sources.

Pace, George B. "Sir Thomas Elyot against Poetry." *Modern Language Notes* LXI, No. 8 (December 1941): 597-99.
Examines conflicting attitudes towards poetry in two of Elyot's works.

Rydén, Mats. *Relative Constructions in Early Sixteenth Century English.* Uppsala, Sweden: Almquist & Wiksells, 1966, 384 p.
Study of the development of English literary prose. Rydén accords preeminence to Elyot's achievements as an author and translator.

Salamon, Linda Bradley. "A Gloss on 'Daunsinge': Sir Thomas Elyot and T. S. Eliot's *Four Quartets.*" *ELH* 40, No. 4 (Winter 1973): 584-605.
Relates Elyot's notion of dancing in *The Governour* to poet T. S. Eliot's metaphoric concept of musical quartets. Eliot, a descendant of the author, was highly conversant with his forebear's work.

Starnes, D. T. "Elyot's *Governour* and Peacham's *Compleat Gentleman.*" *The Modern Language Review* XXII, No. 3 (July 1927): 319-22.
Outlines English author Henry Peacham's indebtedness in *The Compleat Gentleman* (1622) to *The Governour.*

Tillyard, E. M. W. "Sir John Davies: *Orchestra,* 1594." In his *Five Poems, 1470-1870: An Elementary Essay on the Background of English Literature,* pp. 30-48. London: Chatto & Windus, 1948.
Briefly mentions Elyot's thoughts on dancing in *The Governour* within a larger discussion of Sir John Davies's *Orchestra* (1594), a poem on dancing.

Warren, Leslie. "Patrizi's *De Regno et Regis Institutione* and the Plan of Elyot's *The Boke Named the Governour.*" *Journal of English and Germanic Philology* XLIX, No. 1 (January 1950): 67-77.
Establishes Francesco Patrizi's *De Regno et Regis Institutione* (1519), a widely read treatise on education, as a textual source for *The Governour.*

Watson, Foster. Introduction to *The Boke Named the Gouernour,* by Sir Thomas Elyot, pp. xi-xxvi. London: J. M. Dent & Co., n.d.
1907 synopsis of the form and content of *The Governour.*

Wortham, James. "Sir Thomas Elyot and the Translation of Prose." *The Huntington Library Quarterly* XI, No. 3 (May 1948): 219-40.
Details Elyot's fidelity to translational precedents of Dutch scholar Desiderius Erasmus.

(Lady) Ann Fanshawe

1625-1680

English memoirist.

A seventeenth-century English memoirist, Fanshawe is one of a small number of female autobiographers whose works provide a distinctive perspective on the Civil War and Restoration in England. Her sole literary endeavor, *Memoirs of Lady Fanshawe*, is a private chronicle of her married life and service to the Crown during the reigns of Charles I and Charles II. Intended both for the edification of her only son and as a record of her distinguished ancestry, Fanshawe's *Memoirs* vividly portray the devastating consequences of the Civil War upon many members of the British aristocracy.

Virtually every aspect of Fanshawe's adult life was affected by the Civil War. Born in London in 1625, she was the eldest daughter of Sir John Harrison, a wealthy Royalist. As a child Fanshawe led the carefree life of an aristocrat's daughter. Her mother's death in 1640, however, marked the beginning of a drastic decline in the family's fortunes. In 1643, as a result of heightened tensions between parliament and the monarchy, Fanshawe's father was arrested by order of the Parliamentarians for lending money to Charles I. Briefly imprisoned and then stripped of his estates and wealth, Harrison moved the family to Oxford. There they lived above a bakery—a stark contrast to the luxurious surroundings to which Fanshawe was accustomed. Like many other Royalists, Fanshawe's father never recouped his financial losses. Later that same year, Fanshawe's brother William was killed in Oxford in a skirmish defending the Crown. Fanshawe noted that her one positive experience during that time was meeting and then marrying Sir Richard Fanshawe, an aristocratic Royalist whose circumstances paralleled her own. Despite a sixteen-year difference in their ages (she was 19 and he 35), the marriage was extremely happy. Over the twenty-two years of their life together, Fanshawe conceived twenty children, only five of whom survived to adulthood. Remarkably, during these years she travelled extensively throughout Britain and the continent, though pregnancy and illness often prevented her from maintaining Richard's hectic pace. Fanshawe nonetheless followed her husband, who was ever loyal to the monarchy throughout the Commonwealth and Protectorate, as he fulfilled his various official duties as secretary for war, treasurer of the navy, and ambassador for both Charles I and Charles II. Frequently in danger and usually without much money, Fanshawe outwitted her adversaries on more than one occasion. Indeed, in 1559, as hostile Scottish authorities sought to detain her, she disguised herself and, using an alias (her maiden name), secured travel papers with which she escaped to Paris to join her husband.

After the Restoration in 1660, Fanshawe's life was relatively tranquil. From 1661 to 1666 she lived first in Portugal and then in Spain where her husband served as ambassador. Richard died in 1666 after a brief illness, leaving his wife to provide for five children and numerous servants. Upon his death, the queen mother of Spain offered Fanshawe income and a permanent residence as an in-

(Lady) Ann Fanshawe

ducement to remain in Spain and convert to Catholicism. Despite her uncertain future, Fanshawe declined the honor, claiming she could forsake neither her religion nor her country. Thus, after selling most of her valuables to finance the journey, Fanshawe returned home to bury her husband. Three years later, in 1669, her father died, adding to the overwhelming grief she had endured since her husband's death. Little of Fanshawe's life is known beyond this point except that she devoted herself to caring for her children and completed her memoirs in 1676. Fanshawe died in 1680 and was buried alongside her husband and father in the parish church of Ware.

Fanshawe adored her husband and composed her memoirs primarily to acquaint his descendants with their distinguished forbear. The *Memoirs* thus chronicles his life and Royalist career, focusing upon the years from their marriage in 1644 until his death in 1666. The *Memoirs* is divided into several loosely organized sections. It begins with brief ancestral histories of the Fanshawe and Harrison families as well as more detailed biographies of the memoirist and her husband. Fanshawe and her husband were involved in numerous missions and intrigues relating to the Royalist cause. Her work therefore contains colorful stories of shipwreck, clandestine meetings, imprisonment, and daring escapes. Indeed, critics note that sections of the *Memoirs* have the quality of an exciting romance novel. Other lengthy sections, however, reveal that Fanshawe was chiefly concerned with domestic, household affairs. Because she was writing to preserve the memory of her husband, she gave herself a secondary role in the narrative. Her own experiences, when portrayed, are often merely examples of her successful execution of his commands. Once she had written of his death, Fanshawe apparently had little else to say and so ended her work abruptly.

Fanshawe never intended her memoirs to be made public. As a result, though excerpts from the manuscript were circulated prior to the official publication, the complete text was not available in print until 1829. Since that time the *Memoirs* have generated a small but steady stream of criticism. Scholars have compared and variously assessed Fanshawe's prose style and narrative perspective with that of her contemporaries Lucy Hutchinson, Anne Halkett, Margaret Cavendish, and Anne Clifford. Critics have also examined the historical and sociological value of each autobiographer's work. B. G. MacCarthy, according Fanshawe a place among the forerunners of modern literature, claimed that her *Memoirs* is "characterized not only by her complete realism and narrative power, but also by the sincerity of feeling." MacCarthy added that Fanshawe's work contributed toward "that mastery of narrative form and that expression of the inner being which finally fused in the modern novel." Other critics, however, concur with John Loftis's assessment of Fanshawe's writing as "utilitarian prose, rarely ambiguous but stylistically uneven and undistinguished" and agree with his conclusion that Fanshawe "cannot approximate Lady Halkett's stylistic fluency and subtlety in the analysis of emotion." In general, critical opinion of Fanshawe's work has been favorable, with most scholars finding her work technically flawed yet worthy of further study.

It is as an individual that Fanshawe has generated the most interest. Both nineteenth- and twentieth-century scholars have cited her as an exceptional example of a woman who successfully adapted herself to a life of almost constant danger and uncertainty. Critics have further examined her self-perception with regard to this role. More than one modern scholar has condemned Fanshawe's apparent rejection of her individuality in favor of association with her husband's identity. Indeed, Mary Beth Rose has claimed: "at times the violence and self-hatred implicit in Lady Fanshawe's complete identification with male superiority are starkly revealed." Rose further cites Fanshawe's failure to identify with her own sex as indicative of many seventeenth-century views of women and their roles in society. Today, study on Fanshawe's life and work continues. Although she is considered but a minor English literary figure, her work is nonetheless valued for the insight it provides into seventeenth-century daily life and as a mirror of one woman's perspective on issues more commonly treated by men.

PRINCIPAL WORK

Memoirs of Lady Fanshawe, wife of the Right Hon. Sir Richard Fanshawe, bart., ambassador from Charles the Second to the court of Madrid in 1665. Written by herself. To which are added, extracts from the correspondence of Sir Richard Fanshawe (memoirs) 1829.

*This work was written in 1676.

ANN FANSHAWE (essay date 1676)

[*In the following preface to her* Memoirs, *Fanshawe counsels her son, preparing him for the family history she is about to relate.*]

I have thought it convenient to discourse to you (my most dear and only son) the most remarkable actions and accidents of your family, as well as those of more eminent ones of your father and my life, and neceseity, not delight nor revenge, hath made me insert some passages which will reflect on their owners, as the praises of others will be but just, which is my intent in this narrative. I would not have you be a stranger to [it], because by the example you may imitate what is applyable to your condition in the world, and indeavour to avoyd those misfortunes we have passed through, if God pleases.

Indeavour to be innocent as a dove, but as wise as a serpent, and let this lesson direct you most in your greatest extreams of fortune.

Hate idlenesse, and courbe all passions, be true in all words and actions. Unnecessarily deliver not your opinion but when you doe let it be just, and considered, and plaine.

Be charitable in thought, word, and deed, and ever ready to forgive injury don to yourself, and be more pleased to doe good than to receive good. Be civill and obliging to all, dutifull where God and nature command you, but friend to one, and that friendship keep sacred as the greatest tye upon earth, and be sure to ground it upon virtue, for no other is either happy or lasting.

Indeavour always to be content in that estate of life which it hath pleased God to call you to, and think it a great fault not to imploy your time either for the good of your soul or improvement of your understanding, health, or estate, and as these are the most pleasant pastimes, so it will make you a cheerfull old age, which is as necessary for you to designe, as to make provision to support the infirmitys which decay of strength brings, and it was never seen that a vicious youth terminated in a contented, cheerfull old age, but perished out of countenance.

Ever keep the best qualified persons company, out of whom you will find advantage, and reserve some hours daily to examine yourself and fortune; for if you embark yourself in perpetuall conversation or recreation, you will certainly shiprack your mind and fortune. Remember the proverbe, 'Such as his company is, such is the man', and have glorious actions before your eyes, and think what shall be your portion in heaven, as well as what you desire on earth.

Manage your fortune prudently, and forget not that you must give God an account here after, and upon all occasions.

Remember your father, whose true image though I can never draw to the life unless God will grant me that blessing in you, yet because you were but ten months and ten days owld when God took him out of this world, I will for your advantage show you him with all truth and without partiality. (pp. 101-02)

> *Ann Fanshawe, in an excerpt in* The Memoirs of Anne, Lady Halkett and Ann, Lady Fanshawe, *edited by John Loftis, Oxford at the Clarendon Press, 1979, pp. 101-02.*

HORACE WALPOLE (letter date 1792)

[*An English author, politician, and publisher, Walpole is best known for his memoirs and voluminous correspondence, which provide revealing glimpses of life in England during the last half of the eighteenth century. In the following excerpt from a letter written in response to an inquiry of Anne Liddell, Countess of Ossory, concerning Fanshawe's* Memoirs, *he briefly considers Fanshawe's work.*]

The memoirs, about which your Ladyship inquires, are probably those of a Lady Fanshaw, wife, if I do not mistake, of a Sir Richard Fanshaw, who, if I do not again mistake, died minister in Spain. They were shown to me a few years ago, and I had been told they were very curious, which was a little more than I found them, though not unentertaining; they chiefly dwelt on private domestic distresses, and on what the aristocrats of that time were apprehending form their enemies, who however were not such tigers and hyenas as the French of this day. Still so few private letters of the Civil War from 1640 to 1660 have been preserved, probably from the fears of both writers and receivers, that one likes to read any details. (pp. 147-48)

> *Horace Walpole, in a letter to Lady Ossory on July 17, 1792, in his* Horace Walpole's Correspondence with the Countess of Upper Ossory, *Vol. III, edited by W. S. Lewis and A. Dayle Wallace, Yale University Press, 1965, pp. 147-51.*

[FRANCIS JEFFREY] (essay date 1829)

[*Jeffrey was a founder and editor of the* Edinburgh Review, *one of the most influential periodicals in early nineteenth-century England. A liberal Whig, he often allowed his political beliefs to color his critical opinions. In the following excerpt, he compares Fanshawe's* Memoirs *with those of her contemporary, Lucy Hutchinson, referring to the latter women by a variant spelling of her surname, "Hutchison."*]

There is not much in this book [*Memoirs of Lady Fanshawe*], either of individual character, or public story. It is, indeed, but a small affair—any way; but yet pleasing, and not altogether without interest or instruction. Though it presents us with no traits of historical importance, and but few of personal passion or adventure, it still gives us a peep at a scene of surpassing interest from a new quarter; and at all events adds one other item to the great and growing store of those contemporary notices which are every day familiarizing us more and more with the living character of bygone ages; and without which we begin, at last, to be sensible, that we can neither enter into their spirit, nor even understand their public transactions. Writings not meant for publication, nor prepared for purposes of vanity or contention, are the only memorials in which the true 'form and pressure' of the ages which produce them are ever completely preserved; and, indeed, the only documents from which the great events which are blazoned on their records can ever be satisfactorily explained. It is in such writings alone,—confidential letters—private diaries—family anecdotes—and personal remonstrances, apologies, or explanations,—that the true springs of action are disclosed—as well as the obstructions and impediments, whether in the scruples of individuals or the general temper of society, by which their operation is so capriciously, and, but for these revelations, so unaccountably controlled. They are the true key to the cipher in which public annals are almost necessarily written; and their disclosure, after long intervals of time, is almost as good as the revocation of their writers from the dead—to abide our interrogatories, and to act over again, before us, in the very dress and accents of the time, a portion of the scenes which they once guided or adorned. It is not a very striking portion, perhaps, that is thus recalled by the publication before us; but whatever interest it possesses is mainly of this character. It belongs to an era, to which, of all others in our history, curiosity will always be most eagerly directed; and it constantly rivets our attention, by exciting expectations which it ought, in truth, to have fulfilled; and suggesting how much more interesting and instructive it might so easily have been made.

Lady Fanshawe was, as is generally known, the wife of a distinguished cavalier, in the Heroic Age of the civil wars and the Protectorate; and survived till long after the restoration. Her husband was a person of no mean figure in those great transactions; and she, who adhered to him with the most devoted attachment, and participated not unworthily in all his fortunes and designs, was, consequently, in continual contact with the movements which then agitated society, and had her full share of the troubles and triumphs which belonged to such an existence. Her *Memoirs* ought, therefore, to have formed an interesting counterpart to those of Mrs Hutchison; and to have recalled to us, with equal force and vivacity, the aspect under which those great events presented themselves to a female spectatress and sufferer, of the opposite faction. But, though the title of the book, and the announcements of the editor, hold out this promise, we must say that the body of it falls far short of performance: and, whether it be that her side of the question did not admit of the same force of delineation or loftiness of sentiment; or, that the individual chronicler has been less fortunately selected, it is certain that, in point both of interest and instruction; in traits of character, warmth of colouring, or exaltation of feeling, there is no sort of comparison between these gossiping, and, though affectionate, yet relatively cold and feeble, memoranda, and the earnest, eloquent, and graphic representations of the puritan heroine. Nor should it be forgotten, even in hinting at such a parallel, that, in one important respect, the royalist cause must be allowed to have been singularly happy in its female representative. Since, if it may be said with some show of reason, that Lucy Hutchison and her husband had too many elegant tastes and accomplishments to be taken as fair specimens of the austere and godly republicans; it certainly may be retorted, with at least equal justice, that the chaste and decorous Lady Fanshawe, and her sober diplomatic lord, shadow out rather too favourably the general manners and morals of the cavaliers.

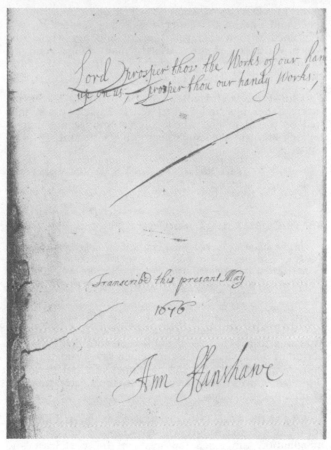

Holograph title page of Lady Fanshawe's Memoirs.

After all, perhaps, the true secret of her inferiority, in all at least that relates to political interest, may be found in the fact, that the fair writer, though born and bred a royalist, and faithfully adhering to her husband in his efforts and sufferings in the cause, was not naturally, or of herself, particularly studious of such matters, or disposed to occupy herself more than was necessary with any public concern. She seems to have followed, like a good wife and daughter, where her parents or her husband led her; and to have adopted their opinions with a dutiful and implicit confidence, but without being very deeply moved by the principles or passions which actuated those from whom they were derived; while Lucy Hutchison not only threw her whole heart and soul into the cause of her party, but, like Lady Macbeth or Madame Roland, imparted her own fire to her more phlegmatic helpmate,—'chastised him,' when necessary, 'with the valour of her tongue,' and cheered him on, by the encouragement of her high example, to all the ventures and sacrifices, the triumphs or the martyrdoms, that lay visibly in her daring and lofty course. The Lady Fanshawe, we take it, was of a less passionate temperament; and her book, accordingly, is more like that of an ordinary woman, though living in extraordinary times. She begins, no doubt, with a good deal of love and domestic devotion, and even echoes, from that sanctuary, certain notes of loyalty; but, in very truth, is chiefly occupied, for the best part of her life, with the sage and serious business of some nineteen or twenty *accouchemens*, which are happily accomplished in different parts of Europe; and, at last, is wholly engrossed in the ceremonial

of diplomatic presentations,—the description of court dresses, state coaches, liveries, and jewellery,—the solemnity of processions, and receptions by sovereign princes,—and the due interchange of presents and compliments with persons of worship and dignity. Fully one-third of her book is taken up with such goodly matter; and nearly as much with the genealogy of her kindred, and a faithful record of their marriages, deaths, and burials. From the remainder, however, some curious things may be gathered. . . . (pp. 75-7)

There is great choice of this sort for those who like it; and not a little of the more solemn and still duller discussion of diplomatic etiquette and precedence. But, independent of these, and of the genealogies and obituaries, which are not altogether without interest, there is enough both of heart, and sense, and observation in these **Memoirs**, at once to repay gentle and intelligent readers for the trouble of perusing them, and to stamp a character of amiableness and respectability on the memory of their author. (p. 85)

> *[Francis Jeffrey], in a review of "Memoirs of Lady Fanshawe," in* The Edinburgh Review, *Vol. L, No. XCIX, October, 1829, pp. 75-85.*

CHARLES L. KENNEY (essay date 1861)

[*In the following excerpt, Kenney extols the historical and entertainment value of the* Memoirs.]

As a learned lady, [Ann Fanshawe] has indeed no pretensions; but that she was a thoroughly well-educated woman, of sound sense and noble and refined sentiments, the memoir which she has left strikingly proves. This memoir was written in 1676, for the instruction of her only surviving son, Sir Richard Fanshawe, who was then a youth, and to him it is personally addressed, the reflections with which the narrative is interspersed breathing the spirit of maternal tenderness and solicitude. Although it had constantly been mentioned in many popular works, and the name of Lady Fanshawe had ever been included among the most notable female characters of England, this remarkable autobiography was never printed till the year 1829. Of its perfect genuineness there has never been a doubt, and indeed it is referred to in the will of Lady Fanshawe; and it is the more surprising that the publication of this manuscript was so long postponed, as it not only reflects the mind of a most noble, devoted, and accomplished woman, in a life-story scarcely inferior in interest to the most thrilling romance, but the references it contains to events which form part of the history of the country have been found to throw a light on some doubtful points of fact, and clear up some commonly received misrepresentations. To these valuable items of historical testimony . . . [is added] Lady Fanshawe's own account of her life,—a life than which I can hope to find none . . . setting a fairer example of womanly excellence, and combining more proudly the softer qualities and tenderer graces peculiarly the appanage of her sex, with the heroic fortitude and endurance which constitute the crowning glory of a perfectly noble woman. (pp. 200-01)

> *Charles L. Kenney, "Daughters of Eve," in* Temple Bar, *Vol. III, August, 1861, pp. 200-14.*

JAMES HUTTON (essay date 1878)

[*In the following excerpt, Hutton briefly praises Fanshawe and the* Memoirs.]

Few nobler footprints have been left on the sands of time than those impressed by the heroic gentlewomen who shared the good and evil fortunes of their husbands during the Civil War, and under the Commonwealth and Restoration. Here and there we obtain a glimpse of sufferings patiently endured, of heart-wringing solicitude tempered by a living faith, and of an active and intelligent co-operation in the dramatic incidents of the times. Never, perhaps, did women show themselves more conspicuously in their natural part of a 'help meet for man' than during that chequered period, nor does any one of them appear in a brighter and purer light than the wife and widow of Sir Richard Fanshawe, Ambassador to the Court of Madrid. (p. 204)

Three years before her death she applied herself to the composition of a memoir of her eventful life, with the single-minded view of setting before her son the bright exemplar of his father's conduct, whether as a loyal servant of the Crown, tried by the extremes of adversity and prosperity, or in his domestic relations as a faithful and affectionate husband. Of herself she always speaks modestly and unaffectedly, as though she had simply endeavoured to do her duty in that state of life in which it had pleased Providence to place her. For that reason, if for no other, her plain, unadorned narrative is a vivid illustration of the genuine worth of a true English gentlewoman. (p. 215)

> *James Hutton, "Lady Fanshawe," in* Belgravia, *Vol. XXXV, No. 138, April, 1878, pp. 204-15.*

CHARLES DICKENS, JR. (essay date 1889)

[*A nineteenth-century English editor, Dickens was the eldest son of the celebrated novelist Charles Dickens. In the following excerpt from* All the Year Round, *a periodical edited by both father and son, Dickens junior deems Fanshawe a heroine for her "wifely love" and "domestic self-sacrifice."*]

In those dark days of English history when King strove with Parliament—the "divine right" of the anointed sovereign with the just liberties of the subject—there were not wanting on either side noble instances of loyal heroism and steadfast self-devotion.

Lord Falkland, Sir John Eliot, Montrose, died on the battle-field, in prison, on the scaffold, for that which each deemed the right. These men, and many others like them, were the heroes of their time; the same spirit animated them, though they met, sword in hand, to fight for opposed principles, rival interests. (pp. 416-17)

England had her heroines, too, in those days of danger and privation: such devoted women as Mrs. Hutchinson and the eccentric Duchess of Newcastle. True, their "heroic actions" were not "performed publicly in the field," as the Duchess puts it, "but privately in the closet." Theirs was the womanly devotion of wifely love, the loyal courage of domestic self-sacrifice.

Such a heroine was Lady Anne Fanshawe, who, all unconsciously, has sketched her own character in her charmingly frank and unaffected *Autobiography*. "It is a character," to quote Mr. Davenport Adams, "which one cannot but respect and admire. A tender and loving disposition was combined with a courageous heart; and her whole life, which was darkened at one time by many dangers and privations, was informed by a spirit of the truest and tenderest piety." (p. 417)

This loyal lady and devoted wife died in 1679-80, having survived her husband several years. Englishwomen may well be proud of one whose simple courage and unpretending heroism shed such lustre on their name. (p. 420)

> *Charles Dickens, Jr., "A Loyal Lady," in* All the Year Round, *Vol. 2, Nos. 44-48, November 2, 1889, pp. 416-20.*

BEATRICE MARSHALL (essay date 1905)

[*In the following excerpt from her 1905 introduction to Fanshawe's* Memoirs, *Marshall appraises the historic value of the text, comparing it with the autobiographies of Fanshawe's contemporaries Lucy Hutchinson and Margaret Cavendish, Duchess of Newcastle.*]

There is a deathless charm, despite the efforts of modern novelists and playwrights to render it stale and hackneyed, attaching to the middle of the seventeenth century—that period of upheaval and turmoil which saw a stately *debonnaire* Court swept away by the flames of Civil War, and the reign of an usurper succeeded by the Restoration of a discredited and fallen dynasty.

So long as the world lasts, events such as the trial and execution of Charles Stuart will not cease to appeal to the imagination and touch the hearts of those at least who bring sentiment to bear on the reading of history.

It is not to the dryasdust historian, however, that we go for illuminating side-lights on this ever-fascinating time, but rather to the pen-portraits of Clarendon, the noble canvases of Van Dyck, and above all to the records of individual experience contained in personal memoirs. Of these none is more charmingly and vivaciously narrated or of greater historic value and interest than the following memoir [*Memoirs of Lady Fanshawe*] of Sir Richard Fanshawe, "Knight and Baronet, one of the Masters of the Requests, Secretary of the Latin Tongue, Burgess of the University of Cambridge, and one of His Majesty's Most Honourable Privy Council of England and Ireland, and His Majesty's Ambassador to Portugal and Spain." It was written by his widow in the evening of her days, after a life of storm and stress and many romantic adventures at home and abroad, for the benefit of the only son who survived to manhood of fourteen children, most of whom died in their chrisom robes and whose baby bones were laid to rest in foreign church-yards.

Two contemporaries of Lady Fanshawe, Mrs. Hutchinson and the Duchess of Newcastle, also wrote lives of their husbands, which continue to live as classics in our literature. But the Royalist Ambassador's wife is incomparably more sparkling and anecdotic than the Puritan Colonel's, and she does not adopt the somewhat tiresome "doormat" attitude of wifely adoration towards the subject of her memoir which "Mad Margaret" (as Pepys called her Grace of Newcastle) thought fitting when she took up her fatally facile pen to endow her idolised lord with all the virtues and all the graces and every talent under the sun.

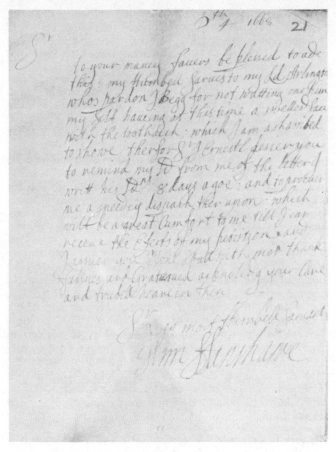

1668 letter by Lady Fanshawe, illustrating the author's phonetic spelling.

Yet with less lavishly laid on colours, how vivid is the portrait Lady Fanshawe has painted for posterity of the gallant gentleman and scholar, one of those "very perfect gentle knights" which that age produced; loyal and religious, with the straightforward simple piety that held unwaveringly to the Anglican Church in which he had been born and brought up.

And of herself, too, she unconsciously presents a series of charming pictures. The description of her girlhood is a glimpse into the bringing up of a Cavalier maiden of quality, of the kind that is invaluable in a reconstruction of the past from the domestic side. In the town-house in Hart Street which her father, Sir John Harrison, rented for the winter months from "my Lord Dingwall," where she was born, her education was carried on "with all the advantages the time afforded." She learnt French, singing to the lute, the virginals, and the art of needlework, and confesses that though she was quick at learning she was very wild and loved "riding, running and all active pastimes."

One can picture the light-hearted "hoyting girl" breaking loose when she found herself at Balls in Hertfordshire, where the family spent the summer, and skipping and jumping for sheer joy at being alive. And then we see her at fifteen suddenly sobered by the death of her mother, a lady of "excellent beauty and good understanding," and taking upon her young shoulders the entire management of her father's household. With naïve satisfaction she tells

of how well she succeeded and how she won the esteem of her mother's relations and friends, being ever "ambitious to keep the best company," which she thanks God she did all the days of her life. (pp. v-viii)

An unfinished sentence gives a pathetic close to these pages, so full of touches of humour, keen observation and racy anecdote. It would seem as if the hand which wielded so descriptive and ready a pen had wearied of its task; as if, at last, the sunny nature was overcast and the merry heart saddened. But surely not another word is needed to make the narrative more perfect. Those who first become acquainted with it in this reprint will meet with many things less familiar than Lady Fanshawe's moving account of her leave-taking from Charles I. at Hampton Court, which has been quoted hundreds of times. They will be thrilled by at least three stories of the supernatural told with the *èlan* and consummate simplicity that exceeds art, and they will be charmed with the ingenuousness of the writer when she writes about herself, and her masterly little sketches by the way of such characters of the time as Sir Kenelm Digby and Lord Goring, son of the Earl of Norwich. Indeed, we venture to think they cannot fail to find the whole book delightful, because, though relating to a long-vanished past, it is as livingly human and fresh as if written yesterday. (pp. xiii-xiv)

> *Beatrice Marshall, in an introduction to* Memoirs of Lady Fanshawe, *edited by Beatrice Marshall, John Lane: The Bodley Head, 1905, pp. v-xiv.*

JOHN MacARTHUR (essay date 1907)

[*In the following excerpt, MacArthur assesses Fanshawe's prose style and considers the historical value of her* Memoirs.]

The autobiography of Ann Lady Fanshawe, first printed in 1829, is well known as one of the most readable memoirs of the seventeenth century. Horace Walpole had sight of the papers and wrote about them to Lady Ossory: "I had been told they were very curious, which was a little more than I found them, though not unentertaining. They chiefly dwelt on private domestic distresses and what the aristocrats of that time were apprehending from their enemies, who, however, were not such tigers and hyænas as the French of this day." This gives a very misleading idea of the narrative; for although Lady Fanshawe, as the wife of a conspicuous cavalier, had plenty of domestic anxiety and vicissitude during the civil war, she was a woman of intelligence beyond the common, deeply interested in public events as they affected the monarchy and the nation. Her husband, Sir Richard, entered diplomacy in 1635 as secretary to the British Embassy at Madrid, and thereafter, saving seven years spent in prison and on parole following on his capture at the Battle of Worcester, was constantly employed in the public service until his death in Spain in 1666. Lady Fanshawe tells how, on an occasion, he gently bridled her curiosity about politics—tells it so prettily, and in a way that reveals so much of the manner of a fashionable English household at that period, that we are tempted to make a somewhat long extract from her narrative. (p. 174)

After the restoration, Fanshawe was appointed Ambassador to the Court of Spain, and his wife gives a delightful account of their journey thither and their reception in Madrid. Very imposing must have been the appearance presented by the new Minister and his suite, which included twenty footmen dressed in liveries (also new) of "dark green cloth with a frost upon green lace." It was the age when men went in fine raiment:—

> "My husband went in a very rich suit of clothes of a dark *fillemorte* brocade laced with silver and gold lace, nine laces, every one as broad as my hand, and a little silver and gold lace laid between them, both of very curious workmanship. His suit was trimmed with scarlet taffeta ribbon, his stockings of white silk upon long scarlet silk ones, his shoes black, with scarlet shoestrings and garters,"

and so on. . . .

Neither in the memoirs nor in nearly 400 pages of notes appended to them is there anything new to the student of the reigns of Charles I. and II., but Lady Fanshawe is a charming writer; her story is full of lively episode and vivid portraiture. It is a boon to have her autobiography in such an agreeable form as the present edition, which, besides many illustrations, has the merit of an excellent index. (p. 175)

> John MacArthur, "Lady Fanshawe's Autobiography," in The Bookman, *London, Vol. XXXII, No. 191, August, 1907, pp. 174-75.*

SIR HENRY M. IMBERT-TERRY (essay date 1922)

[*Imbert-Terry was an English essayist. In the following excerpt, he assesses Fanshawe's writing and relates her impression of the murder of Charles I to the perceived reaction of the British populace.*]

[When Fanshawe] married she easily adapted herself to the cares and responsibilities of matrimony, presenting her partner with six sons and eight daughters, not taking into account half-a-dozen other infants, whom the stress of those stormy years brought to an untimely end or an immature beginning.

It may well be imagined that a lady of this persevering disposition would not rest content unless she participated as much as possible in her husband's pursuits. As Sir Richard occupied a high and confidential position in the King's household occasions arose when reticence became necessary. Reticence, doubtless, is a virtue possessed by both sexes; there appears, however, to be a difference in their methods of practice.

On this occasion the wife asked many questions; the husband smiled and equivocated. She renewed her importunity; he embraced her and talked of other things. At supper she ate nothing and expressed a belief that he did not love her, to which he replied by stopping her mouth with kisses. "So we went to bed; I cried; he went to sleep." The narratrix then recounts that the same procedure continued the next day until Sir Richard took the fair inquisitor in his arms and said. "My dearest soul; nothing on earth can afflict me like this; when you ask me of my business it is wholly out of my power to satisfy thee; my life and fortune shall be thine but my honour is my own which I cannot preserve if I communicate the Prince's affairs. I pray thee with this answer rest satisfied."

The whole episode, as daintily related by Lady Fanshawe, is quite charming, far more so than many like scenes in the comedies of the period, and it gives an excellent example both of the gifts of the authoress and of her right and true disposition. . . . (pp. 93-4)

In relating all the various adventures, Lady Fanshawe habitually punctuates her narrative by interposing the interesting information that either before or after the reported event she contributed an addition to her family, on one occasion producing three infant sons at a fell swoop. In the interval between these periodical visitations she returned to England for the purpose of arranging for a safety pass for her husband so that he might compound with the Parliamentary authorities for his estate, in which enterprise she succeeded sufficiently to allow Sir Richard to remain in London until October, 1647.

The disastrous attempt of Charles I to escape from Hampton Court caused the deepest dejection among the devoted band of followers who remained around the person of their Monarch. Lady Fanshawe visited the King three times during his sojourn in this place. Her account of her final interview is worthy of remembrance: "The last time I ever saw him when I took my leave I could not refrain from weeping. When he saluted me I prayed God to preserve his Majesty with long life and happy years. He stroked me on my cheek and said: 'Child; if God pleases it shall be so, but both you and I must submit to God's will,' and then he added significantly, 'you know in what hands I am.'"

History has recorded the act those hands committed; it is not the place here to discuss that tragedy, but when Lady Fanshawe concludes by mourning "that the deed then done brought grief to the heart of all Christians not forsaken by God," she utters an expression of belief which stirred the souls of thousands of those whose every instinct of loyal allegiance was outraged by the murder of their Sovereign. (pp. 96-7)

> Sir Henry M. Imbert-Terry, "Some Memorialists of the Period of the Restoration," in Essays by Divers Hands, *n.s. Vol. II, 1922, pp. 69-106.*

DONALD A. STAUFFER (essay date 1930)

[*A noted American biographer, poet, and essayist, Stauffer wrote biographical and critical studies of English and American literature. In the following excerpt from* English Biography Before 1700 *(1930), he examines the emotional nature of Fanshawe's* Memoirs.]

One of the best autobiographies by women is to be found in the *Memoirs of Anne Lady Fanshawe*, transcribed under her own supervision in 1676 and disclosing a full picture of a noble man and a noble wife. There are few biographies which present a love as complete and as sympathetic as that between Sir Richard Fanshawe and Anne:

> Glory be to God we never had but one mind throughout our lives, our souls were wrapped up in each other, our aims and designs one, our loves one, and our resentments one. We so studied one the other that we knew each other's mind by our looks; whatever was real happiness, God gave it me in him.

This love is expressed even unconsciously, as when she inserts an innocent adverb in this sentence: "He was married at 35 years of age, and lived with me but 23 years and 29 days."

For her son's betterment she includes at the outset certain general precepts which her own experience had tested [see excerpt dated 1676]:

> Endeavor to be innocent as a dove, but as wise as a serpent; and let this lesson direct you most in the greatest extremes of fortune.... Be civil and obliging to all, dutiful where God and nature command you; be friend to one—and that friendship keep sacred as the greatest tie upon earth. And be sure to ground it upon virtue, for no other is either happy or lasting.

The story progresses without effort, and the fortunes of the two principal figures are traced—the marriage at Wolvercote Church near Oxford, the vicissitudes of the Civil Wars, the travels of the Court of the Scilly Islands and Jersey, a last leave-taking from the king, war in Ireland, and exile in France. She does not scruple to insert the most realistic details, and has decided opinions on such subjects as the Irish fleas or the "very bad cheese" of Nantes. Her anecdotes are sharply cut, as is the story of the ghost she saw while sleeping in a massive old pile in Ireland:

> She spake loud, and in a tone I never heard, thrice 'Ahone'; and then with a sigh more like wind than

Lady Fanshawe and her daughter Mary, by David Teniers, probably painted in the spring of 1660.

breath she vanished, and to me her body looked more like a thick cloud than substance. I was so much affrighted that my hair stood on end and my night-clothes fell off.

Her love for her husband guides the course of the whole narrative. At times she is to be seen in man's garb, standing on deck to be near her husband when their ship, on its way to Spain, is threatened by a Turkish man-o'-war. "But when your father saw it convenient to retreat, looking upon me he blessed himself, and snatched me up in his arms, saying, 'Good God, that love can make this change!'; and though he seemingly chid me, he did laugh at it as often as he remembered that voyage."

Again, with a dark lantern she steals at four o'clock in the morning towards Whitehall to comfort her imprisoned husband: "And I would go under his window and softly call him. He that after the first time expected me never failed to put out his head at first call. Thus we talked together; and sometimes I was so wet with rain that it went in at my neck and out at my heels." She never flatters herself. When she escapes to France in 1658 by feigning to be a common woman, she leaves her maid at the gate, "who," she says, "was much a finer gentlewoman than myself." Again she returns a young lion given her as a present by a Spanish official, "but I desired his Excellency's pardon that I did not accept of it, saying I was of so cowardly a make I durst not keep company with it."

The last half of the autobiography describes Lady Fanshawe's life after the Restoration, in the Embassy at Madrid. In recording "the customs and principles and country" of Spain she is graphic. After these years of splendor as a great lady, she must also record the death of her husband, and, beautifully, she quotes from his own translation of one of Horace's odes, without comment:

> Lollio, thou art a man hast skill
> To fathom things; that being tried
> In either fortune, couldst abide
> In both upright; and Lollio still . . .

The narrative does not survive his death, but breaks off abruptly. Although the biography is objective and anecdotal, Lady Anne and Sir Richard are solid figures; their mutual love colors the entire work and gives it steadiness and unity. (pp. 210-12)

> *Donald A. Stauffer, "The Autobiography," in his* English Biography Before 1700, *1930. Reprint by Russell & Russell Inc., 1964, pp. 175-216.*

B. G. MacCARTHY (essay date 1944)

[*In the following excerpt from* Women Writers: Their Contribution to the English Novel, 1621-1744 *(1944), MacCarthy discusses the composition and structural elements of Fanshawe's work.*]

The arrangement of the *Memoirs* is as follows:

(1) A portrait of her husband, Sir Richard Fanshawe.

(2) An account of his ancestors.

(3) A reference to their marriage, together with the names of their children alive and dead. Of the dead she mentions the burial places.

(4) A few pages dealing with the family of Sir Thomas Fanshawe of Jenkins, who was a near relative of her husband.

(5) An account of her own birth; of her mother, of her mother's death; and of her own brothers and sister.

(6) An account of her father's second marriage; of his birth and relatives.

(7) An account of her own childhood, and upbringing.

(8) A long and detailed account of the adventures which befell her husband and herself during their married life.

It is true that parts (1) to (7) are badly arranged, but this does not greatly matter, as, from the fictional point of view, the main interest is centred in the long narrative which constitutes section (8).

To the composition of the *Memoirs* Anne Fanshawe brought a most energetic, vivid and individual mind. She was a woman of great courage and directness, with a knack of adapting herself to any circumstances and of rising to any situation. We see her, fine and bejewelled, sweeping her curtsey to the Queen, or standing squarely on deck in the tarry clothes of a cabinboy to meet the attack of Turkish pirates; gracing the brilliance of ambassadorial banquets, or gnawing a hunk of rotten cheese when shipwrecked off the coast of France; defending her husband's house from robbers, outwitting the passport authorities at Dover, fleeing through the streets of embattled Cork, or with her hair standing on end at the sight of a fearful ghost. She never wearies. She takes what comes with the simplicity and verve of a child. She remains always the spontaneous and gallant Anne Fanshawe. She retains always her tremendous gusto for living. In the minuteness of her observation, in her interest in clothes, customs, food, she is a very woman. When her husband goes as English ambassador to the Spanish court, she can tell us exactly the width of his coat-lacing, the colour of his shoe-strings and the sort of ribbon which trimmed his gloves. When she flees from Bristol to Barnstaple to escape the plague, she notes (with delightful inconsequence) that "near Barnstaple there is a fruit called a masard, like a cherry, but different in taste, and makes the best pies with their sort of cream I ever eat"; also that at the merchant's house where she lodged there was a parrot a hundred years old. Such Pepysian particularity adds greatly to the realism of the narrative. Like the great diarist she has an insatiable appetite for curious facts. For example, the Spanish women, "all paint white and red, from the Queen to the cobbler's wife, old and young, widows excepted, who never go out of close mourning, nor wear gloves, nor show their hair after their husband's death"; and again, that in Spain "they have a seed which they sow in the latter end of March, like our sweet basil; but it grows up in their pots, which are often of china, large, for their windows, so delicately, that it is all the summer as round as a ball and as large as the circumference of the pot, of a most pleasant green, and very good scent." She loves also anything that is traditional or mysterious, and tells with great relish how the prophecy written over the entrance gate of the Alhambra came to be fulfilled. She describes further that through an iron grate fixed in the side of a hill near the Alhambra, one could distinctly hear the clashing of swords, and she adds that, according to a legend, it could never be opened since the Moors left, and that all perished who attempted it.

But although Anne Fanshawe's attention to detail gave a particular vividness to her narrative, she had a power of natural realism quite independent of such touches. The vigorous simplicity of her style, and its worth as an expression of personality can best be shown by extracts; and a brief resumé of the principal events will show the ability of this biographer to tell a gripping and, at times, a very moving story. (pp. 110-12)

No more is needed to attest the excellence of Anne Fanshawe's *Memoirs*. They are characterised not only by her complete realism and narrative power, but also by the sincerity of feeling. Had she written fiction it could never have been Pastoral or Heroic. To her the world around her was so colourful and so vitally interesting that she could never have found self-expression in fashioning a pale world of shepherds and knights. She knew an exiled Prince and a slain King: she had experienced real wars, real shipwreck, real love, and real grief. She had a firm grip on facts. If she were to create a story, one feels sure that she could never have subscribed to literary conventions which bore no relation to actual life.

As biographers Anne Fanshawe and the Duchess of Newcastle are immeasurably superior to Anne Clifford and Lucy Hutchinson. It is not so easy to compare Anne Fanshawe's work with that of the Duchess. In the construction of a narrative, in realism, in vivid descriptiveness, Anne Fanshawe was the superior, but the Duchess of Newcastle had—how shall one phrase it?—moments of greatness which somehow set her apart. This aspect is most clearly seen in *The True Relation*. It is a subjective aspect, the value of which in the development of fiction is not perhaps so strikingly apparent as the more external qualities of Anne Fanshawe's writing. Nor would it be just too greatly to stress Lady Fanshawe's objectiveness, lest one should seem to deny her that sensitive rightness of feeling so evident in many of the passages we have quoted. One cannot weigh different qualities against each other. It is best to think of the Duchess and Lady Fanshawe as two halves of a future whole—as contributing towards that mastery of narrative form and that expression of the inner being which finally fused in the modern novel.

Our female biographers were alike in one thing: they defied mortality. They were determined that not all of them should die, that they would erect a monument more lasting than brass to those events which were their pride and their heartbreak, which had devoured the years of their lives and demanded all their love, their faith and their endurance. Naturally it was essential for them to show that these sacrifices had been worth while, and so we find them exercising selectivity—not artistic, but merely human selectivity—in the use of their material. Anne Clifford never doubts that the law-suit was worth the contentions of a life-time, and she clenches her teeth on the humiliations of her married life, the Duchess ignores the slanders on the Duke's hasty exile; Lucy Hutchinson omits the details of the Colonel's lapse from valour; Anne Fanshawe refuses to consider that her husband's recall from Spain might have been deserved. Anne Fanshawe was nearest to the technique of fiction, but each woman told the story which she had lived in fact. Thus our female biographers' writings represent a phase in the evolution of the English novel which cannot be ignored. (pp. 120-21)

B. G. MacCarthy, "Biography," in her Women Writers: Their Contribution to the English Novel, 1621-1744, *Cork University Press, 1944, pp. 70-121.*

JOHN LOFTIS (essay date 1979)

[*Loftis is an American essayist and academic. In the following excerpt from the introduction to his 1979 edition of Fanshawe's* Memoirs, *he assesses Fanshawe's writing abilities, unfavorably comparing her with Lady Anne Halkett.*]

Lady Fanshawe's is in a specialized sense a family memoir: a record of her own and her husband's families, of her husband's career, and of their married life. She addressed the *Memoirs* to her only surviving son, Sir Richard Fanshawe (1665-94), as an instructive memorial of the prominence and achievements of his forebears and particularly of his father, who had died when the son was less than a year old. The nature of the *Memoirs* is conditioned by Lady Fanshawe's intention in writing them, an intention in which publication had no part. Those passages which may to us seem boastful should be read with an awareness that she envisaged, not an audience at large, but a family audience who would read the *Memoirs* in manuscript. She intended to provide her descendants with a record of their lineage.

The passages devoted to family history are often tedious. Yet Lady Fanshawe's concern to preserve a comprehensive record of the family in its many branches provides insight into the structure of that level of English society made up of the richer gentry and the lesser nobility. Her concern to describe the family's sufferings, in life and in property, in the Royalist cause reveals in convincing detail the depth of the social upheaval among persons of her rank. If, as has been suggested, the Civil Wars had no great consequences for the English citizenry at large, they had devastating consequences for the social class to which Lady Fanshawe (and Lady Halkett) belonged. Lady Fanshawe's *Memoirs* provide a human dimension to generalized interpretations of the Wars' impact on the gentry and aristocracy. (pp. xiv-xv)

Lady Fanshawe's reliability as a reporter of the events she recounts is not uniform throughout the *Memoirs*. We may accept the impression she conveys of huge Royalist losses without regarding the sums of money she mentions as accurate; and we may more confidently accept her reports of the deaths in battle of friends and relations, some of whom she names. But she is frequently in error about dates, particularly when writing about her husband's life before they were married in 1644, when he was nearly thirty-six years old. Yet in the latter portions of the *Memoirs* devoted to her husband's embassies to Portugal and Spain, she is so precise, so meticulous in specifying dates and sums of money, that we may assume she wrote with personal records before her. Several passages have indeed the discontinuity that would result from the transcription of a diary she had written earlier. The discontinuity of sentences within a single paragraph is occasionally such as to suggest she dictated them to an amanuensis.

Despite the momentous events she witnessed, Lady Fanshawe writes as a woman preoccupied with practical affairs, largely ignoring the ideological conflicts inherent in the Civil Wars. Her closest approach to an expression of the emotional and intellectual convictions held by many of the Royalists appears in her reverence for Charles I. She tells of visiting him in the autumn of 1647, when he was held captive at Hampton Court:

> I went 3 times to pay my duty to him, both as I was the daughter of his servant and wife to his servant. The last time I ever saw him, when I took my leave, I could not refraine weeping. When he had saluted me, I prayd to God to preserve His Majesty with long life and happy years. He stroked me on my cheek and sayd, 'Child, if God pleaseth, it shall be so, but both you and I must submit to God's will, and you know in what hands I am in.'

The King then turned to her husband, addressing him as 'Dick', and gave him oral instructions to be conveyed to the Prince of Wales and letters to the Queen, both of whom were then in France.

Lady Fanshawe's reverence for Charles II, as the Prince became in January 1649, is conveyed rather by silence about his failings—except for a single reference to his indulging his pleasures—than by anything she writes. Her silence did not extend to his Ministers. She omits gossip about licentiousness, but her *Memoirs* are not charitable in their judgement of Englishmen in high office—the Royal family always excepted. She is consistently severe in references to Sir Edward Hyde, the Earl of Clarendon as he became at the Restoration, her animus apparently arising from a conviction that Clarendon was responsible for Charles II's failure to keep a promise to make Sir Richard one of his Secretaries of State. She regards Clarendon 'and his party' as responsible for the English objections to the terms of a peace settlement with Spain negotiated by Sir Richard, and for his recall as ambassador to Spain. She writes acidly about the Earl of Sandwich, who succeeded Sir Richard in Madrid. After alluding to his alleged cowardice, she writes that 'He neither understood the custmes of the [Spanish] court, nor the language, nor indeed anything but a vitious life, and thus was he shuffled into your father's imployment to reap the benefit of his five years' negotiation of the peace of England, Spaine, and Portugall . . .'. This is less than a comprehensive account of a complicated subject.

Lady Fanshawe appears to best advantage in her loving portrait of her husband. The bitterness of her comments on Lord Clarendon, Lord Sandwich, and Lord Shaftesbury arose in part from her partisanship on his behalf. She believed that he—and after his death she—had been treated ungenerously and even unjustly, and in the privacy of her *Memoirs* she expressed resentment at those she considered responsible. She had no reluctance to tell an anecdote to her own disadvantage if it illustrated the good judgement of her husband, as in the episode, not long after their marriage, when at the instigation of a woman of rank she tried to persuade him to tell her confidential information about the Royal family. Her detailed account of her husband's kind but firm response to her indiscretion, a response that in its restraint had a fatherly quality about it, can remind us that he was almost seventeen years older than she. (pp. xv-xvii)

Lady Fanshawe's *Memoirs* are important for the record they provide of persons, events, and places. Hers is a utilitarian prose, rarely ambiguous but stylistically uneven and undistinguished. (p. xviii)

John Loftis, in an introduction to The Memoirs of Anne, Lady Halkett and Ann, Lady Fanshawe, *edited by John Loftis, Oxford at the Clarendon Press, 1979, pp. ix-xviii.*

MARY BETH ROSE (essay date 1986)

[*In the following excerpt, Rose discusses Fanshawe's concept and presentation of her marriage as an "idealized partnership of identical emotions and goals."*]

Unlike the Duchess of Newcastle, Ann Fanshawe succeeds remarkably in subsuming her individuality within her role. Characteristically, the cultural superego through which she defines herself is not the prescribed composite of individualized female character traits with which the Duchess struggles, but rather the seventeenth-century Protestant vision of the perfect wife. Since the British Reformation in the 1530's, the essentially Pauline conception "holy matrimony," wherein "the husband is head of the wife, even as Christ is head of the Church" (Ephesians 5:23) had been refined and reiterated in Protestant moral and religious writing. At the very beginning of her narrative, Lady Fanshawe succinctly presents the image of her desired identity as a fortunate partner in such a union, the "great mystery" in which the husband and wife "shall be one flesh," the husband loving the wife as he loves himself, the wife submitting to the husband, reverencing him (Ephesians 5:21-33): "*Glory be to God* we never had but one mind through out our lives, our soules were wrapped up in each other, our aims and designs one, our loves one, and our resentments one . . . What ever was reall happiness God gave it me in him; but to commend my better half . . . methinks is to commend myself and so may bear a censure."

At no point in her narrative does Lady Fanshawe deviate from her loyal, loving adherence to this idealized partnership of identical emotions and goals. Indeed she recounts the one moment of matrimonial conflict in her autobiography only in order to reveal the ease with which she overcame her need for self-assertion. In this isolated instance she discusses her attempt during the height of the Civil War to extract secret information from her husband, Sir Richard, who was performing crucial services for the beleaguered King Charles: "I that was young, innocent, and to that day had never in my mouth 'What news,' begun to think there was more in inquiring into buseness of publick affaires than I thought off." She wheedles and cries, refuses to eat or sleep until he tells her what he knows; he condescends, kisses her, changes the subject, until finally compelled by her weeping and begging to declare that, though his life, fortune, and "every thought" are hers, yet "my honour is my own." It never occurs to Lady Ann to question either openly or deviously an arrangement in which her husband's knowledge and attachments are so much freer and more various than her own. Instead the unequal logic of patriarchal power relations is revealed to her through the glow of Sir Richard's undoubted affection and, as she watches him, the scales fall from her eyes: "So great was his reason and goodness, that upon consider-ation it made my folly appeare to me so vile that from that day untill the day of his death I never thought fit to aske him any business, but that he communicated freely to me, in order to his estate or family."

The problem for this inquiry becomes: how does a self-defined silent partner manage to generate a narrative unified and enlivened by her integrated conception of her individuality? As Lady Fanshawe continually makes clear, her goal is not to act, as a subject, but to be loved, as an object of devotion. The lack of conflict with which she discards her girlish fondness for physical activity in order gladly to assume her dead mother's modest, subdued role as family caretaker indicates the potentially static quality of her life account. Yet most of her *Memoirs* tell a lively and engaging story.

Surprisingly, in telling her story, Lady Fanshawe eschews two rhetorical strategies that female autobiographers commonly employ when confronting the contradiction between culturally enjoined silence and the need for self-assertion, or between the peaceful, cyclical orderliness assumed to comprise feminine destiny and the linear, suspenseful quest motif required for the construction of conventionally masculine narrative. The first of these strategies, devious self-assertion, takes the form either of self-idealization disguised as self-deprecation or the overt denial of anger and hostility, prominent emotions that, because they cannot really be ignored, form a subversive subtext. The Duchess of Newcastle and . . . Alice Thornton are experts at this double-edged, often self-defeating technique. At times the violence and self-hatred implicit in Lady Fanshawe's complete identification with male superiority are starkly revealed, as in her account of her son Richard's death. "Both my eldest daughters had the small-pox att the same time," she explains, underscoring the virtue of her priorities, "and though I neglected them, and day and night tended my dear son, yet it pleased God they recovered and he dyed, the grief of which made me miscary and caused a sickness of 3 weeks." But the inhumanity in this passage is shocking precisely because it is exceptional; furthermore, no unacknowledged emotional conflicts surface to disturb the author's untroubled identification with the sexual status quo.

A second narrative strategy which female autobiographers commonly use involves the creation of a conventional linear quest motif out of the author's romantic adventures, which culminate in her destiny-as-marriage. Lady Anne Halkett uses this strategy with great success. . . . But, despite her genuine love for her husband and her dramatic location of selfhood in marriage, Lady Ann Fanshawe . . . fails to tell the saga of her courtship. For her, the story of self-creation begins, rather than ends, with marriage.

In Lady Fanshawe's case, it is clearly the Civil War that liberates her from the acquiescence and passivity required by the sexual ideology to which she is profoundly attached; it is therefore the War which gives her story a plot. Because Sir Richard is deeply involved in Royalist intrigue, Lady Ann must frequently act to protect him, along with their joint property interests. Unlike the Duchess of Newcastle, whose ambivalence about public self-assertion and individuality paralyzes her, Ann Fanshawe responds to the call to independent action as a challenge. In three daring episodes, for example, she not only makes danger-

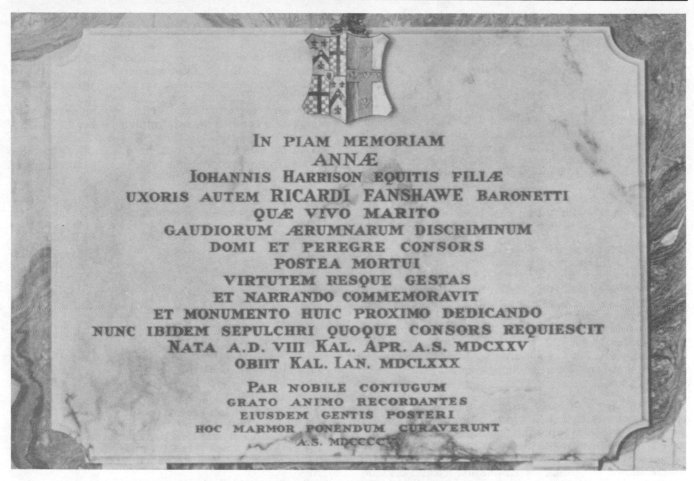

Memorial of Lady Fanshawe, erected at Ware Church in 1805.

ous, clandestine nightly trips to visit her husband in jail, but also intrigues resourcefully for his freedom; imitating romantic tradition, she disguises herself as a man and stands by her husband's side during a shipboard battle with Turkish pirates, inspiring Sir Richard to cry, "Good God, that love can make this change!"; she plots and successfully enacts a courageous escape from Britain, forging her passport in order to join her husband when he is exiled in France. Significantly, the perilous exigencies of Civil War in no way compel the boldly and publicly active Lady Ann to feel conflict about her feminine identity. On the contrary, the war simply lends wider meaning to her role as faithful, obedient, and loving wife. Unlike the Duchess's, her identification with her role is complete and untroubled, enabling her to perform effectively on her husband's behalf. Just as her duty as wife and mother later becomes the rationale for the act of writing her *Memoirs*, so her marriage provides her with a motive and cue for action during the Revolution without requiring her to question prevailing sexual assumptions, which she never does.

For Lady Ann Fanshawe, the female autobiographer's task of integrating potentially conflicting aspects of identity in the creation of a story and a self is thus considerably reduced in difficulty by the Civil War. The external chaos of the Revolution paradoxically releases her from internal conflict by allowing her to merge her private concerns with the larger political environment. Specifically, the ex-

terior strangeness of the political scene enlarges the internal borders of the psychologically familiar, enabling her to act by rendering her vision of the ideal Protestant marriage more expansive and flexible. This point becomes clear when we examine the progress of her narration, which divides neatly between accounts of the Revolution and the Restoration. In her retelling of Civil War experiences, Lady Ann structures her vision of her marriage with a coherent narrative pattern of death and resurrection, disaster and delivery. Replete with echoes from the Gospels and the Book of Acts, her story of holy matrimony plagued by war becomes a secular scripture recounting separation from and reunion with her husband who, going about "his master's business," becomes a type of Christ that she can follow, serve, and adore. This scheme works well to propel the narrative forward but, when the two are permanently reunited at the Restoration, the successful pattern inevitably dissolves.

During peacetime, when Sir Richard serves as ambassador to Portugal and Spain, the flamboyant public drama of war, resonant with the depth of emotional life, dwindles to a shallow catalogue of ceremonies and gifts that is enlivened only by Lady Ann's sensual love for exotic and colorful objects, along with her splendid eye for concrete physical detail. Indeed the depiction of her passionate attachment to money and property alters drastically as her experience shifts from war to peace. The pattern of separation from and reunion with Sir Richard, for example, allows her to unite money with love in a blissful epiphany of bourgeois marital goals: "He with all expressions of joy received me in his arms and gave me an hundred pieces of gold, saying, 'I know that thou that keeps my heart so well will keep my fortune.' . . . And now I thought myself a qween, and my husband so glorious a crown that I more valued myself to be call'd by his name than borne a princess . . . and his soule doted on me." In peacetime Spain, however, this ecstatic merger of affection and property is reduced to representing the once dynamic soldier Sir Richard as a colorful, although lifeless, diplomatic artifact: "His sute was trimed with scarlet taffeta ribbon, his stockings of white silk upon long scarlett silk ones, his shoes black with scarlett shoes' strings and garters, his linnen very fine laced with very rich Flanders lace, a black beavour button on the left side, with a jewell of 1200 lb."

Lady Fanshawe's capacity for reverence has given way to the related but less creative capacity to be dazzled. In the second part of her narrative, her need to be loved is represented in the reiterative rendition of public honors—the banquets, gifts and canon salutes that celebrate her and her husband by diplomatic requirement. It is a static picture of power without desire: she has become absorbed in the institution, rather than the relationship of marriage. It is not surprising that her narrative trails off inconclusively after her husband's death, although she survived him by fourteen years.

Lady Fanshawe's *Memoirs* provide an excellent example of the way in which a chaotic period of history involves a woman whose conventionality and single-minded devotion to her husband would otherwise have restricted her to silence and passivity in an engaging and dramatic story. In Elaine Showalter's terms, the Revolution releases the muted female voice to achieve creative expression within the "allowable forms" of masculine adventure and narration. Yet to read the *Memoirs* is to become increasingly aware of an inhibited, repressed story. It is not simply that Lady Fanshawe's narration dwindles from war to peace, drama to stasis, ceasing entirely with the death of her husband and her role as his wife. Rather there is an essential tale that remains untold, namely, the saga of Lady Ann's body.

During the twenty-two years of her marriage, Ann Fanshawe gives birth to fourteen children, nine of whom die, and this impressive statistic does not encompass the repeated trauma of miscarriages, including one of triplets. In short, while during both war and peace she is almost constantly pregnant, miscarrying, or giving birth, Lady Ann treats these experiences peripherally, merely mentioning rather than exploring them. This astonishing omission cannot be accounted for by attributing to her an anachronistic reticence about sexuality. It is rather that, in her selection of material and her choice of narrative strategies, she assigns a secondary value to this highly individualized aspect of her experience. (pp. 254-59)

> Mary Beth Rose, "Gender, Genre, and History: Seventeenth-Century English Women and the Art of Autobiography," in Women in the Middle Ages and the Renaissance: Literary and Historical Perspectives, edited by Mary Beth Rose, Syracuse University Press, 1986, pp. 245-78.

ADDITIONAL BIBLIOGRAPHY

Delaney, Paul. "Female Autobiographer." In his *British Autobiography in the Seventeenth Century*, pp. 158-66. London: Routledge & Kegan Paul, 1969.
    Considers Fanshawe's place in the development of British autobiography, comparing the *Memoirs* primarily with the autobiography of Lady Anne Halkett.

Findley, Sarah, and Hobby, Elaine. "Seventeenth Century Women's Autobiography." In *1642: Literature and Power in the Seventeenth Century, Proceedings of the Essex Conference on the Sociology of Literature, July 1980*, edited by Francis Barker, Jay Bernstein, and others, pp. 11-36. Essex: University of Essex, 1981.
    Compares Fanshawe's *Memoirs* with the autobiographies of several of her contemporaries, including Anne Halkett, Lucy Hutchinson, Margaret Cavendish, and Mary Rich.

(Sir) Thomas Malory

?-1471

(Also Maleore, Maleorre, Malleorré, and Malorye) English prose writer.

Malory is recognized as a towering figure of medieval English literature. His masterwork, the *Morte Darthur*, is the best-known treatment in English of the Matter of Britain: tales of the exploits and deeds of King Arthur and the knights of the Round Table. The *Morte Darthur* is esteemed on several counts. It is a mirror of medieval culture and manners, a seminal work of English prose, and a narrative of enduring entertainment value. Yet the *Morte* remains an enigma. Scholars are at odds about authorship, source material, authorial intention, narrative structure, and thematic content. Whatever puzzles it presents, however, the *Morte Darthur* is an acknowledged literary milestone. In the words of critic William Henry Schofield, it is "the fountainhead of [English] Arthurian fiction."

The authorship of the *Morte Darthur* has long been hotly disputed. Candidates from Wales, Yorkshire, Lincolnshire, and Huntingdonshire have been advanced and powerfully defended, but it is now generally agreed that the "syr Thomas Maleore knyght" named in the colophon of the 1485 printing of the text may be identified with Sir Thomas Malory of Newbold Revel, Warwickshire. His birth date is uncertain, but it is believed to be just before 1400. He was probably the son of John Malory, esquire, also of Newbold Revel. As a young man, Thomas served with the earl of Warwick's forces in France. He succeeded to his father's estate in 1433 or 1434. Far from being the sort of man likely to write what William Caxton called a "Noble and Joyous book," Sir Thomas was a ruffian of the most extreme kind. He was indicted for theft in 1443 and served in parliament later in the decade. He is next heard of in 1450, when he evidently embarked upon an appalling career of rape, robbery, and brutal violence. All together, this "servant of Ihesu bothe day and nyght" (as he claimed of himself) was to spend years in prison for his crimes.

The most damaging document relating to Malory is the memorandum of an inquisition held at Nuneaton in 1451. Therein it is stated that on 4 January 1450 Malory led an attempt to murder Humphrey, Duke of Buckingham. A few months later (May 23) he raped Joan Smyth of Monks Kirby, and the following week he extorted 100 shillings from Margaret Kyng and William Hales. He raped Joan Smyth again on August 6, stealing £40 in goods belonging to her husband. On 31 August he extorted 20 shillings from John Mylner. Almost a year later, on 4 June 1451, Malory and five others stole seven cows, two calves, a cart worth £4, and 335 sheep from a Warwickshire farm. He was arrested a month later and placed in custody, but he broke out of prison by swimming the moat. The very next day (July 28) he reconvened his band of abettors. That night he led an attack on Coombe Abbey, stealing jewels, cash, religious objects, and other valuables. The next night he returned to Coombe for more booty, this time inciting a riot in which he may have personally beaten the abbot bloody with a stick. In spite of the seriousness of the charges brought at Nuneaton, Malory was never brought to trial for the crimes enumerated in the memorandum, though he was summoned in March 1452 to answer charges not sufficiently explained the year before. For a time he apparently continued his criminal enterprises, jumping bail in 1454 to avoid felony prosecution. He was called before the King's Bench on 16 January 1456. Two years later he was committed to the Marshalsea. Nothing further is known of him until 1468, when he was specifically excluded from Edward IV's general pardon of 24 August. Sir Thomas died in March 1471, probably having completed the *Morte* a year or two earlier. According to the seventeenth-century English antiquary William Dugdale, he was "buried . . . in the Chappell of St Francis at the Grey Friars, near Newgate in the Suburbs of London."

The central story of the *Morte Darthur* consists of two main elements: (1) King Arthur's reign ending in disaster with the dissolution of the Round Table, and (2) the quest for the Holy Grail. The work begins with the adulterous conception of Arthur and the establishment of his kingship by his pulling of the Sword—Excalibur—from the Stone. Arthur and his knights then engage in battles in defense of the realm and the Round Table. After a series of stirring adventures and victories, Arthur conquers Rome and is welcomed into the city by the pope. There follow tales of Arthur's knights: the prowess of Sir Palomides and Sir Lancelot, the pursuit of the mysterious Questing Beast, the rescue of prisoners held by rogue knights, the ventures of Sir Tristram and his paramour, and other accounts. The quest for the Holy Grail is initiated. This vexing and ill-fated undertaking leads to the loss of some of Arthur's finest knights, among them Lancelot's son, the pure-hearted Sir Galahad. During the quest, the beginning of the end of the Round Table is foreshadowed in the shortcomings and spiritual imperfections of men once considered paradigms of knightly virtue. With the return of the knights from the failed attempt to recover the Grail, the dissolution of the Round Table proceeds in earnest. Lancelot evidences moral and spiritual failings, committing adultery with Arthur's consort, Queen Guinevere, while Arthur himself is increasingly thwarted by the challenges of kingship. The conflict between knightly and Christian behavior remains unresolved, precipitating the tragic and bloody collapse of Arthur's society at the treacherous instigation of the king's bastard son, Sir Mordred. In the end, Arthur is dead, Guinevere has entered a nunnery, and the kingdom is in ruins.

According to a statement at the end of the book, the *Morte Darthur* was completed in "the ix yere of the reygne of kyng edward the fourth," that is between 4 March 1469 and 3 March 1470. It first saw print on 31 July 1485 in the workshop of William Caxton. Caxton's edition is divided into 21 books and 506 (numbered 507, one having been skipped near the end of Book I) chapters. Caxton's was the only version known until 1934, when W. F. Oakeshott discovered a manuscript of the *Morte* in the Fellows Library of Winchester College. The Winchester text parallels the Caxton version closely except for the section treating Arthur's war with the Roman emperor Lucius, but it is a decidedly distinct text nonetheless. The manuscript, which was apparently copied during the 1470s or early 1480s, is divided into ten parts forming five larger units, corresponding to Caxton's Books I-IV, V-VII, VIII-XII, XIII-XVII, and XVIII-XXI. The manuscript was edited by Eugène Vinaver in 1947 as *The Works of Sir Thomas Malory*. Its relationship to Caxton's version is not altogether clear and is the subject of ongoing discussion. All that is known for certain is that the manuscript did not serve as printer's copy for Caxton.

The existence of two distinct versions of the *Morte Darthur* has challenged critics who have sought to uncover Malory's original intention. What are the sources of the text? What bearing do they have on the narrative structure? Is the *Morte* a single story or a series of separate tales? These questions, which touch on textual as well as thematic issues, have not been adequately resolved but are vital to an understanding of the *Morte*. Caxton himself claimed that his edition was printed according to a copy that "Syr Thomas Malorye dyd take oute of certeyn bookes of Frensshe and reduced it into Englysshe." It is clear, however, that in addition to French prose romance cycles—*Estoire del Saint Graal, Estoire de Merlin, Lancelot du Lac, Queste del Saint Graal, Roman du Graal,* and *Mort Artu*—Malory also borrowed extensively from at least two Middle English Arthuriads, the alliterative *Morte Arthure* and the stanzaic *Le Morte Arthur*, as well as from *La mort le Roi Artu*, the final segment of the Old French Vulgate Cycle. Malory's use of these and other works is especially evident in the syntax, vocabulary, and prose style of the *Morte*. Alliterative rhythms derived from English accounts of Arthur color much of the text: "As the kynge was in his cog and lay in his caban, he felle in a slumberyng and dremed how a dredfull dragon dud drenche much of his peple and com fleyng one synge oute of the weste partyes." Elsewhere, Gallic vocabulary is strong, and portions of the *Morte* are near-exact translations from French antecedents. While some critics have claimed that Malory's heavy reliance on existing material makes him "unoriginal" in the modern sense, most readers have at least praised his redaction and arrangement of the sources.

The chief controversy in Malory studies concerns the structural unity of the *Morte*. As early as 1894, Sir Walter Raleigh criticized the "inevitably rambling structure" of the work. He claimed: "To attain to a finely ordered artistic structure was beyond Malory's power; the very wealth of legend with which he had to deal put it beyond him, and he is too much absorbed in the interest of the parts to give more than a passing consideration to the whole." Two decades later, George Saintsbury viewed Malory as a "compiler" as far as the narrative of the *Morte* is concerned: "The point is that this *compilator compilans compilative in compilationibus compilandis* has, somehow or other, supplied a mortar of style and a design of word-architecture for his brute material of borrowed brick or stone, which is not only miraculous, but, in the nature even of miraculous things, uncompilable from any predecessor." Elsewhere, Saintsbury added: "Malory alone made of the diverse stories one story, one book." The discovery and publication of the Winchester Manuscript enriched the discussion. In the introduction to his edition of the text, Vinaver set forth revolutionary views. He maintained that, far from being a continuous narrative, the

Morte is a series of eight "separate romances." Caxton, he added, produced it as a single book under a "spurious and totally unrepresentative title." Hence Vinaver formulated the new title, *The Works of Sir Thomas Malory*, to reflect this view. Vinaver's contention set the stage for a scholarly battle that has scarcely let up since. Vinaver himself never wavered from his conclusion, and his many writings on the subject won him powerful supporters. His critics, however, have pointed to Malory's own words as evidence of the unity of the work: "I pray you all, gentlemen and gentlewomen, that read this book of Arthur and his knights from the beginning to the ending...." "This book" and "beginning to the ending" suggest, it has been claimed, a continuous narrative, not a series of independent tales. Internal evidence concerning continuity is often cited, but it is generally ambiguous and has been variously interpreted. Perhaps one of the most balanced approaches is that of C. S. Lewis. Generally favoring the continuous narrative theory, Lewis touched on both textual and aesthetic matters: "Under Malory's work lies that of the French prose romancers; under theirs, that of Chrétien, Wace, and other poets; under that, Geoffrey, and perhaps the Breton *lais*; deepest of all, who knows what fragments of Celtic myth or actual British history? Malory is only the last of many restorers, improvers, demolitionists; if you will, of misunderstanders." Lewis concluded that the *Morte* is not "what any single individual either intended or foresaw.... Though every part of it was made by a man, the whole has rather grown than been made. Such things have a kind of existence that is almost midway between the works of art and those of nature."

The structural unity of the *Morte* is such a dominant critical concern that other matters might seem relatively unimportant, but this is far from being the case. From its first printing onwards, readers and critics alike have embraced the work. Initially, commentators were at pains to demonstrate the historical veracity of Arthur and the Round Table. Caxton devoted nearly half of his preface to this matter, while William Stansby included a brief introduction to his 1634 edition in order to "confute the errours of such as are of an opinion that there was never any such man as king Arthur." Earlier, Roger Ascham took issue with the moral standing of the *Morte* in his posthumously published treatise *The Scholemaster* (1570). "In our forefathers tyme," he wrote, "when Papistrie, as a standyng poole, couered and ouerflowed all England, fewe bookes were read in our tong, sauyng certaine bookes of Cheualrie, as they sayd, for pastime and pleasure, which, as some say, were made in Monasteries, by idle Monkes, or wanton Chanons: as one for example, *Morte Arthure*: the whole pleasure of which booke standeth in two speciall poyntes, in open mans slaughter, and bold bawdrye: In which booke those be counted the noblest Knightes, that do kill most men without any quarell, and commit fowlest adoulteres by sutlest shiftes." It was not until the late nineteenth century that the *Morte Darthur* was "discovered" as a major work of literature. Before then, commentary focused more on the entertainment value of the *Morte* than on anything else. It took the textual pioneer H. Oskar Sommer and the aesthetic critic Andrew Lang to bring the *Morte* into the mainstream of English literary history. Early commentators on the artistry of the *Morte* viewed the work in practically ethereal terms. Schofield wrote in 1912: "The art of Malory's work an injudicious reader, even to-day, is apt to overlook. The writing seems all so natural and simple, so lacking in rhetorical ornament, that one who is unobservant may readily be deluded into thinking that little praise is due the author. But let him compare the *Morte d'Arthur* with any other work of the same kind, ancient or modern, let him attempt to improve on any good passage that attracts him, and he will surely discover that here is art that conceals art, here is distinction that, forgetting itself, evades remark." Later in the decade, Vida D. Scudder, a major early promoter of Malory, concluded: "Malory's style is truly 'the man.' It belongs to no school, is the result of no tradition. It is a gift from above." Since Scudder's time, critics have explored many further aspects of the *Morte*. The "moral paradox" of a criminal author having written a work on "love, curtosye, and veray gentylnesse" has emerged as a major concern, while such smaller issues as novelistic elements, characterization, allegorical imagery, "courtly love," time patterns, formulaic language, neologisms, and dialogue in the work have been treated repeatedly. Hardly a single statement on any of these subjects has yet been approved by all readers, however—a fact sure to keep Malory in the forefront of English literary criticism.

The width and variety of response to the *Morte Darthur* suggests the strong appeal of the work to a variety of readers. As the single greatest repository of Arthurian Legend in English, its influence upon poets, novelists, and scholars has been tremendous. Equally, the *Morte* has stirred the imaginations of generations of readers whose love of the Round Table and all it represents is abiding. Vinaver has commented on the longevity and general popularity of the *Morte Darthur*: "Many writers had worked on the French Arthurian prose romances between the thirteenth and the fifteenth centuries; there had been adaptations of it in Spain and in Germany. All this is now dead and buried, and Malory alone stands as a rock defying all changes of taste and style and morals; not as a grand paradox of nature, but as a lasting work of art."

PRINCIPAL WORKS

The Noble and Joyous book entytled le morte Darthur Notwythstondyng it treateth of the byrth, lyf, and actes of the sayd kyng Arthur, of his noble knyghtes of the rounde table, theyr meruayllous enquestes and aduentures, thachyeuyng of the sangreal, & in thende the dolorous deth & departyng out of thys world of them al (prose) 1485

The Works of Sir Thomas Malory. 3 vols. (prose) 1947; revised edition, 1967

*There is no evidence that Malory gave this work a title. The present title was apparently supplied by William Caxton, the printer of the first edition. This work is also known as *The Booke of the Noble Kyng, Kyng Arthur, Sometyme Kynge of Englonde, of his Noble Actes and Feates of Armes and Chyvalrye, his Noble Knygtes and Table Rounde, The Whole Book of King Arthur and of His Noble Knights of the Round Table, Le Morte d'Arthur, Le Morte Darthur, Morte d'Arthur, Morte Arthur,* and, most commonly, *Morte Darthur.*

WILLIAM CAXTON (essay date 1485)

[*Caxton is revered as the first English printer. In 1475, while living in Bruges, he set up and published* The Recuyell of the Historyes of Troye, *the first book printed in English. One year later, in 1476, he established a press in Westminster, where, during the next decade and a half, he produced over 80 separate works. Caxton was a gifted editor, translator, and author in his own right. He often wrote prefaces to the works he published, supplying information (when available) about authorship, textual history, genre, intended audience, narrative structure, and other critical and aesthetic matters. His most famous publications include Geoffrey Chaucer's* Canterbury Tales *(1478 and 1484), John Gower's* Confessio amantis *(1483), a translation of* The Golden Legend *(1483), and Malory's* Noble and Joyous book entytled le morte Darthur *(1485). In the following excerpt from the preface of the last-named work, Caxton argues that Arthur's reputation is chiefly literary and notices the didactic, historical, and entertainment value of the* Morte Darthur *itself.*]

After that I had accomplysshed and fynysshed dyvers hystoryes as wel of contemplacyon as of other hystoryal and worldly actes of grete conquerours and prynces, and also certeyn bookes of ensaumples and doctryne, many noble and dyvers gentylmen of thys royame of Englond camen and demaunded me many and oftymes wherfore that I have not do made and enprynte the noble hystorye of the Saynt Greal and of the moost renomed Crysten kyng, fyrst and chyef of the thre best Crysten, and worthy, kyng Arthur, whyche ought moost to be remembred emonge us Englysshemen tofore al other Crysten kynges.

For it is notoyrly knowen thorugh the unyversal world that there been nine worthy and the best that ever were, that is to wete, thre Paynyms, thre Jewes, and thre Crysten men. As for the Paynyms, they were tofore the Incarnacyon of Cryst whiche were named, the fyrst Hector of Troye, of whome th'ystorye is comen bothe in balade and in prose, the second Alysaunder the Grete, and the thyrd, Julyus Cezar, Emperour of Rome, of whome th'ystoryes ben wel knowen and had. And as for the thre Jewes whyche also were tofore th'Yncarnacyon of our Lord, of whome the fyrst was Duc Josué whyche brought the chyldren of Israhel into the londe of byheste, the second Davyd, kyng of Jerusalem, and the thyrd Judas Machabeus, of these thre the Byble reherceth al theyr noble hystoryes and actes. And sythe the sayd Incarnacyon have ben thre noble Crysten men stalled and admytted thorugh the unyversal world into the nombre of the nine beste and worthy, of whome was fyrst the noble Arthur, whos noble actes I purpose to wryte thys present book here folowyng. The second was Charlemayn, or Charles the Grete, of whome th'ystorye is had in many places, bothe in Frensshe and Englysshe; and the thyrd and last was Godefray of Boloyn, of whos actes and lyf I made a book unto th'excellent prynce and kyng of noble memorye, kyng Edward the Fourth.

The sayd noble jentylmen instantly requyred me t'emprynte th'ystorye of the sayd noble kyng and conquerour kyng Arthur and of his knyghtes, wyth th'ystorye of the Saynt Greal and of the deth and endyng of the sayd Arthur, affermyng that I ought rather t'enprynte his actes and noble feates than of Godefroye of Boloyne or ony of the other eyght, consyderyng that he was a man borne wythin this royame and kyng and emperour of the same, and that there ben in Frensshe dyvers and many noble volumes of his actes, and also of his knyghtes.

To whome I answerd that dyvers men holde oppynyon that there was no suche Arthur and that alle suche bookes as been maad of hym ben but fayned and fables, bycause that somme cronycles make of hym no mencyon ne remembre hym noothynge, ne of his knyghtes.

Wherto they answerd, and one in specyal sayd, that in hym that shold say or thynke that there was never suche a kyng callyd Arthur myght wel be aretted grete folye and blyndenesse, for he sayd that there were many evydences of the contrarye. Fyrst, ye may see his sepulture in the monasterye of Glastyngburye; and also in Polycronycon, in the fifth book, the syxte chappytre, and in the seventh book, the twenty-thyrd chappytre, where his body was buryed, and after founden and translated into the sayd monasterye. Ye shal se also in th'ystorye of Bochas, in his book De Casu Principum, parte of his noble actes, and also of his falle. Also Galfrydus, in his Brutysshe book, recounteth his lyf. And in dyvers places of Englond many remembraunces ben yet of hym and shall remayne perpetuelly, and also of his knyghtes: fyrst, in the abbey of Westmestre, at Saynt Edwardes shryne, remayneth the prynte of his seal in reed waxe, closed in beryll, in whych is wryton Patricius Arthurus Britannie Gallie Germanie Dacie Imperator; item, in the castel of Dover ye may see Gauwayns skulle and Cradoks mantel; at Wynchester, the Rounde Table; in other places Launcelottes swerde and many other thynges.

Thenne, al these thynges consydered, there can no man resonably gaynsaye but there was a kyng of thys lande named Arthur. For in al places, Crysten and hethen, he is reputed and taken for one of the nine worthy, and the fyrst of the thre Crysten men. And also he is more spoken of beyonde the see, moo bookes made of his noble actes, than there be in Englond; as wel in Duche, Ytalyen, Spaynysshe, and Grekysshe, as in Frensshe. And yet of record remayne in wytnesse of hym in Wales, in the toune of Camelot, the grete stones and mervayllous werkys of yron lyeng under the grounde, and ryal vautes, which dyvers now lyvyng hath seen. Wherfor it is a mervayl why he is no more renomed in his ownc contrcyc, sauf onelye it accordeth to the word of God, whyche sayth that no man is accept for a prophete in his owne contreye.

Thenne, al these thynges forsayd aledged, I coude not wel denye but that there was suche a noble kyng named Arthur, and reputed one of the nine worthy, and fyrst and chyef of the Cristen men. And many noble volumes be made of hym and of his noble knyghtes in Frensshe, which I have seen and redde beyonde the see, which been not had in our maternal tongue. But in Walsshe ben many, and also in Frensshe, and somme in Englysshe, but nowher nygh alle. Wherfore, suche as have late ben drawen oute bryefly into Englysshe, I have, after the symple connynge that God hath sente to me, under the favour and correctyon of al noble lordes and gentylmen, enprysed to enprynte a book of the noble hystoryes of the sayd kynge Arthur and of certeyn of his knyghtes [*The Noble and Joyous Book Entytled Le Morte Darthur*], after a copye unto me delyverd, whyche copye svi Thomas Maloiye dyd take oute of certeyn bookes of Frensshe and reduced it into Englysshe.

And I, accordyng to my copye, have doon sette it in enprynte to the entente that noble men may see and lerne the noble actes of chyvalrye, the jentyl and vertuous dedes that somme knyghtes used in tho dayes, by whyche they came to honour, and how they that were vycious were punysshed and ofte put to shame and rebuke; humbly bysechyng al noble lordes and ladyes wyth al other estates, of what estate or degree they been of, that shal see and rede in this sayd book and werke, that they take the good and honest actes in their remembraunce, and to folowe the same; wherin they shalle fynde many joyous and playsaunt hystoryes and noble and renomed actes of humanyté, gentylnesse, and chyvalryes. For herein may be seen noble chyvalrye, curtosye, humanyté, frendlynesse, hardynesse, love, frendshyp, cowardyse, murdre, hate, vertue, and synne. Doo after the good and leve the evyl, and it shal brynge you to good fame and renommee.

And for to passe the tyme thys book shal be plesaunte to rede in, but for to gyve fayth and byleve that al is trewe that is conteyned herin, ye be at your lyberté. But al is wryton for our doctryne, and for to beware that we falle not to vyce ne synne, but t'exersyse and folowe vertu, by whyche we may come and atteyne to good fame and renommé in thys lyf, and after thys shorte and transytorye lyf to come unto everlastyng blysse in heven; the whyche He graunte us that reygneth in heven, the Blessyd Trynyté. Amen.

Thenne, to procede forth in thys sayd book, whyche I dyrecte unto alle noble prynces, lordes, and ladyes, gentylmen or gentylwymmen, that desyre to rede or here redde of the noble and joyous hystorye of the grete conquerour and excellent kyng, kyng Arthur, somtyme kyng of thys noble royalme thenne callyd Brytaygne, I, Wyllyam Caxton, symple persone, present thys book folowyng whyche I have enprysed t'enprynte: and treateth of the noble actes, feates of armes of chyvalrye, prowesse, hardynesse,humanyté, love, curtosye, and veray gentylnesse, wyth many wonderful hystoryes and adventures. (pp. cxi-cxiv)

> *William Caxton, "Caxton's Preface," in* The Works of Sir Thomas Malory, Vol. I, *edited by Eugène Vinaver, Oxford at the Clarendon Press, 1947, pp. cxi-cxv.*

ROGER ASCHAM (essay date 1568?)

[Ascham was a major sixteenth-century English humanist scholar and poet. He is best known for two works: Toxophilus *(1545), dialogues on the virtues of the English longbow, and* The Scholemaster *(1570), a posthumously published essay that has been described by Michael Jamieson as "a humane, practical treatise on education, showing a lively understanding of the young." In the following excerpt from* The Scholemaster, *Ascham denounces the* Morte Darthur *as a bawdy and brutal book and strongly advises against putting it in the hands of "a yong ientleman, or a yong mayde."]*

S. Paul saith, that sectes and ill opinions, be the workes of the flesh, and frutes of sinne; this is spoken, no more trewlie for the doctrine, than sensiblie for the reason. And why? For, ill doinges, breed ill thinkinges. And of corrupted maners, spryng peruerted iudgementes. And how? there be in man two speciall thinges: Mans will, mans mynde. Where will inclineth to goodnes, the mynde is bent to troth: Where will is caried from goodnes to vanitie, the mynde is sone drawne from troth to false opinion. And so, the readiest way to entangle the mynde with false doctrine, is first to intice the will to wanton liuyng. Therfore, when the busie and open Papistes abroad, could not, by their contentious bookes, turne men in England fast enough, from troth and right iudgement in doctrine, than the sutle and secrete Papistes at home, procured bawdie bookes to be translated out of the *Italian* tonge, whereby ouer many yong willes and wittes allured to wantonnes, do now boldly contemne all seuere bookes that sounde to honestie and godlines. In our forefathers tyme, whan Papistrie, as a standyng poole, couered and ouerflowed all England, fewe bookes were read in our tong, sauyng certaine bookes of Cheualrie, as they sayd, for pastime and pleasure, which, as some say, were made in Monasteries, by idle Monkes, or wanton Chanons: as one for example, *Morte Arthure*: the whole pleasure of which booke standeth in two speciall poyntes, in open mans slaughter, and bold bawdrye: In which booke those be counted the noblest Knightes, that do kill most men without any quarell, and commit fowlest aduoulteres by sutlest shiftes: as Sir *Launcelote*, with the wife of King *Arthure* his master: Syr *Tristram* with the wife of kyng *Marke* his vncle: Syr *Lamerocke*, with the wife of king *Lote*, that was his own aunte. This is good stuffe, for wise men to laughe at, or honest men to take pleasure at. Yet I know, when Gods Bible was banished the Court, and *Morte Arthure* receiued into the Princes chamber. What toyes, the dayly readyng of such a booke, may worke in the will of a yong ientleman, or a yong mayde, that liueth welthelie and idlelie, wise men can iudge, and honest men do pitie, And yet ten *Morte Arthures* do not the tenth part of so much harme, as one of these bookes made in *Italie*, and translated in England. (pp. 134-36)

Roger Ascham, "The First Booke for the Youth," in his The Scholemaster, *edited by John E. B. Mayor, George Bell and Sons, 1895, pp. 71-143.*

WILLIAM STANSBY? (essay date 1634)

[*The following excerpt is from the unsigned preface of the 1634 edition of the* Morte Darthur, *a version based on Caxton's 1485 edition and printed by William Stansby for Jacob Bloome. Here, the critic, commonly believed to be Stansby himself, sketches the historical background of the* Morte Darthur *and considers the didactic value of the tales.*]

After this kingdome had, for the space of above foure hundred and eighty yeares, borne the intolerable yoke of the Romane servitude, which began by the conquest which Julius Cæsar made here in the raigne of Cassibellan, king of the Brittaines, seventeene yeares before the Incarnation of Christ, and ended in the time of Gratian, which was three hundred seventie six yeares after Christ, who had slaine Maximinianus, the Romane emperour; which Gratian after being slaine, Vortiger of the bloud royall of the Britaine king, did, by usurpation and the murther of Constance, the sonne of Constantius, seize upon the crowne. And being by his wicked life and ill gotten soveraignty, grown odious, and hated by most of his subjects, hee was inforced to send into Germany for the Saxons, to aide and support him. The Saxons having got footing here, never gave over their military diligence till they got full possession of the whole kingdome; chasing the British kings beyond the rivers of Dee and Seaverne in North Wales, in the raigne of Carreticus, in the yeare five hundred eighty sixe. The above said Vortigerne the usurper was deposed,

to whom his sonne Vortimer succeeded, but Vortimer was poysoned by Rowan the daughter of Hengist the Saxon, and Vortigerne againe was restored to the crowne; and after nineteene yeares of a troublous raigne, hee and his wife Rowan were burnt in their castle or palace by Aurelius Ambrose, who was of the race of Constance, who formerly had beene murdred by Vortigerne. This Aurelius Ambrose raigned thirty two yeares, to whom succeeded his brother Uter Pendragon, who was the father of Arthur, the great king of Britaine, of whose worthy acts and noble atchievements this history [*Morte Darthur*] makes mention. King Uter Pendragon begat Arthur of the beauteous Igraine, wife to the duke of Cornwall, which lady king Uter afterward rewarded, and, by the helpe of Merlin the great magitian, Arthur was brought up and educated. He raigned king of Britaine in anno five hundred and sixteene. In his raigne he curbed the insolent power of the domineering Saxons, he wanne and subdued Denmarke and Norway. He ordained and instituted the order of the round table at Winchester, which was honoured with the number of one hundred and fifty knights. He was victorious beyond the seas against the Saracens, and by his conquests made many of those misbeleeving Pagans acknowledge the true God. Whilest he was abroad in these noble and heroicall imployments, his nephew, Mordred, whom hee had put in trust with the government of his realme, being puffed up with ambition and possessed with treason, he caused himselfe to be crowned, and usurped the kingdome; which king Arthur hearing of, hee made quicke expedition into this land, and landed at Dover, where the traytor Mordred was with a mighty army to impeach and hinder the kings arrivall. But in spight of all trayterous and rebellious opposition, king Arthur landed his troupes, and after two set battailes he slue Mordred, and with the losse of his owne life, wonne a glorious victory, and being dead, was buried at the towne of Glastenbury in Somersetshire, after hee had raigned sixteene yeares, to whom next succeeded in the Britaine throne Constantine the fifth, being a kinsman to king Arthur, and sonne to Cadors duke of Cornwall.

All this former narration is set downe to confute the errours of such as are of an opinion that there was never any such man as king Arthur, and though historians doe disagree in their chronologies about times and places, some having written partially, some neglectively, and some fabulously and superstitiously, yet in the mayne points which are most materiall, they doe all conclude of the predecessours and successours of king Arthur, according as I have formerly related. It is apparent in all histories that there were nine most famous and renowmed kings and princes, who for their noble acts and worthy atchievements, are stiled the nine worthies, and it is most execrable infidelity to doubt that there was a Joshua, it is wicked Atheisme to make a question if there were a David, it is hatefull to be diffident of a sometime Judas Macchabeus; besides there are none, of any capacitie, but doe believe there was an Alexander. The world is possest with the acknowledgement of the life and death of Julius Cæsar, and the never dying fame of the illustrious Trojan Hector is perspicuous; we must all approve of the being of that magnanimous prince Godfrey duke of Bulloigne, who was the christian generall at the conquest of Jerusalem, in the yeare 1110. Besides, France, Germany, and all the christian world hath in fresh and admired memory the famous emperour Charlemaigne or Charles the Great.

And shall the Jewes and the Heathen be honoured in the memory and magnificent prowesse of their worthies? shall the French and Germane nations glorifie their triumphs with their Godfrey and Charles, and shall we of this island be so possest with incredulitie, diffidence, stupiditie, and ingratitude, to deny, make doubt, or expresse in speech and history, the immortall name and fame of our victorious Arthur. All the honour we can doe him is to honour our selves in remembrance of him. This following history was first written in the French and Italian tongues, so much did the poets and chronologers of forraine nations admire our Arthur. It was many yeares after the first writing of it, translated into English, by the painfull industry of one sir Thomas Maleore, knight, in the ninth yeare of the raigne of king Edward the Fourth, about one hundred and fifty two yeares past; wherein the reader may see the best forme and manner of writing and speech that was in use at those times. In many places fables and fictions are inserted, which may be a blemish to the reputation of what is true in this history, and it is unfitting for us to raze or blot out all the errours of our ancestours, for by our taking consideration of them, wee may be the better induced to beleeve and reverence the truth. It is 1114 years since king Arthurs raigne, which was long before the dayes of Edward the Fourth, whereby it may be mused what speech they used above 1100 yeares agoe, when as it was so plaine and simple in king Edwards time.

And therefore, reader, I advertise thee to deale with this book as thou wouldest doe with thy house or thy garment, if the one doe want but a little repaire thou wilt not (madly) pull downe the whole frame, if the other hath a small spot or a staine thou wilt not cast it away or burne it, gold hath its drosse, wine hath its lees, man (in all ages) hath his errours and imperfections. And though the times are now more accute and sharp-witted, using a more eloquent and ornated stile and phrase in speech and writing then they did, who lived so many yeares past, yet it may be that in the age to come, our successours may hold and esteeme of us as ridiculously as many of our over-nice critickes doe of their and our progenitours, as we are refined in words I wish we were reformed in deeds, and as we can talke better, it were well if wee would not doe worse. Wee perceive their darknesse through our light, let not our light blind us that we may not see our owne ignorance. (pp. xxi-xxv)

As (by the favour of Heaven) this kingdome of Britaine was graced with one worthy, let us with thankfulnes acknowledge him; let us not account it our shame, that he hath bin our countries honour; let us not be more cruell then death to smother or murder his name; or let us not be worse then the grave in burying his favour. Thus, reader, I leave thee at thy pleasure to reade but not to judge, except thou judge with understanding. The asse is no competent judge betwixt the owle and the nightingale for the sweetness of their voices; cloth of Arras or hangings of tapistry are not fit to adorne a kitchin, no more are ketles, pots, and spits to hang in a ladies bed-chamber. Neither is it beseeming for a man to censure that which his ignorance cannot perceive, or his pride and malice will prejudicate or cavill at. (pp. xxv-xxvi)

> *William Stansby? in a preface to* La Mort d'Arthure: The History of King Arthur and of the Knights of the Round Table, *Vol. I by Sir Thomas Malory, edited by Thomas Wright, John Russell Smith, 1858, pp. xxi-xxvi.*

ROBERT SOUTHEY (essay date 1817)

[*A late eighteenth- and early nineteenth-century English man of letters, Southey was a key member of the so-called Lake School of poetry. His poetry consists mainly of short verse, ballads, and epics, many of which are notable for their novel versification and meter. His prose writings, which are generally more highly praised than his poetry, include ambitious histories, biographies, and conservative social commentaries. Today Southey is primarily remembered as a conservative theorist and as the biographer of such figures as Horatio Nelson, Thomas More, and John Wesley. In the following excerpt from the preface to his 1817 redaction of the* Morte Darthur, *he maintains that Malory was a compiler, not an original artist.*]

There are other Romances which I have not met with, from whence materials for the *Morte Arthur* have been drawn; but these are the principal sources, Lancelot, Tristan, and the Sainct Greaal, having furnished nearly two thirds of the whole. Whether this compilation was made originally by Sir Thomas Malory, or translated by him from a French compendium, has not been ascertained; nor is it of importance, as there is no claim to originality on his part. The compiler seems to have altered the incidents as freely as the arrangement, and may perhaps have made some additions of his own; Mr. Douce has suggested that he used manuscripts to the texts of which we may probably always be strangers, and this therefore must remain doubtful. It is probable also that some of his materials have never been printed. "O blessed Lord," says Caxton, "when I remember the great and many volumes of St. Graal, Ghalehot, and Lancelot du Lac, Gawain, Perceval, Lionel and Tristram, and many other, of whom were over long to rehearse, and also to me unknown." Ghalehot may perhaps mean the *hault Prince* Galehault, who figures in the history of Lancelot; or more probably Galahad, who sate in the siege perilous, of whom there certainly existed a separate Romance; it was the favourite book of Nuno Alvarez Pereira, who endeavouring as far as possible to imitate the character which he admired, became himself the fair ideal of a perfect knight, as courteous as he was brave, as humane as he was courteous, as pious as he was humane, uniting in himself the accomplishments of a hero, the feelings of a true patriot, and the virtues of a christian and a saint.

It seems too, from the exclamation of Caxton, that Gawain and Lionel had each their history; but I believe none are known to be in existence, or at least that none have been published. The story of Beaumayns has, from its structure and completeness, the appearance of having been a metrical Romance. I do not know from whence the story of Balin and Balan has been derived; it has finer circumstances in it than any other part of the *Morte Arthur*.

The history of the Round Table Romances may be investigated with better opportunities in France than in England; but it must be sought for also among the remains of the Welsh and Breton fictions, and something may perhaps be discovered in the Walloon tongue, though it is to be feared that many a precious manuscript may have perished during the first frenzy of the revolution in Brabant and the adjoining countries. If a society for this purpose were formed by the lovers of chivalrous literature in all countries, the members, while they procured their own individual gratification, would contribute something toward the restoration of that feeling which formerly prevailed in the republic of letters, but which the convulsions of the political world have so long and so mournfully suspended. The object should be, a faithful republication of all this family of romances, whether in verse or prose, with a careful investigation of the history of each. It would not be difficult to detect, from internal marks, the order in which they were written, though perhaps impossible to ascertain the time. In their present state the productions of very different times are frequently blended together. Much light would be thrown, in the progress of these researches, upon the history of literature and the manners of the middle ages. (pp. xxvi-xxviii)

> *Robert Southey, in an introduction to* The Byrth, Lyf, *and* Actes of Kyng Arthur, *Vol. I by Sir Thomas Malory, edited by Robert Southey, Longman, Hurst, Rees, Orme, and Brown, 1817, pp. i-lxiii.*

ANDREW LANG (essay date 1891)

[*Lang was one of Great Britain's preeminent men of letters during the closing decades of the nineteenth century. He is perhaps best remembered as the editor of the "Color Fairy Books," a twelve-volume series of fairy tales that helped stimulate interest in children's literature in England. The selections in* The Blue Fairy Book (1889), The Lilac Fairy Book (1910), *and the ten volumes in between include stories from various world cultures and are an outgrowth of Lang's meticulous research into early languages and literature—research that called attention to cultural affinities in the folktales, myths, and legends of otherwise disparate societies. In the following excerpt from his introduction to H. Oskar Sommer's 1891 edition of the* Morte Darthur, *Lang compares the* Morte *with the epics of Homer and comments on the style and language of the work.*]

[Malory] was no great clerk in Celtic mythology, and perhaps no very discriminate judge of what was best to choose, what best to omit, in his "French books." He was content to tell of "noble and renowned acts of humanity, gentleness, and chivalry. For herein may be seen noble chivalry, courtesy, humanity, friendliness, hardiness, love, friendship, cowardice, murder, hate, virtue, and sin." These are the elements of our life, these are the *farrago libelli* which Ascham should not have reproached for containing mere "bold bawdry and open manslaughter" [see excerpt dated 1568?]. In the very first page we meet Igerne, "a passing good woman," who "would not consent unto the king," though hers, after all, was Alcmena's fate. Malory is throughout strong on the side of goodness. The Laureate talks of his book as "touched with the adulterous finger" of the time of Edward IV. But assuredly, if we compare the popular romance of that day with the popular romances of any other, we might consider that a golden age which found its favourite reading, and its ideals of conduct, in the **Morte d'Arthur.** Men and women will be men and women; but here, even if the passion be sinful, it is still passion, ardent, constant, and loyal to the grave.

There is no more strange fortune in literature than that which blended wild Celtic myths, and a monastic theory of the saintly life, with all of chivalrous adventure, with all of courtesy and gentleness, that the Middle Ages could conceive, and handed it on to be the delight of the changing ages.

In this respect, in the mingling of remote, scarce decipherable legends with a high theory of human life, in the choice of what was feasible in Celtic legends, in its transmutation into the universally appropriate and excellent, the work of Malory may be compared to the Homeric epics. Both have their distant undiscoverable sources in the high far-off lands of a society to which we can never return. Both gain a mystery and a magic from early imaginings, both have been touched with the colour of many ages, both have the noble melancholy of great deeds done and great enterprises attempted, to end as all human endeavour ends, leaving only a song or a story in the ears of men yet to be born. Studying Malory and Homer together, we are struck by the resemblances and differences of life and of its ideals; we are impressed by the changes that Christianity and the temper of the North have brought into what may be styled the heroic and aristocratic theory of existence, of duty, of enjoyment.

The epic and the romance both start from the conception of the marvellous, the supernatural, but how strangely that conception varies in each under the influence of the new, the Christian, and the Northern ideas. The old capricious Gods have departed, of course, and made way for a deity of mercy and justice. But magic is as powerful in Malory as in Homer. Merlin does such a craft that Pellinore saw not Arthur, as Apollo lightly hides Agenor or Aeneas in a mist. In Nimue, one of the ladies of the lake, we have Malory's Circe, whose wiles are too cunning even for his Odysseus, Merlin. The wide world to the knights, as to the adventurous Ithacan, is an unsubstantial fairy place, and Malory's castles are as enchanted as the isles of the unsailed Homeric seas. The vividness of Malory's pictures has that element of surprise which waits for us as we go up to Circe's house, through the oak coppice and the wild wood. The knight rides over a bridge that is old and feeble, and, coming into a great hall, sees lying a dead knight that was a seemly man, and a brachet licks his wounds, and there comes a lady weeping. Across the moors, and through the darkness of the forests, Arthur rides after the mysterious Morgan le Fay, who shapes herself, by enchantment, into a great marble stone. But in Malory the adventures lead to no end till the Graal has to be won; the knights ride forth for the mere pleasure of the unknown, for the mere interest of what may befall them. One sleeps below an apple-tree, and lo! there come four Queens, and look on his face, and know that it is Lancelot, and contend for his love. Then Morgan le Fay carries him to the enchanted Castle Chariot, and they lay him "in a chamber cold," and tell him that, though no lady can have his love but one, and that Queen Guinevere, "now thou shalt lose her for ever, and she thee, and therefore thee behoveth to choose now one of us four." The knight is more loyal to his love than Odysseus to his wedded wife: "lever had I die in this prison with worship, than to have one of you to my love, maugre my head. . . . And as to Queen Guinevere, she is the truest lady unto her lord living." But all these adventures among chapels perilous, and valleys where stand pavilions of red sandal, are, unlike the Homeric adventures, without an end or aim. The slight unity that we find in the earlier parts, before the Graal becomes an aim and end, before the love of Lancelot brings a doom on all, is in the character and position of Arthur. Like the sleepless Agamemnon, he might complain of the great charge laid on his life; like Charlemagne in the *Chanson de Roland*, he might cry,

Deus! si peneuse est ma vie!

Different as are their ideas of love, and of pure fidelity and constancy unshaken in a man, Homer and Malory draw near each other in their pictures of their great ladies and lovers, Helen and Guinevere. Ruinous they both are, but each might say to her singer and her romancer, in the words of Helen to the dead Hector, "Never yet heard I evil or despiteful word from thee." Both romance and epic are chivalrous here; neither Homer nor Malory preaches nor rebukes, like the Arthur of the *Idylls of the King*. But different are the repentances of the fateful ladies, the sorrows of the North and South. "At the last," says Helen, "I groaned for my blindness that Aphrodite gave me, when she led me to Troy from mine own country, forsaking my child and my bridal chamber, and my lord, that lacked not aught, either of wisdom or beauty." In heroic Greece, the shame is over and past; in Elysium, in the Avalon of Argos, Helen and Menelaus are destined to endless joy. But the spirit of Christianity and of the North, that gave us the passion of Brynhild, demand from Guinevere another penance. "She let make herself a nun, and great penance she took, as ever did sinful lady in this land, and never creature could make her merry, but lived in fasting, prayers, and alms deeds, that all manner of people marvelled how virtuously she was changed." In that last meeting of Lancelot and Guinevere, when she might have gone with him to her own Elysium of Joyous Garde, she cries, "As well as I have loved thee, mine heart will not serve me to see thee; for through thee and me is the flower of kings and knights destroyed." So she parts from "the truest lover of a sinful man that ever loved woman;" "then he sickened more and more and dwined and died away; . . . .sometime he slumbered a broken sleep, and ever he way lying grovelling on the tomb of King Arthur and Queen Guinevere."

Helen and Guinevere are both children of the old world of dreams; both born in the land of myth, each is a daughter of Gods, or a daughter of the moon, as the old story fabled of Helen, or "the white ghost," as Guinevere's name is interpreted; they are not born of men nor of mortal seed: they are as the vision of Beauty on earth among the passions of men. But between the years that sang of Helen and the years that told of Guinevere what a change has come, and how readily the Greek wins to her rest in her home by Eurotas, and how hardly does Guinevere attain to hers. Guinevere is never in later time to be worshipped and sainted, like Helen, for her very beauty's sake. "Une immense espérance a traversée la terre," a hope that brings with it pain and sorrow, and an array of new passions and desires that never vexed or rejoiced the older faith, the older time. In all this conclusion of the faithful and disloyal love,

Whose honour rooted in dishonour stood,

Malory has penned the great and chief romance of his own age and of ours, the story that must endure and must move the *lacrymae rerum* till man's nature is altered again. Homer knows wedded love, which no man has praised with nobler words than he puts the lips of Nausicaa; and he knows light loves of chiefs and captives. But that great charm of a love which is constant as it is sinful, of Lancelot and of Guinevere, does not come into his ken, nor can we fancy him alluring and saddening us with the passion of Clytaemnestra and Aegisthus, "with sheer

doom before their eyes," the doom that they drew on them "beyond what was ordained." Nor does Homer know, or care to dwell on, a hopeless passion like the mortal love of Elaine for Lancelot. We may see one touch of such an affection in the words of Nausicaa when she bids Odysseus a last farewell, a passage the more deeply moving for its reticence. But of Nausicaa we learn no more; tradition even is not busy with her; while the last voyage of the Maid of Astolat is an enduring possession of romance. And yet more remote from Homer, of course, is the chastity of the Sangraal legend. Mr. Rhys has very ingeniously tried to account for the purity of Galahad and Percival, as if it were the inheritance from solar heroes, who had been of much prowess before the age of the passions began. But we may far more plausibly attribute the purity of Galahad to monastic influence in part, and in part to the Germanic chastity of which Tacitus tells, arising from a lofty respect for women. We may contrast it with those views of Thetis, so frankly heathen, which disconcert Mr. Gladstone in the *Iliad*. Malory's ideal in this matter was probably very far from being attained by his readers, yet it remains an attractive picture of a manly purity associated with strength and courage.

Among the many differences of temper which distinguish this great romance of the Middle Ages from the great epics of prehistoric Hellas, perhaps the strongest is to be found in the various theories of courage. In Homer, courage is a very varying quality. When Hector challenges the Achaean princes, dismay and silence fall on them. No man is eager to volunteer. In battle even Achilles (perhaps in an interpolated passage) is adread. Agamemnon is eternally despondent and anxious for flight. Only Odysseus, when cut off by a crowd of Trojans, dares to stand his ground, unaided and alone. "For I know that they are cowards, who flee the flight, but whosoever is a hero in war, him it mainly behoves to stand stubbornly, whether he be smitten, or whether he smite." Even Hector, in his last stand at the Scaean gate, deliberates about making shameful terms with Achilles, though Asteropaeus has just set him the example of a gallant and glorious death. Neither Greek nor Trojan fights a losing battle well; and when Homer makes Hector actually run for his life, he gives us a scene which no romancer nor saga-man dared to write about a hero. Other is the temper of Lancelot in the Queen's chamber, naked and unarmed, and beset by overwhelming numbers: "Wit you well, Madam, I shall sell my life as dear as I may:—And now I had liever than to be lord of all Christendom that I had sure armour upon me, that men might speak of my deeds or ever I were slain."

We cannot doubt that Homer sang to men who shared his theory of courage—who, like him, believed that the bravest had their fighting days, as Paris says of himself, and their days when fighting was not dear to them. All this is doubtless true enough to human nature. But not to believe it, not to acknowledge it, to resist and defy the whispers of fear, is true to the Northern nature, and this creed has given us many an unsung Thermopylæ.

The Celtic legends, passed through the French mind, and rendered in Malory's English, have, what Homer lacks, the charm of mystery and distance, the background of the unknown. In Homer all is beheld in the clearest and most delicate air; about Merlin and Morgan le Fay, and the ladies of the lake, and the strange swords and cups, there is a mist of enchantment. They are relics of an older world, not understood even by the narrators. It is, probably, not the Celtic, but the mediæval fancy which introduces another element of the romancer, much suppressed in Homer—that of broad conventional humour. The epics know of no such warrior as Dinadan among their many types of character. He satisfies the rude mediæval taste in jokes; he preserves the romances from becoming too sentimental. He sets a dish of fish before "the haut prince" because the haut prince "had a custom he loved no fish." So comic is this excellent Dinadan that Lancelot "may not sit in his saddle when that spear hitteth him," that spear with which the humorous knight smote his friends in the ribs. "Then laughed the queen and the haut prince that they might not sit at their table," so "tickle of thes ear" are those beings, children of the mist and of the night as they are.

Thus Malory's book is a very complete and composite picture of a strangely inherited ideal; it is, indeed, "a jumble," but, of all jumbles, the most poetic and the most pathetic. Structureless as it seems, patchwork as it is, the *Morte d'Arthur* ends as nobly as the *Iliad*, deserving the praise which Shelley gives to Homer, and dying away in "the high and solemn close of the whole bloody tale in tenderness and inexpiable sorrow." It is well called "La Morte d'Arthur," for the ending atones for all, wins forgiveness for all, and, like the death of Roland, is more triumphant than a victory. Like the three damoysels, Malory is skilled "to teach men unto strange adventures," to instruct in all courage, chastity, endurance, and true love, nor can we estimate what his influence must have been in training the fathers of Elizabeth's Englishmen. Thus it has somehow befallen that the Arthurian legends, in their third descent, are infinitely more dear and familiar to Englishmen and English boys than the original French romances are to the French, or to any foreign people who borrowed them from the French. In France, the romances are the special possession of scholars only; in England, Malory's *Morte* is a favourite in most school-rooms, and has been the inspiration of our greatest poet since our great poetic age. It is characteristic of our mixed race that we have nothing at all like an ancient Germanic epic in our popular and living literature. *Beowulf* is far too remote from us in every way; we are not fortunate enough to possess anything corresponding to the *Song of Roland*. We owe our national romance first to the Celts, then to the French; but the form and, to a great extent, the spirit are English, are Malory's.

The style of Malory is, of course, based on the fresh and simple manner of his French originals. For an English style of his age, it is particularly fluent. Periods of considerable length and intricacy, especially in speeches, do not give him any trouble. As examples, we might take the dialogue of Lancelot and the Queen when he is surprised in her chamber. The daring, chivalry, and self-restraint of the knight are here admirably and suitably expressed. Perhaps it is just because he does follow a French copy, and so is familiar with words derived from the Latin, that Malory possesses his fluency and facility. The constant advice to use only "Anglo-Saxon" in modern composition is erroneous, and is ungrateful to those great makers of our language, the writers from Spenser to Shakspere. Malory is, of course, much less Latinised than they; such a phrase as

The multitudinous seas incarnadine

cannot be expected from him. But he is almost as remote from the "Wardour Street English" which stands in a false following of the Icelandic. If we take his famous chapter on true love and the month of May, we see how much his language owes to the Latin, or to the Latin through the French. Here we have such Latinised words as "flourisheth," "constrain," "divers causes," "gentleness," "service," "negligence," "deface," "stability," "virtuous," "endure," "accord," and so forth, all in half a page. The language has slipped away from its monosyllables, and is becoming more rapid and more fluent. Here, too, Malory offers examples of a trait common in him—the sudden change to the second person, as if in livelier and more actual address: "There never was worshipful man or worshipful woman but they loved one better than another, and worship in arms may never be foiled, but first reserve the honour to God, and secondly the quarrel must come of thy lady.... Therefore all ye that be lovers call unto your remembrance the month of May, like as did Queen Guinevere, for whom I make here a little mention, that while she lived she was a true lover, and therefore she had a good end." In ordinary spelling, the words all remain good current English. Almost the only obsolete word in the chapter is "lycours." Even when the carter "drove on a great wallop" Malory needs no glossary. His language always explains itself; for example, in the picturesque expression, "I sawe no thynge but the waters wappe and waves wanne." Malory's chief mark of childlike simplicity is in his conjunctions; his narrative is stitched with "so's" and "and's," though this is, of course, less marked in his dialogue and in his reflective passages. The childlike character becomes almost Republican in such a passage as this: "he landed wyth seven kynges, and the nombre was hydous to beholde." On the whole, it may be said of the narrative manner that it is well fitted to the wandering tale; just old enough and quaint enough to allure, and to mark the age, without disturbing or delaying even the youngest reader of the noble and joyous history. Readers enough Malory has, and is likely to have, more probably than any other ancient English author, more even than Chaucer, whose language and prosody offer more difficulty, and who has the perennial disadvantage of writing in verse. Maundeville, probably, can never be popular, in spite of his entertaining matter. Ascham only attracts scholars and the curious. But the manner and matter of Malory make him the most generally known of all old authors, except, of course, the translators of the Bible. (pp. xiii-xxi)

Andrew Lang, "'Le Morte Darthur'," in Le Morte Darthur: Studies on the Sources, Vol. III *by Syr Thomas Malory, edited by H. Oskar Sommer, David Nutt, 1891, pp. xiii-xxv.*

SIR WALTER RALEIGH (essay date 1894)

[*A renowned lecturer and literary critic, Raleigh was the first to be appointed professor of English literature at the University of Oxford. His critical approach to literature, evident in his lectures and in such works as* The English Novel *(1894) and* Shakespeare *(1907), was that of a highly perceptive, urbane commentator. In his literary exegesis he aimed to bring about the non-specialist's understanding of English literature through concise textual commentary. In addition, Raleigh often further illuminated his subject through insightful examination of the personality of the writer under discussion. In the following excerpt from* The English Nov-

el, he considers the prose style and structure of the Morte Darthur.]

The scholars who are unwilling to admit that the Arthur legends grew up on Breton soil have also claimed Sir Thomas Malory, on the authority of Bale, for a Welshman. It is quite certain, at least, that he was, as Bale calls him, "heroici spiritus homo," a man of a heroic temper; the facts of his life are lacking. His book, *Le Morte Darthur*, a compilation mainly from French sources, was finished, as he himself states, in the ninth years of the reign of King Edward IV., that is to say, either in 1469 or 1470. It was secured for posterity by Caxton, who printed it in 1485.

In the preface which he contributed to his edition of the work, Caxton discusses at some length the existence of an historical Arthur [see excerpt dated 1485]. He had delayed printing the noble history of King Arthur because, like Milton later, he was troubled with the doubt whether such a king had ever existed. Divers gentlemen of this realm of England had attempted to conquer his scepticism, alleging, among other things, that in the castle of Dover "ye may see Gawaine's skull." He concludes by remarking that, true or not, the book is exemplary and profitable. "And for to pass the time this book shall be pleasant to read in, but for to give faith and belief that all is true that is contained herein, ye be at your liberty; but all is written for our doctrine, and for to beware that we fall not to vice ne sin, but to exercise and follow virtue; by the which we may come and attain to good fame and renown in this life, and after this short and transitory life to come unto everlasting bliss in heaven."

The words are memorable as marking the beginning of prose fiction; history and fable, so long inextricably entangled, are here drawing apart from one another; literature is proclaiming itself as an art, and declaring a purpose beyond the scope of the humble chronicle.

To attain to a finely ordered artistic structure was beyond Malory's power; the very wealth of legend with which he had to deal put it beyond him, and he is too much absorbed in the interest of the parts to give more than a passing consideration to the whole. His simple forthright narrative is admirably lucid and effective, and makes amends for an inevitably rambling structure, while his flashes of chivalrous feeling illuminate the plains through which his story wanders. He is a master in the telling use of the Saxon speech, although he translates from the French. When Queen Guinevere escaped from the insolent overtures of Sir Mordred, she took the Tower of London and suddenly "stuffed it," says Malory, "with all manner of victual, and well garnished it with men, and so kept it." Sir Launcelot, after her death, "dried and dwined away . . . and ever he was lying groveling on the tomb of King Arthur and Queen Guenever." The Holy Grail descends amidst "cracking and crying of thunder." Sir Bedivere, when he was sent to throw away Excalibur, "saw nothing but the waters wap and the waves wan." And this fascinating simplicity of diction is matched by the clearness of outline that distinguishes Malory's pictures; the figures he employs, few in number, are of the natural and unsought kind dear to Saxon speech. A knight appears in the lists as "bright as an angel," two combatants rush together "like two rams," the children that King Arthur finds the giant roasting are broached on a spit, "like young

birds." The allegorical habit has left traces here and there on Malory's work, but indeed it may be said for allegory that it fosters simplicity in prose narration. Where words are to bear a double meaning it is important that the first should be clearly defined, and perfectly distinguished from the second; the elaborated metaphorical style of a later and more sophisticated age mingles the fact and its figurative associations as early narrative prose never does. The Renaissance troubled the waters, and it was long ere prose ran clear again. There is no better prose style for the purposes of simple story-telling than that which many English writers have at command from Malory to Latimer.

The human emotions enshrined in this style have an irresistible appeal. Pity, anger, love, and pride, speak straight to the heart. The passionate and rebellious cry of Queen Guinevere, "I trust through God's grace after my death to have a sight of the blessed face of Christ, and at doomsday to sit at His right side, for as sinful as ever I was are saints in heaven," has parallels in modern literature. Burns expresses the same hope, but his surmise that after all he may—

> Snugly sit among the saunts
> At Davie's hip yet,

has lost more in pathos than it can make good by its gain in humour.

The work of Sir Thomas Malory became for the following age the embodiment of the ideas of chivalry and the wellhead of romance. It was twice reprinted by Wynkyn de Worde, in 1498 and 1529, and again by William Copland in 1557. The demand continued, and there are later reprints, belonging to the reigns of Elizabeth and Charles I. respectively, by Thomas East and William Stansby. But in the Elizabethan age, as in our own, it became the feeder of poetry rather than of prose; Spenser knew it well and Shakespeare read it; traces of its influence on the greater prose writers, even on Sir Philip Sidney, are scant enough. (pp. 14-17)

> *Sir Walter Raleigh, "The Romance and the Novel," in his* The English Novel: A Short Sketch of Its History from the Earliest Times to the Appearance of "Waverly," *John Murray, 1894, pp. 1-24.*

WILLIAM HENRY SCHOFIELD (essay date 1912)

[*Schofield was a Canadian-born American scholar and critic. He is best remembered as a pioneering student of Arthurian Legend. In the following excerpt from his 1912 study* Chivalry in English Literature: Chaucer, Malory, Spenser *and* Shakespeare, *he discusses Malory's portrayal of chivalry and courtly love in the* Morte Darthur.]

Apart from the language, and in so far as it is only what it purports to be, a narrative of knightly adventure, the *Morte d'Arthur* might almost as well have been written seventy years before Chaucer's birth as seventy years after his death. Yet inquiry shows that "this noble and joyous book" is more than a simple "reduction" of early French romance, as is generally believed. "Notwithstanding it treateth of the birth, life, and acts of King Arthur, of his noble knights of the Round Table, their marvellous quests and adventures, the achieving of the Sangreal, and in the end of the dolorous death and departing out of this world of them all,"—it was evidently called forth by the author's anxiety regarding conditions in England in his own day, and was intended to be influential for good and not merely entertaining then.

Malory makes no effort to conceal the fact that he wrote primarily for the gentle-born. "I pray you all, gentlemen and gentlewomen, that read this book of Arthur and his knights from the beginning to the ending"—thus he addresses his friends when about to lay down his pen. Throughout his work he had taken no thought of any other audience, and he finally appeals only to gentlemen and gentlewomen for their prayers after he is dead. Caxton, moreover, states with emphasis who "came and demanded" him to print the book—"many noble and divers gentlemen of this realm of England" [see excerpt dated 1485]. He hints, to be sure, that the narrative might appeal to other estates and be pleasant for them to read in; but he insists on the station of those to whom he humbly submits the finished volume. "This said book," he says, "I direct unto all noble princes, lords and ladies, gentlemen or gentlewomen." "This said book" is one of the first ever dedicated in England to Gentle Readers, and Caxton's words have a literal significance that soon became attenuated in frequent use.

In many ways the *Morte d'Arthur* must have interested Malory's contemporaries more than it does us. All of the fifteenth century would recognize in it much more clearly than we a true guide for gentlemen's careers; they could understand better the mode of battle and tourney, whereby heroes still won renown; they could hardly fail to be aroused by seeming parallels in the Arthurian past to the events of their own present, which have concerned men little since. On the other hand, we are no doubt attracted to the work by a certain quaintness of style that only the passing of years could produce; and the charm of "far-off, bygone things" in romance, picturing a life which we have now no duty to mend, draws us with unalloyed winsomeness as it could not possibly have done those who felt bound to consider the results of that life when actually devoid of inspiration and vitality. Above all, we see the book in a better perspective from the point of view of art.

The art of Malory's work an injudicious reader, even today, is apt to overlook. The writing seems all so natural and simple, so lacking in rhetorical ornament, that one who is unobservant may readily be deluded into thinking that little praise is due the author. But let him compare the *Morte d'Arthur* with any other work of the same kind, ancient or modern, let him attempt to improve on any good passage that attracts him, and he will surely discover that here is art that conceals art, here is distinction that, forgetting itself, evades remark.

Malory's book has been reproached with lack of unity, not altogether without cause. Whoever reads it as a whole, is certain to be bewildered by the complexities of certain stories, and by the way the numerous adventures in a single tale sometimes follow one another in strange confusion. He will discover also curious inconsistencies in the presentation of character, and contradictions of tone and sentiment. These faults, however, inhered, and were much more manifest, in the sources of the book, and no one can study Malory's methods of composition in connection with those of his predecessors without great admiration for the skill with which he has welded together, and

Balin meets a damsel in the forest. From London, British Library, Add. Ms. 38117.

stamped with a peculiar personal impress, the vast, incongruous body of material which he undertook to mould.

The *Morte d'Arthur* is the fountain-head of Arthurian fiction, so far as most Englishmen of to-day are aware; for the many French and Middle-English documents concerning knights of the Round Table which were current in mediaeval times are now familiar to none but the scholarly few. Malory, more than anyone else, deserves the credit of making modern Englishmen feel that Arthur and his comrades were national heroes. No doubt this had been the tendency of English writers of the alliterative school from the poet Layamon at the beginning of the thirteenth century on; but the great majority among us have never heard mention of these writers of the rural west, let alone attempted to read their artless lines. Save the *Morte d'Arthur*, there was no English book on the same theme widely read until Tennyson produced his *Idylls of the King;* and had it not been for Malory, Tennyson would never have thought of composing these. To English poets, in fact, the *Morte d'Arthur* has ever seemed a palace of manifold dreams. From it one after another of them has emerged greatly enamoured of old romance, eager to perpetuate the aspirations that it reveals and evokes. After Malory,

The mightiest chiefs of English song
Scorned not such legends to prolong.

It was a prejudiced pedant, Roger Ascham, who in the sixteenth century uttered strong condemnation of the *Morte d'Arthur*, which, he asserted, was "received into the prince's chamber," when "God's Bible was banished the court" [see excerpt dated 1568?]. "The whole pleasure of [it]," he said, "standeth in open manslaughter and bold bawdry—in which book those be counted the noblest knights that do kill most men without any quarrel, and commit the foulest adulteries by subtlest shifts." Ascham far overshot the mark at which he aimed. To be, like him, a hater of "papistry" did not really necessitate, as he seemed to think, hatred of everything mediaeval—certainly not of chivalry and the "matter of Britain," the chief if not the whole pleasure of which really consists in its potent stimulus to idealistic endeavour. Milton, though a Puritan, had better judgement, along with finer poetic vision. How willingly his imagination played about the scenes of Malory's, as well as of Spenser's, work! We did not need to have him tell us "whither [his] younger feet wandered;" but still we are glad to have had him frankly state: "I betook me among those lofty fables and romances, which recounted in solemn cantos the deeds of knighthood founded by our victorious kings, and from thence had in renown over all Christendom;" and while we may be far from thinking him unwise to have chosen a "higher argument" for his mature pen, we cannot but long for that wonderful poem which we should now possess if he had fulfilled his first desire and sung "the great-hearted heroes of the unvanquished Table in their bonds of fellowship." But an epic of Arthur, Milton in the end did not see fit to write; and the *Morte d'Arthur* remains still, probably will always remain, that English work which most nearly merits so lofty a name. (pp. 75-80)

When one considers the circumstances of Malory's life—his aristocratic lineage and profession of arms, his training as a gentleman and a soldier, his experience of foreign and civil war, the vicissitudes of his own fortunes, and finally, the fact that he wrote late in life, probably suffering in prison, approaching death—one understands better why the *Morte d'Arthur* is what it is: a work of retrospect, tinged with sadness for the passing of the good old days; a work of idealism, troubled with knowledge of miserable facts daily divulged; a work of patriotism, written when the land was being wasted by civil strife; a work of encouragement to the right-minded, and of warning to the evil-minded, among men of that class in which the author lived and moved. (pp. 87-8)

Malory wrote no preface to his book. Only incidentally does he himself reveal its serious aim, though now and then he becomes frankly hortatory; but the worthy Caxton plainly states what decided him to perpetuate the narrative in type.

The *Morte d'Arthur*, Caxton makes clear, was in his opinion a book of moral edification, as well as one of entertainment, primarily appealing to the aristocracy of the "noble realm" in which he lived. He further exalts the work as patriotic in effect. Englishmen, he declares, were to be reproached because foreigners knew more than they of King Arthur, "which ought most to be remembered amongst us Englishmen, considering that he was a man from within this realm and king and emperor of the same,"—"the most renowned Christian king, first and chief of the three best Christians and worthy"—a king "to whom none earthly prince may compare," who in his time

had "the flower of chivalry of the world with him"—*rex quondam, rexque futurus.*

Many scholars have concerned themselves with the mythical conception of Arthur as a resident of the Otherworld, some time to return to liberate his British folk; but few, if any, have observed that Malory's presentation of this ideal monarch was planned to arouse definite contemporaneous interest by the subtle enforcing of similitude between past and present happenings.

"It befell in the days of Uther Pendragon, when he was king of all England, and so reigned"—these, Malory's opening words, are notable for their definite contradiction of the facts of romance on behalf of the romance of facts. "It befell," like the "once upon a time" of a fairy tale, immediately transports us into the realm of remoteness and fable, and "the days of Uther Pendragon" prepares us to hear tales of the mighty Celtic warriors whom Geoffrey of Monmouth created in glorification of ancient Britain. Yet soon we discover that it is with a king of England we have to do. Malory begins his book as if he were writing about a monarch of the House of Lancaster, whose right to the throne was not quite clear—a king "the which had great war in his days for to get all England into his hand." "All the battles that were done in Arthur's days," from the initial one at St. Albans, have a striking resemblance to those of fifteenth-century England. The first undertakings of the monarch are to defeat his enemies and establish his kingdom; he has a private counsellor; he appeals to the Archbishop of Canterbury; he consults his lords and commons; he holds parliaments; his object is the dignity of the nation. Malory strongly emphasized the idea that Arthur was an *English* king; and we see him make alliances, use strategy, prepare for and carry on war, in the same spirit, and often in the same places, as the English of his day. "All men of worship said it was merry to be under such a chieftain that would put his person in adventure as other poor knights did." (pp. 89-91)

Malory persistently identifies romantic places with English localities. "The city of Camelot," he notes, "is called in English, Westminster." We read of "a town called Astolat, that is now in English Guildford;" of "a castle that is called Magouns and now it is called Arundel, in Sussex;" and of Joyous Gard, where Launcelot lived with Guinevere, "some men say it was Alnwick and some say it was Bamborough." But the assertion that "the country of Logres" is "the country of England" gives us his chief guiding thread. In writing of Arthur and his wars with his nobles, Malory's thoughts were not far from his own land in his own days. "Alas!" we can hear him say like Sir Launcelot: "Alas! that ever I should live to hear that most noble king [Arthur or Henry VI], that made me knight, thus to be overset with his subjects in his own realm." Yet "it is an old said saw, there is hard battle there as kin and friends do battle either against other; there may be no mercy but mortal war." More than once Malory recorded a truth which the world, despite so much experience, never seems to learn: "Better is peace than ever war."

Here he is at one with his sympathetic contemporary, Occleve, who near the close of his *De Regimine Principum* makes a strong statement of the woes of "inward war" in England and France in his days, and pleads with touching earnestness for "the gift of peace, that precious jewel." (pp. 92-3)

Even as, in his account of Arthur's wars, Malory endeavoured to establish pride in united England, and to show the calamity of wavering truth and allegiance, so also, in the portrayal of good and bad knights, he tried to promote the virtue of individual aristocrats, by whose example society might be improved.

King Arthur he pictures as straightforward and frank, with "a great eager heart," ready to put his own body into jeopardy when need called, bountiful in gifts, generous in praise, forgiving of offence, whom "never yet man could prove untrue to his promise." He "had liefer to die with honour than to live with shame." (pp. 95-6)

King Mark of Cornwall is portrayed as Arthur's absolute opposite. Mark is repeatedly spoken of as the most villainous knight (or king) in the world, whose fellowship all good knights eschewed. He is mean, wily, and ill-conditioned, a vile recreant, "a fair speaker and false thereunder," a liar, a traitor, and a murderer. All knights deem him "the most horrible coward that ever bestrode a horse."

Though Arthur's presence is always felt in the background, when he is not conspicuously in the foreground, of the scenes pictured by Malory, the *Morte d'Arthur* is chiefly occupied with the exploits of other members of the Round Table brotherhood, especially of Sir Tristram and Sir Launcelot. Malory did not invent any new episodes, and the exploits of his leading heroes have in general a great sameness, as they had in Old French prose romance. Through conventional feats of arms, the various knights reveal one after another whether they are worthy or unworthy of the high standards of their order. . . . (pp. 96-7)

The reading of Malory shows that if nowadays English-speaking people, high and low alike, respond instantly to the call of fair play, this is merely a part of their chivalric inheritance. Frequently it is emphasized in the *Morte d'Arthur* that there is "no worship" in taking an opponent at a disadvantage. We find Sir Lamorak interrupting an unequal struggle, because, he said, "it was shame, four against one." "Fie for shame," Sir Breuse is rebuked; "strike never a knight when he is on the earth." "Though this knight be never so false," said Pelleas about Gawain, "I will never slay him sleeping; for I will never destroy the high order of knighthood." Sir Launcelot, observing a fight, undertook "to help the weaker party [the under dog, as it were] in increasing of his chivalry." But there are deeper truths in the knightly ideal, which Malory and chivalric writers in general also help us to grasp. Sir Balin said: "Worthiness and good qualities and good deeds are not all only in arrayment, but manhood and worship is hid within man's person." "Humility and patience," a hermit explained to Gawain, "those be the things that be always green and quick; for [to the end that] man may no time overcome humility and patience, therefore was the Round Table founded, and chivalry hath been at all times."

According to the Old French [*Book of the Order of Chivalry*], "God and chivalry concord together." In that work, however, nothing is said of the courtly love which is essential in the matter of Britain. Malory shows no special fondness for this courtly love, but he could not write a *Morte d'Arthur* and leave it out. Though he necessarily dwells on the amours of his chief heroines, he betrays no

quickening enthusiasm for the theme. It would have been difficult, we must admit, so to humanize the ordinary account of Guinevere's intrigue with Launcelot as to fill anyone with tremors of excitement. Even Chrétien de Troyes in the beginning was unable to make it seem other than artificial, and it lost any real life it ever had when elongated in tedious prose. But the same cannot be said of the passion of Tristram and Ysolt. We are thrilled to this hour by the early poems on their unconquerable love. If Malory did not give us something similarly exquisite and moving, it was primarily, of course, because the works of such men as Thomas and Béroul were inaccessible to him, yet also, we can but think, because of his own serious nature and his moral aim in the composition of his book. (pp. 99-101)

On Sir Launcelot Malory lavishes more superlatives than on any other knight. He is the biggest and the best breathed, the worshipfullest, the marvellousest, the courtliest, the noblest, the most honoured of high and low— and this "in all the world." He is the flower of knights, a man of might matchless, peerless of courtesy. Yet, notwithstanding, he also appears in the *Morte d'Arthur*, as in every romance where he is represented as the father of Galahad, and made to participate in the Quest of the Holy Grail, in the rôle of a sad and sorry sinner, because he "trusted more in his harness than in his Maker," but above all because he had done all his great deeds less in honour of God than in adoration of Guinevere. "For, as the book saith, had not Sir Launcelot been in his privy thoughts and in his mind so set inwardly to the queen, as he was in seeming outward to God, there had been no knights passed him in the quest of the Sangreal."

When one reviews the relations of Launcelot and Guinevere, as presented by Malory, it is plain that Launcelot reveals himself in word and deed as much the nobler of the two. Guinevere is altogether lacking in humility, patience, or other Christian virtue. When she heard of her lover's conduct with Elaine, "she writhed and weltered as a mad woman." When she saw him bear in a tourney the sleeve of the Maid of Astolat, "she was well nigh out of her mind for wrath." On this occasion, she at first refused to see Launcelot or to let him explain; then finally, when the facts of his great loyalty were revealed, she still rebuked him, but now for too little "bounty and gentleness" to her rival—who is dead! "This is not the first time," said Sir Launcelot, "that ye have been displeased with me causeless; but, madam, ever I must suffer you, but what sorrow I endure I take no force." It is Guinevere who, when Launcelot would spare her captor, Meliagraunce, gives him a sign to fight to a finish and revenge by death the insult to her. Launcelot is impelled to take every sort of risk for her sake. He recks not for himself; but he is loth to see her dishonoured. His chivalry is in reality only personal idealism, which benefits him morally more than it does the lady he serves.

Launcelot loved but one, and that, according to Malory, by reason of right. "For to take my pleasure with paramours," the hero declares, "that will I refuse, in principal for dread of God, for knights that be adulterous or wanton shall not be happy or fortunate, and who that so useth shall be unhappy and all thing is unhappy that is about them." Yet, despite its perfect fidelity, Malory presents his paragon's love for Guinevere as a grievous offence. It superinduced the great catastrophe of the fall of the Round Table fellowship and the death of the king. (pp. 103-05)

Guinevere was captious and unreasonable to her lover, as well as unfaithful to her husband; Morgain la Fée afflicted Ascolon by her "false lusts;" Vivien deceived Merlin, who was "assotted" upon her; and Ettard brought on herself the scorn of all ladies and gentlewomen because of the pride she manifested towards King Pelleas, who "chose her for his sovereign lady, and never to love other but her." But, on the other hand, there are many beautiful ladies in the *Morte d'Arthur* who seem the incarnation of gentleness, devotion, and truth. Balin bitterly laments that he interfered with the true love of Lanceor and his lady Colombe: by accident he slew "two hearts in one body," for the lady "slew herself with her lover's sword for dole and sorrow" at his death. "I have given," avows Elaine, "the greatest riches and fairest flower that ever I had, and that is my maiden love and faith." She desired Launcelot's presence "liefer than all the gold that is above the earth;" she died of her "fervent love." "Now blessed be God, said the fair Maid of Astolat, that that knight sped so well, for he is the man in the world that I first loved, and truly he shall be the last that ever I shall love."

Throughout Malory's book, true love is exalted as a noble inspiration to valour. "Well I wot that love is a great mistress," spoke his chief hero concerning the fate of Palamides, a mighty warrior, who loved Isolt long and faithfully without guerdon. "She hath been the cause of my worship," declared Palamides, "and else I had been the most simplest knight in the world. For by her and because of her, I have won the worship that I have." "I proffered her no dishonour . . . I offended never as to her person." "I shall love her to the uttermost days of my life." (pp. 107-08)

Finally, in this connection, it deserves note that almost the only instance of happy *wedded* love in the entire *Morte d'Arthur* is that of the wife of King Meliodas, the mother of Sir Tristram; she was "a full meek lady and well she loved her lord, and he her again, and the time came that she should bear a child, so there was great joy betwixt them." Malory, we may well believe, favoured wedded love as much as Chaucer, but his material gave him little chance to make that clear. (p. 110)

The most original part of the *Morte d'Arthur* . . . is that which sets forth the *enfances* of Sir Gareth. . . . It is improbable that this story ever passed through the hydraulic press of late French prose, for it is not sapped of delightful freshness. Malory's words are here specially full of vigour, and his phrases more tinged with homely realism than anywhere else. We gladly applaud young Gareth, because, while bewilderingly successful in arms, he is ever modest, and because, though "he had great labour for his love," he yet so persevered, with astonishing self-restraint, that his love's labour was not lost. "I would fain be of good fame and knighthood," he says; and he conquers every obstacle set in his path—moral obstacles of unfair scorn and undeserved recrimination, as well as the physical impediments of dreary ways, and opponents without mercy and pity. For the sake of his honour and Arthur's, he engages in a fierce succession of fights, and then in a great tournament "paineth himself and enforceth himself to do great deeds" so as to show himself best beloved with his lady. "This Sir Gareth was a noble knight and a well ruled and a fair languaged"—so ends the story of his brilliant career. Certainly, not only by reputation, but also by his conduct in instances recorded, he appears in Malory's book as

Launcelot describes him in maturity—"a gentle knight, courteous, true and bounteous, meek and mild, and in him is no manner of mal-engine, but plain, faithful and true."

The words "meek and mild" applied here to Gareth, as elsewhere to Launcelot, remind us of the persistent union of the phraseology as well as the principles of chivalry and religion. One of the most favoured hymns now sung in English churches opens with the words "Gentle Jesu, meek and mild." There is evidently something of mysticism in Malory's book. Often while reading it, we seem to be within a solemn Gothic cathedral, where processions pass and organ notes resound; incense rises and chants die away; but a great sense of mystery remains. In an atmosphere remote from that of the world, unreal for the body, the soul seems to be lifted up, to perceive the higher verities of life. "By the Round Table," Malory tells us, "is the whole world signified by right." (pp. 114-16)

Malory nowhere gives a hint that there might be any sort of gentleman in the land but one of station. To him the gentleman is exactly the French *gentilhomme*. The commons, or commonalty, are mentioned only a few times in his book, and never with consideration. That he did not leave them out simply because they had little to do with knightly story is evident from the fact that he included certain incidents and reflections, which he might have omitted if he had desired, but with the tone of which he seems, on the contrary, to have been in full sympathy. (pp. 117-18)

Malory believed in the established order of things, the ascendency of the nobles, but not as one indifferent to corruption or injustice. He would have had the lords of his day reform themselves, and he would have conducted the reform on the basis of idealistic principle,—the pressure to change coming from within, spiritual, rather than from without, temporal. He would not have wished to overthrow the constitution of knighthood when it no longer perfectly fulfilled the object of its being: he would have amended it so that it might still prevail for good. Malory was serious, earnest, high-souled. He loved his country, "the noble realm of England," and though inflexible in class feeling, he was undoubtedly a force for righteousness in his day. Because of just such men as he, the English aristocracy has long been honoured, nay beloved.

In England there has never been so definite a cleavage between the different ranks of society as exists on the Continent. In England noble birth seldom ensures a title to others than the eldest born of a family, and there are at present innumerable gentlemen in the realm of better lineage than many of the peers. This fact has been an endless aid to the maintenance of knightly ideals among the people at large. Chivalry has not concerned the titled alone. Commoners and aristocrats alike have striven to exhibit the noble qualities which Malory led them to admire in the heroes of the Round Table. Through the *Morte d'Arthur* the whole nation has come better to comprehend the virtue of chivalry—its beauty and its holiness. (pp. 122-23)

William Henry Schofield, "Malory," *in his* Chivalry in English Literature: Chaucer, Malory, Spenser and Shakespeare, *Cambridge, Mass.: Harvard University, 1912, pp. 75-123.*

GEORGE SAINTSBURY (essay date 1912)

[*Saintsbury was a late nineteenth- and early twentieth-century English literary historian and critic. Tremendously prolific, he composed histories of English and European literature as well as numerous critical works on individual authors, styles, and periods. In the following excerpt from a work originally published in 1912, he closely examines the prose style of the* Morte Darthur.]

I do not know (or at least remember) who the person of genius was who first announced to the world that Malory was "a compiler." The statement is literally quite true (we may even surrender the Beaumains part and wish the receivers joy of it) in a certain lower sense, and exquisitely absurd as well as positively false in a higher. But it does not directly concern us. The point is that this *compilator compilans compilative in compilationibus compilandis* has, somehow or other, supplied a mortar of style and a design of word-architecture for his brute material of borrowed brick or stone, which is not only miraculous, but, in the nature even of miraculous things, uncompilable from any predecessor. Even if that single "French book" which some have used against him from his own expressions, were to turn up, as it has never turned up yet, his benefit of clergy would still remain to him, for no French originals will give English clerkship of this kind and force. Moreover, as shall be more fully shown and illustrated presently, he had certainly English as well as French originals before him, and how he dealt with one at least of these we can show confidently, and as completely as if we had been present in Sir Thomas's *scriptorium*, in the ninth year of the reign of King Edward the Fourth, and he had kindly told us all about it.

"Original" in the only sense that imports to us, Malory can have had none—except perhaps the unknown translator or author of "Mandeville," on whom he has enormously improved. The *idée mère* of both styles—an idea of which in all probability both writers, and the earlier almost certainly, were quite unconscious—is the "*unme*tring" without "*un*rhythming" of the best kind of romance style, with its easy flow, its short and uncomplicated sentences, and its picturesque stock phrases freed from verse- or rhyme-expletive and mere catchword. (pp. 82-3)

[The verse of one of Malory's sources, the verse *Morte d'Artur,* is] emphatically "no great shakes." It is not so bad as the contemporary exercitations of the abominable Herry [*sic*] Lonelich or Lovelich; but it has a great deal of the ever-recurring expletive, the flat and nerveless phrase, and the slipshod rather than flowing movement of the worst verse-romances. Still, it gives a fair "canvas," and this Sir Thomas takes, not even disdaining the retention of a few brighter stitches of his predecessor's, which he patches in, not fearing but welcoming, and mustering them into a distinct prose rhythm—treating them, in fact, just as Ruskin does his doses of blank verse. And so, out of the substance and the general procession of the verse, he has woven a quite new rhythm, accompanying and modulating graceful and almost majestic prose of the best type. There had been nothing in English prose before like the Queen's speech [during her last meeting with Lancelot]; and it had been manufactured, as genius manufactures, out of a very commonplace web of English verse.

The Lancelot dirge . . . may be a later composition, at a time when . . . definite rhetorical devices were attempted.

It has at any rate no parallel in the verse, though this deals with the actual scene. But that, more famous than either of them, of the "throwing of Excalibur," with its immensely interesting addition of Tennyson's re-versing from Malory himself, requires more notice. (pp. 84-5)

We may indeed note [in the passage] . . . how this "compiler" succeeded, as to his mere matter, in compiling *out* Bedivere's silly compromise of throwing the scabbard the second time; but still more the real things—his fashion and manner of style and treatment. These are weaker in the verse than in the original of the Guinevere passage, and he hardly takes anything literal in phrase, altering importantly when he does take something, as in the feeble expletive "deep." But he weaves the whole once more into the most astonishing tissue of pure yet perfect prose rhythm. That it takes but little, as Tennyson showed, to make it once more into splendid verse of character as different as possible from the bald shambling sing-song of the early fifteenth-century man, is nothing against this. That you can get some actual blank verse or fragments of blank out of it is nothing again:

> That has been [*un*]to me so lief and dear . . .
> And thou art named a noble knight . . .
> For thou wouldst for my rich sword see me dead . . .

For these (as such things in the right hands always do) act as ingredients, not as separable parts. They colour the rhythm, but they do not constitute it. They never correspond with each other.

It is not, however, to the great show passages of "the death and departing out of this world of them all," of the Quest of the Graal, of the adventures of Lancelot and the rest, that it is necessary to confine the search for proof of Malory's mastery of style and rhythm. One general symptom will strike any one who has read a fair amount of the *Morte* from our point of view. There are plenty of sentences in Malory beginning with "and"; but it is not the constant go-between and usher-of-all-work that it is in Mandeville. The abundance of conversation gets him out of this difficulty at once; and he seems to have an instinctive knowledge—hardly shown before him, never reached after him till the time of the great novelists—of weaving conversation and narrative together. Bunyan, and certainly most people before Bunyan's day, with Defoe to some extent after him, seem to make distinct gaps between the two, like that of the scenes of a play—to have now a piece of narrative, now one of definite "Tig and Tiri" drama. Malory does not. His narrative order and his dialogue are so artistically adjusted that they dovetail into one another. Here is an instance, taken entirely at hazard, not better than a hundred or a thousand others, and perhaps not so good as some:

> And with that came the damosel of the lake unto the king and said, "Sir, I must speak with you in private." "Say on," said the king, "what ye will." "Sir," said the lady, "put not on you this mantle till ye have seen more, and in no wise let it come upon you nor on no knight of yours till ye command the bringer thereof to put it upon her." "Well," said King Arthur, "it shall be done as ye counsel me." And then he said unto the damosel that came from his sister, "Damosel, this mantle that ye have brought me I will see it upon you." "Sir," said she, "it will not beseem me to wear a knight's garment." "By my head," said King Arthur, "ye shall wear it or it come on my back, on any man that

here is;" and so the king made it to be put upon her; and forthwith she fell down dead, and nevermore spake word after, and was brent to coals.

Here, in a sample as little out of the common way as possible, you may see the easy run of rhythm, the presence of a certain not excessive balance, tempered by lengthening and shortening of clauses, the breaking and knitting again of the cadence-thread; and even (which is really surprising in so early a writer) the selection, instinctive no doubt, but not the less wonderful, of an emphatic monosyllable to close the incident and paragraph. If a more picked example be wanted, nothing better need be sought than the often-quoted passage of the Chapel Perilous. While one of the best of all, though perhaps too long to quote, is that where Lancelot, after the great battle with Turquine (the exact locality of which, by the way, is given in the old histories of Manchester), comes to the Giant's Castle of the Bridge, and slays the bridgeward, but riding into the castle yard, is greeted by "much people in doors and windows that said, 'Fair Knight: thou art unhappy,'" for a close to the chapter.

The dominant of Malory's rhythm, as might indeed be expected in work so much based on French prose and verse and English verse, is mainly iambic, though he does not neglect the precious inheritance of the trochaic or amphibrachic ending, nor the infusion of the trochaic run elsewhere. His sentences, though sometimes of fair length, are rarely periodic enough, or elaborately descriptive enough, to need four-syllable and five-syllable feet: and you may resolve sentence after sentence, as in the last passage noted, into iambs pure, iambs extended by a precedent short into anapæsts and iambs, or curling over with a short suffix into amphibrachs, and so getting in the trochee.

Ănd sŏ | Sīr Lăn | cĕlŏt ănd | thĕ dămsĕl | dĕpārtĕd.

Yet, in some mysterious way, he resists, as has been said, the tendency to drop into poetry.

Now hast thou | thy payment that thou hast so long deserved

is, as a matter of fact, an unexceptionable blank-verse line, preceded by an unexceptionable fragment in a fashion to be found all over Shakespeare, in Milton, and sometimes in all their better followers as well. Yet you would never dream of reading it in prose with any blank-verse rhythm, though the division at "payment" gives a fraction of further blank verse, which Shakespeare in his latest days, or Beaumont and Fletcher at any time, would have unhesitatingly written.

I had thought of giving a few more rhythmical fragments in the way of a *bonne bouche*. But on going through the book (no unpleasant concession to duty) for I suppose nearer the fiftieth than the twentieth time, I found that, to do justice, *mere* fragments would hardly suffice. Quintilian, I suppose, would hardly have appreciated Malory's matter; but he must have admitted that the style was not of that "complexion sprinkled with spots, bright, if you like, but too many and too different," which the sober Roman hated. Every now and then, indeed, there comes a wonderful symphonic arrangement, as in the close of the story of Balin: "Thus endeth the tale of Balin and Balan, | two brothers born in Northumberland, | good knights," | where I have put the double division to mark what we

may almost call the prose-line, making a prose-stanza with no trace of verse in it. More complicated and more wonderful still is the rhythm of the dialogue between the sorceress Hellawes, damsel of the Chapel Perilous, and Sir Lancelot; while the Graal part is crowded with such things. But Malory never seems to put himself out of the way for them; they surge up suddenly in the clear flood of his narrative, and add life and flesh to it for a moment—and the flood goes on.

It must, however, be observed that this prose of Malory's, extraordinarily beautiful as it is, was a sort of half-accidental result of the combination of hour and man, and could never be repeated, save as the result of deliberate literary craftsmanship of the imitative, though of the best imitative, kind. As such it has been achieved in our own days; and in the proper place I may point out that the denigration of Mr. Morris's prose as "Wardour Street" and the like is short-sighted and unworthy. It is then a product of the man directly, but not (or only in an indirect and sophisticated way) of the hour. In Malory's days there was a great body of verse-romance in English, with a half-conventional phraseology, which was not yet in any sense insincere or artificial. This phraseology lent itself directly to the treatment of Malory's subject; while the forms in which it was primarily arranged lent themselves in the same way, though less obviously, and after a fashion requiring more of the essence of the right man, to a simple but extremely beautiful and by no means monotonous prose rhythm, constantly introducing fragments of verse-cadence, but never allowing them to arrange themselves in anything like verse-sequence or metre. That the great popularity of the book—which is attested by such outbursts against it as that of Ascham [see excerpt dated 1568?] from the mere prosaic-Protestant-Philistine point of view, almost as well as by its eight black-letter editions between 1485 (Caxton's) and 1634 (Stansby's)—was to any large, to even any appreciable, extent due to conscious delight in this beauty of prose, it would be idle to pretend. Milton may have seen its beauty when those younger feet of his were wandering in romance, and had not yet deserted it for Philistia and Puritania; when he forgathered with Lancelot, and Pelleas, and Pellinore, instead of with the constituents of "Smectymnuus," and the creatures of Cromwell. Spenser can hardly have failed to do so earlier, for though he has, with an almost whimsical perversity of independence, refused to know anything of Malory's Arthurian *matter*, the whole atmosphere and ordonnance of the *Faerie Queene* are Malorian. But that this popularity did influence Elizabethan prose few competent students of English literature have ever failed to recognise. (pp. 87-92)

George Saintsbury, "From Chaucer to Malory," in his A History of English Prose Rhythm, *1912. Reprint by Indiana University Press, 1965, pp. 56-101.*

E. K. CHAMBERS (essay date 1922)

[Chambers is esteemed as a great historian of the English stage. He wrote groundbreaking scholarly studies of early English drama, notably The Mediaeval Stage *(1903),* The Elizabethan Stage *(1923), and* Shakespeare *(1930), and his* Arthur of Britain *(1927) helped fuel interest in Malory and the* Morte Darthur. *In the following excerpt, he offers a comprehensive overview of the structure of the* Morte

Darthur *and comments on thematic and generic issues relating to the work.*]

Sir Thomas Malory came late to his high theme. The heyday of Arthurian romance was over by the middle of the thirteenth century. Then began the period of scribes and interpolators, with their sequels and *enfances*. The outlines of the old stories were blurred, their movement slowed down under the accumulation of subsidiary adventures, conventional and interminable. They had always been long-winded enough; the evenings in a mediaeval castle, when the day's fighting was over, were long. The alliterative revival of the fourteenth century gave some fresh impulse, but it passed. Then the *Romance of the Rose* brought in the new mode of sentimental allegory, and Chaucer followed with his quicker and more vivid way of telling tales. Moreover, the best of the romances were still in French, and cultivated England was ceasing to talk French. They became old-fashioned, and at the most contributed to balladry. It is the popular literature—ballads, carols, miracle-plays—which counts most in the fifteenth century; except for Malory himself, who has nothing to do with all these. And so when Malory began to turn over the faded manuscripts in the window-seat of some country manor, and to shape them into his strong new prose, he was almost as deliberate an archaist as the writer of *The Faerie Queene* or the writer of *The Defence of Guenevere*. It was not all loss. Detached from the tradition, he had to pour some new wine into the old bottles, to bring his antiquarian findings into some kind of vital relation to the thought and conditions of his own day. I shall come back to that.

Just now I want to remind you how difficult Malory's material was to handle, and to note some weak points in his handling. I am not going to linger over this; it is an intricate subject, for which all the evidence is not yet available, while some of what is available has not always been wisely used. But I think it is clear that the process of 'reducing' out of French into English, of which Caxton's preface [see excerpt dated 1485] to the **Morte d'Arthur** speaks, must have involved not merely the work of an abbreviator and translator, but also a good deal of selection and compilation from different sources. There is no trace of any single French book which remotely resembles Malory's. He must have had several manuscripts at his disposal, perhaps more than one would expect to find kept together, anywhere outside some great household. A few of them contained versions of tales other than those contained in the manuscripts we know, or tales not otherwise known at all. But as a rule we can determine the kind of manuscript he used. He must have had the comprehensive romance of *Lancelot*, of which there are five sections, the Early History of the Grail, the Merlin, the Lancelot proper, the Quest of the Grail, and the Mort Artus. This was itself to some extent of composite origin, although the latest investigation, that of M. Ferdinand Lot, tends to ascribe four of the five sections to a single hand, and to regard only the Merlin as an interpolation. He had the other vast romance of *Tristan*, in a late and debased form. He had, perhaps unfortunately, a variant of the Merlin, written to lead up to a version of the Quest of the Grail, other than that given in the *Lancelot*. And, Caxton notwithstanding, he had English sources, as well as French; the alliterative *Morte d'Arthur*, upon which he based his account of Arthur's wars with Rome, and perhaps the fourteenth-century met-

rical *Morte d'Arthur*, which shares many of Malory's divergences from the *Lancelot* in the last stages of his story. I have said enough to show that the material was complex. The bulk alone was very great; ten times that of the **Morte d'Arthur**. Some of the adventures told were essential to the working out of the main themes; others were incidental, and led nowhere. There was an obvious danger, in a drastic reduction, of taking the incidental and missing the essential. Moreover, the romances had slowly grown into their latest forms. They had influenced and counter-influenced each other in diverse fashions. They had heroes and adventures in common, but the adventures did not always work out in the same way, and the heroes did not always sustain the same characters. Sir Thomas Malory had not, even to the extent to which we have, the clue of scholarship to enable him to thread these mazes. With all deference to a really great writer, I think that, so far as the first half of the **Morte d'Arthur** is concerned, he rather bungled his structural problem. We expect a work of fiction to have a beginning, a middle, and an end; to progress, however deviously, through the medium of consistent personalities, to an intelligible issue. The **Morte d'Arthur** does not satisfy this expectation. That is why, through so much of it, we walk perplexedly. It is, in the phrase of a poet of our own day, 'the dim Arthuriad'. It is full of beginnings which have no end and of ends which never had a beginning. It does not perhaps matter much that knights who have been killed in one book live to fight and be killed again in another. But Merlin comes and goes, and we are never told who or what Merlin is. First Pellinore and then Palamydes pursues the questing beast, but the nature of the quest remains dark. The adventures of Balin bear many suggestions of their significance in relation to the Grail, but when the book of the Grail comes, they are found not to have been significant. Malory has in his hands two of the world's dozen great love stories, and does not succeed in telling either of them completely. The earlier scenes between Tristram and Iseult are hidden in an overgrowth of commonplace chivalric adventures, the chief purposes of which are to pit Tristram against Lancelot, to let Iseult write sentimental letters to Guenevere, and to make King Mark quite unnecessarily contemptible. And then we are told, 'Here endeth the second book of Sir Tristram. But here is no rehearsal of the third book.' And so we are left to hear of Tristram's death by a casual report in the later book, and then it is not the pathetic and imaginative story of the black sail, with which we are familiar from the old poems, but only a treacherous stabbing in the back by Mark. It is not altogether Malory's fault. He did not know the old poems, and the prose *Tristan* was the worst of models. Perhaps he would have done better to have left the *Tristan* alone, and kept to the *Lancelot*. But if he robs us the end of Tristram, he robs us of the beginning of Lancelot. There is nothing of the changeling boyhood, nothing of the coming to court and of Lancelot's trembling at the sight of Guenevere; not even that episode of the first kiss, of which Dante makes such unforgettable use in the *Divine Comedy*. The outcome of Lancelot's relation with Geunevere, as we shall see, is nobly treated; but the relation itself is taken for granted, and is not led up to. It therefore, to some extent, fails to carry us with it. One point more, and I shall be glad to have done with depreciation. A solution of continuity which affects character is more serious than one which merely affects plot. And one important character at least, that of Gawaine, is not maintained on the same plane throughout. In all the earlier Arthurian romances Gawaine is the noblest of Arthur's knights; he is 'Gawane the gay, gratious, and gude', the embodiment of courtesy, always contrasted with Kay the churlish and crabbed. Then somebody, Walter Map or another, invented Lancelot, and made him the queen's lover, and the imagination of the romance writers took hold of Lancelot and he became the leading knight of the Round Table, ousting Gawaine. But for the purposes of the Lancelot romance Gawaine, although relegated to the second place, must remain noble, and Lancelot's true comrade in arms, until some inevitable break comes, which dissolves the high companionship, and precipitates the ultimate tragedy of the Mort Artus. And so it is in Malory's opening and closing books. But so it is not throughout the story. I do not merely mean that Gawaine, as a worldly man and a lover of light ladies, is not thought worthy to achieve the Holy Grail, and, to say the truth, does not much mind whether he achieves it or not. Lancelot himself does not achieve the Holy Grail. But in the Tristram section there is a systematic blackening of Gawaine's character as a knight. He slays the good Sir Lamorak by treachery, and we are told that privily he hated Sir Lancelot and all his kin, and that 'after Sir Gareth had espied Sir Gawaine's conditions, he withdrew himself from his brother Sir Gawaine's fellowship, for he was vengeable, and where he hated he would be avenged with murder, and that hated Sir Gareth'. Malory has forgotten this, when he comes to the Mort Artus, but the reader cannot forget.

What then should be the attitude of criticism in the face of all this structural incoherence? One way is to demonstrate that Malory is much more subtle than we took him for, and that, when he seems most artless, he is really laying the threads of his deliberate design. This is the way adopted in a recent book on the *Morte d'Arthur* which reached me as I was meditating these observations. The other is to accept the facts, and to take Malory for what he can give, and not for what he cannot give. That is, I think, the better way. There are stirring and amusing tales enough in the earlier books, even if they are episodic and do not advance a main theme; the tale of Arthur's fight with the giant on Mont St. Michel, for example, or that of Gareth's adventures with the minx Lynette. Or you may regard the whole thing as a tapestry; half close your eyes and watch a pleasant landscape, full of running waters, and moated castles, and hermitages, and green lawns, and 'plumps' of wood, amongst which move bright little figures in blue and white and red armour, every now and again stopping to lay spears in rest and upset one another, and then swearing eternal friendship and riding away again. Here is a ford perilous, and at the door of a pavilion a dwarf watches a shield, hung there for the challenge of any knight who has a mind to end an ill custom. There a tired knight sleeps under a great apple-tree that stands by a hedge, and presently his horse grimly neighs, and by sweep four queens on white mules under a canopy of green silk, and cast an enchantment upon him. They are Morgan le Fay and her sisters, high-born dames, but 'nigromancers' all. And presently knights and ladies begin to gather from their several adventures, and turn their horses' heads all one way. They are making for the great tournament beside Lonazep. The name sounds full of promise. But it is not worth while following them; the great tournament beside Lonazep is a tournament like any other. And throughout you have the delight of Malory's

admirable prose; as finished an instrument in its way as any prose the sixteenth century can show, but with the freshness of the early world still upon it. A formal analysis of style would be tedious. I choose three points only for illustration. The first is the constant use of vivid words, which have now gone out of the language. A knight rides 'a great wallop' until he comes to a fountain. Another is smitten on a ship and falls down 'noseling' to the shipboard. Lancelot tilts with Gawaine and charges him 'so sore that his horse reversed up so down'. A tall lad is a 'much young man'. Arthur has a dream of a fight in the air between a boar and a dragon, in which 'the dragon flew away all on a height, and come down with such a swough, and smote the boar to powder, both flesh and bones, that it fluttered all abroad on the sea'. Sometimes there is an echo of the alliterative poems. Gawaine comes to battle 'as brim as any boar'. Bedivere sees 'the waters wap and waves wan'. Such phrases are racy of the vernacular, but it is French, although it sounds like English, when Gawaine bids Lancelot 'deliver the queen from thee and pike thee lightly out of the court'. It is both French and English, when Sir Bors sees 'a spear great and long that came straight upon him pointling'. The tempers of the two languages are coalescing. So much for my first stylistic point. The second is that, although there is little word-painting, Malory is alive to the sweet influences of the Pleiades. His adventures are hung about, like English sport, with outdoor sights and sounds. Knights ride to keep their tryst, and 'lodge them in a little leaved wood, beside there the tournament should be'. They fight with such dint of strokes 'that the noise and sound rang by the water and the wood'. A fight lasts all day, and at evensong 'they set them down upon two mole-hills there beside the fighting place, and either of them unlaced his helm and took the cold wind'. A tired man comes to a fair well and puts off his helm 'to drink of that burbley water'. Another is caught in a storm, when there fell 'a thunder and a rain, as heaven and earth should go together'. More elaborate is the picture when Arthur meets a churl at the door of his castle in Sherwood. 'He was all befurred in black sheepskins, and a great pair of boots, and a bow and arrows, in a russet gown, and brought wild geese in his hand, and it was on the morn after Candlemas day.' It is Merlin in disguise, coming across the snows of Candlemas. My third point is a trick of dialogue. Malory can be rhetorical, when a dramatic needs calls for it. But for the most part the knights are of brief speech. They are men of their hands. Arthur has to face the challenge of six kings at once, and asks advice of his barons. 'They could no counsel give, but said they were big enough.' Could a war debate among English lords be better or more briefly rendered?

But a wind-bag will get his answer. 'As for that threatening, said Sir Gringamore, be it as it may, we will go to dinner.' And when Turquine has flung his defiance at the whole of the Table Round, 'That is over much said, said Sir Lancelot.' The phrasing may shape itself in gnomic homespun. 'What nephew, said the king, is the wind in that door?' When Lancelot's time of trouble comes, his fellowship recall that they have had much weal with him and much worship. 'And therefore, Sir Lancelot, said they, we will take the woe with the weal.' These brevities of speech are Malory's nearest approach to humour. Fundamental humour, the humour of a Chaucer, is perhaps incompatible with romance. It shatters the dome of many-coloured glass. Chaucer and Shakespeare between them did not leave much romance about Troilus and Cressida.

Towards the middle of the *Morte d'Arthur*, light breaks over the story. We no longer see men walking as trees darkly. They begin to arrange themselves in definite patterns, and to move through real conflicts of character and passion to a deliberate end. Henceforward everything centres round Lancelot; we get clear of the *Tristan*. Malory is ruthless in abridging his source, taking only so much from the intricate adventures of the French *Lancelot* as will establish, firstly, his hero's priority to all the other knights of the Round Table, secondly, the special link between him and Gawaine and his brother Gareth, thirdly, his love relation with Guenevere, and, fourthly, his parentage of Galahad. Lancelot may not himself see the Grail, but he cannot, in a Lancelot romance, give place to any of his fellows. So the Grail-winner must be his son, and as Lancelot will love no woman but Guenevere, the existence of a son must be explained by bringing Lancelot under a spell. Spells are always legitimate in romance. Galahad is born, grows up, comes to court, and achieves the siege perilous. And so the story slides into the Quest of the Grail. I hope I shall not imperil sympathy if I say that I do not regard the Quest of the Grail as one of the most satisfactory parts of the *Morte d'Arthur*. Again it is not altogether Malory's fault. He follows the French *Lancelot* closely here, and the Quest, as he tells it, was an integral part of the *Lancelot*, perhaps from the beginning, and certainly in the version which came down to him and has come to us. But the much-told tale is told better elsewhere. The Galahad Quest has not the mystery of Chretien de Troyes' original fragment; it may be just because it is not a fragment. It has not the tender melancholy of the *Perlesvaus*, the version translated as *The High History of the Holy Grail*. German scholars find a deeper humanity in Wolfram von Eschenbach's *Parzival*. The introduction of the theme into the *Lancelot* explains itself well enough. It is a quite legitimate attempt to bring romance into the service of religious mysticism. It points from the way of earthly achievement to the way of spiritual illumination. The chivalry of heaven is set against the chivalry of the Round Table. But the initial inspiration, whatever its worth, is insufficient to carry the writer through his long series of symbolic adventures and still more symbolic visions, with a hermit waiting at every crossroads to expound the symbolism in its bitterest detail. The hermit had ill success with the frivolous Gawaine. 'Sir, said Sir Gawaine, and I had leisure I would speak with you, but my fellow here, Sir Ector, is gone, and abideth me yonder beneath the hill. Well, said the good man, thou were better to be counselled.' Do not our hearts, in these long books, sometimes go down the hill with Gawaine? Structurally, too, the Quest makes a false issue in the story. When Galahad comes to court with his unearthly beauty, and all the knights turn to their new avows, Arthur is 'displeased'. He foresees the end of the Table Round.

> For when they depart from hence, I am sure they all shall never meet more in this world, for they shall die many in the quest. And so it forthinketh me a little, for I have loved them as well as my life, wherefore it shall grieve me right sore the departition of this fellowship, for I have had an old custom to have them in my fellowship. And there with the tears fill in his eyne.

The Round Table had worked for the betterment of human life, but of this, as the history of religious thought has shown, the mystic impulse may take hardly more account than of 'the vain glory of the world, the which is not worth a pear'. But if a theme of mysticism was to be the issue of Malory's story, surely it should have ended with this theme. It ends quite differently. The Grail vanishes. The knights who achieve it are those who have least to do with the Round Table. The old motives of life re-establish themselves. Only in Lancelot is a little sting of conscience left; he has been of the Quest, and has failed. And the ultimate debate, upon which the fortunes of Arthur and his fellowship break and are dissolved, is not between the ideals of Camelot and the ideals of Corbenic, but a purely human one, the familiar conflict between human love and human loyalty.

The two books which follow the Quest contain four great adventures of Lancelot. Three of them concern his relations with Guenevere; his services to her in the delivery from the stake and the rescue from Sir Meliagrance; his renunciation for her in the beautiful tale of the fair maid of Astolat. The epilogue hints at the problem which is coming.

> For, Madam, said Sir Lancelot, I love not to be constrained to love; for love must arise of the heart, and not by no constraint. That is truth, said the king, and many knights: love is free in himself, and never will be bounden; for where he is bounden he loseth himself.

There is already tragic irony here. The fourth adventure shows Lancelot at the top of his knightly renown. He alone, of all the Round Table, may touch Sir Urre's wounds and heal them. And when the adventure is over, 'ever Sir Lancelot wept as he had been a child that had been beaten'. That is a fine touch of Malory's. ... [The tragic reversal of fortunes] is upon us. And now, with the last two books, Malory rises to the full height of his epic theme. May I call it epic? Professor Ker, to whom in all things mediaeval we are bound to defer, draws a sharp distinction between epic and romance, between Roland or Beowulf and Lancelot. For him the epic is the heroic. The defence of a narrow place against odds, dramatically told; that is a typical heroic or epic adventure. Well, I do not wish to deny the differences in temper between the *Chanson de Roland* and the *Lancelot*, with a century or more of romance-writing between them; although Lancelot was in a tight place enough when he slew Sir Colgrevaunce at the door of Guenevere's chamber, unarmed against fourteen knights who 'had gotten a great form out of the hall, and therewith they rashed at the door'. But common usage, I think, allows of many different tempers and manners of writing within the notion of epic, insisting only on dignity and scope of treatment, and on the linking up of individual fortunes with those of some greater whole, a house, a nation, an empire, humanity itself. This linking up does not fail in the *Morte d'Arthur*. Professor Ker does not admit that the national or 'ecumenical' theme is of the essence of epic; he finds this rather in 'dramatic representation of the characters'. And he quotes Aristotle—always an excellent thing to do. Aristotle praises Homer because, while other poets 'tell their story straight on', he 'with little prelude, leaves the stage to personages, men and women, all with characters of their own'. It is true. But Aristotle is here contrasting the manner of a good epic poet with the manner of some bad epic poets. He is not trying to define the notion of epic. He does not say whether its theme should or should not have a national or ecumenical aspect. Certainly the *Iliad* is the tale of Troy, as well as the tale of the wrath of Achilles, and the *Odyssey* is not unconcerned with the dynasty of Ithaca. However this may be, Aristotle ought to have approved of the last two books of the *Morte d'Arthur*. Malory follows his precept exactly. There is a little prelude, and then, with rare comments, Malory stands aside and lets his characters speak and act for themselves. Here is the little prelude.

> In May, when every lusty heart flourisheth and bourgeoneth; for as the season is lusty to behold and comfortable, so man and woman rejoicen and gladden of summer coming with his fresh flowers, for winter, with his rough winds and blasts, causeth a lusty man and woman to cower and sit fast by the fire. So in this season, as in the month of May, it befell a great anger and unhap that stinted not till the flower of chivalry of all the world was destroyed and slain; and all was long upon two unhappy knights, the which were named Agravaine and Sir Mordred that were brethren unto Sir Gawaine.

The stage is now set. The action is swift, the conclusion inevitable; there is a full sense of the pity of it. The web of the psychological situation is closely woven. It is not merely the 'eternal triangle'; Lancelot, Arthur, Guenevere. Lancelot is the midmost figure, drawn this way by fidelity to his king, and that way by fidelity to his mistress. But there is also Mordred, the child of Arthur's sin, and destined from birth to be Arthur's undoing, working now actively with Agravaine for Lancelot's overthrow. And there are Gawaine and Gareth, bound to Lancelot by all knightly bonds. He has rescued Gawaine from Carados and Turquine; he has knighted Gareth and loves him. When the crisis comes, Gawaine is for long true to Lancelot. Then, in rescuing Guenevere for the second time from the stake, Lancelot unwittingly slays the unarmed Gareth, and Gawaine's love is turned to hate. His fiercer spirit compels the reluctant king to besiege the lovers in Joyous Gard. At this siege Lancelot's behaviour is perfect in its sad deference to an ancient loyalty. It is long before he will level a spear, and when Bors unhorses Arthur, Lancelot alights and horses him again, and 'the tears brast out of Arthur's eyes, thinking on the great courtesy that was in Sir Launcelot, more than in any other man'. The Pope intervenes and bids Arthur take his queen again and 'accord' with Lancelot. Arthur consents. Lancelot rides with the queen from Joyous Gard, which hereafter shall be Dolorous Gard, to Carlisle, both clothed alike in white cloth of gold tissue, with an hundred knights in green velvet, and every knight 'with a branch of olive in his hand in tokening of peace'. It is his last pageant. He perjures himself, as others in like case have done, and will do again. Guenevere's reputation is to be unstained. And now you think that her adventures at least are ended, and that she will live it out at Carlisle or Camelot, like that Helen whom Telemachus beheld at Sparta, when Troy fires had long been dust . . . , a comely housewife with her distaff among her handmaidens. The story will have it otherwise; but now it goes with Lancelot. Arthur may be reconciled, but Gawaine will not be reconciled. Lancelot must 'pike' him out of that court, of which he had been at once the stay and ornament. Arthur and Gawaine and their host follow him over the seas to Benwick, and there, stung by Gawaine's insults, Lancelot twice lays him low, and twice refuses to take his life. Then Mordred strikes again, raising rebellion in Arthur's absence, and claiming to wed

Guenevere. Arthur returns. Gawaine dies of his old wound at Dover, and relents, but all too late, bidding Arthur send for Lancelot, and begging that Lancelot will visit his tomb. The rest is familiar; the death of Arthur, the pathetic farewell between Lancelot and Guenevere, their edifying ends in their several hermitages, Lancelot's burial at Joyous Gard, and Ector's threnody over his bier. No doubt it is in all the anthologies, but I cannot forbear to quote it.

> Ah Launcelot, he said, thou were head of all Christian knights; and now I dare say, said Sir Ector, thou Sir Lancelot, there thou liest, that thou were never matched of earthly knight's hand; and thou were the courteous knight that ever bare shield; and thou were the truest friend to thy lover that ever bestrode horse; and thou were the truest lover of a sinful man that ever loved woman; and thou were the kindest man that ever strake with sword; and thou were the goodliest person ever came among press of knights; and thou was the meekest man and the gentlest that ever ate in hall among ladies; and thou were the sternest knight to thy mortal foe that ever put spear in the breast.

Such is Malory's music and such his meaning; and now he has nothing to do but to date his book, and bid his readers 'pray for me while I am on live that God send me good deliverance, and when I am dead, I pray you all pray for my soul'. What does he mean by 'good deliverance'? . . . The direct echoes of his life in his book are not many. As I have said, like Homer, he rarely intervenes. But even as blind Homer introduces the blind Demodocus, so Malory, when he has described how Tristram fell into prison, passes to a comment:

> So Sir Tristram endured there great pain, for sickness had undertaken him, and that is the greatest pain a prisoner may have. For all the while a prisoner may have his health of body, he may endure under the mercy of God, and in hope of good deliverance; but when sickness touches a prisoner's body, then may a prisoner say all wealth is him bereft, and then he hath cause to wail and to weep.

This is one of three or four reflective passages which, so far as we can tell, Malory did not find in his sources. The most famous is the chapter on 'How true love is likened to summer', which introduces the tale of Guenevere's Maying. Some blossoming bough has flung itself across the window of his prison, and the old knight stops to muse on spring and love. This, too, is in all the anthologies. Another, and perhaps critically the most significant, is in the account of Mordred's rebellion, when the people were 'so new fangle' that for the most part they held with him.

> Lo ye all Englishmen, see ye not what a mischief here was, for he that was the most king and knight of the world, and most loved the fellowship of noble knights, and by him they were all upholden, now might not these Englishmen hold them content with him. Lo thus was the old custom and usage of this land. And also men say that we of this land have not yet lost ne forgotten that custom and usage. Alas this is a great default of us Englishmen; for there may no thing please us no term.

Here then Malory reads a lesson. And indeed to regard the *Morte d'Arthur* as no more than a piece of archaistic romancing would be to mistake its temper. After all, Malory is writing with his eye on the fifteenth century. The Wars of the Roses were no crusade. Chivalry was not much in evidence when Lord Clifford stabbed young Rutland at the bridge of Wakefield. Lancelot would not have done that. And so Malory, who remembers Agincourt, will set before his countrymen the ideal of a better England, an ideal in which the knights are charged

> never to do outrageously, nor murder, and always to flee treason. Also, by no mean to be cruel, but to give mercy unto him that asketh mercy...; and always to do ladies, damsels, and gentlewomen succour upon pain of death. Also, that no man take no battles in a wrongful quarrel for no law, ne for no world's goods. Unto this were all the knights sworn of the Table Round, both old and young.

Can he bring back the days of King Arthur—or is it the days of King Henry V?

Certainly the *Morte d'Arthur* is a book that makes for righteousness. It was a singular aberration of criticism when Roger Ascham wrote of it that 'the whole pleasure standeth in two speciall poyntes, in open mans slaughter and bold bawdry: in which book these be counted the noblest knights, that do kill most men without any quarrel, and commit foulest adulteries by subtlest shifts' [see excerpt dated 1568?]. I do not claim that Malory sees his way quite clearly through the queer spiritual tangle of the twelfth-century *amour courtois*. Perhaps such casuistry was not for him. He knows that love is good, and therefore of Guenevere he will 'make here a little mention, that while she lived she was a true lover, and therefore she had a good end'. But he knows also that sin brings tragedy. It is not merely that the sinful man will not see the Holy Grail. The tragedy is here and now. 'For as well as I have loved thee' says Guenevere to Lancelot, 'For as well as I have loved thee, mine heart will not serve me to see thee; for through thee and me is the flower of kings and knights destroyed.' Better than by Ascham, the spirit of the book is held by William Caxton, who, after the 'simple cunning' which God hath sent to him, will put it into print for an 'ensample'.

> For herein may be seen noble chivalry, courtesy, humanity, friendliness, hardiness, love, friendship, cowardice, murder, hate, virtue and sin. Do after the good and leave the evil, and it shall bring you to good fame and renommee.

I sometimes wonder what democracy, with its transmutation of all literary as well as all social values, which is before us, will make of the *Morte d'Arthur*. Malory's is a very aristocratic ideal. The churl does not count for much in it. Agincourt was all very well, but I daresay Malory sat holding his spear at the siege of Rouen, when the townsfolk, after living on 'cattis, hors, houndis, rattis, myse, and all that myght be etynne', were driven out of the gates by the garrison 'for spendyng of vitaille', and remorselessly driven back into the moat by Henry's forces. I hope that he was one of the knights told off to take them a Christmas dinner there. In the *Morte d'Arthur* itself, the distinction between noble and churl is fundamental. If there are sparks of nobility in a cowherd's son, like Tor, or a kitchen knave, like Gareth, you may be sure he will turn out to be a king's son in disguise. There is much emphasis on lineage. That Lancelot and his son are 'the greatest gentlemen in the world' is quaintly explained. They are of the lineage of Jesus Christ. Percivale and his brother may not

dwell at home, 'for we be come of king's blood of both parties, and therefore, mother, it is our kind to haunt arms and noble deeds'. Even the hermits in Logres are of gentle birth.

> For in these days it was not the guise of hermits as is nowadays. For there were none hermits in those days, but that they had been men of worship and of prowess, and those hermits held great household, and refreshed people that were in distress.

Malory goes out of is way to give this bit of antiquarian lore. He must have known anchorites in his own time, whose salad even a wandering knight would not want to share. Well, when democracy comes to its own, I suppose that Lancelot will have to go through the crucible, with Plato's wardens and Aristotle's magnanimous man. And yet, after all, the transmutation of values is not the extinction of values. An economic redistribution will not wholly remove the need for chivalry. Even in the New Jerusalem, I think, there will be courtesies to be exchanged, wrongs to be righted, public service to be done. And so, perhaps, the lamps that burnt for our fathers may still glimmer upon our path, and it may still prove true that 'in him that should say or think that there was never a king called Arthur, might well be aretted great folly and blindness'. (pp. 3-15)

> *E. K. Chambers, in his* Sir Thomas Malory, *1922. Reprint by Folcraft Library Editions, 1971, 16 p.*

HERBERT READ (essay date 1929)

[*Read was a prolific English poet, critic, and novelist. In the following excerpt, he discusses the concept of glory in the* Morte Darthur.]

The *Morte Darthur*, like most of the books printed by Caxton, has had an influence on the course of English literature which it would be idle to estimate; and purely as literature Malory's 'miraculous' redaction has not wanted praise. 'Miraculous' was Professor Saintsbury's word, and is to be found in that *History of English Prose Rhythm* which paid such a notable tribute to Malory's originality and mastery in the formation of an English style [see excerpt dated 1912]. Professor Saintsbury did not by any means exhaust the technical virtues of Malory's prose; and now that the spirit of the age cries out for literature justified in action, for books visibly related to experience, we perceive more readily than ever certain subtleties of visual actuality and exact expression in the *Morte Darthur*. The last refinement of all great writing is the selection and isolation of significant detail; and no one is more triumphant in this sense than Malory. In the death scene of the Fair Maid of Astolat, for example, where for once English prose seems to out-reach the range of English verse, we see how a detail noted almost casually in the very last clause can inform the whole narrative with appropriate desolation and melancholy:

> And then she called her father, Sir Bernard, and her brother, Sir Tirre, and heartily she prayed her father that her brother might write a letter like as she did indite it: and so her father granted her. And when the letter was written word by word like as she devised, then she prayed her father that she might be watched until she were dead. And while my body is hot let this letter be put in my right hand, and my hand bound fast with

the letter until that I be cold; and let me be put in a fair bed with all the richest clothes that I have about me, and so let my bed and all my richest clothes be laid with me in a chariot unto the next place where Thames is; and let me be put within a barget, and but one man with me, such as ye trust to steer me thither, and that my barget be covered with black samite over and over; thus father I beseech you let it be done. So her father granted it her faithfully, all things should be done like as she had devised. Then her father and her brother made great dole, for when this was done anon she died. And so when she was dead the corpse and the bed all was led the next way unto Thames, and there a man, and the corpse, and all, were put unto Thames; and so the man steered the barget unto Westminster, and there he rowed a great while to and fro or any espied it.

In spite of these and other great merits, the *Morte Darthur* is to-day in a curious predicament—sometimes a butt for facetious scorn, sometimes a hobby-horse for romanticists, and when it has escaped these fates, a feast to be served in polite selections to schoolgirls. It almost seems that great books must be defamed before they can become popular; I have seen an emasculated edition of *Gulliver's Travels* sold on the bookstalls as one of a series of "Sunny Stories for Little Folks". Malory's genius has not been travestied in marketplace and nursery in quite the same way as Swift's; but certain perversions of the spirit of his work have prevented the true appreciation of its merits.

The first of these might be called the quixotic-perversion. The *Morte Darthur* is really the epitome of the literature of an age—the feudal age. It was written at the break-up of that age by one who shared in its stress and anguish with body and soul—so at least we may conclude if, as now seems likely, the author of the *Morte Darthur* can be identified with the Sir Thomas Malorie of Newbold Revel, in the parish of Monks Kirby, Warwickshire, whose name occurs among those of a number of Lancastrians excluded from a general pardon granted by Edward IV in 1468. The turbulent career of this knight has been reconstructed with a good deal of ingenuity by Mr Edward Hicks [in *Sir Thomas Malory: His Turbulent Career* (1928)]. Malory probably began his adventurous life as a member of the retinue of Richard Beauchamp, Earl of Warwick, and undoubtedly saw many years of active military service in France. Later in his life, in his native country, he became involved in adventures which we might really call 'quixotic', and was charged with insurrection, robbery and rape. He pleaded "in no wise guilty" of all these charges, but his plea was dismissed, and he seems to have spent the remaining twenty years of his life in prison; during that time he composed the *Morte Darthur*.

Malory was formulating for the last time a tradition which had lasted for five hundred years. He was writing of events remote enough to be legendary. The reaction was fast upon him, and when it came it fell foul of what was nearest and handiest—the *Morte Darthur*. The damosels and knights of the Arthurian cycle were fair objects and easy victims for the scorn of an age that had grown wealthy, realistic and cynical. The legendary charm lasted until Spenser, in whom, however, romance has become too ornate and sophistical; and in a more general and yet a more profound way the spirit of Malory is the spirit of the Elizabethans, particularly of that embodiment of all most remarkable in the age, Sir Philip Sidney. But the reaction, fed by a more diffuse and bourgeois spirit, came to

a head in such travesties as *The Knight of the Burning Pestle*. The world has been pleased to see this mockery sanctioned in *Don Quixote*; but that is a superficial view of Cervantes' romance. No thoughtful reader ever came from *Don Quixote* in a cynic or ironic mood against the age of chivalry. (pp. 34-8)

The second obstacle which a reader of the *Morte Darthur* must overcome is the romantic perversion. This is more difficult to avoid because ostensibly we are among friends. But Malory has had no greater enemies than his revivalists. *La Belle Dame Sans Merci* may pass as a momentary reincarnation of the magic of the *Morte Darthur*; but the travesties of Tennyson and Morris, followed by the effeminate and etiolated ornaments of Aubrey Beardsley, have had disastrous effects. They bathe the stark narrative in an atmosphere of milk and honey; they turn romance into romanticism, muscular prose into watery verse. Such pretenders shrink from the vigorous realism of Malory. Tennyson regrets

'One
Touched by the adulterous finger of a time
That hover'd between war and wantonness
And crownings and dethronings',

and improves on Malory by making his Arthur a king of prigs. Even the noble simplicity of Malory's style is translated into the sentimentality of a Victorian valentine. Compare Elaine's last letter:

Most noble knight, Sir Launcelot, now hath death made us two at debate for your love. I was your lover, that men called the Fair Maiden of Astolat; therefore unto all ladies I make my moan, yet pray for my soul and bury me at least, and offer ye my mass-penny: this is my last request. And a clean maiden I died, I take God to witness: pray for my soul, Sir Launcelot, as thou art peerless.

—with Tennyson's versification of it:

Most noble lord, Sir Lancelot of the Lake,
I, sometime call'd the maid of Astolat,
Come, for you left me taking no farewell,
Hither, to take my last farewell of you.
I loved you, and my love had no return,
And therefore my true love has been my death.
And therefore to our lady Guinevere,
And to all other ladies, I make moan.
Pray for my soul, and yield me burial.
Pray for my soul thou too, Sir Lancelot,
As thou art a knight peerless.

To romanticize and sentimentalize the *Morte Darthur* is to sacrifice its finest essence, which is action and intact honour displayed in the midst of all worldly perils—cowardice, murder, hate and sin.

The third obstacle to the modern appreciation of Malory is in the nature of a reaction from the perversion just mentioned. People sick of romantic transcriptions of chivalry turn away without investigating the thing itself. Antiromantic as most of this generation must be, we imagine that all romance is romantic. It is a great error; and if the excuse is not ignorance, it is merely indifference. But an age with so few illusions, with such poor outlets for emotion and reverence, cannot afford to be either indifferent or ignorant, and must in the end go to Malory and his like to recover certain necessary virtues—virtues which Una-muno finds implicit in the figure of Don Quixote.

All such virtues are included in the sentiment of glory. It may seem odd that a generation which has lived to experience the bitterest disillusion of glory should be urged to recover that sentiment from an old romance. But glory itself has been perverted, for many centuries and from many causes. (pp. 39-42)

Glory has usually been associated with war, and in Malory is accompanied by what his first critic, Roger Ascham, called "bold bawdry and open manslaughter" [see excerpt dated 1568?]. That glory has no necessary connection with war is clear after a moment's reflection; for martial glory is not essential glory, and we must still distinguish glory with grace—as in Wolfe and Nelson—from glory with pride—as in Alexander and Napoleon. War occupies a privileged position because it alone has provided a large number of people with an opportunity for disinterested action. That is the burden of many apologies for war, such as those of Proudhon and Ruskin. War allows men to seek glory without pretension, in the shelter of a crowd, with the excuse of a common cause. As Vauvenargues pointed out in one of his maxims, the dominating qualities in men are not those which they willingly allow to appear, but, on the contrary, those which they hide.

> This especially applies to ambition, because it is a kind of humiliating recognition of the superiority of great

Arthur and Mordred meet in the last battle. From London, Lambeth Palace Library, MS. 6.

men, and an avowal of the meanness of our fortune or the presumption of our spirit. Only those who desire little, or those who are on the point of realizing their pretensions, can be openly complacent about such things. What makes people ridiculous is a sense of pretensions ill-founded or immoderate, and since glory and fortune are advantages most difficult to attain, they are for that reason the source of the deepest sense of ridicule in those who lack them. (pp. 43-4)

The glory which Vauvenargues saw in the clear light of reason, and which Cervantes saw in the gentler light of a profound sympathy, Malory saw as the mainspring of action. Vauvenargues finds it necessary to defend glory; Cervantes must approach it obliquely, smother it in hocus-pocus; but Malory takes it as a matter of course: it is the natural thirst of all 'men of worship'. Worship ('worthship') is a word which recurs many times throughout the *Morte Darthur*; the glossaries usually give its meaning as 'honour', but from the context it is evident that it means something more definite. It means active honour, magnanimity, *grandeur d'âme*, glory gained. The tale of Sir Gareth of Orkney "that was called Beaumains"—a part of the *Morte Darthur* which seems to be dependent to an unusual extent on Malory's own genius—illustrates the concept of worship more clearly than most of Malory's tales. (pp. 48-9)

It is easy now to identify Malory's 'worship' with Vauvenargues' and Unamuno's sentiment of glory. The . . . exploits of Beaumains show how he won greater worship, and how he rescued and wedded Dame Lionesse of the Castle Perilous. But one thing is to be observed as typical of this 'path of glory': each triumph is made to contribute to the greater glory of King Arthur, the defeated knights are one by one made to swear fealty to Beaumains' overlord. This, however, is not in any way to be interpreted as an abstraction of the sentiment of glory: the worship is definitely personal to Arthur himself. The King is a knight of knights, a great leader like Charlemagne, but not a symbol; king by the magic test of Excalibur, but not by divine right; king in virtue of his great worship only.

The mention of Charlemagne calls to mind the *Song of Roland*, which might well be named the 'Song of Worship', for in that great epic human glory shines out in pure masculine beauty. In this the *Song of Roland* is superior to the *Morte Darthur*, which pays as the price of its enhanced romance all the confusion and disaster of sexual passion. A militant religion is the mainspring of action in the *Song of Roland*, but the sense of glory is the individual sense. There is no suggestion of gaining glory for a particular body like Church or State; glory is pursued at the expense of flesh:

> Dieu! dit le Roi, que ma vie est peineuse!

There is base treachery in the *Song of Roland*, but the *Morte Darthur* is dark with sexual intrigue. The morals, to an ascetic like Ascham, or to a conventionalist like Tennyson, could not appear as anything but queer. Malory himself excuses the adulterous conduct of Launcelot and Queen Guenever with the naïve remark: "For love that time was not as is nowadays". This makes all the more curious the last chapter of Book XVIII, with its lament for love in the old way. True love is compared to the month of May. . . . (pp. 53-5)

Malory is here moralizing, and expressing his own spirit rather than the spirit of his narrative. He seeks, like Don Quixote, to identify love and glory. It was a paradox more evident to the age of Malory and of Cervantes (for theirs were essentially the same age) than to the legendary age in which Malory found the sources of his romance. We might say that in the interval the moral sense had become finer, that manners had improved, and that a code of honour had been established; we might say such things did not a deeper instinct tell us that mankind has always been the same in such matters, beneficent and cruel by turns, in love chaste and stable one day, harsh and adulterous the next; the true life being lived only by those who, like Sir Beaumains and Don Quixote, see beyond the futility of what is to the glory of what might be. (p. 56)

> Herbert Read, "Malory," in his The Sense of Glory: Essays in Criticism, *Cambridge at the University Press, 1929, pp. 33-56.*

LLEWELYN POWYS (essay date 1936)

[*In the following excerpt, Powys explores Malory's adaptation of Arthurian Legend in the* Morte Darthur *and comments on the prose style of the work.*]

It was the intermingling of the Cymric legends, fantastic and supernatural, with the courtly notions of mediæval chivalry, so strongly appealing to the Normans, which inspired the genius of the Lancastrian knight, Sir Thomas Malory, to compile his tales, tales which have ensorcerised subsequent generations into a very ducdame circle, as though they were being summoned by the echo of Rowland's horn coming to them as clear as ever, over the vineyards of Roncesvalles:

> Roland has gone over the hill forever,
> And Oliver lies beside him on the plain,
> Nothing is left but a horn in the distance blowing,
> Charlemagne . . . Charlemagne. . . .

By Malory's art fragments of the Arthurian legend were woven together as plain as scenes on a tapestry, so that the old book can render the love passions of that dreaming past at one with those that now take place in our own fugitive period.

Never does a troop of Sherborne hunters pass along the straight drives of the Leweston or Honeycombe woods, with the hoofs of their horses treading in the litter of the musty pheasant straw, without these emotions being present, present as inevitably as the smell of the frosts, not severe enough yet to leave any 'bone' under the rain-soaked sods of the tough wintry grasses. Such gay privileged companies riding out into leafless woods from warm breakfast rooms could scarcely hope to be free of it, being a folk who have never known what it is to have an empty pot upon the fire, or indeed to be in any way stinted of their victuals. A nervous hand, deliberately laid upon the arched neck of a high-spirited horse, or a single protracted glance, and, before a field gate swings open, the life of a man is shaken to its foundations. How many Iseults and Queen Gueneveres, leaving their horses to trig subservient stablemen, glide back to their houses as eager for the refreshments of love as they are hungry for food, their tired limbs, white as elder flowers, deep lapped in furs! Do these idle provocative ladies of the West Country who fol-

low so nonchalantly, so unmindfully, the merciless pastimes of a savage ancestry ever give a thought to Sir Tristram and the debt they owe to him? 'For,' as books report, 'Sir Tristram was the noblest blower of a horn of all manner of measures; for of Sir Tristram came all the good laws of venery and hunting, and all the sizes and measures of blowing of an horn that all manner of gentlemen have cause to the world's end to praise Sir Tristram and to pray for his soul.'

How vividly Sir Thomas Malory evokes the legendary stories of these impassioned lovers from the days in Ireland when Tristram 'learned Isoud' as a maid to 'harp and carp'; even to the fatal hour of his death at the hands of King Mark 'as he sat harping afore his lady La Beale Isoud.' And between those two harpings, how many snatched meetings—long winter nights transformed under the ordinance of a fairy space-time 'to the third part of a minute,' hours in screened garden alleys when a whole rose-blown summer afternoon would scarce measure a digit movement on the blithe face of the terrace dial.

Malory's narrations have an innocent way of sliding out from under accepted proprieties. They are profoundly amoral—'Goose if I had you upon Sarum plain I'd drive you cackling home to Camelot.' When King Arthur is besieging Joyous Gard, Sir Launcelot looks down upon him from the castle wall, and though he has 'purfled' his own mantle with the king's beard more wantonly than even King Ryence had threatened to do, calmly assures Arthur that Queen Guenevere is 'a true lady unto your person as any is living unto her lord.'

And what a wealth of poetry there is in the prose account of Tristram and Iseult's drinking of the fatal cup! 'When they were in their cabin; it happed so that they were thirsty, and they saw a little flasket of gold stand by them, and it seemed by the colour and the taste that it was noble wine. . . . Then they laughed and made good cheer, and either drank to other freely, and they thought never drink that ever they drank to other was so sweet nor so good. But by that their was in their bodies, they loved either other so well that never their love departed for weal neither for woe. And thus it happed the love first betwixt Sir Tristram and La Beale Isoud which love never departed the days of their life.' And over and over again after this dramatic prelude to their trance the same ballad-like chime sounds through the book's pages. It is indeed impossible for Iseult to open her lips without her breath—breath fragrant as the garden pinks called sops-in-wine—carrying upon it the indefinable airy spirit of one of the old gestes. In a mood of passionate despair caused by the report of Tristram's death she goes into the orchard of Tintagel intending to kill herself; to stab herself under a plum tree was her plan. Before taking her into his arms to carry her back to her chamber the distracted husband hears her say 'Sweet Lord Jesu, have mercy upon me, for I may not live after the death of Sir Tristram de Liones, for he was my first Love and he shall be the last.' There is something gracious and free about the relations between the two Queens. Who indeed was likely to be more conversant than the Dame Guenevere with complexities incident to emotions gone awry? At each stage of Iseult's story King Arthur's Queen is ready with encouragement or consolation. 'And in this meanwhile La Beale Isoud made a letter unto Queen Guenevere, complaining her of the untruth of Sir Tristram, and how he had wedded the King's daughter of Brittany. Queen Guenevere sent her another letter, and bade her be of good cheer, for she should have joy after sorrow.' And again when Tristram returned secretly to Tintagel and the two lovers were once more together the news of their happiness came as glad tidings to the Court of Camelot. 'Fair damosel,' said Iseult to her messenger, 'how fareth my Lord Arthur, and the Queen Guenevere, and the noble knight, Sir Lancelot? She answered, and to make short tale: Much the better that ye and Sir Tristram be in joy. God reward them, said La Beale Isoud, for Sir Tristram suffereth great pain for me and I for him.' Perhaps we may find Sir Malory's own attitude to such perplexing entanglements reflected in the bold words uttered by Sir Palomides when Sir Tristram 'that daffish knight' began narrowly challenging him concerning his love for Iseult. 'I have done to you no treason, for love is free for all men, and though I have loved your lady, she is my lady as well as yours; howbeit I have wrong, if any wrong be, for ye rejoice her, and have your desire of her, and so had I never, nor never am like to have, and yet shall I love her to the uttermost days of my life as well as ye.' Though he had no disinclination himself to fish in his neighbour's lily pond, such a declaration was not likely to be hospitably received by Sir Tristram. Nor could one so deeply in love be expected to acquiesce when Sir Dinadan, twitted by Iseult for being fancy free, uttered his capital heresy. 'God defend me,' said Dinadan, 'for the joy of love is too short, and the sorrow thereof, and what cometh thereof, dureth over long,' a sentiment hardly in accord, be it said, with the impassioned manners either at Camelot, Tintagel, or Joyous Gard!

Even Merlin, who was wise enough to warn King Arthur 'covertly' that the maiden Guenevere, daughter of Leodegrance 'The gentilest and fairest lady' was not 'wholesome' for him to take to wife, himself became utterly besotted by his love for the enchantress Nimue, 'the damosel of the lake' as soon as ever she set her light and artful foot on the stairway of King Arthur's Court. 'But Merlin would let her have no rest . . . and went with her ever more where so ever she went. . . . And always Merlin lay about the lady to have her maidenhood, and she was ever passing weary of him.'

The case was no better between Sir Lancelot and the Queen. In vain the knight, by making a confession of his madness to a holy hermit, thought to rid himself of the fever in his blood. It was of little avail.

'Then, as the book saith, Sir Lancelot began to resort unto Queen Guenevere again . . . ever his thoughts were privily on the Queen, and so they loved together more hotter than they did to-forehand, and had such privy draughts together, that many in the Court spake of it.'

How often have gleaning-bells and market-bells sounded in Sparkford Vale since those amorous, froward, and aristocratic days! It is in the month of May when the hawthorn is in bloom that true lovers should wander over the green orgulous hill and through every meadow that lies about it; till they come to know each shadowed alder-nook along the banks of the River Camel, and every hedge-shelter of this charmed section of Somerset. Let them leave their lamp-lit cottage lodging after their supper of eggs to drink living water from this paved fountain when the constellation Cygnus hangs high over head through the white nights of Midsummer.

Lovers, haste! the dusk has come;
Why do you waste these pretty hours?
Everything has gone to sleep,
Sheep and lambs, and birds and flowers.

Let them lie together listening to the winds in the ferns and to the midnight murmurs floating up from the wide dewy fields eastward of Avalon.

Leland in his travels questioned the local country people of his day about what they knew of 'this very torre or hill wonderfully enstrengthened of nature,' but they could tell him nothing beyond the fact that a horse-shoe made of silver had been found there not long before, and that they had always heard 'that Arture much resorted to Camalot.'

It has often seemed to me that the finest prose in English literature was written in the seventeenth century, and yet when I read the opening chapter of Sir Thomas Malory's nineteenth book I can scarce imagine sentences better contrived, sentences that can conjure before us with more art those days in early spring most favourable to love-making.

> And thus it passed on from Candlemass until after Easter, that the month of May was come, when every lusty heart beginneth to blossom, and to bring forth fruit for like as herbs and trees bring forth fruit and flourish in May, in like wise every lusty heart that is in any manner a lover, springeth and flourisheth in lusty deeds. For it giveth unto all lovers courage, that lusty month of May. . . . For then all herbs and trees renew a man and woman, and like wise lovers call again to their mind old gentleness and old service. . . . But nowadays men can not love seven nights but they must have their desires. . . . Right so fareth love nowadays, soon hot, soon cold: this is no stability. But the old love was not so; men and women could love together seven years, and no licours lusts were between them. . . . Wherefore I liken love nowadays unto summer and winter; for like us the one is hot and the other cold, so fareth love nowadays; therefore all ye that be lovers call unto your remembrance the month of May, like as did Queen Guenevere, for whom I make here a little mention, that while she lived she was a true lover, and therefore she had a good end. (pp. 491-96)

> *Llewelyn Powys, "Love at Camelot," in* The Nineteenth Century and After, *Vol. CXX, No. DCCXVI, October, 1936, pp. 490-96.*

LOUIS MacNEICE (essay date 1936)

[*MacNeice was an Irish-born English poet, critic, translator, playwright, radio scriptwriter, and novelist. He was connected with the left-wing literary movement of W. H. Auden and his circle in the 1930s and has been much praised for the sensory and visual qualities of his poems. In the following excerpt, he discusses the* Morte Darthur *as a novel.*]

Sometimes in dreams the dream becomes palpably more substantial. The process is like scrambling eggs. From an indefinite froth comes, seemingly instantaneously, something with a recognizable texture, something one can put in one's mouth. When a dream behaves in this way, it is becoming a work of art. The effect is often one of healthy bathos. From a sickly-sweet twilight of indefinite sensations there emerges perhaps the exceedingly familiar, exceedingly detailed, figure of someone one knows, and this at once makes the dialectic of the dream concrete. So it is with Malory.

Malory has sometimes (rightly but not fairly) been censured for misunderstanding of his originals, prosaic outlook, bathos, poor construction and inconsistent portraiture—for his lack, in fact, of those two supposed essentials, method and a point of view. For this we should be thankful. The novel is not a school-exercise, ten marks for construction, five for characterization, three for the moral, two for the style.

The novel is the furthest removed literary form from the philosophical treatise. Even philosophical treatises can benefit from the random element (is it not perhaps its inconsistencies which have fascinated students of the *Critique of Pure Reason?*) but, generally speaking, a philosophical treatise should be completely under the control of the mind of the author, a novel not so. Of course very often a novelist thinks he is controlling his material when he is not. Even with such a self-conscious artist as James Joyce it looks in *Ulysses* as if it is his *material* which is making the running. Joyce is pre-eminently a selector but, as a true novelist, he selects by touch rather than by theory. Malory of course was a selector in a very narrow sense—namely, a redactor. He took a number of books in a foreign language and made out of them one book very much shorter in his own. If he had been a theorist, one-minded, Shavian, he would have gone about his job quite differently. His book would have come from his hands ready to be labelled—an exposition of artificial romantic love *à la* Chrestien de Troyes, or of mediaeval Christian mysticism with the stress on the Grael, or of pure chivalry with a fifteenth-century moral, or maybe a Celtic romance weltering in marvels, or a national epic purged of Gallic accretions and with the emphasis on Arthur's insularity, his hardy impudence against the Roman Emperor. But what reached Caxton's press was none of these things.

None because all. The *Morte d'Arthur* is a divine mix-up. If Miss Jessie Weston could have told Malory that the Grael is the superfoetation of Christianity upon a pagan vegetation myth, he would not have understood her but, if he could have understood her, he would have been very angry. The Grael, with its Cistercian subtleties, was difficult enough to handle as it was. Yet the vegetation myth, whether we call it that or not, is there. The Waste Land and the Wounded King represent something which is vastly old—Jung might call it an archetypal myth—and which the reader appreciates all the better because the symbolism is not explicit. The novelist's job is not to be explicit. To take Joyce once more as an example, Dedalus in *Ulysses* is a failure because it is clear what he is meant to be, Bloom may be meant to be something also but he *is* so incontrovertibly that his meaning is not given a chance to wreck him. Malory's character are like Bloom rather than Dedalus. Which perhaps explains how it was that Ascham missed the point of the book and said that the whole pleasure of it "standeth in two speciall points, in open manslaughter and bold bawdrye." We know what some people think is the whole pleasure of *Ulysses*. It is a virtue in a novelist that his point is able to be missed.

Most people would not classify the *Morte d'Arthur* as a novel, but I cannot see why not. The *Odyssey*, according to T. E. Shaw, was the first European novel. Why not the *Iliad?* Presumably because of that desperate bugbear, "construction." I should prefer to call neither of them novels as they are both in verse. But the *Satyricon* of Petronius was a novel, so was the *Golden Ass* of Apuleius and so

were the Icelandic Sagas. It is foolishly assumed that the novel, like tragedy in Aristotle's *Poetics*, should possess (*a*) plot, (*b*) characterization. But Aristotle's distinction between plot and history will not hold in this *genre;* the psychologists moreover tell us, what we have always felt in our bones, that there are more kinds of continuity than one. As for characterization no one has ever made clear quite how differentiated or quite how substantiated the characters ought to be in a novel. Malory's claims to being a novelist are so minimal in the eyes of the purists that I will digress to go one worse in their eyes.

I believe that it would be possible to write a novel about two cricketers A and B (those might even be all they had for names) and confining oneself to their matches—scores, strokes and style—yet produce a readable book. Plot here would consist merely in cricket match after cricket match, while the character of A would differ from that of B merely in the external difference of their scores, etc., and the more internal difference of their cricketing technique. Note that in any character, in books or in life, it is impossible to draw a rigid line between his external or incidental attributes—what he does, wears, the shape of his face—and the internal or essential ones, what he thinks, feels. Note again that such a "plot" as that of my cricketing novel cannot be dismissed as no plot but mere repetition. One cannot merely repeat. Any enumeration of objects or events will take on a rhythm, as we read it, just as the monotony of the noise of a train takes on a rhythm as we listen to it.

I thought of cricket because I have often found myself taking pleasure day by day in reading the accounts, or merely the batting averages, of players whom I have never seen and do not wish to see. And many people perhaps read everything in the newspapers in this way. Why do they do this? Because, firstly, the newspaper heroes, sportsmen or politicians, are for them dream-figures, *though they know they are real people;* secondly, the repetition with variations of their performances (Mr. Ramsay MacDonald . . . Mr. Ramsay MacDonald . . .) builds up a vast and gentle rhythm in the back of the mind, hypnotizing us into an escape from reality; but it is the sort of escape people are said to find in opium. They see the real objects and they know they are the same but they see them different. Before any greater claims are put in for Malory, I must repeat my opening point and say that his book throughout gives me the same joy that I get in reading the sporting page in the daily papers or that I get when I see something heroically familiar, however banal, in a dream.

Malory got his heroes out of the French books. They were already a conflation of French and English with a dash of Welsh. Some will say (as Professor Vinaver in his charming book on Malory) that he clipped them into fifteenth-century Englishmen. This is an exaggeration. Malory's characters, more than those of most novelists, are knit up with their background and their background is not stable. The varied threads (how often this book is called a tapestry!) are compromised successfully. Malory is a master of half-conscious compromise, typically English. Thus even his *Quest of the Grael* is acceptable, though we must agree with Vinaver both that the mysticism of it was antipathetic to Malory (after all he was a robber of monasteries), that the Chapels Perilous, etc., were not his natural province, and that the Weltanschauung of the Grael, suppressed but not extinguished by Malory, clashes very badly with that of the Round Table. But there is much to be said for a clash, even if it is not intended.

Some years ago I used to be most irritated when I came to Book XIII and had to pass from the harpings and joustings of Tristram to the frigid perfection of Galahad. I see now that without Galahad, Lancelot, his unwilling father, would not be so great, or not so *tragically* great, a figure; just as without the Quests preceding it, the Morte proper, the dissolution of the Round Table, would not be a vast moral catastrophe but merely a crash in the cricket averages.

Professor Vinaver is undoubtedly right when he says that Malory wavers continually in his treatment of Lancelot and Guinevere—Malory's "most cherished ideal is that of happy marriage, and he forgets that marriage and a hero-lover like Lancelot are entirely incompatible." And Vinaver, quoting the passage where Lancelot condemns paramours, points out that it comes oddly from a man who is "the very embodiment of adulterous passion." But is this kind of inconsistency a flaw? It may be that Malory is inconsistent for a purely mechanical reason, that he cannot control his originals. I should prefer to think that he could see two sides of a question, that he could feel with Lancelot in his love as well as in his preaching. But whether he could or not, the fact is that this not too conspicuous vacillating between two or more worlds is something which, whether it is due to skill or accident, is greatly to be desired in novels because it represents, though far more gently, the bitter dialectic of opposites which makes humanity. Any child trained on the Dalcroze system can move two limbs simultaneously in different rhythms. Any civilized man can see simultaneously, or at least in rapid alternation, the point of marriage *à la* Malory and of love *à la* Lancelot.

The main themes and persons of the *Morte d'Arthur* have often been analysed. To illustrate my thesis that Malory to some extent benefited from the difficulties of his task, if not also from the deficiencies of his own mind (it does not hurt a novelist to be something of a zany), I would take the character of Sir Gawaine. Sir Gawaine took my fancy when I first read the book at the age of twelve. I have since tried to find the reason for this. He is not one of the villains, like King Mark or Morgan le Fay, but he more often than not is out of favour with his author. He is a strong knight but not a very knightly one. Perhaps I liked him because I felt that the author had a grudge against him. There are some half-dozen knights who can always beat him, and the reader acquires a sporting hope that he may give one of them a surprise. This sporting interest is a little counterbalanced by the fact that Gawaine has an unfair advantage in that his strength magically increases threefold towards noon. But "his wind and his evil will" increased with it, which gives him a brute attractiveness. The interest in Gawaine, however, is not merely a sporting one. If Gawaine were absent, not only would the mechanism of the catastrophe (Arthur's war with Lancelot and the revolt of Mordred) have to be contrived anew, but the book would lose a recurring *motif* of moral contrast. Of all the more important knights Gawaine is the furthest from being a paragon.

A curious thing is that in the earlier Arthurian literature he was more or less a paragon, a great national champion—Malory's portrait of him is inconsistent, and

how he became as vicious as Malory represents him, I leave to Arthurian scholars. But his viciousness is important. Malory in translating the Queste omitted passages which stressed the opposition of the Grael to the Round Table. He was to the end a hero-worshipper of worldly knights. But Gawaine was one worldly knight, "a passing hot knight of nature," that Malory makes an example of. His chief characteristic is vindictiveness; the vendetta means more to him than chivalry. He is not merciful, he begins his career by killing a lady, and he has other bad blots on his record such as the seduction of the lady Ettard. It is notable that it is he who sets the example to the other knights and starts them on the Quest of the Grael, but this he does out of self-glory, not out of holiness, and it only brings disappointment to himself and injury to the Round Table—"Gawaine, Gawaine, ye have set me in great sorrow. For I have great doubt that my true fellowship shall never meet here more again." Malory concentrates on Gawaine the bitterness which in the original Queste, it seems, was directed against the Round Table in general. Gawaine, in his quest, after a tedious lack of adventure, at last, with two others, is attacked by seven knights, whom he and his companions kill. He did not know that the slain knights were symbols. A hermit, however, reproves him—"ye have used the most untruest life that ever I heard knight live. *For, certes, had ye not been so wicked as ye are, never had the seven brethren been slain by you and your two fellows*" (italics mine). Obviously a new system of values has been slipped into the story. Up till now it had been a good thing to kill knights. We begin to sympathize with Gawaine, who makes no attempt to amend himself and, when the hermit tells him to do penance, refuses—"for we knights adventurous often suffer great love and pain."

Towards the end of the story Gawaine rises to a kind of brute dignity. He never takes advice and he never forgives. His intractable spirit causes the downfall of Arthur. "So upon the morn there came Sir Gawaine as brim as any boar, with a great spear in his hand. . . ." He makes Lancelot fight with him against his will, and when Lancelot struck him down, and he could not stand, "waved and foined at Sir Lancelot as he lay." Lancelot, of course, was too courteous to strike a wounded man. The contrast here is between the knight-errant *par excellence* and a far more primitive type of hero. Gawaine is like some of the Icelandic heroes. His presence gives the *Morte d'Arthur* a necessary taint of earthiness. But it is typical of the beautiful balance of this book that Gawaine is allowed a death-bed repentance—not repentance in general but repentance for his conduct to Lancelot, to whom while dying he writes a practical and dignified letter.

Malory's minor characters are hardly differentiated, but we never question their reality. They are as real as the Wife of Bath though they are not so realistic. Not till Defoe do we get as strong a feeling of reality from English prose fiction. Caxton's preface, by the way, has been taken as evidence that the *Morte d'Arthur* is the first professedly fictitious prose narrative in the language. After Malory's time, of course, many new influences swept away any lingering aversion to non-didactic or unhistoric fiction. But such invented romances as those of Lyly and Sidney show none of the life and solidity of Malory's mere redaction. More important in the history of the English novel were the Elizabethan pamphleteers who anticipated that humour of manners which was later to be so prominent and which, present in Chaucer, was inevitably absent from Malory; Malory shows little humour, though there is a certain folk quality which might be called humour in his story of Beaumains.

In style the Elizabethans produced nothing like Malory's for pure narrative. Lyly's is not, properly, a narrative style at all—"a delicate bayte with a deadly hooke, a sweete Panther with a devouring paunch, a sower poyson in a silver potte." The pamphleteers made more important innovations, their digressive gusto being the same quality that characterizes so many English novels from Fielding to Thackeray.

> The Germaines and lowe Dutch, me thinkes should bee continually keept moyst with the foggie aire and stinking mistes that arise out of their fennie soyle: but as their Countrey is over-flowen with water, so are their heads alwaies over-flowen with wine, and in their bellies they have standing quagmires and bogs of English beere.

Such writing has robustness and clarity, qualities in which the English novel has never been deficient. Malory's style has something else much rarer, a delicate virility which belongs exclusively to narrative.

This quality cannot be analysed. In some places it seems to be attained by understatement. Malory is not a writer whom we feel *writing* all the time as we hear a clock ticking. Witness the first appearance of the Grael, a passage which Professor Vinaver has censured as inadequate:

> so they went into the castle to take their repast. And anon there came in a dove at a window, and in her mouth there seemed a little censer of gold. And therewithal there was such a savour as all the spicery of the world had been there. And forthwithal there was upon the table all manner of meats and drinks that they could think upon. So came in a damsel passing fair and young, and she bare a vessel of gold betwixt her hands, and thereto the King kneeled devoutly, and said his prayers, and so did all that were there. Then said Sir Launcelot, What may this mean? This is, said the King, the richest thing that any man hath living. And when this thing goeth about, the Round Table shall be broken.

This passage is indeed inadequate in that it totally fails to bring out the Grael's significance. As exposition it fails, as mere statement it is magnificent. M. Jean Cocteau says in a note on his play *Orphée*—"Inutile de dire qu'il n'y a pas un seul symbole dans la pièce. Rien que du langage pauvre, du *poème agi*." It seems to me that Malory attained sometimes this peculiar kind of expression which Cocteau is seeking self-consciously. The philosopher makes a judgement, but the poet and the novelist, on their different planes, make statements. Malory is a master of statement. (pp. 19-29)

> Louis MacNeice, "Sir Thomas Malory," in The English Novelists: A Survey of the Novel by Twenty Contemporary Novelists, *edited by Derek Verschoyle, Harcourt Brace Jovanovich, 1936, pp. 19-29.*

CHARLES WILLIAMS (essay date 1944)

[Williams was a writer of supernatural fiction and a poet whose best works treat the legends of Logres (Arthurian Britain). He was also a central figure in the literary group known as the Oxford Christians or "Inklings." The religious, the magical, and the mythical are recurrent concerns in his works, reflecting his devout Anglicanism and lifelong interest in all aspects of the preternatural. Although his writings are not today as well known as those of his fellow-Inklings C. S. Lewis and J. R. R. Tolkien, Williams was an important source of encouragement and influence in the group. In the following excerpt from an essay originally published in the Dublin Review *in 1944, he explores Malory's treatment of the Grail Legend in the* Morte Darthur.*]*

The Twelfth Book of Malory's *Morte D'Arthur* ends with the following words: 'And here followeth the noble tale of the Sangreal, that called is the holy vessel: and the signification of the blessed blood of our Lord Jesus Christ, blessed mote it be, the which was brought into this land by Joseph of Aramathie.' The Seventeenth Book ends: 'Thus endeth the story of the Sangreal, that was briefly drawn out of French into English, the which is a story chronicled for one of the truest and the holiest that is in this world.' The five books between are occupied with Galahad and the achievement of the Quest.

It is not my purpose here to discuss the origins of the Grail story—Celtic, Classical, or Christian. Much attention has been given them. The Grail itself has been traced back to 'heirlooms belonging to the house of Atreus' and to 'the wars of the ancient Irish gods'. The first view was put forward by Mr. Charles B. Lewis; the latest discussion of the second is in the recently published *Origin of the Grail Legend* by Professor Arthur Brown. It is, no doubt, true that Chrétien de Troyes, who seems to have begun the Tale, may have been vaguely influenced from both sources. Writers are apt to take over agreeable ideas from any source. Thus Professor Brown discusses the four-sided fairy cup of plenty in Irish mythology, and points out the insistence on the number four in Chrétien's *Percival*. This is exactly the kind of detail which might easily have appealed to and been taken over by a Christian writer; the Evangelists, the four-sided City, &c. On the other hand, when Professor Brown speaks of a castle surrounded by a river which is crossed by a bridge and writes: 'H. R. Patch has argued that the river and the bridge that often accompanies it are oriental material worked over by the Irish', he gives Mr. Patch too much importance. Houses on islands, even if supposed to be in the Other World, must have been too natural to Chrétien for him to need suggestions from the marvels of the Oriental and the Celt. He could do that sort of marvel by merely looking out of his medieval window.

There is perhaps still room for some consideration of the Tale as it has existed in the English imagination. There are a number of texts, even without involving those of the Middle Ages. They occur mostly in the Victorian poets—Hawker, Morris, Tennyson, Swinburne—and they are mostly unsatisfactory. There is, however, no need to explain this by dragging in religion; it is much more easily and truly explained by saying that none of these poets had the full capacity of the mythical imagination. If we can read the *Idylls of the King* without remembering what critics have said about them, we shall find a great deal of good stuff. But it is true that Tennyson was really writing (and very properly) a modern moral story, as he said he was. He could not—he did not try to—get the Myth. Thus Balin, in the Grail Castle, instead of wounding the King with the Sacred Lance, uses it as a jumping-pole. This is a serious lapse. Morris arranged a highly decorative and highly delicate pageant of Galahad. The poet who, in an occasional touch, gets nearest to the tone of the Myth is Swinburne. This will seem odd unless we realize that the poetic capacity for Myth is quite different from the human capacity for religion; a fact not without relevance to our general belief in religion as well as to our criticism of verse.

But it is, of course, in prose rather than in verse that the thing has remained for us in English; it is in Malory, and in Sebastian Evans's translation of a part of Chrétien's *Percival* under the title of the *High History of the Holy Graal*. The latter book is a very noble piece of work. But it is, as it were, a detail; the whole grand Myth—or at least much of it—is in Malory. There is, however, even in Malory, a certain suggestiveness which Malory does not seem altogether to have understood. The present article does not intend to discuss how far these significances are in Malory's originals; its writer would be incapable, and the discussion would be irrelevant. The point is not where they came from but what they have become.

One main fact, however, must be mentioned. There are, in the history of the European imagination, a few moments when a superb invention of the very first importance takes place. I doubt whether there has ever been one of more real power than that of the invention of Galahad; not even excluding that of Dante's discovery of Beatrice as the theme of the *Commedia*. That, one really feels, must, sooner or later, have happened; there were so many poets in love. But the invention of Galahad as the son of Lancelot might easily not have happened. Someone—M. Vinaver says a Cistercian—at some time in some place thought of it; it was a moment as near to divine inspiration as any not technically so called can be. It is, of course, necessary to speak cautiously here. M. Vinaver himself opposes the idea, put forward by other writers, that there is any 'mystic affiliation' between Lancelot and Galahad. He properly distinguishes between the Court of Arthur and the Court of Heaven. 'The author of the *Queste* [the Galahad romance]', he says, 'was conscious of an acute conflict between the two kinds of chivalry, and never derived the one from the other. Galahad's mysticism can by no means be fathered upon Lancelot.' This is certainly true. But it is equally true that Galahad himself has certainly been fathered upon Lancelot, and that therefore their relation—even in division—is a very particular relation. Their distinction exists in a kind of imaginative union; the greater (however much greater) derives, in that Myth, for ever from the lesser, and something in each of their differing hues illumines the other.

Malory took the tale over. He either took over with it, or else he invented, certain details. It may be objected that my choice of these details is arbitrary, and I entirely agree that there are many insignificant details in Malory. He fills his pages with all sorts of things which may be fascinating but are not (in our sense) mythical. But there are some which are mythical in the sense that they seem to have a profound spiritual relevance. The whole question of Courtly Love may be ruled out at once. Malory was not concerned with that technique, any more than (at least, di-

rectly) with the greater passion and truer vision of the Dantean Romantic Love. Lancelot and Guinevere do not develop that. But they are still passionately and permanently in love. It is almost impossible for either of them to alter the exterior situation. A very little extra touch here and there in the *Morte* would have made it quite impossible—a little heightening of the realistic side of the kingdom of Arthur. The chief man in the kingdom after the King cannot throw up his job at once, and the Queen can certainly not throw up hers. The struggle after virtue, the happiness-unhappiness, the mere infinite tiresomeness, and the beauty, are all in the situation.

But there are (and here we begin the Myth as Malory has it) other people about. One of these is the Saracen knight Palomides. Palomides is in love with the Queen Iseult, but she is married to Mark and in love with Tristram. That, however, is not relevant to the Myth, except that the misery of Palomides accentuates his bitterness. He will not be christened, 'howbeit in my heart I believe in Jesu Christ and his mild mother Mary', till he has done certain great deeds, and overcome the questing beast (which is not without a likeness to the inner agony he suffers). At the seven-days' tournament at Lonazep, in that discourtesy to which he is prone, he commits an outrage against the laws of chivalry, and insults and injures Lancelot. Lancelot forgives him—'Sithen my quarrel is not here, ye shall have this day the worship as for me . . . it were no worship for me to put you from it.' But Lancelot carries his courtesy farther, for soon after the tournament is closed he finds Palomides in the hands of those who are about to put him to death, and rescues him from twelve knights; 'and Palomides kneeled down upon his knees and thanked Sir Lancelot'.

Lancelot in fact had a great many activities besides being in love with Guinevere: 'thou were', said Sir Ector of him, 'the courteousest knight that ever bare shield. And thou were the truest friend to thy lover that ever bestrod horse. And thou were the kindest man that ever struck with sword.' It is immediately after his exhibition of courtesy towards someone who has injured him—this is the significant, if accidental, detail—that we find Lancelot riding towards the mysterious castle of King Pelles, who is the Keeper of the Grail; it is shown between the hands

> of a damozel passing fair and young. O Jesu, said Sir Lancelot, what may this mean? This is, said the king, the richest thing that any man hath living. And when this thing goeth about, the Round Table shall be broken; and wit ye well, said the king, this is the holy Sangreal that ye have seen. . . . The king knew well that Sir Lancelot should get a child upon his daughter, the which should be named Sir Galahad, the good knight, by whom all foreign country should be brought out of danger, and by him the Holy Greal should be achieved.

There is about this a known predestination: 'the king knew well that Lancelot should'. Lancelot is here the predetermined father of the great Achievement; he is the noblest lord in the world, the kindest, the bravest, the truest. But he will not have to do with any woman but the Queen: 'when was Lancelot wanderingly lewd?' And Galahad must certainly be the child of the Grail-princess and certainly not of Guinevere. How is it to be done? It is brought about by holy enchantment and an act of substitution. Lancelot is deluded (as it were, by a courtesy of terrible condescension) into riding 'against night' to another castle, where he is received 'wordhipfully with such people to his seeming as were about Queen Guinevere secret'. He is given a cup of enchanted wine and taken to the room where the supposed Queen is: 'and all the windows and holes of that chamber were stopped that no manner of day might be seen'.

I am not unaware that the substitution of one woman for another is common enough in the romances; it is the kind of substitution that makes this so thrilling. The vision is of 'the best knight', labouring in that threefold consciousness of God, the King, and Guinevere, received into the outlying castle of the Mysteries, and then by the deliberate action of spiritual powers drawn on into a deeper operation. He dismounts: around him are those who seem to be the Queen's servants, but it is not so; the assumed forms, the awful masks, of this sacred mystery attend him; he is taken to a chamber as dark as the dark night of the soul; and there the child who is to achieve the Grail is begotten.

And the next morning? Here, it must be admitted, Malory fell away from what the Myth demanded. He sends Lancelot back to the Court, sends the Princess after him, describes the anger of Guinevere, enchants Lancelot all over again, causes him to meet the Queen, and then drives him mad because of his disloyalty to her. There is some very good writing, but it will not do. What must obviously happen is that immediately on waking in the Castle of the Substitution, Lancelot realizes the deception; which he does—'anon as he had unshut the window the enchantment was gone; then he knew himself that he had done amiss. Alas, he said, that I have lived so long; now I am shamed.' It is then that his mind should be overthrown; it is very proper that he should leap from that window of awful realization 'into a garden, and there with thorns he was all to scratched in his visage and his body; and so he ran forth he wist not whither, and was wild wood as ever was man; and so he ran two years, and never man might have grace to know him'.

So far as I can see, there is no particular reason for two years; nine months would have been a better time. Presently he comes again to the house of the Grail, and there 'by force Sir Lancelot was laid by that holy vessel; and there came a holy man, and unhylled that vessel, and so by miracle and by virtue of that holy vessel Sir Lancelot was healed and recovered'. He remains for some time in disguise and seclusion, calling himself only 'Le Chevalier Mal Fet, that is to say, the knight that hath trespassed'. The trespass is, no doubt, chiefly his unintentional falsity to Guinevere, but then in Malory truth is part of his passion; Lancelot does not believe that he will become true to the King by being untrue to the Queen. He may fail to manage to be true to both, but this is his intention. He is merely overthrown by that element in him which, because of his love and courtesy, is predetermined 'where Will and Power are one' to make him the father of Galahad. There is no compromise with the sin, but there is every charity towards the virtue.

At last Lancelot meets with Percivale and returns with him to the Court. The name of Percivale brings us to the second part of the Myth. Time has gone by, but time is not in Malory very strictly attended to. Galahad is taken to a Convent of White Nuns, where he is brought up. But the tale passes on from Lancelot's return almost directly to the coming to the Court of the High Prince: not indeed

that in Malory 'the High Prince' is Galahad's title at all; it belongs to Galahault, who is quite a different person, and not of much importance. He had once been; it was he who had brought Lancelot and Guinevere to their first kiss in one of the love-romances where the greater interpretations were not imagined. As a result he had gained a literary immortality, for he had been given a famous line in the *Inferno*: 'Galeotto fu il libro e chi lo scrisse.' It is proper that the title should pass from him; in a myth there ought to be more than charm, sweetness, and physical delight to justify such a phrase.

It is Pentecost; the King holds his court. One rite has already been solemnized. Palomides has been reconciled with Tristram and has been baptized by 'the suffragan of Carlisle'. 'And so the king and all the court were glad that Sir Palomides was christened. And at the same feast in came Galahad and sat in the siege perilous.' The second sentence is premature, but the tale passes on to give a full account. A fair gentlewoman who says she has come on King Pelles' behalf (Pelles is the Grail King) asks for Lancelot and carries him off to a nunnery in a forest. It is a brief episode, but very moving, for there Lancelot unknowingly knights his son—'seemly and demure as a dove, with all manner of good features'. 'On the morn, at the hour of prime, at Galahad's desire, he made him knight and said: God make him a good man, for of beauty faileth you not as any that liveth.' Lancelot's consent goes with Galahad's desire; he does not know what he does, but he does what courtesy and largesse demand; and both he and his son are the more advanced in the Way.

In the tale of Galahad himself at Camelot it might be held that there has been since Malory a certain alteration in values. We are not so much affected by the pulling of swords out of stones floating on rivers (besides, there have been too many of them) as by such other things of possible significance as the coming to every knight at the feast of what food he desired, and of the laying to rest of the High Prince in the King's bed. The first and dominating fact is, of course, the sitting of Galahad in the Siege Perilous. But the meaning of this would require a whole thesis of the meaning of the Siege and of its making by Merlin. The magical foreknowledge of Merlin is certainly not ordinary magic; it is not contrary to grace, though Merlin himself is somehow apart from the whole question of sin and grace. He is rather as if time itself became conscious of the future and prepared for it. The sitting of Galahad in the Siege is the condition precedent to all achievement; and Tennyson's phrase may serve for the moment—that he cried: 'If I lose myself I find myself.' At the supper there is a blast of thunder and a beam of seven-times-clear sunlight; all the lords see their companions fairer than before, and all have the meats and drinks that they love best. I have wondered if this second result would not be more convenient if it were taken to mean that what each had actually before him was precisely to his most satisfaction. It would fit the first better; it is what is there that is fairest. The world is in the Grail, which then appears, but it appears covered and carried invisibly. It must, of course, be so, or there would be no further achievement, and the tale would have to stop. But in every great Myth the technique and the meaning are one; only it does us no harm to realize that the tale, as well as the meaning, has to be kept going. This is the world in the Grail, but it is (also and therefore) at first the world clothing the Grail, so that it cannot be seen in itself. Vows are taken by the lords to seek it out, much to the King's sorrow, for he knows that this will break up the great fellowship. The Queen has a brief interview with Galahad in which she declares him to be Lancelot's son, but 'as to that, he said neither yea or nay'. 'And in the honour of the highness of Galahad he was led into King Arthur's chamber, and there rested in his own bed.'

This is a very great sentence, for it is at once the fulfilment and the frustration of the three lordliest personages, whether they like it or not. There lies in the King's bed that which is the consummation and the destruction of the Table. To Lancelot it is the visible defeat of his treasured fidelity, and the success and defeat of his own life. And to the Queen it is her lover's falsity and her lover's glory. The Queen has some glorious phrases: 'I may well suppose that Sir Lancelot begat him on King Pelles' daughter, by the which he was made to lie by enchantment, and his name is Galahad. I would fain see him, said the queen, for he must needs be a noble man, for so is his father that him begat, I report me unto all the Table Round.'

It is then this living, tragic, and joyous Resolution of all their loves that now enters on its own adventure. They had all talked of love; let them now love this. Its quest begins, and must be passed over here. Towards the conclusion the High Prince reaches Sarras with two companions; they are Percivale and Bors. There seems a significant reason, though Malory does not develop it, why it should be so. Galahad, of course, has no relation with human loves (except Lancelot); his whole function is the Quest. But Percivale finds a lady who declares herself to be his sister. Obviously in the tale this is meant literally, but in the Myth it has not so much the significance of kinship in blood as of kinship in spirit. It is a human relationship, but it is one known only in the companionship of the quest; it is conjoined love, but love conjoined in the Grail. The lady is of a holy temper; on the journey she dies by giving her blood for another lady who is sick. 'She said to the lady, Madam, I am come to the death for to make you whole; for God's love pray for me.' This again is an act of substitution, but clear and without deceit. Her body is found again when the three lords reach Sarras, though indeed it might well have been taken with them in the ship that carries them across the last ocean, and have made a fourth to the living three.

But the third, Bors? Bors, one might say, is the ordinary fellow. Malory (and here he allows the Grail fellowship rather more than he need have done) does not say he was married. But he does say he had a son by another Elayne, 'and save for her, Sir Bors was a clean maiden'. The Princess of the Grail was called Elayne, and though it is an unimportant point it is admirably right that a wife, for there is no need to deny her the marriage which the tale implies in principle, should have the same name. But if we allow Sir Bors his marriage and his work in the world and his honest affections, see how perfect the companionship of the three lords becomes! There is the High Prince, wholly devoted to his end in the Grail; and there is Percivale with his devout and self-less spiritual sister; and there is Bors with his wife and child. These are functions each of the others. The High Prince is at the deep centre, and the others move towards him; but also he operates in them towards the world. These are three degrees of love. Their conclusion is proper to them. Galahad is assumed into the Grail. Percivale after that assumption remains a hermit by

the City of Sarras, where that other sacrificed flesh of his sister is buried. Bors returns to Camelot, joins Lancelot, is made a king, goes on a crusade, and in the last sentence of the book dies, with Sir Ector, Sir Blamore, and Sir Bleoberis, fighting against the Turks, 'upon a Good Friday, for God's sake'.

The conclusion of the Quest itself is found in Sarras, which is beyond and across the sea from the house of the Grail. There is a suggestion that though the Grail in Logres is the consummation of the life of Camelot, yet the Grail beyond seas is only the beginning of the life of Sarras. Galahad is the living suggestion of that other life. When he and Percivale and Bors reach Sarras, they are put into prison by 'the king of the city', who is a 'tyrant', but after a year he dies, and Galahad is made king. This might indeed be thought to have a great meaning in religious experience: after the endurance of tyranny comes the time of sovereignty. Another year of this brings them to their end. Joseph of Arimathie says Mass—only he? only he in Malory, but there is a phrase which suggests more: 'a man kneeling on his knees in likeness of a bishop, that had about him a great fellowship of angels *as it had been Jesu Christ himself; and then he arose and began a mass of Our Lady*'. The italics are mine; they will suffice to suggest that at that moment something like the Creation and the Redemption exist at once. Galahad is called; after Communion he parts from his companions; and it is then that one of the greatest phrases in Malory is used. Galahad says to Bors: 'Fair lord, salute me to my lord Sir Lancelot my father, and as soon as ye see him bid him remember of this unstable world.'

If the state of these great mysteries, where one like Christ begins a mass of Our Lady, is recognized, that final salutation has its full value. It is then that the High Prince remembers, recognizes, and salutes his father. The times have been changed since the love of Guinevere and the enchanted darkness of the chamber of Elayne, but Galahad derives from all. 'The unstable world'—yes; but it was thence that he himself came. The rejection of importunate love—yes; Guinevere herself is to say so; but it is through the mystical substitution which lies even there that the High Prince was begotten. Lancelot was a master of courtesy, and it is so that Galahad is fathered on him. He himself never achieves the Grail, but at the point of a greater achievement than any he could have known, his son's greeting (full and ungrudging) reaches him, through another (still and always through another), 'Fair lord, salute me to my lord Sir Lancelot my father.'

Charles Williams, "Malory and the Grail Legend," in his The Image of the City and Other Essays, *edited by Anne Ridler, Oxford University Press, London, 1958, pp. 186-94.*

E. K. CHAMBERS (essay date 1947)

[*In the following excerpt, Chambers explores Malory's use of source material in the* Morte Darthur *and comments on the prose style of the work.*]

It was, perhaps, his nostalgia for a decayed chivalry which led William Caxton to make his greatest gift to English letters, the so-called **Morte Darthur** of Sir Thomas Malory. The printing of this was completed, about a year after the *Order of Chyualry* itself, on 31 July 1485. (p. 185)

It seems clear that the ungrammatical *le morte Darthur* of Caxton's colophon is merely a translation of *The Deth of Arthur*, which properly belongs to the eighth tale, and that Malory's own title for the romance as a whole was *The Book of King Arthur and his noble Knights of the Round Table*. For brevity we may perhaps refer to the individual tales as the *Coming of Arthur*, the *War with Rome*, the *Lancelot*, the *Gareth*, the *Tristram*, the *Sangreal*, the *Knight of the Cart*, which is again on Lancelot, and the *Death of Arthur*. It must be added that Malory's use of the term 'Tale' is not free from ambiguity. It does not always, especially in the earlier part of his story, indicate one of its main divisions. Sometimes there is a tale within a tale. Thus in the *Coming of Arthur* we find a reference to the 'book' of Balyn the Saveage, which later becomes a 'tale of Balyn and Balan' and has an 'Explicit' of its own. So, too, we get an 'Explicit the Wedding of Arthur' at the end of a long passage, which indeed begins with a mention of the wedding, but for the rest deals wholly with sporadic adventures of Sir Gawaine, Sir Torre, and King Pellinore. Many of the tales, indeed, are largely made up of strings of independent episodes, with abrupt transitions between them, which are indicated by recurrent phrases, on the models of the 'Or dit le conte', or more fully, for example, 'Ore laisse li contes à parler du chevalier de la charrete et retourne à parler d'une aultre matière', which are so common in French romance. Such are:

> So leve we sir Tristram and turne we unto Kynge Marke

> Now leve we of sir Lamorak and speke we of sir Gawayne

> Here levith the tale of sir Launcelot and begynnyth of sir Percyvale de Galis

> Now turnyth thys tale unto sir Bors de Ganys

or, more unusually,

> Here this tale overlepyth a whyle unto sir Launcelot.

Alternatively, the beginning of an episode is often indicated by a title for it in a marginal side-note.

It is possible that the opening leaves of the Winchester MS., now lost, may have contained some account of the sources from which Malory derived his material. His colophons to the *Coming of Arthur*, the *Tristram*, the *Sangreal*, and the *Knight of the Cart* make it clear that the chief of these was a 'Freynshe booke', and to this, or more briefly to 'the booke', there are further references in the text of all the tales, except the *War with Rome*. Professor Vinaver has made an elaborate investigation of the extant French Arthurian texts which cover Malory's ground and has come to the conclusion that, while his immediate exemplar cannot be precisely identified, it was probably one of a number of late compilations which were current in France during the fifteenth century, and were derivatives from an original prose cycle as it had developed in the thirteenth. It had a *Merlin*, a *Suite de Merlin* or *Livre d'Artus*, which gave the early history of the hero, a *Lancelot* or parts of one, possibly a *Gareth*, a *Tristan*, a *Queste del Saint Graal*, a *Mort Artu*, into which other parts of the *Lancelot* had been incorporated. Behind the prose cycle itself of course lay much earlier work, Geoffrey of Monmouth's quasihistorical narrative of the British champion, the Round Table contributed by Master Wace, the poems of Chrestien de Troyes, which brought in the Provençal

motive of *amour courtois*, those of Robert de Boron, now mostly lost, the elaboration of the Grail story by the religious mysticism of the Cistercian writers. But Malory's French book was not his only source. He certainly also knew English books on his hero, and also traditions of him surviving in the countryside. In describing the departure of Arthur in a ship with three queens, he says 'I fynde no more wrytten in bokis that bene auctorysed', and he adds:

> Yet som men say in many partyes of Inglonde that kynge Arthur ys nat dede, but had by the wyll of Oure Lorde Jesu into another place; and men say that he shall com agayne, and he shall wynne the Holy Crosse.

So, too, in describing the fate of Lancelot's kin, he adds:

> And somme Englysshe bookes maken mencyon that they wente never oute of England after the deth of syr Launcelot—but that was but favour of makers! For the Frensshe book maketh mencyon—and is auctorysed, that syr Bors, syr Ector, syr Blamour and syr Bleoberis wente into the Holy Lande.

One English book, of which Malory made use, we are able to infer. It has long been thought that his account of the *War with Rome* was taken from a fourteenth-century alliterative *Morte Arthure*, of which a version is preserved in the Thornton MS. This he refers to as 'the Romaunce'. Traces of alliterative diction are apparent in Caxton's text. But it is now clear from the much fuller Winchester MS. that here Caxton has substituted a paraphrase of his own. The Winchester text is much longer and abounds in alliterative passages, evidently taken straight from the source. Malory, however, used a different version from that of the Thornton MS., and towards the end of the tale he abandoned it, since it contained an account of the rising of Mordred against Arthur, which was not to his purpose. It has been suggested that he also used for the *Death of Arthur* an English stanzaic *Morte Arthur*, now Harleian MS. 2252. Here, however, he does cite the French book, and it is more likely that both he and the writer of the English poem drew upon a French original no longer known. The one tale of which no other version, English or French, has been discovered is the *Gareth*. It has been suggested that this is of Malory's own composition, that the name Beaumains, which Gareth assumes, was adapted from that of Richard Beauchamp, Earl of Warwick, and that Malory drew upon a story told by the earl's biographer, John Rous, of a tournament at Calais, in which the earl appeared on three days in three different accoutrements, of which one was that of a Green Knight, and defeated all his opponents. This seems rather far-fetched. In fact Gareth makes no change of costume, although he does, but not in a tournament, successively slay or overthrow a Black, a Green, a Red, and a Blue Knight. Nor am I much impressed by the suggestion that the name of the Duke de la Rowse, who appears in a later episode, was taken from Rous himself. In fact, moreover, here as elsewhere, Malory cites the French book as his source. We can hardly, therefore, regard the request of the colophon that the readers will 'pray for hym that this wrote' as indicating an original composition.

It is possible that Malory began his work by writing the *War with Rome*, and then turned to the French book. There is a slight duplication of the embassy from the Emperor in the *Coming of Arthur*. And a passage in the colophon to this tale may conceivably suggest that at one time he meant to go no further:

> Who that woll make ony more lette hym seke other bookis of kynge Arthur or of sir Launcelot or sir Trystrams.

But the eight tales, as they stand, are clearly meant to be read as the successive chapters of a continuous narrative. There are many references from tale to tale, and to some extent threads dropped in one are taken up in another. What, then, must we regard as the dominating theme which Malory was attempting to develop? It sometimes looks as though there were none at all. The French book was a dangerous model. Of some early mythical elements in its origins little is left beyond Merlin and the sorceries of the bad Morgan le Fay and the good Lady of the Lake. When he reads that every day in the year, from early morning to high noon, Gawaine's might increased unto thrice its strength, the anthropologist may no doubt recognize that originally Gawaine was a sun-hero. But, long before it came to Malory, the narrative had been much elaborated by a succession of *remanieurs*, who had brought in innumerable sporadic adventures on a common model. A knight rides abroad, meets another, overthrows him, and sets free a lady whom he has abducted, and rides away. A Gareth, a Palomides, a La Cote Male Taille, conceived on these lines, easily becomes tedious. Malory cut this element in his sources very freely, but not freely enough. Here are still to the full the *Arturi regis ambages pulcherrimae*, of which Dante writes. Much of the *Tristram*, in particular, which occupies over a third of Malory's pages, is largely irrelevant, and after all the tale, as he tells it, lacks its fine ending of the black and white sails and the deaths of the lovers. Malory begins well with the *Coming of Arthur*, but thereafter are many confusions and inconsistencies. Merlin's prophecies are by no means all confirmed. The origin of Arthur's sword Excalibur is left very obscure. Galahad gets the description of the *haut prince*, which properly belongs to a distinct Sir Galahalt. Bagdemagus dies and is alive again later. There is a 'questing beast', which is pursued by King Pellinor and later by Palomides, but we never learn its nature. There are many references to the murders of Pellinor and his son Lamorak by Gawaine, but the stories of them are never fully told. These are samples only, and some of them may be due to Malory's sources rather than himself. More important is the rift in the characterization of Gawaine. In the *Coming of Arthur* Merlin speaks of him as the man in the world whom Lancelot loves best, and anticipates that Lancelot will slay him with Balin's sword. Lancelot does not, in fact, although Galahad once defeats Gawaine with it. Gawaine was held to be a good knight when he became one of the Round Table, and he did good service in Arthur's wars at home and against the Romans. But already he had slain a lady, although indeed it was by accident, and had been sworn by a quest of ladies to be courteous and always to show mercy. And in the tales that follow, his character is consistently depreciated. The deaths of Pellinor and Lamorak were to his discredit. Even his brother Gareth withdrew from his fellowship, 'for he was evir vengeable, and where he hated he wolde be avenged with murther: and that hated sir Gareth'. Tristram, too, describes his whole family, other than Gareth himself, as 'the grettyste distroyers and murtherars of good knyghtes that is now in the realme of Ingelonde'. It is rather surprising that he is the first knight to swear himself to the quest of the Grail. Galahad, however, refuses to ride with him. When bidden by a hermit, he will do no penance, and when a second hermit also reproves him he rides down the hill and abandons the adventure. But when we come to the *Death of Arthur*, this past reputation seems to have been largely forgotten. He is hostile to Lancelot because he had slain Gareth through an accident. But there is much nobility in the relations between them. He dies of a wound from Lancelot's hand, but writes him a letter, referring to 'all the love that ever was betwyxte us', and Lancelot in his turn weeps by his tomb and describes him as 'a full noble knyght as ever was born'.

The accounts of the Sangreal, again, are full of obscurities and even discrepancies. It has come into the narrative long before the tale devoted to the *Quest* of it. It is kept at Corbyn, which later becomes Carbonek, by a King Pellam, who later becomes Pelles. It contains part of the blood of Jesus Christ, which Joseph of Arimathea brought into the land. In the *Coming of Arthur* Balin comes to Pellam's castle, fights him, and wounds him with a marvellous spear which he found on a table. It was that of Longinus. Malory here refers to the *Quest*, and tells us that Pellam lay many years sore wounded, and might not be whole until Galahad healed him. It was 'the dolorouse stroke'. But when Lancelot visits Corbyn and begets Galahad on Elaine, the daughter of Pelles, and again when he runs mad and is harboured there as a fool, nothing is said of any infirmity. Pelles moves about, like any other king. Galahad, however, when he comes to Camelot, describes him as not yet whole from Balin's stroke. Later he is more than once referred to as the maimed king, but an entirely different account of the maiming is given by Percival's sister. According to her Pelles, while hunting in Ireland, came to a ship and found there a sword, which he drew, and therewith entered a spear, with which he was smitten through both thighs, and never since might be healed, until Galahad came. It is probable that Malory's French book had drawn upon more than one version of the Grail story. And of this there is further evidence in a greeting sent by Galahad from Camelot to 'my graunte-syre kynge Pelles and unto my lorde kynge Pecchere', and in a later passage where Lancelot is said to have seen the Grail in 'kynge Pescheors house'. Malory is not very lucid, again, in distinguishing between Lancelot's imperfect vision of the Grail and the more complete one vouchsafed to Galahad. Both of them see much more than the covered vessel. Of Lancelot, standing outside the door of a chamber, we are told,

> Before the Holy Vessell he saw a good man clothed as a pryste, and hit semed that he was at the sakeringe of the masse. And hit semed to sir Launcelot that above the prystis hondis were three men, whereof the two put the yongyste by lyknes betwene the prystes hondis, and so he lyffte hym up ryght hyghe, and hit semed to shew so to the peple.

The priest looked as if he were overcharged with the weight, but when Lancelot attempted to enter the chamber and help him, a breath of fire smote him, and he fell to the ground insensible.

> 'Sir,' seyde they, 'the queste of the Sankgreall ys encheved now ryght in you, and never shall ye se of Sankgreall more than ye have seen.'

Galahad's experience is a much longer one. Joseph, the first bishop of Christendom, comes in.

> And than the bysshop made sembelaunte as thoughe he wolde have gone to the sakeryng of a masse, and than he toke an obley which was made in lyknesse of brede. And at the lyfftyng up there cam a figure in lyknesse of a chylde, and the vysage was as rede and as bryght as ony fyre, and smote hymselff into the brede, that all they saw hit that the brede was fourmed of a fleyshely man. And than he put hit into the Holy Vessell agayne, and than he ded that longed to a preste to do masse.

The bishop vanished, and out of the Holy Vessell came a man 'that had all the sygnes of the Passion of Jesu Cryste, bledynge all opynly'. He took the Vessell, and from his hands Galahad and his fellows received their Saviour. This experience goes beyond Lancelot's, to whom no word was said by the Divine Person, but both alike have entailed what a theologian would call the Real Presence.

The entanglements are over when the Grail has vanished, and thereafter Malory is free to tell one of the best stories of the world. Lancelot resumes his love of Guenevere, forgetting 'the promyse and the perfeccion that he made in the queste'. Aggravayne spreads the scandal. Lancelot withdraws from Guenevere, to her anger, and leaves the court. Guenevere is falsely accused of poisoning. She must be burnt, unless a knight will do battle for her. Lancelot does, and the lovers are reconciled. Then comes the story of the love of Elaine of Astolat for Lancelot, an episode again, but a gracious one. Malory now allows himself one of his rare comments, in a discourse on May time, and the instability of modern love, as compared with that of King Arthur's days. It was not so with Queen Guenevere, 'for whom I make here a lytyll mencion, that whyle she lyved she was a trew lover, and therefor she had a good ende'. She goes maying, is abducted by Mellyagaunce, and rescued by Lancelot, who drops his dignity to ride in a cart. Both king and queen now cherish Lancelot. Another episode comes to exalt him, in his healing of the wounds of Sir Urre, after which he weeps 'as he had bene a chylde that had been beatyn'. But now tragedy is at hand. It is introduced by an ironical repetition of the May-day theme. Aggravayne is still plotting, and with him his half-brother Mordred, Arthur's illegitimate son. They denounce the amour of Lancelot and Guenevere to Arthur, who indeed already had 'a demyng of hit'. Then they have the luck to find Lancelot in Guenevere's chamber. Lancelot slays Aggravayne and wounds Mordred. Mordred reports the affair to Arthur, who condemns Guenevere to be burnt at the stake. Gawaine refuses to be present, and his brothers Gaherys and Gareth will only go unarmed. Lancelot comes to rescue the queen, and takes her to Joyous Garde. But in the mellay he has the misfortune to slay Gaherys and Gareth. As a result, Gawaine becomes his relentless foe. He instigates Arthur to besiege Joyous Garde. Lancelot, from its walls, asserts the innocence of Guenevere and upbraids Gawaine with the death of Lamorak. Gawaine will not allow Arthur to be reconciled, and a battle follows. Lancelot bids his knights to spare Arthur and Gawaine, and when Arthur is unhorsed, alights to remount him, and Arthur weeps, 'thynkyng of the grete curtesy that was in sir Launcelot more than in ony other man'. Then the Pope intervenes, bidding Arthur take Guenevere again, and accord with Lancelot. Arthur is appeased, but not Gawaine, although Lancelot offers to undertake a pil-

grimage for the souls of his brothers. Lancelot now goes overseas to his realm of Benwick. He suspects that Mordred will make trouble in England. Arthur, instigated by Gawaine, takes an expedition against Benwick, leaving Mordred in charge at home. Gawaine and Lancelot again dispute and fight. Gawaine is wounded, but Lancelot spares him. In a second fight he is smitten by Lancelot on the same wound. Now comes news that Mordred has declared himself king. He would have wedded Guenevere, but she takes refuge in the Tower of London. Arthur returns to England and defeats him. Gawaine is again smitten on his old wound. He writes to Lancelot, bidding him visit his tomb and pray for his soul, and 'for all the love that ever was betwyxte us' rescue Arthur from Mordred. And he bids Arthur cherish Lancelot. Arthur has already defeated Mordred at Dover and Barham Down. But Mordred is strong in the counties around London. The ghost of Gawaine advises Arthur in a dream to put off battle until Lancelot comes. There is a parley between the king and his illegitimate son. But the accidental drawing of a sword to kill an adder provokes a fresh battle in which Mordred falls, and Arthur is stricken to the death. He bids Bedivere throw his sword Excalibur into a water, and a queen, with three ladies in black hoods, arrives and takes him in a barge to be healed of his wound in the Isle of Avilion. Guenevere becomes a nun at Amesbury. Here Lancelot finds her when he returns to England. They part in piety. Lancelot becomes a priest. He visits Amesbury once more to see Guenevere dead. He buries her at Glastonbury, dies himself, and is taken to Joyous Garde, where Ector speaks the famous eulogy over his corpse. Constantine reigns in England.

What, then, was the dominant motive which we may suppose to have inspired Malory in making his careful selection from the very amorphous material of his French book? Professor Vinaver has suggested that he was a practical and righteous fifteenth-century gentleman, who wished to bring back a decadent England to the virtues of 'manhode, curtesye and gentylnesse', which he believed to have inspired the 'custom and usage' of medieval chivalry. This would certainly have appealed to Caxton. Obviously chivalry looms large in the romance. The Knights of the Round Table are sworn:

> Never to do outerage nothir morthir, and allwayes to fle treson, and to gyff mercy unto hym that askith mercy, uppon payne of forfiture othir worship and lordship of kynge Arthure for evirmore; and allwayes to do ladyes, damesels, and jantilwomen and wydowes strengthe hem in hir ryghtes and never to enforce them uppon payne of dethe. Also that no man take no batayles in a wrongefull quarell for no love ne for no worldis goodis.

And chivalrous adventure is the obligation of noble birth. The mother of Aglovale and Percyvale would have them abide at home.

> 'A, my swete modir,' seyde sir Percyvale, 'we may nat, for we be comyn of kynges bloode of bothe partis. And therefore, modir, hit ys oure kynde to haunte armys and noble dedys.'

It is a very aristocratic ideal. Nobody counts for much, except the knights and their ladies, and a sprinkling of pious hermits. And even these are of aristocratic origin.

> For in thos dayes hit was nat the gyse as ys nowadayes; for there were none ermytis in tho dayes but that they

had bene men of worship and of preuesse, and tho er-
mytes hylde grete householdis and refreysshed people
that were in distresse.

The rest are 'churls' and of no account. They take to their
heels when they see a knight coming. And no wonder! A
carter, busy on fetching wood for his lord, refused to stop
his work and give Lancelot a ride to a castle. And then

> Sir Launcelot lepe to hym and gaf hym backwarde with
> hys gauntelet a reremayne, that he felle to the erthe
> starke dede.

I doubt whether Malory has his eye much on the England
of his own day. He does, indeed, stop, in the middle of his
account of the rising of Mordred against Arthur, to make
one of his rare personal comments:

> Lo ye, all Englysshemen, se ye nat what a myschyff here
> was? For he that was the moste kynge and nobelyst
> knyght of the worlde, and most loved the felyshyp of
> noble knyghtes, and by hym they all were upholdyn,
> and yet myght nat these Englysshemen holde them con-
> tente with hym. Lo thus was the olde custom and usay-
> ges of thys londe, and men say that we of thys londe
> have nat yet loste that custom. Alas! thys ys a greate de-
> faughte of us Englysshemen, for there may nothynge us
> please no terme.

But of the England of the fifteenth century, exhausted by
generations of foreign enterprise and dynastic quarrels, of
England as we find it depicted in the *Paston Letters*, of the
complete breakdown of law and order, of the abuses of
maintenance and livery and private warfare, of the corruption of officials, of the excessive taxation, of the ruin of
countrysides by the enclosure of agricultural land for
pasture—of all this we find no consciousness whatever in
Malory's pages. A revival of the spirit of chivalry might
have done something to help matters, but a strong hand in
the central government would have done more.

Malory does not, however, except in this outburst, come
before us as a political thinker, but as a story-teller, intent
on the development of a very dramatic theme. It is the
drama of Arthur and Lancelot, and indeed, as it works
out, it seems to be Lancelot, rather than Arthur, who is
the protagonist. Arthur is prominent at the beginning,
with his triumphant coming, the success of his early wars,
the mystery of Excalibur, and the establishment of the
Round Table. Later his rôle becomes a more passive one.
His begetting of Mordred is significant. Between Arthur
and Lancelot stand Guenevere and later Gawaine. To Arthur belong Merlin, Nimue, and Morgan le Fay. Merlin
drops early out of the story, but he lives long enough to
prophesy of Lancelot, and to see Lancelot himself as a
boy. And among all the entanglement of Malory's earlier
tales, the most notable thing is the constant emphasis on
Lancelot. In the *War with Rome* there are frequent mentions of him, which appear to be Malory's own additions
to the alliterative poem as he found it. Certainly they are
not in the version of the Thornton MS. It is difficult to be
sure, without greater knowledge of Malory's French book
than we possess, but it seems likely enough that the ruthless cuttings of it, which we conjecture, were largely mo-
tived by the desire to bring Lancelot into the foreground.
The third tale is entirely devoted to him, and at the end
of it his pre-eminence among the members of the Round
Table is assured.

At that tyme sir Launcelot had the grettyste name of
ony knyht of the worlde, and moste he was honoured of
hyghe and lowe.

Thereafter he is constantly referred to as the exemplar of
perfect knighthood. In the long-drawn-out earlier part of
the *Tristram* the only significant thing is the friendship
which establishes itself between him and Tristram. 'Of all
knyghtes', says Tristram, 'he bearyth the floure.' It is noteworthy, again, that Malory brings Lancelot as near to the
complete vision of the Grail as he can, and that of those
who ultimately achieve it, one is his son and another his
nephew. Of his part in the final outcome of the drama no
more need be said. But it is relevant that it is on him, and
not on Arthur, that the threnody, which forms its epilogue, is spoken.

If we feel that Malory is slow in getting under way with
his high theme and too often allows the earlier part of his
narrative to be unduly clogged with episodes, there can at
least be no doubt as to the singular beauty of his prose. He
is free from the desire to 'augment' the English language
with 'aureate' terms, which is the bane of so much contemporary writing, and comes nearer to the vernacular tradition which Dr. R. W. Chambers has traced back,
through the pieties of the thirteenth and fourteenth centuries, to its Anglo-Saxon beginnings. But he gives it a wider
scope by applying it to secular material, and here, of
course, he is much under the influence of his French models. Professor W. P. Ker, who has said so many of the best
things about medieval literature, speaks of his 'high imaginative prose', and in elaboration:

> The style of his original has the graces of early art; the
> pathos, the simplicity of the early French prose at its
> best, and always that haunting elegiac tone or under-
> tone which never fails in romance or homily to bring its
> sad suggestions of the vanity and transience of all
> things, of the passing away of pomp and splendour, of
> the falls of princes. In Malory, while this tone is kept,
> there is a more decided and more artistic command of
> rhythm than in the Lancelot or the Tristan. They are
> even throughout, one page very much like another in
> general character: Malory has splendid passages to
> which he rises, and from which he falls back into the
> even tenour of his discourse. In the less distinguished
> parts of his book, besides, there cannot fail to be noted
> a more careful choice of words and testing of sounds
> than in the uncalculating spontaneous eloquence of his
> original.

One may add that Malory, unlike Caxton, does not share
the love of his French predecessors for linking synonymous words in doublets, and that he makes no attempt to
reproduce in English those elaborate periods of carefully
linked subordinate clauses which they favoured. He prefers to proceed, both in narrative and in dialogue, by a
succession of simple sentences, each introduced with an
'And', 'But', 'So', 'Then', 'For', 'Wherefore', or the like,
and to obtain his rhythm by balancing these with longer
ones. He has been accused of occasional breakdowns in
grammatical construction, but a comparison of the Winchester text with that of Caxton suggests that here the
scribes have not always served him well. The diction is
fairly modern. There are a few French words which have
not established themselves in the language, and a few English ones which have died out of it. Dialogue is apt to
come to an abrupt conclusion. The knights are men of
their hands and have no turn for a prolonged debate. Ar-

thur calls them together to plan a coming campaign. 'They coude no counceil gyve, but said they were bygge ynough.' Lancelot is advised to avoid a wrong quarrel. 'As for that,' said Sir Lancelot, 'God ys to be drad.' But a hermit can outdo them in brevities of speech. One has called upon Sir Gawaine to do penance for his sins, but Sir Gawaine refuses. ' "Well", seyde the good man, and than he hylde hys pece.' Malory is fond of vivid words. Knights come into battle 'as hit had bene thunder', or 'hurtling', or with a 'wallop'. They fall to the earth 'flatling' or 'noseling'. A spear comes 'poyntelynge'. There is little deliberate scenic description, but a strong feeling for out-of-door life. An army stands still 'as hit had be a plumpe of woode'. A knight lashes at a shield, 'that all the medow range of the dyntys'. He rides by moonlight, and comes to 'a rowghe watir, which rored', or finds 'an ermytage, whiche was undir a woode, and a grete cliff on the othir syde, and a fayre watir rennynge undir hit'. It has the simplicity of an Italian miniature. And in passages of spiritual exaltation Malory can rise without effort to the level of his theme. Galahad comes to court, and Lancelot looks upon his son, as he knights him. 'God make you a good man, for of beauté fayleth you none as ony that ys now lyvynge.' (pp. 188-99)

> E. K. Chambers, "Malory," in his English Literature at the Close of the Middle Ages, *Oxford at the Clarendon Press,* 1947, pp. 185-205.

E. M. W. TILLYARD (essay date 1954)

[*Tillyard was an English scholar of Renaissance literature whose studies of John Milton, William Shakespeare, and the epic form are widely respected. In the following excerpt from his celebrated study* The English Epic and Its Background *(1954) he contends that the* Morte Darthur *is not an epic.*]

Malory was more than a generation younger than Lydgate and yet he is less touched by the literary happenings in Italy that promoted the Renaissance. He is thus at the very tail-end of a tradition. Not that this is fatal to great literature. Milton, writing around the time of the Restoration, looks to the old humanist not to the new scientific way of thinking and, though fully aware of Copernicus and his followers, can present a Ptolemaic universe with conviction. Malory's chivalric world is not ineffective because by then antique and outmoded. It is indeed highly effective, but only in expressing an individual vision. Set *Morte Darthur* alongside *Piers Plowman* and you will see how little group-feeling Malory possesses. He creates no picture of general life; he almost makes us forget that there are other classes in the world than the knightly. Even his notion of chivalry is less true to his age than is, for instance, Spenser's to the Elizabethan. Spenser's knights are in themselves ridiculously archaic, and yet their quests have a true affinity with the adventurous spirit of the time. Malory's notion of chivalry is nostalgic and not expressive of the actual England of the Wars of the Roses. That is, in the main; for it may be that something of contemporary gloom has got into the account of Arthur's final battle.

This conclusion, that Malory's bent was not towards epic, applies to Caxton's version of Malory (till recently the only version) as well as to the one that has superseded it. But it has been strengthened by W. F. Oakshott's discovery of a new manuscript of Malory in the Library of Winchester College and Eugène Vinaver's edition of Malory based upon it. Vinaver has made the most important demonstration that what Caxton in his edition called **Morte Darthur** was not a consecutive narrative at all but a series of romances constituting Malory's collected works. Previously it had been natural to think of **Morte Darthur** as one thinks of *Piers Plowman,* a single great work on which the author spent his working life. Now we know there can be no question of Malory's applying his will at a single great stretch. There is, Vinaver tells us, great variety among the different romances. Some are very close to their originals, others are free rehandling with much added matter. And Malory grew freer as he went on. At one extreme is his earliest section, the romance of Arthur and the Emperor Lucius, stiff in style and close to its original, the English alliterative *Morte Arthure*; at the other extreme are the romances that follow the episode of the Grail, recounting the story of Elaine of Astolat, the jealousy of Guinevere, Launcelot's accidental killing of Gareth and Gaherys with his consequent breach with Gawain, their brother, the breach between Arthur and Launcelot, and the final battle.

It is then in the stories following the Grail episode that Malory is most himself. There if anywhere we shall discover his true bent. And that bent is towards the basic human passions, those that have least to do with time and that are as apt to the ages of Homer or of Queen Victoria as to the fifteenth century. Guinevere's jealousy makes one naturally think of Anna Karenina, Launcelot's bounty to his friends when banished from England and the Round Table, of Shakespeare's Antony in *Antony and Cleopatra.* Further, it is the passionate cadence of the speeches that now counts for more than any narrative or description. And that cadence, though produced through English of the fifteenth century, belongs to all human passion.

> 'Fy on hym!' seyde the quene [to Sir Bors about Sir Launcelot]. 'Yet for all his pryde and bobbaunce, there ye proved youreselff better man than he.'
> 'Nay, Madam, sey ye nevermore so, for he bete me and my felowys, and myght have slayne us and he had wolde.'
> 'Fy on hym!' seyde the quene. 'For I harde Sir Gawayne say before my lorde Arthure that hit were mervayle to telle the grete love that ys betwene the Fayre Maydyn on Astolat and hym.'

There is also in these last episodes a strong sense of the logic of destiny. The turning-point in Launcelot's career was his killing accidentally two of Sir Gawain's kin, Sir Gareth and Sir Gaherys; and it is significant that Malory specifies Sir Gareth in a way his French original does not. Gareth was especially dear both to Launcelot himself and to his rival Gawain; and his killing meant an irremediable feud between Gawain and Launcelot. But though Launcelot killed Gareth and Gaherys accidentally, it was through his adultery with Guinevere that the occasion arose for the accident to happen. And it was from this accident that the breach between Launcelot and Arthur became such that it could never be healed. And this breach brought with it the ruin of the Round Table and the death of Arthur. Both the timeless passions and the logic of destiny are the marks of tragedy; and the last of Malory's series of romances are tragedy of a magnificence which perhaps has not generally been sufficiently recognised.

But if I have compared Malory's power of depicting the human passions with that shown in *Anna Karenina* and *Antony and Cleopatra* I can only point to contrasts if the comparison is extended to other things. The setting of *Anna Karenina* is all Russia, of *Antony and Cleopatra* the East and the West of the ancient Roman world. Shakespeare and Tolstoi combine tragic narrowness and timelessness with epic breadth and the sense of varied life. Malory is more akin to Webster in his tragic capacities than to Shakespeare. His genius does not extend to epic. (pp. 176-78)

> E. M. W. Tillyard, "The Fifteenth Century," in his The English Epic and Its Background, *Oxford University Press, 1954, pp. 172-78.*

THOMAS C. RUMBLE (essay date 1960)

[*Rumble is an American medievalist best known for his studies of Malory and the* Morte Darthur. *In the following excerpt, he challenges Eugène Vinaver's contention, presented in his 1947 edition of* The Works of Sir Thomas Malory, *that the* Morte Darthur *exhibits numerous textual, thematic, and narrative inconsistencies.*]

Medievalists have frequently commented on the great number of inconsistencies which, real or imaginary, seem to mar Sir Thomas Malory's **Morte Darthur**. It is impossible, of course, to explain away the fact that near the beginning of Malory's work King Arthur fights against King Lot with Excalibur, the magic sword which he does not obtain until considerably later in the book. But such obvious inconsistencies as this are probably fewer than has generally been supposed; certainly they are far fewer than we might reasonably expect in view of what we know about the probable conditions under which Malory wrote.

However much Malory scholarship is indebted to Professor Eugene Vinaver for his recent excellent edition of the Winchester manuscript of the **Morte Darthur** [**The Works of Sir Thomas Malory** (1947)], it seems to me only just to point out that in his accompanying "Commentary" there are a number of inaccuracies which tend to diminish Malory's stature as a writer by attributing to the **Morte Darthur** inconsistencies which do not, in fact, exist. Most of these inaccuracies are matters of interpretation. They result sometimes from Vinaver's misconstruction of the idiom of Malory's language, sometimes from his neglect of the context of the episode he is commenting on, or sometimes simply from a misreading of Malory's text. Whatever the case, since we are not likely soon to get a revision of this part of Vinaver's work, it may be appropriate here to call attention to at least a few of the most questionable of his interpretations and to suggest that in writing the **Morte Darthur** Malory was working a great deal more carefully than Vinaver's conclusions would indicate.

Early in the **Morte Darthur**, after Balin has killed Launceor and after Launceor's "damesell" has "destroyed hirselff for the love of hys dethe," Balin meets his brother Balan, who had earlier set out from Northumberland to find Balin and to deliver him from his "dolerous presonment" in Arthur's court:

> And than was he [Balin] ware by hys armys that there com rydyng hys brothir Balan. And whan they were mette they put of hyr helmys and kyssed togydirs and wepte for joy and pité. Than Balan seyde, "Brothir, I litill wende to have mette with you at thys suddayne adventure, but I am ryght glad of your delyveraunce of youre dolerous presonment: for a man told me in the

Castell of Four Stonys that ye were delyverde, and that man had seyne you in the courte of kynge Arthure. And therefore I com hydir into thys contrey, for here I supposed to fynde you."

Vinaver says of this meeting:

> In *F* [Malory's presumed French source] the speaker is Balin (*Balaain*). *M* [Malory] seems to have confused the two brothers, probably because, contrary to his practice, he has changed a dialogue into a monologue. Another inconsistency is that Balan begins by saying *I litill wende to have mette with you at thys suddayne adventure* and concludes with the words *here I supposed to fynde you.*

Now, first of all, despite some slightly puzzling references of pronouns in the paragraph immediately preceding the dialogue between the brothers in *F* it is nevertheless evident that there, as in Malory, it is *not* Balin (*Balaain*) who speaks first, but Balan, (*Balaan*). In *F* the conversation begins, as Vinaver rightly notes: "Ha! frere, je ne vous cuidai je mais veoir! Par quel aventure estes vous delivrés de la dolereuse prison ou vous estiés?" But that these are Balan's words should be apparent from the fact that it is Balin who had been imprisoned, not Balan, even though in *F* Balin's imprisonment had taken place "en la terre de Norhomberlande" rather than in King Arthur's court. Secondly, just as there is nothing in Malory's text to indicate that he had "confused the two brothers," neither is there any indication that his deviation from his source consisted in having changed a dialogue to a monologue; for a comparison of a larger section of the episode in Malory and in *F* will show that although he compressed the original dialogue greatly, giving Balan little part in it after the opening speech, he by no means changed it to a monologue. Finally, concerning the contention that Balan's speech is in itself inconsistent, we must remember that prior to Balan's opening remark to his brother that he "litill wende to have mette" the latter "at thys suddayne adventure" (*i.e.* "at this sudden chance," or simply "so suddenly"), he had been told by "a man in the Castell of Four Stonys" that Balin had been delivered out of his "dolerous presonment" and had been seen in the court of King Arthur. There is no reason, therefore, why Balan should not conclude his greeting with the words "I com hydir *into thys contrey*, for here I supposed to fynde you," especially since, in Malory's idiom, "thys suddayne adventure" suggests logically enough that Balan had scarcely expected to meet Balin without searching a long time for him throughout Arthur's realm—"thys contrey."

Shortly after the meeting of Balin and Balan, after the brothers have helped put down King Lot's rebellion against Arthur and have parted again, Balin takes up the quest of Berbeus, a knight who, under Balin's safe "conduyte," has been slain by the invisible knight, Garlon, and whose lady "ever . . . bare the truncheon of the spere with hir that Harleus le Berbeus was slayne withall." Balin and Garlon finally meet at a feast in the castle of King Pellam, where Garlon is no longer invisible, but "the knyght with the blacke face," King Pellam's brother. After an exchange of angry words, Garlon "slapped [Balin] on the face with the backe of hys honde" and Balin "rose hym up fersely and clave [Garlon's] hede to the sholdirs." Balin then turns to Berbeus's lady:

> "Now geff me the truncheon," seyde Balyn to his lady, "that he slew youre knyght with." And anone she gaff

Bedivere returns Excalibur to the water. From London, British Library, Add. MS. 10294.

hit hym, for allwey she bare the truncheone with hir. And therewith Balan [*sic*] smote hym thorow the body and seyde opynly, "With that troncheon thou slewyste a good knyght, and now hit stykith in thy body."

Vinaver considers that Malory deviated from his source in this incident:

> In *F* Balin uses his own sword to kill Garlan, and it is not until Garlan is dead that he asks the lady to give him "le tronchon de quoi li chevaliers fu ferus devant les pavillons" and thrusts it through Garlan's body: "et en fiert Garlan qui a terre gisoit mors, si durement qu'il li tresperce les deus costés." *M* makes Balin kill Garlan with the truncheon....

Quite apparently, however, in Malory's version, just as in *F*, Balin *does* kill Garlon with his own sword when he cleaves the latter's head "to the sholdirs." Nowhere else in Malory is a knight still alive after such a blow, and there is no reason to believe that this instance is any exception. It is only *after* Balin has struck Garlon with his own sword, at any rate, that he asks Berbeus's lady for the truncheon, and with that weapon "smote [Garlon] thorow the body." What may prompt a questionable reading of this incident is that, as Balin delivers the second of these two blows, he addresses Garlon, emphasizing dramatically for the benefit of "hys oste and all the knyghtes [who] rose frome the table" the justification of his act: "With that troncheon thou slewyste a good knyght, and now hit

stykith in they body," he says, even though Garlon must certainly be dead by then.

In the "Torre and Pellynore" section of the *Morte Darthur* there occurs an episode which provides another example of what Vinaver regards as an inconsistency. Pellinore is sent from Arthur's court on a quest to free a lady who has been abducted from Arthur's wedding feast by Sir Outelake (Hontzlake) of Wentland. He overtakes Sir Outelake as the latter is jousting with another knight, who has "chalenged that lady of that knyght and seyde she was hys cosyne nere, wherfore he [Outelake] sholde lede hir no farther." After interrupting the struggle between these two knights, and after discovering "the causis why they fought," Pellinore addresses Outelake:

> "... ye com in suddeynly thereas we were at the hyghe feste and toke away thys lady or ony man mught make hym redy, and therefore hit was my queste to brynge her agayne and you bothe, other ellis that one of us to leve in the fylde."

Vinaver comments on this incident that

> "and you bothe" is not in *F*, nor is it consistent with the fact that when Pellinor started on this quest he was not even aware of the existence of the two knights.

But since Pellinore addresses Sir Outelake when he says "hit was my queste to brynge her agayne and you bothe," he clearly means "agayne" in the sense of "back to Arthur's court," and "bothe" in the sense of "too" or "also." The object of Pellinore's quest, as it was designated earlier by Merlin, is set forth in almost precisely the same terms; Pellinore was to "brynge agayne the lady and the knyght, othir ellis sle hym," and there is no mention at that point, nor is there any intended now, of the knight with whom Outelake is fighting for possession of the lady—the knight who at first glance may seem the second of "bothe" knights.

Another of the inconsistencies which Vinaver attributes to the *Morte Darthur* concerns one of Gawain's adventures. In the company of a "scornful damesell," Gawain arbitrates a dispute between a dwarf and a knight over the possession of a lady. Given her choice between the two, the lady chooses to go with the dwarf, who "toke hir up and wente his way syngyng, and the knyght went his way with grete mournyng":

> Than com there two knyghtes all armed and cryed on hyght, "Sir Gawayne, knyght of the courte of kynge Arthur! Make the redy in haste and juste with me!"

Comparing this passage with its parallel in French, Vinaver remarks:

> In *F* two knights appear, but only one of them cries: *Gauvain, Gauvain, a jouster te convient!* This explains the apparent inconsistency in *M* between the plural of the opening sentence and the singular of "juste with me."

The sentences immediately following that with which Vinaver is here concerned, however, resolve Malory's "apparent inconsistency" much more readily than does the parallel passage in *F*. After the two knights have cried their challenge to Gawain,

> so they ran togedirs, that eyther felle downe. And than on foote they drew there swerdis and dud ful actually. The meanewhyle the other knyght went to the damesell and asked hir why she abode with that knyght [Gawain]....

If, as Vinaver supposes, the "they" of these sentences is intended to represent all three knights (Gawain and the two challengers), then *all*, not "eyther," would have to stand as the subject of "felle downe," for nowhere else in the *Morte Darthur* does Malory use the pronoun "eyther" to refer to more than two persons. Moreover, Malory himself goes on to tell us that "the *meanewhyle* [*i.e.* while the jousting between Gawain and one of the two knights is taking place] the *other* knyght went to the damesell." However elliptical it may seem, Malory's idiom implies unmistakably that the challenge, though uttered by both knights, is the expression of *either's* willingness to joust with Gawain, for only one does—not both.

There are several instances in the "Tristram" section of the *Morte Darthur* in which Vinaver attributes inconsistencies to Malory. The first of these concerns the episode in which Tristram is exiled for the second time from King Mark's court. During his first exile, "fayre naked and wood," Tristram had rescued King Marks's knight, Sir Dinaunt, "frome the grymly gyaunt sir Tauleas," and had been brought unrecognized back to Mark's castle. There, after Tristram's recovery and after his recognition by Sir Andred, Mark "lete calle hys barownes to geve jugemente

unto sir Trystramys to the dethe." The barons' judgment, however, is that Tristram shall be "banysshed out of the contrey for ten yere"; and after Tristram has armed himself, "there were many barowndes brought hym unto hys shyp, that som were of hys frendis and som were of his fooys." On the way to the ship ("in the meanewhyle"), Tristram and his escort encounter Sir Dinadan, who challenges Tristram to joust with him. Upon being given a fall, Dinadan "prayde sir Trystram of hys jantylnes to gyff hym leve to go in hys felyshyp." Tristram grants Dinadan's request, and the two "toke their horsys and rode to their shyppys togydir." The passage Vinaver comments on in this episode begins as follows:

> And whan sir Trystramys was in the se he seyde, "Grete well kynge Marke and all myne enemynes, and sey to hem...."

There follows Tristram's long and scathing speech concerning how ill-rewarded have been all of his services to King Mark, immediately after which Malory tells us:

> And furthewithall he toke the see.

> And at the nexte londynge faste by the see there mette with sir Trystram and with sir Dynadan sir Ector de Marys and sir Bors de Ganys....

Vinaver says of this episode that

> Tristram's speech was delivered 'in the se', with Dinadan as the only listener, and it seems odd that Tristram should ask Dinadan to greet Mark when Dinadan has no intention of going back to King Mark's court. The inconsistency is due to the fact that *M* has made two speeches into one: the first addressed in *F* to the Cornish barons *before* sailing; the second, addressed to the sailors *after* the landing at Camelot.

But the "inconsistency" here seems to me to result from interpreting "in the se" too literally and from neglecting the context of Tristram's speech. It is true enough that Malory has made two speeches into one, but there is certainly nothing inconsistent in the episode as a result of this compression. Tristram meets Dinadan, jousts with him, and accepts his "felyshyp" before riding on to his ship—"in the meanewhyle," as Malory puts it. Then, "whan sir Trystramys was in the se," he delivers his speech dramatically and obviously to the barons who have escorted him to his ship—not, as may seem, to Dinadan after they have put out to sea. This reading is borne out in two ways. First, since the barons are charged to bring Tristram "unto hys shyp," we realize that it is they, not Dinadan, who are to return to Mark's court and can thus report to Mark what Tristram has said. Secondly, Vinaver interprets Malory's "in the se" as meaning that Tristram has already set sail when he makes this departing speech, whereas what we are meant to understand is simply that Tristram is "on board" his ship, but not yet under way. The last sentence of the episode substantiates this; for after Tristram has delivered his speech to the barons standing on the shore; "furthewithall he toke [to] the see."

Shortly after his arrival at King Arthur's court, as the "Knyght with the Blacke Shylde," Tristram takes part in the tournament of the Castle of Maidens. When Lancelot is declared the winner of this tournament at the end of the third day, he declines the prize in favor of Tristram, saying,

"Sir Trystram hath won the fylde, for he began firste, and lengyst hylde on, and so hathe he done the firste day, the secunde, and the thirde day!"

At this point Tristram has already left the field; and when Lancelot yields the prize, "than kynge Arthur and sir Launcelot and sir Dodynas le Saveage toke their horsis to seke aftir sir Trystram." Vinaver comments on this episode that

> in *F* Tristram is referred to as the Knight with the Black Shield, and the knights of the Round Table decide to go in quest of him to find out who he is. The moment his identity is disclosed, as it is in *M*, the quest becomes aimless.

Here again, however, the context of the incident is extremely important. Malory makes no great attempt to conceal Tristram's identity throughout this episode; on the first day of the tournament, having taken "such a buffette that he sowned uppon hys horse, . . . anone sir Dynadan cam to sir Trystram and seyde, 'Sir, I know the bettir than thou wenyst'." And, as already seen, after the tournament Lancelot contends that "Sir Trystram hath won the fylde." Thus, far from setting out on an "aimless" quest at this point, Arthur, Lancelot, and Dodinas go in search of Tristram not to find out who he is, but to bring him back to court and bestow upon him "the gre" which Lancelot has disclaimed in his favor. Malory has altered the motivation of this quest; but there is no doubt in the reader's mind as to the identity of the Knight with the Black Shield, and there is no doubt in the minds of those who go in search of him after the tournament. King Arthur makes this clear when, immediately before setting out on their quest, he tells Lancelot and Dodinas of having witnessed one of Tristram's performances in the tournament.

> "Full harde I sye him bestad . . . when he smote sir Palomydes upon the helme thryse, that he abaysshed hys helme with hys strokis. And also he seyde 'here ys a stroke for sir Trystram,' and thus he seyde thryse."

Another incident in the "Tristram" section which will bear a careful consideration of its context is Dinadan's refusal to joust with an "arraunte knyght." Required by this knight to joust, Dinadan says, "I have no wyll to juste"; pressed, he questions the knight, "Whether aske you justys [,] of love othir of hate?" The knight answers "Wyte you well I aske hit for loove and nat of hate." Dinadan then suggests that, this being the case, they meet in King Arthur's court, "and there I shall juste wyth you." The knight asks Dinadan's name and, after being told, says, "A, sir, full well know I you for a good knyght and jantyll, and wyte you well, sir, I love you hertyly." Dinadan answers, "Than shall here be no justys betwyxte us," and the two part. Vinaver says of this meeting:

> In *M*'s version this dialogue makes little sense. Dinadan first refuses to fight, then, without any apparent reason, offers to meet the challenger in single combat at Arthur's court. The unknown knight, on the other hand, after challenging Dinadan, declares that he loves him 'hertely' [*sic*], although he is clearly unaware of Dinadan's identity. Finally, Dinadan's concluding remark, 'than shall here be no justys betwyxte us', is contrary to all chivalric customs, for it does not rest with him to withdraw the unknown knight's challenge. The reason for all these inconsistencies is that. . . .

Despite Vinaver's argument here, and the long quotation which he goes on to cite from *F*, the context of this incident provides "apparent reason" enough for Dinadan's offering to meet the unknown knight in single combat at Arthur's court. The episode really begins some twenty-five pages earlier in Vinaver's text, where Dinadan and Lamorak and other of Arthur's knights leave court to cry "a grete turnement in haste bysyde Camelot, at the Castell of Jagent." During the many adventures which take place before Dinadan's meeting with the unknown knight, Dinadan twice refuses to joust needlessly, suggesting to his challengers that they save jousting for the tournament; as he says to Palomides, the first of these challengers, "I woll not have ado with you but in good manner." Thus, though Malory has again altered the motivation he found in his source, there is no reason to refer to "all these inconsistencies" in commenting on the encounter between Dinadan and the unknown knight. Moreover, in terms of Malory's understanding of the code of chivalry, there is really no breach of "chivalric customs" involved here, either; for before refusing to joust with the unknown knight, Dinadan establishes definitely that the challenge is made "for loove and nat of hate." Under these conditions, we are meant to see, Dinadan can legitimately refuse to joust; in fact, in Malory, at least, any knight can refuse another's challenge, and for any number of reasons, simply by agreeing to the assignment of a specific time and place for a future meeting. More serious than all this, however, is the contention that the unknown knight "declares that he loves [Dinadan] 'hertely', although he is clearly unaware of Dinadan's identity." Malory surely intended a clearer reading to this passage; for, his challenge having been refused, the unknown knight says to Dinadan, "Sytthen ye woll not juste wyth me, I pray you tell me your name." And it is only *after* learning Dinadan's name that the unknown knight claims to know Dinadan "for a good knyght and a jantyll" and to love him "hertyly."

Another instance of a questionable reading of Malory's text concerns the battle between Malagrin and Alexander. Having compared Malory's description of this battle with that of his presumed French source, Vinaver says:

> In *F* . . . Malagrin (Malegryne) and Alexander talk in the intervals of fighting, whereas in *M* the conversation seems to be taking place while they are 'rushing together like two wild boars.'

The following excerpts from the context of this episode, however, suggest unmistakably that in Malory's version, just as in that of his French source, the two knights *do* talk during an interval, not *while* the battle is taking place. After Alexander has unhorsed Malagrin, the two draw swords and fight afoot "longe tyme by the space of three owrys, that never man coude say whyche was the bettir knyght." When finally "they rushed togyders . . . and felle grovelynge bothe to the erthe," Malagrin says, "Now, sir knyght, *hold thyne honde a whyle*, and telle me what thou arte." After exchanging names, and after each has boasted of his past feats and of what he intends to do to the other when they resume their battle, "than they laysshed togydyrs fyersely." Clearly Malory implies in this scene that the conversation between the two knights takes place not *while* they are fighting, but after Alexander "stays his hand" at Malagrin's request and before they again "lash together fiercely." Though Malory has reduced to a single interval in the fighting what was a series of intervals in his source, he is by no means so inconsistent here as to have his knights engage in a lengthy conversation while they do battle.

One more illustration of the kind of inconsistency which Vinaver questionably attributes to Malory will suffice. At the end of the sixth day of King Arthur's tournament at Surluse, while all of the knights and their ladies sit at dinner, "at the myddys of [this] dynar in cam sir Dynadan and began to rayle." As the scene develops, it is clear that Dinadan's clowning amuses the entire company and is purposely meant to do so. After considerable good-natured banter with Sir Galahalt, the "Haute Prince of the Long Iles," Dinadan turns to Sir Lancelot:

> "Well, well," seyde sir Dynadan to sir Launcelot, "what devyll do ye in this contrey? For here may no meane knyghtes wynne, no worship for the."

> "I ensure the, sir Dynadan," seyde sir Launcelot, "I shall no more mete with the, nother with thy grete speare, for I may nat sytte in my sadyll whan thy speare hyttith me. And I be happy, I shall beware of thy boyteous body that thou beryst.... God forbode that ever we mete but hit be at a dysshe of mete!"

Vinaver has elsewhere commented on what seems to him a lack of humor in the *Morte Darthur*, but it is difficult to take this, of all scenes, seriously. He says of the dialogue between Dinadan and Lancelot that

> this [Lancelot's] speech would seem to be more in keeping with Dinadan's behaviour than with Lancelot's, and it is not unlikely that in translating the dialogue *M* mistook one for the other. In *F* Lancelot, far from being afraid of Dinadan, threatens to make him *laissier la cuir* at the next tournament.

To take this dialogue seriously is to overlook not only what precedes it (Dinadan's jesting at the expense of Sir Galahalt), but what follows it as well; for immediately after Lancelot's last words, Malory describes the effect of Dinadan's japing upon the company at dinner:

> Than lowghe the quene and the Haute Prynce, that they myght nat sytte at their table, and thus they made grete joy tyll on the morne.

Moreover, it is significant that, as the direct outcome of Dinadan's playing the fool with Lancelot, on the seventh day of the tournament Lancelot disguises himself in "damesels aray," strikes Dinadan from his horse, and brings him back to court dressed in "womans garmente":

> And whan quene Gwenyver sawe sir Dynadan ibrought in so amonge them all, than she lowghe, that she fell downe; and so dede all that there was.

Scholars interested in Malory are indeed fortunate to have available an edition of the Winchester manuscript of the *Morte Darthur* so soon after its discovery; they are particularly fortunate to have a text of that manuscript which, so far as I can see, is as competently edited as Vinaver's. The points I have brought up in this paper are meant only to suggest that the "Commentary" of Vinaver's edition is in need of considerable revision and that scholars will do well to consider each item of that "Commentary" carefully before accepting it and before basing further conclusions upon it. All things considered—the bulk of Malory's work, the number and variety of its sources, and the conditions under which it was written—the really careful reader of the *Morte Darthur* will be impressed, I think, not with how many are its inconsistencies, but how few. (pp. 59-69)

Thomas C. Rumble, "Malory's 'Works' and Vinaver's Comments: Some Inconsistencies Resolved," in The Journal of English and Germanic Philology *Vol. LIX, No. 1, January, 1960, pp. 59-69.*

CHARLES MOORMAN (essay date 1960)

[*Moorman is an American authority on medieval English literature. In the following excerpt, he discusses the courtly love theme in the* Morte Darthur.]

Taken together, a number of the recent close studies of Sir Thomas Malory's treatment of his French and English sources reveal one unmistakable fact about Malory's purpose in writing the *Morte Darthur*: that Malory intended from the very beginning of his labors to set down in English a unified Arthuriad which should have as its great theme the birth, flowering, and decline of an almost perfect earthly civilization. An analysis of the structure of the *Morte Darthur* reveals also that in order to give unity and coherence to his book, Malory singled out and focussed upon three leit-motifs of the legend—the love of Lancelot and Guinevere, the Lot-Pellinore feud, and the Grail quest—each of which defines one of the causes of the downfall of Arthur's kingdom, the failures in love, in loyalty, in religion.

Of these three controlling motifs, the most immediately compelling is the Lancelot-Guinevere story. For although the final tragedy is the culmination of the disastrous effects of all three and although Malory is careful to trace each of the three plot strands through all eight divisions of his work, Lancelot and Guinevere are, in a manner of speaking, Malory's hero and heroine, and it is natural that the reader's first concern in the *Morte Darthur* should be with them.

For, whatever else it may be, the *Morte Darthur* is the tragedy of two of the world's most popular lovers, and it is clear that their love and their tragedy, which is, of course, the tragedy also of the whole society, are inseparable. Their love, moreover, is in Malory's sources a particular kind of love, *l'amour courtois*, courtly love, and whatever Malory may or may not have understood by the term, courtly love was an aspect of plot and character with which he had to deal in constructing his own version of the tale. The purpose of this paper, then, is to attempt to define the part played by the system of courtly love in the history of Arthur's kingdom as Malory conceived it.

It seems clear first of all that Malory knew all about courtly love and its presence in his sources before he set out to write his book. P. E. Tucker's statements [in the 1953 *MLR* article "The Place of the 'Quest of the Holy Grail' in the 'Morte Darthur'"] that "Malory seems to have taken Lancelot as his exemplar of the knightly ideal without realizing how different his conception of chivalry was" in regard to the role of courtly love and that in "Book III he realizes quite suddenly that he very much dislikes this feature of his sources" thus seem to me to be based on a misconception both of Malory's early knowledge of Arthurian romance and of his total design and plan of composition.

[In the 1950 *Studies in English* article "Malory's Early Knowledge of Arthurian Romance"] R. H. Wilson has demonstrated quite effectively that Malory even before he started to write was familiar with the prose *Tristan* and with the French Vulgate Cycle, both of which texts treat courtly love as a part of the chivalric code. Moreover, Malory's treatment of courtly love in the *Morte Darthur* is so consistent from first to last that one can hardly avoid the conclusion that, far from realizing "quite suddenly" in midstream that he did not approve of what Lancelot and Guinevere were doing, Malory had instead from the beginning taken pains to adapt as far as he was able this aspect of the French chivalric code to his own preconceived notions of the Arthurian characters and drama.

Courtly love as it appears in Malory's French sources reveals the basic paradox which underlies the system in all the works in which it appears. Love, on the one hand, is the source of the best features of the chivalric code. Properly and devoutly followed, the service of the beloved prompts a man to reveal in action the noblest feelings possible to him; he is required to demonstrate the sincerity and depth of his love by displays of unusual courtesy, generosity, and bravery. Love, says Andreas Capellanus, is "omnium fons et origo honorum." Yet courtly love is by definition immoral and adulterous, and it was vigourously condemned as such by the Church. It might even be conjectured that to the unknown thirteenth-century French writers of the Vulgate Cycle and the romances, *l'amour courtois* existed not only as a paradox, a literary ambivalence, but as a fundamental dilemma of life, necessitating as it did a choice between Venus and Christ. Thus Chaucer in the *Troilus and Criseyde* must recant, and even Andreas feels the necessity of making apologies for the laws he has set down.

Malory could hardly fail to be aware of the paradoxical nature of courtly love as he found it in his sources, and it seems to me that instead of ignoring or distorting or even merely reducing the courtly love material he found there, he instead set out to exploit the paradoxical nature of courtly love in order to define and emphasize one of the chief failures of Arthur's court. For Malory was not confused and troubled as were his predecessors; to Malory, the adulterous courtly love of his sources was an evil, and he sets out in the *Morte Darthur* to show how this tragic confusion of earlier times contributes to the destruction of the Round Table civilization. Thus Malory consistently reduces those sections of his sources which extravagantly glorify courtly love lest his reader misconstrue his intent and think him in agreement with the attitudes of the French writers; yet he is careful to preserve the core of such passages in order to demonstrate the tragic effect of courtly love upon his characters. As we shall see, Malory is able by such tactics to focus clearly upon the paradoxical nature of courtly love and thus to sharpen its tragic effect.

Seen from this point of view, one of the great causes of the downfall of Arthur's court is a failure in love, or rather a triumph of the wrong kind of love. The tragic consequences of the Lancelot-Guinevere affair are best seen as resulting from a struggle between the adulterous courtly love of the last days of the court and the fresh, chivalric love of its youth. The passage best illustrating the conflict between courtly and chivalric love occurs late in the *Morte*

Darthur and is clearly Malory's own. After describing the coming of May to Camelot, Malory says:

> For, lyke as wynter rasure dothe allway arace and deface grene summer, so faryth hit by unstable love in man and woman, for in many persones there ys no stabylité: for we may se all day, for a lytyll blaste of wyntres rasure, anone we shall deface and lay aparte trew love, for lytyll or nowght, that coste muche thynge. Thys ys no wysedome nother no stabylité, but hit ys fyeblenes of nature and grete disworshyp, whomsomever usyth thys.
>
> Therefore, lyke as May moneth flowryth and floryshyth in every mannes gardyne, do in lyke wyse lat every man of worshyp florysh hys herte in thys worlde: firste unto God, and nexte unto the joy of them that he promysed hys feythe unto; for there was never worshypfull man nor worshypfull woman but they loved one bettir than another; and worshyp in armys may never be foyled. But firste reserve the honoure to God, and secundely thy quarrell muste com of thy lady. And such love I calle vertuouse love.

This passage cannot be taken in context as praising the present state of affairs between Lancelot and Guinevere. After all, Malory has just told us that following the Grail quest Lancelot "forgate the promyse and the perfeccion that he made in the queste" and that had he not been "in hys mindis so sette inwardly to the quene as he was in semynge outewarde to God, there had no knyght passed hym in the queste of the Sankgreall." Also Lancelot is twice within a few pages to defend Guinevere's adultery, first on the basis of a technicality (she is accused of having slept with one of her attendant knights; actually she has slept with Lancelot) and then with no justification whatsover—hardly instances of first reserving the honor to God. It is noteworthy too that while immediately following the passage quoted Malory manages a few kind words (only a "lytyll mencion") for Guinevere solely on the basis of her fidelity to Lancelot, he does not attempt to praise Lancelot at all.

Taken in context, the quoted passage seems to me to recapitulate here at a moment of crisis the theme that Malory has been emphasizing throughout the *Morte Darthur* in his treatment of Lancelot and Guinevere. "Vertuouse" love is the way things might have been: its virtues are stability and chastity, and it is perfectly compatible with the chivalric ideals of honor and loyalty and with marriage. Courtly love is the way things have gone: its vices are instability (a term continually applied to Lancelot) and adultery, and it is connected throughout Malory's book with a debased chivalry. To Malory's mind, the "olde love was nat so." The whole story of Lancelot and Guinevere is thus seen by Malory as a gradual debasement of what might have been "vertuouse" love into the adulterous relationship he observed in his sources.

There can be little doubt that Malory's presentation of the early history of the lovers is designed to show precisely this point. Malory is careful in his earliest mentions of Guinevere to forecast and thus emphasize the disastrous effect which her love for Lancelot will have upon the court; to a vague source passage in which Merlin warns Arthur of the harm which the queen's beauty may bring him, Malory adds the specific information that "Lancelot scholde love hir, and sche hym agayne." Malory's first presentation of Lancelot in Book III is done in the same manner; in a passage original with Malory, we first see Lancelot as the man who "loved the quene agayne aboven all other ladyes dayes of his lyff and for hir he dud many dedys of armys and saved her from the fyre thorow his noble chevalry."

Yet Malory, unlike his French sources, does not present the adulterous love of Lancelot and Guinevere as a proven fact. R. M. Lumiansky has already pointed out [in the 1953 *MLN* article "The Relationship of Lancelot and Guenevere in Malory's 'Tale of Lancelot'"] how Malory's changes in Book III, the "Tale of Lancelot," all indicate that at this point in Malory's story, "Lancelot loves the Queen . . . but she has as yet given him no indication that she will grant him her love." Malory is clearly interested in informing his reader at the outset of his book of the tragic effect of the love of Lancelot and Guinevere, presumably in order to focus the reader's attention upon the progressive deterioration of that love. Thus we first see Lancelot in Book III as an aspiring young lover, subduing false knights for Guinevere's sake and denying all false reports that he and Guinevere are engaging in an affair. It is important to note that Lancelot protests vigorously any suggestion that he wishes anything other than to admire the queen from a safe distance. In response to a damsel's statement that "hit is noysed that ye love quene Qwenyvere." Lancelot states at some length his belief that knights errant should neither marry nor involve themselves with paramours. Lumiansky regards Lancelot's statement as a "half-truth," spoken presumably in an attempt to disguise his true feeling toward the queen. I should prefer to think that Lancelot is here perfectly sincere. That he is in love with Guinevere he nowhere denies; he speaks of the queen only to defend her honor and to assert the innocence of his own intentions.

Lancelot would seem to be, in short, the perfect embodiment of young "vertuouse" love, worshipping his lady from afar. Yet that lady is married, and the love which he bears her can lead him only into a courtly relationship, the end of which is adultery. He is thus in reality the young courtly lover, even though he has not as yet been accepted as such by Guinevere, who at this point holds him only "in grete favoure aboven all other knyghtis." Although Lancelot has not as yet entered into adultery with Guinevere, he exhibits even here the distinctive marks of the courtly lover, and in altering his sources to indicate Lancelot's early conformity to the code of *l'amour courtois*, Malory would here seem to be forecasting in yet another way the inevitable downfall of the court. For no matter how high-minded his intentions, Lancelot, like Troilus, has in all innocence embarked upon a path which can lead only to adultery and tragedy.

It is significant that, having presented in Book III a picture of the first innocent symptoms of the deadly malady of love, Malory abandons the Lancelot-Guinevere story in order to present in Book IV, the "Tale of Gareth," quite a different kind of love story. Whether or not Malory had an immediate source for his "Gareth" is here of no importance. What is undeniably of Malory's own invention is the placing of the Gareth story within the total Arthurian framework. Coming as it does between the first, deceptively innocent signs of courtly love in Lancelot and the actual adultery of the "Tale of Tristram," the "Tale of Gareth" sheds light forward and backward.

Malory's "Tale of Gareth" is a story of the type called the *belle inconnu*, the fair unknown, and tells the familiar story of the young knight of noble birth who, having been first assigned menial kitchen duties at Arthur's court, asks to accompany a damsel who has come to the court seeking aid for her mistress who is held in captivity. During a series of encounters with unfriendly knights, the young hero's victories are held in contempt by the damsel who mistakenly thinks him to be of inferior birth. Eventually the damsel comes to recognize his true worth, and the knight marries the lady whom he had set out to rescue.

This oft-repeated story is used by Malory as a commentary upon love and the behavior of lovers, the main purpose of which is to present a natural, untutored affection, very different from the artificial, conventionalized *l'amour courtois*. We may safely pass over in this discussion the verbal encounters between Gareth and the Lady Lynet, the damsel who accompanies him on his adventurous journey, in order to concentrate on his behavior toward the Lady Lyones whom he rescues. His remarks upon first seeing her are instructive: having pronounced her "the fayryst lady that ever [he] lokyd uppon," he says to her captor, the Red Knight, that "she lovyth none of thy felyshyp, and thou to love that lovyth nat the is but grete foly," a common-sense principle utterly opposed to that tenet of courtly love which insists that the true lover press his suit in spite of any rebuffs he might receive. As Vinaver says [in his edition of *The Works of Sir Thomas Malory* (1947)], "no protagonist of a French romance of chivalry could have said this, and it is safe to assume that the maxim is M[alory]'s own."

Nor does the Lady Lyones exhibit the hauteur which generally marks the courtly heroine. During the combat which follows immediately upon the lovers' first glimpse of one another, the Lady Lyones makes Gareth "suche countenaunce that his herete waxed lyght and joly." And later, when Lyones attempts to treat Gareth in the accepted courtly fashion by rebuffing his attempt to enter her castle and by telling him that he "shalt nat have holy [her] love unto the tyme that [he] be called one of the numbir of the worthy knyghtes," she is told by Gareth in most uncourtly fashion that he has "nat deserved that [she] sholde shew [him] this straungenesse" since he has "bought [her] love with parte of the beste bloode within [his] body." It is noteworthy that Lyones immediately drops her courtly manner and assures Gareth that his "grete travayle nother [his] good love shall nat be loste" and that she will love only him until death. True, she does insist in courtly style that he "laboure in worshyp this twelve-monthe" but immediately upon Gareth's departure, she undertakes a plan which results in her seeing him almost immediately. Having learned from Gareth's dwarf his true lineage, Lyones disguises herself "lyke a prynces" and flirts with Gareth when he appears at her brother's castle to reclaim his dwarf. Gareth, however, immediately violates the most sacred of the courtly lover's rules by falling in love with this new girl, the disguised Lyones; he even finds himself thinking "many tymes; 'Jesu, wolde that the lady of this Castell Perelus [Lyones] were so fayre as she is!'" Lyones, upon seeing Gareth's fickleness, promptly forgets her courtly stipulation that he wait a year before approaching her again, reveals her identity, and, in the same interview, arranges to come to Gareth's bed that very night. This is hardly the prescribed conduct for courtly ladies.

Their plans, however, are thwarted by Lynet, who feels that "hir sister dame Lyonesse was a lytyll overhasty that she myght nat abyde hir tyme of maryage..." and so twice interferes to preserve her sister's chastity. The tale ends with the marriage of Gareth and Lyones and with their mutual pledges of fidelity:

> 'For, my lorde Arthure,' seyde dame Lyonesse, 'wete you well he is my fyrste love, and he shall be the laste; and yf ye woll suffir hym to have his wyll and fre choyse, I dare say he woll have me.'

> 'That is trouthe,' seyde sir Gareth, 'and I have nat you and welde you as my wyff, there shall never lady nother jantyllwoman rejoyse me.'

If read in context, Gareth is clearly a commentary on *l'amour courtois* and is so placed as to contrast with the adulterous affairs of Lancelot and Tristan. The "Tale of Gareth" works towards the propositions that the true end of love is marriage, not adultery, that young lovers may in fact be fickle, that wise maids had best not tarry, and that young lovers sometimes need restraining. Gareth is a "vertuous" rather than a "courtly" lover; he occasionally spends a sleepless night or goes without eating, but these actions seem dictated by a quite human passion, "his love was so hoote," rather than by the elegant conventions of the code. The Lady Lyones, like Gareth, is direct and frank; her attempts to test Gareth by courtly standards failing, she wastes no time in arranging for their marriage. By contrasting Lyones' action in rebuking Gareth after he has rescued her with Guinevere's similar act in Chrétien's *Knight of the Cart*, Vinaver demostrates that even here in her most unsympathetic action, Lyones has a "kinder heart" than the usual courtly heroine. The contrast between the two women is surely consciously enforced by Malory in order to emphasize the true nature of the Lancelot-Guinevere relationship.

If the "Tale of Gareth" defines the Lancelot-Guinevere relationship by contrast, then the Tristan section works by comparison and allusion to accomplish the same end. Generally speaking, Malory has drastically reduced the courtly material found in his sources mainly in order to reduce the vast size of the sprawling legend, but partly also in order to change somewhat the nature of the Tristan story. As Thomas Rumble has amply demonstrated [in an unpublished 1955 Tulane University dissertation], Malory's only reason for including the Tristan material at all was to provide a "parallel motif" to the Lancelot-Guinevere relationship "lest the adulterous love of Lancelot and Guinevere be thought an anomaly—a single flaw in an otherwise perfect world...." Yet Malory's sources, whatever they may have been, almost certainly glorified courtly love by romanticizing its tragic consequences. In Béroul, Eilhart, Thomas, Gottfried, and the others, the passion of Tristan and Isode is beyond the lover's control; they are driven by a love which transcends ordinary earthly relationships and reponsiblities. Tristan and Isode in the older books are thus sympathetic figures, caught in a tragedy of fate beyond their control.

Needless to say, such a conception hardly fitted Malory's plan. Thus we find Malory systematically robbing the legend of its courtly glamour and yet at the same time preserving the adulterous actions of the lovers in order to enforce a comparison with Lancelot and Guinevere. Time and again, Malory makes Isode a more attractive, a more

human figure by de-emphasizing her stylized characteristics as a courtly heroine; she falls in love with Tristan quite naturally, not through drinking the potion; she does not in Malory institute the plot against Brangwayne; she wants Palomides spared so that he may be christened; she even invites Tristan to bring Isode Blanchemains to court.

Tristan also is made by Malory somewhat less of a courtly hero and more of an ordinary knight than he is in the older legends. Like Isode, Tristan falls in love long before he drinks the potion; he forgets Isode the Fair and marries Isode Blanchemains; as Vinaver states, "his first concern is chivalry, not Isode."

Changes in other characters reinforce Malory's general change in emphasis: Malory blackens Mark; he appears in the *Morte Darthur* as a cowardly, treacherous villian in order to make the adultery of Tristan and Isode more human, more understandable, and less mystical, though none the less excusable. Palomides and Dinadan retain their roles as critics of the courtly pose, though Malory reduces the length of their speeches.

Malory, in short, attempts to strip the courtly glamor from the Tristan-Isode legend by presenting the story of a young knight and a married queen whose sins are all of their own making and who all too obviously resemble Lancelot and Guinevere. There is a little of the Celtic magic left in Malory's "Tale of Tristan" nor is there meant to be; the lovers are no longer fated to love. Yet the essentials of the courtly system are carefully preserved: the youthful innocence, the secret meetings, the pledges, the adultery, the tragedy.

Malory is careful to enforce the parallels between the situation in Cornwall and that at Camelot. As Lumiansky has pointed out, the sixteen passages in Book V which concern the Lancelot-Guinevere affair all "show the commencement of the adultery and its development to a degree that awareness of it has spread widely...." We watch the progress of Tristan and Isode directly, but we are constantly made aware that the love of Lancelot and Guinevere is following a similar path: Tristan writes to Lancelot, Isode to the Queen, and Mark to the King; Morgan sends the symbolic shield to Arthur and almost succeeds in forcing Guinevere to drink from the magic horn from which Isode could not drink; Tristan's prowess is continually compared to that of Lancelot. Over and over the parallels are enforced. The adultery of Lancelot and Guinevere, like that of Tristan and Isode, is public knowledge by the middle of Book V.

Although Malory is sharply criticized by Vinaver for leaving unfinished the tragedy of Tristan and Isode, there would seem to be a number of reasons for Malory's decision to end their story with the christening of Palomides and the preparation for the Grail quest. Malory almost certainly wished to preserve his general chronology and so wished to begin the Grail quest rather than finish the Tristan story; he may have wished, as Rumble suggests, to postpone any account of the Tristan-Isode tragedy in order to make it a part of the general tragedy of the court. But he may also have wished to suppress the romantic pathos of the last days—the dying Tristan, Isode's frantic attempt to reach him, the false message of the sails—and so avoid any glorification of a passion which he saw only as a destructive force.

There is no need to recount in detail the later history of Lancelot and Guinevere as Malory recounts it in Books VII and VIII. Misunderstandings lead to separations and reunions; the pious vows of the Grail quest are forgotten; the adultery cannot be ignored at court and becomes a formidable weapon in the hands of Mordred. To the very end, however, the courtly code exerts its evil influence. Lancelot is the queen's servant while he lives; "and never dud [he] batayle all only [for] Goddis sake, but for to wynne worship and to cause [him] the better to be beloved, and litill or nought [he] thanked never God of hit." Guinevere becomes more and more demanding, more and more the aging courtly heroine, jealous and nagging:

> 'Sir Launcelot, I se and fele dayly that youre love begynnyth to slake, for ye have no joy to be in my presence, but ever ye ar oute of thys courte, and quarels and maters ye have nowadayes for ladyes, madyns and jantillwomen, [more] than ever ye were wonte to have beforehande.'

She first becomes furious that Lancelot has worn Elayne's sleeve, then later rebukes him for his unkindness to Elayne. She orders him to wear her sleeve at the next tourney, even though she knows it will be recognized. She arbitrarily orders him to spare Melegant's life knowing that Melegant alive will be a constant threat to Lancelot.

Lancelot's reactions to these excessive demands show clearly the dilemma he has been forced into by the courtly system. He is too much a man of the world to think that his conduct is going unnoticed; his genuine religious feelings are outraged by his own actions; yet he must obey Guinevere, not because she is the queen, but because he is her pledged lover. In passages largely original with Malory, Lancelot warns Guinevere of what must be the outcome of their affair. "I love nat to be constrayed to love," he tells her and later, in apparent hopelessness, he adds, "but, madame, ever I muste suffir you, but what sorow that I endure, ye take no forse."

The final degradation of the lovers comes when Lancelot is forced, again by the demands of the code which he willingly adopted many years before, to forsake his honor and defend the guilty queen. His action, the action of a courtly lover, results in the accidental killing of Gareth, the "vertuous" lover, and brings crashing down the whole fabric of the Arthurian civilization.

But Malory does not restrict his comments on courtly love to his main narrative line. There is hardly a quest or a conversation that does not contain a passing allusion to love, allusions which Malory, by means of additions to and changes from his sources, uses to advance his attitude toward courtly love. Among the dozens of such reductions and changes, a few may serve as striking indications of Malory's attitude toward courtly love and toward the adultery which springs from it. Arthur, we remember, is himself born of a liason which just misses being adulterous. Mordred is the product of the adulterous union of Arthur and his half-sister Morgause. By a few subtle changes Malory transforms the love of Blamore and his lady, whom Gawain kills, from a conventional courtly relationship into a genuine devotion.

By remarkable set of changes, Malory transforms the whole complexion of the tale of Pelleas and Ettard. Pelleas no longer appears as a courtly lover willing to suffer endless indignities for the sake of a cruel lady whom he will never win. He is instead a young man in love who suffers "in truste at the laste to wynne hir love." His action in placing his sword across the throats of Ettard and the treacherous Gawain is a promise of vengeance to come, not a sign of courtly forgiveness. Instead of allowing Ettard to marry Pelleas, Malory makes the faithless Ettard die of sorrow and provides Pelleas with the Damsel of the Lake.

Again, in the course of a quarrel between Lamerak and Melegant, Lamerak states in a most uncourtly way that it seems to him a useless matter to fight over the virtues of women since "every man thynkith his owene lady fayryste." And surely Lamerak's courtly complaint of his love for the aged Morgause ("O, thou fayre quene of Orkeney, kynge Lottys wyff and modir unto sir Gawayne and to sir Gaherys, and modir to many other, for thy love I am in grete paynys!" is meant as a parody of *l'amour courtois*. The rivalry of Mark and Tristan for the favors of Segwarides' wife is almost certainly intended as an ironic commentary on a degraded courtly affair.

It is thus possible to see in the *Morte Darthur* an attitude toward and treatment of courtly love by means of which Malory is able to foreshadow and suggest at every turn in his plot the tragic implications of his story. We see in the main narrative line—in the young Lancelot, in Tristan, and, by contrast, in Gareth—and in a great number of incidental references to courtly love and lovers signs of the approaching catastrophe. Malory is able, moreover, to solve the great dilemma of courtly love which had confronted the writers of his sources: he unequivocally condemns courtly love throughout his book by emphasizing its tragic consequences and thereby avoids recantation and paradox. Such changes as Malory makes therefore contribute directly to the tragic theme of the *Morte Darthur* and bear witness to the unity of Malory's vision. (pp. 163-76)

> *Charles Moorman, "Courtly Love in Malory," in ELH, Vol. 27, No. 3, September, 1960, pp. 163-76.*

BARBARA GRAY BARTHOLOMEW (essay date 1963)

[*In the following excerpt, Bartholomew analyzes the thematic function of Gawain in the* Morte Darthur.]

Malory's characterization of Gawain is one of the enigmas of the *Morte D'Arthur*. From Jessie L. Weston to T. H. White, critics have puzzled over Malory's treatment of this colorful figure. In portraying Gawain, Malory uses each of the contradictory chronicle and romance traditions of the "bad Gawain." and the "good Gawain." The result is that in the *Morte D'Arthur* Gawain is good-humored, chivalrous, and loyal on some occasions, and spiteful, wicked, and treacherous on others. In short, Malory's Gawain emerges as a character composed of obvious inconsistencies of virtue and evil. The scholarly attention focused upon this characterization indicates agreement that the role of Gawain is central to an interpretation of the *Morte D'Arthur* as a unified work. Gawain is such a complex figure in the *Morte D'Arthur*, however, that complete understanding of his character and of Malory's purpose is almost impossible. This essay does not attempt comprehensive treatment of Gawain. By pointing out an artistic purpose for the contradictory behavior which Gawain exhibits, it outlines what seems to me to be the thematic function of Gawain in the *Morte D'Arthur*. In my opinion, Malory creates Gawain as an inconsistent character in order that the knight may (1) serve as a focal figure, representing a typified image of the Round Table knights and thus (2) provide basis for Malory's judgment upon the failure of the ideal, specifically as it is brought to life in the society of the Round Table. (p. 262)

In many respects, Gawain appears as a sort of embodiment of the Round Table and, by extension, of humanity. He is a part of Arthur's noble fellowship of knights at every significant point in its history, and he reflects the qualities of good and bad which prove the Round Table's strength and its downfall. Since fully a hundred and fifty knights compose the Round Table, the creation of one knight who typifies the company seems almost a necessity. Such a figure functions as a focal character: he gives a measure of direction to any consideration of the great mass of knightly episodes, and he provides a dramatic representation of Malory's major theme.

It seems quite significant that Malory should make Gawain, who is most good and most evil, the only knight who, like Arthur, is associated with the Round Table from the time it is set up in Arthur's kingdom until the time of its destruction. Gawain is made knight and seated at the Round Table on the occasion of Arthur's wedding, when the Round Table is given Arthur as dowry. The myriad adventures which are to proceed from the Round Table fellowship begin with Gawain's quest for the "whyght herte." Also, Gawain strikes the first overt though unintentional blow at the Round Table when he is the first who vows to follow a quest for the Sankgreall. Through his vow for vengeance in the slaying of Gareth and Gaheris, the noble fellowship is shattered. And his death, as will be discussed later, marks the end of Arthur's "Table Rounde."

Equally significant is the fact that Malory never quite grants Gawain the status of a principal actor. Thus, Gawain's role as an almost-major character meshes with Malory's presentation of him as a sort of microcosm of the Round Table. Several scholars have aptly noted Malory's de-emphasizing Gawain's role in order to build up Lancelot. This subordination of Gawain to Lancelot serves to identify Gawain more closely with his fellows. Throughout the *Morte D'Arthur*, as Malory weakens the link connecting Gawain with the principal actors, he strengthens the link which binds Gawain to his fellow knights of the Round Table. His method appears in the frequency with which Malory emphasizes Gawain not in individual exploits but as a member of a group. On his first quest he is one member of a trio, and the individual honor—or dishonor—of his first adventure is tempered by the chiding presence of Gaheris. The *Noble Tale of Arthur and Lucius*, where Malory's aggrandizement of Lancelot takes definite shape, may serve as an overall example. Here Gawain is as consistently linked with the other knights as he is with the principals Arthur and Lancelot. He is not emphasized enough to usurp attention from the principals, but he is endowed with stature enough above the other knights to make his actions stand out as the type of theirs. Thus, the deeds of all Arthur's forces are memorable through the actions of Gawain. When Malory builds up Lancelot, he effects a change not only in Gawain's importance but also in his status. Lancelot is lauded on an indi-

vidual level, but Gawain is praised for his activities as part of a team. For instance, he and Bors are ambassadors; he and Idres are rescuers; and he and "many mo knightes of the Round Table that here be not rehersid" are valiant warriors. Malory grants Gawain one extended individual adventure in this tale in his encounter with Priamus, but even this episode functions as a magnified type of what is happening for the entire Round Table force. When Gawain fights the Saracen, the Round Table warriors are beset also: "Thy pryse men ar sore begone and put undir, for they are oversette with Sarazens mo than five hondred." And when Gawain's opponent switches his loyalty to Arthur, all the other Saracens follow suit.

Malory continues this treatment of Gawain in the *Gareth* section, where Gawain is not so much an individual champion of the kitchen boy "Bewmaynes" as he is a member of a small and thoughtful group. "And so ded sir Gawayne," adds Malory at least twice after speaking of Lancelot's kindnesses to Gareth. In this section, and indeed throughout the work, "... and Gawayne" occurs with startling frequency, linking him as the second half of a pair or as one unit of a longer catalogue. In general, Malory's policy appears to be to couple Gawain with less individualized knights in order to emphasize his bond with them. Gawain stands at their head in importance, but Malory's refrain in assigning him rank time after time is "Gawayne and the others."

Since he creates Gawain as typifying the Round Table knights, perhaps Malory does not resolve the inconsistencies of the two traditions entangling the character of Gawain because he does not need to resolve them. Indeed, he makes effective use of the inconsistency. The most striking single feature of Malory's Gawain is that he is a character of extremes. As [B. J. Whiting indicates in his discussion of Gawain's "epic degeneration" in the 1947 *Mediaeval Studies* article "Gawain: His Reputation, His Courtesy, and His Appearance in Chaucer's *Squire's Tale*"], Malory heightens the extremes by sharply juxtaposing them. Thus Malory turns the disadvantage of inconsistency in traditional treatment to an advantage. Gawain's inconsistency is the inconsistency of humanity, specifically, the humanity who comprise Arthur's noble company, magnified even as the Round Table is larger-than-life. Malory need not emphasize the average and the usual in Gawain's character. Gawain is accorded highest praise and sharpest blame because he combines the best and the worst to be found among Arthur's knights. In him are focused the qualities which propel the Round Table to greatness and the qualities which plummet it to its ruin.

For Arthur, the Round Table is the fulfillment of his dream of an ideal society, grounded in loyalty, honor, nobility, and truth. Gawain shows that ideal in operation. A foreshadowing that the ideal must fail appears at his very admittance to the knightly company. Gawain joins the Round Table with a chip on his shoulder. After Torre is knighted ahead of Gawain and after Pellinor is honored by Merlin in the seating, "Thereat had sir Gawayne grete envy and tolde Gaherys hys brother, 'Yondir knyght ys putte to grete worship, which grevith me sore, for he slew oure fadir kynge Lott. Therefore I woll sle hym,' seyde Gawayne." Concern for a slain father is noble, but "grete envy," no matter how human an emotion, is a mortal sin. True, Gawain's later actions lighten the appearance of his ignoble emotions. He is sympathetic with his unknown brother Gareth; he is an invaluable aid to Arthur's cause in the Roman campaign; he is staunchly loyal to his sworn blood brother Ywain and goes into exile with him; he is gallant and light-hearted in pursuit of adventure, feeling no shame or ill will when defeated by Lancelot or Gareth; he is genuinely interested in helping in the Lancelot-Elaine episode; and he is always fiercely loyal to Arthur. But this behavior, no matter how appealing on human terms, does not elevate Gawain to the level of the ideal. Gawain's evil is as assertive and as pervasive as his good. Malory introduces Gawain's evil nature with characteristic and, in my opinion, intentional abruptness near the end of the *Gareth* section: "for evir aftir sir Gareth had aspyed sir Gawaynes conducions, he wythdrewe hymself fro his brother sir Gawaynes felyship, for he was evir vengeable, and where he hated he wolde he avenged with murther; and that hated sir Gareth."

The evil side of Gawain receives its most pointed expression in the *Tristram* section. In this tale Malory presents Gawain as sometimes good and usually evil, with no middle ground. The character portrayed in this section is obviously inconsistent: Malory does not even attempt to reconcile Gawain's good side with his evil side. It seems to me that in emphasizing inconsistencies, Malory frankly acknowledges the existence of profound evil even within a scheme which is aimed toward the achievement of an ideal. Gawain's character springs from paradoxes of good and evil. On an enlarged scale, the Round Table fellowship of which Gawain is representative manifests the same unrelieved extremes. Critics point to the murder of Lamorak as the ultimate example of Gawain's depravity. There is motivation for the deed besides Gawain's ill will at being defeated in the tournament by Lamorak, since Lamorak has been having "ado" with Gawain's mother Morgawse. Still, Gawain's inciting his relatives to gang murder is discreditable, and his execution of the deed in ambush, as Palomides' account shows, is despicable:

> "sir Gawayne and his three bretherne, sir Aggravayne, sir Gaherys, and sir Modred, sette uppon sir Lamorak in a privy place, and there they slew his horse, and so they faught with hym on foote more than three owrys bothe byfore hym and behynde hym, and so sir Modred gaff hym his dethis wounde behynde hym at his bakke, and al to-hewe hym."

Malory means the deed to be condemned, as comments by Gareth, Tristram, and various other characters demonstrate. By accepting Gawain's blackness here, Malory recognizes that the human soul inclines as strongly toward wickedness as it does toward virtue. Good and evil are contradictory, but they exist together in the individual and in humanity, and hence in the quest for the ideal. In short, Malory accepts the inconsistency as the paradox inherent in the human condition.

In Malory's overall scheme, Galahad and, in a different sense, Lancelot, appear as the ideals in contrast to Gawain, the actual. Lancelot, who, except for his "synne," is "ellys ... more abeler than ony man lyvynge," represents highest human achievement on the secular plane, where Arthur's interest for his Round Table centers. And Galahad, of course, represents spiritual perfection. If the Round Table were composed of knights like Galahad or even Lancelot, Arthur's ideal might continue in reality. But instead it is composed of knights like Gawain, in va-

rying proportions of good and evil. One of Malory's basic points seems the impossibility of such perfection as Lancelot and Galahad exhibit. Even noble humanity is more like Gawain, forged from contradictions and enigmas, than it is like the ideal figures. Bors, blemished by only one spot—but imperfect because of it—is a rarity whom Malory accords frequent praise and high honor (i.e., dying in the Holy Land). The quest for the Grail further illustrates this point. Humanity, when faced with the possibility of achieving perfection, is most likely to behave as Gawain does; in the Grail quest almost the entire Round Table follows his lead. Gawain's vow and the other knights' oaths are deeply felt:

> "I woll make here a vow that to-morne, withoute longer abydynge, I shall laboure in the queste of the Sankgreall, and that I shall holde me oute a twelve-month and a day, or more if nede be, and never shall I returne unto the courte agayne tylle I have sene hit more opynly than hit hath bene shewed here. And iff I may nat spede I shall returne agayne as he that may nat be ayenst the wylle of God."

> So whan they of the Table Rounde harde sir Gawayne sey so, they arose up the moste party and made such avowes as sir Gawayne hathe made.

But the sincerity is sudden and, for the most part, short-lived, and the oaths include an all-too-human escape clause. Gawain, like the mass of knights, is zealous in his pursuit of the Grail until he becomes aware that this quest is beyond his achievement because it differs from his usual blood-and-thunder adventures not in degree but in kind. Ultimately he, like the other knights not characterized on the individual level, admits failure and returns without regret to Arthur's court. Thus Malory realistically pictures the human factor, whose bent toward expediency hinders the ideal.

On the whole, Malory's judgment on the ideal as expressed in the Round Table is neither harsh nor pessimistic. Malory does not condemn Gawain for his humanity, even when he pictures Gawain in his most grievous wrong. Malory's tolerance appears in his treatment of Gawain's vow for vengeance at the slaying of his brothers. Malory gives clear foreshadowing of Gawain as a knight with strong family loyalty, a trait which, in itself, Malory decidedly approves. He is aware, however, that emotions noble in themselves can be completely misdirected. Thus, Gawain's almost insane taunts to Lancelot during the siege of Benwick lend his degeneration a depth of wickedness and despair unsounded throughout the entire *Tristram* section. Malory portrays his acceptance of Gawain's representative humanity, both good and evil, in the reactions of Arthur and Lancelot on the occasion of Gawain's death. Here Gawain is associated with the Round Table for the last time. At the beginning of the Grail quest, Arthur says of his group of knights that "I have loved them as well as my lyff. Wherefore hit shall greve my ryght sore, the departicion of thys felyship.... And therewith the teerys felle in his yen." When Arthur discovers Gawain dying, he makes "greate sorow oute of mesure," takes Gawain in his arms, swoons thrice, and calls him

> "the man in the worlde that I loved moste. And now ys my joy gone! For now, my nevew, sir Gawayne, I woll discover me unto you, tha[t] in youre person and in sir Launcelot I moste had my joye and myne affyaunce.

> And now I have loste my joy of you bothe, wherefore
> all myne erthely joy ys gone fro me!"

In this intense outcry Arthur mourns for more than a kinsman. In the death of Gawain, Arthur sees the death of the
Round Table, his "erthely joy," the end of the noble fellowship to which the king has given his life. Lancelot's reaction to Gawain's death is also significant. His grief at
Arthur's passing is deep though restrained. His sorrow at
the death of Gawain is vehement and prolonged. When he
lies "two nyghtes uppon hys [Gawain's] tumbe, in prayers
and in dolefull wepyng," Lancelot is bidding farewell not
only to Gawain but to a way of life. His grief is for the end
of the life set up by Arthur for his Round Table and represented by Gawain not only in the observance but in the
breach, a noble and stately code which has died as surely
as has Gawain.

Perhaps the key to Gawain as representing Malory's verdict on the ideal is that Gawain is redeemed in death. Attempts like Arthur's to achieve even a non-spiritual ideal
must fail because they are executed by fallible human beings so filled with contradictory good and wickedness that
the ideal is lost in the vagaries of the pursuit. But Gawain's salvation indicates that fulfillment is not necessary.
On the whole, Malory's verdict on the inevitable failure of
an idealistic effort does not condemn but supports idealism. This fact appears in the contrast betwen Malory's
warm and sympathetic regard for Arthur, whose is the
dream, and his hard-bitten treatment of Gawain, whose is
the necessary human failure of that dream. Thus, in Gawain, Malory creates a bold juxtaposition of Cardinal Virtue and Deadly Sin in order to present Gawain as typical
of the best and the worst in the Round Table fellowship,
typical of the human instruments through whom Arthur's
scheme of the ideal must succeed or fail. (pp. 263-67)

> Barbara Gray Bartholomew, "The Thematic
> Function of Malory's Gawain," in College En-
> glish, Vol. 24, No. 4, January, 1963, pp. 262-67.

C. S. LEWIS (essay date 1963)

[*Lewis is considered one of the foremost twentieth-century
authors to write on Christian and mythopoeic themes. Indebted principally to George MacDonald, G. K. Chesterton,
Charles Williams, and the writers of ancient Norse myths,
he is regarded as a formidable logician and Christian polemicist, a perceptive literary critic, and—perhaps most
highly—as a writer of fantasy literature. Also a noted academic and scholar, Lewis held posts at Oxford and Cambridge, where he was a respected authority on medieval and
Renaissance literature. Lewis was a traditionalist in his approach to life and art. He opposed the modern critical movement toward biographical and psychological interpretation,
preferring to practice and propound a theory of criticism
that stresses the author's intent rather than the reader's presuppositions and prejudices. In the following excerpt, he investigates what he considers five key "paradoxes" concerning
Malory's intentions in the* Morte Darthur. *For a response to
Lewis's essay, see the following excerpt by E. Vinaver.*]

I begin by considering certain paradoxes which have been
thrown up by the remarkable discoveries made in the last
fifty years about Malory and the book (or books) which he
translated with modifications, from the French and which
Caxton printed in 1485. They are five in number.

I. The work has long passed for a mirror of honour and
virtue; the author appears to have been little better than
a criminal.

II. The work strikes every reader as a rich feast of marvels,
a tale 'of faerie damsels met in forest wide'; but a comparison of it with its sources seems to show Malory almost
everywhere labouring to eliminate the marvellous and introduce the humdrum.

III. The work seems to many of us the typical specimen
(because it is the first specimen we met) of Interwoven or
Polyphonic narrative. But once again, comparison with
the sources shows everything proceeding as if Malory de-
tested this technique and did his best to pluck the threads
apart.

IV. Its handling of the Grail story sounds deeply religious,
and we have the sense that it is somehow profoundly connected with the final tragedy. But a case can be made out
for the view that Malory evaded the religious significance
and ignored or severed the connexion.

V. Malory seemed to Saintsbury (and doubtless to many)
the man who alone "makes of this vast assemblage of stories one story and one book". The evidence of the Winchester MS. convinces Professor Vinaver that he really
wrote several works which were never intended to form a
whole.

If all these Paradoxes stand, they build up into a single
grand Paradox. It is not of course paradoxical that a man's
work should be other than he intended. What is paradoxical is that a man's work should succeed by its failure to realize every single intention he had when he made it. For
it is as a mirror of honour, as a feast of marvels, as a Polyphonic narrative, as a romance of chivalry haunted by the
higher mystery of the Grail, and as (in some sort) a unity,
that the **Morte Darthur** has pleased. And not only pleased,
but so far outstripped its rivals that it alone of all medieval prose romances has survived as a living book into our
own century. In Malory's case, apparently, nothing succeeds like failure.

The reader should be warned at once that I am not attempting a *reductio ad absurdum*. I am not sure whether
all the Paradoxes, in their sharpest form, will stand; but
neither am I sure that all of them will completely fall. It
therefore may be true that something like this paradoxical
'success by failure' has actually happened. If it has, then
I want to draw a conclusion from it. But that will come
later; in the meantime I will proceed to examine the five
Paradoxes one by one.

I. The apparent discrepancy between the man and the
work has seemed to some so formidable that they seek refuge in the possibility that the wicked Malory of the records is not our author but another man of the same
name. But this is rather a desperate expedient. By all
sound methodological principles a Malory whose Christian name was Thomas, who was a knight, who lived at
the right time, and who was sometimes (like our Malory)
in prison, must be assumed to be the author until any evidence to the contrary turns up. A far more respectable alternative is Professor Vinaver's view [presented in his edition of *The Works of Sir Thomas Malory* (1947)] that the
discrepancy is an illusion because the book (or books) are

not in fact noble; the common belief in their 'morality' is based mainly on Caxton's preface.

Yet I cannot quite accept this. It must of course be admitted that there are in the text untransmuted lumps of barbarism, like Arthur's massacre of the children. And even when we discount these, no one can claim (or should demand) that the general tone conforms to the standards either of the New Testament or of modern, peace-time respectability. But I find in it, sometimes implicit, sometimes explicit, an unforced reverence not only for courage (that of course) but for mercy, humility, graciousness, and good faith. The best way to see it is to compare Malory's heroes, the characters he obviously admired, with those of Homer, Virgil, Renaissance drama, or even our ealier novelists. I cannot conceive that even the best of them—even Hector, Pallas, Othello, or Tom Jones—could ever have been made to understand why Lancelot wept like a beaten child after he had healed Sir Urry. A character from Corneille might understand the scene when Gawain, unhorsed, bids Marhaus to dismount, 'or else I will slay thy horse', and Marhaus, instantly obeying, replies, 'Grammercy, of your gentleness ye teach me courtesy'; I doubt if he could equally have understood Lancelot's unrenspousive endurance of Gawain's challenges. I cannot deny either 'morality' (it is not a word I love) or something better to the imagination that shows us Lancelot refusing to take Gareth's victory from him at the tournament, or Pelleas laying his sword across the throats of Gawain and Ettard, or all Lancelot's contrition in Book XV, or the last message of Galahad, now almost a blessed spirit, to his father, or the final lament of Ector. In such passages, and indeed almost everywhere, we meet something which I chiefly hesitate to call 'morality' because it is so little like a code of rules. It is rather the civilization of the heart (by no means of the head), a fineness and sensitivity, a voluntary rejection of all the uglier and more vulgar impulses. We can describe it only in words derived from its own age, words which will now perhaps be mocked, such as *courtesy, gentleness, chivalry.* It makes the *Morte* a 'noble' as well as a 'joyous' history. I at any rate will never blacken the book to make it match the man.

But was the man so black? At first sight it would seem hard to deny, for he was convicted of cattle-lifting, poaching, extortion, sacrilegious robbery, attempted murder, and rape. The record suggests to Professor Vinaver a man who at the age of forty 'from being a peaceable and presumably well-to-do citizen . . . became a law-breaker'. And if we apply certain habitual conceptions of our own to Malory's record, this result seems inevitable. But are these conceptions possibly too local and modern? 'Citizen', 'law-breaker', and (why has that come in?) 'well-to-do'. I suspect that a man of Malory's class and time would not much have relished the titles 'peaceable' or 'citizen'; and the real question about his actions probably was for him, and should be for us, not whether they broke the law but whether they were cowardly, discourteous, treacherous, and (in a word) unknightly. It is not clear that they need have been. Our record of them comes from lawyers. In that age evidence was not scientifically sifted and accusers laid it on thick. In every county civil war exploited, and was exploited by, local feuds. Legal proceedings, whether civil or criminal, were often primarily moves in family quarrels. We need not assume that he did all the things he was accused of. But even if he did, he need not have been,

by all standards, a villain. Cattle-lifting was a gentlemanly crime. If he killed other men's deer, so did the Douglas at Otterburn. A knightly ambush and encounter could be attempted murder. Rape need mean no more than abduction; from the legal point of view Lancelot committed rape when he saved Guinevere from the fire. If Malory, loving Joan Smyth *par amours*, and knowing her cuckoldy knave of a husband to be little better than a King Mark, carried her off behind him at 'a great wallop' and perhaps thus saved her from a broken head and two black eyes at home, he may have done what a good knight and a true lover ('of a sinful man') should. That he often fell below the highest standards of chivalry, we may well believe; we need not believe that he fell flagrantly below them. He might, on the evidence, have been as good a knight as Tristram; for what should we think of Tristram himself if our knowledge of him were derived only from King Mark's solicitors?

Of course this picture is conjectural; but it is equally conjecture to represent him, on the strength of the records, as the sort of man who in our days becomes a 'criminal'. We don't know what he was really like, and I suppose we never shall.

II. This Paradox, like the next two, of course involves the assumption that differences between Malory's text and the extant MSS. of his originals are due to Malory. I think this is very probably so. I agree with Professor Vinaver that it is monstrous to set out by assuming that Malory had no spark of originality and therefore to trace everything in which he differs from those MSS. to a hypothetical, lost, intermediary. But probability is not certainty. We cannot be absolutely sure that any given passage, peculiar to Malory, or even any given omission, was his own. Everything I say about Paradoxes II, III, and IV must be understood with this *caveat.*

There are fewer marvels in Malory than in the corresponding French romances. There are, to be sure, at least two places where he introduces a marvel which they lack. But one of these seems to me to be almost certainly the (not unhappy) result of a graphic error. In *C* XVII. 19 the *sword* 'arose great and marvellous and was full of great heat that many men fell for dread'. In the French it was a wind (*ung vent*) that so arose. I suppose that either Malory or the scribe of the French MS. he was using, having the sword in his head from the preceding passage, wrote it here, intending to write *wind.* The other is in *C* IV. 6, where a sudden, presumably miraculous light of torches in Malory replaces the French text's ordinary arrival of torches carried by ladies. But this, or both these, amount to nothing against the opposite instances. No one disputes that Malory's text naturalizes, negatively, by the omission of wonders, and positively, by introducing practical, mundane details. When Arthur defeats Damas he makes proper legal arrangements for the righting of the wrongs Damas has done: 'I will that ye give unto your brother all the whole manor with the appurtenance, under this form, that Sir Ontzlake hold the manor of you, and yearly to give you a palfrey'. Similarly (in *C* VII. 35) the defeated knights swear homage and fealty to Gareth 'to hold of him for evermore'. King Anguysh sending Marhaus to Cornwall, assures him that his expenses will be amply covered. When Tristram bleeds over the lady's bed in *C* VIII. 14, we are told the extent of damage almost as if Malory had made up the laundry list—'both the over-sheet and the nether-sheet and the pillows and the head-sheet'. Mordred explains at length, and very sensibly, why young knights are at a disadvantage on horseback. Lancelot's habit of talking in his sleep is noted. Best of all, we are told exactly how much it had cost the Queen (£20,000) to send out knights in search of him.

The Paradox here is not very strong, for it turns on the contrast between Malory's supposed intentions and the known effect of his work. For, clearly, even if we know what he did, we can only guess what he intended. It is possible to imagine a burly, commonsensible man who was always trying to turn the faerie world of the romances into something much more earthy and realistic. Accepting that picture, we may smile at the 'success by failure', the happy frustration of his vain labour which has made his book for centuries the chief delight of all who love 'the fairy way of writing'. But a quite different picture is equally possible. If you write fairy-tales and receive letters from your child readers, you will find that children are always asking the sort of questions that Malory is always answering. A simple and serious delight in marvellous narrative most emphatically does not involve any indifference to mundane details. The more seriously you take the story the more you want to tie everything up and to know how people got from one place to another, and what they had to eat, and how all outstanding issues were settled. Neglect of these points, whether in writer or reader, means that the whole thing is merely conventional or playful. Multiplication of marvels goes with the same attitude. Those who love them, as alone they can be loved, for their suggestiveness, their quality, will not increase their number. Two enchanters, two ghosts, two ferlies are always half as impressive as one. Every supposedly naturalistic change that Malory made in the story might proceed from a far fuller belief and a more profound delight in it than the French authors had ever known. He would not be the less English for that.

Once more, I ask no one to choose between these two pictures. Either, as it seems to me, will fit the facts. We shall never know which is true.

III. The excellent remarks of Professor Vinaver on what I have called Interwoven or Polyphonic narrative will have made it clear to all readers that this is a real technique, not, as an earlier generation supposed, a mere muddle or an accidental by-product of conflation. It is a technique not peculiar to medieval prose romance. We find it fully developed over long stretches of Ovid's *Metamorphoses*. The rudiments of it are there in parts of *Beowulf*. The epic poets of Italy took it over from the romance, and Spenser took it over from them. Sidney re-wrote the *Arcadia* to make it more polyphonic. Milton seems to have toyed with the idea of using it for a great epic; he certainly acknowledged that to depart from Aristotelian unity in a narrative might be an enriching of art.

Quite clearly the method continued to be used for centuries, not in blind obedience to tradition but because it gave pleasure. Dante selected this feature of chivalrous romance for special praise: *Arturi regis ambages pulcerrime*. Tasso confesses that all knights and ladies prefer it; everyone reads Ariosto, and no one reads Trissino. He even records how his father discovered by sad experience that 'unity of action gave little pleasure' The vogue of the Polyphonic in fact lasted longer than that of the modern novelistic technique has yet done. It would be interesting to analyse, and perhaps not difficult to account for, the pleasure it gave. But that would be too long a digression. What matters for the moment is that it did please and can please still. To the present day no one enjoys Malory's book who does not enjoy its *ambages*, its interweaving.

For it is certainly interwoven. Arthur has a war against five kings. To repair his losses he must make new knights. His selection sends Bagdemagus, malcontent, from the court, and the story of his wanderings crosses the latter end of Merlin's story. Arthur meanwhile has got involved in the affairs of Damas and Ontzlake, which in their turn involve both him and Accolon in the machinations of Morgan, which lead to the banishment of her son Uwain, which leads to his joint errantry with Gawain, which brings them both (now in company with Marhaus) to those three damsels at the river-head who fork the story into three ... and so on. Those who dislike this sort of thing will not much like Malory.

Yet it may be, as Professor Vinaver concludes, that Malory 'strongly disliked' it himself. Certainly the evidence that he constantly simplified is irresistible. Whether he wanted to simplify still further and get rid of the Polyphonic altogether, or whether he wanted to go just as far as he has gone and liked the degree of Polyphony which survives under his treatment, we do not know. If he wanted to get rid of it altogether, he has undoubtedly failed. To anyone who comes to his work fresh from modern literature its Polyphonic character will be at first one of the most noticeable things about it. And the work will be liked, where it is liked, not despite of this peculiarity but (in part) because of it.

IV. This Paradox involves us in two subjects: Malory's treatment of the holy quest, and the connexion, if any, between it and other matters in his text.

Professor Vinaver's view on the first subject depends on the interpretation of a great many different passages. I shall refer to them both by the Book and Chapter of Caxton's edition and by the page and line of the Professor's (which I indicate by the letter *W*). They fall into four classes.

1. A passage held to indicate Malory's 'confidence in the unfailing merits of Arthurian chivalry' (*W* 1524). This is *C* XVI. 3 (*W* 946.18) where a Hermit in the French text condemns the Round Table for *luxure* and *orgueil*; but in Malory, for 'sin and wickedness'. I cannot myself see that the substitution of the general for the particular makes the condemnation less severe.

2. Passages where Malory substitutes the worldly for the religious. Thus in *C* XVI. 3 (*W* 945.10) the dying Uwain in the French asks that prayer be made for his soul; in Malory he asks to be remembered to Arthur and the court, 'and for old brotherhood, think on me'. (This phrase itself might imply a request for prayers, but I would not press that.) Again, in *C* XVI. 6 (*W* 955.9) Bors, surprisingly, and without authority from the French, says that he who achieves the Grail will win 'much earthly worship'. Both these, and especially the latter, are strong evidence for Professor Vinaver's view: if it is felt that they are sufficient to colour the whole narrative, then that view will be unassailable. Two other passages which might be quoted here seem to me, on the other hand, to rank as 'worldly'

only if we adopt standards of worldliness which are almost intolerably severe. In *C* XIII. 19 (*W* 896.11) Malory allows the contrite Lancelot to be 'somewhat comforted' when day breaks and he hears the birds sing. In the French (which is finely imagined) the morning and the birds directly produce the conviction of God's anger, which in Malory comes home to Lancelot only when he realizes that he has lost his horse and his armour. This is certainly very practical, homely, English, and (in a word) Malorian; but it does not for me empty the scene of all religious significance. Again in *C* XVII. 13 (*W* 1011.31-1012.1) Malory's Lancelot (not his French equivalent) after a month of fasting on board ship with no one but a dead lady for company, 'was somewhat weary of the ship' and went ashore 'to play him'. (Middle English *play* in such a context is of course a very mild world; we should have said 'to stretch his legs' or 'to relax'.) Now I think a man might have done that and yet be a very good sort of penitent on the whole. Both passages, indeed, are for me specimens of that Malorian realism which brings the story to life; they make Lancelot, not a stained-glass figure, but a real man, though a contrite one. It is proper, however, to point out that the difference between Professor Vinaver and myself may be simply the same difference there was between the French originals and Malory, the difference between the hard lines and rigid schematization of Latin thought, and the softening, compromising temper of us islanders. (For some say our best Christians are all Pelagians, and our best atheists all Puritans, at heart.)

3. The third class is, for me, the hardest to feel sure about. In *C* XIII. 14 (*W* 886.18) the qualification for success in the holy quest is, in the French, *chevaillierie celestiale*; in the English, 'virtuous living'. In *C* XIII. 16 (*W* 891.32) it is again, for Malory, 'knightly deeds and virtuous living'; for the French author it is service to the Creator, defence of Holy Church, and the offering to Christ of the treasure (one's soul) which has been entrusted to one. In *C* XVI. 6 (*W* 956.2) Bors is praised in the French for his 'religious', in Malory for his 'stable', life. In *C* XVI. 13 (*W* 968.11) Lionel is condemned by the French author because *n'a an soi nule vertu de Nostre Seignor qui en estant le tiegne*; by Malory, because 'he is a murderer and doth contrary to the order of knighthood'. These are I think the strongest specimens. That in *C* XV. 5 (*W* 931.25) seems to me weak. It is true that the motive which Malory gives Lancelot for joining in a certain fray is, as Professor Vinaver claims, incongruous with the Quest; but then Malory is fully aware of this and in the very next chapter (*C* XV. 6; *W* 933.32-934.4) makes his recluse tell Lancelot that such 'bobaunce and pride of the world' must be abandoned. The insertion of both these passages by Malory would seem to emphasize the very point which, it is claimed, he was ignoring. We might perhaps add *C* XVI. 17 (*W* 974.15-17) where the edifying mutual forgiveness of Bors and his brother is also peculiar to Malory.

But the earlier passages remain, and I will not for a moment dispute that they all indicate an important change made by Malory and affecting his version throughout. The question is how we are to define it. At first sight I am tempted to say that where the originals used specifically religious, Malory uses ethical, concepts: *virtuous* for *celestial, knightly* and *virtuous* for the offering of the heart to Christ, *stable* for *religious*. This certainly means that the choice before Malory's knights is not that between 'reli-

gion' in the technical sense and active life in the world. They are to go on being knights (*C* XIII. 20; *W* 899.1-5); just as the soldiers who came to the Baptist were told to go on being soldiers. Malory in fact holds the same view as Langland and Gower and many other English medieval moralists. No man need leave the Order to which he has been called, but every man must begin really to fulfil the functions for which that Order exists. The recall is not from knighthood to the cloister, but from knighthood as it has come to be (full of 'sin and wickedness') to knighthood as it was intended to be, grounded in 'patience and humility' (*C* XVI. 3; *W* 945-7). Admittedly, then, the story is ethical, as against mystical. But we must not say 'ethical, as against religious', for the ethical claim and the attempted ethical response, when prompted by a vision, purged by confession and penance, supported and corrected at every turn by voices, miracles, and spiritual counsels, is precisely the religious as it most commonly appears in secular vocations. And *stability* (perseverance to the end, or consistency) is of course essential.

4. Finally, we have those passages which exalt the supremacy of Lancelot over all other knights. There may be some difference of opinion as to which we should include in this class. I certainly would not include *C* XVII. 22 (*W* 1035.11-12) where Galahad, almost at the threshold of Heaven, sends to his father a message bidding him 'remember of this unstable world'. The words are full of knightly courtesy, filial duty, and Christian charity, but of course they are a warning and (by delicatest implication) a reproof. It is Galahad whom they exalt. Nor do I find much 'rehabilitation' of Lancelot in Malory's insertion at the end of *C* XVII. 23 (*W* 1036.19-1037.7). Lancelot does not relate the adventures of the Grail *simpliciter*, but those 'that he had seen'. Bors had seen, and Bors told, what Lancelot had not seen. One would expect the surviving knights each to contribute to the report which Arthur naturally demanded. And the passage repeats Galahad's message, with its grave implication. Another doubtful place is *C* XVI. 1 (*W* 941.20-22). Here Gawain says that 'if one thing were not' (surely beyond all doubt the 'one thing' is his adultery?) Lancelot would be matchless. But as things are, far from rising (for purposes of this Quest) to the level of Galahad, Perceval, and Bors, Lancelot 'is as we be', is just like the rest of us, *nous autres*, Ectors and Gawains—'but if he take the more pain on him'. I cannot imagine a better way of making us feel how Lancelot has sunk than thus to let us hear lesser men exclaiming that at last he's no better than they.

The passages on which the Vinaverian view must finally rest are those where Malory deliberately inserts the praise of Lancelot. A damsel in *C* XIII. 5 (*W* 863.30), a hermit in *C* XV. 4 (*W* 930.14), and a second hermit in *C* XV. 4 (*W* 930-14), and a second hermit in *C* XVI. 5 (*W* 948.27-8) all remind us that Lancelot was the best knight, for a sinful man, that ever lived. The reservation is of course important; but in spite of it, I am prepared to admit that all these passages may be meant to blunt for us the edge of the abasement which Lancelot undergoes in the French text. But it also seems to me equally possible that they were intended to have—and for me they have—a very different effect. It is a question of what may be called the logic of the imagination. If one wanted to exhibit in a novel the theme that intellectual achievements were no passport to heaven, one would not choose for one's protagonist some mediocrity who has 'got a good second'. Only a fool would labour to show the failure, on the highest level, of pretensions which were doubtfully adequate even on their own. Obviously one would build one's protagonist up to the stature of a Porson, a Sherrington, or a Mahaffy. If you want to show that one sort of achievement is inferior to, even incommensurable with, another, then of course the more splendid (in its own kind) your specimen is, the more impressive its failure (in another kind) will be. Every word said in praise of Lancelot as a good knight 'of a sinful man'—as the bravest, most courteous, most faithful in his love, but not seriously hitherto attempting that perfection of chastity and all other virtues which the Christian law demands of the knight, in his own fashion, no less than of the contemplative—serves all the more to drive home the moral of the whole story, makes it all the clearer that with the Quest we have entered a region where even what is best and greatest by the common standards of the world 'falls into abatement and low price'.

But, as before, I end in uncertainty. I am sure that Malory's handling has not on me the effect, and therefore need not have been meant to have the effect, which Professor Vinaver supposes. I know it has the opposite effect on me. I cannot rule out the possibility that it was intended to have this opposite effect. I do not claim to know that it was.

So much for his treatment of the Quest. As regards its relation to other parts of his work, I feel a little more confident. I appears to me to be unmistakably linked with the *Morte*. Before the Quest begins, before Galahad is begotten, when the Grail first appears before Lancelot in the house of Pelles, Malory inserts the prophecy that 'when this rich thing goeth about, the Round Table shall be broken for a season'. (*C* XI. 2; *W* 793.32-36). I do not know what to make of 'for a season', and how right (as often) Caxton was to omit it! But it is Malory who had introduced, even if Caxton perfected, the note of doom: the dreadful hint that the best is fatal to the good. Then in the Quest itself (*C* XIII. 20; *W* 897.27-28) Lancelot promises 'by the faith of his body' never to come in Guinevere's 'fellowship' again if he can avoid it. Then, when the Quest is over, almost immediately, Lancelot 'forgat the promise and the perfection that he made in the Quest'. This is in the French; but as if this were not enough Malory must add that this was the inadequately repented 'bosom-sin' which had led him to fail in that attempt (*C* XVIII. 1; *W* 1045.12-16). Notice too that in thus forgetting his promise Lancelot is verifying the diagnosis ('not stable, but . . . likely to turn again') made upon him by the hermit in *C* XVI 5.—a passage, so far as we know, of Malory's own making. The connexion here, if unintended, is singularly fortunate. But Malory still feels he has not done enough. Returning to *C* XVIII. I, we find a dialogue between Lancelot and Guinivere inserted (*W* 1045.30-1048.14) in which he almost begs the terrible woman to release him, pleading, 'I was but late in the quest,' confessing that 'privy thoughts to return to your love' were the lime-twigs he could not escape, trying to make her understand that such experiences 'may not be lightly forgotten'. Then later (*C* XIX. 10-12) we have what is perhaps the greatest of all passages peculiar to Malory, the healing of Sir Urry. Here Lancelot is proved by infallible signs to be in one sense (he knows too well in what and how limited a sense) the best knight of the world. Hence, while all praise him to the skies, he can only weep like a beaten

child. As he failed on the Quest, so (for the same reason) he is failing now. In him, its highest specimen, the whole Round Table is failing; on it and him, as the result of his illicit love, the prophecies begin to be fulfilled. They are, not doubt, worked out through a tangle of human motives, the spite of Agravain and Mordred, the assumption of the blood-feud by Gawain. Of course. The fulfilment of the prophecies about Oedipus came about through seemingly free agents obeying human motives. That is how prophecies are fulfilled in good stories; no one ever suggested that the motivation somehow abolishes the connexion between the prediction and the event. And when all is nearly over and the doom worked out, Lancelot again recalls to us the source of the whole tragedy: 'For in the quest of the Sangreal I had forsaken the vanities of the world had not your love been' (*C* XXI. 9; *W* 1253.14-15).

And still, though I cannot see how any reader fails to see the connexion, I cannot be certain whether Malory himself saw it or not.

V. Finally, did Malory write one book or eight? Close study of the Winchester MS. has convinced Professor Vinaver that he wrote eight; instead of the *Morte Darthur* we have the 'Works' of Malory, and inconsistencies between them no longer matter—indeed, no longer exist, for independent worlds of invention cannot be inconsistent with one another. This view has been seriously criticized by Mr. D. S. Brewer [in his 1952 *Medium Ævum* article "Form in the Morte Darthur"]. He points out that the eight 'works' are full of backward and forward references, their order not alterable, and 'bridge' passages often supplied. I think I should be on Mr. Brewer's side in this question, if I were not bogged down in a preliminary doubt as to what precisely the question is.

I believe I know fairly well what we mean if we say, '*Pickwick* is one work, but *Pickwick* and *Great Expectations* are two works'. We mean that within *Pickwick,* as within *Great Expectations,* there are characters that continue or recur, and that there are causal connexions, and the later parts presuppose the earlier; whereas there are no common characters and no causal connexions shared by both. But ask me the same questions about *Barchester Towers* and *The Last Chronicle*; already a shade of ambiguity has crept in. Now go to a step further. What of *Paradise Lost* and *Paradise Regained*? Here there are characters common to both, and the later poem presupposes and recalls events in the earlier. Satan's temptation of Christ presupposes his rebellion against God and his expulsion from Heaven. And if Satan, and the whole story, were as purely Milton's invention as Archdeacon Grantly is Trollope's, the two poems would stand in the same not very easily defined relation as the two novels. Actually, however, Satan's career with all its causal and chronological structure already exists in the Fathers and in popular belief, before Milton sets pen to paper, and continues to exist whether he wants us to treat *Regained* as a sequel or as a wholly separate poem. Presupposals of events in *Paradise Lost,* and backward references, are bound to occur. It may be impossible to say whether a given instance of them illustrates the unity of the two poems or whether it merely exhibits at one point the external, pre-existing, non-Miltonic unity of the matter he worked on. Hence we may generalize: wherever there is a matter (historical or legendary) previous and external to the author's activity, the question, 'One work or many?' loses a good deal of its meaning. And of course Malory's matter was of this kind.

On top of this a special difficulty arises from the fact that Malory was a medieval author. If it were possible to question him directly, in what form should we put our question? It would be no use asking him how many books he thought he had written; he would think we meant the material volumes or 'quairs'. If we asked him, 'How many tales?' he might enumerate more than eight. Such expressions as 'Thus endeth the tale of . . .' (*C* II. 19; *W* 92.22), or 'the adventure of' (*C* III. 8; *W* 108.28) or 'the quest of' (*C* III. 11; *W* 113.34) occur within the Vinaverian units. If we talked to him about 'artistic unity', he would not understand. We might finally, in desperation, try to find out whether he was at all worried at the appearance in one passage of some knight whose death had been recorded in an earlier passage. He would, I feel certain, simply refer us to 'the French book' as his authority. For the difficulty between Malory and us would not be merely linguistic. We should by the very form of our questions be presupposing concepts his mind was not furnished with. Did any Middle English author conceive clearly that he was writing fiction, a single work of fiction, which should obey the laws of its own inner unity but need not cohere with anything else in the world? I cannot believe it. They are all, even Chaucer, handing on, embellishing, expanding, or abridging a matter received from some source. They feel free to illuminate it at any number of points with their own vivid imagination, and even to correct what seems to them improbable, improper, or unedifying. But whatever their own degree of actual belief or of scepticism (were they clearly aware of either? did they for the most part even raise such questions?) they all proceed as if they were more or less historians; unscholarly, decorating, and emotional historians to be sure, like Livy or Plutarch, but (by and large) historians still. I do not for a moment believe that Malory had any intention either of writing a single 'work' or of writing many 'works' as we should understand the expressions. He was telling us about Arthur and the knights. Of course his matter was one—the same king, the same court. Of course his matter was many—they had had many adventures.

The choice we try to force upon Malory is really a choice for us. It is our imagination, not his, that makes the work one or eight or fifty. We can read it either way. We can read it now one way, now another. We partly make what we read.

As will be seen, the examination of all five Paradoxes produces in me varying degrees of doubt (weakest as regards the Third, strongest as regards the Second and Fifth) about Professor Vinaver's idea of Malory's intentions; but it produces no confidence in any alternative theory. The net result is that Malory eludes me. Perhaps, then, I shall be able to find him in his style, for they say that a man's style is himself. Unfortunately, Malory turns out to have not a style, but styles. The inverted and alliterative language of the Roman War has little likeness to the limpid, unobtrusive prose in which we follow the adventures of knights errant. And we know why. The one is from the Alliterative *Morte*, the other renders, and copies as closely as English can, the style of the French prose romances. In both, Malory writes such a style as he has most lately read. And we cannot say that this subjection to the model is a prentice weakness which he outgrew in his maturity. At the very end, as soon as the Stanzaic *Morte* comes before him, the tell-tale features, the tags, inversions, and alliterations, creep into his prose: 'while we thus in holes us hide'—'that was wary and wise'—'droop and dare'—'shred them down as sheep in a fold' (*C* XX. 19; *W* 1211-12). And when he leaves his originals altogether to reflect upon the story (*C* XVIII. 25; *W* 1119-20), we have a style different from all these. There are more (ultimately) Latin derivatives close together (*constrain, divers, negligence, stability*, and *rasure*), and doublets like 'bring forth fruit and flourish', 'springeth and flourisheth', 'arase and deface', 'deface and lay apart'. This is quite unlike the prose used in his own (or what we take to be his own) additions to the narrative parts, especially those dialogues which he inserts more freely as he nears the end. These are no doubt admirable; but who, on purely internal evidence, could have picked them out (as almost anyone could pick out the alliterative passage about the dream in *C* v. 4)? They may be better than the surrounding prose which reproduces the French, but they are all of a piece with it. Malory's greatest original passages arise when he is most completely absorbed in the story and realizes the characters so fully that they begin to talk for him of their own accord; but they talk a language he has largely learned from his sources. The very ease with which he wanders away from this style into that of some inferior source or into a language of his own (which he may have thought 'higher') suggests that he hardly knows what he is doing. Thus, while in one sense it would be monstrous to say that he 'has no style' (he has written prose as musical, as forthright, as poignant, as was ever heard in England) it would be true in another. He has no style of his own, no characteristic manner. (If you were searching all literature for a man who might be described as 'the opposite of Pater', Malory would be a strong candidate.) In a style or styles so varied, everywhere so indebted to others, and perhaps most original precisely where it is most indebted, one cannot hopefully seek *l'homme même*. Here also Malory vanishes into a mist.

And this result neither surprises nor disappoints me. I have called this essay 'The English prose *Morte*', because I think we may deceive ourselves by such expressions as 'Malory's **Morte Darthur**' or 'The Works of Sir Thomas Malory'. They sound so dangerously like 'Browning's *Sordello*' or 'The Works of Jane Austen'. But there is no real parallel. Our familiar concept of 'author-and-his-book' is foiled by the composite works of the Middle Ages. Even in *Troilus and Criseyde*, where the whole is much shorter and the last worker's additions are much larger and known more certainly, we are foiled. We can sort out the Boccaccian and the Chaucerian passages. But not the Boccaccian and the Chaucerian element. For of course the surviving Boccaccio is modified by the interpolated Chaucer, and the Chaucer modified (this is less often stressed) by the Boccaccio. In the end we cannot really say that either author, nor even in what proportion each author, is responsible for the total effect. The prose **Morte** is very much more complicated. Whatever Malory's intentions—if he had any intentions—may have been, it is agreed on all hands that he has changed the tale very little. From the nature of the case he could not have changed it much. It is too vast, too filled with its own strong life, to be much affected by alterations so comparatively short and sporadic as his. This does not mean that his contribution is of negligible value. Like so many medieval authors (like, for example, the poet of *Cleanness* and *Patience*), at point after point he adds vividness, throws some figure into bolder relief, cuts away an excrescence, or sweetens some motive that he rightly found odious. The process may be described as 'touching up'. But there is no question of a great artist giving to a pupil's work those strokes of genius 'which make all the difference'. Rather, a deft pupil has added touches here and there to a work which, in its majestic entirety, he could never have conceived; and from which his own skill has been chiefly learned. Though he has in fact improved it, it was (by our standards, not by those of the Middle Ages) rather cheek of him to try. But even if he had done harm, he would not have done much harm.

If some people find it distressing to have a work which cannot be assigned to any single author, let me remind them that in another art we are familiar with this sort of thing. I am thinking of a great cathedral, where Saxon, Norman, Gothic, Renaissance, and Georgian elements all co-exist, and all grow together into something strange and admirable which none of its successive builders intended or foresaw. Under Malory's work lies that of the French prose romancers; under theirs, that of Chrétien, Wace, and other poets; under that, Geoffrey, and perhaps the Breton *lais*; deepest of all, who knows what fragments of Celtic myth or actual British history? Malory is only the last of many restorers, improvers, demolitionists; if you will, of misunderstanders. Meanwhile, the great cathedral of words stands solidly before us and imposes on us a meaning which is largely independent of their varying and perhaps incompatible purposes. Who, if any, first saw or intended the tragic and ironic parallel between Mordred's begetting and Galahad's? Or the necessity that the Grail should bring not peace but a sword? Or the three-storied effect inevitably produced by the intermediate position of the good knights between the villains like Mark and the perfect knights like Percivale? Or the deep suggestiveness of Arthur's relation to that dark family (Morgan, Morgause, and the rest) from whom he emerges, who lie in wait for him, and who mysteriously return in his last hour to take him away?

I said just now that Malory was only the last of the makers of the *Morte*. I should have said, last but one (or even last but two). It follows from the view I am trying to put that Caxton's text is not most usefully regarded as a corruption. He touched up Malory as Malory touched up his predecessors and by the same right. The greatest service that he did the old fabric was one of demolition. Most unluckily (and probably, as Professor Vinaver thinks, early in his career) Malory had come across the Alliterative *Morte*. It is not a first-class poem, not comparable in epic quality to the battle scenes of Layamon, and it treats the dullest and most incredible part of the whole Arthurian legend. It is far easier to suspend one's disbelief in enchantments than in vast contradictions of known history scrawled across a whole continent; and a narrative of unbroken military successes, dull even when true, is insufferable when feigned. It is defeat, or (as in the *Iliad*) discords within one of the armies, that we need for epic. Malory swallowed this poem almost whole, except that by separating it from the *Morte* he deprived it of the tragic close and the moral judgement which had saved it from total paltriness. He also surrendered his style without resistance to the influence of the alliterative metre, which, degenerate even in the original, becomes in prose a noisy rumble. Caxton

wisely abridged the whole dreary business, and removed (he might well have used the knife more boldly) some of the traces of the metre. Thus where Winchester's (and no doubt Malory's) text read

> Now fecche me, seyde sir Pryamus, my vyall that hangys by the gurdyll of my haynxman, for hit is full of the floure of the four good watyrs that passis from Paradyse, the mykill fruyte in fallys that at one day fede shall us all. . . .

Caxton gives

> And Priamus took from his page a vial full of the four waters that came out of Paradise.

Notice that Caxton has made it much more Malorian, more like the best and most typical parts of Malory, than Malory himself had done. This is 'forcing a man to be free', making him himself *C* v. 10; *W* 234.11-14). Again in *C* v. 8 (*W* 219.16-17) we owe to Caxton 'the ground trembled and dindled' instead of 'all the vale dyndled'. The division into chapters, if sometimes unskilfully done, has made the book everywhere more readable. The rubrics he prefixed to the chapters have become as much part of its beauty as the glosses of the *Ancient Mariner's*. Sometimes, as in 'how Lancelot fell to his old love again', they direct us unerringly to the pith of what follows (*C* XVIII. 1); again and again they are evocative in the highest degree.

I am not of course suggesting that Caxton's share in the final effect is remotely comparable to Malory's; only that he too, in his degree, has helped a little, and that it is no misfortune if his text has counted for so much in the English imagination. That is why I have usually quoted not only from Caxton but even from Caxton edited by Pollard; the household book. I enjoy my cathedral as it has stood the test of time and demand no restoration. I have no more wish to discard Caxton for Malory than to discard Malory for the French romances.

It would distress me if anyone took this to imply the slightest depreciation of Professor Vinaver's great edition. It is an indispensable work of which English scholarship may well be proud, and my own debts to it will be obvious. Indeed the view I have taken allows me to give Professor Vinaver a place higher, in my opinion, than scholarship of itself could claim. I hesitated a while ago whether to call Malory last but one, or last but two, of the many who worked at the prose *Morte*. For has not Professor Vinaver some right to be numbered among them? He has not, naturally, allowed himself the liberties of a Malory or even of a Caxton. His chisel has touched no stone of the building. But he has made a new approach, and one which many modern pilgrims will find more congenial. His book smacks of our own century as Caxton's smacked of his. The division into eight romances, and above all the title, *The Works* of Malory, whether right or wrong (or neither), makes it far more digestible by contemporary critical conceptions than the old *Morte*. The *Works*, the Complete Works—that is what our libraries are used to. Already Malory fits more comfortably on the shelf beside the 'works' of everyone else. And the mere look of the pages—the paragraphing and the inverted commas—acclimatizes the book still further. Beyond question, Professor Vinaver has shown the cathedral from a new angle; placed the modern pilgrim where he will enjoy it best. And now that his edition is deservedly reaching the stage of cheap reprints, it may in its turn become the household book; until perhaps *alter Achilles*, some second Vinaver (a little cold to the first one as he is a little cold to Caxton) recalls his generation to the long forgotten book of 1485 or even to the French, and someone like myself puts in a plea for what will then be the old, the traditional, 'Works of Malory'. And all these preferences will be legitimate and none of them 'right' or 'wrong'. The cathedral of words is so large that everyone can find in it the work of his favourite period; and here, as you could not do in a real cathedral, you can always strip that favourite work of later accretions without pulling the whole thing down. What you must not do is to call those bits 'the' or 'the real' cathedral. They might have been. The whole might have been designed by one man and finished in one style. But that is not what happened. Though every part of it was made by a man, the whole has rather grown than been made. Such things have a kind of existence that is almost midway between the works or art and those of nature. (pp. 7-28)

> C. S. Lewis, "The English Prose 'Morte'," in Essays on Malory *by Walter Oakeshott and others, edited by J. A. W. Bennett, Oxford at the Clarendon Press, 1963, pp. 7-28.*

EUGÈNE VINAVER (essay date 1963)

[*Vinaver is recognized as a pioneer in Malory studies. He wrote one of the first comprehensive studies of the author,* Malory *(1929), and edited the three-volume* Works of Sir Thomas Malory *(1947) from the Winchester Manuscript of the text. He is perhaps best known for his sometimes controversial view that the* Morte Darthur *is a collection of related tales but not a continuous narrative. In the following excerpt, he responds to C. S. Lewis's investigation of "paradoxes" in the* Morte Darthur *(see preceding excerpt), focusing on whether Malory conceived the work as a single, unified narrative or as a series of related but discrete tales.*]

MY DEAR LEWIS, Of all the contributors to this volume I am the most fortunate. You have shown me your essay [see excerpt dated 1963] and asked me to write a reply to it or, to quote your own words, 'a development from it'. The privilege is a perilous one, and at first I hesitated to take up the friendly challenge; but the prospect of a dialogue with you on the vital issues you have raised is irresistible.

Everything you say is enlightening and much of it is revealing. I have lived with Malory for many years and I think I know how he impresses me; but I would rather leave the reader with *your* impressions firmly fixed in his mind, for I consider them an acquisition for us all and not a matter for discussion. What might usefully be discussed is not what you feel about Malory, but the way in which you account for your feelings—your interpretation of your reaction to the book.

I find this interpretation debatable, and there you probably agree. You sum it up by saying: 'the net result is that Malory eludes me.' I confess that up to that point, as I went on reading your essay, the familiar but invariably fresh magic of your language and thought lulled me into a delightful state of acquiescence. But when I came to these words I had to pause. Surely, I reflected, if there is one critic whom Malory does *not* elude it is C. S. Lewis; hence, if the 'net result' of his argument is to make him deny so obvious a fact there must be something wrong

with his argument. I did not, and I could not, ask myself *why* Malory 'eluded' you, because he quite clearly had not done so. The only question in my mind was why you *thought* he had eluded you. What was it that gave you the feeling that you were faced with something strange and 'paradoxical': not even with one paradox, but with as many as five? There is no simple and uniform answer to this question. But as I was looking for a possible answer a passage from *A Winter's Tale* came to my mind—the lines spoken by Polixenes in Act IV:

> You see, sweet maid, we marry
> A gentle scion to the wildest stock,
> And make conceive a bark of baser kind
> By bud of nobler race. This is an art
> Which does mend Nature, change it rather, but
> The art itself is Nature.

Art itself is nature. It plays, as Spenser said not long before these words were written, 'second Nature's part', and while it is totally different from Nature in the ordinary sense, which includes the artist's personality, his outlook and his intentions, it is part of a natural process which we can occasionally observe and which would be the greatest paradox of all, were it not 'itself Nature'.

The first of the five 'paradoxes' which you list at the outset is the cleavage between the man and the book. 'The work has long passed for a mirror of honour and virtue; the author appears to have been little better than a criminal.' Let us leave aside for the moment all questions of fact. The evidence on which the notion of Malory's 'immorality' rests is very slight indeed. Considering the state of justice in fifteenth-century England, even a conviction would not have been sufficient to prove that he was guilty of any of the charges brought against him; and there was in fact no conviction, or at least we have no record of one. Your own assessment of Malory's probable misdeeds is as fair a hypothesis as any that can reasonably be advanced in the present state of our knowledge. But even if he were as 'immoral' a character as some of his other biographers want him to be, what difference would this make to our understanding of his work? What except the romantic myth of the work being an expression of the 'whole man' makes you think that there would be anything abnormal about a cleavage between the man and the book? I should have thought that it would be more contrary to the natural course of things if there were no such cleavage, for in that case the two 'natures' would be identical, whereas in fact they hardly ever are: no reader of your *Personal Heresy in Criticism* will ever take their identity for granted. Proust in his *Méthode de Sainte-Beuve* contrasts them as two distinct entities, totally unlike one another.... On this showing it seems singularly fortunate that our knowledge of Malory the man is not only limited but apparently inconsistent with the nature of his work: we are not even tempted to explain one through the other. It is, as you put it, 'a desperate expedient' to question Malory's identity simply because we cannot square the known facts of his life with the meaning and the message of his book; desperate to the extent of being perverse. Malory's biography has its uses: it is entertaining in itself, and it is an interesting sidelight on the social history of his time. But to feel 'disconcerted' about it as, for instance, E. K. Chambers did, is to misuse the results of biographical research, which are no more—and no less—puzzling in this case than such results normally are.

Your second and fourth 'paradoxes' are more difficult to dispose of, if indeed they can be disposed of at all. The problem they raise is a fundamental one. You find a curious contrast between Malory's efforts 'to eliminate the marvellous and introduce the humdrum' and the result of these efforts (Paradox II), and you suggest that there is an equally curious contrast between what seems to be a 'deeply religious' handling of the Grail story and a constant tendency to evade the religious issue (Paradox IV). What you say is not only true, but illuminating and very important. In Malory the feeling of the marvellous is not lessened, but intensified in spite of his 'practical realism'; and again, in his version of the Quest of the Holy Grail, much as he tries to cut down the religious exposition and even substitute the worldly for the divine, he produces a work which makes a more deeply religious impression on one's mind than the strictly orthodox original upon which it is based. How does this come about? I think you have supplied the answer. The work is not 'what any single individual either intended or foresaw'. 'Though every part of it was made by a man, the whole has rather grown than been made. Such things have a kind of existence that is almost midway between the works of art and those of nature.' I hope these words will long be remembered by all those who read Malory and induce others to read him. Perhaps you will allow me to illustrate them by a brief quotation:

> Lorde, I thanke The, for now I se that that hath be my desire many a day. Now, my Blessed Lorde, I wold nat lyve in this wrecched worlde no lenger, if hit myght please The, Lorde.

This is Galahad's last prayer, and perhaps one of the most profoundly religious moments ever recorded in any version of the Grail story. If you look at the corresponding place in Pauphilet's edition of the *Queste del Saint Graal* you will find that every single word used by Malory is there, but that about three-quarters of the French text is missing in Malory. Among the omissions there are some important phrases and sentences which by the strict standards of the author of the French *Queste* the occasion required. And yet when you read the two passages together you realize that one has a power and a greatness totally absent from the other. Is this not, in miniature, the process you are thinking of? But why contrast in this instance 'art' and 'nature'? Why not say with Polixenes that this is 'an art that Nature makes'? The discrepancy between the intention and the result occurs daily in every branch of art, not because nature 'takes over' from the artist, but because the artist's genius takes control of the situation and modifies what we call his intention—his conscious self, his 'design'. It is again art 'playing second nature's part', acting much in the same way as nature is supposed to act, but *within* the artist's mind. Malory the man was certainly not a believer in the supernatural: the simple method of collation shows how consistently he cut it down in adapting his French books. And he was certainly not interested in the complexities of the Grail doctrine, as the same method amply demonstrates. But when we say this we describe the mind—or what happened in the mind—of Sir Thomas Malory when he was thinking about the supernatural and the Grail: we do *not* describe the process of his work, which is something very different and much more difficult to understand. The greater the author and the theme, the more room there is for this inner logic of the work, which alone, in the last analysis, determines the 'result'. It is the logic of the supernatural and the logic of the Grail theme that make the work into 'something which none of its successive builders intended or foresaw', but that logic only becomes active in the artist's hands; when it defeats his intentions and his beliefs the triumph is his: it is the triumph of his art over his conscious self, and each time it occurs he may well experience a 'more profound delight' in the result than the French authors had ever known.

Perhaps for the sake of clarity I ought to put it another way. If I understand your reasoning correctly, it is something like this: there was an excess of the supernatural in Malory's French originals; because he was out of sympathy with the supernatural he reduced the overall amount of it, and because 'two enchanters, two ghosts, two ferlies are always half as impressive as one' the reduction added to the impressiveness of the marvellous. But does this mean that anybody applying the same equation ($2 = \frac{1}{2}$) to the same material might achieve the same result? Surely not. And if you agree, that is to say, if you think as I do that the equation taken by itself is inoperative, would you not say that it became operative in Malory because of something that happened *in* Malory and did not happen elsewhere—something that for want of a better word we call his art? The equation is, of course, a paradox, and a splendid one, but not the process which makes the equation work. The essence of it is the co-existence of two 'natures', the conscious and the creative, one 'mending' the other—clearly something rare, but no more paradoxical or accidental than any art 'which adds to Nature'. This is not a criticism, but a development of your argument. Alone among critics you have perceived the significance of Malory's treatment of the supernatural and the religious, and the interpretation I suggest is simply a means of describing this treatment in more explicit terms while 'walking stumblingly' after you.

The two remaining sections—III and V—are no less illuminating and thought-provoking. You formulate your 'paradox V' as follows:

> Malory seemed to Saintsbury (and doubtless to many) the man who alone 'makes of this vast assemblage of stories one story and one book' The evidence of the Winchester MS. convinces Professor Vinaver that he really wrote several works which were never intended to form a whole.

A thorny problem, and one which has engaged the attention of a considerable number of critics ever since I published my edition of the *Works*. But it seems to me that you have found the answer—if you can bear another paradox—by saying that you are 'bogged down in a preliminary doubt as to what precisely the question is'. Malory would have been 'bogged down' in very much the same doubt. It would be no use asking him, if he came back to life, 'how many books he thought he had written; he would think we meant the material volumes or "quairs".... If we talked to him about "artistic unity" he would not understand.' And you put the entire problem in a nutshell when you say: 'We should by the very form of our questions be presupposing concepts his mind was not furnished with.' But there are two issues we might consider: (*a*) how did Malory intend his romances to be presented to his readers? and (*b*) do these romances *in fact* make one romance? From the editor's point of view the first question is the only one that matters; the critic, on the other hand, is—or should be—interested primarily, if not exclusively, in the second, i.e. in the result, not in the intention. And either question can be answered without prejudice to the other.

What Malory *intended* could have been gathered long ago from his own words had they not been partly distorted in the process of transmission and partly misunderstood—or ignored. The Pierpont Morgan copy of Caxton's edition is the only existing record of what Malory wrote in his last colophon. In the other extant copy—the John Rylands—the last pages are missing. They have been replaced by Whittaker's facsimiles, which Sommer reproduced in his reprint, and everybody has since looked upon Sommer's text as a convenient and entirely reliable substitute for Caxton's. Unfortunately it is not at all reliable and the fault is not Sommer's, but Whittaker's. The Pierpont Morgan copy read as follows:

> Here is the ende of the hoole book of kyng arthur and of his noble knyghtes of the rounde table that whan they were hole togyders there was euer an hondred and forty And here is the ende of the deth of arthur

The word *hoole* is the last word on the last page but one of the text; it is perfectly legible, but if one is a little careless, and especially if one is thinking of the next word (the first on the following page)—*book*—one can easily misread *hoole* as *booke*. This is precisely what Whittaker did. In Sommer we find, as a result, *here is the ende of the booke book*, which all later editors took for a dittography and reduced to *here is the end of the book*. Next came the critics who, looking at the passage, decided, quite naturally, that from Malory's point of view the 'book of King Arthur', & c., was the same as the 'Death of Arthur': that the words after the first *the ende of* were a description of the work of which the words after the second *the ende of* supplied the title. Hence, they concluded, Malory did give his romances one general title, and Caxton did not betray the author's intentions by saying in his own colophon: 'Thus endeth thys noble and Ioyous book entytled le morte Darthur.' There was clearly no harm in 'anglo-normanizing' *the death of*. Who can say, then, that Malory did not intend to write one book or that *Le Morte Darthur* is not its legitimate title?

I am not suggesting that without Whittaker's error critics would not have accepted Caxton's title and all that it involves, or even that the belief in Malory's 'unifying' design, shared by so many and denied by so few, rests to any appreciable extent on Malory's colophon; but I do think that now that we have at last got the correct reading of this colophon we ought to take some notice of it. Its implication seems to me crystal-clear. On the one hand there is 'the whole book', the entire collection, or series, of romances about King Arthur and his knights; and on the other, there is the *Death of Arthur*, the last work in the series, which presumably stands in the same relation to the whole as does each one of the romances—or 'works'—that occur earlier on. If we add to this the fact that, as the Winchester MS. shows, each romance has a separate title given to it in its colophon, that five out of the eight colophons end with the word *Amen*—the medieval equivalent of THE END—that four of these plus one other give the author's name (the equivalent of the signature with which not so long ago authors used to conclude their books), can

The Malory coat of arms.

there be much argument as to what Malory *intended* 'the whole book' to be? I am deliberately refraining for the moment from any discussion of its internal 'unity' or lack of 'unity': I am concerned purely and simply with what the text was meant to be; in other words I am arguing as an editor, not as a critic. And as an editor I feel that Malory has given us as clear an indication as any medieval author has ever done as to how his text should be presented to his readers. The only hesitation one might have concerns the words *the whole book of King Arthur and of his noble knights that when they were wholly together there was ever a hundred and forty*. Is this a title or a description of the series? My own feeling is—but I may be wrong—that both the qualifying adjective 'whole' and the subordinate clause after 'knights' tip the balance against the 'title' theory, and this is why I did not think I would be justified in replacing *Le Morte Darthur* (which, incidentally, *nobody* used as a title after Caxton until Haslewood revived it in 1816) by another title. I called my edition *The Works of Sir Thomas Malory*, which is clearly not a 'title'. You say, quite rightly, 'I do not for a moment believe that Malory had any intention either of writing a single "work" or of writing many "works" as we should understand the expression.' Of course not. But what author ever starts off with the idea of writing 'many works'? Can you honestly say that you ever did? And yet, if at some not distant date there appears a series of volumes entitled *The Works of C. S. Lewis* will you regard it as something contrary to your intentions as a writer?

I now come to the other and perhaps more important aspect of the problem: the 'critical' as distinct from the 'editorial'. I agree entirely with your concluding remarks: 'It is our imagination, not his (Malory's), that makes the work one or eight or fifty. We can read it either way. We can read it now one way, now another. We partly make what we read.' *We partly make what we read* describes a general phenomenon; what matters to us at the moment is the particular phenomenon: *We can read it now one way, now another.* We certainly can, but why? My explanation would be that the kind of 'unity' that people occasionally look for, and find, in Malory's romances is not the essential or the 'binding' kind. It is a kind without which any one of his romances could very well exist and be appreciated to the full. Remove from Malory's text all the occasional references to what is going to happen in a later work or to what has happened already in an earlier one, and nothing of importance will be lost. You are right in saying that some of these references are 'singularly fortunate', and it does not matter at this point in the argument whether they are of Malory's own making or whether they come straight from his sources: we are discussing the effect of the work, not its genesis. But by and large I can see only two 'areas' in which these references occur in a way that is at all significant: between the *Tale of King Arthur* and the *Quest of the Holy Grail* and between the *Quest* and the romance that comes immediately after it, *The Book of Sir Lancelot and Queen Guinevere.* The examples you quote are from the latter area; other critics have made a good deal of those which occur in the former. I cannot help feeling that too much has been read into some of these examples. Does the sentence 'and ever Sir Launcelote wepte, as he had bene a chylde that had bene beatyn' in *The Healing of Sir Urry* really mean that 'as he failed in the Quest, so (for the same reason) he is failing now'? Lancelot has healed Sir Urry after everyone else has failed in the attempt. He and all the 'kings and knights' kneel down and give 'thankynges and lovynge unto God and unto Hys Blyssed Modir'. And tears—not, I think, of sorrow or contrition, but of joy and gratitude, flow down Lancelot's face. What can be more natural? And why think of the Quest at this point, and of Lancelot's failure in it, when there is not the slightest indication in the text that any such thoughts crossed his mind? I mention this example simply because so much has been made of it by the champions of 'unity' (E. K. Chambers was, I think, the first to suggest the interpretation which you have adopted). But there are, of course, others which cannot be dismissed, and which I have no intention of querying. Lancelot certainly refers to the Quest in speaking to Guinevere (*W* 1046.3-14), and Malory in describing the effects of the Dolorous Stroke clearly refers to the Grail theme (*W* 85.27-9). There are other reminders and anticipations of the same kind. But how much do they really mean to Malory's readers? Not to compilers of concordances, nor to Ph.D. candidates who laboriously dig them out and exhibit them as precious finds, but to people who read Malory as he was meant to be read, that is to say for pleasure, as a 'noble and joyous book'? I am sure you have guessed already the thought behind this question, but let me make it clearer still. In a work such as the Arthurian Cycle of romances commonly known as the 'Vulgate'—the great cycle containing the *Estoire del Graal*, the *Merlin*, the *Lancelot* proper, the *Queste del Saint Graal*, and the *Mort Artu*—references and cross-links of this kind not only occur more frequently, but have an entirely different function: without

them the work would not make sense; it could be neither understood nor enjoyed (this, incidentally, is the reason why critics who have not taken the trouble to follow them up find the Vulgate unreadable). Hence there is, I think, some justification for calling such a composition 'one work'; none of it could be appreciated by a reader who did not carry the whole of it in his head. I have often wondered whether the changes in the form of the European novel are not determined, in the last analysis, by the variations in the quantity of things that one *can* carry in one's head: our modern novel does seem to correspond to our present capacity, while the thirteenth-century cyclic novel leaves us far behind, just as it left Malory and his readers far behind. Of course, it is always pleasant to be reminded in passing of something one remembers; but it is also pleasant to know that it does not really matter whether one remembers it or not, and this is what to my mind makes Malory's echoes from one work to another 'singularly fortunate'. It would be disastrous if we made the entire edifice of his romances rest upon them: *Le Morte Darthur* would immediately collapse. If we don't want this to happen we must not let our imagination 'make the work one'; but on the other hand, it would be a pity if we lost altogether the feeling which you describe so well in your Preface to extracts from Spenser in *Major British Writers*, the feeling that 'adventures of this sort are going on all round us, that in this vast forest (we are nearly always in a forest) this is the sort of thing that goes on all the time, that it was going on before we arrived and will continue after we have left'.

Here, then, the achievement, the final result is not in any way contrary to the intention: we read Malory more or less as he thought one ought to read him, and enjoy the arrangement and the somewhat capricious sequence of romances as he intended it to be enjoyed. The difficulty upon which so much thought and effort have been expended in recent years does not arise (and this is indeed a paradox) until we 'presuppose concepts Malory's mind was not furnished with' either at the reflective or at the creative level.

There is much the same relationship between intention and achievement in his narrative technique (Paradox III). You agree that he made a valiant effort to 'straighten out' the unbelievably complex pattern of interwoven narratives which he found in his French books. If he had done this very few people in post-medieval England would have bothered to read him, just as in post-medieval France very few people have bothered to read in the original the great Arthurian Cycle of the thirteenth century. Of course, he did not carry the process of straightening-out to the end; and of course it is true that such 'interweavings' as he left in the text often add to our enjoyment of it. But it is entirely a question of degree: he carried his modifications far enough to make the work 'pleasant to read in' by modern standards. Here again the reader's reaction is conditioned partly by the author's efforts and partly by what he allowed to survive from the earlier state of his stories. With all its component elements and techniques the work has grown, as you say, 'into something strange and admirable', something which none of its successive builders can claim to have foreseen exactly as it is. This great cathedral 'stands solidly before us' and imposes upon us a structure of its own. Nothing else survives. Many writers had worked on the French Arthurian prose romances between the thirteenth and the fifteenth centuries; there had been adaptations of it in Spain and in Germany. All this is now dead and buried, and Malory alone stands as a rock defying all changes of taste and style and morals; not as a grand paradox of nature, but as a lasting work of art. Is it not, then, right that we should be thinking of the work in terms of what *he* did when he called it back to life? To create does not necessarily mean to invent or even to build; it may mean to leave out or to undo what others have done; it may even be something less tangible, which somehow transforms what had no existence into something that has. And our task as interpreters is really much more modest than people think. We can neither define nor explain. But we can point in the direction where were feel the path of genius lies and hope that in this way we may bring ourselves and others a little closer to its understanding. This is what you have done. Hence my gratitude. (pp. 29-40)

> Eugène Vinaver, "On Art and Nature: A Letter to C. S. Lewis," in Essays on Malory *by Walter Oakeshott and others, edited by J. A. W. Bennett, Oxford at the Clarendon Press, 1963, pp. 29-40.*

WILFRED L. GUERIN (essay date 1964)

[*Guerin is an American academic and scholar whose writings cover the spectrum of English and American literature. In the following excerpt, he explores the origin and purpose of the "Tale of Gareth" in the* Morte Darthur.]

The fourth large division of *Le Morte Darthur*, the "Tale of Gareth," presents the arrival of "the goodlyest yonge man and the fayreste" that the court of Arthur has ever seen. Appearing on Pentecost, at the time when Arthur holds "the Rounde Table moste plenoure," the young man humbly asks for three gifts. For the moment he requests only the first: food and drink for a year. Sir Kay scorns the young man as a "vylayne borne" and mockingly names him "Beawmaynes." But Beaumains is "meke and mylde," and as a kitchen knave he endures Kay's abuse for a year.

When Pentecost is next celebrated, a damsel named Lynet arrives at court to request help for her sister, Lyonesse, whose castle is besieged by the Red Knight of the Red Lands. Beaumains now requests his other two gifts: that he be assigned this adventure and that he be knighted by Lancelot. Lynet is insulted when the kitchen knave is assigned to her, but she has no choice. Beaumains identifies himself to Lancelot as Gareth, brother to Gawain, is knighted, and begins a series of encounters of increasing difficulty, during which Lynet is exceedingly unsympathetic toward him. He overcomes six thieves, two knights at a bridge, the Black Knight, the Green Knight, the Red Knight, Sir Persaunt of Inde, and finally the Red Knight of the Red Lands. By his prowess and his gentlemanly qualities, he wins approval from Lynet.

But Lyonesse now requires that he "laboure in worshyp this twelve-monthe" in order to win her love. Subsequent episodes effectively test Gareth's prowess, his determination, and his chastity. He and Lyonesse plan a tournament, the intended result of which is to have Gareth publicly win her as his lady. After the tournament, but before he rejoins Lyonesse, Gareth fights the Brown Knight without Pity, the Duke de la Rouse, and—unknowingly—his own brother Gawain. Lynet stops the final encounter by

making the two brothers known to each other. Arthur then arranges for the marriage of Gareth and Lyonesse, which is celebrated by the whole court with great joy and ceremony.

The "Tale of Gareth" presents particular difficulties to the commentator concerned with originality in *Le Morte Darthur*. Though almost every aspect of the "Tale" is somewhat similar to aspects of earlier romances in French, no actual source has been found for Malory's story.... [Many] scholars have assumed that Malory did have a French source, now lost, for this division of his book. My own view is that Malory borrowed hints for this "Tale" from French romances, but that he is to be credited with great originality for its creation.... In brief, it will be my contention that—through its happy picture of the Round Table at the height of its success, and through its preparation of Gareth for the role he will later play in the collapse of the Round Table—the "Tale of Gareth" contributes importantly to the unity of Malory's book. (pp. 99-100)

It seems clear ... that many similarities exist between earlier French romances and numerous aspects of the "Tale of Gareth." But the fact remains that, so far as we know, Malory had before him in the writing of this "Tale" no "source," at least not in the sense that we use in considering the other segments of *Le Morte Darthur*. Consequently, I suggest that in light of the various relationships which the "Tale of Gareth" has to the remainder of *Le Morte Darthur*, we should grant the possibility—even the probability—that this "Tale" is Malory's original creation, with bits taken from earlier romances, specifically to serve certain functions within the book as a whole. These relationships and functions will be discussed below.

As a preliminary we should note Malory's consistency in the spelling of Gareth's name and in the conception of his age. In the *Vulgate Cycle*, the prose *Tristan*, and the English stanzaic poem *Le Morte Arthur*, all used by Malory, Gareth's name is spelled in numerous ways. Frequently Gareth is confused with his brother Gaheris, whose name in the manuscripts often resembles Gareth's. But in Malory's version the form for the younger brother is consistently *Gareth*. Malory also modified the statements of the French romances concerning Gareth's age. Possibly for better dramatic effect and for smoother integration of the "Tale of Gareth," matters to which I shall return, Malory caused Gareth to be considerably younger than his brothers and to enter the story after it was well under way. The point at present is that Malory maintained this pattern throughout his bulky work, even into the final "Tale," as in Gawain's sourceless comment concerning the youth of both Gareth and Gaheris. Similarly, Malory went beyond the French romances by making Gareth consistently admirable in ideals, personality, and physical attributes. There can be no doubt about Malory's desire to give a more clearly etched picture of Gareth than was present in the French romances.

Such a clarification of the character, and even of the name, of Gareth facilitated one of Malory's major objectives: to use the "Tale of Gareth" in the portrayal of Arthur's Round Table at the height of its power and glory, during the happy period before the inevitable decline. It may be well to recall at this point the oath that Arthur instituted for the members of the Round Table, for in its principles we find the code by which Gareth lives and which, in the "Tale of Gareth," he brings to its clearest manifestation. In the oath, original with Malory, Arthur charges his knights

> never to do outerage nothir morthir, and allwayes to fle treson, and to gyff mercy unto hym that askith mercy, uppon payne of forfiture of their worship and lordship of kynge Arthure for evirmore; and allwayes to do ladyes, damesels, and jantilwomen and wydowes socour: strengthe hem in hir ryghtes, and never to enforce them uppon payne of dethe. Also that no man take no batayles in a wrongefull quarell for no love ne for no worldis goodis.

The oath is presented in the course of the first "Tale"; there and in the second "Tale" Arthur consolidates his power and gathers around him knights who are capable of fulfilling most of the injunctions of the oath. Then, in the "Tale of Lancelot," Lancelot emerges as the protagonist of the developing society.

Once the rise of that society is sufficiently clear, Malory is ready to show the arrival of young Gareth in the "Tale of Gareth"—and to exemplify the spirit and the letter of the oath presented many pages earlier. Thus, Gareth is horrified by the barbaric deeds of the Red Knight of the Red Lands; he befriends Lynet and Lyonesse, "strengthening" the latter in her rights, and he accuses the Red Knight of forcing his attentions upon her; he disavows association with murder and vengeance, even when his brother Gawain is guilty of them. He also illustrates the positive elements of the oath, as when he "endured all that twelvemonthe and never dyspleased man nother chylde, but allwayes he was meke and mylde." Lynet says, " . . . he is curtyese and mylde, and the moste sufferynge man that ever I mette withall. . . . And at all tymes he gaff me goodly and meke answers agayne." After his climactic victory over the Red Knight of the Red Lands, Gareth grants mercy to those who ask it, although his sense of justice dictates that the Red Knight should die; his yielding to the petitions for mercy represents an advance over the harsher requirement of an avenging justice. Gareth's fulfillment of the oath of chivalry, the timing of his arrival at court, and the respect he is given during the "Tale of Gareth" together show that the Round Table has achieved the flowering of chivalry.

In other ways the "Tale of Gareth" reveals the general happiness of Arthur's court. The story emphasizes color, the charm of magic and myth, the bustle of tournaments, the joys of family ties, and, perhaps most of all, the joys of wedded love. Color, both literal and figurative, stimulates the imagination in Gareth's victories over knights in black, green, red, "inde," red again, and brown. Gareth uses the magically changing color of his armor to confuse the audience at the tournament. This sensuous appeal compares with such episodes as that of the mysterious, light-exuding knight who carries a battle-ax and whose head can be replaced on his shoulders. The wedding feast, the procession of knights paying homage to Gareth, and the accompanying jousts make the close of the "Tale" a panorama of the richness and glory of this era of Arthur's reign.

Of deeper significance for the structural emphasis on the flowering of chivalry is the treatment of love. At one level, it exists in the mutual concern shown by the brothers

whom Gareth defeats on his way to the besieged castle. At another, love and respect bring Gareth into varying relationships with Gawain, Arthur, Lancelot, and Morgause. But the height of emotion is in the mixture of passionate love and ideal love that brings together Lyonesse and Gareth. Beginning with Gareth's fighting the Red Knight of the Red Lands, this love at first seems little more than the conventional sudden emotion of the courtly romances, an interpretation strengthened by Lyonesse's request that Gareth "labor" for a year and by the youthful attempts of the lovers to meet at night in Gryngamour's castle. But as Charles Moorman points out [in his 1960 *ELH* article "Courtly Love in Malory"], the "Tale of Gareth" is far from a courtly love romance; instead Malory deliberately makes it "a commentary upon love and the behavior of lovers, the main purpose of which is to present a natural, untutored affection, very different from the artificial, conventionalized *l'amour courtois*." Whatever traces of courtly love there are in the "Gareth" take on an almost ironic meaning.

> If read in context, Gareth is clearly a commentary on *l'amour courtois* and is so placed as to contrast with the adulterous affairs of Lancelot and Tristan. The "Tale of Gareth" works towards the propositions that the true end of love is marriage, not adultery, that young lovers may in fact be fickle, that wise maids had best not tarry, and that young lovers sometimes need restraining. Gareth is a "vertuous" rather than a "courtly" lover. . . .

Thus, when Lynet intervenes to save the love for a fulfillment different from that of the courtly love tradition, she acts with a sense of righteousness and "was a lytyll dysplesed; and she thought hir sister dame Lyonesse was a lytyll overhasty that she myght nat abyde hir tyme of maryage, and for savyng of hir worshyp she thought to abate their hoote lustis. And she lete ordeyne by hir subtyle crauftes that they had nat theire intentys neythir with othir as in her delytes untyll they were maryed." That Lynet's efforts are well directed is later clear when Arthur asks Gareth "whether he wolde have this lady as peramour, other ellys to have hir to his wyff." Both Gareth and Lyonesse insist that marriage is their goal; they explicitly use the words "wife" and "husband"; and Lyonesse protests that Gareth "is my fyrste love, and he shall be the laste." With their marriage and with those of two of Gareth's brothers, Malory brings full stress upon the happiness of all concerned. As with the married love of Pelleas and Nineve in the first "Tale," Gareth's is an index to the noblest elements of the chivalric ideal—and an effective contrast to the loves that will later wither the flower of chivalry. But for the moment, the "Tale of Gareth" shows the Round Table at its highest point: the oath is being fulfilled, there is a sense of well-being and security, and a type of happy love is established at court.

Gareth's role, however, is not limited to the "Tale" which bears his name. Just as the contrast with other loves and lovers in *Le Morte Darthur* reaches beyond the "Tale," Malory's treatment of Gareth includes an interplay of personalities which helps to portray some of Malory's most important figures. Gareth's role in characterization is more significant than that of the Gaheriet of the *Vulgate Cycle*, for Gareth not only shows the complexities of the protagonists but is beloved of the three great knights of the Arthurian world: Gawain, Tristram, and Lancelot.

The relationship between Gareth and his older brother is complex but by no means contradictory. He is proud of Gawain, yet quite capable of speaking out against the latter's faults. This seeming inconsistency has been criticized as an artistic fault, but is defensible when one recalls that while Gareth regularly espouses good and shuns evil, he is also faithful to friends and relatives. The literary relationship derives from the psychological, for Gareth is a foil to Gawain: his actions and statements consistently point up his brother's faults, as in the contrast between Gawain's vengeance (derived from the sources) and Gareth's hatred of vengeance (apparently original with Malory). These contrasts are emphasized by the many times that Malory causes one brother to refer to the other, using expressions such as "my brother Gareth" or "my brother Sir Gawain." But Malory also uses Gareth to portray certain redeeming qualities in Gawain. For instance, Gawain is shown as capable of a lasting affinity with, and of a paternalistic attitude toward, Gareth, the epitome of all the good qualities of the Gawain clan. Gawain is magnanimous: though Gareth is a close friend of Lancelot, Gawain looks upon this friendship as something praiseworthy, not as a cleavage in the family. Since Gareth is the mainstay of his family's best traits, Gawain is ennobled by his appreciation of the worth of such a relative. Furthermore, since Gawain appears more like a father to Gareth in *Le Morte Darthur* than in the sources, his grief and his desire for revenge after Gareth's death are more credible. In short, Gareth is used to demonstrate the depth and breadth of Malory's Gawain.

Comparisons between Gareth and his three other brothers are of a different sort, consistently advantageous for him and disparaging to them. Like the comparison with Tristram, this relationship was inherited from the French; since it served Malory's purpose to perpetuate the contrast, it underwent little change. It should be noted that while Gaheris does not fare so poorly as do Aggravain and Mordred, he never approaches the level of Gareth. Clearly, Malory considered the family of Gawain as a complex of personality traits, with Gareth at its center, epitomizing more admirable qualities than any of his brothers.

Since the relationship between Gareth and Tristram is not radically different from those between Gareth and the other two important knights, it is not necessary to consider it in detail here, with one exception: the relationship achieves more than characterization, for the "Tale of Gareth," with its appearances of Tristram and knights associated with him, helps to fuse the "Tale of Tristram" into the general scheme of Malory's plot. This fusion was important, since Malory was adding to his conventionally "Arthurian" sources the formerly separate prose *Tristan*.

Of greater significance, however, both for characterization and for the increased artistry of Malory's plot, is the stress in the "Tale of Gareth" and elsewhere on Gareth's relationship with Lancelot. That friendship not only constitutes one of the key aspects of Malory's characterization, but intensifies the irony of Lancelot's inadvertent killing of Gareth late in *Le Morte Darthur*. Unlike the Gareth-Gawain affiliation, which often points up the differences between the two brothers, the friendship between Gareth and Lancelot more consistently shows similarities. Mutual love, not kinship, is the essence of this relationship. Lancelot's worth, necessary for Malory's general purpose, is made clearer by his friendship for and fostering of the

young Beaumains. From the time that Lancelot dubs the young man to the end of *Le Morte Darthur*, that friendship prospers. Their affinity and their oneness in ideals and in innate goodness become more important as the book progresses; to show this importance, both before and after Lancelot kills Gareth, Malory adds speeches to stress their ties of mutual love and respect. However, Lancelot, like Gawain and Tristram, suffers by comparison with Gareth: Gareth is outspoken for chastity, whereas Lancelot is adulterous.

Malory also made several modifications in the Gareth-Lancelot relationship. Lancelot's dubbing of Gareth, an episode unique with Malory, is one of the most important. The five allusions to the dubbing which are made late in *Le Morte Darthur* indicate that Malory intended the episode to be instrumental in the unification of the entire book, making the last two "Tales" in a sense dependent upon the interpolated "Tale of Gareth," and stressing Gareth's sense of fealty to Lancelot. This change compares with the reversal of the Lancelot-Gareth relationship from what it was in the *Vulgate*; there an apparently older Gaheriet stands guard over the young Lancelot before the latter is knighted. To effect this change, Malory avoided numerous references to Gareth which are in the early sections of the *Vulgate Cycle*, sections which lie behind the first three "Tales" in his own version. Thus he could present Gareth as the young protégé of Lancelot in the "Tale of Gareth" and could maintain that relationship throughout the rest of the book. [In *Le Morte Darthur of Sir Thomas Malory and Its Sources* (1917)] Vida Dutton Scudder long ago pointed to another modification that fits the pattern just suggested when she said that perhaps the greatest loss from the prose *Lancelot* was Lancelot's friendship with Galahad, le Haut Prince: "But this figure could not have been introduced without weakening both Lancelot's single-hearted passion for Guenevere and his relation with Gareth.... Lancelot's genius for comradeship is sufficiently indicated by his devotion to Gareth, a devotion also essential to the catastrophe."

Because of these modifications and because of the interpolation of the "Tale of Gareth," Malory was singularly successful in providing for that catastrophe a setting which is much more effectively ironic than the comparable French version. When the catastrophe itself comes, his improvements are consistent with those just mentioned. For example, although the *Vulgate* Gaheriet apparently knows of but does not warn Lancelot of the plot against him, Gareth is free of any such duplicity. Also contrary to the *Vulgate*, Gareth is unarmed; by following the stanzaic *Morte Arthur* in this detail, Malory enhances both the drama and the pathos of Gareth's role. Finally, the *Vulgate* Gaheriet strikes the first blow and is struck at first not by Lancelot but by Ector. All of these modifications reflect the earlier characterization of Gareth in the "Tale of Gareth," where his friendship with Lancelot was first introduced and where Malory could say of the young man that "allwayes he was meke and mylde." (pp. 106-17)

[No] source has been identified for the "Tale of Gareth." It has been my purpose to suggest that Malory created the "Tale," borrowing some characters and incidents from earlier romances, to serve specific functions within *Le Morte Darthur* as a whole. Following the accounts in the first three "Tales" of the rise of Arthur and of Lancelot, it presents a happy picture of the Round Table at the height of its effectiveness. This picture serves as background against which the coming evidences of human frailty and of inescapable catastrophe in the later "Tales" will be viewed. Further, the character of Gareth himself serves as a standard against which the behavior of Gawain and his other brothers is to be measured. Perhaps most important is Malory's clear presentation of Gareth at this point in his book as preparation for the later irony when Lancelot inadvertently kills him. (p. 117)

> Wilfred L. Guerin, "'The Tale of Gareth': The Chivalric Flowering," in Malory's Originality: A Critical Study of "Le Morte Darthur," edited by R. M. Lumiansky, The Johns Hopkins Press, 1964, pp. 99-117.

EDMUND REISS (essay date 1966)

[Reiss is an American editor and critic who has written widely on medieval English literature. In the following excerpt from his full-length 1966 study of Malory, he closely studies Malory's treatment of courtesy, love, and honor in the "Tale of Gareth."]

The *Tale of Sir Gareth of Orkeney* (Caxton's Book VII) may be viewed as essentially a continuation of Malory's presentation of the ideal knight. A basic difference between this tale and that of Sir Lancelot, however, is that Gareth, the central figure, is not already known for his excellence. The tale acts, therefore, not as a testing of any previously known worth but as the actual development of the man. The revelation of prowess and courtesy is neither after the fact, as it was in the *Tale of Lancelot*, nor in any way superfluous; for the reader does not know how valiant Gareth is. In fact, at the beginning of the tale the reader does not even know the identity of the main character. He exists for all as Beaumains, a name at first apparently meaning "Great Hands," and one contemptuously given him by Sir Kay.

Even though the reader, along with Lancelot, soon finds out that this unknown man is of noble heritage—youngest son of King Lot and brother of Sir Gawain—he still exists throughout much of the romance as Beaumains, an unproven figure. Through his adventures his innate virtues are revealed both to the reader and to the character himself. Nor can these adventures be considered as mere demonstrations of pre-existing valor. Gareth's nobility cannot be regarded as mainly an inherited possession, since Gawain, his brother, is lacking in courtly virtues. While Gawain may be a gallant warrior, he is not a courteous knight. In fact, throughout the tale, Lancelot, rather than Gawain, acts as Gareth's ideal.

A problem that seems to be suggested in this tale is the late medieval conflict between the higher and the lower nobility, the problem of whether true nobility is passively inherited or actively achieved. Knightly qualities can theoretically be held by anyone; but, as Maurice Valency states [in *In Praise of Love: An Introduction to the Love-Poetry of the Renaissance* (1958)], they "would sit badly on a churl since he would normally be lacking in the qualities requisite to a noble way of life." Gareth has inherited nobility, but he keeps this fact hidden so as to prove himself and to be accepted for himself as knight in his own right and not as son of Lot and brother of Gawain. Here nobility of birth, shown supplementing nobility based on personal

merit, makes meaningful the idea that the two must go together: just as the hero must be ideal warrior and lover, so must he combine within himself all facets of nobility.

The *Tale of Gareth* consequently acts also as a dynamic demonstration of the personal merit of its main character. As such it demonstrates the "new principle of nobility, individualistic in character, which could be deduced solely from a man's bearing and behavior." Nobility is "an aptitude and a process" with self-perfection as its end. Only after the hero is proved as Beaumains can he become Gareth; the nobility is really the identity, and it cannot be taken for granted. Also the tale shows Gareth fighting and defeating knights who are quite different from the evil figures found in the *Tale of Lancelot*. What is mainly wrong with these knights is that they are inadequate: although excelling in prowess, they, like Gawain, are lacking in courtesy. The story of Gareth functions furthermore as a demonstration that the perfect knight must combine prowess with courtesy. Lancelot and Gareth show this combination in themselves; they excel and are unbeatable.

Of Malory's romances, the *Tale of Gareth* is unique in not having a known source. Although Malory refers to a "Freynsh boke" as his source, this French romance is unknown. Nevertheless, the story probably goes back to a French source, perhaps to one that may have been "a French non-cyclic prose romance" in which Malory "introduced a few episodes of his own." At the same time, as Vinaver notes, "practically each important episode of the story has a parallel in medieval French romance." Still, as Vinaver also states, whether or not the story in Malory's source was a self-contained narrative, it was "the type of work which Malory himself endeavoured, with varying degrees of success, to shape out of his long-winded cyclic sources, and for this reason alone it must have been much after his own heart."

In particular, the romance is related to the popular kind centering around the figure of some *bel inconnu* some fair unknown. This man, seeming to be of humble origin, excels as a knight and, as is later discovered, really comes from a noble family. Sometimes the hero is the son of a famous figure, as in a version of the *bel inconnu* story represented, for example, by the English *Libeaus Desconus*, in which the main figure turns out to be the natural son of Gawain. At other times the hero does not know who he is, and his *enfances* are revealed as a kind of comedy, as in, for example, stories centering around the young Perceval. Malory also used a story of the *bel inconnu* kind in the *Book of Tristram* in the section called "La Cote Male Tayle," one which may have some connection with the Gareth story. In the *Tale of Gareth* the hero knows who he is but cloaks his ancestry on purpose. Gareth, perhaps like Prince Hal in Shakespeare's *I Henry IV*, wants to hide his light so that, when he is finally known, "he may be more wond'red at." So too do Hal and Gareth experience all sides of life, and the excellence of both must certainly be based partly on their full experience.

The *Tale of Gareth* begins with Arthur preparing to dine at the Feast of Pentecost, but demanding first to witness a "grete mervayle." It comes in the form of Gareth, shown here as a tall man who, not able to walk by himself, must lean on other knights. Gareth presents himself to Arthur as hungry and lacking in strength. Although this helplessness seems strange and may, as Vida Scudder thinks, be merely sham, there may also be a fuller meaning that is not completely brought out by Malory. Symbolically, Gareth's weakness may be an indication that he is not as yet whole or fully developed, for he must still prove himself. His lack of perfection is thus revealed in terms of physical weakness. Still, even in his unformed state, Gareth stands out as, in Arthur's words. "one of the goodlyest yonge men that ever I saw"; and he also appears to be a man who will, in Arthur's estimation, "preve a man of ryght grete worshyp." But, before Gareth can become such a man and before he can be complete, he must experience adversity.

It is traditional in stories showing the development of heroes that good fortune be preceded by misfortune: the hero must experience some sort of lowering or humiliation that may function as an initial purging or preparation. In the *Tale of Lancelot* that knight experiences a lowering because of his inadvertent sleep but Gareth brings about his misfortune himself. Like any common churl and like a man overly concerned with the gross and earthly, Gareth asks Arthur to give him "mete and drynke" for a year, even though Arthur tells him to "aske bettyr," and even though the knights wonder at his boorishness. Kay, in particular, regards Gareth as merely "a vylayne borne," who belongs only in the kitchen, and continually mocks the man. This derision that Kay levels at Gareth supplies in detail the lowering and humiliation that is symbolically Gareth's first test. Through the insults thrown at him, his humility and patience are being tested. Should he give way to his feelings and reveal himself, he will not be strong. It is not then the "mete and drynke" that will build up Gareth and give him strength to stand by himself; it is the humility and patience he must show in the face of the scorn directed at what seems to be his inordinate concern for food. Also, as Gareth later explains, his own conscious humiliation acts as a test for the Knights of the Round Table; for Gareth in his lowly position is able to see who his real friends are. He can, in particular, differentiate between those who value him for himself and those who do so only for his inherited rank.

Along with the development of Gareth, Malory also continues to emphasize the nobility of Lancelot, who appears principally as the courteous benefactor of the young man. Although Gawain too would like to help Gareth, Malory discounts his courtesy as one based on kinship. Even though Gawain is consciously unaware that any relationship exists between him and Gareth, he is still Gareth's brother, and his response to him is an instinctive one. Lancelot's actions, on the other hand, are presented as coming completely from "his grete jantylnesse and curtesy."

After a year of preparation, Gareth moves from his humiliation and servitude to ask permission to go with a damsel who has come to Arthur's court requesting aid for her lady. Because the damsel will not reveal her lady's name but says only that she needs help against a "tirraunte," the Red Knight of the Red Lands, Arthur refuses to give her a champion from his Knights of the Round Table. When Gareth, however, is allowed to follow this adventure, the damsel is angry that she should get only a "kychyn knave." But Gareth now changes. As if by magic, rich armor appears for him; he fights and easily defeats Kay, who had wanted to know whether Gareth would recognize him "for his bettir"; and, concluding his preliminary preparation at

Arthur's court, he fights to a draw and is knighted by Lancelot, the greatest knight in the world.

The first part of Gareth's story ends with the hero rising from his position of "kychyn knave" and redeeming himself in the eyes of Arthur and his knights. In the second part of his tale Gareth proves himself both to the damsel he accompanies and to the world outside Arthur's court. Although in this section Gareth shows great prowess, he also continues to reveal courtesy. His humility and patience are again put to the test, for the damsel continually berates, insults, and scorns him. For example, when Gareth overtakes her, she asks, "What doste thou here? Thou stynkyst all of the kychyn, thy clothis bene bawdy of the grece and talow.... What art thou but a luske [sluggard], and a turner of brochis [spits], and a ladyll-waysher?" In her scorn, the damsel appears similar to Kay; but her taunts are harder for Gareth to bear. He cannot be revenged on her as he was on Kay; with the damsel, he experiences a real test of his innate courtesy, his *gentilesse.* Even after Gareth rescues a knight bound by "six theffis," kills two knights at a ford, slays the Black Knight, and defeats and receives homage from the Green Knight and the Red Knight, the damsel still treats him with scorn. She states that his victories must have been accidental: "evir thou doste is by mysseadventure and nat by preues [prowess] of thy hondys." Throughout his adventures she condemns him with statements that he succeeds only through "myshappe" and "myssefortune."

There is a kind of paradox in Gareth's situation. Unless the man be noble and worthy, his strength and prowess are in vain. It is, for example, like the strength of giants; and, in fact, when Gareth was earlier fighting Lancelot, Malory described him as fighting "more lyker a gyaunte than a knyght." At the same time, unless the man be an able and strong fighter, he cannot be noble. There is truly a narrow path here, and only the best can walk along it.

It is not Gareth's prowess that makes the damsel recognize his worth and inherent nobility but his patience and endurance. The damsel and her words test him, but the test is not finished even after she acknowledges his nobility. When they come to the Blue Knight, the damsel admits that Gareth has done valorous deeds and acted and spoken well with her. Because he has proved himself, and because he and his horse are tired, she advises him to save himself and not fight the Blue Knight. Gareth, however, replies that he will still fight the man and thus refuses to feel that perfection is something one attains momentarily and then forgets. At this point the damsel, who is truly sorry about her previous scorn, says to Gareth, "so fowle and so shamfully dud never woman revyle a knight as I have done you, and ever curteysly ye have suffyrde me." Gareth modestly replies that "a knyght may lytyll do that may nat suffir a jantyllwoman," and he consequently retains his humility.

While acting symbolically as a test for Gareth, the damsel also exists as a real flesh-and-blood person; she is not merely a creature of the supernatural or of magic evoked to prove him. In her treatment of Gareth she has been rash, too outspoken, and too full of *desmesure.* Gareth's humility shames her, and she develops into a more moderate, tolerant person.

The second part of the tale ends with Gareth's defeating the Blue Knight and receiving homage from him. Gareth has, in effect, proved himself as the hero—specifically, as the man of prowess and the gallant man of courtesy—and he is now allowed to know of his future test: the adventure that is the reason for his being with the damsel and that is the heart of the tale. It is revealed that the damsel is Lynet and that she is taking him to the Castel Daungerous to fight for her sister, Dame Lyones, who is besieged by the Red Knight of the Red Lands. This fight, however, is to be seen as more than a local fight and as more than a proving of Gareth's prowess. This Red Knight has kept up the siege of Lyones in hopes of fighting the noblest knights of the world: Lancelot, Tristram, Lamorak, or Gawain. By fighting for Lyones, Gareth may be regarded as joining these warriors in prestige. Also Gareth fights not as an individual knight but as champion of Arthur's court and of knighthood in general.

The Red Knight of the Red Lands, Sir Ironsyde, is in one sense "a full noble knyght"—Gawain had earlier described him as "one of the perelest knyghtes of the worlde"—but he is also lacking: "he is nother of curtesy, bounté, nother jantylnesse; for he attendyth unto nothyng but to murther." In particular, this knight—like Tarquin in the *Tale of Lancelot*—makes "shamfull warre uppon noble knyghtes"; and, after he defeats them, he hangs them "by the necke, and their shyldis about their neckys with their swerdis and gylte sporys uppon their helys." In other words, although this knight is "a full lykly man and a noble knyght of proues, and a lorde of grete londis and of grete possessions," he is imperfect because "in hym is no curtesy."

The conflicts in the *Tale of Gareth* may so far be seen in terms of three stages of development. First, Gareth himself acts as an *exemplum* of the conflict between hereditary nobility and achieved nobility. Then, when Gareth is in the company of the damsel, the first conflict is resolved; but a new one, a conflict between the man of prowess and the man of courtesy, is revealed and begins to be developed. Third, there appears the necessity of the hero's possessing both prowess and courtesy—the fusion of the two is lacking in the Red Knight of the Red Lands; and the fight between him and Gareth is symbolically a fight between imperfection and perfection, at least perfection as it exists so far in Gareth.

A variety of qualities not emphasized in the preceding *Tale of Lancelot* is brought out in the *Tale of Gareth*. The adventures, moreover, do not exist for their own sake but illustrate various imperfections and perfections and are, furthermore, steps along the way in the development of Gareth from Beaumains, the kitchen boy. Like the damsel Lynet, the Red Knight functions as a test for Gareth. He is, in fact, something of a supernatural creature whose strength, like Gawain's, increases till noon and then decreases. Gareth is told by Lynet that he should wait until afternoon to summon the Red Knight to battle, but Gareth characteristically refuses; and his response shows clearly the extent of his courtesy: "A! fy for shame, fayre damesell! Sey ye nevir so more to me, for and he were as good a knyght as ever was only I shall never fayle hym in his moste myght, for other I wyll wynne worshyp worshypfully othir dye knyghtly in the felde." Gareth would not be a true knight, a noble man, if he did not fight when his opponent had his full strength.

Also, a new development now appears: Gareth's prowess and valor are not wholly for the world of knighthood but are also for the Lady Lyones, with whom he falls in love. When Gareth falters during the fight, he is revived by Lynet's words: "A, sir Bewmaynes! Where is thy corrayge becom? Alas! my lady my sister beholdyth the, and she shrekys and wepys so that hit markyth myne herte hevy." Gareth's renewed strength enables him to defeat the Red Knight, who then begs for mercy. Gareth says he cannot with *worship* spare him because of the shameful way he has treated his former opponents, but the Red Knight explains that he "putte hem to so shameful a deth" because of a promise to a lady and that she is responsible for his doing "vylany unto Arthurs knyghtes." Unlike the evil Sir Tarquin of the *Tale of Lancelot*, the Red Knight has acted unchivalrously only because he has kept his word to someone else; he is not the one seeking revenge. Like Pelleas in the *Tale of Arthur*, the Red Knight is driven to an excess through the evil of someone else. When Gareth hears the arguments of "many erlys and barowns and noble knyghtes" who come forward to beg the life of the Red Knight and say that, if he is killed, "his myssededys that he done may not be undone," Gareth agrees to spare the man. This victory ends the third section of the tale.

The fourth section centers around Gareth's love of the Lady Lyones. When, after defeating the Red Knight, he goes to see her, he finds his way blocked; and the lady tells him that he will not enjoy her love until he is "one of the numbir of the worthy knyghtes." He is therefore supposed to "go and laboure in worshyp this twelve-monthe." This assignment is the fourth step in Gareth's development, his ascent to earthly perfection. To be perfect in combat and in the world of the warrior is not necessarily to be so for love. The warrior and the lover represent not only two different ways of life, but the demands of each are different. One requires an external perfection, while the other insists on an internal worth. One would think that Gareth's courtesy would be enough to show that he is not only a man of prowess, but his courtesy must be demonstrated explicitly in terms of love. Although Gareth says to Lyones that he has already "bought" her love with the blood of his body, the lady adamantly insists that he prove himself further.

There is, however, confusion in the story; for no sooner does Gareth sorrowfully go his way than the lady sends her brother, Sir Gryngamour, after him to abduct Gareth's dwarf whom the lady plans to ask "of what kynrede" Gareth is come. Consequently, notwithstanding her earlier words to Gareth, it seems that what the Lady demands from Gareth is proof not only of an achieved nobility but also of an inherited one. The dwarf is taken, reveals his lord's ancestry, Gareth follows to rescue him, and in a short time the knight and Lyones declare their love. But the dwarf had already revealed to the lady Gareth's identity and ancestry. Despite all the confusion here, the important thing seems to be not that Gareth must prove himself further but that he must suffer the pangs of love before being rewarded with his lady's hand. Once again his patience and humility must dominate; he must, as it were, give his all for love.

Thus, after Gareth sorrowfully leaves Lyones, Malory writes that he is not able to sleep: he "had no reste, but walowed and wrythed for the love of the lady of that castell." As Lynet says, not only is Gareth "curtyese and mylde" but he is also "the moste sufferynge [enduring] man" she ever knew. This suffering is presented as a quality, even as a virtue; and as such it is something new to the Arthurian chivalric order seen in Malory. Earlier, in the *Tale of Arthur* Pelleas had suffered for love, but his woe was presented as an excess and something to be avoided. In the *Tale of Gareth*, on the other hand, suffering means enduring and must of necessity be found in a man worthy of both victory in battle and the love of a noble lady.

But both Gareth and Lyones are so much "in hoote love" that they desire "to abate their lustys secretly" before marriage. This consummation, another example of *desmesure*, is prevented by the "subtyle craufftes" of Lynet, who suddenly appears possessing magic and being similar to Nyneve, the Damsel of the Lake, seen in the *Tale of Arthur*. She causes armed knights to intrude upon the two lovers as they lie together in bed; and, although Gareth keeps killing them, Lynet keeps bringing them back to life. Although Gareth criticizes her action, Lynet, by acting for Gareth as a kind of conscience based on chivalric and Christian ideals, does succeed in preventing the lovers from rashly consummating their love. She tells Gareth that everything she docs "shall be for your worshyp and us all."

The rest of the *Tale of Gareth* is primarily concerned with the hero's demonstrating his perfection, primarily his courtesy, to the world and especially to Arthur and his court. Gareth has Lyones call a tournament in which she will be the prize for the best knight. Gareth obviously expects to win the lady, and the tournament may be seen as the specific proof that will rank him among the best knights in the world. In effect, it is really what Lyones had desired when she sent Gareth away, but now it is Gareth himself who suggests the test.

In this tournament Malory seems more concerned with splendor and combat than with Gareth's development. Whereas the hero's action in declaring this tournament that could theoretically end in his losing the lady might seem rash, proud, and even marked by *desmesure*, no such implications are present. Malory appears to be interested only in the tournament itself, and he glories in his descriptive art. In fact, in the whole *Tale of Gareth* there is a striking play of color, of a quality found, as Vida Scudder says, nowhere else in the *Morte Darthur*.

The tournament may be regarded as a battle of the greatest knights in the world, and the list of participants reads like a rollcall of the most famous of all Arthurian knights. Gareth, receiving the help of the knights he had formerly defeated, takes on all of Arthur's forces except Lancelot, who, out of courtesy, will not fight him. The jousting ends inconclusively, however; for, when Gareth's identity is discovered, he is so disturbed that he rides off by himself into the forest. There he performs more acts of prowess that seem to be largely superfluous and finally, in ignorance, fights Gawain, his brother. Before either is killed, however, Lynet, now described as the "lady Savyaige," suddenly appears to stop the fight. The tale ends with Gareth's receiving fealty from the knights he has conquered, becoming a ruler in his own right, and marrying Lyones. Malory also writes that in the future Gareth draws away from the "evir vengeable" Gawain and comes closer to Lancelot, who still remains his ideal. The imperfection in Gareth's brother, specifically the fact that whenever Ga-

wain hates, "he wolde be avenged with murther," is an imperfection that the good, proved Gareth cannot tolerate.

The closeness of Gareth and Lancelot is not accidental, for this entire tale is properly seen in conjunction with the *Tale of Lancelot*. The two men make up earthly perfection, and their two stories describe it; one complements the other. Also these two tales act in conjunction with *Arthur and Lucius*, in which the perfection of Arthur and his Order is seen; and all together these tales illustrate and create the perfection of chivalry in its various manifestations in this world. (pp. 100-09)

> *Edmund Reiss, in his* Sir Thomas Malory, *Twayne Publishers, Inc., 1966, 223 p.*

R. T. DAVIES (essay date 1967)

[*Davies is a distinguished English authority on medieval English literature. In the following excerpt from his introduction to a 1967 selection from the* Morte Darthur, *he reviews the structure and prose style of the work.*]

Although we do not know what title, if any, Malory intended his work to have, Caxton, in his Epilogue, showed that he regarded what he had printed as one book, about King Arthur and his knights, and, in the tailpiece of the last Book, it can scarcely be any other than Malory himself who refers to this work as 'the whole book of King Arthur and of his noble knights', and envisages our reading from its 'beginning' to its 'ending'. The work comprises, then, eight principal 'books' or 'tales'–terms which are used indifferently and which are used also of constituent stories within these larger divisions . . . . (p. 18)

There are, of course, many and gross imperfections and weaknesses of structure and unity. Although Book Five, of Tristram, keys into the Book that follows it, it is the one Book of them all that might make one wonder if Malory had not intended each Book to be separate to an extent that has caused Professor Vinaver to call his edition *The Works of Malory*. For one thing, it is by no means obvious how its events are related chronologically to those in other Books. But the wonder is not so much that there are defects in general cohesion, as that there is so much cohesion as there is. Chaucer above all, but also, for example, Gower and the poet of *Sir Gawain and the Green Knight*, had, some three-quarters of a century earlier, created works in verse conspicuous for their sophisticated unity. But the vast body of diverse Arthurian lore which Malory tackled has been aptly compared by C. S. Lewis to a great medieval church in which its various parts are of various periods and whatever unity there is is not that of any one artist. We should have been much helped had Malory revised his earlier Books (which there is very little to suggest he did) let alone rewritten them as a novelist would in the light of what he had achieved in the last two, and with the kind of skill he had by practice then acquired. He might have fetched out and developed more thoroughly themes that are undoubtedly present and stimulate the attentive reader, but which, despite the amount of selection and arrangement which comparison with his sources suggests he made, still fail to stand out distinctly. There is, for example, the feud between, on the one hand, King Lot and his sons, Gawain, Gaheris and Aggravaine, and, on the other, King Pellinore and his sons, Lamorak, Agglovale and Percival. This theme includes the connection of the death of Lamorak with that of Tristram, in so much as both were slain treacherously.

Malory's style is remarkable for its time in this kind of literature. We do not know whether he was acquainted with English religious homiletic writing, which enjoyed a tradition continuous from Pre-Norman Conquest to Tudor England, and with other prose narratives of the fifteenth century, such as the didactic preachers' stories of the *Gesta Romanorum* and the *Golden Legend*, or the instructive guide-book, *Mandeville's Travels*. Such works as these were less ambitious but, like his, generally translations, sometimes from French. There are certainly other likenesses between some of this prose and Malory's, but so, too, there are between his literary artefact and, for example, the unpretentious, everyday letters of the time. A number remain and are, presumably, written much as they would have been spoken. The major stylistic difference between Book Two, with its alliterative English source, and the other Books, together with Malory's capacity to accommodate such diverse matter as bloody battles, human passion and the appearances of the Grail, suggest that his chameleon genius took its colour from his sources and immediate purposes. Vocabulary and syntax are generally simple, the one comprising chiefly native English words and the other being loosely articulated with 'and's' and 'so's' and 'but's'. His style is basically unsophisticated, direct, concrete, colourful and vigorous, like English speech and never far from it. It might be hazarded that it was for this reason that Malory's dialogue is outstandingly good, were it not that dialogue is good also in English writers more obviously within a literary tradition, such as Chaucer and the poet of *Sir Gawain and the Green Knight*.

On almost every page some passage arrests and moves and reveals Malory's genius as an imaginative writer. Since medieval artists are so often to be seen as didactic or artificial, he is, perhaps, nearer to John Keats, and to Keats's 'Man of Achievement', than might have been expected, in that he has a capacity for entering into a variety of characters and situations and living them out on the page for their own sake and not to make a point or to instruct or to decorate or even to contribute to a greater artistic whole. Though many of the characters are not differentiated at all, Pellinore, Dinadan, Guenevere, Palomydes, Bors, to mention a few, all have distinctive personalities. But they are not, of course, all Malory's peculiar creation: as usual it is not easy to distinguish the traditional and the new. Certainly, on the one hand, multiplicity of invention is characteristically medieval as many an illuminated manuscript or carving in stone or wood will testify, while, on the other, Malory does not always develop fully the potential of his diverse figures. In reading him, however, we may, at one time, be laughing at some of the extravagances of the chivalric attitude and at another sympathizing with it even when it prompts the loyal rescue of a woman who has been frequently distrustful and petulant. Even at the last Guenevere will say to Launcelot as he vows to live the life of penance and prayer, 'I may never believe you.' And, unkind as this may seem, she has some justice on her side for, with creative percipience of the kind I am here indicating, Malory has Launcelot then request a last kiss!

It was the diversity of Malory's work and its power to please which Caxton remarked in his Preface: 'herein may be seen noble chivalry, courtesy, humanity, friendliness, hardiness, love, friendship, cowardice, murder, hate, virtue and sin. . . . And for to pass the time this book shall be pleasant to read in' [see excerpt dated 1485]. Caxton also expected it to serve a moral purpose, but whether, in this, he had interpreted Malory aright is a matter for discussion. Equally, the extent to which, on the one hand, the author wrote with a preconceived moral design and with his principles fully formed, or, on the other, found his moral values as he met the exigencies of translating and retelling the tales under the immediate compulsion of his imagination, is a question to be asked not only of Malory's work but of that of any creative artist. Were the latter the case it might account, for example, for the several, not obviously connected, causes given for the breaking up of the Round Table–the quest of the Sankgreall, the work of Fortune, the adultery of Launcelot and Guenevere, the ill-will of Aggravaine and Mordred, and Arthur's permitting a situation in which he and Launcelot are divided.

Nevertheless, throughout the immense diversity of the whole book there is implicitly affirmed and variously explored the value of a noble way of life appropriate to 'worshipful' men and women. It is one of the factors unifying the work. Prowess shows itself the first characteristic of a knight, that is to say, his valour, physical strength and combative skill. He keeps faith and is honest. He is merciful and he courteously serves women. Guile, treachery and cowardice are consistently rejected.

Very occasionally Malory makes an overt statement about the 'worshipful way'. For example . . . , in a passage for which no source is known, saying that worshipful men and women will always love one more than another, he distinguishes between love 'in King Arthur's days' and 'love nowadays', and, calling the old-fashioned love 'virtuous', so makes his own characteristically impulsive and simple reconciliation of romantic love and Christianity. Marriage is never mentioned, but this love is loyal to one person, stable, steady and continent, and, in this sense, so righteous that he can say of the adulterous Guenevere, whose love was 'virtuous', that she 'had a good end', that is, died in a state of grace. In fact, of course, Guenevere's final state of grace is achieved by her rejection of love in the practice of penance and prayer: she becomes a religious, and everyone marvels how 'virtuously' she is 'changed'. Moreover, Malory blurs the nature of her intimacy with Launcelot at the moment of her being finally surprised in her room with her lover, saying he does not know whether they were in bed together or not. It is this sort of opacity with which we are so often presented in trying to interpret Malory. But his success in making warmly real and desirable to us the relationship between his lovers implicitly affirms the worth he feels there is in it: it is part of the worshipful way that Launcelot follows which is neither ignoble, like King Mark's way, nor holy, like Sir Galahad's, but the way for a country gentleman and a horsed soldier who has not renounced this mutable and sinful world as a monk but, as the best knight 'of a sinful man', strives to make of the world and the flesh something noble. Indeed, such is the quality of the life he lives 'in the world' that, when he leaves it to seek the Grail, he is able to achieve almost as much spiritually as one who has always rejected it, Galahad the greatest Grail knight himself.

These are the sort of guarded considerations one is led to make about what Malory may have found he was saying with developing authority and consistency in his corpus, or series, of Arthurian tales. It was not something merely topical, growing, perhaps, out of the wars and politics of his time. It is a measure of his greatness that, if knightly armour and hermits' cells are to us picturesque archaisms, what Malory describes going on inside them is as relevant to us today as it ever was. It is a further measure of his greatness that it was not until the eighteenth century that England knew again prose narrative of such stature. (pp. 18-23)

> *R. T. Davies, in an introduction to* King Arthur and His Knights: A Selection from What Has Been Known as "Le Morte Darthur" *by Sir Thomas Malory, edited by R. T. Davies, Faber & Faber, 1967, pp. 13-26.*

KENNETH REXROTH (essay date 1968)

[*Rexroth was a leading pioneer in the revival of jazz and poetry in the San Francisco area during the 1940s and 1950s. Largely self-educated, he early became involved with such left-wing organizations as the John Reed Club, the Communist party, and the International Workers of the World. During World War II he was a conscientious objector, but later he became antipolitical in his work and writing. As a critic, Rexroth's acute intelligence and wide sympathy allowed him to examine such varied subjects as jazz, Greek mythology, the works of D. H. Lawrence, and the Kabbal. As a translator, Rexroth was largely responsible for introducing the West to both Chinese and Japanese classics. In the following excerpt, he examines the genre and structure of the* Morte Darthur.]

There is a kind of ecology of the epic. The necessary social conditions that produce the heroic literature of any culture are of short duration. Although the period of epic creation has always been singularly brief, once written the books have proved the most timeless of all. Thomas Malory's *Le Morte d'Arthur* today is almost five hundred years old, yet it still seems to us—judged on our own terms—not only one of the greatest achievements of English prose style but one of the most absorbing narratives.

If heroic literature is disorder recollected in tranquillity, the tranquillity enjoyed by Sir Thomas Malory seems to have been forced. He wrote the book in prison in a troubled time, the last years of the Wars of the Roses—a time almost as bad as the days of the withdrawal of the Roman Imperium from Britain, of the Saxon invasion and the slow, bloody retreat of the Britons, marked by a succession of tragic last stands, across the island and into the fastnesses of Wales.

Homer's tranquillity, according to legend, was equally enforced—by his blindness—and he too looked back five hundred years from a time of troubles to a period of mass invasion. May be the epic arises out of primitive disorder recollected in a time of sophisticated disorder.

We think of the rhythms of Malory's narrative as being of the very texture of noble chivalric utterance. His style has spawned innumerable absurd imitations of knightly speech. We think of the attitudes of his characters as embodying the very essence of the Age of Chivalry. It's not true. When Malory wrote, in the chaotic beginnings of the English Renaissance, the Age of Chivalry was long over. Its ethic survived only as courtly ceremonial etiquette, in

a very few years to be replaced by the deliberate teaching of the *courtoisie* of the Renaissance gentleman. And of course Malory did not write about a historical Age of Chivalry at all but about one laid in the barbaric times immediately after the collapse of Roman civilization.

The world of *Le Morte d'Arthur* is almost completely shaped by the demands men usually fulfill in dream. Into the narrative of the adventures of Arthur and his court and the originally distinct story of the Quest of the Holy Grail, Malory, working in his prison with his French books about him, poured all the shadow life of bygone Medieval Europe. Those who have found in the Grail story the cryptic revelation of a pagan mystery religion or the obscure gospel or the occult ritual of the Albigensian heretics or the ancestors of the Freemasons and Rosicrucians are not correct in fact, but their interpretations are true to the mood that haunts the narrative.

The mysteries that hide behind these tales of knight-errantry, dueling, warfare, adultery, ruined owl-haunted chapels lost in the forest, and wandering maidens lost in enchantment are the mysteries of the human personality itself. It is not just the Unconscious with its universal symbols and archetypes that sets the stage and garbs and manipulates the characters; it is also the essential doom and pathos of the human condition. We all fight a losing battle. Arthur, Tristram, Launcelot, Gawain—even in the beginning, in the days of feasts and tournaments—are losing. We can hear the pulse of their fate in the rhythms of Malory's prose, like the chant of a ritual march.

The story of Galahad and the Grail Quest may well have been included by Malory as a metaphor of the transcendence of the epic's war and adultery, hate and lust. It serves that function in any theoretical analysis of the book. But in the act of reading and appreciation it does not. It separates itself out as a different story. However carefully Malory strives to connect the main story of Launcelot, Arthur, and Gawain with their failure in the Grail Quest, and however symbolical the relation of Launcelot and his bastard son, Galahad, may be, the two plots are really incongruous. The story of the Grail stands best alone.

In spite of tedious detail and naïve style, the Medieval French Grail romances transmit more of the mystery that has attracted generations of cranky interpreters and spinners of learned fantasy, as well as the whole tribe of occultists, to the Grail legends. However, Malory's version is all most modern readers are likely to read, and it is sufficiently awe-inspiring. In *Le Morte d'Arthur* the major actors in the drama of King Arthur's court will find their transcendence not in supernatural vision, but in the common human illumination that comes with the acceptance of tragedy.

Epic in a sense *Le Morte d'Arthur* may be, but above all else it is the last summation of Medieval romance and the first of all modern romances. If the epic heroes of Greece or Iceland are brought down by the monstrous regimen of women, by the malevolence of wives and mistresses, the epic narrator reserves his sympathy for his falling heroes. His villainesses he treats with fear and contempt; his heroines are adoring lovers, dutiful daughters, and loyal housewives.

Tristram and Iseult, Launcelot and Guinevere are equally possessed, equally enraptured, and equally guilty. By no stretch of the imagination was the motive of the Trojans "All for love and the world well lost"; but it is the first and only commandment of all romantic lovers—whether the queens of an imaginary Britain or the emancipated misses of late-nineteenth-century Scandinavia. Launcelot and Guinevere will be reborn many thousand of times in the pages of pulp magazines or in Thomas Hardy's *Two on a Tower* or Lawrence's *Lady Chatterley's Lover*. Their morality will be the dangerous code by which five hundred years of naïve servant girls and oversophisticated and idle millionairesses will live out their destructive lives. Yet we weep for their follies. When they come together in the gloom-enshrouded last days, when all has been spent for love and all the world has been lost indeed, the pathos of their speech is almost more that can be borne, and Malory's prose rises to create one of the greatest passages of literature.

Possibly what gives Malory's narrative structure is its steady progress toward the final judgments of its leading actors upon themselves. Like Lear, at the end they understand their own folly, and so their tragic and romantic lives acquire at last their own significant form. It is ultimately an aesthetic question. D. H. Lawrence's novel is a truncated structure; it lacks a sequel which might have been called *Lady Chatterley's Second Husband*. (pp. 164-68)

*Kenneth Rexroth, "Malory: 'Le Morte d'Arthur',"
in his* Classics Revisited, *Quadrangle Books,
1968, pp. 164-68.*

P. J. C. FIELD (essay date 1971)

[*In the following excerpt, Field discusses the pictorial element in the* Morte Darthur, *noting especially its relation to Malory's adaptation of his sources.*]

Description is related to narration in literature much as decoration is related to structure in architecture; it is impossible entirely to separate one from the other. There is little description which does not add to narrative, and few words in the baldest narration which have no pictorial content. This is particularly important to a study of the **Morte Darthur** since the book contains little elaborate or set-piece description. Most of what we see, hear, and so forth in the story comes from sentences which function primarily by forwarding the action. Description slows the pace of a story and tends to make each incident more self-sufficient, while narrative invites the question "And what then?"

These simple categories are less inadequate than they would be for a piece of twentieth-century literary impressionism because, by a modern reader's expectations, the pictorial element in the **Morte Darthur** is limited both in amount and in complexity. Medieval romance is less descriptive than the average modern novel, and the **Morte Darthur** in turn is less descriptive than most medieval prose romances. . . . Malory wrote with no sign of self-consciousness or of explicit literary theory. So the greater part of his story is naturally written in the readiest and easiest way, in stock phrases, interrupted by flashes of vision and insight at climactic moments. Such high points

are the more striking against the low tension of the mass of his work, and this has persuaded more than one sensitive critic to think of him as a colourful and descriptive writer. This use of stock words and phrases stylises what little pictorial content his work provides. His ladies are all fair, as Robert Graves remarks (unless we take it by default that those of them who are merely "rychely besene" are not), and they are not distinguished into degrees and types of beauty. Malory's work is full of the anomalies of an unselfconscious writer, and he has one solitary young lady with "fayre yalow here". This only points up the fact that we do not know the colour of Arthur's or Lancelot's or Guenivere's. Again, exceptionally, we know the colour of Arthur's eyes, Gareth's height, and Gawain's taste in fruit, but we do not know these things about anyone else in the story, and we finish the *Morte Darthur* with no idea of what either Lancelot or Guenivere looks like, except that the former has a scar on his cheeks. And this, like the scar on Bors's forehead and Gawain's taste in fruit, is necessary to the action.

This sort of occurrence of physical detail in small memorable incidents of the "man-bites-dog" type is a characteristic of chronicles concerned more with the matter than the manner of their story. For instance, in the most famous of all chronicles, we find a similar unique reference to physical height:

> And behold, there was a man named Zacheus, which was the cheefe among the Publicanes, and he was rich. And he sought to see Jesus who he was, and could not for the prease, because he was litle of stature. And he ranne before, and climed up into a sycomore tree to see him, for he was to passe that way. [Luke xix 2-4(A.V.)]

And so with the hairy hands of Esau (Gen. xxvii 22-23) and the linen cloth worn by the young man in the Garden of Gesthemane (Mark xiv 51). In a chronicle, incidents like these either explain some turn in the action, or catch the attention because they are strikingly odd. They all interrupt with unusual descriptive detail a story which normally has no place for it in the progress of psychology, morality, and action.

This description, like the narrative, is nearly all in stock phrases rather than new-minted epithets. Since stock phrases are common both in the *Morte Darthur* and in its sources, it might at first sight be thought that Malory is merely taking his stock phrases from his sources, particularly from his French sources. This is further suggested by the fact that some of the phrases in the English are literal translations of phrases common in the French. "The best . . . of the worlde" corresponds to "le plus . . . del monde", and "Ce veuille ge bien" to "I wille well." But further consideration suggests that the causes are more complicated. Some of Malory's phrases are taken directly from the corresponding point in his source, but a good many of the French phrases do not appear in his work at all. "Lors huerte li cheval d'esperons" is one phrase common in all the French romances which Malory does not adopt. Some of the phrases are found in original composition in Malory's time and seem to be part of the English language. And others are replaced by English ones which are not even inspired by the French, let alone translated from it. When a French knight charges his enemies, he normally "les fait voler a terre," where the most common phrase in Malory is "smote them over their horses' tails."

Knights joust in the courtyard for the ladies of the castle. From London, British Library, Add. MS. 12228.

This habit of description in stock phrases would seem to have been drawn not so much from the texts in front of him as from the combination of a chronicler's attitude to his story with the composition habits of spoken rather than written prose. (pp. 83-5)

In keeping with the importance of chivalry to his book, Malory's descriptions of people are normally not physical but moral and emotive ones. They force a certain response on us: such are descriptions of Lancelot as "the best knight in the world", and of Arthur as "the most noble king that made me knight" A comparison of the parallel texts edited by Helen Wroten of the **Morte Darthur** and the alliterative *Morte Arthure* shows that one of Malory's most frequent changes is to substitute "noble knights" for the plain "knights" of the alliterative text. He even on one occasion makes the enemy "noble Romaynes". This is his view of his characters and theirs of each other. So we as readers have to create a physical appearance to fit our idea of a noble knight, instead of having some idea of the appearance of the man who plays out his part before us, and deciding for ourselves that he is noble. (p. 86)

Malory calls forth the strongest degree of evoked emotional response to be found in any English author of major literary status, and this response is largely produced by the cumulative effect of description in moral and emotive terms. His characters cannot be separated from the re-

sponse he builds into them. In the action, the reader apprehends the indivisible unit of the "*noble* king" or the "*good* knight". This is the basis of a story whose structure and substance are seen in the same terms: of good and bad, shame and honour, God and conscience.

The overwhelming effect of the **Morte Darthur** comes from the unification of all levels of the story, but in an examination of the style, it is the more immediately verbal elements which concern us. A detailed comparison of a passage of Malory's story with its source will show us how his visual imagination worked.

Quasi-statistical measurements can only act as pointers to literary judgements, and not as substitutes for them. But it is a strong pointer that in the whole tale of Balin, Malory originates no piece of description more striking than "hir mantell . . . that was rychely furred". Almost all his description is inspired by the French and incorporates words and sometimes translates whole sentences from it. In the later parts of the **Morte Darthur**, however, he does add occasional physical details to the story. But Malory is not only unwilling to increase the descriptive element in this story; he also ruthlessly cuts out a great deal of it from his sources. In the tale of Balin, this starts in the first paragraph, where the wounded messenger on his foundered horse is replaced by "ther com a knyght". He does the same in the two major descriptive passages of the

French: the scene of Balin's adventure with the *pensif chevalier*, and the scene where he and his brother attack Royens and his knights. I propose to examine the second of these in detail.

The French is a tense, lucid, and relatively naturalistic account of a particular ambush. It is a much more convincing military incident than any fight in the *Morte Darthur*. A mind which delighted in the immediate details of the chivalric life shows us the knights waiting in the moon-shadows at the roadside, the anxious half-suspicious conversation with their unrecognised guide, a narrow road which makes it possible to attack Royen's knights all at once, and the physical appearance of the wounded Royens regaining consciousness, giving parole at the point of the sword, and finding himself unable to ride. The delight in the practical details of the chivalric life overflows into ironic comment on cowardice and its results:

> Si tornerent erramment en fuies. Et ne voient comment il se puissent eschaper, si se laissent cheoir a val la montagne, car ensi cuident il bien fuir et eschaper; mais l'avalee estoit si roste et si haute qui'il laissent la doutouse mort et emprendent la certainne: car nus qui a val se laisse cheoir ne la puet eskiver qu'il ne muire errauement.

The French incident is a little wordy, but it is competent narration by any standards.

Malory is not at his narrative best, but shows indications of where his later strength will lie. The skilful description which gives a clearly visualised, coherent, and probable course of events is discarded except for a few lines. Not one of the points of detail listed above is retained.

We notice several characteristic kinds of omission. The first is of merely connective detail. The French author puts his characters in the wood to wait for nightfall. "Ensi parloient entre eus trois ensamble de moult de choses." This purely connective detail of little visual or causal value serves in the French to make the progress of the story more solid, but Malory removes it. Such things recur continuously in the French romance from the beginning, and in the English are always drastically reduced and usually cut out, so that the sequence of actions in Malory tends to be abrupt and even disconnected. Similarly in the French prose *Tristan*, two knights prepare to fight one another, and the author describes the process in some detail. The knights exchange their challenges through a squire, and "L'escuier s'empart, et vient a Persides et lui dit les paroles que Palamedes lui mandoit." Malory reports the words of the challenge as they are given to the squire, but gives nothing corresponding to the sentence quoted. We must infer from the resulting actions that the squire has done as he was told. All the French authors give a good deal of this civilised background of behaviour. The details of Lancelot's rising in the prose *Lancelot* are one example:

> Et Lancelot est vestus et appareillies, et orent oy messe entre lui et les .iij. chevaliers qui avec lui estoient. Il envoierent querre lor armes au chastel....

Again, at the end of a day in the *Mort Artu*:

> Au soir quant il fu tens de couchier, Lancelos se parti de leanz a grant compaignie de chevaliers, et quant il furent a lor ostel, Lancelos dist a Boort....

Or a passing phrase earlier in the same book:

> Quant les napes furent levees....

None of the phrases appears in Malory, who is disinclined to be circumstantial at any time, and who shows us next to nothing of the refinements of manner or the details of daily life among his noble knights. Phrases such as these do naturally appear in those English romances which are translated closely from the French. We may instance the following, from Caxton's translation of one of Charlemagne romances:

> Fayr was the courte, and the daye was full fayr and bryght, and fayr was the company, as of xv. kynges, xxx dukes and lx erles. They wente to the chirche for to here the fayr messe that was song; and moche riche was the offeryng. And whan they had herde the messe, they cam ayen to the palays, and asked after water for to wasse their handes; and the dyner was redy, so they wasshed and set theym doun to dyner.

Malory steadily reduces this kind of description in the *Morte Darthur*. He can use flat summary statement similar to "ensi parloient entre eus trois ensemble de moult de choses;" indeed, one of his most characteristic traits of style is to have someone neither visualised nor individualized making great cheer or great dole in a totally formulaic way. But this is rarely filling in time or space. It is almost always the beginning or end of something, establishing the grief for a suicide, the compassion for a burial, or the curiosity for a quest: a structural part of the action.

Secondly, within the action itself, the descriptive detail is cut down, even though it may contribute to the progress as well as to the mood of the story. The French ambush of Balin convinces us because we see the moon rising as the mounted squire thunders past the lurking ambushers, and we see the trees whose shadows conceal them on the side of the road away from the steep slope. The physical circumstances cause and explain much of the action: they are a large part of the reality which the French story gives us. The main structure of Malory's incident is less the physical circumstances of the act and more its central significance, that the two have defeated the forty. This is the kind of story which Malory always tells. (p. 86-9)

A much later ambush of even greater importance to the plot of the *Morte Darthur* is even less circumstantial than the one in the tale of Balin:

> But so, to make shorte tale, they were all condiscended that, for bettir for wars, if so were that the quene were brought on that morne to the fyre, shortely they all wolde rescow her. And so by the advyce of sir Launcelot they put hem all in a wood as nyghe Carlyle as they myght, and there they abode stylle to wyte what the kynge wold do.

The incident concentrates on the personal relations: who holds the initiative? who counters him? not on physical facts.

In the French tale of Balin, Merlin appears "desghisés...d'unc roube d'un conviers toute blanche," but in English only "disgysed so that they knew hym nought." Similarly, Malory does not often bother to recount the particular blows which win a fight. He omits the more brutal facts of the fight between Lancelot and the knights who set on Kay. In his source, Lancelot flays the face off one of his opponents. And this holds generally throughout the *Morte Darthur*. There are, as always with Malory, exceptions; there is no sign that he did not add to the French of his own initiative:

> Arthurs swerde braste at the crosse and felle on the grasse amonge the bloode, and the pomell and the sure handyls he helde in his honde.

But such clear and detailed description is very exceptional, even at climactic moments. He reduces a two-stage fight in the French prose *Tristan* to "by forse". In proportion, the pictorial element of the French sources is cut much more than the dialogue. When Malory keeps or adds descriptions, they are usually connected clearly with meaning. So when he adds "no speare in hys reste" to a fight, it is to justify the good knight Sir Tristram taking a fall. The most striking piece of description in Malory's tale of Balin is Merlin's statuary, which serves to emphasise the central theme of the triumphant knightliness of Arthur. It also provides a clear foreshadowing of the Grail story: a persuasive motive for preserving it, since Malory is particularly interested in the early books of the *Morte Darthur* in establishing forward links with the later ones. One suspects that it is these reasons, and not a desire to visualise, which have persuaded Malory to preserve this notable descriptive passage. (pp. 90-1)

A striking exception to the general lack of description in the *Morte Darthur* is "Lucius", which is much more vivid and colourful than the parts of the book derived from the French. Malory is always affected by his sources, and just as he preserves whole lines of alliterative poetry in his narrative, so he keeps Arthur's dream of the dragon. And part of the description of the giant of the mountain is also preserved. All the physical details in Malory come from the alliterative poem, and he only adds:

> He was the foulyst wyghte that ever man sye, and there was never suche one fourmed on erthe, for there was never devil in helle more horryblyer made.

This is typical of Malory's description; a non-visual negative and superlative. The reader's imagination must respond to its own image. (p. 93)

A considerable amount of colourful positive description in "Lucius" remains. But when we compare Malory's tale with its source in detail, we can see that Malory has in fact drastically excised the descriptive. Clear, rich, set-piece descriptions are among the most striking beauties of English alliterative poetry, and the *Morte Arthure* contains some outstanding ones. Malory makes a clean sweep of them all. The vivid picture of the embarkation for France has vanished without trace. The seventy-line description of the feast for the Roman ambassadors is reduced to three lines, and its descriptive content to one word:

> So they were into chambyrs and served as rychely of *deyntés* that myght be gotyn. So the Romaynes had thereof grete mervayle.

Malory has reduced all the overwhelming catalogue of culinary achievement to a single evocative phrase. Had he had an explicit theory of style, he would presumably have "normalized" the prose of "Lucius", in imagery, rhythm, and syntax. As it is, we can see in the enormous incomplete change which has taken place, a confirmation that his reshaping of the French was not accidental. In the

Morte Darthur, physical detail is not the ultimate reality: we are not given a phenomenological view of life. (p. 94)

Most of Malory's images are stock ones which recur throughout a passage, sometimes throughout the whole book. To rise to acute sensory perception or to a formal simile is rare with Malory, and he repeats the figures which he does use, often several times.

> They twenty knyghtes hylde them ever togydir as wylde swyne, and none wolde fayle other.

> A company of good knyghtes, and they holde them togydirs as borys that were chaced with doggis.

> Smote hym to the colde erth.

> The noble knyghtes were layde to the colde erthe.

> And than they fought togiders, that the noyse and the sowne range by the watir and woode.

> They com in so fersely that the strokis redounded agayne fro the woode and the watir.

> Ever he wepte as he had bene a chylde.

> Ever sir Launcelote wepte, as he had bene a chylde that had bene beatyn.

Some are separated by only a few pages, some by the major part of the *Morte Darthur*. But as one of the few striking elements in a style generally unobtrusive, they serve to bind the whole together. . . . But they do not draw attention to the narrator as an individual, for, however appropriate their use, the comparisons are those of the ordinary man:

> A grete steede blacker than ony beré.

> Sylke more blacker than ony beré.

> Horse and man all black as a beré.

> A stronge blacke horse, blacker than a byry.

These elements of the common speech do not attract attention: we focus on the facts they represent and not on the manner of their expression. They give little hint of physical sensitivity in their author. Even when strikingly just, and the description of Lancelot weeping is of unsurpassed insight, it is not the physical resemblance which impresses the reader, but the psychological and moral comparison.

Linked with this description is a type of action of which the French author is very fond, and which Malory retains to a large degree: the chivalric ritual statement. It has been said that the chivalric romances were "a self-portrayal by feudal knighthood of its mores and ideals". Though this was no doubt more conscious in the sophisticated Chrétien de Troyes who provoked it than in our present author, it may well explain the prevalence of the sort of statement in which "Balin left" becomes "Balyn sente for hys horse and armoure, and so wolde departe frome the courte, and toke his leve of kynge Arthure." The chivalric ritual statement is an expression of a sense of the proper, the feeling that the acts which are the outward signs of the knightly way of life should have a place in expressing knighthood. Everyone *goes*, but only a knight sends for his horse and armour and takes his leave of the king. When Lancelot says:

"Now woll I do by your counceyle *and take myne horse and myne harneyse* and ryde to the ermyte sir Brastias..."

the function of these apparently superfluous words is not to inform Bors of the obvious, nor, as it might be in a different mode of writing, to prepare for some twist in the action for which Lancelot needed to be mounted and armed, but to stress again the knighthood of Lancelot, which is the thesis to be set against the antithesis of his sin, in the dialectic of Malory's story. In the French story of Balin, the author describes the first meeting of the brothers in a formula which Malory gives in very similar words:

And whan they were mette they put of hyr helmys and kyssed togydirs and wepte for joy and pité.

This is the proper, the admirable, the knightly thing. So is Lanceor's pursuit of Balin.... So it is generally that heads should be smitten off lightly, that horses should be ridden a great pace, and that knights should thrust and foin, trace and traverse, in statements with a minimum of descriptive content.

This neglect of physical detail is matched by something of a disregard for human limitations. Malory's knights share with their French originals an intensification of activity above the human norm but rarely quite impossible. The fights are therefore not *quite* realistic, since it is improbable that any man could, for instance, fight all day in armour without resting. The reader blinks when he finds Lancelot *en queste* cleaving one adversary "unto the throte", a second "unto the pappys", and a third "to the navyll". Similarly with the small details of life: squires appear from nowhere when needed and are forgotten when not. But reality is almost the rule. Pumpkins rarely turn into stage-coaches, and when they do, it is not by a knight's contrivance. The problems which King Arthur's knights have to face remain analogous to our own: the final tragedy is simplified but still real. (pp. 98-100)

The omission of connective statement, pictorial description, and inferable fact, the reduction in the number of small incidents revealing character, and the pruning even of the formulaic chivalric statement contribute to a style of unified effect [in the **Morte Darthur**]. These fit in with the increase in pace given by reducing the story to a quarter of its length, with the unobtrusive stock words and phrases, the simple co-ordination of clauses, and the constant tone produced by the repetition of moral and emotive terms of praise. All these factors combine to increase verisimilitude, and to ensure that the reader's attention is given to the facts of the narrative, and not to the narrator or his manner of narration. Insofar as we are aware of the narrator whose *persona* comes off the page to us, our impression is of a somewhat naive man, who cares only for the essential facts, who tells a plain blunt tale, despising all mannered writing which might interfere with the truth. The relation of this *persona* to Sir Thomas Malory is a matter of biographical interest only, but the verisimilitude which it conveys forces the reader to suspend his disbelief in the rather crudely narrated ambush which we have examined. It is this pictorial asceticism which emphasises those moral implications of the story which in the end dominate its effect. Malory's style is the result of a complex of elements too heterogeneous and irregular in their

combination to be the results of conscious art; but the careless yet subtle amalgam into which its elements have been fused will bear comparison with the greatest and most distinctive styles in English prose. (pp. 101-02)

> *P. J. C. Field, in his* Romance and Chronicle: A Study of Malory's Prose Style, *Barrie & Jenkins, 1971, 202 p.*

LARRY D. BENSON (essay date 1976)

[*An American academic and critic, Benson is an authority on Middle English literature. In the following excerpt from his 1976 study* Malory's "Morte Darthur," *he closely examines Malory's account of the death of Arthur in the* Morte Darthur, *noting especially the role of Fortune in the closing pages of the work.*]

The last tale of the **Morte Darthur** presents the convergence of the historical forces that produce the great anger "that stynted nat tylle the floure of chyvalry of alle the worlde was destroyed and slayne," and the narrative method becomes more historical than thematic. The movement of the action is tragic, as we see Lancelot, who was at the height of his career at the end of *Lancelot and Guenevere*, plunged into misery, and the tone becomes one of mourning, tears, pity, and distress. The historical tragedy that began in *The Sancgreal* here reaches its conclusion. Yet the tone of *The Death of Arthur* is also one of forgiveness, of final joy, and it shows the ultimate triumph of virtue over vice, if not in the world at large at least in the protagonists themselves. Arthur, Gawain, Guenevere, and Lancelot all bear part of the guilt for the tragic fall of the Round Table, yet all four are forgiven and we see each for the last time not as a sinful and flawed tragic figure but as an exemplar of virtue finally rewarded for faithfulness to love or chivalry. Though Lancelot is plunged into misery, he rises to the joy of Heaven. This movement is part of the thematic comedy that continues throughout the final three tales, the overall rise of Lancelot from the failure of his Grail quest to the triumph of his end and the affirmation of the values for which he stands. The double movement of Lancelot's fortunes within this tale is a recapitulation of the simultaneous comedy and tragedy that informs the whole last section of the **Morte Darthur**.

As in each of the final tales, the figure of Lancelot provides the main coherence. The narration begins with Lancelot, Arthur, and the Round Table still abiding in prosperity. The treachery of Agravain and Mordred sets the forces of tragedy in motion; Lancelot must flee, Guenevere is sentenced to die at the stake, and Lancelot rescues her, accidentally killing Gareth as he does so. This unfortunate act earns him the implacable hatred of Gawain and brings on the first war between Lancelot and Arthur. The war is temporarily settled when Lancelot returns Guenevere to Arthur and is exiled from England. This brings Lancelot to his lowest point in the tale, a victim, as he says, of Fortune. Arthur remains in relative prosperity even during the siege of Benwick that follows. His tragic fall begins with Mordred's betrayal. Lancelot is left in Benwick, while Arthur returns to England, where both he and Gawain are killed, the Round Table is destroyed, and Guenevere flees to a nunnery. Only then, after the complete narration of Arthur's fall, do we return to the story of Lancelot, who comes back to England to begin the comic movement from the "povre estat" upward to the highest point, borne up by countless angels to Heaven, where, we assume, he still abides in prosperity.

Consequently, although, *The Death of Arthur* is indeed a "most piteous" and tragic tale, it is a very unusual example of that genre. Perhaps most unusual in a fifteenth-century tragedy is the absence, in the story of Arthur's fall, of any reference to Fortune, the force that invariably appears in and defines the genre of late medieval tragedy. Malory mentions Fortune only once in the entire tale, and then only in reference to Lancelot's fall. No doubt all the characters are in Fortune's power, but Malory makes almost nothing of this. His French source, the *Mort Artu*, makes a great deal indeed of the role of Fortune. For example, in the *Mort Artu* Arthur's dream of Fortune is not just a comment on the action, as in the analogous alliterative *Morte Arthure;* it is a symbol of the tragic movement of the entire work. Arthur recognizes this: "A, Fortune! Contrary and varying creature, the most disloyal thing that might be in this world, why were you so courteous and friendly to me if you were to sell it to me so dearly in the end? You who were once my mother have become my step-mother, and to make me die of grief you have brought Death with you, so that you have shamed me in two ways at once, through my friends and through my land." He returns to this theme when he is dying: "Girflet, Fortune, who has been my mother until this but has now become my step-mother, makes me spend the rest of my life in grief, bitterness, and sorrow." Fortune has done as she threatened in Arthur's dream, and in the *Mort Artu* the final battle is the realization of the symbolism of that dream.

Although Malory knew both the dream of Fortune in the *Mort Artu* and the much more elaborate account in the alliterative *Morte Arthure,* he turns for his version to the stanzaic *Morte Arthur* and thus reduces the dream to a brief presage of coming disaster: Arthur dreams that he is seated on a great wheel, above hideous black water in which are all manner of beasts and serpents. The wheel turns, he falls among the beasts, and he awakes crying "Helpe! Helpe!." There is no Dame Fortune to turn the wheel and no direct hint that Fortune controls the events of Arthur's last days.

Certainly this does remove Fortune completely from the work. Though she does not appear in Arthur's dream, her wheel does, and in this context only the most obtuse fifteenth-century reader could have missed its implications. Likewise, although Fortune is mentioned only once in the tale, this occurs in Lancelot's speech after his banishment from England, which marks the moment when the fellowship of the Round Table is broken forever, and the reader must recognize that Arthur's situation as well as Lancelot's is due to the workings of Fortune. Finally, when Lancelot describes himself as a victim of Fortune, he cites as previous examples Hector and Alexander, who are, like Arthur, among the Nine Worthies. In later medieval literature the Nine Worthies are common *exempla* of the workings of Fortune (they so appear in the alliterative *Morte Arthure*), and the mention of two of the pagan Worthies in this context must surely have reminded many of Malory's readers of the first and greatest of the Christian Worthies, as Caxton calls Arthur in his preface to this book [see excerpt dated 1485].

The implications are clear and probably intentional: Arthur is a tragic figure. Malory could hardly have presented him in any other light. However, it is also clear that Malory makes as little as possible of Fortune's power over Arthur. By Malory's time the older, morally neutral idea of the tragedy of Fortune (a fall, deserved or not) was developing toward the more modern idea that the tragic hero, because of some flaw, bears responsibility for his own fall. This is already the case in the *Mort Artu*, where the fall is a punishment for sin, and by the middle of the fifteenth century it was true of an increasing number of tragedies of Fortune. By avoiding any direct mention of Fortune in relation to Arthur, Malory provides as little occasion as possible for suggesting these associations to his readers. Instead, he makes Lancelot the focus of the tragedy, and though he omits every mention of Fortune that he found in the *Mort Artu* he invents that speech in which Lancelot blames Fortune for his fall.

Lancelot's lament on Fortune comes very early in the tale, well before Arthur's last battle. Apparently we are to see Arthur as the victim of Lancelot's tragedy, with Lancelot as the scapegoat for Arthur's fall. Lancelot can bear the blame, for unlike Arthur, whose history required a sudden fall and death, Lancelot's history allowed time for amendment of life, for the comic upward movement that redeems him in our eyes as well as God's. Of course, even Lancelot bears little guilt. Malory spreads the blame so widely that little is left for Lancelot: Gawain and Guenevere claim they are to blame; Mordred and Agravain are indeed guilty of initiating the disaster; and blind destiny, the English people, even the adder, are among the cause of the final catastrophe.

Arthur alone remains relatively blameless. Malory even removes, as much as possible, Mordred from his role as agent of divine retribution for Arthur's incest. This is, of course, a major force in the historical tragedy. In *The Tale of King Arthur* Merlin had foretold that Mordred would kill Arthur as a punishment for his incest, and Mordred does exactly that. In the *Mort Artu* the reader is clearly reminded of this. When Arthur learns of Mordred's rebellion, he says: "Ah, Mordred, now you make me recognize that you were the serpent that I once saw issue from my belly and that burned my land and attacked me. But never did a father do as much to his son as I shall do to you, for I shall kill you with my two hands." And at exactly the moment the mortal blows are exchanged, we are told "Thus the father killed the son, and the son mortally wounded the father." Malory mentions in passing that Mordred was made regent of England because "syr Mordred was kynge Arthurs son," but he never refers to the earlier prophecy, and the only mention of Mordred's sinful engendering is in a context designed to emphasize Mordred's incestuous longings rather than Arthur's. Mordred "Toke quene Gwenyver, and sayde playnly that he wolde wedde her (which was his unclys wyff and his fadirs wyff)."

However, our impression of Arthur as the victim of Fortune rather than the sinful agent of his own destruction arises mainly from the action itself. In the *Mort Artu* Arthur is the ordinary sort of late medieval tragic hero, blinded by pride and heedlessly rushing to his own doom. The dying Gawain begs him to send for Lancelot's help in the coming battle with Mordred, but Arthur steadfastly refuses to do so. After Gawain has died, he appears to Arthur in a dream, and again he begs him to avoid the coming battle.

> Sir Gawain said, weeping: "Sire, avoid fighting Mordred; if you fight him, you will die or be mortally wounded."
>
> "Certainly," said the king, "I shall indeed fight him, even if I must die for it, for I would be a coward if I did not defend my land against a traitor."

Arthur receives further warnings, and Mordred himself offers to negotiate. Arthur rejects Mordred's offer and ignores the warnings. When the archbishop begs him to delay the battle, "the king swore by the soul of his father Utherpendragon that he would never turn back." Even when the archbishop shows Arthur the stone that Merlin erected to prophesy the king's defeat, his pride will not allow him to turn back.

> "Sire," said King Arthur, "I see enough that, if I had come so far forward, I would turn back, whatever desire I had had until now. But now may Jesus Christ help us, for I shall never leave here until Our Lord has given the victory to me or to Mordred; and if it turns out badly for me, that will be through my sin and my excess, for I have a greater number of good knights than Mordred has."

Arthur's army is badly outnumbered, but he is too blinded by pride to recognize this. Too late he realizes that he should have taken Gawain's advice and sent for Lancelot, "For I know well if I had asked him he would have come willingly and courteously." Neither the Arthur of the *Mort Artu* nor its reader is left in any doubt about the king's responsibility for his own fall.

Malory's version is altogether different. In the beginning of the tale Arthur is the headstrong king of the *Mort Artu*, determined to avenge himself upon Lancelot. But his anger is soon tempered; he is eager to forgive Guenevere and take her back to end the first campaign against Lancelot, and he invades Benwick only because Gawain forces him to. He also does all he can to avoid the last battle. When the dead Gawain appears to Arthur and warns him to delay the battle until Lancelot arrives with reinforcements, Arthur immediately sets about arranging a truce. He, not Mordred, offers to negotiate, and he is willing to grant Mordred the most generous terms in order to avoid the battle in which he knows the flower fo chivalry will be destroyed.

That final battle takes place not because of Arthur's blind pride but because of blind chance—the adder that glides forward just at the moment when Arthur and Mordred are about to settle their differences peaceably:

> Ryght so cam oute an addir of a lytyll hethe-buysshe, and hit stange a knyght in the foote. And so whan the knyght felte hym so stonge, he loked downe and saw the addir; and anone he drew hys swerde to sle the addir, and thought none othir harme. And whan the oste on bothe partyes saw that swerde drawyn, than they blewe beamys, trumpettis, and hornys, and shoutted grymly, and so bothe ostis dressid hem togydirs. And kynge Arthur toke hys horse and seyde, "Alas, this unhappy day!" And so rode to hys party, and sir Mordred in lyke wyse.

"Unhappy" has the meaning "ill fortune," and it recurs throughout this tale; but it also means "miserable" and "unlucky," for it is a more ambiguous and less exact term than "Fortune." Clearly the fall of the Round Table is predestined by history, by Providence or Fortune. Those two "unhappy knights" Mordred and Agravain are the immediate agents of the tragic fall, and Arthur's incest, the feud between the houses of Pellinor and Lot, and the love of Lancelot and Guenevere are the ultimate causes. But one cannot escape the feeling that save for a series of unhappy accidents the catastrophe might have been avoided: if Lancelot had not accidentally killed Gareth, if the English people, beyond Arthur's control, had not proved fickle at just that moment, if the adder had not glided forward when it did—all might have ended differently. The *ifs* are of course illusory; the book had to end this way, but the recurring suggestion of accident in Malory's version clearly implies that Arthur is helplessly and innocently caught in forces beyond his or anyone's control.

Nevertheless, Arthur does bear part of the blame for the tragic fall of the Round Table. Therefore, for Arthur, as for all of his protagonists, Malory provides a form of forgiveness, and our last view of the king is one that suggests divine approval. Malory's most striking addition to the history of Arthur is the prophecy of Arthur's return. The ***Morte Darthur*** has so powerfully shaped our own ideas of Arthurian history that many readers believe the prediction of Arthur's return is an inevitable part of the story of his death.

> Yet som men say in many partys of Inglonde that kynge Arthure ys nat dede but had by the wyll of oure Lorde Jesu into another place; and men say that he shall com agayne, and he shall wynne the Holy Crosse. Yet I woll nat say that hit shall be so, but rather I wolde sey: here in thys world he chaunged hys lyff. And many men say that there ys wrytten upon the tumbe thys:
>
> Hic iacet Arthurus; rex quondam rexque futurus.

There is nothing like this in any other version of Arthur's death known to Malory. The manuscript of the alliterative *Morte Arthure* ends with that inscription which "men say" is on Arthur's tomb, but this was added in a later hand and has nothing to do with the poem itself, which ends with Arthur dead and the survivors weeping in despair. Likewise, in the stanzaic *Morte Arthur*, says he will go "a little stounde / Into the Vale fo Avaloun," but there is no hint of his return. In that poem, as in the *Mort Artu* and Hardyng's *Chronicle*, any allusion to Arthur's survival would have weakened the tragic effect at which the authors aimed. Malory seems determined to do just that, to undercut the tragedy by the suggestion that "Arthur by the wylle of oure Lorde Jesu" has "chaunged hys lyff." Malory's point is not that Arthur will return ("I woll nat say that hit shall be so") but that his death is marked by divine approval for the good deeds of his life, which clearly outweigh his human defects.

Malory suggests that the same is true of each of his other characters. Even Gawain, who of the four major characters comes nearest to being the direct agent of the downfall of the Round Table and who is clearly the least virtuous, is rehabilitated in death. Gawain confesses his guilt to Arthur in his dying speech: "Thorow me and my pryde ye have al thys shame and disease, and had that noble knyght, sir Launcelot, ben with you, as he was and wolde have ben, thys unhappy war had never begun." Then Gawain makes amends for his sins. he writes a letter to Lancelot, "flour of al noble knyghtes that ever I harde of or saw be my dayes," and he explains that he alone is responsible for his own death. He begs Lancelot to come to England and pray for his soul help defeat that false traitor Mordred.

Lancelot does come to England, and he prays for three days at Gawain's tomb. Gawain thus received Lancelot's forgiveness, and perhaps the reader's as well. He seems clearly to have had God's forgiveness, for after his death he is allowed to appear to Arthur in a dream in which he warns the king to avoid the coming battle with Mordred (advice which, as we have noted, Arthur does his best to take). This is significant, since it means that our last view of Gawain is of a good knight doing his duty by his king. But more significant is the fact that God allows Gawain to return from death in this manner because of the chivalric deeds he achieved while he was living. Gawain appears to Arthur accompanied by a great crowd of ladies. He explains, "Al thes be ladyes for whom I have foughten for, whan I was man lyvvnge. And all thes ar tho that I did batayle for in righteuous quarrels, and God hath gyvyn hem that grace, at their grete prayer, bycause I ded batayle for them for their ryght, that they shulde brynge me hydder unto you." Gawain, as we know, did many unrighteous battles as well, but apparently his good deeds outweigh his evil, and chivalry avails even in Heaven.

So perhaps does earthly love. We . . . [may remark] that passage in which we learn that Guenevere is destined to have a "good end" because she was a "trewe lover." There is obviously a difficulty here, since her acts as a true lover created the conditions that brought about the fall of the Round Table. She is aware of this and takes the veil to atone for her ill deeds. Like Gawain, she confesses her sin. When Lancelot comes to the nunnery, she tells her fellow nuns, "Thorow thys same man and me hath al thys warre be wrought, and the deth of the most nobelest knyghtes of the worlde, for thorow oure love that we have loved togydir is my most noble lorde slayne. Therefore, sir Launcelot, wyte thou will I am sette in suche a plyght to gete my soul hele." That she does get her soul "hele" is shown by two passages that Malory invented—Guenevere's gift of prophecy, whereby she foretells her own death, and the miraculous vision that announces her death to Lancelot with the divine command that she be buried next to Arthur. Just as our last view of Gawain is of the good knight doing his duty by his king, so our last view of Guenevere is of the good wife, at last reunited with her husband.

Again Malory's version is much different from the French. In the *Mort Artu*, as in most versions of the last days of the Round Table, Guenevere enters the nunnery not out of any sense of penitence but because she fears for her safety. She thinks Mordred will kill her if he wins the last battle, and Arthur will kill her if he wins. She spends a sleepless night, "badly frightened, for she could see no escape anywhere," and she finally decides to flee to a nunnery: "Thus the queen remained there with the nuns because of the fear that she had of King Arthur and of Mordred." As the author of the alliterative *Morte Arthure* tells it, "She kaires to Caerlion and caught her a veil/Askes there the habit in the honour of Crist/And alle for falsede and fraud and fere of her lord!"

Malory's Guenevere is a more admirable character, truly repentent for her sin and yet a "trewe lover." By her good example she brings Lancelot to salvation. And, though she must renounce any possibility of happiness with Lancelot, we are shown in her death scene that she still loves him, knows the power of her love, and therefore dares not look upon him. "Wherfor the quene sayd in heryng of hem al, 'I beseche Almyghty God that I may never have power to see syr Launcelot wyth my worldly eyen!'" Lancelot has become a temptation rather than a joy to her, but this is because her love for him remains true, and she has a good end.

Finally, Lancelot is absolved from blame and has the holy death that the Grail hermit prophesied for him. Lancelot . . . is the one explicitly tragic figure in *The Death of Arthur*; he himself tells us this in his speech of farewell to the "Moste nobelyst Crysten realme, whom I have loved aboven all othir realms": "But Fortune is so varyaunte and the wheele so mutable that there is no constant abydyng. And that may be preved by many old cronycles as Noble Ector of Troy and Alysaunder the myghty conquerour and many mo other; when they were moste in theyr royalté, they alyght passying lowe. And so faryth hit by me." Unlike the usual tragic hero, a Hector or Alexander, Lancelot has suffered neither death nor loss of wealth and prosperity. He remains the king of Benwick, a knight of such prowess that even Gawain with his supernatural strength cannot avail against him. Lancelot is brought passing low by being deprived of his lady and his king. The measure of his tragic fall is the measure of his virtue, for it is only his loyalty to Arthur and to Guenevere that leads him to regard his situation as tragic.

Likewise, his loyalty, the main source of his "worship" throughout the ***Morte Darthur***, underlies his movement upward from this low position to the joy and solace that he attains in the comic plot that brackets the tragic story of Arthur's death. Lancelot never wavers in his loyalty to Arthur, even during their wars. He refuses to fight against the king even when he is besieged at Joyous Garde and Arthur unrelentingly attacks him: " 'God defende me,' seyde sir Launcelot, 'that ever I shulde encounter with the moste noble kynge that made me knyght'." Later, during the same campaign, when Bors has struck down Arthur, he draws his sword and asks Lancelot,

> "Sir, shall I make an ende of thys warre?" (For he mente to have slayne hym.)

> "Nat so hardy," seyde sir Launcelot, "uppon payne of thy hede, that thou touch hym no more! For I woll never see that moste noble kynge that made me knyght nother slayne nor shamed."

During the siege of Benwick, Lancelot does all in his power to avoid shedding the blood of Arthur or his knights, restraining his own men and steadfastly refusing to return evil for evil. He fights Gawain only when he is forced to, and he will not slay him despite Gawain's insulting refusal to surrender. His patience changes Arthur's attitude, and henceforth the king bitterly regrets the war that has come between them. Lancelot spares Gawain and begs Arthur to lift the siege:

> "And therefore, my lorde Arthur, remembir you of olde kyndenes, and howsomever I fare, Jesu be your gyde in all placis."

> "Now, alas!" seyde the kynge, "that ever thys unhappy warre began! For ever he forbearyth me in all placis,

and in lyke wyse my kynne, and that ys sene well thys day, what curteysye he shewed my neveawe, sir Gawayne!"

When Gawain writes to Lancelot, absolving him of any blame in his death and telling him of Mordred's treachery, Lancelot momentarily despairs, but Ector reminds him of his duty to the king. Lancelot thanks him—"for ever ye woll my worshyp." He realizes that his "worship" depends on his loyalty, despite the trials to which he is subjected by Arthur in the sieges of Joyous Garde and Benwick. He immediately sets out for England, eager to serve the king once more.

Lancelot also remains true to Guenevere, and his faithful love for the queen, which prevented his achieving the Grail, becomes the means of his salvation. Guenevere truly repents of her love for Lancelot, and she takes the veil to atone for that sin. Lancelot enters the religious life not because he forsakes his earthly love but because he remains true to it. When he meets Guenevere for the last time, she urges him to remain in the world and take a wife. Lancelot, for the first time in his life, cannot obey his lady, because to do so would be to forsake his love:

> "Well, madame," seyde he, "ye say as hit pleasith you, for yet wyste ye me never false of my promyse. And God deffende but that I shulde forsake the worlde as ye have done! For in the queste of the Sankgreall I had that tyme forsakyn the vanytees of the worlde, had nat youre love bene . . . And therefore, lady, sythen ye have taken you to perfeccion, I must nedys take me to perfection, of ryght. For I take recorde of God, in you I have had myn erthly joye, and yf I had founden you now so dysposed, I had caste me to have had you into myn owne royame. But sythen I fynde you thus desposed, I ensure you faythfully, I wyl ever take me to penaunce and praye whyle my lyf lasteth, yf that I may fynde ony heremyte, other graye or whyte, that wyl receyve me. Wherefore, madame, I praye you kysse me, and never no more."
>
> "Nay," seyde the quene, "that shal I never do, but abstayne you from such workes."

One wonders what the Grail hermits would make of this sort of vocation. It is, to say the least, a curiously worldly way of renouncing the world. And this must surely be Malory's purpose—to provide a means for Lancelot to renounce the world, as the history requires, without renouncing his faithful love for the queen.

Lancelot remains loyal to his chivalric ideals even in and beyond his religious retreat. His last wish is that he be buried at the Joyous Garde. Though he repents of so worldly a vow, like a good knight he remains true to it: "bycause of brekyng of myn avowe, I praye you al, lede me thyder." Likewise, almost the last deed in his life is his taking Guenevere's body to lie next to Arthur's, thus finally proving loyal both to his lady and his king. When Guenevere is buried, Lancelot swoons, and a fellow hermit upbraids him:

> "Ye dysplese God with suche maner of sorow-makyng."
> "Truly," seyd syr Launcelot, "I trust I do not dysplese God, for he knoweth myn entente; . . . my sorrow may never have ende. For whan I remembre of hir beaulté and of hir noblesse, that was bothe with hyr kyng and wyth hyr, so when I sawe his corps and hir corps so lye togyders, truly myn herte wold not serve to susteyne my

careful body. Also whan I remember how by my defaute and myn orgule and my pryde that they were bothe layed ful lowe, that were pereles that ever was lyvyng of Cristen people, wyt you wel," sayd syr Launcelot, "this remembred, of their kyndenes and myn unkyndenes, sanke so to myn herte that I myght not susteyne myself." So the French book maketh mencyon.

The speech is, of course, Malory's own invention, the last of the series of confessions—by Gawain, by Guenevere, and now by Lancelot. The earlier French author would not have presented a Lancelot still as concerned with the things of this world ("whan I remembre of hir beaulté and of hir noblesse"). Malory's Lancelot remains essentially a chivalric knight, and he thus has a good end. He is borne to Heaven, as the hermit bishop says, by "mo aungellis than ever I sawe men in one day," and he dies in the unmistakable odor of sanctity, "wyth the swetist savor aboute hym that ever they felte." His soul goes to heaven, but his body is returned to the Joyous Garde.

This is the end of the history of the Round Table. But Malory's book does not end here. The suggestion that Lancelot remains a true knight even in the saintly last days now becomes explicit in the new conclusion that Malory provides for the whole story of King Arthur. These final pages are of great thematic importance to the work, but they are frequently ignored by critics who concentrate only on the "plot" and who have therefore emphasized since Strachey's day [see Additional Bibliography] their conviction that the book ends with Lancelot and his fellowship "once knights but now hermit priests doing bodily all manner of penance." From this point of view the book does seem to end, as Charles Moorman writes [in his 1965 *Mediaeval Studies* article "Malory's Tragic Knights"], "with the burial of the chivalric ideal." That is true of works such as the *Mort Artu*, but not of Malory's **Morte Darthur**, which ends with a powerful definition and celebration of the chivalric ideal and a clear statement that chivalry survives even the death of Lancelot.

Throughout the last pages of the **Morte Darthur** we witness the slow gathering of the surviving knights of the Round Table. In the *Mort Artu* and the stanzaic *Morte Arthur*, the surviving knights gather to end their days in penance at the hermitage. In the **Morte Darthur** the gathering serves a different purpose. The last of the knights to come to the hermitage is Sir Ector, who arrives immediately after Lancelot's death and delivers his moving tribute to the dead hero:

> "Ah Launcelot!" he sayd, "thou were hede of al Crysten knyghtes! And now I dare say," sayd sir Ector, "thou sir Launcelot, there thou lyest, that thou were never matched of erthely knyghtes hande. And thou were the curtest knyght that ever bare shelde! And thou were the truest frend to thy lovar that ever bestrade hors, and thou were the trewest lover, of a synful man, that ever loved woman, and thou were the kyndest man that ever strake wyth swerde, and thou were the goodlyest persone that ever cam emonge prees of knyghtes, and thou was the mekest man and the jentyllest that ever ete in halle emonge ladyes, and thou were the sternest knyght to thy mortal foo that ever put spere in the reeste."

The speech is a powerful reassertion of the virtues that Lancelot exemplified throughout his earthly life, and because Lancelot achieved his saintly end by remaining a true knight, Ector's threnody is by no means incongruent with Lancelot's holy death.

Nevertheless, holiness is of no concern in Ector's speech. Malory apparently wants his readers' last view of Lancelot to be not of the repentant hermit but of the perfect wordly knight. Ector ignores Lancelot's years in the hermitage certainly not because he fails to admire them but because they are finally not essential to Lancelot's greatness. The world has had many good hermits but only one great Lancelot, and in Ector's speech Malory defines exactly the nature of Lancelot's greatness.

This would merely heighten the sense of tragic loss if Lancelot were the last knight to live by the code of chivalry. However, Malory's final addition to his story assures us that chivalry survives even the death of Lancelot. The knights who gather at the hermitage form the last of the groups of four of which Malory is so fond, and they carry on the life of chivalry:

> Somme Englysshe books maken mencyon that they wente never oute of Englond after the deth of Syr Launcelot—but that was but favour of makers. For the Frensshe boke maketh mencyon—and is auctorised—that syr Bors, syr Ector, syr Blamour, and syr Bleoberis wente into the Holy Lande, thereas Jesu Cryst was quicke and deed. And anone as they had stablysshed their londes, for, the book saith, so syr Launcelot commaunded them for to do or ever he passyd oute of thys world, these foure knyghtes dyd many batoylles upon the myscreauntes, or Turkes. And there they dyed upon a Good Fryday, for Goddes sake.

Of course, the French books mention no such thing, and Malory's insistence upon written authority for this passage, as usual, merely conceals his own invention. In no other French or English version do Arthur's knights leave the hermitage to carry on the chivalric life in this manner.

Lancelot's companions may have been purified by their stay in the hermitage, since they now fight exclusively against the "myscreauntes, or Turkes," but they follow the chivalric way nevertheless, earning worldly rewards ("stablysshed their landes") and dying in a manner that, as we have seen, many a fifteenth-century knight in both life and fiction would have wished. Malory is so intent upon emphasizing for his readers that the history of the Round Table does not end in despair or penance that he forgets, or perhaps simply does not care, that Bors, Blamour, and Bleoberis have taken religious vows. The author of the *Queste del Saint Graal* would not have made such a mistake; since Bors is to return to the world at the end of the *Queste* its author carefully specifies that when Bors stayed at the hermitage with Perceval he did not adopt "religious clothyng": "He chonged never hys secular clothyng, for that he purposed hym to go agayne into the realme of Logrus." Malory includes that in his *Tale of the Sancgreal* just as he includes in his *Death of Arthur* the fact that when Bors comes to Lancelot's hermitage, "He preyed the Bysshop that he myght be in the same sewte. And so there was an habyte put upon hym, and there he lyved in prayers and fastyng." But so far as Malory is concerned, this is of no importance compared to Bors's loyalty to Lancelot's dying command that he continue the worshipful way of knighthood in the world.

The last paragraphs of the *Morte Darthur* epitomize Malory's method of dealing with the problems raised by his in-herited history. He retains the historical facts and the consequent tragic pattern they suggest, just as he retains the fact that Bors takes religious vows. Then he modifies their effects by additions such as Bor's leaving the hermitage to carry on the chivalric life. The result is not a coherent pattern of tragedy but rather what Stephen Miko calls [in his 1966 *Medium Ævum* article "Malory and the Chivalric Order"] a "tragic emulsion," in which the elements of tragedy are held in suspension, never quite coming together to produce a tragic effect. They are held apart by the thematic, essentially comic elements that prevent the historical pattern from coalescing. Consequently, the end is neither completely tragic nor purely comic. As Edmund Reiss writes [in *Sir Thomas Malory* (1966)], we are left in doubt whether to be "wholly delighted or thoroughly disenhearted by what has happened." That doubt can never by completely resolved, for it is this mixture of joy and sorrow that lends the conclusion of the *Morte Darthur* its peculiar force and beauty. Perhaps, after all, Caxton was right; he best characterized this complex book when he humbly beseeched the noble lords and ladies of his audience "That they take the honest actes in their remembrounce, and to folowe the same; wherein they shall fynde many joyous and playsaunt hystoryes and noble and renomned actes of humanyté, gentlylnesse, and chyvalryes. For herein may be seen noble chyvalrye, curtoyse, humanyté, frendlynesse, hardynesse, love, frendshyp, cowardyse, murdre, hate, vertue, and synne. Doo after the good and leve the evyl, and it shal bringe you to good fame and renommee." (pp. 235-48)

> *Lurry D. Benson, in his* Malory's "Morte Darthur," *Cambridge, Mass.: Harvard University Press, 1976, 289 p.*

JAMES W. SPISAK (essay date 1983)

[*Spisak is a Canadian-born American authority on Malory and the* Morte Darthur. *In the following excerpt from his preface to* Caxton's Malory: A New Edition of Sir Thomas Malory's "Le Morte Darthur" Based on the Pierpont Morgan Copy of William Caxton's Edition of 1485, *he describes the sources and composition of the* Morte Darthur, *briefly reviewing textual and aesthetic criticism of the work.*]

As Malory planned and began to write his Arthuriad, he turned to the French prose romance cycles as his primary sources. Nothing could have been more logical. Prose romance had been established on the continent for over two centuries, and it was quickly beginning to replace verse as the fashionable mode in fifteenth-century England, as Caxton's list of translations and publications was to attest. Seated in the English romance tradition, Malory turned to the French cycles, many of which were known to him, as models, both in letter and in spirit. The French romances were comprehensive, and this is a quality that surely made them attractive to Malory. He doubtless found them to be sprawling and at times unwieldy, as we do. But "reducing" them into something manageable was not so formidable a task for Malory as it seems to us—other Englishmen had been doing it, if on a smaller scale.

The series of French romances that influenced Malory most is what we now call the Vulgate Cycle, which consists of five branches written at different times: *Estoire del Saint Graal, Estoire de Merlin, Lancelot du Lac, Queste del Saint Graal*, and *Mort Artu*. The last three of these were written first by three different authors: the *Queste* was added to the *Lancelot*, and the *Mort* to these two. A few years later another writer added the first two tales in order to complete the history of Arthur and his knights.

Though the particular manuscripts he used are not extant, Malory drew extensively from this cycle. He reduced the *Queste* considerably, excising many of the allegorical and exegetical passages, to demonstrate the failure of purely earthly chivalry in his own Grail quest. The Vulgate *Queste* was almost certainly Malory's only source for his Grail. The other branch of the Vulgate Cycle Malory knew thoroughly is the *Mort Artu*, which he used in his last tales as well as in the Roman War episode. Though his redaction of this section is much less faithful than that of the *Queste*, Malory's detailed knowledge of it is apparent in his last books, even though he was drawing on other sources for them as well. Malory also drew widely, though less exhaustively, from the voluminous *Lancelot du Lac*, which he used in Book VI as well as in Books XVIII and XIX. Since he drew only from parts of this branch, we cannot be sure that he had access to a complete version. In fact, since we have no hard evidence that he knew the first two branches, we cannot say with certainty that he knew the entire cycle as we have it. It might well be that Malory's direct source consisted of only the three branches that were written first, perhaps even with an abridged *Lancelot*.

We now know of a second French cycle that Malory knew at least in part, the *Roman du Graal*, thanks to the fine work of Fanni Bogdanow. Though all branches of this cycle are not extant, it probably consisted of an *Estoire del Saint Graal*, a prose *Merlin*, the *Suite de Merlin*, a *Queste*, and a *Mort Artu*. Again, since we know only that Malory drew from the *Suite*, we cannot assume he had access to the whole cycle. Such is probably also the case with the *Tristan*, which Malory used in other sections of the *Morte* than the middle third. As Vinaver's study shows, this was probably a branch of a post-Vulgate cycle whose other members are no longer extant. The particular version Malory used has not been discovered among the many manuscripts that still survive, though Vinaver has used some of the extant ones to reconstruct the content of this romance. While we may be grateful that this task was so skillfully done, we must be cautious when drawing conclusions about Malory's use of this material.

Besides these cycles, which existed in many manuscripts, Malory also knew the *Perlesvaus*, an earlier version of the Grail quest, which he used in Books I and VI. This work, too, may have been planned as part of a cycle, though no external evidence of one remains. This does not detract from the importance of the *Perlesvaus* or any other lone work as a possible source for Malory. Though we can deal directly only with extant works, the predominance of the cyclic form of the French romances Malory used requires us continually to consider those that did not survive.

The great deal of attention given to Malory's French sources has, until recently, overshadowed study of the English works he drew from. Two notable exceptions to this are the alliterative and stanzaic poems, whose influence on Malory was first extensively discussed by Sommer. The alliterative *Morte Arthure* is the primary source for Book V, Arthur's war with Lucius, and the discovery of the Winchester MS. has enabled us to see that Malory made even more extensive use of this poem than had been previously realized. The manuscript version of the Roman War . . . is twice as long as that printed in Caxton's edition, and many of the passages that appear in the manuscript alone were drawn directly from the alliterative poem. The stanzaic *Morte Arthur* is by now familiar to us as the source for certain sections of the closing books. Malory drew directly from it in the last two books, and he also used it occasionally in writing Books IV and XVIII.

These two poems have been extensively re-examined as part of the recent attention given to Malory's English sources. We now know, for example, that Malory turned to the alliterative poem while he was writing the ending of his work, and that he used the stanzaic poem at the beginning. Indeed, the way in which he adapted the stanzaic poem is typical of the method he and other English authors used to adapt English metrical romances. We have further learned, through the recent work of E. D. Kennedy, R. H. Wilson, and especially Larry Benson, that these two poems are not the only English works Malory knew, but are part of a large vernacular romance tradition with which he was very familiar.

Among the English works Malory knew well is Hardyng's *Chronicle*, which he used directly in both versions of the Roman War episode, in the early books whose primary source is the French *Merlin*, and in the last books, which are deftly drawn from several sources. Besides these specific borrowings, Malory was also influenced by Hardyng in more general ways, such as in the overall structuring of his Arthuriad, the adaptation of the Grail quest, and the characterization of Arthur. But he was influenced by other English writers as well, and recent scholarship—made possible in part by the higher survival rate of vernacular manuscripts—has uncovered several fourteenth- and fifteenth-century works that Malory had considerable familiarity with and was probably affected by. Among these are *Ywain and Gawain*, *Sir Gawain and the Carl of Carlisle*, *The Wedding of Sir Gawain*, *The Jeaste of Syr Gawayne*, *Arthour and Merlin*, *Awntyrs of Arthure*, *The Avowing of King Arthur*, *Sir Launfaul*, *Sir Degrevant*, *Lybeaus Desconus*, and *Ipomadon*.

The voluminous work done by Sommer and Vinaver instigated a movement in source studies that has grown steadily—"out of measure," in the view of some scholars. While we must, as textual and literary critics, ultimately work with what Malory left us rather than with what we think he should have left us, the yield of source studies on Malory has been particularly bounteous, primarily because **Le Morte Darthur** represents the felicitous juncture of an established cycle of French Arthurian romances and the English chronicle and romance traditions that comprised the author's heritage. Recognition of the various influences of Malory's sources on his work need not cast doubts on his ultimate inventiveness.

The influence of Malory's sources on his style is a very complex issue. Any "reducing" of French sources would inevitably involve translation to some degree, and at its best Malory's handling of French probably did not allow him perfect bilingual facility. This is not to slight his *knowledge* of French; but reading and selecting details of a story in a foreign language is not the same as adapting the story itself to one's own purposes in a new context.

Since Malory was widely read in the French romances before he began writing, there are certain general influences, positive and negative, that they had on his style. The narrative technique of *entrelacement* is typical of these. At first glance Malory seems to have removed the complex interlacing we find in his French sources; but as Benson has shown, he actually replaced it with a simpler "bracketing" that is also to be found in other English romances with which he was familiar. And the influence of *entrelacement* can also be seen in the more straightforward tales, such as that of Gareth, whose sources are probably even less complex than Malory's adaptation of them.

Another broad influence on Malory's prose style is alliteration. This is obvious in Book V, where his primary source was an alliterative poem, but Matthews and others have shown that Malory was steeped in the English alliterative tradition and seems, in fact, to have been very fond of alliteration. Our awareness of Malory's use of this device has grown as we have learned more about the English sources he used. In Book V, much of what Malory added to his source is alliterative, and in the closing books, based on the English stanzaic poem and the French prose *Mort Artu*, alliteration is frequent. Even in some tales drawn solely from the French, such as that of Launcelot (Book VI), alliteration is a major feature of Malory's prose style.

Besides being swayed by such conventions as these, Malory was undoubtedly influenced in writing particular tales by the style of whatever sources he was using at the time. So in the parts he added to Book V we see inverted word order, in his reduction of the *Queste* we see a heavy use of Gallic vocabulary; and in his version of the Tristram story are many syntactical constructions that were clearly translated directly (and not always felicitously) from the French. But alliteration can be seen frequently in those sections whose French source is known, and Gallicisms pervade even the most English of Malory's tales, the Roman War. On stylistic grounds, one who read through Malory without his sources at hand would be hard put to tell when he set aside a French source or picked up an English one. Indeed, even with the sources at hand such questions sometimes cannot be decided with certainty. And it is the fusion of the two romance traditions that produced and characterizes Malory's style.

Consideration of Malory's style involves another issue, the order in which he composed the various parts of his work. This question also depends somewhat on source study, since Malory probably did not have access to all his sources all the time he was writing. Except for some discussion of the Roman War episode, most scholars have taken for granted that the various parts of the **Morte** were written in the order in which they finally appear, since that order is the same in both versions of the work. While we may assume, for this reason, that the final arrangement of the tales was Malory's, we cannot assume that he wrote them in this order. Few writers have been able to compose a piece of any substance from start to finish without some rearranging. We should expect this all the more from someone who was writing a cycle, since the encyclopedic information he chose to include rarely presented itself in the sequence he had in mind, and since that sequence was less rigid and more apt to change in cyclical romance than in most other genres.

A thorough consideration of the order of composition would need to be the subject of a separate study, since it is connected with so many other issues. Some groundwork on this topic has been done by Terence McCarthy, who has proposed a sequence that is radically different from that of the final arrangement. Basing his arguments on stylistic evidence, allusions, and the appearance of minor characters, he offers the following order of composition: Grail, Roman War, Tristram, Merlin, Launcelot, Gareth, and Morte (both sections). While I agree that the Grail and Tristram probably were early works, and that the last tales were done last, I am uncertain about the middle, particularly the tales of Launcelot and Gareth. The Roman War is a special problem, and always will be, since it exists in two very different versions. But the early books, based on the French *Merlin*, are especially curious and may illustrate the complexity of the issue.

Those who cite the Merlin section of Malory's work as an example of his immature style and lack of experience in handling the cumbersome French sources have worked on the assumption that these were early tales. But many of the allusions to upcoming events are much more specific in Malory than in the corresponding place in the *Suite*, and the source of such details is easily found if we allow that these books were written after some of those that are placed later in the final order. The reference to Percival's sister in Book II, for example, is to be found in the *Suite*, but only in Malory do we have the explicit reference to the Grail story and the added information that she dies in the process of healing the sick damsel. And as R. H. Wilson has shown, the description of the Grail chamber in which Balin smites the dolorous stroke is not to be expected— and in fact is not found—in any version of the French prose *Merlin*.

Whether or not we allow that the tales based on the *Merlin* were written later than some of the others, the layouts of both the manuscript and the printed text prevent us from assuming that these tales were written in the order Malory finally placed them. The explicits in the manuscript suggest that there are three tales here (rather than one or six), corresponding to Caxton's Books I-II, III, and IV. Caxton's division into four books makes perfect sense, however, as the break between Books I and II logically marks the beginning of a new tale. While the layout of both texts raises the possibility that these books were not written in their standing order—and hence probably not at the same time—the difference in the ways Malory used his sources shows that they were not.

Malory's use of his primary source for the first four books, the *Suite du Merlin*, varies considerably. While his handling of all parts of the *Suite* reveals his tendency to replace interlaced stories with more straightforward ones, this seems particularly true of the first two books. The narration of Arthur's birth and the tale of Balin represent a continual modification of the same source. But in Book III, Arthur's Wedding, Malory departs substantially from his source, as T. L. Wright has carefully demonstrated [in the 1964 study " 'The Tale of King Arthur'. Beginnings and Foreshadowings"]. In Book IV, Malory begins with a simple narration of the interlaced tales of his source but adds his own ending—one which shows a detailed knowledge of events recounted later in the Tristram section and, in the manuscript version, suggests that he has already written several stories about Arthur and his knights, including Launcelot and Tristram. Though further subdivision needs to be considered, let us postulate for the moment only that Malory wrote the first four books during two different periods, the first two at one time, the next two at another. Which came first?

Besides general changes in style and structure, there are specific reasons for putting Books III-IV before I-II. For one, Arthur does not receive the Round Table until he marries Guenevere in Book III, but Malory mentions knights of the Round Table in Books I and II. Though this may not be a gross error, it is a puzzling inconsistency. But if we allow that he wrote Book III before the others, we can see how easy it would have been for him to assume we knew about the Round Table knights. In addition, there are no references in Books III-IV to the first two books, while there are specific references in the earlier books to these two. In the tale of Balin, for example, we learn of Morgan's affair with Accolon, her plot to kill Arthur, and the power of the sheath of Excalibur. Malory here significantly alters his source, in whch an anonymous knight and lover of Morgan, privy to her devices, asks for the sheath to protect him in battle. Morgan confuses the sheaths and gives him the wrong one, and consequently he is seriously wounded. Believing that he was betrayed, the knight discloses her devices to Arthur, who kills him, believing Morgan's lie instead. Malory combines the anonymous knight with Accolon and cuts the story drastically, alluding to it rather than rehearsing it, presumably in order to give Morgan's treachery some motivation. And he could not have done this if he had not already written the episode of Arthur's battle with Accolon.

This coupling of Books I and II is also supported by some of the evidence that makes me put these two tales late in Malory's overall order of composition, perhaps directly before the *Morte*. Wilson long ago demonstrated that Malory named many characters that were anonymous in the *Suite* and in his other French and English sources. McCarthy rehearses some of Wilson's evidence and uses the fact that no new characters are introduced into Malory's Grail story to argue that it was his first work. It seems worth noting, then, that most of the new names Malory introduces in the Merlin section, and all of the lists of knights, come in Books I and II. In fact, taken together, these two tales seem to serve as an introduction to all the major and many of the minor characters of the *Morte*— the kind of introduction that can only be written after most of the rest of the work is done. In theme and tone, too, these are like the last tales, containing many references to the Grail, the tale of Tristram, and the Morte, and emphasizing Arthur's overall success as a king. Mordred's birth and Arthur's death are mentioned, and the first book ends with a somber prediction of the downfall of Arthur's kingdom and even a reference to the destructive aspect of the month of May. Both tales are prophetic and generally carefully wrought, and together they form an overture that shows the author in complete control of his work.

Even the thorny Roman War episode offers evidence for placing the first two books of the Merlin section later than the last two. There are several characters—such as Brian des les Isles, Marhalt, and Pelleas—who appear in Books III, IV and V, but not in Books I and II. This suggests that Book V was written after the last part of the Merlin, but not necessarily after the first, whose lists of names Malory

probably drew from another source. Further evidence of the placement of Book V may be found in the opening lines of the manuscript version, in which Malory sums up what he has related in the preceding tales—Arthur's wedding and the establishment of the Round Table—but makes no mention of Arthur's birth, Merlin, or Balin. He also links with the explicit of the preceding tale by repeating the arrival at court of Launcelot and Tristram.

The disparity of the two versions of the Roman War episode raises the question of revision. Matthews' argument for authorial revision . . . , as it becomes generally accepted, is providing the groundwork for a careful examination of the two texts. A few scholars have already extended his theory to other parts of the *Morte* in order to show, as R. M. Lumiansky and his syndicate suggested long ago, that Malory *did* systematically revise certain parts of his work. The question of revision will surely be addressed in future studies of Malory's style, even if the whole issue is a nettlesome one. Given the constraints under which Malory apparently wrote, for example, we cannot assume that he would have finished the whole work before going back to do any revising: any impediment, such as being imprisoned in some way, that would cause him to hurry or leave off at one time, would probably allow him free time for revision at another. For many reasons, not the least of which is the taste of the individual reader, we will never know precisely what Malory did or did not revise; but his practices in the Roman War episode give us at least some basis for comparing the two versions of the other parts of his work.

Whether the theories put forth here be accepted is far less important than are the questions that led to them. Any consideration of an author's style requires us to examine his known sources, the chronology of his works (or, in this case, the parts of his work), and all states of the text that are extant. This task is difficult with Malory since many of his sources are lost and since we have no external evidence for ordering the parts of his work. (pp. 620-27)

James W. Spisak, in an introduction to Caxton's Malory: A New Edition of Sir Thomas Malory's "Le Morte Darthur," *edited by James W. Spisak, University of California Press, 1983, pp. 601-29.*

MURIEL WHITAKER (essay date 1984)

[*In the following excerpt from* Arthur's Kingdom of Adventure: The World of Malory's Morte Darthur *(1984), Whitaker examines the time scheme of the* Morte Darthur.]

The diversity of late medieval temporal patterns is illustrated by Pieter Brueghel's painting 'The Triumph of Time' where a child-devouring Cronus, a serpent with its tail in its mouth, sun, moon, chariot, globe, clock, hourglass, zodiacal signs, church, maypole, leafy woods, bare boughs, the Tree of Life hung with the scales of the Last Judgment, Death with his scythe mounted on a horse that scatters the perishable artefacts of civilisation, and an angel sounding the last trump are combined to express linear, cyclical, and vertical concepts. Like the painting, Malory's *Morte Darthur* is typically medieval in its lack of a consistent historical perspective or a unified iconography. In the most literal sense, the time of Arthur's reign is the fifth century for his grandfather was the historical Constantine who proclaimed himself Roman Emperor at York in 306 AD. The genealogy is revealed and emphasised when Arthur rejects Lucius' claim to tribute. We are also given a fifth century date for the commencement of the Grail Quest: four hundred and fifty-four years after the Crucifixion. Malory says little about the Saxons—they are Mark's enemies rather than Arthur's—for the ethos of his historical vision is that of the high middle ages, evoked not only by political allusions to establishing the succession, the voice of the commons, the role of the Archbishop of Canterbury, trial by combat but also by reference to architecture, costume, arms and armour. Complexities and inconsistencies are partly due to the variety of his sources, partly to his own desire to update traditional material.

Castle architecture ranges from simple Norman towers to the Red Knight's fourteenth-century stronghold, machicolated and double-ditched. The monasteries of white monks so common in the Grail landscape would not have been found much before the thirteenth century. Allusions to clothing and armour are equally unreliable as indications that Arthurian society occupied a specific time. The long scarlet ermine-trimmed gowns of Lancelot, Tristram, and Galahad are typically thirteenth century and, in fact, often appear in illustrated French manuscripts of the period as both male and female garments. By the mid-fourteenth century a great change has occurred, the separation of male and female styles, with the man's surcoat becoming a short tunic, then a close-fitting jacket or doublet worn with hose. When Gawain tells Priamus that he has grown up in the wardrobe department of King Arthur's household where it is his duty to 'poynte all the paltokkys that longe to hymself and to dresse doublettis for deukys and erlys', the reference to doublets comes from Malory's fourteenth century source, the alliterative *Morte Arthure*, but he substitutes for the poet's 'aketoun' a fifteenth century term for the short tight tunic known as a paletot.

Isolde appears wimpled at the tournament at Lonezep, wearing the headgear of a respectable married woman of the thirteenth century, the period of Malory's source, the *Prose Tristan* (ca.1232). Guenevere, too, seems to dress according to the old fashion of wearing two tunics, the *cotte* (kirtle), a long sometimes trailing garment with tight sleeves, and the sleeveless voluminous surcoat. When Lancelot finds the queen standing at the stake in her smock, he casts a kirtle and gown on her. The fact that the kirtle and gown can be put on so quickly suggests that they are loose thirteenth century garments rather than the more elaborate late fourteenth century styles that needed lacing, buttoning, and belting. Malory's depiction is more austere than that of the *Mort Artu* authors who send her out to die in a dress of red taffeta, a tunic, and a cloak. In the case of armour, the hauberk (chain mail shirt), the coif (a tight fitting mail cap), and the helm with ventails are thirteenth century while the helm with vizor, the gauntlet, and the horse armour (peytrels and crowpers) that bursts with the shock of Gareth's attack on the Red Knight are fourteenth century.

To the social milieu of his thirteenth and fourteenth century sources, Malory adds contemporary references. Professor Vinaver makes a case for Arthur's resemblance to Henry V and for similarities between the *Morte Darthur*'s military campaigns and those of the Hundred Years War and the Wars of the Roses in which Malory is thought to have participated. There are business-like commercial details. Guenevere's search for the mad Lancelot costs her twenty thousand pounds; as mourning for Gawain, Lancelot doles out meat, fish, wine, ale and twelve pence to every comer. Mordred uses cannon, the latest military equipment, to attack the Tower of London.

Malorian patterns of time can best be explored by classifying them as linear, cyclical, and vertical. The Judeo-Christian linear scheme envisaging time as a continuous progress from the Creation to the Last Judgment is applicable to the biography of an individual, the history of a nation, and the history of the Church. The history of Arthur is, in fact, inseparable from that of his nation and Church since he exemplifies the *Christianissimus rex*, an idealised type created by medieval historiographers to justify the ambitions of Western successor states claiming the Roman *imperium* and to present a model of Christian kingship which embodied military successes against pagans, the protection and exaltation of the nation, and the upholding of justice.

Arthur's biography is not a day by day account or an annual report but an arbitrarily chosen sequence of events conforming to a hero pattern—royal ancestry, mysterious conception and birth, protected childhood, success in a supernatural test followed by public recognition, preliminary combats, a crucial struggle, climactic victory, and apotheosis.

We see him as a new-born baby bound in a cloth of gold and delivered to Merlin at the postern gate, christened 'Arthur' by a holy man, and nursed by Sir Ector's wife 'with her owne pappe'. 'Yong' Arthur accompanies Ector and Kay to the New Year's Day tournament, succeeds in the sword test but is rejected by the barons as 'a boye of no hyghe blood borne' and as 'a berdles boye' (the noun having implications of social inferiority as well as youth). Youthful inexperience underlies his reliance on Merlin's strategic advice and, one feels, his seduction by Morgause (sent to spy on Arthur's court, as Malory tells us) but by the time of the Roman wars which occur about twenty years after the war with the Five Kings, he is in the prime of life. After the defeat of Lucius and the coronation in Rome, he becomes fixed in the cyclical time of courtly romance, performing strictly ceremonial roles, until Mordred's jealousy and Lancelot's disaffection propel him back into a linear time that recognises the inescapability of age and death. Even so, Malory avoids the *Mort Artu* specification of Arthur's age as ninety-two, dissociating connotations of physical and mental debility from his depiction of a vigorous, decisive monarch.

Other heroes—Lancelot, Galahad, Tristram—provide an impression of passing time for they are glimpsed as infants, as youths about to be knighted, and then as successful knights-errant whose eventual deaths are described directly or reported. Tristram is allowed an 'enfance' superficially realistic (though the seven year periods are archetypal)—a stepmother acquired when he is seven, education in France until he is fourteen, instruction in hunting, harping, hawking and terminology until he is eighteen, when he turns up at his uncle's court.

Individuals are linked to their family's past by genealogy. For example, the historicity of Lancelot's life is asserted by his vision of a man with a crown of gold (Joseph of Arimathea) accompanied by seven kings, Lancelot's ancestors Nappus, Nacien, Hellyas le Grose, Lysays, Jonas,

Lancelot, and Ban. His son Galahad shares not only in this ancestry but in that of his mother who is descended from the Keepers of the Grail and King David.

Memory also connects past and present in a personal way. Gawain's recollections of his father's death motivate the vengeful murders of King Pellinore, Morgause, and Lamerok. Lancelot's grief at the Glastonbury tomb is made almost unbearable by his remembrance of Guenevere's beauty and nobility and of his own sinful pride that has laid low these two who were 'pereles that ever was lyvyng of Cristen people'. Though little used in the earlier books, the individual's ability to recall the past is a poignant device in the chronicle of the Round Table's disintegration and destruction, whether it is Arthur mourning over Gawain's corpse, Lancelot reminding the full court of how he and his friends have upheld the fellowship, or Gawain recalling Gareth's devotion to Lancelot who has slain him.

Another device creating a sense of temporal progress as well as curiosity and suspense is the use of prophecy, an important element in the Christian assimilation of the Old Testament. Merlin functions as an Old Testament prophet, warning, foretelling, and preparing for events that are to come. Some prophecies are specific and personal announcements of the future, a kind of fortune-telling. On the first night that Uther sleeps with Igraine he will beget a child. The child that Arthur has begotten on his sister will destroy him and all his knights. Balin will strike the Dolorous Stroke that will cause great vengeance. In the place where Lanceor and Columbe were slain, Lancelot and Tristram will fight the greatest battle between knights and true lovers ever seen. Balin's sword will never be handled by any except the best knight in the world, Lancelot or Galahad. Lancelot will kill Gawain. The most poignant prophecies concern his own fate which he can foresee but not avoid. Warnings to Arthur have the effect of prophecy; for example, the repeated warning about guarding his scabbard, and the disapproval of Arthur's plan to marry Guenevere, for 'Launcelot scholde love hir, and sche hym agayne'.

A second concentration of warnings and prophecies occurs in the story of the Grail. Hermits are the chief percipient agents, foreshadowing such things as the coming of Galahad and the instability of Lancelot, but diverse sources—Elaine, King Pelles, Josephé, the daughter of Duke Lyanowre, Perceval's sister, and even the tomb at Corbenic and the Ship of Solomon—contribute to the Providential nature of this tale.

The allegorical dream vision not only propels the action forward but creates an emotion of wonder, fear, or curiosity appropriate to the effect that the future event will have on the dreamer. Arthur's dream of the marvellous dragon destroying the diabolical bear presages his dual victory over the giant of St Michael's Mount and the forces of the Emperor Lucius. When the King of the Hundred Knights dreams that the castles and towns of the eleven rebel kings are blown down by a great wind and carried off in a flood, the confidence of Arthur's enemies is shaken and their destruction assured.

In the first two books, Malory's treatment of chronicle material is too often a sequence of actions crudely linked by temporal adverbs ('and then', 'and when'), the paratac-

tic structure boringly emphasising the linearity. Nevertheless, such embellishments as prophecies, dream visions, magic tests and giant-slaying carry us along as Arthur establishes his kingdom and his empire which until the seventeenth century were regarded as his historical realities.

With the Grail material, the reign of Arthur and the lives of his knights are integrated into the larger scheme of Judeo-Christian world history. Galahad himself is a type of Christ, his adventures a re-enactment of Biblical history as he heals the blind king Mordrain, the Maimed King, and the cripple at Sarras or—in Harrowing of Hell parallels—leads the prisoners from the Castle of Maidens and releases the souls from the burning tomb. The Grail is the vessel of the Last Supper, the lance the weapon with which the legendary Longinus pierced Christ's side. The history of these relics is part of an evangelisation myth that attributes to Joseph of Arimathea the founding of the British Church. White knights (angels), holy men, saintly recluses encountered by the Grail knights recreate church 'history' with their stories of King Evelake's war against the Saracens, Josephé's imprisonment in Great Britain and his release by Mondrames, the wounding of Nacien, the alternative version of the Dolorous Stroke and Waste Land.

The most powerful historical artifact, aside from the Grail is the Ship of Solomon, a complex synthesis of Biblical typology. On its side is written 'I am Faythe'. In recounting its history and explaining its artefacts—the bed with its crown and richly mounted sword, the three spindles, one white for the purity of Eve undefiled and of the Virgin Mary, one green for procreation, one red for Abel's blood—Perceval's sister links contemporary history (the Grail Quest) to universal history. Furthermore, the history of an individual, Galahad, is joined to that of his ancestor Solomon who had been assured by a disembodied voice that 'the laste knyght of thy kynred shall reste in thys bedde'. This ship has its existence in time rather than space for it carries the history of man from his creation to the present.

Since the *Morte Darthur* begins in King Uther's time, a little before Arthur's conception, and ends when the last Round Table knights have died in the Holy Land, the linear time occupies about a hundred years. That the period had no exact historical identity would not have bothered Malory or most of his contemporaries who believed with Caxton that 'there was suche a noble kyng named Arthur, and reputed one of the nine worthy, and fyrst and chyef of the Cristen men'.

While a linear time scheme is appropriate to secular and religious history, cyclical time is appropriate to myth and romance for these are genres of renewal. Through the natural process of changeless change, every night, winter and death flows into day, spring and birth. The undiminished beauty of fées, the agelessness of knights and ladies, the terrible but never fatal wounds of heroes, the ability of villains like Tarquin, Carados and Breuze Sans Pyté to return from the dead and fight again testify to the renewal implicit in this pattern which predominates in 'The Noble Tale of Sir Launcelot du Lake,' 'The Tale of Sir Gareth of Orkney' and 'The Book of Sir Tristram de Lyones.' It is wrong to think of 'The Book of Sir Tristram' as later than the other two simply because it follows them. Lamerok, Dinadan, La Cote Male Tayle and Palomides are clearly established knights when they turn up at Lyoness' tournament. The begetting of Galahad in linear time may already have occurred when Lancelot begins the round of activities described in Book III. Critics who attempt to construct a consistent chronology for the **Morte Darthur** fail to recognise that the book accommodates more than one view of time.

Whether diurnal, seasonal, or epochal, withdrawal and return provide the rhythm of adventure. The diurnal cycle reveals antithetical worlds of knighterrantry. In the morning the hero rides into a forest where the daylight hours produce dangerous challenges; at nightfall he inevitably arrives at a castle, pavilion, manor or hermitage that refreshes him with food, entertainment, rest and possibly love.

The seasonal cycle, too, dictates the rituals of his life. New knights are created in the spring; summer (from Whitsun to Michaelmas) is the season of quests; winter is spent in hunting and hawking, jousting and tourneying. Twelve months is the period allowed for completing a task. Knights like Iwain and Marhalt who complete their quests before the appointed time accept the hospitality of a lady or an earl, only returning to Camelot at Pentecost.

The liturgical cycle is introduced not so much for religious as for social reasons. In **Morte Darthur** the great feasts of the Church arc primarily chivalric occasions with the joust of the Diamond occurring at Christmas, the knighting of King Pelles' nephew at Candlemas (February 2) and Alexander the Orphan on Our Lady Day in Lent (March 25); the Great Tournament is held on the Feast of the Purification of Our Lady and the Winchester tournament on Allhallowmas Day (November 1). Since even circles require an ending and beginning (the snake with its tail in its mouth), Arthur's Pentecostal Feast is the point of stasis, combining fulfilment and expectation. At least thirteen separate feasts on this day arc mentioned including those associated with Arthur's coronation, his post-nuptial establishment of the Round Table and the first swearing of the Round Table oath, Lancelot's return to court after the adventures of Book III, the arrival at court of Pelleas and Nyneve, Marhalt, Gareth (who on the following Pentecost is knighted and undertakes the quest of Lady Lyoness), and La Cote Male Tayle (not to mention a whole procession of defeated knights), Galahad's filling of the Sege Perilous and the beginning of the Grail Quest, and finally the Healing of Sir Urry. Urged by Isolde, Tristram attends the significant Pentecostal feast preceding the Grail Quest and during this same festal season Palomides is christened. These two knights alone remain in cyclical time, the one by returning to Isolde at the Joyous Gard, the other by continuing his pursuit of the questing beast, rather than moving into the linear time of the Grail Quest. Through these annual celebrations when the knights renew their oaths and receive public acclaim for their achievements, both they and the reader are restored to a recognizable point in time. Pentecost precipitates by means of *geis*, boons, and challenges another cycle of quest and combat. And, finally, it combines the chivalric and Christian symbolism that characterized much Arthurian romance.

The self-contained 'Tale of Sir Gareth of Orkney' illustrates the uses of cyclical time in chivalric romance. The book begins as Arthur and his court celebrate Pentecost at Kynke Kenadowne 'uppon the sondys that marched nyghe

Walys.' Arthur's *geasa* is satisfied by the appearance of a young stranger who is granted a year's meat and drink and the promise of two more gifts when Pentecost comes round again. The following year during the celebrations in Caerleon, having been awarded a quest and knighted by Lancelot, he sets out to free Lady Lyoness from the Red Knight of the Red Laundes and to prove his worthiness. The third Pentecost, also spent at Caerleon, is marked by the appearance of defeated knights who testify to Gareth's deeds of prowess accomplished during the preceding twelve months. Lady Lyoness' tournament on the following Lady Day (August 15) allows a public demonstration of Gareth's superiority while reuniting him with Arthur's court. The tale concludes with his marriage at Michaelmas (September 29), the end of the questing season. Thus a tale that seems diffuse and erratically episodic is actually controlled by a consistent temporal pattern.

The diurnal cycle is utilised with equal consistency. When Gareth leaves court on the second Pentecost, to follow the guide damsel Lynet, he kills three thieves and releases their prisoner who entertains him that night in his castle. Next morning Gareth rides into the forest, kills two opponents at a ford, approaches the black land at evensong, kills the Black Knight and dons his armour, then meets and defeats the Green Knight who provides him with his second night's lodging. The third morning, after mass and breakfast at the castle, Gareth again rides into the forest, approaches the Red Knight's castle, defeats his opponent after two hours and is again sheltered for the night. On the fourth morning he rides into the forest, approaches the city of Sir Persaunte of Inde, and engages the Blue Knight in the hope of defeating him within two hours after noon so that he can reach Lady Lyoness' castle, seven miles away, while it is still daylight. But the combat is prolonged until suppertime and Gareth spends the night in Persaunte's pavilion. On the fifth day he approaches the Castle Daungerous, spending the night in a hermitage. On the sixth day he fights the Red Knight of the Red Laundes, purposely initiating the conflict early in defiance of his opponent's solar strength which increases as the sun rises to its zenith. This time the jousting lasts an entire day until evensong and later. After the Red Knight's capitulation, ten days are spent resting in a pavilion so that the hero's wounds may heal. Then Lyoness orders Gareth to labour in worship for twelve months to prove his devotion (and to provide time for further adventures).

The regular alternation of day and night, adventure and rest, forest and castle is the continuum of this genre. In 'The Tale of Gareth' and even more in 'The Book of Sir Tristram' there is a temporal amplitude not found in the chronicle material.

The Malory saw Arthurian time as a golden age is evident in his idealisation of courtly life at Camelot in his disparaging comments on the present as compared with the past. Amid the pessimism, social fluidity, feudal disintegration and political uncertainty of fifteenth century England, it would not be strange if he, like his printer Caxton, longed for the return of a time when knights did more than 'go to the Baynes and playe atte dyse'. The essence of his chivalric vision expressed in the oath of the Round Table knights, and in original comments such as that appended to 'The Great Tournament': 'And he that was curteyse, trew, and faythefull to hys frynde was that tyme cherysshed.'

His most famous original comment occurs in 'The Knight of the Cart' where the joyful renewal of nature in May is likened to the blossoming and burgeoning in human hearts:

> for than all erbys and treys renewyth a man and woman, and in lyke wyse lovers callyth to their mynde olde jantylnes and olde servyse, and many kynde dedes that was forgotyn by neclygence.

But love nowadays is not as it used to be. In 'a lytyll blaste of wyntres rasure' we deface and destroy love, for in many people there is no stability. The contrasting imagery of May and winter is ironically reiterated to introduce the account of Agravain's plot against Lancelot which comes to a head a year after Guenevere's Maying.

Perhaps because a circle is aesthetically more satisfying than a line, the biography of Arthur, though essentially linear, reveals some cyclical patterning. The Roman Wars which occupy seven years of linear time are fitted into the liturgical cycle by the coincidence of major events with the sequence of Christian feasts and into the seasonal cycle by references to nature. The Roman legates interrupt the New Year's feast; Arthur's parliament is called after the utas of St Hilary (January 21); Lucius plans to arrive in France by Easter; Arthur rides to St Michael's Mount through a springtime landscape; the Emperor is killed in May; in Tuscany, Sir Florens and his fellowship tie their horses in a flowery meadow; Arthur reaches Lucerne at Lammas (August 1) descending into Lombardy when the vines are loaded with grapes (October); soon afterwards, the Roman senators are granted six weeks to prepare for the coronation which takes place at Christmas.

In the last book, Arthur's dream of falling from a throne on Fortune's Wheel into black water where he is seized by serpents, dragons and wild beasts presages the end of his life cycle as the return of Excalibur to the Otherworld signifies the end of his reign. Finally, Arthur's own journey to Avalon whence 'men say that he shall com agayne' places him in the cycle of eternal return.

Like the Middle English miracle plays, the *Morte Darthur* belongs to the time of grace, the time in which man can prepare himself for eternity. Not only had God entered time to live as man in history, but through His death in time He had won for those men who lived between the Crucifixion and the Last Judgment the possibility of eternal life in bliss. Guenevere's determination to 'gete my soule hole' in the hope of seeing the blessed face of Christ and sitting on His right side at Domesday is perfectly consistent with the medieval relating of time to eternity.

One cannot understand either the Grail material or 'the dolorous death and departing out of this world of Sir Launcelot and Queen Guenevere' without accepting the concept of vertical interventions of the supernatural and timeless in the natural and temporal. Corbenic, like a sacred mountain, is a vertical connection between earth and heaven, time and eternity, while the Grail which it houses but does not confine is a symbol of God's grace, expressing His glory, sweetness, plenitude, healing powers, and accessibility to the devout. Otherworld interventions persist throughout 'The Tale of the Sankgreal' as angels and devils encourage or tempt the questers, strange voices instruct and warn, and a hand without a body suddenly appears, holding a candle and bridle or seizing the Grail and lance for which the world has grown too evil. The healing of Sir Urry, Lancelot's triple vision charging him for the remission of his sins to attend to Guenevere's burial, and the archbishop's view of angels carrying Lancelot's soul to the open gates of heaven are other examples of the divine participating in the human.

Magic may also be seen as vertical intervention. When Lancelot is tricked into sleeping with Elaine to engender Galahad, Malory makes it clear that he is not simply confused by Brusen's drink, as in the French source, but that the enchantress has cast a spell that can only be broken by the light of day. Inasmuch as Galahad's conception is essential to the typological pattern, Brusen is a divine agent. Similarly, Merlin's use of magic to bring about Arthur's conception and the devising of the sword test to establish his claim to the throne are interventions seemingly ordained by God since Merlin counsels the Archbishop to summon the lords of the realm

> that they shold to London come by Christmas upon payne of cursynge, and for this cause, that Jesu that was borne on that nyghte, that He wold of His grete mercy shew some myracle, as He was come to be Kynge of mankynde, for to shewe somme myracle who shold be rightwys kynge of this reame.

It is ironical and for the modern reader moving that despite Malory's acceptance of a conclusion asserting that asceticism, prayer, and withdrawal are preferable to the transient joys of earthly chivalry, nevertheless the author's expression of value remains mundane. The images in Ector's eulogy are entirely temporal and ephemeral—the knight bestriding his horse, bearing his shield, striking with his sword, setting his spear in its rest, sitting in the hall among ladies, making love to his woman, forgiving his opponents, cherishing his friends. All are victims of time. And yet they are what signify the noble and joyous.

The disjunction between the idealistic earlier books, with their confident accounts of secular chivalric adventures, and the realistic final books is caused by a shift in the temporal frame. When Arthur's kingdom becomes a metaphor for fifteenth-century England with its continental wars, dynastic conflicts and disintegrating feudalism, there is a generic change from romance (which Northrop Frye has described as the 'mythos of Summer') to tragedy, the myth of a paradise lost. The 'joy of the court,' an adumbration of the ideal world, is destroyed by envy, hatred, and treachery. In this situation, the only acceptable happy ending for characters living in linear (i.e. historical) time is provided by the allegorical image of human life as a pilgrimage or quest directed towards a heavenly state which Boethius described as 'interminabilis vitae tota simul et perfecto possessio.' This is the solution offered by the authors of the *Vulgate Prose Cycle*. Whether or not Malory preferred *la chevalerie terrienne* to *la chevalerie célestienne*, his *Tale of the Sankgreal* is the *Morte Darthur's* pivot, accounting not only for the destruction of Arthur's earthly *roiaume aventureux* but also for the apotheosis which was the goal of every good Christian. As the Apocalypse promised, 'The kingdoms of this world are become the kingdoms of our Lord, and of his Christ.' (pp. 105-14)

Muriel Whitaker, in her Arthur's Kingdom of Adventure: The World of Malory's Morte Darthur, *D. S. Brewer, 1984, 136 p.*

ANN DOBYNS (essay date 1986)

[*In the following essay, Dobyns examines Malory's presentation of character in the* Morte Darthur.]

Malory's tendency to substitute dialogue for narrative has long been recognized as one of his dominant stylistic characteristics, and while many readers of the *Morte* describe this dialogue as lively and vivid, they also insist on its lack of individuality. The apparent contradiction in the two observations is acknowledged by at least one of these critics who attributes the liveliness of Malory's speeches to their brevity and performative function while maintaining that they remain characteristic of type rather than individual. "Malory is wonderfully good," Mark Lambert argues [in *Style and Vision in "Le Morte Darthur"*], "at making his dialogue both normative and vivid." In a recent challenge to this standard position, Peter R. Schroeder attempts [in his 1983 *PMLA* article "Hidden Depths: Dialogue and Characterization in Chaucer and Malory"] to show that in one particular case Malory has created a character with psychological depth. Examining the speeches of Guinevere in the *Morte*, Schroeder observes variety and incongruity which lead him to conclude that she is "plausible, individual, and inconsistent in the way 'real people' often are." Thus, he argues, "Her speech, concealing as much as it reveals, keeps hinting at something inarticulate but psychologically 'real' beneath its surface." As radically different as these two positions appear, ultimately the findings, if not the conclusions, may be reconcilable. In this paper I propose a third possibility. While recognizing the conventionality of Malory's characters, I find a complexity expressed by dialogue which stretches the traditional notions of typed characters. Like Schroeder, I have observed the apparent non sequiturs in Guinevere's speeches. And yet, while admitting an element of individuality, I find the *Morte*'s dialogue not psychologically revealing, but metaphoric, and Malory's characters thus emblematic.

Guinevere has often been seen to represent all that is wrong with the world of chivalry; she is jealous and covetous, quarrelsome and unfaithful, in short, as Edmund Reiss has called her [in *Sir Thomas Malory* (1966)], the "worldly alternative to the Holy Grail." Such an interpretation, however, considers only one facet of a very complex character. Indeed, it overlooks her essential nobility in the first four tales, most of the fifth, and her final scene. Neither a Morgan le Fay nor a hermit, Guinevere is, as Reiss has argued, quite worldly, but Malory's concept of the worldly is rather more subtle than Reiss's neat antithesis would lead one to conclude. This most worldly woman is, in fact, capable of ideal nobility as well as susceptible to corruption. She thus can be seen as representing both the finest and the most ignoble characteristics of the Arthurian world or, metaphorically, Malory's view of the chivalric ethic.

One way Malory makes Guinevere an emblem of the fellowship is through her speeches, or to be more precise, by creating different discourse styles for different narrative contexts and further by establishing a paradigm of her discourse which mirrors the development, decline, and final view of the chivalric society. By comparing her speeches to those of Isolde, a character whose story is a pale reflection of Guinevere's, I shall try to show Guinevere as a metaphoric representation of the fellowship.

The story of Tristram and Isolde in many ways mirrors that of Lancelot and Guinevere. Indeed, the two tales provide parallel motifs: both Guinevere and Isolde are queens whose paramours are the most noble knights of their respective courts. In addition, their stories have a number of parallel episodes: both are captured by knights; both remain at court while the knights pursue adventures; both are separated from their lovers during a time when the knights, in madness and exile, wander the forest. Whatever Malory's ultimate purpose in narrating two tales of love triangles, the similarities and contrasts between the stories offer a special opportunity to examine his techniques of characterization by means of discourse.

The styles of the two queens' speeches, it turns out, are remarkably similar in diction, formula, and syntax, a finding which should surprise no one, since nearly all Malory's readers have observed the lack of individualization of speech in the *Morte*. What has not been noticed up to now, of course, is that in addition to the general stylistic resemblances, the two queens generally modify their discourse in the same ways in similar narrative situations. Both speak in three principal contexts: they converse with kings, knights, and their lovers. Each setting elicits a particular style. Addressing kings, the queens speak far more formally than in any context and display a brevity and understatement which [in *Romance and Chronicle: A Study of Malory's Prose Style* (1971)] P. J. C. Field associates with the noble syntax of a knight. Each speech addressed to a king is short, its clauses linked by coordinate conjunctions, its nouns unmodified. When Guinevere responds to Arthur's directive to accompany him to battle, for instance, she replies, " 'Sir,' she seyde, 'I am at youre commaundemente, and shall be redy at all tymes.' " Later, under quite a different set of circumstances, she answers Arthur's question of Lancelot's whereabouts with " 'Sir,' seyde, the quene, 'I wote nat where he ys, but hys brother and hys kynessman deme that he be nat within thys realme.' " Similarly, Isolde replies to greetings from Arthur with " 'Sir,' she seyde, 'ye ar wellcom' " and later, with Tristram, " 'Sir, God thanke you!' seyde sir Tristram and la Beall Isode. 'Of youre goodnes and of youre larges ye ar pyerles.' " And when their kings question them about suits brought against them, they respond simply with like formulas: Guinevere replies, "Sir, as Jesu be my helpe," and Isolde, "Hit is as he seyth, so God me helpe!"

Addressing knights, the two queens speak in similar styles as well, and the similarities are even more remarkable in parallel episodes. Compared to the restrained style when they speak to kings, their speeches addressed to knights are generally somewhat longer with greater modification and concentration of nouns. Two examples in which the queens banish knights from their presence show the resemblance in style. Watching Palomides and Tristram battle and seeing Palomides weakening, Isolde stops the fight and sends Palomides away with:

> "This shall be thy charge: thou shalt go oute of this contrey whyle I am [therin]. . . . Then take thy way," seyde La Beale Isode, "unto the courte of kynge Arthure, and there recommaunde me unto quene Gwenyvere and tell her that I sende her worde that there be within this londe but four lovers, and that is sir Launcelot and dame Gwenyver, and sir Trystrames and quene Isode."

And in an earlier episode, Guinevere sends Pediver on a pilgrimage to Rome, saying:

"But this shall I gyff you in penaunce: make ye as good skyffte as ye can, ye shall bere this lady with you on horsebak unto the Pope of Rome, and of hym resseyve youre penaunce for your foule dedis. And ye shall nevir reste one nyght thereas ye do another, and ye go to ony bedde the dede body shall lye with you."

Isolde's speech, in many ways recalls the form of Guinevere's: both speeches begin with clauses containing the demonstrative *this* referring forward to adjunctive clauses. In Isolde's speech "this" refers to "thou shall go out of this country"; in Guinevere's, "Make you as good a skyffte as you can." In addition, the nominal clause in each combines simple imperative and imperative with temporal auxiliary: in Isolde's speech, "thou shalt go," "take," and "tell"; in Guinevere's speech, "make," "ye shall bere," "resseyve," and "ye shall nevir reste." Further, both speeches include prepositional phrases of direction: in Isolde's "unto the courte of kinge Arthure"; in Guinevere's "unto the Pope of Rome." Finally, the two speeches rely heavily on short clauses and a high frequency of nouns. The speeches do, of course, differ, and the differences illustrate the extent to which narrative demands determine discourse style. For example, while Isolde addresses Palomides with the familiar *thou*, Guinevere retains the polite form of the second-person pronoun. In each case, the situation determines the choice of pronoun. Because Guinevere is speaking in her role as Arthur's queen and arbiter of justice, she has no need to justify her authority; Isolde, though, is banishing a suitor and, in doing so, reminding him of the difference in their social status.

While the characteristic styles of the two queens remain similar in speeches addressed to kings and knights, they are distinctly different in the third context. A most remarkable contrast can be seen in their conversations with their paramours. Although both queens vary their style when speaking to their lovers, they change in rather different ways. The contrast can be seen both in their private and public conversations.

Isolde's most intimate conversations with Tristram occur within the seclusion of Joyous Guard, and yet she speaks more like a chiding wife than a lover. A speech which has a parallel in one of Guinevere's in a similar narrative situation illustrates the difference in the two queens' styles. In parallel episodes, Lancelot and Tristram wish to withdraw from knightly functions rather than attend without their lovers. Both Guinevere and Isolde argue that such an act would be a shameful disregard of knightly duty and thus would elicit slanderous gossip:

Isolde:

"God deffende" seyde La Beall Isode, "for than shall I be spokyn of shame amonge all quenys and ladyes of astate; for ye that ar called one of the nobelyste knyghtys of the worlde and a knyght of the Rounde Table, how may ye be myssed at that feste? For what shall be sayde of you amonge all knyghts? 'A! se how sir Trystram huntyth and hawkyth and cowryth wythin a castell wyth hys lady, and forsakyth us. Alas!' shall som sey, 'hyt ys pyté that ever he was knyght, or ever he shulde have the love of a lady.' Also, what shall quenys and ladyes say of me? 'Hyt ys pyté that I have my lyff, that I wolde holde so noble a knyght as ye ar frome hys worshyp.' "

Guinevere:

"Sir, ye ar gretly to blame thus to holde you behynde my lorde. What woll youre enemyes and myne sey and deme? 'Se how sir Launcelot holdith hym ever behynde the kynge, and so the quene doth also, for that they wolde have their plesure togydirs.' And thus woll they say."

Despite the similarity in the form and subject, these speeches' differences in style reflect the difference in the two queens' roles as lovers. Although throughout the *Morte*, Isolde is defined in terms of her relationship with Tristram, her speeches never display the intimacy of Guinevere's private speeches to Lancelot. In fact, Guinevere's speeches display density and economy, while Isolde's have a chatty, informal quality exhibited by looseness and verbosity. For example, Guinevere employs parallel clauses with ellipsis when she warns Lancelot that their enemies will judge their actions: "see how Sir Lancelot holds himself" and "so the queen does also"; the adverbial clause of purpose, "for that they would have their pleasure together," unites the two clauses and the two lovers in the repeated third-person personal pronoun *they* and the intensive adverb *togydirs*. Isolde also uses words and clauses parallel in content and grammatical function but without the tightness and balance of Guinevere's. Isolde anticipates the inevitable gossip of the court in three loosely parallel clauses, clauses parallel in function but not in syntax: "Ah, see how Tristram hunts," "Alas, it is a pity that ever he should have the love of a lady," and "it is a pity that I have my life." Further, Isolde's speeches display a repetitiveness which contrasts with the economy of Guinevere's speeches. While Isolde uses three quotations to illustrate the shameful gossip, in the parallel speech, Guinevere uses only one—and an economical one at that. Finally, whereas Isolde's speech is open-ended, Guinevere's is neatly completed with its concise statement of summation.

Although Guinevere's private speeches to lancelot display a looser and longer period than her public speeches, they never approach the informality of Isolde's. One way Malory distinguishes between informality and intimacy is in the use of pronouns. Unlike Guinevere, Isolde never addresses Tristram with the familiar *thou* in her role as lover. Thus, while she may speak informally, she does not speak intimately. Guinevere, on the other hand, addresses Lancelot with the formal *ye* in public, but with the intimate form in some private conversations. She shifts to the familiar *thou* in four separate episodes, and, in each episode, Malory emphasizes the familiar form by repeating it throughout the speech. Twice, she addresses her lover with the contemptuous *thou*: first, when she discovers Lancelot in Elaine's bed and exclaims, "A, thou false traytoure knyght! Loke thou never abyde in my courte, and lyghtly that thou voyde my chambir! And nat so hardy, thou false traytoure knyght, that evermore thou com in my syght!" In the second episode she questions his fidelity and cries out with anguish and contempt:

"Sir Launcelot, now I well understonde that thou arte a false, recrayed knyght and comon lechourere, and lovyste and holdiste othir ladyes, and of me thou haste dysdayne and scorne. For wyte thou well, now I undirstonde thy falsehede I shall never love the more, and loke thou be never so hardy to com in my syght. And ryght here I dyscharge the thys courte, that thou never com within hit, and I forfende the my felyship, and uppon payne of thy hede that thou se me nevermore!"

The other two instances of the familiar form show affection rather than contempt. In the first, Lancelot prepares to leave Guinevere to fight his accusers when Aggravayne and Mordred discover the lovers in the queen's chamber. Before taking his leave, Lancelot renews his vows of love and assures Guinevere that if he is killed, his kin will rescue and protect her; Guinevere responds, " 'Nay, sir Launcelot, nay!' seyde the quene, 'Wyte thou well that I woll [nat] lyve longe aftir thy dayes.' " Similarly, in her final farewell, Guinevere repeatedly addresses Lancelot with the intimate *thou* as she vows never again to see him and implores him to depart from her.

Besides the use of the second person, the first- and third-person plural pronouns define the differences between the two queens in their roles as lovers. While Isolde never refers to herself and Tristram jointly by the first- or third-person plural pronoun, Guinevere uses the form in three episodes. As in the use of the familiar singular form, Malory emphasizes the plural form by repetition. In the first episode, quoted above, when Guinevere advises Lancelot of his knightly duty, she first refers to *their* pleasure, then intensifies the closeness of their relationship with the adverb *togydirs*. In the second episode, when Guinevere and Lancelot are discovered together in the queen's chamber, she uses both the nominative form and the possessive: "now ar we myscheved bothe!" and "I dred me sore oure longe love ys com to a myschyvus ende." Finally, in the last episode, the pathos resonates through the plural pronouns: "thorow oure love that we have loved togydir is my moste noble lorde slayne." In this final parting from Lancelot, the repetition of the first-person plural pronoun becomes a refrain, a poignant reminder of their love and a recognition of the tragic consequences of that love.

Not only are the two queens dissimilar in parallel episodes in their roles as lovers, they differ in an even more fundamental way, and the contrast illustrates their different functions in the **Morte**. Isolde's discourse style remains constant whether she speaks to Tristram in public or private. Guinevere's style, in contrast, changes remarkably. While she maintains formal decorum in public conversations, in private she expresses her emotional attachment to Lancelot and, indeed, displays a range of emotions.

Although Isolde is technically Tristram's queen by virtue of her marriage to King Mark, she never speaks to him in the ceremonial voice. Likewise, she never speaks to him in the intimacy of her chamber. In fact, the conversations between Tristram and Isolde generally occur in a semiprivate or public context, and these speeches vary little in length or level of formality. In the presence of knights at a tournament, for instance, Isolde expresses her concern for Tristram's safety:

"Myne owne lord" [seyde] La Beall Isode, "for Goddys sake, be ye nat displeased wyth me, for I may none othirwyse do. I saw thys day how ye were betrayed and nyghe brought unto youre dethe. Truly, sir, I sawe every dele, how and in what wyse. And therefore, sir, how sholde I suffir in youre presence suche a felonne and traytoure as ys sir Palomydes? For I saw hym wyth myne yen, how he behylde you whan ye wente oute of the fylde. For ever he hoved stylle uppon his horse tyll that he saw you com agaynewarde; and than furthwy-

Merlin takes the baby Arthur from Igraine. From London, British Library, Add. MS. 38117.

thall I saw hym ryde to the hurte knyght, and chaunged hys harneys with hym, and than streyte I sawe hym how he sought you all the fylde, and anone as he had founde you he encountred wyth you, and wylfully sir Palomydes ded batayle wyth you. And as for hym, sir, [I] was nat gretly aferde, but I drad sore sir Launcelot whyche knew nat you."

And in a semiprivate parting (with only Dame Brangwayne in attendance), she exclaims:

"A, my lorde, sir Tristram! Blyssed be God ye have youre lyff! And now I am sure ye shall be discoverde by thys lityll brachet, for she woll never leve you. And also I am sure, as sone as my lorde kynge Marke do know you he woll banysh you oute of the contrey of Cornwayle, othir ellis he woll destroy you. And therefore, for Goddys sake, myne owne lorde, graunte kynge Marke hys wyll, and than draw you unto the courte off kynge Arthure, for there ar ye beloved. And ever whan I may I shall sende unto you, and whan ye lyste ye may com unto me, and at all tymes early and late I woll be at youre commaundement, to lyve as poore a lyff as ever ded quyene or lady."

The two speeches exhibit many similarities. Both begin with the vocative *my lord* rather than the more formal *sir* or *sir Tristram*. Also both speeches are extended by hypotaxis, and the clauses in each joined loosely by coordinate conjunctions, often with adverbs or adverbial phrases: *truly, therefore, now*, and *and therefore*. Further, both speeches rely heavily upon adverbs or adverbial phrase for modification. The few adjectives are, in the main, past participles: *displeased, betrayed, discoverde,* and so forth. Each speech contains much repetition as well. In the public speech, "I saw" is repeated five times; in the private, "I am sure" occurs twice and "he will" twice.

The dialogue between Lancelot and Guinevere is found sometimes in the formal court, other times in the private intimacy of the bed chamber. Malory has created distinctly different discourse styles for the two settings: one for when Guinevere addresses Lancelot in her role as ceremonial queen, one when she addresses him as paramour. In the presence of other knights at a tournament, for example, Guinevere formally addresses Lancelot with "Sir, I requyre you that and ye juste ony more, that ye juste wyth none of the blood of my lorde kynge Arthur," and after the same tournament with "Sir, well have ye done this day!" In a private parting, however, she addresses him intimately: " 'Alas' seyde she, 'that ever I syghe you! But He that suffird dethe upon the Crosse for all menkynde, He be unto you good conduyte and saufté, and all the hole felyshyp!' " As these representative speeches show, the syntax of her public speeches to Lancelot is tighter and more balanced than that of her private ones. The public speeches contain short clauses with little modification, while the private speech's interjection "Alas" and subsequent nominal clause, "that ever I saw you," suggest the informality of conversational speech, and modifiers lengthen clauses and thereby loosen the structure.

The stylistic disparity accounts for some puzzling passages in the later books. In "The Fair Maid of Astolat" episode, for example, Guinevere refuses to receive Lancelot after he wears the maid's colors in the tournament at Winchester, then formally reprimands him for his treatment of the maid when the cause of her death is revealed: " 'Sir,' seyde the quene, 'ye myght have shewed hir som bownté and jantilnes whych myght have preserved hir lyff.' " Were Guinevere a consistent character, the passage would be puzzling, its tone perhaps ironic. Because Guinevere maintains two very different and mutually exclusive roles, however, both her private rejection of Lancelot and her public judgment of his chivalric behavior are appropriate. Guinevere's style differs not only between public and private speeches but also between her private speeches, where she expresses a range of emotions. In each case, the style changes, from the indignant " 'Than' seyde the quene, 'loke that ye com to me whan I sende for you' " to the jealous "Sir Launcelot, I se and fele dayly that youre love begynnyth to slake, for ye have no joy to be in my presence but ever ye ar oute of thys courte, and quarels and maters ye have nowadays for ladyes, madyns and jantillwomen, [more] than ever ye were wonte to have beforehande," to the tender " 'Truly,' seyde the quene, 'and hit myght please God, I wolde that they wolde take me and sle me and suffir you to ascape.' "

Guinevere's variety in her private style becomes clear when compared with Isolde's relative stability and, further, with Guinevere's own consistency in other roles. Her stylistic inconsistencies suggest a certain ambiguity or even divisiveness in her character. In other words, the pattern of her speeches expresses her condition of being divided against herself, public against private, a condition echoing the flaw in the chivalric society. And yet while this flaw may well be what the reader remembers, neither the queen nor the fellowship is merely flawed. Both begin and end nobly. In fact, the story of Guinevere structurally reflects that of the fellowship of the Round Table, and her style of discourse is illustrative of Malory's view of both.

Malory develops Guinevere's nobility in the early books. She not only is the wife of the king who establishes and keeps the code but also brings the Round Table to Arthur's court as part of her dowry. Moreover, her wedding to Arthur provides the occasion for establishing the fellowship and its code of behavior. She is also the gracious hostess of the court when she greets visiting knights and ladies, oversees the entertainment of guests at banquets, and remains at court when the king and his knights seek adventure. She is in her role as hostess when she meets Arthur and his company in London on their return from the Continent (quite a change from the alliterative *Morte* where she marries Mordred) and also when she welcomes Sir Tristram when he joins the fellowship, the speeches of welcome another of Malory's additions. Further, she acts, in the early tales at least, as a kind of judge of knightly behavior. Three particular instances show her speaking in this capacity. In the first, she pronounces blame-worthy the unknightly behavior of King Pellinor; in the second, she praises Sir Kay's valor in the war with the five kings; in the third, she finds King Pediver guilty of the murder of his wife. None of the pronouncements are found in Malory's French source. Then changes are particularly noteworthy because the speeches in the three episodes function together to identify Guinevere with the knightly code.

In order to underscore the tragic fall of the once-exemplary fellowship, Malory apparently contrasts the later instability of the knights with their essential nobility in the first few books. Likewise, Guinevere's behavior in the early books is virtuous and her language illustrates her nobility. Not merely a figurehead, she even accompanies her king and his retinue to battle during the war with the five kings. She shows her nobility in this episode in both words and deeds, responding to her king with a quiet dignity and the tone of a respectful subject: when Arthur allows her to decide whether to attempt the crossing of the Humber or to remain and face the battle, she chooses the action appropriate for a queen and responds, " 'Yet were me lever to dey in this watir than to falle in youre enemyes handis,' seyde the quene, 'and there to be slayne.' "

In "The Book of Sir Tristram," however, Malory begins to develop her relationship with Lancelot and thus creates a tension between Guinevere in her role as Arthur's queen and her role as Lancelot's paramour. It seems to me that at this point in the tale Malory wishes to leave ambiguous the state of the relationship between Lancelot and Guinevere, and it seems so for two reasons. In the first place, his references to their adultery are explicit in the later books, as is his description of the Tristram-Isolde relationship from its inception. Second, and perhaps more convincing, there is no evidence of Guinevere's private style of speaking until the "Lancelot and Elaine" episode toward the end of "The Book of Sir Tristram." Instead of an explicit relationship then, there are rather forebodings throughout "The Book of Sir Tristram" of the treasonous relationship as Lancelot accompanies Guinevere to the tournament at Surluse, as he tells her that he is harboring Tristram and Isolde at Joyous Guard, as he repeatedly refers to her beauty, and as Tristram and Isolde, whose story parallels that of Lancelot and Guinevere, fall in love and then live openly in adultery.

Despite the forebodings throughout "The Book of Sir Tristram," Guinevere, like the chivalric society, remains essentially noble, and thus her response to Lancelot's infidelity in the "Lancelot and Elaine" episode is startling. Full of wrath, she rebukes Lancelot and calls him a false knight, yet upon hearing his explanation, immediately relents. Eugène Vinaver notes that Guinevere's forgiveness of Lancelot is not found in Malory's source and, further, that it seems out of keeping with his account of subsequent events. That seems to be precisely the point of the addition; Guinevere's response is altogether improbable and out of character. In fact, from this episode until her final farewell to Lancelot, Guinevere's behavior and her style of speaking vacillate from noble, ceremonial, and public to passionate, varied in emotion, and private.

Guinevere's final scene, however, shows her altering her behavior to return to her proper ceremonial and thus noble role. Rather than maintaining the setting in the privacy of the queen's chamber as found in the stanzaic *Morte*, Malory places the lovers in a cloister with the queen attended by her ladies. The more formal setting allows her to begin by addressing the ladies who attend her with a formal, unadorned speech: " 'Ye mervayle, fayre ladyes, why I make thys fare. Truly,' she seyde, 'hit ys for the syght of yondir knyght that yondir stondith. Wherefore I pray you calle hym hyddir to me.' " When she turns to speak to Lancelot, however, she shifts to the style and tone characteristic of her private conversations with her lover. The sentences lengthen immediately; the syntax becomes more complex with extensive embedding. Her use of first-person plural pronoun and second-person singular pronoun also marks the intimacy of the speech: "Thorow thys same man and me hath all thys warre be wrought, and the deth of the moste nobelest knyghtes of the worlde; for thorow oure love that we have loved togydir is my moste noble lorde slayne. Therefore, sir Launcelot, wyte thou well I am sette in suche a plyght to gete my soule [hele]."

The change in style adds a poignant note but also reminds the reader of the public consequences of their private sin. Gradually, as Guinevere recalls the magnitude of their sin, she discards the intimate style of speaking found in her private conversations with Lancelot for the polite style of her formal speeches and, thus, attempts to distance him from her. After repeating, in condensed form, her opening confession of responsibility for the downfall of the fellowship, she begins the process of becoming more formal: "And therefore [go] thou to thy realme, [an]d there take ye a wyff, and lyff with [hir wyth] joy and blys." Her syntax once again becomes simpler, paratactic, the period shorter with little modification, and the polite form of the second-person pronoun begins to appear. In her second speech, her sentences are even shorter, and she has shifted to the polite form of the pronoun with only one exception: " 'A, sir Launcelot, if ye woll do so and holde thy promyse! But I may never beleve you,' seyde the quene, 'but that ye woll turne to the worlde agayne.' " By her third and final speech, her words are brief, and she has abandoned *thou* entirely, shifting irrevocably to the formal *ye*: " 'Nay,' sayd the quene, 'that shal I never do, but absteyne you from suche werkes.' " The change in style marks her attempt to end the adulterous relationship both in fact and in spirit. Though she is for a time divided against herself

and inconstant in her fluctuations in emotions, Guinevere's final speech represents her role as queen. Thus, the paradigm of her discourse, which reflects the development of the fellowship of the Round Table, expresses a positive view of the chivalric society. It may be inevitable that men and women fail to live up to their ideals, but the quest, Malory shows us, is a glorious one, and those who attempt it finally are noble. (pp. 339-50)

> Ann Dobyns, "The Rhetoric of Character in Malory's 'Morte Darthur'," in Texas Studies in Literature and Language, *Vol. XXVIII, No. 4, Winter, 1986, pp. 339-52.*

DEBORAH S. ELLIS (essay date 1987)

[*Ellis is an American academic and scholar. In the following excerpt, she considers Malory's idea of treachery as it is presented in the "Tale of Balin" in the* Morte Darthur.]

Critics of the *Morte Darthur* have long recognized the force and importance of the tale of Balin within the work as a whole. Whether they advocate its significance as a completely self-contained story whose unity reveals Malory's preoccupation with untangling the threads of his French source, or proclaim it as an example of Malory's construction of one complete story, readers consistently respond to what Vinaver has termed [in his edition of *The Works of Sir Thomas Malory* (1947)] the 'relentless destiny' evoked by its tone and plot. Recent attempts to account for the power of the story often hinge on interpretation of the meaning of this sense of destiny within it

The damsel with the sword who begins the story provides our first indications that treachery is a relative term, if only because it is so important both to her and to Balin, who is presented originally as a prisoner recently released from a six-month sentence for killing Arthur's cousin—surely a technical form of treason in itself. The damsel's sword can only be drawn by a man 'withoute velony other treachory and withoute treson', a condition that she repeats with small variation four more times in two pages. To her surprise, none of Arthur's knights succeeds until the poorly-clad Balin offers to try. The damsel's quest for a knight without treachery—the negative expression of this goal is in itself important—becomes identified with a standard appearance/reality contrast, since 'for hys [Balin's] poure araymente she thought he sholde nat be of no worship withoute vylony or trechory'. Balin's success at disenchanting the damsel of her sword thus proves both a general and a particular truth; we learn both that 'worship and hardynesse ys nat in araymente' and that Balin is 'moste of worship withoute treson, trechory or felony'. The structure of these phrases, in which 'worship' is identified as an intrinsic given and 'treson and trechory' are associated with external trappings that are most important when absent, implies a substance-accident relationship important to our understanding of treason as motif and motive.

Balin's initial success in this scene appears as a simple, almost emblematic assertion of Malory's values, and it is structured in an almost fairy-tale pattern that we see later in such episodes as lancelot's healing of Sir Urry. Balin's goodness is only emphasized by our delay in recognizing him as the hero. But discordant elements exist here even before the damsel warns Balin that 'that swerde shall be youre destruccion'. This 'Booke of Balyne le Saveage' has opened with neither Balin nor the sword damsel, but with Arthur's troubles from King Royns of North Wales, a monarch who by medieval standards was both a traitor and a rebel, having 'rered a grete numbir of peple [who] were entred in the londe and brente and slew the kyngis trew lyege people'; the contrast between the last four words and Royns' status is obvious. It does not seem accidental that the damsel with the sword, who sets in train such monumental bloodshed and treachery, comes directly to Arthur's court from Royns', providing an early indication of the contagious nature of treason. Moreover, no one at court is happy at Balin's success; their initial reaction is 'grete mervayle' and 'grete despite', followed by a majority reaction claiming 'that Balyne dud nat this adventure all only by myght but by wycchecrauffte'. The suspicion of sorcery is reinforced by the Lady of the Lake's appearance, which follows hard on Balin's clearly doomed intransigence over the sword. Ideas of loyalty, treachery, and revenge now become entangled in a knot that persists up to Balin's death.

The true curse of Balin's sword, we gradually realize, is that it can only be used in some sort of betrayal, and family deaths—culminating, of course, in Balin's fratricide—figure predominantly in its history. At this point one must try to sort out some of the elements of the revenge feud that provides 'the principal inciting cause of the "Balin" plot'. According to the omniscient Merlin, the sword damsel is in fact 'the falsist damesell that lyveth', who had caused the death of the Lady of the lake's father. We must assume that the death in itself does not prove the falseness, however, since the relatively pure Balin had caused that Lady's brother's death. That Lady herself, on the other hand, had caused Balin's mother's death 'thorow hir falsehode and trechory', and so Balin kills her with the sword. His weapon had been given to the sword damsel in the first place so that she could 'be revenged on hir owne brothir' and so proves to be tainted both in origin and destination. Malory has gone to some trouble to establish Balin as a knight 'withoute trechory other treson', and yet this knight (in a technically treasonous despite to his king) kills a treacherous woman with a sword designed for fratricide. His actions defy his motives, for by killing a traitor, he becomes tinged with treason, just as by using a sword intended for fratricide, he becomes the killer of his brother. It is just this contagious nature of treason that Malory finds most compelling throughout the *Morte*. Indeed, treason is not only the most shameful of sins, but is also one of those least subject to human control. In Malory's definition of chivalry, one of his original interpolations, we recognize treason's ubiquity, for a true knight must remember ' . . . never to do outerage nothir mourthir, and allwayes to fle treson, and to gyff mercy unto hym that askith mercy . . . ' Treason in this warning, in another negative expression, can be neither invoked nor controlled; like the plague, its avoidance depends on flight rather than rectitude.

Balin's as well as Mordred's betrayals take their significance from the whole context of treachery in Malory's work. The entanglement of purity, treachery, and fratricide set up in the opening scenes of 'Balin' have, as [Elizabeth T. Pochoda implies in *Arthurian Propaganda. Le Morte Darthur as an Historical Ideal of Life* (1971)], significance for the whole *Morte* as well as for the rest of the

story: 'For Malory, fratricide seems to be the central symbol of societal dissolution. His whole revision of the Balin story as a moral vignette was centered on the unwitting combat of the two brothers'. But the Balin story is actually structured as a sequence of overlapping 'moral vignettes'. In this sense, the first killing of a woman—Balin's decapitation of the Lady of the Lake in Arthur's court—foreshadows the deaths of other women, deaths that Balin is responsible for despite himself. Balin has a pragmatic attitude towards the knight's duty to protect women: 'the lady that ys dede dud to me grete damage, and ellis I wolde have bene lothe as ony knyght that lyvith for to sle a lady'. This is consistent, on the whole, with Malory's general approach to the question of chivalry towards women; Gawain is shamed, for instance, not so much for accidentally killing Blamour's lady as for not giving mercy to Blamour in the first place. But this tone changes in 'Balin', for the deaths of ladies assume an independent force of betrayal that underlies all Balin's misadventures. Balin is unable to discriminate between help and harm, between the lesser and the greater evil, and so he becomes in his turn both a betrayer and a victim, one who hopelessly recognizes that 'That blast . . . is blowen for me, for I am the pryse, and yet am I not dede'. In his role as the Parsifal-like holy fool who brings on the wasteland, he consistently causes the deaths of innocent women. It is his reluctance to harm Launceor's lady, with its tragic result, that evokes his first sense of remorse, and it is significant that Malory links the Dolorous Stroke to Columbe's death.

> And he went unto hir for to have tane the swerde oute of hir honde; but she helde hit so faste he myght nat take hit oute of hir honde but yf he sholde have hurte hir. And suddeynly she . . . rove hirselff thorowoute the body.

> Whcn Balyne aspyed hir dedis he was passynge hevy in his herte and ashamed that so fayre a damesell had destroyed hirselff for the love of hys dethe. 'Alas!' seyde Balyn, 'me repentis sore the dethe of thys knyght . . .'.

Similarly, Balin brings about the deaths of Garnysh, his lady, and her lover with the same innocence, though this time unmixed with remorse. 'God knoweth I dyd none other but as I wold ye dyd to me', he tells Garnysh, but at the latter's suicide he silently 'dressid hym thensward, lest folke wold say he had slayne them . . . '—an accusation that he himself rejects. Balin has turned the lady's infidelity into his own kind of innocent treachery against all three of them. The dolorous stroke episode in its turn conjoins the idea of treachery and the role of ladies, for Balin must be accompanied by a lady when he goes to Pellam's castle in the pursuit of Pellam's brother Garlon, 'thys traytoure knyght that rydith invisible'. The lady whose presence allows Balin's admission is then destroyed by the Dolorous Stroke, despite Balin's wish that he might 'nat lose the lyff of hir whyle my lyff lastith'. Balin himself suffers a moral wound in this episode that parallels the death of the lady under his protection, for his single-minded attempt to get vengeance on the 'traytoure knyght' inevitably touches him with Garlon's poison. Kelly points out that 'in striking Pellam, whose long-festering wound corresponds to that of the young man [killed by Garlon], Balin becomes in effect another Garlon'. The parallels here go beyond these wounds. Pellam and Garlon are ultimately responsible for the attacks on each other in another instance of fratricide, and Balin is paralleled to Garlon not only through the deaths of ladies and of brothers, but ultimately as another and perhaps deadlier 'traytoure knyght'.

Self-contained episode or not, the tale of Balin expresses frequent links to the rest of the *Morte*, from Royns to Galahad. As Balin wanders in his destructive path, hints of greater destruction act as comments on his adventures. Nero, Lot, Mark, Pellinore, Morgause and Morgan, Accolon and Mordred all appear or are predicted as actors in an initially bewildering array of gloomy events. Treachery links all of them with each other, with Arthur, and with Balin. Throughout this story, Balin's treacherous sword has turned mutual love into mutual death, from that of Launceor and Columbe to that of Balin and Balan, and Merlin's prophecy of the sword's future continues the same theme: 'And Launcelot with thys swerde shall sle the man in the worlde that he lovith beste: that shall be sir Gawayne'. The narrow bridge to the grave that Merlin constructs, not to be crossed except by a man without treachery, links the quest at the beginning of the tale with the future of all Arthur's court. Even if Balin's sword is forgotten, its significance only grows, since the court is ultimately destroyed by the contagion of treason: 'But ever he that faryth with treson puttyth oftyn a trew man in grete daungere'.

To be a traitor, in Malory, is to be the worst kind of anti-social criminal, one whose guilt must taint his world: 'And whan the kynge and quene and all the lordis knew off the treson of sir Mellyagaunte, they were all ashamed on hys behalffe'. To be denounced as a traitor or accused of treason is the worst insult one can hear. Gawain besieges Benwick 'halff a yere' before he succeeds in taunting Lancelot out to fight him, but at last even Lancelot's saintly self-control yields to 'sir Gawayne evermore callyng hym "traytoure knyght" ...'. As Lancelot's kin point out to him, 'Sir, now muste you deffende you lyke a knyght, othir ellis ye be shamed for ever, for now ye be called uppon treson, hit ys tyme for you to styrre!' A treacherous death can never be sufficiently avenged or mourned: '... there was never none so bewayled as was sir Trystram and sir Lamorok, for they were with treson slayne ...'. But side by side with this seeming clarity of ethical values lies an intrinsically ambivalent approach to ideas of treachery. Just as Malory takes pains to establish the innocent Balin as a carrier of evil, so he also is careful to distribute the blame for Arthur's fall to Lancelot and Gawain as much as to Mordred and Aggravaine. Indeed, avoiding Mordred in a deliberate departure from his source, Malory tells us, '... and here I go unto the morte Arthur, and that caused sir Aggravayne'. In Malory it is not the traditionally nefarious Mordred who is called 'traytoure knyght' but the well-intentioned Lancelot, called so not only by Gawain at Benwick but by Mordred and Aggravaine after they have cornered him in Guinevere's room. No one in the long climax of Malory's story directs anything more hostile at Mordred or Aggravaine than a general sense of disgust and regret: ' "A, Aggravayne, Aggravayne!" seyde the kynge, "Jesu forgyff hit thy soule, for thyne evyll wyll thou haddist and Sir Mordred, thy brothir, unto sir Launcelot hath caused all this sorrow" '. In a number of ways, Malory dilutes Mordred's traditional faults and directs us to look at the responsibilities of Aggravaine as agent and Lancelot as cause for the downfall of the kingdom.

Treason, in Malory, is a measurement of that which divides the bad knight from the good one. Thus Lancelot, the archetypal good knight despite his moral lapses, can truthfully announce, '... I fared never wyth no treson, nother I loved never the felyshyp of hym that fared with treson', whereas Mordred is so corrupted by treachery as to be unable to meet the minimum fighting requirements for a knight: '... so sir Mordred gaff hym his dethis wounde behynde hym at his bakke, and all to-hewe hym'. Malory is far more interested in the behavior of his characters than in their motives or origins, so that he carefully suppresses most of the references to Mordred's incestuous origins that he found in the *Suite du Merlin*. Yet Malory's Mordred is not a detached fragment of evil who single-handedly brings down the kingdom. He functions mainly as a relief against which the actions and beliefs of the other characters are starkly focused.

Largely because of Mordred's problematical characterization, critics cannot agree on Malory's own assessment of blame for Arthur's fall. One study, for instance, claims that Malory blames the fall of the kingdom on Arthur's over-partiality to Gawain. Such a theory suggests Malory's recurrent motif of mistaken personal loyalties. Arthur trusts individuals too much, and even when his perceptions of the truth stop him from blind trust in his family, he remains eager to be deceived. The sanctuaries of the Round Table are all personal, and Arthur is most vulnerable to treachery even after he has dismissed faith based on relationships. For instance, King Mark writes to Arthur warning him to look to his own wife:

> Whan kynge Arthure undirstode the lettir, he mused of many thynges, and thought of his systyrs wordys, quene Morgan le Fay, that she had seyde betwyxte quene Gwenyver and sir Launcelot, and in this thoughte he studyed a grete whyle. Than he bethought hym agayne how his owne sistir was his enemy, and that she hated the quene and sir Launcelot to the deth, and so he put that all oute of his thought.

It is as an individual rather than an emblem that Malory's Mordred must be judged, for in Malory's works the true emphasis appears to be not on the formal bonds of loyalty, which are too easily corrupted, but on the essential characters of the protagonists. The knights who distrust Mordred see him as envious rather than treacherous. Gawain tells him, 'for ever unto all unhappynes, sir, ye woll graunte'. Lancelot says, 'For ever I drede me ... that sir Mordred woll make trouble, for he ys passyng envyous and applyeth hym muche to trouble'. They are concerned with the basically perverse nature of Mordred's character, not with his formal disloyalties. In the same way, Sir Gareth avoids his brother Gawain because the latter had a murderous nature: 'for he was evir vengeable, and where he hated he wolde be avenged with murther ...'. It is Gawain, in fact, who in some ways acts as a median between the excesses of Arthur and of Mordred. It is Gawain rather than Arthur who falls victim to misguided family loyalty, and it is Gawain who, like his brother Mordred, is distrusted on the basis of his personality. When Gawain learns of the deaths of his brothers, he invokes all the degrees of fealty that might motivate Arthur, addressing the latter as 'My kynge, my lorde, and myne uncle'. His appeal is legitimate on all three levels, but it comes from a mistaken cause which he later regrets. All of these degrees of loyalty, plus that owed by a son to his father, are violated by Mordred when he obeys formal law in demanding retribution from Arthur; thus, these responsibilities themselves become invested with evil.

Jill Mann's recent perceptive study of Malory ["Malory: Knightly Combat in *Le Morte D'Arthur*," in *Medieval Literature: Chaucer and the Alliterative Tradition* (1982), edited by Boris Ford] argues that his readers should begin 'by banishing from [their] critical vocabulary the word "character" as inappropriate to his representation of human figures, and also by ceasing to impose on his work the opposition between feudal loyalty and romantic love which critics have for so long tried to read into it . . . '. She stresses not the divisiveness but the ultimate wholeness of Malory's works. I would extend her analysis to the ultimate wholeness of Malory's major characters, despite her words of warning:

> The vast numbers of people to whom we are introduced are barely differentiated from each other in terms of individual personality, and what distinguishing traits they have are liable to shift in a disconcerting fashion. Gawain is now a traitor and murderer, now a noble knight, and we cannot see what governs the change from one role to the other.

Yet it is specifically Mordred's and Lancelot's consistency of characterization that enables Malory to present his particular, disillusioned late medieval view of treachery. Mordred and Lancelot do not experience the same conflicts that agonized their earlier counterparts. Lancelot is not torn between impulses of loyalty and of betrayal, just as he does not represent 'the opposition between feudal loyalty and romantic love'. Rather, he is consistently loyal both to Arthur and to Guinevere. His character, as the embodiment of a simple reflex of loyalty within a complex situation, reveals the inadequacy of loyalty itself. Similarly, Mordred is recreant in every activity, so that his ultimate treachery is expected and consistent rather than dramatically striking. The very inevitability of Mordred's betrayal reveals the inadequacy of idealistic expectations of loyalty. Treachery ultimately defines the betrayed as well as the traitors: it has become the only sure link in a deteriorating chain of social relationships.

Malory's chronic distrust of institutions of formal loyalty gives his story a deep structural irony as he unfolds the last days of the betrayed kingdom. The scene of Lancelot's entrapment in Guinevere's bedroom, for instance, is so much a microcosm of the Arthurian theme of violated refuges as to almost parody that theme. The trap is laid not because of treachery as much as malice, and it leads not to treachery as much as to confusion. Right after this episode, Lancelot takes stock of his friends and seems to be in control of a network of personal loyalties, although he is soon to go out and kill one of his best friends, Gareth, and hopelessly alienate the other, Gawain. As the ensuing war develops and Arthur is attacked on two sides, Mordred's army grows to include supporters of Lancelot, and Lancelot's besieged supporters include friends of Lamorok. Here the right personal loyalties are not compensated by personal judgement; knights who, unlike Mordred, are not basically evil, are still deceived by their loyalties. Treachery, and hence Mordred's characterization, depends not so much on the king's misguided appraisal of sanctuary as on Malory's ingrained rejection of all potential sanctuaries, except for that of personal worth. Malory's

ideal of fellowship depends on the knightly characters of the people involved, which can too often turn unstable and bring on a tragedy of personal conflicts. Mordred in this last version of the fall of the kingdom stands for the spiritual perversion and loss of meaning that such instability leads to. (pp. 67-74)

Deborah S. Ellis, "Balin, Mordred and Malory's Idea of Treachery," in English Studies, *Netherlands, Vol. 68, No. 1, February, 1987, pp. 66-74.*

ADDITIONAL BIBLIOGRAPHY

Altick, Richard D. "The Quest of the Knight-Prisoner." In his *The Scholar Adventurers*, pp. 65-85. New York: Macmillan Co., 1950.
   A lively survey of scholarly efforts to establish the identity of the author of the *Morte Darthur*.

Atkinson, Stephen C. B. "Malory's 'Healing of Sir Urry': Lancelot, the Earthly Fellowship, and the World of the Grail." *Studies in Philology* LXXVIII, No. 4 (Fall 1981): 341-52.
   Explores reactions to the healing of Urry's enchanted wounds in the *Morte Darthur*.

Aurner, Nellie Slayton. "Sir Thomas Malory—Historian?" *PMLA* XLVIII, No. 2 (June 1933): 362-91.
   Investigates topical, historical, and topographical references in the *Morte Darthur*.

Bennett, J. A. W., ed. *Essays on Malory*. Oxford: Oxford University Press, Clarendon Press, 1963, 147 p.
   Offers seven articles on aspects of Malory, chiefly treating issues raised by the publication of Eugène Vinaver's edition of the *The Works of Sir Thomas Malory* in 1947.

Benson, Larry D. "Sir Thomas Malory's *Le Morte Darthur*." In *Critical Approaches to Six Major English Works: "Beowulf" through "Paradise Lost,"* edited by R. M. Lumiansky and Herschel Baker, pp. 81-131. Philadelphia: University of Pennsylvania Press, 1968.
   A comprehensive overview of Malory criticism, providing commentary on textual matters, the structural unity of the work, sources, and major themes.

Bradbrook, M. C. *Sir Thomas Malory*. Writers and Their Work, No. 95. London: Longmans, Green & Co. for The British Council and The National Book League, 1958, 40 p.
   A concise study of the *Morte Darthur*, with commentary on authorship, the Round Table, and tragic themes in the work.

Davies, R. T. "The Worshipful Way in Malory." In *Patterns of Love and Courtesy: Essays in Memory of C. S. Lewis*, edited by John Lawlor, pp. 157-77. London: Edward Arnold (Publishers), 1966.
   Examines Malory's treatment of the concepts of nobility and honor in the *Morte Darthur*.

Dillon, Bert. *A Malory Handbook*. Boston: G. K. Hall & Co., 1978, 196 p.
   A systematic annotated guide to primary and secondary materials concerning Malory's life and work, with detailed examinations of individual tales in the *Morte Darthur*.

Erskine, John. "Malory's *Le Morte d'Arthur*." In his *The Delight of Great Books*, pp. 53-71. Cleveland: World Publishing Co., 1941.

A general appreciation of the incidental and episodic merits of the *Morte Darthur*.

Field, P. J. [C]. "Four Functions of Malory's Minor Characters." *Medium Aevum* XXXVII, No. 1 (1968): 37-45.
Reviews criticism of the function of minor characters in the *Morte Darthur*, concluding that Malory was drawing a secular civilization in the work.

Field, P. J. C. "Description and Narration in Malory." *Speculum* XLIII, No.3 (July 1986): 476-86.
A close examination of the narrative style of the *Morte Darthur*.

Hartung, Albert E. "Narrative Technique, Characterization, and the Sources in Malory's 'Tale of Sir Lancelot'." *Studies in Philology* LXX, No. 3 (July 1973): 252-68.
Explores the implications of Malory's narrative technique on his portrayal of proper knightly behavior.

Knight, Stephen. *The Structure of Sir Thomas Malory's Arthuriad.* Sydney: Sydney University Press for Australian Humanities Research Council, 1969, 95 p.
Discovers a structural dichotomy in the *Morte Darthur* that is unsympathetic to polyphonic narrative.

Lambert, Mark. *Malory: Style and Vision in "Le Morte Darthur."* New Haven: Yale University Press, 1975, 225 p.
Examines the prose style of the *Morte Darthur*, noting especially Malory's worldview as revealed by the texture of the narrative.

Lewis, C. S. Letter to Fr. Peter Milward. In his *Letters of C. S. Lewis,* edited by W. H. Lewis, p. 264. London: Geoffrey Bles, 1966.
A 1955 letter in which Lewis comments: "What Malory meant I have no idea. I doubt if he had any clear intention. To use an image I have used before, I think his work is like one of our old English cathedrals to which many generations have contributed in many different styles, so that the total effect was foreseen by no one and must be regarded as something midway between a work of art and a work of nature."

———. "The The Morte Darthur." In his *Studies in Medieval and Renaissance Literature,* edited by Walter Hooper, pp. 103-10. Cambridge: Cambridge University Press, 1966.
A generally favorable review of Eugène Vinaver's three-volume edition of *The Works of Sir Thomas Malory* (1947), noting differences between Vinaver's version and William Caxton's 1485 treatment of the text.

Life, Page West. *Sir Thomas Malory and the Morte Darthur: A Survey of Scholarship and Annotated Bibliography.* Charlottesville: University Press of Virginia for the Bibliographical Society of the University of Virginia, 1980, 297 p.
A comprehensive survey of scholarship and annotated bibliography of Malory and the *Morte Darthur* through 1977.

Loomis, Roger Sherman, ed. *Arthurian Literature in the Middle Ages: A Collaborative History.* Oxford: Oxford University Press, Clarendon Press, 1959, 574 p.
Contains forty-one articles on the evolution of Arthurian literature, including "Sir Thomas Malory" by Eugène Vinaver.

Lumiansky, R. M. "Sir Thomas Malory's *Le Morte Darthur,* 1947-1987: Author, Title, Text." *Speculum* LXII, No. 4 (October 1987): 878-97.
Surveys work on the *Morte Darthur* since the publication of Eugène Vinaver's 1947 edition of *The Works of Sir Thomas Malory.*

Matthews, William. *The Ill-Framed Knight: A Skeptical Inquiry into the Identity of Sir Thomas Malory.* Berkeley: University of California Press, 1966, 262 p.

Assesses arguments concerning the authorship of the *Morte Darthur*, advancing Thomas Malory of Yorkshire as the best candidate.

Moorman, Charles. *The Book of Kyng Arthur: The Unity of Malory's Morte Darthur.* Lexington: University of Kentucky Press, 1965, 106 p.
A book-length expansion of Moorman's 1960 essay "Courtly Love in Malory" (see excerpt above dated 1960), treating love, religion, and chivalry in the *Morte Darthur.*

Pochoda, Elizabeth T. *Arthurian Propaganda: "Le Morte Darthur" as an Historical Ideal of Life.* Chapel Hill: University of North Carolina Press, 1971, 185 p.
Views the *Morte Darthur* as commentary on traditional approaches to the question, What constitutes the ideal of life?

Schroeder, Peter R. "Hidden Depths: Dialogue and Characterization in Chaucer and Malory." *PMLA* 98, No. 3 (May 1983): 374-87.
Maintains that in their works Chaucer and Malory "produce the illusion of characters with unexplained psychological depth by allowing the exterior to suggest the interior."

Scudder, Vida D. *Le Morte Darthur of Sir Thomas Malory: A Study of the Book and Its Sources.* London: J. M. Dent & Sons, 1921, 430 p.
An early study, originally published in 1917 as *Le Morte Darthur of Sir Thomas Malory & Its Sources,* of the artistry and principal themes of the *Morte Darthur.*

Sommer, H. Oskar. Introduction to *Le Morte Darthur,* by Sir Thomas Malory, edited by H. Oskar Sommer, Vol. II. London: David Nutt, 1890, 230 p.
A valuable early study of texts and editions of the *Morte Darthur*, with commentary on the language of the 1485 Caxton printing.

Starr, Nathan Comfort. "The Moral Problem in Malory." *The Dalhousie Review* XLVII, No. 4 (Winter 1967-68): 467-74.
Treats Malory's ethics in the *Morte Darthur*, maintaining that the author's "great moral achievement" lies in his recognition of the "co-existence of good and evil in the noble man and of the ways in which the clash of opposites can be reconciled."

Stone, Brian. "Models of Kingship: Arthur in Medieval Romance." *History Today* 37 (November 1987): 32-38.
Comparative study of the Arthurian Legend in medieval French and English romance, noting Malory's portrayal of Arthur as warrior and general.

Strachey, Sir Edward. Introduction to *Le Morte Darthur: Sir Thomas Malory's Book of King Arthur and of His Noble Knights of the Round Table,* by Sir Thomas Malory, edited by Sir Edward Strachey, pp. ix-lvi. London: Macmillan and Co., 1931.
A comprehensive study, originally published in 1891, of the authorship, theme, and text of the *Morte Darthur.* Strachey singles out Malory's poetry-like prose for special praise.

Takamiya, Toshiyuki, and Brewer, Derek, eds. *Aspects of Malory.* Arthurian Studies, No. 1. Cambridge: D. S. Brewer, 1981, 232 p.
Contains eleven specially commissioned essays on Malory and the *Morte Darthur*, including Edward D. Kennedy, "Malory and His English Sources"; Shunichi Noguchi, "Englishness in Malory"; Terence McCarthy, "The Sequence of Malory's Tales"; Lotte Hellinga, "The Malory Manuscript and Caxton"; and Richard R. Griffith, "The Authorship Question Reconsidered."

Vinaver, Eugène. *Malory.* Oxford: Oxford University Press, Clarendon Press, 1929, 208 p.

An important early biographical and critical study of Malory and the *Morte Darthur*, focusing on the style and narrative technique of the work.

——. Introduction to *The Works of Sir Thomas Malory*, by Sir Thomas Malory, edited by Eugène Vinaver, Vol. I, pp. xiii-cix. Oxford: Oxford University Press, Clarendon Press, 1947.

Provides a comprehensive overview of textual and aesthetic issues concerning Malory's Arthuriad, arguing that the *Morte Darthur* is not a continuous narrative but a series of related yet discrete texts.

Samuel Pepys

1633-1703

English diarist, historian, and letter writer.

Pepys is recognized as one of the greatest diarists in the English language. As a highly placed civil servant and tireless man-about-town in Restoration London, he observed and recorded the goings-on of his age, providing a unique record of what it was like to be alive in the early years of the reign of Charles II. His *Diary* is therefore valued as a historical document of incomparable import. Strikingly candid and replete with anecdote and incident, the *Diary* is also esteemed as an original and finely crafted literary work.

Pepys loved life and lived it to the fullest. He was born in London in 1633 and remained a Londoner all his life. His father, John Pepys, was a tailor and first cousin of Edward Mountagu, first Earl of Sandwich, who was to become Samuel's close friend and patron. His mother, Margaret Kite, was the sister of a Whitechapel butcher. Pepys began school in Huntingdonshire, where his paternal family had lived for centuries as reeves, farmers, and minor landholders. He was then sent to St. Paul's School in London. In 1649 he saw Charles I beheaded: the beginning of the Commonwealth. The next year he went as a sizar to Magdalene College, Cambridge, where he took his B. A. degree in March 1654. Almost nothing is known about his stay at the university except that he was once "scandalously overseene in drink": a serious offense in a decidedly Puritan decade. In 1655, at twenty-two, Pepys married fifteen-year old Elizabeth Marchant de St. Michel, the beautiful but penniless daughter of a Huguenot refugee of good family. The couple moved into Mountagu's lodgings in Whitehall Palace, where Pepys was working as secretary and domestic steward for his well-placed relative, who was about to be made General-at-Sea by Lord Protector Oliver Cromwell. In his diary entry for 25 February 1667, Pepys recalled the privations of early married life: "Lay long in bed, talking with pleasure with my poor wife how she used to make coal fires and wash my foul clothes with her own hand for me, poor wretch, in our little room at my Lord Sandwiches; for which I ought for ever to love and admire her, and do. . . ." On 26 March 1658, Pepys was "cut of the stone at Mrs. Turner's in Salisbury Court" (as he recorded in the *Diary* entry for 26 March 1660). Pepys commemorated the success of this extremely dangerous kidney-stone operation—performed in less than sixty seconds and without benefit of anaesthesia—by resolving "while I live" to keep the day "a festival." The next year Pepys was made a minor clerk in the office of George Downing, a Teller of Receipt in the Exchequer, and carried letters to Mountagu in the Baltic.

1660 was a watershed year for Pepys. Now living in Axe Yard, Westminster, he began the *Diary* on 1 January. He noted in a brief preface to the first entry: "My own private condition very handsome; and esteemed rich, but endeed very poor, besides my goods of my house and my office, which at present is somewhat uncertain." Uncertainty and poverty, however, in time gave way to undreamt of stability and riches. On 9 March Pepys was made Admiral's sec-

Samuel Pepys

retary by Mountagu, and two months later he accompanied Mountagu's fleet to Holland to bring over Charles II for the Restoration. These events, like so many that touched Pepys's life during the remainder of the decade, are treated fully in the *Diary*. On 28 June Pepys resigned his clerkship in the Exchequer. The next day he was appointed Clerk of the Acts to the Navy Board. By 17 July Pepys had moved to comfortable lodgings in the Navy Office in Seething Lane, where he promptly engaged himself a servant and clerk. To his great content, he was now earning upwards of £300 per annum: a handsome salary for a man so young and a considerable advance upon the £50 he had received under Downing. During the next few years Pepys flourished. He took on the duties of justice of the peace, oversaw naval victualling, was admitted as a Younger Brother of Trinity House, the principal maritime corporation, and was appointed to the Tangier Committee. Pepys quickly mastered the niceties of his new offices, moving steadily into positions of increasing authority. During the Second Dutch War of 1665-67, he served the Royal Navy faithfully, courageously remaining at his post in London during the Great Plague of 1665 and helping save the Navy Office from destruction in the Great Fire of

London in 1666. On 31 May 1669, Pepys closed the *Diary* for good, mistakenly believing himself on the verge of blindness: "And so I betake myself that course which [is] almost as much as to see myself go into my grave—for which, and all the discomforts that will accompany my being blind, the good God prepare me." Henceforth, though he prospered mightily and kept extensive business memoranda, Pepys never again attempted to lay bare his life in diary form.

Elizabeth Pepys died of a fever in November 1669, bringing to a close a stormy but essentially happy relationship that had lasted fifteen years. Pepys now threw himself into business with astonishing fervor. By the time the *Diary* closes, Pepys was probably worth about £10,000: a large estate, built chiefly upon perquisites and fees attached to his professional offices. Thirty years later, he had claims to several times that figure. Year by year, Pepys worked to increase his wealth and influence. With the resignation of the Duke of York as Lord High Admiral of the Navy in 1673, Pepys was made Secretary to the Admiralty Commission. He was, in effect, administrative head of the naval department. Later in the year, he was elected member of parliament for Castle Rising, Norfolk. He proved an active and effective legislator and tireless spokesman for the navy. Through legislation and personal intervention, he put down the rampant blatant corruption of the victualling yards and won allowance for thirty new ships, thereby restoring the balance of sea power, which had tilted perilously in favor of France and the Netherlands. In 1679 Pepys was implicated in the Popish Plot. He was detained in the Tower of London for nearly two months, but the proceedings against him were abandoned when it became clear that the "evidence" against him had been fabricated by a malefactor. With the accession of the Duke of York as James II in 1685, Pepys was given a free hand to develop the Royal Navy as he saw fit. He spent wisely and liberally, dramatically increasing the burden of the navy and nearly tripling the number of guns. Pepys retired in 1689, shortly after James II was succeeded by William of Orange in the Glorious Revolution. In the words of Pepys's friend and fellow-diarist John Evelyn, "when James II went out of England, [Pepys] laid down his office, and would serve no more." Free from the stresses of office, Pepys spent the remainder of his life in a comfortable house in York Buildings, London, writing the only work he saw published, *Memoires relating to the State of the Royal Navy of England*, and perfecting and arranging the private library he ultimately left to Magdalene College. He died on 26 May 1703 and was buried beside Elizabeth in St. Olave's Church, London. His best-known epitaph was written by Evelyn in his own diary: "This [day] dyed Mr. Sam: Pepys, a very worthy, Industrious & curious person, none in England exceeding him in the Knowledge of the Navy, in which he had passed thro all the most Considerable Offices..., which he performed with great Integrity.... [He] was universaly beloved, Hospitable, Generous, Learned in many things, skill'd in Musick, a very greate Cherisher of Learned men, of whom he had the Conversation."

Pepys's *Diary* covers the period 1 January 1660 to 31 May 1669: slightly less than ten years in a professional career that lasted nearly thirty-five. The manuscript is preserved in six calf-bound volumes in the Pepysian Library of Magdalene College and contains about 1,250,000 words. Ex-

cept for proper names and occasional words in longhand, it is written in a somewhat modified form of the shorthand invented by Thomas Shelton and described in the 1635 edition of his *Tachygraphy*. The system has raised problems of transcription for editors, but the difficulties are generally minor, and very little of the text is obscure or invites interpretation. Pepys developed his own lingua franca for selected passages, chiefly those of an overtly erotic or especially sensitive nature, based on Spanish but containing a smattering of French, Italian, Dutch, English, Latin, and Greek. An example of such a passage appears in the entry for 23 May 1667: "This afternoon I had opportunity para jouer with Mrs. Pen, tokendo her mammailles and baisando elle, being sola in the casa of her pater, and she fort willing." This may be rendered: "This afternoon I had the opportunity to amuse myself with Mrs. Pen, taking her breasts in my hands and kissing her, being all alone in her father's house, and she most willing." It is usually clear how these passages should be transcribed and rendered, but not always; the meaning of a few such entries is therefore not really evident. The manuscript contains about 4,000 corrections to the shorthand and numerous added words, phrases, and sentences. Virtually none of these emendations presents textual or interpretive problems, however, and nearly all may be put down to one of three causes: 1) afterthought; 2) sense correction, clarification, or alteration; and 3) perceived improvement of style.

The *Diary* is considered one of the most valuable English documents of the Restoration age. According to William Matthews, who coedited the most complete edition of the text, "the diary is one of the principal source-books for many aspects of the history of its period. It is also a repertory of the familiar language of its time, and therefore an important source for historians of the English language. Most importantly, it is one of the great classics of literature." Pepys conceived the *Diary* as a personal journal, a record of his day-to-day comings and goings, but it also served as a quotidian chronicle of public affairs and the men and women behind them. Thus it is both a history of Pepys himself and a history of his country. "The diary serves therefore not only as a mirror but also as a private window giving on to a broad and varied external view—on to court politics and naval administration, or (at the other extreme) on to the simple domesticities of a London household," Robert Latham has written. In the *Diary* Pepys aimed at objectiveness in his reporting. Whatever he judged worth recording, he recorded, cramming his entries with detail and concealing nothing for the sake of decorum or in the interest of self-deceit. The entries, written apparently within days of the events they describe if not hours, are therefore markedly factual in content and immediate in tone: a quality not evident in, say, Evelyn's diary, which was extensively revised and contains numerous afterthoughts, distortions, and (it seems likely) suppressions. Pepys treated high and low themes with equal dignity and interest: all manner of men and women talked, and Pepys listened. Church affairs, navy business, court intrigues, political gossip, diplomatic doings, the activities of the Royal Society, the proceedings of the Privy Council, the Second Dutch War—all figure strongly in the pages of the *Diary*. Equally, Pepys's public, private, and domestic lives are described fully. He enthusiastically chronicled his growing fortune, making much use of figures and statistics; noted the contents of his increasingly elaborate and expensive wardrobe while confessing his private pleasure in outdressing his peers; recorded the countless meals taken outside the house: venue, company present, food served, ales, beers, wines, and spirits consumed; complained about servant problems; and variously heralded and lamented the changing state of his relationship with his wife. Small, telling, incidental details are everywhere: Pepys's delight in his wife's wearing a black patch (4 November 1660); a piercing hangover the morning after Charles II's coronation: "Waked in the morning with my head in a sad taking through the last night's drink, which I am very sorry for" (24 April 1661); penny loaves charged at twopence during the Great Fire and a chimney-bound cat "with the hair burnt off the body and yet alive" (5 September 1666); and the King and the Duke of York winking at each other at the council board (14 February 1668). Moreover, Pepys graphically chronicled the two great London catastrophes of the 1660s—the 1665 Great Plague and the 1666 Fire—and the greatest spectacle of the age, the splendid coronation of Charles II. His account of the Plague is grimly chilling and grisly, amplified by horrifying tales of individual tragedies, while his description of the Fire is enhanced by his having pushed to the rear of the retreating panicky masses to view the devastation at close range. "A most horrid malicious bloody flame," he noted in the entry for 2 September 1666.

The *Diary* is particulary valued by students of the drama and music. "No man of his day was better qualified than Pepys to judge dramatic productions," wrote J. Warshaw in 1920. Richard Ollard later claimed of Pepys: "An irresistible air of bedroom farce clings to him, partly deriving from the candour of the *Diary*, partly from the bawdiness of Restoration comedy that gives so much life and colour to our picture of the age." The *Diary* is replete with criticism of the drama. Pepys was an insatiable playgoer—he considered his fondness for the theater practically an addiction and even took steps to "cure" himself of it—and commented freely on what he liked and disliked. He paid special attention to the acting, believing that a good performance could improve even a mediocre play, and made notes on theater architecture, scenery, lighting, and the general state, mood, and appearance of the audience. He saw new plays and revivals alike, taking his cues from the ever-changing signboards. Thus he commented on the works of Shakespeare as well as many of the chief dramatists of the Restoration. For some plays, in fact, Pepys's comments are the only known contemporary criticism. Pepys also frequented musical performances. He was a musician himself—he sang, played the flageolet excellently and was proficient with other woodwinds, practiced on strings, and even tried his hand at composition—and a keen and knowledgeable music critic. His music criticism is therefore valued both for its insight and fullness and as a rare record of musical tastes not otherwise especially well documented.

During the period of its composition, Pepys's *Diary* was apparently kept locked away in his house or at the office. What use Pepys made of it after 1669, no one really knows, but he did refer to it on 3 September 1663 to check a gypsy's prophecy that he would refuse someone a loan, and he used it at least twice to refresh his memory on business matters. At Pepys's death in 1703, the *Diary* passed with his library to his nephew John Jackson and from him to Cambridge in 1724. There it lay, essentially undisturbed, for nearly one hundred years until edited by Richard Neville (later Lord Braybrooke) from a transcript made by a Cambridge undergraduate, John Smith. *Memoirs of Samuel Pepys, Esq. F. R. S.* was published in two volumes in 1825. Only a selection from the *Diary* was printed, the editor's aim being "to omit nothing of public interest." The *Memoirs* was received with practically unbridled enthusiasm. Francis Jeffrey, writing in the *Edinburgh Review* in 1825, claimed warmly: "[We] can scarcely say that we wish it a page shorter; and are of opinion, that there is very little of it which does not help us to understand the character of his times and his contemporaries, better than we should ever have done without it; and make us feel more assured that we comprehend the great historical events of the age, and the people who bore a part in them. Independent of instruction altogether too, there is no denying, that it is very entertaining thus to be transported into the very heart of a time so long gone by; and to be admitted into the domestic intimacy, as well as the public councils of a man of great activity and circulation in the reign of Charles II." Jeffrey's two themes, the *Diary's* historical import and entertainment value, presaged all future criticism of the *Diary* and were echoed in an 1826 *Quarterly Review* article by Sir Walter Scott. A new edition of the *Diary*, "Considerably Enlarged," appeared in 1848-49, but it was not until the publication in 1893-99 of an only slightly abridged version, edited by H. B. Wheatley, that the text was made available in a form that approximated the original.

Henceforth scholars could comment confidently on the work. In addition to reaffirming the historical value of the *Diary*, critics praised Pepys's self-portrait. Andrew Lang, writing to Pepys in one of his famous "Letters to Dead Authors" in 1893, found in the *Diary* "the only pages among the books of the world which show us a character as it really was," adding, "of bedside books, sir, which may send a man happily to sleep, with a smile on his lips, your egregious *Diary* is by far the best and dearest." Soon commentators began exploring the *Diary* for evidence concerning the development of the English language, the progress of the Restoration drama, and English narrative technique in the late seventeenth century. Others read it simply for the good stories it contains. At the same time, students of the *Diary* sought to reveal Pepys's apparent motive in keeping a journal, his method of composition, and his intended audience. Commenting on the style and method of the *Diary*, Arthur Ponsonby concluded in 1928: "Pepys reflects his mood by the length or brevity of his entries and by the style of his narrative rather than by any deliberate confessions of depression or elation." The full text of the *Diary* was not published until 1983, the year Matthews and Latham completed the 11-volume *Diary of Samuel Pepys: A New and Complete Transcription*. Volume One, published in 1970, offered for the first time a close, careful examination of the manuscript. Matthews wrote: "[The] manuscript makes it fairly certain that Pepys's way of writing was more complex than is usually assumed, and consequently that his great diary is no simple product of nature, thrown together at the end of each succeeding day. In part at least, it is a product fashioned with some care, both in its matter and its style." This statement, questioning the common assumption that the *Diary* is artful more by accident than design, threw new light on Pepys as litterateur. Thus Matthews could add, "Pepys is probably the only diarist who has contributed verbal formulae to the bloodstream of English," and Latham could conclude in a 1985 essay: "In the sheer technique of diary keeping—quite apart from the value of what he wrote—he has no equal."

Pepys's *Diary* is the record of a man and his age, a mirror of soul and state. Between the daily "up betimes" and the familiar peroration "and so to bed," Pepys displayed his tremendous appetite for life—his love of things old and new, common and curious—in words both evocative and informative. As Ollard has stated: "The *Diary* is a great work, as literature, as history, as a psychological document and as a key to what has been known as the English character in an age of national cultures perhaps soon to become extinct. It is thus almost impossible to exaggerate its value and importance."

PRINCIPAL WORKS

*The Portugal History; or, A Relation of the Troubles That Happened in the Court of Portugal in the Years 1667 and 1668 (history) 1677

Memoires relating to the State of the Royal Navy of England, for Ten Years, Determin'd December 1688 (prose) 1690

Memoirs of Samuel Pepys, Esq. F. R. S., Secretary to the Admiralty in the Reigns of Charles II and James II, Comprising His Diary from 1659 to 1669, Deciphered by the Rev. John Smith, A. B. of St. John's College, Cambridge, from the Original Short-Hand MS. in the Pepysian Library, and a Selection from His Private Correspondence. 2 vols. (diary and letters) 1825; revised editions 1848-49, 1854

The Life, Journals and Correspondence of Samuel Pepys. 2 vols. (diaries and letters) 1841

The Diary of Samuel Pepys, M. A., F. R. S., Clerk of the Acts and Secretary to the Admiralty. 10 vols. (diary) 1893-99

Private Correspondence and Miscellaneous Papers of Samuel Pepys, 1679-1703, in the Possession of J. Pepys Cockerell (letters and prose) 1926

Samuel Pepys's Naval Minutes (prose) 1926

Further Correspondence of Samuel Pepys, 1662-79, from the Family Papers in the Possession of J. Pepys Cockerell (letters) 1929

†Letters and the Second Diary of Samuel Pepys (diary and letters) 1933

Shorthand Letters of Samuel Pepys, from a Volume Entitled S. Pepys's Official Correspondence, 1662-1679 (letters) 1933

The Tangier Papers of Samuel Pepys (diary and prose) 1935

Mr. Pepys upon the State of Christ-Hospital (essays) 1939

The Letters of Samuel Pepys and His Family Circle (letters) 1955

Charles II's Escape from Worcester: A Collection of Narratives Assembled by Samuel Pepys (prose) 1966

The Diary of Samuel Pepys: A New and Complete Transcription. 11 vols. (diary) 1970-83

The Shorter Pepys (diary) 1985

*The attribution of this work to Pepys is not universally accepted.

†The "Second Diary" is the text of the diary Pepys kept in Tangier and Spain in 1683 and 1684, first published in 1841 in *The Life, Jour-*

nals and Correspondence of Samuel Pepys.

JOHN EVELYN (diary date 1703)

[*Evelyn was a highly cultivated English dilettante and man of letters. He is best known for the diary he kept covering the years 1641 to 1706, a work that, like Pepys's* Diary, *is admired for its anecdotal and historical value. Pepys and Evelyn were close acquaintances but differed in some respects in their views of the court of Charles II—a fact borne out by Evelyn's abundant and unreserved criticisms of the moral tone the king set. In the following excerpt from his diary entry for 26 May 1703—the day Pepys died—he praises Pepys's character and achievement.*]

This [day] dyed Mr. Sam: Pepys, a very worthy, Industrious & curious person, none in England exceeding him in the Knowledge of the Navy, in which he had passed thro all the most Considerable Offices, Clerk of the Acts, & Secretary to the Admiralty, all which he performed with greate Integrity: when K: James the 2d went out of England he layed down his Office, & would serve no more: But withdrawing himselfe from all publique Affairs, lived at Clapham with his partner (formerly his Cleark) Mr. Hewer, in a very noble House & sweete place, where he injoyed the fruit of his labours in g(r)eate prosperity, was universaly beloved, Hospitable, Generous, Learned in many things, skill'd in Musick, a very great Cherisher of Learned men, of whom he had the Conversation. His Library & other Collections of Curiositys was one of the most Considerable; The models of Ships especialy &c. Beside what he boldly published of an Account of the Navy, [*Memoires relating to the State of the Royal Navy of England*], as he found & left it, He had for divers years under his hand the History of the Navy, or, *Navalia* (as he call'd it) but how far advancd & what will follow of his, is left I suppose to his sisters son Mr. Jackson, a young Gent: whom his Unkle had educated in all sorts of usefull learning, Travell abroad, returning with extraordinary Accomplishments, & worth to be his Heire: Mr: Pepys had ben for neere 40 years, so my particular Friend, that he now sent me Compleat Mourning: desiring me to be one to hold up the Pall, at his magnificent Obsequies; but my present Indisposition, hindred me from doing him this last Office: (pp. 1096-97)

> John Evelyn, in a diary entry on May 26, 1703, in his The Diary of John Evelyn, *edited by E. S. De Beer, 1955. Reprint by Oxford University Press, London, 1959, pp. 1096-97.*

[FRANCIS JEFFREY] (essay date 1825)

[*Jeffrey was a founding editor of the* Edinburgh Review, *a highly influential British periodical noted for its generally Whig bias. In the following excerpt from his review of Lord Braybrooke's edition of the* Diary, *he offers a mixed assessment of Pepys's character while commending the* Diary *as history.*]

We have a great indulgence, we confess, for the taste, or curiosity, or whatever it may be called, that gives its value to such publications as [*Memoirs of Samuel Pepys, Esq.*]; and are inclined to think the desire of knowing, pretty minutely, the manners and habits of former times,—of understanding, in all their details, the character and ordinary way of life and conversation of our forefathers—a very liberal and laudable desire—and by no means to be confounded with that hankering after contemporary slander, with which this age is so miserably infested, and so justly reproached. It is not only curious to see from what beginnings, and by what steps, we have come to be what we are: It is most important, for the future and for the present, to ascertain what practices, and tastes and principles, have been commonly found associated or disunited: And as, in uncultivated lands, we can often judge of their inherent fertility by the quality of the weeds they spontaneously produce—so we may learn, by such an inspection of the moral growths of a country, compared with its subsequent history, what prevailing manners are indicative of vice or of virtue—what existing follies foretell approaching wisdom—what forms of licentiousness give promise of coming purity, and what of deeper degradation—what uncertain lights, in short, announce the *rising*, and what the *setting* sun! While, in like manner, we may trace in the same records, the connexion of public and private morality, and the mutual action and reaction of government and manners;—and discover what individual corruptions spring from political dishonour—what domestic profligacy leads to the sacrifice of freedom—and what national virtues are most likely to resist the oppressions, or yield to the seductions of courts.

Of all these things History tells us little—and yet they are the most important that she could have been employed in recording. She has been contented, however, for the most part, with detailing merely the broad and apparent results—the great public events and transactions, in which the true working principles of its destiny have their end and consummation; and points only to the wrecks or the triumphs that float down the tide of human affairs, without giving us any light as to those *ground currents* by which its central masses are governed, and of which those superficial appearances are, in most cases, the necessary, though unsuspected effects.

Every one feels, we think, how necessary this information is, if we wish to understand what antiquity really was, and what manner of men existed in former generations—how vague and unsatisfactory, without it, are all public annals and records of dynasties and battles—of how little interest to private individuals—of how little use even to philosophers and statesmen! Before we can apply any example in history, or even comprehend its actual import, we must know something of the character, both of the age and of the persons to which it belongs—and understand a good deal of the temper, tastes, and occupations, both of the actors and the sufferers. Good and evil change natures with a change of those circumstances; and we may be lamenting as the most intolerable of calamities, what was scarcely felt as an infliction, by those on whom it fell. Without this knowledge, therefore, the most striking and important events are mere wonders to be stared at—altogether barren of instruction—and probably leading us astray, even as occasions of sympathy or moral emotion. These minute details, in short, which History has so often rejected as below her dignity, are indispensable to give life, certainty or reality to her delineations; and we should have little hesitation in asserting, that no history is really worth anything, unless it relate to a people and an age of which we have also those humbler and more private memorials. It

is not in the grand Tragedy, or rather the Epic fictions, of History, that we learn the true condition of former ages—the real character of past generations, or even the actual effects that were produced on society or individuals at the time, by the great events that are there so solemnly recorded. If we have not some remnants or some infusion of the Comedy of middle life, we neither have any idea of the state and colour of the general existence, nor any just understanding of the transactions about which we are reading. (pp. 23-5)

The work before us relates to a period of which we have already very considerable memorials. But it is, notwithstanding, of very great interest and curiosity. A good deal of what it contains derives, no doubt, its chief interest from having happened 180 years ago: But there is little of it that does not, for that very reason, throw valuable lights on our intermediate history. It consists, as the title shows, of a very minute and copious Diary, continued from the year 1659 to 1669—and a correspondence, much less perfect and continuous, down nearly to the death of the author in 1703. Fortunately for the public part of the story, the author was, from the very beginning, in immediate contact with persons in high office and about court—and, still more fortunately for the private part, seems to have been possessed of the most extraordinary activity, and the most indiscriminating, insatiable, and miscellaneous curiosity, that ever prompted the researches, or supplied the pen, of a daily chronicler. Although excessively busy and diligent in his attendance at his office, he finds time to go to every play, to every execution, to every procession, fire, concert, riot, trial, review, city feast, public dissection or picture gallery that he can hear of. Nay, there seems scarcely to have been a school examination, a wedding, christening, charity sermon, bull-baiting, philosophical meeting, or private merry-making in his neighbourhood, at which he was not sure to make his appearance, and mindful to record all the particulars. He is the first to hear all the court scandal, and all the public news—to observe the changes of fashions, and the downfal of parties—to pick up family gossip, and to retail philosophical intelligence—to criticise every new house or carriage that is built—every new book or new beauty that appears—every measure the King adopts, and every mistress he discards.

For the rest of his character, he appears to have been an easy tempered, compassionate, and kind man, combining an extraordinary diligence and regularity in his official business and domestic economy, with a singular love of gossip, amusement, and all kinds of miscellaneous information—a devoted attachment, and almost ludicrous admiration of his wife, with a wonderful devotion to the King's mistresses, and the fair sex in general, and rather a suspicious familiarity with various pretty actresses and singers; and, above all, a practical sagacity and cunning in the management of affairs, with so much occasional credulity, puerility, and folly, as would often tempt us to set him down for a driveller. Though born with good blood in his veins, and a kinsman, indeed, of his great patron, the first Earl of Sandwich, he had nothing to boast of in his immediate pregenitors, being born the son of a tailor in London, and entering on life in a state of the utmost poverty. It was probably from this ignoble vocation of his father, that he derived that hereditary taste for Dress which makes such a conspicuous figure in his Diary. The critical and affectionate notices of doublets, cloaks, beavers, peri-wigs, and sword-belts, actually outnumbering, we think, all the entries on any other subject whatever, and plainly engrossing, even in the most agitating circumtances, no small share of the author's attention. Perhaps it is to the same blot in his scutcheon, that we should trace a certain want of manliness in his whole character and deportment. Certain it is at least, that there is room for such an imputation. He appears before us, from first to last, with the true temper, habits, and manners of an *Underling*—obsequious to his superiors—civil and smooth to all men—lavish in attentions to persons of influence whom he dislikes—and afraid and ashamed of being seen with his best friends and benefactors, when they are supposed to be out of favour—most solicitous to keep out of quarrels of all sorts—and ensuring his own safety, not only by a too humble and pacific bearing in scenes of contention, but by such stretches of simulation and dissimulation as we cannot easily reconcile to our notion of a brave and honourable man.

To such an extent, indeed, is this carried, that, though living in times of great actual, and greater apprehended changes, it is with difficulty that we can guess, even from this most copious and unreserved record of his inmost thoughts, what were his political opinions, or whether indeed he had any. We learn, indeed, from one passage, that in his early youth he had been an ardent Roundhead, and had in that capacity attended with exultation the execution of the King—observing to one of his companions at the time, that, if he had been to make a sermon on the occasion, he would have chosen for his text the words, "The memory of the wicked shall rot." This, to be sure, was when he was only in his eighteenth year—but he seems afterwards to have accepted of a small office in the Republican Court of Exchequer, of which he is in possession for some time after the commencement of his Diary. That work begins in January 1659, while Monk was on his march from Scotland; and yet, not only does he continue to frequent the society of Harrington, Hazlerigge and other staunch republicans, but never once expresses any wish of his own, either for the restoration of the Royalty, or the continuance of the Protectorate, till after he is actually at sea with Lord Sandwich, with the ships that brought Charles back from Breda. After the Restoration is consolidated, indeed, and he has got a good office in the Admiralty, he has recorded, amply enough, his anxiety for the permanency of the ancient dynasty—though he cannot help, every now and then, reprobating the profligacy, wastefulness, and neglect of the new government, and contrasting them disadvantageously with the economy, energy, and popularity, of most of the measures of the Usurper. While we give him credit therefore, for great candour and impartiality in the *private* judgments which he has here recorded, we can scarcely pay him the compliment of saying that he has any political principles whatever—or any, at least, for which he could ever have dreamed of hazarding his own wordly prosperity.

Another indication of the same low and ignoble turn of mind is to be found, we think, in his penurious anxiety about his money—the intense satisfaction with which he watches its increase, and the sordid and vulgar cares to which he condescends to check its expenditure. Even after he is in possession of a great income, he goes and sits by the tailor till he sees him sew all the buttons on his doublet—and spends four or five hours, of a very busy day, in watching the coach-maker laying on the coats of varnish on the body of his coach! When he gives a dinner, he knows exactly what every dish has cost him—and tells a long story of his paddling half the night with his fingers in the dirt, digging up some money he had buried in a garden, and conveying it with his own hands, with many fears and contrivances, safely back to his house. With all this, however, he is charitable to the poor, kind to his servants and dependents, and very indulgent to all the members of his family—though we find him chronicling his own munificence in helping to fit out his wife's brother, when he goes abroad to push his fortune, by presenting him with 'ten shillings—and a coat that I had by me—a close bodied, light-coloured, cloth coat—with a gold edging on each seam—that was the lace of my wife's best petticoat, when I married her!' (pp. 26-9)

One of the most characteristic, and at the same time most creditable pieces of *naiveté* that we meet with in the book, is in the account he gives of the infinite success of a speech which he delivered at the bar of the House of Commons, in 1667, in explanation and defence of certain alleged mismanagements in the Navy, then under discussion in that assembly. The honourable House probably knew but little about the business; and nobody, we can well believe, knew so much about it as our author,—and this, we have no doubt, was the great merit of his discourse, and the secret of his success:—For though we are disposed to give him every credit for industry, clearness, and practical judgment, we think it is no less plain from his manner of writing, than from the fact of his subsequent obscurity in Parliament, that he could never have had any pretensions to the character of an orator. Be that as it may, however, this speech seems to have made a great impression at the time; and certainly gave singular satisfaction to its worthy maker. (p. 37)

On turning to the political or historical parts of this record, we are rather disappointed in finding so little that is curious or interesting in that earliest potion of it which carries us through the whole work of the Restoration. Though there are almost daily entries from the 1st of January 1659, and though the author was constantly in communication with persons in public situations—was personally introduced to the King at the Hague, and came home in the same ship with him, it is wonderful how few particulars of any moment he has been enabled to put down; and how little the tone of his journal exhibits of that interest and anxiety which we are apt to imagine must have been universal during the dependence of so momentous a revolution. Even this barrenness, however, is not without instruction—and illustrates by a new example, how insensible the contemporaries of great transactions very often are of their importance, and how much more posterity sees of their character than those who were parties to them. . . . [The] author's own political predilections are scarcely distinguishable till he is embarked in the fleet to bring home the King—and the greater part of those with which he converses seem to have been nearly as undecided. Monck is spoken of throughout with considerable contempt and aversion; and among many instances of his duplicity, it is recorded that upon the 21st day of February 1660, he came to Whitehall 'and there made a speech to them, recommending to them *a Common wealth*, and *against* Charles Stuart.' The feeling of the city is represented, no doubt, as extremely hostile to the Parliament, (here uniformly called the Rump); but their aspirations are not said to be directed to royalty, but merely to a free Parliament and the dissolution of the existing junto. So late as the month of March our author observes, 'great is the talk of a single person. Charles, George, or Richard again. For *the last* of which my Lord St John is said to speak very high. Great also is the dispute in the House, in whose name the courts shall sue for the new Parliament.' It is a comfort however to find, in a season of such universal dereliction of principle, that signal perfidy, even to the cause of the republic, is visited with general scorn. A person of the name of Morland, who had been employed under the Protector in the Secretary of State's office, had been in the habit of betraying his trust, and communicating privately with the exiled monarch—and, upon now resorting to him, had been graced with the honour of knighthood. Even our cool headed chronicler speaks thus of this deserter.

> Mr Morland, now Sir Samuel, was here on board, but I do not find that my Lord or any body did give him any respect—he being looked upon by him and all men as a knave. Among others he betrayed Sir Rich. Willis that married Dr F. Jones's daughter, who had paid him 1000*l.* at one time by the Protector's and Secretary Thurloe's order, for intelligence that he sent concerning the King.

And there is afterwards a similar expression of honest indignation against 'that perfidious rogue Sir G. Downing,' who, though he had served in the Parliamentary army under Okey, yet now volunteered to go after him and Corbet, with the King's warrant, to Holland, and succeeded in bringing them back as prisoners, to their death—and had the impudence, when there, to make a speech to 'the Lords States of Holland, telling them to their faces that he observed that he was not received with the respect and observance *now*, that he was when he came from *the traitor and rebell Cromwell!* by whom, I am sure, he hath got all he hath in the world;—and they know it too.'

When our author is presented to the King, he very simply puts down, that 'he seems to be a very sober man!' This, however, may refer only to his dress and equipment, which . . . seems to have been homely enough, even for a republic. (pp. 40-1)

The most frequent and prolific topic in the whole book, next perhaps to that of dress, is the profligacy of the court—or what may fairly be denominated court scandal. It would be endless, and not very edifying, to attempt any thing like an abstract of the shameful immoralities which this loyal author has recorded of the two royal brothers, and the greater part of their favourites. . . . (p. 44)

The mingled extravagance and penury of [the disorderly Court of Charles II] is strikingly illustrated by two entries, not far from each other, in the year 1667—in one of which is recorded the royal wardrobeman's pathetic lamentation over the King's necessities—representing that his Majesty has 'actually no handkerchiefs, and but three bands to his neck'—and that he does not know where to take up a yard of linen for his service!—and the other setting forth, that his said Majesty had lost 25,000*l.* in one night at play with Lady Castlemaine—and staked 1000*l.* and 1500*l.* on a cast. It is a far worse trait, however, in his character, that he was by no means scrupulous as to the

pretexts upon which he obtained money from his people—these memoirs containing repeated notices of accounts deliberately falsified for this purpose—and not a few in particular, in which the expenses of the Navy are exaggerated—we are afraid, not without the author's cooperation—to cover the misapplication of the money voted for that most popular branch of the service, to very different purposes. In another Royal Imposture, our author now appears to have been also implicated—though in a manner far less derogatory to his personal honour, we mean in procuring for the Duke of York, the credit which he has obtained with almost all our historians, for his great skill in maritime affairs; and the extraordinary labour which he bestowed in improving the condition of the Navy. (pp. 48-9)

We do not know whether the citations we have now made from these curious and most miscellaneous volumes, will enable our readers to form a just estimate of their value. But we fear that, at all events, we cannot now indulge them with any considerable addition to their number. There is a long account of the great Fire and the great Sickness in 1666, and a still longer one of the insulting advance of the Dutch fleet to Chatham in 1667, as well as of the settlement at Tangiers, and of various naval actions during the period to which the Diary extends. But, though they all contain much curious matter, we are not tempted to make any extracts; both because the accounts, being given in the broken and minute way which belongs to the form of a Diary, do not afford many striking or summary passages, and because what is new in them, is not for the most part of any great importance. The public besides has been lately pretty much satiated with details on most of those subjects in the contemporary work of Evelyn,—of which we shall only say, that though its author was indisputably more of a gentleman, a scholar, and a man of taste than our actuary, it is far inferior both in interest, curiosity, and substantial instruction, to that which we are now considering. The two authors, however, we are happy to find, were great friends; and no name is mentioned in the latter part of the Diary, with more uniform respect and affection than that of Mr. Evelyn—though it is very edifying to see how the shrewd, practical sagacity of the man of business, revenges itself on the assumed superiority of the philosopher and man of letters. (pp. 49-50)

We meet with the *names* of many distinguished men in these pages, and some characteristic anecdotes,—but few bold characters. He has a remarkable interview with Clarendon—in which the cautious and artful demeanour of that veteran politician is finely displayed, though on a very trivial occasion. (p. 50)

There is no *literary* intelligence of any value to be gained from this work. Play collectors will probably find the names of many lost pieces—but of our classical authors there are no notices worth naming—a bare intimation of the deaths of Waller, Cowley, and Davenant, and a few words of Dryden—Milton, we think, not once mentioned. There is more of the natural philosophers of Gresham College, but not much that is valuable. . . . (p. 51)

And now we have done with Mr Pepys. There is trash enough no doubt in his journal,—trifling facts, and silly observations. But we can scarcely say that we wish it a page shorter; and are of opinion, that there is very little of it which does not help us to understand the character of his times and his contemporaries, better than we should ever have done without it; and make us feel more assured that we comprehend the great historical events of the age, and the people who bore a part in them. Independent of instruction altogether too, there is no denying, that it is very entertaining thus to be transported into the very heart of a time so long gone by; and to be admitted into the domestic intimacy, as well as the public councils of a man of great activity and circulation in the reign of Charles II. Reading this book seems to us to be quite as good as living with Mr Samuel Pepys in his proper person,—and though the court scandal may be detailed with more grace and vivacity in the *Memoires de Grammont*, we have no doubt that even this part of his multifarious subject is treated with far greater fidelity and fairness in the work before us—while it gives us more clear and undistorted glimpses into the true English life of the times—for the court was substantially foreign—than all the other memorials of them that have come down to our own. (p. 54)

> [Francis Jeffrey], in a review of "Memoirs of Samuel Pepys, Esq.," in The Edinburgh Review, Vol. XLIII, No. LXXXV, November, 1825, pp. 23-54.

[SIR WALTER SCOTT] (essay date 1826)

[*Scott was a nineteenth-century Scottish novelist, poet, historian, biographer, and literary critic. He is best known for such historical novels as* Waverley *(1814),* Rob Roy *(1818), and* Ivanhoe *(1819), all of which were great popular successes. In the following excerpt from his review of Lord Braybrooke's edition of the* Diary, *he closely examines the background and content of the work, noticing its historical value and comparing it with other records of the era it treats.*]

There is a curiosity implanted in our nature which receives much gratification from prying into the actions, feelings, and sentiments of our fellow creatures. The same spirit, though very differently modified and directed, which renders a female gossip eager to know what is doing among her neighbours over the way, induces the reader for information, as well as him who makes his studies his amusement, to turn willingly to those volumes which promise to lay bare the motives of the writer's actions, and the secret opinions of his heart. We are not satisfied with what we see and hear of the conqueror on the field of battle, or the great statesman in the senate; we desire to have the privilege of the valet-de-chambre to follow the politician into his dressing closet, and to see the hero in those private relations where he is a hero no longer.

Many have thought that this curiosity is most amply gratified by the correspondence of eminent individuals, which, therefore, is ofter published to throw light upon their history and character. Unquestionably much information is thus obtained, especially in the more rare cases where the Scipio has found a Lelius—some friend in whom he can fear no rival, and to whose unalterable attachment he can commit even his foibles without risking loss of esteem or diminution of affection. But in general letters are written upon a different principle, and exhibit the writers less as they really are, than as they desire their friends should believe them to be. Thus it may be observed that the man who wishes for profit or advancement usually writes in a style of bullying independence—a flag which he quickly strikes to the prospect of advantage; the selfish individual,

on the other hand, fortifies his predominant frailty by an affectation of sensibility; the angry and irritable man attends with peculiar strictness to the formal and ceremonial style of well-bred society; the dissolute assume on paper an air of morality; and the letters of the prodigal are found to abound with maxims of prudence not a whit the worse for the author's own wear.

These discrepancies between epistolary sentiments and the real character of the writer, become of course more marked when the letters, like those of Pope, are written with a secret consciousness that they may one day or other come before the public. It is then that each sentence is polished, each sentiment correct; and that a letter, ostensibly addressed to one private friend, is compiled with the same sedulous assiduity as if it were to come one day flying abroad on all the wings of the press.

The conclusion is that there can be little reliance placed on the sincerity of letter-writers in general, and that in estimating the mass of strange matter which is preserved in contemporary correspondence, the reader ought curiously to investigate the character, situation, and temper of the principal correspondent, ere he can presume to guess how many of his sentiments are real; how much is designed as a gentle *placebo* to propitiate the feelings of the party whom he addresses; how much intended to mislead future readers into a favourable estimate of the writer's capacity and disposition. (pp. 281-82)

Thus much for the faith of familiar letters, which, from the days of Howell downwards we believe, will be found to contain as regular and rateable a proportion of falsehood as the same quantity of given conversation. In private Diaries, like that now upon our table [*Memoirs of Samuel Pepys, Esq.*] we come several steps nearer to the reality of a man's sentiments. The journalist approaches to the situation of the soliloquist in the nursery rhyme.

> As I walked by myself,
> I talked to myself,
> And thus myself said to me.

It is no doubt certain that in this species of self intercourse we put many tricks upon our actual and our moral self, and often endeavour to dress deeds, enacted by the former on very egotistical principles, in such a garb as may in some degree place them, favourably before the other's contemplation. Still there must be more fair dealing betwixt ourself and our conscience, than ourself and any one else;—*here* there is much which can neither be denied or extenuated; *Magna est veritas et prevalebit.* Indeed such seems the force of the principle of sincerity in this sort of self-communing as renders it wonderful how much such records contain of what is actually discreditable to the writers. These confessions may have been made either because the trick was cleverly done, (as many a Newgate knave indites a narrative of his rogueries that at the same time he may preserve some remembrance of his talents,) or because the moral sense of the party in the confessional has become dull and blunted, and insensible of the manner in which his tale is likely to be regarded by men whose sense of right and wrong is undepraved; or, finally, (that case perhaps occurs seldomest of any,) because the narrator feels his secret mind oppressed beneath the same weighty burthen of solitary consciousness which sometimes drives malefactors of a different class to speak out more than had even been laid to their charge. Owing to these and other motives we have ourselves listened to unsolicited avowals made in general society of such a character as served to strike with dismay, and eventually to disperse a gay and unscrupulous company, who shrunk away in disgust, and left the too candid narrator to spend the rest of the evening in reflecting on the consequences of untimely confidence. Those who make such admissions in society are still more ready to record them in their diaries. Nothing indeed can be more natural than the conduct of the barber of king Midas, who relieved his mind of a burthensome secret by communicating to a bundle of reeds the fact that the worthy prince whom he served had the ears of an ass. In modern times a memorandum and a goose-quill would have naturally been the barber's resource, nor are we at all certain that the committing his mystery to the treacherous reeds meant any thing more than that the court-barber of king Midas kept a diary, which fell into the hands of some reviewer of the times.

If there is any one to whom we can ascribe perfect good faith in the composition of his diary, it is certainly the author of that which lies before us. Mr. Pepys was in the fortunate situation that he had no crimes to conceal, and no very important vices to apologize for. We think we can determine to what class the latter belonged: and yet they are so very well glossed over, that we can easily believe the frank gentleman was prevented by the blinding influence of that witch, Vanity, from accurately considering the feelings likely to be excited in the minds of others by certain matters which he has faithfully recorded.

There was an additional ground of security in Mr. Pepys's case; he had, to keep up the parallel of king Midas's barber, dug his pit extremely deep, and secured his record against easy consultation or rapid transcription. His diary was written in a peculiar shorthand or cipher, which he had practised from an early period of life. Undoubtedly he laid considerable stress on this circumstance in considering the possibility of his journal falling into unfriendly hands during his life, or being too rashly communicated to the public after his death. At least it is certain that when he gave up, with much regret, the keeping this daily register of his private thoughts and remarks, it was in consequence of his eyesight being for a time in such a state that he no longer retained the power of writing his cipher.

> And thus ends all that I doubt I shall ever be able to do with my journall, I being not able to do it any longer, having done now so long as to undo my eyes almost every time that I take a pen in my hand; and therefore, whatever comes of it, I must forbear: and therefore resolve from this time forward to have it kept by my people in long-hand, and must be contented to set down no more than is fit for them and all the world to know; or if there be any thing, I must endeavour to keep a margin in my book open, to add here and there a note in short-hand with my own hand. And so I betake myself to that course, which is almost as much as to see myself go into my grave: for which, and all the discomforts that will accompany my being blind, the good God prepare me!

From this touching passage, as indeed from the whole tenor of the diary, it is evident that Mr. Pepys wrote under a feeling of security, and therefore with a frankness not often to be found amongst diarists, who have not the same resources against the risk of inconvenience from malicious or impertinent scrutiny into their private lucubrations. Why, when his eyes recovered (as they must soon have done) their usual strength, he did not resume the diary, no hint is given. Is it quite impossible that he may have done so, and that other volumes may hereafter be discovered?

In the meantime it is to Lord Braybrooke that we owe the possession of these two curious volumes, containing, as we hope presently to show, much that is interesting to the historian and to the antiquary, as well as a treasure of amusing facts for the benefit of the general reader. (pp. 282-84)

We must follow some species of arrangement in the view which we are about to give the reader of the contents of these volumes, and perhaps it will be as natural as any other, first, to consider those passages which affect Mr. Pepys personally, and introduce us to a knowledge of his character; and here we are compelled in some measure to draw a comparison betwixt our journalist and his contemporary Evelyn, who has left a similar, and, at least, equally valuable record referring to the same period.

Evelyn and Pepys were friends, and it is to the credit of the latter that he enjoyed the good opinion of the former. Both were men of sound sense, both were attached to science and the fine arts, both were, generally speaking, of sober and studious habits, both were attached to the crown from principle, and both were grieved and mortified by the unkingly mode in which it was worn by the 'merry monarch, scandalous, and poor,' under whose authority it was their fate to live, and by whom they were, each in his degree, held in estimation. Both writers were, moreover, shrewd and sharp critics of the abuses of the times, had seen the reign of fanaticism and hypocrisy succeeded by that of open profligacy and irreligion, and were mortified and grieved spectators of an extent of licentiousness to which no other age, perhaps, could in England produce a parallel.

But yet the characters of the two diarists were essentially different, and the distinction, it must be owned, is not in favour of Pepys. This may, in some measure, be owing to the difference of their relative situations. Evelyn, highly born and independent in fortune, had been bred up in the principles of the cavaliers, and has been justly said to constitute one of the best and most dignified specimens of the old English country gentleman. The restoration found him in his own place; he had nothing to repent of, nothing to sue for; was willing to view the conduct of his master with lenient eyes, but, having nothing to fear from the resentment of king or minister, was not obliged to wink at such vices as his conscience called on him to condemn. Pepys's original political opinions, on the other hand, though they must be considered as those of a boy, did not quite fit the great change which took place at the restoration;—of which he himself gives us the following naive instance.

> Here dined with us two or three more country gentlemen; among the rest Mr. Christmas, my old schoolfellow, with whom I had much talk. He did remember that I was a great roundhead when I was a boy, and I was much afraid that he would have remembered the words that I said the day the king was beheaded (that, were I to preach upon him, my text should be—'The memory of the wicked shall rot'); but I found afterwards that he did go away from school before that time.

Again, when Sir John Bunch upbraided him that 'it was a fine time for such as he who had been for Oliver to be full of employment, while the old cavaliers got none,' he frankly owns that he answered nothing to the reproach, for fear of making bad worse. This alteration of opinion, which led Pepys to dread the tenacity of his old school-fellow's memory, may serve to indicate a little versatility of principle foreign to the character and practice of Evelyn. We must not, indeed, forget that he began life poor, the son of a mechanic, dependent upon a powerful relative, and was obliged for his own rise to use the prevailing arts of corruption, (for so the giving presents to his superiors must be termed,) and thus early tempted to judge with less severity even vices which he disapproved of, when practised by those on whose efficient services his advance in life must depend. But there was by nature, as well as by situation and habit, a loftier tone about the character and virtues of Evelyn than Pepys seems to aspire to. He was, like Sully at the court of Henry IV., a contemner of the frivolities and foibles exhibited by the king and courtiers. Pepys's abhorrence of vice and of the dissipations of fashion was not of a character so decisive. Like Old Gobbo, he did 'somewhat *smack*, somewhat *draw to*,'—he had a certain degree of indulgence towards the 'upper abuses' of the times, which prevents the full effect of his censures, and would sometimes half persuade us that a quiet secret sip from the cup of Circe was a cordial *haud alienum a Scævolæ studiis*. Thus, we find he kept occasional company with Harry Killigrew, young Newport and others, wild rogues as any about town, whose mad talk made his heart ache. And although he tells us this was only for once, to know the nature of their life and conversation, yet the air of Vauxhall is not very favourable to rigid virtue when breathed in such society, and the question will occur 'whether it is for gravity to play at cherry-pit with Satan.'—Again, a decent degree of censure is no doubt bestowed on those 'Light o' Loves,' who adorned the court and disputed the good graces of Charles, but their beauty is at the same time extolled in such terms as show the journalist's admiration of their persons had sometimes balanced, if not outweighed, his virtuous indignation at their improprieties.

Perhaps a contrast between the different modes in which those two journalists saw similar scenes, will be the best illustration of our meaning. And first remark the severe dignity with which Evelyn passes censure on the witty and worthless sovereign, for the levity of his conduct in public towards our old acquaintance Nell Gwyn.

> I thence walked through St. Jame's Parke to the garden, where I both saw and heard a very familiar discourse between [the king] and Mrs. *Nellie* as they called an impudent comedian; she looking out of her garden on a terrace at the top of the wall, and [the king] standing on the green walke under it. I was heartily sorry at this scene. Thence the king walked to the Dutchess of Cleaveland, another lady of pleasure, and curse of our nation. (pp. 289-90)

Our friend Pepys did not aspire at quite so high a strain of moral feeling as is expressed by Evelyn, although he seems to have come the length of listening with much edification to a learned divine, who proved, 'like a wise man, that righteousness is a surer moral way of being rich, than sin and villany.' He did not approve of the naughty doings of the time, but he appears to have been fully sensible of the seductions which Evelyn held so cheaply. It is true that he seems to have sympathized with Evelyn, when in communing together concerning the 'badness of the government, where nothing but wickedness and wicked men and women command the king,' and concurred in thanking providence that it had put some stop to the prodigalities of Charles in the matter of Lady Byron, the merry king's 'seventeenth mistress,' who had had an order for £4000 of plate to be made for her, 'but by delays, thanks be to God, she died before she had it.' Pepys could, no doubt, speak scholarly and wisely upon these subjects with Evelyn, and his journal echoes back many of the complaints which are to be found in the diary of his more dignified friend. But still, if he did not turn aside to listen to the songs of the Syrens, no more did he stop his ears absolutely against them. Lady Castlemaine appears to have attracted his particular admiration, though Mrs. Stuart (La Belle Stuart of Count Anthony Hamilton) at times seems to have, in his estimation, disputed the palm of beauty. (pp. 290-91)

But albeit the charms of the beautiful Stuart might have power at times to shake Mr. Pepys's allegiance, he seems on the whole to have been loyally devoted to the supremacy of the reigning favourite. To a true knight all emblems and appurtenances of the lady of his admiration are rendered invaluable by their connexion with the idol. Thus, good Mr. Pepys dotes upon certain articles of Lady Castlemaine's dress as well as upon her picture. 'In the Privy-garden saw, the finest smocks and linnen petticoats of my Lady Castlemaine's, laced with rich lace at the bottom, that ever I saw; and did me good to look at them.' On the subject of her picture, our zealous admirer is scarcely less enthusiastic than on that of her petticoats. He saw, at Mr. (afterwards Sir Peter) Lely's, among other portraits, the 'so-much-desired-by-me picture of Lady Castlemaine, which is a most blessed picture, and one that I must have a copy of.' Upon another occasion he is in extasies with her beauty, when talking with 'a person booted and spurred,' the king, doubtless, 'she being in her hair put on his hat, which was but an ordinary one, to keep the wind off, which became her mightily, as every thing else does.' Yet with all his admiration of Lady Castelmaine, Pepys regretted the king's doting folly in his conduct towards her. He is scandalized at learning that Charles had bestowed on her all the Christmas presents made by the peers, and that at the great ball she appeared richer in jewels than the queen and princesses both together. In another passage he mentions her removal to Whitehall, where she occupied an apartment next to that of the king, which, says he, 'I am sorry to hear, though I love her much.' (p. 292)

Pepys in his love of wit and admiration of beauty finds room to love and admire Nell Gwyn, whose name still carries an odd fascination with it after so many generations, and who had certainly, to atone for her misgovernance, talents and principles to which Lady Castlemaine was a stranger. She best pleaded her own case when, in a quarrel with Beck Marshal, a frail sister of the stage, she stated the nature of her parentage and education. When the latter, who was the daughter of Stephen Marshal, the great Presbyterian preacher, upbraided Nell with being Lord Buckhurst's mistress, 'Nell answered her, "I was but one man's mistress, though I was brought up in a brothel to fill strong water to the gentlemen; and you are a mistress to three or four, though a Presbyter's praying daughter!"'

The six volumes of the Diary *manuscript, preserved in the Pepysian Library, Magdalene College, Cambridge.*

Pepys admired her particularly in the part of Florimell, in the Maiden Queen of Dryden, 'both as a mad girl and when she acts a young gallant;' she is in other places 'pretty witty Nelly.' He goes behind the scenes, and though not much pleased with the manners and society he finds there, yet when he comes to the women's shift (dressing-room), where Nell was dressing for her part, he finds her 'very pretty, prettier than he had thought.' On the whole, we think it quite as well that Mrs. Pepys happened to be present at such a scene as follows, which it seems was his introduction to Nelly.

> A most pretty woman, who acted the greater part Cœlia to-day, very fine, and did it pretty well: I kissed her, and so did my wife; and a mighty pretty soul she is.

We learn from Pepys's authority, notwithstanding his general partiality, that Nell played serious characters very ill; and this makes him express his wonder at her excellence in mad characters, which certainly approach the tragic. The truth is, our friend was a general admirer of rank and personal accomplishments in men and women, and appears to have joyed in all circumstances which brought him into close connection with persons so endowed. Thus, he does not conceal his satisfaction when presented to the Duchess of York.—'It was the first time I did ever, or did see any body else, kiss her hand, and it was a most fine white and fat hand.' On the other hand, Pepys was severe in his remarks on those who neglected personal appear-

ance. He declares himself ashamed to walk with an old friend, Mr. Pechel, otherwise a good humoured man, 'on account of his red nose.' He will have his brother put into canonical habiliments that he may be fit to walk with him in the streets; and he marvels at and censures the Treasurer of the Navy for not pairing his nails, when we are of opinion he ought, in those days, to have been quite satisfied with the admitted cleanness of his palms.

It followed, of course, that attentive as he was to beauty and gay attire elsewhere, he was not negligent of those qualities at home, and Mrs. Pepys enjoyed, as was fitting, no small share of his attention and admiration. The following articles are curious, both as they illustrate the temper of the writer, and the customs of the age. Among all the beauties present at Nan Hartlibb's wedding, we learn his wife was thought the greatest. He found her particularly pretty on having allowed her to wear a black patch, and is pleased with two peruques of hair brought for her use by La Belle Pearce. 'They are,' he vauntingly says, 'of his wife's own hair, or else he would not have endured them.' Many other little intimations there are of his pride in Mrs. Pepys's beauty and the dominion which he exercised over her wardrobe; and in the following passage he acquiesces with peculiar dignity in the increase of that species of paraphernalia with which women are usually most gratified.

> This evening my wife did with great pleasure shew me her stock of jewells, encreased by the ring she hath

made lately as my Valentine's gift this year, a Turkey stone set with diamonds: and with this, and what she had, she reckons that she hath above 150*l.* worth of jewells of one kind or other; and I am glad of it, for it is fit the wretch should have something to content herself with.

He is extremely interested as a husband equally and an amateur in the progress of Mrs. Pepys's picture; scarce the by-him-so-much-desired portraiture of Mrs. Lady Castlemaine seems to have interested the worthy man more. We hope and trust there were few serious interruptions of the happiness of this kind couple; and have little doubt that they had cause upon each anniversary of their marriage, as upon the ninth, to 'bless God for their long lives and loves and healths together, and pray to God for the continuance of their mutual affection.'

Nevertheless, he that touches pitch runs a risk of being defiled, and we observe our friend Pepys, for a good and grave man, was rather too fond of frolicsome society, and of conversation that was more entertaining than edifying. Pepys was a poet too, and composed his own songs; an amateur, and sung them to his own music. This task seems to have rendered female assistance necessary to make out a sort of concert, in which Mrs. Mercer, Mrs. Pepys's maid, displayed some talents for music, which Mr. Pepys in all honesty judged worthy of further cultivation. This seems to have displeased Mrs. Pepys, and her husband records the incident and his own defence.

> Thence home; and to sing with my wife and Mercer in the garden; and coming in I find my wife plainly dissatisfied with me, that I can spend so much time with Mercer, teaching her to sing, and could never take the pains with her. Which I acknowledge; but it is because that the girl do take musick mighty readily, and she do not, and musick is the thing of the world that I love most, and all the pleasure almost that I can now take. So to bed in some little discontent, but no words from me.

On our part, we are by no means so jealous of Mrs. Mercer as of a certain slut called Knipp, an actress of some celebrity, and apparently as much to Mr. Pepys's taste as her merry comrade Nell Gwyn. The figure she makes in the *Diary* is somewhat alarming, as for example—

> Comes Mrs. Knipp to see my wife, and I spent all the night talking with this baggage, and teaching her my song of 'Beauty retire,' which she sings and makes go most rarely, and a very fine song it seems to be. She also entertained me with repeating many of her own and others parts of the play-house, which she do most excellently; and tells me the whole practices of the play-house and players, and is in every respect most excellent company.

He sets out with Knipp to be merry at Chelsea too—and she praises (cunning one) his vein of poetry, telling him his song of 'Beauty retire' is mightily cried up, 'which I am not a little proud of,' says Pepys simply, 'and do think I have done "It is decreed" better, but I have not finished it.' He meets at the theatre 'One dressed like a country-maid with a straw hat on, and at first I could not tell who it was, though I expected Knipp: but it was she coming off the stage just as she acted this day in "The Goblins;" a merry jade.' Moreover the celebrated Tom Killigrew seems to have found out the Clerk of the Acts' blind side, when he said 'Knipp was going to become the best actor

upon the stage.' Upon the whole, we are afraid his friend Evelyn would have shaken his head at some of these and similar entries, and so much pleasure does the secretary express in the society of this 'merry jade,' that we cannot but fear the worthy woman, his wife, may have had cause for uneasiness. But—Honi soit qui mal y pense.

In fact Mr. Pepys, like many more, had an acquired character very different from his natural one. Early necessity had made Pepys laborious, studious and careful. But his natural propensities were those of a man of pleasure. He appears to have been ardent in quest of amusement, especially where any thing odd or uncommon was to be witnessed. Thus he expresses, on one occasion, his regret at not being able to join a crowd of boys and girls, in following the crack-brained Duchess of Newcastle, who reached home before he could get up to her. But he gravely promises he will find a time to see her. To this thirst after novelty, the consequence of which has given great and varied interest to his diary, Pepys added a love of public amusements which he himself seems to have considered as excessive, and which he endeavoured to check by a vow—not against seeing plays, but against paying for admission to them. This singular composition between taste and principle had this further advantage, that it brought his economy, which appears to have been pretty rigid, in aid of his resolution. He appears to have been much disconcerted by a young gallant who carried him to the theatre under pretence of treating him, whereas in the event Pepys was obliged to pay for them both, leading him thus at once into a breach of his vow and an expense double the usual entrance-money. His vow, however, does not seem to have excluded him from the Bear-garden, the Cockpit, and other places of popular resort, of which he gives some amusing descriptions, and where he was wont to attend with his cloak drawn round his face, to prevent his being detected. Our grave gentleman in office took the same precaution at the theatre, being 'in mighty pain lest he should be seen by any body to be at a play.' Mr. Pepys's vow against wine, the inordinate use of which was one of the greatest vices of the period, was formed with the same flexible power of accommodating itself occasionally to the inclinations which it was intended to curb. Being at a city feast at Guild-hall.

> We went into the Buttry, and there stayed and talked, and then into the Hall again: and there wine was offered and they drunk, I only drinking some hypocras, which do not break my vowe, it being, to the best of my present judgment, only a mixed compound drink, and *not any wine.* If I am mistaken, God forgive me! but I hope and do think I am not.

Assuredly his piece of bacchanalian casuistry can only be matched by that of Fielding's chaplain of Newgate, who preferred punch to wine, because the former was a liquor no where spoken against in scripture.

We cannot drop our sketch of Mr. Pepys's character without noticing his respect and veneration for fine clothes; and the harmless yet ludicrous vanity which dwells with such mechanical accuracy on each variety of garment wherewith he regales the eyes of the million. This is so very prominent a point of his character that it reminds us of the *humour* of one of Ben Johnson's characters, who estimates the quantity of damage done in a duel, not by wounds sustained in the flesh of the combatants, but by the slits and cuts inflicted on their finery. We cannot help thinking this singularly strong propensity was derived by inheritance from his father's shop-board, and that amidst all his grandeur and all his wisdom the Clerk of the Acts could not, unhappily, *sink the tailor*.

The reader becomes as well acquainted with Pepys's wardrobe, as Prince Henry was with that of Poins, and nothing can be more amusing than the little touches of self-love mingled with the catalogue of coats, cloaks, breeches, and stockings, which of themselves are curious to the antiquary. The minuteness of the description, the petty swelling of the heart which could record with complacence every piece of gaudy pageantry which he adopted, savours strongly of the *parvenu*. But though Pepys had valuable qualities, dignity made no part of his character, any more than stoical or severe morality. On the 3d December, 1660-1, casting his roundhead, he appeared, for the first time, in the dress of a cavalier, with coat and sword; which last, we are happy to say, did not get between his legs, as was to have been expected, for if it had, he would certainly have recorded it. After this happy commencement the spirit of gentility seems to have risen rapidly in his ambitious bosom;

> Put on my first new lace-band; and so neat it is, that I am resolved my great expense shall be lace-bands, and it will set off any thing else the more.

At another time he puts on 'his new scallop, which is very fine.' And again, we are called upon to admire 'his new shaggy purple gown, with gold buttons and loop line;' or the more sober elegance 'of a black cloth suit, with white linings under all to appear under the breeches.' But this, it may be said, is the mere vanity of the man of fashion, the dandy of his time. True; but there is combined in Pepys's case a sense of the importance of fine clothes, with a prudent attention to the cost; the first bespeaking the consciouness of personal vanity proper to the purchaser; the latter, peculiar to one who has regarded the other side of the account, and, no question, derived from the good master fashioner, the father, whose ultimate end in creating fine garments was to make money by them. (pp. 293-97)

There may be something a little childish in all [Pepys's exultatation about his wardrobe], but still, as no one is surprised at an individual sacrificing ease, health, and comfort, for the sole purpose of obtaining the means of supporting such a display, it is always some comfort in finding he actually enjoys that which he has laboured so hard to gain. And after all Mr. Pepys was probably not more vain than was natural to any man who had attained wealth and distinction by his own exertions—he was only trusting to the cipher he used, and more candid than people are used to be in communicating his real feelings. (p. 298)

There are sundry . . . odd littlenesses about Pepys which injure him in comparison with his friend Evelyn. He was too sensible of the influence of the great, and too ready to truckle to it, though we believe honest and fair in his own department. In the course of offence taken against him by the celebrated Lord Chancellor Clarendon, on account of his having marked out some ornamental trees in Clarendon Park for the use of the navy, both he and his principal, Lord Sandwich, retreat vilely from what they seems,

to have (however absurdly) conceived to be a high public duty—with this humiliating confession on the part of Pepys; 'Lord, to see how we poor wretches dare not do the King good service for fear of the greatness of these men!' During an interview, in which he uses all the evasions and excuses which might deprecate the Chancellor's displeasure, he labours under an occasional suspicion that Clarendon is seriously disposed 'to try his fidelity to his king.' The Chancellor disliked, as any other gentleman would do, having fine trees cut down close to his house: but the Clerk of the Acts magnifies the matter most ridiculously. Elsewhere Pepys seems, at least, fully sensible of the necessity of propitiating the great, but the following is a curious instance of the dread he entertained in failing in the least etiquette towards them. He met, it seems, the Duke of York coming along 'the Pell Mell;'

> In our walk over the Parke, one of the Duke's footmen come running behind us, and come looking just in our faces to see who were, and went back again. What his meaning is I know not, but was fearful that I might not go far enough with my hat off.

Our diarist must not be too severely judged. He lived in a time when the worst examples abounded, a time of court intrigue and state revolution, when nothing was certain for a moment, and when all who were possessed of any opportunity to make profit, used it with the most shameless avidity, lest the golden minutes should pass away unimproved. It was said of Charles himself, that he did by Tangiers as Lord Caernarvon said of wood, which he termed 'an excrescence of the earth, provided by God for the payment of debts.' The same might at that time have been said of most of the great employments in England, which were considered by those who filled them, not with reference to the public right and interest, but merely as they could be rendered available to their own private emolument. It is no mean praise, that we find Pepys, at such a period of general abuse, labouring successfully to introduce order and discountenance abuses in his own department. (pp. 300-01)

Our Journalist, besides his grave treatise upon the Mare Clausum—to which, by the bye, he gave a new title at the Restoration, the former being suited to the Republican model—has some pretension to notice as a man of letters,—having written a romance, and, at least, two songs. The former he prudently burned, though not without some regret, doubting he could not do it so well over again if he should try; the latter were rendered mellifluous by the voices of Knipp and Mercer. He does not appear to have got beyond the false taste of his times, as he extols *Volpone* and the *Silent Woman* as the best plays he ever saw, and accounts the *Midsummer Night's Dream* the most insipid and ridiculous. *Othello* he sets down as 'a mean thing;' *Henry VIII*. although much cried up, did not please him, even though he went with purpose to be pleased; it was, in his opinion, 'a simple thing, made of patches;' 'and, besides the shows and processions in it, there was nothing well done.' But the most diverting circumstance is the series of unsuccessful efforts which Pepys made to relish the celebrated poem of Butler, then enjoying all the blaze of novel popularity. Possibly some remaining predilection for the opinions which are ridiculed in that witty satire prevented his falling in with the universal fashion of admiring it. The first part of *Hudibras* cost him two shilling ands sixpence, but he found it so silly an abuse of a presbyterian knight going to the wars, that he became ashamed of it, and prudently sold it for eighteen-pence. Wise by experience, he did not buy the second part, but only borrowed it to read. (p. 303)

It would be unjust to dismiss the personal character of Pepys without noticing his sincere, pious, and thankful disposition. Whatever human weaknesses he may display, and however he may seem at times vain of his worldly advantages, he never fails to return thanks to the Author of good for the blessings which he enjoys; and if we see foibles more clearly, it is because there is neither mystery nor vice to intercept our prospect into his bosom. It is at the bottom of the clear fountain that the least pebbles are distinctly visible.

In point of expression such Memoirs, composed entirely for bringing back events to the writer's own recollection, ought not to be severely criticised. The language is always distinct and intelligible, though sometimes amusingly quaint; as when he says of Harrison, that in the course of being hanged, drawn, and quartered, 'he looked as cheerful as any man could do in that condition:' and again in the following exquisitely limited tribute of sorrow for the death of a predecessor in office.

> Sir William Petty tells me that Mr. Barlow is dead; for which, God knows my heart, I could be as sorry as is possible for one to be for a stranger, by whose death he gets 100*l.* per annum.

The public affairs alluded to in the course of these Memoirs are, of course, numerous and interesting, and Pepys's information, recorded merely for his own satisfaction, and collected, in many instances, from the highest authorities, cannot but be valuable. We are not aware that any evidence occurs of a very new and original character, contradictory of historical facts as usually stated. But there is much that is additional and explanatory of what was formerly known; much that removes all doubt,—that throws a more distinct and vivid light over the picture of England and its government during the ten years succeeding the Restoration. A most melancholy picture it is of the period illuminated by the wit of Hamilton, and sung by Dryden—

> 'The world was then so light,
> I hardly felt the weight;—
> Joy ruled the day, and love the night.'
> *Secular Masque.*

The evidence of this prosaic contemporary places it in a very different view. The conduct of the king, mean, thoughtless, and inconsiderate beyond measure, was such as could not have been pardoned in a prince in the heyday of youth, and nursed in the full enjoyment of absolute command. Yet Charles, in advanced life, and trained in the school of adversity, seems to have possessed neither the power of exerting his own reason nor the submission to be guided by the wisdom of others, but to have flung the reins of his empire among his courtiers at random, or voluntarily and by choice to have imparted them to the most profligate amongst these, as Buckingham and Clifford. Mere good nature is the only virtue which Pepys allows him, for he will not even admit his power of saying the wise things which he never did. He describes him as reading his speech from the throne imperfectly and ill, and repeatedly mentions his conversation as poor, flat, and un-

interesting. His talk with his courtiers, when engaged in visiting the naval magazines, he describes as idle and frothy, misbecoming the serious business on which he was engaged. Perhaps, however, the person who could not see the wit of *Hudibras* may have been blind to that of Charles. (pp. 304-05)

If quitting the broad path of history we seek for minute information concerning ancient manners and customs, the progress of arts and sciences, and the various branches of antiquity, we have never seen a mine so rich as the volumes before us. The variety of Pepys's tastes and pursuits led him into almost every department of life. He was a man of business; a man of information, if not learning; a man of taste; a man of whim; and, to a certain degree, a man of pleasure. He was a statesman, a bel esprit, a virtuoso, and a connoisseur. His curiosity made him an unwearied as well as an universal learner, and whatever he saw, found its way into his tables. Thus his diary absolutely resembles the genial cauldrons at the wedding of Comacho, a souse into which was sure to bring forth at once abundance and variety of whatever could gratify the most eccentric appetite. If, for example, a gastronome, to continue the allusion, desires to know what constituted a good dinner, he will find that a 'very fine' one consisted of

> A dish of marrowbones; a leg of mutton; a loin of veal;
> a dish of fowl, there pullets, and a dozen of larks all in
> a dish; a great tart, a neat's tounge, a dish of anchovies;
> a dish of prawns and cheese.

(pp. 308-09)

If the curious affect dramatic antiquities—a line which has special charms for the present age, no book published in our time has thrown so much light upon plays, playwrights, and playactors. There is an account by Killigrew of the improvements which he himself made upon the stage of his time, bringing it, if we may believe him, from tallow candles to wax lights; from two or three fiddlers to nine or ten capital hands; from the late queen's auspices very rarely vouchsafed, to the constant and regular patronage of royalty. Then there are anecdotes, not only of Knipp and Nell, but of Kynaston and Betterton, and Lacey and Mohun, and passages concerning Dryden and Cartwright, and Sam Tuke, and we wot not whom besides—annotations, in short, for a new edition of the *Roscius Anglicanus.* They cannot, for example, but be delighted to meet with the account of the new play, *Queen Elizabeth's Troubles, and the History of Eighty-eight,* which is very curious, as it seems to have consisted almost entirely in scenery and dumb show. The Queens Elizabeth and Mary appeared dressed in the costumes of their age; and a prolocutor stood on the stage, and explained the meaning of the action to the audience. Pepys was much affected with the sad story of Queen Elizabeth, which he had sucked in from his cradle, but fully as much so to see Knipp dance among the milk-maids, and come out in her night-gown, with no locks on, but her bare face, and hair only tied up in a knot behind; which he thought the comeliest dress he had ever seen her in. The play, as well as the very peculiar mode of representation, seems to have escaped the industry of Isaac Reed.

There is another class of antiquaries, who retire within the ancient enchanted circles, magical temples, and haunted castles, venerated by their forefathers: and here they, too, may find spells against various calamities, as against cramps, thorn-wounds, and the like, and stories respecting spirits, and an account of the ominous tempest of wind which, in the opinion of the Journalist, presaged the death of the queen; but which proved only to refer to that of Sir William Compton; with much more to the same useful purpose.

Those who desire to be aware of the earliest discoveries, as well in sciences as in the useful arts, may read in Pepys's Memoirs, how a slice of roast mutton was converted into pure blood; and of those philosophical glass crackers, which explode when the tail is broken off; of *aurum fulminans*, applied to the purpose of blowing ships out of water; and of a newly contrived gun, which was to change the whole system of the art of war; but which has left it pretty much on its old footing. Notices there are, moreover, of the transfusion of blood; and how many unhappy dogs died in course of the experiment;—in short, we have in this sort the usual quantity of information, partly genuine, partly erroneous, partly perverted and nonsensical, which an amateur man of science contrives to assemble in his head or in his memory. An amateur of the useful arts may also remark that the most successful inventions are not always successful in the commencement. (pp. 310-11)

There exists a class of Old Bailey antiquaries—men who live upon dying speeches, sup full upon the horrors of executions, and fatten on the story of gibbetings like ravens on the mangled limbs. Here such readers will find a cake of the right leaven for their tastes. Here is an account of the execution of Sir Henry Vane, as well as several of his associates; and of Colonel Turner, who was in actual life a personification of Cowley's Captain Cutter. No wonder it should be so; for the reader must recollect, that this was the same reign in which Roger Nash records as the greatest inconvenience of his brother Dudley's office as sheriff, 'the executioner coming to him for orders, touching the abscinded members, and to know where to dispose of them. Once, while he was abroad, a cart with some of them came into the court-yard of his house, and frighted his lady almost out of her wits. And she could never be reconciled to the dog hangman's saying *he came to speak with his master.*' We read an account lately (but have unhappily mislaid the reference), which showed that the salting and pickling which the *abscinded* members, since that is the phrase, underwent before exposure, was quite a holiday in the jail: the executioner presiding on the occasion, and distributing refreshments at his own expense among the spectators.

To the lover of ancient voyages and travels it may especially be hinted, that Pepys, as befitted a member of the Navy-board, was curious in 'questioning every year picked men of countries.' Of course he sometimes met with travellers who had a shade of Sir John Mandeville about them. Such might be the worthy captain who assured him that, as lobsters turn red on being boiled, negroes become white on being drowned; showing that there is at least one extremity of washing which can blanch the Ethiopian. There is also an account of the country above *Queensborough*, meaning, it would seem, the duchy of Courland, in which, though we can recognize some of the peculiarities of that northern latitude, Mr. Harrington and the east-country (i. e. Baltic) merchants, who were is visitors, have rather extended the travellers' privilege. Indeed it may be observed in general, that Mr. Pepys does not appear to be devoid of that spirit of credulity which accompanies in ea-

ger and restless curiosity. He who is willing to listen must naturally be desirous to believe.

If a lover of antique scandal that taketh away the character, and committeth *scandalum magnatum* against the nobility of the seventeenth century, should desire to interleave a Granger, or illustrate a Grammont, he will find in these volumes an untouched treasure of curious anecdote for the accomplishment of his purpose. If the progress of the fine arts is the subject of investigation, the Memoirs abound with circumstances interesting to the amateur; there are anecdotes of Lely and Cooper and Fairthorne, and an account of ill usage offered to Holbein's painting in the ceiling at Whitehall, with notices of medals and coins and medallists, and much more equally to the purpose. If anecdotes of great persons, or of persons of notoriety are in request, you have them untouched by either D'Israeli or Seward, from Oliver Cromwell down to Tom Killigrew. Jests lurk within these two quartos, unprofaned by Joe Miller, notices of sold songs which Ritson dreamed not of.—Here may the ballad-monger learn that Simon Wadlow, vintner, and keeper of the Devil's Tavern, did on the 22d April, 1661, lead a fine company of soldiers, all young countrymen in white doublets; and who knows but that this might have been either

> Old Sir Simon the king,
> Or young Sir Simon the squire;

personages who bequeath names to the memorable ditty beloved of Squire Western. The students of political economy will find a curious treat in considering the manner how Pepys was obliged to bundle about his money in specie, removing it from one hiding-place to another during the fire, concealing it at last under ground, and losing a great deal in digging it up again. Then he hit on the plan of lodging it with a goldsmith; and his delight on finding he was to receive £35 for the use of £2000 for a quarter of a year, reminds us of the glee of Crabbe's fisherman on a similar discovery:

> 'What! five for every hundred will he give
> Beside the hundred?—I begin to live.'—

But his golden visions were soon disturbed by a sad conviction not unlike that which lately passed over our own money-market, that bankers were but mortal men, and that they could not pay interest for money and have the full sum at the same time lying by them ready on demand. (pp. 312-13)

But we stop abruptly, or we might find a difficulty in stopping at all, so rich is the work in every species of information concerning the author's century. We compared the Diary to that of Evelyn, but it is as much superior to the latter in variety and general amusement, as it is inferior in its tone of sentiment and feeling; Pepys's very foibles have been infinitely in favour of his making an amusing collection of events; as James Boswell, without many personal peculiarities, could not have written his inimitable life of Johnson.

We ought to mention some curious and valuable letters which occupy the latter part of the second volume. The reader may be amused with comparing the style of Pepys and his sentiments as brushed and dressed, and sent out to meet company, with his more genuine and far more natural effusions of a night-gown and slipper description.

This, however, he must do for himself; we have not leisure to assist him.

The circumstances which induced Mr. Pepys to discontinue his diary, we lament as a great loss to posterity. True, the days which succeeded were yet more disastrous than those he commemorated. The Popish plot had not, when he ceased his record, dishonoured our annals;—England had not seen her monarch a pensioner to France,—and her nobles and statesmen at home divided into the most desperate factions which sought vengeance on each other by mutual false accusation and general perjury. Yet considering how much of interest mingled even in that degrading contest, considering how much talent was engaged on both sides, what a treasure would a record of its minute events have been if drawn up by 'such a faithful character as Griffiths!' (p. 314)

> *[Sir Walter Scott], in a review of "Memoirs of Samuel Pepys, Esq.," in* The Quarterly Review, *Vol. XXXIII, No. LXVI, March, 1826, pp. 281-314.*

SYDNEY SMITH (letter date 1826)

> [*Smith was an English cleric and journalist who was instrumental in the founding of the* Edinburgh Review *in 1802. In his day he was greatly praised for his conversational wit, a skill only marginally evident in his writings, which nevertheless are enjoyed for their ready humor and strong inclination toward satire. In the following excerpt from an 1826 letter to Lady Holland, he criticizes the Diary as "nonsense." According to D. Pepys Whiteley, writing in the 15 February 1963 issue of the* Times Literary Supplement, *Smith's opinion of the Diary "is not without interest because (so far as I know) it is the only indication in a published work of the reaction of the ordinary reader, as opposed to the professional literary critic, to the Diary as it first appeared."*]

I cannot help (why should I help it?) writing a Line to congratulate you upon your return to the best of all worldly Castles in excellent health.

I was sorry I could not wait to say this in person, but I am always away too long and am always in a hurry. (p. 448)

I do not at all regret the advice I gave to my Brother to retire from parliament, though I was the only one of his friends who agreed with him on that point. Pain is the first thing to be avoided, then Ennui; better to have nothing to do than to groan and suffer. I have been reading Pepys not without some indignation at being obliged to read such nonsense merely because yourself and Allen and other persons have read it. and I must not fall behind. Hardly a drop of water fallen since February; The Country has the appearance of Arabia infelix.— (pp. 448-49)

> *Sydney Smith, in a letter to Lady Holland on June 20, 1826, in his* The Letters of Sydney Smith, Vol. I, *edited by Nowell C. Smith, Oxford at the Clarendon Press, 1953, pp. 448-49.*

SAMUEL TAYLOR COLERIDGE (essay date 1834?)

> [*An English man of letters, Coleridge is considered one of the most significant poets and critics in the English language. As a major figure in the English Romantic movement, he is best known for three poems, "The Rime of the .*

Ancient Mariner" (1798), "Kubla Khan" (1816), and "Christabel" (1816), and one volume of criticism, Biographia Literaria; *or Biographical Sketches of My Literary Life and Opinions (1817). He was the first prominent spokesman for German idealistic metaphysics in England and one of the first proponents of modern psychological criticism. In the following excerpt from undated notes he made in his personal copy of the Diary, Coleridge praises the work as history but finds fault with much of Pepys's dramatic criticism. (The page and volume numbers reprinted below refer to Lord Braybrooke's 1825 edition of the text).*]

Diary, I, 84.

> From fourth line beginning "went by water to my Lord . . ." to the fifteenth line, "which I was not so convinced of before."

Exquisite specimen of dry, grave, irony.

Diary, I, 189.

> Falling into discourse of a new book of drollery in use, called Hudibras, I would needs go find it out: . . . it is so silly an abuse of the Presbyter Knight going to the warrs, that I am ashamed of it.

At p. 167 Pepys pronounces the *Midsummer Night's Dream* the most insipid ridiculous Play he had ever seen. (pp. 486-87)

Diary, II, 13.

> Line 15, "Mrs. Turner do tell me very odde stories," to line 18, "do the business."

Most valuable on many, various, and most important accounts, as I hold this Diary to be, I deem it invaluable, as a faithful Portrait of enlightened (*i. e.* calculating) Self-love and Self-interest in its perihelion to Morality or its nearest possible neighborhood to, or least possible distance from Honour & Honesty. And yet what a cold and torpid Saturn with what a sinister & leaden Shine, spotty as the Moon, does its appear, compared with the principles & actions of the Regicide, Colonel Hutchinson, or those of the Puritan, Richard Baxter (in the autobiography edited by Sylvester), both the Contemporaries of Pepys. (p. 487)

Diary, II, 108.

To initiate a young Student into the mystery of appreciating the value of modern History, or the books that have hitherto passed for such,—First, let him carefully peruse this Diary! and then, while it is fresh in his mind, take up and read Hume's History of England, Reign of Charles the 2nd. Even of Hume's Reign of Elizabeth, generally rated as the best and fullest of the work, I dare assert: that to supply the omissions alone, would form an appendix occupying twice the space alloted by him to the whole Reign, and the necessary rectification of his statements half as much. What with omissions, and what with perversions, of the most important incidents, added to the false portraiture of the Character, the work from the Reign of Henry VIIth. is a Mischievous Romance. But alike as Historian and as Philosopher, Hume has meo saltem judicio, been extravagantly over-rated. Mercy on the Age, & the People, for whom Locke is profound, and Hume is subtle. (pp. 488-49)

Diary, II, 125.

Sixth line from the bottom concerning bear-baiting—"The sport was very good."

Certainly Pepys was blest with the queerest & most omnivorous taste that ever fell to the lot of one man!

Diary, II, 151.

Line 15 from the top, "And there saw Henry the Fourth."

This is, I think, the fifth of Shakspear's Plays, which Pepys found silly, stupid trash, & among them Othello! Macbeth indeed he commends for the *shews* & music, but not to be compared with the 'Five Hours' Adventures'!!! This and the want of *Wit* in the Hudibras, is very amusing—nay, it is seriously instructive. Thousands of shrewd, and intelligent men, in whom and in S. Pepys, the *Understanding* is *hypertrophied* to the necrosis or morasmus of the Reason and Imagination, while far-sighted (yet oh! how short-sighted) Self-Interest fills the place of Conscience, could say the same, if they dared.

Diary, II, 254.

Line 22: "a very excellent & persuasive, good & moral sermon ... He shewed, like a wise man, that righteousness is a surer moral way of being rich, than sin and villany."

Highly characteristic. Pepy's only ground of morality was Prudence, a shrewd Understanding in the service of Self-love, his Conscience. He was a *Pollard* man, without the *Top* (i. e. the Reason, as the source of Ideas, or immediate yet not sensuous truths, having their evidence in themselves; or, the Imagination or idealising Power, by symbols mediating between the Reason & the Understanding), but on this account more broadly and luxuriantly branching out from the upper Trunk. For the sobriety and stedfastness of a worldly self-interest substitute inventive Fancy, Will-wantonness (*stat pro ratione voluntas*) and a humorous sense of the emptiness and dream-likeness of human pursuits—and Pepys would have been the *Panurge* of the incomparable Rabelais. *Mem.* It is incomprehensible to me that this great and general Philosopher should have been a Frenchman, except on my hypothesis of a continued dilution of the Gothic Blood from the reign of Henry IVth. Des Cartes, Malbranche, Pascal, and Moliere, being the *ultimi Gothorum*, the last in whom the Gothic predominated over the Celtic.

Diary, II, 260.

To the fair to see the play 'Bartholomew Fair'; and it is an excellent play.... [Line 5] only the business of amusing the Puritans begins to grow stale and of no use, they being the people that at last will be found the wisest.

Pepys was always a Commonwealth's man in his heart. N. B. Not a Democrat, but even more than the Constitutional Whigs, the very Antipodes of the modern Jacobins, or *Tail-up, Head-down* politicians. A Voluptuary, and without a spark of bigotry in his nature, he could not be a Puritan; but of his free choice he would have preferred Presbyterianism to Prelacy, and a mixed Aristocracy of Wealth and Talent, to a Monarchy or even a mixed Government—such at least as the latter was in his time.

But many of the more enlightened Jacobites were Republicans who despaired of a Republic. *Si non Brutus, Cæsar.* (pp. 489-90)

Diary, II, 348, at the conclusion.

Truly may it be said that, this was a greater & more grievous loss to the mind's eye of his posterity, than to the bodily organs of Pepys himself. It makes me restless & discontented to think, what a Diary equal in minuteness and truth of portraiture to the preceding from 1669 to 1688 or 90, would have been for the true causes, process, and character of the Revolution. (p. 491)

> Samuel Taylor Coleridge, "Samuel Pepys," in his Coleridge on the Seventeenth Century, *edited by Roberta Florence Brinkley, Duke University Press, 1955, pp. 486-92.*

ROBERT LOUIS STEVENSON (essay date 1881)

[*Stevenson was a Scottish novelist, short story writer, poet, essayist, dramatist, and prayer writer. His novels* Treasure Island *(1883),* Kidnapped: Being Memoirs of the Adventures of David Balfour in the Year 1751 *(1886), and* Strange Case of Dr. Jekyll and Mr. Hyde *(1886) were enormous popular and critical successes that helped establish his reputation as an inventive stylist and vivid storyteller. Stevenson is especially noted for his understanding of youth, which is evident both in his early boys' books and in his much-loved* A Child's Garden of Verses *(1885). In the following excerpt from an essay originally published in the* Cornhill Magazine *in 1881, he analyzes the character and intent of the* Diary, *commenting as well on the literary merits of the work.*]

That there should be such a book as Pepys's *Diary* is incomparably strange. Pepys, in a corrupt and idle period, played the man in public employments, toiling hard and keeping his honour bright. Much of the little good that is set down to James the Second comes by right to Pepys; and if it were little for a king, it is much for a subordinate. To his clear, capable head was owing somewhat of the greatness of England on the seas. In the exploits of Hawke, Rodney, or Nelson, this dead Mr. Pepys of the Navy Office had some considerable share. He stood well by his business in the appalling plague of 1666. He was loved and respected by some of the best and wisest men in England. He was President of the Royal Society; and when he came to die, people said of his conduct in that solemn hour—thinking it needless to say more—that it was answerable to the greatness of his life. Thus he walked in dignity, guards of soldiers sometimes attending him in his walks, subalterns bowing before his periwig; and when he uttered his thoughts they were suitable to his state and services. On February 8, 1668, we find him writing to Evelyn, his mind bitterly occupied with the late Dutch war, and some thoughts of the different story of the repulse of the Great Armada:

Sir, you will not wonder at the backwardness of my thanks for the present you made me, so many days since, of the Prospect of the Medway, while the Hollander rode master in it, when I have told you that the sight of it hath led me to such reflections on my particular interest, by my employment, in the reproach due to that miscarriage, as have given me little less disquiet than he is fancied to have who found his face in Michael Angelo's hell. The same should serve me also in excuse for my silence in celebrating your mastery shown in the design and draught, did not indignation rather than courtship urge me so far to commend them, as to wish the furniture of our House of Lords changed from the story of '88 to that of '67 (of Evelyn's designing), till the pravity of this were reformed to the temper of that age, wherein God Almighty found his blessings more operative than, I fear, he doth in ours his judgments.

This is a letter honourable to the writer, where the meaning rather than the words is eloquent. Such was the account he gave of himself to his contemporaries; such thoughts he chose to utter, and in such language: giving himself out for a grave and patriotic public servant. We turn to the same date in the *Diary* by which he is known, after two centuries, to his descendants. The entry begins in the same key with the letter, blaming the "madness of the House of Commons" and "the base proceedings, just the epitome of all our public proceedings in this age, of the House of Lords"; and then, without the least transition, this is how our diarist proceeds:

> To the Strand, to my bookseller's, and there bought an idle, roguish French book, *L'escholle des Filles*, which I have bought in plain binding, avoiding the buying of it better bound, because I resolve, as soon as I have read it, to burn it, that it may not stand in the list of books, nor among them, to disgrace them, if it should be found.

Even in our day, when responsibility is so much more clearly apprehended, the man who wrote the letter would be notable; but what about the man, I do not say who bought a roguish book, but who was ashamed of doing so, yet did it, and recorded both the doing and the shame in the pages of his daily journal?

We all, whether we write or speak, must somewhat drape ourselves when we address our fellows; at a given moment we apprehend our character and acts by some particular side; we are merry with one, grave with another, as befits the nature and demands of the relation. Pepys's letter to Evelyn would have little in common with that other one to Mrs. Knipp which he signed by the pseudonym of *Dapper Dicky*; yet each would be suitable to the character of his correspondent. There is no untruth in this, for man, being a Protean animal, swiftly shares and changes with his company and surroundings; and these changes are the better part of his education in the world. To strike a posture once for all, and to march through life like a drum-major, is to be highly disagreeable to others and a fool for oneself into the bargain. To Evelyn and to Knipp we understand the double facing; but to whom was he posing in the *Diary*, and what, in the name of astonishment, was the nature of the pose? Had he suppressed all mention of the book, or had he bought it, gloried in the act, and cheerfully recorded his glorification, in either case we should have made him out. But no; he is full of precautions to conceal the "disgrace" of the purchase, and yet speeds to chronicle the whole affair in pen and ink. It is a sort of anomaly in human action, which we can exactly parallel from another part of the *Diary*.

Mrs. Pepys had written a paper of her too just complaints against her husband, and written it in plain and very pungent English. Pepys, in an agony lest the world should come to see it, brutally seizes and destroys the tell-tale document; and then—you disbelieve your eyes—down

goes the whole story with unsparing truth and in the cruellest detail. It seems he has no design but to appear respectable, and here he keeps a private book to prove he was not. You are at first faintly reminded of some of the vagaries of the morbid religious diarist; but at a moment's thought the resemblance disappears. The design of Pepys is not at all to edify; it is not from repentance that he chronicles his peccadilloes, for he tells us when he does repent, and, to be just to him, there often follows some improvement. Again, the sins of the religious diarist are of a very formal pattern, and are told with an elaborate whine. But in Pepys you come upon good, substantive misdemeanours; beams in his eye of which he alone remains unconscious; healthy outbreaks of the animal nature, and laughable subterfuges to himself that always command belief and often engage the sympathies.

Pepys was a young man for his age, came slowly to himself in the world, sowed his wild oats late, took late to industry, and preserved till nearly forty the headlong gusto of a boy. So, to come rightly at the spirit in which the *Diary* was written, we must recall a class of sentiments which with most of us are over and done before the age of twelve. In our tender years we still preserve a freshness of surprise at our prolonged existence; events make an impression out of all proportion to their consequence; we are unspeakably touched by our own past adventures, and look forward to our future personality with sentimental interest. It was something of this, I think, that clung to Pepys. Although not sentimental in the abstract, he was sweetly sentimental about himself. His own past clung about his heart, an evergreen. He was the slave of an association. He could not pass by Islington, where his father used to carry him to cakes and ale, but he must light at the "King's Head" and eat and drink "for remembrance of the old house sake." He counted it good fortune to lie a night at Epsom to renew his old walks, "where Mrs. Hely and I did use to walk and talk, with whom I had the first sentiments of love and pleasure in a woman's company, discourse and taking her by the hand, she being a pretty woman." He goes about weighing up the *Assurance*, which lay near Woolwich under water, and cries in a parenthesis, "Poor ship, that I have been twice merry in, in Captain Holland's time"; and after revisiting the *Naseby*, now changed into the *Charles*, he confesses "it was a great pleasure to myself to see the ship that I began my good fortune in." The stone that he was cut for he preserved in a case; and to the Turners he kept alive such gratitude for their assistance that for years, and after he had begun to mount himself into higher zones, he continued to have that family to dinner on the anniversary of the operation. Not Hazlitt nor Rousseau had a more romantic passion for their past, although at times they might express it more romantically; and if Pepys shared with them this childish fondness, did not Rousseau, who left behind him the *Confessions*, or Hazlitt, who wrote the *Liber Amoris*, and loaded his essays with loving personal detail, share with Pepys in his unwearied egotism? For the two things go hand in hand; or, to be more exact, it is the first that makes the second either possible or pleasing.

But, to be quite in sympathy with Pepys, we must return once more to the experience of children. I can remember to have written, in the fly-leaf of more than one book, the date and the place where I then was—if, for instance, I was ill in bed or sitting in a certain garden; these were jottings for my future self; if I should chance on such a note in after years, I thought it would cause me a particular thrill to recognise myself across the intervening distance. Indeed, I might come upon them now, and not be moved one tittle—which shows that I have comparatively failed in life, and grown older than Samuel Pepys. For in the *Diary* we can find more than one such note of perfect childish egotism; as when he explains that his candle is going out, "which makes me write thus slobberingly"; or as in this incredible particularity, "To my study, where I only wrote thus much of this day's passages to this, and so out again"; or lastly, as here, with more of circumstance: "I staid up till the bellman came by with his bell under my window, *as I was writing of this very line*, and cried, 'Past one of the clock, and a cold, frosty, windy morning.'" Such passages are not to be misunderstood. The appeal to Samuel Pepys years hence is unmistakable. He desires that dear, though unknown, gentleman keenly to realise his predecessor; to remember why a passage was uncleanly written; to recall (let us fancy, with a sigh) the tones of the bellman, the chill of the early, windy morning, and the very line his own romantic self was scribing at the moment. The man, you will perceive, was making reminiscences—a sort of pleasure by ricochet, which comforts many in distress, and turns some others into sentimental libertines; and the whole book, if you will but look at it in that way, is seen to be a work of art to Pepys's own address.

Here, then, we have the key to that remarkable attitude preserved by him throughout his *Diary*, to that unflinching—I had almost said, that unintelligent—sincerity which makes it a miracle among human books. He was not unconscious of his errors—far from it; he was often startled into shame, often reformed, often made and broke his vows of change. But whether he did ill or well, he was still his own unequalled self; still that entrancing *ego* of whom alone he cared to write; and still sure of his own affectionate indulgence, when the parts should be changed, and the writer come to read what he had written. Whatever he did, or said, or thought, or suffered, it was still a trait of Pepys, a character of his career; and as, to himself, he was more interesting than Moses or than Alexander, so all should be faithfully set down. I have called his *Diary* a work of art. Now when the artist has found something, word or deed, exactly proper to a favourite character in play or novel, he will neither suppress nor diminish it, though the remark be silly or the act mean. The hesitation of Hamlet, the credulity of Othello, the baseness of Emma Bovary, or the irregularities of Mr. Swiveller, caused neither disappointment nor disgust to their creators. And so with Pepys and his adored protagonist: adored not blindly, but with trenchant insight and enduring, human toleration. I have gone over and over the greater part of the *Diary*; and the points where, to the most suspicious scrutiny, he has seemed not perfectly sincere, are so few, so doubtful, and so petty, that I am ashamed to name them. It may be said that we all of us write such a diary in airy characters upon our brain; but I fear there is a distinction to be made; I fear that as we render to our consciousness an account of our daily fortunes and behaviour, we too often weave a tissue of romantic compliments and dull excuses; and even if Pepys were the ass and coward that men call him, we must take rank as sillier and more cowardly than he. The bald truth about oneself, what we are all too timid to admit when we

are not too dull to see it, that was what he saw clearly and set down unsparingly.

It is improbable that the *Diary* can have been carried on in the same single spirit in which it was begun. Pepys was not such an ass, but he must have perceived, as he went on, the extra-ordinary nature of the work he was producing. He was a great reader, and he knew what other books were like. It must, at least, have crossed his mind that someone might ultimately decipher the manuscript, and he himself, with all his pains and pleasures, be resuscitated in some later day; and the thought, although discouraged, must have warmed his heart. He was not such an ass, besides, but he must have been conscious of the deadly explosives, the gun-cotton and the giant powder, he was hoarding in his drawer. Let some contemporary light upon the Journal, and Pepys was plunged for ever in social and political disgrace. We can trace the growth of his terrors by two facts. In 1660, while the *Diary* was still in its youth, he tells about it, as a matter of course, to a lieutenant in the navy; but in 1669, when it was already near an end, he could have bitten his tongue out, as the saying is, because he had let slip his secret to one so grave and friendly as Sir William Coventry. And from two other facts I think we may infer that he had entertained, even if he had not acquiesced in, the thought of a far-distant publicity. The first is of capital importance: the *Diary* was not destroyed. The second—that he took unusual precautions to confound the cipher in "roguish" passages—proves, beyond question, that he was thinking of some other reader besides himself. Perhaps while his friends were admiring the "greatness of his behaviour" at the approach of death, he may have had a twinkling hope of immortality. *Mens cujusque is est quisque*, said his chosen motto; and, as he had stamped his mind with every crook and foible in the pages of the *Diary*, he might feel that what he left behind him was indeed himself. There is perhaps no other instance so remarkable of the desire of man for publicity and an enduring name. The greatness of his life was open, yet he longed to communicate its smallness also; and, while contemporaries bowed before him, he must buttonhole posterity with the news that his periwig was once alive with nits. But this thought, although I cannot doubt he had it, was neither his first nor his deepest; it did not colour one word that he wrote; and the *Diary*, for as long as he kept it, remained what it was when he began, a private pleasure for himself. It was his bosom secret; it added a zest to all his pleasures; he lived in and for it, and might well write these solemn words, when he closed that confidant for ever: "And so I betake myself to that course which is almost as much as to see myself go into the grave; for which, and all the discomforts that will accompany my being blind, the good God prepare me." (pp. 263-73)

It is generally supposed that, as a writer, Pepys must rank at the bottom of the scale of merit. But a style which is indefatigably lively, telling, and picturesque through six large volumes of everyday experience, which deals with the whole matter of a life, and yet is rarely wearisome, which condescends to the most fastidious particulars, and yet sweeps all away in the forth-right current of the narrative,—such a style may be ungrammatical, it may be inelegant, it may be one tissue of mistakes, but it can never be devoid of merit. The first and the true function of the writer has been thoroughly performed throughout; and though the manner of his utterance may be childishly awkward, the matter has been transformed and assimilated by his unfeigned interest and delight. The gusto of the man speaks out fierily after all these years. For the difference between Pepys and Shelley... is one of quality but not one of degree; in his sphere, Pepys felt as keenly, and his is the true prose of poetry—prose because the spirit of the man was narrow and earthly, but poetry because he was delightedly alive. (pp. 281-82)

There never was a man nearer being an artist, who yet was not one. The tang was in the family; while he was writing the journal for our enjoyment in his comely house in Navy Gardens, no fewer than two of his cousins were tramping the fens, kit under arm, to make music to the country girls. But he himself, though he could play so many instruments and pass judgment in so many fields of art, remained an amateur. It is not given to anyone so keenly to enjoy, without some greater power to understand. That he did not like Shakespeare as an artist for the stage may be a fault, but it is not without either parallel or excuse. He certainly admired him as a poet; he was the first beyond mere actors on the rolls of that innumerable army who have got "To be or not to be" by heart. Nor was he content with that; it haunted his mind; he quoted it to himself in the pages of the *Diary,* and, rushing in where angels fear to tread, he set it to music. Nothing, indeed, is more notable than the heroic quality of the verses that our little sensualist in a periwig chose out to marry with his own mortal strains. Some gust from brave Elizabethan times must have warmed his spirit, as he sat tuning his sublime theorbo. "To be or not to be. Whether 'tis nobler"—"Beauty retire, thou dost my pity move"—"It is decreed, nor shall thy fate, O Rome";—open and dignified in the sound, various and majestic in the sentiment, it was no inapt, as it was certainly no timid, spirit that selected such a range of themes. (pp. 282-83)

When writers inveigh against respectability, in the present degraded meaning of the word, they are usually suspected of a taste for clay pipes and beer cellars; and their performances are thought to hail from the *Owl's Nest* of the comedy. They have something more, however, in their eye than the dulness of a round million dinner-parties that sit down yearly in Old England. For to do anything because others do it, and not because the thing is good, or kind, or honest in its own right, is to resign all moral control and captaincy upon yourself, and go post-haste to the devil with the greater number. We smile over the ascendency of priests; but I had rather follow a priest than what they call the leaders of society. No life can better than that of Pepys illustrate the dangers of this respectable theory of living. For what can be more untoward than the occurrence, at a critical period and while the habits are still pliable, of such a sweeping transformation as the return of Charles the Second? Round went the whole fleet of England on the other tack; and while a few tall pintas, Milton or Pen, still sailed a lonely course by the stars and their own private compass, the cock-boat, Pepys, must go about with the majority among "the stupid starers and the loud huzzas."

The respectable are not led so much by any desire of applause as by a positive need for countenance. The weaker and the tamer the man, the more will he require this support; and any positive quality relieves him, by just so much, of this dependence. In a dozen ways, Pepys was quite strong enough to please himself without regard for others; but his positive qualities were not co-extensive with the field of conduct; and in many parts of life he followed, with gleeful precision, in the footprints of the contemporary Mrs. Grundy. In morals, particularly, he lived by the countenance of others; felt a slight from another more keenly than a meanness in himself; and then first repented when he was found out. You could talk of religion or morality to such a man; and by the artist side of him, by his lively sympathy and apprehension, he could rise, as it were dramatically, to the significance of what you said. All that matter in religion which has been nicknamed other-worldliness was strictly in his gamut; but a rule of life that should make a man rudely virtuous, following right in good report and ill report, was foolishness and a stumbling-block to Pepys. He was much thrown across the Friends; and nothing can be more instructive than his attitude towards these most interesting people of that age.... [When he saw some Quakers] brought from a meeting under arrest, "I would to God," said he, "they would either conform, or be more wise and not be catched"; and to a Quaker in his own office he extended a timid though effectual protection. Meanwhile there was growing up next door to him that beautiful nature, William Pen. It is odd that Pepys condemned him for a fop; odd, though natural enough when you see Pen's portrait, that Pepys was jealous of him with his wife. But the cream of the story is when Pen publishes his *Sandy Foundation Shaken,* and Pepys has it read aloud by his wife. "I find it," he says, "so well writ as, I think, it is too good for him ever to have writ it; and it is a serious sort of book, and *not fit for everybody to read."* Nothing is more galling to the merely respectable than to be brought in contact with religious ardour. Pepys had his own foundation, sandy enough, but dear to him from practical considerations, and he would read the book with true uneasiness of spirit; for conceive the blow if, by some plaguy accident, this Pen were to convert him! It was a different kind of doctrine that he judged profitable for himself and others. "A good sermon of Mr. Gifford's at our church, upon 'Seek ye first the kingdom of heaven.' A very excellent and persuasive, good and moral sermon. He showed, like a wise man, that righteousness is a surer moral way of being rich than sin and villainy." It is thus that respectable people desire to have their Greathearts address them, telling, in mild accents, how you may make the best of both worlds, and be a moral hero without courage, kindness, or troublesome reflection; and thus the Gospel, cleared of Eastern metaphor, becomes a manual of worldly prudence, and a handybook for Pepys and the successful merchant.

The respectability of Pepys was deeply grained. He has no idea of truth except for the *Diary.* He has no care that a thing shall be, if it but appear; gives out that he has inherited a good estate, when he has seemingly got nothing but a lawsuit; and is pleased to be thought liberal when he knows he has been mean. He is conscientiously ostentatious. I say conscientiously, with reason. He could never have been taken for a fop, like Pen, but arrayed himself in a manner nicely suitable to his position. For long he hesitated to assume the famous periwig; for a public man should travel gravely with the fashions, not foppishly before, nor dowdily behind, the central movement of his age. For long he durst not keep a carriage; that, in his circumstances, would have been improper; but a time comes, with the growth of his fortune, when the impropriety has shifted to the other side, and he is "ashamed to be seen in a hackney." Pepys talked about being "a Quaker or some very melancholy thing"; for my part, I can imagine nothing so melancholy, because nothing half so silly, as to be concerned about such problems. But so respectability and the duties of society haunt and burden their poor devotees; and what seems at first the very primrose path of life, proves difficult and thorny like the rest. And the time comes to Pepys, as to all the merely respectable, when he must not only order his pleasures, but even clip his virtuous movements, to the public pattern of the age. There was some juggling among officials to avoid direct taxation; and Pepys, with a noble impulse, growing ashamed of this dishonesty, designed to charge himself with £1000; but finding none to set him an example, "nobody of our ablest merchants" with this moderate liking for clean hands, he judged it "not decent"; he feared it would "be thought vain glory"; and, rather than appear singular, cheerfully remained a thief. One able merchant's countenance, and Pepys had dared to do an honest act! Had he found one brave spirit, properly recognised by society, he might have gone far as a disciple. Mrs. Turner, it is true, can fill him full of sordid scandal, and make him believe, against the testimony of his senses, that Pen's venison pasty stank like the devil; but, on the other hand, Sir William Coventry can raise him by a word into another being. Pepys, when he is with Coventry, talks in the vein of an old Roman. What does he care for office or emolument? "Thank God, I have enough of my own," says he, "to buy me a good book and a good fiddle, and I have a good wife." And again, we find this pair projecting an old age when an ungrateful country shall have dismissed them from the field of public service; Conventry living retired in a fine house, and Pepys dropping in, "it may be, to read a chapter of Seneca."

Under this influence, the only good one in his life, Pepys continued zealous and, for the period, pure in his employment. He would not be "bribed to be unjust," he says, though he was "not so squeamish as to refuse a present after," suppose the king to have received no wrong. His new arrangement for the victualling of Tangier, he tells us with honest complacency, will save the king a thousand and gain Pepys three hundred pounds a year,—a statement which exactly fixes the degree of the age's enlightenment. But for his industry and capacity no praise can be too high. It was an unending struggle for the man to stick to his business in such a garden of Armida as he found this life; and the story of his oaths, so often broken, so courageously renewed, is worthy rather of admiration than the contempt it has received. (pp. 284-90)

Robert Louis Stevenson, "Samuel Pepys," in his Familiar Studies of Men & Books, 1882. Reprint by Eveleigh Nash and Grayson Limited, 1980? pp. 261-94.

EDMUND GOSSE (essay date 1889)

[*Gosse was a distinguished English literary historian, critic, and biographer. He wrote extensively on seventeenth- and eighteenth-century English literature and is credited with introducing the works of Norwegian dramatist Henrik Ibsen to English readers. In the following excerpt from an essay originally published in 1889, he assesses favorably the* Diary's *historical value over its aesthetic value.*]

A certain Mr. Samuel Pepys (1633-1703), who was clerk to the Navy and finally secretary to the Admiralty during the last years of the century, left his library to Magdalen College, Cambridge, where it is preserved intact in a handsome building of the age of Queen Anne. Pepys was nearly forgotten, when in 1825 Lord Braybrooke gave to the world a copious diary, kept from 1660 to 1669, nine years and a half, which he had found in shorthand in the Bibliotheca Pepysiana, and had deciphered. In 1879 Mr. Mynors Bright went over the work again, correcting and enlarging the transcript. Lord Braybrooke's task revealed a new author to English readers. This diary, in which Pepys wrote down his experiences, night by night, with extreme artlessness, is unrivalled as a storehouse of gossip and character-painting. When it begins, the author is still young, and freshly come to town to try his fortunes; before it closes the king has greeted him as "another Cicero." It is scarcely literature—that is to say, there is neither art nor effort at construction; but Pepys has extraordinary picturesqueness and great capacity in describing what he has seen in the best and briefest words. Evelyn's diary has a coldness, a dignity, in its ease, that suggest that he conceived that the world might force it into publication. Pepys believed himself absolutely safe behind the veil of his cipher, and he made no effort to paint the lily. How Pepys spent the afternoon and evening of November 5, 1666, may be taken as a typical instance of his precise and garrulous method:

> After dinner and this discourse I took coach, and at the same time find my Lord Hinchingbroke and Mr. John Crew and the Doctor going out to see the ruins of the city; so I took the Doctor into my hackney coach (and he is a very fine sober gentleman), and so through the city. But, Lord! what pretty and sober observations he made of the city and its desolation; till anon we came to my house, and there I took them upon Tower Hill to show them what houses were pulled down there since the fire; and then to my house, where I treated them with good wine of several sorts, and they took it mighty respectfully, and a fine company of gentlemen they are; but above all I was glad to see my Lord Hinchingbroke drink no wine at all. Here I got them to appoint Wednesday come se'n-night to dine here at my house, and so we broke up and all took coach again, and I carried the Doctor to Chancery Lane, and thence I to White Hall, where I staid walking up and down till night, and then got almost into the play-house, having much mind to go and see the play at Court this night; but fearing how I should get home, because of the bonfires and the lateness of the night to get a coach, I did not stay; but having this evening seen my Lady Jemimah, who is come to town, and looks very well and fat, and heard how Mr. John Pickering is to be married this week, and to a fortune with £5000, and seen a rich necklace of pearl and two pendants of diamonds, which Sir G. Carteret hath presented her with since her coming to town, I home by coach, but met not one bonfire through the whole town in going round by the wall, which is strange, and speaks the melancholy disposition of the city at present, while never more was said of, and feared of, and done against the Papists than just at this time. Home, and there find my wife and her people at cards, and I to my chamber, and there late, and so to supper and to bed.

A memoir so unaffected, drawn up in an age so brutal, might have proved very offensive, but Pepys, though full of human frailty, was a wholesome soul, and undebased by any touch of cynicism. To the humorist and to the antiquarian his faithful Dutch picture of life under Charles II. is invaluable. Pepys was an able administrator in the civil service, and a grave collector of prints, books, maps, and music. In his diary he reveals an emotional side to his character which the world can hardly have suspected. (pp. 97-98)

Edmund Gosse, "Prose After the Restoration," in his A History of Eighteenth Century Literature (1660-1780), *Macmillan and Co., 1889, pp. 73-104.*

ANDREW LANG (essay date 1893)

[*A Scottish folklorist, editor, journalist, critic, poet, historian, essayist, translator, and novelist, Lang was one of Great Britain's preeminent men of letters during the closing decades of the nineteenth century. He is perhaps best remembered as the editor of the "Color Fairy Books," a twelve-volume series of fairy tales that helped stimulate interest in children's literature in England. The selections in* The Blue Fairy Book *(1889),* The Lilac Fairy Book *(1910), and the ten volumes in between include stories from various world cultures and are an outgrowth of Lang's meticulous research into early languages and literature—research that called attention to cultural affinities in the folktales, myths, and legends of otherwise disparate societies. In the following excerpt from his "Letter to Samuel Pepys, Esq.," written as one in a series of imaginary "Letters to Dead Authors," he provides a general appreciation of the* Diary.]

Honoured Sir: It was the saying of a wise man, though a young one, that we do all of us travel through life with a donkey. You kept your donkey in a stable very private. The charger dwelt in that noted *Diary* of yours, a journal written in cipher, which has now for many years been transcribed in plain hand, and given to the world. Mr. Pepys, do not, I pray you, blush so fiery a red; not *all* the *Diary* hath yet been made public, and the world is still a stranger to many of those most private confidences between your donkey and yourself. Matters there be which I could mention, an' I would, but I write for a generation in which they who read not are very modest, and will raise a cry against you and me, if I keep not a bridle on my pen. The record of a whole day in the sad story of Deb is omitted, concerning Knip and Pierce, and *a certain other lady* (oh fie, Mr. Pepys!) the world knows no more than the worthy minister, your editor, chose to tell it.

You, sir, of all men, have been, thanks to the companion of which I spoke, your own Boswell. You know James well, I make no doubt, and have spoken with him and Dr. Johnson, ere now, concerning the *Deuteroskopia,* or Second Sight of the Highlanders. (p. 354)

[Dr. Johnson's] friend, Mr. Boswell, as you know, wrote the life of that great and good man; no better life hath ever been penned. But it cannot have escaped your penetration that Mr. Boswell is something of an ass. I speak it lovingly, for, in part by virtue of his asinine qualities, combined with others, he told tales of himself and his friend such as another would not have narrated. You, too, Mr. Pepys, when you ran to your journal, fell into the mood of Mr. Boswell, therefore it is that we know in you two different men, the Mr. Pepys of the *Diary*; vain, jealous, of a marvellous poor spirit, a pillar of theatres and taverns; and the Mr. Pepys of the Admiralty, a patriot, a great man of affairs, and to a foolish and unhappy king, a servant as loyal as Dundee. The Mr. Pepys who was Evelyn's friend, who was President of the Royal Society, who remade the glorious English navy, and raised it from its

shame; the Mr. Pepys whose "greatness in death was answerable to the greatness of his life," is, alas! forgotten by all but the learned. The Mr. Pepys who was affrighted by his young gibcat, which he "took for a sprite," the Mr. Pepys who joyed in a new coat; who was so proud of being addressed as "Esquire;" who stinted his wife in clothes and pleasure, while he went brave and joyous himself; the Mr. Pepys who courted Knip, and made love to Deb, and took vows and broke them, and had his bellyful of Magdalene beer—that naughty, roguish Mr. Pepys is known, and loved, and read by all men who read at all.

Of bedside books, sir, which may send a man happily to sleep, with a smile on his lips, your egregious *Diary* is by far the best and dearest. Compared with you, Montaigne is dry, Boswell is too full of matter; but one can take you up anywhere, and anywhere lay you down, certain of being diverted by the picture of that companion with whom you made your journey through life. Unlike to that which St. Francis spoke of himself, thou wert *not* "too hard on thy brother, the Ass," rather treating him as one who loved him. Whether you are digging up your treasure, so openly and palpably buried at midday by Mrs. Pepys, or hunting for that other treasure in the tower which you did not find, or boxing the boy Eliezer's ears for spilling the beer over your papers, or going—yourself a boy—to see your king murdered, or meeting Mr. James Sharpe, later murdered himself as our Archbishop, on the voyage to bring back the second Charles, or "in an ill humour of anger with your wife to bed," you are perpetually the most amusing of gossips, and, of all who have gossiped about themselves, the only one who tells the truth. You have such an appetite for life that to read you almost makes a sated student hungry again. There is absolutely no experience but you get some kind of delight in it, keeping the anniversary of that cruel operation which preserved Mr. Pepys to a grateful country. "A flagon of ale and apples drunk out of a wooden cup," lives forever, and "makes all merry" still, because you tasted it and recorded it.

To see an old play over again delights you, "which is the pleasure of my not committing these things to my memory." That is also the pleasure of not committing your *Diary* to our memories; your deeds and misdeeds, your dinners and kisses, glide from our recollections, and, being read again, surprise and amuse us afresh. *Decies repetita placebit,* that *fabula, de te.* In church, Mr. Pepys, however dull the Scot's sermon may be, *you* are never dull. There is generally a pretty face to stare at, a pretty hand to squeeze, while you present it with a hymn-book. Only once we read, in church-time, "not a handsome face in all of them, as if, indeed, there was a curse upon our parish, as Bishop Fuller heretofore said." But what a blunder that was when you "took another pretty woman for Betty Michell, and taking her a clap on the"—back, found out your mistake; Mr. Pepys, was this a gallant and ordinary form of salutation, when "good King Charles" (as my Lord Ailesbury lovingly styles him) was our ruler? And with what face can you blame the Court and praise the Puritans, you who are such a runagate and outlier? Why, you were in love with half of King Charles's beauties, though "my Lady Castlemaine never looked so ill, nor Mrs. Stewart either, as in this plain, natural dress." Yet to a plain, natural dress, as far as you dared, you restricted your wife, poor wretch, scolding and bullying her for some tiny female extravagance in a pair of cheap earrings. This is what

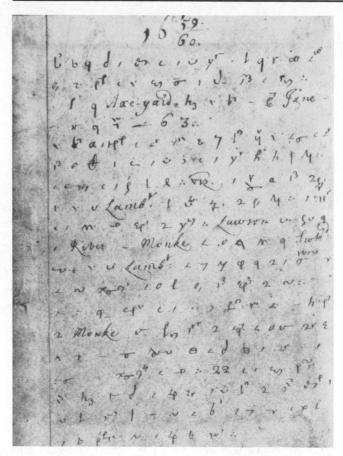

The opening page of the Diary *manuscript. It begins: "Blessed be God, at the end of the last year I was in very good health."*

we like least in you, sir. You had an open hand for your own pleasures; why so surly, then, with Mrs. Pepys? Your hand was open for presents, too, and in our day, though you were indifferent honest in your own, we think you sailed very near the wind in the matter of bribery. But other times, other manners, you did not buy the King bad bargains, if you took a trifling toll by the way. If you loved pleasure, and a pretty maid, and oysters, and ale, and the play, you loved books, too, and wisely; "they were growing numerous and lying one upon another on my chairs," to which trouble, sir, your humble and obliged servant is also a martyr. Indeed, what did you not like—pictures, scientific instruments, ruling your account books, "a song in the garden with your wife and the girl," "flinging fireworks, and mighty merry, smutting one another with candle-grease and soot till most of us were like devils." Simple enjoyments were these. A grave official dresses as a maid, his maid as a boy, Mrs. Pepys and Peggy Pen put on periwigs, they all dance a jig; "thus we spent till three or four in the morning, mighty merry, and then parted and to bed."

The Plague comes, and you cling to your work like a hero; the Fire comes, the Dutch come, the wild westland Whigs march on Edinburgh; young cornets mimic the Scotch covenanting preachers for the entertainment of the Archbishop of Canterbury; gamblers crowd Whitehall; the Restoration rushes to its ruin; through it all you look on, now with a sigh, now with a laugh; you do your duty manfully,

you take your fling like a man; you are wicked, you are found out, you crouch and shiver and repent; you are cowardly, mean, and you know it; generous, daring in your way, all by turns, and every turn you note down as calmly as if you were speaking of a stranger. And it really is of a stranger you speak, of some one who is not the official, sedate Mr. Pepys, but the lively, indiscreet animal, in whose society he marches through revolution, restoration, revolution again, "and so to bed" at last, full of years and honours.

By you, when you reached the land, the awful land where nothing is forgotten, where all our lives lie open to us like a book, perhaps there was little of lost to be recovered. All was written down too distinctly in these ciphered pages, the only pages among the books of the world which show us a character as it really was. It were unchristian to judge you; priggish and foolish to despise you; to admire you is not very easy; but, dear Mr. Pepys, we all truly love you, and what better price can you be paid for the ciphering that so harmed your eyesight? A sad sorrow to you, sir, but even a greater trouble to ourselves. You should have kept that journal your whole life long, and told us of that shameful Popish Plot, wherein you were so wickedly handled; of lying Shaftesbury, and his tattle about your crucifix; of King Charles's death; of Monmouths's rising; of that ill Revolution where James, who was brave as Duke of York, lost his heart as King, and fled; though "a wave of the bonnet of bonnie Dundee" might have dispelled the traitors and sent Marlborough packing after Sunderland. What a chronicle we have lost, what a veracious recorder was spoiled by that malady of your eyesight; how your penitence, which makes us smile while your wife lived to threaten you with the tongs, would have made us weep when she was no more living to be sinned against!

The pearl necklace which you gave (cost you £64) yet adorns a great-great-great-granddaughter of your plain sister, Pal; and your family treasures the silver-gilt flagon which was presented to Mr. Pepys by King James. How our toys do outlast us, bringing living men close to the famous dead, and the fallen dynasty! (pp. 354-56)

Andrew Lang, "A Letter to Samuel Pepys, Esq.," in Scribner's Magazine, *Vol. XIV, No. 3, September, 1893, pp. 354-56.*

CHARLES WHIBLEY (essay date 1896)

[*A prolific English critic and reviewer, Whibley was an authority on sixteenth- and seventeenth-century English literature. In the following excerpt from an essay originally published in the* New Review *in 1896, he studies Pepys's introspection in the* Diary.]

[Above all, Pepys] is the frankest man in history: he is frank even to himself. The veriest fool, the commonest knave can cultivate an appearance of frankness to the world. But Pepys's achievement was far higher and less simple. He looked at himself with absolute straightforwardness, and could understand his own vanities—could measure his own vices without difficulty. He never seeks a fantastic motive; he never excuses the grossest wantonness. He extenuates nothing—not even the faults of his friends. Here, then, is the one man we have been permitted to know, as we shall never know ourselves. Let us, then, make the most of him: let us do homage to the one master of self-revelation that history can furnish forth.

A lust of being and moving, of exercising his senses to their utmost, governed his existence. Unnumbered and innumerable are his crowded hours of glorious life. The man who "is with child to see any strange thing" is neither cynic nor Philistine. Nothing came amiss to him. He was as pleased with Sir George Ent's discourse upon "Respiration" as he was with the peerless beauty of Lady Castlemaine. Only he must always be doing, or hearing, or seeing some new thing. To-day he is singing with Knipp, and listening with a hungry ear to the praise of his famous song, "Beauty, Retire;" to-morrow he is discussing with Dr. Whistler whether masts should be kept dry or damp. Now he goes to Will's to meet "Dryden the poet (I knew at Cambridge)"; now he is chaffering for cloves with some poor seamen in a "blind alehouse." And all the while he is drinking in life at its abundant source. His zest is almost too violent, and you wonder how he could have sustained, through many years of suffering, this ferocious energy of enjoyment; how he remained firm in this dogged determination to miss no minute of lapsing time. But to his industry no transition seemed abrupt: he turned from his mistress to his accounts without weariness or regret, and no sooner had he found an end of his figures than he was ready to play again with all the spirit of a released schoolboy. His philosophy was the most arrogant that ever a man about town imagined. "Read every book," he said in effect, "see every play, empty every wine-cup, kiss every woman." And when he died, in all piety he might have owned that he never missed an opportunity. Alexander conquered the world; but Pepys, with a keener, more selfish understanding of life, conquered a world for every sense. He could not take a boat without singing to the "skuller"; he could not meet a Dutch bellman without taking his clapper in his hand, without noting that "it is just like the clapper that our boys frighten the birds away from the corn with in summer time in England."

But in all his research, in all his desire to penetrate the mysteries of science, there is no touch of pedantry. He was not one to encumber himself with the impediments of useless knowledge. He learnt all that he could with the lightest heart and the merriest smile. For he had but two motives in his life: pleasure and self-advancement. Mr. R. L. Stevenson, the most valiant champion of Pepys and his *Diary*, wrote, maybe in a moment of morbid self-consciousness, that he was happy but once. Samuel Pepys knew only the briefest interludes of displeasure. For ten years he screamed aloud with happiness, in so confident a tone that you wonder that he was not always trying to dodge the nemesis of his own pleasures. "In this humour we sat till about ten at night," he writes, of himself, and Evelyn, and Sir J. Minnes, and my Lord Bruncker—"and so my Lord and his mistress home, and we to bed, it being one of the times of my life wherein I was the fullest of true sense of joy." "True sense of joy"—is it not magnificent? And the phrase may be matched upon every page. Yet says the professional historian of literature: "Pepys lacked enthusiasm"!

Nor was it part of his creed to put off till to-morrow what might be enjoyed to-day. His was the Epicureanism of Horace. "*Carpe diem*" he shouted in his joyous voice. "I do indulge myself a little the more in pleasure," said he by way of excuse to himself, "knowing that this is the proper age of my life to do it; and out of my observation that most men that do thrive in the world, do forget to take pleasure during the time that they are getting their estate, but reserve that till they have got one, and then it is too late for them to enjoy it with any pleasure." So Pepys let not an hour pass unchallenged, and by a youth of pleasure prepared an old age of happiness.

He loved the amenities of life: art, music, a new coat, the songs of birds, the river, the open air were his perpetual delight. But before all things he loved a pretty woman. At the outset he was but a modest wooer. He once—it was on his return from Delft—sat side by side with "a pretty sober Dutch lass," and "I could not fasten any discourse upon her," he declares in a bland confession of failure. During the same journey to Holland he found "a pretty Dutch woman in bed alone," and, "though he had a month's mind, he had not the boldness to go to her." But in a year's space his boldness was invincible. And the *Diary* . . . is a pæan to the triumph of love. He might have said with truth that he never saw a pretty woman that he did not salute. A bright eye lit up for him the darkest sermon. The austerity of Church was but an occasion for the ogling of beauty. For every woman he has a magnificent phrase. "Our noble, brave, fat lady," he calls Madame Lethulier, when he saw her at church. Not even his bitterest enemy could call his patriotism in question, and yet hot upon the defeat of the Dutch fleet he writes: "that which pleased me as much as the newes was to have the fair Mrs. Middleton at our church, who indeed is a very beautiful lady." Two qualities only did he abhor in woman: avarice and that immodesty which sets no barriers in the path of love. So he hated Mrs. Lane with a freely expressed cordiality. For not only was she a too easy mistress, but she borrowed £5 upon the firm security of £4 10s. in gold—a transaction whereat the business habits of the excellent Pepys most properly revolted.

To kiss and tell is righteously esteemed the unpardonable sin. Yet Pepys kissed every day, and confided the exploit to his *Diary*. But by the wittiest inspiration of genius he made this ultimate confidence, not in bald English, but in an infantile jargon, wherein French and Spanish and Latin are unequally blended. And you think that he employed this artifice, lest the secret journal, conscious of his shame, should change its ink to a blushing scarlet. Nowhere else does he reveal so openly the master frailty of his temperament. The record was (let us assume) for himself alone. His vanity insisted that he should remind himself that he passed the evening with Mrs. Bagwell or with Mrs. Martin; his honour whispered that it was monstrous to tell the truth, intended only for his single eye, in plain English. Wherefore he invented a lingo of his own to salve a callous conscience. The contradiction is exquisite and characteristic. In these poor phrases of illegitimate French, you seem to catch the cunning casuistical brain of Samuel Pepys in perfect action. Upon every page he reveals himself with obvious intent; here he lays bare his conscience with an inadvertent subtlety. And the effect is almost too acute. You are not merely looking over his shoulder; you seem to be guiding the hand that writes.

By his own account a more general lover never lived. He made his conquests on the highway or in the kitchen. That he may dally with the wife, he sends the husband forth to purchase wine, and presently offers him a purser's place. When his sister Pall would marry, he recommends Mr.

Harman, the upholsterer, "to whom I have a great love, and did heretofore love his former wife." But to be found out was in his eyes a cardinal sin. And when Creed disgraced himself at Oxford, Pepys was the first to condemn his indiscretion. Now and again a wave of penitence swept over the golden sands of his complacency. "Musique and women," he acknowledges, with regret, "I cannot but give way to, whatever my business is." And again: "I observe the folly of my mind that cannot refrain from pleasure." Even his good resolutions are made but to be broken. "I have made an oathe," says he one day, "for the drinking of no wine, & c., on such penalties till I have passed my accounts and cleared all." And in a week he confesses that he has broken his oath "without pleasure." "Without pleasure"—that is the one phrase in the book that one is persuaded to mistrust. For the first and last time Pepys seems to be posing, to be cutting an antic before a mirror. Had he said the wine was bad, you had understood him. But were the wine good, you know that, oath or no oath, Pepys would have delighted in it.

Yet amidst all the frivolity and selfishness of his time, Pepys remained a patriot. While the Dutch were threatening our coasts, the Secretary's mind was troubled the more if it rained, "to think what the sailors would do on board in all this weather." When the Plague drove all save heroes and paupers from London, Pepys remained at his post in the very best of good humours, serving his country with unbated zeal. In a hopelessly corrupt age, he took no more commissions than should satisfy his necessities; and the glory of the British fleet overcame in his regard the plumpest check, the most provoking eye. (pp. 115-21)

Was Pepys an artist? This is the question which has grimly agitated the critics. Yet the answer seems easy: assuredly he was. He understood the art of life incomparably well. He never opposed his absorbing greed of sensation; he bent all the sterner considerations of time to the full enjoyment of the moment. And the severest critic will hardly detect a single fault in the interpretation of his wishes. He was an artist also in frankness, in that rare quality which, despite (or on account of) its simplicity, is far more difficult of attainment than the highest heaven. The artistic result of which is that he has given us such a picture of a man as is approached nowhere else than in Boswell's *Life of Johnson*. Once it was fashionable to believe, with Macaulay, that Boswell's was an idiot grinning through a horse-collar. It is still popular to assert that Pepys is a garrulous braggart, who has amused the nineteenth century by accident. But in the world of art accidents do not happen, and the peculiar excellence of the *Diary* is as firmly intentioned as a play by Shakespeare or a lyric by Tennyson.

Pepys set out to give himself a finished record of his life, and while his modesty shrank from immediate publication, he doubtless intended posterity to enjoy the fruit of his ceaseless labour. That the manuscript, with its cipher explained, should have been carefully and generously bequeathed to Magdalene College is proof positive that Pepys had a certain conscious respect for his own work. Had the journal been the idle, lazy vapourings of an amiable loafer, it would have been destroyed before its indiscretions could have annoyed a wondering world. But the journal was the one, long, deliberate effort of Pepys's life, and it is idle to deny the title of artist to the man who has drawn the living portrait of a living man.

Even by his style, Samuel Pepys may claim the august title. For its very looseness is perfectly appropriate. He had already made an experiment in literature when, at Cambridge, he began his romance *Love a Cheate*. And if, as he said, he had lost one vein, most assuredly he found another. His mannerisms, his monotony, his constant use of the stereotyped phrases of the day, give to his *Diary* an air of reality which a more deliberate method would have missed. (pp. 121-23)

Charles Whibley, "The Real Pepys," in his The Pageantry of Life, *William Heinemann, 1900, pp. 107-23.*

PERCY LUBBOCK (essay date 1909)

[*Lubbock was an English biographer and critic who served for a time as curator of the Pepysian Library in Magdalene College, Cambridge. In the following excerpt, he discusses the* Diary *as "a book which is not merely the chief of its kind but one of which no other of its kind has nearly approached."*]

Samuel Pepys holds to-day a curiously accidental place in English literature, but it is a place which is all his own. He was not a man of letters; he was a capable official, business-like and trustworthy, with an insatiable taste for life. But the book which he produced without knowing it to be a book, his matchless *Diary*, has been claimed without question for literature. A book which in its unconsidered candour is perhaps the most remarkable portrait of a human being that we possess, a book in which there is no page which is not brim-full of life and character, is not the less a work of art because its author was unaware of it. For such a book a place must be found, if no place already existed; if it seems to belong to no recognized form, a new form must be invented. This, to be sure, has long ago been done; the private letter and the casual diary now compete for fame on equal terms with the tragedy or the epic; and Pepys, no doubt very much to his surprise, has become one of the figures of our literary history. He has indeed become more than this, for the volumes which so picturesque a series of chances has protected for us have a different kind of value as a mere transcript of events, a record of contemporary gossip about people and things; and from this point of view Pepys has also become an historical authority. (pp. 1-2)

[Pepys has] indisputably been made to stand for a type. His name expresses in our day, rightly or wrongly, as marked a conjunction of qualities as the name of Falstaff or of Juan.... Pepys was surely too exuberant, too many-sided, too greedy of all sorts of incompatible aspects of life, to be anything but an extraordinary and isolated individual. Yet it is not for nothing that a name becomes thus consecrated as a universal symbol, and Pepys' torrent of self-revelation, with all its peculiar contrasts, may really reflect habitual and general humanity. It at any rate needed a man who adopted the world's standards and respected its hypocrisies as ingenuously as did Pepys, to give the whole convention away so thoroughly. There is not one grain of irony in any line that he wrote, and after so naked and unconscious an exposure of the tacit compromise upon which our civilized life is based, it should be difficult to treat it solemnly. The difficulty is still somehow solved; but at the same time the world indemnifies itself for its enforced decorum upon this chattering, bustling, self-important man, dead now for more than two hundred years. The place that Pepys occupies in our literature, the place which is all his own, is that, simply and essentially, of the ordinary man. For that place he has, it would seem, as yet no serious competitor. His name is perhaps never mentioned without an indulgent smile, a twinkle, a half-patronizing, half-roguish implication that we are all like that at bottom, that his *Diary* is the kind we should all keep if we were honest with ourselves. Other writers are exceptions, brains of special power, imaginations of out-standing strength; he alone is Everyman, the type of aver-age mortality, the sum of all its desires and efforts. If that is so, no wonder that the accidental book which gives his portrait has found a place of its own in our literature. (pp. 2-4)

Solely for his own personal and private satisfaction, so we are forced to conclude, Pepys... produced one of the most living and extraordinary books in the English lan-guage, a book which is not merely the chief of its kind but one of which no other of its kind has nearly approached. In a sense, no doubt, he may be said to have lacked all lit-erary skill—he had no conscious knowledge, that is, of the process by which he translated his impressions into words—but given his intense relish for life, his copious flow, his vivid vocabulary, that lack only enhanced the ar-tistic value of his work. If a literary self-consciousness were anywhere perceptible, the force of the whole amazing portrait would be impaired, and so its value for art. It is no more than true to say that Pepys loved it as he loved his life. It was, in fact, his life: absorbing, irrepressible, variegated, a thousand strands twisted into one, a life lived among the world, and yet his very own, known only to himself. (pp. 193-94)

Percy Lubbock, in his Samuel Pepys, *Hodder and Stoughton, 1909, 284 p.*

H. B. WHEATLEY (essay date 1911)

[*An English essayist and a founder of the Early English Text Society, Wheatley is remembered chiefly for his multi-volume edition (1893-99) of Pepys's* Diary, *a more complete transcription than any previously published. In the following excerpt from a study prepared for* The Cambridge History of English Literature, *he praises the human side of the* Dia-ry *while comparing Pepys and John Evelyn as diarists.*]

Pepys's diary is so various in its interest that it is not easy in a few words to indicate where its chief distinction lies. The absolute sincerity and transparent truth of the narra-tive naturally explains much, but the vitality of the man and his intense interest in the pageant of life supplies the motive power. Important events gain by the strength of their presentment, and trivialities delight us by the way in which they are narrated. Here is not only a picture of the life and manners of the time, but, also, the dissection of the heart of a man, and the exposure suggests a psycholog-ical problem difficult of solution. We naturally ask how it came to pass that the writer of the diary arrived at a per-fection of style suitable to the character of what he had to relate. Is it possible that he had previously practised the writing of a journal? We see the man grow in knowledge and power as the diary proceeds; but the narrative is equally good at the beginning and at the end. Pepys appar-

ently made notes on slips of paper and then elaborated them without any unnecessary delay. It is remarkable that there should be few or no corrections in the written manu-script. He wrote in secret, and, when he unguardedly (at the time of his detention in the Tower) told Sir William Coventry that he kept a diary, he was immediately after-wards sorry for his indiscretion. It is also matter for won-der that he should have trusted a binder with the precious book. Was the binder brought into the house to bind the pages under the writer's eye?

The brilliancy of the narrative and the intimacy of the confessions so thoroughly charm the reader that, in many cases, he overlooks the fact that, although Pepys was de-voted to pleasure, he was not absorbed by it, but always kept in view the main object of his life—the perfection of the English navy. Pepys was not a man of letters in the same way that Evelyn was one. When the latter was inter-ested in a subject, he wanted to write upon it, and not only wanted to, but did write.... This was not the case with Pepys. Early in his official life, he proposed to write a history of the navy, and collected materials for the pur-pose; but, although he talked about the project, he never got at all forward with it. His *Memoires of the Navy* was prepared under an urgent desire to present his *apologia*, and was only a chapter in the great work that had long been projected. This little book contains a thoroughly ef-fective statement of his case; but it is not lively reading or a work of any literary merit. The question, therefore, arises why the diary is different, and why it is remarkable as a literary effort.

The entries are all made with care, and there is no hurry about any of them; but we must remember that they were written fresh from the heart, and many hard judgments passed on colleagues were the result of temporary indigna-tion. He was himself careful, tidy and methodical, and he was impatient of untidiness and improvidence in those around him. His wife often irritated him by her careless-ness and want for method; but his poor sister, Paulina Pepys, comes off as badly as anyone in the diary. She did not receive much kindness from her brother and sister-in-law, although Pepys did his best to find her a husband, and, when the search was followed by success, gave her a handsome dowry. The pages of the diary are full of partic-ulars respecting Pepys's various servants, and their part in constant musical performances. It is necessary to bear in mind that most of these servants were more properly com-panions or maids of Mrs Pepys.

Pepys's system of vows and the excuses made for not car-rying them out are very singular and amusing. He feared the waste of time that would arise from a too frequent at-tendance at the theatre, and from his tendency to drink. The fines which he levied upon himself had some influ-ence in weaning him from bad habits. It does not appear that he neglected his work, even when taking pleasure; for, although the working day was often irregular in arrange-ment, the work was done either early in the morning or late at night, to make up for occasional long sittings after the midday meal. The diary contains a mine of informa-tion respecting theatres and music; there is much about the buying of his books and book-cases, but it should be borne in mind that the larger portion of the Pepysian li-brary now preserved at Magdalene college, Cambridge, was purchased after the conclusion of the diary.

It has been said that Pepys knew Evelyn a great deal better than we know that stately gentleman, but that we know Pepys a hundred times better than Evelyn did. In illustration of this dictum, two passages from Pepys's diary come to mind. On 10 September 1665, he joined a party at Greenwich, where Sir John Minnes and Evelyn were the life of the company and full of mirth. Among other humours, Evelyn repeated some verses introducing 'the various acceptations of may and can,' which made all present nearly die of laughing. This is certainly a fresh side of his character. On the following 5th of November, Pepys visited Evelyn at Deptford, when the latter read to the former extracts from an essay he had in hand, also a part of a play or two of his making, and some short poems. 'In fine a most excellent person he is and must be allowed a little for a little conceitedness but he may well be so, being a man so much above others.' So Pepys helps us to know Evelyn better and love him none the less; while, as for Pepys himself, we certainly know him better than Evelyn knew him, though we readily accept Evelyn's noble tribute to his merits. His frailties he has himself recorded; but, even were there no other evidence on the subject than is to be found in the diary itself, it would show him to have been a patriot and a true and steadfast friend. (pp. 258-60)

> *H. B. Wheatley, "Memoir and Letter Writers: I. Evelyn and Pepys," in* The Cambridge History of English Literature: The Age of Dryden, Vol. VIII, *edited by Sir A. W. Ward and A. R. Waller, 1911. Reprint by Cambridge at the University Press, 1964, pp. 241-60.*

HELEN McAFEE (essay date 1916)

[*McAfee was an American editor and literary critic best known for her long association with the* Yale Review. *In the following excerpt, she explores the "intrinsic worth and unique interest" of Pepys's dramatic criticism.*]

If, as has been said, Pepys's *Diary* is "a mine of information respecting the history of the stage," no one can complain that it has been indifferently worked. Ever since its first appearance in the incomplete edition of 1825, specialists in Elizabethan plays and in Restoration plays, students of the theatre—of its music and its manners, of the art of staging and the art of acting—have ransacked its pages, each for his particular purpose. As a result, the Diarist's name is today inseparably linked with the names of the actors, the managers, and the dramatists of his time. His casual comments have become a part of the *traditio* of the English stage.

To be specific, what Pepys has given us is a body of closely dated, firsthand evidence as to the history of the theatre in the first decade of Charles the Second's reign. Its value is enhanced by the critical importance of the time it covers. For two reasons the early years of the Restoration period are of especial interest to the student of the stage: first, because with the reopening of the playhouses after the Puritan interregnum, during which they had remained officially closed, the drama and theatre entered upon a new life; and, secondly, because during the decade of 1660-1670, as so seldom has happened, the two arts developed side by side. Fortunately for us, our informal historian was interested in both aspects of the contemporary stage, in the production of plays as well as in the plays

themselves. Thus we find in his journal accounts not only of the rise of rhymed heroic tragedy and the new "society comedy," but also of the innovations in the employment of actresses and movable scenery. He contributes alike to our knowledge of the continued popularity of pre-Restoration plays, the contemporary attitude towards Shakespeare, the minor as well as the major dramatists of the period, the vogue of French and Spanish plays in translation; and to our information about the reopening of the theatres, the personalities of the well-known people in the theatrical world—many of whom he knew intimately—and the manners and customs of the Restoration playhouses. Especially important are his accounts of the years from 1660 to 1663, of which there is elsewhere scant reliable record.

Yet certain objections have been raised from time to time to Pepys as a dramatic historian. There is, first of all, the question, I he accurate? It cannot, of course, be shown that he invariably is. Besides, it would be too much to expect from the *Diary* scrupulous exactness in all things, for in this, no less than in other matters, standards have changed since Charles the Second's reign. Occasionally, there is a disconcerting divergence between the account of an event recorded by Pepys and that recorded by some other supposedly good authority. Thus, in referring to the opening of the Duke of York's playhouse in Lincoln's Inn Fields as having taken place late in June, 1661, the Diarist conflicts seriously with John Downes, who states that it occurred in the spring of 1662—and who had reason to know since he was prompter at this theatre. Again, Pepys twice refers to May 7, 1663, as the date of the first performance at the new King's theatre in Drury Lane, whereas according to this same Downes and a playbill—which R. W. Lowe terms "a not very astute forgery"—this performance took place on April 8. In both these cases, it looks as if either Pepys or Downes must have been misinformed, though facts may yet be brought to light which will reconcile the conflicting statements. Moreover, as rumor did not travel rapidly in an age when there were no daily newspapers, it would be strange if Pepys's information were not at times stale. We know this to be the case, for instance, with his report of Abraham Cowley's death, which he first enters under August 10, 1667, when, as a matter of fact, the poet had been dead thirteen days.

But in how many instances the Diarist's dates are actually wrong, the investigator may well-nigh despair of determining; the difficulty is that nearly all the clues, in the external evidence at least, lead in a circle and so eventually back to Pepys. This is the case with many of the statements about the early Restoration performances made by Genest. Downes and Langbaine cover the same period, it is true, but their material is rarely closely dated. Some slight basis for comparison is, however, afforded by the *Diary* of John Evelyn and a list found among the papers of Sir Henry Herbert—then Master of the Revels—of plays acted by Killigrew's company. In several instances statements in them corroborate Pepys, and in no case do they definitely conflict with him. Pepys saw five performances at the King's theatre which are also mentioned under the same dates in the list just referred to, and records two performances of plays which are also recorded by Evelyn. It is interesting to find both the diarists giving accounts of the presentations of Tuke's *The Adventures of Five Hours*, on January 8, 1663, and of Dryden's *An Eve-*

ning's Love, or The Mock Astrologer, on June 19, 1668; and it is instructive to compare their respective comments. Few as they are, these corroborations cannot but confirm the student in the tendency to accept the dates of Pepys's journal, in the main, without question.

Another charge that has been brought against the Diarist as a dramatic historian is that he does not always give names and titles correctly—even allowing for the laxity of the age in matters of spelling. There is a reference, for example, on September 14, 1667, to a play which he calls *The Northern Castle*. No such play is known, and it seems probable that the title as Pepys gives it may have been a slip for *The Northern Lass*, a comedy by Richard Brome. Possibly, too, in certain instances, the Diarist ascribes plays to the wrong authors. He mentions on September 15, 1668, a play translated "out of French by Dryden called 'The Ladys à la Mode,'"—which may have been a mistake for Richard Flecknoe's *Damoiselles à la Mode*; and in his entry under December 10, 1663, he refers to Shakespeare's *Henry VIII*—before he has seen it, to be sure—as Sir William D'Avenant's "story of Henry the Eighth with all his wives." But anyone who examines into the matter, will soon discover that inaccuracies such as these are, so far as can be judged, the exception.

The unique value of Pepys's comment on the Restoration stage lies, as has been said, as much in the kind as in the mere bulk of material he presents. His was indeed a many-sided interest. In intellectual and moral tolerance, where the theatre is concerned, he stands in striking contrast to his fellow-diarist Evelyn, who speaks of "very seldom going to the publiq theaters for many reasons," his chief complaint being against the "foule and undecent women now (and never till now) permitted to appear and act." Evelyn flattered himself on one occasion that he was "far from Puritanisme"; but he was not so far from it that moral scruples did not stand between him and a whole-hearted appreciation of what the contemporary theatre had to offer. As for Pepys, he could enjoy without let or hindrance everything about it, from Betterton's Hamlet to the orange-girls. "It is in virtue of his own desires and curiosities," says Stevenson, "that any man ... is charmed by the look of things and people." Thus it was with Pepys at the playhouse. His curiosity was unbounded here as elsewhere. He liked to read plays on his trips to and from Deptford on Admiralty business as well as to see them at the theatre. Hence everything and everybody on the stage appealed to him. His accounts of performances are, of course, for this reason peculiarly satisfactory; if there was a single novel or exceptional fact about the play, the players, the scenery, the music, the dancing, the audience, or the theatre itself, we feel certain that he has noted it. Whatever may be said of Pepys's critical acumen, remarks a recent writer, "no one has ever impeached his powers of observation."

The Diarist was not, to be sure, equally competent to judge in all these matters. It has been frequently charged that his criticisms of the plays are not so satisfactory as his criticisms of the acting, which seems often to have mattered to him more. In a certain instance, Pepys realized this himself. When Young, "but a bad actor at best," took Thomas Betterton's famous part in one of Pepys's favorite plays, *Macbeth*, the Diarist exclaims: "Lord! what a prejudice it wrought in me against the whole play!" But this does not mean that he was without literary taste or that he invariably judged a piece solely on its acting qualities. He could thoroughly appreciate a play like Jonson's *Catiline*, which he insisted had "much good sense and words to read," even though it appeared "the worst upon the stage, I mean, the least diverting, that ever I saw any." At any rate, he had his own theories of what was justifiable in tragedy, and of what was proper material for comedy, distinguishing between true "wit" and mere "fooling" or, as he calls it, "mirth fit for clowns." From his criticism of Etherege's *She Would if She Could*, it is evident that "witty" and "roguish" dialogue did not wholly blind him to deficiencies of plot; while in the case of Lord Orrery, whom he admired as a dramatist in many ways, he recognized the limitations which made one of his plays of "just the very same design, and words, and sense, and plot" as every other.

Pepys's literary judgment has been questioned mainly on the ground of his attitude towards Shakespeare, which is betrayed in certain "delicious bits of criticism," as Professor Lounsbury has called them, "whose impudent inappreciativeness later critics have occasionally equalled, but whose charm they have never been able even remotely to rival." In this connection, his wholesale condemnation of *A Midsummer-Night's -Dream* as "the most insipid ridiculous play that ever I saw in my life," and his disparaging comparison of *Othello* with Tuke's *The Adventures of Five Hours* have usually been cited. Now, although, as Stevenson says, the Diarist's failure to appreciate these and other plays of Shakespeare on the stage is not "without either parallel or excuse" [see excerpt dated 1881], there is no need to minimize its import. Yet in passing judgment, two modifying circumstances must at the same time be borne in mind—on the one hand, the nature of the record Pepys kept, which attempted to do no more than jot down among a thousand other matters first impressions of plays, and, on the other hand, the nature of the Shakespearean productions he saw. Some of these were redeemed, we know, by the acting of the Bettertons, but others must have been hopelessly inadequate. Besides, it should not be forgotten in any final appraisal that Pepys never tired of seeing *Hamlet*—even trying at one time to get "To bee or not to bee" "without book"; that he held *Henry IV* "a good play"; and that he was "mightily pleased" with *Henry VIII*. In short, although it may be true that, as Sir Sidney Lee says, he "lived and died in complacent unconsciousness of Shakespeare's supreme excellence," there is little in his references to signify that Pepys wholly shared what has sometimes been assumed to be the conventional Restoration attitude towards Shakespeare, based upon such views as that expressed by Evelyn after seeing *Hamlet*: "Now the old plays began to disgust this refined age since his Majestie's being so long abroad."

As a dramatic historian, it should also be mentioned that Pepys was in two respects free from the prejudices of his time—or possibly, one should say, of the Court circle of his time. There is, first of all, his standpoint on the morality of the stage. This question, like the question of his feeling for Shakespeare, cannot be fairly considered apart from the general theory and practice of the *Diary* as a whole. It must be remembered that Pepys never aims at anything like such completeness or finality in his picture of a play on the stage as we are accustomed to expect from the modern dramatic reviewer. Neither is he writing for the edification of the public. He is only noting for his own private benefit the particular aspects of the production that for one reason or another stood out to him as of especial interest. Hence, quite naturally, we do not find the Diarist putting every play he sees, or indeed every play which might well be examined on this ground, to a rigid moral test. On the other hand, from the comments that Pepys makes from time to time on the moral issue, it would seem hardly justifiable to conclude, as does [John Palmer in *The Comedy of Manners* (1913)], that "Pepys criticises the plays he so loved to frequent from almost every other point of view than the moral," or yet to assert that he is never "distressfully disturbed by the improprieties afterward discovered by Collier and his successors in the theatre." For one thing, he looked with disapproval upon the gross immorality of Thomas Killigrew's *The Parson's Wedding*. Even though all the world commended Dryden's *Mock Astrologer*, he did "not like it, it being very smutty." He came out positively in favor of Brome's *Jovial Crew* as "merry and the most innocent play that ever I saw"; while of Sir Samuel Tuke's *Adventures of Five Hours* he enthusiastically writes: "The play in one word, is the best . . . that ever I saw, or think ever shall, and all possible, not only to be done in the time, but in most other respects very admittable, and without one word of ribaldry." This testimony of Pepys, along with that of Evelyn, would seem to indicate that while the Court of the Merry Monarch countenanced gross immorality on the stage, and even fathered it—as Dryden later charged—the "City" was never wholly reconciled to it.

Again, Pepys's opinion differed from that which the Restoration Court is generally held to have imposed upon the contemporary stage, on the merits of the rhymed couplet for heroic plays. In a reference to *The Indian Queen*, by Dryden and Sir Robert Howard, the Diarist appears emphatically against its use. "The play good," he writes, "but spoiled with the ryme, which breaks the sense."

One habit of Pepys as a playgoer works to the especial good fortune of the modern student. This is his practice of going to see the same play several times over, at intervals varying from two or three days to two or three years. And since he is more concerned with fidelity to the immediate fact than with consistency to former statements, we are thus enabled to see one play from several different angles. Often he did not come to any definite conclusion about it until the second or third performance, meantime testing his preconceived prejudices, if he had any, noting the implication of new impressions, and, in general, keeping an open mind. This is well illustrated in his various accounts of a contemporary tragedy by Thomas Porter called *The Villain*. The first time Pepys saw it, he was "never less pleased with a play in my life"; the second time, he was "better pleased with the play than I was at first, understanding the design better than I did"; and the third time he records, "The more I see it, the more I am offended at my first undervaluing the play, it being very good and pleasant, and yet a true and allowable tragedy." With Dryden's popular comedy, *Sir Martin Mar-all*, his experience was just the reverse. He first saw it on August 16, 1667, the day after its *première*, and "never laughed so in all my life"; then on August 19 and 20, still finding it "a very ingenious play, and full of variety." Six weeks later he witnesses another performance "with great delight, though I have seen it so often"; then once more before the year is out, and three times in 1668. His enjoyment of it never

lessens; the last time he mentions it, he writes: "Though I have seen it, I think, ten times, yet the pleasure I have is yet as great as ever." New details, if not fresh impressions, were generally gathered with each performance, and to his habit of seeing plays repeated, Pepys's record owes much of its value. Indeed, we are in so far indebted to the Diarist for this persistence in attending the theatre that we must even forgive him the absurd casuistry with which he manipulates his frequent vows to stay away.

In short, it cannot be said that Pepys was either a professed literary critic or a typical Restoration playgoer. Beyond the average man, he was open-minded and sincere in his appreciation of various types of plays, and many-sided and indefatigable in his interest in the theatre. Yet while he was too individual to subscribe in every matter to the stage conventions of the period, his power of observing closely others as well as himself, enabled him to body forth with peculiar realism the attitude of his age.

The intrinsic worth and unique interest of the evidence, as a whole, that Pepys has preserved for us can be grasped only by an examination of its full content. But perhaps the significance of a few of the comments on certain important groups of plays should be pointed out. . . . (pp. 17-27)

At first glance, the entries in the *Diary* for the dramas of the pre-Restoration period point to the overwhelming popularity, during the decade succeeding the King's return, of the romances of Beaumont and Fletcher, over twenty-five of which Pepys saw at one time or another. A reading of his criticisms in full will show, however, that he, at least, did not admire them as he did the plays of Jonson. *The Maid's Tragedy* he found on first hearing "too sad and melancholy," though later he thought it "a good play"; and *Philaster* was "far short of my expectations." But when it came to Jonson, his praise was not thus tempered. *The Alchemist* he held to be "a most incomparable play"; he declared that *The Silent Woman* had "more wit in it than goes to ten new plays"; *Volpone* was "the best I think I ever saw." For Shirley, more of whose plays (nine in all) are referred to as being produced than any other dramatist of his period excepting Beaumont and Fletcher and Shakespeare, Pepys cared less, admiring only *The Traitor*, as "a very good Tragedy." Along with this should be mentioned Massinger's *The Bondman*, which from the *Diary* would seem to have been among the most successful plays of the time, perhaps because it provided Betterton with one of his best parts. "To the Opera," writes Pepys after a certain performance, "where we saw 'The Bondman,' which of old we both did so doat on, and do still"; and again, "There is nothing more taking in the world with me than that play." Of the twelve plays of Shakespeare which Pepys saw staged, at least eight seem to have been acted substantially unaltered, four being given in contemporary versions. From the *Diary* we learn that the general popularity of *Hamlet, Henry VIII*, and *Othello*, which were among the unaltered plays, should be set over against the success of D'Avenant's *Macbeth* and Dryden and D'Avenant's *The Tempest* in any consideration of the Restoration view of Shakespeare.

Pepys also supplies us with significant evidence as to the brief day of rhymed heroic drama. He applauds at length the success of the Earl of Orrery's plays—said to have been written at the instigation of Royalty—*The Black*

Prince, Henry the Fifth, and *Mustapha*, this last, "a most admirable poem, and bravely acted." At the same time he dissents from the general opinion about other plays of this type. Besides feeling that *The Indian Queen* was "spoiled with the ryme," he calls the sequel, Dryden's *The Indian Emperor*, "a good play, but not so good as people cry it up." Moreover, on April 16, 1669, he notes a bit of gossip, which in its tone would seem to presage the coming of Buckingham's *Rehearsal* and the beginning of the end of heroic drama: "I did meet with Shadwell, the poet, who, to my great wonder, do tell me that my Lord of [Orrery] did write this play [*Guzman*], trying what he could do in comedy, since his heroique plays could do no more wonders." To certain of the dramatists, that is, it was already clear that the tide had turned.

With contemporary comedy, Pepys was perhaps more in sympathy. He describes among the earliest comic successes Cowley's satirical *Cutter of Coleman Street*, under December 16, 1661, and D'Avenant's *The Wits*, under August 15, 1661. Dryden's *Sir Martin Mar-all, or The Feign'd Innocence* (1667), he esteems "the most entire piece of mirth, a complete farce from one end to the other, that certainly ever was writ"; he records that *Secret Love, or The Maiden Queen* is "mightily commended for the regularity of it, and the strain and wit," though its success was doubtless due in a measure to the "comical part" of Florimel, done by Nell Gwyn. He has a long notice of Etherege's first play, *The Comical Revenge, or Love in a Tub*, January 4, 1665, which he calls "very merry"; and of his second, *She Would if She Could*, February 6, 1668, from the first performance of which "there was 1,000 people put back that could not have room in the pit," and about which the audience thought, so Pepys says, "there was something very roguish and witty." It is especially interesting to see from these entries in regard to Etherege the attitude of his contemporaries towards this first important writer of Restoration "society comedy."

If it is true that we do not understand a period until we know its minor in addition to its major writers, we must acknowledge a still further debt to Pepys's journal; for it has much to say of the lesser contemporary dramatists. The fact is that the work of mediocre men bulks as large in the *Diary* as it usually does in the estimation of the contemporary public. The plays mentioned by Pepys of the three Howards—Edward, James, and Sir Robert—of the Duke of Newcastle, Sir Charles Sedley, Thomas Killigrew, John Lacy—the actor,—Thomas Porter, Richard Rhodes, Sir Robert Stapylton, and Thomas Shadwell—all are cases in point.

The most notable seem to have owed their success largely to contemporary allusions. Such was Edward Howard's *The Change of Crowns* (1667), in which John Lacy acted the part of the country gentleman who had the effrontery to attack "the Court with all the imaginable wit and plainness about selling places, and doing every thing for money." The King, who attended its first performance, was, we are told, so incensed at thus being abused to his face that he ordered the theatre closed and Lacy imprisoned. Finally, another actor got permission to reopen the theatre on condition that this play should not be repeated. Pepys pronounced *The Change of Crowns* "bitter indeed, but very true and witty." Curiously enough, Sir Robert Howard's *The Duke of Lerma* (1668), which, according to the Diarist, was "designed to reproach our King with his mistress-

es," did not arouse similar resentment in the royal spectator. Pepys fully expected that the first performance would be stopped, but although the whole Court was present, the play was allowed to take its course, and fortunately it "ended well, which salved all." Other plays, like Sedley's *The Mulberry Garden* (1668), drew crowded houses because of their author being "so reputed a wit"; and still others because, like James Howard's *All Mistaken* (1667), with its two "mad parts" immortalized by Hart and Nell Gwyn, they provided rôles that suited stage favorites. If these plays themselves have not stood the test of time, it is nevertheless instructive to learn from Pepys on what their popularity in their own day rested.

And here may be mentioned in passing the translations and adaptations referred to in the *Diary*, many from the Spanish, but most from the French, which flourished on the Restoration stage. Of the plays from Pierre Corneille, alone, Pepys saw five, each performed several times over,—*The Cid, Heraclius* ("an excellent play, to my extraordinary content"), *Horace, The Mistaken Beauty*, and *Pompey the Great. The Adventures of Five Hours*, based upon a Spanish play now ascribed to Antonio Coello, was, in Pepys's judgment, "the best, for the variety and the most excellent continuance of the plot to the very end, that ever I saw, or think ever I shall." "And the house," he concludes, "by its frequent plaudits, did show their sufficient approbation."

Pepys and his companions also frequently attended puppet-shows. Of these *Polichinello* (The Italian *Punch*), mentioned nine times in all, seems to have been the most popular. One performance at least was graced by "Young Killigrew" and "a great many young sparks." After seeing *The Surprisal* at the King's theatre, Pepys went one day "to Polichinello, and there had three times more sport than at the play." Other puppet-plays referred to in the *Diary* are *The Modern History of Hero and Leander* (in *Bartholomew Fair*, Act V); "the story of Holofernes"; "Patient Grizill"; and the "show of Whittington." Of the last-named, Pepys remarks: "How that idle thing do work upon people that see it, and even myself too!" (pp. 27-33)

Among the dramatists of the day, we read two or three times of Abraham Cowley, who was at his death "mightily lamented" as "the best poet of our nation, and as a good man"; of Sir William D'Avenant and his difficulties as manager of the Duke's company; and of "Dryden the poet," whom Pepys knew at Cambridge, and whom he saw "at the great Coffee-house," where "all the wits of the town" foregathered. The Diarist furnishes us with portraits of the unpopular Sir Robert Howard, ridiculed by Shadwell in *The Sullen Lovers*; of the popular and profligate Sir Charles Sedley, examples of whose witty repartees as a theatre-goer are carefully set down; of Tom Killigrew "the King's Foole or Jester," with his love of music and his managerial ambitions, his "raillery" and his "merry stories." Thus are the literary "lions" of the Restoration playhouse exhibited in Pepys's pages. (pp. 27-33)

Helen McAfee, in her Pepys on the Restoration Stage, *1916. Reprint by Benjamin Blom, Inc., 1964, 353 p.*

J. WARSHAW (essay date 1920)

[*In the following excerpt, Warshaw studies Pepys as a critic of the drama.*]

Nearly everybody who has discussed Pepys' dramatic impressions has found it necessary to apologize for the immortal diarist. The excuses are offered more in sorrow than as censure. Sir Sidney Lee, whose ideas on Shakespeare Pepys unfortunately and of course, unconsciously crosses, sees in Pepys a matter-of-fact business-man whom *Romeo and Juliet* would hardly enthuse: "Things of the imagination—stood with him on a different footing. They were out of his range or sphere." The best that Robert Louis Stevenson can allege, in spite of his warm admiration for Pepys, is that if he "did not like Shakespeare as an artist for the stage—it is not without either parallel or excuse" [see excerpt dated 1881].

Pepys' chief title to fame will not rest on his perspicacity as a dramatic critic, and it may be of small consequence that his observations should be taken one way or another. Yet it is his privilege, as it is every man's, that he should be presented in a true light; and the drama is too much in his debt to slight him.

Pepys is easily the most faithful drama-lover of whom we have knowledge. His characterization of Colonel Reames as "a man who understands and loves a play as well as I, and I love him for it" is, perhaps, one of the finest tributes to the drama ever written. His "oaths" against going to plays,—often broken, but with what anguish of spirit!—prove how irresistible a fascination the theater exerted on him. The extraordinary amount of space which he devotes in his diary to plays, players, playwrights, and happenings in the theatrical world can probably not be duplicated outside of the work of professional critics and chroniclers. Pepys is beyond compare in the revivification of the dramatic London of Beaumont and Fletcher, Davenant, Dryden, Lord Orrery, Betterton, Kynaston, Hart, Lacy, and Nell Gwynn. Historians of the stage during the reign of the Stuarts owe as much to him as social students of the Victorian Age owe to Dickens. Manifestly, the least we can do in justice to him is to try to understand his dramatic judgments and, above all, the basis for them.

Pepys has drawn on himself the fire of the dramatic critics mainly because of his frank opinions about certain plays of Shakespeare. *Hamlet* he adored, and he and his wife spent part of a day "getting a speech out of *Hamlet*, 'to bee or not to bee' without a book" *Macbeth, The Tempest, Henry the Eighth,* and *The Merry Wives of Windsor* he appreciated in varying degrees, and the more when they were adequately performed. *Othello* he once "esteemed a mighty good play," but revised his judgment after reading Sir George Tuke's adaptation of Calderon's *The Adventures of Five Hours,* and thereupon set it down as "a mean thing." Toward *Twelfth Night, A Midsummer Night's Dream,* and *Romeo and Juliet* he remained consistently unfavorable. The first is "one of the weakest plays that ever I saw on the stage;" the second is "the most insipid, ridiculous play that ever I saw in my life;" the third is "a play of itself the worst that I ever heard, and the worse acted that ever I saw these people do."

Not to mince words, the highest flights of poetic fancy in dramatic form left Pepys cold. He could see no more in them than in *Hudibras,* though he conscientiously reread the latter several times in the hope of fathoming the popularity of a book whose author he knew and regarded as an "eminent man." Some justification, to be sure, may be raised for him on the ground that Shakespeare's plays were commonly acted from wretchedly garbled versions, that few actors except Betterton did full justice to Shakesperian rôles, and that *Romeo and Juliet* was so little a favorite as to permit Theophilus Cibber to state, though erroneously, that the performance on September 11, 1744, was the first "for one hundred years." Nevertheless, Cibber was so near the truth that Mr. H. Barton Baker can oppose to it only Pepys' mention of the acting of *Romeo and Juliet* in March, 1662. Nor can Pepys be cleared by the assumption that he did not read Shakespeare. On the contrary, he owned copies of Shakespeare and unquestionably read more than the *Othello.*

Either Pepys was congenitally incapable of rising above chines of beef, bottles of Rhenish wine, pieces of plate, black cloth suits "trimmed with scarlet ribbon, very neat, with my cloak lined with velvet and a new beaver, which altogether is very noble, with my black silk knit canons I bought a month ago," and "some little French romances" which, "God forgive him!" he read on the Lord's day in the intervals of taking physic, or else he was hemmed in by conditions which made his dramatic preferences the most natural and the most logical thing in the world. Fairplay demands that we examine those conditions.

The years 1660-1670, within which the diary falls, were as different from the Shakesperian period as the years after 1859, the date of Darwin's *Origin of Species,* have been, in literature, from the whole preceding era. The splendid romanticism of the Elizabethans had been swept away by French taste, by a court subservient to French customs, manners, dress, and other modes of invidious distinction, by a wave of rationalism and intellectualism emanating from Aristotle, Bacon, Descartes, Pascal, Huyghens, and Galileo, by a growing national and personal spirit of commercialism, and, in art, by a mania for verisimilitude, if not realism. Shakespeare, though mentioned with admiration by many writers, is not the idol that Ben Jonson and Fletcher are, and when praised is remembered rather for his more human and less fanciful plays. Only genuine poets are entranced by the *Romeo and Juliet* style: and such poets are few. Dryden descants meagerly on Shakespeare, but amply on Ben Jonson and Fletcher. Thomas Rymer inquires, "—would not a rap at the door better express Iago's meaning than 'Call aloud,' etc.—For what ship? Who is arrived? The answer is: ''Tis one, Iago' etc. Is this the language of the Exchange or the insuring office? Once in a man's life he might be content at Bedlam to hear such a rapture. In a play one should speak like a man of business—." This is the belief of the age all over Europe, though rarely so bluntly put. The drama has been divorced from poetry: and the divorce has been made absolute, as an examination of all later drama down to our own times will demonstrate.

It took the French nearly two hundred years to begin to appreciate Shakespeare. Voltaire, under deeper obligations to Shakespeare than he has ever cared to acknowledge, grants him flashes of genius, but treats him, on the whole, as a barbarian (*tout barbare qu'il etait*). Shall we deny dramatic taste to Voltaire and to the entire French nation? Shall we deny dramatic taste to the other nations of Europe among which Shakespeare's vogue has been of slow advancement? Why, then, impugn Pepys' dramatic appreciation? The pure dramas of Shakespeare were relished by Pepys: and Shakespeare's pure poetry so enthralled him that he set several of the poems to music. To the drama, the dramatic; to poetry, the poetic. All that has been proved against Pepys is an aversion for the confusion of *genres*.

In other respects, Pepys' dramatic criticism is sane. The principal fault to be found with it is that it betrays the shorthand writer.

No man of his day was better qualified than Pepys to judge dramatic productions. His training went much farther than the witnessing of a play a week on an average for the ten years of the diary. An amateur actor in his youth, he must have learned something about the structure of plays at first hand. At a performance of *Philaster*, he recalls that he was once booked for the rôle of Arethusa: "and it was very pleasant to me, but more to think what a ridiculous thing it would have been for me to have acted a beautiful woman." His reading of plays was wide, and included *The Duchesse of Malfy, The Mayden Queene, Henry the Fourth, The Madd Lovers, The Custome of the Country, The Indian Emperour, The Adventures of Five Hours,* Cowley's Latin comedy, *Naufragium Joculare,* the Latin writers of comedy, and *Othello.* Many of them were read by Pepys while walking to Woolwich or going by water to Deptford, near which his upright, but dour and drama-fearing friend, John Evelyn, lived. That he was familiar with printed French and Spanish plays may be taken as a matter of course, for he had an excellent reading and speaking ability of both languages.

In addition to his steady attendance at the theater and his continued reading of plays, he had interesting discussions on the drama with men like Colonel Reames, and undoubtedly indulged in his love for information and theatrical news with Dryden, Killigrew, Sir Charles Selden, and other dramatists. Of his minute knowledge of stage gossip, no other evidence is needed than the turning of the pages of his diary. He is privy to all that occurs in the London theaters; he is on terms of intimacy with Mrs. Knipp, to the detriment of his domestic peace; he can retail the latest joke about Orange Moll: he has a chance at the "kissing of Nell" or "Nelly" (Gwynn), which chance, you may be sure, he does not miss; he can tell item by item what improvements have been made in the playhouses, when women first acted in women's parts, when the "lower classes" began to invade the theaters, what actors were deteriorating, and what nobleman was maintaining what actress. One sometimes wonders where he found the time to be such an altogether efficient Clerk of the Acts and later Secretary of the Admiralty!

Out of this variegated experience, even a less intelligent man would have developed into a passable dramatic critic: and Pepys was thoroughly intelligent. He may be naive on occasion, as when he admits that he drinks "I know not how, of my own accord, so much wine, that I was even almost foxed, and my head aked all night; so home and to bed, without prayers—I being now so out of order that I durst not read prayers, for fear of being perceived by my servants in what case I was;" or when he tells us intimately "(Lord's day.) My wife and I lay long, with mighty content; and so rose, and she spent the whole day making herself clean after four or five weeks being in continued dirt;"

or when he is "at a loss to know whether it be my hare's foot which is my preservation; for I never had a fit of the collique since I wore it, or whether it be my taking of a pill of turpentine every morning;" but intellectually alert he always is. We must, therefore, assume that his comment on plays and acting are worth at least as much as the comments of most of his contemporaries.

It is a pity that the deciphering of his shorthand notes could not, in the nature of the case, be accompanied by an elaboration of his dramatic sentences. Pepys jotted down in his "journal," generally in the late hours of the night, his impressions of the day. He made no effort at completeness. His method was selective. Consequently, the diary is an accumulation of "high points:" but with what native art they are displayed! His dramatic verdicts will never satisfy us, because they are almost always a summing-up, and the intervening steps are omitted; yet there is enough in them to enable us to hazard a guess at the process underlying his conclusions.

Judicial sentences such as these are characteristic of the diary: "*The Ghosts*—but a very simple play;" "*The Usurper*, which is no good play;" "*The Knight of the Burning Pestle*," by his favorites, Beaumont and Fletcher—"which please me not at all;" "*The Witts*, which I had already seen twice, and was most highly pleased with it;" "*The Alchymist*, which is a most incomparable play;" "*The Roman Virgin*, an old play, and but ordinary;" "*Cutter of Coleman Street*, a silly play;" "*Sir Martin Mar-all*, which, the more I see, the more I like."

If Pepys had gone no further, we should have scant reason for speaking of him as other than a chronicler of stage events. His definite contribution to dramatic criticism is, however, considerable, and his testimony is invaluable in determining the dramatic spirit of his period. It is much more to our profit that he can enlighten us on his historical environment than that he should have composed antiquarian disquisitions. His diary surpasses Evelyn's in vividness, vigor, and human interest by as much as Boswell's *Life of Samuel Johnson* surpasses any of Johnson's works, though Evelyn and Johnson were indubitably the greater men.

Pepys' dramaturgy is consonant with the soundest dramatic standards of his own and of modern times. It is also liberal, admits excellencies of various kinds, and shies only at the unnatural drama, that is to say, the drama which speaks, like *Romeo and Juliet*, a language never uttered by human lips, no matter how frequent in elevated writing. He does not realize that the lofty poetic diction of Shakespeare subserves an extremely important purpose, namely, that of *creating atmosphere*; and regretful of his obtuseness on this score as we may be, we must admit that Shakespeare's method, as Voltaire has pointed out, is perilous. Pepys evidently felt that it is not safe nor desirable to take the exceptional for a norm.

A play, in Pepys' opinion, is an entertainment. It may be sad or droll or neither, but its aim is "divertisement." It has not, so far as we can learn from Pepys, any social or moral object other than that of bringing people together and interesting them; and, from his attitude toward plays, we could readily have deduced Mr. William Archer's definition (1912): "The only valid definition of the dramatic is: any representation of imaginary personages which is capable of interesting an average audience assembled in a theater." This liberal notion does not mean that a play can outrage the common decencies; indeed, it means, and it meant for Pepys, exactly the opposite; and I am sure that Sir Sidney Lee has exaggerated Pepys' tolerance of coarseness on the stage, as in *The Custom of the Country*, which anticipates the theme of Beaumarchais' *Mariage de Figaro*. In point of fact, Pepys on several occasions expresses disgust at the vulgarity of plays by some of his favorite authors: "—and there I saw this new play (*Evening Love*, by Dryden) my wife saw yesterday, and do not like it, it being very smutty;" "I went to the theatre, and there saw *Bartholomew Faire*, (by Ben Jonson) the first time it was acted now-a-days. It is a most admirable play, and well acted, but much too prophane and abusive." Broad jests and bluff language were the style in England as in France, and it would be as uncharitable in these days of suggestive motion-pictures and plain-dealing in newspapers accessible to any girl of fifteen, to make a boor out of Pepys as it would be to declare Mme. de Sévigné, his contemporary, indelicate and unrefined, because she wrote one day to her daughter, "Pour mes vapeurs, j'ai pris huit gouttes d'essence d'urine." A careful reading of the diary proves that Pepys was always something of a Puritan. He laments, in terms of despair, the loose-living of the higher classes and remarks, apropos of *Bartholomew Fair*, "—only the business of abusing the Puritans begins to grow stale, and of no use, they being the people that, at last, will be found the wisest."

Given such a conception of the drama, and accepting the surroundings in which Pepys was placed, we find that his dramatic views were in accord with the best thought of England and France. Plot that chains the attention he treats as a *sine qua non* of a good drama; and it is the ingenious plot of Calderon's *The Adventures of Five Hours* which elicits his enthusiasm. The Three Unities do not appear to concern him greatly,—and they have seldom bothered Englishmen,—though he comments with approval on the limitation of time in the play just mentioned, and his watchfulness for plot indicates that he mentally demands unity of action or interest. Proper characterization he takes for granted, and improper characterization, as Nell Gwynn's in serious parts, especially in view of her talent in mad parts, or the botched representation of Cromwell and Hugh Peters in *The Usurper*, he condemns strongly. Verisimilitude, as may be expected of a man who was essentially a realist, and the more so, since he moved in the orbit of Dryden, Racine, and Corneille, was regarded by Pepys as the keystone of the drama. His censure of the letter in *The Black Prince*, because it was "so long and so unnecessary," is unstinted; yet he is just enough to state on his next view of the play that it "is now mightily bettered by that long letter being printed, and so delivered to everybody at their going in and some short reference made to it in the play." An unusual aspect of Pepys' belief in the necessity of verisimilitude on the stage is to be seen in his attention to historical accuracy—a rather new notion in the dramatic profession. *Heraclius* charms him with its "garments like Romans very well" and the Emperor's people standing about him "in their fixed and different postures in their Roman habits, above all that I ever saw at any of the theatres;" *Queen Elizabeth's Troubles and the History of Eighty Eight* "shows the true garbe of the Queen in those days just as we see Queen Mary and Queen Elizabeth painted."

With the minor details of the drama Pepys is familiar, and his criticism or commendation is appropriate. If the language is unsuitable, the wit flat, the similes mixed, the sense spoiled by the rhyme, the fun "sorry, poor stuffe, of eating of sack posset and slabbering themselves, and mirth fit for clownes," as in *The Man is the Master*; if the prologue is poor, the epilogue extraordinary, the dialogue strained, the drama "merely a show," the "design" insipid, the ending awkward, the topic too melancholy, the scene admirable, the "fancy" unsatisfying; if the singing is exquisite or disappointing—whether by favorites or no—the pronounciation defective, the dancing graceful, the costuming comely, the acting equal to the part, the rehearsals i. dequate, the scene spoiled by the incongruous behavior of the actors, the great and revered Betterton "out;" you may be sure that none of it has escaped Pepys. You may be sure, too, that, in spite of his multifarious activities, his political and social responsibilities, his continual recapitulation of his financial status, and his meetings with the King, the King's favorites, lords and ladies, ambassadors, distinguished scientists, and foreign notables, he will save space for the drama, no matter how agitated, or nearly blind he may be, in that compressed "journal" of his through which all London passes for ten years.

There can be no doubt that Pepys both "loved" and "understood" a play. He has endeared himself to all dramalovers, and their only regret must be that his other duties and his lack of presumption kept him from leaving the definitive volume on the drama and the stage of the Stuarts. (pp. 209-13)

J. Warshaw, "Pepys as a Dramatic Critic," in Drama, *London, Vol. 10, Nos. 6 & 7, March & April, 1920, pp. 209-13.*

J. R. TANNER (essay date 1925)

[*Tanner was an English naval historian who edited Pepys's private correspondence and wrote extensively on the* Diary *and* Naval Minutes. *In the following excerpt, he discusses the* Diary *as literature.*]

"It is generally supposed," writes Robert Louis Stevenson, "that as a writer Pepys must rank at the bottom of the scale of merit" [see excerpt dated 1881]; and although he argues that this is to place the *Diary* too low, he convicts the author of it by implication of writing in a style that is ungrammatical, inelegant, and full of mistakes. A later writer [H. B. Wheatley in *The Cambridge History of English Literature* (see excerpt dated 1911)] arrives at a sounder conclusion when he assigns distinction to the *Diary*, due partly to "the absolute sincerity and transparent truth of the narrative" and partly to "the vitality of the man and his intense interest in the pageant of life"; and then points out that the supreme merit of his style lies in the fact that it is suitable to the character of what the diarist had to relate. As the author is his only reader, he never writes for effect. He does not emit correct sentiments with one eye on the public, but delivers himself of his real mind. The result is that he writes simply and without effort, in words that exactly express his thoughts about people and things. Any attempt at elegance would have destroyed the characteristic charm of the *Diary*, because it would have disfigured with insincerity a literary work which is absolutely sincere. It is scarcely too much to say that we have here the perfection of style, because it is so entirely appropriate to the purpose for which it is used.

How profoundly the character of style can be modified by the introduction of a public can be seen in the other writings of Pepys himself. The narrative of his voyage to Tangier in 1683, his journal in Spain, and his account of the voyage home, are dull and pedestrian records of daily happenings, only rarely illuminated by the penetrating observations and criticisms which the *Diary* so freely dispenses.

> 1683. August 12. Sunday—Morning, prayers and sermon by Dr. Ken; prayers in the afternoon. Evening, came the Cleveland yacht with the money for Tangier. Sir J. Berry sailed, and we came to anchor again. Mr. Bankes went to Windsor.

How insipid is this entry in the *Tangier Journal* after the lively descriptions of earlier Sundays which are to be found in the *Diary*; and the rest is all of a piece with it, for Pepys is playing up to his reputation as a serious naval administrator. The author is very observant and makes interesting remarks about discipline and navigation. He finds "Spanish onions mighty good"; he is "uneasy with the chinchees or musquittoes"; he suffers from "a mighty cold" that made him dumb; he hears "a silly sermon"; and he writes "a merry, roguish, but yet mysterious" letter,— but the life and sparkle have gone, and the greater part of the *Tangier Journal* might have been written by any dull official.

If the style of this Journal has little in common with that of the *Diary*, still less has Pepys's official correspondence preserved in the *Admiralty Letters*. This is always perfectly clear and business-like, but ponderous and processional. The sentences are long and labyrinthine, in which "the thread of thought winds deviously through an infinity of dependent clauses, but the thread is never lost, and the reader always arrives in the end at the destined goal." One letter contains a single colossal sentence of 333 words, yet the grammatical construction is faultless and the sense is absolutely clear. Pepys's only acknowledged work, the *Memoires of the Royal Navy, 1679-88,* published in 1690, is written in much the same style, and one of the sentences runs to 247 words. The official speaks in quite a different tone to the diarist, but in both cases the style is admirably adapted for its purpose.

When he corresponds as a "virtuoso" with other collectors and men of taste, Pepys adopts yet another literary style, as far removed from that of the *Diary* as it is possible for a style to be. He models himself on his friend Evelyn, and writes letters which are strained, artificial, and full of cryptic allusions and "coagulated compliment." In a letter of September 1693 to Dr. Charlett, Master of University College, Oxford, the earlier Pepys flashes out for a moment through the obscurity of the later style. After apologising for the "clamminess" of his memory, he refers to "Mr. Wood's no-mortification, and the further kicks he means to expose his teeth to from the heels of truth." A later letter to the same correspondent, written on November 9, 1698, concerning Mr. Isted's election as a Fellow of the Royal Society, is however a more typical specimen of the "virtuoso" at his simplest; his more contorted productions are all too long for quotation.

> I did with great pleasure join in the unanimous election of him . . . into our Society at Gresham College; and

that therefore, besides your commands and his own apparent merits, I am now by colleagueship become his humble servant and honourer, and by your leading me to it will as an elder brother take upon me to read to him (as he favours me with opportunities for it) upon the great subject of this world out of a register I carry about me of my own mistakes in it.

Simple and almost homely as the style of the *Diary* is, it sometimes attains a high level of literary distinction, and there are to be found in it not a few gems of English prose. Pepys's account of his first sight of the Fire, on Sunday September 2, 1666, is as a whole extraordinarily impressive. He and his friends took refuge upon the water and found themselves under "a shower of fire-drops."

> When we could endure no more upon the water, we to a little alehouse on the Bankside, over against the Three Cranes, and there staid till it was dark almost, and saw the fire grow; and, as it grew darker, appeared more and more, and in corners and upon steeples, and between churches and houses, as far as we could see up the hill of the City, in a most horrid malicious bloody flame, not like the fine flame of an ordinary fire. . . . We staid till, it being darkish, we saw the fire as only one entire arch of fire from this to the other side the bridge, and in a bow up the hill for an arch of above a mile long: it made me weep to see it. The churches, houses, and all, on fire and flaming at once; and a horrid noise the flames made, and the cracking of houses at their ruine. So home with a sad heart. . . .

In contrast with this is a charming pastoral scene on Epsom Downs on July 14, 1667. Pepys sprained his right foot when leaping down a little bank, but the pain passed off,

> And so the women and W. Hewer and I walked upon the Downes where a flock of sheep was; and the most pleasant and innocent sight that ever I saw in my life— we find a shepherd, and his little boy reading, far from any houses or sight of people, the Bible to him; so I made the boy read to me, which he did, with the forced tone that children do usually read, that was mighty pretty, and then I did give him something and went to the father and talked with him. . . . He did content himself mightily in my liking his boy's reading, and did bless God for him, the most like one of the old patriarchs that ever I saw in my life, and it brought those thoughts of the old age of the world in my mind for two or three days after.

In his account of the funeral of Sir Christopher Myngs, who had been mortally wounded in action on the last day of the great battle with the Dutch off the North Foreland, June 1-4, 1666, Pepys reaches his highest plane. He was present at the funeral in a coach with Sir William Coventry, at which, he tells us,

> there happened this extraordinary case—one of the most romantique that ever I heard of in my life, and could not have believed but that I did see it; which was this:—About a dozen able, lusty, proper men come to the coach-side with tears in their eyes, and one of them that spoke for the rest begun and says to Sir W. Coventry, 'We are here a dozen of us that have long known and loved and served our dead commander Sir Christopher Mings, and have now done the last office of laying him in the ground. We would be glad we had any other to offer after him, and in revenge of him. All we have is our lives; if you will please to get his Royal Highness to give us a fireship among us all, here is a dozen of us,

out of all which choose you one to be commander, and the rest of us, whoever he is, will serve him; and, if possible, do that that shall shew our memory of our dead commander and our revenge.' Sir W. Coventry was herewith much moved (as well as I, who could hardly abstain from weeping), and took their names, and so parted; telling me that the would move his Royal Highness as in a thing very extraordinary, which was done.

No more touching tribute than this has ever been paid to the memory of a great seaman, nor better evidence given of the simple loyalty of sea-faring men which in their descendants has served us so well of late. "The truth is," continues Pepys,

> Sir Christopher Mings was a very stout man, and a man of great parts and most excellent tongue among ordinary men.... He had brought his family into a way of being great; but dying at this time, his memory and name... will be quite forgot in a few months as if he had never been, nor any of his name be the better by it; he having not had time to will any estate, but is dead poor rather than rich.

A writer who was alive to the pathos of this scene and could describe it in a style which comes so near distinction, reflecting with dignity upon the swift passing of human greatness, is something more than the "delightful old diarist" and "garrulous gossip" which he has been called by undiscerning readers; but it is characteristic of Pepys that he should conclude his entry for the day with an anti-climax: "In my way home I called on a fisherman and bought three eeles, which cost me three shillings." (pp. 204-11)

> *J. R. Tanner, in his* Mr. Pepys: An Introduction to the Diary, *G. Bell and Sons, Ltd., 1925, 308 p.*

J. R. TANNER (essay date 1926)

[*In the following excerpt, Tanner considers the method and purpose of Pepys's* Naval Minutes.]

The volume entitled **Naval Minutes** is the only one of the "Sea-Manuscripts" in the Pepysian Library at Magdalene College, Cambridge, which is entirely personal to Pepys. It contains notes made by him, mainly during his two periods of retirement, for his projected History of the Navy, and shews the wide range of his researches, and the progress which he had made in collecting his materials.

The first mention of the scheme occurs in the *Diary*, under date June 13, 1664, when he talked with William Coventry

> of a History of the Navy of England, how fit it were to be writ; and he did say that it hath been in his mind to propose to me the writing of the history of the late Dutch War, which I am glad to hear, it being a thing I much desire, and sorts mightily with my genius; and, if well done, may recommend me much. So he says he will get me an order for making of searches to all records, etc., in order thereto, and I shall take great delight in doing of it.

The History of the Dutch War was undertaken by Evelyn at Arlington's suggestion (Evelyn's *Diary*, February 13, 1669) reinforced by an appeal from the King (June 18, 1670), but the manuscript was unaccountably lost, and only the Preface survived, to be published in 1674 under the title, *Navigation and Commerce, their Original and Progress*. It appears, however, from the **Diary** for January 16, 1668, that Pepys had not abandoned the idea of proceeding with the more ambitious work. He seems to have taken the matter up seriously after his liberation from the Tower in 1679. In January, 1680, Evelyn was impressing upon him the importance of his writing a history of navigation, referring him to Selden's manuscripts and giving him a list of books which he ought to consult. He answers questions propounded to him by Pepys, and from time to time references occur in their correspondence to the progress of the work.

The minutes themselves are fairly copied into the volume by clerks, with occasional additions and corrections in Pepys's own hand; but their arrangement is somewhat chaotic. The earliest dated entry is for July 29, 1680, and, with a few exceptions, they run chronologically until May 23, 1683. A new copyist, writing in a small, cramped hand, then interpolates five pages relating to 1692 in a space in the volume what must have been originally left blank for some other purpose. After this, chronological order is resumed, still with a few exceptions, until the end of 1693, although the period of Pepys's second secretaryship of the Admiralty when official business was absorbing all his attention, is only represented by less than twenty pages. After the end of December, 1693, the entries go back once more to 1679 or 1680.... Chronological order is then resumed with the beginning of 1694, and the last dated minute is for February, 28, 1696. This is some four years before Pepys's health began to fail, and seven years before his death; but we know from his correspondence that as late as January 2, 1700, he was enquiring after Monson's *Naval Tracts*.

The purpose of the **Naval Minutes**, and the conditions under which they were written, prevented the author from applying to them the faculty for methodical arrangement which was one of his special characteristics. His notes were made just as they occurred to him, and they lie in the volume in a confused heap, without any attempt being made to classify them according to subject. Many of the entries are mere memoranda of points to be investigated in the future, and thus problems are stated without being solved, and topics are referred to but are not followed up.

Nevertheless, the contents of the volume constitute an inexhaustible mine of miscellaneous information about sea affairs.... The lines of research which Pepys laid down for himself range from the earliest history of navigation down to the naval problems of his own day, and include a vast variety of subjects. In a couple of colossal sentences he endeavours to take 'a right measure of the knowledge of the ancients in the matter of navigation,' and arrives at the conclusion that the extent of it had been greatly exaggerated. His enquiries into the history of the office of Lord High Admiral begin with 'Marthusius, mentioned by Spelman and others for King Edgar's Admiral', and he has something to say about the Count of the Saxon Shore. He refers to a vast number of ancient and medieval authorities, including Nonnius, Festus, Agellius, and Lilius Gregorius Giraldus. He shews himself impatient of the English claim to the Dominion of the Sea, proposing to collect 'instances of inconveniences which states have suffered by taking to themselves great titles and pretensions beyond what they could maintain'; and in several passages he criticises acutely 'the several strainings of arguments made use of by Mr. Selden for support of his *Mare Clausum*.'

In connexion with shipbuilding, the **Naval Minutes** contain historical information and critical comment of extraordinary interest. In 'Sir Anthony Deane's Observations touching the improvement of the English Navy from foreigners' and elsewhere..., the story is told of the adoption of the frigate, the galley, the galley-frigate, and the yacht; and there are several references to Sir William Petty's experiments with double-bottom vessels. Pepys observes the shipbuilding is no mystery; he quotes with approval a statement by Sir William Petty that two of the best English shipbuilders were incapable of laying down a draught, 'their knowledge lying in their hands so confusedly, so as they were not able themselves to render it intelligible to anybody else'; and he follows Sir Anthony Deane in maintaining 'that no one shape of a ship can be in general said to be the best, for every distinct use requires a different shape.' He also notes that in earlier times ships of war so called 'served only as sea-carriages for the men that went thither to fight in them; whereas now ships are themselves become, by the force of their bodies and guns, instruments both of offence and defence.' The increase in the burthen of ships is assigned to 'within one century or less, namely, upon the invention of great guns, and the employment of them in sea service.' England suffers in her shipbuilding from the neglect of her timber, which is 'suffered to stand about an hundred years too long.... To

Pepys at age 35, by John Hayls. In the author's hand is the manuscript of his song "Beauty Retire."

which let me add, the principal use of the forests being to serve the kings in their pleasures and their ministers to their profits.'

The 'constant and evident hazards of a seaman's life' are compared in parallel columns with those of the land-soldier, to the former's disadvantage; and as 'the seaman's trade' requires 'real drudgery and constant toil,' the English, spoiled by the 'natural plenty' of their country, cannot 'endure it so well as other nations and particularly the Dutch do.' English seamen are unruly and illiterate, and 'love their bellies above anything else,' but their courage 'arises much from the nature and plenty' of their diet. Herrings 'won't go down at this day with our seamen, however I find that they have in former ages done.' 'No kind or degree of the land-education in use among us in England... qualifies a man at all for a sea-employment (as such), or gives him any considerable help towards it,' for 'the very language itself' is 'utterly unintelligible to a land-man.' Why cannot children be taught the use of the compass in schools, 'as slinging was promoted by the mothers among the children of the Baleares'? A voyage or two should 'carry with it the public credit of being one of the first qualifications in a nobleman or gentleman for public trust, in Parliament or elsewhere.'

As we should naturally expect, the **Naval Minutes** contains an abundance of criticism of Pepys's predecessors in office, and especially of the Admiralty Commission of 1679-84, the misdoings of which are exposed in his printed **Memoires of the Royal Navy**. They were 'wholly ignorant' of 'the business of the sea,' and 'would not be obliged by Mr. Pepys's rules.'

> An ignorant pretender to an office has but (by his interest) to get himself put into one, how unfit soever he knows himself, and indisposed for the labour necessary to render him otherwise. For (from all my observation, and more particularly in the Navy) no degree of inexperience or unusefulness, by age or otherways (provided he can but keep himself from making enemies by being troublesome in his office) ever sufficed to turn a man out on't without some provision made for rendering such his removal easy to him by pension or other equivalent, if not advantage.

Even Pepys's own creation, the Special Commission of 1686, did not escape, its members, with the exception of Deane and Hewer, being charged—one with laziness, another with love of pleasure, a third with want of method, and most with lack of zeal.

With these deficiencies Pepys contrasts the knowledge and capacity of Charles II and James, Duke of York. They both 'understood the sea' and were 'mathematical Admirals.' They were easy of access to the builders, and encouraged 'all men of that trade, beginners as well as old practisers, and even assistants and foremen as well as master-builders... to bring their draughts to them' for discussion. They took 'delight to visit the merchant-yards as well as their own,' and to 'honour and assist with their presence no less the merchant builder at his launchings of a new ship of any tolerable consideration, and enquiring after the proofs of them at their return from sea, than [their] own master-builders.' But William III is 'a Prince whose genius seems bent to land-action only.'

In the course of his investigations Pepys is led to father several interesting suggestions: an Order of Sea-

Knighthood, borrowed from Sir Robert Slyngesbie, who had been Comptroller of the Navy at the Restoration; Sir William Petty's idea of an international law of trade, so that 'every man of every nation should find himself at home in any suit, and know how to manage himself therein, as if he were in his own country; just as the Pope, by having his Church service performed in Latin, pretends that every man of his Church knows in every country as well as in his own when he enters into a church what to do and what is in doing'; and a notion discussed with Dr. Plot, that there might be a sort of clearing-house of knowledge set up among the 'Literati and Virtuosi of a nation,' 'by directing him that wants, whither to go for, and him that has, where to communicate what possibly in his hand would remain eternally useless.' Pepys's own suggestions are more prosaic, and more closely concerned with his immediate interest of the sea. He would like an 'express fund' to be 'appropriated by Act of Parliament to the service of the Navy and made indivertible therefrom'; and a permanent council set up for superintending the affairs of the Navy in the intervals of Parliament. He also comments on the want of any proper register of instructions for Ministers sent abroad, 'every Minister of State being almost to begin again to invent instructions for every Minister that is sent abroad to this or that Prince or State, as if it were the first time we had ever sent any thither'; and notes the tendency observable after the Revolution of 1688 for the Cabinet to supersede the Admiralty and send orders direct to the admirals at sea.

The *Naval Minutes* furnish a certain amount of material for the biographer of Pepys, besides that which is associated with his History of the Navy. There is a reference to an idea of his which never took practical shape, of a General Chest on the lines of the Chest at Chatham, but 'to be contributed to from the merchants' service as well as the King's,' and relieving disabled seamen and widows from both services alike. He also had it in his mind to write a Life of Lord Sandwich, and planned the collection of materials for it but he seems to have got no farther. At a great sacrifice of fees due to himself, he suggested the proclamation making unnecessary the renewal of commissions and warrants in the Navy on the Duke of York's surrender of the office of Lord High Admiral in 1673, 'which profits I voluntarily proposed my being prevented of, for the ease of the poor navy officers...And this though the King himself was afterwards to sign all commissions and warrants, whose hand was never before in any age or office made so cheap as to be issued for nothing.' We also learn that Pepys was really the originator of the victualling-contract of 1677, and of the instructions added to the patents of the Comptrollers of the Victualling and the Stores, the Treasurer of the Navy, 'and other Commissioners.' He claims the authorship of the establishments of 1677 for chaplains and for men and guns, and of the proclamation of 1674 forbidding the wearing of the King's flag by merchantmen. He also drafted the new instructions for the office of Lord High Admiral adopted in 1673. He claims credit for his 'personal care' of the Mole at Tangier; for making provision in the Navy Office 'for the collecting and keeping of journals'; and for the 'keeping the guardships by commanders being allowed them.' We find a reference to a scheme for 'the retaining strictly apart the stores laid up for particular ships,' which appears to have been defeated by 'laziness in the yard-officers, impatience and vanity of ship-officers, and the general pretence of

keeping stores from decay.' He prevented 'the provision for maintaining of decayed seamen from Trinity House' from being 'swallowed up by the watermen,' and urged that body 'to the taking into their own hands the sounding of our coasts.' He tells us that he refused to take out a pardon in advance, 'though most of the greatest Ministers of State have and do, and particularly my Lord of Shaftesbury'; and he explains that he took out a patent for the office of Secretary of the Admiralty in 1684 'at the King's own instance and for his only service, by the enabling me to administer an oath.'

It is not unnatural that the *Naval Minutes* should contain a good many references to Pepys's sufferings in Parliament, for these had made a deep impression upon his mind. Although 'few sea-ports in England had two Burgesses to serve them in Parliament qualified like Sir Anthony Deane and me,' he was known there 'under the envious name of Admiral.' He consoles himself, however, with the thought, 'My aim is for the good of futurity, though little deserving it of me.'

Certain characteristic observations remind us of the Pepys of the *Private Correspondence,* and even of the Pepys of the *Diary*. He has no illusions about his countrymen. 'The nature of the English is generally to be self-lovers, and thinking every thing of their own the best, viz. our beef, beer, women, horses, soldiers, religion, laws, etc., and from the same principles are over-valuers of our ships.' He is impatient of inaccurate representations, and complains of 'the ridiculous pageants of ships and trade exposed upon the Lord Mayor's Days,' and the 'scandalous barges made of lighters' that appeared upon the same occasion. The sea is neglected in a country dependent upon it. 'England has taken a knight errant, St. George, for its guardian saint, and not any of the Apostles and other fishermen that would have had more relation to the sea'; but 'the seaman's services' are 'not seen.' 'Art is not an advantage particular to us, it being common to all other nations equal to us, but labour and experience; this making men diligent and painful, whilst art makes them rather idle, proud, and opinionate; and experience it is we must boast of at sea or nothing. More artists miscarry at sea (through their idleness and presumption) than men of experience less knowing.' 'Has any physician in any age offered at a remedy against the sea-sickness?' 'Observe the maliciousness of our English proverb towards the service of the sea, viz. That the sea and the gallows refused nobody. Which is verified too much in our practice of sending none thither but the vicious or poor.'

Critics of the *Diary* have spoken of Pepys as 'credulous,' but in the *Naval Minutes* he is disposed to be sceptical. In what must have been in his day a daring experiment in the Higher Criticism, he dismisses, on technical grounds, the story of Noah's Ark. He also pours contempt upon the report current at the beginning of the Popish Plot that the French had invaded the Isle of Purbeck with 40,000 men, and 'the folly of this nation who should not understand the sea better in so easily swallowing so ridiculous a story.' On the other hand, he refers without comment to the raising of 'a storm at sea by means of witches.'

More personal to himself is the remark that 'The life of a virtuous Officer in the Navy is a continual war defensive, viz. against the Ministers of State, and in particular the Lord Treasurers, in time of peace, and all prejudiced inquisitors and malcontents with the Navy management in time of war.' 'To regulate and reform the Navy seems a work at this day little less than that ascribed to Hercules in his cleansing the Augean stables'; but 'my felicity' is 'known to lie in less room and to be had with less noise (*sub otio literato*) than in the public troubles of life my employment hath been ever exposing me to.'

Perhaps his most striking observation is one that arises out of Pepys's experience as an historian: 'Memoirs are true and useful stars, whilst studied histories are those stars joined together in constellations, according to the fancy of the poet.' (pp. ix-xx)

> *J. R. Tanner, in an introduction to* Samuel Pepys's Naval Minutes, *edited by J. R. Tanner, The Navy Records Society, 1926, pp. ix-xx.*

ARTHUR PONSONBY (essay date 1928)

[*Ponsonby was an English miscellaneous writer who served for a time as private secretary to Queen Victoria. In the following excerpt, he examines the style and substance of the* Diary, *contending that Pepys the diarist merits a high place in the history of English letters.*]

[What] are the chief merits which give [*The Diary of Samuel Pepys*] its unique position among all diaries? First and foremost, Pepys did not write for disciplinary reasons nor . . . for any special reader. He wrote because he enjoyed writing. In this he resembles another very eminent diarist, Sir Walter Scott. Not till he was fifty-six did Scott begin "journalizing", but the obvious enjoyment with which he wrote is the very element which makes his journal such delightful reading. "I am enamoured of my journal," he says, and again, "I think this journal will suit me well".

Nothing is more difficult than the comparison of diaries. Depending as they do on the individuality of the writer, they may be good for very different reasons. A fault in one may amount almost to a merit in another where the treatment is slightly different. Introspection, for instance, can be irritating when it is accompanied by excessive self-depreciation, yet the introspective note is what makes diaries like those of Marie Bashkirtseff and Barbellion specially interesting. Even these, however, are self-conscious and lacking in honesty. Pepys was not introspective and therefore does not suffer from these faults. Amiel was scientific in his self-analysis and quite honest, but no one reads Amiel's journal for entertainment. In the haze of his abnormal analytical self-dissection the atmosphere of his private life is smothered. Learning does not improve a diary. In spite of Evelyn's scholarship his *Diary* is on a very much lower level than that of his friend. This is partly due to his having written it up and epitomised periods. One feels that he registers only what he wanted to be known publicly. It would be interesting to know if in the course of their conversation together either of them had suggested to the other that diary writing was a desirable habit.

Fanny Burney's power of narration is of a higher order than that of Pepys and her capacity of reporting conversations unequalled. But the writer of fiction too often gets the upper hand over the recorder of facts and in the latter part of her diary she becomes diffuse and long-winded. Charles Greville, also an official, confines himself very nearly exclusively to a record of the political history of his day, and, important as his journal is, the colour of individuality is comparatively faint. On the other hand, Benjamin Haydon's diary, one of the most remarkable of English diaries, is charged with his personality. He carries his reader along in amusement at his unrestrained tirades and violent polemics and in amazement at his brilliant pen-portraits of his contemporaries. Known to his friends as a bad painter, a mad eccentric, and an importunate beggar, he was discovered by posterity to be in the midst of all his craziness a very shrewd observer and skilful recorder of the events of his life. But his egotism is excessive, his invective tiring, and his supplications unreadable. The long diary of Lord Shaftesbury gives the man's full life-story; his public spirit and his austerity penetrate in almost every entry. Full and honest as it is, there is no light touch, no entertainment, no observation of the trivialities which give colour and ornament to life, and it is therefore difficult to read. In a lighter vein is Tom Moore's diary. But his pleasant intimate gossip was written for publication.

In some of the diaries of more obscure people we find elements of naïveté and charm which are lacking in the records of those who have had to deal with greater events and have lived among eminent people. Thomas Turner, the Sussex storekeeper, and William Jones, the Vicar of Broxbourne, had special *flair* for diary writing. We get personality and atmosphere, spontaneity and humour unspoiled by any intention of publication. Dr. Edward Dale's few entries of Court life and descriptions of the Princesses Mary and Anne (afterwards Queens) are too scrappy to merit very much attention, but he undoubtedly had something of the Pepysian touch in his gossip. Swift has a witty sparkle, and Byron in his brief attempts an amusing, indiscreet recklessness. Both, however, had readers in view. There is a suggestion of playing to the gallery. In humour and certainly in candour Pepys is their superior.

Pepys in fact can hold his own and surpass all diarists by merits which some of the others have and by merits which none of the others have. . . . [He] was a regular daily writer and his impressions are therefore fresh; his candour is a proof of his honesty, and he had no thought of publication. The genius appears in his power of selecting the incidents and epitomising situations, in the casual jotting of humorous opinions, the marvellous observation of intriguing situations, the restraint in handling the larger events, and the delicacy in which he can lighten them by a whimsical word or phrase, the keen enjoyment in which he reports his good fortune, the optimism and joy which always chases away the gloom of despondency, and the introduction of the intimate, the secret, nay, even the obscene in their proper place with disarming ingenuousness. We laugh with him, we laugh at him, and we are always entertained.

Whether Pepys was moral, scrupulous, learned, or clever has nothing whatever to do with the excellence of his *Diary*. We find all this out when we read it because he tells us everything.

A full and sincere diary is to some extent a revelation. It may be the revelation of expected and characteristic thoughts and opinions; it may be the revelation of unsuspected thoughts and deeds; it may also be the revelation of hitherto unknown qualities, the fact of them being unknown redounding very much to the credit of the diarist. Because of its completeness Pepys's *Diary* is too often judged, so far as he personally is concerned, as a revelation of the weaknesses and moral lapses which were not observed by his contemporaries. But in order to be fair, this nosing out of unsavoury passages and chuckling over his follies and faults must be balanced by the observation of excellent qualities to which he only refers incidentally. He may have been timid and nervous physically; several occasions on which he was frightened are entered perfectly honestly. But in the far more important sphere of moral courage and in kindness to the unfortunate he is shown up in the *Diary* in a very favourable light. For instance when Lord Brouncker, who was no favourite with Pepys, fell into disfavour, Pepys walked with him in Westminster Hall although he "was almost troubled to be seen" with him. He considered him wrongly accused, and declares he is "able to justify him in all that he is under so much scandal for". It was a bold act for a subordinate official to send "a great letter of reproof" to his chief. When Pepys sent his well-reasoned but severe letter to Lord Sandwich on November 18, 1663, he confesses he is "afeard of what the consequences may be". But in discharging what he considered to be an important public duty he had no hesitation.

Again in 1669, when there was question of dismissing officers of the Navy, Pepys writes:

> I have not a mind indeed at this time to be put out of my office if I can make shift that is honourable to keep it; but I will not do it by deserting the Duke of York.

When his cousin Joyce drowned himself Pepys quite unostentatiously took very great trouble to help his widow. He goes and comforts her, "though I can find she can, as all other women, cry, and yet talk of other things all in a breath" At a time when he was under grave suspicion of being a Roman Catholic he almost quixotically invited Cesare Morelli the singer to stay with him as his guest, although Morelli's membership of the Church of Rome told against the Secretary of the Admiralty, who was accused of harbouring a priest.

Other instances could be found, but they must be searched for, because they are never stressed. Pepys was incapable of writing for effect. When he was moved his rapid shorthand correctly conveys his emotion. The description of Sir Christopher Mings's funeral which he attended with Sir W. Coventry is very striking. He gives verbatim the tribute paid to their dead commander by "a dozen able, lusty, proper men" who came to their coach side; and then he adds his own:

> Sir Christopher Mings was a very stout man, and a man of great parts and most excellent tongue among ordinary men.... He had brought his family into a way of being great; but dying at this time, his memory and name will be quite forgot in a few months as if it had never been, nor any of his name be the better for it; he having not had time to will any estate, but is dead poor rather than rich.

The self-conscious writer would have ended there, saying to himself, "I won't spoil that by recording anything else to-day". But Pepys went on. He reports a far from innocent visit to Mrs. Bagwell, and ends up his entry, "In my way home I called on a fisherman and bought three eeles which cost me three shillings". Is it too much to say that the value of what is serious when it occurs is greatly enhanced by a writer who also can admit his incorrigible frivolity?

A sentence in an entry can be very eloquent. An entry of pages may tell you nothing. The length of Pepys's entries varies according to his mood; unlike the over-methodical diarist, he does not confine his report of the day's doings to an equally measured space of page. He writes at some length when in the vein and when events prompt him. But even his short entries reflect his mood and are wonderfully informing. Here is the brief and very comprehensive record of April 10, 1668:

> All the morning at Office. At noon with W. Pen, to Duke of York and attended Council. So to Duck Lane and there kissed bookseller's wife and bought legend. So home, coach, Sailor. Mrs Hannam dead. News of peace. Conning my gamut.

Pepys reflects his mood by the length or brevity of his entries and by the style of his narrative rather than by any deliberate confessions of depression or elation. Often we can picture him writing as when he tells us the candle is going out, "which makes me write thus slobberingly". Or again: "I staid up till the bellman came by with his bell under my window, as I was writing of this very line, and cried 'Past one of the clock, and a cold, frosty, windy morning'"; and could the suggestion of depression be better indicated than it is by the simple word "and" in the concluding sentence on October 9, 1664? "To bed without prayers it being cold and to-morrow washing day."

When he writes at length he is never wearisome. His Sunday outing on Epsom Downs on July 14, 1667, is described at great length. This was purely because he enjoyed it so much, not because anything of importance occurred. As it is one of the prettiest passages in the *Diary*, and as it shows us Pepys not as an official nor as a frivolous townsman, but as an appreciator of simple beauty, a couple of extracts may be given:

> ... the women and W. Hewer and I walked upon the Downes where a flock of sheep was; and the most pleasant and innocent sight that ever I saw in my life—we find a shepherd and his little boy reading, far from any houses or sight of people, the Bible to him; so I made the boy read to me which he did with the forced tone that children do usually read, that was mighty pretty, and then I did give him something, and went to the father and talked with him; and I find he had been a servant in my cozen Pepys's house, and told me what was become of their own servants. He did content himself mightily in my liking his boy's reading, and did bless God for him, the most like one of the old patriarchs that ever I saw in my life and it brought those thoughts of the old age of the world in my mind for two or three days after. We took notice of his woolen stockings of two colours mixed and of his shoes shod with iron both at the toe and heels and with great nails in the soles of his feet which was mighty pretty....took coach, it being about seven at night, and passed and saw the people walking with their wives and children to take the ayre, and we set out for home, the sun by and by going down, and we in the cool of the evening all the way with much pleasure home talking and pleasing ourselves with the pleasure of this day's work....Anon it grew dark, and as it grew dark we had the pleasure to see several glow-worms which was mighty pretty.

A close scrutiniser of diaries will find words in the earlier part of this entry which show that it was not written on the day. They are the words, "for two or three days after". The next two entries are unquestionably written on the day and the explanation comes on the third day, when he writes that he goes to his chamber "to set down my Journall of Sunday last with much pleasure". This shows—and there may be other occasions which cannot so easily be detected—that when he had something very special he reserved the writing of it for a time when he had plenty of leisure, going on meanwhile with the ordinary daily entries.

Another excellent long description of an entirely different scene is the entry on January 1, 1667/68, in which he minutely pictures a gambling scene at "the Groome-Porter's", where all the different types of people and different manners of winning and losing are described. (pp. 81-9)

While the noting of trivialities gives colour to a diary, they can be and are in the case of some diaries insignificant and pointless. With Pepys the trivial note nearly always gives spice and character to his entry. When he meets Sir J. Lawson and has a very short talk with him, this would appear to be an incident not worth recording. But Pepys gives us the reason, "his hickup not being gone could have little discourse with him".

The *Diary* has suffered, as was inevitable, from the extraction of plums, the quotation of snippets, and the abbreviation of entries. Those who have read the full version are better able to judge the painstaking and methodical industry of the man. The full flavour and humanity of a diary can be appreciated only by reading consecutive entries, even though some of them may be devoid of historical interest or even of individual peculiarities. His meticulous recital of the seemingly unimportant has to be studied daily in order that the living man may be clearly discerned. But it is important to remember in attempting to estimate the man from the pages of his *Diary* that we can examine only nine and a half years of the seventy that he lived.

The entries contain no long philosophic or even political disquisitions—just a skilful recital of events. There are no elaborate character sketches with biographical details, but he hits off people in two or three lines certainly without a moment's hesitation as he wrote. A few of these passing comments may be quoted.

> (Major Waters); a deaf and most amourous melancholy gentleman who is under a despayr in love ... which makes him bad company though a most good natured man.

> (Aunt James); a poor religious well meaning, good soul talking of nothing but God Almighty and that with so much innocence that mightily pleased me.

> (Mr. Case); a dull fellow in his talk and all in the Presbyterian manner; a great deal of noise and a kind of religious tone but very dull.

> (Mrs. Horsefield); one of the veriest citizen's wives in the world, so full of little silly talk and now and then a little sillily bawdy.

One can learn a great deal about a man from his observation of other people. Three of these descriptions taken at random from among the many show that he was pleased with simplicity, intolerant of pomposity, and put off by pretentious coarseness. Many fine shades of character may be detected in diary entries always provided that the writer is spontaneous and not consciously describing himself.

Perhaps Pepys's style is not what is called literary; his grammar may be faulty—it often is—his phrasing clumsy. All this does not matter in the smallest degree in diary writing. There are excellent diaries in which phrasing, and even grammar, spelling, and punctuation are all execrable. Charles Russell (1898), a foreman riveter, shows in an unpublished diary that he had no conception of grammar or of spelling, but his lively narrative of his adventures in Africa could not be improved. Your literary man who thinks about his English, his style, his balance, and his epigrams is very unlikely to be a good diarist. There are indeed not many literary men even who are capable of the terse powers of lucid expression sometimes displayed by Pepys. Without sententious epigram he can epitomise an event, a situation, or a character in phrases which would be spoilt by the alteration of a single word. Mother wit often counts more than education.

If diaries are to be classed as literature—and they most certainly ought to be—we must in considering them broaden our judgements and canons of taste with regard to style.

When a man can give you a vivid picture of events and personalities and convey to you his sense of living through his life with all his passing hopes and misgivings, joys and sorrows, petty irritations and high aspirations, and at the same time never weary you but invariably entertain you, his style must have some supreme merit however much it may violate the orthodox standards to which writers are supposed to conform.

There is sometimes a tendency to adopt towards the *Diary* an attitude of patronising amusement, to regard it merely as the effusions of an entertaining scribbler. Such critics seem to suggest that we could all write diaries of this sort if we wanted to or if we tried, and that after a couple of hundred years our records would be read with as much interest and amusement as we find in reading Pepys.

Let anyone try! Many have tried within the last two or three hundred years, and how few in their efforts come within any measurable distance of comparison with Pepys! To write regularly requires discipline. Not all are capable of this to begin with. Always to feel inclination requires a peculiar sort of effort. To epitomise your day so as to give a true picture of it requires special discrimination and power of selection. By power of selection we mean the choice of incident. A mere recital of consecutive incidents is not enough. Certain thoughts and deeds must be detached which may be trivial and not immediately relevant, but they may reflect the outward atmosphere and inward mood and make a reader feel present. This requires skill. After all, every minute of everyone's day is filled. Strother, the York shop assistant, endeavoured to write down *everything* that happened in the day. Of course it was impossible, and he gave up the attempt after two or three days. A sentence or two would have given him in his old age just as vivid an impression of those days as his laborious and almost unreadable effort. But selection, which is perhaps the most important element in a diarist's outfit, cannot be learned. No hard work, preparation, or study will make a man into a good diarist. It is not a matter of conforming to recognised standards. There are none. A good diarist *nascitur non fit*. There is no question of taking advice or of thinking out and cultivating an ingenious method. It all rests with the attitude of mind, the disposition and the instinctive inclination of the writer. Although almost every effort at diary writing has peculiar interest, success depends more on temperament than equipment.

On the other hand, the opposite tendency to regard Pepys as an outstanding extraordinary man and a great wit and observer is equally wide of the mark. As the earlier chapters have shown, he was quite an ordinary man, in no other way exceptionally talented, and as a writer in the literary sense he may quite justifiably be rather severely criticised.

Yet another opinion put forward by those who rightly appreciated Pepys's official pre-eminence is that the *Diary* is a "by-product" of no particular account; that there is nothing remarkable about his writing the *Diary*, that his claim to fame is that he was the "right hand of the Navy", and that such a man should write such a *Diary* if anything detracts from his greatness. There have, however, been many equally admirable, and indeed more admirable, Civil Servants than Pepys whose names are forgotten, whereas in his capacity as a diarist he stands alone. That official work is infinitely more important than writing a diary is a contention that need not be disputed. However, to be merely noteworthy in the one but supreme in the other alters the balance of the comparison.

But in all of these views the central point of interest is missed, a point which is perhaps more psychological than intellectual or literary. It is that an average man, inconspicuous and, although assiduous in his work, by no means specially gifted, should have been able, unsuspected by his contemporaries and even by himself, to perpetrate a work of undoubted genius in a realm which about twenty-five per cent of educated people have privately explored without, except in a very few instances, approaching anywhere near the same result.

So much has been said of the side-lights thrown by Pepys on the events of his day, on the manners, customs, and fashions, and on his own domestic life. But too little has been said of the unsurpassed efficacy of the method in diary writing which his genius adopted and of his temperamental fitness for this self-imposed task.

Pepys's claim to be placed among Men of Letters must rest alone on the *Diary*. The remainder of his literary output is entirely negligible. The claim is well founded, and a by no means inferior position among the immortals has readily been accorded to him. (pp. 90-5)

> *Arthur Ponsonby, in his* Samuel Pepys, *The Macmillan Company, 1928, 160 p.*

R. G. HOWARTH (essay date 1932)

[*Howarth was an Australian literary scholar and poet. In the following excerpt from his 1932 introduction to* Letters and the Second Diary of Samuel Pepys, *he discusses Pepys's*

Second Diary—*the record of Pepys's 1683-84 sojourn in Tangier and Spain—and comments on Pepys's correspondence as a mirror of his post-*Diary *life and personality.*]

Our Mr. Pepys is of course the Pepys of the *Diary*. For us the *Diary* is his personal monument and life's work, although it forms but a portion of his extant writings and covers nine years only—and those not the most important—of his life. It is difficult to realize, with only the *Diary* before us, that life, and the life of Pepys in particular, went on after the tragic conclusion of his daily record; yet it did go on, Elizabeth Pepys died, Samuel advanced in power, respect, and wealth, encountered vicissitudes, made many choice friends, and died in 1703 at an age which might well make the *Diary* what it has been called, "an indiscretion of his youth." For the forty or so other years of his mature life, years for which there is no covert record, what was Pepys doing? What sort of man was he before the *Diary*? What were his experiences, and how did he register and comment on them, after 1669? From the *Diary* itself we should have very lively anticipations. But there we are *inside* the man, looking through the window he had made himself on the world; here, with the letters on which we mainly depend for our knowledge, we are peering through a curtained pane from without. The difference between letters such as Pepys wrote to his friends and *Diary* such as he composed for his own secret self is noticeably wide. But the world intervenes between the *Diary* and the letters.

Still, the just comparison is between *Diary* and letters of the *Diary* period. Beyond that point the divergences are greater, and are only to be explained in the most natural way. We must expect some growth, some differences, to appear in Pepys in the years from 1669 to 1703; we should be prepared to acknowledge the effect of growing public importance and preoccupation with official affairs. We must, in short, be ready to admit that our Pepys of, say, 1689 is not our Pepys of 1669. He cannot be expected to remain constant, except in some ineradicable native qualities. The chances are that the letters of the later period depict Pepys just as truly as the *Diary* of the earlier.... [Indeed, when] he came to keep another diary, he revealed no self differing from the self exposed in his letters. When this is perceived the picture of the mellowed and ageing Pepys emerges, to be set beside that of the wonderfully living figure who enacts before us perpetually the human comedy of the *Diary*. (p. vii-viii)

The difference between the earlier and the later Pepys is well illustrated in the *Second Diary*, which is the record of his observations on his voyage to Tangier in 1683, his travel in Spain, and the return voyage in 1684. The diary is in shorthand, and shorthand might be expected to encourage confidences. Pepys had been forced to give up shorthand in 1669 because of the condition of his eyesight, and though for a short time this improved, there is constant reference to his affliction from 1669 to 1683. Yet occasional recourse was had to shorthand, not for reasons of secrecy, but for speed and convenience. Thus in 1677 he took "Parliament notes" in shorthand, and marked them: "To be transcribed in longhand" On September 13, 1683, at Tangier, he speaks of being "with my Lord in his cabin, for him to write, in long-hand, from my short-hand notes, which I read, my arguments for destroying Tangier" Throughout his life he made occasional copies of letters in shorthand. What, we may well ask, considering the character of the *Second Diary*, was his reason (other than convenience) for employing shorthand in it? It is true that his mission was secret, but he knew little of its importance when he began to chronicle the events following his departure from London:

> 8. *Wednesday.*—Lord Dartmouth returned to Portsmouth, and entertained, on board, Lord and Lady Gaynsborough; I and my company dining at our lodgings, Dr. Goundy's. So we all went on board, for good and all.

It does seem, however, from an entry of October 3, that Pepys regarded his journal in much the same light as his earlier *Diary*, and found pleasure in keeping it and reading it over:

> After dinner, to my chamber, to carry on this my private journal, ever since Sunday last to this time and place; and so to read it, being still very foul weather.

But no stronger proof of the fact that Pepys had lost the spirit in which he carried on for nine years his first *Diary* could be found than that here, where the habit was again formed, where he had the opportunity to digress into personalities, he stuck to his task like an official, and permitted himself few irrelevancies. Indeed, Pepys's journal gradually resolves itself into a mere "collection of instances" of abuses by commanders in the king's service: information which he is storing for future use. As some people write verse with distinction in youth, and later lose the power through disuse or preoccupation with other interests, so, it seems, Pepys lost most of the qualities of the impeccable diarist. It will suffice to quote some typical entries, and endeavour to indicate some of his characteristics as a diarist at this time.

A part of the entry for September 23 runs:

> Dr. Trumbull and I have dined at a table by ourselves, to so little content, that we are resolved to break it off from this day. After dinner with my Lord, again read in my chamber; thence to church, where the parson of the parish preached. Here I first observed, outside the church, lizards sticking in the windows, to bask in the sun. At noon, we had a great locust left on the table. This morning, in my chamber, was the most extraordinary spider I ever saw, at least ten times as big as an ordinary spider. With such things this country mightily abounds. But, above all that was most remarkable here, I met the Governor's lady in the pew; a lady I have long remarked for her beauty: but she is mightily altered, and they tell stories on her part, while her husband minds pleasure of the same kind on his. After sermon, I led her down to her chair. Asking her how Tangier agreed with her ladyship, she told me well enough for the little time she had to stay in it. By which I see she knows the mystery.

Although displaying curiosity, observation, and the old interest in pretty women, this is far from equalling even the most ordinary entries in the great *Diary*. The whole *pace* is slowed down to the pulse of middle age. But Pepys still notes what he has for meals: "Merry at supper with wine in saltpetre. Spanish onions mighty good." He still records the changes in his health. He is as ever interested in the minutest personal affairs: "I this day put on my first stuff suit, and left off socks, after many years." "Shaved myself, the first time since coming from England." Enjoyment of music leads him to note such incidents as: "Evening. Rode

with Mr. Sheres to the Mole, and on the shore: harp, guitar, and dance, with Mr. Sheres, in his garden, with mighty pleasure." It is a matter of no small concern to him that he is "infinitely bit with chinchees"; that he is forced to be "up betimes, being uneasy with the chinchees or musquittoes." The characteristic phrase still comes to his pen: "Home to my Lord to supper, having a mighty cold that made me dumb." There even occurs twice at least in the diary that now classic peroration: "And so to bed." He expresses himself with his old bluntness (in secret) towards associates: "Dr. Trumbull . . . a man of the meanest mind as to courage, that ever was born." "So the fool went away, every creature of the house laughing at him." A touch of the old reminiscent enjoyment comes into such entries as: "This day, to clear my head of matters, I wrote many letters to friends in England; among others, a merry, roguish, but yet mysterious one, to S. H." Finally, as though to enable us to pit him as he is now against himself as he was on July 14, 1667, when he etched with unfaltering hand that charming scene on Epsom Downs, ending: "Anon it grew dark, and as it grew dark we had the pleasure to see several glow-worms which was mighty pretty," he notes prosaically: "Walk by moonshine in the fields under the wall, thinking of our affairs: a glow-worm shining; very small compared with what we have in England." The poetry, the joy in life, have disappeared.

Not many more passages that appeal to the lover of the "merry, roguish" Pepys of the sixties can be found. Yet the journal as a whole is not uninteresting. If there is little intimate self-revelation there is at least a consistent character and point of view. We are puzzled sometimes how to reconcile the apparent disconnections in the Pepys of the earlier *Diary*. But now there is a settled nature, a less fluid, a crystallizing personality displayed. Little doubt can be entertained that in this journal Pepys wrote what was in him. Its main fault as a diary is the preponderance of reflection over narration. An observant, serious, withal a dull and unquickened Pepys it reveals to us indeed, and yet at the time of writing he was but in his fifty-first year and not quite at the height of his career. As a document of his mental progression it is then priceless: it shows us, in agreement with the letters, and in spite of its limitations, the sort of man Pepys grew into, after the "indiscretion of his youth."

Neither in his *Second Diary* nor in his letters did Pepys achieve the literary distinction, unsought and unconscious though it was, of his first *Diary*. The *Second Diary* has no claim to be considered as literature. The letters, written under a restraint and sense of personal dignity that became habitual, suffer in proportion, from a purely literary point of view. Pepys rarely wrote simply and candidly. As he grew older he became more and more a formalist, considering a letter as the vehicle of dignified compliment rather than as self-expression. Anxiety about the social proprieties is one of his dominating characteristics. Yet so individual a man as Pepys cannot be concealed by his politeness—even if he can be separated from it. In the letters of the later period we get the real Pepys, only as he is when older and soberer, with a real charm of manner imposed upon his sturdy qualities, just as truly as we do in the earlier *Diary*. The merging of his inner and his outer self becomes complete. One or two of the earlier and historically valuable letters contain graphic descriptions of events Pepys witnessed, in a style like the manner of the

Diary. But these letters are in every way exceptional. As a whole, the letters of Pepys cannot be regarded as a literary possession to be treasured. Amusing though they often are, playful, forceful, "beautifully turned," shrewd, human, and friendly, with their quirks of idiom and unmistakably individual phrasing, they are not comparable to the letters of a Dorothy Osborne or a James Howell. The contrast is particularly marked between the letters of Pepys and of Evelyn, a series which is most significant for the insight it affords into the tempers of the two men, who from polite acquaintances became the warmest of friends. The letters of Evelyn emanate from a rich and cultivated mind, those of Pepys from a sober, earthy intelligence that sedulously emulated where it admired. As Tanner aptly says, Evelyn "pours out literary and classical allusions in his somewhat involved and contorted style, and Pepys, labouring after him at a considerable distance, imitates the contortions without being able to reproduce the decorative effects." Yet Pepys was not a literary man. He has come to be regarded so purely by accident, and it is unwise to seek for what he proved to be incapable of giving. In a letter to Dr. Charlett on August 4, 1694, he provides his sufficient excuse: "... being (God knows)", he says, "not only noe prætender to, much lesse Professor of, any of the learned Facultys, but on the Contrary, a Person known to have pass'd the greater and more docible part of my Life, in one unintermitted Cours, or rather Tumult of Businesse, I have had very little Selfe-Leasure to read, and as few Temptations therefore, as Opportunitys of lookeing-out for Curiositys on any other Head, then that whereto I have thus singly beene given-up, I meane the Sea." The interest of these letters is and will be, no doubt, the interest of the personality, habits, opinions, inner evolution, and outer relations of their author. That interest, initiated by the *Diary*, is absorbing. It is impossible to have too much of Samuel Pepys. In spite of obvious changes in himself, we would willingly endure his *Diary* stretched to the length of Evelyn's. But in the absence of that consummation we find in the letters the progress we seek, and the little things about himself which he has accustomed us to rate above all his public history.

The total impression that the later Pepys, the fully developed man, leaves upon us is almost entirely the impression which he sought to make and succeeded in leaving upon his contemporaries; and that is summed up in Humfrey Wanley's private tribute and the judicious panegyrics of Evelyn and the anonymous continuator of Jeremy Collier's *Great Historical Dictionary*. In a letter of March 8, 1700-1 to Dr. Charlett, Wanley says: "I dined to-day with Mr. Isted at Mr. Pepys's, who entertained us with that obliging kindness which engages all that he converses with a love and respect for his person, which time that destroys other things, does digest into a habit, and renders it so perfect that it generally lasts as long as a man's life. Of this there has been many examples; several of Mr. Pepys's friends continuing so, notwithstanding all accidents, till death; and the rest are likely to do the same. This I attribute to his judgment in men and things, in placing his friendships, and showing his countenance on those only whose merit gave them some pretensions thereto." On the day of Pepys's death Evelyn writes in his *Diary*. [see excerpt dated 1703]: "This day died Mr. Samuel Pepys, a very worthy industrious and curious person, none in England exceeding him in knowledge of the Navy.... He was universally beloved, hospitable, generous, learned in many things, skilled in music, a very great cherisher of learned men of whom he had the conversation." Lastly, the unknown "hand" in 1705 presents the same view, and it is the judgment of a personal acquaintance: "... he was a Person of Universal Worth, and in great Estimation among the *Literati* and Men of Science, for his unbounded Reading, his sound Judgment, his great Elocution, his inimitable Style, his Mastery in Method, his singular Curiosity, and his uncommon Munificence towards the Advancement of Learning, Arts, and Industry, in all degrees. To which were join'd the severest Morality of a Philosopher, and all the polite Accomplishments of a Gentleman, particularly those of Musick, Languages, Conversation, and Address." A recent attempt to minimize the importance or individuality of Pepys in his own day neglects or depreciates such evidence. Mingled with our more intimate knowledge of the man, this is the impression we carry away from Pepys's correspondence. (pp. xi-xvi)

> *R. G. Howarth, in an introduction to* Letters and the Second Diary of Samuel Pepys *by Samuel Pepys, edited by R. G. Howarth, J. M. Dent and Sons Limited, 1932, pp. vii-xviii.*

CHAUNCEY BREWSTER TINKER (essay date 1934)

[*A distinguished American man of letters, Tinker played a major role in building Yale University's outstanding collection of primary and manuscript materials relating to James Boswell and Samuel Johnson. He was also a renowned authority on seventeenth- and eighteenth-century English literature and an esteemed lecturer and teacher. In the following excerpt, he evaluates the literary and historical merits of the* Diary.]

I remember to have read somewhere in the pages of Mark Twain the account of a youthful attempt to keep a diary, the result of which was the endless repetition of the simple sentence, 'Got up, washed; went to bed.' I forget what the anecdote was meant to illustrate—the fact that there was nothing in a boy's life worth recording, or the fact that the diarist's art is a difficult one. In either case, I submit modestly but firmly that Mark Twain was wrong. A true diarist will be interesting about anything and about everything; whether the dog has ruined the carpet or a king been seated on his ancestral throne, the true journalist is never dull. The Creator has dispensed him from boring his audience.

Take, for instance, the three incidents of the day recited above: one gets up, one washes, and one goes to bed, all processes sufficiently common—even washing—to seem useless to the literary artist; yet who would spare them from the pages of Samuel Pepys? 'Up and to my office'... 'Up betimes, and to St. James's'... 'Lay in bed, it being Lord's Day, all the morning, talking with my wife; then up.' I find that I resent the entries in his *Diary* that lack this familiar beginning, as though something essential had been omitted. As for the companion phrase, consecrated to the close of day, it has in our own time achieved such popularity that it bids fair to be permanently enshrined in the daily speech of men, and cease to be recognized as a quotation: 'And so to bed....' Sentiment will ultimately make an epitaph of it, like 'Say not good-night,' or 'Good-bye, proud world.'

As for bathing, that may be the most exciting of events, as the poets know: 'the cool silver shock of the plunge,' whether it be into the 'pool's living water' or into the chilly waters of the domestic tub. 'One clear, nice, cool squirt of water o'er your bust.'

> Up, and to the office ... where busy till noon, and then my wife being busy in going with her woman to a hot-house to bathe herself, after her long being within doors in the dirt, so that she now pretends to a resolution of being hereafter very clean. How long it will hold I can guess.

> 22nd. Lay last night alone, my wife after her bathinge lying alone in another bed. So cold all night.

> 25th. Thence home to the office, where dispatched much business; at night, late home, and to clean myself with warm water; my wife will have me, because she do herself, and so to bed.

Verily, nothing that is human is alien to the diarist. For him life contains nothing that is common or dull. Let him tell us what he ate for dinner, or how cold he was in bed, or how a duchess smiled on him, or what is his balance at the bank, or how he has lost his faith in God, or regained it, or been snubbed by a rival, or cursed his enemy in his heart, or cast eyes of desire upon the parlor maid—all is grist to his mill. How near is grandeur to our dust! How easily does this mortal put on immortality!

But immortality is bought at a price, even by the diarist. It is a razor edge, as the Mohammedan tells us, across which the aspirant to Heaven must make his way. And the diarist, like the rest of us, is in perpetual danger of damnation for his sins. He may make much of them in his journals, and even delight us by his own delight in them: but he must not take pride in displaying them. He would do well to set down naught in the hope of admiration or in the fear of derision. Thus, if a genuine diarist records that he was cold in bed, he does so with a childlike simplicity, as a grievance, as a count against his wife, or as a humble, human fact; but the gods forbid him to enjoy the sensation of being clever at his work. As soon as he becomes clever, attending to his style and aspiring to smart phrase and graceful posture, he is a self-conscious artist, a skillful operative. He may, with luck, become Shaw or Mencken, but he will never be a Samuel Pepys. The artist seeks, properly enough, success and applause; but the diarist is not concerned with such matters. He is not permitted to anticipate or even to desire them. When once his record is complete, he may realize, I suppose, in some dim fashion that he has prevailed over oblivion, so that he cannot destroy his work, even though he may, so far as the outward and surface part of him is concerned, be unwilling that any eye save his own should ever see what he has written. (pp. 153-54)

Perhaps the most recent diary published is that of the Yorkshire parson, the Reverend Benjamin Newton, a typical sporting clergyman of the early nineteenth century, who was interested in everything about him, except perhaps the souls of his flock. Like Pepys, he was acutely susceptible to the charms of the other sex, and listed handsome women in numerical order, according to their beauty of (*a*) face and (*b*) figure. He is perpetually entertaining because of his unfailing vivacity. This is the quality which endears Pepys to his readers:—

> I home to set my journall for these four days in order, they being four days of as great content and honour and

pleasure to me as ever I hope to live or desire, or think any body else can live. For methinks if a man would but reflect upon this, and think that all these things are ordered by God Almighty to make me contented ... in my life and matter of mirth, methinks it should make one mightily more satisfied in the world than he is.

Neither syntax nor theology here is beyond criticism, but what vitality it reveals, what sincerity, what contentment! I like to think that the gratitude of young Mr. Pepys was acceptable to his Creator.

> So dispatched all my business, having assurance of ... all hearty love from Sir W. Coventry, and so we staid and saw the King and Queene set out toward Salisbury, and after them the Duke and Duchesse, whose hands I did kiss. And it was the first time I did ever, or did see any body else, kiss her hand, and it was a most fine white and fat hand. But it was pretty to see the young pretty ladies dressed like men, in velvet coats, caps with ribbands and with laced bands, just like men. Only the Duchesse herself it did not become. They gone, we with great content took coach again, and hungry come to Clapham about one o'clock, and Creed there too before us, where a good dinner ... and so to walk up and down in the gardens, mighty pleasant. By and by comes by promise to me Sir G. Carteret, and viewed the house above and below, and sat and drank there, and I had a little opportunity to kiss and spend some time with the ladies above, his daughter, a buxom lass, and his sister Fissant, a serious lady, and a little daughter of hers that begins to sing prettily. Thence with mighty pleasure, with Sir G. Carteret by coach, with great discourse of kindnesse, with him to my Lord Sandwich, and to me also; and I every day see more good by the alliance. Almost at Deptford I 'light and walked over to Half-way House, and so home, in my way being shown my cozen Patience's house, which seems, at distance, a pretty house. At home met the weekly Bill, where above 1,000 encreased in the Bill, and of them in all about 1,700 of the plaguc, which hath made the officers this day resolve of sitting at Deptford, which puts me to some consideration what to do. Therefore home to think and consider of every thing about it, and without determining anything, eat a little supper, and to bed, full of the pleasure of these 6 or 7 last days.

All this mighty pleasure in the midst of a plague-stricken city! Terror hangs over the world like an ever-blackening cloud, but the diarist's appetite for existence endures undiminished. And so it remains to the end of the journal, when, with the dread of blindness descending upon him and faced with the necessity of closing his *Diary*, he can still record:—

> Dined at home, and in the afternoon by water to White Hall, calling by the way at Michell's where I have not been many a day till just the other day, and now I met her mother there, and knew her husband to be out of town. And here je did baiser elle, but had not opportunity para hazer some with her as I would have offered if je had had it. And thence had another meeting with the Duke of York, at White Hall, on yesterday's work, and made a good advance: and so, being called by my wife, we to the Park, Mary Batelier and a Dutch gentleman, a friend of hers being with me. Thence to 'The World's End,' a drinking-house by the Park; and there merry, and so home late.

No trace is here of gloom or apprehension; yet the sentences speed forward to the most pathetic utterances of the great *Diary*. Even as he prays for mercy in the blindness which he believes to be coming on him, he does not forget his 'amours to Deb' and all 'other pleasures' which his eyesight now compels him to resign.

This very quality in which Pepys excels was well described by another great writer of journals:—

> The minds of some men are like a dark cellar—their knowledge lies concealed; while the minds of others are all sunshine and mirror, and reflect all that they read or hear in a lively manner.

These are the words of James Boswell, a man who, quantitatively at least, rivals Pepys as a diarist. Pepys covers but nine years; Boswell, who had no trouble with his visual organs, remained an inveterate journalist to the end, and, no doubt, presented himself at the gate of Heaven notebook in hand. Now Boswell was a vastly less healthy person than Pepys; he suffered through life from a recurrent melancholia which introduces the strangest lights and shadows into his journals; but in his happier hours he had to a very high degree indeed the passion of which I have been speaking. Johnson himself described Boswell's fondness for the metropolis as a '*gust* for London.' And there are other powers which Pepys and Boswell share.

Both, for instance, were collectors. Both belong to that hungry set who save things, who gather relics and preserve souvenirs, who love long rows of well-filled shelves and all the paraphernalia of a library. These men leave treasures to posterity.

There is an intimate connection between this mania and the relish of existence which both men display so noticeably. It is because of his gusto that the diarist attempts to preserve some memorial of it, however inadequate. He cannot bear to think that experiences so rich should perish without leaving a rack behind, and he therefore enters into mortal combat with oblivion. The closer his record to the event itself, the more nearly satisfied he will be. Boswell provides many amusing examples of this desire for verisimilitude. Once when he sent his friend Temple as a sort of ambassador to the young lady with whom he was, or thought he was, in love, he provided him with a long series of detailed directions, the most pointed of which is the command, 'Take notes.' By taking notes, you see, the ambassador may hope to preserve not only the *ipsissima verba* of the interview, but even the very atmosphere and tone of it. The incident will be preserved, as book collectors say, 'in the original condition.' As long as the scenes of one's past are dear to the heart, so long will a man try to prepare for his future nostalgia by the writing of diaries and the preservation of relics. A true diarist is like a great portrait painter who takes his own likeness. The *Diary* of Mr. Pepys is, in a way, the greatest *Selbstbildnis* ever painted. 'A man loves to review his own mind,' said Johnson to Mrs. Thrale; 'that is the use of a diary or journal.' To whom Lord Trimlestown, who was present, said, 'True, Sir. As the ladies love to see themselves in a glass, so a man likes to see himself in his journal.' (pp. 155-57)

[There] is no carelessness or inaccuracy, or rhetoric, no heightening and coloring, in Pepys or Boswell. Both men were professionally concerned with recording facts: Pepys was engaged in filing records for the Naval Office—lists of battleships, with their tonnage and personnel, their movements and their whereabouts, and thousands upon thousands of similar details of no special interest to posterity. Boswell, as a Scotch lawyer, had to present his cases to the court in written form. Such work begets in a man a sense of fact, and a respect for the moving finger of time. He is not likely to date an important letter 'Wednesday.'

Much of our pleasure in reading Pepys springs from our conviction of its authenticity. It is this that sweeps us along, page after page, over the names of persons of whom we know nothing. But we do know that they are real, like the persons whom we pass in the street, even though we can tell nothing whatever about them. Some of them are acquainted with Pepys, and we are acquainted with him—that is sufficient. With a few of them we, too, become better acquainted as we read on, so that, if we persevere, we find our pleasure constantly mounting, since our knowledge of what is going on is gradually clarified. We shall never come to a perfect vision of it all—even the most painstaking research will never attain to that—but life as it was three hundred years ago, and Samuel Pepys in his habit as he lived, these we may come to know.

Let us not mistake. Pepys is not great merely because he brings us into contact with the exciting events of his time. True, he lived through the *annus mirabilis* of 1666, and so had intimate personal knowledge of the defeat of the Dutch fleet, the great plague that swept over the city, and the Great Fire which swept over it in a more literal sense. These are important events, as are a thousand others with which Pepys brings us in contact, and so the *Diary* is an invaluable source book for historians. But this is not the reason that Pepys has the devotion of his readers.

The fact is that the man had the fine art of making his record sparkle with vitality. I cannot analyze that gift. I have never met anybody who could. Most essays on Pepys—and there are many delightful ones—rely for their charm on liberal quotations from the *Diary*. The more quotations, the more charm. The essayist usually contents himself, as in the present instance, with a characterization of the man, not with a critical analysis of his style. How shall one show the component parts of anything so artless?

Yet Pepys was an artist, and I believe that he knew it. It would be more accurate to say that he came in time to know it. It seems to me preposterous to try to believe that a man who has produced a vast work of genius should be unaware of what he has done. He may very well have been ignorant of its largest relations and of its permanent value to mankind; but that he should have had no intimation of its pictorial and panoramic quality, no realization of the fact that it plumbs the depths of human nature—this is to me beyond belief. I should as soon expect the builder of the pyramids to be unaware of the shape which he had erected.

And I believe, furthermore, that it was this knowledge of what he had done that prevented Pepys from destroying or ordering the destruction of the *Diary*. He could not do it, nor do I think that another man who had created such a thing (if we may tolerate such an assumption) could bring himself to destroy it. For Pepys it would have been a kind of suicide.

He was aware, of course, that it could be readily decoded,—was not the same code used in his office?—and, indeed, a cipher that cannot be decoded, if such there be, would be simply a form of oblivion. And yet there was a certain protection in it. A cipher does furnish a screen against casual observation; a long diary, like that of Pepys, might hope to survive many years unread. After a lapse of a couple of generations, secrecy was no longer of consequence. This was perhaps, consciously or subconsciously, what Pepys wished. He wanted privacy—protection, that is, from the inquisitiveness and derision of his neighbors; and this the cipher afforded, and would probably continue to afford as long as any of his contemporaries remained alive. To most of us posterity hardly matters. The genial soul of Pepys may very well have been content to meet it, and entrust his reputation to it. I cannot see why any man should shrink from that. It is one's neighbors and relatives whom one wishes to elude. In the masquerade of life a man does not care to give himself away. It is a world in which we are all making a plucky pretense. One takes conscious pride in 'getting away' with one's pose, and none more so than Pepys in public life. But there is solid comfort in making a clean breast of it, whether one is purging the stuffed bosom of the perilous stuff that weighs upon the heart or merely setting down the various devices by which he has succeeded in snatching the pleasures of existence as they fly. But it is so hard to get a hearing and to utter all that one would like to say! Confessors, I have been told, find some difficulty in persuading their penitents to abridge the tale of their sins. 'No excuses, please; no details,' they must be always hinting. But the diarist feels no such restraint, and hears no such monitor. He may go on forever.

And as for being read by posterity, is there not a certain pleasure in that, even though everything has to come out? It is certainly no worse than dying and meeting the Recording Angel, which is the experience that awaits us all. But, thanks be to God, it is an angel, and not our neighbors, our wives, or our professors whom we have to meet. Perhaps it will not be so bad after all. Who knows but there may be a solid satisfaction in it, upon getting a hearing at last? The angel will probably do the best he can for us. It is the way of angels.

Posterity has been friendly to Pepys. Not even an angel, I imagine, could have been more indulgently kind. Where is there an author more beloved by his readers? Boswell is still despised by multitudes, Walpole is disliked, Cowper pitied, and Rousseau distrusted. But Pepys is like Lamb, loved by everybody. I have encountered but one sneer at Pepys, and that was from the pen of a Communist, writing for the *New Masses*, one Michael Gold:—

> Samuel Pepys is esteemed by bourgeois readers because he did the things they do, or want to do: he accepted bribes, he dodged his taxes, he was unfaithful . . . to his wife, he beat his servants.

In the new world of Communism there will, I suppose, be none of these dreadful things, for sin and the knowledge of it will have been abolished (by law), and nobody will care whether he is loved by posterity or not. (pp. 157-59)

Chauncey Brewster Tinker, "The Great Diarist," in The Atlantic Monthly, *Vol. 153, No. 2, February, 1934, pp. 153-59.*

S. C. ROBERTS (essay date 1958)

[*Roberts was a noted English essayist, editor, biographer, and translator. He wrote widely on the lives and literary careers of Samuel Johnson and James Boswell and was known as an investigator of chronology and other matters relating to Sherlock Holmes and Dr. Watson. In the following excerpt, he compares Pepys and Boswell as diarists.*]

Samuel Pepys and James Boswell have frequently provoked comparison. Each was the author of a classic, and the *Life of Samuel Johnson* and the *Diary* have long been admitted to the category of books which no gentleman's library should be without; they also have the much rarer distinction of being two of the most widely read and the best loved narratives in the English language.

The backgrounds of the authors and the circumstances of composition were, of course, widely different. (p. 24)

[The *Diary*] has rightly been hailed as a work of art, but it was a work of unpremeditated, rather than of conscious, artistry.

As he faithfully recorded, day by day, his doings and his misdoings, Pepys had no feeling that he was laying the foundations of a posthumous literary fame. Not that he was without ambition—he was very properly ambitious to be an efficient public servant, to acquire the means to establish a gentleman's household, and to make a good collection of books. In due time all these aims were achieved; but such has been the fame of the *Diary* that it is only in the present century that Pepys's great services to the state, and to the Admiralty in particular, have been fully recognised.

At once this suggests a Boswellian parallel and a Boswellian contrast. Writing in 1874 Lord Houghton remarked that 'it was the object of Boswell's life to connect his own name with that of Dr Johnson'. This is the kind of half-truth which for many years obscured the full range of Boswell's literary and social ambitions. His *Life of Samuel Johnson* was quickly recognised as the greatest biography in the language and has maintained its supremacy; but it is only in the last thirty years that Boswell has been properly estimated as an author in his own right rather than as the faithful follower of the Great Lexicographer. (pp. 24-5)

Pepys's diary is a neat and orderly document embodying the detail of nine and a half years; Boswell's journals, letters and memoranda sprawl over forty years. No longer is it true to say, as Tanner said, that 'we have more intimate knowledge of Pepys than of any other personality of the past'. Pepys's diary has been described as an indiscretion of his youth; Boswell's papers reveal the improprieties of a lifetime.

This is, indeed, the outstanding difference between the careers of the two men: the record of Pepys's later life is the record of supremely successful and valuable service in Parliament and in naval administration; Boswell, too, aimed at distinction at the bar and longed to enter the House of Commons, but in this he failed miserably; it was only in his literary ambitions that he achieved fulfilment—an achievement which is the more remarkable as the full story of Boswell's way of life is revealed. For to the end he persistently failed to resist the allurements of

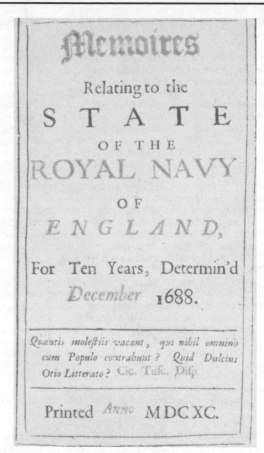

Title page of Pepys's Memoires relating to the State of the Royal Navy of England *(1690).*

wine and women, and it is sometimes difficult to imagine how his hours of sobriety sufficed for the compilation of his biographical masterpiece. Pepys, too, in his younger days frequently drank too much—but not on the Boswellian scale.

> Home and to bed [he recorded on 9 March 1660]. All night troubled in my thoughts how to order my business upon this great change with me that I could not sleep and being over-heated with drink I made a promise the next morning to drink no strong drink this week, for I find that it makes me sweat and puts me quite out of order.

Again on 29 September 1661:

> I drink I know not how, of my own accord, so much wine that I was even almost foxed and my head aked all night; so home and to bed, without prayers, which I never did yet, since I came to the house, of a Sunday night: I being now so out of order that I durst not read prayers for fear of being perceived by my servants in what case I was. So to bed.

So, on the last day of the year, he took a solemn oath to abstain from plays and wine and found himself much better for it, but in February he had reason to fear that 'by my too sudden leaving off wine, I do contract many evils upon myself'.

With the stories of Pepys's infidelities all readers of the *Diary* are familiar. Mrs Pepys was not unnaturally suspi-

cious of Mrs Martin, Mrs Pierce, Mrs Knipp and the rest, and when she caught her husband in October 1668 in the act of embracing Deb, it occasioned the greatest sorrow to Pepys that ever he knew in this world. But three weeks later he contrived to meet Deb again in a coach and told his wife a 'fair tale' when he got home. But Mrs Pepys was not deceived, and after a stormy scene Pepys promised never to offend more, praying God for grace more and more every day to fear him and to be true to his poor wife. But, alas, Pepys's promises were tinged with a Boswellian frailty. Pepys could never resist a pretty face, but he had no feeling for promiscuity. Boswell ranged over a wider field. 'I ought to be a Turk,' he once wrote, 'I believe I should make a very good Sultan', and in the *Journals* already published which record his early adventures in London, Holland, Germany, France and Italy his innumerable affairs, whether with countesses or with drabs are described with a frankness of detail far exceeding the confessions of Pepys.

With Boswell it was no mere sowing of wild oats. He married a good woman and was conscious of her goodness; but except for comparatively short periods he never attained to a self-control sufficient to make him live a decent life. The Edinburgh journal of the 1770's is a wearisome record of drunkenness and debauchery, relieved only by Boswell's extraordinary candour. Thus on 28 August 1776 he writes:

> I drank too much. We had whist after dinner. When I returned to town, I was a good deal intoxicated, ranged the streets, and having met with a κομελυ, φρεσχλοοκιυυ υιγλ, μαδλυ υεντυρεδ to λυε ωιτχ χερ . . . I told my δεαρ ωιφε immediately.

It is the last sentence that is so characteristically Boswellian—and so unlike Pepys. Similarly, on 10 April 1780:

> Dined at Dr Gillespie's with Commissioner Cochrane, Dr Webster and John. Was in sound spirits, but drank so as to be intoxicated a good deal, so that I ranged an hour in the street and dallied with ten strumpets. I had however caution enough left not to run a risk with them. Told my valuable spouse when I came home. She was good humoured and gave me excellent beef soup, which lubricated me and made me well.

Poor Mrs Boswell! She had married with her eyes open, but she can hardly have been prepared for all that she had to endure. She read her husband's journal from time to time and in principle disapproved of it. Even Boswell had doubts sometimes. On 30 July 1779 he wrote:

> Were my Journal to be discovered and made publick in my own lifetime, how shocking would it be to me! And after my death, would it not hurt my chidren? I must not be so plain. I will write to Dr Johnson on the subject.

But whatever Dr Johnson said, Boswell adhered to his policy of self-revelation. 'I have a kind of strange feeling', he wrote, 'as if I wished nothing to be secret that concerns myself.'

Boswell's persistent intemperance in relation both to wine and women must not blind us to the brilliance of his reporting. The diaries that he kept during his visits to London are, in fact, the core of his immortal biography and his description of evenings at the Club, or at the Mitre, or at a dinner-party of which Johnson was the central figure are, by general consent, the high-lights of the work.

Johnson apart, there are many passages in Boswell's earlier journals in which the ingenuousness and the careful observation of detail may well be reminiscent of Pepys.

In 1769 Boswell, fresh from his tour abroad and full of enthusiasm for the cause of Corsican liberty, decided to attend the Shakespeare Festival at Stratford-on-Avon, taking with him the costume of a Corsican chief to wear at the masked ball.

> 6 Sept, 1769: To see a noble band of the first musicians from London, with Dr Arne at their head, Mr Garrick, a number of nobility and gentry and of the learned and ingenious assembled to do honour to Shakespeare in his native place gave me much satisfaction....
>
> At dinner... an Irish lady, wife of Captain Sheldon, a most agreeable little woman, pleased me most. I got into great spirits. I paid her particular attention. I began to imagine that she was stealing me from my valuable spouse. I was most unhappy from this imagination. I rose and went near the Orchestra, and looked stedfastly at that beautiful insinuating creature, Mrs Baddeley of Drury Lane, and in an instant Mrs Sheldon was effaced. I then saw that what I feared was love was in reality nothing more than transient liking. It had no intereference with my noble attachment....
>
> 7 Sept: This was the night of the Ball in Mask, when I was to appear as a Corsican chief. I had begun some verses for the Jubilee in that character. But I could not finish them. I was quite impatient. I went home and forced myself to exertion and at last finished what I intended. I then ran to Garrick, read them to him and found him much pleased. He said the passage as to himself—
>
> 'Had Garrick, who Dame Nature's pencil stole
> Just where old Shakespeare dropt it, etc—'
>
> was both a fine poetical image and a fine compliment. There was a fellow called Fulke Weale here, who advertised printing at an hour's notice, I suppose taking it for granted that Stratford would produce a general poetical inspiration which would exert itself every hour. To him I went. But Mr Angelo's fireworks turned his head, and made him idle. He preferred them to all poetical fire. I then went to the Bookseller and Printer of the Place, Mr. Kaiting. He had a lad from Baskerville's at Birmingham, of Scots extraction, his name *Shank*. I found him a clever active fellow; and set him to work directly. He brought me a proof to the Masquerade Ball about two in the morning. But could not get my verses thrown off in time for me to give them about in my Corsican dress. I was quite happy at the Masquerade. I had been at a Publick Breakfast in the Town Hall, and had tea made for me by my pretty Irish lady, who no longer disturbed me. Tonight she did me the favour to dance with me a minuet while I was in complete armour, and, when I laid aside my arms, a country dance. I got acquainted with Mr Murphy, Mr Colman, Mr Kelly, Mr Foote at this Jubilee... My Corsican dress attracted everybody, I was as much a favourite as I could desire.

It would be difficult to select a happier portrait of the young Boswell than this. At about the same age, on 10 April 1661, Pepys went on an expedition with Sir Wm Batten and others to see the Dockhouses at Chatham. After being hospitably received by Mr Pett and having inspected the good ship *The Prince*, the party went on to Rochester

> and there saw the Cathedrall which is now fitting for use and the organ then a-tuning, Then away thence, observing the great doors of the church which, they say, was covered with the skins of the Danes.... So the Salutacion tavern, where Mr Alcock and many of the town came and entertained us with wine and oysters and other things.... Here much mirth... we had, for my sake, two fiddles, the one a base viall, on which he that played, played well some lyra lessons, but both together made the worst musique that ever I heard.
>
> We had a fine collacion, but I took little pleasure in that, for the illness of the musique and for the intentness of my mind upon Mrs Rebecca Allen. After we had done eating, the ladies went to dance and among the men we had, I was forced to dance too; and did make an ugly shift. Mrs R. Allen danced very well and seems the best humoured woman that ever I saw. About 9 o'clock Sir William and my lady went home, and we continued dancing an hour or two, and so broke up very pleasant and merry, and so walked home, I leading Mrs Rebecca, who seemed, I know not why, in that and other things, to be desirous of my favours and would in all things show me respects. Going home, she would needs have me sing, and I did pretty well and was highly esteemed by them. So to Captain Allen's... and there, having no mind to leave Mrs Rebecca what with talk and singing.... Mrs Turner and I staid there till 2 o'clock in the morning and was most exceeding merry and I had the opportunity of kissing Mrs Rebecca very often...

There is a notable kinship of spirit between these two passages. There is the same pleasure in being a member of a congenial company that is out to enjoy itself; there is the same zest for sightseeing; there is the same appreciation of the pleasures of the table; there is the same enjoyment of flirtation; and there is the same satisfaction in being a popular member of the party. But there is one difference: Pepys, of course, is delighted that Mrs Rebecca should show him such marked favour; but he is quite honest in saying that he did not understand why he should be singled out for such attentions. Boswell, on the other hand, deliberately set out to attract attention. As always, he was dramatising himself. His enthusiasm for Corsican liberty was genuine enough, but he chose to advertise it in a flagrantly ridiculous way. Ridicule he did not mind, provided that he achieved sufficient prominence and that he enlarged his acquaintance with well-known people. 'I was as much a favourite as I could desire'—such was his verdict on the Stratford-on-Avon expedition; for Boswell it was the final, and completely satisfying, verdict and something quite different from Pepys's naïve acceptance of unpremeditated enjoyment.

Not that Pepys was averse from recording his own successes. In his orderly manner he frequently contemplates his steady rise in the world and his record, for instance, of his famous speech in the House of Commons of March 1667/8 bears no mark of false modesty. Having fortified himself with half a pint of mulled sack and a dram of brandy he spoke most acceptably and smoothly for more than three hours, during which many went out to dinner and came back half drunk. But there was a chorus of praise for the speech; the Solicitor-General said that Pepys 'spoke the best of any man in England; the King himself congratulated him; Mr George Montagu said he was another Cicero . . .'. If Boswell had ever approached such success in his career as an advocate, we can well imagine that he would have preserved a similar record of complimentary remarks. But he would not have added, as Pepys did, 'for which the Lord God make me thankful! and that I may make use of it not to pride and vain-glory, but that, now I have this esteem, I may do nothing that may lessen it'.

It was only as an author that Boswell tasted the sweets of universal praise: 'My book has amazing celebrity,' he wrote to Temple after the publication of his book on Corsica in 1768, 'Lord Lyttelton, Mr Walpole, Mrs Macaulay, Mr Garrick have all written me noble letters about it'; and when the *Life* of Johnson had been published in May 1791 he wrote in the following month to John Wilkes: 'You said to me yesterday of my *magnum opus* "it is a wonderful book". Do confirm this to me, so as I may have your *testimonium* in my archives at Auchinleck.'

Pepys, from the very beginning of his public career, was an industrious apprentice and in due time he had his reward. One of his outstanding virtues as a civil servant was his extremely methodical ordering of business; this love of method was similarly evident in the ordering of his household as poor Mrs Pepys found to her cost; and when Pepys gradually secured the leisure and the means to gratify his passion as a collector of books and manuscripts and prints and music, he proceeded in the same orderly manner: 'Up & by & by to my bookseller's, and there did give thorough direction for the new binding of a great many of my old books, to make my whole study of the same binding, within very few' he wrote on 18 January 1665 and three weeks later he noted what a pleasant sight it was to contemplate the uniform appearance of his shelves. But he was not a collector of the omnivorous type. On 2 February 1667 he spent a Sunday morning in setting his books in order and like all collectors he discovered a considerable increase in the course of the year. But he was determined to discipline his library: 'I am fain', he wrote, 'to lay by several books to make room for better, being resolved to keep no more than just my presses will contain.' He was as methodical in destruction as in preservation. At Christmas time 1664 he judged it fit to look over all his books and papers and to tear up all that he found either boyish or not to be worth keeping or fit to be seen, if it should please God to take him away suddenly. Nearly a year before he had made a similar clearance, destroying, in particular, the MS. of *Love a Cheate*, a romance which he had begun ten years before at Cambridge. 'Reading it over,' he writes, 'I liked it very well and wondered a little at myself at my vein at that time when I wrote it, doubting that I cannot do so well now if I would try.'

All this is very unlike Boswell. It is true that occasionally Boswell contemplated some specific field of collecting. Thus on 13 September 1776 he wrote about his trip to Glasgow: 'I went to the College and bought a few little books at Foulis' shop and amused myself with a project of purchasing a compleat collection of the productions of the press of the ingenious brothers, both now dead.' But this was just a passing fancy. What Boswell collected was *Boswelliana*.

The primary point of resemblance between Pepys and Boswell lies in the fact that neither hesitated to enter in his diary the least creditable features of his life and char-

acter, though for the most lurid passages each was driven to a prudent measure of disguise—Pepys to an Anglo-French jargon, Boswell to a Greek transliteration. Each of them was religious in his own way; each of them fell short of the moral standards which his religion enjoined; each of them, when attending divine service, was liable to concentrate his attention upon pretty women. From the social point of view, it is clear that each of them possessed the indefinable and unteachable quality which is commonly called charm. Through his *Diary* Pepys has communicated this charm to generations of readers and there is little need, at this time, to analyse it. Boswell's case is less simple. For many years the paradox of the greatest biography being written by a man of Boswell's character served to baffle the critics. Macaulay's preposterous theory that Boswell wrote a great book because he was a great fool dominated the popular view for many years, but is now very properly discredited. The *Life* of Johnson is, in fact, the product not only of descriptive brilliance, but of patient and industrious research. Despite his drunkenness, despite his frequently nauseating accounts of his sexual licence, there is abundant evidence of Boswell's essentially clubable qualities, of the good humour which made him irresistible in a social milieu. In her famous mark-book Mrs Thrale gave Johnson full marks (20) for Morality and 0 for Good Humour; to Boswell she gave, rather charitably, 5 for Morality, but 19 for Good Humour. As a final fragment of evidence on this point a paragraph from an unpublished letter of Boswell may be cited. It is a letter written to his cousin Robert Boswell from Eton on 30 July 1792, at the end of his son Alexander's last term at school:

> I am here at the delivery of my son Alexander from school. He hastens off to London to-day. But I hover here awhile to contemplate a noble Seminary, which I regret much my not having had the advantage to attend. The Provost and Fellows are wonderfully good to me. This is what is called Election time when the boys are chosen for the foundation at King's College, Cambridge; and there is a deal of feasting in which I share; for they are pleased to hold me as an Etonian by adoption. I own I like the union of luxury and learning.

Boswell was nearing the end of his dissolute life, but it is clear that the Provost and Fellows of Eton were captivated. The charm—a charm of Pepysian quality—was still at work. (pp. 29-39)

> *S. C. Roberts, "Pepys and Boswell," in his* Doctor Johnson and Others, *Cambridge at the University Press, 1958, pp. 24-39.*

PERCIVAL HUNT (essay date 1958)

[*In the following excerpt, Hunt reviews the major themes and subjects of the* Diary, *noting especially the merits of Pepys's prose style.*]

[In the *Diary*] Pepys wrote of his daily affairs. He did not write for the future, or to show wonders and himself to lesser people, or, it seems, even for his own rereading. He wrote a chronicle day by day, a log of his actions, thoughts, and feelings, a direct account of his life, with not many sweeps of philosophy or abstraction. He did philosophize but not usually. He philosophized on his having got his position by favor, on the need that words of a song be left in the language in which they were written, on his lack of lasting sorrow when his brother died, on the conduct of the King and Court ("God knows what will be the end of it!"); on London after the Fire and after the Plague. He wrote of his childhood at Ashted when he went back there at thirty; and he wrote a tremendously effective and self-forgetful account of the Fire. But philosophizing is not the main recurring substance of the *Diary*; it is in the *Diary* because it was part of some day in his life.

Pepys had the luck or the instinct or the determination to be in important places at important times, often in places he has no business to be. Once there, he shoved his way, quite unashamed, to the front. Possibly what he wrote made up for his elbowing. At sixteen he stood close by the scaffold when Charles I was beheaded on a cold January afternoon; and at twenty-six, time having changed his fortune and opinion, he went to see General Harrison, who had signed the King's death-warrant, hanged and drawn and quartered—"a bloody day." He was in London when Oliver Cromwell died; and when Richard Cromwell gave up his ineffectual rule; and while Parliament and the Army struggled; and he watched, one morning in February, 1660, "it being a most pleasant morning and sunshine," General Monk march his men into control of the City ("all his forces . . . in very good plight and stout officers"). He was secretary to the Admiral on the "Royal Charles," which brought Charles II back to England, and he saw him land at Dover and ride away to London "in a stately coach." At the coronation he pushed into the Abbey among the followers of the King's Surveyor-General and from a seat high up under the roof of the North Transept he saw and heard what he could. (At the next coronation, as a baron of the Cinque Ports, he walked close by the King.) When the new Queen (September 21, 1662), whom everybody was curious about, heard her first mass in her Chapel of St. James's, he crowded close up to the altar and to the Queen; and since his cousin was the ambassador and admiral whose ship carried the Queen from Portugal, Pepys heard much about her. He was in London during the Plague, and he watched almost hour by hour the Great Fire. He knew the King, the Duke of York, the Court, and some of the King's ladies. He saw the Established Church return with the Restoration, and the playhouses open, and the old ways come in again, though changed. He had part in the humiliations and triumphs of the endless, intermittent, vital Dutch Wars, and he lived a long time shadowed by the Popish Plot and by the Titus Oates and his like. He had part in the coronation of James II, and four years after that he saw James deposed and William III come. He knew London intimately, places and people, and the quiet English country beyond, and the villages, and the farmlands. He was familiar with workingmen in the City, and the men who kept the little shops and taverns, and their clerks, and the great merchants, and the banker-goldsmiths. He had been at Cambridge with Dryden; for years he talked and often ate with Thomas Fuller of the *Worthies*; he became a friend of "that miracle of a youth Christopher Wren" and of the noble Mr. John Evelyn, and of many such; and he corresponded with Sir Isaac Newton, Sir Hans Sloane, Sir Godfrey Kneller, the Duchess of Newcastle, the Duke of York, and masters and dons at Oxford and Cambridge, and other learned and humane men. Most of them he wrote of in the *Diary*. (pp. 4-6)

Music is a constant topic in the *Diary*. Often for awhile the *Diary* lets music lie unseen below what is told of acts and personalities, yet it soon comes again into expression, for Pepys's interest in music never ended. He writes of his own singing and composing and playing; of listening to the singing and playing of others; of choosing a servant partly because he had a good voice or read music or played the lute; of teaching his wife and his friends and his servants to sing; of studying the science of music—its structure, theory, mathematics; of speculating whether music-charts and other like inventions—were ever a help in composition; of going to hear good music and of his delight when he was surprised by good music heard unexpectedly. At home early and late, and at his friends'; at sea and on the Thames going down to inspect a Shipyard; in his own or in somebody else's garden; at church; at inns and taverns; and in coaches as he traveled on business; in almost every place and in most conditions of mind, Pepys sang or played or heard music, or he talked of it, or read or thought of it. He himself had a pleasant, well-trained voice, and played with skill the flageolet, the lute, and the treble viol. One June evening "it being very hot weather I took my flageolette and played upon the leads [the flat roof of his house] in the garden, where Sir. W. Pen came out in his shirt onto his leads, and there we staid talking and singing, and drinking great drafts of claret, and eating botargo [fish roe "to promote drinking"] and bread and butter till twelve at night, it being moonshine; and so to bed, very near fuddled" (June 5, 1661). There are many such entries, with variations. (p. 119)

Almost nothing has been written about the music in Pepys's prose, about its style. The prose of the *Diary* is admirable. Rhythms (accents heavy and light, and pauses), the sounds of vowels and consonants in the phrasing, the variety and length and arrangement of phrases and sentences and words, all mingle into a fluid whole as the different ideas and feelings follow one another. The reader, unless he is an analyst, does not notice what makes the effect nor does it seem to him that Pepys ever was consciously after an effect. Indeed, Pepys wrote spontaneously; he wrote as he did because he thought and felt as he did and had a great literary gift. Pepys—to put it another way—was absorbed by the facts and by his feelings about them, and he could write prose that carried the facts and the implications, the suggestion, the experience which the facts had for him. His prose has the resonance of his temperament, his character, his abilities. His prose is his personality expressing itself in words.

When he tells a matter dull for him, it becomes dull stuff from the style of telling; when he tells a happy matter, his writing gets the happiness. His Navy Office summaries are sharply business-like; his excitement about a good play carries excitement.

The first Sunday he went to Saint Olave's after the Plague, Pepys walked through the churchyard (326 dead from the Plague, were buried there and in the church). "It frighted me indeed . . . more than I thought it could have done, to see so [many] graves lie so high upon the churchyards where people have been buried of the plague . . . I . . . do not think to go through it again a good while" (January 30, 1666).

In the evening, September 2, 1666, the first day of the Great Fire, Pepys, watching from

a little ale-house on the Bankside . . . saw the fire grow . . . more and more . . . , in corners and upon steeples, and between churches and houses, as far as we could see up the hill of the City, in a most horrid malicious bloody flame, not like the fine flame of an ordinary fire . . . , it made me weep to see it. The churches, houses, and all on fire and flaming at once, and a horrid noise the flames made, and the cracking of houses at their ruins.

In both these, Pepys tells of his fear. The first holds an ominous, almost unlocalised feeling of horror, which Pepys implies but does not name; the second tells his specific terror of the Fire, with specific terms. In the first, the phrases are longer and slower-moving, and heavy with m's and n's and lagging ld's, d's, k's, and t's. The second has shorter phrases and sharper, higher sounds which run on faster.

One meal which Pepys had with the Duke of Albermarle, he did not enjoy: "I find the Duke of Albermarle at dinner with sorry company, some of his officers of the Army; dirty dishes, and a nasty wife at table, and bad meat, at which I made but an ill dinner" (4 April, 1667). In one sentence, three lines of the Diary, Pepys makes the facts quite clear. He gives, too, his feeling, by jagged phrases chopped into short lengths, by omitting many "and's," by the sound of the words "sorry," "dirty," "nasty," by strong alliteration of sharp "t's" and "d's." Pepys had been irritated by this dinner and still was irritated as he wrote those uncomfortable rhythms and the jangled sounds.

Sunday, June 11, 1665, Pepys had quite another sort of meal: "In the evening comes Mr. Andrews and his wife and Mr. Hill, and stayed and played, and sung and supped, most excellent pretty company, so pleasant, ingenious, and harmless, I cannot desire better. They gone we to bed, my mind in great present ease." Mr. Andrews was Pepys's friend before the *Diary* starts, and Mr. Hill he met in 1664 and kept as a good friend long after the *Diary* ends. What he says of the supper has a pervading sense of ease and comfort and rest among old friends, stated in clear facts and sustained in the simplest kind of sentence built upon parallel phrases linked in many "and's." The writing never rises to any sharp description. It flows slowly, yet it never drags because it has in it clear open vowels and liquid consonants—l, m, n, r—and alliteration, and almost rhyming words. Toward the end of the first sentence, the words become longer and more homely; they move on slowly: "excellent pretty company, so pleasant, ingenious, and harmless." The second sentence, which ends the account, is contrastingly short. It shows two moods. The first phrases of five words—bare, short, clipped—tells that the evening is done: "They gone we to bed." The rhythm and sound of the next six words—the last six—carry the earlier mood.

One afternoon, May 22, when he was thirty, he walked with John Creed, secretary of the Tangier Commission, from Greenwich to Woolwich, down along the river, four miles or so. He wrote " . . . by water to Greenwich, and [after] calling at the little alehouse at the end of the town to wrap a rag about my little left toe, [it] being new sore with walking, we walked pleasantly to Woolwich, in our way hearing the nightingales sing." He seems to have written this off-hand. In the half-sentence he gives, quite completely and quite without strain, the tone of the pleasure he had on the walk. He uses short words, innocently actual details, barely two adjectives, a child-like directness of phrasing, and the nightingale for poetry and wonder.

Two long quotations, one from the *Diary*, the other from a letter, are fair examples of wholly different tones in Pepys's writing. The first was written when he was about thirty-two:

> . . . To the 'Change after office, and received my watch from the watch-maker, and a very fine [one] it is, given me by Briggs, the Scrivener. . . . But, Lord! to see how much of my old folly and childishnesse hangs upon me still that I cannot forbear carrying my watch in my hand in the coach all this afternoon, and seeing what o'clock it is one hundred times, and am apt to think with myself, how could I be so long without one; though I remember since, I had one, and found it a trouble, and resolved to carry one no more about me while I lived. So home to supper and to bed [May 13, 1665].

The second is from a letter to Evelyn, written when Pepys was sixty-seven and living in leisure at Clapham.

> I have no herds to mind, nor will my Doctor allow me any books here. What, then, . . . you say, . . . are you doing? Why, truly, nothing that will bear naming, and yet I am not, I think, idle; for who can, that has so much of past and to come to think on, as I have? And thinking, I take it, is working, though many forms beneath what my Lady and you are doing. But pray remember what o'clock it is with you and me; and be not now, by overstirring, too bold with your present complaint, any more that I dare be with mine, which, too, has been no less kind in giving me my warning, than the other to you, and to neither of us, I hope, and, through God's mercy, dare say, either unlooked for or unwelcome. I wish, nevertheless, that I were able to administer any thing towards the lengthening that precious rest of life which God has thus long blessed you, and, in you, mankind, with; but I have always been too little regardful of my own health, to be a prescriber to others. . . . [Chapham, 7 August, 1700]. (pp. 120-23)

The *Diary* was written in an age of great prose. Within, roughly, the hundred and fifty years after 1550, the Book of Common Prayer (1549, 1552) and the King James Bible were published, and North's Plutarch (1579), Donne's devotional prose, Shakespeare, Bacon's *Essays*, Sir Thomas Browne's *Religio Medici*, and much of Milton and Dryden and Fuller and Izaak Walton and Bunyan and others. This English prose had pungency and exactness and comprehensibility, color and beauty and surprise. Unlike earlier writing in English it gave no implied or open apology for not being Latin or Greek. The new science, too, thought English a good language. In 1667 the Royal Society, which Pepys had become a member of in 1665, urged that writers and speakers reject all "swellings of style" that they aim at "a close, naked, natural way of speaking . . . a native ease," and, above all, that they use the speech of common men.

Pepys knew the classics, and much of the best writing of the closer past and of his own time. He valued the older, established writers. Contemporary writing he judged as he did any other sort of work by men he knew. He went to many plays of Dryden ("Dryden the poet I knew at Cambridge"; February 3, 1662), who was about his own age, some of which he cared for not at all and some of which, he wrote, "pleased me mightily." And he read Dryden's prose and did not hesitate to give his opinions of it. "I bought the Mayden Queen, a play newly printed which I like, at the King's house so well. . . . Mr. Dryden, . . . he himself, in his preface, seems to brag of [it] and indeed it

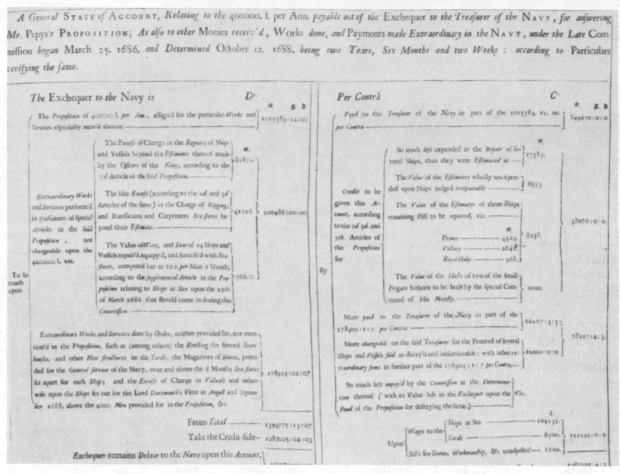

A page in Pepys's Memoires relating to the State of the Royal Navy of England *(1690).*

is a good play" (January 18, 1668). He suggested to Dryden putting Chaucer's *Poor Person* into contemporary verse. Thomas Fuller, twenty-five years older than Pepys, he knew so well that when he "met with Dr. Thomas Fuller" he "took him to The Dog, where he did tell me of his last and great book which is coming out; that is, his History of all the Families in England; and he could tell me more of my own than I knew myself" (January 22, 1661). Once he had a long talk with Fuller about ways of writing, and another time he heard Fuller preach. It was "a dry sermon." Pepys looked at Dryden and Fuller and other writers of his time with a level eye, seeing them not magnified or lessened by distance and accumulated criticism.

The two books Pepys read and heard and valued most were the King James Bible and the Book of Common Prayer. The *Diary* shows this all through it, in big things and little. The Bible, with the Prayer Book, has changing and suitable rhythms, gained it seemed unconsciously; it uses exact and simple words; it prefers to be specific rather than to generalize; and the subject is always clearly dominant, made all the more so by being written of in prose beautifully suited to express it. Such prose, the seventeenth century at its best valued and wrote; and so, at its best, seventeenth century prose has force and clearness and luminous suggestion. Izaak Walton and Sir Thomas Browne and John Bunyan and Pepys, in different styles, wrote that sort of prose. Browne, in the *Religio Medici*,

quite individually wrote: "There is surely a piece of divinity in us, something that was before the elements, and owes no homage to the sun." And "We carry within us the wonders we seek without us; There is all Africa and her prodigies in us." And "We see by an invisible sun within us." Half way through "The Fourth Day" of the *Complete Angler* Walton wrote: "No life, my honest scholar, no life so happy and so pleasant as the life of a well-governed angler; for while the lawyer is swallowed up with business, and the statesman is preventing or contriving plots, then we sit on cowslip banks, hear the birds sing, and possess ourselves in as much quietness as those silent silver streams, which we now see glide so quietly by us." Bunyan, telling the death of Mr. Valiant-for-Truth, ended: "And so he passed over and all the trumpets sounded for him on the other side." "And the Pilgrim they laid in an upper chamber, whose windows opened toward the sun-rising: the name of the chamber was Peace; where he slept till break of day, and then he arose and sang." Browne, Walton, and Bunyan, each speaks in his own way, yet the Bible and the Prayer Book have a part in them all; as the two books have in the quite different writing of the *Diary.* (pp. 123-25)

Percival Hunt, in his Samuel Pepys in the Diary, *University of Pittsburgh Press, 1958, 178 p.*

IVAN E. TAYLOR (essay date 1967)

[In the following excerpt, Taylor suggests reasons for the fame of the Diary.*]*

Pepys's *Dairy* is famous for many reasons: first, it is famous simply by reputation, as are *Hamlet* and *Paradise Lost*. People have heard about these works and talked about them, and they have become household words; but the majority, perhaps, of those who have heard and who talk have never read these works completely. In the case of the *Diary*, it is not necessary to read it all to sample its flavor, and a dozen entries chosen at random may convince the unwary that he knows what is in it. In the second place, the *Diary* is famous because of Mr. Pepys's reputation, a bad one, with the ladies. He is generally thought to be the sexy little man, ill at ease with women of his own class but a cad with housemaids.

If the reader goes a step farther and reads the *Diary* through, he makes the discovery that the first reason for its fame—its reputation based on hearsay or on reading a few entries—has completely misled him. No two entries are alike, for no two of Mr. Pepys's days were alike. Between the entry "up betimes" and the familiar "and so to bed," his average day is crammed with activities so diverse, momentous, and pleasurable that the ordinary man would need a week or two to sort them out and live through them. The average man is satisfied to meet or entertain a friend occasionally—once a day, or a week, or a year. Mr. Pepys met crowds of men daily, and he relates in the *Diary* what they talked about, what they planned, what they ate and drank.

Generally speaking, the *Diary* is a catalogue of little things made to appear portentous. This fact may be still another reason for its fame and freshness; for Mr. Pepys convinces the reader that a catalogue of his own days could be made to appear important. And, indeed, the events of one's own daily round are of as much prodigious and marvelous significance to one's self as a president's or a king's. Everyman feels this to be true—but Mr. Pepys has demonstrated that a man's life can be important and that any man can write the story of his days so that all men would delight in reading it. This promise may not be true in fact; but Mr. Pepys and his *Diary* beguile us to believe it. This disarming beguilement is a central reason for the fame of the *Diary*.

The *Diary* is famous, moreover, because Mr. Pepys tells a good story. Every listener or reader enjoys the narrator who edits the events of a tale, places them in sequential order, and saves a good sting for the tail of his story. A master storyteller, Mr. Pepys makes all incidents appear significant. He is in the class of Chaucer or Bunyan or the best newspaperman. The casual reader remembers, in the foregoing connection, Mr. Pepys's account of The Plague of 1665-1666, the Great Fire of London, or the Coronation of Charles, the attention to significant and personal detail: "to my great trouble hear the plague is come into the city... but where should it begin but in my good friend and neighbor's, Dr. Burnet, in Fenchurch Street: which in both points troubles me mightily." This is the Pepysian method of telling a story, and he is quite aware of what he is doing: The Plague is in the old city, it is close by at a neighbor's house, and the neighbor is friend and physician. He is also at his best in recording the events of the fire:

Everybody endeavoring to remove their goods, and flinging [them] into the river or bringing them into lighters that lay off [shore]; poor people staying in their houses as long as till the very fire touched them.... And among other things, the poor pigeons... were loth to leave their houses, but hovered about the windows and balconys till they were, some of them, burned, their wings, and fell down;...

Or, as he records the events immediately after the coronation of Charles II, he notes the details that have attended coronations time-out-of-mind to the present—details, indeed, attending the court of legendary King Arthur and found in the pages of old romance:

And the King came in with his crown on, and his sceptre in his hand, under a canopy borne up by six silver staves carried by Barons of the Cinque Ports and little bells at every end... and the King's first course carried up by the Knights of the Bath... and my Lord of Albemarle's going to the kitchen and eat a bit of the first dish that was to go to the King's table. But, above all, was these three Lords, Northumberland, and Suffolk, and the Duke of Ormond, coming before the courses on horseback, and staying so all dinner-time....

This passage is a mere sampling of the magnificent details of the coronation dinner presented for all time by Mr. Pepys: the awkwardness of crown and scepter at a time like this; the great lords serving as ceremonial waiters; the one testing the food for poison, who would keel over in the King's stead if there were poison. And, if the patient horses standing by had misbehaved, Mr. Pepys would have recorded the comic contretemps.

And he took sheer delight in recording unmentionable instances such as the time Lady Jemimah Montagu stopped in to visit him. Mr. Pepys, stepping from his office next door, found her sitting on the chamber pot in his dining room—and backed away in embarrassment. Or he tells of the time he was charmed by the ladies perched behind the bushes at Epsom Wells after the medicinal waters of that spa had quickly worked their way; or of the time Mr. Pepys himself rushed out of a wayside outhouse, sword in hand, to face a barking dog and, having left his belt on the toilet seat, nearly lost his breeches. The *Diary* reports a thousand such instances. Mr. Pepys, comic or serious, in big affairs and little, is a master storyteller.

Still another reason for the greatness of the *Diary*, and one close to the gift of narration, is that it contains the poetry of little things; for Mr. Pepys looks at life through the eyes of a poet. Poetry lies in his heart. The poet is the shaper not alone of verses but of events to give them life and meaning. Mr. Pepys arranges the happenings of a day in such terms that they seem to make life significant—his life and Everyman's. Poetry is a way of seeing things with the eye, but the focus of the camera lies in the heart. Mr. Pepys, so to speak, saw all things with the camera of his eye, but the focus of the lens lay within him.

Another reason for the greatness of the *Diary* is its catalogue of those pedestrian virtues that the average puritanical man fancies that he has. And English-speaking peoples, generally, are Puritans at heart; they are inheritors of the Kingdom of Heaven on earth for having earnestly coveted the best gifts set forth in the "dearly beloveds" of Archbishop Laud's Book of Common Prayer and in all the *apologiae pro vitas suas* of seventeenth-century reformers.

The *Diary* is a constant reminder that there is grace abounding to the chief of sinners, grace that echoes down through the hornbooks of England and the memory gems of Isaac Watts and a thousand courtesy books down and through the admonitions of Poor Richard, telling Everyman how to conduct his affairs so that he may win that Puritan pearl of great price—getting ahead in the world.

Mr. Pepys's *Diary* is the greatest embodiment, therefore, of Puritan virtues: early to bed and early to rise makes a man . . . ; a penny saved is a penny earned . . . ; stay the third glass (although Mr. Pepys occasionally broke his vow and awoke next day with his head in a sad state, after vomiting all night); and mind the shop and the shop will mind you. The average man who reads the *Diary* believes that if he, like Pepys, would be faithful in business and constant in prayer, serving whatever lord or king he serves, he, too, like Pepys, could rise from a poor servant and clerk, and by sticking to his desk, could become a ruler of the King's navy, and Secretary of the Admiralty. Getting ahead was a prime virtue in Mr. Pepys, and the *Diary* shows how he did it.

Everyman sees a little, or much, of Mr. Pepys in himself; for the *Diary* is the greatest record extant of average man when unobserved by others. No man has written such an absolutely frank account of his own day-to-day conduct. Diaries, generally, are edited to show the diarist at his best or at least better than he is. No man is as good as his reputation; and, if he wants to find out what he really is, he should read the *Diary*. Everyman does not have the same faults as Mr. Pepys, but every man has his quota of faults; and, if he were as honest with himself as Mr. Pepys, he would set them down unexpurgated. And the story would be Everyman's diary.

Still another reason for the fame of the *Diary* is Mr. Pepys's friendliness and loyalty to his friends. He was at his best in the club with a circle of men. He enjoyed drinking, eating, and singing with his friends. He was also that best of friends, the good listener. Men trusted him, sought his advice, and gave him their confidence. Like many men, he was sometimes ashamed and embarrassed at the contemplation of his low-brow friends. and he was conscious of having outgrown them and of having risen above them. He always treated them well, nevertheless; and he more than compensated for any temporary lapse into snobbishness by the gracious and generous manner of treatment that he accorded those in stations even lower than those of his former friends—his own servants. This account of friendship and friendly consort, of trustworthiness, of loyalty to his inferiors. to his equals, and to his superiors lies at the heart of the *Diary*.

Close to his virtue of the art of friendship is another quality that accounts for the eternal freshness of the *Diary*: Mr. Pepys's love of life. He enjoyed the daily round. He had fun. Staying in bed with Mrs. Pepys on a Sunday morning, remaining home from church to purge himself with laxatives, pinching the girls at church, going to the alehouse, Bartholomew Fair, or the theater—always the theater. In town or in the country, Mr. Samuel Pepys enjoyed himself, went home, and recorded what he had done. The *Diary* reads like an entertainment program, a nine-year schedule of pleasures.

It is a nine-year schedule, too, of the serious struggle that England made to free its mind of error, of political lethargy, of social indifference, and of malfeasance and malfunction in high places. It is the record of the follies and moral feebleness of a good and gracious King who could not put off knighthood and put on kingship. As a result, King Charles had so many mistresses, so wasted his kingdom's substance in riotous living, and managed England with so many cabals and secret dealings that his mismanagement nearly brought her to her knees. The *Diary* records these melancholy events.

The *Diary* is a great book, moreover, because it tells the scholar, the historian, the antiquarian, and the curious reader what England was in the middle years of the seventeenth century. It would be wise, indeed, for the historian of social custom, of religion, of the church, of the theater, of the language of England, or of anything to study the *Diary*; for in it he finds on almost every page a living account of what seventeenth-century men did for a livelihood, how they entertained themselves and were entertained how they preached and listened to sermons, how they talked, and even the very curse words that they used. Pepys, like Chaucer, Shakespeare, and Bunyan, is England's historian. One can think of a score of other books to be written on Pepys, or a hundred, on subjects like seventeenth-century preaching, reading, feeding, childbearing, medical practice, music that stirred men's hearts, dancing, the flowers that were grown, and the cultivation of the trees and orchards of England. All of these matters are revealed to the reader of the *Diary*, often in detail.

But the greatest appeal in the *Diary* lies in meeting Mr. Pepys and coming to know him and to love him: vain, self-conscious little Samuel Pepys; amorous but timid; bold-venturesome but fainthearted. Hardworking, honest, he refused to accept a hand-out from his inferiors, plugged up the ratholes that impoverished the King's stores, but tilted a contract his way for a gift of gold or a silver tankard. Devoted to his father, he was contemptuous of his mother and of his homely freckled sister Paulina. Standing hat-in-hand in the presence of the great ones of England, he held his own and refused to knuckle under to such as the swaggering Sir William Penn and Sir William Batten. A good man, all in all, is Samuel Pepys; and we may never have the chance to look upon the likes of him again. For there surely will never be another *Diary* like his. (pp. 18-23)

The *Diary* brings us into intimate contact with one of the most remarkable men who ever lived and, yet, a truly average man with typical faults as well as virtues. To use of good, if overworked, phrase, Mr. Pepys was the "divine average"; for, in many ways, he was the best of men. When death lurked and danger threatened, he did not run and hide; he stood his ground—in plague and fire and war, and he watched in open-mouthed wonder. He did, though, what average man has done since time began: he took part in things. There were crises in Pepys's day as in ours. Average men today, and always, will face fire and flood, pestilence and deprivation with quiet determination as did Pepys.

The paradox of the *Diary* is that average days to average men are not ordinary at all, for they assume a vast importance to each man. There is no evidence anywhere in the *Diary* that Pepys thought of himself as special or as remarkable in any way. Vain and self-conscious he was, indeed, and lovably and delightfully so; but the sin of pride—of vainglory—was not a sin of Samuel Pepys. The average man who reads the *Diary* may be pleased to recognize himself in Mr. Pepys. When Mr. Pepys viewed the Coronation, he stationed a comely woman next to Mrs. Pepys so that from a distance he could watch her decently; when pestilence came, he rubbed himself with plug tobacco as any man might do to ward off evil by reaching into the dark, backward abyss of time to invoke a charm or to practice a forgotten rite; but Pepys stayed among the comfortless and dying; when fire broke out, Pepys ran to see it but stayed to put it out. These great events happened on average days, for any day is an average day; but Mr. Pepys threaded the events together by taking part in them. The secret of the power of Mr. Pepys and his *Diary* is that Mr. Pepys shows average man that, while doing average things, if he take his part in the daily round, his days, too, are filled with meaning and living wonder.

The literary quality of the *Diary* depends, to a large extent, on its simplicity of style and on the personal grace revealed in Mr. Pepys's way with words. He wrote down what he witnessed and shared of the life about him while the indicents were fresh in his mind. There may be a slight hint here and there in the *Diary* that Mr. Pepys wished some day to edit it for print but it is, in fact, a spontaneous record of things as they happened from day to day. Mr. Pepys's friend and contemporary, John Evelyn, wrote a wonderful diary, too, and always it invites comparison with Pepys's; neither suffers from the comparison. Evelyn's diary represents the edited and thrice-pondered account; Pepys's represents things as they happened, on the spot. (pp. 150-51)

> *Ivan E. Taylor, in his* Samuel Pepys, *Twayne Publishers, Inc., 1967, 160 p.*

WILLIAM MATTHEWS (essay date 1970)

[*Matthews was an English-born American linguist, critic, historian, and biographer. He coedited the eleven-volume* Diary of Samuel Pepys: A New and Complete Transcription *(1970-83) and was a leading authority on diaries written in English. In the following excerpt from the introduction to the eleven-volume text, he closely examines the* Diary *as literature, noting Pepys's methods of composition and commenting on how these methods influence critical perceptions of Pepys the writer.*]

On 16 October 1665 Pepys reports entering his journal for eight days past and expresses the hope that thereafter he will be able to fall into his old way of doing it daily. Frequent notes throughout the diary, even in its first year, that two, three, four, up to ten, twelve, fourteen days were entered at one time indicate, however, that the practice of day-by-day entry was seldom consistent. The phrase 'And so to bed', when it concludes a daily entry, shows that many entries were made late at night, just before Pepys turned in; but this practice, too, was in nowise consistent, for many entries were made during mornings and afternoons, as Pepys himself testifies. Nor does his 'And so to bed' always prove that the entry was made on the day it describes, since many such entries go on, with no break in style, to describe matters that occurred after the diarist was abed or asleep. Much of the diary was written at Pepys's office, for secrecy as some have thought; but the diarist sometimes preferred to work on it in his home, and

sometimes he did so elsewhere, aboard ship, in lodgings, in several places in the country. Where he wrote seems to have been as much a matter of convenience as of secrecy; sometimes he worked in the office simply because his wife was away in the country, rain was coming into the house, or his home was being renovated.

Pepys uses many terms to describe his work on the diary. Some have an air reminiscent of accountancy, and a few imply that the composition may have been more complicated than is usually thought: 'to set right', 'to make good', 'to put in order' and 'to perfect'. The last term is particularly suggestive, for elsewhere Pepys uses it to mean making a fair copy and bringing a draft into publishable form. The appearance of most of the manuscript, the regularity and even spacing of the symbols and lines, the straightness of the lines, the even colour of the ink over large sections, the neat disposition of the daily entries on the pages, all suggest that this is in fact largely a fair copy. And this general visual impression is supported by details in the manuscript itself.

The manuscript provides clear evidence that some parts of the diary were first written as rough notes. That some of the rest once existed in an earlier form (presumably a rough copy or draft) also seems to follow from the fact that in many entries a note on the act of making the entry is followed by notes on activities that happened after the entry was made. These are typical examples:

> I returned home and to my office, setting down this day's passages; and having a letter that all is well in the country, I went home to supper; then a Latin Chapter of Will and to bed.

> ...to the office, there set down my Journall, and so home to supper and to bed—a little troubled to see how my family is out of order by Wills being there, and also to hear that Jane doth not please my wife as I expected and could have wished.

The later material has been added; but that the text as we have it represents a second copy is suggested by various details; the syntax for one thing, and the uniformity of ink and penmanship which characterises the added material and the material which precedes it.

Another kind of evidence that parts of the diary once existed in another form is afforded by the fact that during times of danger Pepys twice mentions entrusting his diary ('which I value much') to other people for safekeeping—for during its absence he continued to keep up the diary, later copying it into the final manuscript. A similar procedure must also have been adopted during his period aboard ship in 1660 or his many trips to Brampton, Portsmouth and elsewhere, for it is highly unlikely he carried his diary-book with him.

Still further support comes from details of the manuscript. Considered as a whole, these details indicate that the composition of the diary was quite complicated.

Differences in ink and penmanship are striking. The ink varies between black and light brown, the shorthand symbols differ from section to section in size, sharpness, and angling, and the lines are spaced differently. These differences often run in blocks, and they tend to suggest that the entries were commonly made by series of days. These series sometimes agree with the blocks of entries mentioned by the diarist himself, but very often they disagree, and the discrepancies seem to indicate that much of the diary may once have existed in two versions: one, a rough copy that Pepys destroyed, possibly section by section as he entered it into the diary-books; the other, the final manuscript.

The case for this hypothesis may be reinforced by several types of error in the manuscript. First, several words, such as 'love' (*recte* 'home') or 'made' (*recte* 'good'), which make nonsense and can best be explained as results of copying from slightly imperfect shorthand. Second, numerous mistakes in pronouns and tenses (e.g. 'his' for 'my' and 'told' for 'tells') which suggest that Pepys was confusing direct and reported forms of speech, which is something very unlikely in a first copy but feasible enough in a second. Third, numerous omissions or *homoeoteleuta*, most of them incipient and corrected but some not, which would not be likely to occur in an original text but are mistakes natural to a second copy, expecially when the eye jumps from one instance of a word to a second, in the next line perhaps. Fourth, many errors, such as 'mother' for 'murder' or 'is' for 'his' or 'state' for 'stayed', of representing one word by another of nearly the same sound. Usually in these pairs the shorthand forms are substantially different, and the only explanation seems to be that the diarist spoke, perhaps in a mutter, as he entered the matter into the manuscript—a practice that is more likely to have resulted from reading from another copy than from original composition. Fifth, a number of statements that Pepys could not see what he was writing or that his writing was slubbering or his hand shaking, which are usually so graphically contradicted by the straight lines and neat penmanship of the entries themselves that it seems evident that the statements must relate to a prior copy. Sixth, many pages in which the symbols are tiny and the lines crowded, in striking contrast with pages that precede or follow. These crowdings suggest that some series of days may have been squeezed into the manuscript later than entries which bear later dates, a practice for which there is direct evidence elsewhere in the manuscript.

Of most of these types of detail the manuscript yields many examples, scattered throughout the diary. Their apparent testimony is that the manuscript at Magdalene must, in part at least, be a fair copy made from a rougher form. And that this was indeed a Pepysian practice is made certain by what the diarist himself tells us about the famous section of the diary that describes the Great Fire. On 11 October 1666 he squeezes in a memorandum that he had taken his journal during the fire and the disorders following (1 September-10 October) in loose papers 'until this very day' and could not get time to enter them in his book until the morning of 18 January.

Further record of the practice, and evidence as to what the earlier copy was like, is afforded by two sets of notes for 10-19 April (at home) and 5-17 June 1668 (in the country). Blank pages are left in the manuscript at these points, and foolscap sheets of shorthand notes, organised by days, are bound in. For 29 September-10 October of the same year there are also blank pages; but here there are no inserted sheets.

The shorthand on these sheets begins with accounts, and the accounting items are struck through and check-marked. In addition to short annotations written on the lines of the accounting items, general observations on the day's activities are appended. These general notes, and also the annotations in the accounts, are cryptic in style, even though they have been copiously revised by excisions and insertions. Very clearly, these are rough notes, first revised, which Pepys meant to enter in his diary-book more meticulously, and perhaps more amply. It is to these materials, possibly, that he refers on 22 November 1668 when he writes of having left his journal for some days 'imperfect'.... [These and other details] suggest that similar rough notes may once have existed for much of the diary.

That may not be the whole story of how Pepys composed his diary, however. During the diary period Pepys kept several manuscript books: among them, a by-book, a 'book of tales', an account-book or books and a 'Brampton book', all of which have been lost; the business journal he called his 'Navy White-Book', which was largely in shorthand, and the great diary itself. The two series of rough notes, and possibly the many terms in the diary which seem to associate it with accounting, suggest that the diary and accounts may have been products of a single process. A similar relationship may also have existed for the other three books, for sometimes the diary refers to entering a *bon mot* in the 'book of tales', occasionally it refers briefly to matters that are set out at length in the Navy White-Book, and once it mentions entering a journal-book out of a by-book. All these records cannot have been composed simply from memory. For the accounts and business records, Pepys must have used invoices and minutes; and the characteristic formulae of the account may be seen here and there throughout the diary. For general observations, Pepys must often have drawn from notes. He speaks of his pocket-papers and of old broken office-notes in shorthand. He also mentions a blacklead pencil he carried with him and the silver fountain-pen that Sir William Coventry gave him: with these, as he states, he reported sermons, took down the very words of conversations and copied in the theatre the echo-song in *The Tempest*. It may therefore be assumed that his rough draft was partly assembled from bills, pocket-papers, minutes and similar basic materials relevant to the various manuscript books. Indeed, on one occasion the diarist refers to this practice when he mentions the difficulty of writing his diary during a time he was kept several days from his lodging, 'where my books and papers are'. Much has been written of Pepys's prodigious memory for detail. But Pepys once consulted his physician about the decay of his memory, and once he speaks of entering a series of days from memory but adds that it troubled him to remember it and that he was forced into doing so by the absence of his papers. It accords better with the evidence, therefore, and takes little away from Pepys's reputation, to assume that some of the diary's fine detail came ultimately from documents and notes.

At the other end there is also abundant witness that Pepys sometimes read over entries he had recently made in the diary-book and revised them. The evidence is the hundreds of instances where longhand has been superimposed upon shorthand, sometimes in ink of different density and colour, and also the many notes that are squeezed into blank spaces at the ends of paragraphs or written in the margin. Except for one occasion apparently, Pepys did not fill in the occasional blanks he left in his manuscript, mostly of names; but for part of the diary at least, one of his processes was a revision of the manuscript itself.

The logic of these details suggests five possible stages in the composition of the diary. First, the accumulation of bills, minutes, official papers, news-books and rough notes on a day's proceedings. Second, the gathering of these into a form which combined accounts with diary-style notes. This process may at times have been skipped, and often it was done in a series of days. Third, the entering of the accounts and business matters into the appropriate manuscript-books, and the first revision of the general entries which were intended for the final manuscript of the diary. Fourth, entry of these general notes into the diary-book. This process must have been slow; the available evidence indicates an average pace of less than twenty words per minute. Pepys seems to have read in a mutter at times as he worked on this stage, and he certainly worked with extreme care, aiming at neatness and evenness comparable with that of a printed book. The process may also be assumed to have entailed selection, occasional expansion and condensation, and a measure of polishing. It was done, judging by writing style and ink, either by days or in blocks of days, and the crowding of certain entries seems to suggest that some blocks may have been entered later than entries that bear later date. The two sections of rough notes bear witness to this procedure, and so does the Great Fire sequence, which, as Pepys states, was entered at various times three months and more after the events, blank pages having been left for it—too few, to judge from the many entries in tiny characters. Judging by his practice of ending a day neatly at the bottom of a page and by the fact that each of the first three volumes ends on the last day of June, it is also likely that Pepys adapted many entries to the available space. The fifth and final process was reading over the entries that had been made shortly before, making small corrections and stylistic improvements, and inserting some further details at the ends of paragraphs and entries.

This series of five stages represents the most extreme form that Pepys's method of composition might take. The cryptic style of some entries suggests that there were at times no rough notes, and the evidence for late changes suggests that any final revision was done somewhat fitfully. Nevertheless, the manuscript makes it fairly certain that Pepys's way of writing was more complex than is usually assumed, and consequently that his great diary is no simple product of nature, thrown together at the end of each succeeding day. In part at least, it is a product fashioned with some care, both in its matter and its style.

This arduous procedure is something one might have expected from the diarist, for it may be doubted that Pepys ever did anything casually. It is a procedure, moreover, that explains many features of the diary. It explains, for example, the unevenness in manner and fullness; bare, notelike entries at one extreme and full, sweeping passages at the other, presumably as Pepys had less or more time or inclination to develop and refine from his basic notes and recollections. It could explain also his remarkable skill in inserting long parenthetical statements into his sentences and still coming out with clean syntax. Impressive as it is, it may be simply a result of combining into one sentence two, sometimes three or more, separate entries from his rough notes. The procedure of composition could also explain Pepys's apparent prodigies of memory and much of the extraordinary detail of the diary; and, taken with his use of shorthand, it might also partly account for

the peculiar happiness of his normal diary-style. In letters and in reports, Pepys tends to the extended sentences and rotund utterance of the public man. Thus, the letter to Sir George Carteret to which he refers in the diary at 14 November 1663 sets out in this way:

> The occasion of this morning's dispute at the Board was not more unwelcome to us all than your frequent mention of Sir William Warren's masts was particularly to me, for that I fear your dissatisfaction in that contract yet remains to my prejudice. The truth is, I blame myself for not giving you long since the account you demanded relating thereunto. But such is my unaptness to encourage any occasion of discontent, that notwithstanding that contract hath received so high a censure, and the compassing of it charged as a particular practice of mine (and that not only in the Office but in other places, where I am concerned to have my actions better understood), yet I have chosen rather to expect the issue of all this than be thought to design reproach to another more than right to myself by seeking justification in a matter little needing any. But since I find you still dissatisfied, and being doubtful how my silence may be interpreted. I have made it my afternoon's work to state the whole matter to you, and thus it is.

Even in private letters to scholarly friends he sometimes speaks like a whale. And every now and then in the diary, especially when it is dealing with important public affairs, there are stretches of this ample manner. But most of it is written in rapid, even impetuous language, simple and limited in its sentence patterns, familiar in its vocabulary, innocent of ornament or rhetoric, a diary-style which is close to ordinary speech, although it is more economical, denser with facts and more elliptical than most men's speaking:

> Then to the Dolphin to a dinner of Mr. Harris's, where Sir Wms. both and my Lady Batten and her two daughters and other company—where a great deal of mirth. And there stayed till 11 a—clock at night. And in our mirth, I sang and sometimes fiddled (there being a noise of fiddlers there) and at last we fell to dancing—the first time that ever I did in my life—which I did wonder to see myself to do. At last we made Mingo, Sir W. Battens black, and Jack, Sir W. Pens, dance; and it was strange how the first did dance with a great deal of seeming skill.

Such a style might proceed naturally from notes; but so might a style heavy and ornate. And since Pepys publicly used the Ciceronian mode, his use of a simple quasi-conversational manner for the diary is a clear sign of either his instinctive or conscious responce to what was proper for a private record. And flecking the pattern of the diary throughout are the traits of actual speech: the rhythms, the verbal usages, the idioms and linguistic fashions of Pepys himself and the people he heard and talked with. This prevailing style, endless detail in the matter, speaking quality in the manner, ellipses of verbs and pronouns appropriate to diary notation, is one of the most extraordinary features of Pepys's diary; and the symbol of its effectiveness is that Pepys is probably the only diarist who has contributed verbal formulae to the blood-stream of English. Most of this success must be attributed to Pepys's feeling for language and occasions and to his sensitivity to the patterns of conversation. But something must also be credited to the rapid composition made possible by the rough notes, written soon after the events, and to the continued use of shorthand which, however slowly it was written, permitted an easy flow into a final form and may also have sanctioned for Pepys a style different from that which he normally used in his longhand.

The procedure may also have facilitated one unusual and brilliant quality of Pepys's style, its peculiar sensitivity to the moment. 'Immediacy' is a word often used in connection with diaries; and it is a fact that among historical chronicles, diaries are valuable because of the shortness of the interval dividing event from record. But this is historical immediacy. Literary immediacy is something quite different: it is an effect of language and imagination. Most diaries, although they may record events only a few hours after they happened, are very far from giving the sense of the living moment that is so frequent in Pepys. In fact, Pepys himself does not always give it. The Tangier journal of 1683, written long after his inspiration had passed, hardly ever makes a reader feel he is present at what is described. Even in the great diary there are stretches that fail to do so. The two sections of rough notes are historically immediate; but they have almost no sense of the moment. On the other hand, what is seemingly the most spontaneous and living series of entries in the diary, the long account of the Great Fire, was, as Pepys himself states, entered into the diary-book three months and more after the events.

There is paradox in the literary immediacy of the diary, and the explanation may lie in the two forms. The rough form provided the immediacy of history. Rewriting from it, Pepys had alternatives. He could simply abstract what he wanted; he could introduce pattern into the material; he could use the notes as a point of departure and go on to maturer reflection and the more solemn manner of a chronicle of the state and himself. Quite often he seems to have transferred mechanically, and the entries are lacklustre, wanting both emotion and variety in pattern. On several occasions he boiled down the material for several days into single entries. And sometimes he expatiated at length as though he were writing a formal chronicle of *res gestae*. But over an astonishingly large part of these nine and more years, Pepys seems to have treated the rewriting as an opportunity for imaginative re-entry into the recent past represented by his rough notes, and also for making all those changes that contribute to immediacy in the literary sense—the selection and combination of details, the effects of conversation, the injection of judgement words, the retention of some details that were reported while he was in the very act of writing the rough notes and the addition of others that occurred while he wrote the fair form.

From composition we may turn to motive. Pepys is rightly regarded as a great civil servant, a remarkable administrator and reformer, the 'Saviour of the Navy' as Bryant styles him. He would not have disputed these praises. But he was disposed to explain his superiority by talents that may strike us as less than heroic: a capacity for mastering his business, attention to detail and zeal in taking pains, punctiliousness and accuracy in minute-taking and bookkeeping. The last in particular is one ground for his contempt for his colleague Povey and one cause of disputes in his household.

The diary is a concomitant of Pepys's delight in bookkeeping. The rough notes from which the existing version may have been written were, as we have seen, partly accounts, and the diary manuscript bears some of the marks of a book-keeper's hand, in its precise spacing and lining, its almost complete freedom from blots. These are externals and they partly reflect the ordinary neatness of the government clerk; but in the matter itself not a little reflects the mind of a man who believes there is a vital correspondence between values and dates. At the end of certain months, and more fully at the end of each year, Pepys presents a balance-sheet for himself and the nation, a concise statement that sets out the debits and credits in politics, morality and finance, particularly in his own finance. This is a procedure which loses distinctiveness in the body of the diary; but it is significant, and it reveals that one of Pepys's chief motives was one that explains the origin of many diaries of his times and later.

This was not his only motivation of course. Many diaries are the product of a puritanical urge to record (and so to correct) the writers' moral backslidings. There may well be an element of this motivation in Pepys, for certainly he was a puritan of a sort. Despite his fondness for pleasures of the flesh, he was a man divided, given to acting as recorder and punitive magistrate over his own inclinations. In his accounts of his amours, in his reports of quarrels with his wife, he is ready to report and condemn his own failings. He imposed on himself a system of fines (to be given to the poor) for going to the theatre, etc., beyond certain limits. With occasional lapses, he steadily fought the battle of labour against pleasure. But it may be doubted whether this puritanism was what motivated Pepys to become a diarist. More likely, it was his taste for history that set him out on his journey and sustained him for over nine years. The urge to be a chronicler of the times is probably the commonest reason for writing diaries. Not least among Pepys's many contributions to scholarship are his several great collections of documents on particular historical subjects: the history of the navy, the adventures of Charles II after his escape from the battle of Worcester, the activities of Captain John Scott, his accuser at the time of the Popish Plot, the development of handwriting and engraving and so on. Much of his collecting was solely for his own pleasure or use, but for some of it Pepys seemed to envisage publication (e.g. for the account of Charles II's escape from Worcester) and one of Pepys's frustrations was not having time to write a history of the Second Dutch War—although in a period of leisure later in his life he did manage to publish a self-vindicating account of naval administration between 1679 and 1688. It is often affirmed that the diary was secret, meant only for Pepys's own eyes. That was probably true for his lifetime. But some things suggest that he may have intended it to be read by future scholars of historical taste. He carefully guarded it, catalogued it in detail and set it in the library that he bequeathed to Magdalene specifically for the benefit of scholars. The diary *ab initio* was of the times: a history of naval and public affairs; a history in which Pepys, though no angel, was clearly on the angels' side.

To the motivations of the accountant, the puritan and the historian might be added an inspiration even more basic. Pepys was a characteristic product of his day, a virtuoso, a man sympathetic to every new trend in science and scholarship. In the diary period he was a friend or acquaintance of some of the chief scholars of that remarkable time—Hooke, Boyle, Wilkins, Petty, Evelyn—and later he was to add others. He displayed a lively interest in the scientific work that was being done at Gresham

College; in 1665 he was elected a fellow of the Royal Society, and before then had attended its lectures and demonstrations. Nineteen years later he was honoured by being made the society's president, and it is his name that in 1687 authorises the imprimatur for what may well be the society's most famous publication, Newton's *Principia Mathematica.* Yet for all his curiosity about the new experiments, for all his fondness for new technical devices and his belief that a good general scholar should know optics and mathematics, in the presence of such giants as Boyle and Hooke, Pepys seems simply a curious tyro. He bought and read scientific books as soon as they came off the press and made them a mainstay of his remarkable library. But sometimes he confesses his inability to understand them. The paradox, however, is more apparent than real. The scope of natural philosophy was then broad enough to include interests that now form no part of natural science: shorthand, for example, or dialects, or the right way of writing. Bacon himself had envisaged the advancement of the new learning by the collection of materials in a great many subjects, and in his *Essay on projects* he called for particular 'histories' of many human activities and of the natural conditions that motivated and shaped them. Pepys's own collections, largely the product of later years but some just begun in the diary period, were to be directed to a remarkably large number of Bacon's specific recommendations: a history of music; a history of painting, sculpture, modelling, etc. (including collections of prints); a history of the printing of books, of writing, of sealing; a history of the art of war and the arts thereto belonging; a history of the art of navigation and of the crafts and arts thereto belonging. Like his friend Evelyn, Pepys was a modern man, and so a Baconian. No work is mentioned more often in the diary than Bacon's *Faber Fortunae,* an essay on self-help that he never tired of reading. His several collections of documents are witness to one phase of his later Baconian zeal; but the diary, too, is moulded in part by Baconian attitudes. The prevalence of facts and details in its history has a Baconian air; and so do many of its preoccupations with science and technology—it might even be argued that the shorthand itself is witness to Pepys's disposition towards the products of the new technology. Even more Baconian is its depiction of the diarist himself.

The most astonishing feature of the whole diary is the fullness and variety of its portrait of the writer, and its almost incredible honesty. No other diarist, not even the puritans or Boswell or Barbellion, lays himself so bare as Pepys does. Something of this may be attributed to Pepys's confidence in the obscurity of his shorthand, something to his egocentricity, something to puritanism, something perhaps to a book-keeper's ordinary honesty. But far more important as a motive than all these is Pepys's passion for microscopic observation of himself as he actually was. Egocentric and charged with feeling as the diary is, it often reads as though it had been written by an *alter ego,* by another man in the same skin, one who watched understandingly but rather detachedly the behaviour and motives of his fellow-lodger. The diary-form lends itself to this kind of duality, since the diarist is at once performer, recorder and audience. But it is some kind of commentary on human nature that very few diarist are able or willing to avail themselves of its opportunity: some throw themselves on their diaries as if in confession; most present themselves at their best, or rationalise, or fit themselves to a pattern, or talk about other matters than themselves. Through large areas of Pepys's diary, however, the diarist is both the observer and the observed, the penitent and the priest, the patient on the couch and the psychiatrist too, the man in the street and the behavioural sociologist. At one place or another almost every variation of his being is represented: waking, dreaming, acting, thinking, feeling, day-dreaming, rejoicing confidently, torturing himself with doubt and self-accusation. In those marvellous long records of quarrels with his wife he is always present as a third party, understanding both sides, but shrewd about both. His long-drawn-out and fascinating account of his successful siege of Deb Willet's virtue, a story that has the makings for a sentimental novelette, is converted into something that a major novelist might envy, a transformation made possible largely by the diarist-clinician's observation of the obsession that grew upon him and by his sociological recording of the degradation that slowly came upon Deb and the near-tragedy that developed in his own home. Much of the matter that is printed for the first time in [*The Diary of Samuel Pepys: A new and Complete Transcription*] might be labelled pornographic and scatological. Since most of it is written in Pepys's own *lingua franca* and hedged with shorthand and dog-Latin devices, it may be judged to deal with behaviour that Pepys himself thought shameful. Yet his presentation of this record of his moral deviations is clinical rather than moral or erotic; much of it reads like material for a scientific report on sexual behaviour in the human male. That Pepys included it, although ashamed, is the most evident testimony to the full objective reporting, the scientific outlook, the Baconianism that went into the diary and the manner in which it was reported.

These are some of Pepys's motives in writing his diary, but although they explain some of its contents and qualities, they do not explain all. Nor do they explain why Pepys's diary is so much more interesting than others. That it is possible for a diarist to be historically minded, scientific, honest, accurate, careful, copious, even to write in shorthand, and yet to be considerably dull, is evident from the diary (1709-12) of an eminent American colonist, Richard Byrd of Westover, Virginia. And even John Byrom's (1722-44), although it is more varied and humane than Byrd's, is not precisely lively. One essential difference was that Pepys was a typical seventeenth-century virtuoso, a man who justified himself by the diversity of his interests. In Pepys, perhaps, they proceed from one single comprehensive quality, vitality; but if so, its manifestations relate to almost all aspects of his life and most features of his times: work, pleasure, friendship, business, public life and private, almost the whole range of society. In his own mild way, John Evelyn touched on a few of them in his words a Pepys's death [see excerpt dated 1703]. But although Evelyn could appreciate his friend's industry and love of learning and music, he was, partly because of the nature of their friendship, partly because of his own nature, not fully cognisant of the intensity of Pepys's nature or the full range and quality of his talents and interests.

There is, for example, Pepys's intense attraction to beauty: that 'strange slavery that I stand in to beauty, that I value nothing near it'. An example is the occasion when he went to church 'and there stood wholly privately at the great doors, to gaze upon a pretty lady; and from church dogged her home, whither she went to a house near Tower-hill; and I think her to be one of the prettiest women I ever saw'. Despite his lechery on other occasions, that represents a passion of platonic kind, and it is one that he also brings to painting, to music and to the remembrance of things past. Housman himself is not more effective in describing the effect of a complete submission to beauty than is Pepys: 'but that which did please me beyond anything in the whole world was the wind-musique when the Angell comes down, which is so sweet that it ravished me; and endeed, in a word, did wrap up my soul so that it made me really sick, just as I have formerly been when in love with my wife; that neither then, nor all that evening going home and at home, I was able to think of anything, but remained all night transported, so as I could not believe that ever any music hath that real command over the soul of a man as this did upon me; and makes me resolve to practice wind-music and to make my wife do the like'. Almost as much delight goes into his recall of his boyhood pleasures during his visit to Ashtead in 1663. With matters intellectual and social, even with business it was much the same: all readers of the diary will surely remember Pepys's delight with the youngster whom he recognised to be so much like himself, 'with child to see any strange thing'.

This zest and energy, this ready delight in things new as well as in old things, are vital in making Pepys the diarist

he is. Of all English writers, perhaps the only one who is his equal in gusto is Chaucer. It is therefore no accident that Pepys should have collected Chaucer and admired him warmly as a poet. Who else among English writers has Pepys's enthusiasm for everyday people, everyday life, or his habit of judging everything he liked the best that ever there was? Who else, even among Elizabethans, is so spontaneous with 'fine', 'rare', 'brave', 'mighty pleasant', 'exceeding good'.

The quality of a man and the quality of his book are not necessarily parallel, however, and when it comes down to bedrock, Pepys's supreme gift was that he was a fine writer. It is our habit when reading diaries to regard them as products of nature rather than of art. And in most cases the preconception is valid. Diaries *en masse* might well be regarded as natural products, and their commonly lumpish matters and styles witness the artlessness of their writers. But it is also true that almost all diaries that give genuine and protracted pleasure to an ordinary reader do so because the diarists possessed, instinctively or by training, some of the verbal, intellectual and emotional talents that characterise the novelist. Diaries are not novels; they are bound to reality, with its deplorable habit of providing excellent story situations and no artistically satisfactory ends. Nevertheless, it is not hard to think of the best diarists as novelists tied for the occasion to reality and the daily round.

Pepys's private library in London.

This is particularly true of Pepys. His diary, as we have seen, was composed slowly and carefully, and subjected to revisions.... [Textual evidence reveals] abundant occasions when Pepys has substituted words more precise, picturesque or tuneful. Far more, one may assume, may have occurred in revision of the rough notes and entering them into the final manuscript. And that Pepys had some bent towards the art of the novelist, albeit of a romance kind, may be argued from an entry for 30 January 1664:

> This evening, being in an humour of making all things even and clear in the world, I tore some old papers; among others, a Romance which (under the title of *Love a Cheate*) I begun ten year ago at Cambridge; and at this time, reading it over tonight, I liked it very well and wondered a little at myself at my vein at that time when I wrote it, doubting that I cannot do so well now if I would try.

That unfortunate victim to Pepys's passion for neatness was, judging from its title, akin to the contemporary French romance. The novelistic qualities that contribute to the delight of the diary are less mannered, more realistic. They are numerous, and it will be enough to list some of the more striking. The great crowd of characters, many sketched by a phrase, an action, a comment, others appearing through long stretches of the diary, growing in depth and variety as detail follows detail and as Pepys's attitude to them hardens—or changes. The abundance and variety of the conversation: some of it bursting in as direct speech, most reported in Pepys's own words but tinged with the tones and idioms of the speakers themselves. The habit of presenting the weather, sometimes even the physical scene, not as a discrete item, as is customary in diaries, but in emotional relationship with people and happenings. The passages of genre-painting: the well-known and delightful pastoral scene on Epsom Downs, 'the most pleasant and innocent sight that ever I saw in my life', for example, or the entries that describe his visit to his poor relations in the Fens, a vivid series of Dutch portraits and landscapes in words. The instinctive habit of recalling fond memories of his boyhood and youth at Durdans, Kingsland and Cambridge. The selection of concrete details which are both vivid and symbolic, a remarkable skill which is shown particularly well in the description of the Great Fire and the Plague but is also evident throughout. The practice of presenting quarrels with his wife as balanced digests of dialogues, and of slipping into the reports small details about dress or the state of the sky. The description of day-by-day happenings in affairs of long duration in such a way as to lose nothing of any accumulating excitement, irony, suspense or climax they may have offered. The long, fascinating story of Deb Willet's seduction and degradation has already been mentioned, and there are shorter sequences of similar kind throughout the diary, among them the story of the shocking illness, the sudden death and the grimly comic burial of Pepys's brother, Tom, the strange infatuation that William Wight the fishmonger, Pepys's uncle, developed for Elizabeth Pepys, and the long defence of the navy that reaches its climax in the diarist's great speech in the Commons.

These practices and habits have been called novelistic. Perhaps it might be better to say that his zest and his literary instinct led Pepys to relate a story excitingly whenever the material gave him a chance. Whatever it is called, however, in the diary it is essentially an artistic gift, and one that

few diarists have possessed. It is probably the lack of that essential gift of art rather than any lack of opportunity that causes diaries in general to be rated low in the literary scale. Diaries, even dull ones, have many virtues: for one thing, they probably bring a reader closer to human actuality than any other form of writing. As life-records they present a natural disorder and emphasis which is artfully rearranged in biography, and so somewhat corrupted. As self-delineations they deal directly with people and events which in the novel are subjected to the stresses and conventions of art and design. And in many ways they are the most natural and instinctive product of the art of writing. But although tens of thousands are called to be diarists, few are chosen to be really good ones. Most diarists do not do any of these things at all well. The uniqueness of Pepys is that for reasons that have been stated and for others that escape definition, he does them all superbly. In his own bailiwick, and at his best, he is as much a nonpareil as are Chaucer and Shakespeare. And in one matter he is unique. No one else has ever composed so brilliant and so full an account of an actual man as he actually was. And that must be because he was not only a great man but because he was also a great writer. (pp. xcvii-cxiii)

> *William Matthews, "Introduction: The Diary as Literature," in* The Diary of Samuel Pepys: 1660, *Vol. I by Samuel Pepys, edited by Robert Latham and William Matthews, University of California Press, 1970, pp. xcvii-cxiii.*

ROBERT LATHAM (essay date 1970)

> [*Latham is an English essayist, editor, and historian. He coedited the eleven-volume* Diary of Samuel Pepys: A New and Complete Transcription *(1970-83) and edited a reduction of the complete edition,* The Shorter Pepys *(1985). In the following excerpt from the introduction to the eleven-volume text, he discusses the* Diary *as history.*]

[Pepys's] diary, although primarily a personal journal, was designed to serve also as a chronicle of public affairs. This dual purpose declares itself in the opening entry, which begins: 'Blessed be God, at the end of the last year I was in very good health...', and continues: 'The condition of the State was thus...'. The two subjects—the history of the man and the history of his country—become fused to a certain extent (or at least the boundaries between them become blurred) with the growth of Pepys's involvement in public life. But they still remain separable, and whenever the diarist breaks into the succession of daily entries in order to sum up—at the end of a volume or of a year—he makes a statement, balanced, like the opening entry, between personal and national affairs.

He was an extrovert, and the public and private themes are both stated in the same key, as it were—are both treated as objective events, with very few passages of introspection and none of reminiscence to mark the differences between them or to hold up the flow of narrative development. The diary material was shaped simply by the fall of events, as in all good diaries. Now one history, now the other, moved to the forefront as its partner moved back. The long war crisis of 1667 left small room for private affairs, just as a domestic crisis (like his brother Tom's illness in 1664, or his affair with Deb Willet in 1668) crowded out public affairs.

It is this mingling of two varieties of record, in a diary executed on a large scale and in minute detail, which is the principal explanation of its character and value as an historical source. By reason of its detail and its length (it is roughly as long as Gibbon), it yields a great mass of information. By reason of the duality of its structure, it is free from some of the limitations of autobiography on the one hand, and of generalised national history on the other. Pepys's concern with the large events of the world outside himself makes it impossible for him to indulge for too long in personal *trivia*, while his concern with himself and the small events of everyday living always gives a human dimension to his account of public affairs. The diary serves therefore not only as a mirror but also as a private window giving on to a broad and varied external view—on to court politics and naval administration, or (at the other extreme) on to the simple domesticities of a London household. There is much else too—in particular, glimpses of the religious and cultural life of London. The view has one obvious drawback—it is impossible to see much of the countryside—but a very large part of his contemporary England is displayed by Pepys. If all records of his period, except this one, were to disappear, it would still be possible to reconstruct much of Pepys's world from the diary alone.

Pepys's interest in public events was a natural one, and it would have been difficult for him to have thought of his life in any other way than in the context of political history. Born nine years before the outbreak of civil war, he had grown up not into the sort of world which could have been predicted at his birth but into the chaos and catastrophes of revolution. Londoners, as front-line witnesses of the upheaval, felt the force of events with particular sharpness. As a boy of sixteen Pepys had stood outside Whitehall Palace and watched—with approval—the execution of his King. Moreover, it was in the political world that he had made his career, serving in the 1650s both Mountagu and the Exchequer. When the diary opens in 1660 it reveals a young man whose mind had already acquired the habit of political reflection. He was hunting out political news, observing parties and interests, making political judgements, concerning himself more and more in the 1660s to discover what good or evil had come out of the 'late times'. It was on politics that his career and livelihood, his social position and a large part of his happiness, all ultimately rested.

The result is that the diary contains both an individual's experience and the multiple experiences of his society. To historians this is a piece of particularly good fortune. Moreover, a good diary—whatever its design—can have a special usefulness to the study of history. It can be—and often is—more honest than letters; more true to events than memoirs composed afterwards; less limited and less uncommunicative than institutional records. At its best it may amount to something approaching a total transcript of experience, and if its author is a man of significant experience, and has the right diary technique, then its value is considerable.

To the historian, the cardinal value of the good diary is perhaps its realism. It will register the impression of events at the moment of their impact, and not as they later appear by hindsight. It will not conceal the author's mistakes or bad judgements. It will repeat itself, contradict itself; it will follow rumours and false clues. It will move not in large sweeps of time, like a history or an autobiography, but at the pace of natural life, set by the rhythm of waking and sleeping. Its diurnal form will mean that its treatment of some events will be spasmodic and episodic, but this is the way in which many events—even processes—happen. Its sole principle of arrangement will be that of chronology. All that the diarist observes he will hold suspended in the same stream of time which carries him and everything else along with it—the large matters with the small, the distant with the intimate. The diarist, although he will comment on events and may well relate some events to others, will not attempt (if he is a good diarist) to isolate them or rearrange them: he will merely mark their passing in the stream. His function is to register the daily flux of change—the weather rather than the climate of his age. And, more than that, if he keeps his diary with a proper fullness, he will recall those things—apparently slight but significant—which no other form of record is so well designed to preserve, and which are often irrecoverable—a dream or a mood, an impulse, a half-suppressed thought, intonations of voices, the gestures and the silences that sometimes do service for speech.

So much for the ideal. Pepys comes as close as anyone to it. His methods are models for the diarist. His narrative, composed from notes a few days after the event, and substantially unaltered thereafter, never suffers from the silent distortions and insidious afterthoughts (all the effect of rewriting long after) which disfigure so much of the diary of his friend Evelyn. He wrote regularly and with a technique which seems assured and fully developed when he starts the diary and rarely flags to its end—cramming it with detail, spending hundreds of words, if necessary, on a single event or conversation. He could never have written, in the manner typical of Evelyn: 'I had discourse with the Dutch Ambassador concerning the present state of Flanders'—and have left it at that—a note as dry and dead as a pressed leaf in the pages of a herbarium. Pepys would have caught and preserved the incident alive. He would have given not only the substance of the conversation but also the chance details—the diarist's clothes or the ambassador's mannerisms—which re-create atmosphere. The men and their encounter (and very likely the state of Flanders) would have been made vivid and memorable.

He never obtruded his views, though he often expressed them. He wrote honestly, concealing nothing. He wrote voluminously, and he dealt mainly in facts. His fondness for statistics is noticeable—not only in his references to public finance and the currency but in his account of naval engagements or of epidemics. The result is a diary which has a high density of hard factual information and an almost absolute freedom from cant and self-deceit. There is much, of course, that is missed from it, even within its own limits, and in some matters Pepys was wrong. But omissions and mistakes are few and on balance unimportant. His version of the daily round of living obviously excluded much that was routine. He often, for instance, wrote about composing the finished version of his diary (an irregular event), but never (as far as may be judged from some cryptic material) about the more regular event of making the preparatory notes. He did not usually mention the prices of purchases, since these went into the account-books which were entered up from the same set of rough notes as the diary itself. He did not normally report sermons at any length—as did Evelyn and other diarists of the period—but dismissed them with a brief phrase or sentence. The only sermon reported fully is the farewell sermon preached by the Presbyterian Dr Bates of St Dunstan-in-the-West on 10 August 1662, shortly before his extrusion a fortnight later, and in that case the diarist's interest was in the public event of the extrusion rather than in the sermon.

It is remarkable how often he misreported, just slightly, the words of the sermon's text. He had a faulty verbal memory, and did not trouble to look up his Bible. He made other verbal slips: 'my lord Chancellor' for 'my lord Chamberlain', 'parliament' for 'House of Commons' are typical examples. He very occasionally gave wrong dates; for example, of a proclamation he had misread, or of parliamentary proceedings he knew of only from hearsay. Writing on 25 May 1669, he misdated the council proceedings of the 21st, probably because he was then catching up with twelve days' arrears. At 12 October 1667 his summary of the Lord Keeper's speech at the opening of the parliamentary session is misleading because he had gleaned his news from four informants two days after its delivery. On other occasions his attempts to compress complicated news items could lead to garbling. But, all told, his accuracy is remarkable.

Of his sources of information, some were commonplace at the time and have often been used since—pamphlets and broadsheets for domestic politics, or newspapers for news of distant parts and of naval engagements. In his hundred or so entries about the Plague he regularly reproduced the figures of deaths published in the weekly bills of mortality. But with these materials he often combined information which is peculiarly his own. For English news, the newspapers were dependent on him rather than he on them. On naval news he was himself a prime authority. He also had access to the manuscript newsletters from Holland or Flanders which reached the Secretary of State giving foreign intelligence, and to which Pepys could add the overseas news he heard from seamen and shippers. As for the Plague, he knew enough about the methods of parish clerks to correct the figures they submitted to the compilers of the official bills of mortality.

The validity of Pepys's information varies with its subject, and general judgements of it ought to be few and guarded. On the daily detail of his own life, he is, of course, the unique authority, and he gives us an account which has certain distinct levels of interest. As a source of facts about everyday affairs, it yields fine detail not easily found elsewhere. As a variety of sub-history (if we may call it so), it may illuminate larger themes: as in early 1660, when Pepys's observation that M.P.'s were stockpiling their firewood reminds us of the Rump's stubborn refusal to dissolve. More generally, this flow of prosaic information exerts, paradoxically, a powerful effect on the imagination. We are never in danger of forgetting that Pepys was in so many ways like ourselves: we can easily imagine ourselves in his situation. We make therefore the more effort to understand what is strange to us in him and his world. We are more interested in a man's politics or religion if we know what he had for dinner.

To the historian, one of the most interesting features of these private and domestic revelations is perhaps the information they give about Pepys's religion—to many of

Pepys's contemporaries the most vital of all issues. We know from his letters that his High Anglicanism in his last years, after 1688, was a facet of his political convictions: a form taken by his loyalty to his old master James II. He had grown up under strong puritan influences, though never becoming in any strict or formal sense a Puritan. These were influences which no one alive in Interregnum England could escape, and Pepys had been directly subjected to them from his mother, his school and his university. There are clear traces of puritanism in Pepys—in his habit of attempting to control his behaviour by taking vows, perhaps also in his dislike of gaming and of swearing. But his ecclesiastical position, clear enough by the time the diary opens, was by then that of a middle-of-the-road Erastian, distrustful of both ritualists and precisians, a loyal son of the Church of England but a strong critic its clergy, staunchly anti-Roman but at the same time only amused by talk of the Pope as anti-Christ. He attended both Presbyterian and Anglican services during the Interregnum, but preferred the Anglican. After the Restoration he went to his parish church with respectable frequency rather than with devout regularity; and if he slept during the sermon he usually had the excuse that it was during the afternoon service. In the whole of the diary period, he apparently never made his communion, at the monthly celebrations at his parish church or elsewhere. His Lents were kept sketchily, and he observed Sunday as best he could, which was sometimes not very well. He read his Bible only a little, and (probably in common with many other householders) regarded family prayers mainly as a method of household management. He was at bottom, in the diary period, a worldling. Yet there can be no doubt of the sincerity of his religious feelings. He turned naturally to God, when alone, to express thanks or to ask for protection and help. His Anglicanism may have been loosely formulated in so far as it was a creed, but as a social discipline it was a cause to which his loyalty was firm. Just as his patriotism led him to support any stable government, republican or monarchical, his Anglicanism was an expression of his attachment to any church which could command the devotion of the nation at large. Living in times of ecclesiastical strife, he looked to statesmen and church leaders to work out the terms of an ecclesiastical peace. He welcomed the proposals made for union between Presbyterians and Anglicans, particularly those of 1667-8, and at all times he favoured toleration. Seeing conventiclers carried off to prison, on 7 August 1664, he wrote: 'They go like lambs, without any resistance. I would to God they would either conform, or be more wise and not be ketched.' Perhaps he was less religious than most men of his class and generation, but his views on toleration—or something like them—were widespread among the educated laity, and it was on ecclesiastical pragmatism of this sort—on the layman's common sense—that the solutions of these problems reached at the Revolution of 1688-9 were largely to rest. The evidence of the diary has at any rate the virtue of offsetting the testimony of the clergy which tends to bulk too large in the minds of most ecclesiastical historians.

Another subject on which the diary has special information is Pepys's career during these years in the service of the state—in the Navy Office primarily, but also in the Exchequer, the Privy Seal Office, the Tangier Committee, and the Royal Fishery. No other civil servant of the seventeenth century kept a diary on such a scale, and its material, particularly that concerning the Navy Office, may be used both to supplement official records and, occasionally, to correct them.

Some official naval papers covering the diary period have disappeared since Pepys's day (e.g. the Navy Office's day-books and minute-books), but many remain—a large body of correspondence (in most of which Pepys was involved), a complete series of contract books, warrant books and Navy Treasury ledgers, an office memorandum book (1660-8), and many miscellaneous papers. Pepys himself kept (mostly in shorthand) a personal memorandum book (his 'Navy White Book', 1663-8), as a memorial of all business which had gone wrong through the shortcomings of his colleagues, and as a means of self-protection against criticism in parliament or elsewhere. At several points it covers the same ground as the diary, but in greater detail. All these official and semi-official records, together with those of the Lord High Admiral, and other government records, form the basis for a study of the work of Pepys's Navy Office, and to them the diary kept by the Clerk of the Acts serves only as an interesting supplement. By itself, it is a wayward, incomplete and prejudiced source for administrative history. It sometimes spends itself on the small transactions which had a special importance to Pepys himself, rather than on the larger matters which had less impact on him personally. But its value is that it can add unique detail, and that in general it provides administrative history with a personal dimension not provided by other sources. It gives an impression of the officials in action—of their daily routines; of their conversations together; of their anxiety to enlarge their functions so that they and their personal clerks could enjoy more fees; of their bargaining with merchants, their comings and goings between Seething Lane and the dockyards. Pepys's version of what happened is partial (in both senses of the word), but it is a vivid and on the whole credible picture of the human scene in which the play of administrative action took place. Pepys's judgements of his colleagues have the reputation of being over-severe. He may well have been a little self-righteous, and prone to the censoriousness which comes from an inflexible regard for professional standards. However, Batten, his principal *bête-noire*, had a poor reputation with Coventry as well as with Pepys, and is known to have left his office papers in disorder; and Penn (another of Pepys's butts) was also criticised by Sandwich and by Gauden.

There are certain office matters on which the diary is particularly useful. It is perhaps at its best in registering the successive stages of an extended event—the process of negotiating a contract, the composition of a long report, the story of a protracted piece of litigation. The crucial subject of naval finance is nowhere better treated in general terms, and although here the diary's statistical material is sparse, this is a weakness fairly easily remedied from other sources. In no other contemporary account are displayed so precisely the practical difficulties of trying to run the navy on inadequate grants and poor credit. In 1665 an experiment was tried which was to provide a solution. A sum of £11/4m. was granted by parliament, but was appropriated to the navy alone. The diary shows in detail how merchants and bankers reacted. The scheme was at first distrusted, by Pepys himself not least, but proved its value and was repeated (with certain changes) in the grants of 1666 and 1667. (Pepys's old master in the Exchequer, Sir George Downing, had much to do with its inception and success.) There is also some information in the diary about the beginnings of Treasury control over government spending, which started with the establishment of the Treasury commission of 1667 of which, Downing, as secretary, was the leading spirit. Pepys's references to his own dealings with the commission, both as Clerk of the Acts and as Treasurer for Tangier, illustrate the beginnings of the story. It was significant of another important constitutional trend of the time, too, that certain controls were also exercised over the Navy Board and Admiralty by parliament. Pepys gives a good account of the enquiries made by parliamentary committees appointed in 1667-8 into the management and conduct of the Second Dutch War, because he was himself in many respects closely involved, and took the lead (as 'the chief mover among them') in the defence of the Navy officials.

On several aspects of administrative history, the diary has the virtue of speaking indiscreetly where other sources are often silent. It can, in a few frank words, make plain the reasons for the appointment of naval commanders or of Navy Board officials. It reveals the lies with which Pepys protected everyone involved in the prize-goods scandal of 1665—including himself and his patron Sandwich. It shows how (with rather better justification) he and Coventry in November 1664 conspired to inflate their estimates of the costs of a naval war against the Dutch as 'a scare to the Parliament, to make them give the more money'. It gives instances of the suppression of evidence by Pepys when under parliamentary scrutiny—e.g. about Warren's timber contract of 1664, or the payment of seamen by tickets. Pepys sinned cheerfully in all these cases, believing that he was acting in the public interest. There were also occasions, as with many other public servants, when private advantage bulked large in his calculations. At least once he disobeyed office rules by trading with the navy on his own account, supplying calico for flags, and time and again he accepted gifts of money and goods for services rendered. In an age when salaries (unaltered for generations) were artificially low, officials were not expected to refuse all gifts, but the practice had its dangers ('so hard it is,' as Pepys reflected, 'for a man not to be warped against his duty'), and it is difficult for the historian to judge of its effects. Pepys's own attitude is made clear enough in the diary. There were some gifts which obviously operated against the public interest, as in Pepys's view did the frequent tributes of cash and goods which Batten took from merchants quite indiscriminately. Such practices Pepys condemned. But he could not see anything wrong in a gift made merely to expedite business or to establish good personal relations. The test, perhaps a more elastic one than he was willing to admit, was that the public service should also benefit. He would never himself 'by anything be bribed to be unjust', but he 'was not so squeamish as not to take people's acknowledgement where I have the good fortune by my pains to do them good and just offices'. The wealth which Pepys accumulated during the diary period (rising from £25 in liquid capital in 1660 to £7000 in 1667) was built up not only from such gifts but also (and perhaps principally) from fees and poundage income from his Tangier post as well as his office in the navy. Nevertheless, proceeds from gifts were not inconsiderable: large sums of hundreds of pounds from big merchants such as Sir William Warren, £500 p.a. from Sir Denis Gauden as victualler of Tangier, and a succession of presents—silver flagons, 'an excellent Mastiffe, his name Towzer', 'a case of very pretty knifes with agate hafts', and so on. This may not have harmed the Crown, but the gifts were often meant to influence decisions (it is noticeable how often the presents arrived in the midst of negotiations for a contract), and would have been awkward to explain to a critical House of Commons. Some civil servants could joke about it. Cooling, a council clerk, told Pepys, admittedly when drunk, that 'his horse was a Bribe, and his boots a bribe; . . . and invited me home to his house to taste of his bribe-wine'. But Pepys had to be more careful. Receiving a letter from Capt. Grove on 3 April 1663, he closed his eyes before opening it, discerning money to be in—'not looking into it till all the money was out, that I might say I saw no money in the paper, if ever I should be Questioned about it'. The best defence of Pepys is that, surrounded as he was by the calculated generosity of merchants, he preserved his independence. He worked hard when there was no prospect of 'bribes' and at matters which brought no profit. He refused gifts if he thought fit, and he returned them to the donors if the service had not been performed. He upheld the criticisms made by an officer of Woolwich yard of the hemp served in by Sir Richard Ford, even though the latter was an influential merchant (and a neighbour of the Navy Office), because he 'would not have the King's workmen discouraged (as Sir W. Batten doth most basely do) from representing the faults of merchants goods, when there is any'. He did not allow his understandings with Warren and others to deter him from criticising them before the Board, or from holding them to severe terms in the King's interest. Pepys, like many other public servants, had mastered the useful art of receiving gifts without becoming corrupt—an art he shared with his King and with many contemporary politicians.

The political world in which Pepys's career was set is in many ways difficult to understand. It is full of contradictions which derive mainly from contradictory elements within the monarchy. The monarchy of Charles II (in process of change from the authoritarianism of his father to the milder form of the post-1688 period) was at one and the same time both strong and weak. It had great reserves of independent power, and yet it was to some extent and in some circumstances forced to accommodate itself to parliament, to a semi-independent local magistracy, and to national feelings. In this situation public opinion was of importance, and perhaps the greatest contribution which Pepys's diary makes to an understanding of political history is that it gives the best available single account of public opinion in the early years of the Restoration. It covers or touches on most topics of significance; its news is often unique and almost always accurate; and it registers spoken rather than written or printed opinion—i.e. the opinion which, being evanescent, easily disappears from the record. Pepys may be said (though admittedly with some exaggeration) to have transcribed the political conversation of London. The town talked; Pepys listened.

Like Paris in the nineteenth century, London in the late seventeenth was a city alive with political excitement. The English then, like the French later, were known for political instability. They had strong views and lived in critical times. Moreover, the physical size of the political community was small. High politics were mostly conducted in a limited area—the capital—by a limited number of people.

They concerned decisions made by an *élite* in Whitehall and Westminster whose members it was often possible for the London public to know, or to know of, as persons. The slowness of communications enlarged distances. Only occasionally (at times of great crisis or in the very infrequent general elections) did the provinces take an important part in political life; Europe and the rest of the world were days, weeks, months away. The scale of the political world, that is to say, did not dwarf the human beings inhabiting it. Issues of the most general sort could be discussed in terms of personalities. Another condition made for the intensity of political interest among Londoners—the fact that conversation was then the commonest mode of communicating political news and opinion. Newspapers, later to be the main carriers of this traffic, were then virtually forbidden to trade in it—they were official publications and by official policy were kept very brief and reticent. There was thus a premium on political talk. On 6 June 1666, when the public learned that the battle fleets of Holland and England had met, forty enquirers flocked to Pepys's office to hear the result. Obviously this method of news-gathering was unsystematic and open only to Londoners, but it worked, and news by this means could travel quickly. Word of the Anglo-Dutch peace of 1667, which arrived at Whiteball at noon on 6 July, had travelled across town to Pepys's house in the city before he could sit down to his midday dinner. There were, of course, dangers in the oral transmission of news. Falsification of facts was easy, and false news could spread as easily as true, or more easily. Pressures of feeling could build up quickly, and were difficult to control in a large crowded city which had no effective police. The two great public panics of Pepys's lifetime were produced in these conditions—the revolutionary riots of 1641 and the Popish Plot scare of 1678-9. On the other hand, the virtue of these conditions was that they stimulated individuals to take an interest in politics. Modern democracies, which endow the citizen with so much more political power than he had in Pepys's day, also involve him in a type of political life so much more complex and impersonal that he may find some difficulty in participating in it.

It is therefore not surprising to find in the diary a great deal of solid political news in the form of what appears to be personal gossip. Pepys by great good fortune happened to be well placed as an eaves-dropper. He had the entry to the royal palace, to government offices, and to parliamentary committees; and the range of his acquaintance comprised almost all types of person from royalty downwards. Of those who governed England, in fact, only the leaders of the established church were unknown to Pepys. He attracted confidences. Statesmen and city councillors alike would divulge their secrets to him, and from a host of informants he would extract political news of varying interest. In those days of a very small civil service even minor civil servants, being close to the heart of government, could tell Pepys the business methods of the Lord Treasurer, or of secret council proceedings. And beyond the governing circles, Pepys went through London spreading a close-meshed net for his daily haul of news. It might be good fish or it might be red herring—but a day without a catch was to Pepys a day lost. He was regarded by Sandwich (and no doubt by others) as an authority on London opinion. He talked with merchants and financiers; with sailors and shopmen, drabs and dons. Thanks to his gift for hobnobbing, he came near to hearing the talk of the whole town.

His diary technique was well suited to the purpose of recording oral news. Despite his reputation among later commentators, he spent at least as much space on important news as on *trivia*. He summarised each item, dated it, and gave its attribution. He went out of his way to cultivate acquaintances he loathed (religious fanatics in particular) if he thought that their opinion might be of political interest. In listening, he would not interrupt an informant, even if he had heard his story before, in case he might pick up a new detail. In reporting a conversation he would suppress his own opinions, with the result that his account of a talk which lasted for two hours—that with Robert Blackborne on 9 November 1663—reads like a monologue.

It is conceivable that he was led by his own interests to exaggerate the amount of political talk, but any exaggeration was not serious, because there are other witnesses to the same phenomenon. De Cominges, the French ambassador, observed in 1665 that in London even the watermen spoke of state affairs to the milords as they rowed them to parliament. De Cominges himself, and most other envoys, thought it worthwhile to relay their impressions of London opinion regularly to their home governments. Their despatches often cover the same ground as Pepys's diary entries, and (although usually inferior in detail and precision in their treatment of opinion) often confirm them. Clarendon's government itself paid coffee-house politi-

cians the compliment in 1666 of attempting to shut down the coffee-houses 'with their calumnies and scandals'. It is also likely that Pepys over-emphasised those views he agreed with. He tended to find in public opinion what he had set out to find—criticism of the court's wastefulness, of parliament's ignorance and so on. He may well have exaggerated also the strength of Presbyterianism, which was not as important in church or state affairs as Pepys and many of his contemporaries thought.

But on the whole Pepys's accounts of news and public opinion bear the stamp of an accurate record, if not always of an exact judgement. There were available to him three principal broadcasting centres of political news: the royal palaces at Whitehall and St James's, for news of court and government; Westminster Hall, for news of parliament; and, for overseas news, the Royal Exchange in the city. Pepys, besides frequenting all these places himself, had in each of them a number of well-placed informants.

His work for the Navy and Tangier took him often to court. Every Monday, with his colleagues of the Navy Board, he waited on the Lord High Admiral, the Duke of York, in his chambers in Whitehall or, in summer, in St James's. He frequently visited government departments (particularly the Treasury) or attended council committees. During the war his visits multiplied, and involved oc-

The coronation of James II in 1685. Pepys is holding the nearer of the front poles supporting the canopy.

casionally attendance at the cabinet itself (which appears to have been the Navy Committee too during wartime), and at the meetings of ministers held a few days before the meetings of the cabinet in order to prepare business. Most of these visits he would prolong by gossiping in the galleries and ante-chambers, or in the highly political taverns near the palace. The King and Prince Rupert knew him, though not as well as did the Duke of York. Albemarle would hand to him, unopened, naval despatches addressed to him as commander. To Clarendon and Arlington, with whom his dealings were rather less frequent, he was known as a prominent and industrious functionary. Pepys knew intimately two officers of state who were often in the inner confidence of the government—Sir George Carteret (Treasurer of the Navy and Vice-Chamberlain of the King's Household), and Sir William Coventry (secretary to the Duke of York). He also learned much from men less eminent but nevertheless well informed, such as Sir Hugh Cholmley, a courtier. His spies for backstairs news were James Pearse (who had a place in the Queen's Household and was Surgeon to the Household of the Duke of York); Sarah, housekeeper to Sandwich, whose official lodgings were next door to Lady Castlemaine's house in King Street; and the courtiers Bab May and Tom Chiffinch.

It was from these palace sources that Pepys gained most of what he knew about the rise and fall of the King's ministers. His material on the subject before 1667 is usually slight or incidental. From time to time he names the 'cabal'—the inner circle of ministers—but the names (given at secondhand) have to be checked carefully. He has some detail about the resignation of Secretary Nicholas in October 1662, which was to lead to Bennet's (Arlington's) appointment as his successor, and to the undermining of Clarendon's position. His information (at 23 December 1662) that Clarendon was (according to James Pearse) 'as great . . . as ever he was with the King' is interesting in view of the controversies that have gathered around the question of Clarendon's responsibility for the royal declaration of 26 December which promised an indulgence to the Dissenters. But it is with the ministerial changes of 1667-8, in which Coventry was involved, that Pepys's evidence attains its greatest authority. Clarendon's fall in the autumn of 1667, for which Coventry was in large part responsible, is fully described in a series of conversations which Pepys had with Coventry himself. It is an account greatly superior to those written afterwards in the memoirs of Clarendon and the Duke of York, and one which later studies have vindicated without material alteration. The collapse in October-November 1668 of the York-Coventry influence and its replacement by that of the Buckingham-Arlington connection (assisted by Lady Castlemaine) can also be traced in Pepys in a detail which is at all major points confirmed by the surviving correspondence.

The history of the Privy Council is another theme illuminated by the diary. The official register of council proceedings gives only the results of debates, not the debates themselves, and has almost no evidence about the committees or informal groups which made the most important decisions. Pepys gives occasional accounts of what was said, or alleged to have been said, in meetings of full council (some of them 'close' meetings from which Council clerks were excluded), and many accounts of committees—all of which add to the official record. He throws some light on the dark matter of how council committees were composed and organised. Characteristically, too, he can quite casually provide a piece of information (probably otherwise unrecorded) which is revealing. At a meeting on 3 July 1667, for instance, at the height of the invasion scare, when news of a landing by the Dutch at Harwich had just reached London, naval business was held up for 'near two hours' while 'the King and the whole tableful of Lords' discussed a private law dispute between an old man 'with a great gray beard' and his son 'for not allowing himself something to live on'. Albemarle was fast asleep before the case had ended.

The diary contains no studied portraits of individuals, but is rich in such snapshots as that of the sleeping Albemarle. There are the King and the Duke of York winking at each other at the council board; Rupert, who at meetings 'doth nothing but swear and laugh a little, with an oath or two'; the slatternly and avaricious Duchess of Albemarle ('Dirty Besse')—a comic figure who might easily have been invented by a satirist. From a succession of small observations a picture often emerges. The King himself appears as lazy and self-indulgent, but also as intelligent, witty, genuinely interested in the navy, and if not himself an administrator, at least capable of galvanising others into efficiency. About the Duke of York, later James II, Pepys gives perhaps the most valuable information of all, since he knew him better than he knew any other great person. In 1661—well before his reception into the Catholic church—James was known as 'a professed friend to the Catholiques', affecting in his worship a height of ceremony which alarmed Pepys, and so unpopular that the news of the death of his only son in May of that year was said to 'please everybody'. He had a penchant for French and Irish favourites; he was a militarist, and reputedly an enemy to parliament. On the other hand, his work as Lord High Admiral in the 1660s appears, according to Pepys's evidence, to have been done well and to have held his interest, though it had to give way sometimes to the stronger attractions of hunting and womanising. Moreover, he showed some capacity for sound judgement. When Pepys's clerk, Thomas Hayter, in 1663, confessed to having been discovered at a conventicle, word came from his Highness, who had been brought up in army camps to value loyalty above religious conformity, that 'he found he had a good servant, an Anabaptist; and unless he did carry himself more to the scandall of the office, he would bear with his opinion till he heard further'. James's concern for religious toleration—hypocritical later when it was meant to lead to Catholic domination—seems to have been in these circumstances quite genuine. James could, also, be judicious in settling pay disputes, and it would be unsafe to assume that he was in these matters merely voicing the views of advisers. Of course, the epoch-making mistakes he later committed as King arose from his interpretation of his functions as an anointed ruler, and the light thrown on them by evidence from the 1660s can only be indirect. But some of his failings and virtues are clear enough in the diary, and Pepys at any rate gives the lie to Macaulay's famous gibe that James was fit only to be a dockyard clerk.

Pepys's parliamentary news from Westminster Hall, being less picturesque, is less well known than his political news from the court. It has sometimes escaped the notice even of serious students of the subject, although it has been in print since Wheatley's edition of the 1890s. The diary covers a period in which facts about parliamentary debates are hard to come by. Of unofficial parliamentary diaries kept by members or officers of the Houses (on which the historian has mostly to rely), there are very few known examples—none at all for the Lords, and none for the Commons during the four sessions of 1663-5. Pepys offers parliamentary notes which are scattered and brief, but none the less very welcome. He would make a point of learning, from members or from hearsay, about important debates, and although both houses debated in secret and forbade publication of votes and proceedings, news of their transactions was soon bruited around by word of mouth. Close by the parliamentary chambers themselves was Westminster Hall—with its shops and lawcourts and crowds, one of the most frequented of London's public places. Pepys had only to go and gossip there—walking 'from one man to another'—to pick up the latest news of parliament. He more than once penetrated into the chambers themselves, although he was not a member of the Commons until 1673. As an official, he waited on parliamentary committees; as a member of the public, he attended trials held before the Lords; and he was not above gatecrashing large gatherings such as conferences between the Houses and end-of-session meetings, when in the press of people it was possible for strangers to gain admittance. Moreover, he had useful contacts among members of both Houses. Several of his colleagues on the Navy Board sat in the Commons for most of the diary period; so did his relatives, Roger Pepys and Sir Thomas Crew. His colleagues usually expressed the views of the government; his relatives (by a happy chance) those of the opposition groups. He heard about debates in the Lords from Sandwich and from Sandwich's father-in-law, Lord Crew. His entries about parliamentary proceedings, culled from these sources, are far from constituting a running summary for all or even most sessions. They are occasional and disjointed notes about what was relevant to his work, or what seemed important or interesting. The most extended and significant series is the run of entries in October-December 1666 dealing with the Commons' debates on finance. Here, and elsewhere, Pepys's accounts of Commons' debates can sometimes be both fuller and more accurate than those of members who were present. They sometimes tell of the unspoken feelings of members; they report a debate, or committee proceedings, not covered by the official journal. Those occasions when Pepys himself appeared before a parliamentary committee are in some ways reported more fully in the diary than anywhere else—certainly with fuller attention to Pepys's own speeches. The most interesting of the Lords' proceedings treated by Pepys are probably Clarendon's proposal to add a liberal proviso to the bill of uniformity (21 March 1662); Bristol's attempt to impeach Clarendon in 1663 (1, 2 July 1663; 23 September 1667); and the debates (4 January 1668) on the bill for establishing a parliamentary commission to examine accounts.

Pepys was also a chronicler of the views held by the general public of London on political matters. The two movements of opinion which receive his greatest attention are that which preceded the Restoration and that which followed the Dutch War. In reporting the former (during January-March 1660), Pepys wrote from a prejudice in the King's favour: his views were those of the civil servants and moderate politicians anxious to be rid of the republic.

But he observed the unfolding of events coolly, noting the alternative schemes put about by rival groups—a republic, a monarchy, a new protectorate under Richard Cromwell, or a military *régime* under Monck. At 6 March he repeated, with approval, Mountagu's cautionary remark that the King if restored, 'would not last long... unless he carry himself very soberly and well'. On the same day Pepys noted that 'everybody now drink the King's health without any fear, whereas before it was very private that a man dare do it'. This alehouse report is as good a definition as any of the moment at which there was an open change in the public attitude to Charles in London. It happens that the city of London and its government played a critical part in the political revolution of early 1660. It was the resistance of the Common Council of the city to taxation which started the movement. Monck and his army arrived in the capital on 3 February; threw in their lot with the city on the 11th and with their support secured on the 21st the return to the Rump of the surviving members excluded by force in 1648. These last—the 'secluded members'—outvoted the Rumpers, put in a new Council of State of moderates like themselves who then went on to call a new, freely elected parliament. The combination of military force with civic protest and parliamentary authority proved decisive: for the first time since 1641, law and the power to maintain order were on the same side in politics. Pepys's history of London in early 1660 is the best contemporary account we have. He noted both events and opinion; he knew Mountagu and his associates who were in power after the *coup* of 21 February; he lived in Westminster and regularly heard parliamentary news; he learned of the city's moves from Valentyne Fyge, a common-councilman who was also his family apothecary. Clarendon's later account of these months in his memoirs is much inferior to Pepys's: it is secondhand and includes only a single reference to public opinion. Other authorities—the letters of royalist agents (on which Clarendon's account was based), or the despatches of the French envoy—do not have the wide range or the daily detail and continuity of Pepys's reports. If one thinks of Pepys as an historian of London one thinks immediately of his eyewitness stories of the Plague and the Fire—and rightly, if the criterion is vividness and artistic effect. But judged by the test of their contributions to knowledge, those famous passages are equalled and perhaps surpassed by this story of London's political revolution in the early months of 1660.

The Dutch War constitutes the central drama of the diary, just as the Restoration constitutes its opening scene and the Plague and Fire its spectacular interludes. In 1664-5 war was not only welcomed but demanded by many politicians, by great numbers of the public and, above all, by those merchants who stood to gain by it. The King appears to have been anxious to avoid it; his ministers were either vehemently against it or ruefully nervous. So were the naval experts, like Pepys and Coventry, who best knew the practical difficulties. Pepys's account of the war forms a large part of the diary and has many points of interest. It includes careful accounts of naval engagements which took place a long way from his desk in Seething Lane. More predictably, it gives, at large, an administrator's view of the war effort, blaming wasteful courtiers and distrustful M.P.'s for the fatal shortage of money. But the diary's special value is in its record of the public mood in the later part of the war, and particularly in the months which followed the Dutch raid up the Medway of June 1667 and the unpopular peace of July. There is no other source which offers such a continuous run of evidence about the effects of the war on public opinion. There had been defeats (which led men to commend Oliver Cromwell, 'so brave things he did and made all the neighbour-princes fear him'); constant fears of invasion from both Holland and France; rumours of peculation; mutinous crowds of starving seamen in the streets—and to all these the Plague and the Fire had added apocalyptic touches of doom. Clarendon was brought down in disgrace in September-October 1667; other ministers took his place; but Pepys gives the impression that to many Londoners it seemed that monarchy itself stood in danger. In August and November Pepys heard prophecies from three sources that a commonwealth, in which 'men ... minded their business' would soon come in again. This was wild talk, but it is clear that a new attitude towards the puritans was setting in. Previously they had been marked down as rebels and regicides—even the Presbyterians had been tarred with the same brush and their services to the King in 1659-60 forgotten. Now a few Presbyterians returned to public office; the Presbyterian group in the Commons was in 1668 courted by Buckingham; and in the winter of 1667-8 proposals were set on foot for ecclesiastical concessions to the Dissenters. The number of Pepys's references to this new situation is striking. On 17 June 1667 he wrote: 'nothing but the reconciling of the presbyterian party will save us'. Over a year later, when Jonson's *Bartholomew Fair* was staged, Pepys observed that the audience no longer had any stomach for its gibes against puritans. This attitude (which was real, although Pepys exaggerated it) was the first sign since the Restoration of an *entente* between Anglicans and Puritans, which, though it had still to pass through many vicissitudes and fluctuations, was one of the most important political re-alignments of the reigns of Charles II and James II.

The vast amount of scattered political news in the diary reflects the character of Pepys's friendships. He was an intimate of many men who like himself were enthralled by politics. The most interesting of them was Sir William Coventry, secretary to the Duke of York as Admiral. He saw Pepys so often and entrusted him with so many of his confidences—we have already noticed those about the fall Clarendon—that Pepys's diary is the best single source we have for Coventry's views. He explained to Pepys his selling of offices and commissions in the navy; his views on parliamentary management; his preference for commissions rather than individual ministers for certain government offices (a contemporary innovation in the Treasury and elsewhere). He told Pepys in full the story of his part in the division of the fleet in June 1666 which led to its defeat in the Four Days Battle—an account much fuller and franker (especially in its criticisms of Albemarle) than the one he thought it prudent to give to parliament or to commit to paper. Another intelligent public servant, Sir Philip Warwick, secretary to the Lord Treasurer, left little in print or manuscript behind him about this period, but some of his opinions on fiscal affairs are preserved in Pepys. In a conversation with Pepys (29 February 1664) he argued (as would most seventeenth-century officials) in favour of the excise as the best of all taxes, and defended the King's management of finances, blaming the deficit on the ignorance and niggardliness of parliament. In its essentials this last contention has been confirmed by historians.

Whitehall and Westminster, where Pepys could pick up the best of his political news, were his principal listening-posts, but he also used a third—the Royal Exchange in the city, frequented by merchants and shippers in touch with many parts of the world. Here (or from his other contacts with the mercantile community) Pepys gathered his overseas news (much distorted when it concerned states with which England was at war), his news of ship movements (usually accurate), and his travellers' tales (usually picturesque). For news of a more political nature from Europe, Pepys relied rather on Whitehall. Among his city acquaintances, Capt. George Cocke, hemp merchant, had a ready fund of political news, but it was usually on domestic politics.

In the end, however, the historian's debt to the diary will not be calculated simply by adding up the subjects on which it can yield significant information. Its total value is something greater than the sum of the value of its parts, and can best be stated by recalling the point with which this ... [essay] started—the diary's dual structure; its combination of public chronicle and private journal. Because the diary tells an historical story in terms of an individual life, the reader is given not only an intellectual understanding of the period but also the means of achieving an imaginative sympathy with it. Reader and subject are united by a common humanity. This is not only one man's version of the history of a decade—this is what it felt like to be alive. (pp. cxiv-cxxxvii)

> Robert Latham, "Introduction: The Diary as History," *in* The Diary of Samuel Pepys: 1660, Vol. I *by Samuel Pepys, edited by Robert Latham and William Matthews, University of California Press, 1970, pp. cxiv-cxxxii.*

RICHARD OLLARD (essay date 1974)

[*Ollard is an English historian and biographer. In the following excerpt from his book-length biography of Pepys, he estimates the importance of the* Diary *as a mirror of its author and its age.*]

It is the secret of Pepys's fascination that one never gets to the end of him. The contrasts, not to say contradictions, of his character, emotions, tastes, opinions, conduct and circumstances challenge our understanding. Partly, no doubt, they can be explained by his extraordinary capacity for absorbing experience and making it nourish the consciousness that neither age nor disease could blunt or blur. Spiritually and mentally his arteries never hardened; the process of growing up did not, as with most people, end with the coming of middle age. His ear for the music of life always kept him in time; he could make a harmony of the trials and infirmities of old age as he had of the hot idleness of youth and the rush-hour traffic of middle age.

Partly the sturdy intellectual honesty of the diarist who wanted to see himself as he really was forced him to recognise the complexity of questions that most men in most ages never so much as ask themselves. But when all is said and done it is the very extent of our knowledge that shows us the range of our ignorance. We know more about Pepys than about any other individual Englishman of his time, far more than we know about Charles II or Clarendon, Sir Isaac Newton or Sir Christopher Wren, James II or Shaftesbury, to name but a few of the eminent contemporaries to whom he was more or less well known. Luckily for us he was one of the most observant and articulate men who ever lived; and by further good fortune his life covered the most exciting and eventful period of English history. And though he is that history's most vivid single witness (the account in the *Diary* of the Fire of London alone is one of the masterpieces of reporting in our language) he was by no means a spectator standing apart from the life of his time. He was at different times a Member of Parliament, a Fellow and President of the Royal Society, and, for nearly all his working life, both a confidential servant of men who were making policy and an expert government official. The Royal Navy owes more to him, is more his handiwork, than that of any other possible claimant from King Alfred downward. The passion for professionalism, the insistence on administrative discipline that his work for the navy exemplified in itself exerted a powerful creative influence on the civil service. Sea power and efficient bureaucracy were the means that had enabled the Dutch to overhaul and surpass the imperial predominance of the Spaniards and the Portuguese. In Pepys's early manhood England had challenged (he thought rashly) the Dutch title to the world championship. If it were to be made good, the same simple formula was required. Pepys more than any man of his time supplied it. In the words of J. R. Tanner, the great scholar, who has put all students of Pepys in his debt, he was 'one of the best officials England ever had'.

It is easy to underestimate the historical importance of Pepys. We are too familiar with the randy bewigged figure whose name, as a symbol of a slightly *risqué* conviviality, has been appropriated by this wine-shipper or that restaurant. An irresistible air of bedroom farce clings to him, partly deriving from the candour of the *Diary*, partly from the bawdiness of Restoration comedy that gives so much life and colour to our picture of the age. As Mr. Tattle scampers across the stage, baulked of the seduction of Miss Prue by an unwelcome intrusion, we are reminded of the furtive and futile lecheries so vivaciously recorded by Pepys and for the moment indentify the great civil servant with a character described by his creator as a half-witted Beau. It is not that we need to believe that great men have no sex life, a feat of historical credulity possible to few: it is that greatness seems incompatible with consciously making an ass of oneself. And yet Pepys was—and did.

To have written the *Diary* clearly sets him apart from the ordinary run of humanity which it reflects and judges with such piercing discernment. Most men can brace themselves to the shock of self-knowledge provided that they can look away again quickly. Moral and intellectual courage of a high order is required for the sustained, relentless, clinical examination of the private world of thoughts and emotions as well as the half public one of actions and words. Why did Pepys keep his *Diary*? Did he know in his heart of hearts that it would become one the great books of our language? Perhaps he did. But there is no evidence of it. Indeed as J. H. Plumb has pointed out so accomplished a writer would not have plunged his reader into a stream of consciousness that rapidly becomes a whirlpool, as persons, places, allusions are dashed in his face with hardly a word of explanation. Was his principal motive religious and moral? Pepys was a Puritan by upbringing and, in the opinion of so great a scholar as J. R. Tanner, always remained a Puritan at heart. Puritans set great store by the keeping of diaries as a systematic form of self-examination. Or was his ultimate purpose aesthetic, the artist's need to impose some order on the untidiness of experience? Certainly this was among his deepest springs of action. Was it accountancy on the grand scale, the apotheosis of those close reckonings in which he took such evident delight? Very possibly. Was it scientific curiosity, an attempt to establish the fundamentals of psychology by the study of the phenomena readiest to hand—namely himself? Such a motive would not be inappropriate to a Fellow and a future President of the Royal Society. Other reasons could be plausibly advanced. As Robert Latham, the greatest Pepys scholar of our day, has written in his introduction to his definitive edition of the diary:

> After all is said, the origins of so deeply personal a document must themselves be personal. One origin is certainly the vanity which is so clearly marked a feature of Pepys's character. Another, equally certainly, is his love of life. The diary is a by-product of his energetic pursuit of happiness. The process of recording had the effect, as he soon found out, of heightening and extending his employment.

It would be surprising if there were an obvious explanation of anything so extraordinary as the *Diary*. Everyone who reads it and who goes on to find out more about its writer will form his own opinion. This in itself suggests something of the mutiplicity of the man, the multiplicity that characterises a classic in which generations of readers catch echoes of sounds that they have heard when no one else was about. Variety, richness, depth: without these qualities no book could have lasted as long as Pepys's has. But how did they get there? Where do they come from? Not, surely, from that devious, shrewd Mr. Worldly Wiseman who is busily totting up his accounts or deceiving his wife in some liaison which by no stretching of language could be called romantic. Shallow, mean and monotonous would, at first sight, more aptly describe the preoccupation of the greedy, pushful, jealous little bureaucrat it reveals. True—as far as it goes. But Pepys possessed to a high degree the power of empathy, of entering into a mind or a milieu very different from his own and, as he did so, changing the colour and the tone of his mentality with the naturalness of a chameleon. Except that unlike the chameleon he was in some way changed and enriched by his experience. Rather, like Ulysses, he was a part of all that he had met. The combination of passionate curiosity about other people with an equally passionate interest in himself reminds one of Boswell. So does the tendency, most marked in early life, but still clearly discernible in old age, to set up a model of taste and conduct. 'Be Lord Kames!' Boswell's frenzied self-adjuration was carrying things too far. Pepys was at once too cautious and too self-reliant to tell himself to 'be' Sir William Coventry or, later in life, to 'be' John Evelyn. The phrase of the Psalmist 'when I awake up after thy likeness I shall be satisfied with it' comes nearer the mark.

If Pepys was in some respects like Boswell, in more important ones he resembled Dr. Johnson, notably in tenacity, decisiveness and independence of mind. The *Diary* and Boswell's *Life of Johnson* both owe to their method of composition an immediacy that transcends time. To both of them, with the necessary substitution, might be applied Stendhal's judgment of Cellini's autobiography: 'C'est le livre qu'il faut lire avant tout si l'on veut deviner le caractère italien.' The similarities of the two men, their moral seriousness, their political scepticism, their love of learning, their hatred of cant, their capacity for and need of affection, their kindness, are profound. Their differences are magnified or distorted by the fact that the close-ups we possess of each of them belong to opposite ends of their manhood. Johnson was fifty-four when Boswell met him and began that series of studies on which the great portrait is based. Had Pepys chosen that moment in life at which to begin his diary we should have had a self-portrait of the President of the Royal Society and Secretary of the Admiralty, Deputy Lieutenant for Huntingdonshire and Master of Trinity House, a Member of Parliament and a great patron of learning and the arts—a very different person from the young man whom we first see dining at home in the garret off the remains of the turkey on January 1st, 1660. And had Boswell by some inspired tinkering with the time machine been enabled to meet Johnson at the corresponding period of life several years before his own birth he would have found a much more Bohemian and dissolute character than the monumental figure who squashed him flat in the back room of Davies's shop that May afternoon in 1763. This is not to deny the contrasts in temperament and talent that would have been marked at any stage in life. It is an attempt, crude but necessary, to put the *Diary* and its author into some kind of perspective, without falsifying the stature of either. The *Diary* is a great work, as literature, as history, as a psychological document and as a key to what has been known as the English character in an age of national cultures perhaps soon to become extinct. It is thus almost impossible to exaggerate its value and its importance. But Pepy's closest friends and most wholehearted admirers would have been dumbfounded if they had been told that posterity would think of him as a diarist. They would not have been surprised that his name should still be as familiar as that of his great contemporaries Newton and Wren. But as a diarist! None of them even knew that he kept one. They did know him as a man of extraordinary parts and of outstanding achievements. It is almost as though we should be told that Sir Winston Churchill will be remembered by his countrymen for a series of philosophical arguments unearthed among the Chartwell papers a century after his death.

The two facts, that Pepys wrote a diary and that its publication in a mutilated and bowdlerised version in 1825, a hundred and twenty years after his death made his name immortal, are common knowledge. Two other facts, that the *Diary* covers only nine years of a lifespan of seventy and that it was written in shorthand under the strictest secrecy, are perhaps less widely known or at least less often remembered. Yet to a proper understanding of the man they are not less important. Historically the *Diary* has been the making of Pepys; in real life the *Diary* was of his making. It is this paradox that helps one to allow for the magnetic pull into anachronism exerted by so highly charged a work. (pp. 17-21)

> *Richard Ollard, in his* Pepys: A Biography, *Hodder and Stoughton, 1974, 368 p.*

MARVIN MUDRICK (essay date 1976-77)

[*Mudrick is a controversial American essayist and literary critic. His most recent work, consisting chiefly of contribu-* tions to literary reviews, has been criticized by some commentators as lowbrow and unscholarly, while others have labeled it highly original and imaginative. According to one commentator, John Leonard, Mudrick is "rude, contentious, incorrigible, comma spliced, headlong, raunchy, scornful and know-it-all." Another critic, Webster Schott, has described Mudrick as "a literary curmudgeon, a randy iconoclast and a delight. He provokes strange high-culture responses: snarls, laughs, hostility. Plus enlightenment." Nevertheless, Schott has argued, "literary egos and reputations need deflation. Criticism needs less fence-sitting. If Mudrick is tough and demanding he also succeeds in making the books he praises seem to require our reading. The woods are full of critics. There's only one Mudrick." In the following excerpt from an essay originally published in the* Hudson Review *in 1976, Mudrick probes selected cryptic passages in the* Diary.]

On October 20, 1663 Elizabeth Pepys sat in a coach outside a London shop waiting for her husband; and while Pepys

> was in Kirtons shop, a fellow came to offer kindness or force to my wife in the coach. But she refusing, he went away, after the coachman had struck him and he the coachman. So I being called, went thither; and the fellow coming out again of a shop, I did give him a good cuff or two on the chops; and seeing him not oppose me, I did give him another; at last, I found him drunk, of which I was glad and so left him and home; and so to my office a while and so home to supper and to bed.

"No other diarist lays himself so bare as Pepys does," declares Professor Matthews in his [1970 introduction to his and Robert Latham's edition of the *The Diary of Samuel Pepys*], reminding the rest of us how equivocal we are, implicating us against our will but for our own good in the bare facts of the all too human. Isn't Pepys our patsy and double (hypocrite readers!), doesn't his "passion for microscopic observation of himself as he actually was" end by exposing us all as we actually are? Sometimes we aren't much. The masher's way with a lady (that was no lady, that was my wife), the way of a man with a maid (chamber-, bar-, upstairs-, downstairs-), is "kindness or force"— if kindness doesn't work the alternative is naturally force—which are the two sides of a man's mettle (brass), because according to Pepys *nulla puella negat* though occasionally for appearance' sake she balks a little (sooner or later she can't say no: e.g. the lady in the coach doesn't rage or swoon, merely "refuses" and summons her handy husband; maybe next time . . .). Chivalry is dead and the Pepysian *coup de grâce* is that gratuitous cuff on the chops, which he delivers when he's sure the masher won't strike back: who else would not only let it fly at the moment but indite it with unembarrassed deliberateness hours or days later, and note besides how invigorating it is to discover that one's adversary is drunk (and therefore *can't* strike back)? Whatever the moral questions that keep popping up, editors understand all and forgive all because the Pepys of their dreams is Everyman except "incredibly honest." [According to Professor Matthews (see excerpt dated 1970)]:

> Much of the matter that is printed for the first time in the present edition might be labelled pornographic and [Pepys is often troubled with wind, one onset of which he describes at considerable length in pungent detail] scatological. Since most of it is written in Pepys's own *lingua franca* and hedged with shorthand and dog-Latin devices, it may be judged to deal with behaviour that

Pepys himself thought shameful. Yet his presentation of this record of his moral deviations is clinical rather than moral or erotic; much of it reads like material for a scientific report on sexual behavior in the human male. That Pepys included it, although ashamed, is the most evident testimony to the full objective reporting, the scientific outlook, the Baconianism that went into the diary and the manner in which it was reported.

But Pepys won't be caught so easily. Why not infer that not just the *lingua franca* but the whole diary—private, secret, written in shorthand, locked away from prying eyes—"deal[s] with behaviour that Pepys himself thought shameful"? Or who knows, perhaps the lingo is just a device for indicating something rich and strange, i.e. the sexy parts, so that when Pepys wants a quick charge he can look them up by skimming for word-clusters characteristic of the lingo, and shame has nothing to do with it: after all, when his sexual relations with his wife take a turn for the better, he uses it to record even those ("Waked betimes, and lay long hazendo doz vezes con mi moher con grande pleasure to me and ella"); and, for anyone who bothered to crack the simple shorthand, this mostly "Spanish" pidgin is so elementary and so peppered with—intentionally eye-catching?—giveaways ("I only did hazer her para tocar my prick con her hand, which did hazer me hazer") that either Pepys is ashamed past the need for concealment (he *needs* to be found out and humiliated!) or he isn't as ashamed as he ought to be for perpetrating such a witless exercise. Anyhow Pepys doesn't begin to use it till far along in the diary, years after his "moral deviations" have become so inextricable from the pattern of his daily life—like the man in Mark Twain's story who falls into a carpet-making machine and gets woven into the carpet—that dalliances and curds and cream and a shilling tip to Nell who lets him rub her thing with his thing and a salmon-pie in the nick of time for sending on to his wife in the country can all be looped together continuously in the crazy carpet:

> thence I back to the King's playhouse and there saw *The Virgin Martyr*—and heard the music that I like so well; and entended to have seen Knipp, but I let her alone; and having there done, went to Mrs. Pierce's back again where she was, and there I found her asleep on a pallet in the dark, where yo did poner mi manos under her jupe and tocar su cosa and waked her; that is, Knipp. And so to talk, and by and by did eat some Curds and cream and thence away home; and it being night, I did walk in the dusk up and down, round through or garden, over Tower Hill, and so through Crutched Friars, three or four times; and once did meet Mercer and another pretty lady, but being surprized, I could say little to them, though I had an opportunity of pleasing myself with them [?]; but left them, and then I did see our Nell, Payne's daughter, and her yo did desear venga after migo, and so ella did seque me to Tower-hill to our back entry there that comes upon the degres entrant into nostra garden; and there, ponendo the key in the door, yo tocar sus mamelles con mi mano and su cosa with mi cosa et yo did dar-la a shilling; and so parted, and yo home to put up things against tomorrow's carrier for my wife; and among others, a very fine salmon pie sent me by Mr. Steventon, W. Hewer's uncle; and so to bed.

This is as idyllic as the gallivanting ever gets, very likely because the women here aren't the low types with whom he dares to push his luck. It's the latter, of course, who provoke the Pepysian unbuttoning that obliges editors to clear their throats and emphasize the "clinical" and "Baconian" qualities of the sexy parts; but mere laymen might be inclined to substitute such epithets as "humorless," "mechanical," probably "anesthetic," possibly "sadistic," and to notice how readily the tone modulates into something like megalomania. Once Pepys discards his Puritan hang-ups and stops invoking God whenever he masturbates in church during a Sunday sermon or "spends" with one or another of his faceless, bodiless, mindless, unimaginable women ("I find myself, both head and breast, in great pain. . . . It is a cold, which God Almighty in justice did give me while I sat lewdly sporting with Mrs. Lane the other day with the broken window in my neck"), once he has the habit, there's no limit to his self-assurance and his sense of impunity. Thus, as a pretext for visiting the man's wife, he befriends a carpenter at one of the naval shipyards (Pepys is a Principal Officer of the Navy Board): "After dinner I found occasion of sending him abroad; and there alone avec elle je tentoy à faire ce que je voudrais, et contre sa force je le faisoy, bien que pas à mon contentment" (i.e. against her physical resistance I did what I would, though not to my satisfaction). Another time with Mrs. Bagwell "I had sa compagnie, though with a great deal of difficulty; néanmoins, enfin je avais ma volonté d'elle"; but the next day he complains of a "mighty pain in my forefinger of my left hand, from a strain that it received last night in struggling avec la femme que je mentioned yesterday." Or, in a coach with another woman and her husband, "did prender su mano with some little violence" and forces her to masturbate him (under a lap-robe? with her husband sitting on the other side of her? Pepys never brings up such trifles) "all the way home," where once they arrive he is surprised to detect that she seems out of sorts:

> there she did seem a little ill, but I did take several opportunities afterward para besar la [to kiss her], and so goodnight. They gone, I to my chamber, and with my brother and wife did Number all my books in my closet and took a list of their names; which pleases me mightily, and is a jobb I wanted much to have done. Then to supper and to bed.

Or plays the rôle of rough trade with his barmaid and shopgirl regulars:

> So to Westminster, where to the Swan; and there I did fling down the fille there upon the chair and did tocar her thigh with my hand; at which she begin to cry out, so I left off and drank, and away to the Hall and thence to Mrs. Martin's to bespeak some linen, and there yo did hazer algo with ella and drank and away. . . . So by coach home, and there find our pretty girl, Willet, come, brought by Mr. Batelier; and she is very pretty, and so grave as I never saw little thing in my life.

That unaccustomed touch of character and interest is really there in Pepys's first sight of Deb Willet, and commentators have always been grateful for the opportunity to carry on about the intensity and pathos of Pepys's involvement with her; but in fact the first sight of her remains the most moving, Pepys's appetite grinds everything down to its usual quick inventory, and his emotional repertoire never expands:

> going down Holburn-hill by the Conduit, I did see Deb on foot going up the hill; I saw her, and she me, but she made no stop, but seemed unwilling to speak to me; so I away on, but then stopped and light and after her, and

overtook her at the end of Hosier-lane in Smithfield; and without standing in the street, desired her to fallow me, and I led her into a little blind alehouse within the walls; and there she and I alone fell to talk and besar la and tocar su mamelles; but she mighty coy ["quiet," "unresponsive"], and I hope modest ["virtuous"]; but however, though with great force, did hazer ella con su hand para tocar mi thing, but ella was in great pain para be brought para it. I did give her in a paper *20s*, and we did agree para meet again in the Hall at Westminster on Monday next; and so, giving me great hopes by her carriage that she continues modest and honest, we did there part....

Pepys is sentimental about those of his women who not only have a virtuous look but, before he lays them out, put up a desperate fight; he tends, understandably enough, to worry about the risks to other people's virtue while in the very act of assaulting it "with some little violence" or "with great force." Vice is what happens to other people: what he himself seeks is "pleasure" (he often reproaches himself for "my love of pleasure") while others are the subjects or the objects of "vice": "how rude some of the young gallants of the town are become, to go into people's arbors where there are not men, and almost force the women—which troubled me, to see the confidence of the vice of the age"; but, on a typical "Lords day," Pepys

> turned into St. Dunstan's church, where I hear an able sermon of the Minister of the place. And stood by a pretty, modest maid, whom I did labour to take by the hand and the body; but she would not, but got further and further from me, and at last I could perceive her to take pins out of her pocket to prick me if I should touch her again; which seeing, I did forbear, and was glad I did espy her design. And then I fell to gaze upon another pretty maid in a pew close to me...

and so on. Vice, however, is something else and mustn't be left unmoralized: Mrs. Martin, his Westminster Hall regular, having married the wrong man, i.e. not the one Pepys urged on her for some special conveniences to Pepys in the arrangement,

> begins a sad story how her husband, as I feared, proves not worth a farding, and that she is with child and undone if I do not get him a place. I had my pleasure here of her; and she, like an impudent jade, depends upon my kindness to her husband; but I will have no more to do with her, let her brew as she hath baked—seeing she would not take my counsel about Hawly.

True, in this instance Pepy's love of pleasure wins out over his moral indignation, and soon and often he returns to the Hall and takes his position again at the old stand, sometimes "backward" for "convenience," sometimes "devante" for variety. Impudent jade or modest maid; su cosa mi cosa. Pepys thinks of himself as a connoisseur of women, by playing the field he is faithful to them all; he piques himself—and editors drop like flies with delight at the vividness of the phrasing—on the "strange slavery that I stand in to beauty": i.e. to any moher's cosa against which, having contended con mucho pièce de résistance, yo did rub mi cosa para hazer in mi hand. Women, on the other hand, are unreliable and fickle even when not yet vicious: *la donna è mobile*, as Pepys might have reflected: "no passion in a woman can be lasting long," as he does reflect, having joked with a woman and made her laugh after she enters the office solemn-faced to ask his help about housing for her family; and, "the best instance of a woman's

falseness in the world," Mrs. Martin's sister is shameless enough to

> come home all blubbering and swearing against one Captain Vandena, a Dutchman of the Rhenish wine-house, that pulled her into a stable by the Dog tavern and there did tumble her and toss her; calling him all the rogues and toads in the world, when she knows that ella hath suffered me to do anything with her a hundred times.

The logic here, though murky, seems to go as follows: If a woman gives way to any one man, doesn't put a desperate fight against him, indeed "suffers" him to do and do with her at his will and pleasure, then she is by such evidence bursting (and in some sense *obligated*) to be done to and done to by all the men in the world.

Other people, not just women, keep disappointing him, "vexing" him, they seldom fail to hurt Pepys more than he hurts them: "I having from my wife and the maids complaints made of the boy, I called him up and with my whip did whip him till I was not able to stir"; "I took a broom and basted her till she cried extremely, which made me vexed"; "Up betimes; and with my salt Eele went down in the parler, and there got my boy and did beat him till I was fain to take breath two or three times"; "became angry and boxed my boy when he came, that I do hurt my Thumb so much, that I was not able to stir all the day after and in great pain." Or consider such a milestone of injured delicacy as this:

> coming homeward again, saw my door and hatch open, left so by Luce our cookmaid; which so vexed me, that I did give her a kick in our entry and offered a blow at her, and was seen doing so by Sir W. Penn's footboy, which did vex me to the heart because I know he will be telling their family of it, though I did put on presently a very pleasant face to the boy and spoke kindly to him as one without passion, so as it may be he might not think I was angry; but yet I was troubled at it.

Small wonder that when in a fit of temper he pulls his wife's nose or blacks her eye, he can't bear to think that people will *know* (he's a very private man), and is "vexed at my heart to think what I had done, for she was forced to lay a poultice or something to her eye all day, and is black—and the people of the house observed it."

Although if worse comes to worst he can usually beat her up, Pepys is well matched with his wife, above all after she catches him *in flagrante* at home under her very nose: "my wife, coming up suddenly, did find me imbracing the girl con my hand sub su coats; and endeed, I was with my main [i.e. Fr. "hand"] in her cunny." What follows is the most interesting episode in the diary. Pepys is the little boy caught playing doctor with the girl next door; Elizabeth is Big Mama, a volcano of latent and sometimes actual hysteria (one night she advances toward him with red-hot tongs), she is enigmatic and implacable, she is demanding (especially in bed: "I have lain with my moher"—what a difference a "t" makes—"as a husband more times since this falling-out," he writes three weeks later, "then in I believe twelve months before—and with more pleasure to her then I think in all the time of our marriage before"), she is Argus-eyed (insists he have a full-time keeper! herself or his young assistant, either or both of whom must accompany him whenever he leaves the house, e.g. for appointments at Whitehall where he dis-

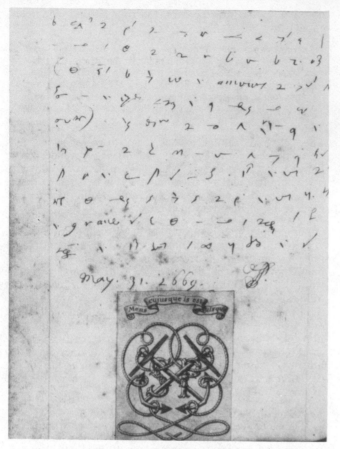

The last page of the Diary *manuscript. Pepys concludes: "[For] all the discomforts that will accompany my being blind, the good God prepare me."*

cusses Navy business with the Duke of York or the King), levitating at last to an ecstasy of omniscience from which she denounces him for having evil *dreams* and passes the night (if Pepys's tangled way of putting it doesn't allow some doubt) keeping a judicial hand ready to check on his unconscious erections: "My wife mighty peevish in the morning about my lying unquietly a-nights, and she will have it that it is a late practice, from my evil thoughts in my dreams; and I do often find that in my dreams she doth lay her hand upon my cockerel to observe what she can."

Professor Matthews has the presumptuousness to rate Pepys with Shakespeare and more particularly with Chaucer, "of all English writers, perhaps the only one who is his equal in gusto.... Who else among English writers has Pepys's enthusiasm for everyday people, everyday life, or his habit of judging everything he liked the best that ever there was?" [See excerpt dated 1970] Pepys does frequently express enthusiasm for one thing and another, for a good dinner he prides himself on giving to friends and eminent acquaintances (especially once he is prosperous enough to be able to show off a handsome house and excellent plate), for music, for dancing; and he can even make a few qualifications and wax philosophical:

> we to dancing and then to a supper of some French dishes (which yet did not please me) and then to dance and sing; and mighty merry we were till about 11 or 12

at night, with mighty great content in all my company; and I did, as I love to do, enjoy myself in my pleasure, as being the height of what we take pains for and can hope for in this world—and therefore to be enjoyed while we are young and capable of these joys.

But which dishes he objected to, or who did what at the party, or how the guests responded to one another, or almost whether anybody but Pepys was there—such matters scarcely ever intrude into the text: Pepys's "pleasure"—as when he is with his women—radiates an aura of self-satisfaction blinding enough to fade out everything in the neighborhood. Pepys is enthusiastic about plays too, goes to them as often as by surrealistic chains of reasoning he can neutralize his Puritan sense of guilt about going, considers himself a connoisseur of plays (on one occasion sits by an acquaintance "who understands and loves a play as well as I, and I love him for it"), but his capsule comments don't inspire a corresponding enthusiasm in the reader: *Romeo and Juliet* is "the worst [play] that ever I heard in my life"; *Sir Martin Mar-all* is "the most entire piece of Mirth . . . that certainly was ever writ"; *The Siege of Rhodes* is "certainly the best poem ever wrote"; *The Adventures of Five Hours* is "the best play I ever saw" (in comparison with which *Othello*, "which I have heretofore esteemed a mighty good play, . . . seems a mean thing"); *Twelfth Night* is "but a silly play and not relating at all to the name or day"; *A Midsummer Night's Dream* is "the most insipid ridiculous play that ever I saw in my life." One might as well be reading the movie reviews in the New York *Times*.

Pepys isn't like Chaucer, rather he's like those of Chaucer's characters who are authorized and camouflaged by a vocation: the Pardoner, the Friar, the Summoner, the Merchant, the Man of Law—

> Nowher so bisy a man as he ther nas,
> And yet he semed bisier than he was.

Chaucer's Man of Law could be Samuel Pepys, Clerk of the Acts of the Navy Board, member of the Fishery Corporation, Treasurer of the Tangier Committee, ubiquitous civil servant trusted and consulted by the Duke of York and the King, confidant to the Earl of Sandwich and Sir William Coventry and Sir George Carteret and Lord Crew, Fellow of the newly established Royal Society, in the prime of his young manhood (he is twenty-six at the beginning of the decade covered by the diary) busy busy busy doing his jobs and maintaining his "interest" with all the right people and accumulating "profits" (bribes) on the side and enjoying convivial dinners and outings almost nightly, yet not so busy that he doesn't have time for a secret life that behind the perfect competence of his rôle grins like an idiot, chasing after housemaids and barmaids and subordinates' wives and petitioners' daughters up and down stairs and all over the shadier sections of town, gorging on awful plays, planning the definitive treatise on the theory of music though he still hasn't got round to asking somebody the difference between concords and discords, trying without luck to follow the lectures and comprehend the experiments at the Royal Society, thrilled by scientific books he can't make sense of (like Boyle's *Hydrostatics*) as he indulges his intermittent determination to become an up-to-date know-it-all (what his age called a "virtuoso"), skeptical about Court gossip but (like Chaucer's old carpenter in *The Miller's Tale* who falls for a cock-and-bull story about the Flood) delighted to get the real dope on the Ark from a book by a Dr. Wilkins, "wherein he doth give a very good account thereof, showing how few the number of the several species of beasts and fowls were that were to be in the arke, and that there was room enough for them and their food and dung; which doth please me mightily—and is much beyond whatever I heard of that subject. And so to bed." The world is his cosa, and with some little violence all the animals fit inside.

Chaucer is the touchstone all right, not because he and Pepys are soul-brothers but because Chaucer is the only writer whose subject is the split between "gusto" and consciousness, the fact that vitality and consciousness ordinarily exist at cross-purposes, that each ordinarily functions at the expense of the other, that vitality is the fundamental good and yet can be incompatible with goodness—Chaucer's "moral vertu," which is the summit of consciousness. Chaucer knows exactly how marvelously vital such characters as the Pardoner and the Wife of Bath are, how full of shrewdness and truth, how interesting and indispensable and generous when their interest isn't at stake (as when Pepys spins out his marvelously detailed account of the Great Fire of London: "a piece of glass of Mercer's chapel in the street, where much more was, so melted and buckled with the heat of the fire, like parchment"), how exhilaratingly sure of themselves, and yet what horrors they would be to confront in the flesh or live with, what freaks and monsters, what liars and moral idiots, how gigantic and invulnerable, how abstract and human. Here is Pepys's Vitality head to head with the Prick of Conscience, on a field of Consciousness Dormant: At his bookseller's he looks into a dirty book which seems to him "the most bawdy, lewd book that ever I saw . . . so that I was ashamed of reading in it"; three weeks later, "to my bookseller's, and there stayed an hour and bought that idle, roguish book, *L'escholle des Filles*; which I have bought in plain binding . . . because I resolve, as soon as I have read it, to burn it"; the next day (Sunday of course), "I to my chamber, where I did read through *L'escholle des Filles*; a lewd book, but what doth me no wrong to read for information sake (but it did hazer my prick para stand all the while, and una vez to decharger); and after I had done it, I burned it, that it might not be among my books to my shame." How cute and *all-zu-menschlich*! chortle the professors, striking a conscious blow for gusto.

There's nobody here but us monsters. For Pepys the Puritan and churchy jerk-off and mad secret fucker and ambitious bureaucrat and lunatic playgoer, Charles II is the ultimate monster—A King and No King—and a wit besides. By his indolence and quite unsecret profligacy Charles has managed to disillusion the populace (and Pepys) in record time and make them yearn for the good old Cromwellian repressions. In March 1668, for instance, there is serious and prolonged rioting in the London streets by mobs of apprentices, who indicate their temper by "pulling down of bawdy-houses, which is one of the great grievances of the nation. To which the King made a very poor, cold, insipid answer: 'Why, why do they go to them, then?' and that was all, and had no mind to go on with the discourse." Pepys, who fancies himself a connoisseur of sermons, no doubt intends the parallel with truth and Pilate; but the King is speaking for Pepys, and neither speaks for Chaucer. Gusto isn't the last word.

Pepys stands up for public order and lies low for private expedience, and many nights before he goes beddy-bye he makes lists of unfinished business that don't distinguish between the two: "so to supper and to bed—vexed at two or three things—*viz.* that my wife's watch [her new timepiece, not her surveillance over him] proves so bad as it doth—the ill state of the office and Kingdom's business—at the charge which my mother's death for mourning will bring me when all paid [his mother had died the week before]." Pepys didn't much care for his mother, he had wept for his brother's death, surely he will weep for his wife's and father's deaths later. Still, Death the Leveler reduces the number of items (categories don't matter) to be ordered and expedited, as when the Lord Treasurer is about to give up the ghost:

> Sir Ph. Warwick doth please himself like a good man, to tell some of the good ejaculacions of my Lord Treasurer concerning the little worth of this world, to buy it with so much pain, and other things fit for a dying man. So finding no business likely to be done here for Tanger, I having a warrant for tallies to be signed, I away to the New Exchange and there stayed a little and then to a looking-glass shop to consult about covering the wall in my closet over my chimney; which is darkish, with looking-glasses . . .

and then and then and then and then "and then to bed, resolving to rise betimes tomorrow to write fair the report."

There is a single exception in the diary: William Coventry, Secretary to the Lord High Admiral, the only person whom Pepys loves, admires, is undeviatingly loyal to, and indeed may be said to reverence from beginning to end. Moreover, on the evidence Pepys gives, it's clear that Coventry deserves Pepys's near-idolatry and it's equally clear that he not only trusts but likes and esteems Pepys:

> and then at noon rise [from a Navy Board meeting] and I with Mr. Coventry down to the waterside, talking; wherein I see so much goodness and endeavours of doing the King service that I do more and more admire him. It being the greatest trouble to man, he says, in the world, to see not only in the Navy, but in the greatest matters of State, where he can lay his finger upon the soare (meaning this man's faults, and this man's office the fault lies in), and yet dare or can not remedy matters.

Pepys's most courageous public act is recorded near the end of the diary—visiting Coventry in the Tower, where he has been committed by the King after being goaded by the Duke of Buckingham into a challenge. Coventry is too conspicuously strong and good to survive in such a government—he seems to have been the only effective, hard-working, brave, far-sighted, and incorruptible official in the inner circle of government policy (Burnet's *History* sums him up as "a man of the finest and the best temper that belonged to the court")—whereas Pepys survives wars and revolutions because he is useful to everybody and not least to himself. Pepys must have been a charmer as well as a useful functionary; at any rate Coventry was charmed and convinced. But Coventry didn't read the diary. (pp. 12-16)

Marvin Mudrick, "Su Cosa Mi Cosa; or, Busy Busy Busy," in his Books Are Not Life, but Then What Is? *Oxford University Press, 1979, pp. 12-26.*

RICHARD LUCKETT (essay date 1983)

[*Luckett is Pepysian Librarian of Magdalene College, Cambridge. In the following excerpt, he scrutinizes the language of the* Diary.]

Hobbes, the most eminent English philosopher in Pepys's day, held that 'The first author of *speech* was God himself, that instructed Adam how to name such creatures as he presented to his sight'. He maintained that speech was 'the most noble and profitable invention of all'; and considered it as essential for any process of self-discovery, as the means by which mankind achieved self-consciousness, and as an index of wisdom or folly: 'as men abound in copiousness of language, so they become more wise, or more mad than ordinary'. Many of the early endeavours of the Royal Society were directed towards the creation of a universal language; these found their fullest, though ultimately unfulfilled, expression in John Wilkins's *Essay towards a real character, and a philosophical language* (1668). Pepys himself is our witness that, with Hobbes, Wilkins maintained that 'were it not for speech, man would be a very mean creature', and the impingement of Wilkins's concerns on Pepys's cast of mind is implicit in his notion of the relation asserted in the title of his book, between language and orthography: Wilkins believed that a universal language would naturally be expressed in a universal shorthand, the two having as their common foundation the Deity's immutable ordering of Nature, philosophically elucidated. Wilkins's aspiration was towards the ideal; a more empirical approach was adopted by his contemporary, the naturalist John Ray, who collected proverbs and dialect usages in the hope that he might adduce from them general principles of human behaviour.

Such concerns were naturally congenial to Pepys. The cognisance of terms of art—such as the 'seamen's manner of singing when they sound the depths'—was a necessary part of his business. In 1660 we find him studying a *Seaman's grammar and dictionary*, and consulting Capt. Cuttance to the same end. But it was pleasure and curiosity that impelled him to 'satisfy' himself from John Bowles 'in some terms of Hunting', and to record his delight in hearing, at his coachmaker's, some 'poor people . . . call their fat child "punch"; which pleased me mightily, that word being become a word of common use for all that is thick and short'. In setting down his reactions to plays and poems he frequently singles out the language for particular comment, distinguishing between the 'conceit, wit, design and language' of a play, concurring with Mennes in his opinion of the 'many fine expressions' in Chaucer, approving Jonson's *Every man in his humour* for its 'propriety of speech', and his *Catiline* for its 'much good sense and language', but finding in Fletcher's *A wife for a month* 'no great wit or language' and displaying evident exasperation at 'a little book . . . concerning English Gentry' which, though written in 'good words', did not contain, from beginning to end, 'one entire and regular sentence'.

This sensitivity went with an acute awareness of the day-to-day importance of an adequate command of language. He took an evident pleasure in commending a letter as 'a very well writ one', and in noting that a woman used 'the best language that ever I heard in my life'. He urged the necessity of good expression on his relatives. In the diary he gave vent to his impatience at 'poor discourse and frothy' and recorded how Mr Bland, the mayor of Tangier,

'spoiled his business' before the Committee for the colony because of his ineptitude 'in the use of grammar and knowledge how to tell a man's tale'. Pepys himself owed his triumphant defence of the Navy Office in 1668 in large measure to the excellence of his language, being told that 'the Sollicitor generall did protest that he thought I spoke the best of any man in England'. Ben Jonson, whom Pepys held in high regard, had asserted that 'Language most shows a man: Speak, that I may see thee. It springs out of the most retired and inmost parts of us, and is the image of the parent of it, the mind. No glass renders a man's form or likeness so true as his speech'. Just such an assumption underlies Pepys's praise of Sir William Petty, 'who in discourse is methinks one of the most rational men that ever I heard speak with a tongue, having all his notions the most distinct and clear'.

Pepys's exercise of language was not restricted to the vernacular. In the diary he displays no false modesty about his ability as a linguist, and as a linguist his natural aptitude had benefited from local advantages, deriving from his education, his family circumstances and his environment. At St. Paul's the teaching of Latin was, as in all grammar schools of the period, the basis of the curriculum; he would also have learned some Greek there (he gave a copy of Stephens's *Thesaurus Graecae Linguae* to the school in 1662); and his residence in Cambridge coincided with a resurgence of interest in the language in the university, exemplified by the scholarship of Henry More of Christ's and Joseph Duport of Trinity and intimately bound up with the influential achievements of the Cambridge Platonists. It is also noteworthy that one of his closest Cambridge friends, Richard Cumberland, subsequently Bishop of Peterborough, was a redoubtable student both of Greek and Hebrew—the latter a subject in which Pepys was sufficiently interested to buy a grammar in 1660. Pepys's Latin was convenient as a vehicle for communication with Admiral Opdam and other foreigners whose native tongue he did not know; it was also the medium for some of the reading that he most relished, above all Bacon's *Faber Fortunae*. His brother John wrote to him in Latin, to Pepys's satisfaction, but his cousin Thomas Pepys, of Hatcham, in his work as a Justice of the Peace, experienced the disadvantages of not knowing the language. Pepys also took an evident pleasure in teaching Latin, and commented tartly on those who attempted more in that language than they could adequately accomplish. He could be equally critical of 'False Greek' in a sermon.

Nevertheless it is probable that Pepys took more pride in his accomplishments in the modern than in the classical languages. In 1669 he dined at the Spanish Embassy and reflected that the Oxford scholar in a Doctor of Law's gown also present, 'though a gentle sort of scholar, yet sat like a fool for want of French or Spanish' and, moreover, spoke Latin 'like an Englishman'; Pepys, by contrast, was able to make much use of his French and Spanish, 'to my great content'. Having a French wife, who evidently continued to use her native language a good deal, must have helped; but it is also significant that his brother Thomas's deathbed ravings were in French. When Sandwich wished to discuss court gossip with Pepys in front of the servants, French was the natural recourse, and Pepys was sufficiently adept at writing French to conduct a correspondence in the language with Lady Wright. His Spanish may seem a more surprising accomplishment; it was undoubtedly one in which he took some pride. He would most certainly not have acquiesced in Samuel Butler's opinion that the study of Greek and Latin affords a man 'a very pitiful Returne of Knowledge in comparison of the intollerable Paines and Industry that is spent upon It . . . ' and that this 'slavery . . . does but render him the more unready at his owne language'; but he no less certainly believed in the value of the 'modern languages', an accomplishment which, according to Anthony Wood, had played a substantial part in the advancement of the early Caroline courtier, Endymion Porter, and which greatly signified in the career of a diplomat who successfully served both Charles I and II, Sir Richard Fanshawe. Pepys was not unusual in his possession of Spanish books; several English collectors and libraries had comparatively large holdings of these, and Spanish literature was also well represented in English translation. Pepys's Spanish gave him at least some understanding of Portuguese. He lacked Italian, but in the 17th century, although Italian was of obvious importance in the world of connoisseurship and the arts, Spanish, supported by the gold, silver and spices of Spain's still vast empire, occupied a commanding position in the mercantile and commercial world. Spain, moreover, retained her Italian possessions, and it is appropriate that, at the very beginning of the diary, we should find Pepys reading a Spanish book on Rome.

Pepys's language in the diary is the immediate and ultimate testimony to the liveliness of his linguistic concerns. Diaries are not always such reliable guides to usage, or indeed habit of mind, as they might at first seem. The degree of self-consciousness implied in the writing of a readable diary carries with it an evident ambivalence. Colonel Byng, in 1789, illustrates the difficulty: 'As I proceed in Tour Writing . . . I get Bold and Vain, Believing that all Diaries become Valuable from Age; tho' I often Revert to some sad Diaries I have read, or heard of, on one of a punctual woman, who wrote:

> Friday. Buried my poor dead Husband.
> Saturday. Turned my *Ass* to Grass.

and tho' this is ludicrous, yet with over Study, and devoid of Nature, what does Tour Writing or any other Writing become?' In his awareness of 'naturalness' as the virtue proper to diary writing Byng unavoidably qualifies the sense of 'natural'. He is extremely conscious of how 'sadly do Recollection and Invention Clash'—a point that will ring true for any reader of Dr de Beer's edition of John Evelyn, where Evelyn's dependence on aids to recollection is repeatedly demonstrated. Evelyn's whole intention in his diary—at least in its final, revised form—that it might contribute to his descendants' knowledge of the world, suggests the preclusion of certain kinds if naturalness. Ralph Thoresby, in 1708, 'read in my dear and pious father's diary in secret' but such discretion in succeeding generations was scarcely to be presumed by any diarist. Pepys's own notion that his diary might come to his aid in the event of an arraignment in Parliament provides an obvious demonstration of the restricted 'naturalness' of the form. Yet his regrets after he had revealed its existence to an acquaintance argue the other way, and some such oscillation is apparent in the next itself. At 19 Oct. 1663 he permits himself a reflection in death which in its literariness recalls Evelyn's set pieces; it is a far cry from the conversational idiom with its characteristic use of 'well' as a resumptive, of 'Well, by and by the child is brought, and christened Katherine'. Yet it is a fact of death that, reflected upon, it tends to present itself in a literary mode, and such passages in Pepys are comparatively uncommon.

In general the evidence for Pepys's style in the diary, so clearly distinct from his official style and from even the most familiar of his letters, as an echo of his speaking voice, is persuasive. There are features to be associated primarily with the pressures imposed by the actual keeping of a diary, above all the frequent ellipses: 'this night my boy Wainman, as I was in my chamber, overheard him let off some Gun-powder'; 'talking and eating and drinking a good ham of English bacon'; 'eat and drank a Jole of salmon at the Rose and Crown'; Knipp 'sings as well and is the best company, in the world' ('as anybody', understood); 'down with' (for 'goes down well with'); 'then home, between vexed and joyed' ('being' understood); 'though the Swedish Agent was there with all the vehemence he could to save the goods . . . '; 'where upon a fine couple of pigeon, a good supper'; 'who is it that the weight of the war depends'; 'but the interest which I wholly lost while in my trunk' (where the inherent absurdity is a demonstration of the lack of self-consciousness). Such ellipses can occur in phrases and even words: 'so' for 'so long as'; 'refrain it' for 'refrain from it'; 'stay' for 'stay for'; 'which' for 'about which'; 'faintness' for 'faintheartedness'. But they do not predominate, and indeed it is their absence that can so often authenticate the ring of the spoken word, the convincing casualness of: 'I protest it is very strange to observe' or 'I never could have thought there had been upon earth a man so little curious in the world as he is'. But it is not the case that redundancy is a defining feature of Pepys's speaking voice: there is the directness of 'I see what he means', the immediacy of 'wrapping myself up warm', the tautological and idiomatic naturalness of 'miserable hot weather all night it was', the frequent and revelatory apostrophes such as 'But Lord', and the unintentional admission of a habit of thought in 'with horrour I speak it', 'I protest it is very strange to observe', or (of a watch) 'and am apt to think with myself: how could I be so long without one?'. When Pepys commended his own performance in speaking in the House of Commons in defence of the Navy Office in 1668 he noted that he had developed his argument 'with full scope and all my reason free about me, as if it had been at my own table', and the excellencies and intimacies of table-talk are never far removed from his most compelling writing in the diary, whether in the ironical observation of others (Balty 'as fine as hands could make him') or himself ('practising to sing which is now my great trade'), the delighted discovery of the apposite word (Mr Milles's 'nibbling' at the Book of Common Prayer), or even an inelegant but effective superfluity of phrase ('a most horrid malicious bloody flame').

The faults of Pepys's style are those of haste and informality. Confusing concatenations of negatives are liable to occur: 'This day my wife killed her turkey that Mr [Sheply] gave her, that came out of Zeeland with my Lord; and could not get her maid Jane by no means at any time to kill anything'; Mr Chetwind who had 'not dined no more than myself'; 'so that I could not sleep hardly all night'; 'The Duke of York gone down to the fleet; but, all suppose, not with intent to stay there—as it is not fit, all men conceive, he should'; and, perhaps a reflection of the extremity of the occasion (and also an illustration of his habit of ellipsis), 'I lacked a pot but there was none, and bitter cold, so was forced to rise and piss in the chimny, and to bed again'. The positive aspect of this tendency is to be detected in Pepys's inventive use of 'un'-forms; in the 17th century 'un' confusingly interchanged with modern 'in', so we find 'uncapable', 'unsufferable', but 'inmethodical'; however, 'unbespeak' and 'uninvite' strongly suggest Pepys's own coinage, and tally with his innovative compounds using over: 'over-working', 'over-wrought', 'over-handsome'. The sequence of tenses sometimes fails to follow truly; the same is true of number, as in: 'And so we dined and was very merry. At 5 a-clock we set out again . . . and were very merry all the way'. Adjectives, adverbs and phrases are on occasion left floating: in 1666 business (and the need to be seen to be minding it) 'is now so great a burden upon my mind night and day, that I do not enjoy myself in the world almost'; during the Fire, 'the poor pigeons I perceive were loath to leave their houses, but hovered about the windows till they were some of them burned, their wings, and fell down'. But redundancy, in general, did not concern Pepys, who was apparently unabashed by 'beautifullest', 'activest' (recorded as nonce by the *Oxford English Dictionary*), or 'the justice himself very hardly escaped'.

Pepys's linguistic criteria, and his linguistic agility, are nowhere better demonstrated than in his epithets for the sermons that he enjoyed or endured. He could admire 'a good plain sermon', 'a most excellent and eloquent sermon', a 'ready, learned, and good sermon', 'the best sermon for goodness—oratory without affectation or study—that ever I heard in my life', 'a very pretty, neat, sober, honest sermon', 'a very good and seraphick kind of sermon', 'a very excellent and persuasive, good and moral sermon'. He could equally be abruptly dismissive of 'a cold sermon', 'a poor dry sermon', 'a dull drowzy sermon', 'a lazy poor sermon', 'a mean sorry sermon', 'a long and sad sermon', a 'flat dead sermon, both from matter and manner of delivery'. These are the comments of a man for whom the linguistic dress of thought was a matter of constant concern, and whose report of Mrs Turner's tirade on 21 May 1667 reveals an unerring ear for the tenor of the spoken word.

It seems probable that, in the course of the last three hundred years, the literary language has been far more variable than the spoken language. Pepys uses a succession of past participles which are instantly recognisable as archaic: 'ris' for 'rose', 'durst' for 'dared', 'lien' for 'layed', 'ketched' for 'caught', 'drow' for 'drew', 'drownded' for 'drowned'. These we can associate with his innumerable spelling variants, which illustrate the arbitrariness of the relation between orthography and pronunciation: 'e' for 'i' in 'engenious', 'enveigh', 'entend', 'endeed', but 'i' for 'e' in 'imbroidery', in 'sense' for 'since', and 'i' for 'a' in 'imbassador'. A similar pattern emerges with 'c', 't' and 's': thus we have 'arbitracion', 'corrupcion', 'objeccions', 'particion', 'stacioner', but 'lissen' for 'listen', 'pention' for 'pension', 'iching' for 'itching' and 'centry' for 'sentry'. Sometimes the spelling indicates a change in pronunciation as in the open vowels of 'guarden' for 'garden' and 'guarrison' for 'garrison', or the three syllables implied in 'Colonell'/'Coll'. Many of the forms suggested by Pepys's spelling still survive in dialect usage, notably 'th' for 'd', as in 'blather' for 'bladder', 'lather', for 'ladder', and its inversion, as in 'farding' for 'farthing'. Other examples are 'fallow' for 'follow', 'perticular' for 'particular', 'fur' for 'far', and 'spile' for 'spoil'. Occasionally the orthography can be etymologically revealing, as in 'Akehorne' which, if some way from the Anglo-Saxon *æcern*, is much further away from the modern form, with its logically attractive but false association with corn, though 'sparrowgrass' for 'asparagus' achieves just the opposite effect. Again a phonetic spelling such as 'piattza' can take us nearer to the actual sound of a foreign word than its correct representation in the conventional orthography of its language of origin, whilst the fact that a word is an importation, though we now would be unlikely to notice it as such, is often signalled orthographically, as in 'attaque' for 'attack', 'choque' for 'shock', or 'banquiers' for 'bankers'. Pepys still on occasion spells out the old form of the genitive, as in 'Mr Philips his chamber' or 'Mr Pepys his meaning', and can prove disconcerting in his use of prepositions, as when he 'dined together with a good pig', or is to be found 'at a haunch of venison' or 'at oysters', or preserves the ancient 'fear of him' for 'fear for him' (that is, 'on his behalf'). Other usages are less archaic than racy, most of all the contraction of 'ily' forms to 'y', that is, of the use of adjective for adverb, as in 'extraordinary' for 'extraordinarily', 'mighty' for 'mightily', 'perfect' for 'perfectly', 'infinite' for 'infinitely'. But Pepys is perfectly capable, on occasion, of using the uncontracted form, as in 'I am mightily taken with them'. Here a linguistic affectation of the Commonwealth and Restoration is at war with Pepys's natural tendency to intensify as much as he is able, the habit exemplified by the 'the justice himself very hardly escaped' where 'very' has to be read in relation to 'hardly', which does not now seem natural, and spelled out (the contracted form triumphantly winning the day) when Pepys records how the captain of the *Naseby* 'treated me huge nobly'; nevertheless the way in which this simply reflects fashionable usage is demonstrated by the occurrence of 'huge gentlemanlike' in a Verney letter of 1653.

Pepys's phrasal inversions are equally a period feature, but he uses them with a frequency that suggests a personal predilection. In part they are due to the redundancy that, for reasons that may superficially appear paradoxical but are in fact perfectly straightforward, is as characteristic an aspect of diary-writing as the ellipsis. It is often in effect a short cut to repeat a phrase, or to neglect its natural place in the sequence of sense. When Pepys writes of calling on 'Mitchell and his wife, which in her night linen appeared as pretty almost as ever to my thinking I saw woman' we come up against just such a failure to anticipate the full run of what he is endeavouring to write. But, as always, its disjunctions are dampened by those natural cadences of a speaking voice that it still contrives to convey. This habit in Pepys (and in his contemporaries) may have been accentuated by the way in which Latin was taught in the period, and, beyond that, by the construction of Latin itself, which is so frequently at odds with the principles governing English usage. The standard Latin dictionary of the day (Philemon Holland's edition of Thomas Thomas's *Dictionarium*, published by the Cambridge University Press) was constructed on a method which offered to the student a repertory of phrases, and these could be put together like building blocks in order to convey a required sense by any student with a sufficiently retentive memory. The inculcation of such an arbitrary habit of phrasal organisation at an early age was not conducive to the spontaneous creation of smooth sequences in English sentences, and the interaction, in educated writing, of Latin and English, can too easily be overlooked. In 1680 John Aubrey, having just completed his life of Hobbes, sent it off to his friend Dr Richard Blackbourne, a Fellow of Trinity College, Cambridge, and in his covering note wrote: 'Pray be my Aristarchus.... First draughts ought to be rude as those of paynters, for he that in his first essay will be curious in refining will certainly be unhappy in inventing... Should mine be in Latin or English?... Is my English style well enough?' In the preceding year John Dryden, urging on the Earl of Sunderland the foundation of a British Academy, had raised the same questions, though with an altered emphasis: 'how barbarously we yet write and speak, your Lordship knows, and I am sufficiently sensible in my own English. For I am often put to a stand, in considering whether what I write be the Idiom of the Tongue, or false Grammar, and nonsense couch'd beneath that specious name of *Anglicisme*. And have no other way to clear my Doubts, but by translating my English into Latine, and thereby trying what sense the words will bear in a more stable Language'. Both Aubrey and Dryden habitually wrote a fine, flowing and natural English, yet neither of them was wholly convinced that this was in fact the case, and both (though not in the same way) had the alternative of Latin running in their minds. The privacy of Pepys's diary obviously protected him from comparable anxieties, but that two such able writers should have such doubts is illuminating, and the readiness of their recourse to Latin significant. Something of the same habit of mind as Aubrey and Dryden evince is arguably a factor contributing to Pepys's stylistic oddities, albeit in an indirect way. This process is more familiar to us in the realm of high and deliberated literary art, notably in the syntactical complexities of Milton. But there is, in any case, more of a connection between the selfconsciously poetic and the unselfconsciously colloquial than might at first be imagined: Milton is Pepys's rival virtuoso (in a competitive field) in the employment of forms with 'un':

> Among innumerable false, unmov'd,
> Unshak'n, unseduc't, unterrifi'd
> His Loyaltie he kept...
>
> (*Paradise Lost*, bk v, 11.897+)

But the differences between Pepys's idiom and our own are less significant than the resemblances. When we hear his speaking voice it is because we recognise the way in which every individual establishes that individuality by slight departures from a norm, and an apprehension of such a norm underlies our sense of Pepys's individuality. He does not search for the sonorous, in the way that Evelyn on occasion does; he does not take Aubrey's evident delight in the pungency of the vocabulary available to him; he does not experience, as Anthony Wood so notably did, pleasure at his own sarcasms. His language is above all a reflection of its objects, not, to Pepys, an object in itself. Its naturalness, its truth to common speech, strikes home because the fundamentals of that speech have changed comparatively little in three hundred years, though in recent years the influence of radio and television has accelerated the process, and in modern England the accents of Pepys are most likely to find their echo amongst the indigenous inhabitants of rural areas and of the few remaining urban districts which have preserved a relatively uniform class structure and avoided redevelopment. In comparable areas of the eastern United States it is probable that the connection is even more immediate.

Pepys's vocabulary may be less exploratory than Aubrey's, but it remains exceptionally vivid in effect. Though Pepys had a liking for apparently novel constructions with 'un-' or 'over-' he was not a neologiser, though neologising has been a habit of mind by no means uncongenial to many private memoirists—the Duc de Saint-Simon, whose high hand with his French vocabulary is notorious, providing the most remarkable example. The *Oxford English Dictionary* records many more first uses from Evelyn than from Pepys, despite Pepys's much greater length, and this in indicative of Pepys's inwardness with the language; Evelyn, whose manner is stiffer, and play of mind within the language more restricted, frequently resorts to foreign terms where Pepys would have had a native word or phrase to hand. Nevertheless the Restoration was a period of linguistic expansion, as it was a period of mercantile and imperial expansion, and there are frequent demonstrations of this in Pepys, and in the words of which he provides our first record. The sea terms, upon a command of which he was professionally dependent, are frequently Dutch in origin; the accounts of meals eaten (which illustrate a different dependence) as frequently involve words deriving from the French. The years after 1660 were, in any case, particularly productive so far as French borrowings were concerned and, given the close connections between the courts and intellectual circles of the two countries, this was scarcely surprising. The utility and availability of French as a second language for Englishmen in the period is demonstrated by the English sojourns of French exiles such as Gramont and St Evremond, who appear never to have needed to learn English, whilst a French newsletter (the *Nouvelles Ordinaires*) appeared in London under the Commonwealth and had a successor (the *Gazette de Londres*) after the Restoration. Huguenot refugees must also have played their part in the anglicising of French vocabulary. It was a tendency that was resisted, frequently by those most fluent in French: Etherege, in *The man of mode* (1676), got great fun out of Sir Fopling Flutter's malapropos excursions into the language, and was merely one amongst the many dramatists who exploited the gag. Yet at the end of the century Aubrey, reflecting on the number of English words used by even so lively a writer as Philemon Holland at its beginning which had by then become archaic, recorded Dryden's opinion that some thirty or forty French words had been naturalised into English in the thirty odd years since the Restoration. It was a subject about which Dryden had been thinking for a long time: as early as 1664 he had expressed the wish that 'we might at length leave to borrow words from other nations, which is now a wantonness in us, not a necessity', though he had gone on to admit that 'so long as some affect to speak them, there will not want others, who will have the boldness to write them'. In 1673 he had again returned to the attack, with a pregnant anticipation of the figure of Sir Fopling, disapproving those 'who corrupt our English idiom by mixing it too much with French: that is a sophistication of language, not an improvement of it: a turning English into French, rather than a refining of English by French. We meet daily with those fops, who value themselves on their travelling, and pretend they cannot express their meaning in English, because they would put off to us some French phrase of the last edition; without considering that, for aught they know, we have a better of our own'.

Pepys would almost certainly have agreed with these sentiments. In 1667 he praised Sir Roger L'Estrange's rendering of Quevedo's *Sueños y discursos* because it did not read like a translation; he evidently regarded English as having a spirit of its own, which good writing should preserve, and his words of French derivation appear to stem less from any proclivity to exploit the resources of that language than from a natural turning to customary usage. When he writes 'volary' (Fr. *volière*), notwithstanding the pre-existence in English of the wholly adequate 'aviary', he is merely following accepted practice. Perfectly good native terms can die out, despite their sufficiency, and be replaced by alien intruders; even so unsophisticated a writer as Edmund Coxere could call on the phrase 'where we lay perdu' without appearing affected. Pepys is equally innocent, and his French borrowings are almost all in essence functional and conventional. They are employed because they are current, and because they serve his purpose: he had had no ambition to be an 'absolute Monsieur'. But he can on occasion turn to French to achieve a witty or pleasing effect, as in his account of his journey to Portsmouth in 1661, where the remark that he had 'this day no other extraordinary rancontre but my hat falling off of my head into the water, by which it was spoiled and I ashamed of it' not only provides an example of a usage ('off of') still to be encountered in N. America though almost extinct in Britain, but also provides an example of a French word deliberately used to suggest the atmosphere of the romances which derived from France and were the staple form of light reading in the mid-17th century; Pepys riding southwards saw himself as a knight errant.

Given the colloquial tenor of the diary, and Pepys's evident liking for classical apophthegms, the relative poverty of proverbial material is revealing. Pepys could not have shared Jane Austen's opinion that proverbs were 'gross and illiberal': he uses them, on occasion, with great effect: 'Though I love the treason I hate the traitor', 'You have brought your hogs to a fair market', 'Sometimes all honey and then all turd', are instances of his feeling for proverbs that were striking and apt. But he employs them sparingly; his natural habit of mind is too individual to incline him to acquiesce in a proverb unless he feels that it really strikes home. He makes, by contrast, considerable play with proverbial phrases, which have an evident appeal both for their economy and their pithiness: there are those that are alliterative (to have 'a back broad enough to bear it', 'mince the matter', 'as supple as a spaniel', 'as drunk as a dog', 'beat one's brains', 'Bridewell birds', 'hang in the hedge'), and the vivid ('take eggs for . . . money', 'be at dagger-drawing', 'worth a fart', 'calm as a lamb', 'pull a crow'); some have passed out of circulation ('take in snuff'—but we still say 'snuffy', 'to keep a quarter', 'have snaps at', have 'a month's mind', to go to one's 'naked bed'), but others remain alive and kicking ('stick at nothing', 'get into the saddle', 'shift for myself', 'take it very well', 'work like a horse', 'cheek by jowl', 'make no bones of it', 'eyes ready to fall out of my head', 'out of play', 'make the pot boyle', to put someone's 'nose out of joint', 'the main chance'). Once again we can perceive a use of language, rather than a subjection to it.

Francis Atterbury, the future Bishop of Rochester, wrote in 1690 a preface to an edition of Edmund Waller's posthumous poems in which he asked what might seem to us the surprising question as to whether it was not the case that 'in Charles the second's reign, English did not come to its full perfection; and whether it has not had its Augus-

tan Age, as well as the Latin. It seems to be already mixed with foreign languages as far as its purity will bear; and as Chymists say of their Moenstruums, to be quite sated with the infusion. But posterity will best judge of this'. Atterbury's estimate of the state of the language under Charles II may be extravagant, and there were many writers during that reign who would have disputed it. But Pepys in the diary provides one good reason for supposing it to be a judgement not far off the mark; it was an instrument supremely able to 'show' both the complexities and simplicities of the man. (pp. 217-28)

Richard Luckett, "Language," in The Diary of Samuel Pepys: Companion, Vol. X, *edited by Robert Latham and William Matthews, University of California Press, 1983, pp. 217-28.*

CHRISTOPHER HILL (essay date 1985)

[*Hill is a distinguished English historian and literary critic who has written widely on aspects of the Puritan Revolution in England. In the following excerpt, he presents a character sketch of Pepys, drawing chiefly on evidence provided by the* Diary *itself.*]

It is an interesting coincidence that two of the most famous of English diarists, Samuel Pepys and Robinson Crusoe, were born into families of the middling sort in the same year—Pepys on 23 February 1632-3, Crusoe "in the year 1632". There is a further similarity: those of us who were brought up on an abridged children's edition of *Robinson Crusoe* know nothing of the hero's life before his shipwreck. In fact Defoe sketches Crusoe's background in some detail, and in the course of the novel frequently refers to his early life. Readers who know Pepys only through the *Diary* find him ready-made at the age of twenty-seven.

We know him—or we think we know him—better than almost any historical character of comparable importance. Thanks to the *Diary* we are more intimate with him than with our colleagues, neighbours and friends. But we tend to allow the endearing young man of the sixteen-sixties to obscure not only the earlier Pepys but also the man who was one of England's greatest civil servants, "the saviour of the navy" and President of the Royal Society. Normally historians can see only the public faces of civil servants—the official despatches, the minutes, the public portrait; they are fortunate if an occasional private letter survives. The great self-revealers of the past—Montaigne, Rousseau, Casanova, De Quincey—show us a carefully prepared persona. None expose themselves so nakedly as the young Pepys does.

He is not concerned to create an image of himself. He is not writing for a public but for himself; and he knows what he is like. So there are no explanations, no justifications, only a dialogue between different aspects of his own personality. The *Diary* does not put before us a single rounded personality, but a broken bundle of mirrors. It is genuine because it is utterly inconsistent. Each of us can select his own Pepys. His *Diary*, like Crusoe's, reveals the course of his adaptation to the new world in which he finds himself thrown up. Crusoe succeeded on his island not only because of his resourcefulness and determination, but also because of the stores and tools which he salvaged from the wreck, and the heritage of ideas and experiences which he brought from his previous life; without these he could not have survived as successfully as he did. (pp. 259-60)

Why, one wonders, did Samuel Pepys start keeping a diary on 1 January 1660? He must have recognized that England was passing from one age to another. Pepys was very aware of the social issues at stake, and his comments are often shrewd and illuminating. He understood by 3 April 1660 that control of the militia by gentry and merchants made rule by "the fanatics" impossible; by 1667 he was assuring himself that "religion will not so soon cause another war".

We must note too Pepys's residual Puritanisms, some of them funny, some serious. His good resolutions, reinforced by solemn vows, helped him to keep play-going and drinking under control, and so to concentrate on his work and on his finances. He paid money into the poor box when he broke his vows. This led to comical evasions and self-deceptions.

> Though my oath against going to plays do not oblige me against this [play-] house, because it was not then in being, yet believing that at the time my meaning was against all public houses, I am resolved to deny myself the liberty of two plays at Court, which are in arrear to me for the months of March and April, which will more than countervail this excess, so that this month of May is the first that I must claim a liberty of going to a Court play according to my oath.

When he was taken to a play at someone else's expense, "I look upon it as no breach to my oath". Four days later he went to another play with his wife, "she giving me her time of the last month, she having not seen any then, so my vow is not broke at all, it costing me no more money than it would have done upon her, had she gone both her times that were due to her". But only five days after that he got Mr Creed to take them both to a play, "lending him money to do it, which is a fallacy that I have found now once, to avoid my vow with, but never to be more practised, I swear". So far as the evidence of the *Diary* goes, he kept this oath. But he resorted to drinking brandy "as an evasion, God knows, for my drinking of wine (but it is an evasion which will not serve me now hot weather is coming, that I cannot pretend, as indeed I really have done, that I drank it for cold), but I will leave it off, and it is but seldom, as when I am in women's company, that I must call for wine, for I must be forced to drink to them".

From the beginning to the end of the *Diary*, Pepys normally refers to Sunday by its Puritan name, "the Lord's Day"—though there are three "Sundays" in September 1660. But he did not always respect the sanctity of the day. On 22 July 1660 he hired a boat on the Sabbath, noting that it was the first time he had done such a thing. On 21 October he asked God to forgive him for stringing his lute on the Lord's day; by the following 9 February he was composing airs on the Sabbath. It seems to have been Pepys's habit to read prayers to his household on Sunday evenings, though on 29 September 1660 he was so drunk that he dared not read them "for fear of being perceived by my servants in what case I was". On 12 January 1664 he made a vow to say prayers twice weekly: on 20 November 1668 he promised his wife to pray each night. In the crisis of September 1666 Pepys's office had to work on Sundays, "which Mr. Hayter had no mind to, it being the Lords day, but, being told the necessity, submitted, poor man".

In words at any rate Pepys was a firm believer in the Puritan work ethic. "It is want of work", he observed in relation to his wife, "that do make her and all other people think of ways of spending their time worse". He had already made a similar comment about "the effect of idleness and having nothing else to employ their great spirits upon" on the King and the Duke of York. It was, Pepys said on 20 August 1663, "against my nature to owe anything to anybody". On 21 May 1663 he made a great scene about his wife using the word devil, though five days later he referred innocently to "my devilish jealousy".

Complicated equivocations enabled him to deny accepting bribes—"not looking into it till the money was out, that I might say I saw no money in the paper, if ever I should be questioned about it". This is indeed the homage that vice pays to virtue—or the post-restoration civil servant to the standards set during the interregnum. (pp. 265-67)

The whole bent of [Pepys's] inquisitive mind was away from superstition, towards science, for the Moderns against the Ancients. In his thirtieth year Pepys began to learn the multiplication table. Twenty-four years later, as President of the Royal Society, he gave his imprimatur to Isaac Newton's *Principia*. In between he praised "mathematick Admirals" and was the moving spirit in founding (with government money) the mathematical school at Christ's Hospital as a nursery for navigators. Pepys was just the sort of enlightened, curious amateur to whom the Royal Society was designed to appeal: his delight in its meetings and especially in his conversations with Wilkins and Hooke is very attractive.

Was Pepys an anti-Trinitarian, like Milton, Locke, Newton, Stubbe and so many more? On 12 October 1668 he bought "William Penn's book against the Trinity", *The Sandy Foundation Shaken*. Pepys had a low opinion of Sir William's son; he found this book so well written that "it is too good for him ever to have written it; and it is a serious sort of book, and not fit for everybody to read". The last comment is very ambiguous. Pepys owned a copy of *Paradise Lost* as well as of Milton's 1645 *Poems*.

Two questions remain about Pepys. Why did he never achieve the knighthood which in the early days of his marriage he set as a target? Many men far less distinguished, and far less well-placed, obtained the honour. At any time between 1684 and 1688, at least, it ought to have been his for the asking. Another mystery is why he never remarried after his first wife's death. He lived with Mary Skinner for the last thirty years of his life, and she was socially accepted even by so priggish a man as John Evelyn. Yet in the *Diary* Pepys had criticized others for precisely this sort of liaison. The great-grand-daughter of Lord Chief Justice Coke was at least the social equal of the tailor's son. Relevant perhaps is the fact that Mary's uncle was Cyriack Skinner, Milton's friend and a former president of the radical Rota Club; and that her brother had got into very hot water indeed in 1676 for trying to publish Milton's desperately heretical *De Doctrina Christiana*. But these prudential arguments no longer applied after 1688. It remains a mystery. Does Mary Skinner account for his failure to receive a knighthood?

St. Olave's Church, London, burial place of Pepys and his wife.

Pepys's **Diary** could provide evidence for an analysis of the position of middle-class wives in this society. The unfortunate Mrs Pepys, who married Samuel when she was fifteen, had nothing to do, apart from looking after the house and the servants: she had no role in her husband's affairs. She was less fortunate than Mrs Bland, who was "as good a merchant as her husband" and "talked like a merchant in her husband's business", or another of Pepys's acquintances, Mrs Pley, who supplied sailcloth to the navy and was "as famous a merchant as you have met with in England". She told Pepys that business was her "sole delight in this world". Elizabeth Pepys was typical of many wives who had lost the self-respect due to a junior partner in the family firm without gaining any real independence as her husband rose in the social scale. Even the jealous Samuel gives no evidence that she was unfaithful to him, as he was regularly to her, even with her servants. The clothes and the patches which Samuel grudgingly allowed her were small compensation for her cooped up, showpiece existence. "Dancing and other pleasures" took her mind off "pleasing of me". It became increasingly difficult for the poor man "to get down her head again" after "giving her too much head heretofore for the year past". He had the sense to recognise that "want of work" was her trouble. But how was that to be remedied? Mrs Pley was to tell him "it is charity to be kept full of employment", but Elizabeth could hardly share Samuel's work. He continually tried to find pastimes for her, provided they did not cost too much. But when she brought her painting teacher to dinner, they had a flaming row, and Pepys, getting the worst of the argument, "resoved all into my having my will done, without disputing, be the reason what it will; and so I will have it". One can see exactly how the exaggerated patriarchal theories of, for instance, the Marquis of Halifax, grew out of this situation; and why some women reacted vigorously when the press became freer in the sixteen-nineties. Mary Skinner was perhaps wise to remain Pepys's mistress. Defoe's Roxana made a philosophy out of the observation that "a wife is looked upon as but an upper servant, a mistress is sovereign". (Halifax however also makes clear the perils of the competitive jungle which was restoration society. Pepys would have been as powerless as Leantio in *Women Beware Women* if some aristocratic wolf had taken a fancy to Elizabeth).

Without his Puritan background Pepys would have got nowhere: it was his diligence that made him, as he recognised. The one thing that the "natural rulers" whom 1660 restored ought to have been able to do was to rule: for centuries it had been their function and their justification. But ruling had got so complex that only the most talented could cope. Even fighting, the traditional job of the aristocracy, had become too professional and—especially at sea—just too hard work. It called for new men, driven by ambition, with a work ethic, self-selected by a career partially open to the talents (like that in Cromwell's New

Model Army). The doors were not so wide open that there were no jobs for "the gentlemen that could never be brought to order, but undid all"; but open enough for the tarpaulins to be able to make the navy the fighting force which Britain's aggressive foreign policy demanded, and for Pepys and his like to be there to get and account for the vast sums of money that the navy spent. Pepys's greatest contribution to English history lay in convincing his superiors that naval wars could be won only if the officer class as a whole was professionalized. After 1677 anyone aspiring to hold a lieutenant's commission must have served for three years at sea, one year at least in the lowly rank of midshipman, and must satisfy three senior officers by "solemn examination" of his mastery of the theory and practice of navigation. Naturally these conditions were not always rigorously enforced; but the standards set were such, Mr Ollard observes [in *Pepys: A Biography* (1974)], as "people may resist but ... will never dare to rescind". The captains, gentlemen or not, were subordinated to the bourgeois civil servants. The successes of the navy in the next century and a half vindicated Pepys. He was less successful in getting regular pay for seamen, lack of which in 1667 made many desert to the Dutch.

Pepys's **Diary** was of course unpublishable in his own time. He wrote it in cypher, and even so kept it existence hidden from everybody except Sir William Coventry, another diarist; and regretted having told him. Yet the care with which he preserved it suggests that Pepys had envisaged the possibility of others ultimately reading it. The **Diary** first appeared in 1825, in the year when Milton's *De Doctrina Christiana*—unpublishable for different reasons—at last saw the light of day. When the world crashed around the republicans at the end of the sixteen-fifties, Pepys was young enough, uncommitted enough, shallow and brash enough to flow with the stream, to adapt himself to a scene which Milton completely rejected. Pepys lived fully and intensely whilst Milton stood apart and put all his life into his last great poems and his *De Doctrina*. Like Milton, Pepys thought he had sacrificed his eyes in the course of duty. But Milton believed he was working for the realization of God's kingdom on earth. For Pepys the whole accent was secular: neither life after death nor the kingdom of heaven on earth interested him much. It was life as it is—corrupt, competitive, cruel, exclusively male-centred; but within these limits it was for him rich, sensuous, rewarding in every sense. Pepys came to terms with reality, with a zest that comes near to being its own justification. He aimed lower, but he achieved his aim—if we can give any precise meaning to "lower" in this context. Elizabeth fared less well: she died in 1669, at the age of twenty-nine. (pp. 268-72)

> *Christopher Hill, "Samuel Pepys (1633-1703)," in his* The Collected Essays of Christopher Hill: Writing and Revolution in 17th Century England, Vol. 1, *The Harvester Press, Sussex, 1985, pp. 259-73.*

ROBERT LATHAM (essay date 1985)

[*In the following excerpt, Latham offers a general critical introduction to the* Diary, *praising it as the most evocative and informative English document of its kind.*]

In his own lifetime Pepys was best known as a great naval administrator. To a select public he was also known as one of the leading amateurs of learning of his day and the owner of a remarkable library. It was not until the nineteenth century that he earned his widest fame—as a diarist. His diary was first published (in a heavily abbreviated form) in 1825. He had written it as a young man without any thought of publication, for diaries, though commonly enough written, were not thought suitable material for the printing press. In the Civil War a few military journals had been printed, and extracts from Archbishop Laud's diary had been published by his enemy William Prynne, but these were publicity exercises and quite exceptional. Diaries were, of their nature, private: Pepys kept his entirely for his own enjoyment. Hence its unselfconscious charm; hence too its frankness. More vividly and more completely than any other diary in the language it reveals both the writer and the world he lived in. (p. xxi)

The practice of keeping diaries seems to have become increasingly common in England from Elizabethan times, and had several specific origins, apart from the growth of literacy in general. In many cases it was a development from the keeping of household accounts. In other cases it reflected an interest in travel—a favourite subject. But perhaps it was the habit of self-examination encouraged by Protestantism, and the growing interest in public affairs, that more than anything else stimulated the practice.

Pepys nowhere states why he kept one. He occasionally mentions his diary's usefulness (for example, in storing information that might help to protect him against parliamentary criticism of his official work, or to remind him of what tip to give to the parish sexton at New Year), but these were incidental benefits and could not have been in his mind when he started it. His reasons, like those of most diarists, are to be inferred from the diary itself. It is plain enough from the opening passages that he has clearly in mind what sort of diary he means to write. It is not to be a series of casual jottings about day-to-day events, or a baring of the soul in confession—two types of diary common enough at the time. It is to be a systematic account of his own affairs and also of what he calls the 'state of the nation'. As the diary continues, the two themes run in counterpoint, as it were, now one, now the other, taking over as the main subject. At each of the summaries he writes at the end of the year or volume, the narrative is halted so that he may sum up the private and public events in turn, in much the same way as he makes up in his monthly and annual accounts of expenses and savings. As a result his diary has a firm and clear structure. One of its origins, therefore, must be the love of order and neatness that was so marked a feature of his temperament, and which shows itself in many forms—in his handwriting, his dress, his carefully arranged library and his taste for formality in the design of buildings and gardens. 'No man in England', Clarendon was once moved to say of him, 'was of more method'. The diary, fully and regularly kept, had the effect of imposing a factitious order on the succession of often random events that made up each day's experience. Besides the diary he kept other personal records, which already by the 1660s included letter-books, memorandum books, account books, a tale book and a book of vows. All were methods of canalising the stream of experience—the diary best of all because it was the most comprehensive and the most intimate.

His decision to start it seems to have been a response to the political excitements of December 1659. He began it immediately afterwards—with an entry for Sunday 1 January 1660: the start of a new week, a new month, a new year and (as he hoped) of a new political era. He bought a notebook bound in simple but rich brown calf, of the sort that stationers sold to customers who wanted something better than an everyday memorandum book, as a commonplace book of some kind. Its pages were ruled in red at the upper and outer margins. On loose sheets, or possibly in a separate book (he later refers to a 'by-book'), he began to make the notes and drafts which often preceded the composition of the diary itself. All this almost entirely in shorthand, in the Shelton system he appears to have learnt at Cambridge. His writing habits were not regular, but he continued to compose it in much the same way, making entries every day or every few days, while his memory of events was still clear and their impact still fresh. Although he had plenty of opportunity to alter his entries if he had chosen to, he refrained, not even filling the rare blank where at the moment of composition he had been unable to recall a name. Being a man of system, he left virtually not a single day without a substantial entry, so that he reveals his daily life from rising to dinner, from dinner to supper and from supper to bed throughout the whole diary period. Moreover, he took the trouble to write in continuous prose. Even when hard pressed for time, he was never content in the final version to make do with mnemonic words and phrases. In the sheer technique of diary keeping—quite apart from the value of what he wrote—he has no equal.

Since he had an exact mind and an unflagging interest in everything that happened (as well as the means of writing quickly), it came naturally and easily to him to write in great detail, whether the subject was a coronation or a country walk or a quarrel with his wife. Evelyn has a graphic description of the Fire, but it is Pepys who notices the pigeons trapped on the window ledges and the cat that took refuge in a chimney-hole. It is this richness of detail that gives the diary its astonishing vividness.

The concern for detail follows from the thoroughness of his technique. Not everything is written down of course, but there is no important aspect of his experience (including his dreams) that is left without some record. No other diarist of his day attempted anything so comprehensive. Evelyn's diary (from 1620 to 1706) covers a lifetime, but is highly selective, being meant to be read by his descendants, and being rewritten to a large extent with that in view. The diary of Robert Hooke, the scientist and architect (1672-83), was regularly kept and covers a wide sweep of ground, but is thin, and often nothing more than disconnected notes. Other diarists, now deservedly forgotten, write irregularly and in the form of brief jottings, often using the printed almanacks whose increasing availability encouraged this sort of diary keeping. Others again might write voluminously, but on only one aspect of their experience—John Ray, John Locke or Celia Fiennes on their travels, Anthony Wood on university events, John Milward and Anchitel Grey on parliamentary debates, Ralph Josselin on village events as seen by a Puritan parson. None of Pepys's contemporaries, as far as we know, attempted a diary in the all-inclusive Pepysian sense and on the Pepysian scale. But thoroughness was second nature to Pepys, and he was as thorough in the writing of his diary as in his work as a public servant or his achievements as a bibliophile.

The small and passing everyday events are set down with great regularity—almost always what he ate and drank, and often what he wore. Although there are no extended passages of introspection, he rarely fails, when the matter warrants it, to record his thoughts. He keeps careful notes on his health, enters the more important of his occasional disbursements and at appropriate intervals summaries of his financial balances, and rarely lets many days go by without an account of his music-making, his reading, and his theatre-going. Little or nothing seems to be left for the Recording Angel to cover. Perhaps the extraordinary frankness and honesty for which the diary is famous is in a way a reflection of this thoroughness. He does not hesitate to admit to the record his fits of bad temper and jealousy, and the occasions when he was guilty of physical (and even moral) cowardice, of dishonesty in the office and of infidelity to his wife. These were facts and the record would be incomplete without them. There was little danger of prying eyes discovering them since they were all concealed in the shorthand, and some (the philandering episodes) concealed still further in a macaronic mixture mainly of English, French and Spanish. Moreover, to confess was also to remind himself of the need to reform. He often, after a lapse, renews his vows against self-indulgence. There was more than a trace of the Puritan in Pepys.

His history of public affairs is marked by similar thoroughness. There is no better contemporary account of the 1660s. His firsthand reports of the Restoration, the Dutch War, the Plague and the Fire have become classical. In addition he recounts the course of political events in close, almost daily, detail. He had had a passionate interest in politics from the days when he had raised a schoolboy's cheer at the execution of Charles I. Now he had the entrée to the court, rubbed shoulders with royalty and knew a wide range of courtiers, ministers and members of parliament. As a result, his diary contains an extremely well-informed though discontinuous history of ministries, parliament and public opinion. His own part in public affairs is naturally in the forefront of the story. He reveals how business was managed in the Navy Office—how he and his colleagues cooperated and quarrelled; how they worked with other departments and with members of the mercantile and shipping community of the City; how they prepared estimates for parliament. It is the only insider's history of the work of the civil service that we have for this period.

A diary so packed with matter, however interesting, might well be unreadable were it not for its manner. But Pepys had a gift for happiness that amounts to genius, and it lights up almost every page. Whenever he pauses to reflect on his condition, it is usually to thank God, despite his troubles, for his good health and his good fortune. Moreover, he had a natural flair for writing, as is clear from his letters and memoranda as well as from his diary. In the diary his method of presentation will often vary with his subject. When recalling the voluminous views of Sir Philip Warwick on public finance, he writes as he would write an office memorandum. When he makes observations on the ordinary events of an ordinary day, his language can be fresh and flexible, so that one can almost catch the inflexions of his voice. 'I to church', he writes at 31 January 1669 (obviously here using no notes) 'and there did hear the Doctor that is lately turned Divine, I have forgot his name—I met him a while since at Sir D. Gawden's at dinner—Dr. Waterhouse'. On other occasions his words are more artfully composed—to describe a scene, such as the Fire, or to express a mood, as in the moving passage with which the diary ends. If he tells a story he tells it well—unhurriedly, giving full value to every significant turn in the story, and holding the reader in delighted suspense. At 29 November 1667 there is for example the tale of his mistaking the chimney sweep for burglars; and in October of the same year the long account of his search for his buried gold in the Brampton garden, when he and Hewer dug around for hours and panned the earth in the summer-house 'just as they do for Dyamonds in other parts of the world'. Best of all in narrative power, his story of those agonising weeks in the autumn of 1668 when Elizabeth discovered his affair with her companion, Deb Willet, drove the young girl from her service and put Pepys under orders as strict as she could make them never to see Deb again. A novelist might envy the sensitivity and understanding with which it is told.

Pepys as a writer has in fact some of the characteristics of a novelist. He is notably observant, often catching his characters in an informal pose—the King weighing himself after tennis, Lord Clarendon nodding off at a meeting. Some of the figures who appear only casually are made unforgettable—the waterman who carried pins in his mouth, the 'mighty fat woman' who sang with 'so much pleasure to herself . . . relishing it to her very heart', and (most memorable of all perhaps) the shepherd on Epsom Downs, with his iron-shod boots and his woollen stockings and his little boy reading the Bible to him—'the most like one of the old Patriarchs that ever I saw in my life'.

A good case could be made for Pepys as the most evocative of English diarists; and an equally good case for his being the most informative. It is the combination of the two qualities which makes him unique. (pp. xxxiii-xxxviii)

Robert Latham, in an introduction to The Shorter Pepys *by Samuel Pepys, edited by Robert Latham, Bell & Hyman, 1985, pp. xxi-xxxix.*

ADDITIONAL BIBLIOGRAPHY

Abernathy, Cecil. *Mr. Pepys of Seething Lane.* New York: McGraw-Hill Book Co., 1957, 384 p.
    A comprehensive biography of Pepys, focusing on "the emergence of a 'new' man at the great moment of transition in English cultural history—nonheroic, efficient, vulnerable."

Bradford, Gamaliel. *The Soul of Samuel Pepys.* Boston: Houghton Mifflin Co., 1924, 262 p.
    A character study of Pepys, with scattered comments on the aesthetic merits of the *Diary.*

Bryant, Arthur. *Samuel Pepys.* 3 vols. Cambridge: Cambridge University Press, 1933-38.
    A well-documented, highly praised biography of Pepys in three volumes: *The Man in the Making, The Years of Peril,* and *The Saviour of the Navy.*

Dale, Donald. "The Greatness of Samuel Pepys." *The Quarterly Review* 275, No. 546 (October 1940): 227-38.
    Review article, treating eight separate works by or about Pepys.

Drinkwater, John. *Pepys: His Life and Character.* Garden City, N.Y.: Doubleday Doran & Co., 1930, 374 p.
    A biography of Pepys aimed at the general reader.

Emden, Cecil S. *Pepys Himself.* London: Oxford University Press, 1963, 146 p.
    A profile of Pepys, offering commentary on the diarist's personal qualities as revealed in the *Diary.*

Lewis, C. S. "Transposition." In his *They Asked for a Paper: Papers and Addresses,* pp. 166-82. London: Geoffrey Bles, 1962.
    Contains a close study of Pepys's diary entry for 27 February 1668, noting the diarist's self-examination of internal sensations.

Lowell, James Russell. "A Great Public Character." In his *My Study Windows,* pp. 83-114. Boston: James R. Osgood & Co., 1871.
    Surveys the life of Josiah Quincy, noting in passing of the *Diary* and Pepys, that "no history gives us so clear an understanding of the moral condition of average men after the restoration of the Stuarts as the unconscious blabbings of the Puritan tailor's son, with his two consciences, as it were,—an inward, still sensitive in spots, though mostly toughened to India-rubber, and good rather for rubbing out old scores than retaining them, and an outward, alert, and termagantly effective in Mrs. Pepys."

Marburg, Clara. *Mr. Pepys and Mr. Evelyn.* Philadelphia: University of Pennsylvania Press, 1935, 156 p.
    Examines correspondence between Pepys and John Evelyn.

Miner, Earl. "Pepys Revived." *The Hudson Review* XXIV, No. 1 (Spring 1971): 171-76.
    Reviews Volumes 1-3 of *The Diary of Samuel Pepys: A New and Complete Transcription,* focusing on the aesthetic qualities of the *Diary* and its likely method of composition.

Moorhouse, E. Hallam. *Samuel Pepys: Administrator, Observer, Gossip.* London: Chapman and Hall, 1909, 327 p.
    An anecdotal biography of Pepys, with chapters on Pepys's personality and Pepys as a man of letters.

Nicolson, Marjorie Hope. *Pepys' "Diary" and the New Science.* Charlottesville: The University Press of Virginia, 1965, 198 p.
    Studies Pepys's interest in science in three chapters: "Samuel Pepys, Amateur of Science"; "The First Blood Transfusions"; and " 'Mad Madge' and 'The Wits'."

Rolland, Romain. "An English Amateur (Pepys' Diary)." In his *A Musical Tour through the Land of the Past,* translated by Bernard Miall, pp. 21-44. New York: Henry Holt and Co., 1922.
    Explores references to music in the *Diary.*

Summers, Montague. *The Playhouse of Pepys.* London: Kegan Paul, Trench, Trubner & Co., 1935, 485 p.
    A survey of the English Restoration theater based on dramatic criticism in the *Diary.*

Tanner, J. R. *Samuel Pepys and the Royal Navy: Lees Knowles Lectures Delivered at Trinity College in Cambridge, 6, 13, 20 and 27 November, 1919.* Cambridge: Cambridge University Press, 1920, 83 p.
    Discusses Pepys's role in the expansion of the Royal Navy.

Trease, Geoffrey. *Samuel Pepys and His World.* New York: Charles Scribner's Sons, 1972, 128 p.
    A lavishly illustrated short biography of Pepys.

Wheatley, Henry B. *Samuel Pepys and the World He Lived In.* 2d ed. London: Bickers and Son, 1880, 311 p.
    A respected early biography of Pepys by the editor of the 1893-99 edition of the *Diary.*

Willy, Margaret. *English Diarists: Evelyn & Pepys.* Writers and Their Work, No. 162. London: Longmans, Green & Co. for The British Council and the National Book League, 1963, 47 p.
    Approaches the *Diary* as a record of "the hopes, fears and gratifications of an obscure, impecunious clerk possessing little but a capacity for hard work and an immense determination to get on."

Wilson, John Harold. *The Private Life of Mr. Pepys.* New York: Farrar, Straus and Cudahy, 1959, 249 p.

Explores the *Diary* as the work of a "normal, reasonably healthy male animal, ruled, as all men are, by passions and appetites."

Winterich, John T. "Samuel Pepys and His *Diary.*" In his *Books and the Man*, pp. 310-25. New York: Greenberg Publisher, 1929.
    A general appreciation of the *Diary*, noting that Pepys was "a remarkably close approximation to the modern conception of a self-made man."

Woodberry, George Edward. "A Word for Pepys." In his *Studies of a Litterateur*, pp. 83-5. 1921. Reprint. Freeport, N. Y.: Books for Libraries Press, 1968.
    Briefly considers Pepys as "one of the most English of his race."

Marie (de Rabutin-Chantal), Marquise de Sévigné
1626-1696

French epistler.

Sévigné is widely regarded as a world master of letter writing. She is credited with helping elevate familiar correspondence to an art form, and her legacy—letters rich in historical ambiance, social commentary, and intimate revelation—is valued as a mirror of seventeenth-century French life. Sévigné presumably wrote with no view toward publication and without particular concern for literary or stylistic refinement: most of the letters were written primarily to express the epistler's love for her absent daughter. Yet while Sévigné's profound maternal devotion has sometimes prompted adverse reaction among critics of her work, Sévigné remains, in Eva Marcu's words, "the letter writer *par excellence*."

Born in Paris, Marie de Rabutin-Chantal enjoyed an upbringing filled with the advantages of noble lineage. She was orphaned at the age of seven and reared by wealthy relatives. A pretty, precocious, and engaging child endowed with a naturally inquisitive mind, Marie delighted all who knew her. She was encouraged to develop an outgoing personality and received an education unusually comprehensive for young ladies of her time. Aside from the academic fundamentals, Marie was exposed to a wide spectrum of literature, was tutored in foreign languages (particularly Italian), and was instructed in singing, dancing, and horseback riding.

In 1644 Marie, by then a beautiful, accomplished woman of eighteen, was wed to Henri de Sévigné, a rich and handsome nobleman. The Marquise de Sévigné was initially very happy in her marriage. She was radiant at court, moved adroitly among the fashionable salons and drawing rooms of Paris, and was welcomed at formal provincial functions in Brittany (her husband's family seat). Her bliss was soon eclipsed, however, by financial difficulties caused by Henri's squandering. Moreover, she was tormented by her husband's repeated infidelity. Henri was killed in a duel over a courtesan in 1651. Left a widow at twenty-five, the marquise was pursued by a string of amorous suitors whose offers she genially but firmly declined. Sévigné devoted herself to her two children, securing for them the educational and cultural benefits she had known. Her daughter, Françoise Marguerite, was two years older than her brother Charles and was especially indulged by the marquise. Françoise Marguerite was a striking beauty but lacked her mother's warm, open disposition. She became the sole recipient of the monumental affection so evident in her mother's most illustrious correspondence. In 1669 Françoise Marguerite married François Adhémar de Monteil, Comte de Grignan. The count promptly went on to fulfill a military appointment, leaving his wife in Paris near her mother. In 1671, shortly after the birth of their first child, Madame de Grignan joined her husband at their home in Provence.

Devastated by her daughter's departure, Sévigné at first shunned visitors and all society. She took solace in her peaceful estate at Livry, discovering greater spiritual balm

Marie (de Rabutin-Chantal), Marquise de Sévigné

in natural surroundings than she had once found in the banter of lively company. In later years she would return often to Livry or to the cherished woodlands of Les Rochers in Brittany, enjoying the species of refreshment she had come to know in her first retirement. Yet Sévigné never really came to terms with separation from her daughter. From the very rattle of the coach initially bearing Madame de Grignan from her, Sévigné was predominantly renewed by unceasing correspondence with her daughter. The marquise came to know the mails intimately, dispatching letters by every available post and growing morbidly anxious if she failed to receive what she believed to be a timely response from Madame de Grignan. Once a casual conduit for news, gossip, and repartee to friends and relations, the letter became a lifeline for the marquise. Although she and her daughter were parted for an aggregate of less than ten years from 1671 to 1696, Sévigné felt each separation keenly and poured out in letters her love and motherly solicitude for her child. Sévigné's effusiveness was often a source of embarrassment and irritation to the reticent Madame de Grignan, who sometimes spurned her mother's elaborate sentiments. The many amusing anecdotes, descriptions of attended functions, and running commentaries on the latest fashions supplied in her mother's letters were all infinitely more to Madame de Grignan's epistolary taste.

Sévigné traveled freely when not visiting her daughter, mixing with the circles of such notables as François de La Rochefoucauld, Madeleine de Scudéry, and Madame de La Fayette. In letters to Madame de Grignan and others she vividly recorded whatever fancy or feeling prompted, nearly always filtering the topic at hand through its maternal associations. Although she was at times saddened by the passage of years and remained troubled by the frequent separations from her daughter, Sévigné retained a robustness for life that belies the contemplative and even somber tone of some later letters. Afflicted with bouts of rheumatism during middle age, she took several laborious cures at Vichy with characteristic good humor. She died of smallpox at age seventy while visiting her daughter's estate.

Letters to Madame de Grignan constitute the bulk of Sévigné's correspondence and are her most widely acclaimed literary achievement. They provide colorful glimpses into major events of the writer's time and are replete with candid, often memorable, portraits of individuals both prominent and obscure. Yet these points are wholly subsidiary to the theme of maternal love. Sévigné included strictly domestic or newsworthy items in the letters—fashions, court scandals, political intrigue, intellectual life in the provinces and the capital, and any number of other topical concerns—to entice her daughter to read them. She feared that without the inclusion of such details her daughter might grow tired of an unbroken stream of pure maternal sentiment. Sévigné's passion is always present, either professed outright when she is swept along on the tides of her emotion and unconcerned with possible adverse reaction, or more subtly stated if she has recently been rebuffed. Anxiety for her daughter's poor health also permeates the missives, along with related advice and admonitions—all understandable in view of Madame de Grignan's repeated pregnancies to accommodate her husband with a male heir.

The enormity of Sévigné's maternal devotion has always nonplussed her followers. Robert Arnauld d'Andilly, a Jansenist and translator of such spiritual classics as St. Augustine's *Confessions*, lectured her on the impropriety and inherent danger of her affection and pronounced her "a pretty pagan" for what he deemed idol worship. Friends and admirers were bemused by the attachment and speculated on its sincerity. The outspoken Marquis de Pomponne remarked: "So it seems that Mme. de Sévigné loves Mme. de Grignan passionately? Do you know what is behind it? Shall I tell you? It is that she loves her passionately." Others have drawn their own conclusions about what has appeared to many a disproportionate love of a mother for her child. Virginia Woolf, for example, warmly commended the letters themselves as "radiant and glowing," fresh even to the modern reader, but attributed their inspiration to "a passion twisted and morbid," one like the adoration of an elderly man for his cruel, young mistress. Later commentators have offered somewhat more clinical observations. Notably, Louise K. Horowitz has asserted that Sévigné's involvement with her daughter was fueled by ideals so unattainable that they necessitated the very absence of the love object and could only be realized on paper—"a means of achieving both a certain liberty and self-constraint through the working over and the manipulation of terms."

Horowtiz's hypothesis suggests another issue commonly raised by critics of the epistler's work: are Sévigné's letters entirely unstudied, a legacy intended solely for her daughter, or were they written, to whatever degree, with posterity in mind? Advocates of the view that Sévigné wrote spontaneously and with no eye toward publication point to Sévigné's own distinctive metaphor for composition—the freely trotting pen unchecked by the writer's "reins"—in defense of their position. Charles Augustin Sainte-Beuve richly praised the artless qualities of the letters. He noticed in them "a profusion of colors, comparisons, images" by which Sévigné, "without trying or suspecting it . . . placed herself in the front rank of . . . [French] writers." Detractors have also bolstered the case for spontaneity. The eighteenth-century English epistler Lady Mary Wortley Montagu averred in a 1754 note to her daughter that Sévigné's "tittle tattle . . . gilt over by airy expressions and a Flowing Style" should be "excus'd as her Letters were not intended for the Press." (Montagu had earlier confided in a 1726 missive to her sister that Sévigné's letters were "very pretty," slyly adding that her own would be "full as entertaining 40 years hence.") But Gaston Boissier, no less an admirer than Sainte-Beuve, has cautioned against taking Sévigné's claim for spontaneity too literally. He believed that the "winning grace of her details, the ingenious turn given to her reflections, her charming variety in the repetition of the same thought . . . seem to betray art and labor."

While Sévigné may well have refined her missives carefully and tailored them to their recipients' tastes, the quality for which her correspondence has been most uniformly applauded is its immediacy. English author and politician Horace Walpole, writing in 1785 to antiquary John Pinkerton, highly recommended Sévigné's correspondence for its historical value and challenged his friend: "Pray read her accounts of the death of Turenne, and of the arrival of King James in France, and tell me whether you do not know their persons as if you had lived at the time." A. B. Walkley, though he discounted the historical pieces and utterly dismissed Sévigné's ever present maternal affection, was yet arrested by the writer's "little intimate, personal touch," her ability to infuse "volumes into a word, and that word whispered, as it were, behind a fan."

The "personal touch" came as naturally to Sévigné as did her love for her daughter. Consequently, critics have viewed the epistler as more than a literary technician whose name is synonymous with artful correspondence. Nearly three hundred years after her death, Sévigné remains a friend to her readers, an individual as vibrant and varied in mood, as distinct in opinion, as any living personality. In this human capacity she has, at times, offended even her warmest enthusiasts by her unquestioning devotion to the aristocratic status quo. Yet more often she privileges the reader with a pensive moment, shares a hilarious sketch of some petty nobleman, or invites him to listen to the first notes of the nightingale's song as though he alone were her intended audience. Sévigné's openness has touched critics deeply. Upon discovering her letters, Scottish philosopher and historian Sir James Mackintosh observed: "She has so filled my heart with affectionate interest in her as a living friend, that I can scarcely bring myself to think of her as being a writer."

PRINCIPAL WORKS

Mémoires de Messire Roger de Rabutin, Comte de Bussy (letters) 1696

Lettres choisies de Mme la marquise de Sévigné à Mme de Grignan sa fille qui contiennent beaucoup de particularités de l'histoire de Louis XIV (letters) 1725

Recueil de lettres choisies pour servir de suite aux lettres de Mme de Sévigné à Mme de Grignan, sa fille (letters) 1751

Lettres de Mme de Sévigné à Monsieur de Pomponne (letters) 1756

Lettres nouvelles ou nouvellement recouvrées de la marquise de Sévigné et de la marquise de Simiane, sa petite-fille (letters) 1773

Lettres de Mme de Sévigné au comte de Bussy-Rabutin (letters) 1775

Lettres inédités de Mme de Sévigné (letters) 1814

Lettres de Mme de Sévigné, de sa famille et de ses amis. 14 vols. (letters) 1862-68

Lettres. 3 vols. (letters) 1953-57

Selected Letters (letters) 1960

Correspondance de Mme de Sévigné. 3 vols. (letters) 1972-78

*Although this work is nominally that of Roger de Rabutin, Sévigné's cousin, it contains letters by Sévigné and marks her first appearance in print.

LADY MARY WORTLEY MONTAGU (letter date 1754)

[*Montagu was an English epistler known for her versatile and sparkling letters, the preponderance of which were written to her daughter, Lady Bute. A cousin and early patroness of novelist Henry Fielding, she was also a close friend of poet Alexander Pope. She is perhaps best remembered for an ongoing bitter quarrel with the latter author, who attacked her viciously in his verse. In the following excerpt from a letter written in 1754 to Lady Bute, she denigrates Sévigné's work.*]

Well turn'd periods or smooth lines are not the perfection either of Prose or verse; they may serve to adorn, but can never stand in the Place of good Sense. Copiousness of words, however rang'd, is allwaies false Eloquence, thô it will ever impose on some sort of understandings. How many readers and admirers has Madame de Sevigny, who only gives us, in a lively manner and fashionable Phrases, mean sentiments, vulgar Prejudices, and endless repetitions! Sometimes the tittle tattle of a fine Lady, sometimes that of an old Nurse, allwaies tittle tattle; yet so well gilt over by airy expressions and a Flowing Style, she will allwaies please the same people to whom Lord Bolingbroke will shine as a first rate Author. She is so far to be excus'd as her Letters were not intended for the Press, while he labours to display to posterity all the Wit and Learning he is Master of.... (p. 62)

> *Lady Mary Wortley Montagu, in a letter to Lady Bute on July 20, 1754, in her* The Complete Letters of Lady Mary Wortley Montagu: 1752-1762, *Vol III, edited by Robert Halsband, Oxford at the Clarendon Press, 1967, pp. 61-5.*

HORACE WALPOLE (letter date 1785)

[*An English author and politician, Walpole is best known for his memoirs and voluminous correspondence, both of which provide revealing glimpses of life in England during the last half of the eighteenth century. In the following excerpt from a 1785 letter to his friend John Pinkerton, he warmly recommends Sévigné's letters.*]

In general, I believe that what I call grace is denominated elegance; but by grace I mean something higher: I will explain myself by instances—Apollo is graceful, Mercury elegant: Petrarch, perhaps, owed his whole merit to the harmony of his numbers and the graces of his style. They conceal his poverty of meaning and want of variety. His complaints, too, may have added an interest which, had his passion been successful, and had expressed itself with equal sameness, would have made the number of his sonnets insupportable. Melancholy in poetry, I am inclined to think, contributes to grace, when it is not disgraced by pitiful lamentations, such as Ovid's and Cicero's in their banishments. We respect melancholy, because it imparts a similar affection, pity. A gay writer, who should only express satisfaction without variety, would soon be nauseous.

Madame de Sévigné shines both in grief and gaiety. There is too much of sorrow for her daughter's absence; yet it is always expressed by new terms, by new images, and often by wit, whose tenderness has a melancholy air. When she forgets her concern, and returns to her natural disposition, gaiety, every paragraph has novelty: her allusions, her applications are the happiest possible. She has the art of making you acquainted with all her acquaintance, and attaches you even to the spots she inhabited. Her language is correct, though unstudied; and, when her mind is full of any great event, she interests you with the warmth of a dramatic writer, not with the chilling impartiality of an historian. Pray read her accounts of the death of Turenne, and of the arrival of King James in France, and tell me whether you do not know their persons as if you had lived at the time. (pp. 392-93)

> *Horace Walpole, in a letter to John Pinkerton on June 26, 1785, in his* A Selection of the Letters of Horace Walpole, *Vol. 2, edited by W. S. Lewis, Harper & Brothers Publishers, 1926, pp. 387-93.*

SIR JAMES MACKINTOSH (journal date 1812)

[*Mackintosh was a Scottish historian and scholar who participated actively in the intellectual life of his day. He wrote* Vindiciae Gallicae—*a rebuttal to English statesman Edmund Burke's* Reflections on the Revolution in France *(1790). In the following excerpt from an 1812 entry in his* Memoirs *(1853), Mackintosh warmly regards Sévigné's appeal.*]

I yesterday read the death of my dear Marie de Rabutin-Chantal; I almost thought it was the death of E—, who certainly resembles her very much, if she had killed J—W— at eighteen, and, instead of Mrs. L— and Aunt —, she had passed her widowhood with the Duc de la Rochefoucauld and the Cardinal de Retz—to say nothing of Madame de la Fayette and Madame de Coulanges. I cannot bear to read these Grignans and Simianes writing to each other after her death, as if she were forgotten, and as if the world could go on without her. I am displeased at not being able to discover the Christian name of Madame de Grignan; and I wish I knew the history of Corbinelli and young Madame de Sevigné the saint. Why am I told nothing of the descendants of the Grignans, either the little Marquis or the adorable Pauline?

It is part of Madame de Sevigné's natural character that she is frank, joyous, and does not conceal her relish for the pleasures and distinctions of life. As she indulges every natural feeling just to the degree necessary to animate her character, and to vary her enjoyment, without approaching vicious excess, she finds no inconsistency in rambling from the vanities of Versailles to admiration, at least, of the austerities of Port Royal; she is devout without foregoing the world, or blaming the ambitious. The great charm of her character seems to me a *natural* virtue. In what she does, as well as in what she says, she is unforced and unstudied; nobody, I think had so much morality without constraint, and played so much with amiable failings without falling into vice. Her ingenious, lively, social disposition gave the direction to her mental power. She has so filled my heart with affectionate interest in her as a living friend, that I can scarcely bring myself to think of her as being a writer, or as having a style; but she has become a celebrated, probably an immortal, writer, without expecting it; she is the only classical writer who never conceived the possibility of acquiring fame. Without a great power of style, she could not have communicated those feelings to others. In what does that talent consist? It seems mainly to consist in the power of working bold metaphors, and unexpected turns of expression, out of the most familiar part of conversational language. (pp. 217-18)

I have just finished the whole Sevigné collection; the last part of it consists of letters from Madame de Simiane to a certain Intendant of Provence. Into what a new world am I fallen! forty years after the disappearance of the goddess! The adorable Pauline become an old country gentlewoman, not so much more lively, as she ought to be, than the wife of any other of the Provençal squires! An impudent country-house, called 'Belombre,' pretends to maintain the honours of Les Rochers! No Sevignés—no Rabutins—no Grignans—no Coulanges! almost all memory of the heroic age is lost. The publication of Madame de Sevigné's letters, and a quotation of one of her sayings, show how the world was before the fall:—'There may, says my grandmother, be such a weight of obligation, that there is no way of being delivered from it, but ingratitude.' (p. 219)

> *Sir James Mackintosh, in a journal entry on February 28, 1812, in his* Memoirs of the Life of the Right Honourable Sir James Mackintosh, Vol. II, *edited by Robert James Mackintosh, 1835. Reprint by Little, Brown and Company, 1853, pp. 217-19.*

CHARLES AUGUSTIN SAINTE-BEUVE (essay date 1829)

[*Sainte-Beuve is considered the foremost French literary critic of the nineteenth century. His best known writings are his literary and historical "lundis"—weekly newspaper articles that appeared nearly every Monday morning over a period of two decades. Sainte-Beuve began his career as a champion of Romanticism but eventually formulated a psychological method of criticism. He considered an author's life and character integral to the comprehension of his work.*

This perspective led him to classify writers into "familles d'esprits," or "families of the mind." Although he usually treated his subjects with respect, he dealt harshly with several, notably François Chateaubriand and Honoré de Balzac. In the twentieth century, Sainte-Beuve's treatment of Balzac provoked the ire of Marcel Proust, who wrote Contre Sainte-Beuve *(1954;* By Way of Sainte-Beuve, *1958) to contest Sainte-Beuve's analytical method. Other twentieth-century critics have praised Sainte-Beuve's erudition and insight but questioned his biographical approach. In the words of René Wellek, "Sainte-Beuve should be described as the greatest representative of the historical spirit in France," who, at his best, "preserves the delicate balance needed to save himself from relativism or overemphasis on external conditions." In the following excerpt from a "lundi" originally published in 1829, he examines Sévigné's work as defined by its social and historical parameters.*]

The critics, particularly those outside France, who have lately judged our two literary centuries with the greatest severity, agree that the dominant characteristics of those periods, their brilliance and attraction, which are expressed in a thousand ways, are the fruits of the spirit of conversation and society—knowledge of the world and men, a keen discernment of what is proper and improper, subtle delicacy of feeling, and graceful piquancy and refinement of language. And indeed, until about 1789, these are, except in the cases of a very few writers, the characteristics that distinguish French literature from the other literatures of Europe. These brilliant qualities have sometimes been held up to us as a reproach; but such a mistake could be made only by persons incapable of appreciating their true meaning.

At the beginning of the seventeenth century, our civilization, and hence our language and literature were anything but mature or firmly established. Europe, after emerging from its religious upheavals and entering upon the Thirty Years' War, was laboriously giving birth to a new political order. France was eliminating the residues of her civil discords. At Court, a few salons, a few *ruelles* or coteries of wits, were already fashionable; but nothing great or original had yet begun to germinate; the monotonous spiritual nourishment was provided by Spanish novels and Italian sonnets and pastorals. Not until after Richelieu, after the Fronde, under the Queen Mother and Mazarin, did there suddenly emerge, as though by miracle, amid the fetes of Saint-Mandé and Vaux, from the salons of the Hôtel de Rambouillet and the antechambers of the young king, three first-class minds, three geniuses diversely endowed, but all of naïve and pure taste, perfect simplicity, and felicitous abundance, nourished by their own native graces and delicacies, and destined to open a glorious age in which none was to surpass them. Molière, La Fontaine, and Mme. de Sévigné belong to a literary generation which preceded that led by Racine and Boileau, and they are distinguished from the latter by various features, rooted both in the nature of their genius and in the date of their coming. We feel that by the turn of their minds as well as by their position they are much closer to the France of before Louis XIV, to the old language and the old French spirit; that they were much more part of these by their education and their readings, and that if they are less appreciated by non-Frenchmen than certain later writers, they owe this precisely to elements in their accent and manner which are the most intimate, the most indefinable, and the most appealing for Frenchmen. We cannot too highly venerate and uphold these immortal writers who first gave French literature its original character, and who have secured for it, down to this day, a physiognomy unique among all literatures.

Molière extracted the strongest and highest poetry conceivable from the spectacle of life, from the living play of human failings, vices, and follies. La Fontaine and Mme. de Sévigné, on a more limited stage, had so fine and true a sense of the things and life of their times, each in his own manner—La Fontaine closer to nature, Mme. de Sévigné to society—and they expressed this exquisite sense so freshly in their writings, that we find it quite easy to consider them as being not too far below Molière. Today we shall speak only of Mme. de Sévigné; it seems that everything has been said about her, and it is true that the details are nearly exhausted; but until now she has been considered too much in isolation, as was long the case with La Fontaine whom she resembles so much. Today, as the society whose most brilliant facet she represents is receding into the past and we can see it in clearer perspective, it is easier and at the same time more necessary to define Mme. de Sévigné's rank, importance, and milieu. It is doubtless for having failed to take into account the difference between her period and ours that many distinguished minds in our own day seem inclined to underestimate one of the most delightful geniuses who ever existed. I should be happy if this article helped to dispel some of these unfair preconceptions.

The excesses of the Regency have been stigmatized a great deal; but before the regency of Philippe d'Orléans, there had been another, not less dissolute, not less licentious, and even more horrible in the cruelty that characterized it—a kind of hideous transition between the excesses of Henri III and those of Louis XV. The immorality of the Ligue, which had smoldered under Henri IV and Richelieu, burst out anew. Debauchery was just as monstrous at that time as it had been at the time of the *mignons* or would be later at the time of the *roués*; but what brings this period closer to the sixteenth century and distinguishes it from the eighteenth, is above all assassination, poisoning, those Italian habits due to the Medicis, and the insane fury of duels, heritage of the civil wars. This is what the impartial reader will see in the regency of Anne of Austria; such is the dark and bloody background against which the Fronde loomed up one fine morning, the Fronde which is often called "a joke with a mailed fist." The conduct of the women of that time—ladies distinguished for birth, beauty, and wit—seems fabulous, and we should like to believe that historians have slandered them. But since excess always begets its opposite, the small number of women who escaped corruption plunged into sentimental metaphysics and became *précieuses*; hence the Hôtel de Rambouillet. This was an oasis of civilized manners in the midst of high society. Eventually it even led to good taste, as exemplified in Mme. de Sévigné who had frequented it. (pp. 119-21)

From the first pages of . . . [her] correspondence we find ourselves in a world very different from that of the Fronde and the Regency; we realize that what is called French society was at last constituted. No doubt (and even if we did not have numerous contemporary memoirs, the anecdotes related by Mme. de Sévigné would be evidence of it), no doubt the young nobility on which Louis XIV imposed dignity, courtesy, and elegance as the price of his favors still indulged in horrible disorders and crude orgies; no doubt, under the brilliant gilded surface, vice was sufficiently rampant to overflow into another Regency, particularly after it was set fermenting by the bigotry at the close of the reign of Louis XIV. But at least the proprieties were observed; opinion began to stigmatize what was unsavory and ignoble. Moreover, as disorder and brutality became less conspicuous, decency and wit were gaining in simplicity. *Préciosité* had gone out of fashion; the former *précieuses* now only smiled at the memory. Gone were the days when people discoursed interminably on the sonnet of Job or of Uranie, on the *carte du Tendre* or on the character of Romain; now they "conversed," they talked, exchanging Court news, evoking memories of the siege of Paris or the war in Guyenne. Cardinal de Retz related his travels, M. de La Rochefoucauld made remarks on human nature, Mme. de La Fayette analyzed feelings, and Mme. de Sévigné interrupted them all to quote a smart saying by her daughter or to recount a prank of her son's or an amusing anecdote about the good d'Hacqueville or M. de Brancas.

In 1829, our utilitarian concerns make it hard for us to imagine what this life of leisure and conversation was really like. The world moves so fast in our day, so many things are by turns brought on the stage, that we scarcely have the time to observe and grasp them all. Our days are spent in studies, our evenings in serious discussions; as for friendly conversations, *causeries*, there are few or none at all. The noble society of our day, which has most largely preserved the leisure habits of the two preceding centuries, seems to be able to do so only by staying aloof from modern ideas and ways. In the period under consideration, this leisurely mode of life was not incompatible with interest in literary, religious, and political events; it was enough to cast an occasional glance at them from the corner of an eye, without leaving one's chair, and the rest of the time one could devote oneself to one's tastes and one's friends. Moreover, conversation had not yet become, as it was to become in the eighteenth century, in the open salons presided over by Fontenelle, an occupation, a business, a social requirement. Wit was not necessarily the aim; geometrical, philosophical, or sentimental subtlety was not *de rigueurhr*; people talked about themselves, about others, about trifles or nothing at all. As Mme. de Sévigné says, there were "endless" conversations. "After dinner," she writes somewhere to her daughter, "we went to talk in the pleasantest woods in the world; we stayed there until six o'clock, engaged in several kinds of conversation, so agreeable, so tender, so friendly, so obliging for both you and me, that my heart is still aglow."

In the midst of this social life, so easy, so simple, so whimsical, and so gracefully animated, a visit, a letter received, insignificant in itself, was an event in which one took pleasure, and which was reported eagerly. The way this was done lent price to the least things; casually, without being aware of it, these people turned living into an art. (Recall, for instance, Mme. de Sévigné's report on Mme. de Chaulnes' visit to Les Rochers.) It has often been said that Mme. de Sévigné went to a great deal of trouble with her letters, that writing them she had in mind, if not posterity, at least the society of her day, whose approval she sought. This is false: the days of Voiture and of Guez de Balzac were a thing of the past. As a rule, she set down whatever sprang to her mind, and as many things as possible; and if she was in a hurry, she scarcely read over what she had written. "The fact is," she says, "between friends we should let our pens trot along as they please; I never pull hard at the reins of mine." But there are days when she has more time and when she feels in better form; then, quite naturally, she takes better care, she arranges and she composes more or less as La Fontaine composed his fables. This is, for example, what she does in her letter to M. de Coulanges on Mademoiselle's marriage, and in the one to him about her lackey Picard, whom she dismissed for having refused to help with the mowing. Letters of this type, artistic and brilliant in form, which did not contain too much malicious gossip or too many little secrets, created a stir in society, and everyone wanted to read them. "I mustn't forget what happened to me this morning," Mme. de Coulanges wrote to her friend. "I was told, 'Madame, a lackey from Mme. de Thianges is here.' I ordered him to be admitted. This is what he had to tell me: 'Madame, I have come from Mme. de Thianges who asks you kindly to send her Mme. de Sévigné's letter about the horse and the one about the meadow.' I told the lackey that I'd bring them to his mistress, and I have passed them on to her. As you can see, your letters make all the noise they deserve; it is certain that they are delightful, and you are like your letters." Thus, correspondence at that time was important, just like conversation; neither was "composed," but people gave all their minds and hearts to them. Mme. de Sévigné continually praises her daughter for her letters: "Your ideas and your style are incomparable." And she reports that "now and then" she reads passages to persons worthy of them: "occasionally I read a little excerpt to Mme. de Villars; she likes the tender passages, and her eyes fill with tears when she hears them."

Just as the candor of Mme. de Sévigné's letters has been doubted, so has the sincerity of her love for her daughter; on this score, too, no allowance has been made for the time she lived in, and for the fact that for persons whose existence is one of luxury and idleness passions may be very much like fancies, just as manias may often become passions. Mme. de Sévigné adored her daughter, and she became known for this; this is why Arnauld d'Andilly called her "a pretty pagan," a worshiper of idols. Separation served only to intensify her affection; she scarcely gave thought to anything else; the questions and compliments of people she saw invariably brought her back to her daughter. In the end, this almost exclusive attachment became the badge of her personality, and she could not do without it, carrying her maternal love about with her as one does a fan. For all that, Mme. de Sévigné was perfectly sincere, frank, an enemy of pretense; she was even one of the first to apply the adjective "real" (*vraie*) to a person, and she might have invented the expression for her daughter if M. de La Rochefoucauld had not forestalled her by applying it to Mme. de La Fayette; at all events she was fond of applying it to persons she loved. After we have analyzed that inexhaustible maternal love from every conceivable angle, we fall back on the explanation given by M. de Pomponne: "So it seems that Mme. de Sévigné loves Mme. de Grignan passionately? Do you know what is behind it? Shall I tell you? It is that she loves her passionately." It would indeed be most ungracious were we to find fault with Mme. de Sévigné for this innocent and legitimate passion, thanks to which we are able to follow step by step the wittiest of all women over twenty-six years of the most delightful period of the most attractive French society.

La Fontaine, painter of fields and animals, was anything but unfamiliar with society, and often portrayed it with subtlety and malice. Mme. de Sévigné, for her part, also greatly loved the country; she went on long visits to Livry, staying with the Abbé de Coulanges, or to her estate of Les Rochers in Brittany, and it is interesting to note how she saw and depicted nature. To begin with, we realize that like our good fabulist she had read *Astrée* at an early date, and that in her youth she had daydreamed under the mythological trees of Vaux and Saint-Mandé. She was fond of taking walks "by the rays of Endymion's beautiful mistress," and of spending a couple of hours alone with the "hamadryads"; her trees were decorated with inscriptions and ingenious devices, such as are found in the landscapes of *Pastor fido* and *Aminta*. . . . [Her] somewhat insipid reminiscences of pastorals and romances come spontaneously from her quill, and her many entirely fresh, original descriptions are all the more charming by contrast. "I have come here [to Livry] for the last good weather in the year, to say farewell to the leaves; they are still on the trees, they have merely changed color; instead of being green, they are now aurora, and so many shades of aurora that they compose a magnificently rich gold brocade, which we try to persuade ourselves is lovelier than green, were it only for a change." And when she is at Les Rochers, she writes: "I'd be very happy in these woods, if only I had a leaf that sings—ah, how pretty, a leaf that sings!" And how she depicts for us "the triumph of the month of May," when "the nightingale, the cuckoo, the warbler usher in the spring in our woods"! How she makes us feel, almost touch "those fine crystalline days of autumn, which are no longer hot, and not yet cold"! When her son, in order to obtain funds for some extravagance, orders the ancient woods of Buron cut, she is upset, distressed at the thought of all the fugitive dryads and dispossessed sylvan deities: Ronsard did not lament more eloquently the fall of the Gastine forest, nor M. de Chateaubriand that of his paternal woods.

Mme. de Sévigné's constant gaiety and playfulness must not be interpreted as the mark of an essentially frivolous, insensitive nature. She was serious, even sad, especially during her stays in the country, and she was given to solitary musings. This is not to say that she indulged in melancholy reveries, strolling along somber paths in the woods, like Delphine or Oswald's sweetheart. That kind of revery had not yet been invented; it was not until 1793 that Mme. de Staël wrote her admirable book, *L'Influence des passions sur le bonheur*. Until then daydreaming had been more natural and more personal, and at the same time less self-centered. To daydream was, for Mme. de Sévigné, to think of her daughter in Provence, of her son in Crete or with the king's army, of absent or dead friends; it was to say: "As for my life, you know it; I spend it with five or six friends whose company I like, and doing a thousand things I am obliged to do, which is no small matter. But I am vexed at the idea that while we do nothing the days go by, and our poor life is made up of such days, and we grow old and die. I think this is very bad."

In those days life was strictly regulated by religion, and it was largely thanks to this that sensibility and imagination, which have since lost all restraint, were kept within sensible bounds. Mme. de Sévigné took good care to "glide over" certain ideas; she explicitly asserts her belief in Christian ethics, and more than once poked fun at her daughter's infatuation with Cartesianism. As for herself, amid the insecurity of this world, she bows her head and takes refuge in a kind of providential fatalism, which bespeaks the influence of Port-Royal and such writers as Nicole and St. Augustine. The tendency to religious resignation increased in her with age, but did not alter the serenity of her disposition, though she expressed herself with greater restraint and her affection acquired a note of gravity. We feel this especially in her letter to M. de Coulanges on the death of the Minister Louvois, where she rises to the sublimity of Bossuet, just as in earlier letters she occasionally equaled the comic verve of Molière.

M. de Saint-Surin, in his meritorious works on Mme. de Sévigné, has lost no opportunity to contrast her advantageously with the famous Mme. de Staël. I, too, believe that the comparison between the two women is interesting and useful, but it must not be made to the detriment of either. Mme. de Staël represents an entirely new society, Mme. de Sévigné one that is a thing of the past; this accounts for the prodigious differences, which we are at first tempted to ascribe solely to the different turns of mind and temperament. However, without denying the profound innate dissimilarity between their two souls—one knew only maternal love, while the other experienced every passion, including the most generous and most virile—closer scrutiny shows that they shared many weaknesses and many qualities, which developed differently only because they lived in different centuries. What spontaneity full of grace and lightness, what pages of dazzling intellectual brilliance in Mme. de Staël, when sentiment does not mar them, when she forgets her philosophy and politics! And does not Mme. de Sévigné sometimes philosophize and discourse? Why else should she make the *Essais de Morale, Socrate chrétien*, and St. Augustine her daily fare? For this allegedly frivolous woman read everything and read well; a mind that finds no pleasure in serious reading, she used to say, acquires "a pale complexion." She read Rabelais and Bossuet's *Variations des églises protestantes*, Montaigne and Pascal, La Calprenède's novel *Cléopâtre*, and Quintilian, St. John Chrysostom, and Tacitus and Virgil, not "travestied," but "in all the majesty of their native Latin." When the weather was rainy, she could read a folio volume "in twelve days." During Lent, she enjoyed the sermons of Bourdaloue. Her conduct toward Fouquet in his disgrace suggests the devotion she would have been capable of in a revolutionary period. If she shows herself vain and boastful when the king dances with her one evening or when, after the performance of *Esther* at Saint-Cyr, he pays her a compliment—would anyone else of her sex have been more philosophical in her place? We are told that Mme. de Staël herself went to a great deal of trouble to wrest a few words and a glance from the conqueror of Egypt and Italy. Surely, a woman who, though associated from early youth with men like Ménage, Godeau, Benserade, kept clear of their pedantries and insipidities by the strength of her good sense, and seemingly without effort evaded the more refined and seductive advances of men like Saint-Evrémond and Bussy; who, though she was a friend and admirer of Mlle. de Scudéry and of Mme. de Maintenon, remained equally aloof from the sentimentalism of the one and the somewhat overdone reserve of the other; who, though connected with Port-Royal and steeped in the works of *ces Messieurs*, had high regard for Montaigne and quoted Rabelais, and desired no other inscription on what she called her "convent" than

"Sacred Freedom" or "Do what you like," as at the Abbey of Thélème—surely, such a woman may be frolicsome and playful, she may "glide over" thoughts, and she may take things by their familiar and amusing side, but for all that she gives evidence of intellectual strength and rare originality.

There is only one occasion when we cannot help regretting that Mme. de Sévigné indulged in her habit of lighthearted mockery, when we absolutely refuse to be amused by her, and, after looking for every possible excuse, still find it hard to forgive her. It is when she relates so cheerfully to her daughter the rebellion of the peasants of Lower Brittany and the atrocities which marked its repression. So long as she confines herself to poking fun at the *Etats*, at the rural squires and their noisy celebrations, at their enthusiasm for voting everything "between twelve and one o'clock," and all the other after-dinner follies of her "next-door neighbors" in Brittany, everything is fine, her jokes have point and substance, and occasionally she brings to mind the touch of Molière. But at a certain point she talks about "a little intestine warfare" in Brittany and "an attack of the stone" in Rennes—this is to report how M. de Chaulnes, the governor of Brittany, was driven back to his house by a hail of stones after he tried to disperse the people. Then she goes on to recount how M. de Forbin arrived with six thousand men, and how those poor devils of mutineers, catching sight of the royal troops from afar, took flight across the fields or fell on their knees, crying *Mea culpa* (the only "French" words they knew). She also relates that, in order to punish Rennes, its parlement was transferred to Vannes; that twenty-five or thirty men were seized "at random" to be hanged, and that the inhabitants of an entire long street, including women in childbed, old men, and children, were driven out and banished, and giving them shelter was forbidden under penalty of death. She speaks volubly of how people were broken on the wheel and quartered, and how the authorities, after they had had their fill of breaking and quartering, confined themselves to plain hanging. In the midst of such horrors perpetrated on innocent people or misguided poor devils, it is painful to see Mme. de Sévigné joke almost as usual. We should like her to display a burning, bitter, generous indignation; above all, we should like to erase from her letters lines such as these: "The rebels of Rennes fled along ago; and so the good will suffer in place of the wicked; but I find all this satisfactory, provided the four thousand soldiers who are at Rennes under M. de Forbin and M. de Vins do not prevent me from taking walks in my woods, which are of marvelous height and beauty." And in another letter: "Sixty burghers have been rounded up; tomorrow the hangings begin. The province will be a fine example to the others, and above all it will remind them that one must respect governors and governesses, that one must not insult them and hurl stones into their gardens"; and finally: "You speak very amusingly about our troubles; but we are no longer broken on the wheel so often; only one man a week, to keep justice functioning; hanging seems now like a treat." The Duc de Chaulnes, who ordered all these horrors to retaliate for the insults hurled at him (the gentlest and most familiar of them was "fat pig") and for the stones that had been thrown into his garden, did not as a result go down even a notch in Mme. de Sévigné's affection. To her and to Mme. de Grignan he remained "our good duke"; more than that, when he is appointed ambassador to Rome and leaves the province, all

Brittany, according to her, "is sad" at his departure. All this certainly suggests many reflections on the customs and civilization of the *grand siècle;* our readers will easily supply these. All I shall say is that on this occasion Mme. de Sévigné's heart unfortunately failed to rise above the prejudices of her time. She might have done so, for her kindness equaled her beauty and her grace. Occasionally she intervened in favor of galley prisoners with M. de Vivonne or with M. de Grignan. Without doubt, the most interesting of her *protégés* was a gentleman of Provence whose name has not come down to us. "This poor boy," she says, "was devoted to M. Fouquet; he was convicted for taking a letter to Mme. Fouquet from her husband; and for this he was sentenced to the galleys for five years. This is a rather unusual case. You know he is one of the finest young men you could see; it is inconceivable that he should be sent to the galleys."

Mme. de Sévigné's style has been so often and so intelligently judged, analyzed, and admired, that it would be hard today to find any appropriate new praise; on the other hand, I do not in the least feel inclined to inject new blood into clichés by means of chicaneries and criticisms. I shall confine myself to one general observation, namely, that the great and beautiful style of the age of Louis XIV can be related to two different techniques, two opposite manners.

Malherbe and [Guez de] Balzac founded, in our literature, the austere, polished, worked, learned style; to achieve it, we proceed from thought to expression, slowly, by degrees, experimenting and erasing. This is the style that Boileau recommends for all purposes; according to him, the writer must go back to his work twenty times, constantly polishing and repolishing it; he boasts of having taught Racine to compose "easy verses with difficulty." Racine is indeed the perfect model of this style in poetry; Fléchier was less felicitous in his prose. But in addition to this kind of writing, always somewhat monotonous and academic, there is another, far freer, capricious and varied, without traditional method, and entirely in conformity with the diversity of talents and geniuses. Montaigne and Régnier had previously given admirable specimens of it, and Queen Marguerite a charming one in her familiar memoirs, the work of a few *"après-disnées."* This is the broad, loose, abundant style, which follows closely the current of ideas; the spontaneous or, as Montaigne himself put it, *prime-sautier* style, that of La Fontaine and Molière, that of Fénelon, of Bossuet, of the Duc de Saint-Simon, and of Mme. de Sévigné. Mme. de Sévigné excels in it: she lets her pen "trot," never "pulling hard on the reins," and as she goes she scatters a profusion of colors, comparisons, images, while wit and sentiment pour from her on all sides. In this way, without trying or suspecting it, she placed herself in the front rank of our writers.

And now, if a few overcritical minds find that I have gone too far in my admiration for Mme. de Sévigné, may I be allowed to ask them one question: Have you read her? And by reading I mean, not perusing a random selection of her letters, not picking out two or three which enjoy a classical reputation—the letters on the marriage of Mademoiselle, on the deaths of Vatel, of M. de Turenne, of M. de Longueville—but plunging into the ten volumes of her correspondence and following her step by step, enjoying everything—in short doing for her as we do for *Clarissa Harlowe* when we have two weeks of leisure and rain in

the country. After that trial, which is anything but terrible, I am sure that you will have forgotten that you ever criticized my admiration. (pp. 123-33)

Charles Augustin Sainte-Beuve, "Madame de Sé-vigné," in his Sainte-Beuve: Selected Essays, *edited and translated by Francis Steegmuller and Norbert Guterman, Doubleday & Company, Inc., 1963, pp. 119-33.*

[LEIGH HUNT] (essay date 1842)

[*Hunt was a nineteenth-century English poet, essayist, and critic. In his criticism, he articulated the principles of Romanticism, emphasizing imaginative freedom and encouraging the expression of a personal emotional or spiritual state. Although his critical works have been overshadowed by those of his friends Samuel Taylor Coleridge, William Hazlitt, and Charles Lamb, his essays are considered both insightful and generous to the fledgling writers he supported. In the following excerpt, Hunt provides a brief critical survey of Sévigné's work and offers a personal assessment of her appeal.*]

Madame de Sévigné, in her combined and inseparable character as writer and woman, enjoys the singular and delightful reputation of having united, beyond all others of her class, the rare with the familiar, and the lively with the correct. The moment her name is mentioned, we think of the mother who loved her daughter; of the most charming of letter-writers; of the ornament of an age of license, who incurred none of its ill-repute; of the female who has become one of the classics of her language, without effort and without intention. (p. 203)

In Boswell's *Life of Johnson* is a reference by the great and gloomy moralist to a passage in Madame de Sévigné, in which she speaks of existence having been imposed upon her without her consent; but the conclusion he draws from it as to her opinion of life in general, worthy of the critic who 'never read books through.' The momentary effusion of spleen is contradicted by the whole correspondence. She occasionally vents her dissatisfaction at a rainy day, or the perplexity produced in her mind by a sermon; and when her tears begin flowing for a pain in her daughter's little finger, it is certainly no easy matter to stop them; but there was a luxury at the heart of this woe. Her ordinary notions of life were no more like Johnson's, than rose-colour is like black, or health like disease. She repeatedly proclaims, and almost always shows, her delight in existence; and has disputes with her daughter, in which she laments that she does not possess the same turn of mind. There is a passage, we grant, on the subject of old age, which contains a reflection similar to the one alluded to by Johnson, and which has been deservedly admired for its force and honesty. But even in this passage, the germ of the thought was suggested by the melancholy of another person, not by her own. Madame de la Fayette had written her a letter urging her to retrieve her affairs, and secure her health, by accepting some money from her friends, and quitting the Rocks for Paris;—offers which, however handsomely meant, she declined with many thanks, and not a little secret indignation; for she was very jealous of her independence. In the course of this letter, Madame de la Fayette, who herself was irritable with disease, and who did not write it in a style much calculated to prevent the uneasiness it caused, made abrupt use of the words, 'You are old.' The little hard sentence came like a blow upon the lively, elderly lady. She did not like it at all; and thus wrote of it to her daughter:—

> So you were struck with the expression of Madame de la Fayette, blended with so much friendship. 'Twas a truth, I own, which I ought to have borne in mind; and yet I must confess it astonished me, for I do not yet perceive in myself any such decay. Nevertheless I cannot help making many reflections and calculations, and I find the conditions of life hard enough. It seems to me that I have been dragged, against my will, to the fatal period when old age must be endured; I see it; I have come to it; and I would fain, if I could help it, not go any further; not advance a step more in the road of infirmities, of pains, of losses of memory, of *disfigurements* ready to do me outrage; and I hear a voice which says, You must go on in spite of yourself; or, if you will not go on, you must die;—and this is another extremity, from which nature revolts. Such is the lot, however, of all who advance beyond middle life. What is their resource? To think of the will of God and of the universal law; and so restore reason to its place, and be patient. Be you then patient, accordingly, my dear child, and let not your affections often into such tears as reason must condemn.

The whole heart and good sense of humanity seem to speak in passages like these, equally removed from the frights of the superstitious, and the flimsiness or falsehood of levity. The ordinary comfort and good prospect of Madame de Sévigné's existence, made her write with double force on these graver subjects, when they presented themselves to her mind. (pp. 230-32)

The two English writers who have shown the greatest admiration of Madame de Sévigné, are Horace Walpole and Sir James Mackintosh. The enthusiasm of Walpole, who was himself a distinguished letter-writer and wit, is mixed up with a good deal of self-love. He bows to his own image in the mirror beside her. During one of his excursions to Paris, he visits the Hôtel de Carnavalet and the house at Livry; and has thus described his impressions, after his half-good half-affected fashion:—

> Madame de Chabot I called on last night. She was not at home, but the Hôtel de Carnavalet was; and I stopped on purpose to say an Ave-Maria before it.' (This pun is suggested by one in Bussy-Rabutin.) 'It is a very singular building, not at all in the French style, and looks like an *ex voto,* raised to her honour by some of her foreign votaries. I don't think her half-honoured enough in her own country.

His visit to Livry is recorded in a letter to his friend Montague:—

> One must be just to all the world. Madame Roland, I find, has been in the country, and at Versailles, and was so obliging as to call on me this morning; but I was so disobliging as not to be awake. I was dreaming dreams; in short, I had dined at Livry; yes, yes, at Livry, with a Langlade and De la Rochefoucauld. The abbey is now possessed by an Abbé de Malherbe, with whom I am acquainted, and who had given me a general invitation. I put it off to the last moment, that the *bois* and *allées* might set off the scene a little, and contribute to the vision; but it did not want it. Livry is situate in the Forêt de Bondi, very agreeably on a flat, but with hills near it, and in prospect. There is a great air of simplicity and *rural* about it, more regular than our taste, but with an old-fashioned tranquillity, and nothing of *colifichet*

(frippery.) Not a tree exists that remembers the charming woman, because in this country an old tree is a traitor, and forfeits his head to the crown; but the plantations are not young, and might very well be as they were in her time. The Abbé's house is decent and snug; a few paces from it is the sacred pavilion built for Madame de Sévigné by her uncle, and much as it was in her day; a small saloon below for dinner, then an arcade, but the niches now closed, and painted in fresco with medallions of her, the Grignan, the Fayette, and the Rochefoucauld. Above, a handsome large room, with a chimneypiece in the best taste of Louis the Fourteenth's time; a Holy Family in good relief over it, and the cipher of her uncle Coulanges; a neat little bedchamber within, and two or three clean little chambers over them. On one side of the garden, leading to the great road, is a little bridge of wood, on which the dear woman used to wait for the courier that brought her daughter's letters. Judge with what veneration and satisfaction I set my foot upon it! If you will come to France with me next year, we will go and sacrifice on that sacred spot together.

Sir James Mackintosh became intimate with the letters of Madame de Sévigné during his voyage from India, and has left some remarks upon them in the Diary published in his Life [see excerpt dated 1812].

> 'The great charm,' he says, 'of her character seems to me a *natural* virtue. In what she does, as well as in what she says, she is unforced and unstudied; nobody, I think, had so much morality without constraint, and played so much with amiable feelings without falling into vice. Her ingenious, lively, social disposition, gave the direction to her mental power. She has so filled my heart with affectionate interest in her as a living friend, that I can scarcely bring myself to think of her as a writer, or as having a style; but she has become a celebrated, perhaps an immortal writer, without expecting it: she is the only classical writer who never conceived the possibility of acquiring fame. Without a great force of style, she could not have communicated those feelings. In what does that talent consist? It seems mainly to consist in the power of working bold metaphors, and unexpected turns of expression, out of the most familiar part of conversational language.'

Sir James proceeds to give an interesting analysis of this kind of style, and the way in which it obtains ascendency in the most polished circles; and all that he says of it is very true. But it seems to us, that the main secret of the *'charm'* of Madame de Sévigné is to be found neither in her 'natural virtue,' nor in the style in which it expressed itself, but in something which interests us still more for our own sakes than the writer's, and which instinctively compelled her to adopt that style as its natural language. We doubt extremely, in the first place, whether any great 'charm' is ever felt in her virtue, natural or otherwise, however it may be respected. Readers are glad, certainly, that the correctness of her reputation enabled her to write with so much gaiety and boldness; and perhaps (without at all taking for granted what Bussy-Rabutin intimates about secret lovers) it gives a zest to certain freedoms in her conversation, which are by no means rare; for she was any thing but a prude. We are not sure that her character for personal correctness does not sometimes produce even an awkward impression, in connexion with her relations to the court and the mistresses; though the manners of the day, and her superiority to sermonizing and hypocrisy, relieve it from one of a more painful nature. Certain we are, however, that we should have liked her still better, had she manifested a power to love somebody else besides her children.... (pp. 232-34)

We may only be allowed to repeat our wish (as Madame de Grignan must often have done) that the 'dear Marie de Rabutin,' as Sir James Mackintosh calls her, had had a second husband, to divert some of the responsibilities of affection from her daughter's head. Let us recollect, after all, that we should not have heard of the distress but for the affection; that millions who might think fit to throw stones at it, would in reality have no right to throw a pebble; and that the wit which has rendered it immortal, is beautiful for every species of truth, but this single deficiency in self-knowledge.

That is the great charm of Madame de Sévigné—*truth.* Truth, wit, and animal spirits compose the secret of her delightfulness; but truth above all, for it is that which shows all the rest to be true. If she had not more natural virtues than most other good people, she had more natural *manners;* and the universality of her taste, and the vivacity of her spirits, giving her the widest range of enjoyment, she expressed herself naturally on all subjects, and did not disdain the simplest and most familiar phraseology, when the truth required it. Familiarities of style, taken by themselves, have been common more or less to all wits, from the days of Aristophanes to those of Byron; and, in general, so have animal spirits. Rabelais was full of both. The followers of Pulci and Berni, in Italy, abound in them.

Madame de Grignan, Sévigné's daughter.

What distinguishes Madame de Sévigné is, first, that she was a woman so writing, which till her time had been a thing unknown, and has not been since witnessed in any such charming degree; and second, and above all, that she writes 'the truth, the whole 'truth, and nothing but the truth;' never giving us falsehood of any kind, not even a single false metaphor, or only half-true simile or description; nor writing for any purpose on earth, but to say what she felt, and please those who could feel with her. If we consider how few writers there are, even among the best, to whom this praise, in its integrity, can apply, we shall be struck, perhaps, with a little surprise and sorrow for the craft of authors in general; but certainly with double admiration for Madame de Sévigné. We do not mean to say that she is always right in opinion, or that she had no party or conventional feelings. She entertained, for many years, some strong prejudices. She was bred up in so exclusive an admiration for the poetry of Corneille, that she thought Racine would go out of fashion. Her loyalty made her astonished to find that Louis was not invincible; and her connexion with the Count de Grignan, who was employed in the *dragonades* against the Huguenots, led her but negatively to disapprove those inhuman absurdities. But these were accidents of friendship or education: her understanding outlived them; nor did they hinder her, meantime, from describing truthfully what she felt, and from being right as well as true in nine-tenths of it all. Her sincerity made even her errors a part of her truth. She never pretended to be above what she felt; never assumed a profound knowledge; never disguised an ignorance. Her mirth, and her descriptions, may sometimes appear exaggerated; but the spirit of truth, not of contradiction, is in them; and excess in such cases is not falsehood, but enjoyment—not the wine adulterated, but the cup running over. All her wit is healthy; all its images entire and applicable throughout—not palsy-sticken with irrelevance; not forced in, and then found wanting, like Walpole's conceit about the trees, in the passage above quoted. Madame de Sévigné never wrote such a passage in her life. All her lightest and most fanciful images, all her most daring expressions, have the strictest propriety, the most genuine feeling, a home in the heart of truth;—as when, for example, she says, amidst continual feasting, that she is 'famished for want of hunger;' that there were no 'interlineations' in the conversation of a lady who spoke from the heart; that she went to vespers one evening out of pure opposition, which taught her to comprehend the 'sacred obstinacy of martyrdom;' that she did not keep a 'philosopher's shop;' that it is difficult for people in trouble to 'bear thunderclaps of bliss in others.' It is the same from the first letter... to the last; from the proud and merry boasting of the young mother with a boy, to the candid shudder about the approach of old age, and the refusal of death to grant a moment to the dying statesman—'no, not a single moment.' She loved nature and truth without misgiving; and nature and truth loved her in return, and have crowned her with glory and honour. (pp. 235-36)

[Leigh Hunt], "Madame de Sévigné and Her Contemporaries," in The Edinburgh Review *Vol. LXXVI, No. CLIII,* October, 1842, pp. 203-36.

[BERNARD CRACROFT] (essay date 1864)

[*Cracroft was an English barrister and author. In the following excerpt, he assesses Sévigné's historical significance.*]

Madame de Sévigné is perhaps the most perfect and beautiful fruit of French civilisation at its highest point. If English life be taken as the best male type of European civilisation, and French life as the best female type, then of this latter Madame de Sévigné is probably the best, the richest, the fullest and fairest, the most unique individual specimen. With the head of a man, and the heart of a woman, admirably clear-sighted, admirably well-judged, impetuous and prudent, uncontrolled as a bird, and as a bird always self-possessed, always graceful, impulsive as a child and wise as a statesman, gracious as a queen, polished as a courtier, witty as a comedian, never trivial in her headlong simplicity, yet unconsciously simple, unconsciously headlong, never looking at herself over her own shoulder, never dreaming, like so many would-be-fine writers, how simple I am, or how eloquent, or how natural, or how affectionate, or how witty, or how acute, or how satirical, or how wise, but simple, eloquent, natural, affectionate, devoted, witty, acute, satirical, wise, under the uncontrollable impulse of a nature polished by splendid education and splendid circumstance into the perfection of itself,— in all things herself always, the slave of no crotchet, or system, or fashion, or sect, never evil in her most cherished aims, a woman, in the best and noblest sense, and only a woman,—Madame de Sévigné is the symbol of all that is best in the best French character, the best apology for the old French monarchy, the pearl of the French aristocracy. The more she is studied the more womanly she seems, and in proportion as she seems more womanly, she appears more admirable. Whether we consider her in her ancestry, in herself, or in relation to her age, the study of her character is one of striking interest to every educated reader. Her letters are an education, and if we had to choose a book which should be the pocket-book of a young girl, with any ambition of becoming a charming woman, it should be the complete collection of Madame de Sévigné's letters. Moreover, these letters are in every particular the true corrective of most of the faults which are apt to beset average English girlhood. They are admirably frank and unconcerned. They are grace incarnate. They are absolutely free from the imbecilities of false reserve and false reticence. They are masculine in sense and matter without roughness, feminine without twaddle, full of feeling without being mawkish, inconceivably buoyant, inconceivably sprightly, yet always above slang and fastness, satirical without the vulgarities of malice, admirably eloquent with the eloquence of an overflowing and polished nature, absolutely absorbed in what they have to say, absolutely free from pedantry, full of the world, open to every breeze of a free, active, and brilliant life, reflecting every ray of the daily sun, untrammelled by sect, or faction, or conceit, simple as nature itself, and rich as art, the very picture of the perfection of liberty. (pp. 181-83)

[Bernard Cracroft], "Madame de Sévigné," in The National Review, *London, n.s. Vol. 1, November, 1864, pp. 181-230.*

[W. D. HOWELLS] (essay date 1869)

[*Commonly known as "the Dean of American Letters," Howells was an American novelist and critic who helped promote realism as a literary movement. Although he wrote nearly three dozen novels, few of them are read today. Yet Howells still stands as one of the major literary figures of his era, having successfully weaned American literature from the sentimental romanticism of its infancy. In the following excerpt from a combined review of separate editions of letters by Sévigné and English epistler Lady Mary Wortley Montagu, Howells treats Montagu briefly and renders a balanced appraisal of Sévigné.*]

"The last pleasure that fell in my way," wrote Lady Mary Wortley Montagu to her sister, "was Madame Sévigné's **Letters**, very pretty they are, but I assert, without the least vanity, that mine will be full as entertaining forty years hence. I advise you, therefore, to put none of them to the use of waste paper." After more than a hundred years, we suppose most people find Lady Mary's self-satisfaction a just, if not a modest one, and are glad that the Countess of Mar and her other friends kept her letters. They form her autobiography, and never was woman's story as maiden, wife, and mother more charmingly written. Rarely, moreover, has any character been more worthy of the portrayal of so brilliant an historian. Mrs. Hale, indeed, laments her want of religious feeling; but this is an indefinite regret which need not greatly trouble anybody till it is determined what religious feeling may be. (p. 518)

But if the editor is not very definite or perfectly fair in regard to Lady Mary, she makes up the deficiency to Madame de Sévigné whom she praises for religious feeling, and who seems from her own testimony to have had chiefly a pretty piety, which led her to read books of devotion and moral discourses at the proper season, and left her free at other times to write scandal to her invalid daughter. We doubt if Mrs. Hale is quite a safe guide in commending the didactic qualities of a lady who in one breath could tell her daughter that M. de la Rouchefoucault said he would be in love with her if he were twenty years younger, and in the next cry with a sprightly air: "After all, we pity you in not having the word of God preached in a suitable manner.... How can one love God if one never hears him properly spoken of?" Madame de Sévigné was a tender and loving mother; but the way in which she speaks of her son's relations with certain "little actresses," is but a worldly way, and that of a Mother of the Period at the best; and her efforts to amuse him and win him away from low company by listening and laughing while he read Rabelais, were not such as to reinforce "every good, just, and noble sentiment" with which she had endeavored to inspire him. She had very probably an "exquisite tenderness of heart," but it is not so much in the tone of a tender-hearted woman as of a sprightly chronicler, willing to turn any event to witty account, that she speaks of the execution of a famous poisoner: "At length it is all over; La Brinvillier's in the air; after her execution, her poor little body was thrown into a large fire and her ashes dispersed by the wind, so that whenever we breathe we shall inhale some small particles of her, and, by the communication of the minute spirits, we may all be infected with the desire of poisoning, to our no small surprise." Madame de Sévigné's "delicate refinement" is not to be found in the gossip of the dissolute court which she recounts, and it must be in the spirit of her time, and not from her own taste, that she repeats such coarse sayings as that of the prince, who "informed the ladies at Chantilly that their transparencies would be a thousand times more beautiful if they would wear them next their skin." Though herself without reproach, she has scarcely a comment upon the profligacy of the society in which she lives, and only a formal sympathy for the truth of Mademoiselle d'Orleans, the king's cousin, when Louis withdraws his permission for her marriage with the Duc de Lauzun. Madame de Sévigné speaks of this passage of guiltless and unhappy love, sole in the annals of that shameless reign, "as a fine dream, a glorious subject for a tragedy or romance, but especially talking or reasoning eternally." The princess, she says in another place, with a neat self-possession which suggests how little comfort could have been got from her, "behaves to me as to a person that sympathizes with her in her distress; in which she is not mistaken, for I really feel sentiments for her that are seldom felt for persons of such superior rank."

"How many readers and admirers has Madame de Sévigné," says Lady Montagu, "who only gives us, in a lively manner and fashionable phrases, mean sentiments, vulgar prejudices, and endless repetitions? Sometimes the tittle-tattle of a fine lady, sometimes that of a nurse, always tittle-tattle; yet so well gilt over with airy expressions and a flowing style" [see excerpt dated 1754]. This is a little unjust, but it is not so unjust and not so ill-advised as Mrs. Hale's high-flown compliments, and prescription of Madame de Sévigné's life and letters as models for the imitation of young ladies. Her letters are to be read for entertainment and instruction by persons of mature judgment. They are a delightful chronicle of the court gossip, when written from Paris, and a bit dull when written from the author's retirement in Brittany; but they always afford a curious study of character and manners. For this reason, or as a kind of sub-history, they are greatly to be valued; but there is so wide a gulf between the interests and conditions of Madame de Sévigné's time and our own, that we think Mrs. Hale very extraordinary indeed, when she says a life like ours "so vulgarizing alike to the mind and to the style, finds its best antidote in the letters of Madame de Sévigné"; and one might well doubt if she had made a faithful study of her author, when she adds that "the tumult of the outer world is faintly heard" in those echoes of fashion and intrigue.

Madame de Sévigné was, like Lady Mary Wortley Montagu, a brilliant and cultivated woman, better than the society in which she lived, but vividly reflecting its spirit in thought and expression; but she had not so open or so liberal a mind as the Englishwoman; she had not such wide and varied experience; and her letters are infinitely less instructive and amusing. Neither is to be proposed as a model in everything, we think; but of the two, by all means let Lady Mary form the young-lady mind. In the mean time, those who are not young ladies, or whose minds are formed, will join us in gratitude to the publishers, who give us in this pleasing form selections from authors who can delight so much. (pp. 518-19)

[W. D. Howells], in a review of "The Letters of Lady Mary Wortley Montagu" and "The Letters of Madame de Sévigné to Her Daughter and Friends," in The Atlantic Monthly, *Vol. XXIII, No. CXXXVIII, April, 1869, pp. 518-19.*

GASTON BOISSIER (essay date 1887)

[*Boissier was a French scholar and critic who wrote extensively on Latin antiquity. His works include* Cicéron et ses amis *(1865),* La religion romaine d'Auguste aux Antonins *(1874), and the biography* Madame de Sévigné *(1887). In the following excerpt from the last-named work, Boissier cites elements contributing to and characteristic of Sévigné's talent.*]

Cousin points out that in the first half of the seventeenth century letter-writing became very fashionable. Letters, with portraits and conversations, take up much space in the romances of the period, and in those of Mademoiselle de Scudéry they are even printed in special type to attract the eye. This fashion is easily understood. A fondness for self-revelation and self-display is a very common infirmity, and in a correspondence this is what is wanted. Egotism here has free course and is perfectly in place; what may be a defect elsewhere becomes a necessity here, an essential feature of the style. People like to write letters because they can be as egotistic as they please, and like to read them because of their delight in fathoming the souls of others. It affords great pleasure to become acquainted with their most secret thoughts, especially when they would not have them known. Thus it is that the epistolary style is sure to please the vain and inquisitive,—and that means almost everybody.

This, doubtless, is why Balzac and Voiture gave to their chief works the form of letters,—though unhappily nothing but the form. (pp. 81-2)

[However] great the success of Voiture's letters, it would seem that in reading them it must have been felt that there was something lacking. Even those most charmed by them would doubtless say to themselves that such compositions would be much more charming still if they were real letters in which the writer, sure of not being betrayed, should give us his confidence, tell us his feelings and his thoughts, instead of expressing conventional sentiments,—in a word, disclose his real self. If, moreover, such a person chanced to write with talent, if by a natural gift he associated with a fluent pen qualities ordinarily due only to labor, there would remain nothing more to be desired. That the intelligent people of this time had such an ideal of a perfect correspondence, and perceived that besides the letters of Voiture, so much read and admired, there were others still more admirable, uniting the merit of sincerity to that of style, is proved by the fact that as soon as Madame de Sévigné's letters were placed in their hands they did not hesitate; they recognized at once that here was perfection. Never, perhaps, has public opinion been so prompt and so unanimous in greeting a masterpiece. When, after the death of Bussy-Rabutin, his daughter had his correspondence published, every one was in raptures over the letters he had received from his cousin. Bayle was so charmed by them that he declared "this woman deserves a place among the famous women of her time." About the same period a Jesuit published a Latin poem entitled "Ratio Conscribendæ Epistolæ" ["The Best Way to Write a Letter"], in which he proclaimed that Madame de Sévigné was the model for that style of composition, and that she wrote with such ease "that one of her letters deserves the expenditure of more time on the part of the reader than it took her to write it."

This Jesuit seems to have imagined Madame de Sévigné as dashing off her letters at a sitting, without taking pains to polish and correct them; and, indeed, this is what she herself gives us to understand when she tells us that she lets her pen run on and gives it free rein. Generally her word has been believed; but there are doubters to whom such a method of composing masterpieces has seemed suspicious. The very merit of her letters makes such critics suspect that they cost her more labor than she pretends. The winning grace of her details, the ingenious turn given to her reflections, her charming variety in the repetition of the same thought, her clever expression of matters pertaining to the affections, seem to betray art and labor. "So much ingenuity," it has been said, "so much care, was probably not expended for one person alone. A lady does not write so elaborately to her daughter. Usually she keeps for her family her ordinary every-day wits, and is seldom very fastidious except for strangers and the public. It is then for these that Madame de Sévigné wrote under her daughter's name, and in being transmitted to us these letters have only reached their real address." Let us find what truth there is in this opinion. It is important to know, if only so as not to be deceived.

In Madame de Sévigné's correspondence there are distinctions to be observed. She does not write in the same way to all her friends, because she has not the same confidence in them all. She is quite aware that some of them do not keep for themselves alone the letters they receive. From Bussy, for instance, anything may be expected. Did he not one day take the liberty to let the king himself into the secret of their intimacy, by sending him his cousin's letters as well as his own? It is natural, then, that in writing to Bussy she should sometimes be constrained. Can she tell what will become of what she sends him in confidence? What Bussy often did for his own sake, Coulanges sometimes did for the sake of Madame de Sévigné; the admiration he felt for her wit was so great that he could not keep it to himself. This she suspected, and so is tempted, in writing to him, to be a little dressy, that the inquisitive may not surprise her unadorned. It ought to occasion no surprise, then, if there is in the first case some constraint, and in the second something perhaps a little studied; but if there is, it does not last long, for it is not a part of her temperament long to retain her self-command. Soon her fancy regains control and hurries her away; she forgets the precautions she wished to take, she surrenders unconditionally; and she does well, for she is never more charming.

In any case, if the thought of this uncertain and unknown public may have exercised some slight influence over her when she wrote to Coulanges and Bussy, in her correspondence with her daughter, at least, she had nothing at all to fear. Here we have the closest intimacy. All that is in the heart is freely uttered. What it would have been dangerous to repeat is related with perfect confidence. Private affairs and affairs of state, the neighborhood gossip, the most scandalous stories, the most compromising revelations,— all are communicated. Madame de Grignan did not, therefore, let her mother's letters get abroad; and if, perchance, she read an extract announcing an important bit of news, she tells us that she took great care that no one should be able to peep over her shoulder and read what ought not to be read. Madame de Sévigné, then, felt sure that the public would never know what she said, and wrote without anxiety. She did not take pains to reflect, to be on her guard, to elaborate a style, "which to her is but a tragic buskin." She abandoned herself to the stream of her thoughts and feelings: "Do you know what I am going to do? Just what I have done hitherto. I always begin without knowing what the end will be; and, ignorant whether my letter will be long or short, I write as much as my pen chooses; it has full sway." . . . Nothing savors more of improvisation than that wealth of details, that fulness and abundance of recital, which are her most delightful quali-

ties, though she sometimes reproached herself with them as faults. When she thought of the weary task her daughter would have in reading "all this gossip," she was vexed with herself, asked her daughter's pardon, and promised faithfully to be henceforth more abstemious. But when once she began chatting with her daughter, all these good resolutions were forgotten, and she knew not where to stop. "I prose away," she said, "with an ease that is fatal to you."

Here, then, is a young, lively, volatile woman, going much into society and much absorbed in pleasure, who has never had the least idea of composing literary works; and yet, as soon as she puts pen to paper, in letters addressed to but one person, without a thought of the public or of posing before it, she writes with the confidence and exactitude of a professional author; she knows how to express her thoughts and feelings; she finds the fitting word; she avoids the hesitation, the repetition, the obscurity, from which those who make a business of writing escape with such difficulty; in short, without seeking it, almost without knowing it, from the very first she is perfect. How has this happened; and by what miracle has she so soon acquired what demands of others so much study and so many efforts?

The answer first occurring to the mind is, that she had received special gifts from Heaven, and that it was her nature to write well; but Nature needs aid from labor. We do not find that those who are born artists know music before they learn it, nor that they play well on an instrument the first time they touch it. In every art there is something in the knack, which must first be learned, and the art of writing is no exception; on the contrary, there is hardly a more difficult one. (pp. 83-90)

In any case, we may be sure that Madame de Sévigné had learned how to write; and it is interesting to know how she received her training. (p. 91)

More than once she spoke with gratitude of "the good teachers she had in her youth." These good teachers taught her French in two ways,—first by making her acquainted with Latin, Italian, Spanish, since there is nothing better than these comparisons with foreign tongues to make us masters of our own; and, moreover, they taught her French directly by the manner in which each of them studied and used it. Both were eminent grammarians, and took an important part in the work then going forward of cleansing the French idiom, of making it purer, more precise, more regular, in order to prepare it for the great literary epoch then beginning. This work may be said to have gone on around Madame de Sévigné; she was familiarly acquainted with almost all of those in charge of it; they were her friends and her teachers. As even the world of rank and fashion had acquired a taste for these researches, she could hear the pupils of Vaugelas, in the society she frequented, discussing the meaning and standing of various expressions, condemning those they considered ill-constructed, and giving others their final form. The women were not merely witnesses of these debates, but were sometimes appealed to as judges. The gallant Father Bouhours thought a great deal of their support, and, hoping to array them on his side, loaded them with eulogy: "There is nothing more correct, more proper, more natural than the language of most Frenchwomen. The words they use, however common, seem quite new, and made on purpose for what they say; so that if Nature herself wished to speak, I believe she would borrow their tongue." (pp. 97-8)

To this education received from her teachers must be added what she derived from her reading. At all times she was "a great devourer of books." Everything interested her. She was very fond of romances, as we have seen, but more serious works did not affright her. Her especial delight was in history, even that of the Turks, in which she found pashas with many Christian virtues. Her inquiring mind found pleasure in everything, from Vergil to Father Maimbourg, spite of the latter's villanous style; and from Nicole who made her quake with fear, to Rabelais who made her die of laughter. It was especially during her leisure intervals at the Rochers estate that she resorted to all kinds of reading to fill up the day: "We still have perfect weather; we read a great deal, and I find what pleasure there is in having no memory, for Corneille's plays and the works of Despréaux, Sarazin, Voiture, all pass again in review before me without wearying me,—quite the reverse. We sometimes dip into Plutarch's *Morals,* which are admirable, or into Arnauld's *Prejudices* or the replies of the ministers, or skim the Koran a little if the fancy takes us; in short, there is no region we do not explore." But when so many regions are explored all at once, none can be thoroughly known. Of this, Madame de Sévigné was well aware; she never posed as a scholar. Speaking of Madame de Kerman, her neighbor in Brittany, who resembled her in being a great reader, she said: "She knows a little of everything, and as I have a like smattering, our superficial areas very well correspond." Perhaps, after all, it is better that a woman should thus range through all authors, from the *Cleopatra* to the Koran, rather than have too profound a knowledge of but one. As a result she may be superficial, but at least she will not be pedantic. (pp. 100-02)

Our education is not the work of our teachers alone; it is carried on also by the society we frequent and the people with whom we are connected. No one escapes altogether the influence of social environment; and Madame de Sévigné must have felt it more than others. We shall see with what ease she adopted in her maturity the opinions of those about her, and how quickly she was affected by their sentiments. This characteristic must have been still more marked in her youth, at an age when all have fewer settled ideas of their own, and are more accessible to the ideas of others.

At first, as we know, she belonged to the Rambouillet coterie, and her place among them was so well assured that Somaize has put her portrait in his *Dictionary of Précieuses.* No one could pass through such a society with impunity; and so some stern critics, convinced that she must have been injured by it, have sought to find traces of affectation in her correspondence. If there are any such traces they are certainly not numerous. The Madame de Sévigné that we know must have appropriated the good qualities of the coterie rather than its bad ones. It was easy enough for her to avoid its defects. By her hearty temperament, her sturdy good sense, the plainness and candor of her mind, and by her relish for extremely free language and merry talk, she was the opposite of a *précieuse.* Let us not forget, moreover, that she was only nineteen when Julie d'Angennes, the daughter of Madame de Rambouillet, married M. de Montausier, and that from this time on the coterie began to scatter. Madame de

Sévigné could have known it only in its decline, when its importance was already much diminished. This, then, was not the place where she completed her intellectual training.

Probably she owed more to the circles which gathered up what was left of the Rambouillet society, and which endeavored to keep up its traditions. She was very much appreciated in these circles; and as early as 1661 one of her admirers speaks of the "high and just renown that her merit gives her in society." These circles, we know, were much occupied with literature; their members liked to talk of recent poems and of new books; authors greatly desired to please them, and made sacrifices to deserve their applause. They accordingly had some influence on the literature of the period; and if we wish to know the special trend of this influence, the theatre, faithful mirror of society, will show us. It is the period of the transition from Corneille to Racine. People were gradually losing their taste for the ideal heroism and magnanimity in fashion since *The Cid*; and instead of those inequalities of style, those haughty colloquialisms, those coarse touches which were not displeasing to less polished spectators, they required more delicacy of portraiture, colors better blended, more scrupulous correctness, sustained nobility, dignity, elegance. Moreover, the idiom is no longer quite the same. Were I not reluctant to establish too abrupt divisions in what took place gradually and by insensible transitions, I should say that a very different kind of French then succeeded the French of Descartes and Balzac. Their language seems the work of scholars, is formed on the model of Latin oratory, and has as its special characteristics, copiousness and majesty. The later French, written and spoken in the second half of the century, continually progressing in refinement and grace from Pascal to La Bruyère, and ever becoming nimbler, more animated, and more buoyant,—the language with which the next century armed itself for its battles,—seems rather to have been formed and fashioned in the conversations of men and women of the world. The literary men of this epoch recognize the drawing-room even more as their school of instruction than as their means of diversion. (pp. 105-08)

How much did Madame de Sévigné owe to this society in which she passed her life? This is hard to determine exactly, but we may be sure that she was indebted to it for something.

We have seen that Madame de Sévigné was prepared to write well by her excellent education, by her reading, and by association with the most distinguished persons in Paris and at the court. She knew her mother-tongue, and spoke it wonderfully well. In that society where intelligent women were met with at every step, she passed for one of the most intelligent and cultivated; her repartees were quoted, her decisions appealed to as authority. At the same time she had the good fortune to witness the blooming of a great literature. In her youth, she read the *Provincial Letters* when first they were furtively circulated; later on, she witnessed the birth of Molière's first comedies, Racine's first tragedies, La Fontaine's first fables; she heard Mascaron, Bossuet, and Bourdaloue; she chatted familiarly with Retz and La Rochefoucauld. With her great intelligence, and her keen delight in all the beauties of literary works, though retaining a secret preference for what she admired in youth, she does not refuse to enjoy the more recent masterpieces; she understands all, profits by all, assimilates all. When the time comes for her soul to be tried and stirred to its depths, all these gathered treasures will be clearly seen. We may be sure that she will know how to express her thoughts and feelings.

Such a time for her was the occasion of her daughter's departure. To be sure, she had before this shown herself a clever woman who knew how to write very agreeable letters, and how to acquit herself in affairs of delicacy with great skill. She had even approached eloquence when she had to defend herself against the cunning and impertinence of Bussy. But all this was comparatively nothing; to bring out her real strength she must be touched in her inmost affections. Her passion then breaks forth from her heart, and it may be said that her whole talent flows out with her tears.

Her daughter has left her, and has gone to join her husband at the world's end, away in Provence. Before reaching this distant land, from which she will return only at rare intervals, she must be exposed to dangers which then used to make the bravest tremble,—the declivity of Tarare, the Rhone, the Bridge of St. Esprit, and what not. The mother thinks of all and dreads all long beforehand. She has continually before her eyes quagmires, precipices, horses running away, boats sinking. Returning to her empty house, where all reminds her of the departed one, she takes her pen and relieves her full heart by writing: "My grief would indeed be commonplace if I could portray it to you, so I shall not undertake it. It is vain for me to seek the dear daughter whom I no longer find, and every step of her horses takes her farther from me. I went to Ste. Marie ceaselessly weeping, and dying with grief; it seemed as if my heart and soul were torn from me; and, in truth, what a cruel parting! I asked the privilege of being left alone; they took me to Madame du Housset's room and made a fire for me; Agnes looked at me without speaking,—this being our bargain; I stayed there till five o'clock, sobbing continually. Every thought stabbed me with grief." Three days later her daughter's first letters are brought to her, and her grief is renewed: "As you received my ring with a burst of tears, so I receive your letters; it seems as if my heart would break.... You make me feel for you all that love can feel; but if you think of me, my poor darling, be sure my thoughts are continually with you; it is what pious people call constant devotion; it is what we ought to feel for God, if we did our duty. Nothing distracts me from it; I am always with you. I see that coach always advancing but never approaching. I am always on the high-road, and sometimes feel almost afraid lest the coach upset. The rains that have continued for the last three days drive me to despair. The Rhone causes me strange apprehensions. I have a map before my eyes, and know every place where you stop over night. To-night you are at Nevers, and Sunday you will be at Lyons, where you will get this letter." (pp. 114-17)

But stop: we must be reasonable. When once we begin quoting Madame de Sévigné we should be glad to keep on. Nothing is more difficult than to break the charm these letters have over one, and regain self-command to study and criticise them. Yet this must be done if we wish to account for our pleasure, and by analysis increase it.

The passages just cited appear so simple, and utter so naturally what we all experience, that they are read the first time without surprise. There seems nothing remarkable about them except this very simplicity and naturalness. Now, these are not the qualities which attract attention. It is difficult to appreciate them in works where they occur, and it is only by reading works where they are lacking that we realize all their importance. But here, as soon as we reflect, we are astonished to perceive that this great emotion is expressed in language strong, confident, and correct, with no hesitation and no bungling. The lively sequence of these complaints implies that they were poured forth all at once, in a single outburst; and yet the perfection of the style seems impossible of attainment without some study and some retouching. It is sometimes said that a strong passion at once creates the language to express it. I greatly doubt this. On the contrary, it seems to me that when the soul is violently agitated, the words by which we try to express our feelings always appear dull and cold; we are tempted to make use of exaggerated and far-fetched expressions in order to rise to the level of our sorrow or joy. Hence come sometimes excessive terms, discordant metaphors. We might be inclined to regard these as thought out at leisure and in cold blood, while on the contrary they are the product of the first impulse, of the effort we instinctively make to find an expression corresponding to the intensity of our passion. There is nothing of this kind in Madame de Sévigné's letters, and however violent her grief may be, it always speaks in accurate and fitting language. This is a valuable quality, and one extremely rare. That we may not be surprised at finding it so highly developed in her, we need only remember what has just been said of the way in which she was unconsciously prepared to become a great writer.

Another characteristic of Madame de Sévigné's letters, not less remarkable, is that generally her most loving messages are cleverly expressed. I do not refer merely to certain isolated phrases that have sometimes appeared rather affected. "The north wind bound for Grignan makes me ache for your chest." "My dear, how the burden within you weighs me down!" "I dare not read your letters for fear of having read them." These are only occasional flashes; but almost always, when on the point of giving way to all her emotion, she gives her phrase an ingenious turn, she makes witty observations, is bright, pleasing, elegant. All this seems to some to proceed from a mind quite self-possessed, and not so far affected by passion as to be inattentive to elegant diction. Just now I placed naturalness among Madame de Sévigné's leading qualities. There are those who are not of this opinion, and contend that naturalness is just the merit she most lacks; but we must define our meaning. Naturalness for each one is what is conformable to his nature; and as each one of us has a nature of his own very different from that of his neighbors, naturalness cannot be exactly the same in every instance. Moreover, education and habit give us each a second nature which often has more control over us than the original one. In the society in which Madame de Sévigné lived, people made a point of speaking wittily. The first few times one appeared in this society it required a little study and effort to assume the same tone as the rest. One had to be on the watch for those pleasant repartees that, among the frequenters of the Rambouillet and Richelieu houses, gave the new-comer a good reputation; but after a while these happy sayings came unsought. To persons trained in such a school, what might at first sight appear subtle and refined is ordinary and natural. Whether they speak or write, their ideas take a certain form which is not the usual one; and bright, witty, and dainty phrases which would require labor of others occur to them spontaneously. To be sure, I do not mean that Madame de Sévigné wrote well without knowing it. This is a thing of which a witty woman always has an inkling; and besides, her friends did not permit her to be ignorant of it. "Your letters are delightful," they told her, "and you are like your letters." It was all the easier to believe this, because she paid to herself in a whisper such compliments as others addressed to her aloud. One day, when she had recently written to her friend Dr. Bourdelot, she said to her daughter: "Bravo! what a good answer I sent him! That is a foolish thing to say, but I had a good, wide-awake pen that day." It is very delightful to feel that one has wit, and we can understand how Madame de Sévigné might sometimes have yielded to this feeling with some satisfaction. In her most private correspondence, that in which she least thought of the public, we might note certain passages in which she takes pleasure in elaborating and decorating her thought, and in adding to it new details more and more dainty and ingenious. This she does without effort, to satisfy her own taste, and to give herself the pleasure of expressing her thought agreeably. It has been remarked that good talkers are not sensitive to the praises of others only; they also wish to please themselves independently of the public around them, and like to hear themselves talk. It might be said in the same sense that Madame de Sévigné sometimes likes to see herself write. This is one of those pretty artifices which in women do not exclude sincerity, and which may be united with naturalness.

Doubtless so fitting and exact a mode of speech, such refinement and wit in the expression of matters of affection, are rare qualities; but they are not the distinguishing characteristics of Madame de Sévigné. She was not the only one who possessed them; we find them, for example, in the correspondence of her friend Madame de Coulanges. What belongs to Madame de Sévigné alone, and places her in the first rank, is her imagination. No one has had a more lively and versatile imagination than hers. She possesses to a wonderful degree that charming gift of seeing what is far away, of travelling in fancy. Need it be said that her daughter's country-seat in Provence was the usual goal of these airy flights? In her moments of bitter sorrow, the thought of that winged horse which in two days travelled the world over, occurred to her mind; and she said, "Oh, if I had the hippogriff at my command!" She really has no need of it; her imagination answers the purpose. From the very first parting she was so well acquainted with the town of Grignan, which she had never seen, that when the daughter leaves it the mother finds herself all abroad. "I believe you to be at Lambesc, my darling, but I cannot see you well from here; there are clouds in my imagination which hide you from my sight. I had become quite at home in Grignan Castle; I saw your rooms, I walked on your terrace, I went to mass in your beautiful church; but now I know not where I am." Another time, after having asked for tidings of the Chevalier de Grignan, whom she highly esteemed, and whose infirmities kept him in Provence, she added: "Tell me in what room you have put him, that I may make him visits." As yet she only knew her granddaughter Pauline by the pleasing descriptions that were sent of her charming countenance, and especially of her beautiful eyes. At these her imagination is kindled, and she cries: "Oh, how pretty they are! I see them." This is not mere talk; she really saw them. To

her absent friends she chats as if they were beside her. Her letters are conversations. She herself says so, and they have all the charms of conversation. And first, we find in them a charming variety and disorder resembling that of familiar talk. She is not like her cousin Bussy, who marshals his thoughts with exemplary regularity. He makes a point of replying to all the observations and even to all the witticisms addressed to him, in perfect order; each is in its place and waits its turn. Madame de Sévigné has no methodical way of writing, and lays no plan beforehand. Her fancy is her guide. She goes out in every direction, and at last tells so many strange things of which at first she did not think, that she becomes a little ashamed of it: "If the postmen knew with what our letters are filled, they would leave them midway." As she sees the events she recounts, no matter at what distance they have taken place, the pictures she gives of them are incredibly true to life. I am a little embarrassed about citing proof, not because instances are wanting, but because these charming narratives are too well known,—they are known by heart. How could I venture to repeat, at this late day, either the death of Turenne, or the story of the Archbishop of Reims returning from St. Germain, or how the game of basset brought about the separation of M. de La Fare and Madame de La Sablière, or the charming gossip about Langlée and Madame de Montespan's dress? But here in a few strokes is a finished picture which seems to me less familiar. It represents the great Condé, who was usually very negligent in his attire, as he appeared to the astonished courtiers on the day when the Prince of Conti married Mademoiselle de Blois: "I will tell you the greatest and strangest piece of news that you could be informed of; namely, that my Lord the Prince of Condé was shaved yesterday; his beard is gone; this is no illusion, nor is it said in jest; it is the truth. All the court beheld it, and Madame de Langeron, seizing her time when the lion had his paws crossed, dressed him in a close-fitting coat decorated with diamonds; and his valet, also taking advantage of his patience, frizzed and powdered his hair, thus reducing him to be the handsomest man of the court, with a head of hair better than any wig. This was the miracle of the wedding feast."

With an imagination so lively and a nature so versatile, it was natural to receive without resistance the impressions that others wished to give her. She adopted the views of her friends, and was quick to share their sentiments. "I always have the same opinion as the person I last listened to." It is evident that she understood her own character. Sometimes she even jested about this weakness. She said of herself: "And I, everybody's dupe, as you are aware;" or again: "You know I follow others, but invent nothing myself." Amusing instances could be cited from her letters of the ease with which her friends induced her to change her mind. This was of course a defect in her character as a woman, but it has added many beauties to her style as a writer. By promptly sharing the emotions of others she added to her own, and her wit is excited and kindled by theirs. When she talks we hear not her alone, but the echo of the great minds she associated with. It seems to me that we can tell by her mode of expressing herself what people she has just left, and from whom she has derived the observations and narratives which she repeats to her daughter. . . . One of her finest letters is that in which she describes the reception of the Knights of the Order of the Holy Spirit in the great promotions of 1674, in which her son-in-law shared. She was not present herself, but Coulanges went to Versailles on purpose to see it, and she tells us that he has just given her an account of it. She really had no need to tell us, for it seems to me that without being informed of it we should readily have perceived his voice, his gestures, his spirit of buffoonery and parody, ever disclosing to him the humorous side of serious matters. It is just like him to seize, and note in passing, the burlesque incidents of this majestic ceremonial,—La Trousse's disordered wig, and the circumstance of M. de Montchevreul and M. de Villars getting so desperately hooked together that no human hand could separate them. "The more they tried, the more of a tangle they made of it, like Roger's rings. Finally, the whole ceremony, all the courtesies, all the manœuvres remaining at a standstill, they had to be violently torn asunder, and main strength won the day.". . . To adapt herself in this way to others, to appropriate their wit and receive from it the stimulus to excite her own, "to invent nothing," but to lend new fascination to ideas coming from other sources, to renew the youth and freshness of these ideas by the keenness of her perception and the ingenuity of her expression,—such is the characteristic charm of woman. In this respect it may be said that Madame de Sévigné was more truly a woman than any other. Her qualities are those which we expect to find, and which please us most, in persons of her sex,—not original powers and creative gifts, but this talent for reflecting those they love, entering into their ideas, and giving these more vigor and animation by reproducing them.

With such qualities, it is not surprising that her style does not essentially differ from that of her contemporaries. She writes as the rest do, though she writes better than they. Even when recounting trifles her diction is flowing and periodic; it is never heavy like that of Madame de Longueville or Madame de Sablé, though it ordinarily has fulness and amplitude. Long explanations are not distasteful to her; she emphasizes her ideas and repeats them; occasionally she knows how to make oratorical flights: this was a common practice with those about her. But she also has her personal modes of speech; she creates expressions which are all her own, and which are freer and livelier than those employed in the seventeenth century by professional authors. When she passes through Burgundy, in amazement at the fertility of the country, she does not hesitate to say, "Everything here is bursting with wheat." Referring to a trip M. de Marsillac made through his domain to repair damages, she says: "He stopped neither for sport nor for excursions; he had with him Gourville, who has not often time to give, and conducted him like a river through all his lands to bring them fatness and fertility." I know of none except her and Saint-Simon who then wrote in so original a way; and they are perhaps the only two who did not trouble their heads about the public. She thought that her letters would never get outside of the private circle to which they were addressed; and as for Saint-Simon, since he had postponed for a century the publication of his *Memoirs*, the fear of his remote readers could not much interfere with his freedom of expression.

When one has just been reading Madame de Sévigné's letters, it is natural that one should be rather surprised that a writer of such talent, who knew she possessed it, should not have been tempted to write some connected work. Why, for instance, did she not compose memoirs like Madame de Motteville, treatises on social ethics like Madame

de Lambert, or novels like Madame de Lafayette? Sometimes such regrets are expressed; and it would at first seem that with her fortunate natural gifts, and her wealth of imagination, she might have left us some great work. Perhaps we are wrong in thinking so. The qualities we admire in her letters are not such as a long work requires. Success in such a work involves the power of self-restraint and self-mastery, ability to take time for reflection, skill in planning and combining beforehand. These are habits difficult of acquirement for one who is accustomed in writing to give up to the impulse of the moment and let the pen run on at random. It has been observed that journalists, who are obliged to improvise an article every day, and who become able to do this with wonderful skill, can at last produce nothing but articles, and are incapable of composing a book. Madame de Lafayette wrote such good novels, just because her temperament did not resemble her friend's, and because she controlled her talents differently. It is easy to see that Nature had intended her to be a professional author. Her letters, irreproachable in their form, full of a discreet and charming intelligence, are generally short and unadorned. Hers is the tone of a woman who makes reserves, and is secretly preparing material for a work she has in view. Madame de Sévigné, on the contrary, pours out all her heart, and when once she has taken her pen, keeps nothing back. It is probable, then, that if it had suddenly occurred to her to write another *Princess of Cleves* in imitation of Madame de Lafayette, she would have found herself devoid of material and ill-prepared, and would perhaps have had less success than we are inclined to suppose. But she has left us her letters; and what more can we ask? (pp. 118-34)

Gaston Boissier, in his Madame de Sévigné, translated by Melville B. Anderson, A. C. McClurg and Company, 1888, 205 p.

S. G. TALLENTYRE (essay date 1899)

[In the following excerpt, Tallentyre delineates the epistler's charm.]

When Napoleon said that reading Madame de Sévigné was like eating snowballs, when Horace Walpole worshipped, as it were, at the shrine of such a grace, softness, and delicacy, when old Mary Montagu characterised the whole correspondence as 'always tittle-tattle,' and My Lord Chesterfield deigned to admire its 'ease, freedom, and friendship,' each critic had no doubt a little right on his side, and the truth lies somewhere between them all. (p. 364)

She writes about everything—and about nothing. About the balls and the comedies at St. Germain; who has asked after Madame de Grignan and has praised her beauty and her disposition. Here is a little criticism of a modish poet or painter and half a page about Madame de Grignan's health. . . . She has a charming little Court scandal to tell her daughter the next morning; or an account to give her of La Vallière at the Carmelites. She confesses to her with a most bewitching humility her passion for 'les vieux romans.' She is 'folle de Corneille,' she says. She has been to hear a 'delicious' sermon (the adjective is perfectly characteristic) of Bourdaloue's this morning, and to Court at night. She has a little argument with her daughter about faith and philosophy—the mother being all for faith, blind, complete, devoted, and the daughter all for independent and reasonable thought. Here she is writing of Madame de Maintenon's unique position . . . or reading St. Augustine 'with transport.' Now she is laughing softly over the peccadilloes of her scapegrace son; or describing the death-bed of the Princess de Conti. The daughter writes solemn maxims on hope and patience and sends them to her mother, and the mother, who, to the end of her life, is much the younger of the two, writes back to lightly chide the daughter about neglecting her dress and appearance. . . . And then again she is talking just as she must have talked in life, of nothing, nothing, nothing; of trifles lighter than air; of things that were great then, or great to her, and are less than trifles now, with an immortal name shining here, and just once or twice a priceless glimpse of history—and again nothing, nothing, nothing. 'Madame cause.'

It is this nothingness which makes Napoleon say with perfect truth that one is no further on when one has read her. But it is also this nothingness which has endeared her to many generations of French people, and by which she still makes her appeal to the heart.

Madame writes, in fact, in the 'little language' of love. She speaks to her daughter about home and children, the trifles of everyday life—and behold! it is what the simplest mother among her readers might say in substance, though not in form, to her own child. Madame's fears for her daughter's health and safety are only the echoes, after all, of anxieties every human being has felt for some one dear to him. In her partings, one re-lives one's own. The desolation of those good-byes, the hopelessness of the long outlook when they are said, the trembling anticipations of reunion (trembling, for fear Fate should be too cruel, and one should meet no more), is there any one so happy—or is it so miserable?—that he has not known these things as she knew them? Does she write of the narrowest coterie only? Does she write pages and pages of the 'tittle-tattle' of 'a fine lady' or an 'old nurse' [see excerpt dated 1754]? Does she write a great deal too fast (her pen has always 'le bride sur le cou,' she says), as well as much too often, and never re-read what she has written? If she had soared to the finest flights of eloquence, if she had only told what would be valuable to the historian and the biographer, if she had omitted volumes almost of her tender feeling for her child, and put in a fuller account of those great spirits among whom she lived, she would have been a much greater genius and much less beloved. Her sensibilities can't but interfere a little with her wit. A great attachment is not with her, any more than with any other woman, a stimulus to great enterprises. She rests in it and is content.

Her letters have been, indeed, well called the 'Book of Repose.' It is into the quiet place of the most natural of all the affections that she leads one through a vicious society

Château des Rochers, Sévigné's estate in Brittany.

and a vicious age, and in the most charming, simple, easy manner imaginable. It is the classic 'des portes fermées' which she has written; the classic of that 'home' for which the Frenchman has no word and such an infinite devotion. Does her soft delicacy bore one now and then? Do those pages of graceful trifles become occasionally a little monotonous, and the easy writing almost irritating in its dainty perfection? It is to be supposed that at times most readers have felt this. And there come other times when that soft and limpid French, when the charm of the writer's personality, her gentle sprightliness, and above all her one long, fond, supreme affection, make the book into a friend who lives. (pp. 370-72)

The passion for Madame de Sévigné is, at least among the French, a passion for the woman as much as for her works. And indeed one knows no more lovable person.

To think of Madame is to think of a fascination beside which beauty leaves one cold. This is the woman who always knows the happiest thing to do, and does it delightfully. She has brilliancy which never offends other people's dulness; and learning which never makes the stupid feel ignorant. She will sympathise with one divinely over a lost toy or a lost hope. She can't help laughing just where she ought to laugh; and dissolves into the most bewitching and the most natural of tears when dull persons read her their dull tragedies. She is so human too—so exquisitely human that when the King dances a minuet with her she immediately discovers him to be the best of monarchs and of men. Wouldn't one like to have met her, to have talked with her, to have looked up into that soft sparkling face, to have been admitted to that kind intimacy, to that impulsive, faithful friendship? There have been greater and better women, no doubt, but in the whole world not one so delightful.

Is Madame profound? By no means. She is light, says one of those biographers who loves her, in all her emotions, save one. She takes her religion even—and she takes a good deal of it—lightly. It affects her sensibilities rather than her soul. She finds, as one has seen, the most awful denunciations of the old preachers 'délicieuses,' life sometimes rather 'désobligeante,' death yet more ill-natured, and ends, 'Mais parlons d'autre chose.' That is her philosophy. (p. 373)

To recall her after more than two hundred years is to recall the perfume of garden roses, or the melody of the most delicious drawing-room music. On every page of those old letters she has left the scent of her robes and the magic of a sweet presence. As to her genius, there may be many opinions; but as to the woman, French of the French, true daughter of that delightful, bright, kind, witty, tactful, and lighthearted nation, there can be but one. (p. 374)

S. G. Tallentyre, "The Great Letter Writers," in Longman's Magazine, *Vol. XXXIV, No. CCII, August, 1899, pp. 364-74.*

GEORGE SAINTSBURY (essay date 1910-11)

[*Saintsbury was a late-nineteenth and early-twentieth-century English literary historian and critic. Hugely prolific, he composed histories of English and European literature as well as numerous critical works on individual authors,*

styles, and periods. In the following excerpt from an essay originally published in the eleventh edition of The Encyclopædia Britannica *(1910-11), he measures the merit of Sévigné's letters within her intellectual milieu.*]

[Madame de Sévigné's letters to her daughter] are of great length. Writing as she did in a time when newspapers were not, or at least were scanty and jejune, gossip of all sorts appears among her subjects, and some of her most famous letters are pure *reportage* (to use a modern French slang term), while others deal with strictly private matters. Thus one of her best-known pieces has for subject the famous suicide of the great cook Vatel owing to a misunderstanding as to the provision of fish for an entertainment given to the king by Condé at Chantilly. Another (one of the most characteristic of all) deals with the projected marriage of Lauzun and Mademoiselle de Montpensier; another with the refusal of one of her own footmen to turn haymaker when it was important to get the crop in at Les Rochers; another with the fire which burnt out her neighbour's house in Paris. At one moment she tells how a forward lady of honour was disconcerted in offering certain services at Mademoiselle's levée; at another how ill a courtier's clothes became him. She enters... at great length into the pecuniary difficulties of her daughter; she tells the most extraordinary stories of the fashion in which Charles de Sévigné sowed his wild oats; she takes an almost ferocious interest and side in her daughter's quarrels with rival beauties or great officials in Provence.

Almost all writers of literary letters since Madame de Sévigné's days, or rather since the publication of her correspondence, have imitated her more or less directly, more or less consciously, and it is therefore only by applying that historic estimate upon which all true criticism rests that her full value can be discerned. The charm of her work is, however, so irresistible that, read even without any historical knowledge and in the comparatively adulterated editions in which it is generally met with, that charm can hardly be missed. Madame de Sévigné was a member of the strong and original group of writers—Retz, La Rochefoucauld, Corneille, Pascal, Saint-Évremond, Descartes and the rest—who escaped the influence of the later 17th century, while they profited by the reforms of the earlier. According to the strictest standard of the Academy her phraseology is sometimes incorrect, and it occasionally shows traces of the quaint and affected style of the *Précieuses*; but these things only add to its savour and piquancy. In lively narration few writers have excelled her, and in the natural expression of domestic and maternal affection none. She had an all-observant eye for trifles and the keenest possible appreciation of the ludicrous, together with a hearty relish for all sorts of amusements, pageants and diversions, and a deep though not voluble or over-sensitive sense of the beauties of nature. But with all this she had an understanding as solid as her temper was gay. Unlike her daughter, she was not a professed bluestocking or philosophess. But she had a strong affection for theology, in which she inclined (like the great majority of the religious and intelligent laity of her time in France) to the Jansenist side. Her favourite author in this class was Nicole. She has been reproached with her fondness for the romances of Mlle de Scudéry and the rest of her school. But probably many persons who make that reproach have themselves never read the works they despise, and are ignorant how much merit there is in them. In purely literary criticism Madame de Sévigné was no mean expert. Her preference for Corneille over Racine has much more in it than the fact that the elder poet had been her favourite before the younger began to write; and her remarks on La Fontaine and some other authors are both judicious and independent. Nor is she wanting in original reflections of no ordinary merit. But to enjoy her work in its most enjoyable point—the combination of fluent and easy style with quaint archaisms and tricks of phrase—it must be read as she wrote it, and not in the trimmed and corrected version of Perrin and Madame de Simiane.

Great part of her purely literary merit lies in the extraordinary vividness of her presentation of character. But her own has not united quite such a unanimity of suffrage as her ability in writing. In her own time there were not wanting enemies who maintained that her letters were written for effect, and that her affection for her daughter was ostentatious and unreal. But no competent judge can admit this view. On the other hand, her excessive affection for Madame de Grignan, her blindness to anything but her daughter's interest; her culpable tolerance of her son's youthful follies on the one hand and the uneven balance which she held in money matters between him and his sister on the other; the apparent levity with which she speaks of the sufferings of Madame de Brinvilliers, of galley slaves, of the peasantry, &c.; and the freedom of language which she uses herself and tolerates from others,—have all been cast up against her. Here the historic estimate sufficiently disposes of some of the objections, a little common sense of others and a very little charity of the rest. If too much love felt by a mother towards a daughter be a fault, then Madame de Sévigné was one of the most offending souls that ever lived; but it will hardly be held damning. The singular confidences which Madame de Sévigné received from her son and transmitted to her daughter would even at the present day be less surprising in France than in England. They are only an instance, adjusted to the manners of the time, of the system of sacrificing everything to the maintenance of confidence between mother and son. Here too, as well as in reference to the immediately kindred charge of crudity of language, and to that want of sympathy with suffering, especially with the sufferings of the people, it is especially necessary to remember of what generation Madame de Sévigné was and what were her circumstances. That generation was the generation which Madame de Rambouillet endeavoured with only partial success to polish and humanize, to which belong the almost incredible yet trustworthy *Historiettes* of Tallemant, and in which Bussy Rabutin's *Histoire amoureuse* did not make him lose all caste as a gentleman and man of honour. It is absurd to expect at such a time, and in private letters, the delicacy proper to quite different times and circumstances. It is not true that Madame de Sévigné shows no sympathy with the oppression of the Bretons, though her incurable habit of humorous expression—of *Rabutinage*, as she says—makes her occasionally use light phrases about the matter. But it is in fact as unreasonable to expect modern political sentiments from her as it is to expect her to observe the canons of a 20th-century propriety. On the whole she may be as fairly and confidently acquitted of any moral fault, as she may be acquitted of all literary faults whatsoever. Her letters are wholly, what her son-in-law said well of her after her death, *compagnons délicieux*; and, far from faultless as Madame de Grignan was, none of her faults is more felt by the reader than her long visits to her mother, during which the letters ceased. (pp. 63-6)

George Saintsbury, "Madame de Sévigné," in his French Literature and Its Masters, *edited by Huntington Cairns, Alfred A. Knopf, 1946, pp. 54-67.*

A. B. WALKLEY (essay date 1923)

[*Renowned for his erudition and urbanity, Walkley was an English essayist and dramatic critic for the* Star, *the* Speaker, *and the* Times *during the late nineteenth and early twentieth centuries. His criticisms were often more literary than theatrical; he once declared that a critic's "instinct is to bring to the play the calm lotus-eating mind with which he daydreams over a book in his library." Several of his articles and essays are included in the collections* Drama and Life *(1907) and* Pastiche and Prejudice *(1921). In the following excerpt from an essay originally published in the* Times *and collected in* More Prejudice *(1923), Walkley accounts for his appreciation of Sévigné's letters.*]

"Lisons *tout* Mme. de Sévigné," said Sainte-Beuve on a wet day in the country [see excerpt dated 1829]. I have just taken his advice and read her through on several fine days. No, not quite all of her, for my edition is 1806, and I believe many more letters have come to light since then. But the 1806 edition contains quite enough to go on with, and has the compensation of being beautifully printed on a fine ribbed paper that you would look for in vain nowadays. I think you should read Mme. de Sévigné in a choice edition; there was a magnificence about her that seems to demand it; for that matter, one likes one's favourite authors to be delicately printed and handsomely bound. I ask myself why, precisely, she is one of my favourites; for the qualities for which a classic author is held up to our admiration are not always those that recommend him to our secret, intimate taste. Your reason assents to the conventional praise; but what really thrills you has nothing to do with reason—"Le cœur a ses raisons, que la raison ne connait pas." Think, for instance, of an author like Hazlitt, so much of whose writing is prolix, improvised, thoroughly bad, and there comes a little intimate, personal touch—a "partridge cooking for his supper" or that volume of "Love for Love" that he read in the old inn at Alton, with its wainscoted room and its silver tea equipage and the dark portrait of Charles II. over the mantelpiece—that sets you hugging yourself with delight.

So I find it is with Mme. de Sévigné. Her maternal affection simply bores me. I cannot help suspecting, too, that it slightly bored her daughter; for the few letters of response we have from Mme. de Grignan are remarkably cool, not to say chilling. And the *bravura* pieces—the Fouquet trial or the death of Turenne—brilliantly written as they are, leave me comparatively cold. With her literary tastes I cannot sympathize, for she preferred Corneille to Racine and Nicole (whom I cannot pretend to have read) to Pascal. Also she has a morbid passion for sermons, which I do not share. What is it, then, that I do like? Well, shameful as the confession is, I'm afraid I like her scandal-mongering, her little discreetly-veiled allusions to the "carryings on" of the Court beauties. They put volumes into a word, and that word whispered, as it were, behind a fan.... What a glimpse ... [one] brief paragraph gives you of the Court of Louis XIV.; the Royal favourite publicly leaning her head on the King's shoulder to let the Court know that she was still in high favour; and in the background, Mme. de Maintenon, quietly awaiting her turn!

One might compile from Mme. de Sévigné's letters a catalogue of Royal favourites almost as long as Leporello's *mille e tre*; but the allusions to them and their varying fortunes are as matter-of-fact as though they were extracts from the Court Circular; there is no moralizing, for Mme. de Sévigné, though a virtuous and really pious woman, was no prude. Indeed, she was immensely flattered and pleased when the universal lover, the Sultan among the odalisques, paid her a little compliment when she went to see *Esther* performed at St. Cyr.

Another thing for which one likes Mme. de Sévigné is her hearty, unaffected love of the country. She fled from Paris, on the slightest pretext, to Livry, her little "place" near Paris she was never tired of praising.... The long journey into Brittany had no terrors for her, and she spent even the winter months in perfect enjoyment at Les Rochers, laughing at her friends in Paris who pitied her. Why should she not be happy there? She had the two prime requisites for life in the country: the love of planting and the love of reading, or, better still, re-reading. She somewhere defends herself against her daughter, who had reproached her for reading the same romances thrice over, with the remark that she reads all her books, serious as well as light, over and over again. That is only possible in the country. (pp. 177-80)

Perhaps, to a man, the subtlest fascination of Mme. de Sévigné's letters is their *odor di femmina*, their essentially feminine outlook on life and concern with the interests peculiar to women. With what satisfaction, when middle-aged, she notes that she still preserves her face and her figure! And with what indignation against her son-in-law she sees her daughter's figure spoiled by yet another *grossesse*! (pp. 180-81)

And the secret of her style? She thinks it is in letting her pen do what it pleases. "I always begin without knowing where I am going; I don't know whether my letter will be long or short; I write as long as it pleases my pen, which governs everything; I believe that to be a good rule, it suits me, and I shall stick to it." She stuck to it for a lifetime of letter-writing—the last letter in my edition of 1806 is numbered 1,100—without self-consciousness, without any eye to posterity, simply talking with her pen; and posterity is still "reading *all* Mme. de Sévigné" with delight. (p. 181)

A. B. Walkley, "A Letter Writer," in his More Prejudice, *William Heinemann Ltd., 1923, pp. 177-81.*

LYTTON STRACHEY (essay date 1924)

[*Strachey was an early twentieth-century English biographer, critic, essayist, and short story writer. He is best known for his biographies* Eminent Victorians *(1918),* Queen Victoria *(1921), and* Elizabeth and Essex: A Tragic History *(1928). Critics agree that these iconoclastic reexaminations of historical figures revolutionized the course of modern biographical writing. Strachey's literary criticism is also considered incisive. In the following excerpt from an essay originally published in the* New Republic *in 1924, he highlights Sévigné's infectious vitality in a fanciful recreation of her relationship with her cousin, Emmanuel de Coulanges.*]

Madame de Sévigné was one of those chosen beings in whom the forces of life are so abundant and so glorious that they overflow in every direction and invest whatever they meet with the virtue of their own vitality. She was the sun of a whole system, which lived in her light—which lives still for us with a kind of reflected immortality. We can watch—with what a marvellous distinctness!—the planets revolving through that radiance—the greater and the less, and the subordinate moons and dimmest asteroids—from Madame de Grignan herself to the dancing gypsies at Vichy. But then, when the central luminary is withdrawn, what an incredible convulsion! All vanish; we are dimly aware for a little of some obscure shapes moving through strange orbits; and after that there is only darkness.

Emmanuel de Coulanges, for instance. He lived a long life, filled his own place in the world, married, travelled, had his failures and his successes ... but all those happenings were mere phenomena; the only reality about him lay in one thing—he was Madame de Sévigné's cousin. He was born when she was seven years old, and he never knew a time when he had not loved her. She had petted the little creature when it was a baby, and she had gone on petting it all her life. He had not been quite an ordinary child; he had had strange fancies. There was a fairy, called *Cafut*, so he declared, to whom he was devoted; this was not approved of—it looked like incipient madness; and several whippings had to be administered before *Cafut* was exorcised. In reality, no one could have been saner than the little Emmanuel; but he had ways of amusing himself which seemed unaccountable to the grandly positive generation into which he had been born. There was something about him which made him no fit contemporary of Bossuet. Madame de Sévigné, so completely, so magnificently, a child of her age, while she loved him, could never take him quite seriously. In her eyes, though he might grow old, he could not grow up. At the age of sixty, white-haired and gouty, he remained for her what, in fact, his tiny pink-cheeked rotundity suggested—an infant still. She found him adorable and unimportant. Even his sins—and in those days sins were serious—might, somehow or other, be disregarded; and besides, she observed that he had only one—it was *gaudeamus*; she scolded him with a smile. It was delightful to have anything to do with him—to talk with him, to laugh at him, to write to him.... [Some] of her most famous, some of her most delicious and life-scattering letters were written to her cousin Coulanges.

He married well—a lady who was related to the great Louvois; but the connection did him little good in the world. For a moment, indeed, an important public office was dangled before his eyes; but it was snapped up by somebody else, and Coulanges, after a few days of disappointment, consoled himself easily enough—with a song. He was very fond of songs, composing them with elegant rapidity to the popular airs of the day; every circumstance of his existence, however grave or however trivial—a journey, a joke, the world's cruelties, his wife's infidelities—he rigged them all out in the bows and ribbons of his little rhymes. His wife was pretty, gay, fashionable, and noted for her epigrams. Her adorers were numerous.... Decidedly the lady was gay—too gay to be quite to the taste of Madame de Sévigné, who declared that she was a leaf fluttering in the wind.... But Coulanges was indifferent to her lightness; what he did feel was her inordinate success at Court. There she gadded, in a blaze of popularity, launching her epigrams and hobnobbing with Madame de Maintenon; he was out of it; and he was growing old, and the gout attacked him in horrid spasms. At times he was almost sad.

Then, gradually and for no apparent reason, there was a change. What was it? Was the world itself changing? Was one age going out and another coming in? From about the year 1690 onwards, one begins to discern the first signs of the petrifaction, the *rigor mortis* of the great epoch of Louis XIV; one begins to detect, more and more clearly in the circumambient atmosphere, the scent and savour of the eighteenth century. Already there had been symptoms—there had been the fairy *Cafut*, and the Abbé Têtu's vapours. But now there could be no more doubt about it; the new strange tide was flowing steadily in. And upon it was wafted the cockleshell of Coulanges. At fifty-seven, he found that he had come into his own. No longer was he out of it—far from it: his was now the popularity, the inordinate success. He was asked everywhere, and he always fitted in. His songs particularly, his frivolous neat little songs, became the rage; they flew from mouth to mouth; and the young people, at all the fashionable parties, danced as they sang them. At last they were collected by some busybody and printed, to his fury and delight; and his celebrity was redoubled. At the same time a wonderful rejuvenation came upon him; he seemed to grow younger daily; he drank, he guzzled, with astonishing impunity; there must have been a mistake, he said, in his birth certificate—it was antedated at least twenty years. As for his gout, it had gone for ever; he had drowned it by bathing, when he was over sixty, all one summer in the Seine. Madame de Sévigné could only be delighted. She had given a great deal of thought to the matter, she told him, and she had come to the conclusion that he was the happiest man in the world. Probably she was right—she almost always was. But, oddly enough, while Coulanges was undergoing this transformation, a precisely contrary one had befallen his wife. She had, in sober truth, grown old—old, and disillusioned, and serious. She could bear the Court no longer—she despised it; she wavered between piety and stoicism; quietly, persistently, she withdrew into herself. Madame de Sévigné, philosophizing and quoting La Fontaine, found—it was surprising—that she admired her—the poor brown leaf; and, on her side, Madame de Coulanges grew more and more devoted to Madame de Sévigné. Her husband mildly amused her. As she watched him flying from country-house to country-house, she suggested that it would save time and trouble if he lived in a swing, so that he might whirl backwards and forwards for the rest of his days, without ever having to touch the earth again.... Coulanges, adored by beautiful young Duchesses, disputed over by enormously wealthy Dowagers, had nothing left to wish for. The gorgeous Cardinal de Bouillon took him up—so did the Duc de Bouillon, and the Chevalier—all the Bouillons, in fact; it was a delightful family. The Cardinal carried him off to his country palace, where there was music all day long, and the servants had the air of noblemen, and the *ragouts* reached a height of ecstatic piquancy—*ragouts* from every country in Europe, it seemed—how they understood each other when they came together on his plate, he had no idea—but no matter; he ate them all.

In the midst of this, the inevitable and the unimaginable happened: Madame de Sévigné died. The source of order,

light, and heat was no more; the reign of Chaos and Old Night descended. One catches a hurried vision of Madame de Grignan, pale as ashes, elaborating sentences of grief; and then she herself and all her belongings—her husband, her son, her castle, with its terraces and towers, its Canons, its violins, its Mistral, its hundred guests—are utterly abolished. For a little longer, through a dim penumbra, Coulanges and his wife remain just visible. She was struck down—overwhelmed with grief and horror. Was it possible, was it really possible, that Madame de Sévigné was dead? She could hardly believe it. It was a reversal of nature. Surely it could not be. She sat alone, considering life and death, silent, harrowed, and sceptical, while her husband—ah! even her husband felt this blow. The little man wrote a piteous letter to Madame de Grignan's daughter, young Madame de Simiane, and tears blotted the page. He was only a shadow now—all too well he knew it; and yet even shadows must obey the law of their being. In a few weeks he wrote to Madame de Simiane again; he was more cheerful; he was staying with Madame de Louvois in her house at Choisy, a truly delicious abode; but Madame de Simiane must not imagine that he did not pass many moments, in spite of all the company, in sad remembrance of his friend. A few weeks more, and he was dancing; the young people danced, and why should not he, who was as young as the youngest? All the Bouillons were in the house. The jigging vision grows fainter; but a few years later one sees him at the height of his felicity, having been provided by one of his kind friends with a room in the Palace at Versailles. More years pass, he is very old, he is very poor, but what does it matter?... On his seventy-sixth birthday he sings and dances, and looks forward to being a hundred without any difficulty at all. Then he eats and drinks, and sings and dances again. And so he disappears.

But Madame de Coulanges, ever sadder and more solitary, stayed in her room, thinking, hour after hour, over the fire. The world was nothing to her; success and happiness nothing; heaven itself nothing. She pulled her long fur-trimmed taffeta gown more closely round her, and pushed about the embers, wondering, for the thousandth time, whether it was really possible that Madame de Sévigné was dead. (pp. 50-8)

Lytton Strachey, "Madame de Sévigné's Cousin," in his Portraits in Miniature and Other Essays, *Harcourt Brace Jovanovich, 1931, pp. 50-8.*

LOGAN PEARSALL SMITH (essay date 1925)

[*A twentieth-century American critic, essayist, and biographer, Smith is best known for his incisive writings on literary and sociocultural issues. Included among his representative volumes are* Trivia *(1902) and* Afterthoughts *(1931). He also wrote longer works, most notably his autobiographical* Unforgotten Years *(1938), the biography* The Life and Letters of Sir Henry Wotton *(1907), and such critical studies as* On Reading Shakespeare *(1933) and* Milton and His Modern Critics *(1940). In the following excerpt from an essay originally published in the* Dial *in 1925, Smith commends Sévigné's range of expression.*]

In traveling across France the train sometimes passes a formal park, through which a great avenue, opening its vista for a second, reveals at the end of that perspective the mansard roofs and stately façade of some seventeenth-century château; and in the imagination of the traveler this little glimpse may awaken the thought of the great age of French history—that vainglorious reign, so famous in arts and arms, of Louis XIV, the *Roi-Soleil*. To an American or English traveler at least there may be something pompous and cold in the vision, thus suddenly evoked, of this vanished France; he may not be able easily to imagine what the personages were really like for whom these parks were laid out and these stately houses erected. But, on the other hand, it is possible that our traveler may feel himself curiously at home in this period—more at home there, indeed, than in the democratic France of the date of his railway journey. (p. 251)

If then our Anglo-Saxon traveler can enter there at ease, can feel himself happy and at home in that society, it must be because a more intimate access, a more personal introduction, has been his privilege: he must have made the acquaintance, and have won the friendship, we may safely hazard, of the lady of genius who stands ready with her golden key to open that escutcheoned gate to those who love her. This magic instrument, the wand which this enchantress wielded (though without the slightest consciousness of its power) was nothing more than the feathered quill with which Mme. de Sévigné scribbled her almost countless letters to her daughter—letters which, in spite of their old dates and spellings, come to us across the centuries like contemporary documents, and read indeed as if they had been written hardly more than a day or two ago. With almost all the upholstered figures of past epochs it is a constant effort to believe that they once actually existed, did once indubitably breathe the air and walk in the sunshine of this earthly scene; but with Mme. de Sévigné, so limpid is the sound of her voice, so lively her glance, so inextinguishable the spirit of life that shines and sparkles in her letters, that we find it hard to believe—we cannot really believe—that she has been, for more than two centuries, dead.

When we get to know her best, at the beginning of her correspondence with her daughter, Mme. de Sévigné was approaching the age of fifty, but her face still retained the coloring of girlhood; she enjoyed, she said, the fine blood that ran so agreeably and lightly through her veins, almost believing that she had discovered some fountain of perpetual youth—for how otherwise could she account for her splendid and triumphant health? This "divine Marquise," with her fair complexion, her blue eyes and golden hair, was a lady of rank and high distinction, who was famous for her wit and grace and beauty. She played no insignificant part in the society of her time, and her biographers have for the most part written of her as a woman of the world, a great lady of Parisian society, a wit and *raconteuse* of worldly gossip. The temptation, indeed, to write of this aspect of her life is a strong one: she loved the world, and appreciated in a curiously conscious way all that was magnificent in the stately age she lived in—the rejoicings for victories, the pomp of great marriages, and the splendor of Versailles as it shone new-built and brilliant in contemporary eyes; the torches and gold costumes of the fêtes there, the confusion without confusion of the courtiers and music, the stately figure of the Grand Monarch, and the triumphant beauty of his mistresses, with their thousand ringlets, their lace and pearls. How diversified everything was, how gay and gallant; and surely, she said, writing before its disastrous eclipse, never had there been a star so brilliant as the King's!

But interesting as is Mme. de Sévigné's account of the Court and fashion, she herself is more delightful than any good society—the "fine creature," as her English lover, Edward FitzGerald, called her, was, as he said, all genuine, "all Truth and Daylight"; and it is the picture she unconsciously gives us of her own frank, generous-hearted nature, her "good Sense [to quote FitzGerald once more], Good Feeling, Humor, Love of Books and Country Life," which is the greatest charm of this correspondence.... We see into this crystal heart perhaps most clearly in the long letters written in the solitude and leisure of her country days. Athough her home was in Paris, she had a retreat at Livry, in the midst of a forest not many miles away. Sometimes in the spring she would drive thither in her coach and six, merely for the afternoon, to refresh her spirit with the young green of the trees and the songs of the nightingales; and often she would live for weeks or months there, especially in the autumn, finding in that autumnal forest a solitude, a melancholy, and a silence which, she often felt, she loved better than anything else in the world. (pp. 252-55)

That love of wild nature which we regard as a modern passion, that blending of mood and landscape which so deeply colors our modern consciousness, is generally supposed—and supposed with much truth—to date from the time when sunsets and lakes and woods and mountains first mirrored themselves, with all the splendor and richness of their coloring, in the romantic eyes of Jean-Jacques Rousseau. But Rousseau had his predecessors: there were lovers of nature before his birth, and among them Mme. de Sévigné, with her passion for trees, must be counted; for although, like her contemporaries, she was blind to the beauty of lakes and moors and mountains, and although her woods were not the savage and dark forests in which Chateaubriand entombed his inexplicable despair, but arranged plantations, with mottoes on the trees, and dry and pleasant walks, and labyrinths, and artificial echoes; yet her melancholy delight in the solitude, the mystery, the *sainte horreur*, as she called it, of these lofty groves, her passion for wandering at night in their dark recesses, were moods of *romantisme avant la lettre*, as the French call it. Nor have any romantic writers of a later period noted with greater sensitiveness the changing aspects and hours of forest scenery; the frosty stillness of winter days, with faint sunlight making the distance dim and misty; the beauty of the leafless trees in March, with a confused noise of birds that foretold the spring; the triumph of May with the nightingales; the coolness of the woods in torrid weather, the sweetness of the summer nights there, with their soft and gracious air; the beauty of the sunsets at the ends of the great avenues, or the enchantment of the moon, silvering the shadowy spaces of their long perspectives. "*Nous avions entendu un cor dans le fond de cette forêt*"—we rub our eyes: can this haunting sentence have been penned, so long before Alfred de Vigny's birth, by a lady of fashion in the bewigged reign of Louis the Fourteenth?

A foreigner who might attempt to define for himself the charm of these seventeenth-century letters, although he might not be able to analyze into its elements this liquid and harmonious French, flowing on through volume after volume with the inexhaustible vivacity of a fountain of clear water, could not but note the felicity of the many translucent phrases which mirror with such limpidity the woodland lights and shadows, as they colored Mme. de Sévigné's meditations and tinged her varying moods, while she paced those avenues, hour after hour and day after day. Heaven only knew, she said, what thoughts she didn't think in that Breton forest: there were pleasant memories and hopes and day dreams; and there was a great spectacle of contemporary history, which she watched from her woods, and over which she moralized with unfailing interest. She liked great events, great changes of fortune pleased her; and there were certain strokes of Providence which, although they took her breath away, delighted her with their suddenness and grandeur.

But the general conclusion of all her thoughts was a sad one; almost all her meditations led to a melancholy moral. Kings, and the lovely mistresses of kings, princes, and courtiers, as she thought of them in her somber forest, all seemed to her examples of human misery and weakness. And none of these actors, playing their parts, great or small, on the world's stage, was contented; and not one of them—and she found in the thought a melancholy kind of consolation—was really happy. And she herself? For her too there were many black thoughts lurking in the forest which she tried to hurry past without regarding. Her humor was indeed a happy one; she was easily amused, and could accommodate herself, she said, to almost anything that happened; and all that was essentially cruel in human conditions, the mockery of hope, the swift passing of time—the very shadows of the great trees she had planted reminding her that she too was growing old—even the nearness of hideous and degrading old age, and of death, which she feared and hated—all this she could bear without repining; it was the common lot. But thus to be growing old and perishing so far from the person she loved with so strange a passion—this was a thought to which neither religion nor philosophy could reconcile her; nothing could cure her bitter tears.

Mme. de Sévigné's letters to the daughter she loved with this vehemence of passion have so much the character of love-letters that many readers have been repelled from them by the tiresome monotony which seems inseparable from effusions of this kind. There is indeed in all extreme affection an element of unreason—a divine madness, it may be, but still a madness—which disconcerts us: the elixir of love is a divine potation, but it is most serviceable for literature after it has been tempered and transfused by art—decanted, it may be, into the crystal chalice of a lyric, or cooled in the ornamented jars of a sonnet-sequence; and impetuous love-letters, fervid with the ebullitions of unmoderated feeling, are apt to pall, in the end, upon the unenamored reader. Even Edward FitzGerald, who in his later years became so devoted to his "blessed Sévigné" that he composed, as a labor of love, a big dictionary of the places and persons mentioned in her letters, confesses that he had been kept aloof from them for many years by "that eternal daughter of hers"; and others of her admirers cannot but be wearied at times by her praises of Mme. de Grignan's perfections and her laments over their ever-recurring separations, especially since posterity has enviously, and perhaps unjustly, agreed to look upon this Countess as an unamiable and sophisticated prig, who was by no means a worthy object of so ardent a maternal passion.

But then they remind themselves that this fine excess has after all its pathetic beauty, and that without its inspiration Mme. de Sévigné would never have written these golden letters, in which she made use of all her resources to amuse and entertain not only her daughter, but posterity as well—gathering the pick, as she said, of all the baskets, the flower of her wit and thoughts and eyes and pen. And after all, they remember, the poor lady, unlike most lovers, was more or less aware of her own folly, and tried to moderate its vehemence and vary its expression in a hundred humorous and graceful ways. Still it was her song, as inevitable and natural to her as the nightingale's descant; and she repeats its phrases over and over with the musical reiteration of that woodland chorister. "*Ah! la jolie chose qu'une feuille qui chante!*" she wrote of the nightingale in a phrase which has become famous; and as she reiterates her longing for the being whose image was her inseparable companion, her voice echoes from the formal forests of seventeenth-century France with something of the pathos and beauty of that fabled parent's musical lament. For the thought of Mme. de Grignan was, she said, the center and depth of all her meditations; around it everything else slid and vanished; and should ever, by some miracle, that thought desert her, it would leave her like a wax figure, hollow and empty and with nothing within. So all day long, and day after day, her imagination, outdistancing the swift couriers who were carrying her letters to the South, would wing its way across the breadth of France to the terraces and triumphant view of that great mountain castle in Provence, where, amid an uproar of music and guests and servants, and a perpetual storm of wind, the lovely philosophic Countess lived and reigned.

Mme. de Grignan piqued herself upon her mastery of the modern and fashionable philosophy of Descartes; her mother was of the older, more human, and homely school of Montaigne, whose essays she was so fond of reading; and curiously enough she remains, with Montaigne, one of the human beings of the past with whom posterity is most intimately acquainted—being indeed, as FitzGerald said of her, much more living to us than most of the living people whom we see about us. Writing long ago those hasty epistles to which she attached not the slightest importance, letting her pen gallop at its will with the reins upon its neck, as she set down amid her woods her meditations on mortality and on the cruel lapse of time, which was bearing her away, with all she loved, so swiftly upon its resistless stream, yet in her very complaints of his invincible power she was, though she had no notion of it, splendidly triumphing over this old enemy. And indeed Time himself, busied as always with his great work of ruin and obliteration, has for once proved himself a chivalrous opponent, turning away his scythe to preserve with delicate care the slightest records of Mme. de Sévigné's moods and fancies. Many writers have longed for durable renown, laboring with no success to win an immortality in the thoughts of succeeding ages; but this splendid gift of Fame was vouchsafed to Mme. de Sévigné in answer to no request of hers. That easy, graceful, smiling defeat of oblivion, that effortless and unconscious victory, we might almost call it, over Death, which is the magic and marvel and the ultimate interest of her writing, was the outcome of a genius she never knew she possessed; nor had she indeed the slightest notion that, in a life in which nothing happened, she was turning into immortality everything she touched, weaving out of her ephemeral thoughts a delicate but enduring tissue which has proved untarnishable by time. And amid the destruction of so much of ancient France, the scene and background of her country meditations still remains, with its formal gardens, its architecture, and the great avenues of its environing forests, so inviolate, so unblemished by the ineffectual and defeated years, that the tourist from another age who makes a pilgrimage to Les Rochers will almost ask himself at last, with a kind of eerie wonder, whether he may not be himself more of a ghost than the spirit he has come to visit—an evanescent shadow or *revenant* out of the chaos of a future much more doubtful than the immortality of that lifetime which is destined to outlast his own—that golden past which shines in these unfading letters, and seems indeed actually to gleam before his eyes, illuminating the circle of sunny space within the enclosure of those Breton woods. (pp. 258-64)

> Logan Pearsall Smith, "Madame de Sévigné in the Country," in American Criticism: 1926, edited by William A. Drake, Harcourt Brace Jovanovich, 1926, pp. 251-64.

RICHARD ALDINGTON (essay date 1927)

[*An English poet, novelist, and critic, Aldington is perhaps best known as the editor of the Imagist periodical the* Egoist *and as an influential member of the Imagist movement. His work with the Imagists was cut short by World War I, however, after which, his mental health damaged by battlefield service, he virtually stopped writing poetry and took up prose. As a novelist he achieved some success with penetrating studies of war, while as a literary critic and biographer he combined his skills as a poet, his sensitivity as a reader, and his personal reminiscences to produce criticism considered creative as well as informative. In the following excerpt, he finds Sévigné's work indicative of her society.*]

In a doubtless praiseworthy effort to recommend the authors of their preference, critics and commentators have been led to exaggerate their value. The books which everyone must read do not fill many shelves; the books which anybody may read with pleasure and profit are ranged by furlongs in the British Museum. The *Letters* of Mme de Sévigné must be read by a Frenchman; but for Americans and English people they belong to the second category, and one of the duties of that minor sort of impresario who pens introductions is to try to point out why such a book is worth picking out from the huge mass of candidates for attention. But nothing is to be gained by adopting the strident methods of news journalism or by energetic attempts to "boost Mme de Sévigné's *Letters* to a peak quotation". Something of the kind, unluckily, has happened both in this and similar cases. One set of cheerleaders insists on Mme de Sévigné's pre-eminence as a prose artist, and, like Gargantua weeping for his dead wife, exclaims that she was the most this and the most that ever seen in the world. A larger class adopts an attitude of fulsome patronage and adulation for her person. This is the sort of writer who speaks of the youthful Shakespeare as "little William", who would love to call Lamb "Charlie", and cannot refrain from the familiarity of "Marie" when relating the life of Mme de Sévigné. The commentator identifies himself wholly with his victim's interests, makes himself one of the family, defends it against all aspersions and criticisms, exults in its triumphs, mourns its griefs and failures, throws rice at every wedding, presses forward to hold the child at every christening, and attends the funeral as a loquacious chief mourner. Mme de Sévigné has posthumously suffered from both sorts of parasite, and it is consequently rather difficult to offer a judgment of her work and personality at this date without reacting too strenuously from these atrocities or unconsciously echoing them. (pp. xi-xii)

Comment has exhausted itself in praise of the *Letters* of Mme de Sévigné; and yet it is a fact that many foreign readers not only find it difficult to share the admiration so widely and loudly expressed in France, but even think the letters in bulk a little tiresome. Not many English-speaking readers, it may be wagered, have followed the heroic example of the late A. B. Walkley [see excerpt dated 1923], who took literally Sainte-Beuve's advice [see excerpt dated 1829] and read *all* the ten large volumes of letters in the *Grands Ecrivains de la France* edition. But the *Letters* would be far more popular and much more readily enjoyed if it were realized that they belong to a type of literature which has been eminently brilliant and fertile in France, comparatively little practised in England and not at all in America. French literature of the seventeenth and eighteenth centuries is sociable, the product of groups among the aristocracy and their *entourage*, the expression of an ideal of leisured life among wealthy and more or less cultured people. The drawing-room, whether in the Royal palaces or in noble houses, was the nursery and trial-ground of authors, and consequently much of the prose of this period is made up of Memoirs and Letters, echoes of conversation, the whispers and whims of fine society. Side by side with the great professional authors, patronizing them and learning literary lessons from them, were a host of distinguished amateurs. Now, the *Letters* of Mme de Sévigné are the very essence of that society, and appreciation of them depends to a great extent upon understanding and sympathizing with its habits and ideals.

The ideal of French society in the seventeenth century was the *honnête homme*, whose literary origins must be sought in the treatises of the Italian Renaissance, such as the *Cortegiano* of Baldassare Castiglione. But the French rapidly modified Italian ideas to suit their own requirements, and mingled with Italian precepts, the traditions of their own mediaeval culture and a strain of Spanish chivalry. The scope of this ideal was far-reaching: it regulated not only such practical affairs as dress, equipage, and even table-manners, but also the duel, gallantry, and all matters affecting taste and society; it determined what drama and literature should receive polite admiration, the use of language which should be cultivated, and all the minor accomplishments of gentlemen and their ladies. How necessary all this was in the early seventeenth century in France may be realized by reading any competent work on the French nobility at the time when Henri IV ended the civil wars. The turbulence, grossness, and ignorance of even the most celebrated personages of that time make an amusing contrast with the highly-coloured pictures of the age drawn by romantic novelists and royalist doctrinaires. (pp. xxi-xxii)

Perhaps a considerable share of the credit for creating the *honnête homme* in Bourbon France must go to Mme de Rambouillet and her salon. She was not the first or the only lady of her time to establish this disguised school for manners, but all observers are agreed that her influence was of the first importance. At the age of twenty, in spite of her youth, her beauty, and her rank, she refused to attend the Louvre. She disliked Louis XIII intensely, and would not mix in his society of huntsmen. She was passionately in love with the beauty of the world, a student of Italian and Spanish, enough of an artist to be her own architect. In forming her society she aimed not at making a centre for authors and artists, though they were warmly welcomed, but at creating a kind of social life which united all the indefinable charms of good company. No doubt her reaction against grossness and ignorance was in some respects carried too far, so that she and her guests became liable to the reproach of preciosity and over-subtle refinement, especially in delicacies of language. But, seeing the task she had undertaken, it is obvious that some affectations and over-refinement were inevitable. In general the society collected by Mme de Rambouillet exerted a very useful influence, and its prestige became so considerable that those who were admitted to her salon were instinctively respected, admired, and copied. In satirizing *Les Précieuses Ridicules* Molière was partly jesting at provincial and out-of-date imitators of the Rambouillet salon, partly slaying an organization which had outlived most of its usefulness, and partly—it must be admitted—flattering a powerful remnant of sporting barbarity.

No one would accuse Mme de Sévigné of preciosity, but, it is a fact that she frequented the second generation of *précieuses* who were gathered under the command of Julie de Montausier. Moreover, her friend and tutor, Ménage, was one of the chief literary figures of the Rambouillet salon. Italian and Spanish, the favourite languages of the *précieuses*, were familiar to her, especially Italian. As Sainte-Beuve tells us, she read Rabelais and Saint Augustine, Montaigne and Pascal, the novel *Cléopatre* and Quintilian, Tacitus and Virgil, "in all the majesty of Latin and Italian" [see excerpt dated 1829]. There are plenty of cultivated women in our time who do all this and more, but not perhaps many in the most fashionable society. While Louis XIV himself was extremely ignorant, he was wise enough to see that literature and the arts, all the charm of fine manners and polite conversation, embellish a despotism and may even console for the loss of liberty. For once in the world's history the most fashionable society and the intellectual life were in harmony; and what is so charming about these people is their ability to enjoy all the finer things of life entirely without pedantry and without any loss of gaiety or even frivolity.

This civilized society furnished Mme de Sévigné with her friends, her point of view, her intellectual virtues, and her prejudices. In spite of her education and her serious reading, she was far from being a blue-stocking. That sense of measure which was so highly prized at the time preserved her from excesses; and even traits which surprise and shock us, like her strange unconscious contempt for the lives of common people, were merely the accepted views of the society she represents, in general so amiably and pleasantly. For them France was a few thousand persons, mostly descended from feudal landlords and warriors. France? No—the world; for it was agreed that no other aristocracy could equal the "*agréemens*" of the French, no foreign monarch compare with Le Roi Soleil. These aristocrats possessed a life and almost a language of their own; and one of their most admirable representatives is Mme de Sévigné. The exclusiveness of their life, the concentration of their interests, make her letters rather allusive, and

that is one more reason why they become more enjoyable as one studies the history, the life and the literature of her age. But they form a vivid record of a brilliant, educated, fastidious, proud, gay, brave, and sociable aristocracy, a monument of "polite life" which is peculiar to France and scarcely likely to be repeated in our own times. (pp. xxiv-xxvi)

> *Richard Aldington, in an introduction to* Letters of Madame de Sévigné to Her Daughter and Her Friends, Vol. 1, *edited by Richard Aldington, 1927. Reprint by Brentano's, 1928, pp. ix-xxvi.*

VIRGINIA WOOLF (essay date 1941?)

[*A British novelist, essayist, and short story writer, Woolf is considered one of the most prominent literary figures of twentieth-century English literature. Like her contemporary James Joyce, with whom she is often compared, she is remembered as an innovative stream-of-consciousness novelist. Concerned primarily with depicting the life of the mind, she rejected traditional narrative techniques and developed her own highly individualized style. Also a discerning and influential critic, Woolf began writing reviews for the* Times Literary Supplement *at an early age. Her critical essays, termed "creative, appreciative, and subjective" by Barbara Currier Bell and Carol Ohmann, cover almost the entire range of English literature and contain some of her finest prose. Along with Lytton Strachey, Roger Fry, Clive Bell, and others, Woolf and her husband Leonard formed the literary coterie known as the "Bloomsbury Group." In the following essay originally published in the essay collection* The Death of the Moth *in 1942, one year following her death, she luxuriantly sketches facets of Sévigné's personality.*]

This great lady [Madame de Sévigné], this robust and fertile letter writer, who in our age would probably have been one of the great novelists, takes up presumably as much space in the consciousness of living readers as any figure of her vanished age. But it is more difficult to fix that figure within an outline than so to sum up many of her contemporaries. That is partly because she created her being, not in plays or poems, but in letters—touch by touch, with repetitions, amassing daily trifles, writing down what came into her head as if she were talking. Thus the fourteen volumes of her letters enclose a vast open space, like one of her own great woods; the rides are crisscrossed with the intricate shadows of branches, figures roam down the glades, pass from sun to shadow, are lost to sight, appear again, but never sit down in fixed attitudes to compose a group.

Thus we live in her presence, and often fall, as with living people, into unconsciousness. She goes on talking, we half listen. And then something she says rouses us. We add it to her character, so that the character grows and changes, and she seems like a living person, inexhaustible.

This of course is one of the qualities that all letter writers possess, and she, because of her unconscious naturalness, her flow and abundance, possesses it far more than the brilliant Walpole, for example, or the reserved and self-conscious Gray. Perhaps in the long run we know her more instinctively, more profoundly, than we know them. We sink deeper down into her, and know by instinct rather than by reason how she will feel; this she will be amused by; that will take her fancy; now she will plunge into melancholy. Her range too is larger than theirs; there

Sévigné's bedroom at the Château des Rochers.

is more scope and more diversity. Everything seems to yield its juice—its fun, its enjoyment; or to feed her meditations. She has a robust appetite; nothing shocks her; she gets nourishment from whatever is set before her. She is an intellectual, quick to enjoy the wit of La Rochefoucauld, to relish the fine discrimination of Madame de La Fayette. She has a natural dwelling place in books, so that Josephus or Pascal or the absurd long romances of the time are not read by her so much as embedded in her mind. Their verses, their stories rise to her lips along with her own thoughts. But there is a sensibility in her which intensifies this great appetite for many things. It is of course shown at its most extreme, its most irrational, in her love for her daughter. She loves her as an elderly man loves a young mistress who tortures him. It was a passion that was twisted and morbid; it caused her many humiliations; sometimes it made her ashamed of herself. For, from the daughter's point of view it was exhausting, was embarrassing to be the object of such intense emotion; and she could not always respond. She feared that her mother was making her ridiculous in the eyes of her friends. Also she felt that she was not like that. She was different; colder, more fastidious, less robust. Her mother was ignoring the real daughter in this flood of adoration for a daughter who did not exist. She was forced to curb her; to assert her own identity. It was inevitable that Madame de Sévigné, with her exacerbated sensibility, should feel hurt.

Sometimes, therefore, Madame de Sévigné weeps. The daughter does not love her. That is a thought so bitter, and a fear so perpetual and so profound, that life loses its savour; she has recourse to sages, to poets to console her; and reflects with sadness upon the vanity of life; and how death will come. Then, too, she is agitated beyond what is right or reasonable, because a letter has not reached her. Then she knows that she has been absurd; and realizes that she is boring her friends with this obsession. What is worse, she has bored her daughter. And then when the bitter drop has fallen, up bubbles quicker and quicker the ebullition of that robust vitality, of that irrepressible quick enjoyment, that natural relish for life, as if she instinctively repaired her failure by fluttering all her feathers; by making every facet glitter. She shakes herself out of her glooms; makes fun of "les D'Hacquevilles"; collects a handful of gossip; the latest news of the King and Madame de Maintenon; how Charles has fallen in love; how the ridiculous Mademoiselle de Plessis has been foolish again; when she wanted a handkerchief to spit into, the silly woman tweaked her nose; or describes how she has been amusing herself by amazing the simple little girl who lives at the end of the park—la petite personne—with stories of kings and countries, of all that great world that she who has lived in the thick of it knows so well. At last, comforted, assured for the time being at least of her daughter's love, she lets herself relax; and throwing off all disguises, tells her daughter how nothing in the world pleases her so well as solitude. She is happiest alone in the country. She loves rambling alone in her woods. She loves going out by herself at night. She loves hiding from callers. She loves walking among her trees and musing. She loves the gardener's chatter; she loves planting. She loves the gipsy girl who dances, as her own daughter used to dance, but not of course so exquisitely.

It is natural to use the present tense, because we live in her presence. We are very little conscious of a disturbing medium between us—that she is living, after all, by means of written words. But now and then with the sound of her voice in our ears and its rhythm rising and falling within us, we become aware, with some sudden phrase, about spring, about a country neighbour, something struck off in a flash, that we are, of course, being addressed by one of the great mistresses of the art of speech.

Then we listen for a time, consciously. How, we wonder, does she contrive to make us follow every word of the story of the cook who killed himself because the fish failed to come in time for the royal dinner party; or the scene of the haymaking; or the anecdote of the servant whom she dismissed in a sudden rage; how does she achieve this order, this perfection of composition? Did she practise her art? It seems not. Did she tear up and correct? There is no record of any painstaking or effort. She says again and again that she writes her letters as she speaks. She begins one as she sends off another; there is the page on her desk and she fills it, in the intervals of all her other avocations. People are interrupting; servants are coming for orders. She entertains; she is at the beck and call of her friends. It seems then that she must have been so imbued with good sense, by the age she lived in, by the company she kept—La Rochefoucauld's wisdom, Madame de La Fayette's conversation, by hearing now a play by Racine, by reading Montaigne, Rabelais, or Pascal; perhaps by sermons, perhaps by some of those songs that Coulanges was always singing—she must have imbibed so much that was sane and wholesome unconsciously that, when she took up her pen, it followed unconsciously the laws she had learnt by heart. Marie de Rabutin it seems was born into a group where the elements were so richly and happily mixed that it drew out her virtue instead of opposing it. She was helped, not thwarted. Nothing baffled or contracted or withered her. What opposition she encountered was only enough to confirm her judgment. For she was highly conscious of folly, of vice, of pretension. She was a born critic, and a critic whose judgments were inborn, unhesitating. She is always referring her impressions to a standard—hence the incisiveness, the depth and the comedy that make those spontaneous statements so illuminating. There is nothing naive about her. She is by no means a simple spectator. Maxims fall from her pen. She sums up; she judges. But it is done effortlessly. She has inherited the standard and accepts it without effort. She is heir to a tradition, which stands guardian and gives proportion. The gaiety, the colour, the chatter, the many movements of the figures in the foreground have a background. At Les Rochers there is always Paris and the court; at Paris there is Les Rochers, with its solitude, its trees, its peasants. And behind them all again there is virtue, faith, death itself. But this background, while it gives its scale to the moment, is so well established that she is secure. She is free, thus anchored, to explore; to enjoy; to plunge this way and that; to enter wholeheartedly into the myriad hu-

mours, pleasures, oddities, and savours of her well nourished, prosperous, delightful present moment.

So she passes with free and stately step from Paris to Brittany; from Brittany in her coach and six all across France. She stays with friends on the road; she is attended by a cheerful company of familiars. Wherever she alights she attracts at once the love of some boy or girl; or the exacting admiration of a man of the world like her disagreeable cousin Bussy Rabutin, who cannot rest under her disapproval, but must be assured of her good opinion in spite of all his treachery. The famous and the brilliant also wish to have her company, for she is part of their world; and can take her share in their sophisticated conversations. There is something wise and large and sane about her which draws the confidences of her own son. Feckless and impulsive, the prey of his own weak and charming nature as he is, Charles nurses her with the utmost patience through her rheumatic fever. She laughs at his foibles; knows his failings. She is tolerant and outspoken; nothing need be hidden from her; she knows all that there is to be known of man and his passions.

So she takes her way through the world, and sends her letters, radiant and glowing with all this various traffic from one end of France to the other, twice weekly. As the fourteen volumes so spaciously unfold their story of twenty years it seems that this world is large enough to enclose everything. Here is the garden that Europe has been digging for many centuries; into which so many generations have poured their blood; here it is at last fertilized, bearing flowers. And the flowers are not those rare and solitary blossoms—great men, with their poems, and their conquests. The flowers in this garden are a whole society of full grown men and women from whom want and struggle have been removed; growing together in harmony, each contributing something that the other lacks. By way of proving it, the letters of Madame de Sévigné are often shared by other pens; now her son takes up the pen; the Abbé adds his paragraph; even the simple girl—la petite personne—is not afraid to pipe up on the same page. The month of May, 1678, at Les Rochers in Brittany, thus echoes with different voices. There are the birds singing; Pilois is planting; Madame de Sévigné roams the woods alone; her daughter is entertaining politicians in Provence; not very far away Monsieur de Rochefoucauld is engaged in telling the truth with Madame de La Fayette to prune his words; Racine is finishing the play which soon they will all be hearing together; and discussing afterwards with the King and that lady whom in the private language of their set they call Quanto. The voices mingle; they are all talking together in the garden in 1678. But what was happening outside? (pp. 51-7)

Virginia Woolf, "Madame de Sévigné," in her The Death of the Moth and Other Essays, *Harcourt Brace Jovanovich, Inc., 1942, pp. 51-7.*

W. SOMERSET MAUGHAM (essay date 1955)

[Maugham was an English dramatist, short story writer, and novelist who is considered a skilled, cynical satirist. Best known for his autobiographical novel Of Human Bondage *(1915), he also achieved popular success with such plays as* Caesar's Wife *(1922),* The Breadwinner *(1930), and* Our Betters *(1923). In the following excerpt, he sketches Sévigné in relation to her historical context.]*

Well over a hundred years ago, Sainte-Beuve wrote that everything that could be said about Madame de Sévigné had already been said [see excerpt dated 1829]. Since then, however, a great deal more has been said. Such being the case, the reader of these lines must not expect me to tell him anything new. All I can hope to do is to remind him of certain facts that he may have forgotten. (p. 13)

Madame de Sévigné was a stylist of high quality. She was fortunate in the time of her birth. This took place at the very beginning of the second quarter of the seventeenth century. The best prose-writers of the preceding century, Montaigne, for instance, wrote with charm and naturalness; but, as George Saintsbury justly remarked, their prose, "though exuberant and picturesque, was not planned or balanced, sentences were ill-formed and the periods haphazard. It was a conversational prose and had the diffusiveness of conversation." Jean Guez de Balzac, who lived through the first half of the seventeenth century, created the literary language of French prose, and (I am again quoting George Saintsbury) "taught French authors to write a prose which is written knowingly instead of a prose which is unwittingly talked". Voiture, his contemporary, had a lighter touch than Balzac, and "helped to gain for French prose the tradition of vivacity and sparkle which it has always possessed as well as that of correctness and grace".

Thus Madame de Sévigné had to her hand a perfected instrument which she had the tact, taste and talent to make admirable use of. Critics have noted that sometimes her grammar was faulty; but style does not depend on syntax, it depends, I venture to suggest, on character; and Madame de Sévigné had charm, unfailing humour, sympathy, affectionateness, common sense and keen observation. She wrote neither a treatise nor an history; she wrote letters, and she knew very well that they must have a personal touch. Hers are as easy, and as apparently spontaneous, as those Jane Austen wrote to her sister Cassandra; but she had the advantage of having subjects to write about of wider interest than had our own Miss Austen.

Newspapers then were few and dull. Letters provided people living away from Paris with the news of the day. Madame de Sévigné was in a good position to give it to her correspondents, since by her birth and connections she moved in high society. The subjects that excited the attention of the world she lived in were the sermons of eminent preachers, criminal trials, and the rise and fall of the King's favourites. When she went to Court she was graciously received. Once, Louis XIV danced a minuet with her, and afterwards she found herself standing beside her kinsman, Bussy de Rabutin. "One must acknowledge," she said to him, "that we have a great King." "Yes, without doubt," he answered. "What he has just done is truly heroic." But whether that witty, sarcastic man was laughing at her or at the monarch is not plain. On another occasion, Louis XIV, to the admiration of all present, talked to her for several minutes. But it was not often that Madame de Sévigné went to Court: she depended then for the latest news on an intimate friend. This was the Duc de La Rochefoucauld, the author of the imperishable maxims. He was a highly cultivated man, extremely intelligent, with a wide knowledge of the world. This knowledge had left him with few illusions. Sentimentalists have reproached him because, as a result of a lifetime's experience, he came to the conclusion that self-interest is the

mainspring of men's behaviour. There is truth in that, but it is not the whole truth. The extraordinary, and heartening, thing about men is that though, in fact, self-interest *is* the mainspring of their conduct, they are capable on occasion of self-sacrifice, disinterestedness and magnanimity. The picture Madame de Sévigné draws of La Rochefoucauld is that of a good, high-minded and generous man; and she never tires of remarking on his good nature, sweetness, amiability, and on his wish to please and to be of service.

During the seventeenth century in France persons of quality took a laudable interest in literature. They read Virgil with delight, and argued intelligently over the respective merits of Corneille and Racine. They discussed the niceties of style, and were ravished by a well-turned phrase. It was, in fact, a time of high civilisation. La Rochefoucauld was in the habit of passing some hours every day with Madame de La Fayette, author of the charming *Princesse de Clèves*, and in her house, in the Faubourg de Vaugirard, they would be joined by Madame de Sévigné and the witty Cardinal de Retz. In summer they sat in the garden, "the prettiest thing in the world", with its flowers, its fountains and its arbour. What would one not give to have heard the conversation of those four cultured, brilliant and well-bred creatures! Never can there have been talk of such savour before or since. Conversation in those happy days was cultivated as an art, and to talk well and entertainingly gave anyone, however modest his origins, an entry into that closed, aristocratic society. Voiture, the son of a vintner, was sought after for his caustic humour. The Duc d'Enghien said of him: "If Voiture were a gentleman (*de notre condition*) one couldn't put up with him." There was Madame Cornuel, daughter of the steward or agent of the Duc de Guise, who was famous for her wit and so was received in exclusive circles. At this great house or at that, Corneille could sometimes be induced to read an unpublished play, or La Fontaine his latest fables; La Rochefoucauld's maxims would be admired or decried and a recent letter of Madame de Sévigné's be read aloud.

The malicious said that her letters were written for effect. What if they were? If you have something to say, which you know will raise a laugh, or if you have a story to tell, which you think will interest, you put it as effectively as you can. I can see nothing blameworthy in that. Madame de Sévigné knew that her letters were passed from hand to hand, and there can be little doubt that she enjoyed writing them and enjoyed the pleasure they gave others. She could be serious enough when the occasion warranted, as, for example, when she gave an account of the death of Turenne; but she had a wonderful sense of fun, and when she had something amusing to relate, she made, as the humorist does, the very most of it. . . . She claimed with justice that her letters were not studied. She might well have said what Jane Austen wrote to Cassandra: "I have now attained the true art of letter-writing, which we are always told is to express on paper exactly what one would say to the same person by word of mouth. I have been talking to you almost as fast as I could the whole of this letter." Madame de Sévigné's letters were written conversation, and the conversation of a woman who talked with wit, humour and spontaneity. (pp. 13-16)

During one of her sojourns at Les Rochers the peasants and the townspeople of Brittany, downtrodden and illegally taxed, revolted. They were punished by the Duc de

Chaulnes, governor of the province, with barbarity. They were hanged, drawn and quartered by the hundred. Men, women and children were driven out of their houses into the street, and no one was allowed, under pain of death, to succour them. Madame de Sévigné wrote: "The mutineers of Rennes have run away long ago; so the good will suffer for the wicked; but I find it all for the best, so long as the four thousand soldiers who are at Rennes, under MM. de Forbin and de Vins, don't prevent me from walking about in my woods, which are very fine and marvellously beautiful." And again: "They've taken sixty bourgeois; they'll begin to hang them tomorrow. This province is a good example to the others; above all it will lead them to respect their governors, not to abuse them and not to throw stones in their garden." It has shocked Madame de Sévigné's readers to see with what complaisance she wrote of these wretched people's sufferings. It is indeed shocking. It cannot be excused, it can only be explained.

The seventeenth century in France was, as I have said, a time of high civilisation; but it was also a brutal time. Men were hard, cruel and unscrupulous. Fine gentlemen cheated freely at cards and boasted of it when they had cozened a fool out of his money. M. de Lenclos, a gentleman of Touraine and father of a famous daughter, ran the Baron de Chabans through the body with his sword as he was stepping out of his coach and could not defend himself. It is true that he had to flee from France, but I do not know that anyone thought the worse of him for the cowardly action. These cultured aristocrats, these elegant ladies—who were reduced to tears by Racine's pathos, who admired Poussin and Claude, who crowded to listen to the sermons of Bourdaloue and Massillon, who were so delicately sensitive to the sadness and beauty of the country—looked upon the peasants as hardly human. They used them as they would never have used their horses or their dogs. Madame de Sévigné shared the common opinions of her day. That the brutes should be hanged seemed to her only fitting, and when the Duc de Chaulnes was removed from the province to rule another that brought in a larger income, she wrote that she was heartbroken to lose her dear good Duke. I suppose the best one can say is that it is unfair to judge those of one generation by the standards of another. Perhaps it is well not to censure Madame de Sévigné too harshly for her indifference to the sufferings of these ill-used creatures when we remember how short a while ago we discovered that men, supposedly civilised, were capable of the cruelties we know of. It looks as though man, when his interest, his fear, his ambition, his pride, are concerned, remains very much what he always was.

The Comte de la Rivière, a relation of the lady's, and himself a voluminous letter-writer, said somewhere: "When you have read one of Madame de Sévigné's you feel a slight pang, because you have one less to read." (pp. 18-19)

W. Somerset Maugham, in a preface to Letters from Madame la Marquise de Sévigné, *edited and translated by Violet Hammersley, 1955. Reprint by Harcourt Brace Jovanovich, 1956, pp. 13-19.*

ANTHONY POWELL (essay date 1956)

[*Powell is a prolific English novelist, playwright, and critic best known for his masterful irony in social comedy. In the following excerpt, he links Sévigné with Dorothy Osborne, her English contemporary in correspondence, and deprecates both writers.*]

To attempt to write objectively of Madame de Sévigné (1626-1696) would be, at this stage, absurd. As Mr. Maugham points out . . . , everything that could be said about her was already thought to have been said even a century ago [see excerpt dated 1955]. Sainte-Beuve himself stated that fact [see excerpt dated 1829]. There remains only to give one's own opinion, and, speaking for myself, I am immune to Madame de Sévigné's charm. I can see that she wrote with extraordinary fluency, that she took a cool, somewhat humorous view of the world, and that in an age when there was no limit to what someone in her position might have allowed herself in the way of bad behaviour, she conducted her life with good sense and dignity. The fact remains that I do not like her. Indeed, it comes as no surprise to me that her husband, before his death in a duel in 1651, lived a life of profligacy with Ninon de l'Enclos and not a few others.

In fairness to Madame de Sévigné I must admit to possessing a similar distaste for the letters of her English contemporary, Dorothy Osborne (1627-1695). Here, too, in Miss Osborne, we find the same ghastly literary facility, the same rather professional gaiety, the same correctness of personal behaviour. One feels that if either lady had lived in our own day, each would have written enormously successful middlebrow novels. Yet Dorothy Osborne, from Macaulay onwards, has been ceaselessly lauded to the skies for the charm of her writing. It is very rare to find anyone she irritates.

Neither of these two ladies seems to me to possess the good points of the seventeenth century as exemplified, in one manner, in France, for example, by La Rochefoucauld and Saint-Simon, or, in quite another, in England by Aubrey and Pepys—a general approach which might perhaps be summarized, though inadequately, by saying that they all appreciate the discovery of the individual. No doubt it would be unfair to Madame de Sévigné and Miss Osborne to say that they have no eyes beyond their own prejudices. This, in itself, would not be a valid objection to their writing. It would at least be attractively feminine. It is something of the cold fish about both of them that repels. The good humour, the well-bred cynicism, the interest in life, fashionable or local, all comes pouring out like a torrent of claret cup, and all expressed in the best possible manner. Yet at the end of it all one feels depressed. Did either of them really have any grasp of what individual life was about? Perhaps this view is merely the consequence of some innate prejudice in myself against the writings of the opposite sex. I record it only to make my position plain.

Pepys, oddly enough (as I read last week), notes in his diary that he dipped in to *Histoire Amoureuse des Gaules*, in which Madame de Sévigné's witty cousin, Bussy de Rabutin, somewhat improperly lampooned her and other of his friends and relations; but, so far as I know, there is no evidence that the diarist knew anything of Madame de Sévigné herself. It is interesting to speculate what his entry about her in his journal might have been.

Most of the Sévigné letters were written to her daughter, married to Comte de Grignan, who, as Governor of Provence, had under his charge the Man in the Iron Mask. For this daughter, Madame de Sévigné cherished an uncomfortable, indeed morbid passion, writing to her as she might have written to a husband or lover. The terms in which she addresses Madame de Grignan suggest some deep maladjustment in the mother's nature that can hardly be explained by reference to Monsieur de Sévigné's goings-on. Her son ended in a monastery after a rakish life (with the episodes of which he used to regale his mother), but a career apparently without much enjoyment owing to a chilliness of temperament inherited from her.

Anthony Powell, "Catching the Post," in Punch, Vol. CCXXX, No. 6019, January 11, 1956, p. 100.

ALFRED NOYES (essay date 1956)

[*Noyes was a twentieth-century English poet and prose writer temperamentally and stylistically wed to the poetry of an earlier age, particularly that of William Wordsworth and Alfred, Lord Tennyson. Although a prolific writer popular with the reading public, Noyes was never recognized as an important poet by most critics. In the following essay, he puzzles over disparate aspects of Sévigné's character as prompted by his reading of Violet Hammersley's edition of* Letters from Madame La Marquise de Sévigné *(1955). The excerpt by Somerset Maugham dated 1955 is taken from a preface to this volume.*]

The new selection from the letters of Madame de Sévigné edited and delightfully translated by Mrs. Hammersley, raises a number of interesting psychological problems. The simplest and first of these is whether we like or dislike Madame de Sévigné, and it is perhaps for this reason that Mr. Somerset Maugham, at the outset of his deft and charming preface [see excerpt by Maugham dated 1955], picks out a symbolic little story of an occasion when Louis XIV danced a minuet with Madame de Sévigné. At its conclusion she found herself standing near her cousin, Bussy de Rabutin. "One must acknowledge" she said to him, "that we have a great King." "Yes, without doubt," he answered. "What he has just done is truly heroic." With that characteristic impartiality which has so endeared the author of *Cakes and Ale* to discerning readers Mr. Maugham adds: "But whether that witty, sarcastic man was laughing at her or the monarch is not plain." Let us at once resolve the doubt. Bussy de Rabutin had a rooted dislike of Madame de Sévigné, and in a *vilain livre* drew what Sainte-Beuve calls a bloody (*sanglant*) and cruel portrait of her. Although later he pretended to make amends, the rooted dislike continually peeps above the ground and continually breaks into leaf and flower. On the occasion of the minuet it peeped. Many others have shared his dislike, but many more, like Horace Walpole, have been strongly drawn to her if only because she was the author of some of the most famous letters in literature.

Mrs. Hammersley's delectable volume, as it is so deservedly called by Mr. Maugham, raises many questions about the truth of the portraits hitherto given to the world, and for this reason, as well as for the fine quality of the translation, it has an unusual interest. Mr. Maugham, in his reminder that it is unfair to judge one generation by the standards of another, lays his finger on the chief difficulty in arriving at a true picture, and it is

particularly difficult when this has to be done through personal letters which express the emotions of the writer in terms that, as Sainte-Beuve said, even in his generation would have seemed ridiculous. When Madame de Sévigné writes to her daughter: "Farewell, my dear blessing. I am wrapped up in the thought that I shall see you, welcome you, clasp you to my heart with a fervour and wealth of affection far surpassing what is common to mankind," she is not necessarily insincere or even extravagant in terms of the language and social manners of her day. A future generation may find amusement in the misuse by our own of words and phrases like "excruciatingly funny," or "frightfully glad." It is indeed upon the combination of naturalness with grace of style that the reputation of Madame de Sévigné is founded, and this because, as Mr. Maugham says with especial justice in her case, "the style is the character of the writer." Voltaire called her the most illustrious exemplar of epistolary style in her age.

What, then, was that character? Madame de Sévigné differs from most of the other famous letter writers in the extreme difficulty of making just that discovery. There have been only four or five other letter writers in the last 400 years whose intrinsic qualities challenge her own. Of these perhaps the chief are Voltaire, Madame du Deffand and Horace Walpole, and of these three Voltaire stands first, not only by the vitality of his wit, but by the extraordinary range of his correspondents—Diderot, Rousseau, Frederick the Great, Madame de Pompadour, Benedict XIV and a host of others—fifteen volumes of the most remarkable letters the world has ever seen. Horace Walpole and Madame du Deffand might tie for second place, but with all three we have a very clear picture of the character behind the letters.

With Madame de Sévigné the case if very different. It is complicated by the fact that in earlier editions the text has been expurgated or toned down to suit the taste of another generation. It seems by no means certain that we now have all the published letters in their pristine form. It makes a good deal of difference, for example, if we take the version adopted by Mrs. Hammersley concerning a bequest to Madame de Grignan:

> "I believe the Chevalier is leaving you his fortune and I entreat you not to follow the dictates of your heart in this matter and give it all away,"

or the version given in a French selection which may be translated thus:

> "I believe he is bequeathing to you whatever he has. Treasure it as a mark of his tenderness, however little it may be."

The puzzling thing is that both versions are true to different sides of Madame de Sévigné's character, and in this respect, as Mrs. Hammersley says, "she was not a Frenchwoman for nothing." It should be said here that both in the Introduction and in the translation Mrs. Hammersley has avoided the pitfall of a too literal interpretation, and has given, in sensitively idiomatic English, a very faithful equivalent of the original. Only once may one detect what seems an unnecessary expansion of a single word when she renders "*sotte vie que je mene*" by "empty vacuity of our days." She is of course right in the context to reject the obvious, and the tautology clearly arises from her desire to give the exact shade of meaning. This is the only instance in 380 pages which the most meticulous criticism could question.

Some of the problems raised are amusing enough. We have on the one hand the Madame de Sévigné whose educational value for young ladies was highly esteemed in the strictest Victorian times; and on the other hand the Madame de Sévigné of whom, with a touch of jealous malice in a letter to Horace Walpole, Madame Du Deffand wrote: "*Ce que je voudrais savoir, c'est si vous y voyez des obscénités cachées dans ses tendresses pour sa fille, et dans ses lettres à M. de Pomponne.*"

In this Madame du Deffand was referring to a directness of language which would nowadays be called "frank realism." Her criticism was really a protest against the canonization of Madame de Sévigné by Horace Walpole, who called her Notre Dame de Livry. In this he might have found support in the statement of Sainte-Beuve, who called her "la plus vertueuse des Grâces."

The wit of Madame du Deffand—a friend of Voltaire—was keener and more sophisticated than that of Madame de Sévigné. Horace Walpole was afraid that his voluminous correspondence with Madame du Deffand, who was so much older than himself, might be misunderstood and incur the ridicule of his contemporaries. Madame du Deffand, the blind sibyl of Paris, saw through this clearly enough, and one of the shrewdest thrusts of that wonderful old lady was her charming threat to her Horace that if he were not careful she would write to him in the strain of Madame de Sévigné's letters to her daughter.

Madame de Sévigné's humour, on the other hand, has been compared with that of Moliere. The comparison is exaggerated but it is not without foundation. Here is an example:

> The Archbishop of Rheims was returning yesterday from St. Germain in hot haste like a tornado. Doubtless he thinks himself the first in the land but then so does everyone else. They were driving through Nanterre,—gallop-a-gallop-a-gallop, when they encountered a man on horseback,—have-a-care, have-a-care, have-a-care. The rider tried to avoid a collision, not so the horse, and the coach and six went straight into them, the rider went head over heels, the coach went over the rider and to such purpose that it overturned into the ditch. The rider, far from being maimed for life, then and there sprang into the saddle and was off like a streak of lightning, and is still galloping, the while the Archbishop's footmen and coachman yell out: "stop him, stop the thief, beat him till he drops." In telling the story the Archbishop adds: 'If I'd caught the rogue I'd have broken both his arms and cut off his ears.'

This is an excellent example of Mrs. Hammersley's translation, with its amusing onomatopoeic reproduction of the original hoof-beats.

Apparently Madame de Sévigné's sense of humour was not shared by her daughter, who indeed had little ground for it at Grignan; but the prodigal son Charles sometimes displayed it with a neat touch of his own, as when he wrote "My compliments to M. de Grignan and his beard, since the one adorns the other."

In her religion Madame de Sévigné managed to combine something like a Greek belief in destiny with a Christian belief in Providence, a reconciliation which is about as difficult in theology as the attempt by the fallen angels to reconcile free will with foreknowledge absolute. But Madame de Sévigné on this article was by no means lost in "wandering mazes." She called the combination the "Ordre de Dieu" and went as straight to her mark as the cannon ball in her description of the death of Turenne, on which she wrote: "Can one doubt the law of predestination; and that the cannon-ball which picked M. de Turenne out from all those who surrounded him, was indeed inscribed with his name from all eternity?" The description of the actual death, in Mrs. Hammersley's translation, is as vivid as the original. In the description of the consternation caused by it, while adhering strictly to the text, she successfully prevents the reader from being misled by the language of the period. In less accomplished hands and by a less idiomatic pen the reader might have been asked to take as literally true Madame de Sévigné's statement that the groans of the grief-stricken soldiers could be heard for several leagues, while the Palace re-echoed with the thuds of swooning Court ladies and lamentations wild enough to have accompanied the fall of Jerusalem.

But how can we measure these intensities of a by-gone period? On one occasion the King escorted his daughter to her bridal-bed. On the following morning he jestingly told his son-in-law that there was a flaw in the marriage contract, whereupon the young man fell in a swoon at the King's feet and remained there in complete oblivion until resuscitated by the conjugal embraces of the bride, a picture surely from *The Rose and the Ring*.

But the extreme emotionalism of Madame de Sévigné's letters to her daughter may have been due to a psychological complex of a somewhat deeper origin which appears to have escaped consideration. It is not clear at what date Madame de Sévigné realised the disastrous consequences of the marriage which she had arranged between her daughter, "the prettiest girl in France," and a middle-aged man suffering from a loathsome disease. She must at least have had strange thoughts about the deformed and defective children and the disfigured wife for whose tragedy Madame de Sévigné was primarily responsible. Surely this would account for the frantic appeals for reassurance about her daughter's health and happiness, and for some, at least, of what are called her realistic appeals to the husband to spare his wife. What other explanation can we give to the statement that her daughter was "walking in grandeur hand in hand with unfathomable wretchedness"? (Not quoted by Mrs. Hammersley). On one occasion she even compares her daughter with Iphigenia.

It seems to me that many of these letters reveal a stricken conscience, and perhaps an appalled recollection of her own triumphant announcement of the marriage which had brought so grim a retribution: "All his wives are dead, and by extraordinary good fortune his father and son as well, so that he is richer than ever before." It seems extraordinary that a stricken conscience—surely the key to the gnawing anxiety, as distinct from what commentators call maternal passion—has been completely passed over.

Finally, it is something more than a mere accident in her pedigree that his worldly woman was the grand-daughter of Sainte Jeanne-Francoise-Fremydt Baronne de Chantal, in whose abandonment of the world and her family for the cloister there are emotional aspects which seem to reappear, misdirected and flowing through other channels, in the life of her grand-daughter. The Sainte Chantal who founded a great religious order and established some eighty religious houses could hardly have been without some effect on her grand-daughter, who certainly shared some of her religious instincts and all the social graces which distinguished Sainte Chantal before she took the veil. The badinage of Horace Walpole and Madame du Deffand about "Notre Dame de Livry" may have been smoke but it indicated at least a smouldering fire. The extraordinary, and most people would think abnormal, emotion of the grand-mother, who, in a chateau resounding with lamentations, prayed that God would take one of her own daughters in order to save the life of little Jeanne de Sales, is repeated in Madame de Sévigné but turned in the opposite direction. This has been described as a *grande passion* by some rather crude anticipators of Freud when, missing all the deeper implications, in his more flatfooted moments as detective-sergeant of the psychology squad, he looked for invisible finger prints on the invisible anatomy of a ghost, or demonstrated to his own satisfaction that the innocent cord of an unconscious mother's dressing-gown was the very rope with which Jocasta hanged herself. But what they mistook for abnormality or indecency in Madame de Sévigné's phrases about the physical beauty of her daughter may well have been due to a mother's consciousness of that beauty's tragical disfigurement through her most grievous fault. It is the cry of a penitent and does not differ essentially from those extravagances of devotional language which Newman deprecated in a famous essay.

These are only my own shots in the dark. I do not feel sure that Madame Sévigné, in her love for gardens and woods, was drawn to them in quite the same way that Mrs. Hammersley so charmingly suggests. It is the Abbey in the background which gives the fragrance to the honeysuckle at Livry; and when Madame de Sévigné walks in the colonnaded woods at Les Rochers she is over-arched by a cloistral seclusion. She is in fact a saint who has missed her way. The emotion in many of her letters goes wide of its mark; it is as though Sainte Chantal had thrown off the veil and returned to the world with all her religious devotion and aspiration streaming in other directions. The result is aptly symbolised by the incident at Vichy, when Madame de Sévigné found it unnecessary to take the waters because she had drunk so much wine. In reparation for this she sat as a model for a statue of the Madonna, which she presented to the XIIth Basilica of St. Andoche at Saulieu.

Mrs. Hammersley is to be congratulated, not only on the fine idiomatic quality of her translation, but on her illuminating and comprehensive introduction. Her book gives us a truer portrait of Madame de Sévigné than has hitherto been accessible in English, all the truer perhaps because she still leaves us with a fascinating enigma. (pp. 149-53)

Alfred Noyes, "The Enigma of Madame de Sévigné," in Contemporary Review, *Vol. CLXXXIX, No. 1083, March, 1956, pp. 149-53.*

EVA MARCU (essay date 1960)

[*In the following excerpt, Marcu considers what made Sévigné's relationship with her daughter distinctive and comments on its epistolary manifestations.*]

It is in the nature of letter writers to reveal much about themselves. And Madame de Sévigné, the letter writer *par excellence*, has left a trail so generously strewn with hints and clues that the impression of her personality has become quite precise and stable. And this in spite of the extraordinary reserve she demonstrated in speaking about herself. It may be said that these letters are the most un-Rousseaulike, the most involuntary confessions imaginable.

Generations of readers have admired the Marquise's unusually flexible, communicative, tolerant, graceful and—above all—well-balanced nature. As to the daughter about whom we know so much less, whatever her qualities might have been, she most certainly lacked her mother's brilliance . . . . The letters tell us much about shortcomings in the daughter, shortcomings that were clearly felt by both but at the same time assiduously wrapped in exaggerated praises on the part of the mother.

From first to last, in all of Madame de Sévigné's letters to her daughter—and only in those to her daughter—there is a strange note, entirely out of tune with the general manner. What motives can be said to lie behind the deviation from the Sévigné norm? How can we reconcile her celebrated mental equilibrium, her common sense and exceptional perspicacity, her capacity for irony and self-mockery, with the extravagant protestations of love sustained over twenty-five years, with the unending flatteries, with those rivers of tears we hear about in every letter, tears shed at the thought of the absent daughter? Not all readers, it is true, have been aware of this disturbing note in her general serenity. Some have, no doubt, been preoccupied with other aspects of the correspondence: the stories of the chronicler, the excellence of the style itself. Others may have been carried away by sheer sentimentality, moved to tears by so grandiose a mother-love. That most penetrating observer of human frailties, Marcel Proust, so attentive a reader of the letters, has nowhere taken exception to the direct declarations of love. And it was he who said in *A la recherche du temps perdu:* "C'est celui qui n'aime pas d'amour qui dit les choses tendres, l'amour ne s'exprimant pas directement."

Perhaps the very particular mother-child relationship in Proust's own family made the Sévigné-Grignan love more credible, as if his own ties had been, so to speak, prefigured in the seventeenth century. But, unlike such readers, there were those who sensed a dissonance, those who wondered at the unwonted turbulence that escaped from the letters. (pp. 182-83)

[It seems safe] to seek explanation for the temper of Madame de Sévigné's letters to her daughter on several levels. We shall have to untangle a skein of diverse agitations and, after having taken them apart, let them grow together again, as they lay helter-skelter—known to her or not—in the living person. There was in her, certainly, a fundamentally sympathetic feeling for, and easy communication with, people. It came naturally to her to make and keep friends—many friends. There was love for her children mingled with a parent's normal share of hopes and vanities. But we also detect an outspoken solicitude to uproot from her daughter a deep-seated feeling of insufficiency, and a burning desire to overcome an opposition in the only person who—with the possible exception of her own husband—ever resisted her charm and wisdom. We also come upon a curious ambition to erect a *monumentum aere perennius* to a unique mother-daughter relationship, as well as an uncharted residuum of sadness. Lastly and importantly, a literary-artistic undercurrent which needed formulation and dramatization of emotions has to be taken into account.

The Marquise's sympathy for, and ease with, fleeting acquaintances and old friends, or, if we wish, her natural gift for conquering all around her, is easily discernible in the correspondence. No less clear is the uncomplicated relationship with her son. We mention the obvious only to rule out any suspicion of lack of feeling, motherly or otherwise, which might have caused difficulties with the daughter.

Yet when we read in one of the first letters following the separation, "Je ne vuex pas que vous disiez que j'étais un rideau qui vous cachait," we understand that the daughter felt just this, and that we have surely come upon one of the roots of the complication. How could the attractive girl not have been painfully paralyzed in society next to her magnetic mother? We know the drama of innumerable sons of famous fathers. Who looks at them, who wants to listen to them while the fascinating parent is present? Fathers, in general, make little effort to have their children forget their superiority, while Madame de Sévigné spent part of her life in praising and flattering her daughter's beauty, wit, intelligence, social graces and—letters. As far as beauty was concerned, she was simply "la plus belle fille de France." Examples in which her various endowments are extolled are so frequent that it is difficult to choose from the abundance.... There would seem to be no need to have the daughter's distraught letter which brought about this reassuring list of perfections. Countless passages through the years repeat the loving reproach: you are wrong to be dissatisfied; you are ungrateful for your gifts. It is amusing to see also a rivalry in reverse between the two correspondents as to their style, each one deprecating her own sorry attempts and praising those of the other. ... (pp. 185-86)

There are literally hundreds of instances where the consuming grief over the separation cannot be explained by rational causes. Madame de Sévigné was anything but old and lonely when her daughter left for Provence. Manifestly Madame de Grignan resisted the taxing fervor of her mother. And yet, this sensible woman who had her daughter's well-being uppermost in her mind, makes it a point to overpower her by showing in letter after letter, and more than once in each, her bleeding heart, her unparalleled veneration, her helplessness before the magnitude of the loss and the task of expressing her passion adequately. Her pleading to be loved in return, her humble or triumphant gratitude for a kind word—all this makes it quite clear that she was engaged in a battle for a resisting heart. ... (p. 187)

Later, after long years, the battle was partly won. Madame de Grignan had mellowed, had perhaps become resigned. Her many sicknesses, her financial disaster, her mother's indefatigable intervention on the Grignans' behalf must have helped to soften the antagonism. But the old habit, "à sa proie attachée," never ceases; there is no letter without complaint and a reminder of undying love, but the distress is now relegated to the past and is so felt less acutely. ... [Madame de Sévigné] does not wish to repeat

herself, but she does; she hopes, almost believes, that her daughter loves her; and if it were true she would be happy. The wooing had become an obsession.

Was it part of the wooing, or was it from another corner of her mind and heart that sprang the colossal effort to prove to Madame de Grignan, to herself, perhaps to the world at large how incomparable the attachment was? (p. 188)

Such a marvel of love—sustained by the most regular correspondence—might have left room for regret at being separated, but it will never explain the irrational threnodies during separations which actually lasted no longer than the mutual visits of mother and daughter. For her own part, Madame de Grignan tried valiantly—at least from a distance—to appease and praise and reassure the unreasonable mother. The despairing note must have deeper causes, some sadness she preferred not to speak about. Here again we have to remember the truly "classic" modesty which she showed in all other questions of her personal life. It is futile to speculate on what we do not know; some anxiety or disappointment simply must be at the bottom of such a disproportion between the "harm" inflicted and the "suffering" expressed. Unavowed causes of strong emotions are not new to our time. In Homer we read this memorable example: When the women in Achilles' tent cried for Patroklos, and when Briseis had said farewell to the dead friend, the poet explains: "So she spoke, lamenting, and the women sorrowed around her / Grieving openly for Patroklos, but for her own sorrows / each."

There are always reasons enough to darken the happiest soul. Several events in Madame de Sévigné's life would account for less than glowing satisfaction on her part. There is the early death of her parents, the undignified end of her marriage—Henri de Sévigné died in a duel fought for another woman after six years of matrimony—and the later details we have from her own hand: the daughter's poor health, and, as it seemed to the mother, her all too numerous pregnancies; the upbringing of the grandchildren, of which she often disapproved; the waste and forseeable disaster at Grignan. There was the son's difficulty in finding a secure footing in life; there was sickness and death around her, and the approach of her own old age which, here and there, she so movingly mentions. She was also sufficiently acquainted with injustice in higher spheres: the notorious "Affaire des poisons," cruel suppression of rebellion in the provinces, the ravages of war. But all this was to come later, while the frantic tone is there from the beginning; and so there must be other, earlier causes. It would seem that the little we know—and some things we do not know—were channeled into the open lament for Patroklos, that is into the despair of being separated from her beloved child.

Her solicitude for the daughter's sensibility, her compulsion to overcome the unwonted resistance—this thorn in her side—her pride in a privileged attachment, largely a fiction, and perhaps some concealed distress, would be sufficient motives to account for a feverish strain in an average person. But in the case of Sévigné there is a lingering suspicion that part of the exaltation might be no more than "literature." Undoubtedly she simply "followed her pen," as she often asserts. But the almost three-thousand published pages we possess, though far from the whole output, demonstrate in her an urge to write that would be remarkable even if the results had not been so good. She has been praised enough for her capacity to describe situations which she herself had not seen. Is it not this power to imagine, and to steady a fleeting impression, to heighten a feeling or an event, the satisfaction of arranging a phrase, of sidetracking the expected, and of finding a cadence, which makes the writer? If all poets are "liars," and since one lies best on a small foundation of truth, could not Madame de Sévigné's fantasy have overflowed at certain points, could not reality have lost its contours, could not a pleasure in dramatization, in eloquence, have taken over? How else are we to understand this opening sentence of a letter: "Quel jour, ma fille, que celui qui ouvre l'absence!" Unpremedidated? Most likely, but the literary "nerve" vibrated and worked sadness into the sober solemnity of some classical tragedy.... If there is a melancholic strain in ... [this], we should not make a tragic Mother-figure out of her. The daughter may indeed have brought problems into her life, but she became the stimulus for her mother's emotions and served as a repository and medium for her literary gifts. The lamentations and protestations are one element only of the Thousand and one Tales that are her letters. The shrill and repetitious declamations are not their most appealing aspect; indeed they might be called the heroine's tragic flaw. The lady does protest too much. But exaltation, too, lay at the source of the writer's most astonishing performances. (pp. 188-91)

> Eva Marcu, "Madame de Sévigné and Her Daughter," in The Romanic Review, Vol. LI, No. 3, October, 1960, pp. 182-91.

HARRIET RAY ALLENTUCH (essay date 1963)

[*Allentuch is an American educator, lecturer, and the author of* Madame de Sévigné: A Portrait in Letters *(1963). In the following excerpt from this work, she discusses Sévigné's ties to immediate experience as they are reflected in her correspondence.*]

Many modern critics feel a temptation to write about Madame de Sévigné as if she were still alive. Virginia Woolf, for example, remarked in her essay on Madame de Sévigné that using the present tense seemed natural [see essay dated 1941?]. Edward FitzGerald, a curious Victorian devotee of the Marquise (best known for his translation of the *Rubáiyát of Omar Khayyám*), voiced a similar opinion when he exclaimed in one of his letters: "The fine Creature! much more alive to me than most Friends." And Lytton Strachey, in his *Portraits in Miniature*, wrote: "Madame de Sévigné was one of those chosen beings in whom the forces of life are so abundant and so glorious that they overflow in every direction and invest whatever they meet with the virtue of their own vitality" [see excerpt dated 1924].

What makes Madame de Sévigné seem, even now, unquenchably alive? What fosters this illusion of living in her presence which has haunted readers for almost three centuries? A trick of the pen? The natural expression of her personality in her letters?

Virginia Woolf suggested an answer when she described with what zest Madame de Sévigné threw herself into the immediate moment:

> She is free ... to explore; to enjoy, to plunge this way and that; to enter wholeheartedly into the myriad humors, pleasures, oddities and savours of her well nourished, prosperous, delightful present moment.

It is true, of course, that letter writers (and especially inveterate letter writers) are usually caught up in current realities, and extract from them every last nuance. But Madame de Sévigné draws special notice by the extraordinary value she set on immediate experience, reaching out for the here and the now as if it alone were real and everything else insignificant. Compared to the moment being lived, there was no past; nor could she think of the future: they faded and disappeared from her consciousness.

When, for example, Madame de Grignan reached Provence in 1671 and sent her mother an account of the perils she had weathered in crossing the Rhone River for the first time, Madame de Sévigné responded not to the fact that the crossing was long passed, nor to the knowledge that her sentiments would appear ridiculous by the time her letter reached the Château de Grignan, but exclusively to the fright which startled her nerves at that very instant. (pp. 60-1)

Such a lament runs through her correspondence like a leitmotif. For letters sometimes spent two weeks or more on the way (particularly from Brittany to Provence). When they arrived, their contents jangled amidst new fears and hopes. While this disheartened her, she saw no alternative. (p. 62)

French characterologists, or to be more precise, those influenced by the work of Otto Gross, consider such absorption in the present, such attentiveness to the moment as it is being lived, a distinguishing feature of personality, which they call "primarité." In their view, some people ("secondaires") live under the influence of the past and future; others ("primaires") turn their thoughts, their feelings, their lives toward the moment. This (according to Gross and his successors) is because sensations and impressions passing through the mind of a "primaire" exhaust their effect at once, or while still in the conscious mind; in the consciousness of a "secondaire," however, impressions go on resonating for a very long time.

Carl Jung, in studying pyschological types, has gone on to link "primarité" with extraversion—a turning outward toward the given (since the past and future are entirely interior). Here is his description of a "primaire," couched in the technical parlance of psychologists:

> The psychological picture, in such a case, would show a constant and rapidly renewed readiness for action and reaction, hence a kind of capacity for deviation, a tendency to a superficiality of associative connections, a certain incoherence, therefore, in so far as significance is expected of the association. On the other hand, many new themata crowd up in the unit of time, though not at all deeply engaged or clearly focused, so that heterogeneous ideas of varying values appear....

Among the many critics interested in Madame de Sévigné, by far the largest group has described her in terms reminiscent of Jung's "primaire." They emphasize, in particular, her rapid tempo of life and the disparate, incompatible ideas and images which arrest her attention and then succeed one another without visible transition. (pp. 62-3)

Living in the moment means, of course, perpetual metamorphosis. As sensations and impressions change and flicker past, the "primaire," fully attuned, changes with them. He is, to use Bussy's term, "inégal": never the same. This means, of course, that his experiences stand apart from one another. Or, to vary the terms, "primaire" time (if such an expression can be ventured) differs from Bergsonian *durée*; it is no continuous stream of feelings and perceptions, one flowing into the next, but rather a series of successive instants, each one separate and distinct.

In describing her philosophy of life (which she recognized to be largely temperamental), Madame de Sévigné spoke of taking the moment as it comes, accepting and enjoying it to the full, and letting it go once the new moment had succeeded the old. (pp. 64-5)

Thus both by nature and intent she refused to cling to the past. But if she turned away from the past, it, in turn, left little trace on her "well nourished, prosperous, delightful present moment." What happened in her life before 1671, the beginning of her correspondence with Madame de Grignan? Why do the details of her childhood disappear into obscurity? Her correspondence confides so many of her thoughts; it is voluminous and intimate; scholars in abundance have worked to establish the facts of her early life (Mallevoue, Depping, Lemoine, and Gérard-Gailly, for example).

The truth is that Madame de Sévigné's richly detailed correspondence has little to say about her youth, even less than legal certificates, family papers, account books, and the casual remarks of her contemporaries. Who would know from her letters, for example, that after her parents died she was raised amidst the family of Emmanuel de Coulanges, that his parents, in fact, acted, until her marriage, as father and mother to her? Their names never appear in her correspondence. Madame de Sévigné mentions her own mother once in eleven hundred letters, and then confuses the facts of her mother's life. Henri de Sévigné, who narrowly escaped ruining her life, is mentioned in a few casual asides, as is her father (whom she never knew). What passes for fact in one literary manual or Sévigné biography after another is speculation (e.g., Gérard-Gailly's contention that she did not feel the loss of her mother) and outright error (e.g., she was brought up at Livry; she never saw her paternal grandmother, Sainte Chantal). What is more, the speculations and errors have hardened into the kind of legends which die hard: for, after all, there is almost nothing to put in their place.

Clearly, Madame de Sévigné began recording experiences (i.e., began to have a past) only when her daughter left Paris; whatever happened to her before then left little impress on her thoughts.

The same discontinuity expresses itself in her way of writing a letter. She was no enemy of interruptions. On the contrary, she liked to set things down in bits and pieces, compose her letters *à plusieurs reprises*, rather than at one sitting. In the morning, after dashing off a few paragraphs, she would set them aside to make her rounds in Madame de La Fayette's *faubourg*, where the latest news and gossip were to be gathered. Sometimes a letter begun early in the day and continued at different moments snatched from her varied activities would be concluded late in the evening after she had taken supper with Coulanges, La

Rochefoucauld, or Madame de Lavardin and her well-informed brother-in-law, the Bishop of Le Mans. Such rambling leads inevitably to letters specked with redundancies and bereft of transitions. Madame de Sévigné resigned herself to these ills. Why go against nature? she asked. (pp. 65-7)

Curiously these very repetitions, which made her wince so uncomfortably, seldom sound like repetitions at all. Infinite variety clothes her expression, even when the same thoughts and feelings are expressed. Indeed, a favorite pastime of Sévigné admirers is embroidering upon the startling diversity of her outpourings of love for Madame de Grignan, which sound as impassioned after twenty years as they did after two. Similarly, when she wrote whole groups of letters about the same events, she put new spark into each one. Under the influence of Turenne's tragic death, for example (more than eighteen letters speak of it), she displayed an inexhaustible capacity to renew herself.

All this in no way contradicts what has been described as "primarité." Previous experiences faded quickly from her consciousness and left her free to benefit from the fresh, untarnished, immediate moment. And so, whenever she heard a retelling of Turenne's death and the grief of his followers (or the indifference of the court), it seemed more a discovery than a repetition or an addition to what she already knew. New feelings, new impetus, spurred her to write one more affecting passage on the same theme.

Thus also, familiar pleasures did not easily turn stale for her. The sight of Livry's deep woods evoked, after many years, a fresh flush of joy, as if she had never seen her well-cherished *abbaye* before. And books she had once dearly loved were on second reading, strange and new. (pp. 67-8)

Madame de Sévigné sometimes mistook "primarité" for a faulty memory. "Mistook" is the proper word, for her memory, rather than faulty, was enviably precise. She could quote almost to perfection the most various of authors (including Bourdaloue himself) and filed away innumerable snippets of gossip and information for Madame de Grignan's entertainment. What seems likely is that she made a distinction between memory as "recall" of information, on the one hand, and memory as "carry-over" of feelings and thoughts, on the other.

For, to go one step further, rather than carry over experiences, she felt that her current impressions recovered the past, opened it up, brought it to life. Verbs like "renouveler" and "réveiller," abound in her letters. Each departure of Retz "revived" the anguished memory of separation from Madame de Grignan and, after his death, that of his nephew, the Duc de Lesdiguières, "m'a renouvelé celle de ce pauvre Cardinal." A letter from Ménage in 1656 "reawakens" the charm of their earlier friendship. A portrait, a place, a letter powerfully evoke Madame de Grignan's presence. This is memory, but it is "primaire" or discontinuous memory: separate incidents flash through the mind when the present, for the moment, disinters the past.

Another of Madame de Sévigné's "primaire" traits (one she confessed with delightful candor) was her openness to suggestion. She caught her moods and sometimes her opinions as well from the all-powerful present moment.

Madame de Sévigné.

In fact, it is hard to imagine anyone more malleable. One can guess from the tone of her letters what book she was reading, whose house she had just visited, whether the sun had shone that day. (pp. 69-70)

Her opinions, inconsistent and diverse, changed with startling abruptness, contradicted each other, and reflected the influence of her wide range of friends. She could reconcile Jansenism with sympathy for human frailty, *frondeur* independence with reverence for the pomp of Versailles. (pp. 70-1)

Madame de Sévigné sometimes changed her mind about people with . . . disconcerting abandon. As in Proust's *A la recherche du temps perdu*, so too in the pages of her correspondence, the dramatis personae undergo startling changes. One is led to believe, in the course of Fouquet's trial, that no greater hypocrite nor no more foolish sycophant existed than the Chancellor Séguier. Suddenly he died and became a saint. . . .

When the much pilloried Madame de Marans (Madame de Grignan's erstwhile "enemy" and supposedly nothing but a bundle of pretenses) "converted" to religion, who was there to make assurances of her sincerity? (p. 73)

Even Monsieur de Forbin-Janson (who suffered more from Madame de Sévigné's pen than anyone else) came in for some warm praise when he changed his bishopric from Marseilles to Beauvais. . . . (p. 74)

Madame de Sévigné's emotions generally flared quickly, shifted, contradicted each other at a brisk tempo. She was seldom the same from one minute to the next, as she had to confess when the Abbé La Mousse tried instructing her in Christian equanimity. (p. 75)

Hanging on to a grudge, for example, was beyond her powers. When Fouquet compromised her and set off a scandal by including her letters among those of his conquests, she had every reason to cut him out of her life. Yet despite the unpopularity of his cause, and warnings from her solicitous old tutor Chapelain (scandalized by Fouquet's conduct), she was among Fouquet's most ardent and audacious supporters. Indeed she addressed heated letters (which could easily have been intercepted) to a man dragged down in Fouquet's disgrace.

Her up-and-down relations with Bussy are an even clearer illustration. One day in 1670, for example, as she sat rummaging through family papers, she came upon something that reminded her of Bussy's *Histoire amoureuse des Gaules* and the subsequent scandal. On a sudden impulse she dispatched a hurtful letter; a few minutes later, remorse got the better of her anger. . . . (pp. 75-6)

Disquieted by the merest trifle, she was just as easily reassured. Once she took it into her head to worry about the effect on her daughter receiving and reading letters before retiring for the night. How would Madame de Grignan fall asleep? After a few letters on this theme, one word from Madame de Grignan sufficed to remove forever this "petit dragon."

And the flimsiest bagatelle could amuse and distract her. An irresistible, darting curiosity, sudden whimsical gaiety, a brief spell of melancholy, succeed one another with no visible sign of transition. In a single letter she can run through the gamut of emotions, reporting everything from frivolous nothings to affecting death scenes. (pp. 76-7)

Perhaps it was the very restlessness of her emotions which made Madame de Sévigné so responsive to the changing moods and diverse temperaments of others. For unlike the introvert with his "heavy, sticky affect" (as Jung put it), she was free to follow and assimilate variations of sensibility and manner. Indeed sometimes she carried this freedom to the extreme and disappeared behind her companion. Thus it was that on her first trip to Provence in 1672 (though herself full of expectation), the mood that emerges from her letters is that of the drowsy, stodgy uncle who accompanied her. . . . (p. 77)

In letters, she adapted her style to her correspondent. When she wrote to the *chansonnier* Coulanges, it was on a note of gay frivolity. . . . Her letters to the sympathetic Comte de Guitaut, on the contrary, read almost as movingly as those meant for Madame de Grignan. Bussy got elegant badinage or saucy railleries, sometimes with a mordant twist. At times she played along with his vanity and prejudices, even to the point of expressing aristocratic indifference to things which really touched her.

Furthermore, though sociable in the extreme, she accepted a *villégiature* far from Paris quite tranquilly. Most of her friends considered such retreats "le désert"; but adjustments were painless for Madame de Sévigné: she could live almost as agreeably at Les Rochers as in the great world of society. . . .

Once, in 1680, Madame de Sévigné examined her past and noted how at odds it was with her exuberant nature; almost as if some great *quid pro quo* had been committed, she wrote. For by natural disposition, she, rather than Madame de Grignan, should have had the active, gregarious life. Yet cost what it might, she adjusted to this, too, gracefully. (p. 79)

And yet perhaps Madame de Sévigné had the best of the bargain. For interweaving a secluded life at Les Rochers and Livry with her convivial activities in Paris satisfied a pronounced need for change. (p. 80)

Certainly she enjoyed a change of scene, if her many different residences, in Paris alone, mean anything. She lived in at least six, and probably more, different houses between the time of her marriage (1644) and her settling at l'Hôtel Carnavalet (1677). This is, of course, in addition to the jaunts which at frequent intervals interrupted her stay in Paris, sometimes for as much as a year or more.

In natural scenery, too, change and diversity fascinated her. Her favorite seasons were those of transition—spring and fall. At Les Rochers she insisted on a growing, changing landscape, even if it meant chopping down fine old trees and replacing them with new sprouts. The trees of Provence, on the other hand, bored her: they refused to change from their endless shade of green.

Even her religious practices had to be varied. She would often interlard her prayers with texts from the ancient fathers to avoid monotonous, if orthodox, regularity. (pp. 80-1)

Curious about everything new from card games to promenades and intellectual fads, she kept in touch with all the recent innovations in Paris. Ménage sent her his latest books and all the interesting works being published while she was away. During the exciting period when Pascal launched his *Provinciales* on the Paris public, Madame de Sévigné awaited each letter impatiently. She was to be found among the curiosity seekers at the Hôtel de Nevers sympathetic to the Jansenist cause. (p. 81)

So inquisitive was she about all the latest novelties, that despite her aversion for metaphysics, she plunged into the works of Descartes and even Malebranche (if not his *Recherche de la vérité*, at least his *Conversations chrétiennes*). She would frequent the fairs to see the sideshow attractions, and, when a comet appeared in the skies of Paris, she was among those who stayed up late into the night to watch its curious path.

System and method were as foreign to her as change was native. Though naturally active and pragmatic, she aimed for immediate results and lacked long-range endurance. (p. 82)

One of the reasons she so enjoyed life at Livry and Les Rochers was that there no system reigned; she could indulge her state for freedom. It was pleasant to shun all set patterns and social duties. *Fantaisie* or chance governed the activities of the day. Rabelais' "Fais ce que voudras," she said, was the motto of her domain. And if some suffocating troupe of bores drew up in their carriage at the front gate, she could escape from the back of her house to the woods.

She loved fancy better than order. The supple whimsy of La Fontaine and the *fantaisiste* poets, their graceful elegance, she defended with passion against dull, heavy minds. (p. 83)

Madame de Sévigné approached letter writing with the same abandon.... Indeed, she exploited her "primaire" propensities to good end. When she wrote without organization, pursuing the unique experience of each separate moment, she obtained the most felicitous effects from her pen. Yet she often mocked her own impulsive, zigzag approach to composition.... Bussy got impatient with her. For him a letter was something neatly laid out: you answered in order every observation received from a correspondent, referring carefully, by a date, to the letter in question. Madame de Sévigné paid him no heed. (p. 84)

Juxtaposition and dissonance, rather than logical linking, distinguish her style. Frequently she piled together chaotic groups of variegated impressions.... The effect is often cinematographic, particularly when she ticked off at an accelerated pace these unlinked, sharply focused images. (pp. 85-6)

[There] is no inventory à la Balzac, no explanation of the impression, nor even an attempt to be complete—merely a rapid winding off of disparate images which appeal directly to the imagination and create the sensation of movement in time. (p. 86)

Impulsive, alert, flexible, "primaire"—she was a genius of improvisation. A few critics, it is true, have held her letters to be labored—it is hard, after all, to imagine someone dashing off a masterpiece! But if nothing else, the repetitions, negligences, and irregularities which shocked her first editor, the Chevalier de Perrin, into "repairing" the text, underline her spontaneity. Nor is it conceivable, active as she was, that she could have found the time to labor painstakingly all those hundreds of letters which, in fact, she did not always take the trouble to reread. When Madame de Grignan praised a particularly felicitous passage, her mother had difficulty recollecting just what it was she had written. Though the desire to please and titillate urged her on (with driving insistence when her daughter was the audience), Madame de Sévigné did so by following to the full the inspiration of the moment. It dictated the shape and form of what she wrote....

Proust has said that style is a clue to an artist's inner nature and personal vision. Madame de Sévigné's way of writing is an especially faithful mirror.

And there is a wonderful harmony here between the genre she cultivated—which flourishes on rapid passage from one idea to the next (even abrupt illogical passage)—and her own personality so mobile, so impressionable, and so alive. (p. 87)

Harriet Ray Allentuch, in her Madame de Sévigné: A Portrait in Letters, *The Johns Hopkins Press, 1963, 219 p.*

LOUISE K. HOROWITZ (essay date 1977)

[*In the following excerpt from a revision of a work originally presented as a doctoral dissertation in 1973, Horowitz reviews criticism of Sévigné's correspondence and extrapolates a particular "life-view" from the author's letters to her daughter.*]

[Do the letters of Mme de Sévigné] offer a general view of man in his universe—both immediate and cosmic? Do they propose a code or style of living? Does the introduction of "je" alter the basic intention of the seventeenth-century moralists: an impersonal negating and subsequent reconstruction of social patterns most necessary to the fundamental well-being of the individual and his society? In reply it must be said that a very powerful view of life, of living, does emerge from the letters of Mme de Sévigné; and in fact, it is one that goes counter to the philosophical and religious thinking of the day. Mme de Sévigné identified living with loving.

The Jansenist, Epicurean, and *mondain* codes are all violated by this other life-view: Jansenism by Mme de Sévigné's heavy emphasis on human love; Epicureanism by her willingness to plunge into a total, highly intense involvement with another, thereby sacrificing repose and emotional liberty; and finally *la mondanité* by her refusal to establish an idiom allowing for the superficial transfer of sentiment without loss of inner control. Unlike the great majority of classical moralists, Mme de Sévigné opted, through her letters, for a radical approach to life, radical in that it embraced the passions without fear.

Nevertheless, her stance is not without ambiguity. Life as love is not exactly what Mme de Sévigné chose, or it is precisely what she chose if living can be completely synonymous with writing. There is a distinction between stressing her passion or stressing the writing that interpreted it, between Mme de Sévigné primarily as active "lover" or passive poet. Recent criticism has tended to emphasize one side at the expense of the other, sometimes forgetting that the feelings and their expression can be separated only with great difficulty. Roger Duchêne in his *Madame de Sévigné et la lettre d'amour* accentuates her passion as a living force, so strong that she had to express it constantly. Left without any other means to do so, she opted for the letter. His study traces the history of Mme de Sévigné's passionate love for Mme de Grignan. Letter-writing is seen as a means to filling in the terrible gap that Mme de Grignan's departure for Provence had created. (pp. 92-3)

Whereas Duchêne is interested primarily in the curve of Mme de Sévigné's love for her daughter and in examining the reasons for such fluctuation, Gérard-Gailly, in his introduction to the Pléiade edition of the letters, offers a Freudian analysis of the passion itself. Duchêne describes from the outside; Gérard-Gailly from the inside. His reading centers primarily upon certain semi-erotic passages of the letters.... (p. 93)

For other critics, notably Jean Cordelier, the love relationship between Mme de Sévigné and Mme de Grignan is viewed as the means through which the former was best able to fulfill a calling as a writer. Cordelier seeks to prove that the passion she experienced was only indirectly tied to Mme de Grignan, via the necessity of writing. Thus she loved the person who allowed her to realize her vocation. Interpreting the question of language in a different vein, Bernard Bray explains that the erotic language Mme de Sévigné frequently used in the letters to her daughter was the result of a linguistic impasse.... This interpretation is

diametrically opposed to the Freudian analysis of Gérard-Gailly, and the center of focus shifts from the psychological to the socio-linguistic.

All the methods used to analyze the correspondence both succeed and fail in their attempts to understand the strange letters. Roger Duchêne's exhaustive study maintains too strict a parallel between living and writing. He is so interested in the gaps between letters, in what mother and daughter were feeling at all times, that he forgets that Mme de Sévigné's primary identity is through letter-writing, and hence through the domain of the summary, the deliberate exclusion, not through any consecutive, all-inclusive pattern.

As for Gérard-Gailly's Freudian study, it too fails at a certain point. Without a doubt his perceptions do open doors, for very frequently Mme de Sévigné's "maternal" love appears ambiguous. The rivalry with M. de Grignan for control over her daughter, the fascination with Mme de Grignan's physical beauty, the references to kisses and embraces far beyond polite convention, point to a situation that seemingly reflects desires of incest and sapphism. Mme de Sévigné herself, on occasion, found it useful to clarify that her love was *maternel*, as if other thoughts had indeed crossed her mind at some point. But the Freudian bent ultimately fails to tell the whole story, for the letters show that writing was a clear alternative—in fact, even sometimes a clear preference—to physical presence, and their love seemed to express itself most satisfactorily for both parties when the written word could interpret it. Thus a study of psyches and motives cannot reflect the entire problem, for it neglects the very crucial question of the necessity to remain in the domain of written communication, and, going one step further, in the domain of the imagination.

On the other hand, the theories stressing the writing experience are belied by Mme de Sévigné herself. Although in reality her great passion may have fared far better when on paper than at any other time, she nevertheless did believe that writing was a substitute for Mme de Grignan's presence, that it was only second best....That writing emerges eventually as a superior alternative to being together is clear through the letters, but only at rare moments was it viewed as such by Mme de Sévigné. Most of the time, she yearned for her daughter's presence. Finally, Bernard Bray, in emphasizing that linguistic patterns alone dictated Mme de Sévigné's expression, cannot sufficiently take into account either the nature of the relationship or the view of living that Mme de Sévigné sought to communicate. Ultimately, all aspects involved in Mme de Sévigné's relationship with her daughter must be studied, not only the fundamental ties but also how and why this alliance expressed itself as it did.

It is difficult to ascertain the precise nature of Mme de Sévigné's feeling for her daughter prior to the latter's departure for Provence, shortly after her marriage. In the face of scholarship suggesting that Mme de Sévigné's love for her daughter was an outgrowth only of Mme de Grignan's marriage and subsequent departure, and thus of a loss of a person who for so many years had been dominated and dependent, other critics have attempted to show that the separation of the two women marked only a heightening of an already forceful passion.

There is really no strong evidence either way. But does an understanding of the years that preceded the 1671 departure to Provence shed much light on the correspondence itself? The only important question—that of Mme de Sévigné's possible desire to dominate her child—can be gleaned readily through the letters themselves, and references to past patterns of behavior do little to clarify that problem. However, by no means was the dependence-independence syndrome the sole, or even primary, reason for Mme de Sévigné's faithful correspondence, a view that might be suggested by an overly detailed account of the years previous to Mme de Grignan's departure.

What is significant is that the departure of Mme de Grignan for Provence on 5 February 1671 (where she was to follow her husband, who had just been named *lieutenant-général* by the court) was an abrupt move and a shock that was to release an expression of intense passion that, during the *grand siècle*, was paralleled perhaps only by the *Lettres portugaises*. (pp. 94-6)

Each subsequent separation following a period of reunion evokes a similar outcry; and although as she becomes accustomed to the absence of her daughter Mme de Sévigné consciously attempts to modify her acute misery and to modulate her tone, the letters are nevertheless, with varying degrees of intensity, primarily the vivid expression of the anguish engendered by the "eternal" separation. Through a process of *défiguration* that a collection of letters such as these cannot help but create, the reader is left with the impression that the periods of separation far surpassed in length the number of days when the two women were reunited. It is, however, the reverse that is true; sixteen years, nine months together, eight years, four months apart. But it is not time together or apart, more of one than of the other, that is really at stake here. The nature of the feeling was such that each period of separation seemed "forever" to Mme de Sévigné.

The motives governing Mme de Sévigné's correspondence with her daughter are no clearer than the precise nature of their relationship prior to 1671. At times it appears that the marquise was "engaged in a battle for a resisting heart," that she sought to maintain her daughter in a state of dependency inconsistent with the newly acquired freedom that marriage and distance had bestowed upon Mme de Grignan. Her frequently haughty, commanding tones suggest that this was at least partially responsible for the highly intense exchange of letters. At certain times—for example, when she unsuccessfully exhorts Mme de Grignan to join her at Vichy and then to return to Paris together for the remainder of the year—it is obvious that a battle of wills was a definite part of their relationship.

In a variation of the above theme, it could be postulated that Mme de Sévigné's obsessive passion for Mme de Grignan illustrates perfectly the fascination with an "absent" person, the fascination that Proust described at such length. Thus Mme de Grignan represents the creature who ultimately escapes total possession, what Albertine was for the *narrateur* of the *Recherche*. (pp. 96-7)

But if precise motivation cannot be determined (for doubtless Mme de Sévigné was moved to write by several reasons), other questions can be more readily resolved. Reading through the letters consecutively, one perceives two important points: (1) the letters to Mme de Grignan do not fit in at all with the ongoing trends of *la mondanité* and *la galanterie*; and (2) on the writing level at least, Mme de Sévigné's involvement with her daughter was strikingly absolute and total.

That the marquise's relationship with Mme de Grignan, as she expressed it in her letters, far transcends any notions of simple gallantry or artificial social structures has been most thoroughly documented by Roger Duchêne in his recent comprehensive study of the letters. *La lettre galante* enjoyed much favor in seventeenth-century French society, where the salon life cultivated various socially acceptable "masks." Thus it emerges as an extremely well-perfected means to avoid the more fundamental sentiments of a primarily erotic base. (p. 98)

Such a code is evident in the letters of the marquise, although not in those to her daughter. Rather, it is in her correspondence with her male admirers that she readily introduces *la galanterie*, particularly in that addressed to Ménage and to Bussy-Rabutin, her cousin. Those letters are filled with wit and teasing grace, with joking ambiguities and puns. Especially in the letters to her cousin, Mme de Sévigné demonstrates a proclivity for a certain equivocal note, where frequent references of a sexual nature contrast with her very restrained, indignant manner when her cousin, provoked by her banter, steps beyond social rules. In the correspondence with her cousin, up until 1658 (in later years this tone is wholly absent from their commerce), the young marquise employs an art of adept word manipulation with great flair.... (pp. 98-9)

The letters addressed to her daughter never joke about love or passion. Of course, Mme de Sévigné was writing then to someone of her own sex, and even if latent incestuous desires were present, the male-female element was absent. Hence there is an immediate reduction in any form of *la coquetterie*. But whereas quarrels or misunderstandings with Bussy-Rabutin or Ménage gave rise to a semi-serious, semi-teasing lilt, any disagreement between Mme de Grignan and her mother was a constant source of pain and bitterness....

Mutual jealousy did indeed exert a strong influence throughout the letters—Mme de Sévigné's envy of Grignan; Françoise-Marguerite's antipathy toward Retz and Corbinelli, close friends and confidants of the marquise. Mme de Sévigné persistently lashed out at M. de Grignan, feeling that it was indeed her right to regulate even when he slept with his wife, to say nothing of the visits to Paris. (p. 99)

In the opposite vein, there were moments of great tenderness—Mme de Sévigné's pleas to her daughter to take better care of her health; the frequent self-denigration ... that alternated with periods of frenzied worry when letters failed to arrive on time or when the marquise believed that Mme de Grignan was somehow in danger, anguish that was frequently without cause. Mme de Sévigné's imagination, her almost masochistic pleasure in torturing herself by creating dreaded adventures, demonstrate that the mood of the letters cannot compare with the cajoling, teasing tone of the correspondence with Ménage and Bussy. Mme de Sévigné's letters to her daughter testify to an overwhelming absorption, which had nothing in common with the orchestrations of *la galanterie*.

Time after time, the marquise writes that her love, her obsession, for her daughter, is in a realm separate from any other domain of her life. To permit the development of such emotion, to allow the feelings to attain a purer state, she frequently sought out absolute solitude.... Solitude, however, necessarily depended upon the absence not only of all who were irrelevant to the passion but also of *l'objet aimé*. Doubtless, a certain amount of fictionalization occurred. What the solitude and the free reign of the imagination offered was the preferred formulation of her sentiments. Being alone allowed for the satisfaction of both the emotional need (constant attention focused on Mme de Grignan) and of the artistic one (perfection of the means of expression). Either way, what is important is the desire to isolate in order to concentrate best on the obsession to the exclusion of all else.

Countless times throughout the long period from 1671 to 1696, Mme de Sévigné explicitly states the degree to which the passion possesses her.... Even the infrequent recourse to *précieux* expression ... cannot detract from the totality of involvement that left little room for other emotional demands. The preoccupation with Mme de Grignan, or perhaps more precisely with the image of Mme de Grignan, the almost deification of that image, is one of the most remarkable aspects of the entire correspondence. One perceives that the extreme concentration upon her daughter, the quasi-religious fervor with which she endows the other woman's very being, was fundamentally vital to Mme de Sévigné, that this extraordinary effort and immersion was linked to the life flow.

Consciousness of her own body was very much a part of the marquise's passion. The love for her daughter is repeatedly tied to her own respiration ... and she "experienced it as consubstantial with her being, with her own identity." What the mail brings and takes away is life itself. As Harriet Ray Allentuch has shown in her study [*Madame de Sévigné: A Portrait in Letters* (1963)], separation was seen as a period of mourning, of physical pain.... Reunion, on the other hand, was viewed as spiritual and physical rebirth.... (pp. 100-02)

In this identification of her love with the life process itself, Mme de Sévigné violates the precepts offered by the Jansenists, the Epicureans, and the *mondain* writers, all of whom placed another ideal—love of God, ataraxia, social perfection—above the intense emotional involvement absolutely vital to the marquise's sense of well-being. Even if, in part, the recourse to letter-writing reveals a decided preference for an attachment to what is absent, rather than a predilection for a permanent, "present" relationship, (a second marriage, perhaps), the commitment is, nonetheless, of a different nature from those proposed by the other writers of the age.

The totality of the involvement, however, created certain problems, the most significant of which is the degree to which Mme de Sévigné altered reality—consciously or subconsciously—to conform to her emotional demands. Time, space, people, all undergo a radical transformation within the context of the letter.

The present is a nonexistent moment in the marquise's writings to her daughter. The passage of time is viewed within her own special confines, dependent upon her own private relativity.... But more is involved than simply an art of eloquent expression; for Mme de Sévigné the present assumes form and meaning only in relation to the past or the future, and is colored completely by either remorse or anticipation. Particularly in the earlier letters to Mme de Grignan, the ones written between 1671 and 1676, she alludes frequently to such states of mind. Thoughts that revolve upon the past are inevitably filled with great sadness of time lost.... She turns next to the future, since the past has not fulfilled and the present is suspended, a nonmoment.... (pp. 102-03)

The future reveals itself also as the undisputed answer to all problems, and, in fact, as a strong counterforce to a reality that is not only unsatisfying but frequently bitter. Even after a period of reunion that was particularly acrimonious, the future assumes a rosy glow, as Mme de Sévigné almost desperately invests time with qualities of transfiguration. The most recent reunion may have been a disaster, but time alone will change that, installing a reign of "truth" that the past has failed to achieve.... The problem, of course, lies in determining whether the reunion ... or the promise of another encounter (judged successful in advance) is the disfiguration of the truth. Living versus writing. The essential truth of the relationship, as Mme de Sévigné saw it, was revealed through the letters. That which did not adhere to the image was somehow inaccurate, false, *défiguré*.

Space, too, acquires new perspectives. That which is "dead" is really most alive. Through the resuscitative powers of memory, places that have a particularly strong association with Mme de Grignan and the past are those sites that most powerfully live within the marquise.... (p. 104)

But letter-writing achieves an even stronger transformation of reality. It was necessary, of course, in the correspondence with Mme de Grignan, to have recourse to the outside world, that is, to the world beyond Mme de Sévigné and her daughter. But did the marquise's references truly reflect ongoing reality? On a double level, it appears that by her particular selection of those to be mentioned in her letters, she conferred identity, existence even, to a choice few alone, and that her choice was ultimately guided by her passion for her daughter. As Bernard Bray has shown, the correspondence is a closed work, a perfect reflection of the closed society at its root; and the letters refer constantly to the same basic group of friends, acquaintances, and family, common to both Mme de Sévigné and Mme de Grignan.

And yet the distinction of who enjoys favor—naming—does not stop there. Particularly those friends who are most deeply involved with Mme de Grignan—or who at least give that appearance to her mother—are included in the letters. Mme de Sévigné attempted to render her passion a collective one, to give it a sense of social primacy that it did not, could not, have. She sought to extricate her obsession from the strictly individual by endowing it with qualities of communal preoccupation.... (p. 105)

This is the problem central to the correspondence, and one that at times did not escape Mme de Sévigné herself. Which is "more real"? Living or writing? Furthermore, is it through writing or being together that a more satisfactory version (vision) of life emerges? Although constantly seeking her daughter's presence, on a conscious level at least, as that which would achieve the greatest fulfillment for herself, Mme de Sévigné, on perhaps a deeper plane, was aware that letter-writing offered a viable and perhaps more sustaining alternative to living together. (pp. 105-06)

In a paradoxical way, then, absence allowed for a more satisfactory expression of love than did presence; and it can be said that writing did emerge as superior to being together, although on the conscious level the latter was the expressed, desired goal. But writing was heavily relied upon to communicate "true" feelings, those superior emotions free of any bitterness, which Mme de Sévigné judged to be the real mark of the relationship with her daughter. That she saw the possibility of achieving the perfection she had mentally established as inherent in her involvement with Mme de Grignan is evident in the unusual recourse to writing even when her daughter was in or nearby Paris. Expressing herself via the written word was a means of achieving both a certain liberty and self-constraint through the working over and the manipulation of terms.... In choosing to communicate via writing, Mme de Sévigné implicitly states that although the relationship may seem imperfect, especially to Mme de Grignan, in essence it is sublime. The rest is appearance, sham, misunderstanding, a failure to relate. If the communication can be made more satisfactory, so too can the relationship; hence, the recourse is to writing. (pp. 106-07)

This problem of what is "more real" is paramount in the letters. There is an ambiguity between absence and presence, imagination and reality, that is difficult to resolve. Aware of the possibility of *défiguration*, Mme de Sévigné proceeded, nevertheless, to (re)construct an elaborate, complex relationship far more successfully on the written level than on the "living" one. At the center of the correspondence is the altering of time, space, and the entire system of relating. Mme de Sévigné stressed the satisfaction of the individual psyche as the preeminent element in the structuring of a life "project," and consequently was governed only by that which could conform to it. The organization of her mental world had to fit the emotional demands she imposed upon it. Moreover, her fantasizing, her reconstruction of the world around her through the use of the written word, was exactly the option of an Esprit, of a Saint-Evremond, or of a La Rochefoucauld, although her demands differed considerably from each of those writers. If we feel more keenly her attempt to transform the universe to certain needs, it is perhaps because her effort was so obviously an intimate one, painted as such, with no recourse to an anonymous *on*. The dream somehow seems more fragile, the attempt to rebuild more vulnerable, because she left herself so exposed.

If, however, the marquise's struggle resembles in structure those of other classical moralists, particularly in the firm belief in the power of the word, her desire to live through her love, and the incessant expression of it, was not at all consistent with the three prevailing "moralist" currents: Jansenism, Epicureanism, and *la mondanité*. The latter two were challenged by her refusal—conscious or subconscious—to be guided by desire for repose or social adaptability. The letters to Mme de Grignan are far too intense ever to be considered as part of the gallant code, and in her refusal to live a present-oriented life, uninvolved and *disponible*, she clearly violated the precepts of Saint-Evremond and the Epicureans. In both cases it was the overwhelming totality of her passion—one that left little room for anyone or anything else—that was in opposition to the current vogues.

Nor do either of the codes seem to have obviously affected her. This was definitely not the case, however, for Jansenism, which appears, at first, to have been the greatest obstacle to Mme de Sévigné's involvement with her daughter. Clearly, her love for her child could never be tolerated by the Jansenists, for whom terrestrial love was viewed as a direct rival to man's love of God. However, the marquise's intellectual battle with Jansenism can be seen as the socialized form of her own private guilt, and as the sole force—sufficiently structured and well developed—able to control what she undoubtedly saw as a violent, potentially self-destructive passion. Recourse to the Jansenist ideals was her only means of counter-balancing her obsession, and although its tenets could not destroy her feelings, at least she could use them as a moderating power.

Mme de Sévigné experienced a vague, nebulous guilt concerning her passion for her daughter, although it is impossible to describe the precise source of that feeling. She had grave concern over the emotional demands and sacrifices that the relationship had placed upon both Mme de Grignan and herself. There are allusions to her own anxieties over the nature of her love, for example, when she finds it necessary to clarify for Françoise-Marguerite (and perhaps for herself as well) that when she says "amour" she means "amour maternel." In any case, whatever the exact cause of the guilt, which runs through the letters, its most satisfactory expression was in religious terms.

The marquise thus came to perceive that her sentiments for her daughter were a violation of God's law. Mme de Sévigné was fully aware that in loving, in adoring, her daughter as she did, she was going counter to the stern Jansenist principles and therefore was not truly surprised when Arnauld d'Andilly scolded her for "idolatry" toward her daughter, or when a priest refused her absolution and communion during Pentecost. How deeply she was concerned over the reprimands is questionable, as is the entire question of her involvement with Jansenism. What can be said is that the rigorous, Jansenist code served as a slight braking force on what would otherwise have been a totally uncontrolled passion. That she felt guilty, as most critics view the situation, for violating the Jansenist principles is not certain; what seems far more probable, judging from certain tones in the letters, is that she experienced a rather strong sense of guilt, and that Jansenism was a sound philosophy for tempering, even only moderately, her obsessive passion.

But the long, emotional struggle with this braking force was not a very successful one. Aware that her feelings bordered on deification, Mme de Sévigné nevertheless failed to make use of the Jansenist tenets in any substantial way. Ultimately, she opted for idolatry and for the free expression of her emotions. By judging and conceding her failure in advance, by stating multifold times that she was too weak to oppose her passion, she thereby allowed for the liberty of living and expressing herself as passionately as she did.... Jansenism was there to serve as a constant reminder to her of the extent of her involvement, to temper the tendencies toward uncontrol, but it was also prejudged unsuccessful.

The only substantial comfort she obtained from the precepts of Jansenism was through the idea of a Providence that she came to see as "willing" the separation of mother and daughter. But this too offered only a means to emotional equilibrium that she could not easily realize. An increasingly strong reliance upon submission to Providence can be detected over the span of twenty-five years, thus giving rise to a theory of religious conversion. Nevertheless, it seems most accurate to conclude, as has Harriet Ray Allentuch, that the heavy dependence upon the ways of Providence was not only "a substitute for painful thoughts" but also a means to absolve both herself and especially Mme de Grignan of any responsibility. "If Madame de Sévigné conceived the suspicion that her daughter might not be doing her utmost to arrange the Grignans' permanent return to Paris, she need only push the phantasm aside."

Too much time has been devoted, however, to the problem of Jansenism in Mme de Sévigné's life and letters. The strict tenets were primarily a means to self-control. The central problem of the correspondence still remains one of penetrating the nature of its origins and expression. A definite choice of structuring life was made, along grounds that were at once personal and general. The obsession with Mme de Grignan was individual, try as the marquise did to endow it with a sense of collective concern. But to base an entire adult life upon this passion, to write about it, to interpret it again and again, to explain, to justify, are needs whose limits are precisely and persistently intertwined in the double domains of love and language. (pp. 107-11)

> *Louise K. Horowitz, "Madame de Sévigné," in her* Love and Language: A Study of the Classical French Moralist Writers, *Ohio State University Press, 1977, pp. 91-111.*

ELIZABETH C. GOLDSMITH (essay date 1984)

[*In the following essay, Goldsmith probes Sévigné's art of "epistolary dialogue."*]

"In our age [she] would probably have been one of the great novelists," Virginia Woolf remarked in her essay on Madame de Sévigné [see essay dated 1941?]. Written at a time when the familiar letter was accorded the status of a literary genre, Sévigné's vast body of letters was much admired by her contemporaries and, while not published during her lifetime, had a readership far surpassing the actual number of her correspondents. For Woolf, Sévigné's skill lay in her ability to capture the spoken voice in the written word: "It is natural to use the present tense, because we live in her presence. We are very little conscious of a disturbing medium between us—that she is living, after all, by means of written words. But now and then with the sound of her voice in our ears and its rhythm rising and falling within us, we become aware ... that we are, of course, being addressed by one of the great mistresses of the art of speech."

Alleviating the reader's awareness of this "disturbing medium" has long been a principal goal of the epistolary writer. Seventeenth-century authors of epistolary manuals regularly tell their readers that in writing a letter they must imagine they are speaking. In his introduction to a collection of model letters published in 1689, Pierre Richelet insists that "when one wants to write a letter, one must convince oneself that writing and speaking to an absent person, amounts to the same thing." Like other authors of epistolary manuals, however, Richelet recognizes that letters and speech are also different, since we have recourse to the written medium when our interlocutor is absent and speech is precluded. Because of this, he continues, "It is necessary to imagine that words in speech are lost in the air, and that they remain in writing on paper, so that one must be more careful about what comes from the pen than from the mouth, because the person who reads has all the time s/he wants to notice mistakes, while they easily escape the ear of the listener."

A more permanent form of expression, epistolary discourse is also more challenging than speech, even when the spoken word achieves the level of conversational art. For as seventeenth- and eighteenth-century theoreticians of epistolary style emphasize, conversational speech lacks the integrity of written discourse because it owes its effects in part to non-verbal forms of expression. "A spoken conversation may be pleasing in part because of the advantages accompanying pronunciation, while a written discourse can only please by its essential graces," writes Vaumorière, in his 1689 letter manual. Unlike letter readers who have a palpable object to examine at will, listeners find that words addressed to them escape their grasp: "What we see on paper remains exposed to our critical eye, and most things that are said to us slip away from our thoughts." Notwithstanding the more complex nature of letters, the writer should consider conversation as the model for epistolary rhetoric and strive to create an ongoing, reciprocal commitment to dialogue with the interlocutor.

The differing dynamics of conversational exchange and letter writing are a central preoccupation in Madame de Sévigné's letters, the most renowned of private correspondences of the seventeenth century. In this epistolary corpus, the metaphor of correspondence as conversation is repeatedly examined and ceaselessly manipulated in the author's commentary on the act of letter writing. This is especially true of the letters to her daughter, for which Sévigné is best known today, although with the loss of Madame de Grignan's half of the correspondence, these are, ironically, the letters whose replies are no longer extant. And yet, it is precisely in this now one-sided mother-daughter dialogue that the reader observes Sévigné's strongest, most passionate preoccupation with the principles of reciprocity and exchange.

Madame de Sévigné's intense love for her daughter provoked much commentary in de Sévigné's own lifetime, and it continues to preoccupy her readers today. One reader has recently argued that Sévigné's devotion to Madame de Grignan was an attempt to re-create her attachment to her own mother, who had died when she was a young girl. More typically, since Saint-Simon the daughter has been viewed as an undeserving idol who aroused in her mother, as Woolf put it, "a passion that was twisted and morbid," and that "caused her many humiliations." In this vein, other readers have seen in Sévigné's attachment to her daughter a Proustian obsession with the person who loved her the least. The question of whether the daughter "deserved" the adoration expressed in the letters is impossible to resolve and ultimately irrelevant to the letters as text. More important, perhaps, is the inscribed feeling of conflict between the mother's love for her daughter and her love of writing: "I find, in writing this, that nothing is less tender than what I am saying: What? I love to write you! Then that is a sign that I love your absence, my daughter; and that is what is horrible." This conflict can never be totally resolved in Sévigné's written representations of her daughter. But her letters bespeak a persistent effort to efface the distance between language and love, absence and presence, by recreating the conditions of speech in written conversation.

Chief among the thematic structures that highlight Sévigné's desire to transform the letter into a spoken dialogue is her obsessive attention to the mechanics of receiving messages. The schedule of mail delivery, the arrival of a courier, the physical appearance of a letter, the sound of opening an envelope, these material features of letter writing are all noted with apparent fascination. From the beginning of her correspondence with Madame de Grignan she ritualizes postal routines and insists on a regular rhythm of exchange. Careful to arrange the continued delivery of her daughter's letters during her travels, she views their arrival at a preestablished location as a personal accomplishment, the successful test of a system she has created: "I arrive here, where I find a letter from you, so well have I managed to give order to our exchanges." She often determines her itinerary by the places where she will receive a letter, or where mail is frequently delivered: "The mail arrives here three times a week, I feel like staying here . . . ." It's a shame to leave such a beautiful and charming place, where one finds this consolation." When she moves from Paris for her prolonged visits to her country estate, her system is reordered to assure a regular rhythm of exchange, and if the routine is disrupted she theorizes over its effect on the quality of her writing.

Through the repeated disruptions and rearrangements of the postal schedule, Sévigné gradually recognizes that her missives fall into two types of discourse: the letter of response to a recently received message, on the one hand, and on the other, the "provisional" letter (*la lettre de provision*), which is often apologetic in tone and articulates a stronger sense of isolation from the addressee: "I think that you see that I am responding Wednesday to your two letters," she writes her daughter, "and Friday I . . . depend on my own resources, which sometimes makes for a poor letter." The letters with no mention of a recently received response are written, she says, "on the point of a needle," for her anxiety puts her at a loss for words: "I am unhappy, I am poor company. When I have received your letters, my words will come to me again." But the loss is never total, since it is still with a verbal message that she announces her verbal powers have been reduced by her daughter's silence. More often, Sévigné draws attention to the excessively self-absorbed quality of her "provisional" letters, which, lacking the referential context of her daughter's message, turn inward from interlocution to monologue. She deems them self-indulgent, written only out of personal needs: "I write provisionally . . . it's that I'm very worried about you, and I love to converse with you all the time; and this is my only consolation right now." Without her daughter's letter to anchor her own message, Sévigné sees her text as superfluous, transgressing the limits of their epistolary system and violating their agreed-upon code of restraint: "I'm taking advantage of you, my dear girl, today I wanted to allow myself this letter in advance; my heart needed it. I won't make a habit of it." In fact,

these letters *are* habitual, products of her daughter's prolonged silences, which generate a feeling of dissociation and despair: "I look for you everywhere and all the places where I saw you hurt me. You see, my daughter, that the smallest things having to do with you make an impression on my poor brain. I wouldn't tell you of these weaknesses, which I'm sure you laugh at, except that today's letter is somewhat up in the air, since I have not yet received news from you." Cut off from the reassurance of interlocution, Sévigné perceives a vast realm of probability, which gives shape to vague and undefined fears: "Those are the horrors of separation. One is at the mercy of all these thoughts. One can think, without being mad, that all that is possible can happen. All unhappy moods are forebodings, all dreams are omens, all forethought is warning." At the same time, a letter written without reference to a previous reply gives her a special power over her addressee. "I have an advantage over you when I write you; you don't answer at all, and I push my words as far as I want to." By that token, her unhappiness, caused by her daughter's silence, is transformed through the act of letter writing into a pleasure that *requires* solitude and silence to be properly enjoyed. Sévigné discovers, then, that written dialogue allows her pleasurable freedoms that she does not experience in conversation. At a distance, the daughter is always listening.

In Sévigné's letters, epistolary dialogue with her daughter assumes a privileged status with respect to speech, all the more so when compared with the conversation of less worthy listeners. From her earliest letters to Grignan, the world of speech and the epistolary world are described as two economic systems governed by different codes of trade and exchange, which grant different values to her own verbal resources. She is, by her own admission, a thoroughly gregarious individual, dependent for affirmation on verbal interchange and social visibility. She declares herself extremely impressionable and easily swayed by the current of linguistic exchange: "I always share the opinion of the person I last hear speak." However she sometimes regards social conversation as wasteful, requiring words to be spent prodigiously, an excess that dissipates instead of nourishing the participants. The language of society at Rennes, for instance, is consumed as immoderately as the food, thus preventing the possibility of gaining true sustenance from either of these activities. In the same letter describing this linguistic excess she suggests that it results in a kind of madness: "Coming, going, complimenting, exhausting oneself, becoming totally mad, like a lady-in-waiting; that is what we did yesterday, my dear." Sévigné contrasts the feasting and verbalizing at Rennes with the silence and moderation of her own country estate, to which she would like to escape: "I am extremely hungry for fasting and silence. I don't have much wit, but it seems that I'm spending what I do have in loose change, which I throw away and dissipate in silliness . . . ." A week later she writes from her country home that she is finally enjoying "silence and abstinence," the sign of a retreat into an exclusive system of written communication where the value of words that had begun to escape her control is reinstated. By withholding verbal investments from the world of speech she is able to give more to her letter correspondent: "What I save on the public, it seems to me that I give it back to you."

Sévigné's willful flights from speech to writing are most dramatic when they coincide with her physical moves from Paris to Les Rochers. The rural environment promotes an intensified self-consciousness, through a paring down of social ties, while moving back to Paris allows her, as she writes, "to empty my head of myself a bit," but it also means a dissipation of the self. In Paris, "the diversity of objects dissipates too much, and distracts and diminishes passion." Leaving a crowded salon represents an attempt to "collect" herself: "I needed this moment of rest to put my head back on a bit, and to regain a kind of composure." At Les Rochers, where she is isolated, her verbal energy is channeled into her preferred correspondence with her daughter, and acquires special linguistic traits: less focused on the referential function and third person narration, it is markedly structured around the first- and second- person axis of dialogue.

In this epistolary dialogue, Grignan's language can provide the most affirming reflection of her mother. In an early letter written from her country estate, for instance, Sévigné weighs her daughter's approval against the flattery of a provincial neighbor:

> You say too many kind things about my letters, my dear. I count absolutely on all of your endearments. I have said for a long time that you are true.... The divine Plessis is simply and precisely false; I do her too much honor to even deign to speak ill of her. She plays the capable lady, the fearful one, the best girl in the world, but above all she counterfeits *me*, so that she

also gives me the sort of pleasure I would get if I saw myself in a mirror that made me ridiculous, and if I spoke to an echo that answered me with nonsense.

As the favored interlocutor, the daughter is the "true" counterpart to her mother, in contrast with the annoying mimicry of the provincial Mademoiselle du Plessis. Both Grignan, in her letters, and Plessis, in her conversation, attempt to offer a gratifying reflection of their interlocutor, and present her with a complimentary exchange of words. But the daughter's epistolary echo is deemed the "true" one, while the irritating neighbor simply debases her partner through an unconvincing imitation of her voice. For flattery, as a mode of communication, poses a serious threat to the stability of verbal exchange. La Rochefoucauld, like Madame de Sévigné, terms it "a false coin," which is given currency only by our vanity, a counterfeit language disrupting the image of perfect reciprocity essential to the ideal of sociability. As Jean Starobinski has written in studying the impact of flattery on the aristocratic elite to which Madame de Sévigné belonged, "when the granting of favors is solicited by artful speaking, imbalance is established, equality disappears, and the law of 'interest' is substituted for or is added to the law of pleasure." For Sévigné, the correspondence with her daughter is an ongoing trade between purportedly equal partners in which the "value" or meaning of words is both immediately comprehensible and durable over time. This idealized

Hôtel de Carnavalet, sometime residence of Sévigné in Paris.

vision of communication sustains her claim that her daughter's words are rare, durable truths in a world of false, insubstantial "paroles": " . . . they have that character of truth which, I always maintain, imposes itself with authority, while falsehood remains weighed down under a load of words without having the power of persuasion." She draws attention to this special value which she ascribes to her daughter's written expressions of sentiment: "Cruel girl! why do you sometimes hide from me such precious treasures? . . . let me enjoy this wealth without which my life is hard and unpleasant; these are not words, they are truths."

These precious "treasures" are revealed more often in writing than in speech, however, for according to Sévigné's letters both women feel they cannot always display their "true" selves in each other's presence, and both cite an inequality in their relationship as the cause. "I don't want you to say that I was a curtain that hid you," Sévigné writes, protesting her daughter's accusation that her presence could be stifling. Through the distance and absence that the letter signifies, however, the most passionately loving self can emerge. Waiting for a letter to appear, Sévigné writes: "The thought of that moment when I will have the yes or no of having letters from you, fills me with an emotion I cannot control. . . . It is the same feeling that makes me fear my own shadow every time your affection is hidden under your temperament; it's the mail that hasn't arrived."

Ultimately, of course, it is only by appropriating her daughter's written words in her own discourse that Sévigné can claim a privileged sincerity for epistolary expression. The authority of Grignan's words is established only in her mother's reply; the interpretive and repossessive function of a response is necessary to determine the value of the letter's message. Sévigné fully exploits the privilege of the letter *reader* who has, as Richelet remarks, "all the time s/he wants." The power of the interlocutor's words can be enhanced or diminished by the reader, as they are woven into the other's epistolary text. "If you think that these words pass superficially into my heart, you are wrong" writes Sévigné; "I feel them sharply, they establish themselves there, I say them and repeat them to myself, and I even take pleasure in repeating them to you, so as to renew your vows and your promises. Sincere people like you give a great weight to their words." The "weight" of these words is measured by the extended play of repetition and leisurely meditation, acts that are not possible in spoken dialogue and that, for Madame de Sévigné, "renew" and strengthen the reciprocal commitment that is the basis of all communication. (pp. 107-14)

> *Elizabeth C. Goldsmith, "Giving Weight to Words: Madame de Sévigné's Letters to Her Daughter," in* The Female Autograph, *edited by Domna C. Stanton and Jeanine Parisier Plottel, New York Literary Forum, 1984, pp. 107-15.*

JO ANN MARIE RECKER (essay date 1986)

[*In the following excerpt, Recker posits Sévigné's affinity with certain comic techniques of French dramatist Molière.*]

[Molière's] *Lettre sur l'Imposteur* contains the admission that it is a "discours du ridicule," an argument concerning the comic in which the term *ridicule* is defined as the visi-

ble and audible shape of what is unreasonable. This notion depends, of course, on an act of intelligent judgement, on a rather accurate perception of what constitutes the normatively reasonable. If by the concept "reasonable" one means that which is fitting or in accord with the nature of a thing or situation, then that which can be shown to be in contradiction with this true nature of an action or person is unreasonable. Hence it can become the source of a comic spectacle.

In a society which valued an aesthetic sense of proportion and which developed a highly defined theatrical code of *bienséance*, the unseemly, indecorous, or disproportionate was immediately recognized by the spectator/reader as a violation of "la raison essentielle." A true wit or *esprit* would be on its judgement seat in its perception of the obvious.*disconvenance* of unreason masquerading as reason. (p. 81)

[The] *dédoublement* of the person, whether by language, disguise, or both, is perceived to be so out of harmony with his/her true as to be ridiculous. The mask, or *paraître*, stands in an absurd relationship to the *être*, and these two facets of reality, when viewed simultaneously in their lack of equilibrium, become ludicrous.

The concept of scene for Molière became an anatomy of dissimulation or trickery, an exposition of the struggle between the deceiver and the deceived, "la peinture de la bêtise et de la ruse." However, unlike the *commedia*, the rogue and the fool in a scene from one of Molière's plays may be aspects of a single personality. When there exists a stark contrast between words and actions, one's mind and reality, there is decidedly in evidence a "manque de raison . . . l'essence du ridicule." This unreasonable disproportion exists in the relationship between the mask and the face, and the plot or action is merely a means to expose and destroy that mask.

Both Molière and Mme de Sévigné could be termed "ironic contemplators," distanced observers of incongruous situations, words, and images. Both view things from that angle of perception which displays facets of the absurd against an assumption of the normal. Both offer the reader/spectator a poetic presentation of an abstract issue in concrete pictures.

Pivotal to the notion of scene, *ridicule* pertains to the unexpectedly incongruous, to something entirely unforeseen and surprising. This idea of the comic as the unreasonable may or may not cause laughter, but it does provide a critique of human activity at the point where it seems to conflict with judgement, reason, normality. . . .

Some examples from the **Correspondance** of Mme de Sévigné serve to illustrate her affinity to *comédie moliéresque* as detailed in the **Lettres,** her use, like his, of irony as a comic weapon. (p. 82)

A comic scene, being more the poetic presentation of an attitude, or of that gulf that separates the mind from reality, depicts those who live more in their own fantasy worlds; these beings are the true "scene stealers." Ironically, Molière is said to have promulgated a theater of reason, and yet he seemed to have a keen understanding of irrationality. As René Bray states, "The power of his imagination gave him kinship with the vagaries he put on the stage. To create them, he had to sympathize with the irrational beings who populated his theatre. He was a poet: his creation is the proof."

The same kind of sympathy mixed with raillery is present in Mme de Sévigné's portrayal of those who lived removed from reality. One such creature is Brancas, the *distrait*. His "occupational hazards" were always sure to provide the laughter which left reason refreshed....

Some, however, elicited less sympathy and more mockery, especially when the choice of attitude sprang from personal vanity or illusions of grandeur. Mme de Brissac was one such person. Whatever she did or underwent took on dramatic proportions, and she made herself the prima donna of any circumstance in life.... (p. 84)

Mme de Sévigné made several excursions into the province of Brittany during the years of correspondence with her daughter. Though much has been said, pro and con, regarding her own attitude toward the people of this region, one cannot help but be struck with the way she described the excessive wining and dining of the governors amidst the background of increasing poverty due to the taxes demanded by the King and the quartering of troops sent there after a consequent insurrection. In itself this situation could be said to be tragic, but the comic element consists in the very perception of extremes.... (p. 85)

The unexpected and the incongruous pertained to the comic, as described in the *Lettre sur l'Imposteur*, as well as to the ironic. Expectations of normalcy are frustrated; outcome does not correspond with event. Such a circumstance is described, for example, in the famous letters which relate the suicide of the King's chef, Vatel, who could not face what he considered to be the supreme dishonor of not having the perfect dinner ready for his sovereign at Chantilly. He deserved to die, he thought, as the fresh fish had not arrived on time!...

One letter which was among those few eventually "nommée" was that which came to be entitled the "Lettre des Chevaliers." A much touted event for weeks prior to the actual date, this investiture of new members into the Order of the Holy Spirit conferred on its knights the distinctive insignia of a blue ribbon. The Count of Grignan had been admitted to the Order, but his official duties in Provence prevented him from attending this solemn ceremony on New Year's Day of 1689. The hilariously incongruous aspect of the actual occurrence contrasted sharply with the anticipation of awesomeness and provides an excellent example of the notion of scene which has its essence in *ridicule*.... (p. 86)

The comic spirit of *ridicule* teases and surprises. With feigned innocence it leads one into its poetic realm, then begins to take the presumably normal only to twist it, distort it into its extreme positions so that the spectator is left with a refurbished concept of what constitutes the normatively reasonable. This is the spirit which seems to describe best the French sense of wit of the "Lettre des chevaliers" and in various other French art forms. A Ravel displays such a comic tendency in a composition like *La Valse*. The listener is lured by waltz rhythms and melodies into what seems to be a Viennese ballroom resounding with lilting Strauss-like strains. There is a mounting volume of sound which builds into an intense frenzy, bordering on chaos. Waltz rhythms take on a relentless power as the music rushes toward its conclusion—a heavy and ironic four beats of the drum.

The play metaphor as a paradigm for life is particularly appropriate to the second half of the seventeenth century as questions concerning illusion and reality were reflected in all literary genres. That this society was especially enamored with the theater every student of theatrical history is aware. Not only was this a society which produced the dramaturgical geniuses of a Corneille, a Racine, and a Molière, to mention only the more prominent, but authors such as Descartes, Pascal, Retz, and La Rochefoucauld, who explored the vertiginous nature of the *paraître*. Many of the latter's wittily coined maxims alone bear testimony to this preoccupation.... (pp. 87-8)

The theatrical metaphor is one which is apt for analyzing even the nondramatic productions of the period. And it is a metaphor which asserts itself in the **Correspondance** of Mme de Sévigné. Life's more naturally "dramatic" moments almost demanded such a way of describing themselves. (p. 88)

Life, however, does not always follow the nicely structured rules of a well-balanced play. Truth does not always have the proportions of the true-seeming, and even the latter, as La Rochefoucauld well knew, requires a consummate skill to maintain. Like Molière, and with an eye and a wit for *ridicule*, Mme de Sévigné saw the scene to be made when the rule of *bienséance* was transgressed and when the unexpected turn of events caused masks of conventional behavior to crack under the force of nature's less-tamed and tameable emotions.... (pp. 88-9)

There are dangers contingent on "playing" life as if it were a series of scenes on a stage. The consequent risk, run by any actor in a poor theatrical performance, is that of suffering the hisses and boos of a perspicacious audience.... (p. 89)

A person who lacks a strong sense of self runs the risk of going through life donning a series of masks, playing in a variety of scenes, without any inner coherence. Tragic? Yes, except to that angle of perception which ferrets out the *ridicule* of such a dichotomy with the personality.... (pp. 89-90)

The apparently spontaneous recurrence of theatrical of terminology in Mme de Sévigné's **Lettres** evidences the adoption on her part of the contemporary outlook which such terminology implies. The theatrical metaphor is not so much a conscious rhetorical device as it is an example of a linguistic construct betraying an unconscious *mentalité*.

Another aspect of the conflict between illusion and reality is present in the idealistic conception of life as depicted in the novels of the day. The *précieux* milieu found in these literary works a depiction of life as they would wish it to be. It is no small wonder, then, that these same *précieuses* admired the theatrical idealism of Corneille, whose characters had so much in common with those of the novel.

Between the theater and the novel in the seventeenth century, there exists a rapport which goes further than an affinity of theme and characters, of great passions and emotions. In both, a language is found which is able to discern and give expression to these feelings. This post-Fronde society suffered a profound disillusionment and, traumatized, lost a sense of self. It looked to book and stage to provide an alternative existence and one which came eventually to supplant a reality that seemed at best demeaning and dull.

It was not left to the theater *per se* to create an illusion. One played at living another life by inventing imaginary situations. People were even given new names to correspond to this new "existence," as is evidenced, for example, in the *portraits*.

The transference of the mundane to a more lofty register could take an ironic twist when related by one who saw the inherently comic incongruities between the everyday and the extraordinary. Mme de Sévigné ... [for example], transforms the victim of a dog-bite into a mythological beauty. In so doing she satirizes the extremes of this precious tendency and debases through parody the would-be heroine.... (pp. 90-1)

Not quite a month later she again saw the queen of this adventure, and not forgetting the mythological context, she maliciously adds to the scene.... The modern Andromeda, probably looking for her Perseus-Tréville, all too quickly dropped her mask of affection for Mme de Sévigné—an inconsistency of behavior which made her the subject of bemused sniggers.

Love as a motif runs the literary gamut. Like Marivaux, who later would have the amorous struggles of the *jeune premier/première* be mirrored in those of the servants, ... [a] passage of the **Correspondance** sees in the adventures of the gardner's widow both literary analogies as well as a *dédoublement* of the Marquise and her daughter. (pp. 91-2)

Life was also a stage where ritual *galanterie* was assiduously practiced and which presupposed a relationship of critical distance. When one lost this distancing and began to take too seriously the illusion of life being lived on another plane, one became ridiculous. It was this very lack of perspective that provided the comic elements in the "courting" of Magdelon and Cathos of *Les Précieuses ridicules* or of Bélise in *Les Femmes savantes*. Though the Marquise, like her contemporaries, saw much of the mundane in theatrical or *romanesque* terms, she maintained the ironic distance of a *moraliste* who always strove to distinguish *être* from *paraître*. Accepting the latter as a necessary social disguise, she nonetheless was enough of an *honnête femme* that she believed likewise in keeping to the normatively reasonable with intelligence as guide. To achieve this, one needed to keep oneself and others under continual scrutiny, to develop the politics of the *regard*.

Conscious of herself as spectator of the social scene, she gives a critique of her own performance in one of the most well known of her letters, that of herself viewing a presentation of Racine's *Esther* at Saint-Cyr.... (p. 95)

This self-awareness in the interests of *galanterie* has several dimensions.... As a member of the audience at Saint-Cyr, she was also an actress with her own role to play. As author of ...[a] letter she gives a spectator's account of her performance on the night of February 19, and, in so doing, is a self-conscious writer-in-performance. (p. 96)

The portraits of Mme de Sévigné were as varied as those one might find in any eclectic art collection. So the comic scenes from her letters offer a kaleidoscope of images, personalities, and situations. What holds them together, however, is the ironist's perception of the inherent *ridicule* and the witticist's ability to display this vision in an arrestingly clever style.

Some of the most amusing scenes she offers are those in which she herself features. (p. 97)

Situations become particularly delectable to the Sévigné minx when she has the opportunity of exposing pretentious foolishness....

Other scenes which would seem to be taken directly from the *commedia* tradition are those which, with the addition of special auditory effects, have the sounds as well as the sights of an old farce.... (p. 98)

A particularly enlightening account puts in relief two diametrically opposed attitudes towards the nuns of Port-Royal who recanted their profession of Jansenistic doctrines. A letter written to Pomponne in 1664 concerns his religious relatives and the latest *signataire*, his niece, Marie-Angélique de Sainte-Thérèse. Here the ironist's double vision of a double world leads to a rational *moraliste's* conclusion after a contemplation of the laughable inconsistency of human behavior.... (p. 100)

It is the double vision which keeps one's eyes open to the ridiculous. One is quick to "spy out" the *Imposteurs* of this world. As Molière had done in his *Tartuffe*, Mme de Sévigné gives a colorful and comic portrayal of some of Tartuffe's feminine counterparts. Where only one dominated the boards of the Théâtre du Palais-Royal, she has a whole gallery of imposters come tripping across the stage in a single scene.... (p. 101)

Ridiculing everything deserving it, Mme de Sévigné cheers herself and Mme de Grignan with humor which has a temperamental and intellectual affinity with *comédie moliéresque*. *Ridicule* seems to appear on every page as, in Williams's words, "for the two correspondents sharing Mme de Sévigné's distaste and amusement over 'bad copies of better originals,' both the principle and the symptoms set in the **Lettres** offer comedy as diverse as Molière's own."

Shared amusement was seen to be part of the seductive wiles of a mother whose happiness, as she so frequently affirmed, depended on her epistolary connectedness with this most treasured daughter and correspondent. Ironic wit in mask, speech, and scene served to display and reinforce that intuitively perceived union. The pain of absence and distance may have been attenuated by this literary *supplément*. Time, however, proved to be a more powerful "stage director" and "script writer," and its effects are apparent in the curve of development which passes from a textual "rire de supériorité" to a "rire grave." The self-portrait of the witty *mondaine*, as mirrored in her letters, changed to that of a daughter of a Provident Father who tried to come to terms with life's mysterious dualities. (p. 102)

Jo Ann Marie Recker, in her "Appelle-moi 'Pierrot':" Wit and Irony in the "Lettres" of Madame de Sévigné, *John Benjamins Publishing Compa-*

ny, 1986, 128 p.

ADDITIONAL BIBLIOGRAPHY

Aldis, Janet. *The Queen of Letter Writers: Marquise de Sévigné, Dame de Bourbilly, 1626-1696.* New York: G. P. Putnam's Sons, 1907, 313 p.
  Biography of Sévigné that includes colorful historical background.

Anderson, Edward Playfair. Introduction to *The Best Letters of Madame de Sévigné,* by Madame de Sévigné, edited by Edward Playfair Anderson, pp. 7-23. Chicago: A. C. McClurg and Co., 1891.
  Contends that Sévigné possessed intellectual depth beyond that common to her peers.

Bradford, Gamaliel. "Madame de Sévigné." In his *Portraits of Women,* pp. 113-31. Boston: Houghton Mifflin Co., 1916.
  Glowing depiction of the writer that emphasizes her human qualities.

Brooks, Geraldine. "Madame de Sévigné." In her *Dames and Daughters of the French Court,* pp. 1-32. 1904. Reprint. Freeport, N. Y.: Books for Libraries Press, 1968.
  Fanciful biographical sketch of Sévigné.

Bussom, T. W. "Mme de Sévigné and La Fontaine." *Modern Language Notes* XLI, No. 4 (April 1926): 239-42.
  Treats Sévigné's use of three fables by French poet Jean La Fontaine in her letters.

Farrell, Michèle L. "Patterns of Excellence: Sévigné in the Classical Maternal Tradition." *Papers on French Seventeenth Century Literature* XIII, No. 25 (1986): 27-38.
  Cites three mythological maternal figures alluded to by Sévigné in correspondence with her daughter. Farrell asserts that "Sévigné moved in a world that recovered its meaning regularly through appeal to classical tradition."

FitzGerald, Edward. *Dictionary of Madame de Sévigné.* Edited by Mary Eleanor FitzGerald Kerrich. 2 Vols. London: Macmillan and Co., 1914.
  Contains thumb-nail sketches of individuals figuring in the writer's correspondence. An English poet and translator, FitzGerald was an ardent admirer of Sévigné.

Horowitz, Louise K. "The Correspondence of Madame de Sévigné: Letters or Belles-Lettres?" *French Forum* 6, No. 1 (January 1981): 13-27.
  Finds unifying structural and stylistic elements throughout Sévigné's letters.

Labat, Alvin. "Proust's Mme de Sévigné." *L'Esprit Créateur* XV, Nos. 1-2 (Spring-Summer 1975): 271-85.
  Considers Sévigné's apparent influence on the work of French novelist Marcel Proust.

Lewis, W. H. *The Splendid Century,* pp. 23ff. New York: William Sloane Associates Publishers, 1954.
  Numerous brief references to Sévigné as a representative of French life during the reign of Louis XIV.

Moore, Virginia. "Madame de Sévigné." In her *Distinguished Women Writers,* pp. 31-41. New York: E. P. Dutton & Co., 1934.
  Sentimental sketch of the writer.

Mossiker, Frances. *Madame de Sévigné: A Life and Letters.* New York: Alfred A. Knopf, 1983, 538 p.
  Biography of Sévigné based on her letters.

Nicolich, Robert N. "Life as Theatre in the *Letters* of Madame de Sévigné". *Romance Notes* XVI, No. 2 (Winter 1975): 376-82.
  Discusses the theatrical character of the writer's correspondence.

Ojala, Jeanne A. "Madame de Sévigné: Chronicler of an Age (1626-1696)." In *Female Scholars: A Tradition of Learned Women before 1800,* edited by J. R. Brink, pp.101-18. Montréal: Eden Press Women's Publications, 1980.
  Biographical and critical portrait that places Sévigné squarely within "the values and views of her society."

Stanley, Arthur. *Madame de Sévigné: Her Letters and Her World.* London: Eyre & Spottiswoode, 1946, 351 p.
  Biography that quotes extensively from Sévigné's letters.

Tancock, Leonard. Introduction to *Selected Letters,* by Madame de Sévigné, translated by Leonard Tancock, pp. 7-17. Harmondsworth, England: Penguin Books, 1982.
  Characterizes Sévigné as "a writer of supremely articulate 'averageness'."

Tilley, Arthur. "Mme de Sévigné and Her Books." In his *Madame de Sévigné: Some Aspects of Her Life and Character,* pp. 110-53. Cambridge: Cambridge University Press, 1936.
  Explores Sévigné's diverse reading tastes as they are reflected in her letters.

Williams, Charles G. S. *Madame de Sévigné.* Boston: Twayne Publishers, 1981, 167 p.
  Detailed biographical and critical study of Sévigné.

Edward Taylor

1642?-1729

English-born American poet, sermon writer, and diarist.

Known chiefly for his poetry collection *Preparatory Meditations before My Approach to the Lords Supper* and the metrical epic *Gods Determinations Touching His Elect*, Taylor was an American Puritan divine whose poetry is widely considered among the first rank of American colonial verse. Though now acknowledged an important early American poet, Taylor was practically unknown until the present century, his works having remained in manuscript for centuries after his death. American scholar Thomas H. Johnson, who discovered and ultimately published the bulk of Taylor's work in 1939, has affirmed that "it is questionable ... whether the depth of his poetic imagination and the vigor of his inventive fancy were equaled in verse by any of his countrymen until the nineteenth century." While not always in agreement with Johnson's high estimation of Taylor's importance, succeeding commentators have demonstrated a keen and abiding interest in Taylor's work, especially its place within the Puritan aesthetic and the correspondingly broader spectrum of American literature.

Taylor was born around 1642 (although some scholars have designated the year 1645) in the hamlet of Sketchley, Leicestershire. One of several children of a yeoman farmer, he received a strict Protestant upbringing and was educated under a noncomformist schoolmaster during a time of unmolested Puritan influence in England. It is believed, though unsubstantiated, that Taylor spent some years at the University of Cambridge. He taught school briefly at Bagworth until his refusal four years after Oliver Cromwell's death to comply with the Act of Uniformity of 1662, which severely restricted the freedoms of Dissenters. Taylor's earliest verse reflects a lifelong adherence to Puritanism and its frequently concomitant anti-Anglican and anti-Roman Catholic sentiment. Unable to teach or to worship in peace, he emigrated to the Massachusetts Bay Colony in 1668.

In Boston Taylor attended Harvard College, where he studied Greek, Hebrew, logic, and metaphysics and continued to write poetry, now mainly elegies on principal Harvard figures. Although he was made a resident scholar shortly after receiving his Bachelor of Arts degree in 1671, he was persuaded by several individuals (among them eminent author and clergyman Increase Mather) to accept a ministry in the small town of Westfield one hundred miles west of Boston. Taylor found the eight-day journey on horseback in the winter of 1671 arduous, but no less difficult was daily life in the wilderness community once he arrived. Aside from physical privation and threats of Indian attack, Westfield presented problems to the young minister in terms of bolstering both his own spiritual well-being and that of his congregation. That the struggle was great is evidenced in a letter Taylor wrote to American diarist and jurist Samuel Sewall in Boston: "I am far off from the Muses' copses, and the foggy damps assaulting my lodgen in these remotest swamps from the Heliconian quarters, where little save clonian rusticity is à la mode, will plead my apology."

Edward Taylor

In 1674 Taylor met and married Elizabeth Fitch, the daughter of a Connecticut minister. During their fifteen years of marriage Elizabeth bore Taylor eight children, five of whom died in infancy. Their union was a happy one, and its stability enabled Taylor to become even more firmly rooted in the frontier town. He had by now won the respect and trust of Westfield, having managed to keep the community intact during the Indian skirmishes of 1675 and 1676 known as King Philip's War. With the town secured, Taylor devoted himself to the permanent organization of his church and was ordained in 1679. When unoccupied with his ministerial obligations, which included preaching once or twice a week in his own community and occasionally in Boston, he farmed, cared for his family, and, having evinced an interest in medicine at Harvard, attended Westfield's sick and elderly. Three years after Elizabeth's death in 1689, he married Ruth Wyllys, the daughter of a prominent Hartford family, and fathered six more children.

While esteemed by his congregation and many outside of it, Taylor did not compromise his religious convictions in order to evade the censure of his fellow clergymen or to mollify his own parishioners. His aim, above all else, was to conform to Christ's scriptural standard and thereby mold his flock. Taylor believed that as a saint of the visible church he was obligated to exhibit (particularly to those whose salvation appeared tenuous) his inner state of grace through outward actions. He was traditional in the interpretation and execution of certain church doctrines and opposed more liberal divines on several fronts. His most significant conflict was with Solomon Stoddard of nearby Northampton over administering communion to unregenerate persons. It became Stoddard's custom to admit any well-behaved Christian to the Lord's Supper, for, he contended, no one could know with absolute certainty that he or she had been saved. Stoddard also argued that the sacrament might well convert an unresolved individual and therefore should not be withheld. Taylor objected bitterly to use of the Lord's Supper as a converting ordinance. In numerous sermons, headed in 1679 by *A Particular Church is Gods House*, he waged what proved to be a losing battle against Stoddard's practice and, to his perception, other potentially dangerous innovations within the church. Not until middle age, however, did Taylor embark upon his most comprehensive and widely recognized written legacy. In 1682 he began the *Preparatory Meditations*, verses composed in anticipation of his monthly communion services over a period of forty-four years. It is believed that Taylor also commenced his other major work, *Gods Determinations*, a lengthy dramatic poem concerning predestination and redemption, around 1682. Ill and enfeebled in his final years but conservative to the last, he died in 1729. His passing was oddly marked by the adoption in Westfield of Stoddardeanism, which itself reflected increasingly liberal religious thought throughout the early American colonies.

The *Preparatory Meditations* derives from the believer's faith in a spiritual union with Christ through the Lord's Supper. The verses, which number over two hundred, are grouped in two series, each poem the subject of a scriptural text but all united by their link to the communion sacrament. Meditations on the love of God, the benefits of redemption, and mankind's sinfulness had long been literary staples before Taylor's time and were esteemed as religious exercises; even those devoted to such specifics as the Lord's Supper were common to a younger Protestant tradition. Conventional, too, were other devices used by Taylor, including matrimonial diction patterned after the Song of Solomon (or Canticles) conveying Christ's mystical marriage to His elect and a language of food and drink mirroring the communion supper itself. The work parts from precedent in its distinctive verse form (meditations were customarily written in prose) and singular use of imagery. Progressions of thought are confined, without variance, to six-line stanzas, resulting in an awkwardness and angularity for which Taylor has been almost uniformly censured. But some critics have viewed these jarring metrics less as imposition than as integral to the poet's process and, further, his worldview. Karl Keller has noted that while the stanza is certainly a rigid structure, Taylor "finds a way of moving, of being moved, within the frame." The critic further remarked that "preparation of oneself for finding an acceptable place in the pattern of the sacrament of the Lord's supper suggests how poetry served Taylor as illusion: as he wrote he was imagining himself undergoing change in a predetermined universe." Imagery throughout the poet's work and particularly in the *Preparatory Meditations* has sparked ongoing preoccupation with Taylor's poetic ancestry. Placed in metaphysical, baroque, and transcendental traditions—all of which have, in some measure, been seen to conflict with the generally accepted Puritan aesthetic—Taylor's works have defied conclusive definition. Although the meditations clearly evidence the legacy of John Donne, Richard Crashaw, Henry Vaughan, and George Herbert (the last of whom is most frequently allied with Taylor), Taylor's grasp of the potential of figurative language is unique. For example, while imagery taken from field and woods, the village streets, and familiar objects is hardly exclusive to Taylor, commentators have found his reliance on such figures of speech in preaching to a semiliterate audience both understandable and appropriate. However, as Albert Gelpi has observed, "Taylor pressed his homely images more forcefully and at greater length than either Donne or Herbert. The more sophisticated Englishmen would have found some of his images distasteful and uncouth, as when he dwells on excremental details or on a conceit of circumcision or of the seed's activity in the womb. At times he pushed a single metaphor too hard; at other times he compounded his metaphors into confusion. But even this irrepressibility suggests not so much the indulgent excesses of the minor metaphysical poets as the earnestness of the Puritan-amateur poet."

Of lesser critical acclaim, *Gods Determinations* is a dramatization of Puritan doctrine. This poem of epic proportions treats creation, predestination, the nature of God and of original sin, redemption through faith in Christ, and the division of mankind into the damned and the elect. Like the *Preparatory Meditations*, *Gods Determinations* draws on a rich heritage of related works but reflects none of them absolutely. As in John Milton's *Paradise Lost* (1667) and John Bunyan's *The Holy War* (1682), the clash between personified virtues and vices is depicted, yet *Gods Determinations* is essentially closer to Michael Wigglesworth's *The Day of Doom* (1662) in its exposition of Puritan thought. Uneven in meter and varying in style from colloquial to ornate, *Gods Determinations* contains, according to Herbert Blau, "a few impressive poems" but is, on the whole, "fairly tedious, inconsistent theologically, and neither a good narrative nor a good *débat*." Though readily admitting that "there is no drama, no dialectic, in *Gods Determinations*," Roy Harvey Pearce has argued that its continuity becomes manifest "as elements of earthly experience are found to be analogues of spiritual experience." Finally, while disclaiming for *Gods Determinations* the universal and timeless appeal of Milton's epic, Donald E. Stanford has called it "the best long poem written in seventeenth-century America."

According to a story that originated with his heirs, Taylor had prohibited the publication of his manuscripts, which passed from his grandson to great-grandson and were circulated among several private libraries before Johnson discovered them at Yale University and eventually published them in 1939. Critics were initially attracted by the rare opportunity to study a body of poetry that had lain dormant and unknown for over two centuries, especially one to which a cryptic (albeit alleged) suppression of publication was attached. For a time commentators were prone to construe Taylor's poetry as an anomaly within a rigid religious context, but they later found themselves compelled to reevaluate preconceptions concerning the Puritan mind. Not merely stern moralists, the Puritans have come to be seen as having possessed an austere but very definite aesthetic. Consequently, with all its unabashed expression of feeling, its lack of artificial piety or pretense, even its employment of the most intimate metaphors to describe the poet's relationship with his Lord, Taylor's verse, in Pearce's words, has been deemed "of a piece with a strenuously, self-consciously orthodox Puritan culture" in which "poetry rises immediately from . . . the need for discovering God in His world." Attempts to sift Taylor's work for qualities indigenous to Puritanism or for affinities with metaphysical and baroque poetry have inspired some critics—struck by Taylor's spirited colloquialisms and exuberant diction—to ally his verse with the mainstream of American poetry. Yet even here Taylor's poetry has defied conclusive analysis, compelling commentators to reexamine the fundamental nature of poetry itself. Hyatt H. Waggoner has labeled certain technical characteristics of the poet's work truly American. He has, for example, pointed to Taylor's quest for self-knowledge, a quest which includes "the chief American poets, from Emerson to Roethke." Gelpi has drawn basic analogies between the *Preparatory Meditations* and works of Walt Whitman and Ezra Pound in terms of "translating a vision of reality into a coherent poetic creation." Yet Keller has suggested that Taylor's poetic language, upon which his critical position is strongly predicated, "has been overrated for its Americanness. It might be thought possible to turn to Taylor's earthy diction, his homely images, his natural speech, his neologisms, and see there the qualities of an American vernacular. . . . But while Taylor's ideolect is highly nonstandard, it is in a number of ways fossilized speech."

Singleminded in his art as in his ministry, Taylor was driven to write poetry by a desire to glorify his Lord. To this end he harnessed all means of technique. Taylor's work, while ultimately not of major stature in the broad context of American literature, continues to tantalize critics who would firmly establish its place in the history of letters and who are, in particular, baffled by the poet's personal vernacular. Of the latter, Mark Van Doren has commented simply that Taylor's "love of God enlisted the service of every word he knew, and he would not have cared had he been warned that some of his words were to grow obsolete."

(See also *Dictionary of Literary Biography*, Vol. 24: *American Colonial Writers, 1606-1734*.)

*PRINCIPAL WORKS

Gods Determinations Touching His Elect: And the Elects Combat in Their Conversion, and Coming Up to God in Christ: Together with the Comfortable Effects Thereof (poetry) 1682
†*Preparatory Meditations before My Approach to the Lords Supper. Chiefly upon the Doctrin Preached upon the Day of Administration* (poetry) 1682-1726
Treatise Concerning the Lord's Supper (sermons) 1693-94
‡*Christographia, or a Discourse Touching Christs Person, Natures, the Personall Union of the Natures, Qualifications, and Operations Opened, Confirmed, and Practically Improved in Severall Sermons Delivered upon Certain Sacrament Dayes unto the Church and People of God in Westfield* (sermons) 1701-03

§*The Poetical Works of Edward Taylor* (poetry) 1939
The Poems of Edward Taylor (poetry) 1960
A Transcript of Edward Taylor's Metrical History of Christianity (poetry) 1962
The Diary of Edward Taylor: An Atlantic Voyage, Life at Harvard College, and Settlement at Westfield, 1668-1672 (diary) 1964

*Because Taylor's works long existed only in manuscript, the dates given here, with the exception of modern editions, are composition and not publication dates.

†Prior to 1960, critics referred to the *Preparatory Meditations* as *Sacramental Meditations*, a title that early scholars erroneously believed was Taylor's but which was later discovered to be an interpolation by Ezra Stiles, Taylor's grandson.

‡The sermons contained in this work correspond to certain of the *Meditations*.

§This edition prints only a selection of the *Meditations*; the 1960 edition of Taylor's poems prints them in their entirety.

EDWARD TAYLOR (poem date 1701)

[*In the following excerpt from one of the* Meditations, *Taylor regards his poetic skill relative to God's position.*]

When, Lord, I seeke to shew thy praises, then
Thy shining Majesty doth stund my minde,
Encramps my tongue and tongue ties fast my Pen,
That all my doings, do not what's designd.
My Speeche's Organs are so trancifide
My words stand startld, can't thy praises stride.

Nay Speeches Bloomery can't from the Ore
Of Reasons mine, melt words for to define
Thy Deity, nor t'deck the reechs that sore
From Loves rich Vales, sweeter than hony rhimes.
Words though the finest twine of reason, are
Too Course a web for Deity to ware.

Words Mentall are syllabicated thoughts:
Words Orall but thoughts Whiffld in the Winde.
Words Writ, are incky, Goose quill-slabbred draughts,
Although the fairest blossoms of the minde.
Then can such glasses cleare enough descry
My Love to thee, or thy rich Deity?

Words are befould, Thoughts filthy fumes that smoake,
From Smutty Huts, like Will-a-Wisps that rise
From Quaugmires, run ore bogs where frogs do Croake,
Lead all astray led by them by the eyes.
My muddy Words so dark thy Deity,
And cloude thy Sun-Shine, and its Shining Sky.

Yet spare mee, Lord, to use this hurden ware.
I have no finer Stuff to use, and I
Will use it now my Creed but to declare
And not thy Glorious Selfe to beautify.
Thou art all-God: all Godhead then is thine
Although the manhood there unto doth joyne. . . .

Be thou my God, and make mee thine Elect
To kiss thy feet, and worship give to thee:
Accept of mee, and make mee thee accept.
So I'st be safe, and thou shalt served bee.
I'le bring thee praise, buskt up in Songs perfum'de,
When thou with grace my Soule hast sweetly tun'de.

(pp. 159-60)

Edward Taylor,"Preparatory Meditations (second series)," in The Poems of Edward Taylor, *edited by Donald E. Stanford, Yale University Press, 1960, pp. 83-386.*

JOHN LANGDON SIBLEY (essay date 1881)

[*Sibley was an editor, assistant librarian and then librarian at the Harvard College Library from 1841 to 1877 and the author of* Biographical Sketches of Graduates of Harvard University *(1873-85). In the following excerpt from that work, he offers a brief sketch of Taylor based on information provided by Taylor's great-grandson, Henry Wyllys Taylor.*]

Rev. Edward Taylor, M.A., who took his second degree in 1720, was born in England, at "*Sketchley* (near *Hinckley*) in *Leicestershire*; had his Education there under a Nonconformist Schoolmaster, and was himself qualified to keep a School, which he did for about a Quarter of a Year at *Bagworth* in the same county; and to such good Acceptance that some Gentlemen in the Neighbourhood took pains to procure him a Licence, which was offer'd him in case he would take the Oaths then requir'd, which he conscienstiously scrupl'd, and so was oblig'd to quit his School to the Grief of the neighbouring Gentry . . . ; otherwise (we may suppose) this Part of the World had never known him."

His great-grandson, Henry Wyllys Taylor, says he was "educated for the ministry, studied seven years in one of their universities,"—Edwards says it was at the University of Cambridge,—"but the ejection of 2,000 dissenting clergymen in 1662, and the persecutions which that class of Christians suffered, induced him to a voluntary exile.

"It seems he was then an ardent anti-monarchist, and his early writings are said to breathe, in no doubtful terms, his strong aversion to the rulings of the existing dynasty." (p. 397)

[Later, as] was the case with many of the early ministers of New England, Taylor discharged the duties of a physician, ministering alike to the bodily and spiritual wants of the population, scattered over an extensive territory.

The *New England Journal* states that he was "very constant and diligent in his Preaching till of late about a year and a half."

A communication from Westfield in the *Boston News-Letter* says he died 14 June, 1729, "in the 85th year of his age. . . . And what a rich blessing GOD sent us in him almost Fifty eight Years Experience has taught us. . . . He was eminently holy in his Life, and very painful and laborious in his Work till the Infirmities of a great old Age disabled him; and continued to have the sole Oversight of this Flock till October 26, 1726, when the Rev. Mr. Bull was ordain'd among us; in which solemn Action he bore his Part." After this "he declin'd preaching publickly, tho' always before very loth to be prevented on any account. And when about two or three Months after, he was by much Intreaty prevailed on (the only Time he was so) he did as it were preach his own Funeral Sermon, from Zechariah i. 5. Your fathers, where are they? and the prophets, do they live for ever?" (pp. 407-08)

Judge [Samuel] Sewall writes: "He and I were Chamber fellows, & Bed fellows in Harvard College Two years: He being admitted into the College drew me thither. I have heard him preach a Sermon at the Old South upon Short warning, which, as the phrase in England is, might have been preached at Paul's Cross." (p. 408)

Taylor had through life a passion for writing poetry. There are extant specimens covering a period of about sixty-seven years; not of a very high order, though some have considerable merit. He gave orders that his heirs should never publish any of his writings. (p. 410)

John Langdon Sibley, "Edward Taylor," in his Biographical Sketches of Graduates of Harvard University in Cambridge, Massachusetts: 1659-1677, Vol. II, *Charles William Sever, 1881, pp. 397-412.*

MARK VAN DOREN (essay date 1939)

[*Van Doren, the younger brother of the poet Carl Van Doren, was one of America's most prolific and diverse twentieth-century writers. His criticism, which is aimed at the general reader rather than the scholar or specialist, is noted for its lively perception and wide interest. In the following excerpt from his review of Thomas H. Johnson's 1939 edition of Taylor's poetry,* The Poetical Works of Edward Taylor, *he commends Taylor's verse.*]

Edward Taylor is a new American poet only in the sense that his work has now for the first time been published. It lay in manuscript for longer than two centuries before Mr. Johnson discovered it at Yale, one of whose presidents, Ezra Stiles, had been Taylor's grandson. Taylor was a Puritan minister with a charge at Westfield, Mass., where he died in 1729 after fifty-eight years of quiet preaching and writing. He had come from England as a young man in 1668, bringing with him for literary equipment a thorough understanding of George Herbert's way with verse, to mention only one pre-Restoration English poet among the several from whom he may be supposed to have taken his start. The way of Herbert was old-fashioned in 1668. By 1729 it was certainly antiquated. But Taylor never followed any other; his original impulse seems never to have been spent, he never changed his mind about his subject—the beauty and goodness of Christ—and presumably there was nothing in his environment to silence him. Here then, more than two hundred years after his death, is a liberal selection from his poems [*The Poetical Works of Edward Taylor*], published by a kind of logic too late once again to be precisely in fashion. For the "metaphysical" rage has passed in contemporary poetry, and Taylor's work must support itself without benefit of school.

It will do so, for it is excellent and interesting. Anne Bradstreet, the best of his American contemporaries, was possessed of a much slighter talent; and Michael Wigglesworth had nothing at all resembling his art. The metaphysical mode does not appear at its best in Taylor, but it fully and surely appears, both in the theological dialogues of *God's Determinations* and in the thirty-two lyrics which Mr. Johnson has selected from *The Sacramental Meditations*. Mr. Johnson commends his poet for developing, as he usually does, a single figure throughout a given poem [see excerpt dated 1939]. Taylor did better, however, when he did otherwise. The mechanics of the "conceit" overwhelmed him too often, landing him in monotony. When he forgot them, or rather mastered them, as for instance in the forty-ninth "**Meditation,**" the result was perhaps a riot of metaphor, but it was also a lively and convincing poem. In such pieces, and generally throughout the vigorous dialogue of *God's Determinations,* Taylor wrote what will doubtless come soon to be considered the most interesting American verse before the nineteenth century. Here is a representative stanza:

> Should I with silver tooles delve through the Hill
> Of Cordilera for rich thoughts, that I
> My Lord, might weave with an angelick skill
> A Damask Web of Velvet Verse, thereby
> To deck thy Works up, all my Web would run
> To rags and jags; so snick-snarled to the thrum.

The vernacular in the last line is characteristic both of Taylor and of his tradition, and sorts in his own case quite naturally with a passionate and melodious piety. His love of God enlisted the service of every word he knew, and he would not have cared had he been warned that some of those words were to grow obsolete.

> Mark Van Doren, "*Poetry Long in Waiting,*" in
> New York Herald Tribune Books, *October 29,*
> *1939, p. 24.*

THOMAS H. JOHNSON (essay date 1939)

[*An American educator and editor, Johnson discovered and published Taylor's unpublished manuscripts, sparking a critical interest in the poet that continues today. In the following excerpt from the introduction to his seminal edition of Taylor's work,* The Poetical Works of Edward Taylor *(1939), Johnson favorably assesses the poet's work within a context of devotional literature and addresses specifics of* Gods Determinations *and the* Meditations.]

The ardor of Taylor's love for Christ is displayed best in the songs which conclude *Gods Determinations* and in the *Meditations,* but the reader need not search afield for analogues among the verses of the seventeenth-century conceitists to explain Taylor's choice of subject. It is true that the manner and devices of his poems especially suggest the example of George Herbert, the Anglican poet beloved so much by Puritans. Five of the unusual metrical patterns of *Gods Determinations* exactly correspond to forms in Herbert's *The Temple.* There are, too, the same rhetorical devices of question, refrain, apostrophe, and direct address. There is an observable correspondence in the length of their songs, and it is further apparent that Taylor believes with Herbert that nothing is so mean but that it can be ennobled by figures from common life, from medical and chemical knowledge. He likewise draws heavily upon metaphors of taste, smell, color, and sound. But there are qualities as well in the verse which ally him more closely with Richard Crashaw than with Herbert: the moods of seraphic exaltation, in which the language of amorous poetry is adapted to religious ends; the prodigality of fanciful tropes; and the complete, almost physical, abandonment to Christ. Yet clearly Taylor does not merely imitate. He was possibly not conscious of the similarities, and in fact is unlikely to have read a line of Crashaw's poetry.

The spirit which animated Taylor's devotion was fully as central in Puritan as in Anglican or Catholic thought. Within Puritanism itself, though not often displayed in verse, is to be discovered all the spiritual fervor that found utterance in his poems. His intense love for Christ sup-

plied the matter; delight in conceits, somewhat belated in point of time, determined the manner. Taylor's debt to other poets, if debt there be, is less obvious. One thinks naturally of Quarles, the laureate among Puritans, whose *Emblemes,* starting from some text of Scripture on which he finds a meditation, may well have furnished a model for the *Sacramental Meditations.* One would like to know whether a copy of Sir John Davies's *Nosce Teipsum* may not have passed through Taylor's hands. Davies's combination of poetry and metaphysics, his discourses on the longing, grief, and destiny of the soul, somewhat parallel *Gods Determinations* and certain of the *Meditations.* No suggestion of the influence of Wither, so often the Puritan's inspiration, is anywhere apparent. On the whole, one's impression is that Taylor struck out for himself. The wealth of colloquial, indigenous terms, adopted from the language of everyday life, often recalled from the technical phrases used by the weavers of his native Warwickshire, produces an effect, when combined with the vigor of his thought and the sensitivity of his ear, that leaves no doubt of his originality. Taylor's delight in the sound and shading of language, a further Elizabethan characteristic, is emphasized by his word coinages: there seems to be no recorded example to match substantives like "squitchen," "glore," "reech," "pillard," and "hone."

The *Meditations* lack the stanzaic variety of *Gods Determinations* in that they uniformly employ the six-line stanza. Their diction, like that found in the lines of the "conceitists" generally, is partly learned and Latinic, partly homely. The lines are concentrated and angular, sometimes rough: an inevitable tendency of verse called metaphysical, wherein the conceit is inspired by a philosophical concept. But at his best Taylor achieves a striking unity of design by developing one figure. He is always the object through which Christ transmits his influence, now as a garden exhaling odor, or as a pipe conveying liquid, or a loom whereon the spirit weaves, or a mint in which God coins his image. By thus developing one single figure in a poem. Taylor avoids a fault to which almost all sacred poets are commonly prone, that is, of strewing metaphors throughout their verses with prodigal abandon. For instance, the figure of Christ as attorney pleading man's cause *sub forma pauperis* before God, the Judge, in Meditation Thirty-Eight, is carefully built up without extraneous imagery. The legal phraseology, so often seized upon to express the covenant idea, is consistently employed and brought to a climax without wrenched or tortured figures. Indeed, it becomes plain by 1685 that Taylor has enriched and deepened his concept of the poetic art to the point where thereafter his *Meditations* are often firmer and sometimes more brilliant statements of his theological position.

Puritans were especially eager to find "types," that is, analogies or correspondent realities between events or persons in the Old Testament and in the New. By such means did they feel that God's word was illuminated and man's emotions stirred. Christ, the antitype, was foreshadowed by whatever prophetic similitude the reader might discover. Thus in a few of the *Meditations* Taylor narrates Old Testament stories as "types" of Christ's advent and suffering, and at moments is able to create striking effects by the speed and concreteness of his narrative summary.

> Jonas did type this thing, who ran away

From God and, shipt for Tarsus, fell asleep.
A Storm lies on the Ship: the Seamen they
Bestir their Stumps, and at wits end do weep:
'Wake, Jonas:' who saith, 'Heave me over deck;
The Storm will Cease then; all lies on my neck.'

Occasionally Taylor composed elegies in frigid decasyllabics. But such "effusions" are not stamped with the image of his personality. In his devotional poetry, on the other hand, he is thoroughly at home, and the fire of that devotion abates very little with the passage of years. His last meditation, written in 1725, when he was past eighty, is as ardent in its expression of love for God as his earlier verses. The text is from Canticles, II:5: "I am sick of love," and opens with the cry: "Heart sick, my Lord, heart sick of Love to thee."

The poet's taste had been formed early, perhaps in Harvard College, perhaps in England before he sailed for Massachusetts Bay; and it never changed. He lived remote from the sources of poetry and from the currents and fashions of a new era. Yet, in view of his exclusive devotion to religious poetry, it is doubtful whether new fashions would have interested him, even supposing he was aware of them. The inventory of his library does not furnish a real clue, for oddly enough it contains only one book of English poetry: Anne Bradstreet's verses. Perhaps the most teasing of all questions that remain unanswered is why he directed his heirs never to publish his verse. Of the many possible answers that suggest themselves, none seems more consistent with the glimpse one catches of his quiet life, his abiding love for his Redeemer, than such as argues a modesty and a sense of human unworthiness that was thorough-going. Taylor seems to have been free from the last infirmity of noble minds.

Of Taylor's contemporaries, one is in the habit of praising "The Tenth Muse" for her charming sincerity, the very local Benjamin Tompson for smoothness, and the well remembered Michael Wigglesworth for historic importance and an occasional stanza of power. The flaws of Taylor's metrics are plain; yet here was a provincial minister and physician who chose poetry the more radiantly to honor the free and boundless mercy of Christ; one who, loving poetry for its own sake, wrote in homely language with a delicacy and brilliance unparalleled in colonial letters.

• • • • •

"I love to Sweeten my mouth with a piece of *Calvin*, before I go to sleep," John Cotton is reported to have said, and in his own day Cotton's remark would have caused no bewilderment. His taste for knotty problems of theology was not the curious whim of an obscure divine, and it is vain to hope for understanding of Puritan literature without realizing that Cotton's predilection was shared by nearly all seventeenth-century gentlemen. Indeed, as we know today, theological dogma, passing through the alembic of Milton's genius, is not unlovely; and in Taylor's verse sequence, dwelling as it does on election, reprobation, free grace, and church fellowship, Puritan doctrine can at times take on a radiant sweetness. Stripped of its specialized theology, Taylor's theme is one that has taxed men's profoundest creative faculties through the ages. It is moral in the sense that all great stories essentially must be, whether written or sung or painted. It is the story of man's struggle to understand himself in his relation to God. The particular "fable" with which Dante or Milton, Wiggles-

worth or Taylor chooses to clothe a moral truth becomes tedious only when the art of its presentation or the spirit behind its conception fails to convince. Yet none of the four, the great together with the lesser, can be understood until the philosophic pattern is displayed. Taylor, as much as Milton, was writing to justify God's ways to man, but his emphasis is different. He did not purpose to give epic effects to Chaos, Heaven, and Hell, but to justify Covenant theology by way of poetic exposition in highly wrought imagery. The limits that he set himself brings *Gods Determinations* more closely into line with the *The Day of Doom* than with *Paradise Lost,* though it is actually quite unlike either. But within the limits, Taylor displays a talent more akin to that of the greater poet for dressing old concepts in memorable language.

To the extent that *Gods Determinations* is written with speaking characters it resembles a morality play, but the speakers develop no dramatic individuality. In all, six are presented: Mercy, Justice, Christ, Satan, the Soul, and a Saint, that is, the "Pious Wise" man, who has experienced reversion to faith. In delineation Satan, even as with Milton, is the most nearly dimensional, though even the shadowy Satan achieves no dramatic entity. The thirty-five sequences have lyric, rather than dramatic, unity, and the seven paeans which conclude the poem move with splendid swiftness to a finish that raises the whole sequence far above mere versified expositions. The color and tone rarely sink into bathos. Taylor carries to his Saviour "wagon-loads" of love; Satan appears with "goggling eyes," inducing sinners as "Jayle Birds" to ride "pick-pack." The metaphoric extravagances seldom strain the reader's sense of the appropriate, and the imagery is drawn from the homely experiences of a pastor and physician; from the world which Taylor knew, not from literary conventions. It is in such characteristics that the charm of Taylor's individuality finds scope.

Gods Determinations opens with a "Preface" celebrating God as the Creator who molded the world, laid its cornerstone, spread its canopies, made its curtain rods, bowled the sun in a cosmic bowling-alley, and above the whole hung the stars as "twinckling Lanthorns." Man was created, sinned, and thereby lost the world. In the short "Prologue" following, man, a "Crumb of Earth," will glorify this "Might Almighty," and Taylor, breathing a hope that his pen may move aright, invokes God's aid lest his "dull Phancy" stir, not mercy, but scorn. The story begins with a brief account of man's fall, and his consequent fear of divine retribution. Justice and Mercy, seeing the creature "Sculking on his face" fall to debate, in language couched in the legal phraseology so often adopted by Covenant theologians, over the question whether man deserves salvation. Mercy argues that

Though none are Sav'd that wickedness imbrace,
Yet none are Damn'd that have Inherent Grace.

He points out that Christ, as scapegoat, took upon himself the sins of mankind, purchasing for the creature His "milkwhite Robe of Lovely Righteousness." But the creature is still crippled by his fall. Mercy pities his infirmity, but realistically concludes that, though man has "broke his Legs, yet's Legs his Stilts must bee." The pity goes further still, for grace will mend the injury, yet man has blindly and foolishly rejected it. Mercy's gift is scorned:

But most he'l me abuse, I feare, for still
Some will have Farms to farm, some wives to wed:
Some beasts to buy; and I must waite their Will.
Though while they scrape their naile or scratch their head,
Nay, though with Cap in hand I Wooe them long,
They'l whistle out their Whistle e're they'l come.

Justice advises that the best way for man to achieve happiness is to obey the moral law, the Ten Commandments; for he can never win salvation on his own merits.

Whos'ever trust doth, to his golden deed
Doth rob a barren Garden for a Weed.

But Mercy's plea wins Justice over, for by the terms of the new covenant of grace God's mercy supersedes His justice. Man therefore is bound over to Mercy, who knows that salvation is promised by God to all who have faith in Christ, whose purchase procured man's pardon.

For Justice nothing to thy Charge can lay;
Thou hast Acquittance in thy surety.

The significance of the debate and its conclusion is lost on man, who peeps about "With Trembling joynts, and Quivering Lips," aware only of his lapsed estate, fearing the consequences of the compact which he broke.

Thus man hath lost his Freehold by his ill:
Now to his Land Lord tenent is at Will,
And must the Tenement keep in repare,
Whate're the ruins and the Charges are.

Crippled and footsore, mankind is invited by God to a "mighty sumptuous" repast, and for the journey thither "the Sinfull Sons of men" are provided a royal coach. But most of them regard the feast of graces spread before them as mere "Slobber Sawces." So froward are they in their dullness that they "hiss piety" and scant all graces. Mercy and Justice are angered into a pursuit of men, to bring them to the table by force, but the congregation divides into ranks and flees from God's presence. Soon captured, the "poor souls" sue for pardon, while Satan appears to taunt them. In their despair they address Christ for aid, and his reply cheers them, until Satan, who "Doth winnow them with all his wiles" charges them with apostasy, saying that no hope exists for men so steeped in villainy and sin. In extended debate between Satan and the Soul, both the inward and the outward man are accused of deadly sins. The Soul cries out in agony to Christ again, and is answered with lines that radiate a graciousness so real, so poignantly touching, that the reader cannot fail to experience with Taylor his devout emotion. The ecstasy of joy prompted by Christ's reply brings to an end the part of the poem dealing with the second rank: those who, seriously regenerate, have found salvation by faith.

At this point a third rebellious rank, who have progressed but a short way in their regeneration, come under Satan's lashing sophistry, and are moved to bewail their helplessness in a threnodial dialogue. But even though they fully anticipate eternal death, they look about once more to be comforted by their former champion Mercy, for "If dy we must, in mercy's arms wee'l dy." The Soul is now prepared to receive assistance from one who has truly experienced sanctification; one who is properly regenerate and knows how to sympathize with as well as instruct unregenerate man. In the person of such a "Pious Wise" one, or Saint, the Soul finds help, and with him enters into dia-

logue. The Saint knows how to resolve the doubts which the Soul raises.

But muster up your Sins, though more or few:
Grace hath an Edge to Cut their bonds atwo.

Satan, he explains, is impotent in the face of Christ's limitless grace. Even after we are reborn we tend to revert to our natural state, and such flaws as appear even in saints darken or stain the color of "that thrice Ennobled noble Gem," the Soul:

Are Flaws in Venice Glasses bad? What in
Bright Diamonds? What then in man is Sin?

But the grace working in us is the needlework of Providence, sometimes weather beaten, and never fully unrolled. It is therefore not to be judged now, when we would be able to see and understand so little of it. We know only that the grace within *does* work. Above all, the Saint reminds his listener, that

If in the golden Meshes of this Net,
(The Checkerwork of Providence) you're Caught,
And Carri'de hence to Heaven, never fret:
Your Barke shall to an Happy Bay be brought.

And finally, the Saint advises, lose yourself in contemplation of the happiness which is the end for which God designed his creature. Give over the questioning whether God cares for you.

Call not in Question whether he delights
In thee, but make him thy Delight.

It is at this point that the arguments for grace and faith and regeneration in terms of Covenant theology, neatly presented as they have been, give way to an art that raises the poem by a lyrical outburst into a place far beyond anything achieved by Americans until long after Taylor's day. The Soul is now convinced of its sin, the first step in regeneration, and moves rapidly through the stages toward glorification, that final state of felicity which can never be completed on earth. The last seven lyrics, each conceived in a different metrical pattern, animate religious doctrine with creative fire. Though they can stand as authentic lyrics by themselves, viewed as a climax to the whole sequence, their effect is symphonic. The awakening Soul's discovery of its power is uttered timidly at first, but as realization turns to conviction, its cry is triumphantly flung out:

methinks I soar
Above the stars, and stand at Heavens Doore.

From this point to the end, the joy of achievement finds glowing expression in the illuminated faith of the poet, set forth with metaphoric brilliance.

• • • • •

We cannot read Taylor's *Sacramental Meditations* without a deep awareness of his overwhelming devotion to Christ's love, and his absorption in the being of his Savior. He expresses himself with autobiographic intimacy. At first we may wonder that a Puritan would abandon himself so fully to a passionate religious exaltation. Such an ardor as he felt may lead the unwary to conclude that Puritans were sacramentalists, or that Taylor was in some degree unorthodox; that somewhere here is displayed an extreme view of the efficacy of the sacraments; the view that the sacraments themselves by Christ's institution confer grace upon the recipient by direct spiritual efficacy. But the truth is otherwise. The *Meditations* need no analogues among Anglo-Catholic sacramentalists to explain their adoration of Christ. At the core of Puritanism, as it was practiced in seventeenth-century New England, are to be found all the humility and all the passionate love for Christ that are necessary.

In common with members of all Christian churches, Puritans observed the sacraments of baptism and the Eucharist, or Lord's Supper, as they preferred to call it. But the seventeenth-century Puritans of New England had an especially compelling reason for assigning to the ordinance of the Lord's Supper an importance which elsewhere it did not always achieve. The foundation of their religious belief was Covenant theology, and of this form Taylor was a thoroughly orthodox exponent. Covenant theology postulated an agreement or compact between God and Adam whereby God freely promised Adam, and through him all his posterity, eternal happiness, providing only that Adam obey God's injunction. But mankind forfeited God's promise when Adam broke the compact, the Covenant of Works, and thereby were subject to God's wrath and condemnation. Nevertheless, God, of His own free will, instituted a new Covenant of Grace, by which all men were given reason to hope for salvation, on condition only that they believe in Christ. Since it was only through Christ's supreme and willing sacrifice of himself that men could now hope to win eternal bliss, they had therefore an even more compelling reason to live up to the terms of the agreement, and to honor the memory of Christ's death and resurrection. Though the Puritan had no dispute with his Anglican brethren about the meaning of the Lord's Supper, his approach to it was undertaken with full knowledge that for him there was no salvation unless he could actively participate in the humility which he must feel toward himself for the first broken covenant, and could rejoice at the thought that Christ stood sponsor for him in the second. If only he might seal his part of the compact!

Thus it becomes clear that, though the manner in which Puritans observed the ordinance of communion remained strictly Calvinistic, and conformed essentially to that which obtained in the Anglican church, the intensity of their observance was more keenly motivated. To the Puritan, mankind had barely escaped a most terrible damnation solely because God had willingly and with supreme loving-kindness instituted a new covenant. He had designed it entirely for man's happiness, since, as Milton said:

> God doth not need
> Either man's work or his own gifts.

Mankind had forfeited all reasonable expectation of salvation by breaking the terms of the first covenant, and God's sealing of a new one was unparalleled kindness. Throughout, God had treated men with perfect justice, but he had gone still further. Having looked upon men as reasonable creatures from whom he did not expect mere blind obedience, God above all desired their happiness, since they alone of all creatures were able to achieve it. They possessed such stock of inherent grace as, by improvement, could win for them felicity. "What is Vanity," exclaimed Samuel Willard, "but a missing the End?" Thus

it was with a heart made especially humble by the immediacy of God's free grace and Christ's boundless love that the Puritan approached the Lord's table.

Except for the exalted place which Puritans gave to the Scriptures, and their covenantal doctrine of man's relation to God, together with certain less central questions of ritual and polity, they were in almost total agreement with the Anglican creed. The emigrations to Massachusetts during the decade of the 1630's were not composed of Separatists, but of Episcopalians fleeing Archbishop Laud's "innovations in religion," since his changes in ritual tended toward Roman practice. In all ways Puritanism had stemmed from Anglicanism, and it therefore recognized in the matter of sacraments only baptism and the Eucharist. On this point both sects were Sacramentarians, that is, opposers of the Roman Catholic doctrine of transubstantiation and the Lutheran theory of consubstantiation. They maintained that Christ ordained those two sacraments and none other, disputing with learned casuistry the Latin doctors who contended that Christ had instituted all seven. The violence which Anglicans felt toward the Roman Catholic doctrine was carried over into the Puritan churches of New England with fierce intensity, and at no point do their objections appear more cogently argued than in their defence of the Lord's Supper. To orthodox Puritans it was explicitly not a converting ordinance, though it was a means whereby men were helped to a state of salvation by conversion. There was no "cultism" in their theory of sacraments, nor is there the least indication of any in Taylor's *Meditations*.

The best New England spokesman on these points was Samuel Willard, vice president of Harvard College, and minister of the Old South Church in Boston from 1676 till his death in 1707. Once a month from January 31, 1687/8, until April 1, 1707, Willard gave a series of public lectures on the Assembly's Shorter Catechism, that body of doctrine on which both Puritan and Anglican faith was founded. The fame of Willard's sermons drew large numbers, and a demand for their publication was finally answered by the posthumous issue of a nine-hundred-page folio volume. Its exposition of the ordinance of the Lord's Supper as it was practiced in the Puritan churches establishes the ardor and humility of Taylor's *Meditations* as thorough-going and essentially Puritan qualities. God had made a promise, so the doctrine is expounded, and the sacrament was a seal to the instrument. How invigorating, then, how glorious was the assurance thus given to all participants!

The idea of the seal, as an actual wafer authenticating the royal charter, is stressed both in the general Puritan theory and in Taylor's poetry. The sacrament thus became a writ or warrant, a *sacramentum*, given under the security of God's explicit pledge "to signify the outward Signs and Seals of the New Covenant," binding both the sovereign and the recipient. To be sure, the terms of the charter did not postulate the sacrament as a converting ordinance: that is, it did not make men Christians. It was a means toward conversion by way of the Word of God, the Scriptures, the principal medium; and to that it was annexed. Its efficacy was confirmed in the Covenant of Grace. At this point the Puritan and Catholic theory of the Eucharist differs centrally, for to the Puritan the operation of the sacrament is moral, not physical or "natural". The bread and wine of the Lord's Supper, the Puritans maintained, was the real spiritual presence of Christ, as Calvin had taught, but it was not the physical Christ. There was no mysterious transubstantiation of the Eucharist into Christ's physical body. The fact that by Roman Catholic doctrine the laity should be denied the wine, which was reserved for the priesthood, seemed blasphemous. Other details of Catholic administration were deemed objectionable: the bread placed in the mouth, rather than the hand; the giving of it unbroken.

The Puritan's constant analysis of his emotions and understanding, his searching of his heart and mind, are well-known characteristics. They were never demanded with more importunity than at the sacred rite of the Lord's Supper. Taylor's *Meditations* but heighten and configure the terms which Willard employs in describing the necessary preparation.

> And if none be admitted but such as are Knowing and Orthodox in Principles, make a Profession of Subjection to Christ, and their Conversations are as becometh Christians, or if they have been Scandalous, testify [their] Repentance and Reformation; there will be no blame upon the Churches of Christ who entertain them.

Though men must examine their worthiness and "preparedness," yet its presence does not "at all intend a Personal Merit, . . . for when in a Legal sense we are most sensible of, and affected with our own Unworthiness, we are Evangelically most Worthy; and the word itself properly signifies, *meet for a thing*. . . . And it is certain, that a Man may be Habitually prepared, and yet Actually unprepared, and be very unfit for present Communion in it, and so lose the benefit of it. And the reason of this is, because of the remaining Corruption which in this Life abides in the best of God's People, which puts a woful impediment to their receiving of Spiritual good by any Ordinance." Thus the heart must be searched, each man looking into his own, "to find enough to humble us, by reason of so much Corruption that we shall discern to be stirring in us, and so much Infirmity attending on all our Graces."

With the heart prepared, then, the partaker was ready to experience the chief design of the ordinance, which is to set forth Christ's love; and the act of eating and drinking gives men "an heart-affecting representation of it." Willard's exposition reveals that the Puritan emphasis, in administering communion, directed men to experience the ardent intensity of Christ's redeeming love. The very images themselves by which Willard clothes the figure of that love are so essential to Puritan thought that Taylor's adoption of them in the *Meditations* was inevitable. Willard says that those are wrong who partake unless they believe the benefit comes because of Christ's "Mediatorial Sufferings, which he suffered in his Humane Nature, to make Satisfaction to offended Justice."

> This Ordinance is called a Feast, and Feasts are made for friendship; which supposeth Love, and that without dissimulation. . . . In a Word, it is to be a Commemoration of the greatest Love, which cannot be done as it ought to be, without the reciprocation of our most ardent and intense Love. . . . If there be any thing that we love better, or equally with him, we do not Love him at all. So that tho' there is a Love which we owe to the Creature, yet when it comes in competition with this, it is comparatively hatred. . . . If we Love him as we ought, he is our all. . . . If we do not come to enjoy him,

and lie in his Embraces, we do not come with a right design, nor can we expect to profit.

Thus does Willard make clear that an ardent humility is basic in Puritan faith. It is that quality precisely which Taylor carried over into the *Sacramental Meditations*; he but enriched and expanded the figures. His intensity was shared, though surely not equaled, by every Puritan partaker of the holy ordinance. (pp. 16-28)

> *Thomas H. Johnson, "His Poetry,"in* The Poetical Works of Edward Taylor, *edited by Thomas H. Johnson, Rockland Editions, 1939, pp. 16-28.*

WALLACE CABLE BROWN (essay date 1944)

[*In the following excerpt, Brown allies Taylor's poetry with metaphysical verse.*]

The Poetry of the early American Edward Taylor, recently published for the first time, has received some critical evaluation—notably by Professors Thomas H. Johnson and Austin Warren. Mr. Johnson emphasizes the historical and ideological aspects of Taylor's work [see excerpt dated 1939]; Mr. Warren, esthetic and technical. Both have remarked the "metaphysical" qualities of this poetry; and Mr. Warren in particular identifies it with the "baroque" in the English metaphysical tradition. The term "baroque," however, describes only one aspect of that tradition, and, I believe, only one aspect of Taylor's work. At his best he went beyond this limitation and became a fullfledged, if minor, metaphysical poet.

The simplest and most obvious relationship between Taylor and the English metaphysicals appears in the characteristic of metrical roughness, which Jonson declared Donne should be hanged for having so much of! Metrical roughness of various kinds is a commonplace in Taylor's verse. (p. 186)

All of Taylor's published poems are, for better or worse, a poetry of "wit" in the seventeenth-century sense. As used by the metaphysical poets, this term must include at least the *discordia concors* of Dr. Johnson and the "sensuous apprehension of thought" of Mr. T. S. Eliot, in both of which intentional ambiguity and a specialized vocabulary are highly significant. In some of Taylor's poems the "wit" attains a level no higher than that of a Benlowes or a Cleveland; but in his best work Taylor's "wit" is genuinely metaphysical.

The "heterogeneous ideas," first emphasized by Dr. Johnson as characteristic of metaphysical poetry, appear throughout Taylor's work. On one level, heterogeneity takes the form of the serious pun, the oxymoron, and the deeper and more thoughtful paradox, each using intentional ambiguity as the relational device. . . . (p. 188)

On a more complex level, heterogeneity of ideas appears in the language of sharp contrasts between the abstract erudite and the concrete commonplace, and in the imaginative distance between the focal points of the imagery. Thus one of Taylor's prayers for the spiritual life takes the following form:

> Lord, ope the Doore: rub off my Rust, Remove
> My sin, And Oyle my Lock: (Dust there doth shelfe).

My Wards will trig before thy Key: my Love
Then, as enliven'd, leape will on thyselve.

• • • • • • •

Adorn me, Lord, with Holy Huswifry:
All blanch my Robes with Clusters of thy Graces:
Thus lead me to thy threashold: give mine Eye
A Peephold there to see bright glories Chases.
Then take mee in: I'le pay, when I possess
Thy Throne, to thee the Rent in Happiness. . . .

The most important effect of these contrasts in metaphysical poetry is the shock or surprise that comes from the domesticating of the Infinite: like Herbert, Taylor looked on God's "furniture so fine, And made it fine to me."

When, however, we go deeper and attend to the significance of the contrasts, we approach the essence of the metaphysical esthetic. First, there is the peculiar effect on the imagination of the great distances between the focal points of the imagery. In one passage Taylor pictures the means of salvation as "the Chariot of the King of Kings," moving among people who treat it as "Some rare Commodity," the price of which they refuse to pay:

It is the Chariot of the King of Kings:
That all who Glory gain, to glory brings;
Whose Glory makes the rest, (when spi'de) beg in,
Some gaze and stare, some stranging at the thing,
Some peep therein; some rage thereat, but all,
Like market people seing on a stall
Some rare Commodity, Clap hands thereon,
And Cheapen 't hastily, but soon are gone
For hearing of the price, and wanting pay,
Do pish thereat, and Coily pass away.
So hearing of the terms, whist! they'le abide
At home before they'l pay so much to ride.

The contrasts in this passage are striking and original, but they are not wholly successful. The ideas, although heterogeneous, are too often merely "yoked by violence together." They give the impression of having been fabricated into a pattern instead of having organically grown into one. Furthermore, there is an intellectuality about the picture that cools rather than fires the imagination.

To be successful, the heterogeneous ideas must be compounded into a synthesis—a process attributed by Coleridge to the power of the imagination. Such "reconcilement of opposite or discordant qualities" occurs, I believe, in the following stanza:

Oh! I always breath'd in such an aire
As I suck't in, feeding on sweet Content!
Disht up unto my Soul ev'n in that pray're
Pour'de out to God over last Sacrament.
What Beam of Light wrapt up my sight to finde
Me neerer God than ere Came in my minde?

Here the imaginative distance between the supernatural communion with God and the natural imagery "breath'd," "suck't in," "feeding," "Disht up," "Beam of Light," etc.) is enormous; yet a synthesis between the two is achieved by the imaginative device of intentional ambiguity. The heterogeneous ideas are suddenly brought together and fused through the power of their multiple meanings. The soul, for example, is normally a metaphysical entity; yet in context it partakes of the physical by having something "disht up" to it. And in the last two lines the beam of light, normally a physical phenomenon, has "wrapt" the poet's physical sight into a metaphysical state beyond even the powers of the mind. Furthermore, the key word "wrapt" functions in the double sense of "wrapped" and "rapt."

Through the characteristic of "sensuous apprehension of thought," we make an even closer approach to the essence of the metaphysical esthetic, an approach that continues to employ heterogeneity of ideas and intentional ambiguity as means to this larger end. Here the thinking not only is perceptual, but becomes a quality of the feeling, just as the feeling becomes a quality of the thought. Such a relationship is difficult to prove logically, but I think it can be sensed when illustrated:

What, shall the frosty Rhime upon my locks
Congeale my braine with Chilly dews, whereby
My Phansie is benumbd: and put in stocks,
And thaws not into steams of reeching joy?

• • • • • • •

Lord, let thy Glorious Body send such rayes
Into my Soule, as ravish shall my heart,
That Thoughts how thy Bright Glory out shall blaze
Upon my body, may such Rayes thee dart.
My Tunes shall dance then on these Rayes, and Caper
Unto thy Praise: when Glory lights my Taper.

The sensuous terminology ("frosty," "Congeale," "benumbd," "thaws not into steams of reeching [reeking] joy") carries the burden of the meaning in the first four lines, and is followed by the vivid sensuous contrasts of "Glorious Body," "ravish," "Tunes shall dance," and "lights my Taper" in the concluding stanza. Thus the thought in this passage is communicated through sensuous imagery; and it seems to me that, for the most part, the thought and feeling are instantaneously apprehended, the sensibility unified.

At its best the sensuous apprehension of thought builds up a complex of interrelated meanings and emotion on different levels. The total effect is rich and dramatic, and takes into account the music, thought, and feeling all at once. (pp. 189-92)

Probably the most distinguishing characteristic of metaphysical poetry is its intellectuality in the presence of strong personal emotion—its extreme emphasis, in these circumstances, upon fundamental brainwork. One aspect of this characteristic is of course the sensuous apprehension of thought which we have just considered. But in its best and fullest sense this kind of intellectuality must encompass the whole poem: it must fuse the poem into a tight logical structure. For this reason the imagery in such poetry is functional rather than decorative, and the thought proceeds with a dynamic logic rather than by successive accretions. It is this characteristic of metaphysical poetry—the tight logical structure—that we do not find in "baroque" poetry, which otherwise may be metaphysical.

Much of Taylor's poetry is baroque in that its imagery is a fanciful, if brilliant, elaboration of a theme. But some of his poems are, I believe, metaphysical in the nonbaroque sense. And it is these poems that place Taylor in the full tradition of metaphysical poetry.

"Meditation One" of the First Series is a strongly emotional poem, yet its tight logical structure keeps the emotion under control and enhances its effects. The subject is God's "Matchless Love." The three stanzas are arranged in degrees of decreasing generality from the viewpoint of the poet. In the first stanza God's love is conceived as uniting the finite and the infinite:

> What Love is this of thine, that Cannot bee
> In thine Infinity, O Lord, Confinde,
> Unless it in thy very Person see
> Infinity and Finity Conjoyn'd?

The concluding couplet makes this concept perceptual by means of the Donne-like image:

> What! hath thy Godhead, as not satisfi'de,
> Marri'de our Manhood, making it its Bride?

In the second stanza this love is pictured, in a series of farflung images, as filling heaven, the earth, and even "Overflowing Hell." The final image continues and narrows down the idea behind "Marri'de our Manhood, making it its Bride"—the dual nature (human-divine) of Christ—with this difference: instead of encompassing all mankind, the idea is limited in this second stanza to God's Elect: in hell,

> For thine Elect, there rose a mighty Tide!
> That there our Veans might through thy Person bleed,
> To quench those flames, that else would on us feed.

The third stanza (beginning "Oh! that thy Love might overflow my Heart!") presents the final narrowing down of the subject to the poet himself. Thus from the abstract concept of God's love as "Infinity and Finity Conjoyn'd" we are led through successive stages of decreasing generality to the centering of the problem in the poet's own heart: "Lord, blow the Coal: Thy Love Enflame in mee." (pp. 193-95)

With all of its roughness and extravagance, Taylor's work is surprisingly effective. Its startling vitality is due, in no small measure, to the characteristics of metaphysical poetry which this paper has examined. With the exception of tight logical structure, which he does not always manage to achieve, Taylor's work exhibits all the "earmarks" (as he himself would say) of the metaphysical esthetic. Certainly after all reservations are made, Taylor remains the best American poet before Freneau and the first (and perhaps only) American Metaphysical. (p. 197)

> *Wallace Cable Brown, "Edward Taylor: An American 'Metaphysical'," in* American Literature, *Vol. 16, No. 3, November, 1944, pp. 186-97.*

AUSTIN WARREN (essay date 1948)

[*Warren was an American educator, literary theorist, and critic who wrote widely on religious and philosophical trends in literature. In the following excerpt from* Rage for Order: Essays in Criticism, *he provides a balanced overview of Taylor's work.*]

Uneven . . . is the poetry of Edward Taylor . . . , published for the first time in 1939 under the editorship of Thomas H. Johnson. Taylor, who migrated from Warwickshire to Massachusetts in 1668 and graduated from Harvard in 1671, must be accounted not only the least negligible American poet before Bryant but the latest of known poets writing in the English baroque.

Taylor has his minor ingenuities—for example, his tributes to Harvard's late president: in a quadruple acrostic, the 'trible' is an anagram, "Charles Chauncy—Call in the Churches," while the left-hand initials spell out "President Dyed"; an acrostic chronogram spells out the date of Chauncy's death and his age. Most elaborate in this kind is Taylor's verse letter to his prospective wife, an alphabetic acrostic containing a triangle which in turn encloses a circle. The triangle spells out:

> The ring of love my pleasant heart must bee
> Truly confined within the Trinitie,

and such, by the equivalence of Triangle and Trinity, the ring is; while the circle translates into:

> Loves Ring I send
> That hath no End.

These instances of what the century called "shaped verses" are simple extensions of the 'emblem,' the visualization of a metaphor.

In all his poetry Taylor is a wit. Like Andrewes and Crashaw, he puns in work of serious intentions. He can write: "This cur that is so curst"; Christ "died upon the cross to cross out sins." Nor is he unfamiliar with the more recondite oxymoron, the "dying life and living death," to be met with in Quarles and the Fletchers.

But his chief instrument is the conceit: the homely conceit. The imaginative distance between its terms is the distance between philosophical theology and anthropomorphic piety, and again between anthropomorphic piety and animism. It is not the hyperbolic and honorific use but the domesticating: the shock comes from the modernization, the provincializing, of the Infinite. Taylor's figures for the spiritual life, his constant matter, come from brewery or wine cellar; or from the stalls in the market place at Coventry; or from weaving, the familiar craft of his native Warwickshire; or from the traffic of sedans and coaches; or from the games played, in his youth, by the ungodly:

> Mine Heart's a Park or Chase of Sins: Mine Head
> 'S a Bowling Alley: sins play Ninehole here.
> Phansy's a Green: Sin Barly-breaks in't led.
> Judgment's a pingle: Blindeman's Buff's plaid there.

Taylor's most ambitious piece, *God's Determinations,* opens with a 'preface' in which, like Sylvester and Benlowes, Taylor, reversing the romantic procedure, analogizes nature to the crafts.

> Who Lac'de and Fillitted the earth so fine,
> With Rivers like green Ribbons Smaragdine?
> Who made the Sea's its Selvedge, and it locks
> Like a Quilt Ball within a Silver Box?
> Who Spread its Canopy? Or Curtains Spun?
> Who in this Bowling Alley bowld the Sun?

The obvious comment to make on this kind of writing is that, granted a certain auctorial inventiveness and charmed persistence, it could go on, like Whitman's naturalistic catalogues, without any reason for stopping. Beyond that, one sees that, within the general mode of 'nature = the artificed,' the poet feels no responsibility to arrange his tropes: they go outdoors, indoors, into my lady's chamber, into her wardrobe, without planned movement of parallelism or contrast. And from this absence of more than most general pattern, one sees the poet is scarcely conscious of his pattern's implications. What they are is clear. God, in creating the earth, did not operate like an architect whose responsibility limited itself to blueprints or like a Newtonian Engineer calculating masses and thrusts and pressures; he worked out his designs with the same manual detail with which a dressmaker puts together a dress or a carpenter makes a box. But the poet seems unaware how far his aesthetic refers back to his theology and, so, uncertain of what he is trying, in words, to do.

This 'preface' is not unfairly characteristic of what follows, a long poem partly in the set dialogue of the moralities, partly in lyric strophes. Its modest but indubitable success is in its logic, still more in its psychology. Taylor—even after reference to *Ductor Dubitantium* and *Treatise on the Religious Affections*—is a respectable, a sensitive, casuist.

After a preluding dialogue between Justice and Mercy, Taylor briefly represents the rebellion, from Satan's army, of the elect; and then the drama—an inner drama—begins. Satan is furious at the defection from his ranks and begins a series of dialectic onslaughts calculated to weaken the morale of the recusants. The converts are divided into three 'ranks' or categories; and Satan addresses himself in turn, with psychiatric shrewdness, to the situation of each. As in Herbert's "The Collar," the subtle argumentation is entirely directed against the reality of the religious experience. It is precarious to represent God as a dialectician; and Taylor has the modest advantage over Milton of not making his God a "school-divine." Satan argues; Christ replies with the simple affection of a father. Satan tries all the ambiguities: sin is too slight to bother about, too gross for God to forgive; Grace is "but an airy notion or a name"; doubtful phantasms are the existence of God, of Heaven, and of Hell.

But Taylor reserves his subtler analysis for the dialogues between the soul of the convert and the 'saint,' the more experienced Christian, who knows the sophistries of Satan and the growing-pains of the regenerate. The Soul suffers from scrupulosities: it fears that only fear of Hell, not love of God, motivates it; it fears "under each Duty done, Hypocrisy"; it is troubled by the philosophical objection that the Christian God is but "a Heape of Contradictions high"; it is disturbed by the misconduct of professed Christians. Finally the saint succeeds in reassuring the novice that the devout life is struggle and gradual progress, and the piece ends with seven lyrics expressive of spiritual triumph and rapture. It is characteristic of Taylor's nature (as everywhere discovered in his poetry) that the drama concerns itself with the souls of the elect: this Puritan poet nowhere contemplates the situation of the damned or touches his lips to the minatory trumpet.

The problem of the 'long poem' presents itself all simply to Taylor. He probably never saw *Paradise Lost,* published the year before he left England; his instances would be *The Divine Weeks, Christ's Victory,* and *The Purple Island,* Anne Bradstreet's *Four Elements.* Within his scope were the sustained allegory of Phineas Fletcher or the graceful Spenserian texture of Giles or the simple, unfigured, unpretentious Tudor verse of the Tenth Muse; but he elected none of them. The piece suggests drama, though it attempts no adjustment of speech to speaker. Of course, Spenser and Milton make none either; but then there is an

epic style to be established, a style consistent in its elegance or opulence. The conceitist method, admirably suited either to the lyric, which it provides with initial structure, or to the short piece, satiric or elegiac, in which constant metaphoric explosion can operate brilliantly, is ill suited to the continuum of the epic or the dramatic. Taylor did not attempt it as seriously as did Du Bartas. Only the lyrics within *Determinations* have tolerable poetic success: the dialogue and narrative oscillate between unreconciled manners in a fashion not to have been tolerated by Giles Fletcher. Without adjustment, the style is now rhetorical or juristic, now colloquial; the diction now theologic, now provincial. Unaware of the stratifications in his vocabulary, Taylor does not know how to expose them with intent and for an effect. And his handling of the trope has equal uncertainty. The "Effects of Mans Apostacy," the first section, opens with an extended if not very original conceit of sin storming the fortress of the heart, which is pursued, with tolerable application, for something like thirty lines, then dropped for straight narrative. There follows a Dantean simile, quite alien in tone and technique:

> Then like a Child that fears the Poker Clapp
> Him on his face doth on his Mothers lap
> Doth hold his breath, lies still for fear least hee
> Should by his breathing lowd discover'd bee....

Taylor is seen to better advantage in his lyrics, within and without the *Determinations.* Between 1682 and 1715 he composed over two hundred **"Sacramental Meditations"** (of which Johnson's selection prints thirty-one). It was the poet's custom to celebrate the Lord's Supper about five times a year and to write for each observance a poem based upon some passage of Scripture. Though the majority of the texts are taken from the Gospels, more than seven come from the Song of Songs, which Taylor, following the traditional practice of Christendom and the immediate precedent of Quarles in Book IV of his *Emblems,* interprets allegorically.

A better than average example of his lyrics is **"Meditation Eight,"** from the Johannine hint, "I am the living bread."

> I kenning through Astronomy Divine
> The Worlds bright Battlement, wherein I spy
> A Golden Path my Pensill cannot line
> From that bright Throne unto my Threshold ly.
> And while my puzzled thoughts about it pore,
> I find the Bread of Life in't at my doore.
>
> When that this Bird of Paradise put in
> This Wicker Cage (my Corps) to tweedle praise
> Had peckt the Fruite forbid: and so did fling
> Away its Food, and lost its golden dayes,
> It fell into Celestiall Famine sore,
> And never could attain a morsell more.
>
> Alas! Alas! Poore Bird, what wilt thou doe?
> This Creatures field no food for Souls e're gave:
> And if thou knock at Angells dores, they show
> An Empty Barrell: they no soul bread have.
> Alas! Poore Bird, the Worlds White Loafe is done,
> And cannot yield thee here the smallest Crumb.
>
> In this sad state, Gods Tender Bowells run
> Out streams of Grace: And he to end all strife,
> The Purest Wheate in Heaven, his deare-dear Son
> Grinds, and kneads up into this Bread of Life.
> Which Bread of Life from Heaven down came and stands

Disht in thy Table up by Angells Hands.

Did God mould up this Bread in Heaven, and bake,
Which from his Table came, and to thine goeth?
Doth he bespeake thee thus: This Soule Bread take;
Come, Eate thy fill of this, thy Gods White Loafe?
Its Food too fine for Angells; yet come, take
And Eate thy fill! Its Heavens Sugar Cake.

What Grace is this knead in this Loafe? This thing
Souls are but petty things it to admire.
Yee Angells, help: This fill would to the brim
Heav'ns whelm'd-down Chrystall meele Bowle, yea and
higher,
This Bread of Life dropt in thy mouth doth Cry:
Eate, Eate me, Soul, and thou shalt never dy.

Taylor's curious coupling of "thing" and "brim," matched in other poems, shows not only that he did not sound terminal *g* but that he accounted nasals a satisfactory rhyme; and elsewhere he allows loose consonances and assonances to count as rhyme. These latitudes share with his Warwickshire provincialisms, his downright coinages, his inversions and other awkward, sometimes unconstruable constructions (like that in the opening stanza) in giving to this poem and his others a primitive vigor and naïveté irrelevant to the baroque aesthetic and unparalleled in other 'metaphysical' verse of the period.

Donne's celebrated prosody in the Satires, like that of other free writers of pentameter iambic, provides its approximate pattern by offering, in a line, either five strong stresses, without calculation of weak syllables, or ten syllables, without calculation of stresses, trusting that the two latitudes will balance to a conversational verse. But Taylor, though he had an iambic rhythm in his memory, seems chiefly to have counted the syllables; and his characteristic practice is to write a line slowed up by its extra stresses. "They no soul bread have" requires an equal weight to each syllable. The line of monosyllables, "What Grace is this knead in this Loafe? This thing," is best read as spondaic. Like other poets, ancient and contemporary, who reduce the flexible music of their rhythms, Taylor compensates by supplying rather copious alliteration—not as structure but as pure and simple phonetic pleasure.

The stiffness of Taylor's lines must not be attributed merely to prosodic awkwardness. Unquestionably he preferred a packed line; like greater poets—Donne, Hopkins, and Crane he was impatient of space given to prepositions and articles and other poetic neutralities. Taylor's "Heav'ns whelm'd-down Chrystall meele Bowle" is less rare in kind for him than, for George Herbert, is the "Christ-side-piercing Spear" of "Prayer."

The poem, which in spite of its inversions seems modern, has the force of its compression, its density. But its chief character is its metaphorism. Taylor is capable—one sees from **"The Ebb and Flow"** and **"Huswifery"**—of working out, neatly and precisely, a conceit: the latter poem tidily analogizes the Christian life to all the instruments and processes of cloth-making—the spinning wheel, the distaff, the reel, the loom, the web, the fulling mills, until the robes of salvation are ready for the pious wearing. Such poems, better called short allegories than extended conceits, are, however, less typical of Taylor and poetically less impressive than the poem before us, of which the method, more bold, is less surely prosecuted.

"Meditation Eight" has the advantage of ending with its two best stanzas. Taylor begins uncertain of direction and with trite locutions (like "golden path" and "bright throne"), locutions bad exactly in the wrong way for baroque poetry. Then the bird figure occurs to him: the soul is bird of Paradise in a double sense—child of heaven and heir of Eden's Adam, who was put in the 'cage' of the Garden as the Soul has been put into that of the Body, to sing God's praises, but who (like his descendant soul) has instead eaten of the forbidden fruit. Taylor manages this equivalence neatly for three lines: the "wicker" cage can well stand for the tree-shaded garden; "peckt" properly modifies bird as well as man. But after that he has his difficulties: while, for a stanza more, evoking the soul as bird, he has really ceased thinking in terms of the figure, without knowing how to return to the narrative "I" of the first stanza; and, before he shapes the "I" into a "thou," he takes in transit a scriptural enough figure of God's running bowels which, however scriptural, is too strong a trope to be thrust, briefly and unsignificantly, into a poem with its own central boldness. "To end all Strife" seems pure aid to the rhyme, since (though there is famine) no conflict has been mentioned.

Then, happily, Taylor finds his tone and theme, already sounded (under the accidental protection of the 'bird') in the third stanza: the translation of Supersubstantial Bread, the *panis angelicus,* into domestic and animistic terms. Even in the last stanzas, the method is too libertine for Donne or Herbert: but the devices associate themselves, in baroque fashion, about surprises—surprises of bearing down with a poet's literalness upon the propositions that Christ is the Bread (therefore subject to all the accidents and comparisons to which bread is subject). The total effect of the poem is amateurish but—by virtue of persistent episodic interest and a theme most efficiently defined as the poem nears its end—powerful.

"The Reflexion," upon the text, "I am the rose of Sharon," is a brilliant piece. In accordance with Taylor's frequent fashion, each stanza is allotted its own conceit, while the textual image, the rose, appears and reappears.

Once at thy Feast, I saw thee Pearle-like stand
'Tween Heaven and Earth, where Heavens Bright glory all
In streams fell on thee, as a floodgate and,
Like Sun Beams through thee on the World to Fall.
Oh! Sugar sweet then! My Deare sweet Lord, I see
Saints Heaven-lost Happiness restor'd by thee.

Shall Heaven and Earth's bright Glory all up lie,
Like Sun Beams bundled in the sun in thee?
Dost thou sit Rose at Table Head, where I
Do sit, and Carv'st no morsell sweet for mee?
So much before, so little now! Sprindge, Lord,
Thy Rosie Leaves, and me their Glee afford.

Christ, as the Rose, offers his sacramental presence; he "sits Rose at Table Head" and carves a morsel of what is at once meat, bread, flower, and supreme value. Sometimes we can visualize Taylor's conceit, after the fashion of an Italian or Flemish primitive, in two or three strong colors against a flat gold background, or of a seventeenth century 'emblem,' an engraving which literally translates into graphic terms a literary figure: so one can read the Pearl, through which sun-beams stream down upon a terrestrial globe; so one can read the opening of another poem of Taylor's, a 'song of innocence';

My shattered Phancy stole away from mee
(Wits run a Wooling over Edens Parke)
And in Gods Garden saw a golden Tree,
Whose Heart was All Divine, and gold its barke:
Whose glorious limbs and fruitfull branches strong
With Saints and Angells bright are richly hung.

But "Dost thou sit Rose" is more complex: it at once invites and repels visualization. Exciting by its compression, it is, and is not, connected with the figures which precede and follow it. Is the preceding "thee," compact with bright glories, the anthropomorphic figure of Christ as the Rose? Whichever, it is difficult not to avoid a connotative overlapping of Christ, the Rose, and the Sun of Righteousness: "in the sun in thee" consists of two disjunct phrases, one of which goes with "bundled," the other with "lie," but juxtaposed as they are, one takes "thee" also as appositive of "sun." And then in the last couplet, have we left the Table for the Garden? The answer has to be indecisive, for the "rosie leaves" equate the "sweet morsels" of the sacred feast, yet the figure of distribution takes a new and garden turn: "springde" (spread) your leaves, and spreading them share with me their "Glee"—their joy, mirth, music. The "rosie leaves" must be the petals: the rose is to open, tendering its petals and their glee, which is perhaps first their equivalence of music, their "sugar sweet" fragrance, then their spiritual delight, their mystical joy. Thus to explicate the stanza is to show Taylor's fancy moving playfully in a mode nearer to *symbolisme* than to the logical prosecution of a conceit.

Something like seven of Taylor's poems have whole virtue; of the others, there are few without a signal stanza or a brilliant line. The work is very uneven; exciting to look into, disappointing to read with consecutive patience. The equivalent can be said of *Theophila*'s Edward Benlowes; of Du Bartas and his translator, Sylvester. Conceitist poetry is never simply commonplace. Bad classical poetry is worn, threadbare, insipid; bad baroque poetry is either a succession of labored ingenuities or a series of uncontrolled conflagrations, spasmodic eruptions, meaningless violences: its worst is a kind of coldly calculated fury. Taylor is sometimes a neat little artisan but more often an unsteady enthusiast, a naïve original, an intermittently inspired Primitive. He is rarely uninteresting, on some level; but his taste—and there is a baroque taste as well as a classical—is unschooled, unsteady. Even Cleveland has taste—of an equilibristic sort: he moves at the pitch of keen intellectual vaudeville; he is a kind of erudite version of the *New Yorker*'s poets. But Taylor is nearer to being an ancestor of another uneven village poet, Emily Dickinson.

Of the poets with whom Taylor invokes comparison—Crashaw, Blake, Dickinson, Hopkins, Crane—all are greater and all are frequent and more sure in their successes. But is it enough to say of Taylor that, like the others, he is at worst still a poet. (pp. 7-18)

> Austin Warren, "Edward Taylor," in his Rage for
> Order: Essays in Criticism, *1948. Reprint by the*
> *University of Michigan Press, 1959, pp. 1-18.*

KENNETH B. MURDOCK (essay date 1949)

[*Murdock was an American educator, editor, and author whose works were almost entirely devoted to colonial literature. In the following excerpt from* Literature and Theology *in Colonial New England, he finds that Taylor's verse derives from but is not hidebound to Puritan poetry.*]

No other poet in early New England had Taylor's talent and no other followed so closely the pattern of the English metaphysical poets of the seventeenth century. Those poets, mostly Anglicans and not Puritans, had built their verse on metaphor and simile, using the figures both for their intellectual and emotional suggestions and endeavoring to convey the full sense of an experience by the evocative power of their images. The result was poetry which was often harsh in music and difficult intellectually, but was at its best amazingly successful in expressing concretely religious emotion and the ineffable values of faith. At its worst it was only rhetorical gymnastics or an elaborately carved but still hollow shell of hyperbole, paradox, strained metaphor, and word-play; in the hands of artists as imaginative as John Donne and George Herbert it became the perfect medium for their feeling for the divine. Donne was not popular among the Puritans, partly no doubt because as Dean of Saint Paul's he was a high officer in a church whose officers they distrusted, but probably chiefly because his religious poems were too sensuously conceived, too crowded with imagery savoring rather of this world than of the next. George Herbert the Puritans liked because the central note of his work was the emotion of an individual believer, dependent upon God and sincerely zealous in devotion to Him. His imagery was often drawn from Anglican forms and practices but was, compared to Donne's, restrained, and there are few of his lines that even a strict Puritan could consider dangerous in their appeal to man's vagrant passions.

Edward Taylor was not born until after Donne's death and until the type of poetry which he and Herbert wrote was largely out of fashion, but throughout his own career, lasting well into the neoclassic period of English poetry, he stuck to the forms and devices of the "metaphysical school." So did some other New Englanders before him and contemporaneous with him, but in their work the forms and devices are usually only external patterns, adopted in deference to convention. Taylor's use of the "metaphysical" metaphor and his reliance on the image combining intellectual and emotional appeal as the primary source of poetic effect, seem to represent not subservience to fashion but the choice of a poetic method integrally related to the nature of his emotion and thought. He was by no means merely an imitator, and in spite of the points of likeness between his work and Herbert's or Donne's, Taylor's poems differ essentially from theirs. The major differences stem from his Puritan beliefs. His work is not typical of New England Puritan poetry, because it is richer in insight and more expert in technique, but it is made of characteristically Puritan elements.

He constantly emphasizes the inadequacy of poetry to express the divine and the hopelessness of the religious poet's task unless God's grace has been breathed into him and his work. This note is common in religious poetry, Puritan or not, but the Puritan gave it special emphasis in his desire to keep clear the distinction between the essential truth which was divine and intangible, and the concrete and finite material with which the poet was forced to work. Taylor disparages his own talents:

> My tatter'd Fancy; and my Ragged Rymes
> Teem leaden Metaphors: which yet might Serve

To hum a little, touching terrene Shines.
But Spirituall Life doth better fare deserve.

(pp. 153-55)

Although Taylor goes farther than most Puritans in his use
of sensuous images, he is careful to draw a sharp line between the senses and the spirit, between what allures man
carnally and what saves him from the snares of this world.

Alas! my Soule, product of Breath Divine,
For to illuminate a Lump of Slime.
Sad Providence! Must thou below thus tent
In such a Cote as strangles with ill s[c]ent?
Or in such sensuall Organs make thy stay,
Which from thy noble end do make thee stray?

(p. 157)

Such passages illustrate two important qualities in Taylor.
One is his startling realism in diction and imagery, his
love for the homeliest of colloquial words and for figures
out of the most commonplace aspects of life, in contexts
where the subject seems to demand dignity in vocabulary
and image. Sometimes the effect is merely incongruous;
sometimes it makes vividly dramatic what otherwise
might be tame. The second quality is Taylor's constant use
of speech tone and his constant tendency toward direct
discourse. His poems are usually declamations, spoken addresses, or prayers. The individual believer, the personified Soul, Satan, or even God and Christ are in Taylor less
often described than made to speak for themselves. Here
too the effect is sometimes incongruous and perhaps, in
the case of speeches put into the mouths of God and the
Saviour, shocking, but surprisingly often the utterance is
moving and the dramatic quality intense.

Taylor's longest work was a poetic sequence called *Gods
Determinations Touching His Elect*. It is the story, told in
a series of poems, of God's choosing some men to salvation, of the conflicts the elect go through in order to
achieve assurance through faith, and of the mercy shown
to them. The subject is characteristic of the Puritan, one
more variant on his central theme of the individual pilgrim's progress toward God. But the treatment is not that
of the formal theologian. The ideas are dramatized; the
whole structure is that of drama. Justice and Mercy argue
in a long dialogue about the best treatment of man. Then
comes a narrative interlude of four poems on man's perplexity when called to account for his sins, God's love in
selecting those to be saved, the intransigence of the chosen
in the face of God's decree, and Satan's fury at their escape from his grasp. (pp. 158-59)

The next poem in the sequence is an address of the tormented soul to Christ, its "Honour'd Generall," and this
is followed by Christ's speech in reply. After another short
narrative interlude comes a long dialogue between Satan
and the Soul, and all but four or five of the other poems
in *Gods Determinations* are speeches of Satan, the Soul,
Christ, or God, or dialogues between characters in the divine drama. The remaining verses are lyric outbursts commenting on, and marveling at, what to the poet is the
beauty of the wayfaring soul's search for blessedness and
God's mercy to it. In its structure, then, *Gods Determinations* is essentially a play, with a kind of chorus which
comments on the action or explains parts of it in dramatic
narrative.

A good example of Taylor's skill in capturing the effect of
colloquial and earthy speech is Satan's opening speech in

his dialogue with the Soul. He ridicules the elect, insisting
that their conversion cannot last and that they have left
him for trifling rewards. They are like dogs answering a
whistle:

Soon ripe, soon rot. Young Saint, Old Divell. Loe!
Why to an Empty Whistle did you goe?
What! Come Uncall'd? And Run Unsent for? Stay,
It's Childrens Bread. Hands off: out, Dogs, away.

To this the Soul replies:

It's not an Empty Whistle: yet withall,
And if it be a Whistle, then a Call:
A Call to Childrens Bread, which take we may.
Thou onely art the Dog whipt hence away.

The movement and tone of both speeches is admirably
contrived for purposes of characterization. Satan's is stac-
cato and harsh—the speech of an angry man, using
phrases like whips. The Soul replies more calmly, in
smoother cadences, and the effect is of gentleness opposed
to rage.

Even more striking is Christ's reply to the anguished soul,
which has cried for aid. The first four stanzas are in their
diction and phrasing nothing but a Puritan lullaby or love
song couched in just such language as Puritan fathers and
mothers must often have used to console frightened children, or lovers to comfort each other.

Peace, Peace, my Hony, do not Cry,
My Little Darling, wipe thine eye,
Oh Cheer, Cheer up, come see.
Is anything too deare, my Dove,
Is anything too good, my Love,
To get or give for thee?

If in the severall thou art,
This Yelper fierce will at thee bark:
That thou art mine this shows
As Spot barks back the sheep again,
Before they to the Pound are ta'ne,
So he, and hence 'way goes.

But if this Cur that bayghs so sore,
Is broken tootht, and muzzled sure,
Fear not, my Pritty Heart.
His barking is to make thee Cling
Close underneath thy Saviours wing.
Why did my sweeten start?

And if he run an inch too fur,
I'le Check his Chain, and rate the Cur,
My Chick, keep close to mee.
The Poles shall sooner kiss and greet,
And Paralells shall sooner meet,
Than thou shall harmed bee.

Except for the last three lines about the poles and about
parallels which come perhaps from Taylor's reading of
Donne, these verses are keyed to the simple emotions and
simple language of simple folk. However startling it may
be to have Christ call the soul by pet names, or refer to the
ways of sheep-dogs, or use New England dialect, Taylor's
lines convey poignantly the honesty and warmth of a genuine religious emotion. Few poetic treatments of the same
theme, however dignified their language and imagery, are
more moving than his.

Apart from *Gods Determinations*, most of Taylor's best
work was done in a long series of *Sacramental Medita-*

tions, each written on the occasion of a celebration of the sacrament of the Eucharist. (pp. 161-63)

The imagery of the *Meditations* is throughout warmer, more sensuous, and more sharply pictorial than that of most Puritan poetry. There is a bird of Paradise, there are roses and other flowers, and jewels. There is Taylor's "Kit"—his little violin—and other musical images; there is a special emphasis on perfumes; and there is, in one case, even incense in a censer. For most of this there is Biblical precedent, but Taylor's tendency, as his devotion to The Song of Solomon reveals, is to select the metaphors and similes which have most direct sensuous appeal. The suggestion is that although he was an orthodox Puritan, he felt as a poet a sense of constraint within the bounds of the ordinary plainness and sobriety of Puritan literary style. No one knows why he asked his heirs not to publish his verses, but he may well have felt that in some of them his passionate expression, his delight in color and fragrance, and his sometimes erotically suggestive imagery would offend his graver colleagues. It is probable, too, that he knew that his work, in its more complex passages, would only puzzle the poetically inexpert Puritan audience. (pp. 166-67)

Taylor's poems reveal both the defects and the virtues of the Puritan's literary creed when applied to poetry. His drastically realistic colloquialisms, his constant use of imagery drawn from the most commonplace activities of everyday life—for example, his poem beginning "Make me, O Lord, thy Spin[n]ing Wheele compleat" in which the whole operation of spinning yarn and weaving the cloth becomes an extended metaphor for man's spiritual progress—and his use of events, characters, phrases, and images from the Bible, show the Puritan's reasoned belief in plain language, in material comprehensible to the Puritan audience, and in the supreme authority of Holy Writ. Taylor proves that this belief need not keep a truly gifted artist from writing good, or even great, poetry. On the other hand, his consistent selection of the Biblical imagery richest in color and in sensuous or even erotic effect, and his use in the *Meditations* of the Song of Solomon more often than any other book of the Bible, suggest that as a poet he unconsciously moved away from the relative asceticism of the Puritan toward the Catholic acceptance of the role of the senses in worship. So also the complication and obscurity of some of his verse indicate a rebellion of sorts against the cardinal Puritan doctrine of clarity in expression, a rebellion dictated by a feeling that the fundamental spiritual verities were too mysterious for logical or prosaic exposition and demanded instead all the rich emotional and intellectual suggestiveness of complex "metaphysical" poetry. When he stays on the level of straightforward theological reasoning of the sort of so common in Puritan writing, Taylor is tame and often awkward; when the "quick Passions," which his grandson said he possessed, took command, he became a poet.

The Puritans' loving humility before God, their vision of spiritual beauty, the grandeur of their conception of the divine, and the glory they felt was represented by their individual and collective services as soldiers and pilgrims of Christ, were themes fit for poetry. Taylor made good use of them. The substance of his work is the way of life and the faith of Puritan New England; his poetic method is the expression of his conviction that faith and life were one and that neither the spiritual nor the material had meaning except when they were united. In his finest lines, the union is achieved. Doctrine takes on life and the reader is warmed by the central fire of Puritan piety. (pp. 169-70)

Kenneth B. Murdock, " 'A Little Recreation of Poetry'," in his Literature & Theology in Colonial New England, *Cambridge, Mass.: Harvard University Press, 1949, pp. 137-72.*

ROY HARVEY PEARCE (essay date 1950)

[*Pearce is an American educator, editor, and the author of* Colonial American Writing *(1951) and* The Continuity of American Poetry *(1961). In the following excerpt, he maintains that Taylor's poetry, "if we take it in and for itself, is finally to be comprehended within its matrix in Taylor's Puritan culture."*]

Today some ten years after the discovery and publication of his *Poetical Works,* we know Edward Taylor to be incomparably the best of our colonial poets. Still, we have not been inclined to read him as a colonial poet—as a man whose work was informed by his Puritan culture, as a man whose vocation it was to set down God's Way with Man in the Massachusetts Bay Colony. We have not, that is to say, been much concerned with Taylor's work as a whole, with its very wholeness. Rather we have looked mainly at its surface—caught its metrical roughness, its syntactic complexity, its heterogeneity of materials, its extended conceits, its bold figures and antitheses—and have read Taylor as a baroque (or metaphysical) poet. And herein, certainly, we have achieved something positive. We have been able to find a place for Taylor in that world of seventeenth-century letters—the world of a Herbert, a Quarles, and a Crashaw—which our critics and historians have mapped out for us. But there yet remain Taylor's own New England world and the substance, the wholeness, of a poetry which takes its immediate and particular life from that world. Taylor's poetry, if we take it in and for itself, is finally to be comprehended within its matrix in Taylor's Puritan culture.

The great bulk of Taylor's poetry consists in this: visions of the world of sinful men as it partakes of God and God's order. The attempt in the poems is not to study human experience of order in the world, but rather simply to show how and wherein that order exists. Thus Taylor is fond of discovering analogies of Biblical doctrine in his immediate and imagined surroundings; thus he is constrained everywhere to find an earthly counterpart—however poor and dim—of that which is ineffably holy. For him the problem is not one of demonstrating or dramatizing this equivalence, but of discovering it. For most certainly—and herein, as we shall see, Taylor is most a Puritan—he knows it is there.

This is the pattern in one of the simplest and best known of his poems, **"Huswifery":**

Make me, O Lord, thy Spinning Wheele compleat;
Thy Holy Worde my Distaff make for mee.
Make mine Affections thy Swift Flyers neate,
And make my Soule thy holy Spoole to bee.
My Conversation make to be on thy Reele,
And reele the yarn thereon spun of thy Wheele....

The poet, his human attributes, and part of his immediate world are seen systematically and integrally to body forth

God's way with man. In another poem ("**Upon a Spider Catching a Fly**") there is figured Satan tangling Adam's race. In another ("**The Ebb and Flow**") man's heart is seen first as a tinder box and then as a censer for the holy fire of God's spirit. (pp. 31-2)

Taylor's achievement in such lyrics as these is explicitly one of discovery, most often the discovery of God-informed unity in man's experience in and of his world. Whatever struggle is involved in making such a discovery, however, is not in the poem; it is external, anterior to the poem. For the poet seems assured always that analogies and evidences of God's order are everywhere around him and are to be discovered if only he can bring himself, with God's Grace, to the point of discovery. At his best, the poet registers such analogies and evidences with clarity and precision. The emotional quality of his poems derives from the excitement at the degree of clarity and precision, and focuses directly on those analogies and evidences. What is primary in the poems is not the poet's experience—the poet as man speaking to men—but rather the meaning and understanding—the discovery—which is the end of that experience.

For all his concern with cosmic *discordia concors,* paradox interests Taylor little. Trained in our time on the paradoxes of metaphysical and baroque poetry, we would perhaps give them much more importance than does Taylor. For his world cannot be paradoxical. Dealing with paradox only casually, he appears to dismiss it with ease; he never really treats it as something to be capitalized on, something to be dramatized.... The positive achievement in both ["**Meditation Six**"] and in "**Huswifery**" lies in the adequacy and precision of poetic images to the task of communicating to us the quality of a wholly meaningful, wholly ordered world.

And so it is in *Gods Determinations Touching His Elect,* Taylor's late morality play. Actually, *Gods Determinations* is a series of dialogues which have little or no dramatic effect. If in the debate over the fate of Man, Christ, Satan, Mercy, Justice, and the Soul are made to speak as individuals, there is yet no conflict, no tension, set up between one individuality and another. Mainly, Taylor would show how each figure can be seen analogically in human terms; this is another way of discovering God and God's order in the world the poet knows. Taylor's characteristic poetic method here is identical with the method of the lyrics. (pp. 33-5)

Everywhere in *Gods Determinations* meaning is discovered as elements of earthly experience are found to be analogues of spiritual experience. Taylor's achievement here as elsewhere lies in the fullness and richness of the analogues he discovers for us. Realization of that fullness and richness is, in a way, realization of Taylor's God—realization, that is to say, of the God of Taylor's poetry. Properly speaking, there is no drama, no dialectic, in *Gods Determinations.* There is just discovered evidence, felt to be ready-made, God-made, logically primary and self-explanatory, there for the discovering. This is the way in all of Taylor's poetry.

This is the way, too, in our Puritan poetry in general, in the implicit esthetic of that poetry, and in Puritan cultural theory and practice. Indeed, with the work of intellectual, social, and literary historians in our time, we can begin to comprehend, to locate historically, Taylor's poetry in its context of New England poetry and New England poetics, and these in turn in their context of New England culture. For the Puritan, poetry could not be an end in itself; it was a means to the universal end of Puritan culture—the Glory of God. And there were for the Puritan, certainly, better, more direct means to this end. Not until the later eighteenth century are there in Puritan writing significant evidences of concern with matters of expression and technique, with specifically human meaningfulness in poetry. In Taylor's time (the late seventeenth and early eighteenth centuries) the old Puritan way still held on. For, as Kenneth Murdock has said [in the Introduction to *Handkerchiefs from Paul* (1927)]:

> The Puritan was not hostile to art, but he was relatively indifferent to it. Poetry, music, fine prose, painting, architecture—all these were well enough in their way, but for him, higher than any other reward was the beauty of holiness, the reward of a patient search for God's will and a diligent effort to perform it unflaggingly and with self-forgetful sacrifice. This attitude thrusts the arts into the realm of pastimes, and the Puritan's adventure with God was so thrilling, and, to him, so beautiful, that there were few hours left for pastime.

An artist—a poet—might discover God's will evidenced in the world about him. He would record his discovery, perhaps. And he would proceed to live according to that will, to discover it elsewhere, not to estimate its human significance.

So the great bulk of Puritan poetry that is being exhumed and edited in our time is of a piece with a strenuously, self-consciously orthodox Puritan culture. That poetry might be a "practical" poetry, a poetry which consists of things-to-be-remembered versified that they might be the more easily remembered—verses ranging from the *Bay Psalm Book,* through elegies on the deaths of pious persons, to records of remarkable providences. Or it might be (from our point of view) a "purer" poetry, verses directly involved in praising God—verses ranging from Mistress Bradstreet's imitations of Du Bartas through the work of Wigglesworth, Fiske, and Colman, to the lyrics and morality play of Taylor. Yet everywhere that poetry rises immediately from what I have termed the need for discovering God in His world. (pp. 37-9)

Operating from such a position, reading the book of the world along with the Bible (the two were most certainly complementary, integrated works of God), the Cambridge- or Harvard-trained Puritan might work out the pattern of his culture. It was a logical pattern, a static pattern—there for the observing and judging, there for the discovery.

And this logical pattern of Puritan culture is clearly the logical pattern of Puritan poetry. Recently, in this connection, Rosemund Tuve has shown (in her *Elizabethan and Metaphysical Imagery*) how literally logical is the language and imagery of sixteenth- and seventeenth-century poetry and how the special quality of much seventeenth-century poetry in particular is to be understood historically as that poetry comes under the impress of Ramist logic. For us what Miss Tuve's work comes to is this: that English poets in the sixteenth and seventeenth centuries were concerned with a reality which was necessarily "intelligible" but not necessarily "visible"; that this poetry was thus "logical" and was thus concerned with an immanent principle of meaning in human experience; that training in Ramist logic, especially in the seventeenth century, pushed these tendencies to an extreme, as that logic broke free from the principles of abstract deduction, made dialectics one with poetics, and pictured the world as one in which a fixed, concretely embodied logical scheme could be observed. Thus, in Miss Tuve's words, "a poem . . . has but to examine and state . . . in order to argue the truth or advisability of something." Or, more generally, in [Perry Miller's words in *The New England Mind* (1939)]: "Ideally, all good judgments—sermons, reflections, poems—ought to be . . . a series of self-evident axioms, arranged in artistic sequence." Now, as we must remember, Ramus was the "official" logician in theocratic, insular New England as he could never have been in Old England. And (implicit) Ramist poetics—a poetics of discovery, of examining and stating, of coming upon, of laying open to view—was in effect New England poetics. Puritan poetry here is an extreme case. But Puritan culture, in all its high orthodoxy, was an extreme culture.

It is the very fact that Puritan culture was thus extreme that makes Edward Taylor so much the poet as Puritan. The neatness of the case makes one suspicious, as it should. The suspicion is allayed only when one concludes that the neatness of the case stems ultimately from the neatness, the high orthodoxy, the oppressively self-conscious ordering and integration, of Puritan culture itself. That culture, indeed, cut Taylor down (or should one say, built Taylor up?) to its size. However adequate that culture might have been for major religious experience, it was yet inadequate for major poetry; for it allowed for little play of the individual will—in the last analysis, for little real human drama. Even in the best of Taylor's poetry the value put on specifically human experience is minimal; he concerns himself with just so much human experience as will make communication possible. It is the meaning of the God-ordered world, of God Himself, which is important, not the fact that a man faces that meaning. Taylor sees the man-made wonders of the visible world as little when compared to natural wonders and as nothing when compared to God:

> Nature doth better work than Art, yet thine
> Out vie both works of nature and of Art.

Art is a human product and as such is lowest in the scale of being. Taylor, we recall, felt his own Art to be so low, so much humanly limited, that he gave orders that his heirs should publish none of his writings.

All this we must understand if we are fully to realize the special quality of Taylor's poetry. Certainly we may grant his achievement simply by reading that poetry; yet in order to comprehend it we must see it in its special Puritan milieu. For Taylor, as Puritan poet, the end of the poem is the thing. Whereas for us—and I think properly—the thing is the act of the poem, the poem as composed and communicating. What we see everywhere in Taylor's work is that the end of the poem inhibits the act of composition, and ultimately the act of the poem itself. (pp. 41-3)

As the complexities of specifically human experience come to little as subjects of Taylor's poetry, so the complexities of a reader's experience appear to have come to little as a problem in Taylor's composing. He seems to have written what he knew with as much eloquence as possible; but he

seems equally to have been confident that that eloquence lay immanent in what he knew, not in the telling of it—in the object of discovery, not in the drama of discovering that object. His achievement is in his rendering the quality of the discovered object, of God's order in His world, with such precision and power as only such confidence in that order could make possible. Reading Taylor's poetry, we read his Puritanism. (pp. 45-6)

> *Roy Harvey Pearce, "Edward Taylor: The Poet as Puritan," in* The New England Quarterly, *Vol. XXIII, No. 1, March, 1950, pp. 31-46.*

RICHARD D. ALTICK (essay date 1950)

[*Altick is an American educator, editor, literary scholar, and author whose many titles include* The Scholar Adventurers *(1950),* The Art of Literary Research *(1963), and* Deadly Encounters: Two Victorian Sensations *(1986). In the following excerpt from the first-named work, Altick draws a correlation between Taylor and his contemporary, the English poet Thomas Traherne.*]

Edward Taylor was, in a sense, the American Traherne. Although his poetry has few resemblances to Traherne's he was a younger contemporary of the long neglected English poet, and his dramatic rediscovery came about through another curious accident of literary scholarship. (p. 306)

[When Thomas H. Johnson unearthed Taylor's manuscript volumes in the Yale University Library,] Taylor proved to have been a poet of no mean gifts, although they were not of the kind of which his fellow Puritans could have approved. He had an intense religious emotion which carried him over into mysticism, as it had carried some of the great Anglican religious poets of his century. But what sets him conspicuously apart from other colonial American poets is his use of richly sensuous imagery, almost in the manner of the Roman Catholic poet Richard Crashaw, and of homely, realistic metaphors suggestive sometimes of John Donne and sometimes of George Herbert. Taylor had to express his devotional feeling in terms of the delights of earthly life. It was no doubt because he feared his contemporaries would be outraged by his frank sense of the physical that he refused to publish what he had written. At all events, the rediscovery has been one of the most discussed events of the last decade among students of American literature, and a substantial critical and appreciative literature is growing up about him. In the frequently heard statement that he was "the greatest poet of New England before the nineteenth century" may be the same incautious enthusiasm which for a time inflated the reputation of Traherne. But it has been a happy development, this unlooked-for finding of poetry full of color and vivid imaginativeness in an era which was thought to have produced nothing better than the dull verses of Anne Bradstreet and Michael Wigglesworth. (pp. 307-08)

> *Richard D. Altick, "Discoveries," in his* The Scholar Adventurers, *Macmillan, New York, 1950, pp. 298-318.*

HERBERT BLAU (essay date 1953)

[*Blau is an American educator, theatrical producer, and author on the theater. In the following excerpt, he considers the sacramental imagery in Taylor's poetry and reviews criticism of Taylor's versification and literary aesthetic.*]

Among the dilemmas caused by Calvin's rejection of the orthodox conception of original sin was that regarding sacramental grace. To the congenitally depraved, the satisfactions of communion were simply inaccessible. Whereas the Anglican, whose universal law (according to Hooker) was the law of reason, could make a voluntary movement toward God, the Calvinist, whose universal law was that of predestination, could at best stand and wait. This was true in theory. In fact, however, the Calvinists and especially the American Puritans were in the habit of contradicting the letter of the law. Had Jonathan Edwards interpreted rigorously the doctrine of God's decrees, he could not have preached repentance. Had Edward Taylor remembered it properly his *Sacramental Meditations* might have been considerably different from what they are.

In explaining the importance with which the Puritans regarded the Lord's Supper, Professor Thomas H. Johnson writes of the excessive humility which the Puritan had to feel toward himself for his generic participation in the breaking of the first covenant, and the concomitant joy he could feel at the thought that "Christ stood sponsor for him in the second" [see excerpt dated 1939]. It is this joy which motivates the sacramentarianism of Taylor. In other metaphysical poets, such as George Herbert, we can observe an affective quality of the communion that is very strong; but Herbert was an Anglican and had a theologically legitimate motivation in the doctrine of the Real Presence. Though the Church of England had repudiated the Catholic transubstantiation, it did at least believe that Christ was present at the communion in his spiritual nature. For Taylor, on the other hand, there is no excuse. His celebration of the sacraments is motivated by nothing except an intense feeling for the ritual as ritual. It is the poetic testimony of his illimitable obligation to God. Professor Johnson discusses in this connection the doctrine of justification by faith alone, which to the Anglicans involved an infusion of grace, a movement of free choice towards God and away from sin, and the eventual remission of guilt. For the Puritans, however, there was always the millstone of predestination. The Puritans could hope to win eternal bliss, but they had no way of knowing whether in the original dispensation of grace they were chosen to be saved or damned.

The best they could do, therefore, was to look for signs:

> Nature was instructive to them only in so far as it suggested the hidden mysterious operations of designing agents. God and devil were both active, scheming, hidden powers, each pursuing his own ends by various ministrations, and natural events were therefore to be understood only in so far as they showed evidence of some divine or diabolical plot.

Cotton Mather's diaries give us some idea of the extremes to which this tantalizing game could be carried; and Taylor's *Sacramental Meditations* though they were written for the annual feast of the Lord's Supper, suggest that Taylor himself, like Mather and the later Hawthorne, may have been susceptible to the habit. The concentration on detail, the inordinate fascination for things of the senses, the magnification out of all proportion of the commonest object are perhaps the most salient features of his poetry. And indeed, several of his *Meditations* begin almost as

though he were emerging—albeit exultantly—from a Hawthorne-like trance.

Mr. Roy Harvey Pearce is certainly correct in defining the central experience of Taylor's poetry as that of *discovery*, the "coming upon" or "laying open to view" the "analogies and evidences of God's order" [see excerpt dated 1950]. This is the very essence of Taylor's method and is derived in part from the Ramist logic accepted by the theocratic Puritans. But it is this same process of discovery, of guessing at signs, which on occasion seriously damages the poetry of Taylor by involving him in a quest for limitless particular perspectives, a series of quickly shifting images which, instead of strengthening the logic of the poem, pulls it apart. Moreover, Mr. Pearce's depreciation of the importance of paradox in Taylor's poetry—"(The danger is that we will make this slight paradox into something larger by substituting our logic for the logic of the poem)"—overlooks the fact that paradox in Taylor, as in all Puritan writers, is more pervasive than a consideration of imagery alone would indicate. For the paradox in Taylor is fundamental, going beyond imagery to theology, and is rooted in the basic Calvinistic dichotomy between "free will" and "fixed fate."

"An artist—a poet," Mr. Pearce writes, "might discover God's will evidenced in the world about him. He would record his discovery, perhaps. And he would proceed to live according to that will, to discover it elsewhere, not to estimate its human significance." But, according to the doctrine of predestination, it was impossible for the artist to make such an adjustment, "to live according to that will," to shape his life in just measure to his perceptions, or, as a matter of fact, to make any perceptions at all. The Puritan could guess, but he could not really discover. Now it is true that in practice most Puritans proceeded to ignore their theoretical incapacities. The circumstances of their existence, urgent and arduous, demanded from them, to an extreme degree, those very powers of percipience and volitional action which their dogma denied. But they would not, in conscious utterance, deny their dogma. Consequently, what appears frequently to be a reliance by Taylor upon the less rigorous rationalizations of the Anglican Church must not be deemed purposeful on his part. A minister rather than a theologian, Taylor never cracked his dialectic over the immovable rock of the free will-fixed fate dilemma.

Like Herbert, who in "Divinitie" expressed no inclination to cavil and animadverted on the needle-point logistics of the theologians, Taylor recommended the acceptance of the illusion of good works (no illusion for Herbert, but definitely one for a sound Puritan). In *God's Determinations,* for example, the Saint—one of the justified elect—urges the doubting Soul to repent his sins, despite the implication of the doctrine of predestination, that man has not the power to repent:

> Perform the Duty, leave th'event unto
> His grace that doth both in and outside know.
> Beg pardon for your sins: bad thoughts defy,
> That are cast in you by the Enemy.
> Approve yourselfe to God, and unto his,
> And beg a pardon where you do amiss.
> If wronged, go to God for right, and pray
> Hard-thoughted Saints black-thoughted thoughts away.
> Renew your acts of Faith: believe in him

Who died on the Cross to Cross out Sin.
Allow not any Sin, but if you sin
Through frailty, Faith will a new pardon bring.
Do all Good Works, work all good things you know,
As if you should be sav'd for doing so.
Then undo all you've done, and it deny,
And on the naked Christ alone rely.
Believe not Satan, unbelieve his tales
Lest you should misbelieve the Gospell bales.
Do what is right, and for the right Contend;
Make Grace your way, and Glory'll be your End.

This goes further even than such works as Jonathan Edwards' highly influential *Justification by Faith* in neglecting the ambiguity of the original allocation of grace and stressing the ultimate possibility of man's redemption. Moreover, it is probably this shift in emphasis which prompted Taylor in *God's Determinations* to deal mainly with the uncertainty of the Elect, rather than like Hawthorne in *The Scarlet Letter*, with the tortured souls of the damned.

The most striking characteristic of *God's Determinations* is its compassion. Though the predicaments of the apostate and the doubting Soul are awful to contemplate, the New Testament God is invariably quick to console. In the following passage, for instance, which has the lyrical simplicity of Henry Vaughan's "The Retreat," or even of Blake's *Songs of Innocence*, Christ descends almost to the stature of a sympathetic housewife:

Peace, Peace, my Hony, do not cry,
My Little Darling, wipe thine eye,
Oh Cheer, Cheer up, come see.
Is anything too deare, my Dove.
Is anything too good, my Love,
To get or give for thee?

(pp. 337-41)

Though it is Taylor's most ambitious work, *God's Determinations* does not contain as great poetry generally as one can find in the *Sacramental Meditations*. Some commentators have remarked the similarity of structure and technique to the morality play tradition and the Theocritan song contest. Few, however, have bothered to point out that it is fairly tedious, inconsistent theologically, and neither a good narrative nor a good *débat*. There are a few impressive poems to which I shall refer, but it is noteworthy mainly because of the great variety of metrical forms—possibly the result of the influence of Herbert's *The Temple*—and because it parallels to a large extent the religious ideas of Wigglesworth's *Day of Doom*.

The incorporation of the various techniques of the morality plays into the poem, which is composed of separate lyrics thematically connected, seems to me no great advantage. Nathalia Wright stresses the morality principle behind the variations in the poem, the verse changes being designed to fit the different persons and situations. These changes are not, she says, the result of exuberance nor of a desire for experimentation [see Additional Bibliography]. Yet the characterizations are slight, and the action is never sustained. Taylor shows signs in the poem of great rhetorical ingenuity and the capacity for tropical language that exalts, and on occasion degrades, the numerous *Sacramental Meditations;* but its fault is that of the *débat* as a poetic form. Although some of the poems late in the sequence may be taken as independent lyrics, most of them bear upon the context and gain their effectiveness partially from antecedent material. But there is no real action to invite participation; the vehicle loses momentum as it goes along. Taylor may not have intended to write a narrative poem, but in that case he would have done better to retain not only the fluid metrical patterns, but also the procedure of *The Temple*.

The *Sacramental Meditations* are better suited to Taylor's genius. They are very nearly pure contemplative poems, and Taylor's instinct for the particular, for the localized sign as evidence of unity in God's ordered universe, affords him a myriad of exemplifications and analogies for the rather condensed set of generalizations which the *Meditations* expound. The sacrament itself, being an allegory, provides him with a ready-made vehicle, and the details which he extracts abundantly from daily life serve as amplifications and reinforcements of his theme, or as alternative possibilities for allegory.

In the *Meditations,* Taylor remains aware that the sacraments do not convert, that they lead to conversion only by referring the recipient to the Word of God. As in *God's Determinations,* Christ's atonement is cause for joy and exultation. But even more: **"The Experience"** exploits the conception that Christ acted *mediately* in human guise for man's redemption, to abrogate the Thomistic hierarchy of intellectual souls. There is a reversal of precedence, and man no longer holds the lowest place:

I'le Claim my Right: Give place ye Angells Bright.
Ye further from the Godhead stande that I.
My nature is your Lord; and doth Unite
Better than Yours unto the Deity.
Gods Throne is first and mine is next: to you
Onely the place of Waiting-men is due.

Despite this presumption, Taylor is still keenly aware of the degeneration of man's nature as a penalty for the fall. In Edwardean theology there is little mention of the degradation of the Reason—all is referred to original sin. In poems like **"Meditation 77,"** second series, the consciousness of original sin and man's present state becomes especially acute:

A State, a State, Oh! Dungeon State indeed,
In which mee headlong, long ago Sin pitcht:
As dark as Pitch; where Nastiness doth breed:
And filth defiles: and I am with it ditcht.
A Sinfull State: this Pit no Water's in't.
A bugbare State: as black as any ink.

The ejaculation, the long cesuras, and the tone suggest Donne, but there is a definite distinction to be made: when Donne becomes repentant, as he does in the *Holy Sonnets*, he discards most of his eccentricities and assumes a fairly straight-forward, unpretentious style. Taylor does the same elsewhere, but in the passage just quoted the "ditcht" of line four, the "bugbare" in the last line, and the concluding phrase are unfortunate, the first two being inappropriately colloquial, the last merely trite.

Another distinction between the two poets is that the sense of personal sin is not so powerful in Taylor as it is in Donne. Taylor, we might conjecture, has less reason for it. As far as we can determine, his character in everyday life was irreproachable.... In Donne one cannot mistake the egocentricity of guilt; he abuses himself, devours himself with his shame, and begs to be ravished by God. Taylor, on the other hand, wants to be remembered. In **"The Reflexion"** he asks:

> Shall Heaven and Earth's bright Glory all up lie,
> Like Sun Beams bundled in the sun in thee?
> Dost thou sit Rose at Table Head, where I
> Do sit, and Carv'st no morsel sweet for mee?
> So much before, so little now! Sprindge, Lord,
> Thy Rosie Leaves, and me their Glee afford.

"The Reflexion" is, with some reservations, one of Taylor's most successful poems. It is packed with his syntactical and metrical idiosyncrasies, but they are absorbed in the swift flow of metaphor. The inversions, the ellipses, the rhetorical questions, the coinages, and the conventional exhortations, like those in the last two lines of the first stanza, are suitable to the setting and theme. The heaven-lost happiness of the Saints having been restored, there is reason for rejoicing. But, the poet reflects, should the Lord pass over him, should He fail to pour His grace into the expectant trencher, then:

> Oh! sweat mine Eye:
> O'erflow with Teares: Oh! draw thy fountains dry.

The conversion here of a Petrarchan conceit to the purposes of devotional poetry has its precedents, of course, in Crashaw and Vaughan, and occasionally in Herbert. We have in these poets, too, the quick leaping amongst images which is responsible for the mixed metaphor in the stanza quoted above: God sits "Rose at Table Head," carving sweet morsels. But the poet cries: "Sprindge, Lord, / Thy Rosie Leaves, and me their Glee afford." The mind is agile enough to make the translation, to recognize that the sweet morsels and the Glee of the Rose are one and the same thing; but it nevertheless prefers more distinction among images. The fault is almost forgotten, however, in the brilliance of the pictures and the sheer rhetorical exuberance. (pp. 342-46)

Taylor seems to have learned from Donne how to manipulate the monosyllables in his verse. One need only compare **"Meditation 30,"** first series, with Donne's "Batter my heart . . . " to establish the influence. The power achieved by the strings of one-syllable words is undeniably great. The theme of Taylor's poem, one of his best, is stated fully in the final stanza, but appears first in the following:

> Thou Rod of Davids Root, Branch of his Bough:
> My Lord, repare thy Palace, Deck thy Place.
> I'm but a Flesh and Blood bag: Oh! do thou
> Sill, Plate, Ridge, Rib, and Rafter me with Grace.
> Renew my Soule, and guild it all within:
> And hang thy Saving Grace on ery Pin.

Taylor uses simple diction here in the development of an elaborate trope. Donne employs his monosyllables as an introduction to the protracted simile, which begins in the second quatrain and carries to the end of the sonnet. I might call attention here to the image in the last two lines of stanza two of Taylor's poem, which seems to me to be peculiarly Taylorian, yet among the best of its kind produced by any of the metaphysicals. The figure is a fitting climax to the excited rhetoric and the pervading ellipses of the first two lines. The meter tugs throughout the stanza and the concluding lines bring the whole to equilibrium:

> What Pittie's this? Oh Sunshine Art! What Fall?

> Thou that more glorious wast than glories Wealth!
> More Golden far than God! Lord, on whose Wall
> Thy scutcheons hung, the Image of thyselfe!
> It's ruinde, and must rue, though Angels should
> To hold it up, heave while their Heart Strings hold.

Mr. Warren has called attention to Taylor's alliteration: "As with other poets, ancient and contemporary, who reduce the flexible music of their rhythms, Taylor compensates by supplying . . . copious alliteration—alliteration not as structure but as pure and simple phonetic pleasure" [see excerpt dated 1948]. Taylor is in other poems susceptible to such censure, but in the above stanza the alliteration is integral to the rhythmic pattern and helps to sustain it. (pp. 348-49)

With an instinct for the particular that is a legacy from his faith (the Puritans, remember, were born allegorists), Taylor draws his imagery from diverse sources: from medicine, the law, the sea, from Petrarchan poetry, and from the most prosaic activities of ordinary life. Generally these details have been subtly diffused throughout the poem, or bluntly but brilliantly developed into extended analogies or into allegory. In **"Meditation 19,"** there is an elaborate trope which combines medical with legal terminology, the trope itself being introduced by an exclamation suitable to the ecstasies of courtly love, but which, as we see in Crashaw, has long been standard in metaphysical poetry:

> Oh! Sweet, sweet joy! These Rampant Fiends befoold:
> They made their Gall his Winding sheete; although
> They of the Heart-ach dy must, or be Cool'd
> With Inflammation of the Lungs, they know.
> He's cancelling the Bond, and making Pay:
> And ballancing Accounts: its Reckoning day.

The shift in embodiment here from the vengeful doctor to the hard-hearted lawyer or bookkeeper, though simple enough to follow, has no particular value or justification. In **"Huswifry"** there is a perfectly logical argument in terms of the spinning wheel and the woven cloth; in **"Meditation 7"** the poet develops consistently the figure of God as a Golden Still refining grace. The selection of details in both cases is adequate and apposite; we are reminded of Herbert's intergrated analogies and allegories. (pp. 351-52)

Metaphor, according to the rhetoricians of the ancient world and of the Renaissance, directs the mind inward to supply from remembered experience aids to clear statement. Metaphors were not mere visual embellishments, but rather *economical* compensations for the inadequacies of language. In a later period, and up to the present day, the exponents of Imagism felt that metaphor should arrest the reader and force him to concentrate on the particular. Their theories were derived from the Lockean doctrine that all knowledge results from sensory perception and that, consequently, all truth resides in the physical world. Modern imagery tends to exist, therefore, as the most accurate transcription of the object itself, and as a substitute for the abstract process.

With the metaphysical poets, however, the particular existed for the thought, the image for the idea. The metaphor pushed the reader into and guided him through the abstract process. In the metaphysical image, if we fasten our attention on the concretion, the idea may leave us behind; for the concretion is only a vehicle—for amplification, for clarification, and in the case of the supra-rational (as in such poets as Vaughan and the American Jones Very) for mere statement. It is true that metaphors in some poems were protracted and tortured to the point that they became no more than ornaments and distractions, but the conception of imagery just outlined was nonetheless that which governed the construction of most traditional poetry, including the metaphysical.

The critic who has perhaps done most to alter this outlook on metaphysical verse is T. S. Eliot, whose theory of the objective correlative, "the sensuous apprehension of thought," is now more or less generally applied to the poets of the school. Mr. Wallace Cable Brown, for example, writing on Taylor, makes this assertion [see excerpt dated 1944]:

> Through the characteristic of "sensuous apprehension of thought," we make an even closer approach to the essence of the metaphysical aesthetic, an approach that continues to employ heterogeneity of ideas and intentional ambiguity as means to this larger end. Here the thinking not only is perceptual, but becomes a quality of the feeling, just as the feeling becomes a quality of the thought. Such a relationship is difficult to prove logically, but I think it can be sensed when illustrated.

He then quotes these lines from Taylor:

> What, shall the frosty Rhime upon my locks
> Congeale my brains with Chilly dews, whereby
> My Phansie is benumbd: and put in stocks,
> And thaws not into steams of rccching joy?
>
> • • • • • • •
>
> Lord, let thy Glorious Body send such rayes
> Into my Soule, as ravish shall my heart,
> That Thoughts how thy Bright Glory out shall blaze
> Upon my body, may such Rayes thee dart.
> My Tunes shall dance then on these Rayes, and Caper
> Unto thy Praise: when Glory lights my Taper.

And then he comments:

> The sensuous terminology . . . carries the burden of the meaning in the first four lines, and is followed by the vivid sensuous contrasts of . . . the concluding stanzas. Thus the thought in this passage is communicated through the sensuous imagery; and it seems to me that, for the most part, the thought and feeling are instantly apprehended, the sensibility unified.

Now it may be true that the thought is apprehended quickly, but it is danger of being just as quickly absorbed in a rush of sensuous detail too complex and too burdensome for the idea, a kind of tropical fireworks whose sparks have to wear themselves out before we realize the significance of the figure they have traced. The progression of this passage is qualitative and associative, rather than syllogistic in the conventional manner, as in the compass image consummating Donne's "A Valediction: Forbidding Mourning."

The critic here, like Eliot in his poetry, seems too much affected by the image and not sufficiently by the idea. What seems to modern critics the operation of Eliot's "sensuous apprehension of thought" in metaphysical poetry is not really that at all. Taylor, Herbert, and Donne, in their best poems, are not merely *feeling* their thought, they are *thinking out* their feeling, trying to arrive at a precise comprehension of the given experience. And in this process the images stand not as objective correlatives substituting for the idea, nor as intentional ambiguities; they stand only in coördination with the logical composition of the poem. The danger of the metaphysical image, which we notice more in Taylor and Crashaw than in Donne, more in Donne than in Herbert (and more in Eliot than in any of these), is that we pay more attention to the nature of the image, its singularity, than to its function, its integrity.

Mr. Brown, like Cleanth Brooks, seems to favor a multiplicity of meanings in a given image; he speaks favorably of a synthesis of heterogeneous ideas through the imaginative device of intentional ambiguity. But the purpose of imagery is not to give multiple meanings: its purpose is to simplify, to clarify, to reinforce. In "Church Monuments" in Donne's compass image, in Taylor's **Christ's Reply,** the meaning is precise and the images are precise. Any meanings read into an image above and beyond the poet's intentions may lead to confusion.

Such poetry does not, as Mr. Pearce suggests in arguing that Taylor's poetry "reflects in its nature and function the very logic of orthodox New England culture, the logic of Peter Ramus—Platonic, unitive, realistic,"—abolish the abstract categories of Aristotelian logic and make the syllogism secondary. Such poetry depends on traditional modes of reasoning; there is no equivalence of image and idea. The sensory object may be the source of the thought, but the process of writing poetry is much more than the mere "distinguishing and organizing of entities." There is in good metaphysical poetry a fusion of abstract idea and concrete image, a carefully defined relationship between motive and emotion. Metaphysical poets have, moreover, a tendency to point their images, to label their metaphors before they even appear in the poem. We see this in many of Taylor's **Meditations,** and in Donne too; but in much modern poetry the image merely appears and the reader is lcft to shift for himself. It is not unlikely that the image will have no explicit locus, as in the various pseudo-references of "Gerontion," and in most of Ezra Pound.

Taylor, unlike the moderns, is not afraid of conceptual language. The trouble with some of his images, however, is not that the vehicle does not carry the tenor, but that the vehicle is too great for the tenor, or, on other occasions, does not have the dignity of the tenor, as though a diamond were to be set in lead or an emperor were to fare forth on a bicycle. There is, as has been indicated, a possible explanation for this last. With the Puritans, as it rarely is with us, God was a household word. He existed for them everywhere, in church and in the bristles of the meanest scrub brush. Their instinct was to search out signs of His decrees, and there was little attempt made to evaluate, to make distinctions, to grade these signs.

As a result, many of Taylor's images do not meet the demands of poetic decorum. They are brilliant perceptions, perhaps, but too menial or too shocking: they attract the attention away from the idea which they are supposed to convey. Mr. Brown states: "The most important effect of these contrasts in metaphysical poetry is the shock or surprise that comes from the domesticating of the Infinite: like Herbert, Taylor looked on God's 'furniture so fine, And made it fine to me' " Other critics speak of the technique as a virtue, but Mr. Brown fortunately recognizes the fallacy in it. The fact of the matter is that the disparity between the things compared is too wide for the mind to bridge with appreciation. The effect is the same as that received from Hardy's realistic burial of the Immanent Will.

Faults of this kind can become quite serious, and they become so in Donne and Crashaw, as well as Taylor. But in Taylor, more so than the others, they exist side by side, in the same poem, with some of his foremost virtues. We rarely question the sincerity of the man; and when he does not speak of the sacramental wafer as "Heaven's Sugar Cake," or does not ask to have his "Pipkin" filled with Christ's "blood red wine," he is as great as these poets, and one of the greatest poets this country has ever produced. (pp. 355-60)

> Herbert Blau, "Heaven's Sugar Cake: Theology and Imagery in the Poetry of Edward Taylor," in The New England Quarterly, *Vol. XXVI, No. 3, September, 1953, pp. 337-60.*

HAYES B. JACOBS (essay date 1960)

[*Jacobs is an American editor, reporter, and feature writer who has contributed short stories, articles, and reviews to the* New Yorker, Harper's Magazine, *and the* Saturday Review. *In the following excerpt, he appraises Taylor's work in glowing—and entirely facetious—terms.*]

I have been busy, frantically so to be exact, in recent weeks, addressing form letters to old college friends, clergymen, booksellers, poets, editorial writers, the American Medical Association's directors, and others whose aid I hope to enlist for the preservation of the literary reputation of Edward Taylor, who, readers of *Harper's Magazine* will hardly need reminding, was one of our most illustrious Puritan poets. Replies to my letters have thus far been somewhat discouraging. People are busy with P.T.A., zoning, fighting jet airports, constructing cold frames, and with disease collections and drives of one sort or another; but I am not disheartened. I still have high hope of putting down what appears to be an all-out campaign, being waged both here and abroad, to belittle and disparage the extraordinary literary output of one of the finest little writers the modern world has known.

First it was a grudging reference to Taylor by an English essayist, hiding in the anonymity of the London *Times Literary Supplement*, who wrote that "Edward Taylor . . . is a not uninteresting minor poet."

Then, *The New Yorker* joined in the attack. It chose a sly, oblique tactic, passing at first over Taylor himself to quibble with the *Times* essayist. It conjectured that he had had some difficulty putting together his article. It pictured him "sitting in his study, poking up the fire in his grate now and then," and hesitating before making his final judgment of Taylor. "Was there a possibility," it asked, "that he might be wrong? . . . There was nobody he could consult, nobody he could turn to, because nobody on either side of the Atlantic had ever heard to Edward Taylor." That is the kind of thing, you will surely agree, that those of us who love Taylor must not take lying down.

I am willing to concede that lines from Taylor's poems are probably not on the very tip of every American schoolboy's tongue, but I am nonetheless certain that nine per-

sons out of ten carry some imprint—farther back, perhaps, toward the soft palate and the uvula—of familiarity with his work. And that cannot be said of very many English-born pastor-physician-poets who came over to live in western Massachusetts during Taylor's life span (1645?-1729).

Who can forget, once he has mined it, the glint of pure, poetic gold in, say, *Gods Determinations touching his Elect: and The Elects Combat in their Conversion, and Coming up to God in Christ: together with the Comfortable Effects Thereof*? I suggest you try asking the next person you meet if he knows who wrote: "Yet let my Titimouses Quill Suck in Thy Graces milk Pails Some small drop . . . " and if he doesn't say instantly, why, Edward Taylor, then I'll eat my mortarboard. And I'll wager that phrases like "Heav'ns whelm'd-down Chrystall meele Bowle," and "Mine Apples ashes are in apple Shells And dirty too," and "Make me, O Lord, thy Spinning Wheele compleat," will continue to go on, forever ringing in our ears, like it or not. Once you get a dirty Apples ash and a Chrystall meele Bowle and a Spinning Wheele in your ear, they're bound to stay there for a while, don't you think? (p. 71)

None of the screeds that would assign a minor reputation to Taylor has acknowledged the fact that for some time now a limited amount of the poetry has been available in *hard covers*. This is the result of the scholarly zeal of my erstwhile professor, Perry Miller, and of [Thomas H.] Johnson, who joined hands to publish *The Puritans*. . . . That thick, blue volume of 846 pp. was required reading in Professor Miller's English 7a (American Literature from the Beginning to Emerson), though as I recall we were allowed to skip around some after Cotton and Increase Mather. Right after Miller and Johnson joined hands, they put their collective finger on the qualities that would insure Taylor's immortality. Would it not be difficult for anyone now, more than twenty years later, to gainsay the prediction (p. 552) that Taylor was the one Puritan poet "whose stature may well develop as time reveals him"? They pay tribute to Taylor's "image-making, his rapture, his tenderness, delicacy, and intense devotion." Taylor's detractors would do well to go back to school, or at least enroll in an evening course, and re-read Miller and Johnson. They would sing a quite different tune on discovering that it was Taylor being singled out to illustrate the point that "the indigenous Puritan muse, even when tied down to the fashions of an earlier style, soared with metaphoric brilliance."

Taylor was as much at home in prose as in poetry. Can anyone match the directness, the simple, ringing clarity as expressed in some of his letters? One thinks particularly of the love letter he posted to Elizabeth Fitch of Norwich in 1674, in which there occurs this passage:

> For you having made my breast the Cabbinet of your Affections (as I yours, mine) I know not how to vse a fitter Comparison to set out my Love by, than to Compare it vnto a Golden Ball of pure Fire rowling vp and down my Breast, from which there flies now, and then a Sparke like a Glorious Beam from the Body of the Flaming Sun.

I look at that passage and all I can say is that I wish I had written it—everything but that comma there after "flies now." . . .

And finally, the amazingly incendiary quatrain:

> But oh! my streight'ned Breast! my Lifeless Sparke!
> My Fireless Flame! What Chilly Love, and Cold?
> In measure Small! in Manner Chilly! See.
> Lord blow the Coal: Thy Love Enflame in mee.

Those lines, and the ones immediately preceding, are of course from . . . *Sacramental Meditations*, and I find my fingers quite hot just from writing them out. The impassioned message they carry will, I trust, enlist support for my Save Taylor project, and if anyone wishes Further Proofe of the True Werth of the dere Fellow's Werke, I shall be glad to Tell him where he can look it up. (p. 72)

> Hayes B. Jacobs, "Stop Picking on Edward Taylor!" in Harper's Magazine, *Vol. 220, No. 1320, May, 1960, pp. 71-2.*

LOUIS L. MARTZ (essay date 1960)

[*Martz is an American educator, editor, and the author of the literary studies* The Wit of Love: Donne, Carew, Crashaw, Marvell *(1969) and* Poet of Exile: A Study of Milton's Poetry *(1980). In the following excerpt from a foreword to Donald E. Stanford's 1960 edition of Taylor's poetry,* The Poems of Edward Taylor, *he compares Taylor's verse to that of George Herbert.*]

Edward Taylor's major work, the *Preparatory Meditations*, [consists] of 217 poems, written from 1682 to 1725, while Taylor was serving as minister to the frontier settlement of Westfield, Massachusetts. Since 128 of these *Meditations* have never before been published, the full range and power of the work have not been manifested; and, as a result, students of Taylor have tended to give at least equal attention to his long doctrinal allegory, *Gods Determinations*, which has been completely available in Thomas Johnson's valuable selection from Taylor's poetry. *Gods Determinations* is a significant work, unique in English poetry; it reveals the workings of the Puritan doctrine of Grace through a framework derived from the old devices of medieval allegory; and it develops, by the blunt insistence of its verse, a certain crude and battering strength. Yet when all is said, *Gods Determinations* remains, I think, a labor of versified doctrine; only a few of its lyrics can approach the best of the *Meditations* in poetical quality. In the end, Taylor's standing as a poet must be measured by a full and careful reading of the *Meditations*.

Such a reading leaves no doubt that Taylor is true poet, and yet it is a strange experience, hard to evaluate and explain. For Taylor leads us, inevitably, to compare his achievement with the consummate artistry of George Herbert, whose poetry Taylor echoes throughout the *Meditations,* as well as in his other poems. The example of Herbert appears with special force at the beginning of the present volume; in the "Prologue" Taylor five times repeats Herbert's phrase "crumb of dust":

> Lord, Can a Crumb of Dust the Earth outweigh,
> Outmatch all mountains, nay the Chrystall Sky?

It seems a clear echo of Herbert's "The Temper" (I), which also deals with the speaker's sense of inadequacy in attempting the praise of his Lord:

> Wilt thou meet arms with man, that thou dost stretch

> A crumme of dust from heav'n to hell?

And the whole conception of Taylor's poem is perhaps influenced also by a stanza from Herbert's "Longing":

> Behold, thy dust doth stirre,
> It moves, it creeps, it aims at thee:
> Wilt thou deferre
> To succour me,
> Thy pile of dust, wherein each crumme
> Sayes, Come?

The "Prologue" thus prepares us for the strongly Herbertian mode of the first Meditation, with its theme of Love and its familiar exclamations in the presence of the Lord: "Oh! that thy Love might overflow my Heart!" Then, shortly after, we have the three poems that Taylor entitled **"The Experience," "The Return,"** and **"The Reflexion"**— the only poems in the sequence thus entitled—with their clear reminiscence of the many titles of this kind among Herbert's poetry: "The Answer," "The Reprisall," "The Glance." But these and the other particular echoes of Herbert pointed out in Mr. Stanford's annotations are only the most evident aspects of a pervasive influence. Like Henry Vaughan, Edward Taylor appears to have had a mind saturated with Herbert's poetry, and the result is that a thousand tantalizing echoes of Herbert remain for the most part untraceable because the meditative voice of Herbert has been merged with Taylor's own peculiar voice. (pp. xiii-xiv)

Yet the full effect of any single poem by Taylor is never quite Herbertian.

Taylor has, first of all, very little of Herbert's metrical skill. In *Gods Determinations* and in the series of short poems on various "occurrants" Taylor attempts to deal with a great variety of stanza forms, in Herbert's way, but with only moderate success. In his *Meditations* no such variety is tried: every poem is written in the popular six-line stanza used in Herbert's "Church-porch." Taylor's handling of this stanza seldom rises above competence, and all too often he gives a lame effect of counting syllables and forcing rimes:

> I needed have this hand, that broke off hath
> This Bud of Civill, and of Sacred Faith.

>   until my Virginall
> Chime out in Changes sweet thy Praises shall.

> To view those glories in thy Crown that vapor,
> Would make bright Angells eyes to run a-water.

This sort of clumsiness, in some degree, is found in most of the poems.

Another problem arises when we compare the language of Herbert and Taylor, especially their use of terms from daily speech. As the above examples indicate, Taylor frequently attains the neat and flexible delicacy of Herbert's conversations with God, where the poet speaks in the presence of a familiar friend, as in Herbert's "Easter":

> I got me flowers to straw thy way;
> I got me boughs off many a tree:
> But thou wast up by break of day,
> And brought'st thy sweets along with thee.

This is colloquial, but chastened and restrained: Herbert's language never strays far from the middle way of educated conversation. Herbert was bred in courtly circles, and though he knows that "Kneeling ne'er spoil'd silk stocking," he does not allow slang, dialect, or "low" terms to spoil his neatness. If he allows a line like. "The workydaies are the back-part," this is exceptional: it is at once absorbed into a more discreet context. But consider these lines by Taylor:

> Thus my leane Muses garden thwarts the spring
> Instead of Anthems, breatheth her ahone.
> But duty raps upon her doore for Verse.
> That makes her bleed a poem through her searce.

Terms like "ahone" and "searce" bring us up abruptly; they lie outside the mainstream of the language, along with dozens of other terms scattered profusely throughout the poetry: *I'st, bedotcht, brudled, crickling, flur, frim, gastard, glout, keck, paintice, riggalld, skeg, slatch, snicksnarls, tantarrow'd, weddenwise, an hurden haump.* Words like these, whether coinages, phonetic spellings, or Leicestershire dialect, require a sizable glossary, such as that provided at the end of the present volume. And the problem is compounded by the fact that Taylor's range runs at the same time to the far end of the learned spectrum: *epinicioum, dulcifi'de, enkentrism, enucleate, officine, fistulate, obsignation, aromatize, theanthropie, bituminated.* Even John Donne, who likes to mingle learned and colloquial terms, does not display in his poetry so wide a range as this; and for Herbert, of course, extremes in either direction are to be avoided: he follows Ben Jonson's dictum: "Pure and neat language I love, yet plain and customary."

The problems presented by Taylor's strangely assorted diction are inseparable from a third difficulty: his use of the homeliest images to convey the most sacred and reverend themes. Here again Herbert leads the way, with his "Elixir":

> All may of thee partake:
> Nothing can be so mean,
> Which with his tincture (for thy sake)
> Will not grow bright and clean.
>
> A servant with this clause
> Makes drudgerie divine:
> Who sweeps a room, as for thy laws,
> Makes that and th' action fine.

But with Herbert these homely images are handled with a bland understatement, a deft restraint:

> You must sit down, sayes Love, and taste my meat:
> So I did sit and eat.
>
> And in this love, more then in bed, I rest.
>
> This day my Saviour rose,
> And did inclose this light for his:
> That, as each beast his manger knows,
> Man might not of his fodder misse.
> Christ hath took in this piece of ground,
> And made a garden there for those
> Who want herbs for their wound.
>
> ("Sunday")

Herbert thus succeeds by the total poise of his poem: where every syllable is taut, we cannot doubt the speaker's word. But what shall we say of Taylor's treatment of Jonah as the "type" of Christ?

> The Grave him swallow'd down as a rich Pill
> Of Working Physick full of Virtue which
> Doth purge Death's Constitution of its ill.
> And womble-Crops her stomach where it sticks.
> It heaves her stomach till her hasps off fly.
> And out hee comes Cast up, rais'd up thereby.

Or this treatment of the sinner's state?

> Mine Heart's a Park or Chase of sins: Mine Head
> 'S a Bowling Alley. Sins play Ninehole here.
> Phansy's a Green: sin Barly breaks in't led.
> Judgment's a pingle. Blindeman's Buff's plaid there.
> Sin playes at Coursey Parke within my Minde.
> My Wills A Walke in which it aires what's blinde.
>
> (pp. xv-xvii)

A brief acquaintance with Taylor's poetry might easily lead us to dismiss him as a burlap version of Herbert, a quaint primitive who somehow, despite the Indians, managed to stammer out his rude verses well enough to win the title of "our best Colonial poet." Such a judgment would be utterly wrong. Taylor is not a primitive: he is a subtle, learned man who kept his Theocritus and Origen, his Augustine and Horace, with him in the wilderness. We have the inventory of his library: it would have done credit to a London clergyman, and for one on the Westfield frontier it is all but incredible—until we realize that the Puritan minister of New England did not come to make terms with the wilderness: he came to preserve the Truth in all its purity and wonder. Taylor's *Meditations* represent a lifelong effort of the inner man to apprehend that Truth.

As we read more deeply and more widely in his poetry, we gradually become aware of the tenacious intelligence that underlies these surface crudities: a bold, probing, adventurous intellect that deliberately tries to bend the toughest matter toward his quest for truth. Consider closely, as a representative example, Meditation 32 of the first series, on the text: "1 Cor. 3.22. Whether Paul or Apollos, or Cephas." We need the whole context of those names: *For all things are yours; whether Paul, or Apollos, or Cephas, or the world, or life, or death, or things present, or things to come; all are yours; and ye are Christ's; and Christ is God's.*

> Thy Grace, Deare Lord's my golden Wrack, I finde
> Screwing my Phancy into ragged Rhimes,
> Tuning thy Praises in my feeble minde
> Untill I come to strike them on my Chimes.
> Were I an Angell bright, and borrow could
> King Davids Harp, I would them play on gold.
>
> But plung'd I am, my minde is puzzled,
> When I would spin my Phancy thus unspun,
> In finest Twine of Praise I'm muzzled.
> My tazzled Thoughts twirld into Snick-Snarls run.
> Thy Grace, my Lord, is such a glorious thing,
> It doth Confound me when I would it sing.

There is an effect of deliberate roughness here, of struggling for adequate expression, climaxed in the vigorous line: "My tazzled Thoughts twirld into Snick-Snarls run." And now, to work his way out of this ragged state, the speaker in the next two stanzas turns to analyse the meaning of God's Love and Grace in lines that gradually become clear, more harmonious, more fluent:

> Eternall Love an Object mean did smite

Which by the Prince of Darkness was beguilde,
That from this Love it ran and sweld with spite
And in the way with filth was all defilde
Yet must be reconcild, cleansd, and begrac'te
Or from the fruits of Gods first Love displac'te.

Then Grace, My Lord, wrought in thy Heart a vent,
Thy Soft Soft hand to this hard worke did goe,
And to the Milke White Throne of Justice went
And entred bond that Grace might overflow.
Hence did thy Person to my Nature ty
And bleed through humane Veans to satisfy.

There, in the middle stanza of the poem, the central act of
Grace is brought home, with perfect clarity and cadence,
to the speaker's mind. As a result, his "Snick-Snarls" disappear, and he bursts forth into spontaneous praise:

Oh! Grace, Grace, Grace! this Wealthy Grace doth lay
Her Golden Channells from thy Fathers throne,
Into our Earthen Pitchers to Convay
Heavens Aqua Vitae to us for our own.
O! let thy Golden Gutters run into
My Cup this Liquour till it overflow.

(pp. xviii-xx)

The poem, I believe, creates a total effect of rough integrity, moving from a ragged opening to the smooth Herbertian phrasing of the close. The rough phrasing, the colloquialism, the vividly concrete imagery, the Herbertian
echoes all play their part in a total pattern. I will not argue
that such a control is always present in Taylor's *Meditations:* there is, as I have implied, a frequent clumsiness
that has no function; and one cannot defend his excesses
in developed imagery, as when he shows the prisoners of
sin thus released by "the Blood of thy Covenant":

And now the Prisoners sent out, do come
Padling in their Canooes apace with joyes
Along this blood red Sea, Where joyes do throng...

But frequently, even in poems with grave flaws, the underlying control is greater than we might at first think, and
sometimes the flaws recede into insignificance as the
whole poem comes into focus.

At the same time, we must reckon with the fact that the
Meditations are written in sequences, sometimes with tight
links between the poems. (pp. xx-xxi)

Thus, as the full effect of an individual Meditation often
enfolds and sustains a number of flaws in detail, so a weak
poem may be enfolded and sustained by the part it plays
in a developing sequence. The flaws are there, and we do
not overlook them; yet the poems, in the large, succeed in
creating a highly original world, designed upon a special
plan. It is a world where the Puritan doctrine of Grace operates to consecrate, within the soul of one of the Elect,
every object, every word, every thought that passes
through his anguished, grateful, loving mind. (p. xxiii)

Louis L. Martz, in a foreword to The Poems of
Edward Taylor, *edited by Donald E. Stanford,
Yale University Press, 1960, pp. xiii-xxxvii.*

NORMAN S. GRABO (essay date 1962)

[*Grabo is an American educator, editor, and the author of
the full-length study* Edward Taylor *(1962). In the following*

*excerpt from that work, he surveys Taylor's earliest literary
efforts, particularly his elegies.*]

[The] early and occasional poems are significant to a study
of Taylor's poetry: as apprentice work, they often anticipate his later and better efforts, and they always illuminate the process by which the poet comes into being.

Six poems, attributed to Taylor with fair certainty, probably date from before his arrival in New England. Two—a
verse acrostic sent to his brother Joseph and his wife Alice
and the verse compliment sent in a letter to his "school-
fellow, W. M."—are personal; the other four are attempts
at controversy. Political and ecclesiastical warfare in the
seventeenth century was as vicious when conducted on paper as on the battlefield. Scurrility, personal vilification,
and gross raillery poured from the pens of some of England's most distinguished writers. Taylor, who was born
at the very beginning of the Puritan domination and who
grew up during the Commonwealth and the Protectorate
of Oliver Cromwell, was approaching maturity when King
Charles II was recalled to the throne. Taylor's parents and
their friends had undoubtedly known at first hand what
Archbishop William Laud's persecution meant. Dissenting
and non-conforming preachers who managed to elude
Laud and make their way to New England were still, to
certain elements in England, heroes of a sort. And so Taylor, in sympathy with the heroic exodus to America, tried
several times to write a "Nipping epigram" that he remembered having seen by "some poetaster" who could not
abide Laud, though Taylor could not have been older than
three when Laud died.

Taylor's relishing this particular piece of doggerel is symbolic not only of the tenacity with which he held to the Independent position in England but of the hopelessness he
must have felt when Charles returned there. By 1661 a
largely pro-royalist Parliament was seated, and it succeeded within four or five years in completely reversing
the political and ecclesiastical fortunes of the Puritans.
Taylor saw a series of acts come into effect that strikingly
altered the political face of the land and that put his ecclesiastical and theological polity to the test. The Municipal
Corporations Act effectively eliminated conscientious Puritans from many public offices by requiring officeholders
to take communion in the Anglican church. In 1662 the
Act of Uniformity required subscribing to the prayer
book, which, since Taylor could not bring himself to it,
cost him, along with nearly two thousand others, positions
in churches, universities, and schools. The Conventicle
Act (1663) prohibited religious worship outside of an Anglican church; and the Five Mile Act (1665) ejected ministers from their congregations if they would not accept the
Act of Uniformity, and it prohibited them from coming
closer than five miles to their former congregations.

The shoe of intolerance was back on the Puritan political
foot now, and the Anglicans were determined to make it
pinch. Taylor's reaction to the Act of Uniformity is a 208-
line satire titled "**The Layman's Lamentation upon the Civil Death of the Late Laborers in the Lord's Vineyard, by
way of Dialogue between a Proud PRELATE and a Poor
PROFESSOUR Silenced on Bartholomew Day, 1662.**" The
decasyllabic couplets begin with the poet-layman, who is
no doubt Taylor, undertaking a mock elegy for the "civil
death" of the silenced ministers. Since they are as good as
dead, the poor professor of the true faith writes their final

epitaph for the lawyers, physicians, divines, soldiers, and builders of the true faith. Echoing John Cotton, he laments, "There's not a sup / Of milk for babes: our spiritual fathers thrust / Quite out of doors; poor children, starve we must". But the proud prelate—who interrupts him with "Leave these complaints, you whining sectary!"—then explains that the change brought about by the Act of Uniformity is certainly no disaster; it will prove a blessed change even for the layman, whom he describes as a "Foolish, fanatic, silly schismatic, / Round-headed fury, crack-brained lunatic." (pp. 108-10)

Another dialogue—this time between a writer and a Maypole dresser—occupies Taylor's attention for some ninety-four lines of undistinguished decasyllabic couplets. He makes no attempt to capture, either by vigorous dialogue or by narrative, a dramatic situation for the poem, though the writer has presumably arrested a gamester in the act of decorating a Maypole. He accuses the gamester of setting up Dagon in God's place by dressing the Maypole, but the gamester can not see how this is so: "What though we do make fine the fine Maypole?" he argues, "We love God's Ark and Dagon we control." But the writer answers that one can not have it both ways; for Maypoles are a pagan celebration of the Goddess Flora. Jeremiah has warned men not to follow the ways of the heathen, and so the writer reminds the gamester. (pp. 111-12)

The poem is interesting because it indicates that sterner side of Taylor—his steady view because he is so stiff-necked. He is in it not only Puritan, but puritanical; and he is quite different from the poet of mysticism which he becomes in the New World. The two facets of his personality are not, however, completely separate; for in many of the later meditations the image of sinfulness as a playground of the devil dominates. The **"Dialogue between the Writer and a Maypole Dresser"** anticipates, therefore, one of his favorite later devices.

Similarly in his last poem of controversy, an answer to a **"Popish Pamphlet cast in London streets not long after the city was burned,"** Taylor anticipates another less wholesome aspect. The pamphlet interprets the London fire as a sign of God's anger with Protestantism and as a kind of prefiguration of the day of doom. London is equated with Babylon, and its destruction is God's warning to Protestants to return to the Church of Rome to avoid eternal fires.... Taylor answers the pamphlet's couplets with his own octosyllabics and with a brand of vulgar sexuality that the Popish publication hardly warrants:

> The devil rode (as it appears)
> Your mother hackney as thousands years.
> She's yet his hag without control,
> For he and she sit cheek by jowl.
> His seed within her lap is sown,
> As testifies your dad, Pope Joan.
> Let bastards, then, and all such crew
> Lie in your mother's lap with you.
> You known't your father's house, therefore
> Your Holy Mother is a whore.
> And bastard like you do retain
> Your mother's, not your father's name.
> We have a Father dear at home,
> Who favors us when so're we come,
> Whose name we do retain, to wit,
> Christian, not Roman Catholic....

Common though it was among Puritans to consider the Church of Rome as the Antichrist and the Whore of Babylon and for Taylor to denounce Catholicism in his sermons—particularly in the **"Christographia"**—there is more to this nasty rejoinder than doctrinal rejection. Taylor enjoys this kind of verbal infighting; he seems postively to have delighted in the invective of whoredom.

The allusion to Pope Joan is especially significant in this regard, for Taylor, who attempted to versify the bawdy legend, left five drafts—or partial ones—among his manuscripts; and the most complete one was "probably composed when Taylor was over eighty years of age." Originating in the Middle Ages, the story of the English girl who became Pope and died after giving birth to a monstrous bastard during a Papal procession enjoyed widespread popularity. In Taylor's own time Dryden mentions the legend in his "Prologue at Oxford, 1680," and apparently refers to Elkanah Settle's *The Female Prelate: Being the History of the Life and Death of Pope Joan*, a London play of 1679. The legend peeks into John Trumbull's *M'Fingal* in American literature; and, for that matter, it received full dramatic treatment as recently as 1930 in Arthur Porter's *Pope Joan*. Taylor finds the coarse story a kind of "jokery," as typical of Papal actions, and as splendid fuel with which to feed the scurrilous fires of the times.

But, to return to the juvenile poems, though they are all three in dialogue or debate form, none has a real dramatic setting; only **"The Layman's Lamentation"** approximates dramatic conflict in the abruptness with which speeches are interrupted and passions raised. Even in it, however, the two speakers receive only the broadest of characterizations—humble sincerity opposed to proud authority—and they speak rather than act. Moreover, Taylor's early poetry is the product of wit rather than of the later realization that power comes from beauty, as well as from reason and vituperation. As a satirist he belongs among the railing rhymers, scorned by Dryden, who wield their satirical wit more like a bludgeon than a rapier.

The other two poems, poetically as inept as these satirical sallies, are both greeting-card compliments. In the one which he sends his love to his brother Joseph and his wife after visiting them, he expresses such sentiments as

> The which I trust will find your health as sound } E
> As (blest be Israel's God) mine doth abound.

He exercises his wit to double the effect of his sentiments by spelling them out acrostically. That is, the first letters of each line and the last letters of each line spell out "EDWARD Taylor TO HIS BROTHER AND HIS SISTER JOSEPH AND ALICE Taylor." The habit of acrostics was a widespread Puritan vice and one which Addison damned as "false wit" along with shaped poetry—but Taylor used it with more complication in his later elegies than any other New England Puritan.

The other poem, which Taylor says he included "in a letter I sent to my schoolfellow, W. M.," echoes the one to his brother and sister-in-law. Not an acrostic itself, it begins by offering his love to one from whom he is separated by fortune's bustling wind and "the cloudy time," by asking after his health, and by promising to include a code or alphabet of love. Once decoded, it presumably reaffirms his love for his friend. . . . His complex love letter to Elizabeth Fitch employs the same device of an alphabet, but this time it is employed as a kind of acrostic, the letters running down as the first letters of each line. This is certainly his most quaint and complicated form, for the lines are so arranged that within the general acrostic two figures are described—a ring inside a triangle, tangential with the triangle at three points. By carefully displacing the lines of his alphabet acrostic, Taylor allows certain letters to fall within the triangle; and, read separately, these letters yield the message: "The ring of love my pleasant heart must be, Truely confin'd within the trinity." The ring within the triangle uses the same letters at points of tangent, spelling out "Love's ring I send, that hath no end." The whole is delightfully confused, and must have afforded Miss Fitch plenteous enjoyment. Most astonishing is the fact that Taylor makes poetry out of the entire business—not very good poetry, but respectable nonetheless.

Puritans seem to have been irresistibly drawn to such exercises of wit in commending the persons of others, especially at the time of their death. Thus the funeral elegy nailed to the hearse of the deceased, passed about at the funeral gathering, or even sent in letters as a way of publicly announcing a death employed the acrostic and anagram abundantly. (pp. 112-16)

Taylor wrote eight elegies in the New England mode; and, just as his meditations excel any lyric poetry attempted in the first century of American settlement, so are his elegies the best of their kind. Three of them were written in his senior year at Harvard; and they may have been composed at the request of the college since there is no other record of Taylor's connection with these persons, all three of whom were eminent New Englanders or at least closely connected with Harvard. The first elegy—"upon the death of that holy man of God Mr. Sims, late Pastor of the Church of Christ at Charlestown"—opens with this general lament:

> Ah me! Ah me! Could grief but make a poet,
> Surge after surge of sorrow sure would do it,

And it becomes hardly more specific in tracing the virtues of Zechariah Symmes. Comparing the earliest New Englanders to the Nazarites driven into the wilderness, Taylor commends Symmes as both a builder and a pillar of God's house in New England, which, since he had been pastor at Charlestown from 1636, is an appropriate figure to describe him. But Taylor seems not to have known him personally, for he can only say of him that he "wrought hard" in the quarry of hard hearts "with pickaxe, wedge, and maul, God's Word." (p. 118)

Two months after Symmes's death another plant was taken from New England soil "and set in glory's flowering pot." Though no more personally acquainted with Francis Willoughby, then deputy governor of Massachusetts, than with Symmes, Taylor constructed a much more elaborate elegy. Grief causes him to surrender his studies:

> Begone, begone, my books, start from my hand,
> Stand off, or offer verse up as you stand.
> Bleed tears, mine eyes; weep blood, my pen; my heart,
> Beat up for volunteers in every part
> To march in sorrow's regimental plot,
> For Willoughby, Oh! Willoughby IS NOT.

The fact stated, Taylor calls the country, court, churches, and college to acknowledge its woe:

> Rise, Harvard, rise; stand up with wat'ry eyes,
> Until a second Willoughby arise.

The second part of this elegy is a very interesting acrostic. Taylor runs the letters "FRANCIS WILLOUGHBY" vertically as the first and the last letters of each of thirty-four decasyllabic lines. This would spell out the name four times, but Taylor complicates the trick by placing the couplets side by side, thereby cutting the thirty-four lines to seventeen doubled lines. The first line, for example, thus reads "F ull fraught with grace, well fit for glory's shel F irmly in glory now enrich thysel F". The middle "F" functions portmanteau-like as both the last sound of the first rhyme word, and the first sound of the second line of the couplet. This cuts the number of times the name is actually spelled out to three.

Unlike the acrostic letter to his brother Joseph, this elegy exploits much more successfully the poetic possibilities of the occasion for which it was written. Ignoring the acrostic, we find the idea that a noble gem deserves a weighty and worthy setting. (p. 119)

Within ten years . . . after the red death that was King Philip's War had strutted across the frontier, after the responsibility for the lives of his community must have weighed as heavily upon him as upon any young wilderness physician, and after he had lost two of his own children, Taylor's personal involvement appears in his poetry. His poetic reflections about death gain in depth, and he forsakes the artifices of acrostic, anagram, and chronogram. (p. 119)

Representative of this change is his fine "**Upon Wedlock, and Death of Children,**" composed probably late in 1682, since it seems to have been occasioned by the death of his daughter Abigail in August of that year. The poem is not technically an elegy, since its purpose is not to commemorate the death of Abigail herself, but it is certainly related to the elegies as Taylor writes them subsequently. Coming in the same year as the first of his *Preparatory Meditations*, these reflections avoid decasyllabic couplets and fall into the stanzaic pattern of the *Meditations*—iambic pentameter lines rhyming *ababcc*. The stanza provides units of thought and image that structure his reflections much more rigidly than the elegiac couplets did. The result is an almost classical restraint, similar to Ben Jonson's, against which the personal anguish of the experience Taylor describes creates a tension he rarely matches. The sense of strain and tension produces a powerful statement, but it is controlled by the strength of the poet's religious faith and by his compliance with God's demanding will.

In this attitude Taylor steps midway between Donne and Herbert. Donne, who solves his spiritual conflicts by fiat, leaves one feeling that the solution provided has not actually resolved the question in his soul. Herbert echoes Donne's struggles vociferously, as in "Love" and "The Collar"; but, when he submits to God's will at the end of the poem, we realize that the sound and the fury have been merely a rhetorical device to accentuate the final, child-like submission. In "**Upon Wedlock, and Death of Children,**" Taylor submits to the Lord's will as fully as Herbert; but Taylor's struggle, while not so loud in expostulation as Donne's, is no mere rhetorical or intellectual quibble but an intensely personal and human one. (pp. 124-25)

"**Upon Wedlock, and Death of Children**" belongs among Taylor's finest accomplishments. Among them it stands unique; for it is the only poem prompted by no specific occasion as were the elegies, by no sense of regular duty like the **Meditations**, and by no literary motive like **God's Determinations**. The "I" of the poem is not the representative soul or the church as it so often seems to be in the larger poems; it speaks for Edward Taylor, frontier minister and physician who has lost two children and who seeks relief from his sorrow in poetry. The intense personal involvement and the universality of his problem elevate the poem from among his elegiac verse. The poet-physician touches the open wound in his spirit with a salty finger, but only to apply a healing balm. He never again writes elegies exactly as he did before. (p. 128)

His most ambitious elegy—"**Upon the Death of that Holy and Reverend Man of God, Mr. Samuel Hooker**"—was written in 1697. Unlike the poem to his wife, which, though it ends with the statement that "she fear'd not death," seems somehow unfinished, this one about Hooker's death is the most polished, rounded poem of its type. This accomplishment is due in part to its division into five sections: each is directed to a different group of mourners, which creates a sense of completeness—the feeling that all parties have been accounted for. And partly its success is due to the fact that the gnawing uneasiness of the earliest elegies about the thinning of Israel's glory becomes its major concern. In fact, Hooker's death is really used to preach a verse Jeremiad against apostasy in New England. Hooker himself is merely a point of focus—an occasion for Taylor to declare his deepest ecclesiastical concerns, or an eminence from which he can descry and rout the enemies of Congregationalism. Partly because it is not basically an elegy but a public edict, it shows Taylor speaking publicly at his best. (p. 130)

[The] commemoration of Samuel Hooker is Taylor's finest elegy, and it is also one of the finest in the New England metaphysical style. It is, therefore, an excellent representative of all the devices of the elegy, except for the classical allusion, which Taylor prefers to avoid. It also represents the summation and refinement of his abilities in the form—puns and biblical allusion; the speech of the deceased and the *exemplum*; the personification of country, colony, and town; the carefully inwrought text from Jeremiah to support his own Jeremiad; and the fully accomplished organization of the whole.

His later elegy about Increase Mather (1723) is interesting for being not only a statement about New England's foremost intellectual leader for more than a quarter of a century and Taylor's close friend but also an echo of his dialogue with Maypole dressers who seem now to have moved to New England and to have displaced Mather, who chose rather to play at "Gospel games, which is an heavenly race." And his elegy on Mehetable Woodbridge, his sister-in-law (1698), has been given the honor of having sketched "the most effective death scene" in the form. Neither is equal to the Hooker elegy; but these and the six other elegies form a minor theme in Taylor's developing skill as a poet. They are also a kind of sketchbook in which he practiced initially the celebration of his golden

theme in the **Meditations**, and they reflect his growing skill in verse. Finally, they represent Taylor's growing concern with the state of God's cause in the New World, and his progressive fear and discouragement with the ecclesiastical and social decline there. (pp. 134-35)

Norman S. Grabo, in his Edward Taylor, *Twayne Publishers, Inc., 1962, 192 p.*

EVAN PROSSER (essay date 1967)

[*In the following excerpt, Prosser examines the structure and imagery of Taylor's work reflections of the author's basic theology.*]

One of the most important underlying themes in Taylor's verse is evident in the very presentation of the **Preparatory Meditations**. That each poem is preceded by a scriptural passage upon which it is based indicates that the poet is not engaged in independent inquiry so much as in contemplation of an already revealed truth. The universe of this poet is closed to searching after novel interpretations of reality. The truth behind the world and his experience is given him in the Bible; he takes as his task the explication of scriptural revelation in terms of daily life on earth. Taylor's conviction that analogies of Biblical doctrine can be found in his immediate surroundings is founded on a generally held Puritan idea that, as John Cotton put it, the world is a "mappe and shaddow of the spiritual estate of the soules of men." As far as Taylor's poetry indicates, the discovery of analogies was only as difficult as reading a map. By and large, any struggle involved in the discovery of the unity of doctrine and experience remains outside the poem. What we are given in the verse is a vision of a world in which God, Nature, and man are in blessed harmony.

Intimacy with God is shown to exist on many levels. Taylor is enough in tune with God to be part of an immediate cause-and-effect relationship with Him, as in "**The Return,**" where Taylor refers to his "Rich Grace, thy Image bright, making me pray," or, more extravagantly:

> When thou dost shine, a Sunshine day I have:
> When I am cloudy then I finde not thee:
> When thou dost cloud thy face, thy Face I crave.
> The Shining of thy face enlivens mee.
> I live and dy as Smiles and Frowns take place:
> The Life, and Death of Joy Lodge in thy face.
>
> (pp. 375-76)

Intimacy is the natural relationship between man and God in the closed world where, in Taylor's theology, man and God necessarily interact at close quarters. The "container" theme in Taylor's imagery is the most persistent one running through the poetry that serves to create a closed-world atmosphere. Probably the best-known instance of this imagery is the coach in "**The Joy of Church Fellowship rightly attended**":

> For in Christs Coach they sweetly sing;
> As they to Glory ride therein.
>
> (pp. 376 77)

Taking its inspiration largely, though not exclusively, from the Canticles, another of the prominent container themes, that of the garden, is also expressive of the life that can go on within a world whose basic organization is not to be questioned. Particularly in a Christian context, where "garden" calls to mind the Garden of Eden, "garden" is an appropriate container image for Taylor, carrying with it the idea of an enclosed plot carefully organized and tended by an agent from the outside. Just as the static quality of the box-lock themes is often relieved by a "key's" introducing change and interplay,

> Christs Key of grace this Cabinet unlocks
> And offers thee,

so with the garden theme the feeling of growth imparts vitality to the concept. (pp. 377-78)

In a universe contained and organized by God, Taylor seeks to discover truths about God's universe by explicating isolated elements of God-given reality.... Characteristic of the minute consideration that Taylor gives these revelations of truth is his tendency to linger over his texts. It is as though he were inlaying his closed universe with fragments from the scriptures, laboriously pasting them up piece by piece.... He writes a series of seven Meditations on I Corinthians 3: 21-23. Each of these Meditations, 31-37(I), takes as its basis a single phrase from the short scriptural passage; and even then the bulk of the quotations are from one of the three verses only. Similarly in the Second Series, three Meditations (96-98) are based on Canticles 1:2, "Let him kiss me with the kisses of his mouth: for thy love is better than wine." (p. 379)

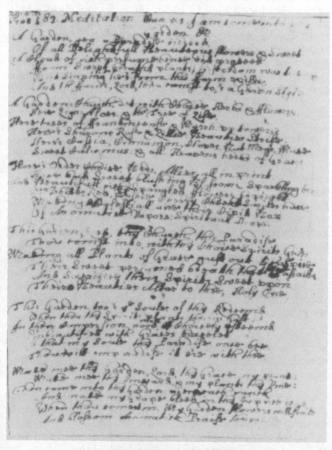

Manuscript page from Preparatory Meditations.

Taylor's use of typology, whereby events and personages of the Old Testament are interpreted as prefigurations of events in the New Testament, is straightforward and thoroughgoing. The main body of the specifically typological poems begins with the Second Series and takes up most of the series through the Thirtieth Meditation. While the particular aim of each of the Meditations in this group is to bring out foreshadowings of Christ in such Old Testament figures as Moses, Abraham, Jonah, and Isaiah, Taylor suggests that the real focus of typology and allegorical reading in general is the mystery of God. Types reach beyond their immediate subject to give evidences of a glory they cannot actually present:

> The glory of the world slickt up in types
> In all Choise things chosen to typify,
> His glory upon whom the worke doth light
> To thine's a Shaddow, or a butterfly.
>
> • • • • • • •
>
> The glory of all Types doth meet in thee.
> Thy glory doth their glory quite excell.
>
> (p. 380)

Allegorical reading is not confined to the Scriptures. In some of the "Miscellaneous Poems" Taylor interprets natural events just as he does those of the Bible and winds up with the same kind of partial vision we have just seen. In **"Upon a Wasp Child with Cold,"** Taylor hopes to "view thy Divinity" through observation of the wasp "In whose small Corporation wee | A school and a schoolmaster see." **"Upon a Spider Catching a Fly"** contains descriptions that have the same kind of allegorical application as is usual in a typological comparison. The spider's web is said

> To tangle Adams race
> In's stratigems
> To their Destructions, spoil'd, made base
> By Venom things
> Dam'd Sins.

Taylor's use of the typological approach both in typology proper and in the allegorical reading of nature introduces a central problem in the poetry. God has provided man with truths of existence that apply to both his everyday life and his relations with the divine. He presents these to man in the Book of the Bible and the Book of Nature for him to read. The only problem is, is man able to read these accounts accurately? Taylor answers that without grace man cannot interpret God's revelations. It is possible to mistake Taylor's position here if we fail to see the two distinct frames of reference within which Taylor speaks. Sometimes he speaks from the world as seen by the sinner, and sometimes he speaks of the world as seen by the saint. Confusion between these two can lead to a misunderstanding of the respective roles of man and God in man's salvation.

Statements made from the point of view of the definitely saved soul necessarily feature visions of close coöperation between man and God. Partly because of the inevitable limitations of human language and partly because of Taylor's special doctrine, which we shall see outlined in the *Christographia*, it is also necessary for Taylor to describe their coöperation in anthropomorphic imagery... :

> Here thus is Entertainment sweet on this.
> Thou feedst thyselfe and also feedest us,

> Upon the spiced dainties in this Dish.
> Oh pleasant food! Both feed together thus;
> Well spicde Delights do entertain thee here.
> And thou thine entertain'st with thy good Cheare.

When such intimacy is indicated by what appears to be an actual bargaining between man and God, as later in the same Meditation, it is particularly difficult not to begin to believe that for Taylor God was not very much exalted above man:

> If I'm thy lilly made by Grace's Art
> I shall adorn thy Palace fragrantly.
> And when thou mee thy spic'de bed interst in
> I'le thee on my Shoshannim Spic'de Songs sing.

But we should bear in mind that such expressions of joy are made by a soul who either has a vision of the graceful state or for some reason has very high hopes.

Representative passages form parts of the poetry where Taylor is in less exalted moods make clear that anthropomorphic imagery is dictated more directly by the necessities of language than by a feeling of natural affinity to God. Especially in a passage dealing with divine as opposed to human wisdom we get a glimpse of the tremendous gap that can exist between God and a sinner, a gap that can be closed only by supplication.

> Unlock thy Locker, make my faith Key here
> To back the Wards. Lord ope the Wicket gate
> And from thine Emerald Shelves, and Pinchase there
> A beame of every sort of Wisdom take
> And set it in the Socket of my Soule
> To make all day within, and night controle.

In the *Christographia* Taylor states explicitly the relation between human apprehension and apprehension aided by grace. In this series of sermons Taylor discourses on the dual nature of Christ, his humanity, and his divinity. It is because of Taylor's strict belief in the humanity of Christ that in the poetry he applies human attributes to God's actions, a habit which, as we have seen, can be a source of some confusion. The doctrinal basis for this habit is expressed in the first sermon, **"The Human Nature,"** where Taylor explains the importance for man of God's assuming a human form:

> For instead of rendering of Humane Nature by
> Sin less than a Worm, and viler than the Earth,
> it prooves the opening of a doore to Advance
> it higher than Angells, and into a Personality
> with the Son of God. Oh! then how is mans
> nature hereby advanced, when a body is prepared
> of it for the Son of God? . . . Here then is
> unspeakable advantage brought to our nature in
> that God prepares of it a Body for his Son.

In the third sermon, **"The Personal Union,"** Taylor describes the Fall of man as the occasion by which man was exalted even over his innocent glory in Paradise. He speaks of the personal union that took place in the salvation of man:

> whereby it (human nature) is as much advanced
> above its first Glory in innocency, in
> brightness of Honor, and highness of excellency, as
> it was cast below that State in darkness of Sin,
> and dolefulness of Sorrow.

This exaltation of humanity can mislead one to minimize the role of grace in Taylor's thought. It may seem that man by his own rational efforts, by way of wisdom, can attain to blessedness. However, the wisdom that Taylor refers to is complete only with the aid of the divine. He says of the wisdom that is Christ's:

> . . . all Created Wisdom is in Christ: This Created
> Wisdom is that light that is Seated in the Intellectual
> Faculty filling the Eye of the Soul with a Cleare Sight
> into all things that are the proper Objects therof.
>
> (pp. 380-83)

To emphasize the importance of humanity's efforts over the grace of divine intervention in the struggle for salvation is to distort Taylor. Taylor is always sensitive to the perilous balance that exists between man's efforts and God's gift of unmerited grace. One result of the combination of this sensitivity with the intimacy with God that Taylor feels is that he is very much aware of the comings and goings of grace and worries about this:

> Yet pardon, Lord, give me this word again:
> I feare to wrong my self, or Gracious thee.
> This I can say, and can this say mentain,
> If thou withdrawst, my heart soon sinks in mee.
> Though oftentimes my Spirits dulled, grow,
> If so, I am, I am not always soe.
>
> (pp. 384-85)

[The] seeing of metaphoric truth in the Bible or in nature necessitates that divine and human apprehension aided by grace differ only in degree and not in kind. The universe cannot be discontinuous, but must be a contained whole unified by the dual nature of Christ. It is as though divine truth were a communicable virus. Man with grace is constitutionally similar enough to God to receive and nurture a germ of truth when Christ carries it from God to saved man. In other words, there is a continuum of inspiration and response that keeps the world unified. (pp. 385-86)

Usually it is quite clear whether Taylor is speaking as a sinner or a saint. What confusion there is comes not from any deliberate obscuring of the point of view, for Taylor usually gives clear indications of the speaker's position at any point in a poem. . . . Confusion is more likely to arise from the constant juxtaposition of the two voices in the verse. Such juxtaposition is functional in Taylor's poetry, as the opposition between voices is the main source of dramatic tension. The two points of view are constantly being opposed and then brought into a resolution. Because both are seen as a part of a continuous system, the resolution of their conflict is always in terms of a flow from one to the other. In this opposition and its resolution we have the basic pattern behind the reciprocal processes of man's supplication for grace and his receiving of it, as Taylor sees them.

The supplicating element, so evident in all of Taylor's verse, is given dramatic quality primarily by means of contrasts based on the opposition of the earthly and the heavenly. (p. 387)

One of the most pervading image themes of the poetry, that of the conduit, plays a large part in presenting the ideas of supplication and response. Essentially it is a metaphor for any means by which flow between man and God is facilitated. The great frequency and variety of its use give a sense of the great possibility that Taylor sees of communication between the human and the divine. (p. 390)

"Filling" imagery provides a transition from the conduit concept to the idea of a "Fullness" of existence, wherein man and God's grace perfectly and completely interact to form a heavenly image of the truly contained and continuous world. With the "fullness" theme we have in a way been brought full circle and can see the kind of existence there would be in God's created contained world if the supplication made for grace were completely responded to. (p. 391)

Evan Prosser, "Edward Taylor's Poetry," in The New England Quarterly, *Vol. XL, No. 3, September, 1967, pp. 375-98.*

WILLIAM J. SCHEICK (essay date 1974)

[*Scheick is an American educator, author, and editor of* Texas Studies in Language and Literature *whose critical works include* The Will and the Word: The Poetry of Edward Taylor *(1974) and* The Slender Human Word: Emerson's Artistry in Prose *(1978). In the following excerpt from the first-named work, he explores Taylor's conception of the human body and the way it relates to the soul.*]

Too often New England Puritan writings have been read in the light of a Platonic or a stoical conception of the human body. It is true that their sermons and diaries focus on the necessity of restraining the body's unruly appetites and passions. According to their psychology, however, the corrupted flesh actually represents a symptom or sign of sin, a view which does not deem the body as the root of evil and the locus of sinfulness. Puritan divines generally refer to the body in a manner similar to their use of the term *nature*; in both instances they primarily stress the *fallen condition* of nature and the body in order to confront sin in its most evident manifestation, that is to say, in the daily lives of their parishioners. A consideration of their Augustinian and Scholastic heritage, with its respect for the human body, argues in fact for a more integrated conception of the body and the soul.

Edward Taylor did not affirm the Platonic belief that the union of flesh and spirit results in discomfort and harm to the soul, which, as a prisoner of the body, longs to return to its heavenly abode. Nor did he advocate the suppression of the body's senses and affections as a prerequisite for a rational life. . . . [His] belief in God's emanation of degrees of perfection or glory counters any idea of a dualism or dichotomy between the natural (flesh) and the heavenly (spirit) orders. As the link between animals and angels, as the very center and crown of creation, man was destined to use his body as an instrument of his soul. (pp. 27-8)

Taylor's rejection of a dualism between the temporal and divine orders is relevant to his conception of the body and the soul. For him the fact that men and angels are fellow servants of God is evident in the angelical nature of the human soul. Indeed, the nature of angels and that of men are so essentially related that "Some are ready to thinke that the Glory of man at the first was Such as did attract the Angells to gaze at him; and the Devells to Envy, and malice him."

Adam possessed a body, second in perfection only to that of Christ. In every way his sensory and affective motions were in harmony with the dictates of his rational soul. It was the divine purpose "that all those Glorious Qualifications, and all those admirable Organs of the Bodie of man, so curiously made, and that imortall Soule, that is Seated in the Whole of these, should in a most regular way act to the glory of God." Adam's "Whole fabrick Consisting of Body and Soule" displayed a beautiful harmony not only between flesh and spirit but also between Adam, the universe, and God.

This harmony was contingent on the body's inherent goodness. As long as it was subordinate to the soul, the body's excellence would manifest itself. . . . Man's senses, as the windows of the soul, originally received divine instruction from nature, instruction which was consistent with right reason and which urged man to respond affectionately to God. Adam, in other words, led a life in which "the Rationall Soule in the body of man, acts the Sensitive body to live a rationall life, by means of its personall Union to it."

In spite of his perfection, Adam's "affections were liable to erre in their Naturall motions." This does not mean that the capacity for sin lay in the senses or affections of Adam's "Spotless Body" Rather, man's flesh, which possesses less perfection than and exhibits a dependence on the higher goodness of the soul, is unstable without rational guidance. But the body itself, as an aspect of God's phenomenal manifestation, remains free from any natural or inherent tendency to sin, for even "Fallen Nature is not Sinfull Nature before it is Rationall nature." Sin is readily manifested in the spirit's bodily agent, but it is solely the product of the rational soul.

The Fall disrupted the initial harmony between the body and the soul. Sin prevented Adam and any of his descendants from benefiting from the divine image once reflected by man's whole being. This loss diminished the excellency of the human body's motions because it impoverished the rational soul by which those motions are animated; both "were Spoiled, and broke to pieces by the Fall." Formerly the temple of the Holy Spirit, the whole man, now shattered and threatened by an apparent dualism between the body and the soul, becomes a tenement in ruins. In respect to his body, man finds himself "turnd out of Doors, and so must stay, / Till's house be rais'd against the Reckoning day."

Nowhere, however, does Taylor say that the body is objectively evil. (pp. 33-5)

Despite his frequent reference to the soul's yearning for heavenly joys, Taylor does not contend that the spirit aches for emancipation from the body. The soul's desire for eternal life stems from that inherent inclination toward perfection found throughout creation. It longs for heaven because there it will be restored to its rightful place in the psychological hierarchy, because as long as the senses and affections remain undisciplined and swayed by carnal gratification, the body appears to oppose the greater good of the soul.

While on earth, the saint is engaged in an unrelenting struggle to realign his body and soul. In the postlapsarian world the senses (which inform reason) and the affections (which give vent to the will's motions) often interfere with and even hinder man's search for truth and wisdom. They are now animated by a sin-ridden soul. "Flesh and Blood, are Elementall things," and in their unnatural insubordination to the soul they gravitate toward the satisfaction of mere carnal appetites. It is in this sense—and only in this sense—that life can be death, that the human body seems a coffin for the soul. The restoration of the body to its rightful place and dignity as the spirit's agent first requires the rectification of the soul, especially the will. With grace the sinful soul and the fallen body—"Nature's Alembick," with "all its pipes but Sincks of nasty ware"—will evince a partially renewed solidarity. Sin . . . is a moral state and thus not inherent in nature or in the flesh. Indeed, what lures man to sin is not his body but his "want of Originall Righteousness together with a strong inclination unto all actuall evill flowing from the guilt of Adams first Sin over all his posterity." Taylor considered the Incarnation, albeit at every moment a gracious gift and an unprecedented act, a natural event. I am not suggesting that the Son was in any way coerced by nature to become incarnate, for both his act of creation and his Incarnation were strictly voluntary. I mean that the body, as a part of nature and as a fundamental component of the whole man, consorted from the first with the order of grace and that the Incarnation increases the degree of its participation in the higher realm. Such an interpretation counters the misleading notion, more accurately attributed to such poets as George Herbert and Richard Crashaw, that the Incarnation shocks nature by suddenly yoking it to the transcendent heavenly order. If the two realms are always intertwined, as Taylor's understanding of nature and of the body suggests, then the Incarnation cannot be construed as an *unnatural* occurrence. (pp. 36-7)

The Incarnation, moreover, was a natural event in another sense. It was from the first a part of the Father's creative plan. God, to be sure, did not ordain the commission of sin in order to necessitate Christ's redemptive sacrifice, but his omniscience anticipated man's actions and providentially allowed for sin in the original scheme. (p. 37)

Because Christ became true man, the whole being of the saint is renewed by divine grace. This means, among other things, that the dignity of the saint's body is reaffirmed. The Incarnation rejuvenates and elevates the essential tie between the flesh and the spirit. Although after the Fall man's being is a mere "Mortall Chip," it never loses, despite the effects of sin, its fundamental connection to God, the "Eternall Plank." When Christ, the "Eternall Plank" or the tree of life, reasserted this essential relation and joined immortal God-head and mortal manhood, human nature—the body and soul, the whole man—was reconverted into "Choice Timber Rich."

The saints are the branches of this fruit-bearing tree. They are specially elected (though only God knows why) and, like timber, are destined to serve a purpose: the glorification of God. Their souls have been rescued by Christ from eternal damnation and their entire being has been freshly retimbered by grace. (p. 40)

[Grace] influences the affections of the body. Taylor emphasized the affections, especially love, because as mental and physical expressions of the soul they are an index to a man's moral state. Although he certainly realized that no single, satisfactory means existed to determine his moral condition with certitude and although he humbly resigned himself to God's mysterious will, Taylor looked to his affective responses for an indication of his standing with God. (pp. 41-2)

[It] is, I think, erroneous to interpret Taylor's conception of the human body from a Platonic point of view. Though he certainly lamented the corrupt state of the flesh, he did not see the body as the prison of a soul yearning for release. It is somewhat misleading to conclude about Taylor that by "spreading out his devotion, by giving it a wider base in his entire life, by denying as strenuously as he could in his whole behavior the duality of body and spirit, and by making himself personally and socially, in his family, church, and community, the whole creation of God, he somewhat relieved the tension that nearly undid John Donne." In Taylor's works, as in those of Donne, there exists no real or objective conflict between the natural and heavenly orders. Taylor emphasized the whole man. This is why he abjured a mere mental or contemplative response to God, why he looked even beyond his *Preparatory Meditations* and to his affections for a sign of the effects of converting grace on his entire being: "Oh! that I ever felt what I profess." In spite of the fact that he deplored the rebellious state of fallen flesh and that he thought Original Sin was transmitted through "Spermatick Principalls," Taylor did not advocate the stoical suppression of the senses and affections. Human nature becomes sinful nature only when it becomes rational nature; though it manifests itself through the soul's bodily agent, sin nevertheless lies solely in the rational soul.

With this perspective it is not difficult to reconcile Taylor's tirades against the flesh. By the word *flesh* he meant the body's moral or subjective condition resulting from sin. This word, as Paul used it and as Edwards explained it in his essay of the Trinity, became a shorthand expression signifying the corrupted state of the body. That is to say, it meant the postlapsarian condition in which the body, bereft of proper guidance, appears to be in tension with the soul. Taylor, as did other Puritan ministers, spoke harshly of the flesh, in this sense, in order to convey to his parishioners the necessity of renouncing the present carnal emphasis of their bodies; then they might strive for a more proper alignment between the body and the soul. They were to seek for the subordination of the flesh "under the conduct of the Spirit." And when, upon occasion, Taylor berated the body in his meditations, he did so for the same reason; he employed the poetic device of meiosis in order to impress upon himself an image not of the inherent evil of the body but rather of its corrupted moral condition. The only real resolution of the apparent conflict between the spirit and the flesh resulting from the postlapsarian moral state of the soul lies in grace, which reinvigorates the soul and reinstates the defiled body to its rightful place. . . . (pp. 46-8)

> *William J. Scheick, in his* The Will and the Word: The Poetry of Edward Taylor, *University of Georgia Press, 1974, 181 p.*

KARL KELLER (essay date 1975)

[*Keller is an American educator, editor, and the author of* The Example of Edward Taylor (1975) *and* The Only Kangaroo among the Beauty: Emily Dickinson and America

(1979). In the following excerpt from the former work, he considers the perceived Americanness of Taylor's poetry and comments on the scatological and erotic imagery fundamental to the Preparatory Meditations.]

The neglect and the discovery of Edward Taylor's poetry have been made more interesting by the desire to believe the Taylor family's story about his injunction against publication. Having willed himself into anonymity, Taylor's unexpected emergence in the twentieth century has been almost as interesting as the poetry itself and the gap that it fills in American literary history. The phenomenon of finding Taylor at that point in American literary history where we were sure so good a poet could not appear has become integral to the poetry itself. The find romanticizes him for us; the wooden preacher takes on a little color thereby.

Shortly before his death in 1729, so the family story goes, Taylor "enjoined it upon his heirs never to publish any of his writings." Though the existence of his poetry was to be reported a number of times, it was lost to us for over two centuries. The unpublished manuscripts fell first into the hands of Taylor's grandson Ezra Stiles through Taylor's son-in-law Isaac Stiles, then into the hands of his great-grandson Henry W. Taylor and others in the Taylor family, and finally to Yale University, the Westfield and Redwood Athenaeums, and other libraries, whence it has been recovered and now published. It has taken over 35 years to locate, transcribe, and publish his poetical work—and some poems and much of his prose remain unpublished. None of this was intended; we invade his privacy as we read him today.

Yet publication *was* on Taylor's mind. He was an incessant student and an industrious writer, producing in the course of 67 years works totalling about 3,100 manuscript pages. As far as his descendants knew, he had "an abiding passion for writing poetry during his whole life."

A number of these writings he apparently intended for the public in one form or another. He wrote a 485-page *Commentary on the Four Gospels,* for example, which was so well thought of that Cotton Mather wrote to Dr. John Woodward and other wealthy persons in the Royal Society of London trying to induce them to publish it. The *Christographia* sermons were circulated separately and then later gathered and revised for publication; too complex for the ear, they were to have been printed and read. Eight other sermons, now titled *Treatise Concerning the Lord's Supper*, were his contribution to the public debate over the Stoddardean heresy. There is also supposed to have been a quarto volume containing many short occasional poems prepared for publication, and quite a number of Taylor's funeral elegies, acrostic love verses, and poems for special occasions were read by the bereaved, the beloved, and interested audiences from Westfield to Boston. Even the poems of *Gods Determinations* and his *Metrical History of Christianity* smack of widely read genre pieces of the period used for soteriological and educational purposes; they show that Taylor did not write in a social vacuum but had a sense of audience, a sense of what was happening in the religious experience of declining New England.

All of this should show that for the archetype of a private poet in our literary history, Taylor had intents and purposes that were noticeably public. Only the *Preparatory Meditations,* a few of the more meditative sections of *Gods Determinations,* and several of his miscellaneous poems seem to have been composed for purely private rather than public ends. Though Taylor copied out a few of them for slight revision, the form in which they have come down to us suggests intermediacy and private satisfaction rather than finality and publication. Where the more public poems are didactic, even dogmatic, the meditative poems are dramatic. The one type is for the most part in drier, more constrictive decasyllabic couplets, the other in the freer, more dramatic sestet of Robert Southwell, George Herbert, and Christopher Harvey (a stanza form which Taylor called "A brisk Tetrastich, with a Distich sweet"). Most of his poems turn outward and are descriptive, narrative, stilted, and technical, but the private poems turn inward, their substance lost in their inward action. Even the full title of Taylor's *Meditations* suggests a privacy about them: *Preparatory Meditations before* My *Approach to the Lord's Supper . . . .* He spoke publicly, but his private poetry made it another world with a language of its own. It would appear that in not making these poems public, Taylor may have been asking, as Emily Dickinson was later to do, How do you publish a piece of your soul?

To account for the privacy of such poetry, it has been a temptation to turn to Taylor's personality and find there a modesty and humility that would have prevented publication. Items from his biography encourage this for a reason: his choice for his ministerial labors of the humbler, remote Westfield over Boston, the publishing center, or Cambridge, the intellectual center; his notoriously rigid piety and reputation for sweetness, personality, and selfless service; his emphasis on the psychological and occult side of Puritanism. Though we know his life poorly, it appears to have been self-sufficient, defensive, insignificant, inward, and thereby one for which a public was not needed. He simply seems to have lacked the vanity of desiring fame, especially at the end of his life when he was no longer interested in writing.

Yet he was at the same time a thorny, proud, contentious personality, a man of quick passions, a man who kept an interest in the public affairs of the area and the colony and who maintained an association and correspondence with the leading public figures of the period. He was a vigorous advocate of unpopular causes, a curious, constant, powerful man, a man abreast of the issues of his time and sure that God had raised him up in hard times to defend the faith. No one who knew him or knew of him thinks to attribute to him the qualities of modesty and humility of the sort that would have prevented him from baring his soul publicly. So it is unconvincing to presume in him an indifference to his writing, a life too lofty to communicate, an exclusiveness with no responsibility to the world. Because of the Puritan suspicion of the incomprehensible and uncommunicative, to find a modesty and humility behind his injunction against publication is to see his spirituality as schizophrenic, even heterodox.

And though Taylor's orthodoxy is unassailable, at least as he revealed it to congregation and community, in his private life, the inward life which his meditative poetry parallels, he may have been something else—noncovenanting Calvinist, vulgarizer of the faith, secret antinomian, arminian enthusiast, esthetically an Anglican or even Catholic, liberal neoplatonist or humanist, sensualist and mystic, even pagan. For such positions (take your choice), he might have had to hide his private thoughts and passions from soberer eyes, and so withheld his poetry from publication. He knew an incompatibility between his style and his belief.

But in a way, the discovery of Taylor's writings did not so much find a skunk in the garden as point up the carelessness of much of the gardening; we were, perhaps, not well prepared for the sensuously meditative, the joyously logical, the humanistically knowledgeable, and the appropriately personable in high Puritanism, and Taylor has in part forced the adjustment. In view of a life devoted to the hard labor of justifying the status quo, a mind sharpened in a very narrow theological groove, and esthetics that could not possibly be distinguished from dogma, it seems clear that if Taylor would not publish his poems, it would have to have been because of his *devotion* to Calvinist principles, not because he was afraid of them.

That his devotion to dogma overwhelmed and limited his skill with his art—and that he knew it—might be seen as a more convincing reason for his not publishing. A man of wide reading and esthetic sensitivity, he might have seen how flawed his verse was by comparison and therefore suppressed it. His meiotic sensibility, as well as his sensitivity to criticism, would have discouraged him. His lack of polish may have embarrassed him, his verses' complexity and obscurity may have warned him, his lack of confidence in his own theory and practice may have humbled him. He may have been simply still another example of a writer conscious of having written something inferior and anxious to forget the fact.

But if Taylor could sense all of this about the unacceptability of his poetry, then he would also have had a sense that the American Puritans would have found his poetry exciting and instructive. He would have known that his work was superior to *The Tenth Muse Lately Sprung Up in America* or *The Day of Doom* or *New England's Crisis*, collections of verse that the first century of Puritans had taken pride in. If he were simply stoical about his lack of ability to write well, he would not have been the meticulous craftsman that he often attempted to be—conscious of technique, working hard to achieve different effects, reworking his lines until they were as dramatic as he could make them—only to do little or nothing to prevent their loss.

It is also possible that Taylor knew he was artistically and intellectually always a little out of touch with his times. His fervor, his style of thought, and his form of verse were all fairly dated. He wrote and thought in 1725 the same as he had written and thought in 1682, as if literary history had been suspended; he was, oddly, a contemporary of Dryden and Swift. The baroque mode that he loved was old fashioned by at least fifty years; his use of it is a relic. By the eighteenth century the meditative tradition had few apologists and few literary uses, even on the Massachusetts frontier. The year 1700 is too late for a morality-play-cum-versified-theological-sermon like **Gods Determinations**. His **Christographia** sermons are imitative of Increase Mather's sermons *The Mystery of Christ Opened and Applied* (1686) and behind them by two decades; his **Metrical History** is imitative of Matthias Flacius' *Magdeburg Centuries* (1516) and John Foxe's *Actes and Monuments* (1563) and behind them well over a century. And

all of the verse and prose that Taylor wrote in the Stoddardean controversy was written in defense of a cause that was unpopular, untenable, and already pretty well lost.

But, though almost everything about him fits an earlier world better, there is nothing to convince one that Taylor had any concern whatever for literary fashion or fashionability of thought—or in fact any reason to concern himself. His call was to the defense of the New England Way and he fulfilled that call with whatever verbal skills he had. That his defense was a strong and almost lone one would hardly be reason for not publishing.

It now seems that these are all reasons without much foundation, reasons that look to Taylor's personality and temperament or to an external world that did not touch his, rather than to his esthetics or to the lasting qualities of his poetry. Self-effacing, alarmingly personal, botched, and archaic as his poetry is, there is yet something about the nature of Taylor's approach to poetry that justifies its privateness.

In its privateness Taylor's poetry was bound to take on some of the personality of a life lived in the New World, and so a related issue is how his poetry belongs to an *American* tradition of letters rather than simply to a Puritan tradition. Louis L. Martz answers to this in the negative: "Is there anything in Taylor's poetry that could be called distinctively American?" How to justify Taylor at the head of American poetry, and not merely as a transitional figure, a link with the heritage, a bridge to what evolved, is a question of historical interest.

To be sure, Taylor was a man of two cultures. He was educated at both an English academy and Harvard. He both taught at Bagworth, Leicestershire, and preached at Westfield on the American frontier. The books he read, the hymns he sang, and the sermons he heard were produced in both London and Boston, and the writers he learned from were British and American. Also, in his loyalism he saw English and New England polity as one, and the confessions of faith on the American frontier were to him no different from those in Puritan England. He appears to have transplanted himself without disturbing his roots, to have become a colonial without dislocation.

The very fact of his writing his more meditative poetry out of personal experience—with that personal experience having its referents, its color, its issues and forms from these shores—could superficially show him to be a provincial. And the earnestness with which he sees his person, his personality, his personal experience as the proper subject for his best poetry perhaps sets him squarely in a tradition of American letters with Walt Whitman and Emily Dickinson. From one point of view, his poetry may indeed be seen as a personal diary which has its symbolism from an involvement in a New Zion (a symbolism that was to inform a tradition from Edwards to Faulkner); a diary with its extravagances of metaphor bringing heaven down to New England *huswifery* and husbandry (a realistic, vernacular metaphoric mode that from Emerson to Frost was to become an American way of poetry); a diary of a self-conscious and lonely poet in the wilderness whose poetry is the fruit of isolation (a recurrent motif in American letters from Anne Bradstreet and Philip Freneau through Hawthorne and Emily Dickinson).

Yet these are mere surface connections with what was to be an identifiable American culture. From his poems one could not, I think, really reconstruct his personal life in Westfield, nor the daily Puritan life, nor an attitude toward time and place. Was his verse rugged and raw because he moved to Massachusetts? his metaphors hyperbolic and humor exaggerated because he lived on the frontier? his language excited and engaging because he wrote alone? Was it the environment that made him more than one expects from a devout man of the time who used his imagination and biblical lore and ordinary skill in rhyme to concentrate his attention on the aweful ideas suggested by his faith? Simply because he was here does not mean that the spirit of his work was.

His language too has been overrated for its Americanness. It might be thought possible to turn to Taylor's earthy diction, his homely images, his natural speech, his neologisms, and see there the qualities of an American vernacular. Or one might see in his privateness a freedom to invent and play with the provincial words of his native country. But while Taylor's idiolect is highly nonstandard, it is in a number of ways fossilized speech. Much of Taylor's usage is of course difficult to the modern reader though common in his time, but a part of Taylor's diction was obsolete at use (words like *attent, flurr, pillard, pistick, dub, tittle-tattle*), another part was made up of archaic survivals in America not current in standard British English but entrenched in regional English dialects (*jags, lugg, frob, grudgens, nit, frim, womble-crops, fuddling, ding clagd, bibble*), and still another part was made up of highly specialized, technical terms derived from Taylor's reading but not in general use (*anakims, mictams, calamus, catholicons, catochee, surdity, syncopee, barlybreaks, noddy, ruff-and-trumpt*). Charles W. Mignon has identified in Taylor's usage diction from several English and Welsh dialects which fossilized in the colonies but which has become obsolete, and in all of Taylor's writings he has found only three Americanisms (*Cordilera, dozde, Netop*). All of which, instead of substantiating the local character of his speech, makes Taylor obscure and relatively much more remote than any other colonial writer. He relies as heavily on the unfamiliar as on that which would communicate with others in his own time and place, and what has often passed for fresh, coined, homely, realistic in him is in large part, it would appear, verbal obscurity and intended for his eyes alone. Instead of speaking New Englandly, Taylor wrote in a personal idiom that was in many ways uncommunicative. Taylor's language was unique but not because he was on these shores.

More than in his personal experience and his language, it may be that Taylor's real importance as an *American* poet is in his defense of the New England Way of theology. Since that way required him to link his piety with community polity and his introspectiveness with citizenship in the New Israel in America, it might follow that the extent to which Taylor was an ardent defender of New England covenant theology is the extent to which he was an American poet. Taylor's life and writings may indeed be seen as having their main motivation in the idea of the self prepared for grace as a test of visible sainthood, for to Taylor the meditative preparationism required by the Half-Way Covenant justified the whole purpose of the emigration to America, safeguarded the purity of gathered churches, and helped to fulfill God's unique covenant with New England. Therefore, in almost everything he wrote—sermons arguing against Stoddardean liberalism, historical verses tracing the evolution of religion toward New England purity, poetry dramatizing the personal value of preparing oneself for membership in church and community—he was, it would appear, a kind of nationalist. His meditative poetry may be almost completely dominated by the peculiarities of the New England situation. On no other shores would he have had to be so passionately patriotic in his piety.

But like the usual reasons for his injunction against publication, these reasons for his relevance to American culture seem imposed with hindsight on the poetry and not derived from any sight that Taylor himself had. While demonstrating something of a New England life, a New England tongue, a New England mind, his poetry still remains apart and aloof from any relationship with the external world. So instead of looking to Taylor's personality—his self-consciousness, his naturalness, his reactionariness—we need to look to his works. In his works themselves lies a more convincing reason, a reason that at one and the same time establishes Taylor as an important private poet and an important American poet.

When it comes to both issues of publication and nationality, it is important to emphasize that Taylor was concerned not so much with poems as products as he was with the production of poems; that is, not so much with the product as with the process, not so much with Meditations as with meditating. He was, as Roy Harvey Pearce has noted, a man "in action," and a Taylor poem is "the act of a man whose imagination is *now* engaged in *creating* something."

For the most part, Taylor deprecates his poems *as products*:

> I fain would praise thee, but want words to do't:
> And searching ore the realm of thoughts finde none
> Significant cnough and therefore vote
> For a new set of Words and thoughts hereon
> And leap beyond the line such words to gain
> In other Realms, to praise thee: but in vain.

As finished products his poems seem to him mere "blottings," "wordiness," a "sylabicated jumble," "ragged Nonsense," "Languague welded with Emphatick reech." . . . Yet in spite of the impossibility of producing anything of worth, Taylor sees importance in the process of using language as a means of meditating on meaning. In fact, he is obsessed with the need to write. Though the purposelessness of a poem itself ought to inhibit the act of composition, it doesn't, for Taylor finds joy in the duty of going through the process. He seems even to accept from the outset the futility of his efforts, but he nonetheless longs to express himself:

> I am this Crumb of Dust which is design'd
> To make my Pen unto thy Praise alone,
> And my dull Phancy I would gladly grinde
> Unto an Edge on Zions Pretious Stone.
> And Write in Liquid Gold upon thy Name
> My Letters till thy glory forth doth flame.

(pp. 81-90)

This is not to say that glory eludes Taylor, for he has glory *as* he sings rather than *in* his song. The opportunity of carrying out his duty to sing praise to God is for him enough; and the result of his singing, his poems, is largely irrelevant. If he is moved to write, he knows that by some divine favor his life has been made dynamic, and it is that spiritual momentum which is important. Without such a process, the product (his life, his poem) is worthless. (p. 91)

Taylor's orthodoxy itself demanded a concern with process rather than product. The condition of the Fall is static and man has mobility only as he works to discover his predetermined spiritual status. His life becomes dynamic as he engages in this process of self-discovery. Nature is in flux and by concentrating on *process*, the Puritan participates, if only through his imagination, in the nature of things as they lie beyond the condition of the Fall. Through thinking of his writing as a process, Taylor, like many of Reformed persuasion, could reenact the process of salvation and live in the illusion of a spiritual development of oneself.

Through introspective meditation the Puritan engaged in a process of transferring truth from the memory and intellect to the affections and the heart and will. In Taylor's predestinarian cosmology, this process was the only thing in which a Puritan could willfully engage in the whole act of salvation: he moved through a series of interior stages of contrition and humiliation, affection and repentance, examining himself mercilessly, arousing in himself a longing desire for help, and thereby predisposing himself for the possibility of saving grace. Without this process, he could not experience the transformation determined for him or even anticipate it, nor would his consciousness be involved in it. But because of the process, he could discover the determined direction of his life. In this there is a careful distinction between the movement and the thing moved, between God in action in a man's life and the man himself, between the process and the product.

This intensely personal process of anticipating salvation dominates the esthetics of Taylor and lies behind his injunction against publication as well as his relevance to American culture. As a poet, language helped Taylor to achieve the condition of "preparedness" he desired. Meditation was for Taylor, as for many Puritans, a *verbal* art. Concentration on the means (language) of arriving at meaning (salvation), he finds his life becoming meaningful (the purpose of praise that he finds himself created for). To be sure, to concentrate on such devices of language as sound, syntax, and imagery is to end up with a poem, a product, but it is the process of working at one's praise that is most important to him, not the result.

Taylor's private poems are themselves for the most part accounts of the process that Taylor went through in preparing himself to be disposed for saving grace. They are not poems *about* the process, but poems showing Taylor *in the process* of preparation. They are miniature dramas in which Taylor is reenacting over and over again that which was to him the most meaningful process of man's life. In fact, the form of a number of the Meditations is so close to the experience dramatized that it can legitimately be called imitative. The form of his poems is fully organic to the ideas in them.

And because he was concerned mainly about the process of writing his poetry, I think that Taylor would have considered as largely irrelevant the modern charges against him of bungling ingenuity, lapses of taste, and awkward

performance. It was a perfect preparation that he was after, not a perfect poem. The writing of poems no doubt helped Taylor get to that point of self-realization desired, and after that objective had been achieved, they were no longer needed. There would have been no reason whatever to publish them. They were useful as devices, as part of the process, of preparing to preach upon and partake the sacrament of the Lord's Supper.

For that reason, a dominant subject in Taylor's poems is Taylor's poems. He is obsessed with writing about writing. He is the Puritan poet's poet, for the poet's worth becomes to him an important metaphor for talking about the business of salvation. Just as he must deprecate himself as a fallen creature of a fallen world, so he depreciates his poems as products. But in addition, just as he accepts the necessity of his existence, so he values the process of writing poetry. Most of the Meditations, and some of the sections of *Gods Determinations*, show Taylor involved dutifully in this process, cursing the results and yet relishing his spiritual activity and hoping for acceptance of his disposition. (pp. 91-3)

Ultimately Taylor's poems do not *mean* very much. They instead show a man watching himself in his worthlessness desiring worth. The meaning of his life therefore lies not in his self nor in his desires (nor even in the object of his desires, God and salvation), but in *the act of desiring*. If he can continually convince himself of the ability to act out his desires, then he can continually reassure himself that God, in His activating love of man, is drawing him to Him. The meditation on one's worthlessness thereby becomes in Taylor's poems the meditation on the process of God's love. In this way the masochistic process of Hookeresque meditation becomes a positive program of conviction of divine love—a moving through the dark self to the realization of light, of worth. This is a reenactment in miniature of the human condition, giving a spatial condition (the Fall) a time dimension (eternal salvation). In being self-destructive, the process of Puritan meditation, at least as Taylor performs it in his *Meditations*, is therefore life-giving. When Taylor's writing stops, his faith also lags, and when his faith is weak his writing stops. The process of one is the process of the other.

What I am trying to suggest is that because he was interested in the process of writing rather than in his writings themselves, Taylor's private poetry makes one more example of what John A. Kouwenhoven calls "the national preoccupation with process." Kouwenhoven finds this fascination to be a central quality which those artifacts that are peculiar to American culture have in common. The American skyscraper, with its effect of transactive upward motion, arbitrary cutoff, and repeatable upward thrust; the American gridiron town plan, with its unfinished completeness, its infinitely repeatable units; jazz, with its freedom of innovation within a rhythmic pattern, its bounds-ignoring momentum, its unresolved harmony; the Constitution, as an infinitely extendable framework; Mark Twain's fiction, with its irreverence for proportion and symmetry, its river-like momentum, and its characters who are, as was Huck Finn, ready to "light out" again; Whitman's *Leaves of Grass*, with its restless, sweeping movement on long lines, its openness at the end; comic strips and soap operas, with their lack of ultimate climax, their emphasis on the continued facing of problems without resolution; assembly-line production, with its timed operations, repetitive work, intermediacy, unfinishedness; chewing gum, with its nonconsumability, its value for action but valuelessness as commodity—all such things unique to American culture have, when judged esthetically, the central quality of *process*. To Kouwenhoven, "America is process." This quality involves mobility, ever-changing unity, mutability, development, and other facets which militate against the idea of man's (and society's) permanence and perfection and pitches him instead into a condition where change, progress, impermanence, and unfulfilled desire have almost moral value.

Indigenous too to Taylor's esthetics is this principle of process. He has a rigid pattern, a cage or skeleton, within which he works (for the most part, the decasyllabic line, the six-line stanza, the fear-hope-desire pattern or the certainty-despair pattern for a structure, and these repeated over and over again as a process of consecutive occurrences without climax, without conclusion, without concern for time, without finish, without resolution), but he finds a way of moving, of being moved, within the frame. Through imaginative use of language, he has freedom within fate, freedom of movement within the determined framework of covenant theology. This redramatizing of his search for signs of salvation suggests vitality within unity, movement in conflict with stasis, desire vs. the human condition. And to do this in preparation of oneself for finding an acceptable place in the pattern of the sacrament of the Lord's supper suggests how poetry served Taylor as illusion: as he wrote he was imagining himself undergoing change in a predetermined universe.

It may be a temptation to think that Taylor's purpose was to try to produce poems that would be so finely wrought, so carefully formed, so fully representative of his mind and spirit that they might serve as signs to Taylor of his election, proving over and over again to himself, like a Puritan merchant realizing proof of his election through his business success, how success with poetic devices is a sign of his justification. But this view must be modified by Taylor's rejection of the products of his pen and the joy he takes in the process alone.

To think of Taylor as conceiving of his poems as great poetry (an assumption that debunkers of Taylor begin with) is the same as saying he lacked critical ability or esthetic sensitivity or knowledge of poetry. He knew how bad his poems were, just as he knew how insufficient he himself was. But to think of Taylor as thinking primarily of the value of the process he was going through each time he wrote a Meditation is to admit significance in him (to be sure, a different kind of significance) as a poet.

In this light, one begins to see purpose even in the "flaws" of his poetry—purpose in his choice of old-fashioned baroque for his metaphors; purpose in his annoying insistence on anaphora, anacoluthon, ploce, polyptoton, and other disruptive scholiastic rhetorical devices; purpose in his corny borrowings from Ramist logic, Biblical typology, and the poetry of Herbert and Quarles; purpose in the erratic mechanics of his punctuation, rhymes, syntax; even purpose in his boring repetitiveness, his awkward unevenness, his outmoded fervor, his banality and bathos. They all must have appeared to Taylor effective devices for moving himself to that depth of soul that he desired, and therefore artistically justified, even esthetically functional. Because he was writing for himself alone and not for oth-

ers, Taylor was free to write of his soul and his God in the language he wanted. How these devices look and sound to us is not as important as how they moved Taylor.

In these ways, Taylor is the exemplary private poet. That he should so greatly enjoy the process of meditating by means of the language of poetry is evidence of its centrality to his esthetics. And being central, it works to include him centrally in American culture as, I feel, no other feature of his thought or style does. Ironically though, his humble love of the poetic process as he knew it almost lost his writings for us. How many other poets were there in early New England who, in being American in the same way, are, as Taylor once was, lost, neglected, undiscovered?

Whether Taylor intended his poetry to provide an example for others to follow we may never know. But by seeing how the process of writing was important to Taylor where the products of his pen were not, I think it is possible to justify his injunction against publication and at the same time make him relevant to the American tradition in literature. (pp. 94-7)

• • • • •

The art with which Taylor pursued his ideas in the *Preparatory Meditations* is seen best in his imagery. A significant esthetic emerges from his metaphors, but more valuable to Taylor would have been the fact that an important eschatology is what his imagery reveals. That the *Preparatory Meditations* was intended by Taylor to be a unified work, in both thought and style, shows up in an exploration of its image patterns.

Among the various kinds of images of salvation in his poems, that scatological and erotic imagery that peppers Taylor's *Meditations* is most fundamental to his thought and most unifying to his art as a Puritan. Taylor obviously felt that his orthodox Puritan eschatology was best explored in such terms, for of all the various types of images in his poetry these are the most dominant. Taylor's vision of the fallen world and of sinful man often finds form in excremental language. . . . (p. 191)

It has been an embarrassment to some of the readers of the *Preparatory Meditations* that Taylor was so worldly in his imagery and a comfort to others that he can be so colorful in his orthodoxy. But rather than being embarrassed or comforted by Taylor's "bawdy" imagery, I would like to argue the extent to which Taylor's excremental view of life and erotic view of salvation *are* his Puritanism. And in the process, one can become convinced of the artful unity of the *Preparatory Meditations*. The descriptions of flatulence, defecation, diseases, seductions, and sensual pleasures in meditation on the Holy Supper are not nods, slips, heresies, or sublimations, but simply honest talk (in rather conventional Biblical/Protestant/Puritan symbols) of how God's grace works.

It cannot be said of such imagery in Taylor's poems, as it can of, say, Shakespeare's bawdry, that the poet is thereby proclaiming his manhood, revealing that he is worldly-wise, or showing himself simply frank and capable of compromise with "the world's slow stain." Though Taylor's individual excremental and erotic images are used by and large in the Meditations as if they are merely facets of cold dogma, the very choice of such language by Taylor suggests a sense of human balance and normalcy of sensibility of the sort that one enjoys (much more fully, to be sure) in Shakespeare. Taylor is withdrawn, intensely dogmatic, and private, however, rather than broad, healthily coarse, and unsqueamishly natural in his use of such language.

Nor can it be said of Taylor's images of salvation, as it can of Donne's grotesque and erotic imagery, that it reveals that underneath the skin he was both sinner and saint, idealist and realist, or a man gradually reforming his life. Taylor is, instead, consistently austere and overwhelmingly eschatological; the joy and sap of life did not fill him in the same way.

Also, where a writer like Swift used conventional Christian symbols of vilification to emphasize his misanthropic view of the depravity of man and the repulsiveness of contemporary life, as well as symbols of sexuality as expressions of hope, a writer like Taylor uses the same symbols for sin and salvation, but for a more plainly soteriological purpose. Swift damns the human race with its "strange Disposition to Nastiness and Dirt" in order to effect a catharsis, and Taylor, with a different theology, makes man stink so that salvation will smell sweet to him.

In the Meditations, Taylor's excremental vision of life and erotic vision of salvation are characterized by existential endurance, evangelical introspection, and infallible hope. That makes him a different kind of writer. From the point of view of the psychoanalysis of history, Taylor is a Protestant fundamentalist of the purest, most analytical and honest kind. And his scatological and erotic imagery proves that fact better than anything else.

As Taylor would have one believe in the Meditations, the world is a "Dunghill Pitt" where man in his fallen state has been corrupted by irrevocable and inscrutable guilt, and is therefore "with filth . . . all defilde." Such scatological imagery is not peculiar to Taylor, however. It is part of world culture from the Bible and Augustine through Calvin, Luther, and Puritan theological discourse. All of these taught Taylor to characterize man's condition in the language of filth. (pp. 192-93)

From the beginning of the *Preparatory Meditations*, Taylor analyzes his difference from the Divine in terms of foulness, and the contrast in the images, while demeaning man, magnifies the glory of God to Taylor's mind, just as to Jonathan Edwards' mind man's total dependence on God magnifies the absolute and arbitrary will of God. . . . While man smells like "stincking Carrion" and "Dunghill Damps," God is by contrast "A Pillar of Perfume" and "Sweetness itselfe." Man's flatulence makes God's hard grace smell sweet. Man is "Becrown'd with Filth" in contrast to the flowers and herbs that crown God's works, and the ugly sight makes the flowers of grace look the more beautiful. Taylor furthermore characterizes himself as sick and diseased by the Lord's grace as having saving salves and medicines, and the sickness makes the Christian plan of salvation seem all the more a redeeming remedy for his sins. The divine is thus defined by its opposites. (pp. 200-01)

To construct this human difference from the divine, Taylor draws on three sources for his terms (apparently the lowest and foulest he knew): barnyard and swamp imagery, toilet images, and the language of bodily disease. The structure of his thought is often defined by the way he moves in the course of a Meditation or a series of Meditations from a barnyard scene to a garden scene, from a privy to a washroom, or from a sickroom to a physician's apothecary. Each move is a definition—by contrast—of saving grace. (pp. 201-02)

The foulest of barnyards, the filthiest of ordure, and the most severe of diseases all construct the desperation of that need and celebrate by contrast the power and benevolence of God. From his human point of view, if he is put off "as Offal," then to Taylor, "Life would be Death." But from a divine point of view, the excremental state is necessary to the process of salvation, for to be bedunged by God is *part of God's grace*. Such a scatology of grace was for Taylor a way of probing through metaphor the necessary anality of rebirth. The symbolic manipulation of excrement or substitutes for excrement is therefore apocalyptic: dunghills produce gardens, excrement purges, sores bring salvation. (pp. 204-05)

Hope in the form of love-longing is the other half of Taylor's imagery of salvation: gold weds dung, Christ embraces dirt, Eros wins over Thanatos.

> I know not how to speak't, it is so good:
> Shall Mortall, and Immortall marry? nay,
> Man marry God? God be a Match for Mud?
> The King of Glory Wed a Worm? mere Clay?
> This is the Case. The Wonder too in Bliss.
> Thy Maker is thy Husband. Hearst thou this?

In this regard, Taylor's metaphoric approach in the *Preparatory Meditations* is an important theme, showing affirmation amid despair and trying to make a garden of bliss out of the dunghill. "Love," Yeats writes, echoing the Augustinian imagery of salvation we find in Taylor, "has pitched his mansion in/The place of excrement." This is the archetypal paradox of love in a fallen world.

When Taylor strikes an erotic note as he discusses his salvation—

> Lord, let thy glorious Body send such rayes
> Into my Soule, as ravish shall my heart,
> That Thoughts how thy bright Glory out shall blaze
> Upon my body, may such Rayes [to] thee dart.

—we are assured that the repression of life/world/self is replaced in his thinking by affirmation and desire. Yet such erotic imagery pervading the Meditations is not cathartic (that is, not a device for releasing sexual tension) nor ascetic (Taylor is not diverting his emotions into sensuous devotions), nor is it mystical and theoleptic (Taylor does not seek to be literally God-possessed). Rather it is semi-Dionysian—Christ the Lover is a god of joy, of healing, of fulfillment—in a way thoroughly consistent with Puritan theology. This erotic imagery is the sensuous apprehension of the possibility of new life—which was, after all, the true calling of a Puritan minister-poet. (pp. 206-07)

The scheme of Taylor's love meditations is simple; he tells it in his first poem in the *Preparatory Meditations*. God's love is so overwhelming that it "Cannot bee/In thine Infinity, O Lord, Confinde." It is a pent-up flood. But this love is not satisfied until God, through Christ, has "Marri'de our Manhood, making it its Bride." Then, as in a marriage union, it finds release. The love desires of God are satisfied only when, after filling heaven up and overflowing hell, the veins of God the Seducer are conjoined with the veins of Man the Beloved. Then the love that God passionately finds outlet for in man through Christ can be repaid by man's passionate love of God. All the factors of Taylor's erotic scheme of salvation are here: God as Lover, mankind as the Beloved One, the seduction, and loving reaction in man that amounts to regeneration. Through such erotic terms, the doctrine of atonement is turned into poetic metaphor.

Taylor tells the whole story of atonement once again in Meditation I.23, and again in erotic terms. So that he might be passionately "inflamde," Taylor says (now playing the role of a desirous woman, as he does in most of his Meditations), he prays for permission to peep into the "Golden City" of heaven to see how "Saints and Angells ravisht are in Glee." Yet he thinks that *his* affairs, *his* love of God, would teach them a thing or two: "'Twould in fresh Raptures Saints and Angells fling." He proceeds to tell how passionate his own love is. Yet he has great doubts that "Man [can] marry God," for it is improper and unnatural that "The King of Glory Wed a Worm." So all that is left for him is "the Wedden in our Eyes"; that is, the passion, the desire, the flirtation. It is the lot of fallen man that his desires go unfulfilled. The reason is that the desires cannot be consummated simply as the result of man's passion; he is depraved, filthy, a worm. It is not until "Christ doth Wooe" and compels the earth-bound Loved One to true love that the two can be joined. God must first be a lover of man before man can be a lover of God. Then their love is consummated. (pp. 213-14)

When Taylor's metaphors of yearning go beyond fleshly descriptions of the Christ who is the source of spiritual beauty and descriptions of the idealized loved one with whom Taylor identifies his spiritual desires, Taylor comes to a use of the language of sexual consummation in a joyous celebration of the conversion from worthless selfhood to divine acceptability and regeneration. "Christ loves to lay the Beloved down" and with "lovely arms ... Circle [her] about, with great Delight." It is as if the soul goes into "Raptures of Joyes" until, as he says, "My Ravisht heart on Raptures Wings would fly." Yet this is not erotic mysticism, but the expression of joy and delight in the possibility of salvation from man's condition. Taylor's desire for love is so intense that it is *like* sexual intercourse: "Thy Person mine, Mine thine, even wedden-wise." So he continually pleads for salvation in sexual terms: "Make thou mee thine that so/I may be bed wherein thy Love shall ly," for he knows that the only way for him to be saved is through the "down laying of myself"; that is, either through abject humility that is like being seduced, or in death as a kind of union with the divine. Such "down laying" is a joyous experience, however, for it is the only way given to man to fulfill his desire for salvation. The language of seduction therefore assists Taylor in reminding himself of the joy, the pleasure, the dynamism of his spiritual desires.

Taylor's erotic images are varied as he seeks to suggest the joy of the love communion: a pearl put into a cabinet, wine poured into a cup, fiery arrows shot through the heart, bag-pipes filled with divine air, sparks of heavenly fire dropped into a tinder box, bellows blowing a fire, or key and oil in a rusty lock:

> Lord, make thy Holy Word, the golden Key
> My Soule to lock and make its bolt to trig
> Before the same, and Oyle the same to play
> As thou dost move them off and On to jig.

For much of such suggestive imagery in the Meditations, Taylor finds it easy to make an erotic metaphor out of innocent Bible idioms, as he does with John 6:53 in Meditation 2.80: "Except you eate the flesh of the Son of Man, etc., ye have no Life in you." To Taylor "having life" suggested the appropriateness of the language of conception in explaining how God gives man a spiritual life. In the poem, Taylor is again the seduced Loved One, who, he says, has no life in her until she "be brought to bed" and "outspred" in the attitude of lovemaking. Then when seduced by the aggressive God that John preaches about, the soul is the womb and Christ is "the Spermadote" and "Saving Grace [is] the seed cast thereinto." Or in other words, God through Christ has holy intercourse with man, "Making vitality in all things flow" until in the womb of the soul "The Babe of Life" is conceived. If the Lord, Taylor concludes, does not make life in him (the seed cast into grace's garden), then his soul is "Spiritual[ly] Dead." Thus man is a fertile garden plowed by the Lord!

Concurrent with Taylor's hopes for God's enravishing love, however, are his more realistic fears that he is rejected as the Beloved of God. He is seldom "hugd," he says, and can "seldom gain a Kiss." He is worried when Christ has kissed him but will not allow him to return the kiss; his emotions are aroused but frustrated:

> let mee lodge in thy Love.
> Although thy Love play bow-peep with me here.
> Though I be dark.

The fault for this lies in himself, he concludes, for though his "ardent love in Christ [has] enfire[d] the Heart," his "Spirituall Eye" is "wholy dark / In th'heart of Love." He yearns for love, yet his fallen nature prevents it. He therefore often fears that Christ might lose his "ardent Flame of Love" for him, his "passionate affection," his "true Love's passion" with "its Blinks or Blisses," for he (Taylor) admits his inclination to love the dunghill of the world more than the Lord. He can find no evidence in his heart at times to "prove his marriage knot to Christ." It is a one-sided love affair, for Taylor finds himself incapable of true love. So he prays that in spite of his debased state, the Lord might make love advances to him continually.

The moment of conversion to God's love is, within Taylor's symbolic scheme, the moment when God the Lover, "Heartsick" for man, ejaculates "in Rapid Flashes" and "bleed[s] out o're Loveless mee." Then man breaks out "in a rapid Flame of Love," repaying the affection. When espoused (chosen) by the Lord, man is "inravisht with thy Beauty's glorious glee," and then "Christ doth Come and take thee by the hand, / And to himselfe presents thee pleasantly [as]/A glorious bride." When Christ has brought beauty to man (that is, elected him) he is then fit "for Christ's Bed" (the communion). Christ proceeds to "Cover thee with's White and Red." In this kind of triple entendre, Taylor's conceits bring together the imagery of sexual union, the signification of the communion, and the dogma of the atonement in a form expressive of the joy of his spiritual desires.

Just as the human and divine combined to create the Christ, so the love between God and man, as in sexual union, combines to make a new being out of excremental man: "One made of twoness Humane and Divine" in order to "compose a Third." This is accomplished when, as Taylor puts it in one poem, Christ's phallic bellows blow on Taylor's coal "till / It glow" and "send Loves hottest Steams" on him. This warms him into intense affection, as to a new life. Then Christ fills his arms and Taylor's worship takes the form of "Embraces." The Lord, as in a bawdy Renaissance scene, "coms tumbling" on man and makes love "in golden pipes that spout/In Streams from heaven." And man is born spiritually. (pp. 216-19)

Most important in Taylor's imagery of salvation that helps to unify the **Preparatory Meditations** is the contrast of the erotic with the scatological. The juxtaposition of the two throughout his Meditations makes an archetypal scheme contrasting, in personal terms, a man's desires vs. his humility before his estate, and, in cosmic terms, spiritual life vs. spiritual death. As Taylor sums it up in Meditation 2.120, because of the "Earthy Dunghills" and "dirty Earth" that dominate man's fallen state, it is necessary for the Lover-Christ to come "Enravishing" mankind, making the world "sweet and Beautious." (pp. 219-20)

In playing both sides of this archetypal scheme against each other and then resolving them in metaphoric forms that amount to a description of the conjuncture of the severe justice of God and the love-longings of man in the process of salvation, Taylor is following the admonition of Paul to the Colossians: You must first "Mortifie . . . your members which are on the earth"; then "as the elect of God, holie & beloved," you must "put on tender mercie"; then will "the peace of God rule in your hearts."

When seen as a unified work after the manner illustrated here, the **Preparatory Meditations** becomes a powerful affirmation of the eschatology of Augustine: "Inter urinas et faeces nascimur." To be sure, the Meditations are individual poems written on particular occasions in language that is varied and on a number of religious subjects. Yet throughout, there is a unity of imagery and tone in all of the separate poems in the series. They were written over a period of thirty years, and yet they work together as a whole to celebrate—even to create—that scheme of salvation which was Taylor's faith. (p. 220)

> *Karl Keller, in his* The Example of Edward Taylor, *The University of Massachusetts Press, 1975, 319 p.*

ALBERT GELPI (essay date 1975)

[*Gelpi is an American educator and the author of* The Poet in America: 1650 to the Present *(1974) and* The Tenth Muse: The Psyche of the American Poet *(1975). In the following excerpt from the last-named work, he addresses distinctive patterns in Taylor's imagery and compares the poet's verse to that of John Donne and George Herbert.*]

Although Edward Taylor left no treatises on poetic theory or practice and even forbade the posthumous publication of his poems, he is the first major poet in America. His boldness and originality can be appreciated more dramatically if his poetry is made to resonate against the sounding board of conventional Puritan literary theory, a position

clearly thought out and tersely propounded in parenthetical remarks, prefatory notices, and occasional essays. The literary principles of the Puritans could be axiomatic, at least for the first generations, because the written word was intended to be all of a piece with the theological vision strong enough to propel a handful of people across the seas to a wilderness to found the City of God. Anne Bradstreet was voicing the courage and the fear of them all when she remembered coming "into this country, where I found a new world and new manners, at which my heart rose." To the minds and tastes of Anglicans like John Donne and George Herbert or of Catholics like Richard Crashaw, the aesthetic attitudes of these colonials would have seemed narrowly and rigidly prescriptive, but these attitudes grew out of their special conception of human nature and man's place in the scheme of things just as much as did Donne's and Crashaw's. Read against the background of the Puritan notion of poetry and language, Edward Taylor's poems stand out in vivid relief, foreshadowing an indigenous American poetic tradition.

William Bradford prefaced his history with the reminder that the story would be rendered "in a plain style, with singular regard unto the simple truth in all things." In the meeting-house, attention to art and artistry—pictures and statues, or music and vestments and ritual—distracted from the essential concern: the focus of God's creatures should be in all things on God's truth. Scholars and historians have long since demolished the caricature of the Puritan as boorish philistine hostile refinement or taste. One need only look at an old New England church for evidence of the Puritans' sense of grace and beauty expressed in simple forms. And they imposed similar limits on literary composition: the style of the artist, his approach to his materials and his medium, must be scrupulously suited (and it was a matter of conscience) to the usefulness of the creation under God in the society, not to the artist's indulgence in the imaginative flights of his titillated senses.

The presuppositions about the written word became a matter of pressing concern and so of precise specification, because if the Puritans produced understandably little music or painting or sculpture, they immediately and copiously began to write book after book. Before anything but a few patches of forest had been cleared for habitation, a printing press was set up in the New World. Since they were a remarkably literate and intellectual group, their leaders, most of whom had received a classical education and training in rhetoric at Cambridge, felt the compulsion, indeed the religious obligation, to write and publish. Their words conveyed God's Word—spoken from the pulpit, sung from the hymnal, preserved between the covers of a book. The purpose and end of writing had, therefore, to be explicit: that writing is best which makes the clearest and most effective translation of God's Word into human speech for the community. No wonder that much of their verse was in fact translation from Scripture. The author's ideas and responses, his talents and invention, were quite irrelevant to the unravelling of complicated matters to the ordinary understanding of ordinary men and women. Though a poet, Anne Bradstreet wanted to make it clear to her children that "I have not studied in this you read [a manuscript book of prose meditations and poems] to show my skill, but to declare the truth, not to set forth myself, but the glory of God."

Needless to say, such assumptions would encourage expository and didactic prose over belles lettres. Even in intellectual prose, however, the writer had to move the reader to the truth of his words, and in order to compel the reader's will he had to move his emotions through affective images and concrete examples. But this emotive appeal of language particularly had to be controlled with a purposeful hand; no ornamental excrescences, no merely human fable, no merely personal touch, no merely individual response should tease the writer's and reader's direct and outward gaze. At the root of this notion of language lay the conviction that the truth or meaning of the written word existed independent of the written word, beyond the skill and personality of the writer, whose task was to investigate objective reality, ferret out the inherent truth and convey it to others less perspicacious than he. (pp. 13-16)

It was in the verse of Edward Taylor . . . that the Puritan spirit received its majestic (and uncharacteristic) poetic statement. (p. 21)

Since Taylor was known as the stern voice raised in the Commonwealth against any abrogation of the covenantal ties, the poetry seems all the odder: written in secret and so private that he would forbid publication even after his death. He would have known the established literary guidelines as he would have known the orthodox position on infant baptism and the Real Presence. Yet he wrote, preserved, and passed on the 400 manuscript pages of poetry marked by personal idiosyncrasy, rhetorical intricacy, elaborate conceits, alliterative and onomatopoetic effects, a thick profusion of images, and an intellectual and emotional intensity that would have jolted the wits of the ordinary reader, had Taylor seen his way to exposing himself thus by publication. The discovery of the manuscripts forty years ago demanded a critical reassessment of the Puritan character and of Puritan poetry. In its evolution Puritanism was for some time resilient enough to contain and nourish its supreme and questioning intellects—Roger Williams and Jonathan Edwards, for example—but not without permanent consequences. By the force of their word and presence these geniuses explored new possibilities in the name of their very Puritanism, thereby expanding its previous formulation and undermining to some extent the substance of Puritanism and its notion of itself. Taylor's poems issued no public challenge to the old order which the poet otherwise staunchly upheld, which indeed he affirmed in his unusual poems; in fact, they present the Puritan consciousness confronting itself in the privacy of its isolation (in the words of Edwards' own resolution) "with all the power, might, vigour, and vehemence, yea violence, I am capable of."

Taylor's sequestration on the outskirts of the colony undoubtedly contributed to the theological conservatism which set him off more and more from the larger community, but in this case intellectual conservatism led to what the community could only consider radical experiments in language. The same conviction that led him to live out in his orthodox fastness the experience of faith issued in poems whose unorthodox language violated not only the restrictions of Bradford and Hooker but also the neoclassic norms of Mather Byles and thereby created the first distinctive poetic style in America.

By the time Taylor arrived from England, his education and poetic tastes had been thoroughly formed. He had read the Renaissance poets, more particularly the metaphysical poets, and most especially George Herbert (judging from the many lines echoed and adapted from Herbert). Among the Puritans in general even the devotional poets of the seventeenth century were little read and imitated because Puritans viewed with alarm Catholicism and its vestiges in Anglicanism as base pandering to the senses and passions of men: "the senses are seduced by Objects, these help to abuse Imagination, which excites disorders in the inferior parts of the soul, and raiseth Passions." Only the otherworldliness of Herbert spared him from the distrust which fell on Donne and Crashaw, with their strongly erotic appeal through imagery and rhythm to the physical senses and the passions.

In a Foreword to Donald Stanford's edition of Taylor's *Poems,* Louis Martz pointed out the many parallels between Taylor and Herbert and also made the equally important observation that substantial differences in sensibility, diction, and technique set Taylor off from the English predecessors to whom he is indebted—from Herbert on the one hand and from Donne and Crashaw on the other [see excerpt by Martz dated 1960]. Taylor's poems consist principally of two long sequences: one (part lyrics, part allegorical morality play) depicting the drama of salvation under the title *God's Determinations Touching His Elect* and two Series of *Preparatory Meditations.* In the poems which make up *God's Determinations* Taylor tried to imitate Herbert's versatility with meters and stanzas but fell far short of Herbert as a virtuoso performer; he simply lacked Herbert's subtlety and adaptability at versification. At the other extreme, the 221 *Preparatory Meditations,* which comprise the bulk of Taylor's work, are all written in the same stave of six (the quatrain and couplet of Herbert's longest poem, "The Church Porch"). Over the decades, during which he wrote "a Meditation" in the same stanza form every six weeks or so, there is notably little limbering or variation; the units remain on the whole sturdy and separate building blocks stacked into a poem.

The real liveliness and originality of Taylor's poetry reside not in prosody but in the qualities of the language, diction, and imagery. Taylor's ear and tongue have a rougher, coarser edge than Herbert's, and the language moves into blunter, more toughgrained effects. At the same time Taylor's language does not recall the more strenuous metaphysical poets. The phrasing and texture suggest neither the baroque energy of Crashaw's best passages nor the nervous athleticism of Jack Donne nor the sinewy strength of Dean Donne but, instead, the bulging muscularity of Edward Taylor of Westfield. At its worst his language can tie itself into knots, the syntax muscle-bound, the word order awry; but no passage of Taylor—good or bad—would be mistaken for lines by any of the English metaphysicals.

The range of Taylor's diction is greater by far than Herbert's, greater even than Donne's: from learned and pedantic terms to expressions from his Leicestershire dialect to words coined for the occasion to colloquial expressions, many of which are obsolete and require a glossary at the back of Professor Stanford's edition. Moreover, many of the unfamiliar and colloquial words have the heavily monosyllabic and consonantal thickness of the Germanic roots of the language, so that the words have the lumpish shape and weight of objects on the tongue: squitchen, springde, hurden, haump, panchins, hift, chuffe, frim, blin, tills, quorns, poother, thrumping, pipkin, cades, crickling, flur, gastard, glout, keck, rigalled, skeg, snick-snarls, and so on. After Herbert's calm limpidity Taylor's diction sounds out with a rude eccentricity and almost primitive power.

Although Herbert frequently applied domestic metaphors to sacred subjects, Taylor pressed his homely images more forcefully and at greater length than either Donne or Herbert. The more sophisticated Englishmen would have found some of his images distasteful and uncouth, as when he dwells on excremental details or on a conceit of circumcision or of the seed's activity in the womb. At times he pushed a single metaphor too hard; at other times he compounded his metaphors into confusion. But even this irrepressibility suggests not so much the indulgent excesses of the minor metaphysical poets as the earnestness of the Puritan-amateur poet. His own sole judge and critic, he was determined at least to exhaust his materials and push his powers to their limits; he would pursue an idea relentlessly rather than risk abandoning it with possibilities unplumbed. (pp. 21-4)

Taylor was no crude and misplaced shadow of Herbert. There is nothing in English metaphysical poetry like either *God's Determinations* or the two Series of *Preparatory Meditations.* In fact, it is the first instance of what may be a distinctly American genre: the open-ended poem written over years, perhaps even over a lifetime, in separate but interacting segments. At any rate, there is nothing like Taylor's *Preparatory Meditations* until Whitman's *Leaves of Grass*, Pound's *Cantos* and Williams' *Paterson.* For all the uneven quality of the particular poems and all the repetitiousness in theme, tone, and imagery, Taylor remains a poet of power and scope, not only in the excellence of particular poems and passages but in the huge harmony of the whole work, and the same is true of Whitman, Pound, and Williams. It is a corpus because its slow progression formulates the terms for translating a vision of reality into a coherent poetic creation. Religious and moral convictions do not make an artist; only the ability to find the symbols for one's convictions lifts utterance into art. Each Meditation elaborates a generating idea or conceit to a personal application at the end. The poetic vitality arises from the metaphorical imagery: not so much from single or individual metaphors (many of which are usual enough) as from the patterns they assume. Certain key metaphors, repeated until they become related, gather themselves into clusters and designs of clusters, evolving a dynamic structure within the uniform regularity of the stanza and the uniform structure of the poems. Images recur and begin to associate themselves with other recurrent images until they accrete as focal symbols which in concert with one another make a kind of figurative *pointillisme.* Point by related point, image by reiterated image, context by analogous context, Taylor draws out the imaginative correlatives for his sense of things. Pound wrote in an early essay, in his own effort to define himself as a poet, that out of the discovery of his unique quality and virtù "the artist may proceed to the erection of his microcosmos"—a very American notion. (pp. 32-3)

Taylor wrote the Meditations as a spiritual and emotional preparation for receiving and administering the Lord's Supper in his church. The Sacrament memorialized the Divine Presence in the individual and joined him thereby to the Communion of Saints—that is, in Calvinist terms, to the Community of the Elect. But that determination rested on personal, subjective confirmation. Consequently, before his appearance at the altar in front of his flock the pastor wrote poems in secret. His only surviving prose is a sequence of sermons called *Christographia* propounding from Scripture and doctrine the significance of the Word's dual nature, God and man, for our mixed existence, body and soul. By extension, in searching his inner heart his words return again and again to the fundamental question that lies beyond question: "But how it came, amazeth all Communion/God's onely Son doth hug Humanity,/Into his very person"(I, 10); "Shall Mortall, and Immortall marry? nay, /Man marry God? God be a Match for Mud?" (I, 23). The answer is incredible Truth: "Thy Maker is thy Husband. Hearst thou this?"

Marriage, hugging embrace, manhood wed as bride—from the start Taylor describes the incarnational mystery in sexual terms. He is, of course, working from a long tradition; the great mystics and religious poets have always invoked sexual passion as the closest human analogue for the impossible but experienced union of opposites. But the sexual mystery is more complex than that: it works both ways. It is not only that man cites the most ecstatic natural union as his inadequate-best way of talking about something more-than-natural. From the human perspective we are faced with the sublime paradox of Spirit freely choosing to express Himself in the human body. Without surrendering transcendental unity He projected Himself into division, submitting to the rhythm of time-space; He entered the sexual dimension and turned us towards the wholeness which is Himself. Time-space moves by the beat of the clock, the pulse of the pendulum, and God is the force beating in every pulse. Once God had become flesh, the duality which is the law of matter and of human sexuality could be resolved, by His own design, only in our integration and perfection as human beings.

Taylor's theology was a firmly founded intellectual structure, but his emotional life was just as strong and just as surely based. For the Christian the paradox of the Incarnation is further complicated by the fact that human nature is fallen, and either the cause or the result of the fall is sexual temptation and sexual sin. Passionate and sensual by nature, even more passionate and sensual than most men (the poetry would suggest), Taylor had constantly to remind himself that the body was, in itself, the unregenerate corpse of fallen man; the opening lines of many poems dwell on the filth, diseases, and vices that afflict the flesh. However, a radical and pervasive sense of the Incarnation such as his would not lead him to rest in a manichaean opposition of body and spirit; precisely to the contrary, he would want to see them as "conjoyn'd" and thereby redeemed. Even an orthodox Calvinist had to distinguish between the corruptible body, weak and prone to sin, and the glorious body, rapturous in ecstasy, which the Incarnation made possible.

Seventy-six of the *Meditations*, including all written between 1714 and 1720 and between 1722 and 1725, take as their scriptural text verses from *The Song of Solomon*, which Taylor refers to as *Canticles.* Its explicit sexuality and erotic imagery have always made fastidious exegetes nervous, but Taylor takes the *Song* as the chief biblical source for his poetry. For Solomon's love-song is not just a spiritual allegory for the marriage of Christ the Bridegroom to His Church, long before His birth; it celebrates the fact that spiritual rapture possesses us not despite the flesh but in the flesh, and the consequent fact that true erotic love is a movement of the spirit. Taylor's Communion meditations do not explore this second proposition, as Whitman's poems would, but they are based on the first conviction. Far from denying Eros, Jesus incorporates and inspires Eros; therein lies the distinction between the sexless angels on the one hand and men and women on the other. We experience all things, including redemption, in the terms of our humanity.

Earlier ... we heard the Puritan concern that "the senses are seduced by Objects, these help to abuse Imagination, which excites disorders in the inferior parts of the soul, and raiseth Passions"; that scruple enforced the plain style. Aware as Taylor was of human frailty and the effects of original sin in the absence of grace, he emphatically agreed with these prohibitive words in most situations. But not in the context of grace and in the privacy of the heart rapt by God; there inhibitions could signify the heart's obdurate coldness. If God chose to come to us, it could only be to possess us in the totality of our human nature, and we ought to strive to respond in the totality of our human nature. So, with *The Song of Solomon* providing the rubrics, Taylor joined the Christian poets who saw their manhood broken by God's holy lust: a line extending in modern poetry from John Donne to a contemporary like William Everson (Brother Antoninus). Donne ended the fourteenth Holy Sonnet with "I, / Except You enthrall me, never shall be free, / Nor ever chaste, except Thou ravish me"; Everson prayed, "Annul in me my manhood, Lord, and make / Me woman-sexed and weak," and wrote a poem titled "The Song the Body Dreamed in the Spirit's Mad Behest," which opens "Call Him the Lover and call me the Bride" and concludes "His great Godhead peels its stripping strength / In my red earth." What links these vastly different poets, one so British and the other so American in sensibility and speech, is the incarnational conviction that in the human fusion eros and agape are inseparable and that man is woman before God.

It is true that Taylor's imagination was restrained by the Calvinist distrust of the unregenerate body and that a poet like Everson, coming after Whitman as well as after Freud and Jung, is blunter and freer because of a deeper, more open engagement with sexuality. As a result, Taylor translates much of the erotic dimension of his imagination into metaphors less overtly sexual and often derived from his reading in Scripture, literature, and science. Nevertheless, the sexual implications are there, felt and admitted, and the strategy of Taylor's first Meditation is to establish the sexual basis for the subsequent figures of speech depicting his experience of grace.

The second poem introduces the metaphor of boxes and containers ... :

> Oh! that my Soul, Heavens Workmanshop (within
> My Wicker'd Cage,) that Bird of Paradise
> Inlin'de with Glorious Grace up to the brim
> Might be thy Cabbinet, oh Pearle of Price.
> Oh! let thy Pearle Lord, Cabbinet in mee.
> I'st then be rich! nay rich enough for thee.
>
> My Heart, oh Lord, for thy Pomander gain.
> Be thou thyselfe my sweet Perfume therein.

> Make it thy Box, and let thy Pretious Name
> My Pretious Ointment be emboxt therein.
> If I thy box and thou my Ointment bee
> I shall be sweet, nay, sweet enough for thee.

And later: "Yet may I Purse, and thou my Mony bee. / I have enough. Enough in having thee." The body cages the soul, its bird of Paradise, but the bird is itself filled with grace, which is like the precious pearl in the soul's cabinet. And so with the pomander and the perfume, the box and the ointment, the purse and the money. Many other Meditations repeat these and related images: castles enclosed by ramparts, cities encircled by walls, man's images for the New Jerusalem which is the City of God.

Why such profuse imagery of containing and being contained? As the pattern builds from poem to poem, the accumulation of images begins to suggest that for Taylor each thing must exist within fixed bounds and limits, that finally the cosmos itself is clasped round in an order which fulfills the creatures it holds in place. God is the absolute who completes each circumference—the self, its sphere of activity, at last the entire system of spheres—yet God is the center of each sphere as well. Man's lot is to contain God by being contained by Him; the omnipotent Deity must come to possess, sometimes by force, his sometimes fractious creatures. Each creature is cast in the archetypally feminine role: the vessel (container, box, walled city, and so on) which opens for entrance in order to close round the quickened life. (pp. 34-8)

Our human nature is dual and paradoxical, but by His own choice God entered a dual existence. In His person the paradox is resolved, and by extension the paradox of our existence can be individually resolved. With the imagination anticipating and responding to grace, Taylor's poems represent his attempt to pitch himself beyond the paradoxes and divisions of our natural experience, epitomized in the sexual polarity, into a transpolar, transsexual, androgynous wholeness of mind and heart and soul posited in the images of God husbanding human nature and manhood brided to Godhead: "Shall Mortall, and Immortall marry?" Consequently the busy kinetics of the poems, the stresses and tension of the language, move toward a still completion, often depicted as a meal or feast bestowed on a starving man. There are many poems on the theme of fullness, and in the 27th, which stems from the scriptural text "In Him shall all Fulness dwell," Taylor substantiates the abstract notion by linking it with several of the principal metaphorical patterns of the Series: a box of gold, a case of rubies, a cabinet of pearls, golden pipes spilling to clay vessels, fire, streams, flowers.

Even this brief sketch of the interwoven metaphors in the ***Meditations*** should demonstrate that the texture of the verse is carefully and richly wrought beyond anything the plain style would tolerate. Why would a conservative Puritan divine embroider a tapestry more splendid by far than the "cloth of gold ... stuck with as many jewels as the gown of a Russian ambassador," a style which Cotton Mather was also so bold as to sanction? To begin with, the stereotype of the Puritan as a clammy and sexless creature will not bear close examination: Anne Bradstreet was no frigid woman nor Taylor afraid of his senses. Moreover, his mighty sense of the Incarnation makes him perceive spirit immanent in flesh and matter. Even so, why should Taylor's fancy turn so frequently to gold, gems, perfumes, liquors, brocades, incense—things which were clearly not part of his life at Westfield? The question implies the answer: exactly because his rich and convoluted imagination dwelt in a wilderness. Because neither the forest filled with beasts and Indians nor the grim austerity of the Westfield community represented to his imagination the garden in the City of God, his imagination compensated from its own resources. The insufficiencies of nature and society drove him into the privacy of his imagination where his passionate nature could articulate the Puritan vision of the city on the hill which John Winthrop had voiced to the first ship-load of Puritans in the misery and anxiety of their earthly condition.

Behind Taylor's poems lies a theological framework, but the poems record the budding of his spiritual life. . . . The recurrence of metaphorical images makes up the fiber and texture of the sequence. By circling back again and again, they envision a world which is, microcosmically as well as macrocosmically, predestined yet creatively in process. Taylor is a poet adequate to his vision, and his achievement lies at last not in particular poems, even the better or best poems, but in the corpus. All the elements of the First Series of *Meditations* are given in the first poem or poems; then the poet associates, elaborates, builds, connects, spatializing the implications of the initial vision. There is little or no temporal development from one point to another, as there is in much of Donne's and some of Herbert's verse; the movement is not linear and progressive but circular and self-defining. The analogy has already been made between the *Meditations* and other American open-form poems like *Leaves of Grass* and the *Cantos*. In some ways—certainly in religious vision and in the sense of a structured cosmos—a better analogy is Eliot's *Four Quartets*, whose circular movement brings us to the point of recognizing that "the end of all our exploring / Will be to arrive where we started / And know it for the first time." In fact, there . . . [is] nothing like Taylor's poems of Christian meditation in our poetry until the *Quartets*. Like Eliot's, Taylor's poems embody the process of realization; the conclusion of the work returns by circuitous indirection to the point of origin: "Infinity, and Finity Conjoyn'd," the mystery itself fleshed in his experience and figured forth in his imaginative symbols. (pp. 41-3)

> Albert Gelpi, "Edward Taylor: Types and Tropes,"
> *in his* The Tenth Muse: The Psyche of the American Poet, *Cambridge, Mass.: Harvard University Press, 1975, pp. 13-54.*

BARBARA KIEFER LEWALSKI (essay date 1979)

[*Lewalski is an American educator and author whose works include* Typology and Poetry: A Consideration of Herbert, Vaughan, and Marvell *(1973) and* Protestant Poetics and the Seventeenth-Century Religious Lyric *(1979). In the following excerpt from the latter work, she posits that Taylor's verse is shaped not by a school or common style but by a Protestant poetics of Christian life.*]

That Edward Taylor's literary debts to Herbert are both profound and pervasive is a critical commonplace. Taylor's editor Donald Stanford declares that *The Temple* was probably the greatest single poetic influence on Taylor, and Louis Martz observes that "like Henry Vaughan, Edward Taylor appears to have a mind saturated with Herbert's poetry" [see excerpt by Martz dated 1960]. There

are several more or less obvious allusions and echoes: Herbert's phrase, "crumme of dust" from "The Temper (I)" occurs five times in Taylor's **"Prologue,"** and the opening lines, "Lord, Can a Crumb of Dust the Earth outweigh, / Outmatch all mountains, nay the Chrystall Sky?" especially recall the Herbert poem. Taylor's refrain "Was ever Heart like mine?" from *Preparatory Meditations* (I.40) seems to echo Herbert's refrain from "The Sacrifice," "Was ever grief like mine?" The few titled poems in Taylor's meditative sequences—**"The Experience," "The Return,"** and **"The Reflexion"**—recall Herbert's titles, and Taylor's stanza form throughout is that of Herbert's "The Church-porch." As Martz notes, several of Taylor's apostrophes to the self or to God might almost be mistaken for lines from Herbert: "My Dear, Deare, Lord I do thee Saviour Call": "Lord speake it home to me, say these are mine"; "Oh! that I ever felt what I profess"; "What rocky heart is mine?"; "Dull, Dull indeed! What shall it e're be thus?" Again, Taylor's analysis of the manifold properties of the Rose of Sharon (I.4) and his witty figure of the Church as Rose seated at the banquet table (**"The Reflexion"**) strongly recall very similar metaphoric procedures in Herbert's "The Rose" and "Church-rents and Schisms." Moreover, Taylor's poems, like Herbert's, often explore his own uncomfortable situation as a Christian poet who owes God worthy praise he cannot provide, because his human limitations and fallen condition preclude any fitting treatment of God's infinite and unimaginable perfections.

By such echoes and allusions Taylor claims some relation to Herbert and his kind of poetry, inviting a comparison which usually leads to critical judgments about Taylor's insufficiencies, Puritan rigidities, or poetic ineptitudes. But the interesting question is what to make of such resemblances, given the obvious differences in diction, in the uses of poetic figures, in metrical smoothness, in poetic craftsmanship. Is Taylor a belated American Metaphysical, using bold conceits, colloquial language, and daring paradoxes, although in a more naïve, uneven, and sometimes poetically inept manner? Is he indeed a practitioner of what Karl Keller calls a "wilderness baroque," utilizing the elements of metaphysical wit—conceit, catachresis, radical metaphor, pun, dramatic exaggeration—as a way of expressing his passionate joy and delight in the beauty of Christ and the things of God? Or does he exhibit a specifically Puritan poetics, differing radically from that of Donne, Herbert, and Vaughan, and characterized by meiosis, repudiation of art, and an emblematic rather than a genuinely symbolic or sacramental conception of language and nature?

This Metaphysical-Puritan dichotomy pointed up by the critics is, I think, a false one for Taylor, who stands in the line of Donne, Herbert, Vaughan, and Traherne as a Protestant poet practicing a Protestant poetics. In her stimulating and suggestive essay, Kathleen Blake has begun to assimilate Taylor to such a tradition, grounding her argument in the Calvinist doctrine of the sacrament shared by the English Protestant poets as well as Taylor. In contradistinction to that metamorphosis of physical into spiritual reality which is formulated in the Catholic doctrine of transubstantiation and which may lead to religious and poetic stances expressive of mysticism or of sheer carnality, Blake finds a special reliance upon metaphor at the core of Protestant poetics, metaphor being the verbal communicator across the ever-present gap between earthly and heavenly reality. Taylor does indeed incorporate all the familiar elements shaping the seventeenth-century Protestant religious lyric in England—Protestant meditative modes, biblical genre theory, biblical metaphor and typology, Protestant emblem methods, Protestant concerns about artful language—though of course he employs these common elements in a quite distinctive fashion. Taylor's Puritanism brought him to the New World, and pointed him in new poetic directions, but for all that it did not finally lead him to a new poetic country.

Though all the poets . . . [studied in Lewalski's *Protestant Poetics and the Seventeenth-Century Religious Lyric*] (except Traherne) are Calvinists on the essential doctrinal points, and none is a crypto-Catholic in regard to the sacrament, some theological emphases do help shape Taylor's particular version of the Protestant poetics. As a covenanted member, and leader, of a Puritan gathered church of "visible saints" in Westfield, Connecticut, Taylor held a rigorous and unambiguous conception of the five points of the Synod of Dort—total depravity, unmerited election, limited atonement, irresistible grace, and perseverance of the saints. Interpretation of these doctrines with Puritan rigor produced in Taylor an intense consciousness of the immense gulf between God and man, to be bridged only and entirely by God's grace and in no smallest degree by anything in nature or in the responses of the elect. (pp. 388-90)

[The] title affixed to Taylor's meditative lyrics, written over a period of forty years—*Preparatory Meditations before my Approach to the Lords Supper. Chiefly upon the Doctrin preached upon the Day of administration*—testifies to the absolute centrality of the Lord's Supper to Taylor's imaginative life, even as his long dispute with Solomon Stoddard opposing any liberalization of requirements for admission to the Supper does to its centrality in his theology. As his *Treatise Concerning the Lord's Supper* makes clear, the sacrament is important to Taylor as the seal of the covenant, the divine gift offered only to the elect whom God has called, regenerated, and clothed with the "wedden garment" of sanctification. According to Taylor's *Treatise*, sacrament days should provoke meditations on God's overwhelming benefits to us and on our own total unworthiness, but also upon the evidences of election and regeneration produced by his grace; the sacrament also lays upon us the obligation to render the tribute of praise. Precisely these themes are treated in poem after poem, and the sacramental focus probably accounts for the rather surprising tone sounded in many of them. The speaker is curiously serene: he writes as one sufficiently assured of election and regeneration to have decided to approach the sacrament, and this assurance dispels a good deal of the tension which might be expected to accompany his profound awareness of personal worthlessness, the unfathomable distance between himself and God, and the failures of his art. Though he laments these conditions he can do nothing to remedy them and so does not actively grapple with his psyche or his art as do Donne, Herbert, Vaughan, and even Traherne; rather, his poetry deliberately enacts failure, as a means to glorify God. Any adequate response to God on his part, in life or in art, must await the glorification God will bestow upon him in the life to come. But as an aspect of his assurance he has some confidence that his poetic attempts can be accepted in lieu of achieve-

ment, and so prays God to "Accept this Lisp till I am glorifide."

The sacrament is also the seal of full membership in the gathered church of elect saints, and this fact also had an effect upon Taylor's imaginative life. Like Herbert and to some extent Vaughan, Taylor wrote sequences of lyrics which present a record of life within the Church—the ever-changing spiritual emotions, tribulations, and experiences attendant upon such a life. But his portrayal of the experience of entering the Church differs from theirs, as does his conception of the Church itself. In Herbert's first poem, "The Church-porch," the promising young man is "lessoned" by a preacher in the externals of the Christian life and thereby brought to the portal of entry into the Church proper, the realm of the inner, sanctified spirit. In Vaughan's first poem, "Regeneration," the speaker is led away from fruitless moral efforts (climbing Mount Sinai) into the garden of the Church where he finds some Christians responsive to grace (the marigolds and the lively stones) but others unresponsive—the unregenerate. Both these versions of entry into the Church postulate a clear separation but not a cataclysmic divide between nature and grace, moral goodness and the life in grace, since the visible Church contains souls in both states, and there seems to be no clear way to identify them in this world. For Taylor the situation is otherwise, as is evident in his long dialogic poem—really a kind of morality play—*God's Determinations*. The action centers upon the difficulties experienced by the various classes of the elect, those who come early and rather easily to Christ and those who resist his call, in believing that they have a part in the promise. Satan's temptations, Christ's consolations, and the good advice and counsel of those already in Church fellowship as visible saints all bear hard upon the late-comers, and the chariot of the Church, sent forth from God to gather up the elect, pursues them throughout the poem. The final short lyrics celebrate the situation of the elect soul—as Bride; as flower planted in Christ's garden (which contains some buds and some blooming flowers but none unresponsive); and as member of the choir of saints "Encoacht for Heaven," joyously and sweetly singing praises produced in them by grace rather than art. Herbert also insists that praises must be a response to grace, but with the significant difference that for Herbert, grace lays upon the Christian poet's lute the responsibility to "struggle for thy part / With all thy art" ("Easter," ll. 7-8) whereas for Taylor the elect remain wholly inadequate to the task of artful praise in their lifetime.

In addition to his two numbered sequences of *Preparatory Meditations*, Taylor also wrote a few miscellaneous lyrics. Some of these are among his finest poems, displaying greater diversity in stanzaic form, greater economy, acuteness, and precision of language and imagery, and a more varied and more intense palette of tones and emotions than do most of the *Preparatory Meditations*. These poems utilize the metaphoric, emblematic, and meditative techniques common to the tradition and characteristic of Taylor, but with a sharp focus upon a particular image or emblem, a given occasion, or a strong emotion. (pp. 390-92)

Especially remarkable and complex are certain emblem-like poems. **"Upon a Spider Catching a Fly"** is reminiscent of several emblem plates, though the poem is more intricate and less overtly didactic than the usual emblem poem. The speaker addresses a spider with a fly in his web, evidently just captured and immediately killed, and he recalls a similar scene (another emblem plate?) in which the spider gently stroked a captured wasp lest he "in a froppish, waspish heate" (l. 18) should tear the web. He then interprets the emblems; Hell's spider spins nets "To tangle Adams race" but God affords grace to some "to breake the Cord" (ll. 36, 43). **"Upon a Wasp Child with Cold"** is also emblem-like, though I have not found close emblem analogues. The *pictura* presents a wasp blasted by the north wind, but holding up all her limbs and head to the sun and exercising all her faculties, until she is finally able to fly away; the application is to the nimble spirit containing sparks of rationality and divinity which control its actions. The poet recognizes this divinely ordered emblem in nature as a "schoolmaster" and a ladder leading him to God (11. 34, 42). Somewhat reminiscent of several Herbert poems, and also Vaughan's initial emblem poem on the flashing flint, Taylor's **"The Ebb and Flow"** effectively explores the speaker's spiritual experience by contrasting two "emblems" for his heart. Just after regeneration it was a tinderbox within which his affections often caught sparks of heavenly fire and flamed forth; now it is a trim censer seldom feeling the sparks from God's "Holy flint and Steel." The speaker's fear that his fire might be an *ignis fatuus* is resolved by the realization that when the Spirit blows away the ashes in the censer, "then thy fire doth glow" (l. 18).

"Huswifery" is perhaps Taylor's best-known poem. Structured as an emblem poem interpreting two figures—a spinning wheel and a loom—it presents the key equations by means of three parallel petitions. The speaker first begs to be made Christ's spinning wheel, with the holy Word his distaff, his affections the flyers, his soul the holy spool, his conversation the reel. Then he urges the Lord to make him a loom on which the Holy Spirit winds quills and the Lord weaves the web, beating it in the "Fulling Mills" of his ordinances (l. 10) and dyeing it in heavenly colors. Finally, he begs God to clothe him with the web so woven— "Understanding, Will, / Affections, Judgement, Conscience, Memory / My Words, and Actions" (ll. 13-15). This is a complex emblem of regeneration and sanctification, presenting God's use and control of all the speaker's faculties so as to make from him and place upon him "Holy robes for glory"—the "wedden garment," which is so pervasive as concept and image in Taylor.

Taylor's two sequences of *Preparatory Meditations* (some 217 poems, a few of them, in two versions) display little variety in genre or form. All are written in the same stanza form (a six-line iambic pentameter stanza rhymed *ababcc*) and most are between thirty and seventy lines in length. These poems owe little to theories regarding the biblical lyric genres, or to the poetic books of the Bible themselves. Though Taylor occasionally alludes to instruments or tunes mentioned in the Book of Psalms in petitioning Christ or the Holy Spirit to play upon him as passive instrument, he wrote no Psalm paraphrases, or New Covenant psalms in creative imitation of David as did Herbert and Traherne, and he based only a handful of his meditations upon psalm texts. Moreover, though Taylor placed the Book of Canticles under contribution for texts and allusions far more often than any other source, he seldom drew upon it for generic models. In fact, as their title indicates, the two sequences are meditations, and specifically, sacramental meditations. They are also, as is indicated by

the biblical text headings supplied to almost all of the poems, conceived as Protestant "deliberate meditations" upon biblical texts, and are thereby closely aligned to sermons. Present evidence hardly warrants the certitude with which Norman Grabo has described Taylor's habits of composition—that the poems were written for the regular monthly sacrament days, after the sermon for the day was composed and before it was preached. But it is clear from Taylor's *Christographia* sequence (where we have both sermon and poem for fourteen such occasions) that there are close relations in imagery and theme between sermon and poem, and that, except in one striking instance, the biblical text used as point of departure and title is the same for both. Yet in this sequence the poems do not epitomize or recapitulate or reformulate the argument or doctrine of the sermon: rather, as we would expect from Protestant meditative theory, the poetic meditations undertake an "application to the self" of whatever aspect of text or argument or doctrine is seen to address the speaker's own condition most forcefully. And since these are poems, they focus most often upon an image, trope, epithet, or other term offered by the biblical text, analyzing or commenting upon or expanding that term in relation to the underlying theological idea it points to, and probing the speaker's responses to its implications. (pp. 394-95)

Though Taylor's poems are in large measure discrete exercises, as the circumstances of their composition would seem to dictate, the First Series of *Preparatory Meditations* (1-49) may have been conceived in terms of, or at any event accommodated to, the meditative program suggested in his *Treatise Concerning the Lord's Supper*. That program calls for a train of meditations focusing upon the sacrament as epitome of the covenant of redemption, and considering the following topics: the glory and beauty of the Bridegroom; the happiness and preferment of the Bride; the Bridegroom's purchase of his Bride with all his estate; the Bridegroom's suffering, death, conquest over death, and ascent to heaven; the benefits and gifts bestowed upon the Bride; the contract celebrated in the "wedden feast" of the sacrament. The poems do in fact seem to follow such a pattern, whose completion is indicated by the fact that Taylor begins a new sequence after number 49. The dominant theme of this first sequence, Christ's love, is sounded by the initial poem, and the next four poems show the speaker personally experiencing and responding to that love. Meditations 4-13 celebrate through consideration of appropriate biblical texts (often from Canticles) the beauty, excellence, and glory of the Bridegroom and the sacramental feast. Meditations 14-22 focus on Christ's mediatorial role (his offices, his passion, his exaltation and enthronement in heaven). Meditations 23-40 develop the benefits the soul enjoys through the Covenant of Grace (it is espoused by Christ; it enjoys forgiveness of sins and fullness of grace; it is adopted by God, made a new creature, made heir to all things present and to come). The last poems (41-49) present the heavenly kingdom as the final benefit of the Covenant—the throne the elect will occupy, the various crowns they will wear, their white robes, their participation in the joys of the Lord—but suggest also the foretastes of that joy in the prospect, and in the consciousness of God's love and grace here.

The second series of *Preparatory Meditations*, in very general terms and perhaps through inadvertent assimilation of the classic Protestant paradigm, reflects the speaker's spiritual growth and development. He begins by approaching Christ through Old Testament types of the Covenant (1-30); proceeds to the direct apprehension and description of Christ the Redeemer in his many aspects (31-56); explores in several short, disparate sequences his doubt-plagued efforts to claim the major benefits of the New Covenant (57-114); undertakes in the Canticles sequence (115-153) a long and probing examination of his participation in Christ's spousal relation to his Church; and concludes with an occasional and partial assumption of the persona of the Bride (154-165). In its broadest terms, this scheme resembles the pattern William Epperson has discerned in Taylor's poems, but I do not find the conformation he suggests to the classic paradigm of Catholic mysticism. As with the other collections of Protestant religious lyrics examined here, Taylor's sequence avoids presenting the spiritual life as a steady progress through fixed stages, and portrays instead, through recurring themes, problems, and vacillations, a continuing spiritual struggle which does not end in this life. In Meditation II.156, Taylor does seem to reach (as do Herbert and Vaughan) something like a plateau of assurance, displaying thereafter a greater delight in and confidence in the relation with the Bridegroom. But even in the last poems that relation is portrayed as very tentative and partial.

Indeed, even this general intimation of spiritual progress is undermined by the fact that virtually every poem in Taylor's two meditative sequences enacts in little the essential spiritual dilemma as he perceived it—a dilemma he cannot resolve on earth. On the one hand, God's glory and love and benefits to the speaker are beyond all measure in their greatness and magnificence. On the other hand, his vileness and utter insignificance prevent his sharing in, or approaching, or comprehending, or in any way responding properly in his life or in his verse to that goodness and greatness. He is utterly dependent upon God's approaches—in the types, in Christ, in the emblems and sacraments and ordinances and other manifestations of grace—for the preparation of the "wedden garment" of sanctification required of the Bride. Whatever the topic, then, the issue in all the poems is always the same: has the speaker the right to apply to himself the spiritual promises and goods described? He poses that question to himself again and again, in terms seldom agonized but almost always tentative, conditional, petitionary: he finds grounds for assurance, and indeed for great wonder and joy, in contemplating the honors and privileges accorded the elect by God; but there is no settling the matter and moving on to some higher state of sanctity or mystical union. The question must be, and is, confronted every time he considers any topic relating to the spiritual life.

This central issue dictates the structure of almost all the meditations. Most are designed according to a simple, contrastive scheme or, perhaps more properly, according to a logic of thesis, antithesis, and resolution. Perhaps most often, the speaker begins by celebrating the greatness, glory, and benefits of the Lord. He then portrays his own vileness and unworthiness to receive such benefits, and the impossibility of rendering proper praise for them. At length he petitions for God's gracious acceptance of him and his praises, despite his vileness—while often looking forward to his transformation in heaven from vileness to glory. Alternatively, the speaker may begin with

his own vileness, then contrast the divine goodness and magnificence, and proceed to the same resolution. Like the stanzaic pattern of these poems, this structural design recurs with monotonous regularity.

Taylor calls upon a much wider range of biblical metaphors and figures, and uses them more constantly, than do the other poets . . . [studied in *Protestant Poetics and the Seventeenth-Century Religious Lyric*]. His poems often focus upon a particular biblical trope or figure for Christ, developing it through association with clusters of related or contrasting images or figures—sometimes biblical, sometimes emblematic, often homely and colloquial, sometimes deliberately base—in order to exhibit the gulf between the speaker and his God. This way with biblical metaphor differs significantly from that of the other poets. Though Taylor recurs often to familiar ranges of imagery—the descriptions of Bridegroom and Bride from Canticles and the sacramental metaphors of Christ as bread and as vine or wine—he usually does not, like Donne, unify individual poems in terms of a single striking image or metaphor. Nor does he, like Herbert and Vaughan, attempt to unify a collection of lyrics by appropriating and developing creatively in his own terms a few dominant biblical metaphors. Nor, like Traherne, does he undertake to forego tropes in order to reveal the naked truth behind the verbal sign or name. He is in some ways closest to Donne in his joyous response to the figurative richness of the Spirit as biblical poet, and indeed he expresses great admiration for the metaphorical texture of scripture in Sermon IX of the *Christographia*. . . . But whereas Donne finds in the Spirit's metaphors a warrant for his own imitation of such poetic richness, Taylor announces in poem after poem that he cannot in this life engage in such competition. He can only appropriate, analyze, comment upon, and thereby enrich his text with large numbers of biblical figures, praising God in his own terms. Often he sets these biblical figures over against others which are colloquial, homely, or base, as if such as these are the only creation possible from his vile and worthless creaturely self.

Many poems are developed through analysis of or commentary upon a principal metaphor or term pertaining to Christ or his salvific, mediatorial role, usually taken from or suggested by the poem's biblical text heading. Key tropes governing a succession of such poems identify Christ as an ointment, the Rose of Sharon, the lily of the valley, the living bread, a feast of fat things, the sun of wisdom, the Spouse, an advocate with the Father, the tree of life, the head of his body, the sun of righteousness with healing in his wings. Other text headings highlight more abstract theological terms, which also admit of and receive metaphorical development: Christ is high priest, great prophet, king of kings, his visage is marred in the passion; he is exalted in his resurrection, ascension, and enthronement in heaven; he is all fullness; he is the Love which gives his life for his friend; he gives life to his elect in the Sacrament.

One primary method of developing such figures and terms is analytic or associative: the speaker works out the implications and aspects and ramifications of the figure, or moves from it by rather free association to other figures and concepts. In such poems the speaker is essentially a commentator or paraphraser, elaborating upon the key figures and terms by means of related figures of a similar kind, or through plainstyle exposition—and always with application to himself. (pp. 396-400)

Another and perhaps more common mode of development is by meiosis—a recasting of God's metaphors in homely, colloquial terms. By this means the poet represents the immense gulf between himself and God's glory and greatness, and enacts the utter impossibility of proper description and worthy praise. He uses this method most often in connection with the sacrament, describing the indescribable feast with kitchen metaphors. Meditation I.8 on John 6:51, "I am the Living Bread," begins with a somewhat extraneous image of the bread of life tracing a golden path from heaven to his door, but then introduces the dominant imagery of bread-famine-cookery through a quasi-allegorical description of fallen man as a starved bird—reminiscent of several bird-in-cage emblem plates:

> When that this Bird of Paradise put in
> This Wicker Cage (my Corps) to tweedle praise
> Had peckt the Fruite forbad: and so did fling
> Away its Food; and lost its golden dayes;
> It fell into Celestiall Famine sore:
> And never could attain a morsell more.
>
> (11.7-12)

Unable to find soul's food here—the creatures' fields have none, angels have none, and the "Worlds White Loafe is done"—the bird-soul is fed by the bread of life, which metaphor Taylor literalizes in graphic and rather shocking ways. God is a baker who takes "The Purest Wheate in Heaven, his deare-dear Son"; who "Grinds, and kneads [him] up into this Bread of Life"; and then bakes and sends that bread forth as "Heavens Sugar Cake" (11. 21-22, 30). (pp. 401-02)

A more radical technique, and perhaps the most common, is metaphoric antithesis. In poems using this technique the speaker sets over against biblical metaphors embodying God's glory and God's promises deprecatory images and figures for himself most often chosen from the base vocabulary of scatology and disease. He is, in a series of poems, a dirt ball, a muddy sewer, a dung-hill, a pouch of passion, a lump of loathsomeness, a bag of botches, a sink nastiness; he is candied over with leprosy, pickled in gall, wrapped in slime. The contrast between God's greatness and his own nothingness is often pointed through precisely drawn antithetical figures: he is a "Crumb of Dust" beside God's glory; he is "Dead Dust" wondrously made to eat "Living Bread"; his soul has an ague thirst assuaged by the red wine of Christ's blood; he is a sluggish servant "More blockish than a block" while his Lord is glorious; he is a "Leaden Oritor" given the "Golden Theame" of Christ's love to sing; his "Clay ball" will be dressed in God's "White robes"; Christ's love is the apple of the Tree of Life while he is a "Wormhol'de thing"; Christ's head contains profoundest wisdom and his contains "addle brains."

In a variation on this method the speaker sometimes sets up his metaphoric antitheses within the same field of imagery so that, finally, the metaphors argue a relationship between himself and Christ as well as a contrast. In this vein he presents his heart as a "poore Eggeshell" or box to hold the precious ointment that Christ is; he wishes to be (in several poems) the valley of which Christ is the lily, or a flowerpot to hold Christ the flower; he would be a vessel to catch Christ's blood, and his "Pipkin" or "Acorn Cup"

overflows with Christ's fullness; he is a prisoner in a darksome, noisome pit without water but sails forth on the Red Sea of covenant blood. (pp. 402-03)

In Taylor's ways with metaphor there is a sense of exuberance, daring, and outrageousness more nearly resembling Donne than any other poet we have considered. But the springs of this curious excess are radically opposed in the two poets. Donne finds his creative freedom in the challenge to imitate the inexhaustible poetic richness of the Spirit; Taylor finds his in recognizing the utter impossibility of such an undertaking, which allows him to invent a new idiom, a meiotic, secular language of non-praise which is nevertheless devoted to the glory of God. As Karl Keller observes, Taylor exhibits constant delight in language, as is perhaps most clearly evident in his persistent wordplays and puns (another point of contact with Donne): the speaker would be Christ's gold, minted by him, and thereby an Angel (I.6); Christ the Rose of Sharon rose up again in his resurrection (I.4); Christ is Almighty and the speaker a "mightless" mite (II.48). Taylor also plays on words through the devices of ploce and traductio—as in the forms of *love* in Meditation I.12:

> My *Lovely* One, I fain would *love* thee much
> But all my *Love* is none at all I see,
> Oh! let thy Beauty give a glorious tuch
> Upon my Heart, and melt to *Love* all mee.
> Lord melt me all up into *Love* for thee
> Whose *Loveliness* excells what *love* can bee.
>
> (ll.43-48)

But Keller's argument that this delight in language springs from Taylor's all-pervasive spiritual joy and delight demands some qualification, for though Taylor did not doubt his election he was often dismayed by his inevitable failures in spiritual attainment and in praise. The delight arises rather from his discovery of an area, however humble, in which he could exercise his creativity freely, in God's honor.

Types are strewn about in Taylor's poems as prodigally as biblical metaphors. His approach to typology is generally conservative and inclusive, relating a large number of personal and ritual Old Testament types to their antitype, the incarnate Christ. In Sermon IX of the *Christographia* series, Taylor states, with reference to Calvin's engraving metaphor, his orthodox Calvinist understanding of the types as foreshadowing and presenting Christ:

> He is the Object of all the Old Testament Prophesies, and Metaphoricall Descriptions of the Messiah. He was variously foretold in the Old Testament even from Adam to the latter end of Malachy.... As he is foretold in the Type, God doth as it were pensill out in fair Colours and [ingrave] and portray Christ and his Natures and Properties.... He is the Truth of all the Prophesies, and Types of the Old Testament.... The types, and Ceremonies were shadows of Good things to come, but the body is of Christ. Col. 2. 17.

In Taylor's poetic sequence on the types (II.I-30), the biblical text titles are almost always from the New Testament, focusing attention sharply upon Christ the antitype, and the speaker's wished-for association with him. In summary form, the sequence incorporates almost the entire range of Old Testament typology as schematized in Samuel Mather's compendium. The opening poem (II.I) points to this range: the speaker's frozen heart, dull spirits, and deep stains are set in opposition to "The glory of the world slickt up in types" (I. 13)—all which glory meets in and is excelled by Christ. The first group of poems (II.I-II.13 and also II.30) deals with the so-called personal types—Adam, Noah, Abraham's seed, Isaac, Jacob, Joseph, Moses, Joshua, Samson, David, Solomon, Jonah. The next group (II.14-II.27) deals with Israelite offices and rituals as types (prophetic types, kingly types, priestly types, Nazarites; altars, tabernacles, festivals, sacrifices, ceremonies). Number 29 deals with one "typical" object, Noah's ark. The typology of events such as the Exodus and the Covenant, and the typology of the Church as antitype of the garden of Canticles serve as subjects of later poems.

Karl Keller has noted that Taylor attempts in various witty ways to include himself in the typological process; in this . . . he stands in the mainstream of Protestant typological exegesis. Taylor found his justification for extending typological reference to the individual Christian precisely where others did, in the notion that the types also refer to Christ's mystical body, his members: "Tho' they may Speake out particular things that are not to be founde in Christ personally considered, yet they are in Christ Mystically Considered." But from the plethora of types he includes, it is clear that Taylor does not, like Herbert, Vaughan, and Traherne, identify himself imaginatively with some one or some few particular Old Testament types such as David the Psalmist or Jacob the pilgrim. He locates himself in the course of typological history by insistent and constant identification with Christ the antitype.

Taylor's typological poems begin, characteristically, with a depiction of his own sinfulness, worthlessness, and inability to praise. He then develops, sometimes very briefly and sometimes in elaborate detail, the ways in which a particular type adumbrates some aspect of Christ's redemptive mission. Very occasionally he associates himself with that type after the manner of correlative typology, but most often he at once claims relation to Christ, the antitype of all the types, through whom he often asserts something of an antitypical role for himself—seeking a better Canaan, finding a new Ark in the Church, and enjoying the garden of the Church, the antitype of Solomon's garden and Isaiah's vineyard. He relates himself to Christ the antitype primarily through the vehicle of language, writing himself into the typological equation by assigning himself a humble, ancillary role in Christ's antitypical redemptive act. In II.2, celebrating Christ as "First Born of Every Creature" (Col. 1:15), he begs inclusion in the familial relationship implied: "Make mee thy Babe, and him my Elder Brother" (l. 37). In II.4, which treats a classic text in typological theory—(Gal. 4:24) comparing Hagar and Sarah, the bondmaid and the free woman—he prays to embody the antitype rather than the type: "Blesst Lord, let not the Bondmaids type / Take place in mee. But thy blesst Promised Seed" (ll. 25-26). As Jacob sought and found a spouse, he prays to be the Spouse found by Christ (II.6). As Aaron caught the sacrificial blood in his vessel, so his soul will be the "Vessel" to catch Christ's blood, (II.23, ll. 37-38). He needs to wash in Christ's blood, the "Choice Fountain" whose type was the purificatory washings of the Old Testament (II.26, l. 31). He must be "Arkd in Christ" the antitype of Noah's Ark (II.29, l. 32).

The poem on Joseph (II.7, on Psalm 105:17, "He sent a man before them, even Joseph, who was sold etc.") is a particularly effective example of this method. The speaker begins by lamenting his flat and dull spirits, his dim ink and blunt pencil, and therein contrasts himself with both the type and the more glorious antitype: "Is Josephs glorious shine a Type of thee? / How bright art thou?" (ll. 7-8). He then recounts the typological parallels as one finds them in Mather: Joseph was betrayed, cast into a pit, sold by his brothers, endured temptation, was cast into jail, was restored to power and glory, and effected the salvation of his starving people with bread—all which have antitypes in Christ, whose glorious image is "pensild out" in Joseph's (l. 35). At this point, characteristically, the speaker writes himself into the relation: his dull skin requires the "brightsome Colours" of Joseph's coat but more especially of Christ's blood and glory. (pp. 405-08)

With Taylor as with Herbert, the issue of how to praise God in poetry is paramount. As we have seen, Taylor enacts through metaphoric procedures of meiosis and antithesis his poetic assumptions about the impossibility of rendering true praise, but he also addresses the issue of praise directly throughout his poems. Standing astonished before the manifestation of God's love in the sacrament or before his wisdom, or his glory, Taylor characteristically exclaims, "How shall I praise thee then? My blottings Jar / And wrack my Rhymes to pieces in thy praise" (I.10, ll. 31-32). Or again, "My Phancys in a Maze, my thoughts agast, / Words in an Extasy; my Telltale Tongue / Is tongue-tide, and my Lips are padlockt fast / To see thy Kingly Glory" (I.17, ll. 13-16). (p. 410)

To this dilemma he offers two kinds of resolutions—in the subjunctive mood and the future tense. He prays, on the one hand, that God will so restore his faculties that they will produce praises made acceptable by grace. The issue here is sanctification, not art: because his heart and faculties are as yet imperfectly restored, more appropriate praises must wait upon the advancement of that process. In **"The Experience"** he prays that his heart might become "thy Golden Harp . . . / Well tun'd by Glorious Grace" (ll. 25-26), and he promises better praise if the experience of "sweet content" and nearness to Christ in the Sacrament is repeated. In **"The Return"** he begs Christ to play upon him as instrument and petitions the Spirit to "keepe my Strings in tune, / . . . Till I sing Praise in Heaven above with thee" (ll. 52-54). In I.27 he promises that when God's fullness dwells in his heart, "I then shall sweetly tune thy Praise" (l. 47). In I.41 he begs Christ to produce in him the love and the skill "To tend thy Lord in all admiring Style" until he is able "to pay in glory what I owe" (ll. 38, 48). In these terms, he alludes at times to the Davidic instruments and tunes—but he is rather an instrument upon which the Spirit plays than an artful imitator of David. In I.18 he prays to be made such an instrument—his breast the virginals, his affections the strings, his panting heart the stops and falls on which the Spirit plays its psalm, "AL-TASCHATH MICHTAM, in Seraphick Tune" (l. 48).

But though more loving praise may be made possible by further sanctification of the heart, this resolution does not meet the problem of the woeful inadequacy of all human art in the praise of God. When art is in any way the issue, Taylor moves to a second resolution—a prayer that God will accept his feeble and inept attempts as tokens of his faith and duty, usually promising to provide fit and appropriate praise when he is translated to the only realm where that is possible—heavenly glory. (p. 411)

The fourteen poems (II.42-56) which parallel the sermons Taylor conceived and bound together under the title *Christographia,* invite special attention as a unified series. The special interest of these poems derives not only from the sermon links, which invite important inferences about Taylor's understanding of the specific domain of the meditative lyric, but also from the superior quality of several of these poems and their diverse poetic strategies. By their title, the *Christographia* sermons claim to present the emblem or portrait of Christ, incorporating, according to the subtitle of the sermon volume, the following aspects: "Christs Person, Natures, the Personall Union of the Natures, Qualifications, and Operations." Each of the poems concerns itself with the particular aspect of Christ which is central to the parallel sermon—Christ's human body, his divinity, the Word made flesh, his wisdom, his fullness, his life, his almightiness, his grace, his truth, his fullness in the Church, his power as priest, his power as prophet and king, his mediatorial power joining all these offices, and finally, his glorious works. But in the poems the procedure is appropriately metaphorical rather than logical: the poems develop the various aspects of Christ not by doctrinal argument but through tropes, epithets, or terms rich in connotation and significance.

In virtually every case the metaphors associated with a specific aspect of Christ are sharply contrasted with tropes pointing up the human speaker's antithesis to Christ in the quality noted, and the resolution begs for the speaker's salvation through, or for his participation in, that quality. The focus is on Christ, but also on the speaker as he applies one or another aspect of Christ closely to his own situation. And since the speaker is a poet, the problem of writing verses looms very large indeed in this series. Having undertaken to depict Christ graphically, to draw his picture, Taylor must confront his human inadequacy and fallenness in virtually every poem. Responding to this pressure, he links even more closely than elsewhere the salvation which he prays to find in Christ and the acceptable praises that will flow from it. Again, this salvation will not make the praises artful or in any degree adequate to the task of depicting Christ, but they will be "sweet" because perfumed by grace and played by Christ himself on the instrument (Taylor) which Christ will tune. (pp. 414-15)

Perhaps the wittiest and most remarkable of the series is II.48, on two words from Revelation I:8, "The Almighty." Here the principal terms are "might" and "mite," homophones which are at the same time antitheses, and which afford large opportunity for pun and wordplay and paradox as Taylor points up the opposition between Christ's might and his own mite, and at the same time suggests the union of the two through the identity of sound. The poem begins with the simple contrast between human might matched with right (the source of strength in earthly sovereigns) and Christ's Almightiness; he then introduces the speaker as the absolute antithesis to any such might—"But what am I, poor Mite, all mightless thing!" (l. 13). Nevertheless, and paradoxically, this mite lays claim to some might in serving the Almighty Christ who accepts widows' mites: it would spend "its mitie Strength for thee / Of Mightless might, of feeble strong delight" (ll. 20-21). And in so doing, this mite mocks earthly or hellish might and

Taylor's gravestone in Westfield, Massachusetts.

power: "Their Might's a little mite, Powers powerless fall" (l. 27). Upheld by the Almighty, he abandons trust in his own might, but yet trusts because his mite is so upheld. The final stanza rings still more changes on the paradoxical union, achieved so wittily through pun and incessant wordplay, which has bridged the antithesis of Christ and the speaker, might and mite:

> If thy Almightiness, and all my Mite
> United be in sacred Marriage knot,
> My Mite is thine: Mine thine Almighty Might.
> Then thine Almightiness my Mite hath got.
> My Quill makes thine Almightiness a String
> Of Pearls to grace the tune my Mite doth sing.
> (ll. 37-42)
> (p. 416)

Taylor's meditations on Canticles texts invite consideration as a group: they comprise sixty-six poems in all, almost one-third of his production in this kind. Moreover, as the first and last few poems in Taylor's total *œuvre* are based on Canticles, and the longest unified sequence (II.115-153) is on consecutive verses from Canticles 5:10 to 7:6, that biblical work may fairly be said to encompass and dominate Taylor's poems. The metaphors and images of Canticles—the spousal relationship of Bridegroom and Bride, the physical beauty of the spouses, the gardens of nuts and spices, the luxuriant feasts, the jewels, perfumes, flowers, colors, and textures—are the very substance of these poems. This pervasive imagery, together with the traditional medieval explication of Canticles as an allegory of mystical experience and love-union with Christ, has led some critics to postulate a strong strain of mysticism and ecstatic religious experience in Taylor. However, though Taylor revels in the Canticles' language and always refers the Canticles texts in some way to his own spiritual life, only very occasionally does he identify his religious experience with the love experiences recounted by the Spouse—and when he does so the experiences described are hardly mystical. He does not, as if he were a Puritan Crashaw or St. Teresa, take on the persona of the Spouse as sexual-spiritual lover.

On the other hand, Taylor's treatment of Canticles departs from the usual Protestant conception of it as an allegorical narrative of the history of the Church and the process of regeneration. His approach is exegetical, directed to the language of the particular biblical verses which serve as headings to his poems. Yet the assumptions of the familiar Protestant allegorical narrative lie behind almost all these poems. For Taylor, the Bridegroom is of course Christ and the Spouse is, most often, the Church as the entire company of the elect: "thy Spouse . . . doth consist of all / Gods blesst Elect regenerate within / The tract of time from first to last" (II.136, ll. 31-33). At times Taylor relates himself to the spousal metaphor by begging association with and incorporation within the Spouse; at other times he does so by exploring whether the Bridegroom's words to the Spouse apply in the particular sense to himself as elect soul. He reads the other primary metaphor of Canticles, the Garden, in terms of the same conventional allegorical symbolism: "This Garden, Lord, [is] thy Church"; "The Garden too's the Soule, of thy Redeem'd" (II.83, ll. 19, 25). The speaker's stance in such poems is to seek plantation and cultivation within the garden-Church (to be a flowerbed, vine, or lily in the garden), and sometimes to ask that the garden be planted and tilled within him. In most of these poems, Taylor probes intensively the metaphors and emblems of Canticles to produce praises for the Bridegroom and Spouse, and to clarify the theological basis of the speaker's relation to both. The few poems in which the speaker relates his own experience of Christ's love to that of the Spouse, or takes on her persona to describe such experiences are not mystical in any precise sense, but display the spiritual affections often treated at length in the Protestant allegory of Canticles. (pp. 416-18)

Most interesting, perhaps, is the lovely poem on Canticles 2:3, "His fruit was sweet to my Tast" (II.163). The term "sweet" is the focus of the poem, and the speaker unhesitatingly assumes the Bride's voice in amplifying the key term: Christ is "all sweet from top to bottom all"; he is sweet in all the stages of his life—"Sweet in the Virgin wombe and horses Manger"; he is all sweet metaphors and emblems—"My Love, my Lilly, my Rose and Crown / My brightest Glory, and my Hony sweet" (ll. 1, 14, 19-20); he is sweet in all his functions—mediatorial actions, righteousness, holiness. The metaphors pour forth thick and fast to explicate this sweetness:

> A Cabbinet of Holiness, Civit box
> Of Heavenly Aromatick, still much more,
> A treasury of Spicery, rich knots,
> Of Choicest Merigolds, a house of Store
> Of never failing dainties to my tast
> Delighting holy Palates, such thou hast.

> A sugar Mill, an Hony Hive most rich
> Of all Celestial viands, golden box
> Top full of Saving Grace, a Mint house which
> Is full of Angells, and a cloud that drops
> Down better fare than ever Artist could,
> More pleasant than the finest liquid Gold.

(ll. 43-54)

Then, recurring to the larger context of the verse—"I sat under his shadow with greate delight and his fruit was sweet to my taste"—the speaker without qualification expresses his own experience of this sweetness in the Bride's words:

> While I sat longing in this Shadow here
> To tast the fruite this Apple tree all ripe
> How sweet these Sweetings bee. Oh! sweet good Cheere
> How am I filld with sweet most sweet delight.
> The fruite, while I was in its shady place
> Was and to mee is now sweet to my tast.

(ll. 61-66)

With Edward Taylor an era in the writing of religious lyric poetry ended, an era which began in England with Wyatt and Coverdale and reached its apogee with Donne and Herbert. The poets I have concentrated upon [in *Protestant Poetics and the Seventeenth-Century Religious Lyric*] did not constitute a distinct school or write in a common style; rather, despite their variousness and individuality they developed and shared what was in large part a common poetics. This poetics derived its major impetus from Protestant conceptions of the Christian life, of the language and poetic genres of scripture, and of the role of art in religious expression. Furthermore, it drew upon a common body of materials (biblical tropes, typological symbolism, divine emblems, biblical lyric models, Protestant meditation, and Protestant sermon theory). Though certain emphases in Taylor's Puritan theology kept him from assuming (as others did) that he could produce worthy divine praises on the basis of this Protestant poetics, he was able to release a new vein of creativity in himself by using the familiar materials and paradigms of that poetics as a counterpoint to his own deliberately homely style.

After Taylor Protestant poetics was radically undermined by an attenuation of faith in dogmatic Christianity and in its sacred Book, which had served in so many ways as poetic model and resource. Some lesser poets whose concerns and achievements were rather devotional than artistic continued to write in these terms, and biblical imagery and typological reference remain generally important in later literature. But major poets seeking to give lyric expression to religious impulses looked elsewhere for the grounds of a religious aesthetics—in universal religious principles, in romantic pantheism, in personal moral imperatives, in private mythologies, in ecclesiastical ritual, in existential *angst*. However, for sixteenth- and seventeenth-century English poets, and especially for Donne, Herbert, Vaughan, Traherne, and Taylor, the Protestant poetics . . . provided a powerful stimulus to the imagination by promoting a profound creative response to the written word of scripture and inviting a searching scrutiny of the human heart. The consequence was a body of religious lyric unrivaled in our literature. (pp. 424-26)

Barbara Kiefer Lewalski, "Edward Taylor: Lisps of Praise and Strategies for Self-Dispraise," in her Protestant Poetics and the Seventeenth-Century

Religious Lyric, *Princeton University Press, 1979, pp. 388-426.*

HYATT H. WAGGONER (essay date 1984)

[*Waggoner is an American educator, editor, and the author of numerous studies, several of them devoted to Nathaniel Hawthorne. In the following excerpt from his most recent work,* American Poets from the Puritans to the Present *(1984), he attempts to fix Taylor's poetry within a definite literary tradition.*]

Of all the Puritan poets, only Edward Taylor makes much use in his poetry of what the Puritans called "carnal" things, and even he is generally only *using* them as transparent signs, not valuing them for what they are in themselves. Though he is by far the best of the Puritan poets and though many of his traits as a writer, particularly the way he uses homely imagery, justify the label "metaphysical" that has been given him, yet he often exhibits the bigotry and idolatry that characterize so much of Puritan verse. Only when we think of his style in the largest sense—of the purely poetic aspect of his poetry—are we likely to think of him as belonging in the company of the chief American poets.

When we do think of him this way—when we close the book and remember only certain lines and phrases—we are likely to decide that he occupies a minor but respectable place in our main tradition. For in his attitude toward language and poetic forms Taylor shows us what will later become recognizable as the peculiarly American attitude, an attitude compounded of perhaps equal parts of Puritan eschatology and Transcendental seeking. Taylor's verbal coinages, archaisms, and often personal meanings, his readiness to drop the meter when the thought demands it, his way of twisting, ignoring, or distorting any convention that gets in his way—all this and more makes us think of Emerson and later American poets. If his doctrines are Puritan, his attitude toward language and forms of verse might just as well be called Transcendental.

Even at his poorest, when he seems to be doing little more than rhyming doctrine or history, he suggests traits we find more fully exhibited later in Emerson, Whitman, Dickinson, William Carlos Williams, and Cummings, traits of American Transcendental poetry, in short. His cavalier attitude toward the conventions with which he was acquainted foreshadows Emerson's definition of what true poetry should be, "metre-making argument." Even thematically, there is a sense in which he is in the main stream of American verse. His central question, "Oh, what a thing is man! Lord, who am I?" has been asked over and over by the chief American poets, from Emerson to Roethke. Like Robinson's, his only real interest in man comes when he sees him against the sky; like R. P. Warren, he is interested in definition of the nature of man's sin and his glory.

But all this is very abstract. When the modern reader turns back to the poems themselves, apart from the half a dozen or so best, he is likely to be more disappointed than pleased by most of what he finds. He finds, for instance, relatively little of that tension between attachment to things temporal and longing for things eternal that characterizes most religious poetry of a high order. In the bulk of his poetry Taylor does not have to face the problem of

trying to wean himself from a loved but dying world. Most of his poems open with that problem already solved by the Puritan theology and ethos. If the tension between love of the things of this world and longing for Heaven existed in the man, as presumably it must have, it does not generally get into the poetry, except sporadically, and when it does it is denigrated.

One of the best of the *Preparatory Meditations*, written as devotional exercises before Taylor's monthly administrations of the Lord's Supper, will illustrate the point. Meditation 33, First Series, is often considered one of the finest poems Taylor ever wrote, partly at least because in it there seems to be an acknowledgment of the conflict between the temporal and the eternal; but even here, Taylor does not grant the attachment anything like equal value with the detachment. According to Taylor's dating, the poem was written the day his first wife died. There are evidences in the poem of Taylor's grief at the loss—perhaps the anticipated loss—of his "true love," his "deare," but chiefly Taylor takes this occasion to upbraid himself for loving a mere "Toy" instead of giving all his love to Christ.

The poem is keyed to First Corinthians, 3:22, which Taylor quotes as including "Life is youres," (Actually, he took only a little liberty with the text, condensing to get at what was for him the heart of the matter: "Whether Paul, or Apollos, or Cephas, or the world, or life, or death, or things present, or things to come; all are your's.") The important point, as Taylor saw it, was that the Faithful are inheritors of eternal life, so that, in effect, Christ *is* their life. Grief then, even grief for one's wife, would be inappropriate. Not attachment but detachment would seem to be our proper relation to the things of this world. For Taylor, this *contemptus mundi* theme must have seemed to be enforced by the preceding verse, "Therefore let no man glory in men. For all things are your's." Prompted by the occasion and habituated as he was to the Puritan tendency toward literalism in interpreting Scripture, Taylor would have read this, "Let no man glory in *men*," that is, in the "things of this world," the "mites" and "Toys" mentioned in the poem. To make this interpretation Taylor had only to ignore the larger context, which makes it clear that Paul was here advising the quarreling churchmen in Corinth to put aside disputes about whose followers they were and concentrate on the essentials of the faith they had received, from whatever source. Judging from the poem that follows, Taylor seems to have felt that the chief meaning of the passage was that he should not be grieved by the thought of his wife's death.

That he actually was grieved the poem makes very evident, especially in the lines:

> Nature's amaz'de, Oh monstrous thing Quoth shee,
> Not Love my life? What Violence doth split
> True Love, and Life, that they should sunder'd bee?

In these lines loss and promise remain in tension. But if his "true love" for his wife conflicts with his love of Christ, Taylor sees this as a sign of a weakness he should try to conquer. What his *real* "life" is, he has already declared, in his opening stanza:

> My Lord my Life, can Envy ever bee
> A Golden Vertue? Then would God I were
> Top full thereof untill it colours mee

With yellow streaks for thy Deare sake most Deare,
Till I be Envious made by't at myselfe,
As scarcely loving thee my Life, my Health.

The play on "deare" suggests that the unruly affections are not yet fully under control, but if the heart is torn, the mind knows what the heart *ought* to feel: Christ is the Lord, the Life, the Health—the true "deare." The second stanza implicitly acknowledges the reality of the conflict by the very vehemence of its denial that there should be a conflict:

Oh! what strange Charm encrampt my Heart with spite
Making my Love gleame out upon a Toy?
Lay out Cart-Loads of Love upon a mite?
Scarce lay a mite of Love on thee, my Joy?

Toward the end of the poem, as Taylor hopes for reunion with his wife in Heaven, "life," which had seemed until now perfectly clear—the promise of eternal life to the faithful—becomes ambiguous: "I and my Life again may joyned bee." In Heaven, he will be able to love Christ as he should, without ceasing to love his wife. Only the assurance of immortality can prevent his being distracted by attachment to mere mites and toys from complete devotion to Christ—"Oh! Graft me in this Tree of Life . . . that I may live." In the end, Taylor is reconciled to his loss, assured that in the light of faith it is really no loss: He has given his wife to be the bride of Christ:

Give me my Life this way; and I'le bestow
My Love on thee my Life, and it shall grow.

He has made a kind of promise—*not* to be grieved, *not* to be further distracted from things eternal. We are a long way here from Anne Bradstreet's poem on the burning of her house, in which the conflict of values was almost completely suppressed, but the same theology may be seen at work, denying the significance of a conflict actually felt. One way to state the superiority of Taylor's poem over Bradstreet's is to say that in the earlier poem, except for one line, we have to *guess* that the poet felt grief at the loss of her worldly goods and so turned to God all the more strongly, while in Taylor's poem a real conflict is implicitly acknowledge even while it is being explicitly denied. At his best, Taylor does a great deal more than merely versify doctrine.

But only a handful of Taylor's poems are as good as this one. Generally they tend to be both clotted and incoherent, sometimes incoherent even as statement. A good deal of the time he seems to be making his poems simply by collecting every possible illustrative image he can think of and simply adding them all up. The famous and justly praised **"Huswifery"** does not prepare us for the bulk of the work in this respect. For the most part, he picks up and drops his metaphors without showing much real concern for them. Meaning is what matters, and this world gets its meaning wholly from outside.

One of his best known, and best, poems will illustrate the point. His **"Preface"** to *God's Determinations* celebrates the greatness of God, the Creator, in imagery that is, for the most part, effective:

Upon what Base was fixt the Lath, wherein
He turn'd this Globe, and riggalld it so trim?
Who blew the Bellows of his Furnace Vast?

Or held the Mould wherein the world was Cast?

Throughout the first dozen lines the images used to convey Taylor's wonder at God's making the world are all drawn from *man's* activities in making things—pottery, ironwork, buildings, clothing. But then Taylor turns from making to other activities ("Who in this Bowling Alley bowld the Sun?," perhaps his greatest line) and to objects that in one way or another image the power of a God who

Can take this mighty World up in his hande,
And shake it like a Squitchen or a Wand.

The most tightly knit part of the poem, lines three through fourteen, has sometimes been printed as a separate poem. So presented, no explanation is needed, for the excerpt is in no way dependent on what precedes or what follows. And even within these twelve lines, the organizing principle is chiefly external, being supplied by the story of the creation in Genesis. Within the poem—either the whole poem or the excerpt—there is no reason why housebuilding should precede sewing and follow iron-making. And the most memorable line of the group, drawn from bowling, would seem to have no connection with anything that precedes or follows.

There is a kind of curious and perverse appropriateness about Taylor's usual way of organizing his poetry. Taylor uses images allegorically, and from the point of view of the intrinsic quality of the images themselves, often incoherently because "nothing Man" and his world have no meaning, no reality even, except as they point to God. Taylor's images for the most part are not symbols but signs, pointers, for by definition symbols have intrinsic interest and implicit meaning. From Taylor's point of view, interest in fallen man and his activities or in nature, which had been blasted along with man by the Original Sin, could very easily become excessive. To value highly things carnal was evidence that one was not one of the Elect. "For here have we no continuing city, but we seek one to come."

Taylor's longest poem of those that have been transcribed from his manuscripts, his *Metrical History of Christianity,* is about as unreadable as a doggerel poem can be. For more than four hundred crowded pages it versifies the legendary history of those who persecuted, and those who suffered for, the faith. Only occasionally does it rise from verse to poetry, in the normative sense, and then chiefly either to praise God for the wisdom He displays in arranging history as he has, or to dwell with loving interest on the sufferings of persecutor or martyr. Thus the fate of Herod:

But God goes on and Justice doth thus smite
Him with a Slow and burning Fire that makes
His bowells rot, a greedy Apetite,
Worms eating him alive, sore Belly akes
A nasty Priapism doth abound
In him, and he doth stinck above the ground.

Such passages as this have their own sort of macabre interest, but they are relatively rare, certainly not typical of the poem as a whole. As a whole, this poem is, I think, the dullest poem I have ever tried to read.

Compared with the *Metrical History, God's Determinations* is easy going. It is in no sense dramatic, as we should expect it to be from the fact that it consists of speeches assigned to various character—the saint, the unregenerate soul, Christ, and others. It is not dramatic because the content of the speeches is determined by purely doctrinal considerations, not at all by any individualizing of the speakers. And neither is it marked by any special lyric intensity or vividness. But it is more coherent than many of the Meditations, and its exposition of the whole range of Christian doctrine is sometimes marked by interesting psychological insights. Some of the speeches by the soul who fears he is not Elect, for instance, along with the replies of the assured saint, contain very perceptive notations of the dynamics of religious belief. As a whole, though, the poem is just dull.

Taylor's elegy on the death of Samuel Hooker seems to me one of his best organized and sustained poems of any length. It is a dignified and sometimes moving poem, except in the passages where Taylor's bigotry takes over. (Why does everyone comment on Wigglesworth's bigotry and no one on Taylor's? Their theology is the same, and the rigor with which both held to it seems equal.) When Taylor praises Hooker for his "orthodoxy," the poem becomes unintentionally funny. Almost everyone, it seems, except Taylor and Hooker and a tiny group of the faithful—almost everyone is damned, doomed to unending God-inflicted torment—for New England is already, in 1697, in "Declension" from earlier orthodoxy. Not only (of course) all non-Christians, not only Christians with the bad luck to be born "Papists" or Anglicans, but Presbyterians (apostasy) and even liberal Congregationalists (Stoddardeans)—not to mention Quakers, Baptists, Antinomians, and others—all these and more are damned. One would think that it ought to have depressed Taylor at times to consider how few, how very few, were those whom God in His infinite power and justice had been able to save. Hawthorne wrote the proper comment on all this in his "The Man of Adamant": the righteousness of the Puritans, he said in effect in the story of the man whose heart finally turned to stone, was indistinguishable from self-righteousness. Theologically, though not, to be sure, in their polity, Puritans were immersed in caves of self the better, as they supposed, to pursue their separate salvations.

Taylor's very best poems are not weakened, as the elegy on Hooker is, by bigotry. The well-known and justly praised **"Prologue"** to the *Preparatory Meditations,* a half dozen or more of the Meditations themselves, **"The Glory of and Grace in the Church Set Out,"** from *God's Determinations,* and a few of the miscellaneous poems, of which **"Upon a Spider Catching a Fly"** and **"An Address to the Soul Occasioned by a Rain"** are perhaps the best, deserve and reward more than one reading. In them Taylor is more than a devotional poet and more than the writer of lines useful for illustrating the nature and consequences of Puritan belief. He is the initiator of a great tradition.

Taylor's anticipations of what was destined to become the main tradition in American poetry—insofar as American poetry is not simply a rather inferior branch of British poetry—are somewhat more apparent in the way he uses language and his attitude toward poetic forms than they are in the substance of his poems. Philosophically, the way from Taylor to Emerson is considerably longer than that "from Edwards to Emerson," to borrow Perry Miller's classic phrase. (Reading Taylor, I have often found myself wishing that he had had Edwards' mind, or that Edwards had had his poetic gift, and had been a poet.)

"Upon a Spider Catching a Fly" will sufficiently illustrate Taylor's foreshadowing of Emerson's most typical and effective manner—as well as his theory—in the matter of poetic style. Taylor's short lines, the absence of all ornament and flourish, the impression he creates of a *mind* at work concerned to *say* something important, the colloquialisms combined with syntactical inversions—all this and more suggests Emerson's practice at his best. Taylor's lines "This goes to pot, that not/ Nature doth call," for instance, are recognizably close in *manner* to Emerson's closing lines in "Merlin I":

> There are open hours
> When the God's will sallies free,
> And the dull idiot might see
> The flowing fortunes of a thousand years;—
> Sudden, at unawares,
> Self-moved, fly-to the doors,
> Nor sword of angels could reveal
> What they conceal.

Taylor's style in **"Upon a Spider"** is perhaps even closer to these lines from Emerson's "Bacchus." Note the inversion in Emerson's last line:

> Water and bread,
> Food which needs no transmuting,
> Rainbow-flowering, wisdom-fruiting,
> Wine which is already man,
> Food which teach and reason can.

It is at once curious and suggestive that many of the features of Taylor's verse that make him seem inferior to George Herbert, whom he so often parallels and apparently echoes, bring him closer to Emerson. Where Herbert is smooth, Taylor is rough; where Herbert is coherent, Taylor is often seemingly, or perhaps really, incoherent; where Herbert works within recognized forms and standard meanings of words, Taylor often seems impatient with form, even the form he has chosen, and quite ready when necessary to bend language to his purposes, even if he has to make up a word or invent a new meaning for an old one. Clearly, Taylor is a lesser poet than either Herbert or Emerson, for entirely different reasons, but comparison of his work with Herbert's tends to lead to the conclusion that Taylor's is hardly worth reading, being only a very inferior imitation; while comparison with Emerson makes him seem a sort of poetic pioneer.

Comparisons are strategic as well as instructive. Whether Taylor ought to be thought of as a late and provincial metaphysical or an early practitioner in a poetic tradition that later diverged more and more widely from British tradition until it produced Whitman and Dickinson—this is a question everyone will want to answer for himself, in his own way. (pp. 16-24)

Hyatt H. Waggoner, "Puritans and Deists," in his American Poets: From the Puritans to the Present, *revised edition, Louisiana State University Press, 1984, pp. 3-32.*

MICHAEL SCHULDINER (essay date 1986)

[*In the following excerpt, Schuldiner links Taylor's spiritual development in the* Preparatory Meditations *with both Cal-*

vinist growth in assurance and the Christianized version of the hero's classical journey.]

Among the more striking characteristics of the "First Series" of Edward Taylor's *Preparatory Meditations* are the levels of spiritual exhilaration and anxiety that appear in the poem. That statements about Taylor's spiritual condition appear at all in his meditations is no doubt due to that self-examination, which, as Norman Grabo points out, accompanied for Taylor the act of meditation. But that self-examination and meditation should produce such intense expressions of spiritual hopes and fears is perhaps due to the relative isolation of the Massachusetts frontier, where no world of art existed into which to escape from the terrors of conscience nor audience of artists for whom to mitigate the pure joys of the Spirit. But perhaps equally striking, at least from the point of view of the student of Taylor's work, is that Taylor continued to write poetry about the spiritual conflicts within him for so long a period of time and with such regularity. The "First Series" alone extends some ten years and is comprised of poems written at roughly two- to three-month intervals—almost all of them dated.

Unquestionably, the account these poems present of the soul's condition provides as fine a record of an individual's spiritual vacillations over an extended period of time as any that exists in verse, and significant statements have in recent years appeared about Taylor's spiritual development as it is reflected in the "First Series" of *Preparatory Meditations*. Donald Stanford and Charles Mignon have provided, for example, important insights into the motivations behind the writing of these poems. Stanford has suggested that the meditation was a means by which Taylor attempted to return to an earlier religious experience. Such experiences, of course, served Taylor as tokens of God's good will toward him. And Mignon has noted that Taylor discerned a relationship between his ability to praise God effectively through meditation and his state of Grace. From this one can infer, as one infers from Stanford's remarks, that Taylor is seeking evidence of his election even as he writes these poems. Insofar as the success of Taylor's search is concerned—the actual progress that appears in the *Preparatory Meditations*—the key insights are provided by Norman Pettit and Louis Martz. Pettit points out that Taylor is already converted by the time the *Preparatory Meditations* are started and so the search for evidence of election is to establish assurance of salvation. And assurance, according to Louis Martz, is established toward the close of the "First Series" of *Preparatory Meditations.* But while such insights into the development taking place in the *Preparatory Meditations* do exist, they are in the form of brief statements—made in passing, and designed, one might think, for others to follow up.

This paper will show in some detail how Taylor's spiritual development as reflected in the "First Series" of *Preparatory Meditations* can be understood in terms of the paradigm for the first stage of spiritual growth—growth in assurance. The thesis of this study, however, is that Taylor's "First Series" of *Preparatory Meditations,* even as they tell of Taylor's development through the first stage of spiritual growth, also recount the first stage of the classical journey of the hero as it had earlier been Christianized. My hope here is to provide alternative and secular means of access to the complex Christian drama of the soul's progress that is conveyed in Taylor's "First Series." (pp. 113-14)

Christian Liberty, of which growth in assurance is the first stage, is a process in which the believer is repeatedly confronted by what Calvin calls "conscience." According to Calvin, when an individual is converted, there develops, apart from faith in God, a new inclination to the performance of good works. But the believer's works are invariably flawed and imperfect, and these flaws and imperfections suggest to him that his works are not motivated by regenerate inclinations but by some hidden sin that still inhabits the flesh. It is this sense of sin, which is in a manner persistent throughout the believer's development, that troubles the conscience. And it is the development toward Christian Liberty that is the means by which the anxiety produced by conscience is allayed. (pp. 114-15)

This development by which one attains to assurance of salvation is comprised of four sequential events. There is first of all the conversion experience in which the Holy Spirit "illumines" the mind and regenerates the will, producing in the believer the sense that all his actions are motivated by the regenerate desire to please God and perform good works. But the believer does not so easily escape from the tendency to sin that he was born with. In fact, the second event in the growth toward assurance is the conscious recognition on the part of the believer that the regeneration of the will has not been entire—that base affections for the things of the world do still exist in him. The third event, the crucial one in the larger scheme, is the "faith-doubt" or "hope-fear" dilemma which appears as the believer begins to reason about his motives. On the one hand, the believer's sincere desire to be serviceable to God suggests to him that he is of the faithful, or at least has reason to hope he is; on the other hand, his inclination to sin produces doubts and fears that he is not of the faithful who are saved by Christ's redemptive act. Eventually however the believer is freed from the reasoning process which holds the dilemma in place. Through contemplation and meditation upon Christ, a communion or identification with Christ takes place, during which time the tensions which hold the reasoning processes in place, as well as the reasoning processes themselves, dissipate. At that point, according to Calvin, the believer is said to arrive at full assurance of salvation. It is important to note however that for Calvin there is no element of pride or arrogance associated with the existence of full assurance. The term full assurance connotes no more than a release from those tensions that had held in place the reasoning processes which yielded doubts and fears that one was not saved.

Edward Taylor's spiritual growth as it appears in the "First Series" of the *Preparatory Meditations* exhibits these same four sequential developments described by Calvin. Taylor undergoes, first of all, an illumination by the Spirit which produces in him regenerate inclinations but which does not free him from base worldly desires and ambitions. Taylor then, in the second place, comes to the conscious recognition that these ambitions and base affections still exist in him. Thirdly, Taylor begins to reason, based upon both the godly and natural affections that appear in him, about whether or not he is saved, and this reasoning produces articulated faith and hope, as well as doubt and fear. Finally, through meditation upon Christ, the tensions that hold the faith-doubt or hope-fear dilemma in place dissipate, and the believer is said to arrive at assurance of salvation.

But, of course, there is a good deal more to Taylor's development from conversion to assurance of salvation than just a poetic version of what Calvin describes. With regard to the first development Taylor undergoes, conversion is, as Calvin had suggested, illumination of the mind. In the meditation entitled "**The Experience,**" Taylor speaks of the "light" of illumination that brought him closer to God, as he asks "What Beam of Light wrap up my sight to finde / Me neerer God than ere Came in my minde?" It is, however, the next meditation, entitled "**The Return,**" in which Taylor identifies this light he has partaken of. It is the light that arrays Christ in heaven, seated in Glory, which has been conveyed to him; a Christ who is, in Taylor's words, "Bright Glories blaze," whose "Shine fills Heaven with Glory" and whose "Smile Convayes / Heavens Glory." Further, in Taylor's view there is a reciprocal relationship between illumination and his regeneration, which for Taylor manifests itself in his ability to perform his own special godly work, his songs of Christ in Glory—the very *Meditations* themselves. First, in an image that likens his "Heart" to a "Golden Harp . . . / Well tun'd by Glorious Grace," Taylor identifies a causal relationship between his ability to hold that bit of Christ's Glory with which he has been illumined and his ability to sing of Christ's glorification: "I praise thee, Lord, and better praise thee would / If what I had, my heart might ever hold" ("**The Experience**").

But the relationship between illumination and the meditation is not only causal; it is reciprocal. As Taylor finds himself growing more distant from the illumination experience of Christ in Glory—his source of inspiration for his attempts to write of Christ in Glory in his *Meditations*—he begins to look to the meditation and meditative process as the means by which to regain something of the experience of illumination. The meditations numbered five through twenty-two, which were written in the four-year period from 1683 to 1687, present Taylor's attempts to use the meditative process to recapture that light which had shown forth from Christ in Glory so that he can once again sing the Glorification. Specifically, Taylor's aim in these meditations is to present an image of Christ's glory to which he can respond much as he did to the glory of Christ during illumination, and thus regain something of the original experience of conversion. In keeping with the regimen of meditation, the first step, after the presentation of the image, is rumination or reasoning about the image. This is followed by the appearance of holy affections—the same affections that would appear in the real presence of the subject of the image. (pp. 115-17)

Some five months after the writing of Meditation 22—in Meditation 24, dated November 1687—Taylor experiences the second important development in the believer's journey toward assurance, the extended confrontation with pride and the baser affections in general. Here, in Meditation 24, Taylor is unable to escape from the argument that his residual affections for the things of the world, which leave little love left for God, prevent him from writing the successful meditation, the one which will recapture for him the illumined frame of mind in which he can write the poem of Christ in Glory. Even as he envisions heaven and addresses his God, Taylor finds "mine Affections Quick as Lightning fly / On toys," but "they Snaile like move to kiss thy hand." And it is because his affections have not been entirely weaned from the world

that Taylor is unable to regain the experience of illumination and his "handy Works," his attempts to describe God's glory in verse, amount to no more than "Words, and Wordiness." This is not to say that Taylor will, at this point, give up his desire to recapture the experience of illumination and write a poem about the Glorification. Placing himself through meditation in that illumined state of mind would, as Taylor understands it, eradicate those unregenerate affections that still exist, as well as provide the inspirational state in which the poem of Christ in Glory can be written. This is to say, however, that Taylor is now taking his inclination to sin seriously and will continue to do so for the next two years, until, in Meditation 36, it evolves into the faith-doubt dilemma—the third development in the progress toward assurance.

In Meditation 36, Taylor commits the error that Calvin had warned against. He abandons the prospect of recapturing the state of illumination and begins to reason about his unregenerate affections, the existence of which suggests to him that he was never really converted. He starts with the assumption that he has, indeed, been justified. But if this is the case asks Taylor, how is it that his sin looms so large before him? "This reason saith is hard to reconcile," confesses Taylor. But Taylor does not admit of the rational conclusion that he is not saved. He asserts that his faith is such that this rational conclusion need not be entertained: "My Faith therefore doth all these Pleas disdain, . . . Upon this banck it doth on tiptoes stand / To ken o're Reasons head at Graces hand." But despite this assertion of faith, doubts of justification continue to appear. "But am I thine?" Taylor asks of God later in Meditation 36. Here Taylor, in a vain attempt rationally to clarify his state, has, as Calvin anticipated, fallen into the faith-doubt dilemma. He cannot, in light of his affections for the world, firmly maintain his faith, and he dare not allow doubts of justification to turn to despair. This vacillation between doubt and faith continues for two years, until in February 1691 Taylor does, by his own admission, come close to despairing of salvation: "I wonder, split I don't upon Despare," says Taylor.

It is at the same time, however, that Taylor arrives at this low point in his dilemma in Meditation 40 that he hits upon a basis for identification with Christ, which, when its implications are fully realized in Meditation 41, will release him from the faith-doubt dilemma and yield what Calvin refers to as full assurance. The crucial passage in Meditation 40 is that in which Taylor recognizes that despite his natural affections for the world, "Christs name / Propitiation is for sins," and asks,

> Lord, take
> It so for mine. Thus quench thy burning flame
> In that clear stream that from his side forth brake.
> I can no Comfort take while thus I see
> Hells cursed Imps thus jetting strut in mee.

This passage is comprised of two images. The first is an image of Christ on the Cross, his side speared by the lance of a Roman soldier. It is by such suffering, as Taylor indicates, that God's justice is appeased, His "burning flame" of anger "quench'd," and Christ atones for the sin of man. The next image is of Taylor who, like Christ, suffers at the hands of "Hells cursed Imps," although in Taylor's case the sufferings take the form of doubts of election and fears of reprobation. In the past, Taylor has looked to Christ's purity as a register by which to judge of his spiritual state; and he has not fared well by comparison. Here however Taylor has found a basis for identification with Christ. Taylor suffers for his sin as Christ had suffered for the sins of mankind. (pp. 118-20)

It is not at all clear how Calvin's doctrine of Christian Liberty, of which growth in assurance is the first stage, evolved or where it evolved from. Martin Luther's doctrine of Christian Liberty, to which one might look for precedent, does not speak of a sequence of events taking place within the conscience or mind of the believer as Calvin's doctrine does. And Melanchthon, who is sometimes identified as the source of Calvin's doctrine of Christian Liberty, precisely because Melanchthon does speak of a sequence of psychological events, does not include among those events assurance of justification. But while it is not clear whether Calvin had a source for the particular design he gave to the doctrine of Christian Liberty it is clear that he had access to discussions of those developments that comprise the stage of growth in assurance. Guillaume Budé's *De transitu Hellenismi ad Christianismum*, for one, presents discussions of each of the three developments that take place prior to assurance of salvation. Moreover, Budé's *De transitu*, as is true of other writings Calvin would have known, reads the particular spiritual development into a particular event of the classical journey-myth. That those spiritual developments which later appear in Calvin's paradigm for growth in assurance had earlier been discerned in certain episodes of classical myth is important here. It suggests that Taylor's development in the "First Series" of *Preparatory Meditations*, which can be read in terms of Calvin's paradigm for growth in assurance, can also be read in terms of the classical journey-myth. (p. 121)

The first development the believer undergoes in Calvin's view is, as we have seen, the conversion experience which illumines the mind and at least partially regenerates the will. The believer is newly inclined to obey God's law and is, in some measure although not entirely, disaffected from the things of the world. In fact, it is when the believer recognizes that he still exhibits affections for the world that the sense of sin appears which marks the second development in the stage of growth in assurance. But the passage from the first to the second development—from the partial regeneration of the affections at conversion to the recognition that regeneration has been, at best, partial—is not always automatic. The believer, despite his conversion, may remain for a time so much a thrall of the duplicitous world that he does not recognize that his actions are motivated, at least in part, by residual natural affections. And it is this interim condition that the Calypso episode of *The Odyssey* speaks of, according to Budé. This is the episode in which Odysseus is stranded on the island of Calypso, whose passion for him is such that, despite his pinning to be off, she is loath to let him leave.

In Budé, "the lodging place of Calypso" is the world where everything is actually "upside-down." It is the place where "arrogance dislodges a sense of shame; slyness, sincerity of speech; swaggering talk, truth; iniquity and dishonesty, goodness and equity." It is the place where deceit reigns, "where veracity remains unnoticed and even incurs displeasure." But it is here that the hero is found, held in place by his natural affections, which, precisely because it is an upside down world, he does not recognize as sinful.

Before he can journey forward, the hero must acknowledge his affections for the world and recognize that they are a product of that sin which, despite conversion, still resides within him. Taylor too is held in place by unacknowledged affections for the world and therefore unable to journey forward until Meditation 24. The particular unacknowledged affection that ties Taylor to the world takes the form of a desire to win renown as a poet, which, at least in part, motivates his attempts at a poem about Christ in Glory. Up to Meditation 24, Taylor has apparently been able to ignore the existence of worldly ambition within him and assume that his poetic efforts have been motivated solely by the desire to praise God. But having recognized in Meditation 24 the existence of unregenerate affections, the remnants of sin within him, Taylor has escaped from the island of Calypso and can now go forward in his journey and examine his sin. It is worth pointing out, however, that Taylor remains on Calypso's island—unable, because of his ambition, to see his sin—for some five years.

The classical myth which was allegorized to reveal the second development of growth in assurance, confrontation with sin, was the Sirens episode of *The Odyssey*. In this episode Odysseus and his crew must sail by the island of a species of being whose song enchants men and lures them to the island where they waste away and die. Odysseus is warned of this by Circe who counsels him to have his men stop their ears with "sweet wax of honey." Odysseus may choose to listen to the song of the Sirens, but only if he will have his men bind him to the mast of his ship so that he is unable to escape. Odysseus does choose to hear the Siren's song, is fastened to the mast, and despite the sensory appeal of the Sirens, his ship passes by to safety. The hero, unlike his companions, confronts with open ears what are, of course, his own affections and passions. And it was as symbols of objects that arouse man's affections for the world, as well as those natural affections themselves, that theologians such as Guillaume Budé viewed the Sirens.

Among the sinful affections for the world identified with the Sirens by Budé was "an active ambition always urging oneself" the sort of ambition that creates the desire to write great poems. Against these Sirens, the unregenerate—who to Budé are represented by the companions of Odysseus—are advised to stop their ears: "the inexperienced, bound by no law of right reason, escape the dangers of the sea without a memorable offense only if they remain free from the sensation of seductions which drag travelers into destruction. For the above mentioned Sirens . . . tie up the charmed ears of listeners and their senses. . . ." By contrast, the faithful individual—the hero—must confront his affections directly: "Just as Ulysses of old . . . heard, as if through a lattice, those extremely sweet and pleasant songs of the Sirens . . . , so in precisely the same manner it is necessary that a man . . . binds the command of his own mind to the mast of the boat by means of the chains of the law of the gospel." In this manner—bound by the gospel to the Cross—the hero confronts the passions and eventually moves forward into the faith-doubt or hope-fear dilemma.

The third development in this first stage of spiritual growth from conversion to assurance, the hope-fear dilemma, is revealed, according to Budé, in the myth of Aeolus whose unpredictable winds act upon a vessel producing "at one time a not doubtful hope, at another a desperate expectation... alternating in the same breast." More commonly however it was the Scylla and Charybdis episode of *The Odyssey* that was allegorized by Christian theologians to reveal the hope-fear dilemma. In that episode, one recalls, Odysseus must pass through narrow straits on one side of which the monster Scylla lurks on high ready to snatch men up in her jaws, and on the other side of which Charybdis, in the form of a whirlpool, waits to suck men down to the bottom of the sea. There is no escaping some destruction for the hero. If he sails close to Scylla to avoid Charybdis, death comes from above; and if he sails by Charybdis to avoid Scylla, death awaits from below. Thus it is a dilemma for which reason has no solution—the simultaneous appearance of equally threatening forces from opposite directions, which the hero must not only contemplate but pass between.

Among the allegorical treatments of the Scylla and Charybdis myth is that provided in the spurious version of *The Soliloquies* attributed to St. Augustine. There, in a prayer that asks for salvation, the author beseeches "Graunt to us O Lord, that wee may hold soe even away, betweene *Sylla*, and *Caribdis*, that haveing escaped the daunger of them both, wee may securely arryve, in the port, with our ship, and our adventure safe." The spiritual journey too is one in which the Christian confronts his Scylla and Charybdis, but for the Christian these monsters take the form of extreme doubt of salvation—despair—and false hopes of being saved—presumption. As *The Soliloquies* point out, our life is spent "in danger," our "end in doubt, for wee know not our end...," and such doubt is occasion for despair of salvation. On the other hand, while Christ is "the hope of all the ends of the earth," such hope of salvation may not be warranted. It may be only a "false delight allureing"—in a word, presumption. And just as the hero looks forward to passing between the threatening forces to safety, so too the Christian looks forward to going beyond doubt and hope, or despair and presumption, to "a supreame, and certain security, secure Tranquility, a quiet joy...." And this of course is Taylor's situation by the time Meditation 39 is written: "Sin's poyson swell my heart would till it burst," confesses Taylor, "Did not hope hence creep in't thus, and nurse't."

The passage through the hope-fear dilemma to the final development of the first stage of spiritual growth, assurance of salvation, has its best classical formulation, for the purposes of this study, in the Theseus myth recounted by Ovid. There it is Ariadne, who, acting as protectress, provides Theseus with the spool of thread that he unravels as he enters the Labyrinth inhabited by the Minotaur, and so is able to find his way out again. Ariadne's idea, imparted to Theseus, allows the hero to escape the imminent death that awaits. And this myth was employed to similar effect by no less than John Calvin himself. The Theseus myth appears at least twice in the *Institutes*. In one instance, he uses the myth to explain the physical suffering that the elect endure on earth, which for Calvin is a participation in the sufferings of Christ. "We share Christ's sufferings," says Calvin, "in order that as he passed from a labyrinth of all evils into heavenly glory, we may in like manner be led through various tribulation to the same glory." Here it is the will of providence that Christ and the elect endure hardships, but are brought safely to glory. In another instance, however, Calvin uses the Theseus myth and specif-

ically the spool of thread in order to indicate the kinds of difficulties the rational soul confronts when it attempts to understand the nature of God's will. The contemplation of God, Calvin warns, "is for us like an inexplicable labyrinth unless we are conducted into it by the thread of the word...." And here of course it is "the thread of the Word" that guides the elect out of their perplexity—out of the paradox confronted by the soul which has reason to both doubt and hope that it is saved.

This same Theseus myth moreover is actually employed by Taylor in Meditation 41 to describe that revelation which had led him out of his dilemma to assurance of salvation. When Taylor, having found a basis for identification with Christ in His sufferings, exclaims at the opening of Meditation 41, "A Clew of Wonders!" he speaks not only having found a "clue" to his dilemma. This "clew" that Taylor has found, he maintains, is that from which Christ's "Web of Flesh," His man-nature, was woven. In effect, Taylor is declaring here that he has found the spool which contains the thread that leads him back to Christ's man-nature with which he is able to identify. In Ovid's story it is Ariadne who, performing the function of guide, provides Theseus with the spool of thread; the clew of thread that Taylor receives is provided by the Holy Spirit operating in the Scripture. Taylor is employing here an allegorization of the Theseus myth, which resembles allegorizations presented by Calvin, to identify his progress out of the hope-fear dilemma. Taylor was apparently somewhat fond of the Theseus myth. He would later present it in the *Christographia* sermons in a much more explicit fashion, although to a different purpose. And, of course, Taylor was fond of Ovid generally—his translation of a fragment from the story of Daedalus still survives.

Taylor's first series of *Preparatory Meditations* can thus be read in terms of both Calvin's paradigm for growth in assurance and the classical journey-myth. (pp. 122-26)

Michael Schuldiner, "The Christian Hero and the Classical Journey in Edward Taylor's 'Preparatory Meditations. First Series'," in The Huntington Library Quarterly *Vol. 49, No. 2, Spring, 1986, pp. 113-32.*

KAREN E. ROWE (essay date 1986)

[*In the following excerpt, Rowe traces Taylor's perspective on the established doctrine of theological types.*]

The eulogizing of magistrates and ministers in New England, whether as Moses, Joshua, or Nehemiah, played an important role in the formation of American culture. Initially an effort to consecrate the leaders of the mission into the wilderness, attributions of biblical identities together with qualities peculiar to that figure enhanced the confidence of Puritan followers. Visualizing a journey over a treacherous ocean to a reputedly uninviting land might overwhelm the most stalwart separatist, were it not for his faith in God's providential care, that is, an unshakable belief in the chosenness of this New Israel. But that trust also derived from a further perception of Puritan leaders, such as John Winthrop and John Cotton, as designated emissaries—men who like prophets and priests in the Old Testament had received their visions from God. Anointed by God, they would appear invulnerable, their strength not subject to geographical accidents or obstacles.

Much like Washington, Lincoln, Kennedy, and King, who became the secular visionaries and heroes of later American epochs, these colonizing fathers achieved the status of folk heroes. But the folk were the small band of Puritan Elect, and the heroes were heralded as historical descendants, if not antitypes, of the Old Testament prophets, priests, and kings. (p. 53)

[Despite the plethora of] contemporary recapitulative uses of biblical types, in *Upon the Types of the Old Testament* and the *Preparatory Meditations* Taylor's mode is not one of cultural identification, but a more exegetically stringent and devotional approach. He does not range far beyond the Old-to-New Testament correspondences, nor in Meditations II.2-15 and 30 does he overtly use biblical persons as historical exempla for his Puritan colleagues. Instead, the sermons and meditations take an exegetically conservative turn toward a schematic examination of the major biblical types, chronologically distributed from Adam through Moses and Joshua onward to David and Solomon. Modeling his selected types on the scriptural order of their descent, Taylor views all Old Testament fathers as foreshadowers of the ultimate Son in Christ. Thus, the Christological emphasis, which so often disappears or remains implicit in historical chronicles and elegies, retains center stage in Taylor's poetry. In part, this exegetical rather than historical bias is determined by Taylor's close reliance on equally Christocentric sources, *Christ Revealed* and *The Figures or Types*. Neither Thomas Taylor nor Samuel Mather indulge in wholesale historical applications of types; indeed, Mather may have been the catalyst to bring his errant brother Increase Mather back from extravagances of recapitulative typology which permeated his jeremiads of the seventies. But the predilection for a Christocentric typology seems also to grow out of Edward Taylor's own personality and his homiletic and meditative aims. Less willing, after the Harvard elegies, to envision himself or his contemporaries as a leader, antitype, or cultural hero, Taylor turns to devotional rather than historical applications. Whereas Cotton Mather focuses upon geographical and temporal realities, Taylor concentrates on moral and spiritual patterns of the Christian life, prefigured by Old Testament priests and prophets but epitomized by Christ's life. Consequently, the meditations reflect his exegetical approach and often mirror the rational explications of his sermons. But just as one would expect homiletic doctrine to culminate in moral improvements, so too the meditations repeatedly close with Taylor's personal requests for guidance—that he might imitate the typal personages in his spiritual strivings. Although he ultimately seeks inspiration from the lives of these patriarchs, Taylor travels by way of the figural parallels set forth so intellectually in his sermons *Upon the Types of the Old Testament*. (pp. 55-6)

[His] analysis of Abraham . . . reveals the several levels at which Taylor, in both homilies and poems, unfolds scriptural meanings. Extracting his raw matter from the Bible and traditional glosses, Taylor perceives Abraham as a type of two different orders, from one perspective adumbrating Christ's relationship with His church as a historical phenomenon and a mystical relationship. Hence, Abraham's paternity of his flock and transmittal of God's promises foreshadow Christ's mission, in which He assumes a mystical headship of the body which is the church of all believers. But the exegesis holds implications not only for the collective church but also for each individual saint, defined as one who renounces works for Christ's saving grace. Taylor thus exegetically construes Abraham in this double way, as a prophetic figure for a later historical dispensation and for an ongoing spiritual process. Once, however, he sets the scriptural explication within the context of a publicly preached sermon, he implicitly acknowledges a further historical continuum which makes the New Testament church mystical one and the same with his Westfield congregation, to whom Jesus' promises are as spiritually as they were literally real to the apostles. Unlike Cotton Mather or contemporary historians, Taylor does not elaborate these connections into a recapitulative typology, because he seeks not so much to sustain the glorious emigration as to preach an enduring inward journey. His homiletic applications speak immediately to the troubled saint who seeks freedom from Hagar's curse of bond-slavery and craves nurture instead from a spriritual fount, represented by Sarah's promise through Isaac that the Savior will deliver men from sin. Removed one step further from the pulpit's public oratory, Edward Taylor delves yet more deeply into the personal by making his meditation an example of incorporation, of Abraham's figural prophecies and Christ's fulfillment absorbed by his own soul. In Meditation II.4 covenant theology becomes realized not as a theory of the chosen nation in New England, but rather as a repeated act of internalized belief essential to support Taylor, the elect saint, in his worldly progress. Taylor both stands so removed from the contingencies of temporal life that historical recapitulations become irrelevant, and yet strikes so close to the heart of figural meaning (one saint rather than a nation, a gospel covenant to supersede the Old Testament, grace not works) that his poem embodies the essence of what Allan Charity calls typology's existential claim of faith. (pp. 63-4)

Taylor's analysis of Abraham exemplifies his exegetical scaffolding, that is, the multiple frames that structure the sermons, yet just as inevitably lead from rational understandings toward exhortatory applications and finally to intensely felt prayers in the meditations. Isaac reveals Taylor's search for connections, whether through imagistic associations (promised seed), biblical "begats" as sons succeed their fathers, or conglobations, either traditional or newly created by Taylor, which place the personal figures in an overarching schema. Although Taylor presents these patterns as inherent in Scripture and reflective of God's prophetic intentions, we cannot escape the sense that the categories (mediator, mystical headship, promised seed, Christ's progress) become occasionally artificial, though admittedly of service to the exegete, preacher, and audience. Jacob also illustrates the extent to which Taylor, like other seventeenth-century figuralists, relies upon *manifest* analogies between the Old and New Testaments, thereby mirroring in method the fundamental principles of Puritan typology—its historicity, pattern of prophecy and fulfillment, and celebration of Christ's superiority *forma perfectior* over ancient persons. Because of the close relationship between sermons and poems, Taylor's exegetical methods inevitably influence the structure of his meditations. But the meditations also reveal Taylor's fascination with imagery, with his personal need to translate didactic teaching into felt learning, and with a poetic medium in which the private man speaks directly to his God. (p. 67)

In much the same way that Taylor adopts prophets, priests, and kings to create a bridge between individual types and the ranks, so also he later redesigns the Israelite nation into a suitable transition to the ceremonial law, for the house of Jacob foreshadows Christ's kingdom to come under the gospel. Consequently, he emphasizes Christ's royal lineage, inherited through Israel:

> Thou art, my Lord, the King of Glory bright.
> A glory't is unto the Angells flame
> To be thy Haurald publishing thy Light
> Unto the Sons of Men: and thy rich Name.
> They are thy Subjects. Yea thy realm is faire.
> Ore Jacobs House thou reignest: they declare.
>
> Their brightest glory lies in thee their king.
> My Glory is that thou my king maist bee.
> That I may be thy Subject thee to sing
> And thou may'st have thy kingdoms reign in mee.

From Luke's account of the annunciation, Taylor evolves a reading consistent with his previous themes in the sermons and meditations on personal types. Descended from the ancient house of Jacob (Israel), Christ assumes his kingship—to reign not literally on earth but spiritually enthroned in believers' hearts. Just as Taylor had praised the Son's glorious kingship adumbrated by Old Testament individuals (David, Solomon) and by ranks in Meditation II.14, he again recalls the messianic promise and its substantial accomplishment through Christ's incarnation. Christ is predestined to redeem men, indeed Taylor himself, from "Sins mutiny," "tawny Pride, and Gall," and "base Hypocrisy" which infect the "rotten heart." Through Christ's sacrifice alienated sinners become grafted into "thy Olive tree / The house of Jacob," a spiritual implantation which enables a thorny human "Bramble bush" to bear instead "sweet Roses then for thee." Taylor often assimilates material from the Bible and preceding expositions, as in his repeated use of Mather's configurations, details, and themes, but he also far surpasses his teachers with innovative realignments of the figural categories and imagistic recreations of traditional themes.

Originality was not a quality highly valued by Puritan theologians, since the mandate to read the Bible literally led to standardly acceptable glosses. Although expositors might vary in style and manner of presentation, nonetheless, the basic scriptural matter and Puritan exegetical approach to figural persons and ranks remained much the same. Thomas Taylor, Samuel Mather, and Edward Taylor held steady to the Christological focus or, as Mather stated the criterion, "an aptness to restrain all the Types to the *Person* of Christ," although with an Abraham or Moses they would countenance the prefiguring of a broader "Gospel Truth or Mystery." For most personal figures, the typological accounts are strikingly congruous, even though each exegete builds upon preceding versions by adding biblical details, reorganizing categories, adopting a new framework, or as in Edward Taylor's case creating evocative images and metaphors for his meditations. (pp. 78-9)

Taylor...employs a system best termed "Christomimetic," because he seeks to make biblical figures relevant in spiritual, not ceremonial or legalistic, ways to his experiences as a seventeenth-century Puritan saint. He nowhere in the *Preparatory Meditations* falls prey to the fallacy of a recapitulative typology whereby some New England historians declare their leaders as veritable antitypes of Moses, Joshua, or Nehemiah and ignore or merely imply Christ's centrality in the figural scheme. Imitation does not mean (to Edward Taylor) adopting a Moses or Joshua to exalt contemporary men; rather, imitation means modeling one's spiritual life on those moral qualities and spiritual deeds adumbrated by Old Testament types, but fulfilled in all truth and light by Jesus himself. Taylor may plead to partake of Solomon's wisdom or Samson's courage or a Nazarite's asceticism, only because such qualities are shadowy versions, human manifestations, of Christ's infinite, less accessible, less visible attributes. Taylor does, however, identify with the kingliness of Solomon, perceiving that role as reserved for Christ alone. Not so circumscribed by historical period, geographical locale, or the leadership of cultural heroes, Taylor chooses to align himself within a totally spiritual, inward realm of experience. Specifics of history, landscape, or culture have little relevance to the spiritual progress of individual souls, since all men are engaged in fundamentally the same journey through this earthly wilderness to the New Canaan of heaven. When Taylor chooses personal types as guides to the inner way of faith, as paradigms for the moral life, as humans in God's service, he grants them a due, but a more modest role than the historians do. Less concerned with inspiring parishioners with august visions of their cultural destiny, Taylor preaches *Upon the Types of the Old Testament* as instructions in the spiritual destiny of each saint, as do Thomas Taylor and Samuel Mather. Likewise, the meditations reflect his intimate psychic needs for spiritual exempla in the Old Testament figures, but more so for a pattern from Christ who perfectly fulfills and supersedes all types. Engaged doubly in a process of *imitatio figura* and Christomimesis, Taylor applies the personal types to the private soul, not to the public arena of history. (p. 86)

> *Karen E. Rowe, in her* Saint and Singer: Edward Taylor's Typology and the Poetics of Meditation, *Cambridge University Press, 1986, 341 p.*

ALAN LEANDER MacGREGOR (essay date 1988)

[*In the following excerpt, MacGregor defends "metaphorical strain" in the preface and prologue to* Gods Determinations.]

All the major critics of Edward Taylor's poetry and poetics are agreed that his use of metaphor makes him stand out among other American Puritan poets. But some have also complained about his rude poetics, charging that his metaphors "attract the attention away from the idea which they are supposed to convey" because the "disparity between the things compared is too great for the mind to bridge with appreciation" and that his attempt to celebrate God's creativity ends up as a lavish and impious tribute to the poet's own power of making.

But the strain felt in Taylor's metaphors is essential to the work they do in his "machinery of transcendence." The disparity of the images is constitutive, not disruptive, of their meanings. Further, Taylor's power of making is overmatched by his dissolution of the artifact and his ritual self-effacement; both of these tactics function as parts of his production of transcendence effects. And both the metaphorical strain and the ritual self-effacement enable Taylor in accomplishing his social role as *pontifex*, bridger and interpreter of cosmological distances on behalf of his community.

I suggest that Paul Ricoeur's theory of metaphor is especially pertinent in evaluating Taylor's poetic practice because he transcribes Aristotle's *mimesis* as "redescription" rather than as "copy." He privileges poetic discourse by marking its referent as speculative rather than denotative. Such discourse puts into play *heuristic fictions*, which deny realistic reference in order to redescribe reality. The metaphors of poetic diction then function imaginatively in the same way that scientific discourse makes use of models for explanation. Though their reference is speculative, metaphors function cognitively and constitute meanings. Thus, "a theory of metaphorical statements will be a theory of the production of metaphorical meaning." Taylor's metaphors "model" his beliefs, enabling him as a spiritual teacher or doctor and making these models available to his implied or imagined audience.

As comparison to scientific models makes clear, Ricoeur's is an operational theory of metaphor: metaphor operates on a conceptually distant object or concept by redescribing it in terms of a more familiar field of meaning(s). Thus can metaphor operate on reality and generate a new (kind of) truth. Such metaphorical redescription depends on a "tensional conception of truth, between subject and predicate, between literal and metaphorical interpretation, between identity and difference." Ricoeur's focus is not on the substitution of one word (vehicle) for another (tenor), but on the new predication, the "transaction between contexts" which metaphorical statement calls into being. When semantic fields are brought together in a metaphor, a new *ad hoc* polysemous field is generated; the meaning of the metaphor is constituted by both the new semantic proximity of the disparate semantic fields and by the residual effect of conceptual distance. The heuristic fiction of semantic proximity thus created allows us (as writers or readers) to operate on and in the world by using the emotions and intellect for cognitive redescription.

"The Preface" and "Prologue," the two poems which open Taylor's religious epic, *God's Determinations*, are heuristically useful, both for Taylor's purposes and for my own. Like his Meditations, both are in a sense occasional, providing the framework within which the poet tests the readiness of his soul to perform its task before he begins. They may also be read as enacting on a small and private scale the main "plot" of the larger and more public work, the demonstration of God's Justice and Mercy in determining the Elect. Further, Emory Elliott has said that the "process of development of the Puritan sermon from the 1660s to the 1690s is the process of the exchange of one dominant archetype—the image of the angry and wrathful father—to another archetype—the figure of the gentle, loving, protective Christ." "The Preface" evokes the archetype of God's judgment, while the "Prologue" hints at the enlivening breath of inspiration, insistently modeling mediation between man and God. Taken together, the two poems announce Taylor's cosmology, enact his aesthetic, and raise major questions about self, language, and social role.

In his almost dramatic exposition of Calvinist election in the body of the work, Taylor identifies two motives for "God's Determinations": the rectitude of His absolute power to condemn (Justice) tempered by His absolute power to save (Mercy). These two equally divine attributes are personified and debate the fate of souls, their arguments and decisions providing a logical framework for the doctrine expounded. Although these first two poems announce these same themes, the poet seems to speak without the dramatic indirection of the body of the work. These poems also offer concentrated evidence of Taylor's characteristic method of representing spiritual truth through metaphor—a method which itself becomes part of the theological theme.

The purpose of "The Preface" is cosmographic. The first lines establish the poles within which the universal drama of *God's Determinations* will unfold:

> *Infinity*, when *all* things it beheld,
> In *Nothing*, and of *Nothing all* did build,
> Upon what base was fixed the Lath, wherein
> He turned this Globe and rigalld it so trim?

The poem "outlines the structure of the Puritan universe in terms of simple extremes (high and low, light and dark, all-sufficiency and insufficiency)." Also established is a movement by paradox, a sense of contradiction which only the Infinity capable of creating All from Nothing can contain. This sense of paradox arises from the need to describe the poles so that readers will experience the cosmological distance between All and Nothing more intensively because the words which refer to the concepts are brought into such jarringly close proximity. From this new semantic proximity, Taylor will create a new semantic pertinence.

The scale of "The Preface" is vast and we see God as Architect and Builder (and other Craftsmen) of the Universe, whose Creation is compared to the building-blocks of human artistry. The natural features which seem marvels from our perspective (globe, rivers, sea) are, from the perspective of God's power, mere bric-a-brac (furnace, ribbons, silver box, curtains). An early critic is disturbed by the conceptual distance between the terms compared (and Taylor's motives for producing this difference): "Though he sets out (as a penitent) to celebrate God's creativity, he ends (as a creator) by paying lavish tribute to his own. . . . metaphor liberates Taylor, only to involve him in what, for the Puritan, was the most serious offense the artist could commit. In effect, two worlds are brought together in 'The Preface': the world God made, and the one which is reshaped by the poet." This interpretation quite rightly points to the implicit comparison the poem asserts between God's Creation and man's, that is, the poet's. The playful treatment of the infinite power of God by the poet from line nine to eighteen (including perhaps the implied usurping *tailor* who laces and fillitts with words and images) at first confirms the charge of poetic *hubris*, but the conceit is not an end in itself, but rather the means to the poet's meaning.

Blake argues that Puritans felt that "Man's duty is to seek and to emulate God, which he can do by a kind of reverse metaphorical process, though full symbolic embodiment is beyond human power. The method of the artist is to tender the glories of the physical world as metaphors for the divine." Taylor's metaphors, be they allegory or conceit, call attention to themselves, I will argue, not simply to flaunt poetic power but, simultaneously and somewhat paradoxically, to abase themselves before the infinitely superior metaphors created by God. The poet's power is co-terminous with his creation, metaphor, while God's power is only inferred or reflected in the Creation visible to man: "Undoubtedly a mighty work, the world glorifies its Maker, but it always remains apart from him. Unlike Jonathan Edwards' God, Taylor's never becomes so intricately a part of his own creation." The poet cannot describe God's grandeur directly, but through metaphor he can demonstrate it negatively, approximating the insignificance of created All when viewed from God's perspective: the Earth becomes a Quilt Ball and Creation, God's Knitting. He remains infinite, but His Works, which are All to men, are reduced to Nothing when imaginatively compared to their Author. Thus the same words express the poet's power and the limits of that power. It is the limit of language—of specific metaphor or poetry itself—to convey spiritual truth. This double perspective is continually reinforced, particularly in the striking line, "Who in this Bowling Alley bowld the Sun?". We are clearly meant to be awed at the immensity of the natural object evoked and chastened by its comparison to Infinitude.

Ricoeur says that metaphorical construing requires "stereoscopic vision," which in this case would mean the ability to see the Universe as both God's Creation and a Bowling Alley simultaneously. By bringing the two terms of the metaphor into a new semantic proximity to each other, Taylor forces on the reader a new pertinence, which Ricoeur aptly calls a "semantic *im*pertinence." Consistent with his view of metaphor as constitutive, he says of this moment: "the multiple meaning does not merely consist of a semantic clash but of a *new* predicative meaning which emerges from the collapse of the literal meaning."

Further, though the natural object is awesomely immense, it is figured (and thus rendered comprehensible) through comparison to the "homely," not only in its range of reference but in the Heideggerean sense of making the reader at home in the world. For his implied community, Taylor *makes ours* what even a sermon might put at a distance. And Taylor has a distinctively *tensional* notion of distance, conscious of the soul's distance from God and desperate to bridge that abyss. As Ricoeur says, poetic feeling's function "is to abolish the distance between knower and known without canceling the cognitive structure of thought and the intentional distance which it implies. Feeling is not contrary to thought. It is thought made ours. This felt participation is a part of its complete meaning as a poem." We can see such "homely" semantic impertinence as a characteristic practice in other Taylor poems as well, such as **"Housewifery"** and **"Thy Human Frame, My Glorious Lord, I Spy."** (pp. 337-42)

Following the scene-setting, Genesis-oriented material and its Job-like treatment in **"The Preface,"** the **"Prologue"** is, as its title declares, a preparatory discourse—a speaking part. The speaker is the poet and he is addressing God. This second poem begins by naming what was left unsaid in the first: the source, the subject, "Lord." We have left the recounting of cosmography and ontology behind and are now listening to a specific, though representative, man in a personal supplication to his Maker. He begins by asking . . . [a] seemingly unanswerable, paradoxical question: "Can a Crumb of Earth the Earth outweigh?" The speaker desires to connect self (here, though rhetorically personal, also functioning as a representative fiction) once again with God, to recover "that lightsome Gem." By framing the prayer as a rhetorical question, the speaker suggests that the answer could conceivably be "yes," thus very discreetly invoking man's privileged position in Creation. This time, however, the riddle is solved within the poem—by a poetic conceit. The poet imagines a Pen capable of returning glory to the source of all Glory, a Pen "whose moysture doth guild ore / Eternall Glory with a glorious Glore."

Continuing **"The Preface"**'s method of inflating and deflating materialistic images simultaneously, Taylor first surrounds his imagined "Pen" with the preciousness of all Creation. The figure "Pen" has multiple references. Most literally interpreted, the pen is Taylor's own pen, which he hopes God will fill with a literally golden ink ("glorious glore"), a metaphor for inspiration. But the pen is also a metonymy for the poet, who is thus represented as God's instrument, whose purpose is, in the language of another poem, to "tweedle praise." And moving to another level of correspondence, the pen is an emblem of the Christian soul: to function as its maker intended, it must be filled with the ink of God's grace. Again Taylor has used metaphor to evoke understanding of the levels of Being, this time as they co-exist in the life-experience of an individual with a calling.

This seeming-All, including "Pen and Scribener," is immediately reduced to nothing however, unless inspired ("made") by God. Just as the "who" questions in **"The Preface"** could only be answered by "who else but God," so these "how can I connect with God" questions can receive only the answer "by receiving His Grace and turning towards Him." Throughout the poem, the mechanism of inspiration is God-centered, rather than poet-centered. Like the pen which represents him, the poet is a passive instrument "mov'de by skill" not entirely or primarily his own.

The third stanza rejoins the initial figure of self-representation to that of the Pen: "I am this Crumb of Dust which is design'd / To make my Pen unto thy Praise alone." This "crumb" refers us back to ending of **"The Prologue,"** with its contrast between man's soul as "the brightest" and "that lightsome Gem," in its pre-lapsarian state, versus "any Coalpit Stone," the image of exile and abnegation which closes the poem. In the **"Prologue,"** the Crumb of Dust, another image of sterility, this time contrasted with the pen full of ink, dominates the plea for inspiration and allows Taylor to represent the self in a heuristic fiction which demonstrates how successfully he can combine his theology with his poetics.

Taylor enacts this complex combination in the last two stanzas. The third stanza completes the Pen-conceit by spelling out the analogies and practical purpose of the supplication: the speaker is specifically a poet, but one who views his calling as representative. His need for poetic *and* spiritual inspiration makes the poet representative of his culture. He wants to

> write in Liquid Gold upon thy Name
> My Letters till thy glory forth doth flame.

The relatively material terms of stanza two are translated into spiritual equivalents in stanza three, from "Liquid Gold" to "thy glory." The material All of Creation in **"The Preface"** is translated into the spiritual All of God's Grace, by which a Crumb of Earth (man, the poet) can the Earth outweigh. While the created world is a gift of God, it is useful only as an analogy to the spiritual gift of Grace. As Jonathan Edwards later said: "It is with regard to this image or resemblance which secondary beauty has of true spiritual beauty, that God has so constituted nature, that the presenting of this inferior beauty, especially in those kinds of it which have the greatest resemblance of the primary beauty, as the harmony of sounds and the beauties of nature, have a tendency to assist those whose hearts are under the influence of a truly virtuous temper to dispose them to the exercises of divine love and enliven in them a sense of spiritual beauty." God has provided man with clues in His Works (including the designs which the first stanza says are imbosomed in the Crumb of Earth) which enliven the virtuous man with the desire to seek God. These are also the materials with which man bridges the gulf between Nothing and All described in **"The Preface,"** between himself and God. Man reverses God's metaphorical creation by using these inferior beauties to construct spiritual analogies, making his own "harmonies of sound," his songs, his poems, as imitations of God's works. But man has only fallen tools ("Letters," language, metaphors) with which to make of fallen nature (images) a bridge to God. What hope is there for this apprentice-craftsman, man?

The poet's earlier call for poetic inspiration, like the other terms of the argument, now moves one increment higher: the speaker is poet, man, and soul. The fourth and finest stanza calls for God's Mercy, the inspiration of faith. The soul asks pardon for its failings, which God will overlook (or, in this case, look *through*): his poems and metaphors are "Slips slipt from thy Crumb of Dust." "Slips" may be used here playfully in the sense of "slip" as an error, perhaps referring to lesser "Falls" than the original, even slips of the poet's pen. The poems themselves may be garden slips, each blossoming in praise, like the flowers in the final stanza. A further possibility is that the word refers to ceramic slips, a glaze of sin which God in His Mercy would see through. In any case, Taylor here imagines God as the perfectly generous stereoscopic Reader, a reader who will understand the love of spiritual beauty which motivates man's (the poet's) production of secondary beauties (metaphors, poems) with all their assertion of self (not soul) and will read their semantic impertinences aright, in the light of the new pertinence towards which the poet gropes.

The seemingly worthless Crumb of Dust contains under its slips the soul, which reflects and is a reflection of God's glory. God is both inside and outside the image, with only the Crumb of Dust intervening. He breathes ("inspires") through the membrane, Man or Poet, to give it literal life and, in this poem of translations, everlasting life. Taylor frequently creates circular patterns of cause and effect in such passages. God, as both cause and effect, seems a particularly static agent of change, while writing / being is the active process intervening which tests the poet's faith.

Taylor's orthodoxy itself demanded a concern with process rather than product. The condition of the Fall is static and man has mobility only as he works to discover his predetermined spiritual status. His life becomes dynamic as he engages in this process of self-discovery. Nature is in flux and by concentrating on *process*, the Puritan participates, if only through his imagination, in the nature of things as they lie beyond the condition of the Fall. Through thinking of his writing as a process, Taylor, like many of Reformed persuasion, could reenact the process of salvation and live in the illusion of a spiritual development of oneself [see excerpt by Keller dated 1975].

This process is the enlivening by God, the inspiration of the poet: equivalent perhaps to God's breathing life into His crumb of dust, Adam. The poet writes, the man lives, the soul is saved—all by the grace of God. (pp. 346-49)

"The Preface," emphasizing the power of God and the potential of His Justice, ends with the image of a diamond grown darker by far than any coalpit stone, "the effect of man's apostacy." **"Prologue,"** in contrast, enacts the process of inspiration, of Grace, nestled within a call for revitalization. It demonstrates the same machinery of transcendence as the Meditations and of Protestant worship: praise, confession of personal repentance or abnegation, absolution, uplift and reconciliation, concluding with a new personal (and, in this work, implicitly social) Covenant in the final stanza. The **"Prologue"** shows a representative man (poet) recognizing the spiritual nature of the universe and emphasizes God's Mercy and Grace. Taken together, these two prefatory poems set up the thematics for *God's Determinations* as a whole. As heuristic fictions, these short, dense, intense poems also train the reader in the hermeneutic which will be required for reading Taylor's great book, which is itself but a hermeneutic for the Great Book of the World, from Creation to Judgment Day. (p. 351)

Alan Leander MacGregor, "Edward Taylor and the Impertinent Metaphor," in American Literature, *Vol. 60, No. 3, October, 1988, pp. 337-58.*

ADDITIONAL BIBLIOGRAPHY

Allen, Judson Boyce. "Edward Taylor's Catholic Wasp: Exegetical Convention in 'Upon a Spider Catching a Fly'." *English Language Notes* VII, No. 3 (March 1970): 257-60.
    Illuminates Taylor's reliance on medieval biblical interpretation in "Upon a Spider Catching a Fly."

Barbour, James W. "The Prose Context of Edward Taylor's Anti-Stoddard Meditations." *Early American Literature* X, No. 2 (Fall 1975): 144-57.
    Discusses Taylor's objections to the views of his contemporary, Solomon Stoddard, as evidenced in his sermons.

Boll, Robert N., and Davis, Thomas M. "Saint Augustine and Edward Taylor's Meditation 138 (2)." *English Language Notes* VIII, No. 3 (March 1971): 183-85.
    Demonstrates Taylor's indebtedness in "Meditation 138 (2)" to St. Augustine's scriptural interpretations.

Callow, James T. "Edward Taylor Obeys Saint Paul." *Early American Literature* IV, No. 3 (1969): 89-96.
    Notes the influence of one of St. Paul's epistles on the *Preparatory Meditations*.

Clendenning, John. "Piety and Imagery in Edward Taylor's 'The Reflexion'." *American Quarterly* XVI, No. 2 (Summer 1964): 203-10.

> Close reading of "The Reflexion" emphasizing sexual imagery in the poem.

Curtis, Jared R. "Edward Taylor and Emily Dickinson: Voices and Visions." *Susquehanna University Studies* VII, No. 3 (June 1964): 159-67.

> Compares Taylor's verse to that of Emily Dickinson.

Daiches, David. "The American Experience: From Puritanism through Post-Puritanism to Agnosticism; Edward Taylor, Emily Dickinson, Wallace Stevens." In his *God and the Poets: The Gifford Lectures, 1983*, pp. 153-75. Oxford: Clarendon Press, 1984.

> Mentions Taylor in tracing the development of poetry in New England.

Davie, Donald. "Edward Taylor and Isaac Watts." *The Yale Review* LXV, No. 4 (June 1976): 498-514.

> Compares Taylor's religious thought to that of Isaac Watts, a Dissenting minister and hymn writer thirty years his junior.

Gatta, John Jr. "Edward Taylor and Thomas Hooker: Two Physicians of the Poore Doubting Soul." *Notre Dame English Journal* XII, No. 1 (October 1979): 1-13.

> Discloses parallels between *Gods Determinations* and Thomas Hooker's *The Poor Doubting Christian* (1635).

Grabo, Norman S. "Edward Taylor's Spiritual Huswifery." *PMLA* LXXIX, No. 5 (December 1964): 554-60

> Close examination of Taylor's poem "Huswifery."

Hammond, Jeff, and Davis, Thomas M. "Edward Taylor: A Note on Visual Imagery." *Early American Literature* VIII, No. 2 (Fall 1973): 126-31.

> Traces nearly identical death images in three of Taylor's poems to a common Puritan aesthetic.

Howard, Alan B. "The World as Emblem: Language and Vision in the Poetry of Edward Taylor." *American Literature* XLIV, No. 3 (November 1972): 359-84.

> Addresses Taylor's perceived paradoxical nature by examining the author as an emblemist rather than a metaphysical poet.

Johnson, Parker H. "Poetry and Praise in Edward Taylor's *Preparatory Meditations*." *American Literature* 52, No. 1 (March 1980): 84-96.

> Maintains that Taylor's *Preparatory Meditations* "express a religious sensibility bent heavenward, not a crabbed self-consciousness absorbed in introspection."

Junkins, Donald. " 'Should Stars Wooe Lobster Claws?': A study of Edward Taylor's Poetic Practice and Theory." *Early American Literature* 3, No. 2 (Fall 1968): 88-116.

> Links Taylor's references to the practice of writing in the *Preparatory Meditations* to poetic theory and Puritan culture.

Lind, Sidney E. "Edward Taylor: A Revaluation." *The New England Quarterly* XXI, No. 4 (December 1948): 518-30.

> Finds Taylor's work especially interesting when it departs from traditional Puritan verse.

Martin, Carter. "A Fantastic Pairing: Edward Taylor and Donald Barthelme." In *The Scope of the Fantastic—Theory, Technique, Major Authors: Selected Essays from the First International Conference on the Fantastic in Literature and Film*, edited by Robert A. Collins and Howard D. Pearce, pp. 183-90. Contributions to the Study of Science Fiction and Fantasy, No. 10. Westport, Conn.: Greenwood Press, 1985.

> Discusses technical similarities in Taylor's *Meditations* and the work of American short story writer Donald Barthelme.

Parker, David L. "Edward Taylor's Preparationism: A New Perspective on the Taylor-Stoddard Controversy." *Early American Literature* XI, No. 3 (Winter 1976-77): 259-78.

> Asserts that Taylor's position on religious communion—evident in his verse—is more liberal than that of his opponent, Solomon Stoddard.

Patterson, J. Daniel. "*Gods Determinations*: The Occasion, the Audience, and Taylor's Hope for New England." *Early American Literature* 22, No. 1 (Spring 1987): 63-81.

> Explores "the theological strategies and pastoral aims" of *Gods Determinations*, attempting to assess the makeup of Taylor's congregation.

Rowe, Karen E. "Sacred or Profane?: Edward Taylor's Meditations on Canticles." *Modern Philology* 72, No. 2 (November 1974): 123-38.

> Places the *Preparatory Meditations* within standard Puritan exposition.

Scheick, William J. "Typology and Allegory: A Comparative Study of George Herbert and Edward Taylor." *Essays in Literature* 2, No. 1 (Spring 1975): 76-86.

> Compares Taylor's and poet George Herbert's use of scriptural symbolism.

——. "The Jawbones Schema of Edward Taylor's *Gods Determinations*." In *Puritan Influences in American Literature*, edited by Emory Elliott, pp. 38-54. Illinois Studies in Language and Literature, No. 65. Urbana: University of Illinois Press, 1979.

> Suggests that the structural and thematic unity of *Gods Determinations* derives from a jawbones design in which the soul is caught between specific adverse forces.

——. "Edward Taylor's Optics." *American Literature* 55, No. 2 (May 1983): 234-40.

> Posits that the conflicting optical theories informing the *Preparatory Meditations* exhibit their author's reconciliation of science and religion.

Stanford, Donald E. "Edward Taylor and the 'Hermophrodite' Poems of John Cleveland." *Early American Literature* VIII, No. 1 (Spring 1973): 59-61.

> Claims that Taylor was influenced by English poet John Cleveland's "hermophrodite" imagery.

Thorpe, Peter. "Edward Taylor as Poet." *The New England Quarterly* XXXIX, No. 3 (September 1966): 356-72.

> Maintains that the irregularities in Taylor's poetic technique are an essential feature of the *Preparatory Meditations*.

Turco, Lewis Putnam. "The Pro-Am Tournament." In his *Visions and Revisions of American Poetry*, pp. 8-15. Fayetteville: The University of Arkansas Press, 1986.

> Briefly notes Taylor's significance as an American poet foreshadowing Ralph Waldo Emerson.

Weathers, Willie T. "Edward Taylor, Hellenistic Puritan." *American Literature* 18, No. 1 (March 1946): 18-26.

> Traces to Theocritus the pattern of dialogue in *Gods Determinations*.

——. "Edward Taylor and the Cambridge Platonists." *American Literature* 26, No. 1 (March 1954): 1-31.

> Posits that Taylor embraced both the doctrines of New England theologians and those of the English Platonist-Puritans.

Wright, Nathalia. "The Morality Tradition in the Poetry of Edward Taylor." *American Literature* 18, No. 1 (March 1946): 1-17.

> Relates aspects of Taylor's poetry to the drama.

Thomas à Kempis

1380?-1471

(Born Thomas Haemerken; also Hamerken, Hammercken, Hämmerken, Haemerlein, Hammerlein, and Malleolus) German devotional writer, biographer, historian, sermonist, hymn writer, and tract writer.

An Augustinian monk, Thomas à Kempis is widely recognized as the author of *De Imitatione Christi* (*The Imitation of Christ*), a devotional treatise regarded as the most widely translated work in Christian literature beside the Bible. *The Imitation* was written as a series of meditations on how to know and love God. As such, it has comforted, challenged, and inspired millions of readers since first appearing in 1418. Translated into many languages, *The Imitation* moved Samuel Johnson to comment upon its popularity among the devout, saying that it "must be a good book, as the world has opened its arms to receive it."

The known facts of Thomas's life are few and simple, for, though full and long, it was fairly uneventful. Born in the Rhineland town of Kempen near Düsseldorf, Thomas was the younger of two sons born to John and Gertrude Haemerken, the former a peasant artisan, the latter the keeper of a local dame school. In his early years Thomas was schooled in Kempen. At age 13 he, like his brother before him, was sent to Deventer in the Netherlands to continue his education. There he was taken under the charge of Florentius Radewyn, superior of the Society of the Brothers of the Common Life. This lay Augustinian devotion, founded in Deventer earlier in the fourteenth century by Gerard Groote, attempted to imitate closely the fellowship, humble simplicity, prayerfulness, and holiness of the first-century Christian church. Associates of the devotion were expected to earn their livelihood not by mendicancy but by using whatever skills they possessed, and for clerics—to whose vocation Thomas was drawn—this meant writing, transcribing, translating, and teaching. Under Radewyn's personal direction, Thomas proved himself an able student, especially as a transcriber of church treatises. He completed his studies in 1399 and applied for admission into the Canons Regular of Windesheim at Mount St. Agnes near the Dutch city of Zwolle. The Windesheim congregation, a priestly ministry connected with the Brothers of the Common Life, had as its prior Thomas's elder brother, John, who welcomed him. From that time until his death, but for a brief few years, Thomas spent his life at the Windesheim monastery.

Thomas was clothed as a novice in 1406 and ordained a priest in 1413. From then on he devoted his time to teaching novices, saying mass, hearing confessions, translating the Bible and other works, copying missals for use by the Brothers, and writing histories, biographies, hymns, sermons and devotional works. Thomas gained a reputation among his fellow monks as a kindly though retiring man, a deep thinker who preferred the solitude of his cell and the company of books to being among his more gregarious fellows. Respecting what they considered his great mind, Godly spirit, and unspoken wishes, the other monks early on ceased approaching him for casual conversation or advice on everyday concerns. In the years after his death in

Thomas à Kempis

1471, his remains were removed to a series of reliquaries, eventually being enshrined within a monument in St. Michael's Church, Zwolle.

From the early fifteenth century onward, the name of Thomas à Kempis has been linked with *The Imitation of Christ*, which was written over the course of several years in the early 1400s. The work contains the essence of Groote's teachings on the Christian life and outlines what Groote (and Thomas) considered the life most pleasing to God and most fulfilling to the Christian pilgrim. As Albert Hyma has put it, *The Imitation* "contains the teachings of Groote in the same way as the Four Gospels in the New Testament contain the sayings of Jesus of Nazareth." *The Imitation*, written in four parts, emphasizes focusing one's every thought upon God, rendering every action in divine service, and following a life of disciplined asceticism. All ambitions, mundane desires, preconceived notions of divine love and divine justice, and seeking for personal gain and worldly knowledge must be discarded that the soul may be free to commune unhindered with God. Identifying this as "the dominant note" of the work, Gamaliel Bradford has written, "The author of the *Imitation* found this reality in God, and all his life was concerned with nothing else: 'Consider that God and you are alone in the universe, and you will have great peace in your heart.' "

From the first *The Imitation* has been widely read and valued, with most readers embracing the work not in its entirety but in portions amenable to life outside monastic walls, to life in the world at large. The work has been otherwise reproached by some readers as being too otherworldly. In the words of Coventry Patmore, "There is a hot-house, egotistical air about much of its piety." And in a letter to a friend, C. S. Lewis wrote, "The *Imitation* is very severe; useful at times when one is tempted to be too easily satisfied with one's progress, but certainly not at times of discouragement. And of course it is written for monks, not for people living in the world like us." Other readers, though, have found the book to read like most other devotional works, "as if it had been written," according to Edgar Allison Peers, "not for fifteenth-century monks, but for twentieth-century housewives or business men catching the 8:30 to town." In any case, the challenge to a disciplined life Thomas poses to the Christian pilgrim is great. Michael Novak has written that the admonitions of *The Imitation* "are not words to flatter us. Many of these words are hard. Many sentences in this book clash against everything our present civilization teaches us. Is that their purpose? They were also hard in the fifteenth century."

The most significant critical controversy surrounding Thomas's works concerns the very authorship of *The Imitation*. From the first unsigned, it was widely acknowledged for many years as from the hand of Thomas. But within two centuries this belief came into question because of alleged differences in style between *The Imitation* and other works undeniably by Thomas (though these other works were also originally unsigned). Jean Gerson of France was forwarded in some quarters as the real author of *The Imitation*, as was the Italian John Gerson and Groote himself. Critical debate rose to its highest during the nineteenth and early twentieth centuries, when close examination of internal evidence as well as the discovery of an apparently autograph copy of *The Imitation* lent increasingly strong support to claims for Thomas's authorship. By the mid-twentieth century the debate seemed over, and today Thomas is recognized as certainly the editor if not the actual author (or one of several authors) of *The Imitation*.

Thomas also wrote over a dozen hymns, several biographies and histories, and numerous sermons, treatises, and tracts. None of these works, however, has received substantial critical examination in English-language studies, though Thomas's insightful and informative *History of the Canons Regular of Mount St. Agnes* is generally considered the most notable of the lot. Still, little criticism has been devoted to any of these works.

Matthew Arnold, who read and reread Thomas's signal work throughout his life, once called *The Imitation* the "most exquisite document in Christendom after the New Testament." Questions of authorship aside, *The Imitation* has been translated (by, among others, John Wesley, the founder of Methodism), read, and contemplated for centuries, attaining the status of a spiritual classic. The key to understanding its popularity lies, perhaps, in its melding of intense spiritual insight and heartfelt honesty: what Francis Thompson called, "the combination of wisdom

and simple practicality, meditative gravity and deep truth of emotional experience, and . . . the breath of humble fraternal love which gives a fragrance to it all. . . . It is not only a voice from the cloister, it is also the beating of a heart."

PRINCIPAL WORKS*

†*De imitatione Christi* (devotional treatise) 1418
[*A full devout and gostely treatyse of the Imytacion and folowynge of the blessed Lyfe of oure moste mercyfull Savyoure criste*, 1503-04]
Hortulus rosarii de valle lachrymarum continens egreias & devotas sentencias (treatise) 1499
["The Little Garden of Roses" published in *Works of the Reverend and Pious Thomas à Kempis*, 1801]
Opera omnia ad autographa eiusdem emendata, atque etiam tertia fere ex parte nuno anota. 3 vols. (sermons, hymns, letters, biographies, and devotional treatises) 1601
[*Works of the Reverend and Pious Thomas à Kempis*, 1801]
"The Valley of Lilies" and "The Soliloquy of the Soul" (treatise) 1807; originally published as "Vallis liliorum" and "Soliloquim animae" in *Opera omnia*, 1601
Opera omnia. 7 vols. (sermons, hymns, letters, biographies, and devotional treatises) 1902-22

*All of Thomas à Kempis's works were circulated in manuscript long before their formal printing.

†The year 1418 is commonly assigned as the composition date of this work, though at the time of its initial circulation it was but three-quarters completed. The title of this work has also been translated as *The Following of Christ*, *The Christian's Pattern*, and, most commonly, *The Imitation of Christ*.

RICHARD WHITFORD (essay date 1556)

[*The self-styled "Wretch of Syon," Whitford was a sixteenth-century Roman Catholic monk who was received into the Order of St. Bridget at Sion Monastery in Middlesex. He wrote treatises on the disciplines of the Christian life and translated* The Golden Epistle *of St. Bernard and* The Imitation, *affixing an introduction to the 1556 printing of the latter. In the following excerpt from the introduction, Whitford commends the value of* The Imitation *as a palliative for the spirit.*]

Amonge manye Treatises, which have bene put out both in Latin and Englishe, in this perillous worlde, to seduce the simple people, & to bring them from the unitie of the Catholike Churche into pervers and abbominable errours, there hath bene also in tyme past before made by divers learned and vertuous men many good Treatises, which yf men woulde be so diligent to looke upon, as they are curious to looke on the other, they shoulde not so soone falle from the true knowledge of Christes doctrine, and the right sense of holie Scripture, which ever hath bene taught by continuall succession in his holie Churche, of the holie ghost, the spirite of truth, who shall ever remayne with it. And amonge many of these Treatises, there is one called, the **Imitation** or **Followinge of Christe**, whiche in my judgement is excellent: and the more it is seriouslie and advisedlie reade and looked upon, the more it shall like every Christian Reader, who will let his minde earnestlie to folow Christ his steppes. Let them prove by reading every day a chapter when they have best leasure, and I doubt not, but they shall finde my sayinges true. I have reade it over very many times, and the more I reade, the more I like it and finde profite to my soule health. It teacheth the true mortification of the fleshe to the spirite, according to the right sense of holie Scripture, and the doctrine of S. Paul. (pp. iii-iv)

> *Richard Whitford, in an introduction to* The Following of Christ *by Thomas à Kempis, translated by Richard Whitford, 1556. Reprint by Scholar Press, 1977, pp. iii-iv.*

SAMUEL JOHNSON (conversation date 1778)

[*Johnson is one of the outstanding figures in English literature and a leader in the history of textual and aesthetic criticism. Popularly known in his day as the "Great Cham of Literature," he was a prolific lexicographer, essayist, poet, and critic. His lucid and extensively illustrated* Dictionary of the English Language *1755 and* Prefaces, Biographical and Critical, to the Works of the English Poets *(10 vols., 1779-81; reissued in 1783 as* The Lives of the Most Eminent English Poets) *were new departures in lexicography and biographical criticism, respectively. Once while lying ill, Johnson attempted to teach himself the Dutch language by translating* The Imitation. *In the following excerpt from a conversation recorded by James Boswell in 1778, he speaks highly of the popularity and practicality of the famous devotional work.*]

Thomas à Kempis ([Dr. Johnson] observed) must be a good book, as the world has opened its arms to receive it. It [*The Imitation of Christ*] is said to have been printed, in one language or other, as many times as there have been months since it first came out. I always was struck by this sentence in it: "Be not angry that you cannot make others as you wish them to be, since you cannot make yourself as you wish to be."

> *Samuel Johnson, in a conversation in 1778, in* The Life of Samuel Johnson *by James Boswell, 1791. Reprint by Dent, 1976, p. 165.*

[FRANCIS PARKMAN] (essay date 1830)

[*Parkman is recognized as one of the greatest historians the United States has yet produced. His multivolume* France and England in North America *(1865-91), which treats the struggle between France and England for control of North America, is celebrated for its probing scholarship, consummate narrative skill, and unified construction. In the following excerpt from a review of Thomas Chalmers's 1829 edition of* The Imitation, *Parkman offers high praise for the work, taking issue only with Chalmers's editorial inferences.*]

[Of *The Imitation of Christ*, translated by Dr. Thomas Chalmers,] it might be difficult to say anything, that has not been said before. Nor is it any part of our purpose to enter largely into its character. Few books of this class have been so long, or so extensively circulated; it having been once and again translated into almost every language of Christendom. It has usually been ascribed to Thomas à

Kempis, the Catholic recluse, whose name it bears; nor does the editor of this present edition intimate any doubt of its genuineness. But notwithstanding common consent, the learned among Catholics as well as Protestants, have by no means been agreed upon the subject; and some, as appears from Dupin, have offered reasons, which go to show even the impossibility of his having been the author. We do not consider the question at this distant day as material; much less as affecting in the slightest degree, the value of the work. But it is right, in giving any account of the various editions of a book so remarkable, as well as of its writer, to separate what is doubtful from what is known. (pp. 174-75)

The introductory essay by Dr. Chalmers, who, after many like honors, is, we believe, now promoted to the professorship of divinity in the University of Edinburgh, will undoubtedly be considered by his admirers, as greatly enriching this edition. It is written with the usual ability, and with somewhat of the peculiarities also, of that popular divine. It is designed to relieve the work from an objection grounded on its supposed deficiency in an article of Orthodox faith; an objection naturally to be expected from men, who, first assuming the point that nothing good or spiritual can spring from any other than an Orthodox stock, find themselves at a loss to account for any evidences of a serious spirit, or even any approaches to a due standard of christian virtue, where there is not some decided recognition of their favorite dogmas. (p. 175)

It is the same charitable spirit, which we sometimes hear inferring in favor of any serious preacher, who, though well known for his attachment to liberal views of religion, is also distinguished by his persuasive and earnest methods of presenting them, 'O! that man is a Calvinist, though he may not know it, or may not choose to avow it to his friends.' And it is much in this mode of inference, that the Professor of Edinburgh thus kindly maintains the soundness of Thomas à Kempis.

> The doctrine of our acceptance, by faith in the merits and propitiation of Christ, is worthy of many a treatise, and many are the precious treatises upon it which have been offered to the world. But the doctrine of regeneration, by the Spirit of Christ, equally demands the homage of a separate lucubration—which may proceed on the truth of the former, and, by the incidental recognition of it, when it comes naturally in the way of the author's attention, marks the soundness and the settlement of his mind thereupon, more decisively than by the dogmatic, and ostentatious, and often misplaced asseverations of an ultra orthodoxy. And the clearer revelation to the eye of faith of one article, will never darken or diminish, but will, in fact, throw back the light of an augmented evidence on every other article. Like any object, that is made up of parts, which we have frequently looked to in their connexion, and as making up a whole—the more distinctly one part of it is made manifest, the more forcibly will all the other parts of it be suggested to the mind. And thus it is, that when pressing home the necessity of one's own holiness, as his indispensable preparation for heaven, we do not dissever his mind from the atonement of Christ, but in reality do we fasten it more closely than ever on the necessity of another's righteousness, as his indispensable plea for heaven.

> Such we apprehend to be the genuine influence of a Treatise that is now submitted anew to the Christian public. It certainly does not abound in formal and di-

rect avowals of the righteousness which is by faith, and on this account we have heard it excepted against. But we know of no reading that is more powerfully calculated to *shut us up* unto the faith—none more fitted to deepen and to strengthen the basis of a sinner's humility, and so reconcile him to the doctrine of salvation in all its parts, by grace alone.

Now, to the view of some, there may be somewhat of candor, but, we confess, there is to our apprehension not a little of assumption and unwarrantable inference in all this. It is giving a name, or imputing opinions to a man, which he himself might refuse, or never think of. Nor do we believe, that Thomas à Kempis, or whoever may have been the writer of this treatise, would, at an interval of more than three hundred years, prefer to have himself or his books 'shut up,' as the Professor expresses it, within the limits of a technical faith, when his far wider and nobler object was, to recommend a practical imitation of Jesus Christ. His work, in this view, is deserving of the exalted praise it has received, and of the wondrous circulation it has obtained. His design was, and he could not have proposed a nobler, to portray and to encourage a life of christian piety and virtue. And though some of his views of christian perfection were undeniably drawn from the spirit of the church of which he was a faithful priest, or from the seclusions of his cloister; and though in accordance with the established creed and symbols of that church, he takes for granted, and not seldom presents, the doctrine of the trinity with its consequences, the deity and worship of Christ, still, with a generous elevation above what is merely ritual or doubtful, above feasts and fastings, rites and images, and much, too, of what is to be ranked with these among the points of doubtful disputation, does he press those simple principles of piety and true goodness, those great duties of imitating Christ and of obeying God, which far beyond, and wholly independent of the vain doctrines of men, in every true church and in every true heart, are the source and life of godliness. What is peculiar to the writer as a Catholic, may indeed, as in the present edition, be omitted. But the reader need only cast an eye over the titles of the chapters, to mark how eminently and exclusively practical, how free from the mystical and the doubtful, are the topics of which he treats. The personal and the social virtues; humility with respect to our attainments; prudence with regard to opinions and actions; danger of rash judgments; patience with the infirmities of others; the evil of superfluous talking; the beauty of charity; the due consideration of human misery; with suggestions for a right intercourse with the world, as well as for reading the scriptures and other holy books, for meditations of death, and diligence in the reformation of life,—will be found among the subjects of the first part; and they are all exhibited with a simplicity, tenderness, and energy of feeling, which make for them a way to every heart, and at the same time with a sobriety and just qualification, which recommend them to every judgment. (pp. 176-78)

[Francis Parkman], in a review of "The Imitation of Christ," in The Christian Examiner and General Review, *Vol. VIII, No. XXXVIII, May, 1830, pp. 174-79.*

THOMAS DE QUINCEY (essay date 1847)

[An English critic and essayist, De Quincey used his own life as the subject of his best-known work, Confessions of an English Opium Eater *(1822). He contributed reviews to a number of London journals and earned a reputation as an insightful if occasionally long-winded literary critic. At the time of his death, his critical expertise was underestimated, though his talent as a prose writer had long been acknowledged. In the twentieth century, some critics still disdain the digressive qualities of De Quincey's writing. Others, however, find that his essays display an acute psychological awareness. In the following excerpt from an essay originally published in* Tait's Edinburgh Magazine *in 1847, De Quincey offers mixed impressions of* The Imitation *in a discussion that balances a sense of awe at the work's impressive publication history with sarcasm—at "Tom" à Kempis's expense.]*

[In his *History of France*] M. Michelet thinks to lodge an arrow in our sides by a very odd remark upon Thomas à Kempis: which is, that a man of any conceivable European blood—Finlander, suppose, or a Zantiote—might have written Tom; only not an Englishman. Whether an Englishman could have forged Tom must remain a matter of doubt, unless the thing had been tried long ago. That problem was intercepted for ever by Tom's perverseness in choosing to manufacture himself. Yet, since nobody is better aware than M. Michelet that this very point of Kempis *having* manufactured Kempis is furiously and hopelessly litigated, three or four nations claiming to have forged his work for him, the shocking old doubt will raise its snaky head once more—whether this forger, who rests in so much darkness, might not, after all, be of English blood. Tom, it may be feared, is known to modern English literature chiefly by an irreverent mention of his name in a line of Peter Pindar's (Dr. Wolcot) fifty years back, where he is described as

> Kempis Tom,
> Who clearly shows the way to Kingdom Come.

Few in these days can have read him, unless in the Methodist version of John Wesley. Amongst those few, however, happens to be myself; which arose from the accident of having, when a boy of eleven, received a copy of the *De Imitatione Christi* as a bequest from a relation who died very young; from which cause, and from the external prettiness of the book,—being a Glasgow reprint by the celebrated Foulis, and gaily bound,—I was induced to look into it, and finally read it many times over, partly out of some sympathy which, even in those days, I had with its simplicity and devotional fervour, but much more from the savage delight I found in laughing at Tom's Latinity. *That*, I freely grant to M. Michelet, is inimitable. Yet, after all, it is not certain whether the original *was* Latin. But, however *that* may have been, if it is possible that M. Michelet can be accurate in saying that there are no less than *sixty* French versions (not editions, observe, but separate versions) existing of the *De Imitatione*, how prodigious must have been the adaptation of the book to the religious heart of the fifteenth century! ["*If M. Michelet can be accurate*":—However, on consideration, this statement does not depend on Michelet. The bibliographer Barbier has absolutely *specified* sixty in a separate dissertation, *soixante traductions*, amongst those even that have not escaped the search. The Italian translations are said to be thirty. As to mere *editions*, not counting the early MSS. for a half-a-century before printing was introduced, those in Latin amount to two thousand, and those in French to one thousand. Meantime, it is very clear to me that this astonishing popularity, so entirely unparalleled in literature, could not have existed except in Roman Catholic times, nor subsequently have lingered in any Protestant land. It was the denial of Scripture fountains to thirsty lands which made this slender rill of Scripture truth so passionately welcome.)] Excepting the Bible, but excepting *that* only in Protestant lands, no book known to man has had the same distinction. It is the most marvellous bibliographical fact on record. (n. pp. 409-10)

> *Thomas De Quincey, in a footnote to "Joan of Arc," in his* The Collected Writings of Thomas De Quincey, *edited by David Masson, A. & C. Black, 1897, n. pp. 409-10.*

GEORGE ELIOT [PSEUDONYM OF MARIAN EVANS] (essay date 1860)

[*An English novelist, essayist, poet, editor, short story writer, and translator, Eliot was one of the greatest English novelists of the nineteenth century. Her work, including the novels* The Mill on the Floss *(1860) and* Middlemarch: A Study of Provincial Life *(1871-72), is informed by penetrating psychological analysis and profound insight into human character. Played against the backdrop of English rural life, Eliot's novels explore moral and philosophical issues and employ a realistic approach to character and plot development. In the following passage taken from the authorial narration in* The Mill on the Floss, *Eliot seeks to explain the appeal of* The Imitation.]

I suppose that is the reason why the small old-fashioned book [*The Imitation of Christ*], for which you need only pay sixpence at a book-stall, works miracles to this day, turning bitter waters into sweetness, while expensive sermons and treatises, newly issued, leave all things as they were before. It was written down by a hand that waited for the heart's prompting; it is the chronicle of a solitary hidden anguish, struggle, trust, and triumph, not written on velvet cushions to teach endurance to those who are treading with bleeding feet on the stones. And so it remains to all time a lasting record of human deeds and human consolations; the voice of a brother who, ages ago, felt, and suffered, and renounced, in the cloister, perhaps, with serge gown and tonsured head, with much chanting and long fasts, and with a fashion of speech different from ours, but under the same silent far-off heavens, and with the same passionate desires, the same strivings, the same failures, the same weariness. (p. 291)

> *George Eliot [pseudonym of Marian Evans], "A Voice from the the Past," in her* The Mill on the Floss, *W. Blackwood and Sons, 1860, pp. 280-94.*

WILLIAM MACCALL (essay date 1866)

[*Maccall was a Unitarian clergyman and essayist. In the following excerpt from an essay in which the question of* The Imitation's *authorship is examined, he praises the famous work and deduces the author's identity.*]

For more than four centuries [*The Imitation of Christ*] has been the chief manual of devotion for Christian lands— inspiration, purification, instruction, food, to all pious souls, consolation to millions of lonely and afflicted hearts. It is strength, it is counsel, it is prayer, it is peace; it is love, and light, and life. In its mysticism there is nothing enervating; in its unction there is nothing cloying; and

it is emotional, sympathetic, no further than it can give force to its maxims, precepts, entreaties. Contrition, humility, self-abnegation, brotherly affection, the glad and holy surrender of the whole being to God, as manifested in Jesus,—these are less the virtues which it teaches to the Christian, than the graces wherewith it clothes him. Perfection is to be the sanctification of sorrow; and tears of penitence are to be the best offering to Him whose name and nature are Mercy. How rare a thing is a purely devotional book, though thousands pretendedly devotional are continually appearing! What is required in a truly devotional book? That the cry of a wounded, weary, solitary breast, should become the wail of a great multitude; and that the didactic, the reflective—all generalizations should be absolutely excluded. Where edification is paraded and pursued, there is no edification. But where, as in the Psalms, there is the lyrical cry of pain and remorse, each suffering bosom that joins responsive finds its own yearnings expressed in nobler language, more potent, more poetic than it could itself employ. In the *Imitation* there is somewhat of formal arrangement; yet the substance is lyrical. There are no moralizings, no abstractions, no dogmatisms, no rhetorical appeals. A brother speaks to brethren of the Divinest Brother, and of the Almighty Father in heaven. Pangs, common to myriads of the faithful, pass from confession into worship. Mighty miracle: Christendom stirred to ardent and perennial adoration by a modest cloistral murmur!

From what sacred lips did that cloistral murmur flow? (pp. 72-3)

[If] internal probabilities and external evidence are to be held of the same value here as in other cases, Thomas à Kempis was, and John Gerson was not, the author of the *Imitation*, and the *Imitation* is forthwith struck out from the list of books whose authors are unknown. We should exceedingly rejoice if our earnest attempt to put an undisputed crown upon a great man's brow, should tend, in a degree however small, to kindle an interest about Thomas à Kempis, his works, and those deep mystical movements in the bosom, or by the side, of the Catholic Church, which have a far richer meaning than the events which ecclesiastical history is in the habit of recording. (p. 98)

> *William Maccall, "The Authorship of the 'Imitation of Christ'," in* Contemporary Review, *Vol. III, No. I, September, 1866, pp. 71-98.*

REV. S. KETTLEWELL (essay date 1882)

[*An English clergyman, Kettlewell wrote several works on church history as well as two studies concerning Thomas à Kempis:* The Authorship of the "De Imitatione Christi" *(1877) and the highly sympathetic* Thomas à Kempis and the Brothers of Common Life *(1882). In the following excerpt from the latter, he discusses* The Imitation *and a number of the author's lesser-known works.*]

[*De Imitatione Christi*], which has reflected so much honour on the name of Thomas à Kempis, is in itself a wondrous production, as it has been elsewhere shown, especially considering the age in which it was written. It exercises a peculiar and powerful influence upon devout minds, which has doubtless been the cause of its marvelous and almost universal popularity ever since it appeared. I do not, however, now purpose to inquire into its intrinsic merits, and what led to its singular fame and the just esteem in which it is held, further than allude to one point, to which I would in passing call attention, as it is here deserving of notice. There was, at the time when it first appeared, a wide-spread yearning to know more of Divine truth, and how men ought to live so as to please God, which this book supplied. This arose in a great measure from the discountenance given to the reading of the Bible by the laity; a covering had, as it were, been thrown over the lamp of life and the full diffusion of its rays discouraged, for men were taught by those then in authority in the Church to regard it as a thing forbidden, or at least fraught with danger to the soul. This, whilst it shut out the light from many souls, made others to long the more for it. And the *Imitatio* carried conviction to numerous souls that in it the echoes of Divine truth were to be found, and men could learn therein how they might approach God and obtain His favour without the intervention of others; for it will be seen that this devotional book is suffused with the spirit of the Holy Volume, though it does not generally adopt its very words. There are numberless instances where a truth or precept from God's Word is inculcated or alluded to, as can be clearly shown, where the exact Scriptural phraseology is not used, and this inculcation of the Divine Will was doubtless, among other causes, the principal reason for its wide diffusion and the ready welcome it received. (I, pp. 10-11)

There may be a few points on which we may not agree with him. The ideal of the Christian life may seem to some pitched too high, and the religion presented to our view too severe. There often appears a suppression of the natural affections in the endeavour to subjugate self—a separation of the religious from the secular life which seems carried too far—and there is a clinging to a few doctrinal errors and superstitious customs which all cannot hold with. Those of us who have been brought up within the bosom of the English Church have happily a form of doctrine resting on the firm basis that nothing is to be required as necessary to salvation but what can be proved by Holy Scripture; and we are naturally jealous of anything that has not this warrant, and are firmly opposed to whatever is repugnant to it. And it may be we are so satisfied with the fruit as to think little of the tree that bore it, and how those aforetime had to grope their way in darkness and to struggle with a terrible thraldom. Making allowance, however, for the times in which these men lived, and the social conditions of their outward life, differing from our own, we may often behold in their lives and teaching a closer conformity to the example of Christ, and a more literal interpretation and attention to His precepts, than is presented to our view in this too sceptical and self-indulgent age. But as regards à Kempis those points on which we differ from him may easily be eliminated amid so much that is good and profitable for our spiritual advancement and worthy of our attention; for though living in a dark and superstitious age, he became an ardent student of Holy Scripture when it was much neglected, and sought not only to be enlightened by it, and to shed its bright rays on all around him, but strictly endeavoured to make it the rule and guide of his life, and not less the foundation of his teaching. (I, pp. 29-30)

There are a few other works [by à Kempis] which have not been as yet particularly noticed, and seem to call for some remarks. (II, p. 428)

Sommalius's edition of the works of à Kempis is that which most modern compilers have taken as their authority for what he has written. And from the little information which he vouchsafes to give respecting the sources from whence he derives the several Treatises of à Kempis we may learn these particulars. On the title-page, he says, the original author (à Kempis) had himself borne witness to having written many of them. On the first leaf, just before the dedication to the Abbot of the St. Trudo, there is an index of the conténts, with the remark, that those works prefixed with a star are edited from the original manuscripts; the others only from old copies of the same, found in St. Peter's Library, at Ghent.

Sommalius then divides the works of Thomas à Kempis into three volumes. In the first he gives what may be termed the homiletical writings of à Kempis; namely, his *Sermons to Novices*; of these there are three parts or series; there is, moreover, another part to the Brethren (ad Fratres): then follow his thirty-six *Conciones et Meditationes* on the Life and Passion of Our Lord. In these all the chief points of the Gospel History are taken up in order, from the Incarnation of Christ to the presentedoutpouring of the Holy Spirit, and the founding of the infant Church at Jerusalem. (II, pp. 429-30)

In the second volume Sommalius has the four books of the *De Imitatione Christi*: the *Soliloquium Animæ*. Then come two of the most valued works of à Kempis which rank next after these, the *Hortulus Rosarum*, and the *Vallis Liliorum*. They do not appear among those treatises in the volume dated 1441, written by Thomas, but they do in the other. And they were probably composed at a later period to the other works, for the style is somewhat different, and has consequently led some persons to think that they were not written by the author of the *De Imitatione Christi*. There is greater connection of thought in the sentences; moreover the passages are not so short and terse as many of his other writings, and take a more extended view of the work of Christ. Yet these points can hardly be taken as a proof that they are not the writings of Thomas, but rather that they were written under somewhat different circumstances, or at another period to what the others were. There is no doubt that in some of his works he made use of the teaching of his early instructors, and the notes that he retained of their discourses. . . . The two books, viz. the *Garden of Roses* and the *Valley of Lilies*, moreover, apparently belong to one another, for the one seems to be like the continuation of the other: and the author might have made one book out of the eighteen chapters of the first, and the thirty-one chapters of the second, and given one or other title to the whole. It is quite unimportant that neither the first book treats of Roses nor the second of Lilies; though allusions are made to these flowers, for the author has the instruction of earnest-minded Christians in view. They are excellent treatises on religious ethics, with suitable meditations or soliloquies. When he wrote them he had evidently been made a Priest. And from what is said in the twelfth chapter of the *Garden of Roses* it was evidently in the time of war, for he says, 'Seldom is good news heard; everywhere many battles rise up; within are fears, without are fightings. No day is there without labour, no hour free from the fear of death, Wars and fires arise, according to the just judgment of God, because of men's sins, that they may be urged on as with scourges to seek after heavenly things. Therefore unceasing prayer is above all necessary against all the dangers of the world; as a strong breast-plate against the darts of the enemy.' Most probably these words refer, says Mooren, to the devastations caused by the campaign of the Dukes of Burgundy and Gelderland against Utrecht, when the monasteries had much to suffer.

In this second volume also we have *De Tribus Tabernaculis*, and *De Disciplina Claustralium*; the latter work refers to the regulations and duties of the cloister life among the Brethren, and has been by some reckoned a fifth book of the *De Imitatione Christi*. Next to this comes *De Fideli Dispensatore*, in which the duties of a faithful steward are set forth, under the character of Martha; who, whilst discharging her duties faithfully and in love to the Saviour, must learn not to despise the character of her sister Mary, whose service, though more silent and hidden, is very acceptable before God. And he shews that both have their place in the Church of Christ, and must highly esteem each other. (II, pp. 431-33)

In addition the second volume contains the *Hospitale Pauperum*, which does not, as the title would lead us to suppose, refer to Christian benevolence towards the suffering poor; but, like the *De Disciplina Claustralium*, it speaks more of the conventual life among them, and how they are both inwardly and outwardly to embrace a life of poverty in the place where they dwell. Thomas often finds delight in recalling the teaching of Gerard Groote and Florentius, to whom the Brothers of Common Life owe their origin. In the nineteenth chapter of this work, a real treasure is to be found in the shape of brief ejaculatory prayers for the devout, which he terms versicles. The *Dialogus Novitiorum* explains the purpose and style of the work in its title. The old venerable Frieslander Priest who is brought forward in the fifth chapter was a favourite hero with Thomas.

In the introduction a young man having resolved to lead a religious life, inquires how he can more fully do the will of God, escape the temptations of the world, and at length attain eternal blessedness with the faithful in Christ Jesus; and the whole of the subsequent instructions are addressed to him, being as it would seem chiefly drawn from the memorable sayings and counsels of the early fathers of the Brotherhood. The *Doctrinale seu Manuale Juvenum* is of a similar character to the former book: but is more in the form of a short directory for leading a devout life. And it is to be noticed that Thomas begins by recommending a diligent study of the Holy Scriptures, to be followed by an attentive regard to the voice of conscience within us. The book *Exercitia Spiritualia* comes after this, and is followed by another of like title; both of which relate to those things which will promote the soul's welfare. *De vera Compunctione Animæ* bears more upon the early life of the convert, and how his contrition of heart is carried on with God in secret. Then follow two books, entitled *De Solitudine et Silentio*, in praise of the solitary life and of silence, which appear to have been written after he was relieved from the office of Procurator, that he might the better apply himself to a life of contemplation.

In another part of the second volume, Sommalius introduces several of Thomas's minor works, among which *De Elevatione Mentis ad acquirendum Summum Bonum*, may be considered one of his choicest pieces. In this part also

we have some prayers by him, and some Hymns or Canticles.

In his third volume, Sommalius gives us the historical or *biographical* works of à Kempis, but without adding the *Chronicles of Mount St. Agnes*, of which he makes no mention, though the work is undoubtedly by Thomas, and has never been questioned.

The Lives written by Thomas are in three books, the first containing that of Gerard, the great; the second, that of Florentius, and the third that of nine of the earlier members and fathers of the Brothers of Common Life. As Henry Brune lived the longest of these persons whose memoirs are recorded, and died in the year 1439, it is thought probable that they were written after this time. To these there is added another biography, namely that of the sainted Dutch maid, Lidwine, which is dedicated to the Brethren, Canons Regular of the Monastery of St. Elizabeth, near Briel, Zeland, by one who calls himself Frater N., pauper et peregrinus. As this memoir does not find a place in the earlier editions of Thomas's work, it has been accounted spurious: and the letter N. seems to point to some other person rather that to Thomas. It is rather a lengthy memoir, and contains towards the close an account of three miracles; the last of which took place in the year 1448, from which it appears that it must have been written after this date. But, whether Thomas was the compiler of it or no, we learn from the prologue that the work had been sent to Brother N. for correction and criticism, and must therefore have been originally from another source.

At the end of the third volume we have some letters of Thomas, which have been preserved, and to which we have already largely drawn attention, written on various occasions. To these succeed some more prayers on the Passion of our Lord. Then other prayers, chiefly addressed to the Virgin Mary and other Saints, concluding with a few more sacred Canticles. With regard to these Canticles, it may here be mentioned that in the Burgoyne Library at Brussels there is still to be seen a Codex written by Thomas, which was formerly the property of a Jesuit of Cortryck, which, besides other little works, contains some of the Hymns of Thomas, with music appended to them. (II, pp. 434-36)

The enthusiastic commendation of Prior Pirkhamer in his letter to Peter Danhausser, the publisher of the first edition of Thomas à Kempis's works in 1494, to encourage him in his project, will form a fitting conclusion to these few remarks; it especially applies to his best known writings. 'Nothing more holy,' he says, 'nothing more honourable, nothing more religious, lastly, nothing more for the Christian common-weal, can you ever do, than to take care that these books of Thomas à Kempis be made public; which, though hitherto not taken notice of, may, as fire hidden in the veins of a flint, be very useful and serviceable to the Christian religion.' Then he tells us how some had with these writings put to flight the powers of darkness; and, having given a character of the author upon his own knowledge of him, he addresses his friend again in these words: 'It will be well and considerately done by you, if you bring them out of dust and obscurity into light, that they may be generally read, since they either lead minds disposed and prepared to the search after their Eternal happiness, and to the contemplation of useful learning and solid wisdom, and this after an easy, swift, and compendious method; or else they do fortify those who are already devout and spiritual, liberating them from the shameful ignorance and inexperience which is so extremely dangerous. And of how great edification these works are likely to be for all Christians, even to the greatest and most learned, it is impossible to speak or write. Therefore do not slight them, courteous Peter.' &c. (II, pp. 436-37)

> *Rev. S. Kettlewell, in his* Thomas à Kempis and the Brothers of Common Life, *Vols. I & II,* Kegan Paul, Trench, & Co., *1882, 449 p.; 484 p.*

AUGUST J. THEBAUD (essay date 1883)

[*Thebaud was an American Roman Catholic clergyman and educator. In the following excerpt from an essay examining the question of* The Imitation's *authorship, he offers high praise for the work and for its author.*]

After the Gospel, the *Imitation* undoubtedly is the book that reflects with the greatest perfection the light which Jesus Christ brought us down from heaven. It eminently contains the Christian philosophy. Humility, poverty, meekness, purity of heart, sorrow for sins, forgiveness of injury, joy in the midst of persecution, were held by the Saviour, in the sermon on the mount, as the characteristics of His disciples. Nowhere else do we find the same doctrine inculcated with a more persuasive eloquence and simplicity than in the unpretending little volume that all of us have a hundred times perused.

Nothing certainly is more opposed to our corrupt nature; still all, even non-Christians, have admired and praised the book. Filled with the spirit of Christianity it is most uncongenial to the *animalis homo*; still not a single voice has ever dared to protest against it,—precisely as in our day the men least inclined to submit to the Saviour are often the loudest in professing their admiration for his moral precepts. Such is at all times the power of true virtue!

Hence, after the Bible, and particularly the New Testament, the editions of the *Imitation* have been far more numerous than those of the noblest productions of the human mind. (p. 650)

Still, for the last two hundred years and more, a violent controversy has arisen and continues at this moment in the literary world on the simple question, Who wrote the *Imitation of Christ*? . . .

At this moment learned men in Italy are openly in favor of Thomas. Twenty years ago this would have been considered extraordinary, if not impossible. A number of Benedictine fathers in Germany and France have also abandoned the cause of Gersen, in spite of the efforts of their *confrère*, Dom C. Wolfsgruber, in the book he published at Augsburg in 1880. Everything is evidently preparing for a universal acknowledgment of the claims of à Kempis, and for the final success of the powerful and numerous advocates he has counted on his side during the last three hundred years. (p. 671)

> *August J. Thebaud, "Who Wrote the 'Imitation of Christ'?" in* The American Catholic Quarterly Review, *Vol. VIII, No. 32, October, 1883, pp. 650-71.*

LIONEL JOHNSON (essay date 1891)

[*Johnson was one of the principal members of the group of English artists and writers described by W. B. Yeats as the "tragic generation" of the 1890s. The lives and careers of members of this group, most notably Oscar Wilde, Aubrey Beardsley, and Arthur Symons, span the fin-de-siècle period: an era of controversy and transition in all the arts during which the Decadent movement in art and letters flourished. Influenced by the doctrine of "art for art's sake," the Decadent movement is characterized by experimentation with new aesthetic theories and an eagerness to explore all of human experience, including subjects perceived to have been proscribed by Victorian mores. Members of the "tragic generation" (so called for its high incidence of poverty, sickness, alcoholism, homosexuality, and mental illness) were generally drawn to the Roman Catholic Church; Johnson himself converted to Catholicism in 1890. In the following excerpt from an essay originally published the year after his conversion, he praises Thomas à Kempis and* The Imitation.]

The saints from the Doubting Apostle onward, who bear the name of Thomas, form a remarkable company. To take but three, there is the Angelic Doctor of Aquin, prince of theologians, consecrator of Aristotle to the service of Christian philosophy; there is the indomitable Thomas of Canterbury, martyr for the rights of the Church; there is Thomas More, Lord Chancellor, martyr for the supremacy of the Holy See. But there is one Thomas whose influence has extended over the world, who has sunk into the hearts of innumerable Christians outside his Church; whose chief work can be read in the tongues of the Near East and of the Far: his full name is Thomas à Kempis. (p. 276)

Thomas à Kempis is uncanonized yet; he has not been "raised to the altars of the Church," and no public devotion may be addressed to him. It is to be lamented; and yet it is in keeping with the humility and self-withdrawal of him whose favourite precept, for himself and others, was *Ama nesciri*, "Love to be unknown." The majority of persons if asked what they do know of him, would answer that he wrote *The Imitation of Christ*. Many of them, if told for the first time that the authorship of no work ever written has been so much contested, might be disposed to say that if à Kempis did not write it he ceased to interest them, he had no longer a claim upon their love or upon a special place in their memory. But the man and his way of life were infinitely touching and sweet, quite apart from the authorship of the *Imitation*, now quite settled for all scholars who can appreciate evidence. . . . It is a beautiful life: a life with its spiritual troubles and bodily trials, but a life of mutual charity, of entire simplicity, of gentle order. There is nothing to offend even the least reasonable haters of asceticism and the monastic ideal; Thomas and his brethren had common-sense and a sense of humour, two things without which piety can become distressing and even perilous. . . . His genuine humanity has won for à Kempis his universal hearing. A "religious," writing solely for followers of the monastic life, he yet appeals to the noisy world beyond the cloister, making felt his message of peace through renunciation. Doubtless, he has his danger for the unwary reader, who forgets that men and women in the world must read him for their own purposes, with a difference, *mutatis mutandis*. For lack of this understanding, the *Imitation* has been called "a manual of sacred selfishness"; and even Mr. Coventry Patmore is somewhat inconsistent, when he writes, learned in mysticism and the contemplative life though he was:—

It has struck me often lately that à Kempis, whom you are daily reading now, cannot be read with safety without remembering that he wrote this book expressly for the use of monks. There is much that is quite unfit for and untrue of people who live in the ordinary relations of life. I don't think I like the book quite so much as I did. There is a hot-house, egotistical air about much of its piety. Other persons are ordinarily the appointed means of learning the love of God, and to stifle human affections must be very often to render the love of God impossible.

And yet, what thousands of human souls, alien from the creed of à Kempis, and dissimilar to one another, have loved his gentle and stern wisdom! The *Imitation*, said Dr. Johnson, "must be a good book, as the world has opened its arms to receive it" [see excerpt dated 1778]. No two human beings could well be less like each other than Rachel, the great and terrible actress, and Gordon, the "soldier saint" of Khartoum. Yet the *Imitation* was his study under the shadow of a fierce death; and Rachel awaited death,

Soothing with thy Christian strain forlorn,
A Kempis! her departing soul outworn,
While by her bedside Hebrew rites have place.

(pp. 278-80)

A gentle beauty, with an essential sternness as its secret, belongs to the man—very much a man—who did not, like Savonarola, fly to the cloister, with a great line of Virgil upon his lips, bidding him cast off the dust of his shoes against a degraded world, but who sought it in ardent humility, and lived in it a life which has resulted in spiritual joy to thousands. We do not claim for Thomas à Kempis that he was a great man; yet, in Browning's words:

The little less, and how much it is!
The little more, and what worlds away!

Thomas à Kempis has that "little more," and how high it places him among the saints! "what worlds away" from us! (pp. 282-83)

Lionel Johnson, "Thomas à Kempis," in his Post Liminium: Essays and Critical Papers, *edited by Thomas Whittemore, Elkin Mathews, 1911, pp. 276-83.*

THE SPECTATOR (essay date 1905)

[*In the following excerpt from a general essay on* The Imitation, *the anonymous critic explores the enduring popularity of the work—a popularity that endures despite what the critic deems the work's unfeasible expectations of non-monastic twentieth-century readers.*]

The Imitation of Christ is admitted on all hands to be the finest embodiment of the monastic ideal. That ideal has, we should say, no hold upon the minds of modern Englishmen, yet no book of devotion, setting aside the Bible and the Prayer-book, is, we suppose, so widely read. (p. 665)

The interest of the *Imitation* is purely religious. Unlike St. Augustine, Thomas à Kempis does not confess his sins to his readers, though he tells them of his aspirations and his inclinations, of the meditations which afforded him spiritual consolation, and the rules which regulated his conduct in the community. Apparently it is impossible to escape from the friction of life. Shut out by the highest monastic walls, we find it again self-generated within. "It is no small matter," he writes, "to dwell in community, or in a congregation, and to converse therein without complaint, and to persevere therein faithfully until death." Years ago, he tells us—writing in the beginning of the fifteenth century—the conventual life satisfied those who sought it more completely, and fervour was more common, but "now he is greatly accounted of, that breaketh not the rule, and that can with patience endure that which he hath professed." There are some, he says, "that neither are in peace themselves, nor suffer others to be in peace: they are troublesome to others, but," he adds with kindly tolerance, "always more troublesome to themselves." Evidently the community, in his eyes, judged too much after appearances, and had lowered their earlier standard. "We ask how much one hath done: but how virtuous his actions are, is not so diligently considered. We inquire whether he be strong, rich, beautiful, handsome, a good writer, a good singer, or a good labourer: but how poor he is in spirit, how patient and meek, how devout and spiritual is seldom spoken of." This instinctive ascetic gives much counsel how best to live the monastic life, which seems to him the best worth living. "Never be altogether idle," he says, "but either reading or writing, or praying, or meditating, or labouring something of profit for the common good." Waste of time is one of the snares against which he warns his brethren with the most insistence. "If thou withdraw thy self from superfluous talk, and idle wandring about, as also from hearing of news and tales; thou shalt find sufficient, and fit time to think of good things." Much talking is, his readers are constantly assured, a source of spiritual danger. "The talk of worldly affairs hindreth very much, although they be recounted with sincere intention," is his stern conclusion. "Why do we so willingly speak, and talk one with another," he asks, "when notwithstanding we seldom return to silence, without hurt of conscience?" He thinks it is because we "desire to ease our mind overwearied with sundry thoughts: and we talk willingly, and think of those things which we love best, and most desire; of those, which we feel most contrary unto us." In these days it is difficult to conceive wherein lay the sin of this natural wish for sympathy. Thomas à Kempis, however, dreaded all roads which led to friendship, and had, indeed, very little abstract belief in it. "A friend is rare to be found, that continueth faithful in his friend's distress," he declares. "A friend going from thee or dying shall not grieve thee," he writes. "Thou oughtest to be so dead to such affections of beloved friends, that (forasmuch as appertaineth unto thee) thou shouldst wish to be without all company of men." "Our Lord," he thinks, "bestoweth his blessings there, where he findeth his vessels empty." No doubt this fear of free talk and strong human feeling belonged to the conventional standpoint of monasticism; but we cannot help suspecting that it was intensified by the skinless sensitiveness which the writer from time to time betrays. He regards "injurious words" as one of the heaviest of trials, and the desire to resent them as one of the greatest of temptations. Such sensitiveness he takes to be universal: "part of the ancient corruption of our nature." He is always reminding himself that it is foolish to dwell upon an unkind speech, for "what are words, but words?" and "Let not thy peace be in the tongues of men." Whenever he writes of nature and grace it is impossible not to imagine that he is confiding to us his personal struggles.

As he treats of these opposite human tendencies he seldom mentions actual temptations to sin. His was not the temperament which inclines to any lawlessness; and it is pathetic to read of the sensitiveness he could not overcome, the attention he could not keep, the repugnances he could never root out, and the interest in things human and secular which he never learned wholly to thwart. "Nature seeketh to have those things that be curious and precious, abhorreth that which is mean and base: but Grace delighteth in plain and humble things, despiseth not coarse and mean, nor refuseth to wear that which is old and torn," he writes sadly, and the heart of the reader is moved to defend the instinctive fastidiousness of the scholar against the onslaughts of a peevish and overwrought conscience. He regrets deeply that he is "so watchful to tales, so drowsy to watch in the service of God, so hasty to the end thereof." Perhaps it occurred to him sometimes that a man might be too strict even with himself, for we find him admitting that "those things that a man cannot amend in himself or in others, he ought to suffer patiently until God ordain otherwise"; and again: "I offer up also unto thee whatsoever is good in me, although it be very little."

The charm of such writing is patent. But why it is considered specially suited to young people at a moment when they are entering the lists of life we confess is not so clear. Thomas à Kempis has a horror of ambition, which he presents always upon its worst side, and describes as "gaping after honours"; a great fear of independence, which appears to him nothing but revolt; and a suspicion that all wish for happiness is evil. "Go whither thou wilt, thou shalt find no rest, but in humble subjection under the government of a Superior," he assures us; and "if there had been any better thing, and more profitable to the health of man then suffering, surely Christ would have shewed it by word, and example." Now few people desire to crush all ambition in the young, knowing from how many worse things it is likely to free them, and still fewer would wish them to "find rest" all their lives "under the government of a Superior." Again, most Christians firmly believe that Christ, both by word and example, worked daily and hourly to relieve the sufferings of men. How is it that, in spite of all these drawbacks, all this impracticability and loyal adherence to an ideal which, in this country at least, is dead, the words of Thomas à Kempis are, to use Matthew Arnold's expression, "true and living yet"? The unthinking will point to the title-page, and say: Because he shows us how to imitate Christ. But in all reverence for so great a book, we would ask: Is the "Master" who speaks to the disciple in the words of Thomas à Kempis the same whom the Evangelists have revealed to us? Honestly, we cannot help saying that He is not. Or to be less dogmatic, should we say that the figure of Christ as here displayed is so covered up in Church draperies as to be barely recognisable? How strange, how entirely out of character, do these words sound in the mouth of our Lord:—"I have bestowed all, and will all be returned to me again: and with great severity I require thanks." Again, in speaking of the saints:—"They glory not of their own merits, for they ascribe no good unto themselves, but attribute all to me, who of my infinite charity have bestowed my blessings upon them. They are replenished with so great love of my Godhead."

In the belief of the present writer, the continued life of the book depends not on its ethical teaching—so far as that teaching belongs to itself, and is not common to every form of Christianity—not on the picture which it offers of Christ. It depends upon the fact that Thomas à Kempis taught, and no one can read his book without learning that religion is not a dead science, a dogma to be learnt from books or accepted upon ecclesiastical authority, but something as vital to-day as in the time of the Psalmist or St. Paul. "I (saith our Lord) have taught the Prophets from the beginning, and cease not continually to speak to every one: but many are deaf," he writes. "Let all Doctors hold their peace; let all creatures be silent in thy sight; speak thou alone unto me." He realised to a degree impossible to most natures the direct influence of God upon the human soul, and this is what every religious man of every creed desires to realise, and why he will read any book which can give him an exceptionally vivid account of such an experience, whether the writer be an Augustinian monk or a Bedford cobbler.

Thomas à Kempis heard a voice saying, "I teach without noise of words, without confusion of opinions, without ambition of honour, without contention of arguments." He had the perception of the supernatural which marks religious genius; and however the religious world may doubt his peculiar theology and mistrust his cramped rule of life, they will always want to hear what he has to say. "He to whom the Eternal Word speaketh, is delivered from multitudes and diversities of opinions," he said; and the appeal of his book to men of every variety of creed and doubt is a sufficient proof of the truth of his words. (665-66)

Part of the opening chapter of an early fifteenth-century manuscript of The Imitation of Christ.

A review of "The Imitation of Christ," in The Spectator, *Vol. 94, No. 4010, May 6, 1905, pp. 665-66*

FRANCIS THOMPSON (essay date 1907)

[*Thompson was one of the most important poets of the Catholic Revival in nineteenth-century English literature. Often compared to the seventeenth-century metaphysical poets, especially Richard Crashaw, he is best known for his poem "The Hound of Heaven" (1893), which displays Thompson's characteristic themes of spiritual struggle, redemption, and transcendent love. Like other writers of the fin de siècle period, Thompson wrote poetry and prose noted for rich verbal effects and a devotion to the values of aestheticism. In the following excerpt from a 1907 Athenaeum review of J. E. G. de Montmorency's biographical and critical study* Thomas à Kempis: His Age and Book *(1906), he seeks to define the lasting appeal of* The Imitation.]

[Had] à Kempis been merely a mystic, he would have had no more readers among us than other and greater mystics. His power is in his profound humanity. His appeal to the English mind is, in a way, somewhat like the appeal of Herbert's poetry. Both, in their diverse ways, bring mysticism down to earth, or leaven daily life with mysticism: they blend the subtleties of spirituality with a homely practicality, a Teutonic common sense, which seems in other hands alien to mysticism, and is conspicuously absent from the recognised type of Teuton mystic. Hence their twofold appeal alike to the most acrial and the most practical minds. A Kempis is in more than one way a singular union of opposites. As Mr. de Montmorency shows [in his *Thomas à Kempis: His Age and Book*], he rested absolutely on the past and present of Christianity, he anticipated no future developments; yet he remains quick and vital to a generation which has drifted far from the moorings of the past. His book [*The Imitation of Christ*], as Mr. de Montmorency again shows, is elaborately structural, formal, artificial, and unspontaneous in composition and plan; it is written in a cunning species of rhythmic or semi-metrical prose (whence the English copies style it *Musica Ecclesiastica*), with a kind of musical notation to show the cadence; yet it has all the effect of the simplest and most unmeditated spontaneity, of a spiritual diary straight from the heart. It is often (in this respect like most of the mediæval Doctors) almost a cento from Scripture, and draws freely on a variety of sources; yet its language has a profound impress of direct personality. In the miracle which welds these opposites to a homogeneity, in the combination of wisdom and simple practicality, meditative gravity and deep truth of emotional experience, and in the breath of humble fraternal love which gives a fragrance to it all, lies the grip of the book on all generations. It is not only a voice from the cloister; it is also the beating of a heart. (pp. 33-4)

> *Francis Thompson, "Biography: Thomas à Kempis," in his* Literary Criticisms, *edited by Rev. Terence L. Connolly, S.J., E. P. Dutton and Company, Inc., 1948, pp. 31-4.*

J. T. L. MAGGS (essay date 1908)

[*A British writer on Christian themes, Maggs was the author of* An Introduction to the Study of Hebrew *(1891) and* The Spiritual Experience of St. Paul, and Other Devotional Papers *(1891). In the following excerpt, he posits Thomas à Kempis's place in the history of Christian thought.*]

[Thomas à Kempis] was not a philosopher like Eckhardt, in whose Christianity the dividing line from Pantheism seems at times almost crossed. He was not disposed to the suppression of personality and the introduction of fanciful interpretation as we find these in Ruysbroek. He was not poetic and sensuous as Suso. He represents the non-metaphysical, non-sensuous; to put it positively, the personal, sane, practical, evangelical elements that mark the noblest mysticism. His book stands at the end of an evolution in which these less desirable elements were dropped; it leads on to a yet more evangelical period in which the doctrine of man's immediate and personal relation to his Creator and Saviour—which is of the very essence of mysticism—found a new and more emphatic utterance in the Reformation.

For it can scarcely be denied that the movement in the Netherlands, of which à Kempis may be regarded as the flower, tended, if not to *the* Reformation as it shaped itself on the stage of history, at least to *a* Reformation in doctrine and life.... Brought up in a circle where the devotional element was stronger than the intellectual, where beneath the surface of things accepted and conventional there moved a vigorous personal devotion, where the current practices, some semi-superstitious, were at least in part neutralized by a more abundant spiritual life, à Kempis, who was not a man of action or of restless spirit, was content to save his soul under the conditions to which he was born. He accepted the creed without criticism, and found in the Living Incarnate One, righteousness, peace and joy. Yet as it is possible for a Protestant to read into his book on the Holy Communion a more evangelical meaning than the words present, so is it possible that à Kempis read into the rites, customs and phraseology of his time a more scriptural and spiritual meaning than most of his contemporaries; though he did not go on, as more logical and reforming spirits did, to investigate these errors and to reject the phraseology that embodied them. It can hardly be denied that out of the company of which à Kempis is the best known name, there issued influences which found in the Lutheran Reformation their goal. The Brothers of Common Life multiplied the circulation of Scripture, advocated and vindicated its translation into the common tongue. The habit of popular vernacular preaching, which seems to have been favoured by the pre-Reformation mystics both in England and on the Continent, became a mighty power when Luther made his appeal to the German people. It was in the Brothers' schools that Erasmus and John Wessel were educated. The latter, a most considerable factor of the new movement, was personally acquainted with à Kempis, and owed to the *Imitation* the first impulses to a true spiritual life. The Brotherhood's conception of religion, as inward, spiritual and experimental, found its natural fruition in the German Reformation. (pp. 260-62)

> *J. T. L. Maggs, "Thomas à Kempis," in* The London Quarterly Review, *Vol. CIX, No. 14, April, 1908, pp. 254-63.*

GAMALIEL BRADFORD (essay date 1931)

[*A prolific biographer, Bradford is best known as the father of the genre of "psychography": the depiction of subjects through a collage of anecdotes and quotations which togeth-er (Bradford believed) reveal the essence of the characters ex-amined. From 1912 to 1932 he produced biographical studies of this nature of some 114 individuals, ranging from Casanova to Calvin Coolidge. Notable among Bradford's works are* Lee the American *(1912) and* The Soul of Samuel Pepys *(1924). In the following excerpt from an essay origi-nally published in the* Catholic World *in 1931, Bradford elucidates the major themes and precepts of* The Imitation.]

'Consider that God and you are alone in the universe, and you will have great peace in your heart.' That is the domi-nant note of the *Imitation of Christ* and of its reputed au-thor, Thomas à Kempis. The outer world is of no conse-quence whatever, and all our thought, all our effort, all our love, should be concentrated upon the inner. The frag-ile, glittering splendor of the outer world is fading, elusive, and transitory, unless you can find some enduring reality beneath it. The author of the *Imitation* found this reality in God, and all his life was concerned with nothing else: 'Consider that God and you are alone in the universe, and you will have great peace in your heart.' (p. 113)

The question arises whether the *Imitation of Christ* may rightly be included among these works of à Kempis. There has been an unceasing controversy on the subject and the controversy shows no signs of coming to an end. But on the whole the solid scholarship of Hirsche and others would seem to throw the balance in favor of Thomas, and none of the other suggested authors has anything like such a substantial claim. The mere apparent superiority of the *Imitation* to à Kempis's other writings would not seem to mean more than the superiority of the *Elegy* or *Don Qui-xote* to the other writings of Gray and Cervantes. And an extensive perusal of the seven Latin volumes makes this superiority in à Kempis's case seem much less than is of-ten asserted. At the same time there is no disputing that the *Imitation* is the distilled quintessence of à Kempis's life and work, if he really wrote it, and its enormous popu-larity in all languages and with all sorts of readers, profane as well as religious, makes it the supreme manual of the religious life and of the subdual of the human soul to the God who made it.

To begin with, there is the simple, direct, general subdual of self, the overcoming, the putting down, the eliminating of that turbulent impulse to assert and maintain one's own ego which necessarily means the suppression, the injury, the limiting of others. As à Kempis puts it, 'Know that the love of yourself harms you more than anything else in the whole world.' The foundation, the root, of this love of self is the desire of things, that fatal wanting which Saint Fran-cis all his life proclaimed to be so deadly, and à Kempis, like Saint Francis, insists that desire must be rooted out altogether if perfection is to be attained. Desire is not only selfish in conception and cruel in execution, but it never brings contentment, and instead only unhappiness and restlessness: 'Whenever a man desires anything inordinate-ly, he at once becomes disquieted.' (pp. 119-21)

The summing up, the acme, the concentrated essence of self is in the conception of sin, and it is the apparently complete disappearance of that conception at the present day that makes it so difficult for us to enter into much of à Kempis's attitude. . . . Sin is always busy with the plea-sures of this life, and à Kempis and the *Imitation* wage eternal war upon these pleasures, as being transitory, delu-sive, and in the end full of bitterness and disgust. 'Oh,

what a comforting conscience would he have who never pursued the joys which fade, who never occupied himself with the fleeting pleasures of this world!' And it must be remembered that the substantial background to these trivi-al enjoyments which vanish away is the sure and solid per-manence of the heavenly reward for those who eschew the others and in à Kempis's equal conviction the solid per-manence of hell. (pp. 121-22)

As the author of the *Imitation* battles with desire in gener-al, so he over and over analyzes and specifies the varied details and aspects of it, and brands and lashes them with his simple, unescapable condemnation. There is riches. Brought up as à Kempis had been, in the conventual, com-munity life, in which personal possessions played no part, it might seem as if he could know nothing about riches. But here, as elsewhere, he shows a strange comprehension of the larger movement of the outside world. Riches and possessions burden and weary even those who seem to grasp them most securely. They distract not only from your eternal welfare, but from the ease and serenity of life led here: 'The more a man gathers things to himself, the more he is hampered and distracted.' Riches corrupt those who have them and those who have them not, for those who have want more and those who have not want what the others have. They corrupt even the saints, who are un-consciously led to flatter and bow down and have to be cautioned most earnestly: 'Do not flatter the wealthy, and be not eager to show yourself among the magnates of the world.' The whole attitude towards possessions is made plain, as so often, in one perfect sentence: 'Give up all things, and you shall find all things; give up desire, and you shall find repose.'

Take another almost equally general and equally insidious aspect of worldly interest, the love of reputation and flat-tery and applause. Again à Kempis understands perfectly how universal this is, how it affects not only the sinners but the saints, with its thousand creeping, insinuatingman-ifestations. . . . À Kempis, living all his life in quiet shad-ow, avoiding honors, avoiding dignities, even such minor ones as were offered him, preaches everywhere the vanity of worldly honor and the futility of worldly praise: 'Fly praise as if it were poison. . . . Vain and foolish are those who delight in the commendations of men.' And the grand words of the *Imitation* sum it up even more impressively: 'The cheat deceives the cheat, the vain the vain, the blind the blind, the weak the weak, whilst they extol them, and in truth one rather puts another to confusion whilst he vainly praises him.'

As praise and glory are to be despised and rejected, so also is the vain pursuit of knowledge. It is evident that à Kem-pis himself was no wide or persistent scholar; both the *Im-itation* and his other works make this clear enough. He was a most assiduous reader of the Bible. Biblical allu-sions and turns and suggestions appear in all his writings constantly. Also there is more or less knowledge of the mystics and generally devotional writers who had preced-ed him. But worldly learning and the love of study for it-self get little favor. He knows the charm of them. With all those quiet hours of thought and reflection, such a temper-ament could not be unaware of the charm of books of all sorts or any sort. He recognizes the occasional profit of such studies and the legitimacy of them when kept in proper limits: 'Science is not to be found fault with, nor the simple knowledge of things as they are, which is good considered in itself, and is ordained of God; but these are of much less consequence than a good conscience and a virtuous life!'

The trouble with worldly learning is that it puffs a man up, exalts his opinion of his own gifts and powers, and destroys humility. The saying of Aristotle is all very well, à Kempis thinks. 'Every man naturally desires to know; but what is knowledge worth if it does not carry with it the fear of God?' And he urges and enjoins a persistent caution in such matters. . . . (pp. 122-25)

Nor is this firm and consistent God-lover any more tolerant of beauty than he is of knowledge. There is not one gleam of the arts and their passionate seduction in all his writing. Are not the arts, one all of them, intimately bound up with human passion and human sin? Is not their witchery too nearly related to unholy impulses of indulgence or despair? Painting, to be sure, may illustrate sacred themes, but danger is always perilously inherent in it. At any rate, the quiet monk feels a good deal safer without it. Music is and always has been a prominent element of worship. As such you must accept it and even participate in it. But the rapture of music if for God and not for you. To you it is merely the performance of a religious duty.

Even the love of the exquisite outdoor world, which seems so simple and innocent, is at least distracting. À Kempis cherishes nothing of the charming vagabondage of Saint Francis. The birds and the fishes may be our brothers, but let them pursue their own salvation as their instincts guide them. And he condemns idle strolling, which may lure the eyes so far out of the way: 'The inclinations of sensuality lead you to walk abroad, but when the hour is past, what do you bring back but a burdened conscience and a scattered heart? A joyous setting forth often brings a sad returning home, and a gay evening may be the prelude to a melancholy morning. . . . What can you see anywhere that you do not see here? Here is the sky, and the earth, and all the elements, and of these are all things made. . . . Leave vain things to the vain, and do you attend to those things which God has prescribed for you'

So in everything there is the urgent, ardent injunction to avoid mere curiosity, the flitting and fluttering of soul in external details which divert and distract it from the weightier business that should be its whole vital concern. There were no Sunday papers in the Monastery of Mount Saint Agnes, and it is easy to imagine what à Kempis would have thought of them. 'Leave all curiosity behind you.' It would not be the motto for a Sunday paper.

It goes without saying that the grosser forms of desire are not to be tolerated for a moment in this scheme of things. The body must be nourished and cherished after a fashion, while we have it, more's the pity, but let us deplore the necessity, not encourage it or foster it: 'Oh, if we never needed to eat, or drink, or sleep, but could praise God all the time and give ourselves only to spiritual studies!' It is to be feared that this program would not altogether commend itself in modern educational institutions. But à Kempis gives his view of the matter with his usual marvelous precision and point: '*Sint temporalia in usu, aeterna in desiderio*, Use the temporal, desire the eternal.'

It should be said, however, that, with these principles of extreme apparent austerity, à Kempis, naturally gently and

kindly, does not seem disposed to insist upon the harsher methods of self-discipline which were so often resorted to in the desperate effort to make the spirit overcome the flesh. He does occasionally refer to such things, but his emphasis and his insistence are rather upon spiritual pressure, the urgency and agency of prayer and meditation upon those higher, more eternal themes which make the temptations and distractions of this world seem insignificant. (pp. 125-27)

So far the direct subdual of self in immediate wants and desires. But there is further the subdual of self with reference to other human beings. À Kempis here insists constantly upon the habit of solitude, upon the love of your own cell and abiding place, not merely the rule of it, but the love of it. And of course it is not your cell for yourself, but for the presence of God in it, with the incessant reiteration of the reminder: 'Consider that God and you are alone in the universe, and you will have great peace in your heart.'

Naturally this does not mean that duty to others should be neglected. There should be consideration, there should be courtesy, there should be thoughtfulness, always. You have your duty to others and you should see that it is done. But the duty to God comes first and is more satisfying in its fulfillment. (p. 128)

Certainly it would appear that no one could have cultivated the cell habit much more strictly all his life than did à Kempis. Indeed this solitude has led some lovers of the *Imitation* to dispute his authorship of the book. Every page of it seems to indicate a profound, searching knowledge of the human heart in all its depth and intricacy, which could hardly have been acquired within the walls of a conventual prison. In answer to which we may perhaps suggest the remark of Sénancour, 'If I have not experienced everything, I have at least imagined everything.' Imagination and sensibility, as we can see clearly that à Kempis possessed them, enable a man to divine the secrets of the world's soul in the secrets of his own. At any rate, no one has ever preached the charm of solitude— with God—more insistently and more persuasively than the author of the *Imitation*: 'To leave your cell is always perilous, and to dwell quietly within it is the peaceful haven of a religious life.'

The chief temptation with regard to others is the desire to rule and control them, and in dominating spirits this desire may assert itself as vehemently in the cloister as in the palace. The saint and the servant of God is quite as apt to seek the leadership of others, always for their good of course, as the soldier or the statesman. To à Kempis himself this form of temptation seems to have made little appeal. . . . Help others, serve others, minister to others, as far as you can, he urges, but leave the control of others to those who care for it, and let them remember that there is danger to themselves and to others also in every step they take.

Another form of the relation to others which requires the utmost watchfulness is temper, wrath, anger, whether justified or not. Here again à Kempis would seem to have had himself a gentle and quiet disposition to which such stormy outbursts would have been peculiarly foreign. Yet under the calm aspect there is sometimes more furious tumult than appears, and more effort is needed to secure and maintain the calm than would go into a tempestuous victory: 'There are those,' says the *Imitation*, 'who keep themselves in peace and also have peace with others. And there are those who neither have peace themselves nor leave others in peace; such are a burden to others and always a still more grievous burden to themselves.' And elsewhere à Kempis indicates his judgment of quarrelers in no uncertain terms: 'When thou art proud or angry, when thou backbitest, murmurest, deceivest, liest, and disturbest others, rejoicest at their evil, and repinest at their good . . . then thou followest the Devil.' What more can be said?

But besides actual loud wrath and quarreling, there is the vague aversion and dislike, the distaste we form for our neighbors, often with no reasonable or even conscious ground, but which, if it is indulged, grows irritating and hateful, and often poisons our own lives more than theirs. Get rid of all such harmful instincts, tear them out, root them up, cries à Kempis. Do not dwell upon the faults, or defects, or weaknesses, of others, do not urge them or amplify them: 'You are not yet in heaven with the holy angels, but in the actual world, with men good and evil, and the evil will never be wanting in this region of the shadow of death.' The one sure cure for criticism and fault-finding is to remember that you yourself have probably just such defects and certainly plenty of others: 'For as your eye judges others, so in your turn will others judge you.' Or, as it is put by the Orlando of Shakespeare, who was in many ways so close to à Kempis, for all the difference in their lives, 'I will chide no breather in the world but myself, against whom I know most faults.'

As animosity, bitterness, and hostility are to be rooted out, so also is the idle curiosity which sometimes under the guise of kindly interest diverts its own emptiness by prying and intruding into the affairs and lives of others. There is always the excuse of being active and useful, but the activity too often gets nowhere and the utility is apt to be futility. (pp. 129-32)

The remedy, the sure refuge, which the author of the *Imitation* has to offer for all these temptations and misleading complications with others is silence. What we seek so desperately—and too well he knows it—is somehow to get out of, to escape from, ourselves: 'It is for this that we talk so widely and so freely, because by the exchange of words we seek to console one another, and to cheer our hearts when they are wearied by many thoughts.' Then we learn—though some of us never learn—that such effort for escape is vain, that we cannot get out of ourselves, do what we will, and that the wide waste of words is the most empty delusion of all. So we come to appreciate the blessing and the fruitfulness of silence. To keep still rarely injures anyone. We are so often damaged by what we say, so rarely by what we do not say. If we sit silent and let the world go by, we are at least safe as regards others, and we have the positive advantage of having time and fresh attention to give to the matters that concern our own souls: 'It is the part of prudence to keep silent in evil days, to turn our thoughts inward, and not to be troubled by the judgments of men.'

But, it will be said, though we should avoid strife with others and even vain chatter about them, we should at least seek their support and friendship and affection. These things are very well, à Kempis admits; friends and friendship are useful and allow of our being useful in our turn. They should be recognized and cultivated, within limits. But they are terribly distracting, and at best they are uncertain. (pp. 133-34)

This mistrust of human support extends even to the natural ties of blood and family: 'He who clings to the created falls with that which is prone to fall.' (p. 134)

With this attitude towards earthly affection generally, it is hardly necessary to emphasize à Kempis's view of the love for woman. There are, indeed, vague touches here and there which intimate that he knew what the desires of the flesh might be. But he disposes of the subject concisely when he says, 'Nothing so soils and entangles the heart of man as an impure passion for any created thing'; and the monastic attitude was never better summed up than in the sentence, 'Be not familiar with any one woman, but commend all good women in general to God.'

What is most important to the author of the *Imitation* in this matter of relations to other human beings is, as with Saint Francis, the exquisite virtue of implicit obedience, where the law of God calls for it. It is not of the least consequence that you should command others, but it is of the utmost consequence that you should learn to obey without questioning. 'It is a great sign of wisdom not to be precipitate in action, nor to persist obstinately in your own purposes.' You should obey, not only for the immediate object, but for the mere benefit of the virtue in itself: 'Study to do the will of others, rather than your own.' The precept may seem a long way off from twentieth-century America, but perhaps it has its value, all the more for that reason.

And none knows better than à Kempis that the deeper root of obedience is humility. If you want to subdue yourself, the first principle is to have a poor opinion of yourself, not to display such an opinion, with a mere Uriah Heep hypocrisy, but really to understand the vast weakness and inadequacy and incompetence of human nature, as it may be found in others, but as you know, at any rate, it is to be found in you.

The climax of the overcoming of self lies in the subdual of self with regard to God, the absolute subordination to him of all your needs and passions and desires. In other words, the final triumph of this essential struggle of life is the conquest of the will and the complete union of the frail human will with the all-dominating will of God. (p. 136)

One of the most difficult and haunting elements of self to be overcome in these dealings with God is the instinct of intellectual research and investigation. There is the honest but exaggerated and uneasy effort to get at the truth. So many endless questions suggest themselves. There is such a vast reaching out of curious analysis to the end of the world, and beyond. How did we come to be, how did the universe come to be, how did God come to be, and where is it all tending to? There are questions of the Trinity, questions of the Atonement, questions of Christ's nature, questions of God's nature, and who shall answer them? To all which à Kempis's simple reply is, put these things aside and forget them. You have God's word, clear and intelligible, if you approach it in the right spirit: 'What shall it profit you to dispute loftily about the Trinity, if you lack humility, and so displease the Trinity?' (pp. 137-38)

The remedy for all the uneasiness and all the restlessness and all the vain intellectual aspiration is the simple, quiet repose of faith. '*Fruitive quiescere:*' it is impossible to translate it, but it appears that it is possible to feel it, with boundless spiritual peace. 'To abstain from vain spiritual wanderings and unprofitable arguments for the love of inward quietness.' Surely one whose soul has been torn for years by such wanderings and arguments may appreciate the eternal significance of that, and inward quietness may be the greatest of the gifts of God.

Only, when you think you have established such quietness, when you joyously hope that the supreme sacrifice has culminated, you so often find, in this imperfect and perishable world, that the peace has slipped away from you. The struggle is to be forever renewed, the battle is never finally won: 'Alas, alas, what bitterness of soul it brings, to labor and strive daily against one's self for the reward of eternal life.' The best of the saints, the most self-composed, the most serene, will sometimes cry with à Kempis: 'There is no love that is exempt from grief.' (pp. 138-39)

Accept these trials, as you accept others, as sent by God in his infinite wisdom for your good, wrap love and prayer about you like a comforting garment, and let the storm pass by.

So in a moment, perhaps when you least expect it, the sudden splendor of God overcomes you and fulfills you, and doubts and fears and anxieties are swept away: 'For, rapt out of themselves and swept beyond all merely personal pleasure, they plunge deep into the love of God and there are fruitfully at peace: there is nothing which can discourage or depress them, since they who are filled with eternal truth burn with the fire of inextinguishable love.'

It is true that those who are familiar with the abstract ecstasy of the more especially mystical saints may feel that à Kempis is somewhat too concrete. Though he everywhere and at all times regards Jesus as synonymous with God and as simply shepherding the soul to God, yet one may grow impatient with the persistent intrusion of Jesus as a personal figure, above all in that fourth book of the *Imitation*, with which one would sometimes hope that à Kempis had nothing to do. Also, there is a rather too frequent introduction of a very concrete heaven, that wearisome and uncomfortable vision of the future in which a huge aggregation of monastic and monotonous saints are eternally engaged in singing hymns which might in the end wear out the most devoted piety.

In other words, lovers of the high-wrought, perplexing ecstasy of Eastern Pantheism and of mystics like Saint Catherine, or Molinos, or Madame Guyon, those who take delight in the curious attempt to merge multiplicity in Unity and the distracting many in the eternal One, will sometimes find à Kempis a little unsatisfying. Certainly he does not indulge in the complicated raptures and speculations of Molinos: 'So that the soul must find itself dead to its will, desire, endeavour, understanding, and thought; willing as if it did not will; desiring as if it did not desire; understanding as if it did not understand; thinking as if it did not think; without inclination to anything; embracing equally contempt and honours, benefits and corrections. O what a happy soul is that which is thus dead and annihilated! It lives no longer in itself, because God lives in it.'

And it may well be, as many of his admirers contend, that à Kempis is more sane and reasonable than those who go to such intellectual and spiritual excesses. Yet, all the same, if you watch him carefully, you will find that he too has his moments when the personal and the concrete are burned away and desire and thought and life are dissolved in more intimate union: 'Then the soul begins to pant and long after and vehemently to be in love with this Good, wherein is all and every good, and with this Joy, wherein is all and every joy; with this One, wherein are all things both great and small, high and low; and yet this One is not any one thing of all the things that are created, but is supereminently beyond the form of any human conception whatsoever; it is the beginning and the end of all those goods and felicities that have been created thereby.'

What can be grander than to believe that the whole solid fabric of the universe is built up upon this enduring One? Only, if the One fades away, what is there left?

Yet even for the profane, to whom mystical rapture, however alluring, is a little unsubstantial, the *Imitation*, and in a less degree the other writings of à Kempis, retain a singular enchantment, because of their extraordinary qualities of literary beauty, which make the *Imitation* one of the masterpieces of the world. It is style that makes books live, and though style is inextricably bound up with thought and matter, thought and matter rarely have enduring significance without it. Assuredly in the *Imitation of Christ* every device and resource of literary art is employed to accomplish the one object which the author feels to be above every other.

There is the mere arrangement of the words, which makes so much of the charm and subtle impressiveness of the older Latin. Mediæval Latin is far freer and simpler and more modern than that of the Augustan Age, but à Kempis takes the language and moulds and fashions it to his purposes with a daring and a facility unusual to his contemporaries. Consider a sentence like this, which Cicero would never have written, yet which is so astonishingly effective: '*Vere ineffabilis dulcedo contemplationis tuae, quam largiris amantibus te.*' And again, there is the rhythm; always simple. brief, direct sentences, yet with a clinging sweetness of cadence that gives to prose almost the magic of poetry. And there are strange effects of rhyme, of assonance, also, so elaborate and complicated that they misled the German scholar Hirsche into the attempt to prove that the author of the *Imitation* was often writing actual verse. Hirsche shows all the exaggerations of German erudition, though his work is of extreme value as demonstrating the identity of authorship in à Kempis's various writings. But if à Kempis was not writing deliberate poetry, he at least understood all the subtlest secrets of literary effect. How skillful is his use of antithesis, of repetition, of the crowding, hammering accumulation of words, only oftentimes to conclude with a single light touch which goes as straight to its mark as a feathered arrow!

The remarkable thing is that, with all this skill and variety of artistic resource, the book cannot in any possible way be called artificial. On the contrary, it is the most perfect model of simplicity and naturalness, because the author, artist as he may be by instinct, is so possessed and overpowered by his passion for conveying God to others and to the whole wide world. Most characteristic of this simplicity is the structure of the books and of the chapters and the way they are built up. There is no elaborate or systematic argumentation, no attempt to work out an organized thesis to a definite and preconceived end. A simple topic is selected for each chapter, and the imagination and the feelings play about it and about it with infinite wayward subtlety and grace. And the same inspired, instinctive grace appears everywhere in the turn of the phrases, which have so often a felicity that cannot be reduced to any artistic formula whatever: *'In cruce infusio supernae suavitatis,' 'fruitive quiescere,' 'qui adhaeret creaturae cadet cum labili,' 'cella continuata dulcescit et male custodita taedium generat'*—you can hardly say what makes these and so many others cling in the memory with such compelling charm. And this combination of art and simplicity suggests comparison with another prose masterpiece, distinguished by these same elements, though differing from à Kempis in spirit as widely as one book can differ from another. The Daphnis and Chloë of Longus is a monument of Pagan naturalism, but the delicate rippling cadences of the Greek and the simple human touch all through the book often remind one of the *Imitation*.

Where one finds such extraordinary literary achievement, one cannot help asking one's self how far it is conscious and intentional, how far the writer thought of literary reputation, or at any rate of literary ability and cleverness. It is hardly necessary to say that à Kempis disclaims and condemns any such preoccupation with the utmost energy. He realizes keenly the danger of it: 'If anyone does well, if he reads well, or sings well, or writes well; if he prays well, or studies well, or preaches well, or celebrates well; behold, the Devil at once hovers about him with vainglory.' But all the more does he insist upon the necessity of getting rid of that danger: 'Unhappy indeed is the man who has made a name for himself in this world and who makes fame his object.' These aims must be rooted out and forgotten like every other earthly desire. And in a way there is a certain splendor in the thought that such a supreme flower of human performance as the *Imitation* should remain in the shadow of a dubious authorship, like the great Gothic cathedrals, which it so much resembles in spirit.

But it is impossible to feel that such a master of words as à Kempis should not have been conscious of his mastery. You get the same impression with other great religious writers. Paul was thinking of Christ first, but he was preaching Christ with a marvelous gift of words, and he knew it, whether he believed it came from the Holy Spirit or not.... When à Kempis speaks of the *'apices litterarum,'* 'the tips of letters,' he seems, whether he knew it or not, to suggest the delicate phrase with which Quintilian sums up all the magic of style, in speaking of beauty *'apicibus verborum ligata,'* clinging to the tips of words. And it must have been a perpetual revel to the solitary monk to spread God abroad with all the resources of splendor that the splendid Latin language could possibly be made to yield.

Yet back of all the beauty, whether conscious or not, there was always that profound, intriguing mystery of God, and the tender, solemn, entrancing fall of these magical phrases is like the choiring of the cherubim and seraphim in heaven. God is the secret, the supporting, the indispensable basis of it all. (pp. 140-46)

Gamaliel Bradford, "Alone with God: Thomas à Kempis," in his Saints and Sinners, *Houghton Mifflin Company, 1932, pp. 113-46.*

EDGAR ALLISON PEERS (essay date 1948)

[*Peers was a British educator, biographer, and essayist who specialized in the Spanish Christian mystics and Romantics. His works include* St. John of the Cross *(1932) and* The Romantic Movement in Spain: A Short History *(1968). In the following excerpt from another work,* Behind That Wall: An Introduction to Some Classics of the Interior Life *(1948), Peers seeks to explain the continuing appeal of* The Imitation, *offering a critical overview of the work, as well.*]

With the exception of the Bible, I suppose the *Imitation of Christ* has been read by more people, and is cherished by more people, than any other Christian book in the world. It is said to have been translated from its Latin original into more than fifty languages, and to have gone into six thousand editions. Perhaps before we have gone much farther we shall realize why. But there are two other things that I want to say about it first.

One is that Thomas à Kempis, or whoever its author may have been, was quite clearly writing for people living in the cloister: any number of phrases and passages in it show that. And yet, until you come up against these passages, you never think of such a thing: you read the book, as you would read any modern book of devotion, as if it had been written, not for fifteenth-century monks, but for twentieth-century housewives or business men catching the 8:30 to town. And the other thing about the book is the extraordinary way it grows on you. You begin it quite casually. It doesn't take hold of you with a few arresting opening sentences, or anything like that. But, before you are half-way through, it has become your companion for life. Before long I think the reason for that will be clear too.

Let us begin by looking at the title. *The Imitation of Christ* does not express a fraction of what the book really is. Still less does the title which a sterner age used to give it: *Contemptus mundi*—"Contempt of the world." Both those titles were apparently taken from the heading of the first chapter: "Of the imitation of Christ and the contempt of all the vanities of the world." There are other allusions in the book to the idea of "imitating" Christ, but the dominant idea is, not of imitation, but of closeness, intimacy, communion. I should like to see it renamed *The Book of Friendship with Jesus*. Not only because that is its real subject, but because, as you read it, you seem gradually to come nearer to Christ. (pp. 59-60)

And now let us study the arrangement of the *Imitation*. There are four books, or sections, in it. The fourth is about the Holy Communion—and very much more suitable it is as a guide for self-examination and preparation than a good many modern manuals, beside being profitable for devotion at other times. As this book stands quite by itself, however, I am not going to say anything about it here: I shall confine myself to the other three.

The first book is written for the ordinary, not very ambitious Christian—the sort of person who has to be well shaken up before he makes any sort of progress at all. Watch the author shaking him: "Why wilt thou defer thy

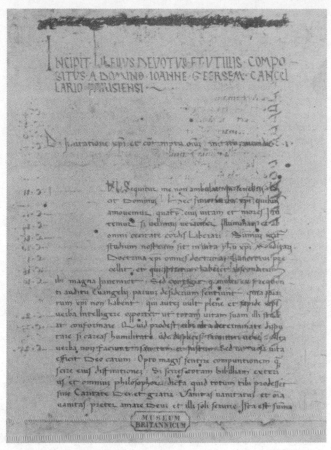

Part of an early manuscript of The Imitation of Christ, *now in the British Museum.*

good purpose from day to day? Arise and begin this very moment, and say 'Now is the time to be doing, now is the time to be striving, now is the fit time to amend thyself.' Unless thou doest violence to thyself, thou shalt never get the victory over sin." Well, there are plenty of us who can do with being talked to like that—and not only those of us who are Christians. As a matter of fact, there is a good deal in Book I of the *Imitation* which would be accepted by the sort of person who "doesn't hold with religion." That is, if you merely read it on the surface.

But what Book I is really doing is preparing the ground. With consummate tact, and with a devastating knowledge of human nature, the author leads you on to something better. . . . He suggests, for example, that you should try to have a few minutes' quiet every day. And then he tells you what to do with it: "In the morning fix thy good purpose; and at night examine thyself what thou hast done." And during the day: "Never be entirely idle, but either be reading, or writing, or praying, or meditating, or trying to do something for the public good."

And so on. Quite useful, you might think, and quite well put, but just a little ordinary, even a little trite. Yes; but here and there we come upon some phrase which thrills us, which sets us on fire, which sends us hurrying on to see what is coming next. Here, for example, in Chapter 20, in the middle of a succession of maxims about the vanity of created things, the thought suddenly bursts into flame:

Shut thy door upon thee, and call unto thee Jesus, thy Beloved.

For me those words mark the real beginning of the *Imitation*. It never seems quite the same again. And when we get out of Book I, in which the tender and intimate name "Jesus" is hardly used at all, into Book II—"Concerning inward things"—we realize where it is taking us. Now we begin to see the interior life:

He that knoweth how to live inwardly, and to make small reckoning of things without, neither requireth places nor awaiteth times for performing of religious exercises.

A spiritual man quickly recollecteth, because he never poureth out himself wholly to outward things.

Now, for the first time, we read of the "lover":

A lover of Jesus and of the truth, and a true inward Christian, and one free from inordinate affections, can freely turn himself unto God and lift himself above himself in spirit.

And now come some of those words which have been a comfort to millions:

If thou canst not contemplate high and heavenly things, rest thyself in the passion of Christ and dwell willingly on His sacred wounds.

For if thou fly devoutly unto the wounds and precious marks of the Lord Jesus, thou shalt feel great comfort in tribulation: neither wilt thou much care for the slights of men, and wilt easily bear the words of those that reproach thee.

Then, little by little, the author builds up that unsurpassable picture which he elaborates in Book III—of the faithful soul retreating to the upper room, watching for the coming of Jesus, giving admittance to Him alone, closing its ears to the raging clamour of the world, but intent to catch the faintest "pulse of the Divine whisper." (pp. 60-3)

Book III, entitled "Of inward consolation," is in effect a series of dialogues between Lover and Beloved. Right at the beginning of Book I we had read: "Let all doctors hold their peace; let all creatures be silent before Thee; speak Thou alone unto me." Was the author, then, leading all the time up to those sublime chapters of Book III? Or did they just come to him as he wrote? Or did he even set down the things which had passed between God and his own soul? We cannot say; but, as we read, we are caught up into the heavens, and we talk with one who himself has walked and talked with God.

Now, I think you will see why the *Imitation* grows upon everyone who loves the Lord Jesus in sincerity. And that gradualness with which it leads you into the Divine intimacy is also one of the reasons why it has become so famous. But there are also other reasons; and here, to end with, are one or two of them.

First, like all great Christian books, the *Imitation* is, rooted in Holy Scripture. True, there is only one chapter on Holy Scripture, and, though every sentence in that chapter is well known, it is a very short one. But you can see that both language and teaching are Biblical through and through.

Secondly, it is intended for simple and humble people. It never despises learning, but it holds up other things as more important.... (pp. 64-5)

Thirdly—again like all great Christian books—it is realistic. Never merely eloquent. Never sentimental. It says a great deal about what St. John of the Cross was later to call the "Dark Night of the Soul." Just before the beginning of that wonderful Book III comes one of the most searching pieces of writing in existence—the chapter called "Of the royal way of the holy Cross." It is an iron tonic, that chapter, a magnificent stimulus to the will. The author can be stern, even with his fellow-lovers. None but is the stronger for reading him, for nowhere is he anything but bracing.

Lastly, there is the greatness of the book's language. As a rule, it is brief, direct, forceful:

> He is truly great who hath great love.

> Fire trieth iron, and temptation the just man.

> Love all for Jesus, but Jesus for Himself.

None of its hard sayings is wrapped up for us. And that is what we all prefer: truth without trimmings:

> We are all frail: but esteem none to be frailer than thyself.

> It were better to avoid sin than to escape death.

> What are words but words? They fly through the air, but they hurt not the rock.

And yet, interspersed with these concise maxims are rhythmical passages of the greatest beauty, unspoiled even by translation. (pp. 65-6)

> Edgar Allison Peers, " 'The Imitation of Christ'," in his Behind That Wall: An Introduction to Some Classics of the Interior Life, 1948. Reprint by Books for Libraries Press, 1969, pp. 59-66.

LEO SHERLEY-PRICE (essay date 1952)

[*Sherley-Price is an English Roman Catholic priest who has written extensively on the lives of the Christian saints and the great literary works of Catholicism. In the following excerpt from his introduction to the Penguin edition of* The Imitation, *he offers a book-by-book critical outline of the work.*]

Thomas à Kempis is not only a master of the spiritual life, he is a master writer as well; consequently we have in the *Imitation* a classic that richly repays careful study and re-reading. As with the Scriptures, the more familiar we are with this book, the fairer the riches we discover in its pages, and the more it becomes a part of ourselves. Open it where one will; on every page will be found something to instruct, to inspire, to give ample food for thought.

It is hardly surprising that a man of Thomas's spiritual and mental powers was widely and soundly read in the best both of pagan and Christian literature. Every page glows with the reflected light of holy Scripture, which he knows so intimately; but he loves also to draw from the wisdom of the Christian Fathers, and from the great philosophers of Greece and Rome, in order to confirm and illustrate his teaching. Anyone familiar with the writings of

S. Bernard, S. Augustine, and S. Thomas Aquinas can readily detect the thought of these great theologians, while Thomas also draws from Ovid, Seneca, and Aristotle. Like the householder of the Gospels, 'he brings out of his treasure things new and old', to illustrate the great truths of God, man, and life.

[BOOK ONE: *Counsels on the Spiritual Life*] Here Thomas seeks firstly to wean the soul from preoccupation with solely material interests, successes and failures, and from dependence on its fellows, and to set before it the Christian teaching on life, on human nature, and on its essential need of God. He shows how, by winning control of our passions, and by overcoming conceit and complacency, we may, like S. Paul, become spiritual athletes, and enter upon the way of purgation, which is the first stage of the soul's progress towards its divinely appointed destiny of union with God. Sincere self-knowledge will bring the soul to a realization of its own nothingness and need of God. The humble following of Christ, and the power of His grace alone can transform our lives, 'for if you rely on your own reasoning and ability rather than on the transforming power of Jesus Christ, you will seldom and only slowly attain wisdom. For God wills that we become perfectly obedient to Him, and that we rise above cold reason on the wings of a burning love for Him.' The Book continues with counsels addressed primarily to Religious, but which are also of value to all who pursue perfection. It concludes by urging the disciple to complete the good work of purgation now begun and sets before him considerations on true contrition, on man's last end, on God's judgement of sinners and man's need of amendment.

[BOOK TWO: *On the Inner Life*] This sets forth the second stage of the spiritual life–the way of illumination–in which the disciple, having made some progress in self-conquest, is gradually illumined by the divine light of the knowledge of God. Here Thomas sets forth the Christian standards of value, spiritual and material: we are shown how the spiritual and eternal is to be prized above the material and transitory, 'for men soon change, but Christ abides for ever, and stands firmly by you to the end' (Ch. I). Through purity of heart and simplicity of purpose, man is raised and cleansed (Ch. 4); and by self-knowledge he is freed from the temptation to pass judgement on others (Ch. 5). The book continues, to speak of the wonders of the love of Jesus, and the glory of His friendship, that only His loved ones know (Chs. 7, 8): and shows that the only road to this desired consummation is that which Jesus Himself has revealed, the road of the Cross, so meaningless to the world, so powerful to the faithful pilgrim. Many fear to tread this hard road (Ch. II), which is the sole road to God. Yet 'See, how in the Cross all things rest, and how in dying upon it all things depend. There is no other way to life and true inner peace than the way of the Cross, and of daily self-denial: ... our merit and spiritual progress do not consist in enjoying great delight and consolation, but rather in the bearing of great burdens and troubles' (Ch. 12). But the love of Jesus will amply outweigh all sacrifices, and light the steep upward path.

[BOOK THREE: *On Inward Consolation*] In the third and longest book, Christ calls on the disciple to seek Him alone, and shows him the way of union and true peace. Aware of the perils that beset the steep ascent of the Mount of God, and seeing all things in their true light, the disciple is led to choose God as his true and only goal (Ch. 3). He is shown how, by the light of grace, he can gradually win free from the entanglements of the world, the flesh, and the devil, and come freely to Christ. In response, the disciple sings the joys and glories of the love of God, and prays: 'Deepen Your love in me, O Lord, that I may learn in my inmost heart how sweet it is to love, to be dissolved, and to plunge myself into Your love. Let Your love possess me, and raise me above myself with a fervour and wonder above all imagination. Let me sing the song of love. Let me follow You, my Beloved, into the heights. Let my soul spend itself in Your praise, rejoicing for love. . . .' (Ch. 5). There follow chapters of practical counsels on the Christian life: on the gradual conquest of self; on the divine virtues of love, obedience, patience, humility, and trust, which must be cultivated as the soul advances with God's help on the road towards perfection (Chs. 7-15). We are shown how holiness is not to be sought as an end in itself, but that we must rest in God alone above all other good, 'above all health and beauty, above all glory and honour, above all power and dignity, above all joy and gladness . . . and above all that is not Yourself, O my God' (Ch. 21). Christ then reveals (Ch. 23) four ways to obtain freedom and peace of spirit, 'the whole secret of perfection', and the disciple offers a most beautiful prayer for mental light. He is then shown (Ch. 25) how the true source of peace and progress rest 'in complete surrender of the heart to the will of God, not seeking to have one's own way either in great matters or small, in time or eternity'. Freedom of mind is not to be achieved by study so much as by prayer and direct contact with the Source of all light and life (Ch. 26). In the ensuing chapters the disciple is warned that obedience to Christ does not imply that he will be freed from sorrow, distraction, or temptation: rather will the Devil redouble his efforts to deter the spiritual athlete, who can expect no ease in this life, but is comforted by the assurance of final victory through perseverance and faith. 'Wait for the Lord: fight manfully and with high courage. Do not despair, do not desert your post; steadfastly devote yourself, body and soul, to the glory of God. I will give you a rich reward, and will be with you in all your troubles' (Ch. 35). The disciple cannot rely on his fellow men for help; God alone can order his affairs aright, and bring good out of ill. He must therefore fix his heart and mind on God in all and above all, as did the holy martyr Agatha, who cried, 'My mind is firmly established and grounded in Christ' (Ch. 45). The disciple is next shown how no evils that the ingenuity of the Devil or man can inflict have power to do real injury to the soul who trusts and lives wholly in Christ (Chs. 46, 47), and who looks steadfastly towards its heavenly home. Nor is the disciple to be overmuch concerned with success or failure, honour or dishonour; 'Let this be your constant desire, that whether in life or death, God may at all times be glorified in you' (Ch. 50). The only way to overcome the corruption of human nature is by self-discipline, that the power of grace may have full play in us; 'for grace is a supernatural light, and the special gift of God, the seal of His chosen, and the pledge of salvation, that raises man from earthly things to love the heavenly, and from being worldly, makes him spiritual. Therefore the more nature is controlled, the richer the graces bestowed' (Ch. 55). The Third Book concludes by urging the disciple to banish all discouragement (Ch. 57); to cultivate humility (Ch. 58); to avoid controversy; and to place his entire trust in God; 'for where You are, there is Heaven; and where You are not, there is Death and Hell. . . . You alone are the End of all good things, the fullness of life, and the depth of wisdom; and the greatest comfort of Your servants is to trust in You above all else' (Ch. 59).

[BOOK FOUR: *On the Blessed Sacrament*] This begins with 'A devout exhortation to Holy Communion', but does far more than encourage the faithful to regular and devout Communion. It deals also with the theological and historical background of the Eucharist, and shows this sacred rite to be the central sun around which all the worship and sacraments of the Church revolve. Here Thomas, true to the doctrine and experience of the Church, shows this sublime Sacrament to be both the effectual pleading of the sacrifice of Christ's death on the Cross, and the fulfilment of His last loving command at the Last Supper, and also the covenanted means of grace and unique act of Christian worship. In this Sacrament the Christian knows Christ Himself to be truly and actually present, hiding His glory beneath the simple forms of bread and wine. Here Christ pleads His sacrifice before the eternal Father: here His Church lifts up holy hands in sacrifice and intercession; here Christ feeds the faithful with His very Self, Body, Blood, Soul and Divinity. The altar is the vital link between God and man, heaven and earth, where angels and men join in adoration of the crucified and risen Christ.

Thomas therefore begins by emphasizing the simple and direct invitation of Christ to the faithful, who desire to have part in Him. He shows the prophetic nature of the ancient sacrifices of the Law, and the need of even greater devotion towards the Sacrament of Christ than that so amply displayed by the great kings and prophets towards the Ark, the Temple, and the sacrifices of old: 'for how great a difference is there between the Ark of the Covenant with its relics, and Your most holy Body with its ineffable powers; between the sacrifices of the old Law that foreshadowed the Sacrifice to come, and the true Victim of Your Body, which fulfils all the ancient rites' (Ch. I). The generosity, goodness, and condescension of God are richly shown in this Sacrament (Ch. 2), which is to be regularly and devoutly received, with a deep sense of unworthiness (Ch. 3). In Chapter 4, the disciple acknowledges his unworthiness, and prays for the transforming graces of this Sacrament. Chapter 5 is addressed in particular to priests, as guardians and dispensers of the Most Holy Sacrament, and calls on them to couple the supreme privilege and dignity of the priesthood with the highest possible standard of life and devotion, since 'a priest should be adorned with all virtues, and show an example of holy life to others . . . for when a priest celebrates the Eucharist, he honours God and gives joy to the Angels; he edifies the Church, aids the living, obtains rest for the departed, and makes himself a sharer in all good things.' Chapters 6 and 7 deal with preparation for Communion, which should include careful self-examination, confession, and sincere purpose of amendment. In Chapters 8 and 9, Christ calls on the disciple for complete surrender to the will of God: 'Naked I hung on the Cross with arms outstretched, offering Myself freely to God the Father for your sins, My whole Person a sacrifice to appease divine displeasure: you, also, must willingly offer yourself daily to Me in the Eucharist, with all your powers and affections as a pure and holy offering. . . . I do not seek your gifts, but yourself.' The disciple responds to this plea, asking pardon for his sins, and praying for the needs of the faithful: 'I offer to You whatever is good in me though it be little and imperfect, that You may strengthen and hallow it, make it dear and acceptable to You, and raise it continually towards perfection.' Christ then warns the disciple (Ch. 10) against the temptation to regard Holy Communion as reserved for the holy, since it is the fountain of grace and mercy for penitent sinners. In Chapters 11 and 12, the disciple speaks of his insatiable longing for God alone above all His gifts and graces, and for Christ as his heavenly food. I acknowledge my need of two things–food and light. You have therefore given me in my weakness Your sacred Body as the refreshment of my soul and body, and have set Your Word as a light to my feet. Without these two, I cannot rightly live; for the Word of God is the light of my soul, and Your Sacrament is the Breath of my life.' The disciple is filled with longing for Christ his Beloved (Ch. 13); he recalls the boundless love shown by other devout souls towards Christ in His Sacrament (Ch. 14); and grieves at the inadequacy of his love as compared with theirs. In Chapter 15, Christ reveals how this grace of devotion can be won by humility and self-denial, and is the gift of God alone. The disciple then makes renewed acts of love and desire for Christ (Ch. 16); and recalling the glorious lives of the Saints, cries (Ch. 17): 'Although I am not fit to enjoy such feelings of devotion as they, yet I offer You all the love in my heart . . . and whatever a pious heart can conceive or desire, that I offer You with all reverence and love.' The Book concludes with Christ warning the disciple against 'curious and unprofitable inquiries' into the manner of His Presence in this Sacrament, since 'God can do more than man can comprehend'. The requirements of God are 'faith and a holy life'. 'All reason and research must follow faith, but not precede or encroach upon it. For in this most holy and excellent Sacrament, faith and love precede all else, working in ways unknowable to man.' (pp. 14-20)

> *Leo Sherley-Price, in an introduction to* The Imitation of Christ *by Thomas à Kempis, translated by Leo Sherley-Price, Penguin Books, 1952, pp. 11-25.*

C. S. LEWIS (letter date 1961)

[*Lewis is considered one of the foremost twentieth-century authors to write on Christian and mythopoeic themes. Indebted principally to George MacDonald, G. K. Chesterton, Charles Williams, and the writers of ancient Norse myths, he is regarded as a formidable logician and Christian polemicist, a perceptive literary critic, and—perhaps most highly—as a writer of fantasy literature. Also a noted academic and scholar, Lewis held posts at Oxford and Cambridge, where he was a respected authority on medieval and Renaissance literature. Lewis was a traditionalist in his approach to life and art. He opposed the modern critical movement toward biographical and psychological interpretation, preferring to practice and propound a theory of criticism that stresses the author's intent rather than the reader's presuppositions and prejudices. During his life Lewis received letters from many of his readers, asking his advice on matters literary and spiritual. To one correspondent, a recent convert to Christianity who write to him in 1941, Lewis recommended* The Imitation *as a good source for daily devotional reading—along with Martin Luther's* Theologia Germanica, *the Psalms, and the New Testament. But in the following excerpt from a 1961 letter to his lifelong friend Arthur Greeves, he qualifies his regard for Thomas à Kempis's work.*]

My dear Arthur,

Yes. The *Imitation* is very severe; useful at times when one is tempted to be too easily satisfied with one's progress, but certainly not at times of discouragement. And of course it is written for monks, not for people living in the world like us.

A good book to balance it is Traherne's *Centuries of Meditations*, wh. I expect you know (*Not* to be confused with his poems, which I don't recommend.) There is all the gold & fragrance! (p. 560)

> *C. S. Lewis, in a letter to Arthur Greeves on November 12, 1961, in* They Stand Together: The Letters of C. S. Lewis to Arthur Greeves (1914-1963), *edited by Walter Hooper, Collins, 1979, pp. 560-61.*

MICHAEL NOVAK (essay date 1974)

[*Novak is a contemporary American educator and man of letters whose political and religious beliefs have spanned the spectrum from left to right. A respected Roman Catholic thinker whose early work included* A Theology for Radical Politics *(1969), Novak served on the staff of liberal Sen. George McGovern during the latter's unsussesful bid for the Presidency in 1972. Novak moved to the right during the mid-1970s. For a time during the late 1970s and early '80s he contributed a regular column on religion, "Tomorrow and Tomorrow," to the conservative periodical* National Review. *Currently Novak is the director of Social and Political Studies at the American Enterprise Institute and holder of the George Frederick Jewett Chair in Religion and Public Policy. In the following excerpt, he comments upon the enduring relevance of and spiritual challenge posed by* The Imitation.]

In 1952, when I was nineteen, I wrote in my copy of the *Imitation* that it contained everything necessary for becoming a saint; "and yet the hardest problems it leaves unanswered." Its relations to human society, to study, to activity, to affluence, and to entertainment troubled me then (according to my notes.)

Now that I am forty-one, my reflections take another tack. In 1952, it seemed good to break out from the monastic pattern, to enter into "the modern world." In 1974, it seems that the abnegation, the obedience, the insight that progress and the future are illusions, and the stress on suffering and death in à Kempis are invitations to break out from the contemporary pattern.

No illusions have a stronger grip upon our minds than those of the age in which we live—and not those of the common people, nor of the conventional wisdom, but those precisely of the most enlightened and intellectual critics of the decade. It is these, which, because more rare and more heroic, most commend themselves to seekers after truth; and those, as well, which—being most salient— later seem to date.

Thus, those who long to represent Catholicism at its best today, must, it seems, undergo two painful tests. We must test ourselves against the Catholicism of our forebears, like à Kempis. We tend to disdain them. But did they see reality more unflinchingly than we?

Secondly, we must, like them, diagnose the exact "spirit of our age"—and detach ourselves from it. We are not saved by progressive notions, nor by patriotic notions. We are not saved by ethnicity, nor by liberation, nor by radical witness, nor by any of the other "options" we so tightly cherish.

> Run hither or thither, thou wilt find no rest but in humble subjection under the government of a superior.
>
> A fancy for places and changing of residence has deluded many.
>
> It is true, everyone is desirous of acting according to his own way of thinking, and is most inclined to such as agree with him in opinion. . . .
>
> Who is so wise, as to be able fully to know all things?

These are not words to flatter us. Many of these words are hard. Many sentences in this book clash against everything our present civilization teaches us. Is that their purpose? They were also hard in the fifteenth century. (p. 169)

> Michael Novak, "Man for Our Time?" in Commonweal, Vol. CI, No. 6, November 15, 1974, pp. 168-70.

LAWRENCE S. CUNNINGHAM (essay date 1977)

[*Cunningham is an American educator, translator, and essayist who has written prodigiously on Roman Catholic themes and concerns. He is the author of the Twayne study* St. Francis of Assisi *(1976) and* The Catholic Heritage: Martyrs, Ascetics, Pilgrims, Warriors, Mystics, Theologians, Artists, Humanists, Activists, Outsiders, and Saints *(1983). In the following excerpt, Cunningham offers an introductory interpretation of the meaning and importance of* The Imitation.]

As a literary remain, the *Imitation* presents us with a series of problems and precious little positive information about its origins. . . . At the age of 19 Thomas of Kempis entered the Augustinian monastery at Zwolle and lived there for 66 years, dying in 1471 at the age of 90. We know also that Thomas studied in the classrooms of the Brethren of the Common Life, so we can deduce that he was in close contact with the *devotio moderna* then gaining the attention and allegiance of many. In fact the spirit of the *devotio moderna*, with its emphasis on ethics, interior piety, individual perfection and evangelical conformity, suffuses much of the *Imitation*.

The *Imitation* as a literary unity presents its own problems. Does it have unity as a single work, or are its four parts actually quite distinct treatises bound together under a single title? The preponderance of scholarly evidence would argue for the distinct nature of the treatises later put into a single volume as the collected works of one author.

Scholarly debates about the unity of the *Imitation* need not detain us here. It is the character of the *Imitation* as a devotional work that should focus our attention. First, it appears clear to the casual reader that the *Imitation* reflects a good deal of open criticism of the conventional religion of the day. There is a distrust of the theological work of the schoolmen: "I would rather feel contrition than know how to define it," the first chapter declares,

while a later chapter on the doctrine of truth asks rhetorically: "What matter is it to us of genera and species?"—thus dismissing the obsession with Aristotelian categories so much loved in that time.

While the *Imitation* has this strong streak of anti-intellectualism, the turn from the intellectual component of religion was not mere obscurantism but a desire to exalt affective knowledge, to heal what a later writer in another context would call the "dissociation of sensibility." Learning, in the technical sense of acquiring knowledge, was not an end in itself for Thomas; it was a method to get closer to God. This spirit of learning is best summed up in the title of LeClerc's great study of monastic learning: *The Love of Learning and the Desire for God*. Intellectual activity was to be oriented to seeking the Source of Truth: "Let not the authority of the author be in thy way, whether he be of great or little learning; but let love of simple truth lead thee to read."

Closely allied with this attitude of intellectual simplicity is the notion of withdrawal and retirement from the world. This emphasis can be explained partially in that the *Imitation* is primarily addressed to those who lived the conventual life of monasticism; indeed, some chapters explicitly treat the question of living under a religious rule or in a house of spiritual formation. Beyond that, however, is an attitude typical of the *devotio moderna*: a profound sense of disquiet with the highly externalized and ritualized life of late medieval religion. Thomas à Kempis completely endorsed the ancient ascetical dictum that as often as one went abroad among men, one returned less a man. He expressed this in a series of paradoxes: "No man can safely appear in public except he who loves seclusion. No man can safely speak except he who loves silence. . . . No man can be a superior but he who obeys well." And so on.

This all may be a bit much for the modern temper. It is unlikely that many people would endorse Matthew Arnold's observation that the *Imitation* is the "most exquisite document in Christendom after the New Testament." Still, the somewhat individualistic and dour nature of the *Imitation*'s author should not prejudice the reader against its considerable merits. It is a book quite free of sentimentality; at times it expresses basic religious truth with the economy of an aphorism, while at other moments it can reach for a poetic horizon.

Beyond that, it is a book not only of devotion but written in devotion. The author speaks not only to the reader but to God. There are many direct, simple, eloquent and scriptural prayers in the text that make it a *vade mecum* of spirituality. With a certain degree of discernment even today's reader can see how well Thomas has opened "before thee the pleasant field of the scriptures that thy heart may be enlarged so thou canst run in the way of Christ's commandments."

> Lawrence S. Cunningham, "Thomas à Kempis: 'The Imitation of Christ'," in The Christian Century, Vol. XCIV, No. 10, March 23, 1977, p. 270.

WILLIAM J. PETERSEN (essay date 1982)

[*Petersen is an American biographer of prominent Western Christians. He has demonstrated a particular interest in the married lives of his subjects, publishing such works as* Martin Luther Had a Wife *(1983),* C. S. Lewis Had a Wife *(1985), and* Catherine Marshall Had a Husband *(1987). In the following excerpt from a 1982 edition of* The Imitation, *he praises the work's value as a guide to the Christian life and speculates about the reasons for its popularity.*]

Of the Imitation of Christ has been described as "the most influential book in Christian literature." It has been translated into more than fifty languages. Few books have found such universal acceptance among both Protestants and Catholics. Perhaps because its language is very simple and forcefully direct. Or because Scripture is woven so intricately into every page. One scholar claims that more than a thousand Bible passages are alluded to in the text.

Or it may be so popular because of such quotations as "God takes into account not so much the thing we do as the love that went to the doing of it." At any rate, this powerful little book has become part of the lives of millions who refer to it constantly for guidance, consolation, spiritual strength and inspiration. (p. xvii)

> *William J. Petersen, in an introduction to* Of the Imitation of Christ *by Thomas à Kempis, Keats Publishing, Inc., 1982, pp. xv-xvii.*

ADDITIONAL BIBLIOGRAPHY

Fitzgerald, Percy. "The Worldly Wisdom of Thomas à Kempis." *The Dublin Review* 142, No. 285 (April 1908): 262-77.
  Illustrates nuggets of practical wisdom in *The Imitation,* comparing Thomas's dictums with those of Thomas Carlyle and Samuel Johnson.

Hopkins, Frederick M. "A Saint and His Immortal Book." *The Publishers' Weekly* CXVIII, No. 20 (15 November 1930): 2288-90.

Catalogues many early editions of *The Imitation* and provides a short historical overview of critical praise of the work.

Hyma, Albert, ed. Introduction to *The Imitation of Christ,* by Thomas à Kempis, pp. vii-xxxviii. New York: Century Co., 1927.
  Textual examination that determines that *The Imitation* "contains the teachings of [Gerard] Groote in the same way as the four Gospels in the New Testament contain the sayings of Jesus of Nazareth." According to Hyma, Thomas was one of several authors of the famous work commonly ascribed to him and was certainly the compiler and transcriber of it.

Jones, Rufus M. "A Great Spiritual Diary." *The Commonweal* XXVI, No. 8 (18 June 1937): 210-11.
  Credits Thomas not as the author but as the editor of *The Imitation,* a work composed, according to Jones, by Gerard Groote.

Pick, Bernhard. "Thomas à Kempis as Hymnographer." *The Open Court* XXVIII, No. 697 (June 1914): 376-79.
  Identifies 17 anonymous hymns written by Thomas.

Rix, H. "Luther's Debt to the *Imitatio.*" *Augustiniana* 28 (1978): 91-107.
  Demonstrates that Martin Luther was familiar with *The Imitation,* drawing upon parallel passages in Luther's writings for evidence.

Sebouhian, George. "Thomas à Kempis and Emerson's First Crisis." *American Transcendental Quarterly,* No. 31, Part I (Summer 1976): 2-5
  Illuminates Ralph Waldo Emerson's references to *The Imitation* in the sermons he wrote early in his career, especially those composed around the time of his wife's death.

Young, William J., S. J. "The Imitation of Christ." In *Masterpieces of Catholic Literature in Summary Form: Vol. 1—c. 90 to 1613,* edited by Frank N. Magill, pp. 491-94. New York: Salem Press, 1965.
  Brief biography of Thomas and discursive survey of the four books of *The Imitation.*

Literature
Criticism from
1400 to 1800
Cumulative Indexes

This Index Includes References to Entries in These Gale Series

Contemporary Literary Criticism

Presents excerpts of criticism on the works of novelists, poets, dramatists, short story writers, scriptwriters, and other creative writers who are now living or who have died since 1960. Cumulative indexes to authors and nationalities are included, as well as an index to titles discussed in the individual volume. Volumes 1-54 are in print.

Twentieth-Century Literary Criticism

Contains critical excerpts by the most significant commentators on poets, novelists, short story writers, dramatists, and philosophers who died between 1900 and 1960. Cumulative indexes to authors, nationalities, and titles discussed are included in each new volume. Volumes 1-33 are in print.

Nineteenth-Century Literature Criticism

Offers significant passages from criticism on authors who died between 1800 and 1899. Cumulative indexes to authors, nationalities, and titles discussed are included in each new volume. Volumes 1-22 are in print.

Literature Criticism from 1400 to 1800

Compiles significant passages from the most noteworthy criticism on authors of the fifteenth through eighteenth centuries. Cumulative indexes to authors, nationalities, and titles discussed are included in each new volume. Volumes 1-11 are in print.

Classical and Medieval Literature Criticism

Offers excerpts of criticism on the works of world authors from classical antiquity through the fourteenth century. Cumulative indexes to authors, titles, and critics are included in each volume. Volumes 1-3 are in print.

Short Story Criticism

Compiles excerpts of criticism on short fiction by writers of all eras and nationalities. Cumulative indexes to authors, nationalities, and titles discussed are included in each new volume. Volumes 1-3 are in print.

Children's Literature Review

Includes excerpts from reviews, criticism, and commentary on works of authors and illustrators who create books for children. Cumulative indexes to authors, nationalities, and titles discussed are included in each new volume. Volumes 1-18 are in print.

Contemporary Authors Series

Encompasses five related series. *Contemporary Authors* provides biographical and bibliographical information on more than 90,000 writers of fiction, nonfiction, poetry, journalism, drama, motion pictures, and other fields. Each new volume contains sketches on authors not previously covered in the series. Volumes 1-127 are in print. *Contemporary Authors New Revision Series* provides completely updated information on active authors covered in previously published volumes of *CA*. Only entries requiring significant change are revised for *CA New Revision Series*. Volumes 1-24 are in print. *Contemporary Authors Permanent Series* consists of updated listings for deceased and inactive authors removed from the original volumes 9-36 when these volumes were revised. Volumes 1-2 are in print. *Contemporary Authors Autobiography Series* presents specially commissioned autobiographies by leading contemporary writers. Volumes 1-9 are in print. *Contemporary Authors Bibliographical Series* contains primary and secondary bibliographies as well as analytical bibliographical essays by authorities on major modern authors. Volumes 1-2 are in print.

Dictionary of Literary Biography

Encompasses three related series. *Dictionary of Literary Biography* furnishes illustrated overviews of authors' lives and works and places them in the larger perspective of literary history. Volumes 1-84 are in print. *Dictionary of Literary Biography Documentary Series* illuminates the careers of major figures through a selection of literary documents, including letters, notebook and diary entries, interviews, book reviews, and photographs. Volumes 1-6 are in print. *Dictionary of Literary Biography Yearbook* summarizes the past year's literary activity with articles on genres, major prizes, conferences, and other timely subjects and includes updated and new entries on individual authors. Yearbooks for 1980-1988 are in print. A cumulative index to authors and articles is included in each new volume.

Concise Dictionary of American Literary Biography

A six-volume series that collects revised and updated sketches on major American authors that were originally presented in *Dictionary of Literary Biography*. Volumes 1-3 are in print.

Something about the Author Series

Encompasses two related series. *Something about the Author* contains heavily illustrated biographical sketches on juvenile and young adult authors and illustrators from all eras. Volumes 1-56 are in print. *Something about the Author Autobiography Series* presents specially commissioned autobiographies by prominent authors and illustrators of books for children and young adults. Volumes 1-8 are in print.

Yesterday's Authors of Books for Children

Contains heavily illustrated entries on children's writers who died before 1961. Complete in two volumes. Volumes 1-2 are in print.

Literary Criticism Series
Cumulative Author Index

This index lists all author entries in the Gale Literary Criticism Series and includes cross-references to other Gale sources. References in the index are identified as follows:

AAYA: *Authors & Artists for Young Adults,* Volume 1
CAAS: *Contemporary Authors Autobiography Series,* Volumes 1-9
CA: *Contemporary Authors* (original series), Volumes 1-127
CABS: *Contemporary Authors Bibliographical Series,* Volumes 1-2
CANR: *Contemporary Authors New Revision Series,* Volumes 1-27
CAP: *Contemporary Authors Permanent Series,* Volumes 1-2
CA-R: *Contemporary Authors* (revised editions), Volumes 1-44
CDALB: *Concise Dictionary of American Literary Biography,* Volume 1-3
CLC: *Contemporary Literary Criticism,* Volumes 1-54
CLR: *Children's Literature Review,* Volumes 1-18
CMLC: *Classical and Medieval Literature Criticism,* Volumes 1-3
DLB: *Dictionary of Literary Biography,* Volumes 1-84
DLB-DS: *Dictionary of Literary Biography Documentary Series,* Volumes 1-6
DLB-Y: *Dictionary of Literary Biography Yearbook,* Volumes 1980-1988
LC: *Literature Criticism from 1400 to 1800,* Volumes 1-11
NCLC: *Nineteenth-Century Literature Criticism,* Volumes 1-22
SAAS: *Something about the Author Autobiography Series,* Volumes 1-8
SATA: *Something about the Author,* Volumes 1-56
SSC: *Short Story Criticism,* Volumes 1-3
TCLC: *Twentieth-Century Literary Criticism,* Volumes 1-33
YABC: *Yesterday's Authors of Books for Children,* Volumes 1-2

Aragon, Louis 1897-1982 .... **CLC 3, 22**
See also CA 69-72; obituary CA 108;
DLB 72

Arbuthnot, John 1667-1735 ...... **LC 1**

Archer, Jeffrey (Howard)
1940- .... **CLC 28**
See also CANR 22; CA 77-80

Archer, Jules 1915- .... **CLC 12**
See also CANR 6; CA 9-12R; SATA 4

Arden, John 1930- ...... **CLC 6, 13, 15**
See also CAAS 4; CA 13-16R; DLB 13

Arenas, Reinaldo 1943- ...... **CLC 41**

Arguedas, Jose Maria
1911-1969 .... **CLC 10, 18**
See also CA 89-92

Argueta, Manlio 1936- .... **CLC 31**

Ariosto, Ludovico 1474-1533 .... **LC 6**

Arlt, Roberto 1900-1942 ...... **TCLC 29**
See also CA 123

Armah, Ayi Kwei 1939- .... **CLC 5, 33**
See also CANR 21; CA 61-64

Armatrading, Joan 1950- ...... **CLC 17**
See also CA 114

Arnim, Achim von (Ludwig Joachim von
Arnim) 1781-1831 .... **NCLC 5**

Arnold, Matthew 1822-1888 .. **NCLC 6**
See also DLB 32, 57

Arnold, Thomas 1795-1842 .... **NCLC 18**
See also DLB 55

Arnow, Harriette (Louisa Simpson)
1908-1986 .... **CLC 2, 7, 18**
See also CANR 14; CA 9-12R;
obituary CA 118; SATA 42, 47;
DLB 6

Arp, Jean 1887-1966 .... **CLC 5**
See also CA 81-84; obituary CA 25-28R

Arquette, Lois S(teinmetz) 1934-
See Duncan (Steinmetz Arquette), Lois
See also SATA 1

Arrabal, Fernando 1932- .. **CLC 2, 9, 18**
See also CANR 15; CA 9-12R

Arrick, Fran 19??- .... **CLC 30**

Artaud, Antonin 1896-1948 .... **TCLC 3**
See also CA 104

Arthur, Ruth M(abel)
1905-1979 .... **CLC 12**
See also CANR 4; CA 9-12R;
obituary CA 85-88; SATA 7;
obituary SATA 26

Artsybashev, Mikhail Petrarch
1878-1927 .... **TCLC 31**

Arundel, Honor (Morfydd)
1919-1973 .... **CLC 17**
See also CAP 2; CA 21-22;
obituary CA 41-44R; SATA 4;
obituary SATA 24

Asch, Sholem 1880-1957 ...... **TCLC 3**
See also CA 105

Ashbery, John (Lawrence) 1927- .. **CLC 2,
3, 4, 6, 9, 13, 15, 25, 41**
See also CANR 9; CA 5-8R; DLB 5;
DLB-Y 81

Ashton-Warner, Sylvia (Constance)
1908-1984 .... **CLC 19**
See also CA 69-72; obituary CA 112

Asimov, Isaac 1920- ..CLC **1, 3, 9, 19, 26**
See also CLR 12; CANR 2, 19;
CA 1-4R; SATA 1, 26; DLB 8

Astley, Thea (Beatrice May)
1925- .... **CLC 41**
See also CANR 11; CA 65-68

Aston, James 1906-1964
See White, T(erence) H(anbury)

Asturias, Miguel Angel
1899-1974 .... **CLC 3, 8, 13**
See also CAP 2; CA 25-28;
obituary CA 49-52

Atheling, William, Jr. 1921-1975
See Blish, James (Benjamin)

Atherton, Gertrude (Franklin Horn)
1857-1948 .... **TCLC 2**
See also CA 104; DLB 9

Atwood, Margaret (Eleanor)
1939- .... **CLC 2, 3, 4, 8, 13, 15, 25,
44; SSC 2**
See also CANR 3; CA 49-52; DLB 53

Aubin, Penelope 1685-1731? .... **LC 9**
See also DLB 39

Auchincloss, Louis (Stanton)
1917- ....**CLC 4, 6, 9, 18, 45**
See also CANR 6; CA 1-4R; DLB 2;
DLB-Y 80

Auden, W(ystan) H(ugh)
1907-1973 ..CLC **1, 2, 3, 4, 6, 9, 11,
14, 43**
See also CANR 5; CA 9-12R;
obituary CA 45-48; DLB 10, 20

Audiberti, Jacques 1899-1965 .. **CLC 38**
See also obituary CA 25-28R

Auel, Jean M(arie) 1936- ...... **CLC 31**
See also CANR 21; CA 103

Austen, Jane 1775-1817 .. **NCLC 1, 13,
19**

Auster, Paul 1947- .... **CLC 47**
See also CA 69-72

Austin, Mary (Hunter)
1868-1934 .... **TCLC 25**
See also CA 109; DLB 9

Avison, Margaret 1918- ...... **CLC 2, 4**
See also CA 17-20R; DLB 53

Ayckbourn, Alan 1939-..CLC **5, 8, 18, 33**
See also CA 21-24R; DLB 13

Aydy, Catherine 1937-
See Tennant, Emma

Ayme, Marcel (Andre)
1902-1967 .... **CLC 11**
See also CA 89-92; DLB 72

Ayrton, Michael 1921-1975 ...... **CLC 7**
See also CANR 9, 21; CA 5-8R;
obituary CA 61-64

Azorin 1874-1967 .... **CLC 11**
See also Martinez Ruiz, Jose

Azuela, Mariano 1873-1952 ...... **TCLC 3**
See also CA 104

"Bab" 1836-1911
See Gilbert, (Sir) W(illiam) S(chwenck)

Babel, Isaak (Emmanuilovich)
1894-1941 .... **TCLC 2, 13**
See also CA 104

Babits, Mihaly 1883-1941 .... **TCLC 14**
See also CA 114

Bacchelli, Riccardo 1891-1985 .. **CLC 19**
See also CA 29-32R; obituary CA 117

Bach, Richard (David) 1936- .. **CLC 14**
See also CANR 18; CA 9-12R;
SATA 13

Bachman, Richard 1947-
See King, Stephen (Edwin)

Bacovia, George 1881-1957 .... **TCLC 24**

Bagehot, Walter 1826-1877 .... **NCLC 10**
See also DLB 55

Bagnold, Enid 1889-1981 ...... **CLC 25**
See also CANR 5; CA 5-8R;
obituary CA 103; SATA 1, 25;
DLB 13

Bagryana, Elisaveta 1893- .... **CLC 10**

Bailey, Paul 1937- .... **CLC 45**
See also CANR 16; CA 21-24R;
DLB 14

Baillie, Joanna 1762-1851 .... **NCLC 2**

Bainbridge, Beryl 1933- .. **CLC 4, 5, 8,
10, 14, 18, 22**
See also CA 21-24R; DLB 14

Baker, Elliott 1922- .... **CLC 8**
See also CANR 2; CA 45-48

Baker, Russell (Wayne) 1925- .. **CLC 31**
See also CANR 11; CA 57-60

Bakshi, Ralph 1938- .... **CLC 26**
See also CA 112

Baldwin, James (Arthur)
1924-1987 ..CLC **1, 2, 3, 4, 5, 8, 13,
15, 17, 42, 50**
See also CANR 3; CA 1-4R; CABS 1;
SATA 9; DLB 2, 7, 33;
CDALB 1941-1968

Ballard, J(ames) G(raham)
1930- .... **CLC 3, 6, 14, 36; SSC 1**
See also CANR 15; CA 5-8R; DLB 14

Balmont, Konstantin Dmitriyevich
1867-1943 .... **TCLC 11**
See also CA 109

Balzac, Honore de 1799-1850 .. **NCLC 5**

Bambara, Toni Cade 1939- .... **CLC 19**
See also CA 29-32R; DLB 38

Banim, John 1798-1842 and Banim,
Michael 1798-1842 ...... **NCLC 13**

Banim, John 1798-1842
See Banim, John and Banim, Michael

Banim, Michael 1796-1874
See Banim, John and Banim, Michael

Banim, Michael 1796-1874 and Banim,
John 1796-1874
See Banim, John and Banim, Michael

Banks, Iain 1954- .... **CLC 34**

Banks, Lynne Reid 1929- ...... **CLC 23**
See also Reid Banks, Lynne

Banks, Russell 1940- .... **CLC 37**
See also CANR 19; CA 65-68

Banville, John 1945- .... **CLC 46**
See also CA 117; DLB 14

Banville, Theodore (Faullain) de
1832-1891 .... **NCLC 9**

Baraka, Amiri 1934-.. **CLC 1, 2, 3, 5, 10,
14, 33**
See also Baraka, Imamu Amiri; Jones,
(Everett) LeRoi
See also DLB 5, 7, 16, 38

Benedikt, Michael 1935- .... **CLC 4, 14**
See also CANR 7; CA 13-16R; DLB 5

Benet, Juan 1927- .... **CLC 28**

Benet, Stephen Vincent
    1898-1943 .... **TCLC 7**
See also YABC 1; CA 104; DLB 4, 48

Benet, William Rose
    1886-1950 .... **TCLC 28**
See also CA 118; DLB 45

Benford, Gregory (Albert)
    1941- .... **CLC 52**
See also CANR 12, 24; CA 69-72;
    DLB-Y 82

Benn, Gottfried 1886-1956 .... **TCLC 3**
See also CA 106; DLB 56

Bennett, Alan 1934- .... **CLC 45**
See also CA 103

Bennett, (Enoch) Arnold
    1867-1931 .... **TCLC 5, 20**
See also CA 106; DLB 10, 34

Bennett, George Harold 1930-
See Bennett, Hal
See also CA 97-100

Bennett, Hal 1930- .... **CLC 5**
See also Bennett, George Harold
See also DLB 33

Bennett, Jay 1912- .... **CLC 35**
See also CANR 11; CA 69-72; SAAS 4;
    SATA 27, 41

Bennett, Louise (Simone)
    1919- .... **CLC 28**
See also Bennett-Coverly, Louise
    Simone

Bennett-Coverly, Louise Simone 1919-
See Bennett, Louise (Simone)
See also CA 97-100

Benson, E(dward) F(rederic)
    1867-1940 .... **TCLC 27**
See also CA 114

Benson, Jackson J. 1930- .... **CLC 34**
See also CA 25-28R

Benson, Sally 1900-1972 ...... **CLC 17**
See also CAP 1; CA 19-20;
    obituary CA 37-40R; SATA 1, 35;
    obituary SATA 27

Benson, Stella 1892-1933 ...... **TCLC 17**
See also CA 117; DLB 36

Bentley, E(dmund) C(lerihew)
    1875-1956 .... **TCLC 12**
See also CA 108; DLB 70

Bentley, Eric (Russell) 1916- .. **CLC 24**
See also CANR 6; CA 5-8R

Berger, John (Peter) 1926- .. **CLC 2, 19**
See also CA 81-84; DLB 14

Berger, Melvin (H.) 1927- .... **CLC 12**
See also CANR 4; CA 5-8R; SAAS 2;
    SATA 5

Berger, Thomas (Louis) 1924- .... **CLC 3, 5, 8, 11, 18, 38**
See also CANR 5; CA 1-4R; DLB 2;
    DLB-Y 80

Bergman, (Ernst) Ingmar
    1918- .... **CLC 16**
See also CA 81-84

Bergson, Henri 1859-1941 .... **TCLC 32**

Bergstein, Eleanor 1938- .... **CLC 4**
See also CANR 5; CA 53-56

Berkoff, Steven 1937- .... **CLC 56**
See also CA 104

Bermant, Chaim 1929- .... **CLC 40**
See also CANR 6; CA 57-60

Bernanos, (Paul Louis) Georges
    1888-1948 .... **TCLC 3**
See also CA 104; DLB 72

Bernhard, Thomas 1931- .... **CLC 3, 32**
See also CA 85-88

Berriault, Gina 1926- .... **CLC 54**
See also CA 116

Berrigan, Daniel J. 1921- ..... **CLC 4**
See also CAAS 1; CANR 11;
    CA 33-36R; DLB 5

Berrigan, Edmund Joseph Michael, Jr.
    1934-1983
See Berrigan, Ted
See also CANR 14; CA 61-64;
    obituary CA 110

Berrigan, Ted 1934-1983 ...... **CLC 37**
See also Berrigan, Edmund Joseph
    Michael, Jr.
See also DLB 5

Berry, Chuck 1926- .... **CLC 17**

Berry, Wendell (Erdman) 1934- .. **CLC 4, 6, 8, 27, 46**
See also CA 73-76; DLB 5, 6

Berryman, Jerry 1914-1972
See also CDALB 1941-1968

Berryman, John 1914-1972 .. **CLC 1, 2, 3, 4, 6, 8, 10, 13, 25**
See also CAP 1; CA 15-16;
    obituary CA 33-36R; CABS 2;
    DLB 48; CDALB 1941-1968

Bertolucci, Bernardo 1940- ..... **CLC 16**
See also CA 106

Besant, Annie (Wood)
    1847-1933 .... **TCLC 9**
See also CA 105

Bessie, Alvah 1904-1985 ...... **CLC 23**
See also CANR 2; CA 5-8R;
    obituary CA 116; DLB 26

Beti, Mongo 1932- .... **CLC 27**
See also Beyidi, Alexandre

Betjeman, (Sir) John 1906-1984 .. **CLC 2, 6, 10, 34, 43**
See also CA 9-12R; obituary CA 112;
    DLB 20; DLB-Y 84

Betti, Ugo 1892-1953 .... **TCLC 5**
See also CA 104

Betts, Doris (Waugh) 1932- .. **CLC 3, 6, 28**
See also CANR 9; CA 13-16R;
    DLB-Y 82

Bialik, Chaim Nachman
    1873-1934 .... **TCLC 25**

Bidart, Frank 19??- .... **CLC 33**

Bienek, Horst 1930- .... **CLC 7, 11**
See also CA 73-76

Bierce, Ambrose (Gwinett)
    1842-1914? .... **TCLC 1, 7**
See also CA 104; DLB 11, 12, 23, 71;
    CDALB 1865-1917

Billington, Rachel 1942- ...... **CLC 43**
See also CA 33-36R

Binyon, T(imothy) J(ohn)
    1936- .... **CLC 34**
See also CA 111

Bioy Casares, Adolfo 1914- .. **CLC 4, 8, 13**
See also CANR 19; CA 29-32R

Bird, Robert Montgomery
    1806-1854 .... **NCLC 1**

Birdwell, Cleo 1936-
See DeLillo, Don

Birney (Alfred) Earle 1904- .. **CLC 1, 4, 6, 11**
See also CANR 5, 20; CA 1-4R

Bishop, Elizabeth 1911-1979 ....**CLC 1, 4, 9, 13, 15, 32**
See also CA 5-8R; obituary CA 89-92;
    CABS 2; obituary SATA 24; DLB 5

Bishop, John 1935- .... **CLC 10**
See also CA 105

Bissett, Bill 1939- .... **CLC 18**
See also CANR 15; CA 69-72; DLB 53

Biyidi, Alexandre 1932-
See Beti, Mongo
See also CA 114

Bjornson, Bjornstjerne (Martinius)
    1832-1910 .... **TCLC 7**
See also CA 104

Blackburn, Paul 1926-1971 .. **CLC 9, 43**
See also CA 81-84;
    obituary CA 33-36R; DLB 16;
    DLB-Y 81

Black Elk 1863-1950 .... **TCLC 33**

Blackmore, R(ichard) D(oddridge)
    1825-1900 .... **TCLC 27**
See also CA 120; DLB 18

Blackmur, R(ichard) P(almer)
    1904-1965 .... **CLC 2, 24**
See also CAP 1; CA 11-12;
    obituary CA 25-28R; DLB 63

Blackwood, Algernon (Henry)
    1869-1951 .... **TCLC 5**
See also CA 105

Blackwood, Caroline 1931- .... **CLC 6, 9**
See also CA 85-88; DLB 14

Blair, Eric Arthur 1903-1950
See Orwell, George
See also CA 104; SATA 29

Blais, Marie-Claire 1939- .. **CLC 2, 4, 6, 13, 22**
See also CAAS 4; CA 21-24R; DLB 53

Blaise, Clark 1940- .... **CLC 29**
See also CAAS 3; CANR 5;
    CA 53-56R; DLB 53

Blake, Nicholas 1904-1972
See Day Lewis, C(ecil)

Blake, William 1757-1827 .... **NCLC 13**
See also SATA 30

Blasco Ibanez, Vicente
    1867-1928 .... **TCLC 12**
See also CA 110

Blatty, William Peter 1928- ...... **CLC 2**
See also CANR 9; CA 5-8R

Blessing, Lee 1949- .... **CLC 54**

Blish, James (Benjamin)
    1921-1975 .... **CLC 14**
See also CANR 3; CA 1-4R;
    obituary CA 57-60; DLB 8

Blixen, Karen (Christentze Dinesen)
    1885-1962
See Dinesen, Isak
See also CAP 2; CA 25-28; SATA 44

Author Index

Brecht, (Eugen) Bertolt (Friedrich)
    1898-1956 .... **TCLC 1, 6, 13**
    See also CA 104; DLB 56

Bremer, Fredrika 1801-1865 .. **NCLC 11**

Brennan, Christopher John
    1870-1932 .... **TCLC 17**
    See also CA 117

Brennan, Maeve 1917- .... **CLC 5**
    See also CA 81-84

Brentano, Clemens (Maria)
    1778-1842 .... **NCLC 1**

Brenton, Howard 1942- ...... **CLC 31**
    See also CA 69-72; DLB 13

Breslin, James 1930-
    See Breslin, Jimmy
    See also CA 73-76

Breslin, Jimmy 1930- ...... **CLC 4, 43**
    See also Breslin, James

Bresson, Robert 1907- .... **CLC 16**
    See also CA 110

Breton, Andre 1896-1966 .. **CLC 2, 9, 15,**
                                              54

    See also CAP 2; CA 19-20;
        obituary CA 25-28R; DLB 65

Breytenbach, Breyten 1939- .. **CLC 23, 37**
    See also CA 113

Bridgers, Sue Ellen 1942- .... **CLC 26**
    See also CANR 11; CA 65-68; SAAS 1;
        SATA 22; DLB 52

Bridges, Robert 1844-1930 .... **TCLC 1**
    See also CA 104; DLB 19

Bridie, James 1888-1951 ...... **TCLC 3**
    See also Mavor, Osborne Henry
    See also DLB 10

Brin, David 1950- .... **CLC 34**
    See also CA 102

Brink, Andre (Philippus)
    1935- .... **CLC 18, 36**
    See also CA 104

Brinsmead, H(esba) F(ay)
    1922- .... **CLC 21**
    See also CANR 10; CA 21-24R;
        SATA 18

Brittain, Vera (Mary)
    1893?-1970 .... **CLC 23**
    See also CAP 1; CA 15-16;
        obituary CA 25-28R

Broch, Hermann 1886-1951 .... **TCLC 20**
    See also CA 117

Brock, Rose 1923-
    See Hansen, Joseph

Brodkey, Harold 1930- .... **CLC 56**
    See also CA 111

Brodsky, Iosif Alexandrovich 1940-
    See Brodsky, Joseph (Alexandrovich)
    See also CA 41-44R

Brodsky, Joseph (Alexandrovich)
    1940- .... **CLC 4, 6, 13, 36, 50**
    See also Brodsky, Iosif Alexandrovich

Brodsky, Michael (Mark)
    1948- .... **CLC 19**
    See also CANR 18; CA 102

Bromell, Henry 1947- .... **CLC 5**
    See also CANR 9; CA 53-56

Bromfield, Louis (Brucker)
    1896-1956 .... **TCLC 11**
    See also CA 107; DLB 4, 9

Broner, E(sther) M(asserman)
    1930- .... **CLC 19**
    See also CANR 8; CA 17-20R; DLB 28

Bronk, William 1918- .... **CLC 10**
    See also CA 89-92

Bronte, Anne 1820-1849 ...... **NCLC 4**
    See also DLB 21

Bronte, Charlotte 1816-1855 .. **NCLC 3,**
                                                8

    See also DLB 21

Bronte, (Jane) Emily
    1818-1848 .... **NCLC 16**
    See also DLB 21, 32

Brooke, Frances 1724-1789 ...... **LC 6**
    See also DLB 39

Brooke, Henry 1703?-1783 ...... **LC 1**
    See also DLB 39

Brooke, Rupert (Chawner)
    1887-1915 .... **TCLC 2, 7**
    See also CA 104; DLB 19

Brooke-Rose, Christine 1926- .. **CLC 40**
    See also CA 13-16R; DLB 14

Brookner, Anita 1928- .. **CLC 32, 34, 51**
    See also CA 114, 120; DLB-Y 87

Brooks, Cleanth 1906- .... **CLC 24**
    See also CA 17-20R; DLB 63

Brooks, Gwendolyn 1917-.. **CLC 1, 2, 4,**
                                              5, 15, 49
    See also CANR 1; CA 1-4R; SATA 6;
        DLB 5; CDALB 1941-1968

Brooks, Mel 1926- .... **CLC 12**
    See also Kaminsky, Melvin
    See also CA 65-68; DLB 26

Brooks, Peter 1938- .... **CLC 34**
    See also CANR 1; CA 45-48

Brooks, Van Wyck 1886-1963 .. **CLC 29**
    See also CANR 6; CA 1-4R; DLB 45,
        63

Brophy, Brigid (Antonia) 1929- ..**CLC 6,**
                                                11, 29
    See also CAAS 4; CA 5-8R; DLB 14

Brosman, Catharine Savage
    1934- .... **CLC 9**
    See also CANR 21; CA 61-64

Broughton, T(homas) Alan
    1936- .... **CLC 19**
    See also CANR 2; CA 45-48

Broumas, Olga 1949- .... **CLC 10**
    See also CANR 20; CA 85-88

Brown, Charles Brockden
    1771-1810 .... **NCLC 22**
    See also DLB 37, 59;
        CDALB 1640-1865

Brown, Claude 1937- .... **CLC 30**
    See also CA 73-76

Brown, Dee (Alexander) 1908-.. **CLC 18,**
                                                  47
    See also CAAS 6; CANR 11;
        CA 13-16R; SATA 5; DLB-Y 80

Brown, George Douglas 1869-1902
    See Douglas, George

Brown, George Mackay 1921- .... **CLC 5,**
                                                  28

    See also CAAS 6; CANR 12;
        CA 21-24R; SATA 35; DLB 14, 27

Brown, Rita Mae 1944- .... **CLC 18, 43**
    See also CANR 2, 11; CA 45-48

Brown, Rosellen 1939- .... **CLC 32**
    See also CANR 14; CA 77-80

Brown, Sterling A(llen) 1901- .... **CLC 1,**
                                                      23

    See also CA 85-88; DLB 48, 51, 63

Brown, William Wells
    1816?-1884 .... **NCLC 2**
    See also DLB 3, 50

Browne, Jackson 1950-........ **CLC 21**

Browning, Elizabeth Barrett
    1806-1861 ....**NCLC 1, 16**
    See also DLB 32

Browning, Robert 1812-1889 .. **NCLC 19**
    See also DLB 32

Browning, Tod 1882-1962 .... **CLC 16**
    See also obituary CA 117

Bruccoli, Matthew J(oseph)
    1931- .... **CLC 34**
    See also CANR 7; CA 9-12R

Bruce, Lenny 1925-1966 ...... **CLC 21**
    See also Schneider, Leonard Alfred

Brunner, John (Kilian Houston)
    1934- .... **CLC 8, 10**
    See also CANR 2; CA 1-4R

Brutus, Dennis 1924- .... **CLC 43**
    See also CANR 2; CA 49-52

Bryan, C(ourtlandt) D(ixon) B(arnes)
    1936- .... **CLC 29**
    See also CANR 13; CA 73-76

Bryant, William Cullen
    1794-1878 .... **NCLC 6**
    See also DLB 3, 43; CDALB 1640-1865

Bryusov, Valery (Yakovlevich)
    1873-1924 .... **TCLC 10**
    See also CA 107

Buchanan, George 1506-1582 .... **LC 4**

Buchheim, Lothar-Gunther
    1918- .... **CLC 6**
    See also CA 85-88

Buchwald, Art(hur) 1925-...... **CLC 33**
    See also CANR 21; CA 5-8R; SATA 10

Buck, Pearl S(ydenstricker)
    1892-1973 ....**CLC 7, 11, 18**
    See also CANR 1; CA 1-4R;
        obituary CA 41-44R; SATA 1, 25;
        DLB 9

Buckler, Ernest 1908-1984 .... **CLC 13**
    See also CAP 1; CA 11-12;
        obituary CA 114; SATA 47

Buckley, William F(rank), Jr.
    1925- ....**CLC 7, 18, 37**
    See also CANR 1; CA 1-4R; DLB-Y 80

Buechner, (Carl) Frederick 1926-.. **CLC 2,**
                                                      4, 6, 9

    See also CANR 11; CA 13-16R;
        DLB-Y 80

Buell, John (Edward) 1927-.... **CLC 10**
    See also CA 1-4R; DLB 53

Buero Vallejo, Antonio 1916- .. **CLC 15,**
                                                  46

    See also CA 106

Bukowski, Charles 1920- .. **CLC 2, 5, 9,**
                                                41

    See also CA 17-20R; DLB 5

Bulgakov, Mikhail (Afanas'evich)
    1891-1940 ....**TCLC 2, 16**
    See also CA 105

Bullins, Ed 1935- .... CLC 1, 5, 7
See also CA 49-52; DLB 7, 38

**Bulwer-Lytton, (Lord) Edward (George
Earle Lytton)** 1803-1873 .. NCLC 1
See also Lytton, Edward Bulwer
See also DLB 21

Bunin, Ivan (Alexeyevich)
1870-1953 .... TCLC 6
See also CA 104

Bunting, Basil 1900-1985 .... CLC 10, 39,
47
See also CANR 7; CA 53-56;
obituary CA 115; DLB 20

Bunuel, Luis 1900-1983 ...... CLC 16
See also CA 101; obituary CA 110

Bunyan, John 1628-1688 ...... LC 4
See also DLB 39

Burgess (Wilson, John) Anthony
1917- ..CLC 1, 2, 4, 5, 8, 10, 13, 15,
22, 40
See also Wilson, John (Anthony)
Burgess
See also DLB 14

Burke, Edmund 1729-1797 ...... LC 7

Burke, Kenneth (Duva) 1897- .... CLC 2,
24
See also CA 5-8R; DLB 45, 63

Burney, Fanny 1752-1840 .... NCLC 12
See also DLB 39

Burns, Robert 1759-1796 .... LC 3

Burns, Tex 1908?-
See L'Amour, Louis (Dearborn)

Burnshaw, Stanley 1906- .. CLC 3, 13, 44
See also CA 9-12R; DLB 48

Burr, Anne 1937- .... CLC 6
See also CA 25-28R

Burroughs, Edgar Rice
1875-1950 .... TCLC 2, 32
See also CA 104; SATA 41; DLB 8

Burroughs, William S(eward)
1914- ...... CLC 1, 2, 5, 15, 22, 42
See also CANR 20; CA 9-12R; DLB 2,
8, 16; DLB-Y 81

Busch, Frederick 1941-.. CLC 7, 10, 18,
47
See also CAAS 1; CA 33-36R; DLB 6

Bush, Ronald 19??- .... CLC 34

Butler, Octavia E(stelle) 1947-.. CLC 38
See also CANR 12; CA 73-76; DLB 33

Butler, Samuel 1835-1902 .. TCLC 1, 33
See also CA 104; DLB 18, 57

Butor, Michel (Marie Francois)
1926- .... CLC 1, 3, 8, 11, 15
See also CA 9-12R

Buzzati, Dino 1906-1972 ...... CLC 36
See also obituary CA 33-36R

Byars, Betsy 1928- .... CLC 35
See also CLR 1, 16; CANR 18;
CA 33-36R; SAAS 1; SATA 4, 46;
DLB 52

Byatt, A(ntonia) S(usan Drabble)
1936- .... CLC 19
See also CANR 13; CA 13-16R;
DLB 14

Byrne, David 1953?- .... CLC 26

Byrne, John Keyes 1926-
See Leonard, Hugh
See also CA 102

**Byron, George Gordon (Noel), Lord
Byron** 1788-1824 ......NCLC 2, 12

Caballero, Fernan 1796-1877 ..NCLC 10

Cabell, James Branch
1879-1958 .... TCLC 6
See also CA 105; DLB 9

Cable, George Washington
1844-1925 .... TCLC 4
See also CA 104; DLB 12

Cabrera Infante, G(uillermo)
1929- .... CLC 5, 25, 45
See also CA 85-88

Cage, John (Milton, Jr.)
1912- .... CLC 41
See also CANR 9; CA 13-16R

Cain, G. 1929-
See Cabrera Infante, G(uillermo)

Cain, James M(allahan)
1892-1977 .... CLC 3, 11, 28
See also CANR 8; CA 17-20R;
obituary CA 73-76

Caldwell, Erskine (Preston)
1903-1987 .... CLC 1, 8, 14, 50
See also CAAS 1; CANR 2; CA 1-4R;
obituary CA 121; DLB 9

**Caldwell, (Janet Miriam) Taylor
(Holland)** 1900-1985.. CLC 2, 28, 39
See also CANR 5; CA 5-8R;
obituary CA 116

Calhoun, John Caldwell
1782-1850 ....NCLC 15
See also DLB 3

Calisher, Hortense 1911-.. CLC 2, 4, 8,
38
See also CANR 1, 22; CA 1-4R; DLB 2

Callaghan, Morley (Edward)
1903- .... CLC 3, 14, 41
See also CA 9-12R

Calvino, Italo 1923-1985 .. CLC 5, 8, 11,
22, 33, 39; SSC 3
See also CANR 23; CA 85-88;
obituary CA 116

Cameron, Peter 1959- .... CLC 44

Campana, Dino 1885-1932 .... TCLC 20
See also CA 117

Campbell, John W(ood), Jr.
1910-1971 .... CLC 32
See also CAP 2; CA 21-22;
obituary CA 29-32R; DLB 8

Campbell, (John) Ramsey
1946- .... CLC 42
See also CANR 7; CA 57-60

Campbell, (Ignatius) Roy (Dunnachie)
1901-1957 .... TCLC 5
See also CA 104; DLB 20

Campbell, Thomas 1777-1844 ..NCLC 19

Campbell, (William) Wilfred
1861-1918 .... TCLC 9
See also CA 106

Camus, Albert 1913-1960.. CLC 1, 2, 4,
9, 11, 14, 32
See also CA 89-92; DLB 72

Canby, Vincent 1924- .... CLC 13
See also CA 81-84

Canetti, Elias 1905- ...... CLC 3, 14, 25
See also CA 21-24R

Canin, Ethan 1960- .... CLC 55

Cape, Judith 1916-
See Page, P(atricia) K(athleen)

Capek, Karel 1890-1938 ...... TCLC 6
See also CA 104

Capote, Truman 1924-1984 .. CLC 1, 3,
8, 13, 19, 34, 38; SSC 2
See also CANR 18; CA 5-8R;
obituary CA 113; DLB 2;
DLB-Y 80, 84; CDALB 1941-1968

Capra, Frank 1897- .... CLC 16
See also CA 61-64

Caputo, Philip 1941-.......... CLC 32
See also CA 73-76

Card, Orson Scott 1951- ....CLC 44, 47,
50
See also CA 102

Cardenal, Ernesto 1925- ...... CLC 31
See also CANR 2; CA 49-52

Carducci, Giosué 1835-1907.... TCLC 32

Carey, Ernestine Gilbreth 1908-
See Gilbreth, Frank B(unker), Jr. and
Carey, Ernestine Gilbreth
See also CA 5-8R; SATA 2

Carey, Peter 1943- ...... CLC 40, 55
See also CA 123, 127

Carleton, William 1794-1869 .. NCLC 3

Carlisle, Henry (Coffin) 1926-.. CLC 33
See also CANR 15; CA 13-16R

Carlson, Ron(ald F.) 1947- .... CLC 54
See also CA 105

Carlyle, Thomas 1795-1881 ....NCLC 22
See also DLB 55

Carman, (William) Bliss
1861-1929 .... TCLC 7
See also CA 104

Carpenter, Don(ald Richard)
1931- .... CLC 41
See also CANR 1; CA 45-48

Carpentier (y Valmont), Alejo
1904-1980 .... CLC 8, 11, 38
See also CANR 11; CA 65-68;
obituary CA 97-100

Carr, Emily 1871-1945........ TCLC 32
See also DLB 68

Carr, John Dickson 1906-1977 .. CLC 3
See also CANR 3; CA 49-52;
obituary CA 69-72

Carr, Virginia Spencer 1929- .. CLC 34
See also CA 61-64

Carrier, Roch 1937- .... CLC 13
See also DLB 53

Carroll, James (P.) 1943-...... CLC 38
See also CA 81-84

Carroll, Jim 1951- .... CLC 35
See also CA 45-48

Carroll, Lewis 1832-1898...... NCLC 2
See also Dodgson, Charles Lutwidge
See also CLR 2; DLB 18

Carroll, Paul Vincent
1900-1968 .... CLC 10
See also CA 9-12R;
obituary CA 25-28R; DLB 10

Carruth, Hayden 1921- .. **CLC 4, 7, 10, 18**
See also CANR 4; CA 9-12R;
SATA 47; DLB 5

Carter, Angela (Olive) 1940- .... **CLC 5, 41**
See also CANR 12; CA 53-56; DLB 14

Carver, Raymond 1938-1988 .. **CLC 22, 36, 53, 55**
See also CANR 17; CA 33-36R;
obituary CA 126; DLB-Y 84, 88

Cary, (Arthur) Joyce (Lunel)
1888-1957 .... **TCLC 1, 29**
See also CA 104; DLB 15

Casares, Adolfo Bioy 1914-
See Bioy Casares, Adolfo

Casely-Hayford, J(oseph) E(phraim)
1866-1930 .... **TCLC 24**

Casey, John 1880-1964
See O'Casey, Sean

Casey, Michael 1947- .... **CLC 2**
See also CA 65-68; DLB 5

Casey, Warren 1935-
See Jacobs, Jim and Casey, Warren
See also CA 101

Casona, Alejandro 1903-1965 .. **CLC 49**
See also Alvarez, Alejandro Rodriguez

Cassavetes, John 1929- ...... **CLC 20**
See also CA 85-88

Cassill, R(onald) V(erlin) 1919- .. **CLC 4, 23**
See also CAAS 1; CANR 7; CA 9-12R;
DLB 6

Cassity, (Allen) Turner 1929- .... **CLC 6, 42**
See also CANR 11; CA 17-20R

Castaneda, Carlos 1935?- ..... **CLC 12**
See also CA 25-28R

Castro, Rosalia de 1837-1885 .. **NCLC 3**

Cather, Willa (Sibert)
1873-1947 .. **TCLC 1, 11, 31; SSC 2**
See also CA 104; SATA 30; DLB 9, 54;
DLB-DS 1; CDALB 1865-1917

Catton, (Charles) Bruce
1899-1978 .... **CLC 35**
See also CANR 7; CA 5-8R;
obituary CA 81-84; SATA 2;
obituary SATA 24; DLB 17

Cauldwell, Frank 1923-
See King, Francis (Henry)

Caunitz, William 1935- ...... **CLC 34**

Causley, Charles (Stanley) 1917- .. **CLC 7**
See also CANR 5; CA 9-12R; SATA 3;
DLB 27

Caute, (John) David 1936- .... **CLC 29**
See also CAAS 4; CANR 1; CA 1-4R;
DLB 14

Cavafy, C(onstantine) P(eter)
1863-1933 .... **TCLC 2, 7**
See also CA 104

Cavanna, Betty 1909- .... **CLC 12**
See also CANR 6; CA 9-12R; SATA 1, 30

Cayrol, Jean 1911- .... **CLC 11**
See also CA 89-92

Cela, Camilo Jose 1916- .... **CLC 4, 13**
See also CANR 21; CA 21-24R

Celan, Paul 1920-1970 .. **CLC 10, 19, 53**
See also Antschel, Paul
See also DLB 69

Celine, Louis-Ferdinand
1894-1961 .... **CLC 1, 3, 4, 7, 9, 15, 47**
See also Destouches, Louis-Ferdinand-
Auguste
See also DLB 72

Cellini, Benvenuto 1500-1571 .... **LC 7**

Cendrars, Blaise 1887-1961 .... **CLC 18**
See also Sauser-Hall, Frederic

Cernuda, Luis (y Bidon)
1902-1963 .... **CLC 54**
See also CA 89-92

Cervantes (Saavedra), Miguel de
1547-1616 .... **LC 6**

Cesaire, Aime (Fernand)
1913- .... **CLC 19, 32**
See also CA 65-68

Chabon, Michael 1965?- ...... **CLC 55**

Chabrol, Claude 1930- .... **CLC 16**
See also CA 110

Challans, Mary 1905-1983
See Renault, Mary
See also CA 81-84; obituary CA 111;
SATA 23; obituary SATA 36

Chambers, Aidan 1934- ...... **CLC 35**
See also CANR 12; CA 25-28R;
SATA 1

Chambers, James 1948-
See Cliff, Jimmy

Chandler, Raymond
1888-1959 .... **TCLC 1, 7**
See also CA 104

Channing, William Ellery
1780-1842 ....**NCLC 17**
See also DLB 1, 59

Chaplin, Charles (Spencer)
1889-1977 .... **CLC 16**
See also CA 81-84; obituary CA 73-76;
DLB 44

Chapman, Graham 1941?-
See Monty Python
See also CA 116

Chapman, John Jay
1862-1933 .... **TCLC 7**
See also CA 104

Chappell, Fred 1936- .... **CLC 40**
See also CAAS 4; CANR 8; CA 5-8R;
DLB 6

Char, Rene (Emile) 1907-1988 .. **CLC 9, 11, 14, 55**
See also CA 13-16R; obituary CA 124

Charyn, Jerome 1937- .... **CLC 5, 8, 18**
See also CAAS 1; CANR 7; CA 5-8R;
DLB-Y 83

Chase, Mary Ellen 1887-1973 .... **CLC 2**
See also CAP 1; CA 15-16;
obituary CA 41-44R; SATA 10

Chateaubriand, Francois Rene de
1768-1848 .... **NCLC 3**

Chatterji, Bankim Chandra
1838-1894 ....**NCLC 19**

Chatterji, Saratchandra
1876-1938 .... **TCLC 13**
See also CA 109

Chatterton, Thomas 1752-1770 .. **LC 3**

Chatwin, (Charles) Bruce
1940- .... **CLC 28**
See also CA 85-88

Chayefsky, Paddy 1923-1981 .. **CLC 23**
See also CA 9-12R; obituary CA 104;
DLB 7, 44; DLB-Y 81

Chayefsky, Sidney 1923-1981
See Chayefsky, Paddy
See also CANR 18

Chedid, Andree 1920- .... **CLC 47**

Cheever, John 1912-1982 .. **CLC 3, 7, 8, 11, 15, 25; SSC 1**
See also CANR 5; CA 5-8R;
obituary CA 106; CABS 1; DLB 2;
DLB-Y 80, 82; CDALB 1941-1968

Cheever, Susan 1943- ...... **CLC 18, 48**
See also CA 103; DLB-Y 82

Chekhov, Anton (Pavlovich)
1860-1904 .. **TCLC 3, 10, 31; SSC 2**
See also CA 104, 124

Chernyshevsky, Nikolay Gavrilovich
1828-1889 .... **NCLC 1**

Cherry, Caroline Janice 1942-
See Cherryh, C. J.

Cherryh, C. J. 1942- .... **CLC 35**
See also DLB-Y 80

Chesnutt, Charles Waddell
1858-1932 .... **TCLC 5**
See also CA 106; DLB 12, 50

Chester, Alfred 1929?-1971 .... **CLC 49**
See also obituary CA 33-36R

Chesterton, G(ilbert) K(eith)
1874-1936 ...... **TCLC 1, 6; SSC 1**
See also CA 104; SATA 27; DLB 10, 19, 34, 70

Ch'ien Chung-shu 1910- ...... **CLC 22**

Child, Lydia Maria
1802-1880 .... **NCLC 6**
See also DLB 1

Child, Philip 1898-1978 ...... **CLC 19**
See also CAP 1; CA 13-14; SATA 47

Childress, Alice 1920- ...... **CLC 12, 15**
See also CLR 14; CANR 3; CA 45-48;
SATA 7, 48; DLB 7, 38

Chislett, (Margaret) Anne
1943?- .... **CLC 34**

Chitty, (Sir) Thomas Willes 1926-
See Hinde, Thomas
See also CA 5-8R

Chomette, Rene 1898-1981
See Clair, Rene
See also obituary CA 103

Chopin, Kate (O'Flaherty)
1851-1904 ....TCLC 5, 14
See also CA 104, 122; DLB 12;
CDALB 1865-1917

Christie, (Dame) Agatha (Mary Clarissa)
1890-1976 .. **CLC 1, 6, 8, 12, 39, 48**
See also CANR 10; CA 17-20R;
obituary CA 61-64; SATA 36;
DLB 13

Christie, (Ann) Philippa 1920-
See Pearce, (Ann) Philippa
See also CANR 4

Christine de Pizan 1365?-1431? .. **LC 9**

Eberstadt, Fernanda 1960- .... CLC 39

Echegaray (y Eizaguirre), Jose (Maria
    Waldo) 1832-1916 ...... TCLC 4
    See also CA 104

Echeverria, (Jose) Esteban (Antonino)
    1805-1851 .... NCLC 18

Eckert, Allan W. 1931- ...... CLC 17
    See also CANR 14; CA 13-16R;
    SATA 27, 29

Eco, Umberto 1932- .... CLC 28
    See also CANR 12; CA 77-80

Eddison, E(ric) R(ucker)
    1882-1945 .... TCLC 15
    See also CA 109

Edel, Leon (Joseph) 1907- .. CLC 29, 34
    See also CANR 1, 22; CA 1-4R

Eden, Emily 1797-1869 ...... NCLC 10

Edgar, David 1948- .... CLC 42
    See also CANR 12; CA 57-60; DLB 13

Edgerton, Clyde 1944- .... CLC 39
    See also CA 118

Edgeworth, Maria 1767-1849 .. NCLC 1
    See also SATA 21

Edmonds, Helen (Woods) 1904-1968
    See Kavan, Anna
    See also CA 5-8R; obituary CA 25-28R

Edmonds, Walter D(umaux)
    1903- .... CLC 35
    See also CANR 2; CA 5-8R; SAAS 4;
    SATA 1, 27; DLB 9

Edson, Russell 1905- .... CLC 13
    See also CA 33-36R

Edwards, G(erald) B(asil)
    1899-1976 .... CLC 25
    See also obituary CA 110

Edwards, Gus 1939- .... CLC 43
    See also CA 108

Edwards, Jonathan 1703-1758.... LC 7
    See also DLB 24

Ehle, John (Marsden, Jr.)
    1925- .... CLC 27
    See also CA 9-12R

Ehrenbourg, Ilya (Grigoryevich)
    1891-1967
    See Ehrenburg, Ilya (Grigoryevich)

Ehrenburg, Ilya (Grigoryevich)
    1891-1967 .... CLC 18, 34
    See also CA 102; obituary CA 25-28R

Eich, Guenter 1907-1971
    See also CA 111; obituary CA 93-96

Eich, Gunter 1907-1971 ...... CLC 15
    See also Eich, Guenter
    See also DLB 69

Eichendorff, Joseph Freiherr von
    1788-1857 .... NCLC 8

Eigner, Larry 1927- .... CLC 9
    See also Eigner, Laurence (Joel)
    See also DLB 5

Eigner, Laurence (Joel) 1927-
    See Eigner, Larry
    See also CANR 6; CA 9-12R

Eiseley, Loren (Corey)
    1907-1977 .... CLC 7
    See also CANR 6; CA 1-4R;
    obituary CA 73-76

Eisenstadt, Jill 1963- .... CLC 50

Ekeloef, Gunnar (Bengt) 1907-1968
    See Ekelof, Gunnar (Bengt)
    See also obituary CA 25-28R

Ekelof, Gunnar (Bengt)
    1907-1968 .... CLC 27
    See also Ekeloef, Gunnar (Bengt)

Ekwensi, Cyprian (Odiatu Duaka)
    1921- .... CLC 4
    See also CANR 18; CA 29-32R

Eliade, Mircea 1907-1986 .... CLC 19
    See also CA 65-68; obituary CA 119

Eliot, George 1819-1880 .. NCLC 4, 13,
                                    23
    See also DLB 21, 35, 55

Eliot, John 1604-1690 .... LC 5
    See also DLB 24

Eliot, T(homas) S(tearns)
    1888-1965 .... CLC 1, 2, 3, 6, 9, 10,
                13, 15, 24, 34, 41, 55
    See also CA 5-8R; obituary CA 25-28R;
    DLB 7, 10, 45, 63; DLB-Y 88

Elkin, Stanley (Lawrence) 1930- .. CLC 4,
                        6, 9, 14, 27, 51
    See also CANR 8; CA 9-12R; DLB 2,
    28; DLB-Y 80

Elledge, Scott 19?? .... CLC 34

Elliott, George P(aul) 1918-1980 .. CLC 2
    See also CANR 2; CA 1-4R;
    obituary CA 97-100

Elliott, Janice 1931- .... CLC 47
    See also CANR 8; CA 13-16R; DLB 14

Elliott, Sumner Locke 1917- .. CLC 38
    See also CANR 2, 21; CA 5-8R

Ellis, A. E. 19?? .... CLC 7

Ellis, Alice Thomas 19?? ...... CLC 40

Ellis, Bret Easton 1964- ...... CLC 39
    See also CA 118

Ellis, (Henry) Havelock
    1859-1939 .... TCLC 14
    See also CA 109

Ellis, Trey 1964- .... CLC 55

Ellison, Harlan (Jay) 1934- .. CLC 1, 13,
                                    42
    See also CANR 5; CA 5-8R; DLB 8

Ellison, Ralph (Waldo) 1914- .... CLC 1,
                            3, 11, 54
    See also CANR 24; CA 9-12R; DLB 2;
    CDALB 1941-1968

Ellmann, Richard (David)
    1918-1987 .... CLC 50
    See also CANR 2; CA 1-4R;
    obituary CA 122

Elman, Richard 1934- .... CLC 19
    See also CAAS 3; CA 17-20R

Eluard, Paul 1895-1952 ...... TCLC 7
    See also Grindel, Eugene

Elvin, Anne Katharine Stevenson 1933-
    See Stevenson, Anne (Katharine)
    See also CA 17-20R

Elyot, (Sir) Thomas 1490?-1546 ..... LC 11

Elytis, Odysseus 1911- ...... CLC 15, 49
    See also CA 102

Emecheta, (Florence Onye) Buchi
    1944- .... CLC 14, 48
    See also CA 81-84

Emerson, Ralph Waldo
    1803-1882 .... NCLC 1
    See also DLB 1; CDALB 1640-1865

Empson, William 1906-1984 ... CLC 3,
                        8, 19, 33, 34
    See also CA 17-20R; obituary CA 112;
    DLB 20

Enchi, Fumiko (Veda)
    1905-1986 .... CLC 31
    See also obituary CA 121

Ende, Michael 1930- .... CLC 31
    See also CLR 14; CA 118; SATA 42

Endo, Shusaku 1923- .. CLC 7, 14, 19,
                                    54
    See also CANR 21; CA 29-32R

Engel, Marian 1933-1985...... CLC 36
    See also CANR 12; CA 25-28R;
    DLB 53

Engelhardt, Frederick 1911-1986
    See Hubbard, L(afayette) Ron(ald)

Enright, D(ennis) J(oseph)
    1920- .... CLC 4, 8, 31
    See also CANR 1; CA 1-4R; SATA 25;
    DLB 27

Enzensberger, Hans Magnus
    1929- .... CLC 43
    See also CA 116, 119

Ephron, Nora 1941- ...... CLC 17, 31
    See also CANR 12; CA 65-68

Epstein, Daniel Mark 1948- .... CLC 7
    See also CANR 2; CA 49-52

Epstein, Jacob 1956- .... CLC 19
    See also CA 114

Epstein, Joseph 1937- .... CLC 39
    See also CA 112, 119

Epstein, Leslie 1938- .... CLC 27
    See also CA 73-76

Erdman, Paul E(mil) 1932- .... CLC 25
    See also CANR 13; CA 61-64

Erdrich, Louise 1954- ...... CLC 39, 54
    See also CA 114

Erenburg, Ilya (Grigoryevich) 1891-1967
    See Ehrenburg, Ilya (Grigoryevich)

Eseki, Bruno 1919-
    See Mphahlele, Ezekiel

Esenin, Sergei (Aleksandrovich)
    1895-1925 .... TCLC 4
    See also CA 104

Eshleman, Clayton 1935-........ CLC 7
    See also CAAS 6; CA 33-36R; DLB 5

Espriu, Salvador 1913-1985 ...... CLC 9
    See also obituary CA 115

Estleman, Loren D. 1952- .... CLC 48
    See also CA 85-88

Evans, Marian 1819-1880
    See Eliot, George

Evans, Mary Ann 1819-1880
    See Eliot, George

Evarts, Esther 1900-1972
    See Benson, Sally

Everson, Ronald G(ilmour)
    1903- .... CLC 27
    See also CA 17-20R

Everson, William (Oliver) 1912- .. CLC 1,
                                    5, 14
    See also CANR 20; CA 9-12R; DLB 5,
    16

Gardner, John (Champlin, Jr.)
1933-1982 .... CLC 2, 3, 5, 7, 8, 10,
18, 28, 34
See also CA 65-68; obituary CA 107;
obituary SATA 31, 40; DLB 2;
DLB-Y 82

Gardner, John (Edmund)
1926- .... CLC 30
See also CANR 15; CA 103

Garfield, Leon 1921-.......... CLC 12
See also CA 17-20R; SATA 1, 32

Garland, (Hannibal) Hamlin
1860-1940 .... TCLC 3
See also CA 104; DLB 12, 71

Garneau, Hector (de) Saint Denys
1912-1943 .... TCLC 13
See also CA 111

Garner, Alan 1935- .... CLC 17
See also CANR 15; CA 73-76;
SATA 18

Garner, Hugh 1913-1979 ...... CLC 13
See also CA 69-72

Garnett, David 1892-1981 ..... CLC 3
See also CANR 17; CA 5-8R;
obituary CA 103; DLB 34

Garrett, George (Palmer, Jr.)
1929- .... CLC 3, 11, 51
See also CAAS 5; CANR 1; CA 1-4R;
DLB 2, 5; DLB-Y 83

Garrigue, Jean 1914-1972 .... CLC 2, 8
See also CA 5-8R; obituary CA 37-40R

Gary, Romain 1914-1980 ...... CLC 25
See also Kacew, Romain

Gascar, Pierre 1916- .... CLC 11
See also Fournier, Pierre

Gascoyne, David (Emery)
1916- .... CLC 45
See also CANR 10; CA 65-68; DLB 20

Gaskell, Elizabeth Cleghorn
1810-1865 .... NCLC 5
See also DLB 21

Gass, William H(oward) 1924- .. CLC 1,
2, 8, 11, 15, 39
See also CA 17-20R; DLB 2

Gautier, Theophile 1811-1872 .. NCLC 1

Gaye, Marvin (Pentz)
1939-1984 .... CLC 26
See also obituary CA 112

Gebler, Carlo (Ernest) 1954- .. CLC 39
See also CA 119

Gee, Maurice (Gough) 1931- .. CLC 29
See also CA 97-100; SATA 46

Gelbart, Larry (Simon) 1923- .. CLC 21
See also CA 73-76

Gelber, Jack 1932- ...... CLC 1, 6, 14
See also CANR 2; CA 1-4R; DLB 7

Gellhorn, Martha (Ellis)
1908- .... CLC 14
See also CA 77-80; DLB-Y 82

Genet, Jean 1910-1986.. CLC 1, 2, 5, 10,
14, 44, 46
See also CANR 18; CA 13-16R;
DLB 72; DLB-Y 86

Gent, Peter 1942- .... CLC 29
See also CA 89-92; DLB 72; DLB-Y 82

George, Jean Craighead 1919-.. CLC 35
See also CLR 1; CA 5-8R; SATA 2;
DLB 52

George, Stefan (Anton)
1868-1933 .... TCLC 2, 14
See also CA 104

Gerhardi, William (Alexander) 1895-1977
See Gerhardie, William (Alexander)

Gerhardie, William (Alexander)
1895-1977 .... CLC 5
See also CANR 18; CA 25-28R;
obituary CA 73-76; DLB 36

Gertler, T(rudy) 1946?- ..... CLC 34
See also CA 116

Gessner, Friedrike Victoria 1910-1980
See Adamson, Joy(-Friederike Victoria)

Ghelderode, Michel de
1898-1962 .... CLC 6, 11
See also CA 85-88

Ghiselin, Brewster 1903- ...... CLC 23
See also CANR 13; CA 13-16R

Ghose, Zulfikar 1935- .... CLC 42
See also CA 65-68

Ghosh, Amitav 1943- .... CLC 44

Giacosa, Giuseppe 1847-1906 .. TCLC 7
See also CA 104

Gibbon, Lewis Grassic
1901-1935 .... TCLC 4
See also Mitchell, James Leslie

Gibbons, Kaye 1960- .... CLC 50

Gibran, (Gibran) Kahlil
1883-1931 .... TCLC 1, 9
See also CA 104

Gibson, William 1914-........ CLC 23
See also CANR 9; CA 9-12R; DLB 7

Gibson, William 1948-........ CLC 39

Gide, Andre (Paul Guillaume)
1869-1951 .... TCLC 5, 12
See also CA 104

Gifford, Barry (Colby) 1946- .. CLC 34
See also CANR 9; CA 65-68

Gilbert, (Sir) W(illiam) S(chwenck)
1836-1911 .... TCLC 3
See also CA 104; SATA 36

Gilbreth, Ernestine 1908-
See Carey, Ernestine Gilbreth

Gilbreth, Frank B(unker), Jr. 1911- and
Carey, Ernestine Gilbreth
1911- .... CLC 17

Gilbreth, Frank B(unker), Jr. 1911-
See Gilbreth, Frank B(unker), Jr. and
Carey, Ernestine Gilbreth
See also CA 9-12R; SATA 2

Gilchrist, Ellen 1935- ...... CLC 34, 48
See also CA 113, 116

Giles, Molly 1942- .... CLC 39

Gilliam, Terry (Vance) 1940-
See Monty Python
See also CA 108, 113

Gilliatt, Penelope (Ann Douglass)
1932- .... CLC 2, 10, 13, 53
See also CA 13-16R; DLB 14

Gilman, Charlotte (Anna) Perkins
(Stetson) 1860-1935 ...... TCLC 9
See also CA 106

Gilmour, David 1944-
See Pink Floyd

Gilroy, Frank D(aniel) 1925- .... CLC 2
See also CA 81-84; DLB 7

Ginsberg, Allen 1926- .. CLC 1, 2, 3, 4,
6, 13, 36
See also CANR 2; CA 1-4R; DLB 5,
16; CDALB 1941-1968

Ginzburg, Natalia 1916- .. CLC 5, 11, 54
See also CA 85-88

Giono, Jean 1895-1970 .... CLC 4, 11
See also CANR 2; CA 45-48;
obituary CA 29-32R; DLB 72

Giovanni, Nikki 1943- ...... CLC 2, 4, 19
See also CLR 6; CAAS 6; CANR 18;
CA 29-32R; SATA 24; DLB 5, 41

Giovene, Andrea 1904- .... CLC 7
See also CA 85-88

Gippius, Zinaida (Nikolayevna) 1869-1945
See Hippius, Zinaida
See also CA 106

Giraudoux, (Hippolyte) Jean
1882-1944 .... TCLC 2, 7
See also CA 104

Gironella, Jose Maria 1917- .. CLC 11
See also CA 101

Gissing, George (Robert)
1857-1903 .... TCLC 3, 24
See also CA 105; DLB 18

Gladkov, Fyodor (Vasilyevich)
1883-1958 .... TCLC 27

Glanville, Brian (Lester) 1931- .. CLC 6
See also CANR 3; CA 5-8R; SATA 42;
DLB 15

Glasgow, Ellen (Anderson Gholson)
1873?-1945 .... TCLC 2, 7
See also CA 104; DLB 9, 12

Glassco, John 1909-1981 .... CLC 9
See also CANR 15; CA 13-16R;
obituary CA 102

Glasser, Ronald J. 1940?- .... CLC 37

Glendinning, Victoria 1937-.... CLC 50
See also CA 120

Glissant, Edouard 1928- ...... CLC 10

Gloag, Julian 1930- .... CLC 40
See also CANR 10; CA 65-68

Gluck, Louise (Elisabeth) 1943-.. CLC 7,
22, 44
See also CA 33-36R; DLB 5

Gobineau, Joseph Arthur (Comte) de
1816-1882 ....NCLC 17

Godard, Jean-Luc 1930- ...... CLC 20
See also CA 93-96

Godden, (Margaret) Rumer
1907- .... CLC 53
See also CANR 4, 27; CA 7-8R;
SATA 3, 36

Godwin, Gail 1937- .... CLC 5, 8, 22, 31
See also CANR 15; CA 29-32R; DLB 6

Godwin, William 1756-1836 .. NCLC 14
See also DLB 39

Goethe, Johann Wolfgang von
1749-1832 ....NCLC 4, 22

Gogarty, Oliver St. John
1878-1957 .... TCLC 15
See also CA 109; DLB 15, 19

Gogol, Nikolai (Vasilyevich)
1809-1852 ....NCLC 5, 15
See also CAAS 1, 4

Grey, (Pearl) Zane 1872?-1939 . . TCLC 6
See also CA 104; DLB 9

Grieg, (Johan) Nordahl (Brun)
  1902-1943 . . . . TCLC 10
See also CA 107

Grieve, C(hristopher) M(urray) 1892-1978
See MacDiarmid, Hugh
See also CA 5-8R; obituary CA 85-88

Griffin, Gerald 1803-1840 . . . . NCLC 7

Griffin, Peter 1942- . . . . CLC 39

Griffiths, Trevor 1935- . . . . . . CLC 13, 52
See also CA 97-100; DLB 13

Grigson, Geoffrey (Edward Harvey)
  1905-1985 . . . . CLC 7, 39
See also CANR 20; CA 25-28R;
  obituary CA 118; DLB 27

Grillparzer, Franz 1791-1872 . . NCLC 1

Grimke, Charlotte L(ottie) Forten
  1837-1914
See Forten (Grimke), Charlotte L(ottie)
See also CA 117

Grimm, Jakob (Ludwig) Karl 1785-1863
  and Grimm, Wilhelm Karl
  1785-1863 . . . . NCLC 3
See also SATA 22

Grimm, Jakob (Ludwig) Karl 1785-1863
See Grimm, Jakob (Ludwig) Karl and
  Grimm, Wilhelm Karl

Grimm, Wilhelm Karl 1786-1859
See Grimm, Jakob (Ludwig) Karl and
  Grimm, Wilhelm Karl

Grimm, Wilhelm Karl 1786-1859 and
  Grimm, Jakob (Ludwig) Karl
  1786-1859
See Grimm, Jakob (Ludwig) Karl and
  Grimm, Wilhelm Karl

Grimmelshausen, Johann Jakob Christoffel
  von 1621-1676 . . . . LC 6

Grindel, Eugene 1895-1952
See also CA 104

Grossman, Vasily (Semenovich)
  1905-1964 . . . . CLC 41

Grove, Frederick Philip
  1879-1948 . . . . TCLC 4
See also Greve, Felix Paul Berthold
  Friedrich

Grumbach, Doris (Isaac)
  1918- . . . . CLC 13, 22
See also CAAS 2; CANR 9; CA 5-8R

Grundtvig, Nicolai Frederik Severin
  1783-1872 . . . . NCLC 1

Grunwald, Lisa 1959- . . . . CLC 44
See also CA 120

Guare, John 1938- . . . . CLC 8, 14, 29
See also CANR 21; CA 73-76; DLB 7

Gudjonsson, Halldor Kiljan 1902-
See Laxness, Halldor (Kiljan)
See also CA 103

Guest, Barbara 1920- . . . . CLC 34
See also CANR 11; CA 25-28R; DLB 5

Guest, Judith (Ann) 1936- . . CLC 8, 30
See also CANR 15; CA 77-80

Guild, Nicholas M. 1944- . . . . CLC 33
See also CA 93-96

Guillen, Jorge 1893-1984 . . . . . . CLC 11
See also CA 89-92; obituary CA 112

Guillen, Nicolas 1902- . . . . CLC 48
See also CA 116

Guillevic, (Eugene) 1907- . . . . . . CLC 33
See also CA 93-96

Gunn, Bill 1934- . . . . CLC 5
See also Gunn, William Harrison
See also DLB 38

Gunn, Thom(son William) 1929- . . CLC 3,
  6, 18, 32
See also CANR 9; CA 17-20R; DLB 27

Gunn, William Harrison 1934-
See Gunn, Bill
See also CANR 12; CA 13-16R

Gurney, A(lbert) R(amsdell), Jr.
  1930- . . . . CLC 32, 50, 54
See also CA 77-80

Gurney, Ivor (Bertie)
  1890-1937 . . . . TCLC 33

Gustafson, Ralph (Barker)
  1909- . . . . CLC 36
See also CANR 8; CA 21-24R

Guthrie, A(lfred) B(ertram), Jr.
  1901- . . . . CLC 23
See also CA 57-60; DLB 6

Guthrie, Woodrow Wilson 1912-1967
See Guthrie, Woody
See also CA 113; obituary CA 93-96

Guthrie, Woody 1912-1967 . . . . CLC 35
See also Guthrie, Woodrow Wilson

Guy, Rosa (Cuthbert) 1928- . . . . CLC 26
See also CANR 14; CA 17-20R;
  SATA 14; DLB 33

Haavikko, Paavo (Juhani)
  1931- . . . . CLC 18, 34
See also CA 106

Hacker, Marilyn 1942- . . . . CLC 5, 9, 23
See also CA 77-80

Haggard, (Sir) H(enry) Rider
  1856-1925 . . . . TCLC 11
See also CA 108; SATA 16; DLB 70

Haig-Brown, Roderick L(angmere)
  1908-1976 . . . . CLC 21
See also CANR 4; CA 5-8R;
  obituary CA 69-72; SATA 12

Hailey, Arthur 1920- . . . . CLC 5
See also CANR 2; CA 1-4R; DLB-Y 82

Hailey, Elizabeth Forsythe
  1938- . . . . CLC 40
See also CAAS 1; CANR 15; CA 93-96

Haley, Alex (Palmer) 1921- . . CLC 8, 12
See also CA 77-80; DLB 38

Haliburton, Thomas Chandler
  1796-1865 . . . . NCLC 15
See also DLB 11

Hall, Donald (Andrew, Jr.)
  1928- . . . . CLC 1, 13, 37
See also CAAS 7; CANR 2; CA 5-8R;
  SATA 23; DLB 5

Hall, James Norman
  1887-1951 . . . . TCLC 23
See also SATA 21

Hall, (Marguerite) Radclyffe
  1886-1943 . . . . TCLC 12
See also CA 110

Hall, Rodney 1935- . . . . CLC 51
See also CA 109

Halpern, Daniel 1945- . . . . CLC 14
See also CA 33-36R

Hamburger, Michael (Peter Leopold)
  1924- . . . . CLC 5, 14
See also CAAS 4; CANR 2; CA 5-8R;
  DLB 27

Hamill, Pete 1935- . . . . CLC 10
See also CANR 18; CA 25-28R

Hamilton, Edmond 1904-1977 . . . . CLC 1
See also CANR 3; CA 1-4R; DLB 8

Hamilton, Gail 1911-
See Corcoran, Barbara

Hamilton, Ian 1938- . . . . CLC 55
See also CA 106; DLB 40

Hamilton, Mollie 1909?-
See Kaye, M(ary) M(argaret)

Hamilton, (Anthony Walter) Patrick
  1904-1962 . . . . CLC 51
See also obituary CA 113; DLB 10

Hamilton, Virginia (Esther)
  1936- . . . . CLC 26
See also CLR 1, 11; CANR 20;
  CA 25-28R; SATA 4; DLB 33, 52

Hammett, (Samuel) Dashiell
  1894-1961 . . . . CLC 3, 5, 10, 19, 47
See also CA 81-84

Hammon, Jupiter 1711?-1800?. . NCLC 5
See also DLB 31, 50

Hamner, Earl (Henry), Jr.
  1923- . . . . CLC 12
See also CA 73-76; DLB 6

Hampton, Christopher (James)
  1946- . . . . CLC 4
See also CA 25-28R; DLB 13

Hamsun, Knut 1859-1952 . . TCLC 2, 14
See also Pedersen, Knut

Handke, Peter 1942-. . CLC 5, 8, 10, 15,
  38
See also CA 77-80

Hanley, James 1901-1985 . . CLC 3, 5,
  8, 13
See also CA 73-76; obituary CA 117

Hannah, Barry 1942- . . . . . . CLC 23, 38
See also CA 108, 110; DLB 6

Hansberry, Lorraine (Vivian)
  1930-1965 . . . . CLC 17
See also CA 109; obituary CA 25-28R;
  DLB 7, 38; CDALB 1941-1968

Hansen, Joseph 1923- . . . . CLC 38
See also CANR 16; CA 29-32R

Hansen, Martin 1909-1955 . . . . TCLC 32

Hanson, Kenneth O(stlin)
  1922- . . . . CLC 13
See also CANR 7; CA 53-56

Hardenberg, Friedrich (Leopold Freiherr)
  von 1772-1801
See Novalis

Hardwick, Elizabeth 1916- . . . . CLC 13
See also CANR 3; CA 5-8R; DLB 6

Hardy, Thomas 1840-1928 . . . . TCLC 4,
  10, 18, 32; SSC 2
See also CA 104, 123; SATA 25;
  DLB 18, 19

Hare, David 1947- . . . . CLC 29
See also CA 97-100; DLB 13

Herbert, Frank (Patrick)
1920-1986 ...... **CLC 12, 23, 35, 44**
See also CANR 5; CA 53-56;
obituary CA 118; SATA 9, 37, 47;
DLB 8

Herbert, Zbigniew 1924- .... **CLC 9, 43**
See also CA 89-92

Herbst, Josephine 1897-1969 .. **CLC 34**
See also CA 5-8R; obituary CA 25-28R;
DLB 9

Herder, Johann Gottfried von
1744-1803 .... **NCLC 8**

Hergesheimer, Joseph
1880-1954 .... **TCLC 11**
See also CA 109; DLB 9

Herlagnez, Pablo de 1844-1896
See Verlaine, Paul (Marie)

Herlihy, James Leo 1927- ...... **CLC 6**
See also CANR 2; CA 1-4R

Hernandez, Jose 1834-1886 .... **NCLC 17**

Herriot, James 1916- .... **CLC 12**
See also Wight, James Alfred

Herrmann, Dorothy 1941- .... **CLC 44**
See also CA 107

Hersey, John (Richard) 1914- .... **CLC 1,
2, 7, 9, 40**
See also CA 17-20R; SATA 25; DLB 6

Herzen, Aleksandr Ivanovich
1812-1870 .... **NCLC 10**

Herzog, Werner 1942- .... **CLC 16**
See also CA 89-92

Hesse, Hermann 1877-1962 .. **CLC 1, 2,
3, 6, 11, 17, 25**
See also CAP 2; CA 17-18

Heyen, William 1940- .... **CLC 13, 18**
See also CA 33-36R; DLB 5

Heyerdahl, Thor 1914- .... **CLC 26**
See also CANR 5, 22; CA 5-8R;
SATA 2, 52

Heym, Georg (Theodor Franz Arthur)
1887-1912 .... **TCLC 9**
See also CA 106

Heym, Stefan 1913- .... **CLC 41**
See also CANR 4; CA 9-12R; DLB 69

Heyse, Paul (Johann Ludwig von)
1830-1914 .... **TCLC 8**
See also CA 104

Hibbert, Eleanor (Burford) 1906-.. **CLC 7**
See also CANR 9; CA 17-20R; SATA 2

Higgins, George V(incent) 1939- .. **CLC 4,
7, 10, 18**
See also CAAS 5; CANR 17; CA 77-80;
DLB 2; DLB-Y 81

Highsmith, (Mary) Patricia
1921- .... **CLC 2, 4, 14, 42**
See also CANR 1, 20; CA 1-4R

Highwater, Jamake 1942- .... **CLC 12**
See also CAAS 7; CANR 10; CA 65-68;
SATA 30, 32; DLB 52; DLB-Y 85

Hikmet (Ran), Nazim
1902-1963 .... **CLC 40**
See also obituary CA 93-96

Hildesheimer, Wolfgang 1916-.. **CLC 49**
See also CA 101; DLB 69

Hill, Geoffrey (William) 1932-.... **CLC 5,
8, 18, 45**
See also CANR 21; CA 81-84; DLB 40

Hill, George Roy 1922- ...... **CLC 26**
See also CA 110

Hill, Susan B. 1942-............ **CLC 4**
See also CA 33-36R; DLB 14

Hilliard, Noel (Harvey) 1929- .. **CLC 15**
See also CANR 7; CA 9-12R

Hilton, James 1900-1954 ...... **TCLC 21**
See also CA 108; SATA 34; DLB 34

Himes, Chester (Bomar)
1909-1984 .... **CLC 2, 4, 7, 18**
See also CANR 22; CA 25-28R;
obituary CA 114; DLB 2

Hinde, Thomas 1926- ...... **CLC 6, 11**
See also Chitty, (Sir) Thomas Willes

Hine, (William) Daryl 1936- .. **CLC 15**
See also CANR 1, 20; CA 1-4R;
DLB 60

Hinton, S(usan) E(loise)
1950- .... **CLC 30**
See also CLR 3; CA 81-84; SATA 19

Hippius (Merezhkovsky), Zinaida
(Nikolayevna) 1869-1945 .. **TCLC 9**
See also Gippius, Zinaida
(Nikolayevna)

Hiraoka, Kimitake 1925-1970
See Mishima, Yukio
See also CA 97-100;
obituary CA 29-32R

Hirsch, Edward (Mark) 1950- .. **CLC 31,
50**
See also CANR 20; CA 104

Hitchcock, (Sir) Alfred (Joseph)
1899-1980 .... **CLC 16**
See also obituary CA 97-100; SATA 27;
obituary SATA 24

Hoagland, Edward 1932- ...... **CLC 28**
See also CANR 2; CA 1-4R; SATA 51;
DLB 6

Hoban, Russell C(onwell) 1925- .. **CLC 7,
25**
See also CLR 3; CA 5-8R; SATA 1, 40;
DLB 52

Hobson, Laura Z(ametkin)
1900-1986 .... **CLC 7, 25**
See also CA 17-20R; obituary CA 118;
SATA 52; DLB 28

Hochhuth, Rolf 1931- .... **CLC 4, 11, 18**
See also CA 5-8R

Hochman, Sandra 1936- ...... **CLC 3, 8**
See also CA 5-8R; DLB 5

Hochwalder, Fritz 1911-1986 .. **CLC 36**
See also CA 29-32R; obituary CA 120

Hocking, Mary (Eunice)
1921- .... **CLC 13**
See also CANR 18; CA 101

Hodgins, Jack 1938-.......... **CLC 23**
See also CA 93-96; DLB 60

Hodgson, William Hope
1877-1918 .... **TCLC 13**
See also CA 111; DLB 70

Hoffman, Alice 1952- .... **CLC 51**
See also CA 77-80

Hoffman, Daniel (Gerard) 1923- .. **CLC 6,
13, 23**
See also CANR 4; CA 1-4R; DLB 5

Hoffman, Stanley 1944- .... **CLC 5**
See also CA 77-80

Hoffman, William M(oses)
1939- .... **CLC 40**
See also CANR 11; CA 57-60

Hoffmann, Ernst Theodor Amadeus
1776-1822 .... **NCLC 2**
See also SATA 27

Hoffmann, Gert 1932- .... **CLC 54**

Hofmannsthal, Hugo (Laurenz August
Hofmann Edler) von
1874-1929 .... **TCLC 11**
See also CA 106

Hogg, James 1770-1835 ...... **NCLC 4**

Holberg, Ludvig 1684-1754 ...... **LC 6**

Holden, Ursula 1921- .... **CLC 18**
See also CANR 22; CA 101

Holderlin, (Johann Christian) Friedrich
1770-1843 .... **NCLC 16**

Holdstock, Robert (P.) 1948- .. **CLC 39**

Holland, Isabelle 1920- ...... **CLC 21**
See also CANR 10; CA 21-24R;
SATA 8

Holland, Marcus 1900-1985
See Caldwell, (Janet Miriam) Taylor
(Holland)

Hollander, John 1929- .. **CLC 2, 5, 8, 14**
See also CANR 1; CA 1-4R; SATA 13;
DLB 5

Holleran, Andrew 1943?- .... **CLC 38**

Hollinghurst, Alan 1954- ...... **CLC 55**
See also CA 114

Hollis, Jim 1916-
See Summers, Hollis (Spurgeon, Jr.)

Holmes, John Clellon
1926-1988 .... **CLC 56**
See also CANR 4; CA 9-10R;
obituary CA 125; DLB 16

Holmes, Oliver Wendell
1809-1894 .... **NCLC 14**
See also SATA 34; DLB 1;
CDALB 1640-1865

Holt, Victoria 1906-
See Hibbert, Eleanor (Burford)

Holub, Miroslav 1923-.......... **CLC 4**
See also CANR 10; CA 21-24R

Homer c. 8th century B.C. ..... **CMLC 1**

Honig, Edwin 1919- .... **CLC 33**
See also CANR 4; CA 5-8R; DLB 5

Hood, Hugh (John Blagdon)
1928- .... **CLC 15, 28**
See also CANR 1; CA 49-52; DLB 53

Hood, Thomas 1799-1845 .... **NCLC 16**

Hooker, (Peter) Jeremy 1941- .. **CLC 43**
See also CANR 22; CA 77-80; DLB 40

Hope, A(lec) D(erwent) 1907- .... **CLC 3,
51**
See also CA 21-24R

Hope, Christopher (David Tully)
1944- .... **CLC 52**
See also CA 106

Hopkins, Gerard Manley
1844-1889 .... **NCLC 17**
See also DLB 35, 57

Hopkins, John (Richard) 1931- .. **CLC 4**
See also CA 85-88

Khodasevich, Vladislav (Felitsianovich)
 1886-1939 . . . . TCLC 15
 See also CA 115

Kielland, Alexander (Lange)
 1849-1906 . . . . TCLC 5
 See also CA 104

Kiely, Benedict 1919- . . . . . . CLC 23, 43
 See also CANR 2; CA 1-4R; DLB 15

Kienzle, William X(avier)
 1928- . . . . CLC 25
 See also CAAS 1; CANR 9; CA 93-96

Killens, John Oliver 1916- . . . . CLC 10
 See also CAAS 2; CA 77-80; DLB 33

Killigrew, Anne 1660-1685 . . . . . . LC 4

Kincaid, Jamaica 1949? . . . . . . CLC 43

King, Francis (Henry) 1923- . . . . CLC 8,
             53
 See also CANR 1; CA 1-4R; DLB 15

King, Stephen (Edwin) 1947- . . CLC 12,
          26, 37
 See also CANR 1; CA 61-64; SATA 9;
 DLB-Y 80

Kingman, (Mary) Lee 1919- . . . . CLC 17
 See also Natti, (Mary) Lee
 See also CA 5-8R; SATA 1

Kingsley, Sidney 1906- . . . . CLC 44
 See also CA 85-88; DLB 7

Kingsolver, Barbara 1955- . . . . CLC 55

Kingston, Maxine Hong 1940- . . CLC 12,
           19
 See also CANR 13; CA 69-72;
 SATA 53; DLB-Y 80

Kinnell, Galway 1927- . . CLC 1, 2, 3, 5,
          13, 29
 See also CANR 10; CA 9-12R; DLB 5

Kinsella, Thomas 1928- . . CLC 4, 19, 43
 See also CANR 15; CA 17-20R;
 DLB 27

Kinsella, W(illiam) P(atrick)
 1935- . . . . CLC 27, 43
 See also CAAS 7; CANR 21;
 CA 97-100

Kipling, (Joseph) Rudyard
 1865-1936 . . . . TCLC 8, 17
 See also YABC 2; CA 20, 105;
 DLB 19, 34

Kirkup, James 1918- . . . . CLC 1
 See also CAAS 4; CANR 2; CA 1-4R;
 SATA 12; DLB 27

Kirkwood, James 1930- . . . . CLC 9
 See also CANR 6; CA 1-4R

Kizer, Carolyn (Ashley) 1925- . . CLC 15,
          39
 See also CAAS 5; CA 65-68; DLB 5

Klausner, Amos 1939-
 See Oz, Amos

Klein, A(braham) M(oses)
 1909-1972 . . . . CLC 19
 See also CA 101; obituary CA 37-40R

Klein, Norma 1938- . . . . CLC 30
 See also CLR 2; CANR 15; CA 41-44R;
 SAAS 1; SATA 7

Klein, T.E.D. 19?? . . . . CLC 34
 See also CA 119

Kleist, Heinrich von
 1777-1811 . . . . NCLC 2

Klima, Ivan 1931- . . . . CLC 56

Klimentev, Andrei Platonovich 1899-1951
 See Platonov, Andrei (Platonovich)
 See also CA 108

Klinger, Friedrich Maximilian von
 1752-1831 . . . . NCLC 1

Klopstock, Friedrich Gottlieb
 1724-1803 . . . . NCLC 11

Knebel, Fletcher 1911- . . . . CLC 14
 See also CAAS 3; CANR 1; CA 1-4R;
 SATA 36

Knight, Etheridge 1931- . . . . . . CLC 40
 See also CA 21-24R; DLB 41

Knight, Sarah Kemble
 1666-1727 . . . . LC 7
 See also DLB 24

Knowles, John 1926- . . CLC 1, 4, 10, 26
 See also CA 17-20R; SATA 8; DLB 6

Koch, C(hristopher) J(ohn)
 1932- . . . . CLC 42

Koch, Kenneth 1925- . . . . CLC 5, 8, 44
 See also CANR 6; CA 1-4R; DLB 5

Kochanowski, Jan 1530-1584 . . . . LC 10

Kock, Charles Paul de
 1794-1871 . . . . NCLC 16

Koestler, Arthur 1905-1983 . . CLC 1, 3,
        6, 8, 15, 33
 See also CANR 1; CA 1-4R;
 obituary CA 109; DLB-Y 83

Kohout, Pavel 1928- . . . . CLC 13
 See also CANR 3; CA 45-48

Konigsberg, Allen Stewart 1935-
 See Allen, Woody

Konrad, Gyorgy 1933- . . . . . . CLC 4, 10
 See also CA 85-88

Konwicki, Tadeusz 1926- . . CLC 8, 28, 54
 See also CA 101

Kopit, Arthur (Lee) 1937- . . CLC 1, 18,
          33
 See also CA 81-84; DLB 7

Kops, Bernard 1926- . . . . CLC 4
 See also CA 5-8R; DLB 13

Kornbluth, C(yril) M.
 1923-1958 . . . . TCLC 8
 See also CA 105; DLB 8

Korolenko, Vladimir (Galaktionovich)
 1853-1921 . . . . TCLC 22
 See also CA 121

Kosinski, Jerzy (Nikodem) 1933- . CLC 1,
      2, 3, 6, 10, 15, 53
 See also CANR 9; CA 17-20R; DLB 2;
 DLB-Y 82

Kostelanetz, Richard (Cory)
 1940- . . . . CLC 28
 See also CA 13-16R

Kostrowitzki, Wilhelm Apollinaris de
 1880-1918
 See Apollinaire, Guillaume
 See also CA 104

Kotlowitz, Robert 1924- . . . . CLC 4
 See also CA 33-36R

Kotzwinkle, William 1938- . . CLC 5, 14,
          35
 See also CLR 6; CANR 3; CA 45-48;
 SATA 24

Kozol, Jonathan 1936- . . . . CLC 17
 See also CANR 16; CA 61-64

Kozoll, Michael 1940?
 See Bochco, Steven and Kozoll,
 Michael

Kramer, Kathryn 19?? . . . . CLC 34

Kramer, Larry 1935- . . . . CLC 42

Krasicki, Ignacy 1735-1801 . . . . NCLC 8

Krasinski, Zygmunt
 1812-1859 . . . . NCLC 4

Kraus, Karl 1874-1936 . . . . TCLC 5
 See also CA 104

Kreve, Vincas 1882-1959 . . . . . TCLC 27

Kristofferson, Kris 1936- . . . . . . CLC 26
 See also CA 104

Krleza, Miroslav 1893-1981 . . . . . . CLC 8
 See also CA 97-100; obituary CA 105

Kroetsch, Robert 1927- . . . . . . CLC 5, 23
 See also CANR 8; CA 17-20R; DLB 53

Kroetz, Franz Xaver 1946- . . . . CLC 41

Krotkov, Yuri 1917- . . . . CLC 19
 See also CA 102

Krumgold, Joseph (Quincy)
 1908-1980 . . . . CLC 12
 See also CANR 7; CA 9-12R;
 obituary CA 101; SATA 48;
 obituary SATA 23

Krutch, Joseph Wood
 1893-1970 . . . . CLC 24
 See also CANR 4; CA 1-4R;
 obituary CA 25-28R; DLB 63

Krylov, Ivan Andreevich
 1768?-1844 . . . . NCLC 1

Kubin, Alfred 1877-1959 . . . . . . TCLC 23
 See also CA 112

Kubrick, Stanley 1928- . . . . CLC 16
 See also CA 81-84; DLB 26

Kumin, Maxine (Winokur) 1925- . CLC 5,
         13, 28
 See also CANR 1, 21; CA 1-4R;
 SATA 12; DLB 5

Kundera, Milan 1929- . . CLC 4, 9, 19, 32
 See also CANR 19; CA 85-88

Kunitz, Stanley J(asspon) 1905- . . CLC 6,
         11, 14
 See also CA 41-44R; DLB 48

Kunze, Reiner 1933- . . . . CLC 10
 See also CA 93-96

Kuprin, Aleksandr (Ivanovich)
 1870-1938 . . . . TCLC 5
 See also CA 104

Kurosawa, Akira 1910- . . . . CLC 16
 See also CA 101

Kuttner, Henry 1915-1958 . . . . TCLC 10
 See also CA 107; DLB 8

Kuzma, Greg 1944- . . . . CLC 7
 See also CA 33-36R

Labrunie, Gerard 1808-1855
 See Nerval, Gerard de

Laclos, Pierre Ambroise Francois Choderlos
 de 1741-1803 . . . . NCLC 4

La Fayette, Marie (Madelaine Pioche de la
 Vergne, Comtesse) de
 1634-1693 . . . . LC 2

Longfellow, Henry Wadsworth
1807-1882 .... NCLC 2
See also SATA 19; DLB 1;
CDALB 1640-1865

Longley, Michael 1939- ...... CLC 29
See also CA 102; DLB 40

Lopate, Phillip 1943- .... CLC 29
See also CA 97-100; DLB-Y 80

Lopez Portillo (y Pacheco), Jose
1920- .... CLC 46

Lopez y Fuentes, Gregorio
1897-1966 .... CLC 32

Lord, Bette Bao 1938- .... CLC 23
See also CA 107

Lorde, Audre (Geraldine)
1934- .... CLC 18
See also CANR 16; CA 25-28R;
DLB 41

Loti, Pierre 1850-1923 .... TCLC 11
See also Viaud, (Louis Marie) Julien

Lovecraft, H(oward) P(hillips)
1890-1937 .... TCLC 4, 22; SSC 3
See also CA 104

Lovelace, Earl 1935-.......... CLC 51
See also CA 77-80

Lowell, Amy 1874-1925 .... TCLC 1, 8
See also CA 104; DLB 54

Lowell, James Russell
1819-1891 .... NCLC 2
See also DLB 1, 11, 64;
CDALB 1640-1865

Lowell, Robert (Traill Spence, Jr.)
1917-1977 .. CLC 1, 2, 3, 4, 5, 8, 9,
11, 15, 37
See also CA 9-12R; obituary CA 73-76;
CABS 2; DLB 5

Lowndes, Marie (Adelaide) Belloc
1868-1947 .... TCLC 12
See also CA 107; DLB 70

Lowry, (Clarence) Malcolm
1909-1957 .... TCLC 6
See also CA 105; DLB 15

Loy, Mina 1882-1966 .... CLC 28
See also CA 113; DLB 4, 54

Lucas, George 1944-.......... CLC 16
See also CA 77-80

Lucas, Victoria 1932-1963
See Plath, Sylvia

Ludlam, Charles 1943-1987 .. CLC 46, 50
See also CA 85-88; obituary CA 122

Ludlum, Robert 1927- ...... CLC 22, 43
See also CA 33-36R; DLB-Y 82

Ludwig, Otto 1813-1865 ...... NCLC 4

Lugones, Leopoldo 1874-1938 .. TCLC 15
See also CA 116

Lu Hsun 1881-1936 .... TCLC 3

Lukacs, Georg 1885-1971...... CLC 24
See also Lukacs, Gyorgy

Lukacs, Gyorgy 1885-1971
See Lukacs, Georg
See also CA 101; obituary CA 29-32R

Luke, Peter (Ambrose Cyprian)
1919- .... CLC 38
See also CA 81-84; DLB 13

Lurie (Bishop), Alison 1926- .... CLC 4,
5, 18, 39
See also CANR 2, 17; CA 1-4R;
SATA 46; DLB 2

Lustig, Arnost 1926-........ CLC 56
See also CA 69-72; SATA 56

Luther, Martin 1483-1546 ...... LC 9

Luzi, Mario 1914-........ CLC 13
See also CANR 9; CA 61-64

Lynn, Kenneth S(chuyler)
1923- .... CLC 50
See also CANR 3; CA 1-4R

Lytle, Andrew (Nelson) 1902- .. CLC 22
See also CA 9-12R; DLB 6

Lyttelton, George 1709-1773 .... LC 10

Lytton, Edward Bulwer 1803-1873
See Bulwer-Lytton, (Lord) Edward
(George Earle Lytton)
See also SATA 23

Maas, Peter 1929- .... CLC 29
See also CA 93-96

Macaulay, (Dame Emile) Rose
1881-1958 .... TCLC 7
See also CA 104; DLB 36

MacBeth, George (Mann) 1932- .. CLC 2,
5, 9
See also CA 25-28R; SATA 4; DLB 40

MacCaig, Norman (Alexander)
1910- .... CLC 36
See also CANR 3; CA 9-12R; DLB 27

MacDermot, Thomas H. 1870-1933
See Redcam, Tom

MacDiarmid, Hugh 1892-1978 .. CLC 2,
4, 11, 19
See also Grieve, C(hristopher) M(urray)
See also DLB 20

Macdonald, Cynthia 1928- .. CLC 13, 19
See also CANR 4; CA 49-52

MacDonald, George
1824-1905 .... TCLC 9
See also CA 106; SATA 33; DLB 18

MacDonald, John D(ann)
1916-1986 .... CLC 3, 27, 44
See also CANR 1, 19; CA 1-4R;
obituary CA 121; DLB 8; DLB-Y 86

Macdonald, (John) Ross
1915-1983 .. CLC 1, 2, 3, 14, 34, 41
See also Millar, Kenneth

MacEwen, Gwendolyn (Margaret)
1941-1987 .... CLC 13, 55
See also CANR 7, 22; CA 9-12R;
obituary CA 124; SATA 50; DLB 53

Machado (y Ruiz), Antonio
1875-1939 .... TCLC 3
See also CA 104

Machado de Assis, (Joaquim Maria)
1839-1908 .... TCLC 10
See also CA 107

Machen, Arthur (Llewellyn Jones)
1863-1947 .... TCLC 4
See also CA 104; DLB 36

Machiavelli, Niccolo 1469-1527 .. LC 8

MacInnes, Colin 1914-1976 .. CLC 4, 23
See also CA 69-72; obituary CA 65-68;
DLB 14

MacInnes, Helen (Clark)
1907-1985 .... CLC 27, 39
See also CANR 1; CA 1-4R;
obituary CA 65-68, 117; SATA 22,
44

Macintosh, Elizabeth 1897-1952
See Tey, Josephine
See also CA 110

Mackenzie, (Edward Montague) Compton
1883-1972 .... CLC 18
See also CAP 2; CA 21-22;
obituary CA 37-40R; DLB 34

Mac Laverty, Bernard 1942- .. CLC 31
See also CA 116, 118

MacLean, Alistair (Stuart)
1922-1987 .... CLC 3, 13, 50
See also CA 57-60; obituary CA 121;
SATA 23

MacLeish, Archibald 1892-1982 .. CLC 3,
8, 14
See also CA 9-12R; obituary CA 106;
DLB 4, 7, 45; DLB-Y 82

MacLennan, (John) Hugh 1907- .. CLC 2,
14
See also CA 5-8R

MacLeod, Alistair 1936- ...... CLC 56
See also CA 123; DLB 60

MacNeice, (Frederick) Louis
1907-1963 .... CLC 1, 4, 10, 53
See also CA 85-88; DLB 10, 20

Macpherson, (Jean) Jay 1931-.. CLC 14
See also CA 5-8R; DLB 53

MacShane, Frank 1927- ...... CLC 39
See also CANR 3; CA 11-12R

Macumber, Mari 1896-1966
See Sandoz, Mari (Susette)

Madach, Imre 1823-1864 ...... NCLC 19

Madden, (Jerry) David 1933- .... CLC 5,
15
See also CAAS 3; CANR 4; CA 1-4R;
DLB 6

Madhubuti, Haki R. 1942- ...... CLC 6
See also Lee, Don L.
See also DLB 5, 41

Maeterlinck, Maurice
1862-1949 .... TCLC 3
See also CA 104

Mafouz, Naguib 1912-
See Mahfuz, Najib

Maginn, William 1794-1842 .. NCLC 8

Mahapatra, Jayanta 1928- .... CLC 33
See also CANR 15; CA 73-76

Mahfuz Najib 1912-........ CLC 52, 55
See also DLB-Y 88

Mahon, Derek 1941- .... CLC 27
See also CA 113; DLB 40

Mailer, Norman 1923- .. CLC 1, 2, 3, 4,
5, 8, 11, 14, 28, 39
See also CA 9-12R; CABS 1; DLB 2,
16, 28; DLB-Y 80, 83; DLB-DS 3

Maillet, Antonine 1929- ...... CLC 54
See also CA 115, 120; DLB 60

Mais, Roger 1905-1955 ...... TCLC 8
See also CA 105

Maitland, Sara (Louise) 1950-.. CLC 49
See also CANR 13; CA 69-72

Major, Clarence 1936- .... **CLC 3, 19, 48**
See also CAAS 6; CANR 13;
CA 21-24R; DLB 33

Major, Kevin 1949- .... **CLC 26**
See also CLR 11; CANR 21;
CA 97-100; SATA 32; DLB 60

Malamud, Bernard 1914-1986 .... **CLC 1,
2, 3, 5, 8, 9, 11, 18, 27, 44**
See also CA 5-8R; obituary CA 118;
CABS 1; DLB 2, 28; DLB-Y 80, 86;
CDALB 1941-1968

Malherbe, Francois de
1555-1628 .... **LC 5**

Mallarme, Stephane
1842-1898 .... **NCLC 4**

Mallet-Joris, Francoise 1930- .. **CLC 11**
See also CANR 17; CA 65-68

Maloff, Saul 1922- .... **CLC 5**
See also CA 33-36R

Malone, Louis 1907-1963
See MacNeice, (Frederick) Louis

Malone, Michael (Christopher)
1942- .... **CLC 43**
See also CANR 14; CA 77-80

Malory, (Sir) Thomas ?-1471 .... **LC 11**
See also SATA 33

Malouf, David 1934-......... **CLC 28**

Malraux, (Georges-) Andre
1901-1976 ...... **CLC 1, 4, 9, 13, 15**
See also CAP 2; CA 21-24;
obituary CA 69-72; DLB 72

Malzberg, Barry N. 1939- ...... **CLC 7**
See also CAAS 4; CANR 16; CA 61-64;
DLB 8

Mamet, David (Alan) 1947-.. **CLC 9, 15,
34, 46**
See also CANR 15; CA 81-84; DLB 7

Mamoulian, Rouben 1898- .... **CLC 16**
See also CA 25-28R

Mandelstam, Osip (Emilievich)
1891?-1938? .... **TCLC 2, 6**
See also CA 104

Mander, Jane 1877-1949 ...... **TCLC 31**

Mandiargues, Andre Pieyre de
1909- .... **CLC 41**
See also CA 103

Manley, (Mary) Delariviere
1672?-1724 .... **LC 1**
See also DLB 39

Mann, (Luiz) Heinrich
1871-1950 .... **TCLC 9**
See also CA 106

Mann, Thomas 1875-1955 .. **TCLC 2, 8,
14, 21**
See also CA 104

Manning, Frederic 1882-1935 .. **TCLC 25**

Manning, Olivia 1915-1980 .. **CLC 5, 19**
See also CA 5-8R; obituary CA 101

Mano, D. Keith 1942- ...... **CLC 2, 10**
See also CAAS 6; CA 25-28R; DLB 6

Mansfield, Katherine
1888-1923 .... **TCLC 2, 8**
See also CA 104

Manso, Peter 1940- .... **CLC 39**
See also CA 29-32R

Mapu, Abraham (ben Jekutiel)
1808-1867 .... **NCLC 18**

Marat, Jean Paul 1743-1793 .... **LC 10**

Marcel, Gabriel (Honore)
1889-1973 .... **CLC 15**
See also CA 102; obituary CA 45-48

Marchbanks, Samuel 1913-
See Davies, (William) Robertson

Marie de l'Incarnation
1599-1672 .... **LC 10**

Marinetti, F(ilippo) T(ommaso)
1876-1944 .... **TCLC 10**
See also CA 107

Marivaux, Pierre Carlet de Chamblain de
(1688-1763) .... **LC 4**

Markandaya, Kamala 1924-.. **CLC 8, 38**
See also Taylor, Kamala (Purnaiya)

Markfield, Wallace (Arthur)
1926- .... **CLC 8**
See also CAAS 3; CA 69-72; DLB 2, 28

Markham, Robert 1922-
See Amis, Kingsley (William)

Marks, J. 1942-
See Highwater, Jamake

Marley, Bob 1945-1981 ...... **CLC 17**
See also Marley, Robert Nesta

Marley, Robert Nesta 1945-1981
See Marley, Bob
See also CA 107; obituary CA 103

Marmontel, Jean-Francois
1723-1799 .... **LC 2**

Marquand, John P(hillips)
1893-1960 .... **CLC 2, 10**
See also CA 85-88; DLB 9

Marquez, Gabriel Garcia 1928-
See Garcia Marquez, Gabriel

Marquis, Don(ald Robert Perry)
1878-1937 .... **TCLC 7**
See also CA 104; DLB 11, 25

Marryat, Frederick 1792-1848 .. **NCLC 3**
See also DLB 21

Marsh, (Dame Edith) Ngaio
1899-1982 .... **CLC 7, 53**
See also CANR 6; CA 9-12R; DLB 77

Marshall, Garry 1935? .... **CLC 17**
See also CA 111

Marshall, Paule 1929- .. **CLC 27; SSC 3**
See also CANR 25; CA 77-80; DLB 33

Marsten, Richard 1926-
See Hunter, Evan

Martin, Steve 1945? .... **CLC 30**
See also CA 97-100

Martin du Gard, Roger
1881-1958 .... **TCLC 24**
See also CA 118

Martinez Ruiz, Jose 1874-1967
See Azorin
See also CA 93-96

Martinez Sierra, Gregorio 1881-1947 and
**Martinez Sierra, Maria (de la
O'LeJarraga)** 1881-1947 .. **TCLC 6**

Martinez Sierra, Gregorio 1881-1947
See Martinez Sierra, Gregorio and
Martinez Sierra, Maria (de la
O'LeJarraga)
See also CA 104, 115

**Martinez Sierra, Maria (de la
O'LeJarraga)** 1880?-1974
See Martinez Sierra, Gregorio and
Martinez Sierra, Maria (de la
O'LeJarraga)
See also obituary CA 115

**Martinez Sierra, Maria (de la
O'LeJarraga)** 1880?-1974 and
Martinez Sierra, Gregorio 1880?1974
See Martinez Sierra, Gregorio and
Martinez Sierra, Maria (de la
O'LeJarraga)

Martinson, Harry (Edmund)
1904-1978 .... **CLC 14**
See also CA 77-80

Marvell, Andrew 1621-1678...... **LC 4**

Marx, Karl (Heinrich)
1818-1883 .... **NCLC 17**

Masaoka Shiki 1867-1902 .... **TCLC 18**

Masefield, John (Edward)
1878-1967 .... **CLC 11, 47**
See also CAP 2; CA 19-20;
obituary CA 25-28R; SATA 19;
DLB 10, 19

Maso, Carole 19?? .... **CLC 44**

Mason, Bobbie Ann 1940- .. **CLC 28, 43**
See also CANR 11; CA 53-56; SAAS 1

Mason, Nick 1945-
See Pink Floyd

Mason, Tally 1909-1971
See Derleth, August (William)

Masters, Edgar Lee
1868?-1950 ....**TCLC 2, 25**
See also CA 104; DLB 54;
CDALB 1865-1917

Masters, Hilary 1928- .... **CLC 48**
See also CANR 13; CA 25-28R

Mastrosimone, William 19?? .. **CLC 36**

Matheson, Richard (Burton)
1926- .... **CLC 37**
See also CA 97-100; DLB 8, 44

Mathews, Harry 1930-...... **CLC 6, 52**
See also CAAS 6; CANR 18;
CA 21-24R

Mathias, Roland (Glyn) 1915-.. **CLC 45**
See also CANR 19; CA 97-100;
DLB 27

Matthews, Greg 1949- .... **CLC 45**

Matthews, William 1942-...... **CLC 40**
See also CANR 12; CA 29-32R; DLB 5

Matthias, John (Edward) 1941- .. **CLC 9**
See also CA 33-36R

Matthiessen, Peter 1927- .. **CLC 5, 7, 11,
32**
See also CANR 21; CA 9-12R;
SATA 27; DLB 6

Maturin, Charles Robert
1780?-1824 .... **NCLC 6**

Matute, Ana Maria 1925- .... **CLC 11**
See also CA 89-92

Maugham, W(illiam) Somerset
1874-1965 .... **CLC 1, 11, 15**
See also CA 5-8R; obituary CA 25-28R;
DLB 10, 36

Maupassant, (Henri Rene Albert) Guy de
1850-1893 .... **NCLC 1; SSC 1**

Meyer-Meyrink, Gustav 1868-1932
   See Meyrink, Gustav
   See also CA 117

Meyers, Jeffrey 1939- .... **CLC 39**
   See also CA 73-76

**Meynell, Alice (Christiana Gertrude
      Thompson)** 1847-1922 .... **TCLC 6**
   See also CA 104; DLB 19

Meyrink, Gustav 1868-1932.... **TCLC 21**
   See also Meyer-Meyrink, Gustav

Michaels, Leonard 1933- .... **CLC 6, 25**
   See also CANR 21; CA 61-64

Michaux, Henri 1899-1984 .. **CLC 8, 19**
   See also CA 85-88; obituary CA 114

Michener, James A(lbert) 1907- ..**CLC 1,
                                      5, 11, 29**
   See also CANR 21; CA 5-8R; DLB 6

Mickiewicz, Adam 1798-1855 .. **NCLC 3**

Middleton, Christopher 1926- .. **CLC 13**
   See also CA 13-16R; DLB 40

Middleton, Stanley 1919- .... **CLC 7, 38**
   See also CANR 21; CA 25-28R;
      DLB 14

Migueis, Jose Rodrigues
   1901- .... **CLC 10**

Mikszath, Kalman 1847-1910 .. **TCLC 31**

Miles, Josephine (Louise)
   1911-1985 .... **CLC 1, 2, 14, 34, 39**
   See also CANR 2; CA 1-4R;
      obituary CA 116; DLB 48

Mill, John Stuart 1806-1873 ..**NCLC 11**

Millar, Kenneth 1915-1983
   See Macdonald, Ross
   See also CANR 16; CA 9-12R;
      obituary CA 110; DLB 2; DLB-Y 83

Millay, Edna St. Vincent
   1892-1950 .... **TCLC 4**
   See also CA 104; DLB 45

Miller, Arthur 1915-.... **CLC 1, 2, 6, 10,
                                 15, 26, 47**
   See also CANR 2; CA 1-4R; DLB 7;
      CDALB 1941-1968

Miller, Henry (Valentine)
   1891-1980 .. **CLC 1, 2, 4, 9, 14, 43**
   See also CA 9-12R;
      obituary CA 97-100; DLB 4, 9;
      DLB-Y 80

Miller, Jason 1939? .... **CLC 2**
   See also CA 73-76; DLB 7

Miller, Sue 19?? .... **CLC 44**

Miller, Walter M(ichael), Jr.
   1923- .... **CLC 4, 30**
   See also CA 85-88; DLB 8

Millhauser, Steven 1943- .... **CLC 21, 54**
   See also CA 108, 110, 111; DLB 2

Millin, Sarah Gertrude
   1889-1968 .... **CLC 49**
   See also CA 102; obituary CA 93-96

Milne, A(lan) A(lexander)
   1882-1956 .... **TCLC 6**
   See also CLR 1; YABC 1; CA 104;
      DLB 10

Milner, Ron(ald) 1938-........ **CLC 56**
   See also CANR 24; CA 73-76; DLB 38

Milosz Czeslaw 1911- .. **CLC 5, 11, 22,
                                 31, 56**
   See also CA 81-84

Milton, John 1608-1674 .... **LC 9**

Miner, Valerie (Jane) 1947-.... **CLC 40**
   See also CA 97-100

Minot, Susan 1956- .... **CLC 44**

Minus, Ed 1938- .... **CLC 39**

Miro (Ferrer), Gabriel (Francisco Victor)
   1879-1930 .... **TCLC 5**
   See also CA 104

Mishima, Yukio 1925-1970 .. **CLC 2, 4,
                                 6, 9, 27**

   See also Hiraoka, Kimitake

Mistral, Gabriela 1889-1957 .. **TCLC 2**
   See also CA 104

Mitchell, James Leslie 1901-1935
   See Gibbon, Lewis Grassic
   See also CA 104; DLB 15

Mitchell, Joni 1943-.......... **CLC 12**
   See also CA 112

Mitchell (Marsh), Margaret (Munnerlyn)
   1900-1949 ....**TCLC 11**
   See also CA 109; DLB 9

Mitchell, W(illiam) O(rmond)
   1914- .... **CLC 25**
   See also CANR 15; CA 77-80

Mitford, Mary Russell
   1787-1855 .... **NCLC 4**

Mitford, Nancy 1904-1973 .... **CLC 44**
   See also CA 9-12R

Mo, Timothy 1950- .... **CLC 46**
   See also CA 117

Modarressi, Taghi 1931- ...... **CLC 44**
   See also CA 121

Modiano, Patrick (Jean)
   1945- .... **CLC 18**
   See also CANR 17; CA 85-88

Mofolo, Thomas (Mokopu)
   1876-1948 ....**TCLC 22**
   See also CA 121

Mohr, Nicholasa 1935-........ **CLC 12**
   See also CANR 1; CA 49-52; SATA 8

Mojtabai, A(nn) G(race) 1938-.... **CLC 5,
                                     9, 15, 29**

   See also CA 85-88

Moliere 1622-1673 .... **LC 10**

Molnar, Ferenc 1878-1952 .... **TCLC 20**
   See also CA 109

Momaday, N(avarre) Scott 1934-.. **CLC 2,
                                     19**
   See also CANR 14; CA 25-28R;
      SATA 30, 48

Monroe, Harriet 1860-1936 .... **TCLC 12**
   See also CA 109; DLB 54

Montagu, Elizabeth
   1720-1800 .... **NCLC 7**

**Montagu, Lady Mary (Pierrepont)
      Wortley** 1689-1762 .... **LC 9**

Montague, John (Patrick)
   1929- .... **CLC 13, 46**
   See also CANR 9; CA 9-12R; DLB 40

Montaigne, Michel (Eyquem) de
   1533-1592 .... **LC 8**

Montale, Eugenio 1896-1981 ....**CLC 7,
                                     9, 18**
   See also CA 17-20R; obituary CA 104

Montgomery, Marion (H., Jr.)
   1925- ....**CLC 7**
   See also CANR 3; CA 1-4R; DLB 6

Montgomery, Robert Bruce 1921-1978
   See Crispin, Edmund
   See also CA 104

Montherlant, Henri (Milon) de
   1896-1972 .... **CLC 8, 19**
   See also CA 85-88;
      obituary CA 37-40R; DLB 72

Montisquieu, Charles-Louis de Secondat
   1689-1755 .... **LC 7**

Monty Python .... **CLC 21**
   See also Cleese, John; Gilliam, Terry
      (Vance); Idle, Eric; Jones, Terry;
      Palin, Michael

Moodie, Susanna (Strickland)
   1803-1885 ....**NCLC 14**

Mooney, Ted 1951- .... **CLC 25**

Moorcock, Michael (John)
   1939- ....**CLC 5, 27**
   See also CAAS 5; CANR 2, 17;
      CA 45-48; DLB 14

Moore, Brian 1921- .. **CLC 1, 3, 5, 7, 8,
                              19, 32**
   See also CANR 1; CA 1-4R

Moore, George (Augustus)
   1852-1933 .... **TCLC 7**
   See also CA 104; DLB 10, 18, 57

Moore, Lorrie 1957-........ **CLC 39, 45**
   See also Moore, Marie Lorena

Moore, Marianne (Craig)
   1887-1972 .. **CLC 1, 2, 4, 8, 10, 13,
                             19, 47**

   See also CANR 3; CA 1-4R;
      obituary CA 33-36R; SATA 20;
      DLB 45

Moore, Marie Lorena 1957-
   See Moore, Lorrie
   See also CA 116

Moore, Thomas 1779-1852 .... **NCLC 6**

Morand, Paul 1888-1976 ...... **CLC 41**
   See also obituary CA 69-72

Morante, Elsa 1918-1985.... **CLC 8, 47**
   See also CA 85-88; obituary CA 117

Moravia, Alberto 1907- .. **CLC 2, 7, 11,
                                 18, 27, 46**
   See also Pincherle, Alberto

More, Henry 1614-1687 .... **LC 9**

More, Thomas 1478-1573 ...... **LC 10**

Moreas, Jean 1856-1910 ...... **TCLC 18**

Morgan, Berry 1919- .... **CLC 6**
   See also CA 49-52; DLB 6

Morgan, Edwin (George)
   1920- .... **CLC 31**
   See also CANR 3; CA 7-8R; DLB 27

Morgan, (George) Frederick
   1922- .... **CLC 23**
   See also CANR 21; CA 17-20R

Morgan, Janet 1945- .... **CLC 39**
   See also CA 65-68

Morgan, Robin 1941- .... **CLC 2**
   See also CA 69-72

**Morgenstern, Christian (Otto Josef
      Wolfgang)** 1871-1914 .... **TCLC 8**
   See also CA 105

Author Index

Salama, Hannu 1936- .... **CLC 18**

Salamanca, J(ack) R(ichard)
1922- .... **CLC 4, 15**
See also CA 25-28R

Salinas, Pedro 1891-1951...... **TCLC 17**
See also CA 117

Salinger, J(erome) D(avid) 1919- ..**CLC 1,
3, 8, 12, 56; SSC 2**
See also CA 5-8R; DLB 2;
CDALB 1941-1968

Salter, James 1925- .... **CLC 7, 52**
See also CA 73-76

Saltus, Edgar (Evertson)
1855-1921 .... **TCLC 8**
See also CA 105

Saltykov, Mikhail Evgrafovich
1826-1889 ....**NCLC 16**

Samarakis, Antonis 1919- ...... **CLC 5**
See also CA 25-28R

Sanchez, Luis Rafael 1936- .... **CLC 23**

Sanchez, Sonia 1934- .... **CLC 5**
See also CA 33-36R; SATA 22; DLB 41

Sand, George 1804-1876 ...... **NCLC 2**

Sandburg, Carl (August)
1878-1967 .... **CLC 1, 4, 10, 15, 35**
See also CA 5-8R; obituary CA 25-28R;
SATA 8; DLB 17, 54;
CDALB 1865-1917

Sandburg, Charles August 1878-1967
See Sandburg, Carl (August)

Sanders, (James) Ed(ward)
1939- .... **CLC 53**
See also CANR 13; CA 15-16R;
DLB 16

Sanders, Lawrence 1920- ...... **CLC 41**
See also CA 81-84

Sandoz, Mari (Susette)
1896-1966 .... **CLC 28**
See also CANR 17; CA 1-4R;
obituary CA 25-28R; SATA 5;
DLB 9

Saner, Reg(inald Anthony) 1931- .. **CLC 9**
See also CA 65-68

Sannazaro, Jacopo 1456?-1530 .... **LC 8**

Sansom, William 1912-1976 .. **CLC 2, 6**
See also CA 5-8R; obituary CA 65-68

Santiago, Danny 1911- .... **CLC 33**

Santmyer, Helen Hooven
1895-1986 .... **CLC 33**
See also CANR 15; CA 1-4R;
obituary CA 118; DLB-Y 84

Santos, Bienvenido N(uqui)
1911- .... **CLC 22**
See also CANR 19; CA 101

Sappho c. 6th-century B.C. .... **CMLC 3**

Sarduy, Severo 1937- .... **CLC 6**
See also CA 89-92

Sargeson, Frank 1903-1982 .... **CLC 31**
See also CA 106

Sarmiento, Felix Ruben Garcia 1867-1916
See also CA 104

Saroyan, William 1908-1981 ....**CLC 1,
8, 10, 29, 34, 56**
See also CA 5-8R; obituary CA 103;
SATA 23; obituary SATA 24;
DLB 7, 9; DLB-Y 81

Sarraute, Nathalie 1902- .. **CLC 1, 2, 4,
8, 10, 31**
See also CA 9-12R

Sarton, Eleanore Marie 1912-
See Sarton, (Eleanor) May

Sarton, (Eleanor) May 1912- ....**CLC 4,
14, 49**
See also CANR 1; CA 1-4R; SATA 36;
DLB 48; DLB-Y 81

Sartre, Jean-Paul (Charles Aymard)
1905-1980 .. **CLC 1, 4, 7, 9, 13, 18,
24, 44, 50, 52**
See also CANR 21; CA 9-12R;
obituary CA 97-100; DLB 72

Sassoon, Siegfried (Lorraine)
1886-1967 .... **CLC 36**
See also CA 104; obituary CA 25-28R;
DLB 20

Saul, John (W. III) 1942- ...... **CLC 46**
See also CANR 16; CA 81-84

Saura, Carlos 1932- .... **CLC 20**
See also CA 114

Sauser-Hall, Frederic-Louis 1887-1961
See Cendrars, Blaise
See also CA 102; obituary CA 93-96

Savage, Thomas 1915- .... **CLC 40**

Savan, Glenn 19??............ **CLC 50**

Sayers, Dorothy L(eigh)
1893-1957 .... **TCLC 2, 15**
See also CA 104, 119; DLB 10, 36

Sayers, Valerie 19?? .... **CLC 50**

Sayles, John (Thomas) 1950- ....**CLC 7,
10, 14**
See also CA 57-60; DLB 44

Scammell, Michael 19?? ...... **CLC 34**

Scannell, Vernon 1922-........ **CLC 49**
See also CANR 8; CA 5-8R; DLB 27

Schaeffer, Susan Fromberg
1941- .... **CLC 6, 11, 22**
See also CANR 18; CA 49-52;
SATA 22; DLB 28

Schell, Jonathan 1943-........ **CLC 35**
See also CANR 12; CA 73-76

Scherer, Jean-Marie Maurice 1920-
See Rohmer, Eric
See also CA 110

Schevill, James (Erwin) 1920- .... **CLC 7**
See also CA 5-8R

Schisgal, Murray (Joseph) 1926- .. **CLC 6**
See also CA 21-24R

Schlee, Ann 1934-............ **CLC 35**
See also CA 101; SATA 36, 44

Schlegel, August Wilhelm von
1767-1845 ....**NCLC 15**

Schlegel, Johann Elias (von)
1719?-1749 .... **LC 5**

Schmidt, Arno 1914-1979...... **CLC 56**
See also obituary CA 109; DLB 69

Schmitz, Ettore 1861-1928
See Svevo, Italo
See also CA 104

Schnackenberg, Gjertrud
1953- .... **CLC 40**
See also CA 116

Schneider, Leonard Alfred 1925-1966
See Bruce, Lenny
See also CA 89-92

Schnitzler, Arthur 1862-1931 .. **TCLC 4**
See also CA 104

Schorer, Mark 1908-1977 ...... **CLC 9**
See also CANR 7; CA 5-8R;
obituary CA 73-76

Schrader, Paul (Joseph) 1946- .. **CLC 26**
See also CA 37-40R; DLB 44

**Schreiner (Cronwright), Olive (Emilie
Albertina)** 1855-1920 .... **TCLC 9**
See also CA 105; DLB 18

Schulberg, Budd (Wilson) 1914- ..**CLC 7,
48**
See also CANR 19; CA 25-28R;
DLB 6, 26, 28; DLB-Y 81

Schulz, Bruno 1892-1942 ...... **TCLC 5**
See also CA 115

Schulz, Charles M(onroe)
1922- .... **CLC 12**
See also CANR 6; CA 9-12R; SATA 10

Schuyler, James (Marcus) 1923- ..**CLC 5,
23**
See also CA 101; DLB 5

Schwartz, Delmore 1913-1966 ....**CLC 2,
4, 10, 45**
See also CAP 2; CA 17-18;
obituary CA 25-28R; DLB 28, 48

Schwartz, Lynne Sharon
1939- .... **CLC 31**
See also CA 103

Schwarz-Bart, Andre 1928- .... **CLC 2, 4**
See also CA 89-92

Schwarz-Bart, Simone 1938- .... **CLC 7**
See also CA 97-100

Schwob, (Mayer Andre) Marcel
1867-1905 ....**TCLC 20**
See also CA 117

Sciascia, Leonardo 1921- .. **CLC 8, 9, 41**
See also CA 85-88

Scoppettone, Sandra 1936- .... **CLC 26**
See also CA 5-8R; SATA 9

Scorsese, Martin 1942-........ **CLC 20**
See also CA 110, 114

Scotland, Jay 1932-
See Jakes, John (William)

Scott, Duncan Campbell
1862-1947 .... **TCLC 6**
See also CA 104

Scott, Evelyn 1893-1963 ...... **CLC 43**
See also CA 104; obituary CA 112;
DLB 9, 48

Scott, F(rancis) R(eginald)
1899-1985 .... **CLC 22**
See also CA 101; obituary CA 114

Scott, Joanna 19?? .... **CLC 50**

Scott, Paul (Mark) 1920-1978 .... **CLC 9**
See also CA 81-84; obituary CA 77-80;
DLB 14

Scott, Sir Walter 1771-1832 .. **NCLC 15**
See also YABC 2

Scribe, (Augustin) Eugene
1791-1861 ....**NCLC 16**

Scudery, Madeleine de
1607-1701 .... **LC 2**

Sealy, I. Allan 1951- .... **CLC 55**

Seare, Nicholas 1925-
See Trevanian; Whitaker, Rodney

Trilling, Lionel 1905-1975 . . **CLC 9, 11, 24**
See also CANR 10; CA 9-12R; obituary CA 61-64; DLB 28, 63

Trogdon, William 1939-
See Heat Moon, William Least
See also CA 115

Trollope, Anthony 1815-1882 . . **NCLC 6**
See also SATA 22; DLB 21, 57

Trotsky, Leon (Davidovich)
1879-1940 . . . . **TCLC 22**
See also CA 118

Trotter (Cockburn), Catharine
1679-1749 . . . . **LC 8**

Trow, George W. S. 1943- . . . . **CLC 52**
See also CA 126

Troyat, Henri 1911- . . . . **CLC 23**
See also CANR 2; CA 45-48

Trudeau, Garry 1948- . . . . **CLC 12**
See also Trudeau, G(arretson) B(eekman)

Trudeau, G(arretson) B(eekman) 1948-
See Trudeau, Garry
See also CA 81-84; SATA 35

Truffaut, Francois 1932-1984 . . **CLC 20**
See also CA 81-84; obituary CA 113

Trumbo, Dalton 1905-1976 . . . . **CLC 19**
See also CANR 10; CA 21-24R; obituary CA 69-72; DLB 26

Tryon, Thomas 1926- . . . . . . **CLC 3, 11**
See also CA 29-32R

Ts'ao Hsueh-ch'in 1715?1763 . . . . **LC 1**

Tsushima Shuji 1909-1948
See Dazai Osamu
See also CA 107

Tsvetaeva (Efron), Marina (Ivanovna)
1892-1941 . . . . **TCLC 7**
See also CA 104

Tunis, John R(oberts)
1889-1975 . . . . **CLC 12**
See also CA 61-64; SATA 30, 37; DLB 22

Tuohy, Frank 1925- . . . . **CLC 37**
See also DLB 14

Tuohy, John Francis 1925-
See Tuohy, Frank
See also CANR 3; CA 5-8R

Turco, Lewis (Putnam) 1934- . . **CLC 11**
See also CA 13-16R; DLB-Y 84

Turgenev, Ivan 1818-1883 . . . . **NCLC 21**

Turner, Frederick 1943- . . . . . . **CLC 48**
See also CANR 12; CA 73-76; DLB 40

Tutuola, Amos 1920- . . . . **CLC 5, 14, 29**
See also CA 9-12R

Twain, Mark 1835-1910 . . **TCLC 6, 12, 19**
See also Clemens, Samuel Langhorne
See also DLB 11, 12, 23

Tyler, Anne 1941- . . **CLC 7, 11, 18, 28, 44**
See also CANR 11; CA 9-12R; SATA 7; DLB 6; DLB-Y 82

Tyler, Royall 1757-1826 . . . . . . **NCLC 3**
See also DLB 37

Tynan (Hinkson), Katharine
1861-1931 . . . . **TCLC 3**
See also CA 104

Tytell, John 1939- . . . . **CLC 50**
See also CA 29-32R

Tzara, Tristan 1896-1963 . . . . . . **CLC 47**
See also Rosenfeld, Samuel

Uhry, Alfred 1947? . . . . **CLC 55**
See also CA 127

Unamuno (y Jugo), Miguel de
1864-1936 . . . . **TCLC 2, 9**
See also CA 104

Underwood, Miles 1909-1981
See Glassco, John

Undset, Sigrid 1882-1949 . . . . . . **TCLC 3**
See also CA 104

Ungaretti, Giuseppe 1888-1970 . . **CLC 7, 11, 15**
See also CAP 2; CA 19-20; obituary CA 25-28R

Unger, Douglas 1952- . . . . **CLC 34**

Unger, Eva 1932-
See Figes, Eva

Updike, John (Hoyer) 1932- . . **CLC 1, 2, 3, 5, 7, 9, 13, 15, 23, 34, 43**
See also CANR 4; CA 1-4R; CABS 2; DLB 2, 5; DLB-Y 80, 82; DLB-DS 3

Urdang, Constance (Henriette)
1922- . . . . **CLC 47**
See also CANR 9; CA 21-24R

Uris, Leon (Marcus) 1924- . . **CLC 7, 32**
See also CANR 1; CA 1-4R; SATA 49

Ustinov, Peter (Alexander) 1921- . . **CLC 1**
See also CA 13 16R; DLB 13

Vaculik, Ludvik 1926- . . . . **CLC 7**
See also CA 53-56

Valenzuela, Luisa 1938- . . . . . . **CLC 31**
See also CA 101

Valera (y Acala-Galiano), Juan
1824-1905 . . . . **TCLC 10**
See also CA 106

Valery, Paul (Ambroise Toussaint Jules)
1871-1945 . . . . **TCLC 4, 15**
See also CA 104, 122

Valle-Inclan (y Montenegro), Ramon (Maria) del 1866-1936 . . . . **TCLC 5**
See also CA 106

Vallejo, Cesar (Abraham)
1892-1938 . . . . **TCLC 3**
See also CA 105

Van Ash, Cay 1918- . . . . **CLC 34**

Vance, Jack 1916? . . . . **CLC 35**
See also DLB 8

Vance, John Holbrook 1916?
See Vance, Jack
See also CANR 17; CA 29-32R

Van Den Bogarde, Derek (Jules Gaspard Ulric) Niven 1921-
See Bogarde, Dirk
See also CA 77-80

Vanderhaeghe, Guy 1951- . . . . . **CLC 41**
See also CA 113

Van der Post, Laurens (Jan)
1906- . . . . **CLC 5**
See also CA 5-8R

Van de Wetering, Janwillem
1931- . . . . **CLC 47**
See also CANR 4; CA 49-52

Van Dine, S. S. 1888-1939 . . . . **TCLC 23**

Van Doren, Carl (Clinton)
1885-1950 . . . . **TCLC 18**
See also CA 111

Van Doren, Mark 1894-1972 . . . . **CLC 6, 10**
See also CANR 3; CA 1-4R; obituary CA 37-40R; DLB 45

Van Druten, John (William)
1901-1957 . . . . **TCLC 2**
See also CA 104; DLB 10

Van Duyn, Mona 1921- . . . . . . **CLC 3, 7**
See also CANR 7; CA 9-12R; DLB 5

Van Itallie, Jean-Claude 1936- . . **CLC 3**
See also CAAS 2; CANR 1; CA 45-48; DLB 7

Van Ostaijen, Paul 1896-1928 . . **TCLC 33**

Van Peebles, Melvin 1932- . . **CLC 2, 20**
See also CA 85-88

Vansittart, Peter 1920- . . . . **CLC 42**
See also CANR 3; CA 1-4R

Van Vechten, Carl 1880-1964 . . **CLC 33**
See also obituary CA 89-92; DLB 4, 9, 51

Van Vogt, A(lfred) E(lton) 1912- . . **CLC 1**
See also CA 21-24R; SATA 14; DLB 8

Varda, Agnes 1928- . . . . **CLC 16**
See also CA 116

Vargas Llosa, (Jorge) Mario (Pedro)
1936- . . **CLC 3, 6, 9, 10, 15, 31, 42**
See also CANR 18; CA 73-76

Vassilikos, Vassilis 1933- . . . . . **CLC 4, 8**
See also CA 81-84

Vazov, Ivan 1850-1921 . . . . **TCLC 25**
See also CA 121

Veblen, Thorstein Bunde
1857-1929 . . . . **TCLC 31**
See also CA 115

Verga, Giovanni 1840-1922 . . . . **TCLC 3**
See also CA 104

Verhaeren, Emile (Adolphe Gustave)
1855-1916 . . . . **TCLC 12**
See also CA 109

Verlaine, Paul (Marie)
1844-1896 . . . . **NCLC 2**

Verne, Jules (Gabriel)
1828-1905 . . . . **TCLC 6**
See also CA 110; SATA 21

Very, Jones 1813-1880 . . . . **NCLC 9**
See also DLB 1

Vesaas, Tarjei 1897-1970 . . . . . . **CLC 48**
See also obituary CA 29-32R

Vian, Boris 1920-1959 . . . . **TCLC 9**
See also CA 106; DLB 72

Viaud, (Louis Marie) Julien 1850-1923
See Loti, Pierre
See also CA 107

Vicker, Angus 1916-
See Felsen, Henry Gregor

Vidal, Eugene Luther, Jr. 1925-
See Vidal, Gore

Vidal, Gore 1925- . . . . **CLC 2, 4, 6, 8, 10, 22, 33**
See also CANR 13; CA 5-8R; DLB 6

Viereck, Peter (Robert Edwin)
1916- . . . . **CLC 4**
See also CANR 1; CA 1-4R; DLB 5

Wilde, Oscar (Fingal O'Flahertie Wills)
1854-1900 .... TCLC 1, 8, 23
See also CA 104; SATA 24; DLB 10,
19, 34, 57

Wilder, Billy 1906- .... CLC 20
See also Wilder, Samuel
See also DLB 26

Wilder, Samuel 1906-
See Wilder, Billy
See also CA 89-92

Wilder, Thornton (Niven)
1897-1975 .. CLC 1, 5, 6, 10, 15, 35
See also CA 13-16R;
obituary CA 61-64; DLB 4, 7, 9

Wiley, Richard 1944- .... CLC 44
See also CA 121

Wilhelm, Kate 1928- .... CLC 7
See also CAAS 5; CANR 17;
CA 37-40R; DLB 8

Willard, Nancy 1936- ...... CLC 7, 37
See also CLR 5; CANR 10; CA 89-92;
SATA 30, 37; DLB 5, 52

Williams, Charles (Walter Stansby)
1886-1945 .... TCLC 1, 11
See also CA 104

Williams, C(harles) K(enneth)
1936- .... CLC 33, 56
See also CA 37-40R; DLB 5

Williams, Ella Gwendolen Rees
1890-1979
See Rhys, Jean

Williams, (George) Emlyn
1905- .... CLC 15
See also CA 104; DLB 10

Williams, Hugo 1942- .... CLC 42
See also CA 17-20R; DLB 40

Williams, John A(lfred) 1925- .... CLC 5,
13
See also CAAS 3; CANR 6; CA 53-56;
DLB 2, 33

Williams, Jonathan (Chamberlain)
1929- .... CLC 13
See also CANR 8; CA 9-12R; DLB 5

Williams, Joy 1944- .... CLC 31
See also CANR 22; CA 41-44R

Williams, Norman 1952- ...... CLC 39
See also CA 118

Williams, Paulette 1948-
See Shange, Ntozake

Williams, Tennessee 1911-1983 .. CLC 1,
2, 5, 7, 8, 11, 15, 19, 30, 39, 45
See also CA 5-8R; obituary CA 108;
DLB 7; DLB-Y 83; DLB-DS 4;
CDALB 1941-1968

Williams, Thomas (Alonzo)
1926- .... CLC 14
See also CANR 2; CA 1-4R

Williams, Thomas Lanier 1911-1983
See Williams, Tennessee

Williams, William Carlos
1883-1963 .. CLC 1, 2, 5, 9, 13, 22,
42
See also CA 89-92; DLB 4, 16, 54

Williamson, David 1932- ...... CLC 56

Williamson, Jack 1908- ...... CLC 29
See also Williamson, John Stewart
See also DLB 8

Williamson, John Stewart 1908-
See Williamson, Jack
See also CA 17-20R

Willingham, Calder (Baynard, Jr.)
1922- .... CLC 5, 51
See also CANR 3; CA 5-8R; DLB 2, 44

Wilson, A(ndrew) N(orman)
1950- .... CLC 33
See also CA 112; DLB 14

Wilson, Andrew 1948-
See Wilson, Snoo

Wilson, Angus (Frank Johnstone)
1913- .... CLC 2, 3, 5, 25, 34
See also CA 5-8R; DLB 15

Wilson, August 1945- ...... CLC 39, 50
See also CA 115, 122

Wilson, Brian 1942- .... CLC 12

Wilson, Colin 1931- .... CLC 3, 14
See also CAAS 5; CANR 1; CA 1-4R;
DLB 14

Wilson, Edmund 1895-1972 .. CLC 1, 2,
3, 8, 24
See also CANR 1; CA 1-4R;
obituary CA 37-40R; DLB 63

Wilson, Ethel Davis (Bryant)
1888-1980 .... CLC 13
See also CA 102

Wilson, John 1785-1854 ...... NCLC 5

Wilson, John (Anthony) Burgess 1917-
See Burgess, Anthony
See also CANR 2; CA 1-4R

Wilson, Lanford 1937- .... CLC 7, 14, 36
See also CA 17-20R; DLB 7

Wilson, Robert (M.) 1944- .... CLC 7, 9
See also CANR 2; CA 49-52

Wilson, Sloan 1920- .... CLC 32
See also CANR 1; CA 1-4R

Wilson, Snoo 1948- .... CLC 33
See also CA 69-72

Wilson, William S(mith)
1932- .... CLC 49
See also CA 81-84

**Winchilsea, Anne (Kingsmill) Finch,
Countess of** 1661-1720 ...... LC 3

Winters, Janet Lewis 1899-
See Lewis (Winters), Janet
See also CAP 1; CA 9-10

Winters, (Arthur) Yvor
1900-1968 .... CLC 4, 8, 32
See also CAP 1; CA 11-12;
obituary CA 25-28R; DLB 48

Wiseman, Frederick 1930- .... CLC 20

Wister, Owen 1860-1938 ...... TCLC 21
See also CA 108; DLB 9

Witkiewicz, Stanislaw Ignacy
1885-1939 .... TCLC 8
See also CA 105

Wittig, Monique 1935?........ CLC 22
See also CA 116

Wittlin, Joseph 1896-1976 .... CLC 25
See also Wittlin, Jozef

Wittlin, Jozef 1896-1976
See Wittlin, Joseph
See also CANR 3; CA 49-52;
obituary CA 65-68

Wodehouse, (Sir) P(elham) G(renville)
1881-1975 .... CLC 1, 2, 5, 10, 22;
SSC 2
See also CANR 3; CA 45-48;
obituary CA 57-60; SATA 22;
DLB 34

Woiwode, Larry (Alfred) 1941- .. CLC 6,
10
See also CANR 16; CA 73-76; DLB 6

Wojciechowska, Maia (Teresa)
1927- .... CLC 26
See also CLR 1; CANR 4; CA 9-12R;
SAAS 1; SATA 1, 28

Wolf, Christa 1929- .... CLC 14, 29
See also CA 85-88

Wolfe, Gene (Rodman) 1931- .. CLC 25
See also CANR 6; CA 57-60; DLB 8

Wolfe, George C. 1954- ...... CLC 49

Wolfe, Thomas (Clayton)
1900-1938 .... TCLC 4, 13, 29
See also CA 104; DLB 9; DLB-Y 85;
DLB-DS 2

Wolfe, Thomas Kennerly, Jr. 1931-
See Wolfe, Tom
See also CANR 9; CA 13-16R

Wolfe, Tom 1931-.. CLC 1, 2, 9, 15, 35,
51
See also Wolfe, Thomas Kennerly, Jr.

Wolff, Geoffrey (Ansell) 1937-.. CLC 41
See also CA 29-32R

Wolff, Tobias (Jonathan Ansell)
1945- .... CLC 39
See also CA 114, 117

Wolitzer, Hilma 1930- .... CLC 17
See also CANR 18; CA 65-68;
SATA 31

Wollstonecraft (Godwin), Mary
1759-1797 .... LC 5
See also DLB 39

Wonder, Stevie 1950- .... CLC 12
See also Morris, Steveland Judkins

Wong, Jade Snow 1922- ...... CLC 17
See also CA 109

Woodcott, Keith 1934-
See Brunner, John (Kilian Houston)

Woolf, (Adeline) Virginia
1882-1941 ....TCLC 1, 5, 20
See also CA 104; DLB 36

Woollcott, Alexander (Humphreys)
1887-1943 .... TCLC 5
See also CA 105; DLB 29

Wordsworth, William
1770-1850 .... NCLC 12

Wouk, Herman 1915- .... CLC 1, 9, 38
See also CANR 6; CA 5-8R; DLB-Y 82

Wright, Charles 1935- .... CLC 6, 13, 28
See also CAAS 7; CA 29-32R;
DLB-Y 82

Wright, Charles (Stevenson)
1932- .... CLC 49
See also CA 9-12R; DLB 33

Wright, James (Arlington)
1927-1980 ....CLC 3, 5, 10, 28
See also CANR 4; CA 49-52;
obituary CA 97-100; DLB 5

Wright, Judith 1915- ...... CLC 11, 53
See also CA 13-16R; SATA 14

Author Index

LC Cumulative Nationality Index

LC Cumulative Title Index

Title Index

Title Index

Title Index

Title Index

Title Index

Title Index

Title Index

Title Index

Title Index

Title Index

"To the Memory of My Beloved, the Author, Mr. William Shakespeare, and What He Hath Left Us" (Jonson) **6**:348, 350

"To the New Yeere" (Drayton) **8**:17, 27

"To the New Yeere" (Drayton) See "Ode on the New Year"

"To the Nightingale" (Winchilsea) **3**:441-42, 444, 447, 451, 454

"To the Nightingale" (Finch) See "The Nightingale"

"To the Pious Memory of the Accomplisht Young Lady Mrs. Anne Killigrew" (Dryden) **3**:186, 216, 223

"To the Pious Memory of the Accomplisht Young Lady Mrs. Anne Killigrew" (Dryden) See "Anne Killigrew"

"To the Pious Memory of the Accomplisht Young Lady Mrs. Anne Killigrew" (Dryden) See "Ode on Anne Killigrew"

"To the Pious Memory of the Accomplisht Young Lady Mrs. Anne Killigrew" (Dryden) See "Ode to the Memory of Mrs. Killigrew"

"To the Queenes most Excellent Majestie" (Lanyer) **10**:183

"To the Reader of These Sonnets" (Drayton) **8**:37

"To the Right Honorable William, Earl of Dartmouth, His Majesty's Principal Secretary of State for North America" (Wheatley) **3**:415, 423, 427, 429, 434

"To the Same (i.e., to Celia)" (Jonson) **6**:349

"To the Toothache" (Burns) **3**:67, 85

"To the Toothache" (Burns) See "Address to the Toothache"

"To the University of Cambridge, in New England" (Wheatley) **3**:413, 415-16, 423, 427, 429

"To the University of Cambridge, in New England" (Wheatley) See "Cambridge"

"To the Vertuous Reader" (Lanyer) **10**:181-82, 184, 190

"To the Vertuous Reader" (Lanyer) See "Epistle to the Vertuous Reader"

"To the Virginian Voyage" (Drayton) **8**:18, 25-7, 30, 42-5

"To the Virginian Voyage" (Drayton) See "Virginian Ode"

"To the Virginian Voyage" (Drayton) See "Virginian Voyage"

"To the Woodlark" (Burns) **3**:81

Tom Jones (*The History Of Tom Jones, a Foundling*) (Fielding)

"Tom May's Death" (Marvell) **4**:439

"Tom Thumb" ("Le petit poucet") (Perrault)

Tombeau de Marguerite de Valois (Ronsard) **6**:434

"Le Tombeau du feu Roy Tres-Chrestien Charles IX" (Ronsard) **6**:437

Tombo-Chiqui; or, The American Savage (Cleland) **2**:51, 53

The Topsy-Turvy World (*Die Verkehrte Welt*) (Grimmelshausen)

"Torticolis" (Rousseau) **9**:345

A Tour through the Whole Island of Great Britain (Defoe) **1**:173-74

Tour to Corsica (*An Account of Corsica, The Journal of a Tour to that Island; and the Memoirs of Pascal Paoli*) (Boswell)

Tour to the Hebrides (*Journal of a Tour to the Hebrides with Samuel Johnson*) (Boswell)

"The Tournament" (Chatterton) **3**:124, 135

The Town and Country Mouse (*The Hind and the Panther, Transvers'd to the Story of the Country and the City-Mouse*) (Dryden)

Town Eclogues (*Court Poems*) (Montagu)

The Town Fop; or, Sir Timothy Tawdrey (Behn) **1**:33, 39, 46-7

Los trabaios de Persiles y Sigismunda (Cervantes) **6**:142-43, 151, 169-70, 174-76, 178, 180

Los trabaios de Persiles y Sigismunda (Cervantes) See *Persiles y Sigismunda*

Los trabaios de Persiles y Sigismunda (Cervantes) See *Travails of Persiles and Sigismunda*

Los trabaios de Persiles y Sigismunda (Cervantes) See *The Troubles of Persiles and Sigismunda*

"Tract on the Popery Laws" (Burke) **7**:46

Tractatus theologico-politicus continens dissertationes all quot, quibus ostenditur libertatem philosophandi non tantum salva pietate, & reipublicae (Spinoza) **9**:393, 397-98, 402, 408-09, 418-19, 423-24, 431, 436, 438-40

Tractatus theologico-politicus continens dissertationes all quot, quibus ostenditur libertatem philosophandi non tantum salva pietate, & reipublicae (Spinoza) See *Theological-Political Treatise*

Tractatus theologico-politicus continens dissertationes all quot, quibus ostenditur libertatem philosophandi non tantum salva pietate, & reipublicae (Spinoza) See *Theologico-Political Treatise*

Tractatus theologico-politicus continens dissertationes all quot, quibus ostenditur libertatem philosophandi non tantum salva pietate, & reipublicae (Spinoza) See *A Treatise Partly Theological, and Partly Political, Containing Some Few Discourses*

"The Tradgedy of Ælla" ("Ælla: A Tragycal Enterlude") (Chatterton)

The Tragedy of Jane Shore (Rowe) **8**:285, 287, 292-97, 299-302, 304-08, 314, 316

The Tragedy of Jane Shore (Rowe) See *Jane Shore*

The Tragedy of Lady Jane Gray (Rowe) **8**:293, 297, 300, 302, 305, 307-08

The Tragedy of Lady Jane Gray (Rowe) See *Jane*

The Tragedy of Lady Jane Gray (Rowe) See *Lady Jane Gray*

The Tragedy of Tom Thumb (Fielding) **1**:203, 239

Traité des devoirs (Montesquieu) **7**:339, 356, 360

Trampagos, the Pimp Who Lost His Moll (Cervantes) **6**:190-92

A Translation of the Psalms of David, Attempted in the Spirit of Christianity, and Adapted to the Divine Service (Smart) **3**:371, 376-78, 382, 395, 398

"A Translation of the Psalms of David, Attempted in the Spirit of Christianity, and Adapted to the Divine Service" (Smart) See "Psalms"

"A Translation of the Psalms of David, Attempted in the Spirit of Christianity, and Adapted to the Divine Service" (Smart) See "Psalms of David"

Translator's Preface (*Vorrede des Uebersetzers zu Der Ruhmredige*) (Schlegel)

El trato de Argel (Cervantes) **6**:177-78, 180-81

El trato de Argel (Cervantes) See *Los tratos de Argel*

Los tratos de Argel (*El trato de Argel*) (Cervantes)

Travails of Persiles and Sigismunda (*Los trabaios de Persiles y Sigismunda*) (Cervantes)

Travel Journal (*Journal du voyage de Michel de Montaigne en Italie par la Suisse et l'Allemagne en 1580 et 1581*) (Montaigne)

The Traveller (Goldsmith) **2**:66, 68, 71-5, 80-2, 94-5, 97, 102, 104-05, 112-15, 128-31

Travels, Chiefly on Foot, through Several Parts of England in 1782 (*Reisen eines Deutschen in England im Jahr 1782*) (Moritz)

Travels in England (*Reisen eines Deutschen in England im Jahr 1782*) (Moritz)

Travels into Severul Remote Nations of the World (Swift) See *Gulliver's Travels*

Travels into Several Remote Nations of the World, in Four Parts; By Lemuel Gulliver (Swift) **1**:426-29, 432-37, 439-42, 444-52, 456, 460-79, 483-91, 497-502, 504-10, 513-17, 519, 527-29

Travels through France and Italy (Smollett) **2**:322, 329, 331, 344, 363, 365-67

The Treasure (Lessing) **8**:112

The Treasure of the City of Ladies, or, The Book of the Three Virtues (*La trésor de la cité des dames; or, Le livre des trois vertus*) (Christine de Pizan)

Treatise (Taylor) See *Treatise Concerning the Lord's Supper*

Treatise Concerning Enthusiasm (More) **9**:318

A Treatise concerning Religious Affections (Edwards) **7**:94, 96, 101-02, 118-21

A Treatise concerning Religious Affections (Edwards) See *Religious Affections*

Treatise Concerning the Lord's Supper (*Treatise*) (Taylor) **11**:373, 385-86

A Treatise Historical containing the Bitter Passion of our Saviour Christ (More) **10**:370

Treatise of Civil Government (Locke) **7**:269, 273

A Treatise of Human Nature: Being an Attempt to Introduce the Experimental Method of Reasoning into Moral Subjects (Hume) **7**:136-41, 154-55, 157-58, 160-61, 163, 165-66, 168, 171, 174, 176, 178, 183, 188, 197-99, 202

Title Index